KU-021-389

Oxford

The world's most trusted dictionaries

School
French
Dictionary

Editors
Valerie Grundy

Nicholas Rollin
with the assistance of Natlie Pomier

OXFORD
UNIVERSITY PRESS

OXFORD
UNIVERSITY PRESS

Great Clarendon Street, Oxford OX2 6DP

Oxford University Press is a department of the University of Oxford.
It furthers the University's objective of excellence in research,
scholarship, and education by publishing worldwide in

Oxford   New York

Auckland Cape Town   Dar es Salaam Hong Kong Karachi
Kuala Lumpur Madrid Melbourne Mexico City Nairobi
New Delhi Shanghai Taipei Toronto

With offices in

Argentina Austria Brazil Chile Czech Republic France Greece
Guatemala Hungary Italy Japan Poland Portugal Singapore
South Korea Switzerland Thailand Turkey Ukraine Vietnam

Oxford is a registered trade mark of Oxford University Press
in the UK and in certain other countries

First published 1997
Revised first edition 2002
Second edition 2004
Third edition 2005
Fourth edition 2007
Fifth edition 2012
This edition 2017

British Library Cataloguing in Publication Data
Data available

ISBN: 978-0-19-840801-7

10 9 8 7 6 5 4 3 2 1

Printed in China by Golden Cup

Introduction

This dictionary has been specially written for students who are in their first years of learning French all the way through to preparing for exams. We have paid particular attention to making the dictionary user-friendly. With the help of colour headwords, alphabet tabs, easy-to-follow signposts and examples, the right translation can quickly be found. French verbs on both sides of the dictionary are numbered to direct the student to the appropriate verb table in the centre pages.

Throughout the writing of this dictionary we have worked in close consultation with students, teachers, inspectors, and examining boards. We gratefully acknowledge the examining boards AQA, OCR, and EDEXCEL, who have read and commented on the dictionary text. Since the first edition of this dictionary there have been many changes in French life. This new edition takes full account of these changes and many new words and examples have been included in order to provide the best possible learner's dictionary of French.

How a bilingual dictionary works

A bilingual dictionary has two languages in it. When you look up a word in one of the languages, it gives the translation for that word in the other language. This dictionary is divided into two halves separated by a section of verb tables. In the first half you look up French words, which are in alphabetical order, to find out what they mean in English and in the second half you look up English words, also in alphabetical order, to find out how to say them in French. The verb tables are explained further on in this section.

At the entry you will find translations but also other information that will help you get the right translation and use the word correctly. Here is a guide to the different things you will find in an entry:

headword   a word you look up in the dictionary

translation   In this dictionary all the French words are in blue and all the English words are in black

NOUN   word class (part of speech): tells you whether the word you are looking up is a noun, a verb, an adjective, or another word class. One headword can be more than one word class.
For instance, **book** can be a noun **she was reading a book** or a verb **I've booked the seats**

(informal)	helpful information: to guide you to the right translation, to show you how to use the translation, or to give you extra information about either the headword or the translation
example	a phrase or sentence using the word you have looked up. You should read through them carefully to see if they are close to what you want to understand or say
MASC	gender: after a French noun, to tell you that it is masculine
FEM	or feminine
•	indicates a phrasal verb such as • **to carry on** or an idiomatic expression such as • **to be over the moon**
[27]	verb number – tells you which verb pattern to look at in the central pages of the dictionary

Using the dictionary

To find out what a French word means

Suppose you want to find out what the French word **bouton** means. You need to use the first half of the dictionary to find the French words that you are looking for. To help you do this, the guide words at the top of each page show the alphabetical range of words on the pages you have open. Notice that hyphens, spaces between words, and accents on letters in French words make no difference to the alphabetical order.

When you find the entry for **bouton** you will find the translation. But you will also see that **bouton** is a noun and because all nouns are either masculine or feminine in French, you are given the gender MASC or FEM (MASC = masculine gender, FEM = feminine gender).

However, it often happens that a French word has more than one English translation so you will see that the translation for **bouton** is divided into sections numbered ❶ and ❷.

bouton *NOUN MASC* ❶ button ❷ spot, pimple

The first translation is **button** and the second is **spot** or **pimple**. You will need to look at both translations to work out which one fits the French sentence you are trying to understand. So:

il y a quatre boutons sur ma veste *means* there are four buttons on my jacket

but

j'ai un bouton sur le nez *means* I've got a spot on my nose

The plurals of most French nouns are formed by adding an -s, as in **boutons** in the first sentence. Exceptional plural forms can be found after the headword:

animal NOUN MASC (PLURAL **animaux**)
   animal

French like English has certain words that you would use when chatting with friends but not in more formal situations. French words like this are marked *(informal)* in the dictionary, like **bouquin**

here:

bouquin NOUN MASC *(informal)* **book**

Note that the usual word for **book** is **livre**.

To find an English word and how to say it in French

You can see that it is quite easy once you know how the dictionary works to look up a French word and find out what it means. Students usually find it harder to use the dictionary to find out how to say something in French. This dictionary is written specially to help you do this and to make it easy to find the right way of saying things in French.

Suppose you want to know how to say **garden** in French. Look up the word in the second part of the dictionary. If you follow the same method of going through the alphabetical order of the headwords as you did when you were looking up a French word, you will find **garden** on page 434.

garden NOUN jardin MASC

Now you can see that the French word for **garden** is jardin. But if you want to make a sentence using a noun like jardin you need to know whether it is masculine or feminine. The MASC after jardin tells you that it is masculine so **in the garden** is dans le jardin. It is not always as easy as this to know which French word you need. Sometimes there will be more than one French word for the English word you are looking up. When the dictionary entry gives you more than just one translation, it is very important to take the time to read through the whole entry. If you look up **plug** the entry looks like this:

plug NOUN ❶ *(electrical)* **prise** FEM
   ❷ *(in a bath or sink)* **bonde** FEM; **to**
   pull out the plug retirer la bonde

You can see that ❶ tells you that the French word for an electrical plug is prise and ❷ tells you that the word for a bath plug or a sink plug is bonde.

Remember that information which is either in brackets or italics or both is there to help you, but it *will never* be the translation itself. Wherever there is more than one translation, depending on what meaning of the English word you are looking for, the dictionary will always help you to choose the right one. Often it is not enough to find the translation of one word. In the case of more common words the dictionary also gives you a selection of common phrases you will often want to use. In the entry for **hair** below you can find out how to use the translation in different expressions:

hair *NOUN* ❶ cheveux *MASC PLURAL*; **to have short hair** avoir les cheveux courts, **to brush your hair** se brosser les cheveux, **to wash your hair** se laver les cheveux, **to have your hair cut** se faire couper les cheveux, **she's had her hair cut** elle s'est fait couper les cheveux ❷ **a hair** *(from the head)* un cheveu, *(from the body)* un poil

How to use the verb tables numbers

On the French side of the dictionary all the headwords which are verbs look like this:

faire *VERB* [10]

On the English side of the dictionary all the verbs given as translations of English verbs look like this:

frighten *VERB* effrayer [59]

If you look at the pages in the centre of the dictionary, you will find tables showing you how to use the different types of French verbs.

The verb **faire** above has the number [10]. If you look at number [10] in the verb tables, you will see that because **faire** is a very common and very irregular verb it has a whole page to itself giving you all the tenses you will need. The verb **effrayer** has number [59] after it. When you look up verb table number [59], you will see the verb **payer**. This means that the verb endings given for payer will also be the endings for **effrayer**. So **payer** is there to show you the pattern that other verbs like it, such as **effrayer**, will follow.

With practice you will soon be able to find your way easily around the dictionary and identify what you are looking for in an entry. Some entries may seem long and complicated at first glance. Reading carefully through the signposts and examples will lead you to the translation you need.

Aa

a VERB ▸ SEE **avoir**

à PREPOSITION ❶ (note that 'à + le' becomes 'au' and 'à + les' becomes 'aux') **at**; à la maison at home, à l'école at school, au bureau at the office, à deux heures at two o'clock ❷ **in**; à Londres in London, à la campagne in the country, au printemps in the spring ❸ **to**; aller à Londres to go to London, donner quelque chose à quelqu'un to give something to somebody ❹ **by**; à la main by hand, à vélo by (or on a) bicycle ❺ **with**; une petite fille aux yeux bleus a little girl with blue eyes ❻ à trois kilomètres d'ici three kilometres from here ❼ ce bracelet est à Natalie this bracelet is Natalie's

abandonner VERB [1] ❶ **to give up**; elle a abandonné les maths she has given up maths, j'abandonne I give up ❷ **to abandon**; un enfant abandonné an abandoned child

abat-jour NOUN MASC **lampshade**

abats PLURAL NOUN MASC les abats **offal** (liver, kidneys, heart, etc)

abattoir NOUN MASC **slaughterhouse**

abattre VERB [21] ❶ **to shoot down**; deux policiers ont été abattus par des gangsters hier two policemen were shot down by gangsters yesterday ❷ **to slaughter** (an animal) ❸ **to demolish** (a building)

abbaye NOUN FEM **abbey**; l'abbaye de Cluny Cluny Abbey

abbé NOUN MASC **priest**

abcès NOUN MASC **abscess**

abeille NOUN FEM **bee**; une piqûre d'abeille a bee sting

abîmer VERB [1] ❶ **to damage**; la pluie avait abîmé la porte the rain had damaged the door, tu vas t'abîmer les yeux you'll ruin your eyesight, des fruits abîmés fruit which is going bad ❷ s'abîmer to get damaged, les pommes vont s'abîmer the apples are going to go bad, la viande s'abîme vite meat goes off quickly

aboiement NOUN MASC **barking**; on entendait des aboiements we could hear dogs barking

abolir VERB [2] **to abolish**

abominable ADJECTIVE **abominable**

abondance NOUN FEM une abondance de plenty of, lots of, il y a des fruits en abondance there's plenty of fruit

abonné, abonnée NOUN MASC, FEM ❶ **season ticket holder** ❷ **subscriber** (to a magazine, journal, etc)

abonné ADJECTIVE être abonné to have a subscription (to a magazine, journal, etc), to have a season ticket (for the bus, train, theatre, etc)

abonnement NOUN MASC ❶ **subscription** ❷ **season ticket**

abonner VERB [1] s'abonner à to subscribe to, je me suis abonné pour un an I have a year's subscription

abord NOUN MASC ❶ d'abord first, tout d'abord first of all, je vais d'abord faire du thé I'll make some tea first ❷ d'abord at first, j'ai d'abord cru qu'il était français I thought at first that he was French ❸ les abords the surroundings

abordable ADJECTIVE ❶ des prix abordables affordable prices ❷ une personne abordable an approachable person

aborder VERB [1] ❶ to tackle (a problem, a piece of work, a subject, etc) ❷ to approach

aboutir VERB [2] ❶ aboutir à to lead to, la rue aboutit à une petite place the street leads to a little square ❷ aboutir à to end up in, nous avons abouti à Paris we ended up in Paris ❸ to succeed, to be successful (of discussions or negotiations)

aboyer VERB [39] to bark

abrégé NOUN MASC summary

abrégé ADJECTIVE la version abrégée the abridged version

abréger VERB [15] to shorten

abréviation NOUN FEM abbreviation

abri NOUN MASC ❶ shelter; trouver un abri to take shelter, les sans-abri the homeless ❷ shed ❸ à l'abri de sheltered from, à l'abri du vent sheltered from the wind, out of the wind, à l'abri de la lumière in a dark place

abricot NOUN MASC apricot; de la confiture d'abricots apricot jam, une tarte aux abricots an apricot tart

abricotier NOUN MASC apricot tree

abriter VERB [1] ❶ to shelter ❷ s'abriter to take shelter

abrupt ADJECTIVE ❶ steep; une pente abrupte a steep slope ❷ abrupt

abrutir VERB [2] ❶ to deafen ❷ to stupefy

absence NOUN FEM ❶ absence; pendant mon absence while I was out, while I was away ❷ l'absence de the lack of

absent ADJECTIVE ❶ être absent to be out, to be away, je serai absent pendant une heure I'll be out for an hour, elle a été absente tout le mois de mai she was away for the whole of May ❷ absent ❸ absent-minded

absenter VERB [1] s'absenter to go out, to go away, je m'absente quelques minutes I'm just popping out for a few minutes

absolu ADJECTIVE absolute

absolument ADVERB absolutely

absorbant ADJECTIVE ❶ absorbing; un livre absorbant an absorbing book ❷ absorbent (material)

absorber VERB [1] ❶ to absorb ❷ to take (food or drink)

abstenir VERB [81] s'abstenir de to refrain from

abstrait ADJECTIVE abstract

absurde ADJECTIVE absurd

absurdité NOUN FEM absurdity; dire des absurdités to talk nonsense

abus NOUN MASC abuse; l'abus d'alcool alcohol abuse

abuser VERB [1] ❶ abuser de to misuse, abuser de l'alcool to drink too much *(regularly)* ❷ abuser de to take advantage of, to exploit, elle abuse de ta gentillesse she's taking advantage of your kindness

abusif, **abusive** *ADJECTIVE MASC, FEM* ❶ **excessive** ❷ **unfair**

acajou *NOUN MASC* **mahogany**; une table en acajou a mahogany table

accablant *ADJECTIVE* **overwhelming**

accabler *VERB* [1] **to overwhelm**

accéder *VERB* [24] ❶ accéder à to reach, to get to, pour accéder à la salle de bains, il faut passer par la chambre to get to the bathroom you have to go through the bedroom ❷ accéder au pouvoir to come to power

accélérateur *NOUN MASC* **accelerator**; appuyer sur l'accélérateur to accelerate

accélération *NOUN FEM* **acceleration**

accélérer *VERB* [24] ❶ **to speed up** *(the rhythm, process, etc)* ❷ **to accelerate** *(in a car)*

accent *NOUN MASC* ❶ **accent**; un accent étranger a foreign accent, parler français sans accent to speak French without an accent ❷ **accent** *(on a letter in written French)*; un accent aigu an acute accent, un accent grave a grave accent, un accent circonflexe a circumflex ❸ mettre l'accent sur quelque chose to put the emphasis on something

accentuer *VERB* [1] **to emphasize**

acceptation *NOUN FEM* **acceptance**

accepter *VERB* [1] ❶ **to accept**; accepter une invitation to accept an invitation ❷ accepter de faire

to agree to do, elle a accepté de m'aider she agreed to help me

accès *NOUN MASC* ❶ **access**; accès interdit no entry ❷ un accès de colère a fit of anger

accessible *ADJECTIVE* ❶ **accessible**; un livre accessible a book which is easy to read ❷ des prix accessibles affordable prices

accessoire *NOUN MASC* **accessory**; les accessoires accessories *(gloves, handbags, etc)*

accessoire *ADJECTIVE* **incidental**

accident *NOUN MASC* ❶ **accident**; avoir un accident to have an accident, un accident de la route a road accident ❷ **hitch**; il y a eu un petit accident there's been a slight hitch

accidenté *ADJECTIVE* ❶ **injured** ❷ **damaged** ❸ 'chaussée accidentée' 'uneven road surface'

acclamations *PLURAL NOUN FEM* **cheering**

accommodant *ADJECTIVE* **easy-going**

accompagnateur, **accompagnatrice** *NOUN MASC, FEM* ❶ **tourist guide** ❷ **courier** *(for a group on a package holiday)* ❸ **accompanying adult** *(with a child)* ❹ **accompanist** *(for example, a pianist accompanying a singer)*

accompagner *VERB* [1] ❶ **to accompany**; je t'accompagne I'll go with you, I'll come with you, je t'accompagne jusqu'à chez toi I'll see you home ❷ accompagné de accompanied by, elle est partie accompagnée de son frère she

A
B
C
D
E
F
G
H
I
J
K
L
M
N
O
P
Q
R
S
T
U
V
W
X
Y
Z

left accompanied by her brother ❸ **to accompany** (on the piano, for example)

accomplir VERB [2] **to carry out** (a task, project, mission, etc)

accord NOUN MASC ❶ **agreement** ❷ **d'accord** all right, OK, **je suis d'accord** I agree, **je suis d'accord avec Rosie** I agree with Rosie, **Paul est d'accord pour venir avec nous** Paul's agreed to come with us, **se mettre d'accord** to come to an agreement, **ils se sont mis d'accord sur le prix** they came to an agreement over the price ❸ **chord** (in music)

accordéon NOUN MASC **accordeon**; **jouer de l'accordéon** to play the accordeon

accorder VERB [1] ❶ **to grant** (a favour, permission, etc) ❷ **to tune** (a musical instrument) ❸ **s'accorder** to agree

accotement NOUN MASC **verge** (on the edge of the road), **hard shoulder** (on the motorway); 'accotements non stabilisés' 'soft verges' (as road sign)

accouchement NOUN MASC **childbirth, delivery**

accoucher VERB [1] **to give birth**

accoutumé ADJECTIVE ❶ **usual** ❷ **accoutumé à** used to, accustomed to

accoutumer VERB [1] **s'accoutumer à** to become accustomed to

accro NOUN MASC (informal) **addict**

accro ADJECTIVE (informal) **être accro de quelque chose** to be hooked on something

accroc NOUN MASC ❶ **tear**; **tu as un accroc à ta jupe** you've got a tear in your skirt ❷ **hitch**; **sans accroc(s)** without a hitch

accrocher VERB [1] ❶ **to hang**; **accrocher un tableau au mur** to hang a picture on the wall, **accroché au mur** hanging on the wall ❷ **to catch, to snag** (something on a nail or thorn, for example)

accroupir VERB [2] **s'accroupir** to crouch (down), to squat

accueil NOUN MASC ❶ **welcome**; **un accueil chaleureux** a warm welcome, **ma famille d'accueil est très sympathique** my host family is very nice ❷ **reception desk**; **Madame Jones est priée de se présenter à l'accueil** would Ms Jones please go to the reception desk

accueillant ADJECTIVE ❶ (of a person) **hospitable, welcoming** ❷ (of a place) **inviting, friendly**

accueillir VERB [35] ❶ **to welcome** ❷ **to receive, to greet**

accumuler VERB [1] ❶ **to collect** ❷ **s'accumuler** to pile up

accusation NOUN FEM **accusation**

accusé de réception NOUN MASC **envoyer une lettre avec accusé de réception** to send a letter recorded delivery

accuser VERB [1] **to accuse**; **il m'a accusé d'avoir volé son stylo** he accused me of stealing his pen

acharner VERB [1] **s'acharner à faire** to persist in doing

achat NOUN MASC **purchase**; **je te montre mes achats** I'll show you what I've bought

acheter VERB [16] ❶ **to buy**; je vais acheter du pain I'm going to buy some bread ❷ acheter quelque chose à quelqu'un to buy somebody something, je t'achète un sandwich? shall I buy you a sandwich?, je lui ai acheté un cadeau I bought him (or her) a present ❸ acheter quelque chose à quelqu'un to buy something from somebody, j'ai vendu ma voiture – c'est Lisa qui me l'a achetée I've sold my car – Lisa bought it from me

acheteur, **acheteuse** NOUN MASC, FEM **buyer**

achever VERB [50] ❶ **to finish** (a piece of work) ❷ **to finish off** (meaning 'kill')

acide NOUN MASC **acid**

acide ADJECTIVE **sharp**, **sour**

acier NOUN MASC **steel**

acné NOUN FEM **acne**

acoustique NOUN FEM **acoustics**

acquérir VERB [17] **to acquire**

âcre ADJECTIVE **pungent**

acrobate NOUN MASC & FEM **acrobat**

acrobatie NOUN FEM **acrobatics**

acte NOUN MASC **act**

acte de naissance NOUN MASC **birth certificate**

acteur, **actrice** NOUN MASC, FEM **actor, actress**

actif, **active** ADJECTIVE MASC, FEM **active**; la vie active working life

action NOUN FEM **action**, **act**; une bonne action a good deed

activement ADVERB **actively**

activer VERB [1] ❶ **to speed up** ❷ s'activer **to hurry up**

activité NOUN FEM **activity**

activité professionnelle NOUN FEM **occupation**

actualité NOUN FEM ❶ **current affairs** ❷ les actualités **the news**

actuel, **actuelle** ADJECTIVE MASC, FEM **present**, **current**; la situation actuelle the present situation

actuellement ADVERB **at the moment**; elle est actuellement à Rome she's in Rome at the moment

adapté ADJECTIVE ❶ **suitable**; adapté à suitable for, suited to ❷ **adapted**

adapter VERB [1] ❶ **to adapt** ❷ s'adapter à **to adapt to**, **to get used to**

additif NOUN MASC **additive**

addition NOUN FEM ❶ **addition** ❷ **bill** (in a restaurant); l'addition, s'il vous plaît can I have the bill please

additionner VERB [1] **to add up**

adhésif, **adhésive** ADJECTIVE MASC, FEM **adhesive**; ruban adhésif sticky tape

adieu NOUN MASC (PLURAL **adieux**) **goodbye**, **farewell** (the usual expression is 'au revoir' since 'adieu' is properly used to mean 'goodbye for ever')

adjectif NOUN MASC **adjective**

adjoint, **adjointe** NOUN MASC, FEM ❶ **assistant** ❷ **deputy**

admettre VERB [11] ❶ **to admit**; j'admets qu'elle a raison I admit that she's right ❷ admettre dans to admit to (a restaurant, a club, etc)

a
b
c
d
e
f
g
h
i
j
k
l
m
n
o
p
q
r
s
t
u
v
w
x
y
z

administratif, administrative
ADJECTIVE MASC, FEM **administrative**

administration NOUN FEM
administration

admiratif, admirative ADJECTIVE
MASC, FEM **admiring**; des regards
admiratifs admiring glances

admiration NOUN FEM **admiration**

admirer VERB [1] to admire

adolescence NOUN FEM **adolescence**

adolescent, adolescente NOUN
MASC, FEM **teenager, adolescent**

adolescent ADJECTIVE **teenage,
adolescent**

adopter VERB [1] to adopt

adoptif, adoptive ADJECTIVE MASC, FEM
un enfant adoptif an adopted child

adoption NOUN FEM **adoption**

adorable ADJECTIVE **adorable**

adorer VERB [1] to adore, to love

adresse NOUN FEM ❶ **address**; quelle
est ton adresse? what's your
address?, se tromper d'adresse to
get (or go to) the wrong address
❷ **skill**; elle l'a fait avec beaucoup
d'adresse she did it very skilfully
❸ **speech, address**

adresser VERB [1] ❶ adresser
une lettre à quelqu'un to send
somebody a letter ❷ adresser
la parole à quelqu'un to speak
to somebody ❸ s'adresser à to
enquire at, adressez-vous à la
réception enquire at reception
❹ s'adresser à to be aimed at, le
film s'adresse aux adolescents the
film is aimed at teenagers

adroit ADJECTIVE **skilful**

adulte NOUN MASC & FEM, ADJECTIVE **adult**

adverbe NOUN MASC **adverb**

adversaire NOUN MASC & FEM
opponent

adverse ADJECTIVE **opposing**

aération NOUN FEM **ventilation**

aérer VERB [24] to air

aérobic NOUN MASC **aerobics**

aéro-club NOUN MASC **flying club**

aérogare NOUN FEM **(flight) terminal**
(in an airport)

aéronautique NOUN FEM
aeronautics

aéroport NOUN MASC **airport**; à
l'aéroport at (or to) the airport

aérosol NOUN MASC **aerosol**

affaire NOUN FEM ❶ **matter, business**;
c'est une drôle d'affaire it's a funny
business, c'est une autre affaire
that's another matter ❷ **affair,
political crisis**

affaires PLURAL NOUN FEM ❶ les affaires
business, un homme d'affaires
a businessman, une femme
d'affaires a businesswoman, un
voyage d'affaires a business trip
❷ **business**; occupe-toi de tes
affaires! mind your own business!
❸ **belongings, things**; tu peux
laisser tes affaires dans la chambre
you can leave your things in the
bedroom

affamé ADJECTIVE **starving**

affamer VERB [1] to starve

affecter VERB [1] ❶ to affect
❷ affecter de faire to pretend to do

affection NOUN FEM **affection**; j'ai
beaucoup d'affection pour lui I'm
very fond of him

affectueusement _ADVERB_
affectionately

affectueux, **affectueuse** _ADJECTIVE MASC, FEM_ **affectionate**

affiche _NOUN FEM_ ❶ **poster** ❷ **notice**

afficher _VERB_ [1] **to put up** (_a poster or a notice_)

affliger _VERB_ [52] ❶ **to distress, to grieve** ❷ affliger de **to afflict with**

affluence _NOUN FEM_ **crowds**; aux heures d'affluence at peak times

affolant _ADJECTIVE_ (_informal_) **frightening**

affoler _VERB_ [1] ❶ affoler quelqu'un to throw somebody into a panic ❷ s'affoler to panic, ne t'affole pas don't panic

affreux, **affreuse** _ADJECTIVE MASC, FEM_ **awful, dreadful** ❷ **hideous**

afin _PREPOSITION_ ❶ afin de faire in order to do ❷ afin que in order that

africain _ADJECTIVE_ **African**

Africain, **Africaine** _NOUN MASC, FEM_ **African**

Afrique _NOUN FEM_ **Africa**; en Afrique in (_or_ to) Africa

agaçant _ADJECTIVE_ **annoying**

agacer _VERB_ [61] **to annoy**

âge _NOUN MASC_ **age**; quel âge as-tu? how old are you?, à l'âge de cinq ans at the age of five, je ne sais pas son âge I don't know how old he (_or_ she) is, il a l'âge de mon père he's the same age as my father

âgé _ADJECTIVE_ ❶ **old**; les personnes âgées old people ❷ âgé de aged, une femme âgée de trente ans a woman aged thirty

agence _NOUN FEM_ ❶ **agency** ❷ **branch** (_of a bank_)

agence de voyages _NOUN FEM_ **travel agent's**

agence immobilière _NOUN FEM_ **estate agent's**

agenda _NOUN MASC_ **diary**

agenouiller _VERB_ [1] s'agenouiller to **kneel down**

agent _NOUN MASC_ ❶ **official** ❷ **agent**

agent commercial _NOUN MASC_ **sales representative**

agent de police _NOUN MASC_ **police officer**; une femme agent de police a woman police officer

aggraver _VERB_ [1] ❶ **to make worse**; aggraver la situation to make things worse ❷ s'aggraver to get worse, la situation s'aggrave the situation is deteriorating, things are getting worse

agir _VERB_ [2] ❶ **to act** ❷ **to behave** ❸ il s'agit de it is about, il s'agit de ton frère it's about your brother, de quoi s'agit-il? what's it about?

agitation _NOUN FEM_ ❶ **hustle and bustle** ❷ **unrest** ❸ **restlessness**

agité _ADJECTIVE_ ❶ **restless, agitated** ❷ **rough** (_sea_) ❸ **bustling** (_street_) ❹ mener une vie agitée to lead a hectic life

agiter _VERB_ [1] **to shake**; agiter la main to wave your hand

agneau _NOUN MASC_ (_PLURAL_ agneaux) **lamb**; un gigot d'agneau a leg of lamb

agrafe _NOUN FEM_ ❶ **staple** ❷ **hook** (_on a garment_)

a
b
c
d
e
f
g
h
i
j
k
l
m
n
o
p
q
r
s
t
u
v
w
x
y
z

agrafer VERB [1] ❶ to staple ❷ to fasten

agrafeuse NOUN FEM **stapler**

agrandir VERB [2] **to enlarge**

agrandissement NOUN MASC **enlargement** (of a photo)

agréable ADJECTIVE **pleasant, nice**

agréé ADJECTIVE ❶ registered ❷ authorized

agréer VERB [32] ❶ to agree to ❷ veuillez agréer l'expression de mes sentiments distingués Yours faithfully, Yours sincerely (this is one of a number of fixed expressions used to end any formal or business letter)

agresser VERB [1] ❶ to attack ❷ to mug

agresseur NOUN MASC **attacker**

agressif, aggressive ADJECTIVE MASC, FEM **aggressive**

agression NOUN FEM ❶ attack ❷ mugging

agressivité NOUN FEM **aggressiveness**

agricole ADJECTIVE **agricultural**

agriculteur, agricultrice NOUN MASC, FEM **farmer**

ahuri ADJECTIVE **amazed, stunned**

ai VERB ▸ SEE **avoir**

aide¹ NOUN FEM ❶ help; avec l'aide de Claire with Claire's help, venir à l'aide de quelqu'un to help somebody ❷ aid (financial aid given to a person or a country)

aide² NOUN MASC & FEM ❶ assistant ❷ helper

aider VERB [1] ❶ to help; il m'a aidé à mettre la table he helped me set the table, est-ce que je peux t'aider? would you like some help? ❷ to give aid to (financial aid to a person, group, or country)

aigle NOUN MASC & FEM **eagle**

aiglefin NOUN MASC **haddock**

aigre ADJECTIVE ❶ sour ❷ sharp

aigu, aigue ADJECTIVE MASC, FEM ❶ high-pitched ❷ acute

aiguille NOUN FEM ❶ needle; une aiguille à coudre a sewing needle, une aiguille à tricoter a knitting needle ❷ hand (of a clock or watch); dans le sens des aiguilles d'une montre clockwise, ça tourne dans le sens des aiguilles d'une montre it turns clockwise

aiguilleur du ciel NOUN MASC **air traffic controller**

aiguiser VERB [1] **to sharpen**

ail NOUN MASC **garlic**

aile NOUN FEM **wing**
• voler de ses propres ailes to stand on your own two feet (literally: to fly with your own wings)

ailleurs ADVERB ❶ elsewhere, somewhere else ❷ d'ailleurs besides, moreover ❸ par ailleurs also, in addition

aimable ADJECTIVE **kind, nice**; vous êtes très aimable that's very kind of you

aimant NOUN MASC **magnet**

aimer VERB [1] ❶ to like; est-ce que tu aimes les fraises? do you like strawberries?, **aimer faire quelque chose** to like doing something, **elle aime aller au cinéma** she likes going to the cinema, **elle aimerait aller au cinéma** she'd like to go to the cinema ❷ **aimer mieux** to prefer, **j'aime mieux les fraises que les framboises** I prefer strawberries to raspberries, **I like strawberries better than raspberries**, **j'aimerais mieux aller au cinéma** I'd prefer to go to the cinema, I'd rather go to the cinema ❸ **to love**; **je t'aime** I love you ❹ **s'aimer** to like each other, to love each other

aîné, **aînée** NOUN MASC, FEM **l'aîné(e)** the eldest, the oldest (child)

aîné ADJECTIVE **elder**, **older** (of two), **eldest**, **oldest** (of more than two); **leur fille aînée** their elder (or eldest) daughter

ainsi ADVERB ❶ **thus** ❷ **in this way** ❸ **ainsi que** as well as, along with

aïoli NOUN MASC **garlic mayonnaise**

air NOUN MASC ❶ **air**; **aller prendre l'air** to go out and get some fresh air ❷ **un courant d'air** a draught ❸ **avoir l'air (...)** to look (...), **avoir l'air bon** to look good, **avoir l'air fatigué** to look tired ❹ **avoir l'air de** to look like, **il a l'air d'un policier** he looks like a policeman ❺ **avoir l'air d'être** to look as if you are, **elle a l'air d'être perdue** she looks as if she's lost ❻ **avoir l'air de faire** to look as if you are doing, **il a l'air de comprendre** he looks as if he understands ❼ **sourire d'un air heureux** to smile happily ❽ **tune**

air bag NOUN MASC **airbag** (in a car)

aire de jeu NOUN FEM **playground**

aire de pique-nique NOUN FEM **picnic area**

aire de services NOUN FEM **motorway service station**

aise NOUN FEM **être à l'aise** to be comfortable, to feel at ease, **être mal à l'aise** to feel uncomfortable

aisselle NOUN FEM **armpit**

ajout NOUN MASC **addition**

ajouter VERB [1] **to add**; **ajoutez un œuf** add an egg

alarme NOUN FEM **alarm**; **sonner l'alarme** to sound the alarm

album NOUN MASC **album**

album de bandes dessinées NOUN MASC **comic book**

album de photos NOUN MASC **photograph album**

album de timbres NOUN MASC **stamp album**

alcool NOUN MASC **alcohol**

alcoolique NOUN MASC & FEM, ADJECTIVE **alcoholic**

alcoolisé ADJECTIVE **une boisson alcoolisée** an alcoholic drink, **une boisson non alcoolisée** a non-alcoholic drink

alcootest NOUN MASC **Breathalyzer**

alcôve NOUN FEM **alcove**

alentours PLURAL NOUN MASC ❶ **surroundings** ❷ **aux alentours de** in the vicinity (or neighbourhood) of

algèbre NOUN FEM **algebra**

Algérie NOUN FEM **Algeria**

a
b
c
d
e
f
g
h
i
j
k
l
m
n
o
p
q
r
s
t
u
v
w
x
y
z

algérien, **algerienne** ADJECTIVE MASC, FEM **Algerian**

algues PLURAL NOUN FEM **seaweed**

alibi NOUN MASC **alibi**

aliment NOUN MASC **food**

alimentaire ADJECTIVE des produits alimentaires food products, l'industrie alimentaire the food industry

alimentation NOUN FEM ❶ **groceries** ❷ **diet**

allée NOUN FEM **path**, **drive**

alléger VERB [15] ❶ **to lighten** ❷ **to reduce**

Allemagne NOUN FEM **Germany**

allemand NOUN MASC **German** (language)

allemand ADJECTIVE **German**

Allemand, **Allemande** NOUN MASC, FEM **German** (person)

aller¹ VERB [7] ❶ **to go**; aller à Paris to go to Paris, je vais à Paris I'm going to Paris, I go to Paris ❷ (used with another verb in much the same way as 'going to' is used in English) je vais écrire à ma mère ce soir I'm going to write to my mother this evening ❸ (comment) ça va? how are you?, ça va bien I'm fine, comment va ta mère? how's your mother?, elle va bien she's fine ❹ **to suit**; cette robe te va bien that dress really suits you, est-ce que jeudi te va? does Thursday suit you? ❺ s'en aller to leave, je m'en vais! I'm off!

aller² NOUN MASC ❶ faire des allers et retours to go to and fro ❷ un aller simple a single ticket, un aller-retour a return ticket, Avignon aller simple, s'il vous plaît a single to Avignon please

allergie NOUN FEM **allergy**

allergique ADJECTIVE être allergique à to be allergic to, elle est allergique aux chats she's allergic to cats

alliance NOUN FEM ❶ **wedding ring** ❷ **alliance**

allié, **alliée** NOUN MASC, FEM **ally**

alligator NOUN MASC **alligator**

allô EXCLAMATION **hello** (only used on the telephone)

allocation NOUN FEM **benefit**, **allowance**

allocation chômage NOUN FEM **unemployment benefit**

allocations familiales PLURAL NOUN FEM **family allowance**

allonger VERB [52] ❶ **to lengthen** ❷ **to extend** ❸ s'allonger to lie down

allumer VERB [1] ❶ **to light**; allumer le feu to light the fire ❷ **to switch on**; allumer la lampe to switch on the lamp ❸ **to switch on the lights**

allumette NOUN FEM **match**; une boîte d'allumettes a box of matches

allure NOUN FEM ❶ **speed**; à toute allure at top speed ❷ **appearance** (of a person)

alors ADVERB ❶ **then**, **at that time**; elle travaillait alors à Paris she was working in Paris then ❷ **so**; alors, comment ça va? so how are you? ❸ alors que while, alors qu'elle faisait ses devoirs while she was doing her homework

alouette NOUN FEM **skylark**

Alpes NOUN FEM les Alpes the Alps

alphabet *NOUN MASC* **alphabet**

alphabétique *ADJECTIVE*
alphabetical; dans l'ordre
alphabétique, par ordre
alphabétique in alphabetical order

alpin *ADJECTIVE* **alpine**

alpinisme *NOUN MASC*
mountaineering

alsacien, alsacienne *ADJECTIVE MASC,*
FEM **from Alsace, Alsatian**

Alsacien, Alsacienne *NOUN MASC,*
FEM **Alsatian**

alternatif, alternative *ADJECTIVE*
MASC, FEM **alternative**

altitude *NOUN FEM* **altitude**

alu *NOUN MASC (informal)* **aluminium**;
du papier alu kitchen foil

aluminium *NOUN MASC* **aluminium**

amalgame *NOUN MASC* **mixture**

amande *NOUN FEM* ❶ **almond**
❷ **kernel** (of a fruit stone)

amant *NOUN MASC* **lover**

amateur *NOUN MASC* **enthusiast**; un
amateur de musique a music lover

amateur *ADJECTIVE* **amateur**; un
photographe amateur an amateur
photographer

ambassade *NOUN FEM* **embassy**;
l'ambassade de France the French
Embassy

ambassadeur *NOUN MASC*
ambassador

ambiance *NOUN FEM* **atmosphere**;
une bonne ambiance a good
atmosphere

ambigu, ambigue *ADJECTIVE MASC,*
FEM **ambiguous**

ambitieux, ambiteuse *ADJECTIVE*
MASC, FEM **ambitious**

ambition *NOUN FEM* **ambition**

ambulance *NOUN FEM* **ambulance**

ambulancier, ambulancière
NOUN MASC, FEM **ambulance driver**

âme *NOUN FEM* **soul**

amélioration *NOUN FEM*
improvement

améliorer, s'améliorer *VERB* [1] to
improve

aménagé *ADJECTIVE* ❶ **equipped**;
une cuisine aménagée an equipped
kitchen ❷ **converted**

aménager *VERB* [52] ❶ to convert,
to do up (a building, a room, etc)
❷ to develop (an area) ❸ to
construct, to improve (a road or
road system)

amende *NOUN FEM* **fine**; une amende
de 500 euros a 500-euro fine

amener *VERB* [50] ❶ to bring; elle
a amené son cousin she brought
her cousin (with her) ❷ to take;
amener un enfant à l'école to take
a child to school

amer, amere *ADJECTIVE MASC, FEM*
bitter

américain *ADJECTIVE* **American**

Américain, Américaine *NOUN MASC,*
FEM **American**

Amérique *NOUN FEM* **America**

ami, amie *NOUN MASC, FEM* **friend**; un
ami à moi a friend of mine, un ami à
Lisa a friend of Lisa's

ami *ADJECTIVE* **friendly**

amiante NOUN MASC **asbestos**

amical ADJECTIVE MASC (PLURAL amicaux) **friendly**

amicale NOUN FEM **association**

amicalement ADVERB ❶ **in a friendly way** ❷ **Best wishes** (at the end of a letter)

amitié NOUN FEM ❶ **friendship**; faire quelque chose par amitié to do something out of friendship ❷ amitiés **love** (at the end of a letter)

amortisseur NOUN MASC **shock absorber**

amour NOUN MASC **love**

amoureux, amoreuse ADJECTIVE MASC, FEM **in love**; être amoureux de to be in love with

amour-propre NOUN MASC **self-esteem**

amovible ADJECTIVE **detachable**

amphi NOUN MASC (informal) **lecture theatre** (in a university)

amphithéâtre NOUN MASC ❶ **amphitheatre** ❷ **lecture theatre**

ample ADJECTIVE ❶ **loose-fitting** (jacket, dress, etc) ❷ **ample** (quantity)

ampleur NOUN FEM **size, scope**

ampli NOUN MASC (informal) **amplifier**

amplificateur NOUN MASC **amplifier**

ampoule NOUN FEM ❶ **light bulb** ❷ **blister**

amusant ADJECTIVE ❶ **funny**; une histoire amusante a funny story ❷ **entertaining**

amuse-gueule NOUN MASC des amuse-gueule nibbles (crisps, nuts, etc)

amuser VERB [1] ❶ **to amuse** ❷ **to entertain** ❸ s'amuser **to play** ❹ s'amuser **to enjoy oneself, to have a good time**, on s'est bien amusé we really enjoyed ourselves, we had a really good time

an NOUN MASC **year**; elle a dix ans she's ten (years old), le jour de l'an New Year's Day, il va en Normandie tous les ans he goes to Normandy every year
• bon an, mal an year in, year out (literally: good year, bad year)

analgésique NOUN MASC **analgesic, painkiller**

analphabète ADJECTIVE **illiterate**

analyse NOUN FEM ❶ **analysis** ❷ une analyse de sang a blood test

analyser VERB [1] **to analyse**

ananas NOUN MASC **pineapple**

anatomie NOUN FEM **anatomy**

ancêtre NOUN MASC & FEM **ancestor**

anchois NOUN MASC **anchovy**

ancien, ancienne ADJECTIVE MASC, FEM ❶ (coming before a noun) **former**; l'ancien président the former president, the ex-president, mon ancienne école my old school, un ancien élève a former pupil ❷ (coming after a noun) **old**; une maison ancienne an old house, une table ancienne an antique table

ancien combattant NOUN MASC **war veteran**

ancre NOUN FEM **anchor**

âne *NOUN MASC* **donkey**

anémone *NOUN FEM* **anemone**

anesthésie *NOUN FEM* **anaesthesia**;
une anesthésie an anaesthetic

anesthésiste *NOUN MASC & FEM*
anaesthetist

ange *NOUN MASC* **angel**
• être aux anges to be over the
  moon, to be absolutely delighted
  *(literally: to be at the level of the
  angels)*

angine *NOUN FEM* **throat infection**;
avoir une angine to have a throat
infection

anglais *NOUN MASC* **English**
(language); parler l'anglais to speak
English

anglais *ADJECTIVE* **English**

Anglais, Anglaise *NOUN MASC, FEM*
Englishman, Englishwoman;
les Anglais the English, il y a une
Anglaise dans notre classe there's
an English girl in our class

angle *NOUN MASC* **❶ angle**; un angle
droit a right angle **❷ corner**; à
l'angle de la rue at the corner of the
street, le magasin qui fait l'angle
the shop on the corner

Angleterre *NOUN FEM* **England**; en
Angleterre in *(or to)* England, aller
en Angleterre to go to England

Anglo-Normande *ADJECTIVE* les îles
Anglo-Normandes the Channel
Islands

anglophone *NOUN MASC & FEM* **English
speaker**

anglophone *ADJECTIVE* **English-
speaking**

angoisse *NOUN FEM* **anxiety**

angoissé *ADJECTIVE* **anxious**

anguille *NOUN FEM* **eel**

anguleux, angeleuse *ADJECTIVE
MASC, FEM* **bony**

animal *NOUN MASC (PLURAL* animaux*)*
animal

animateur, animatrice *NOUN MASC,
FEM* **❶ group leader ❷ organizer
❸ presenter**

animation *NOUN FEM* **❶ liveliness,
life**; il y a beaucoup d'animation
dans le quartier le soir there's a
lot going on in the area at night
❷ organization *(of a group, a
programme, etc)*

animé *ADJECTIVE* **❶ lively** *(person or
discussion)* **❷ busy** *(place)*

animer *VERB [1]* **❶ to run** *(a course)*
❷ to lead *(a group)* **❸ to present**
(a programme or a show) **❹ to liven
up** *(an occasion)* **❺** s'animer to
liven up

anis *NOUN MASC* **aniseed**

anneau *NOUN MASC (PLURAL* anneaux*)*
ring

année *NOUN FEM* **year**; l'année
prochaine next year, l'année
dernière last year, les années 70
the seventies, Bonne année Happy
New Year

annexe *NOUN FEM* **❶ appendix** *(of
book)* **❷ annexe** *(of building)*

anniversaire *NOUN MASC*
❶ birthday; fêter son anniversaire
to celebrate one's birthday, Bon
anniversaire, Joyeux anniversaire
Happy Birthday **❷ anniversary**

a
b
c
d
e
f
g
h
i
j
k
l
m
n
o
p
q
r
s
t
u
v
w
x
y
z

annonce NOUN FEM
❶ advertisement; les petites annonces the small ads *(in a newspaper)* ❷ announcement ❸ sign

annoncer VERB [61] ❶ to announce ❷ to forecast; ils annoncent de la neige pour demain snow is forecast for tomorrow

annuaire NOUN MASC **directory**; l'annuaire téléphonique the telephone directory

annuel, annuelle ADJECTIVE MASC, FEM **annual, yearly**; un événement annuel a yearly event

annuler VERB [1] **to cancel**; le vol a été annulé the flight has been cancelled

anonyme ADJECTIVE **anonymous**

anorak NOUN MASC **anorak**

anorexie NOUN FEM **anorexia**

anormal ADJECTIVE MASC *(PLURAL anormaux)*

anse NOUN FEM **handle** *(of a basket, cup, jug, or teapot)*

Antarctique NOUN MASC l'Antarctique the Antarctic

antenne NOUN FEM ❶ **aerial** *(for a radio or television)* ❷ **antenna** *(of an insect, a radio mast, or a spacecraft)*

anthropologie NOUN FEM **anthropology**

antibiotique NOUN MASC **antibiotic**; prendre des antibiotiques to be on antibiotics

antichoc ADJECTIVE **shockproof**; un casque antichoc a crash helmet

anticiper VERB [1] **to foresee, to anticipate**

antidérapant ADJECTIVE **nonslip, nonskid**

antidote NOUN MASC **antidote**

antigel NOUN MASC **antifreeze**

antillais ADJECTIVE **West Indian**

Antillais, Antillaise NOUN MASC, FEM **West Indian**

Antilles PLURAL NOUN FEM les Antilles the West Indies

antilope NOUN FEM **antelope**

antipathique ADJECTIVE **unpleasant**

antiquaire NOUN MASC & FEM **antique dealer**

antiquité NOUN FEM **antique**

antiseptique NOUN MASC, ADJECTIVE **antiseptic**

antitabac ADJECTIVE **antismoking**

antiterroriste ADJECTIVE **antiterrorist**

antivol NOUN MASC **anti-theft device**

anxieux, anxieuse ADJECTIVE MASC, FEM **anxious**

août NOUN MASC **August**; en août, au mois d'août in August

apercevoir VERB [66] ❶ **to catch sight of** ❷ s'apercevoir de to notice, s'apercevoir que to notice that

aperçu NOUN MASC ❶ **insight** ❷ **glimpse**

apéritif NOUN MASC **drink** *(usually alcoholic, before a meal)*

aphte NOUN MASC **mouth ulcer**

aplatir VERB [2] ❶ **to flatten** ❷ **to smooth out**

apostrophe NOUN FEM **apostrophe**

apparaître VERB [57] **❶ to appear**
❷ to seem; il apparaît que it seems
that

appareil NOUN MASC **❶ device**,
appliance, piece of equipment
❷ telephone; c'est Paul à l'appareil
it's Paul speaking **❸ un appareil**
(dentaire) a brace (for teeth)

appareil photo NOUN MASC **camera**

apparemment ADVERB **apparently**

apparence NOUN FEM **appearance**

apparent ADJECTIVE **❶ visible**,
obvious ❷ apparent

apparition NOUN FEM **appearance**

appartement NOUN MASC **flat**;
'appartement à louer' 'flat to let'

appartenir VERB [81] appartenir à
to belong to, est-ce que ce stylo
t'appartient? does this pen belong
to you?, is this pen yours?, à qui
appartiennent ces chaussures?
who do these shoes belong to?

appel NOUN MASC **❶ call, appeal**; un
appel d'aide a call for help **❷ un**
appel (téléphonique) a telephone
call **❸ faire appel à** to appeal to
❹ faire l'appel to take the register
(at school)

appeler VERB [18] **❶ to call**; ils l'ont
appelé Roger they called him Roger
❷ s'appeler to be called, il s'appelle
Frank he's called Frank, his name is
Frank, je m'appelle Anne my name
is Anne, comment t'appelles-tu?,
tu t'appelles comment? what's
your name? **❸ to phone ❹ to call**;
appeler un taxi to call a taxi

appendice NOUN MASC **appendix**
(organ)

appendicite NOUN FEM **appendicitis**

appétissant ADJECTIVE **appetizing**

appétit NOUN MASC **appetite**; 'bon
appétit' 'enjoy your meal'

applaudir VERB [2] **to applaud**

applaudissements PLURAL NOUN
MASC **applause**

application NOUN FEM **❶ care**
❷ application

appliquer VERB [1] **❶ to apply**
❷ s'appliquer to take care
❸ s'appliquer à to apply to, cela ne
s'applique pas à vous that doesn't
apply to you

apporter VERB [1] **to bring**

apprécier VERB [1] **to appreciate**

appréhender VERB [1] **❶ to arrest**
❷ to dread

apprenant, apprenante NOUN
MASC, FEM **learner**

apprendre VERB [64] **❶ to learn**;
apprendre à lire to learn to read
❷ to hear; j'ai appris que tu vas
partir I hear you're leaving **❸ to
teach**; apprendre quelque chose
à quelqu'un to teach somebody
something, elle leur apprend
le français she's teaching them
French, elle leur apprend à parler
français she's teaching them to
speak French

approche NOUN FEM **approach**

approcher VERB [1] **❶ to move**
(something) closer; approche
ta chaise move your chair closer,
approche ta chaise de la table
move your chair closer to the table
❷ approcher quelqu'un to go up
to somebody **❸ s'approcher de**
quelque chose to go (or come) near
to something

approprié ADJECTIVE **appropriate**

approuver VERB [1] ❶ to approve of ❷ to approve (a document, project, budget, etc)

approximatif, approximative ADJECTIVE MASC, FEM **approximate, rough**

approximativement ADVERB **approximately, roughly**

appui NOUN MASC **support**

appuyer VERB [41] ❶ appuyer sur quelque chose to press something, appuie sur le bouton press the button ❷ to lean; appuyer quelque chose contre le mur to lean something against the wall

après ADVERB **afterwards, later**; une heure après an hour later, peu après shortly afterwards, longtemps après a long time later

après PREPOSITION ❶ after; après dix heures after ten o'clock, après l'école after school ❷ après avoir fait after doing ❸ après que after

après-demain ADVERB **the day after tomorrow**

après-midi NOUN MASC & FEM **afternoon**; cet après-midi this afternoon, demain après-midi tomorrow afternoon, hier après-midi yesterday afternoon, tous les après-midi every afternoon

après-rasage NOUN MASC **aftershave**

aptitude NOUN FEM **aptitude**; son aptitude pour le dessin his aptitude for drawing

aquarelle NOUN FEM **watercolours**; une aquarelle a watercolour (painting)

aquarium NOUN MASC ❶ **fish tank** ❷ **aquarium**

arabe NOUN MASC **Arabic**

arabe ADJECTIVE ❶ **Arab** ❷ **Arabic**

Arabe NOUN MASC & FEM **Arab**

araignée NOUN FEM **spider**; une toile d'araignée a spider's web

arbitraire ADJECTIVE **arbitrary**

arbitre NOUN MASC **referee, umpire**

arbre NOUN MASC **tree**

arbre généalogique NOUN MASC **family tree**

arc NOUN MASC ❶ **bow** (as in 'bow and arrow') ❷ **arch**

arc-en-ciel NOUN MASC **rainbow**

archéologie NOUN FEM **archeology**

archéologue NOUN MASC & FEM **archeologist**

archet NOUN MASC **bow** (for a musical instrument such as a violin)

archevêque NOUN MASC **archbishop**

architecte NOUN MASC & FEM **architect**

architecture NOUN FEM **architecture**

Arctique NOUN MASC l'Arctique the Arctic

ardoise NOUN FEM **slate**

arène NOUN FEM ❶ **arena** ❷ **bullring**

arête NOUN FEM **fishbone**; ce poisson est plein d'arêtes this fish is full of bones

argent NOUN MASC ❶ **money**; dépenser de l'argent to spend money ❷ **silver**; une cuillère en argent a silver spoon

argent de poche *NOUN MASC* **pocket money**

argile *NOUN FEM* **clay**

argot *NOUN MASC* **slang**

aristocrate *NOUN MASC & FEM* **aristocrat**

aristocratie *NOUN FEM* **aristocracy**

arithmétique *NOUN FEM* **arithmetic**

arme *NOUN FEM* **weapon**

armé *ADJECTIVE* ❶ **armed** ❷ armé de armed with, equipped with

arme à feu *NOUN FEM* **firearm**

armée *NOUN FEM* **army**

armée de l'air *NOUN FEM* **Air Force**

armée de terre *NOUN FEM* **Army**

armoire *NOUN FEM* ❶ **cupboard** ❷ **wardrobe**

arobase *NOUN MASC* **at, @** *(in email addresses)*; jean-point-dupont-arobase-mondecom-point-com jean-dot-dupont-at-mondecom-dot-com

aromates *PLURAL NOUN MASC* **herbs and spices**

aromathérapie *NOUN FEM* **aromatherapy**

aromatisé *ADJECTIVE* **flavoured**

arôme *NOUN MASC* ❶ **flavouring** ❷ **aroma**

arracher *VERB* [1] ❶ arracher quelque chose à quelqu'un to snatch something from somebody ❷ **to rip out, to rip off** *(a page or pages)* ❸ **to pull up** *(weeds or vegetables)*

arrangement *NOUN MASC* **arrangement**

arranger *VERB* [52] ❶ **to arrange**; arranger une réunion to arrange a meeting ❷ **to arrange** *(flowers, books, etc)* ❸ **to sort out** ❹ **to fix** ❺ s'arranger to get better, ça va s'arranger it will sort itself out ❻ s'arranger avec quelqu'un to sort it out with somebody, tu t'arranges avec Paul sort it out with Paul

arrestation *NOUN FEM* **arrest**

arrêt *NOUN MASC* ❶ **stop**; un arrêt de bus a bus stop ❷ sans arrêt non-stop

arrêter *VERB* [1] ❶ **to stop**; arrêter la voiture to stop the car ❷ **to switch off** *(an engine, a machine, etc)* ❸ arrêter de faire to stop doing, il a arrêté de fumer he's stopped smoking, elle n'arrête pas de travailler she never stops working ❹ s'arrêter to stop, on va s'arrêter à la boulangerie we'll stop at the baker's

arrhes *PLURAL NOUN FEM* **deposit**; verser des arrhes to pay a deposit

arrière *NOUN MASC* **back**; à l'arrière in the back *(of a car)*, regarder en arrière to look back

arrière *ADJECTIVE* **back** *(door, pocket, etc)*

arrière-goût *NOUN MASC* **aftertaste**

arrière-grand-mère *NOUN FEM* **great-grandmother**

arrière-grand-père *NOUN MASC* **great-grandfather**

arrière-grands-parents *PLURAL NOUN MASC* **great-grandparents**

arrière-petits-enfants *PLURAL NOUN MASC* **great-grandchildren**

arrivage NOUN MASC ❶ **delivery** (of goods) ❷ **batch** (of students)

arrivée NOUN FEM **arrival**

arriver VERB [1] ❶ **to arrive**; arriver à Londres to arrive in London, to get to London, je suis arrivé à cinq heures I arrived at five o'clock, I got there (or here) at five o'clock, j'arrive! just coming! ❷ **to happen**; un accident est arrivé an accident has happened, tu sais ce qui m'est arrivé? do you know what happened to me? ❸ arriver à faire to manage to do, je n'arrive pas à tourner la clef I can't manage to turn the key

arrogant ADJECTIVE **arrogant**

arrondi ADJECTIVE **rounded**

arrondissement NOUN MASC **arrondissement**; elle habite à Paris dans le neuvième arrondissement she lives in Paris in the ninth arrondissement (large French cities are divided into numbered administrative areas called 'arrondissements')

arroser VERB [1] **to water**; arroser les plantes to water the plants, on va arroser l'anniversaire de mon frère we're going to have a few drinks to celebrate my brother's birthday

arrosoir NOUN MASC **watering can**

art NOUN MASC **art**; une galerie d'art an art gallery, l'art de faire the art of doing

art dramatique NOUN MASC **drama**

artère NOUN FEM ❶ **artery** ❷ **arterial road** ❸ **main road**

arthrite NOUN FEM **arthritis**

artichaut NOUN MASC **artichoke**

article NOUN MASC ❶ **article** (in a newspaper, magazine, etc) ❷ **item** (for sale); articles de sport sports equipment, articles de toilette toiletries ❸ **article** (in grammar); l'article défini the definite article, l'article indéfini the indefinite article

articulation NOUN FEM **joint**; articulation du coude/de la hanche elbow/hip joint

artificiel, artificielle ADJECTIVE MASC, FEM **artificial**

artisan NOUN MASC **craftsman**

artisanal ADJECTIVE MASC (PLURAL artisanaux) ❶ **traditional** ❷ **hand-crafted**

artisanat NOUN MASC **arts and crafts**

artiste NOUN MASC & FEM ❶ **artist** ❷ **performer**

as[1] VERB ▸ SEE **avoir**

as[2] NOUN MASC **ace**

ascenseur NOUN MASC **lift**; prendre l'ascenseur to take the lift

asiatique ADJECTIVE **Asian**

Asie NOUN FEM **Asia**

asile NOUN MASC ❶ **refuge** ❷ le droit d'asile political asylum

aspect NOUN MASC ❶ **aspect** ❷ **appearance**; d'un aspect bizarre strange-looking ❸ **side**; l'aspect positif the positive side

asperger VERB [52] **to sprinkle**

asperges PLURAL NOUN FEM **asparagus**

asphyxier, s'asphyxier VERB [1] **to suffocate**

aspirateur NOUN MASC **vacuum cleaner**

aspirine NOUN FEM **aspirin**

assaisonnement NOUN MASC ❶ **seasoning** ❷ **dressing**

assaisonner VERB [1] ❶ **to season** ❷ **to put the dressing on** (a salad)

assassin, **assassine** NOUN MASC, FEM **murderer**

assassinat NOUN MASC **murder**

assassiner VERB [1] **to murder**

assemblée NOUN FEM **meeting**

assembler VERB [1] ❶ **to put together**, **to assemble** (a kit, a machine, etc) ❷ **to gather together** ❸ s'assembler **to gather** (of a group, crowd, demonstration, etc)
• qui se ressemble s'assemble **birds of a feather flock together** (literally: those who are similar gather together)

asseoir VERB [20] s'asseoir **to sit down**, s'asseoir sur une chaise **to sit down on a chair**, assieds-toi **take a seat**, asseyez-vous **do sit down** ▸ SEE **assis**

assez ADVERB ❶ assez de **enough**, assez de pain **enough bread** ❷ **enough**; elle ne mange pas assez **she doesn't eat enough** ❸ **enough**; est-ce que l'eau est assez chaude? **is the water hot enough?** ❹ **quite**; leur maison est assez grande **their house is quite big**, assez souvent **quite often**, assez joli **quite pretty** ❺ j'en ai assez (de) (informal) **I'm fed up (with)**

assiette NOUN FEM **plate**; une assiette plate **a dinner plate**, une assiette

creuse, une assiette à soupe **a soup plate**
• je ne suis pas dans mon assiette aujourd'hui **I'm not my usual self today**

assis ADJECTIVE être assis **to be sitting**, elle était assise dans un fauteuil **she was sitting in an armchair**, rester assis **to remain seated**

assistance NOUN FEM ❶ **audience**; dans l'assistance **in the audience** ❷ **assistance**

assistant, **assistante** NOUN MASC, FEM **assistant**

assister VERB [1] ❶ **to assist** ❷ **to aid** (a country, the poor, etc) ❸ assister à **to be present at**, **to be at**, j'ai assisté à leur mariage **I was at their wedding**

association NOUN FEM **association**

associé, **associée** NOUN MASC, FEM **associate**, **partner**

associer VERB [1] ❶ associer quelqu'un à quelque chose **to include somebody in something** ❷ s'associer à un groupe **to join a group** ❸ s'associer pour faire **to get together to do**

assommer VERB [1] ❶ assommer quelqu'un **to knock somebody senseless** ❷ assommer quelqu'un (informal) **to bore somebody stiff** ❸ être assommé par une nouvelle **to be stunned by a piece of news**

assorti ADJECTIVE **matching**; rideaux et coussins assortis **matching curtains and cushions**, une veste assortie à sa robe **a jacket to match her dress**

assortiment NOUN MASC **assortment**, **selection**

assortir VERB [2] **❶** to match **❷** s'assortir à to match

assouplissant NOUN MASC fabric softener

assourdir VERB [2] **❶** to deafen **❷** to muffle

assourdissant ADJECTIVE deafening

assumer VERB [1] assumer la responsabilité de quelque chose to take responsibility for something, assumer une fonction to hold a position

assurance NOUN FEM **❶** confidence; avec assurance confidently **❷** insurance

assurance automobile NOUN FEM car insurance

assurance maladie NOUN FEM health insurance; est-ce que vous avez une assurance maladie? do you have health insurance?

assurance voyage NOUN FEM travel insurance

assuré ADJECTIVE **❶** confident **❷** insured

assurer VERB [1] **❶** to assure; je vous assure que c'est vrai I assure you it's true **❷** to insure; assurer sa voiture to insure one's car **❸** to provide (a service) **❹** to carry out (a task or a responsibility) **❺** s'assurer to make sure

astérisque NOUN MASC asterisk

asthmatique ADJECTIVE asthmatic

asthme NOUN MASC asthma

asticot NOUN MASC maggot

astiquer VERB [1] to polish

astrologie NOUN FEM astrology

astrologue NOUN MASC & FEM astrologer

astronome NOUN MASC & FEM astronomer

astronomie NOUN FEM astronomy

astronomique ADJECTIVE astronomical

astuce NOUN FEM **❶** cleverness **❷** une astuce a trick (for managing to do something), il doit y avoir une astuce there must be a trick to it

astucieux, **astucieuse** ADJECTIVE MASC, FEM clever; c'était très astucieux de sa part de faire ça it was very crafty of her to do that

atelier NOUN MASC **❶** workshop **❷** studio (of an artist, a sculptor, etc) **❸** work group

athée NOUN MASC & FEM atheist

Athènes NOUN Athens

athlète NOUN MASC & FEM athlete

athlétique ADJECTIVE athletic

athlétisme NOUN MASC athletics

Atlantique NOUN MASC l'Atlantique the Atlantic

atlas NOUN MASC atlas

atmosphère NOUN FEM atmosphere

atome NOUN MASC atom

atomique ADJECTIVE atomic

atomiseur NOUN MASC spray, atomizer

atout NOUN MASC **❶** trump card; c'est atout pique spades are trumps **❷** asset, advantage

atroce ADJECTIVE **dreadful**, **terrible**

atrocité NOUN FEM ❶ **atrocity** ❷ **monstrosity**

attachant ADJECTIVE **lovable**

attache NOUN FEM ❶ **tie**, **string**, **strap** ❷ attaches familiales **family ties**

attacher VERB [1] ❶ attacher ses cheveux **to tie** (or **fix**) **your hair back** ❷ s'attacher **to stick** (to the pan)

attaque NOUN FEM **attack**

attaquer VERB [1] ❶ **to attack** ❷ **to tackle** (a job)

attarder VERB [1] s'attarder **to linger**

atteindre VERB [60] ❶ **to reach** ❷ **to achieve**

atteint ADJECTIVE être atteint d'une maladie **to be suffering from an illness**

attendant IN PHRASE en attendant **meanwhile**, **in the meantime**

attendre VERB [3] ❶ **to wait**; tu peux attendre deux minutes? **can you wait two minutes?** ❷ **to wait for**; j'attends le bus **I'm waiting for the bus**, je t'attends dehors **I'll wait for you outside** ❸ s'attendre à **to expect**

attendrissant ADJECTIVE **touching**

attentat NOUN MASC ❶ un attentat (à la bombe) **a bomb attack**, **a bombing** ❷ **assassination attempt**

attente NOUN FEM **wait**; une attente de vingt minutes **a twenty-minute wait**

attentif, **attentive** ADJECTIVE MASC, FEM ❶ **attentive** ❷ **careful**

attention NOUN FEM ❶ **attention** ❷ faire attention à **to be careful of**, faites attention aux pickpockets! **look out for pickpockets!** ❸ attention! **watch out!**, attention au chien! **beware of the dog!**

atterrir VERB [2] **to land**

atterrissage NOUN MASC **landing**

attirant ADJECTIVE **attractive**

attirer VERB [1] **to attract**; attirer l'attention de quelqu'un sur quelque chose **to attract** (or **draw**) **somebody's attention to something**

attitude NOUN FEM **attitude**

attraction NOUN FEM **attraction**

attraper VERB [1] ❶ **to catch** ❷ attraper un rhume **to catch a cold** ❸ **to catch hold of**

attrayant ADJECTIVE **attractive**

attrister VERB [1] **to sadden**

au ▸ SEE **à**

aubaine NOUN FEM **godsend**

aube NOUN FEM **dawn**; à l'aube **at dawn**

aubépine NOUN FEM **hawthorn**

auberge NOUN FEM **inn**
- on n'est pas sorti de l'auberge **our problems are not over yet** (literally: we're not out of the inn)

auberge de jeunesse NOUN FEM **youth hostel**

aubergine NOUN FEM **aubergine**

aucun ADJECTIVE **no**; en aucun cas **under no circumstances**, sans aucun doute **without any doubt**

A
B
C
D
E
F
G
H
I
J
K
L
M
N
O
P
Q
R
S
T
U
V
W
X
Y
Z

aucun *PRONOUN* **none**; aucun des deux neither of them, aucun d'entre eux none of them

aucunement *ADVERB* **in no way**

audace *NOUN FEM* **daring**

audacieux, **audacieuse** *ADJECTIVE NOUN, FEM* **daring**

au-delà de *PREPOSITION* **beyond**

au-dessous *ADVERB* ❶ **underneath** ❷ **below** ❸ au-dessous de underneath, au-dessous de la table underneath the table ❹ au-dessous de below, au-dessous de la limite below the limit

au-dessus *ADVERB* ❶ **above** ❷ au-dessus de above

audience *NOUN FEM* **audience**

audiovisuel, **audiovisuelle** *ADJECTIVE MASC, FEM* **audiovisual**

auditeur, **auditrice** *NOUN MASC, FEM* **listener**

audition *NOUN FEM* **audition**

augmentation *NOUN FEM* **increase**; l'augmentation des prix the increase in prices, une augmentation de salaire a pay rise

augmenter *VERB* [1] ❶ **to raise**, **to increase**; augmenter les prix to raise prices ❷ **to rise**, **to go up**; le prix a augmenté the price has gone up

aujourd'hui *ADVERB* **today**; nous sommes lundi aujourd'hui today is Monday

auparavant *ADVERB* **before**, **beforehand**

auprès de *PREPOSITION* **beside**, **next to**

auquel *PRONOUN* le garçon auquel je parle the boy I'm talking to

aura, **aurai**, **auras**, **aurez**, **aurons**, **auront** *VERB* ▸ SEE **avoir**

au revoir *EXCLAMATION* **goodbye**

aussi *ADVERB* ❶ **also**, **too**; moi aussi me too, j'ai aussi invité ton frère I also invited your brother, I invited your brother as well ❷ aussi ... que as ... as, mon panier est aussi lourd que le tien my basket is as heavy as yours ❸ aussi bien que as well as, les enfants aussi bien que les adultes children as well as adults

aussi *CONJUNCTION* **so**, **therefore**

aussitôt *ADVERB* **immediately**

Australie *NOUN FEM* **Australia**

australien, **australien** *ADJECTIVE MASC, FEM* **Australian**

Australien, **Australienne** *NOUN MASC, FEM* **Australian**

autant *ADVERB* ❶ **as much**, **so much**; je n'ai jamais mangé autant I've never eaten so much ❷ autant que as much as, as many as, tu en as autant que moi you have as much (or as many) as me ❸ autant de ... que as much ... as, as many ... as, tu as autant de problèmes que moi you have as many problems as I do

autel *NOUN MASC* **altar**

auteur *NOUN MASC* **author**

authentique *ADJECTIVE* **genuine**

auto *NOUN FEM* **car**

autobiographie *NOUN FEM* **autobiography**

autobus *NOUN MASC* **bus**

autocar *NOUN MASC* **coach**

autocollant NOUN MASC **sticker**

autocollant ADJECTIVE **self-adhesive**

autodéfense NOUN FEM **self-defence**

auto-école NOUN FEM **driving school**

automate NOUN MASC **robot**

automatique ADJECTIVE **automatic**

automatiquement ADVERB
automatically

automne NOUN MASC **autumn**; en
automne in autumn

automobile NOUN FEM **car**

automobile ADJECTIVE l'industrie
automobile the car industry

automobiliste NOUN MASC & FEM
motorist

autoradio NOUN MASC **car radio**

autorisation NOUN FEM
❶ permission ❷ permit

autoriser VERB [1] **❶ to allow, to
authorize ❷** autoriser quelqu'un à
faire to allow somebody to do

autoritaire ADJECTIVE **authoritarian,
strict**

autorité NOUN FEM **authority**

autoroute NOUN FEM **motorway**;
l'autoroute de l'information the
information super-highway

auto-stop NOUN MASC **hitchhiking**;
faire de l'auto-stop to hitchhike

auto-stoppeur, auto-stoppeuse
NOUN MASC, FEM **hitchhiker**

autour ADVERB **❶ around ❷** autour
de round, around, autour de la
table round the table

autre ADJECTIVE **❶ other**; l'autre

couteau the other knife, l'autre
jour the other day **❷** un/une autre
another, tu peux me passer un
autre verre? can you pass me
another glass? **❸** quelqu'un d'autre
somebody else, personne d'autre
nobody else

autre PRONOUN **❶** un/une autre
another one, donne-moi un autre
give me another one **❷** les autres
the others, où sont les autres?
where are the others?

autrefois ADVERB **in the past, in the
old days**

autrement ADVERB **❶ differently**;
autrement dit in other words
❷ otherwise

autre part ADVERB **somewhere else**

Autriche NOUN FEM **Austria**

autrichien, autrichienne ADJECTIVE
MASC, FEM **Austrian**

Autrichien, Autrichienne NOUN
MASC, FEM **Austrian**

autruche NOUN FEM **ostrich**

aux ▸ SEE **à**

auxiliaire NOUN MASC & FEM, ADJECTIVE
auxiliary

auxquelles PRONOUN les filles
auxquelles je parlais the girls I was
talking to

auxquels PRONOUN les garçons
auxquels je parlais the boys I was
talking to

avalanche NOUN FEM **avalanche**

avaler VERB [1] **❶ to swallow ❷ to
inhale**

avance NOUN FEM **❶ advance,
progress ❷** je suis arrivé dix

minutes en avance I arrived ten minutes early, avoir dix minutes d'avance to be ten minutes early ❸ être en avance to be early ❹ à l'avance in advance

avancer VERB [61] ❶ to move forward, to advance ❷ avancer quelque chose to move something forward ❸ ma montre avance de cinq minutes my watch is five minutes fast

avant ADVERB ❶ before; longtemps avant a long time before ❷ forward; plus avant further forward

avant PREPOSITION ❶ before; avant Noël before Christmas, avant six heures before six o'clock, elle est arrivée avant moi she arrived before me ❷ avant de faire before doing, avant de partir je vais téléphoner à ma mère before leaving (or before I leave) I'll phone my mother ❸ avant que before

avant NOUN MASC front

avant ADJECTIVE front; la roue avant the front wheel

avantage NOUN MASC advantage

avantageux, avantageuse ADJECTIVE MASC, FEM ❶ des prix avantageux attractive prices ❷ des conditions avantageuses favourable conditions

avant-bras NOUN MASC forearm

avant-dernier, avant-dernière NOUN MASC, FEM l'avant-dernier the last but one

avant-dernière ADJECTIVE second last, last but one

avant-hier ADVERB the day before yesterday

avare NOUN MASC & FEM miser

avare ADJECTIVE mean, miserly

avec PREPOSITION with; avec Marie with Marie, avec un couteau with a knife, avec ça? anything else? (in a shop)

avenir NOUN MASC future; l'avenir the future, à l'avenir in the future

aventure NOUN FEM adventure

avenue NOUN FEM avenue

averse NOUN FEM shower

avertir VERB [2] ❶ to inform ❷ to warn

avertissement NOUN MASC warning

aveuglant ADJECTIVE blinding

aveugle ADJECTIVE blind

aveuglément ADVERB blindly

aveugler VERB [1] to blind

avez VERB ▸ SEE avoir

aviation NOUN FEM ❶ aviation ❷ aircraft industry ❸ flying ❹ air force

avion NOUN MASC aeroplane, plane; aller à Paris en avion to go to Paris by plane, to fly to Paris, par avion by airmail

aviron NOUN MASC ❶ rowing; faire de l'aviron to row ❷ oar

avis NOUN MASC ❶ opinion; à mon avis in my opinion ❷ changer d'avis to change one's mind ❸ notice

avocat¹, avocate NOUN MASC, FEM ❶ solicitor ❷ barrister

avocat² NOUN MASC avocado (pear)

avoine NOUN FEM oats; des flocons d'avoine porridge oats

avoir VERB [5] ❶ **to have (got)**; elle a trois frères she has (or she's got) three brothers, tu as beaucoup de livres you have (or you've got) a lot of books ❷ *(talking about age)* avoir dix ans to be ten, Claudie a dix ans Claudie's ten, quel âge a-t-il? how old is he? ❸ avoir chaud to be hot, j'ai chaud I'm hot, j'ai froid I'm cold ❹ *(used with another verb, like 'have' in English, to form past tenses)* j'ai perdu mon stylo I have lost my pen, j'ai vu ta mère hier I saw your mother yesterday ❺ j'en ai pour dix minutes it'll take me ten minutes ❻ il y a there is, there are, il y a un livre sur la table there's a book on the table, il y a trois livres sur la table there are three books on the table ❼ il y a ago, il y a trois ans three years ago ❽ qu'est-ce qu'il y a? what's the matter?

avons VERB ▶ SEE **avoir**

avortement NOUN MASC **abortion**

avouer VERB [1] **to confess, to admit**

avril NOUN MASC **April**; en avril, au mois d'avril in April

azalée NOUN FEM **azalea**

azote NOUN MASC **nitrogen**

Bb

babouin NOUN MASC **baboon**

baby-foot NOUN MASC **table football**; jouer au baby-foot to play table football, on va faire une partie de baby-foot we're going to have a game of table football

bac NOUN MASC ❶ *(informal) (short for baccalauréat)* ❷ **tub**

bac à glace NOUN MASC **ice tray**

bac à sable NOUN MASC **sandpit**

baccalauréat NOUN MASC **baccalaureate** *(school-leaving certificate sat at the age of 17-18 and giving access to higher education)*; passer le baccalauréat to sit the baccalaureate, réussir au baccalauréat to pass the baccalaureate

bâche NOUN FEM **tarpaulin**

badaud, badaude NOUN MASC, FEM **passerby, onlooker**

baffe NOUN FEM *(informal)* **slap**

baffle NOUN MASC **speaker** *(on a music system)*

bagage NOUN MASC un bagage a piece of luggage, des bagages luggage, où sont tes bagages? where is your luggage?, j'ai fait mes bagages I've packed

bagarre NOUN FEM **fight**

bagarrer _VERB_ [1] se bagarrer to fight

bagnole _NOUN FEM_ (informal) **car**

bague _NOUN FEM_ **ring**

baguette _NOUN FEM_ ❶ **baguette, French bread stick** ❷ **stick** ❸ **drumstick** ❹ **chopstick**

baguette magique _NOUN FEM_ **magic wand**

Bahamas _NOUN FEM PLURAL_ les îles Bahamas the Bahamas

baie _NOUN_ ❶ **bay** (on the sea) ❷ **berry** ❸ une baie vitrée a picture window

baignade _NOUN FEM_ **swimming**; 'baignade interdite' 'no swimming'

baigner _VERB_ [1] se baigner to go swimming

baignoire _NOUN FEM_ **bath**

bail _NOUN MASC_ (PLURAL baux) **lease**; un bail de trois ans a three-year lease

bâiller _VERB_ [1] **to yawn**

bain _NOUN MASC_ **bath**; prendre un bain to have a bath

baiser _NOUN MASC_ **kiss**; bons baisers love and kisses (at the end of a letter)

baisse _NOUN FEM_ **drop, fall**; être en baisse to be falling, la température est en baisse the temperature is falling

baisser _VERB_ [1] ❶ **to lower**; baisser le store to lower (or pull down) the blind, baisser le volume to turn down the volume, baisser la lumière to turn down the lights, baisser les prix to cut prices ❷ se baisser to bend down

bal _NOUN MASC_ **dance**; un bal populaire a village dance (or disco)

balade _NOUN FEM_ **walk, drive**; faire une balade (à pied) to go for a walk, faire une balade (en voiture) to go for a drive, faire une balade à la campagne to go for a walk (or drive) in the country

balader _VERB_ [1] ❶ se balader to go for a walk (or drive), se balader en Écosse to tour around Scotland ❷ balader quelque chose to carry something around

baladeur _NOUN MASC_ **Walkman, personal stereo**

balai _NOUN MASC_ **broom, (long-handled) brush**; passer le balai to sweep the floor

balance _NOUN FEM_ **scales**; une balance de cuisine kitchen scales

Balance _NOUN FEM_ **Libra** (sign of the Zodiac)

balancer _VERB_ [61] ❶ **to sway** ❷ **to swing** ❸ (informal) **to throw, to chuck**; balance-moi les clés! chuck me the keys! ❹ (informal) **to chuck out**; je vais balancer tous ces vieux bouquins I'm going to chuck out all these old books

balançoire _NOUN FEM_ ❶ **swing** ❷ **seesaw**

balayer _VERB_ [59] ❶ **to sweep**; balayer la cuisine to sweep the kitchen floor ❷ **to sweep up**; balayer les miettes to sweep up the crumbs

balayeur, balayeuse _NOUN MASC, FEM_ **roadsweeper**

balbutier _VERB_ [1] **to mumble**

balcon *NOUN MASC* **balcony**

baleine *NOUN FEM* **whale**

baliser *VERB* [1] **❶ to signpost ❷ to mark out**

balle *NOUN FEM* **❶ ball ❷ bullet**

ballerine *NOUN FEM* **❶ ballerina ❷ ballerina shoe ❸ ballet shoe**

ballet *NOUN MASC* **ballet**

ballon *NOUN MASC* **❶ ball ❷ balloon ❸** *(informal)* **Breathalyzer**
- souffler dans le ballon to be breathalyzed

ball-trap *NOUN MASC* **clay pigeon shooting**

balnéaire *ADJECTIVE* **seaside**; une station balnéaire a seaside resort

bambou *NOUN MASC* **bamboo**

banal *ADJECTIVE* **ordinary**; peu banal unusual

banane *NOUN FEM* **❶ banana ❷ bumbag**

banc *NOUN MASC* **bench**; assis sur un banc sitting on a bench

bancaire *ADJECTIVE* **❶ banking ❷** une carte bancaire a bank card

bancal *ADJECTIVE* **❶ rickety ❷ wobbly**

bande *NOUN FEM* **❶ group**; une bande de jeunes a group of young people **❷ gang**; une bande de criminels a criminal gang **❸ strip** *(of fabric or paper)* **❹ tape** *(for recording)* **❺ bandage**

bande-annonce *NOUN FEM* **trailer** *(for a film)*

bandeau *NOUN MASC (PLURAL* bandeaux*)* **❶ headband ❷ blindfold**

bande d'arrêt d'urgence *NOUN FEM* **hard shoulder** *(on motorway)*

bande de fréquence *NOUN FEM* **wavelength** *(on radio)*

bande dessinée *NOUN FEM* **❶ comic strip ❷ comic book**

bande publique *NOUN FEM* **Citizen's Band, CB radio**

bande rugueuse *NOUN FEM* **rumble strip** *(on motorway)*

bande sonore *NOUN FEM* **❶ soundtrack** *(of film)* **❷ rumble strip** *(on motorway)*

bandit *NOUN MASC* **bandit**

banditisme *NOUN MASC* **crime**

banlieue *NOUN FEM* la banlieue the suburbs, une banlieue a suburb, une maison de banlieue a house in the suburbs, un train de banlieue a commuter train

banque *NOUN FEM* **❶ bank**; aller à la banque to go to the bank **❷ banking**; travailler dans la banque to work in banking

banquet *NOUN MASC* **banquet**

banquette *NOUN FEM* **❶ wall seat** *(in a cafe or restaurant)* **❷ seat** *(in a car, bus, or train)*

banquier *NOUN MASC* **banker**

baptême *NOUN MASC* **christening**

baptiser *VERB* [1] **❶ to christen ❷ to name ❸ to nickname**

baquet *NOUN MASC* **tub**

bar *NOUN MASC* **bar**

baraque *NOUN FEM (informal)* **house**

Barbade *NOUN FEM* la Barbade Barbados

barbadien, **barbadienne** ADJECTIVE MASC, FEM **Barbadian**

Barbadien, **Barbadienne** NOUN MASC, FEM **Barbadian**

barbant ADJECTIVE (informal) **boring**

barbe NOUN FEM **beard**
- c'est la barbe! what a drag!
- faire quelque chose à la barbe de quelqu'un to do something behind somebody's back (literally: to do something in somebody's beard)

barbe à papa NOUN FEM **candyfloss**

barbecue NOUN MASC **barbecue**

barbelé NOUN MASC **barbed wire**

barbouiller VERB [1] ❶ to **smear**; tu es tout barbouillé de confiture you've got jam all over your face ❷ to **daub**; barbouillé de slogans daubed with slogans

barbu NOUN MASC un barbu a man with a beard

barbu ADJECTIVE **bearded**

barème NOUN MASC **scale**

barmaid NOUN FEM **barmaid**

barman NOUN MASC **barman**

baromètre NOUN MASC **barometer**

barque NOUN FEM **rowing boat**

barquette NOUN FEM **tub, container**; une barquette de fraises a punnet of strawberries

barrage NOUN MASC ❶ **dam** ❷ **roadblock**

barre NOUN FEM **bar**; une barre de fer an iron bar, une barre de chocolat a chocolate bar

barreau NOUN MASC (PLURAL **barreaux**) **bar**; derrière les barreaux behind bars (in prison)

barrer VERB [1] ❶ to **block**; 'route barrée' 'road closed' ❷ to **cross out**; barrer trois mots to cross out three words ❸ se barrer (informal) to clear off, to leave, je me barre! I'm off!
- on est mal barré (informal) we're in trouble

barrette NOUN FEM **hairslide**

barrière NOUN FEM ❶ **fence** ❷ **gate**

bar-tabac NOUN MASC **cafe** (selling cigarettes, tobacco, and stamps as well as drinks and snacks)

bas NOUN MASC ❶ **bottom, lower part**; en bas de la page at the bottom of the page ❷ **stocking**

bas, **basse** ADJECTIVE MASC, FEM **low**

bas ADVERB ❶ **low**; plus bas further down, parler plus bas to lower one's voice ❷ en bas at the bottom, down below, downstairs, les voisins d'en bas the neighbours in the flat below

bas-côté NOUN MASC **verge** (on the roadside)

basculant ADJECTIVE un camion à benne basculante a dump truck

bascule NOUN FEM ❶ **rocker**; un fauteuil à bascule a rocking chair, un cheval à bascule a rocking horse ❷ **seesaw**

basculer VERB [1] to **topple over**

base NOUN FEM ❶ **basis**; être à la base de quelque chose to be at the root of something ❷ **base**; à base de chocolat chocolate-based ❸ de base basic, les ingrédients de base the basic ingredients

base-ball NOUN MASC **baseball**

base de données NOUN FEM
database

baser VERB [1] **to base**; basé sur
based on

basilic NOUN MASC **basil**; une sauce au
basilic a basil sauce

basket NOUN MASC ❶ **basketball**
❷ **sports shoe, trainer**
• lâche-moi les baskets! (informal)
get off my back!

basketteur, basketteuse NOUN
MASC, FEM **basketball player**

basque NOUN MASC **Basque** (language)

basque ADJECTIVE **Basque**

Basque NOUN MASC & FEM **Basque**
(person)

basse NOUN FEM **bass** (in music)

basse ADJECTIVE ▶ SEE **bas**

bassin NOUN MASC ❶ **pond** ❷ **pelvis**

bassine NOUN FEM **bowl**

bassiste NOUN MASC & FEM **bassist**

bataille NOUN FEM ❶ **battle**; la
bataille de Trafalgar the Battle of
Trafalgar, la bataille du pouvoir the
battle for power, une bataille de
boules de neige a snowball fight
❷ **a card game** (similar to beggar-
my-neighbour)
• avoir les sourcils en bataille to have
bushy eyebrows
• elle avait les cheveux en bataille
her hair was all over the place

bateau NOUN MASC (PLURAL **bateaux**)
boat, **ship**; faire du bateau to go
boating (or sailing)

bateau à moteur NOUN MASC
motorboat

bateau de plaisance NOUN MASC
pleasure boat

bateau-mouche NOUN MASC
pleasure boat (a large river boat for
sightseeing trips)

bateau pneumatique NOUN MASC
rubber dinghy

bâti ADJECTIVE **built**; bien bâti well-
built

bâtiment NOUN MASC ❶ **building**;
les bâtiments de l'école the school
buildings ❷ le bâtiment the
building trade, travailler dans le
bâtiment to work in the building
trade ❸ **ship**

bâtir VERB [2] **to build**

bâtisse NOUN FEM **building**

bâton NOUN MASC **stick**

bâton de ski NOUN MASC **ski stick**

bâtonnet NOUN MASC **stick**

bâtonnet de poisson NOUN MASC
fish finger

bâtonnet ouaté NOUN MASC **cotton
bud**

batte NOUN FEM **bat** (for cricket,
baseball, etc)

batterie NOUN FEM ❶ **battery**
❷ **drum kit, drums**

batterie de cuisine NOUN FEM **pots
and pans**

batteur NOUN MASC ❶ **drummer**
❷ **whisk**

batteur électrique NOUN MASC
(electric) mixer

battre VERB [21] ❶ **to beat** (in a
game); Nicole m'a battu au tennis
Nicole beat me at tennis ❷ **to beat,**

a
b
c
d
e
f
g
h
i
j
k
l
m
n
o
p
q
r
s
t
u
v
w
x
y
z

to batter; battre un chien to beat a dog **❸ to beat** (a mixture); battre les œufs to whisk the eggs, battre la crème to whip the cream **❹** se battre to fight **❺** battre des mains to clap your hands **❻** le cœur bat the heart beats **❼** la porte bat the door bangs

bavard ADJECTIVE **talkative**

bavarder VERB [1] **to chat, to chatter**

baver VERB [1] **to dribble**

bavure NOUN FEM **❶ smudge ❷ blunder**

bazar NOUN MASC **❶ general store ❷** (informal) **mess**

BCBG (short for bon chic bon genre) **chic and stylish** (in appearance)

B.D. NOUN FEM **comic strip** (short for bande dessinée)

beau ADJECTIVE MASC (bel before a vowel or silent 'h'), **belle** FEM (PLURAL beaux) **❶ beautiful, lovely**; une belle maison a beautiful house, un bel homme a handsome man, fais de beaux rêves! sweet dreams! **❷** il fait beau it's a nice day
• faire le beau to sit up and beg (of a dog)

beaucoup ADVERB **❶ a lot**; tu m'en as donné beaucoup you've given me a lot, tu ne m'en as pas donné beaucoup you haven't given me much, cinquante euros c'est beaucoup fifty euros is a lot **❷ a lot**; il lit beaucoup he reads a lot, il ne lit pas beaucoup he doesn't read much **❸ very much**; j'aime beaucoup ta robe I like your dress very much, I really like your dress, j'aime beaucoup aller au cinéma I really like going to the cinema

❹ beaucoup de a lot of, beaucoup d'argent a lot of money, elle a beaucoup d'argent she has a lot of money, elle n'a pas beaucoup d'argent she doesn't have much money, il a beaucoup d'amis he has a lot of friends, il n'a pas beaucoup d'amis he doesn't have many friends **❺** beaucoup plus much more, beaucoup moins much less, beaucoup trop far too much, beaucoup trop court far too short

beau-fils NOUN MASC (PLURAL beaux-fils) **❶ son-in-law ❷ stepson**

beau-frère NOUN MASC (PLURAL beaux-frères) **brother-in-law**

beau-père NOUN MASC (PLURAL beau-péres) **❶ father-in-law ❷ stepfather**

beauté NOUN FEM **beauty**

beaux-arts PLURAL NOUN MASC **fine arts**; école des beaux-arts art school

beaux-parents PLURAL NOUN MASC **parents-in-law, in-laws**

bébé NOUN MASC **baby**

bec NOUN MASC **beak**

bêche NOUN FEM **spade**

bégayer VERB [59] **to stammer**

beige ADJECTIVE **beige**

beignet NOUN MASC **❶ fritter ❷ doughnut**

bel ADJECTIVE ▸ SEE **beau**

belette NOUN FEM **weasel**

belge ADJECTIVE **Belgian**

Belge NOUN MASC & FEM **Belgian**

Belgique *NOUN FEM* **Belgium**

bélier *NOUN MASC* **ram**

Bélier *NOUN MASC* **Aries** (sign of the Zodiac)

belle *NOUN FEM* ❶ ma belle darling ❷ la Belle au bois dormant Sleeping Beauty

belle *ADJECTIVE* ▸ SEE **beau**

belle-famille *NOUN FEM* **in-laws**

belle-fille *NOUN FEM (PLURAL* belles-filles) ❶ **daughter-in-law** ❷ **stepdaughter**

belle-mère *NOUN FEM (PLURAL* belles-mères) ❶ **mother-in-law** ❷ **stepmother**

belle-sœur *NOUN FEM (PLURAL* belles-sœurs) **sister-in-law**

bénédiction *NOUN FEM* **blessing**

bénéfice *NOUN MASC* **profit**; faire un bénéfice de dix mille euros to make a profit of ten thousand euros

bénéfique *ADJECTIVE* **beneficial**

bénévole *NOUN MASC & FEM* **voluntary worker**

bénévole *ADJECTIVE* **voluntary, unpaid**

bénir *VERB* [2] **to bless**

benne *NOUN FEM* **skip** (for rubbish)

béquille *NOUN FEM* **crutch**

berceau *NOUN MASC (PLURAL* berceaux) **cradle**

bercer *VERB* [61] **to rock** (a baby)

berceuse *NOUN FEM* ❶ **lullaby** ❷ **rocking chair**

béret *NOUN MASC* **beret**

berge *NOUN FEM* **bank** (of a river or canal)

berger, **bergère** *NOUN MASC, FEM* **shepherd, shepherdess**

berger allemand *NOUN MASC* **Alsatian (dog)**

besoin *NOUN MASC* **need**; avoir besoin de quelque chose to need something, j'ai besoin d'un marteau I need a hammer, avoir besoin de faire to need to do, j'ai vraiment besoin de me reposer I really need to take a rest

bestiole *NOUN FEM* (informal) **creepy-crawly**

bétail *NOUN MASC* ❶ **livestock** ❷ **cattle**

bête *NOUN FEM* **animal**

bête *ADJECTIVE* **stupid**

bêtise *NOUN FEM* **stupidity**; faire une bêtise to do something stupid

béton *NOUN MASC* **concrete**

bétonnière *NOUN FEM* **cement mixer**

betterave (rouge) *NOUN FEM* **beetroot**

beurre *NOUN MASC* **butter**
• un œil au beurre noir a black eye (literally: an eye with black butter)

beurrer *VERB* [1] **to butter**

bibelot *NOUN MASC* **ornament**

biberon *NOUN MASC* **(feeding) bottle**

bible *NOUN FEM* **bible**; la Bible the Bible

bibliothécaire *NOUN MASC & FEM* **librarian**

bibliothèque *NOUN FEM* ❶ **library** ❷ **bookcase**

a
b
c
d
e
f
g
h
i
j
k
l
m
n
o
p
q
r
s
t
u
v
w
x
y
z

bic NOUN MASC un stylo bic a Biro

biche NOUN FEM doe

bicyclette NOUN FEM **bicycle**; faire de la bicyclette to cycle

bidet NOUN MASC **bidet**

bidon NOUN MASC **can**

bidon ADJECTIVE (informal) **phoney**

bidonville NOUN MASC **shanty town**

bidule NOUN MASC (informal) **whatsit, thingamajig**

bien NOUN MASC ❶ **good**; le bien et le mal good and evil, ça te fera du bien that'll do you good ❷ **possession**; tous leurs biens all their possessions

bien ADJECTIVE ❶ **good, nice**; des gens bien nice people, ce sera bien de le revoir it will be nice to see him again ❷ **well**; je ne me sens pas bien I don't feel well ❸ **happy, comfortable**; on est bien ici it's nice here, on est très bien dans ce fauteuil this chair's really comfortable

bien ADVERB ❶ **well**; elle chante bien she sings well, bien joué! well done!, tu vas bien? are you well? ❷ **well**; bien habillé well dressed, cette couleur te va bien that colour suits you ❸ **very, really**; bien triste really sad, bien chaud really hot ❹ **very much**; j'aime bien ta robe I like your dress very much, I really like your dress, j'aimerais bien savoir I'd really like to know, j'aimerais bien aller au cinéma I'd really like to go to the cinema, 'veux-tu du thé?' – 'oui, je veux bien' 'would you like some tea?' – 'yes, I'd love some', 'tu aimes le poisson?' – 'oui, je l'aime

bien' 'do you like fish?' – 'yes, I do', je veux bien le faire I'm quite happy to do it ❺ **much**; bien mieux much better, bien plus chaud much hotter ❻ bien de **many, a number of**, bien des gens many people

• c'est bien fait pour elle! serves her right!

bien entendu ADVERB **of course**

bien-être NOUN MASC **well-being**

bien que CONJUNCTION **although**

bien sûr ADVERB **of course**

bientôt ADVERB **soon**; à bientôt see you soon

bienvenu, bienvenue[1] NOUN MASC, FEM, ADJECTIVE **welcome**; soyez le bienvenu (or la bienvenue)! welcome!

bienvenue[2] NOUN FEM **welcome**; bienvenue! welcome!, bienvenue en France! welcome to France!, souhaiter la bienvenue à quelqu'un to welcome somebody

bière NOUN FEM **beer**; boire de la bière to drink beer, trois bières, s'il vous plaît three beers, please

bière blonde NOUN FEM **lager**

bière brune NOUN FEM **brown ale**

bifteck NOUN MASC **steak**

bifurcation NOUN FEM **fork** (in the road)

bigoudi NOUN MASC **hair curler**

bijou NOUN MASC (PLURAL bijoux) **jewel, piece of jewellery**

bijouterie NOUN FEM **jeweller's (shop)**

bijoutier, **bijoutière** NOUN MASC, FEM **jeweller**

bilan NOUN MASC **balance sheet**
- faire le bilan de quelque chose to assess something

bilingue ADJECTIVE **bilingual**

billard NOUN MASC ❶ **billiards**; jouer au billard to play billiards ❷ **billiard table**

billard américain NOUN MASC **pool**

billard anglais NOUN MASC **snooker**

billard électrique NOUN MASC **pinball machine**

bille NOUN FEM ❶ **marble**; jouer aux billes to play marbles ❷ **billiard ball**

billet NOUN MASC ❶ **note**, **banknote**; un billet de cent euros a hundred-euro note ❷ **ticket**; un billet de train a train ticket

billion NOUN MASC **billion**

bio ADJECTIVE **organic**

biochimie NOUN FEM **biochemistry**

biographie NOUN FEM **biography**

biologie NOUN FEM **biology**

biologique ADJECTIVE ❶ **biological** ❷ **organic**

biologiste NOUN MASC & FEM **biologist**

bip NOUN MASC **beep**; 'après le bip sonore' 'after the tone' (on an answering machine)

biscotte NOUN FEM **continental toast**

biscuit NOUN MASC **biscuit**

bise NOUN FEM (informal) **kiss**; faire la bise à quelqu'un to kiss somebody on the cheek, grosses bises lots of love

bissextile ADJECTIVE une année bissextile a leap year

bistro, **bistrot** NOUN MASC **bistro**, **cafe**

bizarre ADJECTIVE **odd**, **strange**

blague NOUN FEM (informal) ❶ **joke**; sans blague! no kidding! ❷ **trick**; faire une blague à quelqu'un to play a trick on somebody

blaguer VERB [1] (informal) **to joke**

blaireau NOUN MASC (PLURAL blaireaux) ❶ **badger** ❷ **shaving brush**

blâmer VERB [1] ❶ **to criticize** ❷ **to blame**

blanc NOUN MASC ❶ **white**; peint en blanc painted white ❷ **white meat**, **breast** ❸ **white wine** ❹ **blank**; laisser un blanc to leave a blank

blanc, **blanche** ADJECTIVE MASC, FEM ❶ **white** ❷ **blank**; une feuille blanche a blank sheet of paper

Blanc, **Blanche** NOUN MASC, FEM **white man**, **white woman**

blanche ADJECTIVE ▸ SEE **blanc**

blanchir VERB [2] **to whiten**

blanchisserie NOUN FEM **laundry**

blé NOUN MASC **wheat**

blessé, **blessée** NOUN MASC, FEM **injured person**, **casualty**

blessé ADJECTIVE **injured**

blesser VERB [1] ❶ **to hurt**, **to injure** ❷ se blesser to hurt oneself, tu t'es blessé? did you hurt yourself?

blessure NOUN FEM ❶ **injury** ❷ **wound**

bleu¹ *NOUN MASC, ADJECTIVE* **blue**; peint en bleu painted blue, bleu marine navy blue

bleu² *NOUN MASC* **bruise**

bleuet *NOUN MASC* **cornflower**

bloc *NOUN MASC* ❶ **block**; un bloc de ciment a block of cement ❷ un bloc de papier à lettres a writing pad

bloc-notes *NOUN MASC* **notepad**

blond *ADJECTIVE* **blonde, fair-haired**

bloqué *ADJECTIVE* ❶ **blocked** ❷ **jammed** ❸ **stuck**

bloquer *VERB* [1] ❶ **to block** ❷ **to jam**

blouse *NOUN FEM* **overall**

blouson *NOUN MASC* **jacket**

blue-jean *NOUN MASC* **jeans**; j'ai acheté un blue-jean I bought a pair of jeans

bobine *NOUN FEM* **reel**

bocal *NOUN MASC (PLURAL* **bocaux***)* **jar**

bœuf *NOUN MASC* ❶ **bullock** ❷ **beef**; est-ce que tu aimes le bœuf? do you like beef?

bof *EXCLAMATION (informal)* 'c'était bien hier soir?' – 'bof!' 'did you have a good time last night?' – 'nothing special'

bohémien, bohémienne *NOUN MASC, FEM* **gipsy**

boire *VERB* [22] **to drink**; qu'est-ce que tu veux boire? what would you like to drink?, il n'y a rien à boire there's nothing to drink

bois *NOUN MASC* **wood**; une table en bois a wooden table

avoir la gueule de bois *(informal)* to have a hangover *(literally: to have a mouth made of wood)*

boisson *NOUN FEM* **drink**; une boisson fraîche a cold drink

boîte *NOUN FEM* ❶ **tin**; une boîte de sardines a tin of sardines ❷ **box**; une boîte d'allumettes a box of matches ❸ *(informal)* une boîte de nuit a nightclub, aller dans une boîte to go to a club ❹ *(informal)* **firm, company**

boîte aux lettres *NOUN FEM* **post box**

boiter *VERB* [1] **to limp**

bol *NOUN MASC* ❶ **bowl**; un bol de riz a bowl of rice ❷ *(informal)* **luck**; un coup de bol a stroke of luck
- en avoir ras le bol *(informal)* to be fed up *(literally: to have a bowlful)*
- j'en ai ras le bol d'attendre I'm fed up with waiting

bombarder *VERB* [1] ❶ **to bombard** ❷ **to bomb, to shell**

bombe *NOUN FEM* ❶ **bomb** ❷ **spray can** *(containing hairspray, fly spray, etc)*

bôme *NOUN FEM* **boom** *(of a sail)*

bon, bonne *ADJECTIVE MASC, FEM* ❶ **good**; un bon repas a good meal, bon en français good at French ❷ un bon kilomètre a good kilometre, at least a kilometre ❸ **right**; le bon numéro the right number, la bonne adresse the right address, c'est bon it's OK, it's fine

bon *NOUN* ❶ **voucher** ❷ cela a du bon that has its good points, pour de bon for good

bon ADVERB sentir bon to smell good (or nice), il fait bon aujourd'hui it's a nice day today, il fait bon dans mon appartement it's lovely and warm in my flat

bon anniversaire GREETING happy birthday

bon appétit EXCLAMATION enjoy your meal

bonbon NOUN MASC sweet

bonbonne NOUN FEM ❶ une bonbonne à gaz a gas cylinder ❷ demijohn

bond NOUN MASC leap; se lever d'un bond to leap to your feet

bondé ADJECTIVE crowded, packed; bondé d'étudiants packed with students

bondir VERB [2] to leap; bondir de joie to jump for joy

bonheur NOUN MASC ❶ happiness ❷ pleasure; avoir le bonheur de faire to have the pleasure of doing

bonhomme NOUN MASC (PLURAL bonshommes) fellow, man

bonhomme de neige NOUN MASC snowman

bonjour GREETING hello, good morning, good afternoon
• être simple comme bonjour to be really easy, to be as easy as pie (literally: to be as simple as hello)

bon marché ADJECTIVE cheap

bonne NOUN FEM maid

bonne ADJECTIVE ▸ SEE bon

bonne année GREETING happy New Year

bonne chance EXCLAMATION good luck

bonne heure IN PHRASE de bonne heure early

bonne nuit GREETING goodnight

bonnet NOUN MASC hat, bonnet

bon retour EXCLAMATION safe journey back

bon sens NOUN MASC common sense

bonsoir GREETING good evening

bonté NOUN FEM kindness

bon voyage EXCLAMATION have a good trip

boom NOUN MASC boom (time of prosperity)

bord NOUN MASC ❶ edge (of a table, cliff, etc) ❷ rim (of a glass, cup, vase, etc) ❸ side, edge (of a road, path, etc); au bord de la route on the edge of the road ❹ bank (of a stream or lake) ❺ au bord de la mer at the seaside

bordeaux ADJECTIVE maroon

border VERB [1] ❶ to line; bordé d'arbres tree-lined ❷ to edge, to trim

bordure NOUN FEM ❶ border ❷ edge ❸ en bordure de on the edge of

borne NOUN FEM ❶ kilometre marker (the equivalent of a milestone) ❷ bollard

Bosnie NOUN FEM Bosnia

bosse NOUN FEM bump

bosser VERB [1] (informal) to work

French—English

A
B
C
D
E
F
G
H
I
J
K
L
M
N
O
P
Q
R
S
T
U
V
W
X
Y
Z

botanique *NOUN FEM* **botany**

botanique *ADJECTIVE* les jardins botaniques the botanic gardens

botte *NOUN FEM* ❶ **boot**; des bottes de cuir leather boots, des bottes de caoutchouc wellington boots ❷ une botte de foin a bale of hay

bottine *NOUN FEM* **ankle boot**

bouc *NOUN MASC* **billy goat**

boucan *NOUN MASC (informal)* **din, racket**

bouc émissaire *NOUN MASC* **scapegoat**

bouche *NOUN FEM* **mouth**

bouche-à-bouche *NOUN MASC* **mouth-to-mouth resuscitation**

bouche d'égout *NOUN FEM* **manhole**

bouchée *NOUN FEM* **mouthful**

boucher¹ *VERB* [1] ❶ **to cork** *(a bottle)* ❷ **to block up**, **to fill** *(a hole, gap, or crack)* ❸ se boucher to get blocked up ❹ se boucher le nez to hold one's nose

boucher² *NOUN MASC & FEM* **butcher**

boucherie *NOUN FEM* **butcher's (shop)**

bouchon *NOUN MASC* ❶ **cork** ❷ **screw-cap** ❸ **traffic jam**

boucle *NOUN FEM* ❶ **buckle** ❷ **curl**

bouclé *ADJECTIVE* **curly**

boucle d'oreille *NOUN FEM* **earring**

Bouddha *NOUN MASC* **Buddha**

bouddhisme *NOUN MASC* **Buddhism**

bouder *VERB* [1] ❶ **to sulk** ❷ bouder quelque chose to stay away from something

boudin *NOUN MASC* **black pudding**

boudin blanc *NOUN MASC* **white pudding**

boue *NOUN FEM* **mud**

bouée *NOUN FEM* ❶ **rubber ring** ❷ **buoy**

bouée de sauvetage *NOUN FEM* **lifebelt**

boueux, boueuse *ADJECTIVE MASC, FEM* **muddy**

bouffe *NOUN FEM (informal)* **food**

bouffée *NOUN FEM* une bouffée d'air frais a breath of fresh air

bouffer *VERB* [1] *(informal)* **to eat**

bougeoir *NOUN MASC* **candlestick**

bouger *VERB* [52] **to move**

bougie *NOUN FEM* ❶ **candle** ❷ **spark plug**

bouillabaisse *NOUN FEM* **Mediterranean fish soup** *(made with several varieties of fish and vegetables)*

bouillant *ADJECTIVE* **boiling**; faire cuire à l'eau bouillante cook in boiling water

bouillir *VERB* [23] **to boil**; faire bouillir le lait to boil the milk, le lait bout the milk is boiling

bouilloire *NOUN FEM* **kettle**

bouillon *NOUN MASC* **stock** *(made with meat, fish, or vegetables)*

bouillon-cube *NOUN MASC* **stock cube**

bouillotte *NOUN FEM* **hot-water bottle**

boulanger, boulangère NOUN MASC, FEM **baker**

boulangerie NOUN FEM **bakery, baker's**

boule NOUN FEM ❶ **bowl**; jouer aux boules to play bowls ❷ **scoop** (of ice cream); vous voulez combien de boules? how many scoops would you like?

bouleau NOUN MASC (PLURAL bouleaux) **birch tree**

boule de neige NOUN FEM **snowball**

boulette NOUN FEM **pellet**

boulette de viande NOUN FEM **meatball**

boulevard NOUN MASC **boulevard**

boulevard périphérique NOUN MASC **ring road**

bouleverser VERB [1] ❶ **to overwhelm, to shatter**; être bouleversé (or shattered) ❷ **to disrupt** (a schedule, plans, etc) ❸ **to turn upside down**

boulot NOUN MASC (informal) ❶ **work**; j'ai trop de boulot I've got too much work to do, c'est un boulot immense it's a huge amount of work ❷ **job**; elle cherche du boulot she's looking for a job

boum NOUN FEM (informal) **party**

bouquet NOUN MASC **bunch, bouquet** (of flowers or herbs)

bouquin NOUN MASC (informal) **book**

bouquiner VERB [1] (informal) **to read**

bouquiniste NOUN MASC & FEM **secondhand bookseller**

bourdon NOUN MASC **bumblebee**

bourg NOUN MASC **market town**

bourgeois, bourgeoise NOUN MASC, FEM **middle-class person**

bourgeois ADJECTIVE **middle-class**

bourgeon NOUN MASC **bud**

Bourgogne NOUN FEM **Burgundy**

bourratif, bourrative ADJECTIVE MASC, FEM **very filling**

bourré ADJECTIVE ❶ bourré de crammed with, stuffed with ❷ **drunk**

bourrer VERB [1] **to cram**

bourse NOUN FEM **grant**

Bourse NOUN FEM **stock exchange**

bousculer VERB [1] **to push, to jostle**

boussole NOUN FEM **compass**

bout NOUN MASC ❶ **end**; au bout de at the end of ❷ **tip** (of nose or finger) ❸ un bout de papier a scrap of paper, un petit bout de fromage a little bit of cheese ❹ au bout de after, au bout d'une demi-heure after half an hour

bouteille NOUN FEM **bottle**

boutique NOUN FEM **shop**

bouton NOUN MASC ❶ **button** ❷ **spot, pimple**

bouton d'or NOUN MASC **buttercup**

boxe NOUN FEM **boxing**

boxeur NOUN MASC **boxer**

bracelet NOUN MASC ❶ **bracelet** ❷ **bangle**

bracelet-montre NOUN MASC **wristwatch**

braise NOUN FEM **embers** (of a fire)

brancard NOUN MASC **stretcher**

branche NOUN FEM **branch**

branché ADJECTIVE (informal) **trendy**

brancher VERB [1] ❶ **to plug in** (an iron, a television, etc) ❷ **to connect** (electricity, gas, water, telephone)

bras NOUN MASC **sleeve**; en bras de chemise in one's shirtsleeves

bras de fer NOUN MASC **arm wrestling**

brasse NOUN FEM **breaststroke**

brasserie NOUN FEM ❶ **brasserie, cafe-restaurant** ❷ **brewery**

brave ADJECTIVE **nice** (person)

bravo EXCLAMATION **well done**; Bravo, tes notes sont excellentes! Well done, your marks are excellent!

break NOUN MASC **estate car**

brebis NOUN FEM **ewe**

bref, brève ADJECTIVE MASC, FEM **short, brief**

Brésil NOUN MASC **Brazil**

brésilien NOUN MASC **Brazilian Portuguese** (language)

brésilien, brésilienne ADJECTIVE MASC, FEM **Brazilian**

Brésilien, Brésilienne NOUN MASC, FEM **Brazilian**

Bretagne NOUN FEM **Brittany**

bretelle NOUN FEM ❶ **strap** ❷ **slip road** ❸ des bretelles **braces**

breton NOUN MASC **Breton** (language)

Breton, Bretonne NOUN MASC, FEM **Breton**

breton, bretonne ADJECTIVE MASC, FEM **Breton**

brevet NOUN MASC **certificate**

bribes PLURAL NOUN FEM **bits, fragments**

bricolage NOUN MASC **DIY, do-it-yourself**

bricoler VERB [1] **to do DIY**

bricoleur, bricoleuse NOUN MASC, FEM **DIY enthusiast**

brièvement ADVERB **briefly**

brillamment ADVERB **brilliantly**

brillant ADJECTIVE ❶ **shiny** ❷ **brilliant**

briller VERB [1] **to shine**

brin NOUN MASC **sprig** (of herb or plant); un brin d'herbe a blade of grass

brindille NOUN FEM **twig**

brioche NOUN FEM **brioche, bun**

brique NOUN FEM ❶ **brick** ❷ **carton** (of fruit-juice, milk, etc)

briquet NOUN MASC **lighter**

brise NOUN FEM **breeze**

briser VERB [1] **to break**

britannique ADJECTIVE **British**

Britannique NOUN MASC & FEM **British person**; les Britanniques the British

brocante NOUN FEM ❶ **junk shop** ❷ **second-hand goods**

broche NOUN FEM ❶ **brooch** ❷ **spit** (for roasting)

brochet NOUN MASC **pike**

brochette NOUN FEM ❶ **skewer** ❷ **kebab**; une brochette de viande a meat kebab

brochure NOUN FEM ❶ **booklet** ❷ **brochure**

brocolis *PLURAL NOUN MASC* **broccoli**

broder *VERB* [1] **to embroider**

broderie *NOUN FEM* **embroidery**; des broderies embroidery

bronchite *NOUN FEM* **bronchitis**; avoir une bronchite to have bronchitis

bronzage *NOUN MASC* **suntan**

bronzer *VERB* [1] **to tan**

brosse *NOUN FEM* **brush**

brosse à cheveux *NOUN FEM* **hairbrush**

brosse à dents *NOUN FEM* **toothbrush**

brosser *VERB* [1] ❶ **to brush** ❷ se brosser les dents to brush your teeth

brouette *NOUN FEM* **wheelbarrow**

brouillard *NOUN MASC* **fog**

brouillon *NOUN MASC* **rough draft**

bru *NOUN FEM* **daughter-in-law**

brugnon *NOUN MASC* **nectarine**

bruit *NOUN MASC* ❶ **noise**; entendre un bruit to hear a noise, entendre le bruit d'une voiture to hear the sound of a car ❷ **rumour**

brûlant *ADJECTIVE* ❶ **boiling hot** ❷ **burning hot**

brûlé *NOUN MASC* un goût de brûlé a burnt taste, ça sent le brûlé there's a smell of burning

brûler *VERB* [1] ❶ **to burn** ❷ se brûler to burn yourself

brûlure *NOUN FEM* **burn**

brume *NOUN FEM* **mist**

brun *ADJECTIVE* ❶ **brown** ❷ **dark-haired**

brushing *NOUN MASC* **blow-dry**; se faire faire un brushing to have a blow-dry

brut *ADJECTIVE* ❶ **raw** *(material)* ❷ **crude** *(oil)* ❸ **gross** *(income)* ❹ **dry** *(champagne)*

brutal *ADJECTIVE MASC (PLURAL* brutaux*)* ❶ **violent, brutal** ❷ **sudden**

brutalement *ADVERB* ❶ **suddenly** ❷ **violently**

Bruxelles *NOUN* **Brussels**

bruyant *ADJECTIVE* **noisy, loud**

bruyère *NOUN FEM* **heather**

bu *VERB* ▸ SEE **boire**

bûche *NOUN FEM* **log**

budget *NOUN MASC* **budget**

buffet *NOUN MASC* ❶ **sideboard** ❷ **buffet**

buisson *NOUN MASC* **bush**

buissonnière *ADJECTIVE* faire l'école buissonnière to play truant

Bulgarie *NOUN FEM* **Bulgaria**

bulle *NOUN FEM* **bubble**

bulletin *NOUN MASC* **report, bulletin**

bulletin de salaire *NOUN MASC* **payslip**

bulletin scolaire *NOUN MASC* **school report**

bureau *NOUN MASC (PLURAL* bureaux*)* ❶ **desk**; elle est à son bureau she is at her desk ❷ **office**; au bureau at *(or* to*)* the office

A
B
C
D
E
F
G
H
I
J
K
L
M
N
O
P
Q
R
S
T
U
V
W
X
Y
Z

bureaucratie *NOUN FEM*
bureaucracy

bureau de poste *NOUN MASC* **post office**

bureau de tabac *NOUN MASC* **tobacconist's**

bureau de tourisme *NOUN MASC* **tourist information office**

burin *NOUN MASC* **chisel**

bus *NOUN MASC* **bus**

buse *NOUN FEM* **buzzard**

buste *NOUN MASC* **bust**

but *NOUN MASC* **❶ goal, aim, purpose ❷ goal** *(in football, hockey)*; marquer un but to score a goal **❸ target**

buté *ADJECTIVE* **stubborn**

buvable *ADJECTIVE* **drinkable**

buvard *NOUN MASC* **blotter**; du papier buvard blotting paper

buvette *NOUN FEM* **bar** *(at a dance, village fair, etc)*

buvez, buvons *VERB* ▸ SEE **boire**

ça *PRONOUN* **❶ that, this**; donne-moi ça give me that, ça c'est un moineau that's a sparrow **❷** comment ça va?, ça va? how are you?, ça va bien merci I'm fine thanks **❸** c'est ça that's right, ça ne fait rien it doesn't matter

çà *ADVERB* çà et là here and there

cabane *NOUN FEM* **hut, shed**

cabas *NOUN MASC* **shopping bag**

cabillaud *NOUN MASC* **cod**

cabine *NOUN FEM* **❶ cubicle**; cabine de douche shower cubicle, cabine d'essayage fitting room *(in a clothes shop)* **❷ cabin** *(on a ship)* **❸ cab** *(on a lorry)*

cabinet *NOUN MASC* **❶ office** *(of a solicitor)* **❷ surgery** *(of a doctor or dentist)* **❸** cabinet de médecins medical practice

cabine téléphonique *NOUN FEM* **phone box**

cabinets *PLURAL NOUN MASC* **toilet**

câble *NOUN MASC* **❶ cable ❷ rope**

câblé *ADJECTIVE* être câblé to have cable television

cabosser *VERB* [1] **to dent**

cacahuète *NOUN FEM* **peanut**; des cacahuètes grillées roasted peanuts

cacao NOUN MASC **cocoa**

cache NOUN FEM **hiding place**

caché ADJECTIVE **hidden**

cache-cache NOUN MASC jouer à cache-cache to play hide and seek

cachemire NOUN MASC ❶ **cashmere** ❷ motif cachemire paisley pattern

cache-nez NOUN MASC **(thick) scarf**

cache-pot NOUN MASC **flowerpot holder**

cacher VERB [1] ❶ **to hide**; cacher quelque chose to hide something, elle a caché son portefeuille dans un tiroir she's hidden her wallet in a drawer ❷ se cacher to hide, il s'est caché derrière la porte he hid behind the door

cachet NOUN MASC ❶ **tablet**; un cachet d'aspirine an aspirin ❷ **official stamp** (made with a rubber stamp) ❸ le cachet de la poste the postmark

cachette NOUN FEM ❶ **hiding place** ❷ en cachette secretly, on the sly

cachot NOUN MASC **dungeon**

cactus NOUN MASC **cactus**

cadavre NOUN MASC **corpse, body**

caddie NOUN MASC **trolley** (in the supermarket)

cadeau NOUN MASC (PLURAL **cadeaux**) **present**; faire un cadeau à quelqu'un to give somebody a present, du papier cadeau wrapping-paper, je vous fais un paquet-cadeau? shall I gift-wrap it for you?

cadenas NOUN MASC **padlock**

cadence NOUN FEM **rhythm**

cadet, cadette NOUN MASC, FEM **younger child, youngest child**

cadet, cadette ADJECTIVE MASC, FEM **younger, youngest**

cadran NOUN MASC ❶ **face** (of a watch or clock) ❷ **dial** (on an instrument such as the speedometer in a car)

cadran solaire NOUN MASC **sundial**

cadre NOUN MASC ❶ **frame** (of a picture, mirror, or window) ❷ **surroundings, setting** ❸ **executive** (a person with a management job in a company) ❹ **frame** (of a bicycle)

cafard NOUN MASC ❶ **cockroach** ❷ **depression**; avoir le cafard to be down in the dumps

café NOUN MASC ❶ **coffee**; café instantané, café soluble instant coffee, café moulu ground coffee, café en grains coffee beans, café au lait coffee with milk, prendre un café to have a coffee ❷ **cafe**

café-crème NOUN MASC **white coffee**

caféine NOUN FEM **caffeine**

cafétéria NOUN FEM **cafeteria**

cafetière NOUN FEM ❶ **coffee pot** ❷ **coffee maker**

cage NOUN FEM **cage**

cageot NOUN MASC **crate**

cagibi NOUN MASC **store cupboard**

cagnotte NOUN FEM ❶ **kitty** (of money) ❷ **jackpot**

cagoule NOUN FEM **hood**

cahier NOUN MASC ❶ **exercise book** ❷ **notebook**

caille NOUN FEM quail

cailler VERB [1] to curdle

caillou NOUN MASC (PLURAL **cailloux**) pebble, stone

caisse NOUN FEM ❶ till, cash register ❷ cash desk ❸ checkout (in a supermarket) ❹ box, crate

caisse à outils NOUN FEM toolbox

caisse d'épargne NOUN FEM savings bank

caissier, caissière NOUN MASC, FEM ❶ checkout assistant ❷ cashier

cajou NOUN une noix de cajou a cashew nut

cake NOUN MASC fruit cake

calamité NOUN FEM disaster, calamity

calcaire NOUN MASC ❶ limestone ❷ furring (the sediment which clogs up kettles, steam irons, etc)

calcaire ADJECTIVE eau calcaire hard water, l'eau ici est très calcaire the water here is very hard

calcium NOUN MASC calcium

calcul NOUN MASC ❶ calculation ❷ arithmetic

calculatrice NOUN FEM pocket calculator

calculer VERB [1] to calculate, to work out

calculette NOUN FEM pocket calculator

caleçon NOUN MASC ❶ boxer shorts ❷ leggings

calembour NOUN MASC pun, play on words

calendrier NOUN MASC ❶ calendar ❷ schedule

calepin NOUN MASC notebook

caler VERB [1] ❶ to wedge ❷ to prop up ❸ ma voiture a calé my car stalled

calibre NOUN MASC ❶ size, grade (of eggs, fruit, or vegetables) ❷ calibre, bore (of a gun)

câlin NOUN MASC cuddle; fais-moi un câlin give me a cuddle (usually said to a child), fais un calin à ta grand-mère give your gran a cuddle

câlin ADJECTIVE affectionate

câliner VERB [1] to cuddle

calmant NOUN MASC sedative

calmant ADJECTIVE soothing

calmar NOUN MASC squid

calme NOUN MASC peace and quiet

calme ADJECTIVE ❶ calm ❷ quiet

calmement ADVERB calmly

calmer VERB [1] ❶ calmer quelqu'un to calm somebody down ❷ se calmer to calm down, calme-toi calm down ❸ to soothe; l'aspirine a calmé la douleur the aspirin soothed the pain

calorie NOUN FEM calorie

calque NOUN MASC un calque a tracing, papier-calque tracing paper

calvados NOUN MASC calvados (apple brandy made in Normandy)

camarade NOUN MASC & FEM friend; camarade de classe classmate

cambriolage NOUN MASC **burglary**

cambrioler VERB [1] cambrioler une maison to burgle a house, ils ont été cambriolés they were burgled

cambrioleur, **cambrioleuse** NOUN MASC, FEM **burglar**

caméra NOUN FEM **cine-camera**

caméscope NOUN MASC **camcorder**

camion NOUN MASC **truck**, **lorry**

camion-citerne NOUN MASC **tanker lorry**

camionnette NOUN FEM **van**

camionneur NOUN MASC **lorry driver**, **truck driver**

camp NOUN MASC **camp**

campagnard, **campagnarde** NOUN MASC, FEM **country person**

campagnard ADJECTIVE **country**; la vie campagnarde country life

campagne NOUN FEM **❶ country**, **countryside**; à la campagne in the country, in the countryside, aller se promener à la campagne to go for a country walk **❷ campaign**

camper VERB [1] **to camp**

campeur, **campeuse** NOUN MASC, FEM **camper**

camping NOUN MASC **❶ camping**; faire du camping to go camping **❷** un camping, un terrain de camping a campsite

camping-car NOUN MASC **camper van**

camping-gaz NOUN MASC **camping stove**

Canada NOUN MASC **Canada**; au Canada in (or to) Canada

canadien, **canadienne** ADJECTIVE MASC, FEM **Canadian**

Canadien, **Canadienne** NOUN MASC, FEM **Canadian**

canal NOUN MASC (PLURAL **canaux**) **canal**

canapé NOUN MASC **sofa**

canapé-lit NOUN MASC **sofa bed**

canard NOUN MASC **duck**

canari NOUN MASC **canary**

cancer NOUN MASC **cancer**; avoir un cancer to have cancer

Cancer NOUN MASC **Cancer** (sign of the Zodiac)

candidat, **candidate** NOUN MASC, FEM **❶ candidate ❷ applicant**

candidature NOUN FEM **poser sa candidature à un poste to apply for a job**

cane NOUN FEM **female duck**

caneton NOUN MASC **duckling**

canevas NOUN MASC **canvas**

caniche NOUN MASC **poodle**

canicule NOUN FEM **❶ scorching heat ❷ heat wave**

canif NOUN MASC **penknife**

caniveau NOUN MASC (PLURAL **caniveaux**) **gutter**

canne NOUN FEM **walking stick**

canne à pêche NOUN FEM **fishing rod**

canne à sucre NOUN FEM **sugar cane**

cannelle NOUN FEM **cinnamon**

cannette NOUN FEM **une cannette de bière a small bottle of beer**

a
b
c
d
e
f
g
h
i
j
k
l
m
n
o
p
q
r
s
t
u
v
w
x
y
z

canoë NOUN MASC ❶ **canoe** ❷ **faire du canoë** to go canoeing

canon NOUN MASC ❶ **gun** ❷ **barrel** (of a gun) ❸ **cannon**

canot NOUN MASC **small boat**, **dinghy**; **un canot pneumatique** a rubber (or inflatable) dinghy

canot de sauvetage NOUN MASC **lifeboat**

cantatrice NOUN FEM **opera singer**

cantine NOUN FEM **canteen**; **manger à la cantine** to have school lunch

caoutchouc NOUN MASC ❶ **rubber**; **des bottes en caoutchouc** wellington boots ❷ **rubber band**

cap NOUN MASC ❶ **cape**, **headland** ❷ **course** (of a ship)

capable ADJECTIVE **capable**; **être capable de faire** to be capable of doing

capacité NOUN FEM ❶ **ability** ❷ **capacity**

cape NOUN FEM **cape**, **cloak**

capitaine NOUN MASC **captain**; **le capitaine des pompiers** the chief fire officer

capital NOUN MASC (PLURAL **capitaux**) **capital** (financial)

capital ADJECTIVE ❶ **d'une importance capitale** of major importance ❷ **une question capitale** a key question ❸ **la peine capitale** capital punishment

capitale NOUN FEM **capital city**; **la capitale française** the French capital

capot NOUN MASC **bonnet** (of a car)

câpre NOUN FEM **caper**

caprice NOUN MASC ❶ **whim** ❷ **tantrum**; **faire un caprice** to throw a tantrum

Capricorne NOUN MASC **Capricorn** (sign of the Zodiac)

capsule NOUN FEM ❶ **cap**, **top** (of a bottle) ❷ **capsule**

capter VERB [1] ❶ **capter une chaîne (de télévision)** to get a (television) channel ❷ **capter l'attention de quelqu'un** to catch somebody's attention

captif, **captive** NOUN MASC, FEM **captive**

captivant ADJECTIVE ❶ **fascinating** ❷ **gripping**, **riveting**

captivité NOUN FEM **captivity**; **être gardé en captivité** to be kept in captivity

capturer VERB [1] **to capture**

capuche NOUN FEM **hood**

capuchon NOUN MASC ❶ **hood** ❷ **top**, **cap** (of a pen)

capucine NOUN FEM **nasturtium**

car¹ CONJUNCTION **because**

car² NOUN MASC **coach**, **bus**; **voyager en car** to travel by coach, **un voyage en car** a coach journey

carabine NOUN FEM **rifle**

caractère NOUN MASC ❶ **character**, **nature**; **avoir mauvais caractère** to be bad-tempered ❷ **character**; **leur maison a beaucoup de caractère** their house has a lot of character ❸ **character**, **letter**; **en gros caractères** in large print

caractéristique NOUN FEM, ADJECTIVE **characteristic**

carafe NOUN FEM **carafe**, **jug** (for wine or water)

Caraïbes NOUN PLURAL FEM les îles Caraïbes the Caribbean Islands, aller aux Caraïbes to go to the Caribbean

caramel NOUN MASC ❶ **caramel** ❷ **toffee**

caravane NOUN FEM **caravan**

carbone NOUN MASC ❶ **carbon** ❷ **carbon paper**

carbonisé ADJECTIVE **burnt to a cinder**

carburant NOUN MASC **fuel**

carburateur NOUN MASC **carburettor**

carcasse NOUN FEM **carcass**

cardiaque ADJECTIVE une crise cardiaque a heart attack

cardinal NOUN MASC (PLURAL cardinaux) ❶ **cardinal** ❷ **cardinal number**

carême NOUN MASC **Lent**

caresser VERB [1] **to stroke**, **to caress**

cargaison NOUN FEM **cargo**

caricature NOUN FEM **caricature**

caricaturiste NOUN MASC & FEM **caricaturist**, **cartoonist**

carie NOUN FEM la carie dentaire tooth decay, avoir une carie to have a hole in your tooth

carillon NOUN MASC ❶ **church bells** ❷ **wind chimes**

caritatif, **caritative** ADJECTIVE MASC, FEM **charitable**; une association caritative a charity

carnaval NOUN MASC **carnival**

carnet NOUN MASC ❶ **notebook** ❷ **book** (of tickets or stamps)

carnet de chèques NOUN MASC **chequebook**

carotte NOUN FEM **carrot**

carpe NOUN FEM **carp**

carpette NOUN FEM **rug**

carré NOUN MASC, ADJECTIVE **square**; un mètre carré a square metre

carreau NOUN MASC (PLURAL carreaux) ❶ **floor tile** ❷ **wall tile** ❸ **windowpane** ❹ du tissu à carreaux checked fabric ❺ du papier à carreaux squared paper ❻ **diamonds** (suit of playing cards); le roi de carreau the king of diamonds

carrefour NOUN MASC **crossroads**, **junction**

carrelage NOUN MASC ❶ **tiled floor** ❷ **tiling**, **tiles**

carrelet NOUN MASC **plaice**

carrément ADVERB **downright**, **completely**; c'est carrément malhonnête it's downright dishonest

carrière NOUN FEM ❶ **career** ❷ **quarry**

carrosserie NOUN FEM ❶ **bodywork** (of car, etc) ❷ **bodywork repairs**

cartable NOUN MASC ❶ **satchel**, **schoolbag** ❷ **briefcase**

carte NOUN FEM ❶ **card** ❷ **playing card**; jouer aux cartes to play cards, un jeu de cartes a pack of cards, a card game **❸** map **❹** menu

carte à jouer NOUN FEM playing card

carte à mémoire NOUN FEM smart card

carte à microprocesseur NOUN FEM smart card

carte à puce NOUN FEM smart card

carte bancaire NOUN FEM bank card

carte d'abonnement NOUN FEM season ticket

carte d'anniversaire NOUN FEM birthday card

carte de crédit NOUN FEM credit card

carte de fidelité NOUN FEM loyalty card

carte d'embarquement NOUN FEM boarding card

carte de séjour NOUN FEM resident's permit

carte des vins NOUN FEM wine list

carte de téléphone NOUN FEM telephone card

carte de visite NOUN FEM business card

carte de vœux NOUN FEM greetings card

carte d'identité NOUN FEM identity card

carte postale NOUN FEM postcard

carte routière NOUN FEM road map

carte SIM NOUN FEM SIM card

carte téléphonique NOUN FEM phonecard

carton NOUN MASC **❶** cardboard; une chemise en carton a cardboard folder, carton ondulé corrugated cardboard **❷** cardboard box

cartouche NOUN FEM cartridge

cas NOUN MASC **❶** case; au cas où tu oublierais in case you forget, en aucun cas on no account, en tout cas in any case, at any rate **❷** case; trois cas de rougeole three cases of measles

cascade NOUN FEM **❶** waterfall **❷** stunt

cascadeur, cascadeuse NOUN MASC, FEM stuntman, stuntwoman

case NOUN FEM **❶** square (on a board game) **❷** box (on a form) **❸** hut

casher ADJECTIVE kosher

casier NOUN MASC **❶** pigeonhole **❷** locker **❸** rack

casino NOUN MASC casino

casque NOUN MASC **❶** crash helmet **❷** safety helmet, hard hat **❸** headphones, headset

casquette NOUN FEM cap; une casquette de base-ball a baseball cap

casse-croûte NOUN MASC snack

casse-noisettes NOUN MASC nutcrackers

casse-pieds ADJECTIVE (informal) elle est casse-pieds! she's a pain in the neck!

casser VERB [1] **❶** to break; casser un verre to break a glass **❷** se casser to break, le verre s'est cassé the glass broke **❸** se casser la jambe to break your leg

se casser la tête to go to a lot of trouble *(literally: to break your head)*;
• ne te casse pas la tête! don't go to a lot of trouble!

casserole NOUN FEM **saucepan**

casse-tête NOUN MASC ❶ **puzzle** ❷ **problem**

cassis NOUN MASC **blackcurrant**; sirop de cassis blackcurrant cordial

cassoulet NOUN MASC **oven-baked beans** *(with meat and sausage)*

castor NOUN MASC **beaver**

catalogue NOUN MASC **catalogue**

catastrophe NOUN FEM **disaster**, **catastrophe**

catch NOUN MASC **wrestling**

catcheur, **catcheuse** NOUN MASC, FEM **wrestler**

catégorie NOUN FEM **category**

cathédrale NOUN FEM **cathedral**

catholicisme NOUN MASC **(Roman) Catholicism**

catholique NOUN MASC & FEM, ADJECTIVE **(Roman) Catholic**

cauchemar NOUN MASC **nightmare**; faire un cauchemar to have a nightmare

cause NOUN FEM ❶ **cause**; la cause du problème the cause of the problem ❷ à cause de because of ❸ la cause de quelque chose the reason for something, fermé pour cause de maladie closed for reasons of illness ❹ **cause**; une bonne cause a good cause

causer VERB [1] ❶ to cause ❷ to talk, to chat; causer de quelque chose to talk (or chat) about something, causer avec quelqu'un to talk (or chat) to somebody

caution NOUN FEM ❶ **deposit** *(when renting a flat or house)* ❷ **bail**

cavalier, **cavalière** NOUN MASC, FEM **rider**

cave NOUN FEM **cellar**

caveau NOUN MASC (PLURAL **caveaux**) **vault**

caverne NOUN FEM **cave**

CDI NOUN MASC **school library**

ce[1] *(cet before a vowel or mute 'h')* cette FEM ADJECTIVE ❶ **this**, **that**; ce stylo ne marche pas this pen doesn't work, cette semaine this week, ce couteau-ci this knife ❷ **that**; passe-moi cette assiette pass me that plate, cette chaise-là that chair ❸ cette nuit last night, tonight

ce[2] *(c' before an 'e')* PRONOUN ❶ **this**, **that**, **it**; qui est-ce? who is it?, c'est moi it's me, qu'est-ce que c'est? what is it?, c'est la première maison à gauche it's the first house on the left ❷ **he**, **she**, **they**; c'est un médecin he's a doctor, ce sont les enfants de Paul they're Paul's children ❸ ce qui what, mange ce qui reste eat what's left ❹ ce que what, prends ce que tu veux take what you want ❺ c'est tout ce qui reste that's all that's left, prends tout ce que tu veux take everything you want

ceci PRONOUN **this**; ceci n'est pas à moi this is not mine

cécité NOUN FEM **blindness**

céder VERB [24] ❶ **to give in** ❷ 'cédez le passage' 'give way' *(at a road junction)* ❸ céder sa place to give up your seat ❹ céder à quelque chose to give in to something

cédille NOUN FEM **cedilla**

cèdre NOUN MASC **cedar**

ceinture NOUN FEM ❶ **belt** ❷ **waistband** ❸ **waist**

ceinture de sauvetage NOUN FEM **lifebelt**

ceinture de sécurité NOUN FEM **seatbelt**

cela PRONOUN **this, that, it** *('cela' is used in the same way as 'ça' but is more formal)*; cela ne me concerne pas that does not concern me, cela ne fait rien that doesn't matter

célébration NOUN FEM **celebration**

célèbre ADJECTIVE **famous**

célébrer VERB [24] **to celebrate**

célébrité NOUN FEM ❶ **fame** ❷ **celebrity**

céleri NOUN MASC **celery**

célibataire NOUN MASC & FEM ❶ **bachelor** ❷ **single woman**

célibataire ADJECTIVE **single**; elle est célibataire she's single

celle PRONOUN ▸ SEE **celui**

celle-ci PRONOUN ▸ SEE **celui-ci**

celle-là PRONOUN ▸ SEE **celui-là**

celles PRONOUN ▸ SEE **ceux**

celles-ci PRONOUN ▸ SEE **ceux-ci**

celles-là PRONOUN ▸ SEE **ceux-là**

cellule NOUN FEM ❶ **(prison) cell** ❷ **cell** *(in biology and medicine)* ❸ **unit**

celui, celle PRONOUN **the one**; 'quel livre?' – 'celui qui est sur la table' 'which book?' – 'the one on the table', 'quelle casserole?' – 'celle qui est sur la cuisinière' 'which saucepan?' – 'the one on the cooker'

celui-ci, celle-ci PRONOUN MASC, FEM **this one**

celui-là, celle-là PRONOUN MASC, FEM **that one**

cendre NOUN FEM **ash**; les cendres the ashes

cendrier NOUN MASC **ashtray**

Cendrillon NOUN **Cinderella**

censé ADJECTIVE **supposed**; être censé faire/être to be supposed to do/be, je suis censé être là à dix heures I'm supposed to be there at ten o'clock

cent¹ NUMBER **a hundred, one hundred**; trois cents personnes three hundred people, deux cent cinquante personnes two hundred and fifty people *(note that there is no 's' on 'cent' when it is followed by another number)*

cent² NOUN MASC **cent** *(one hundredth of a euro or dollar)*

centaine NOUN FEM une centaine de personnes a hundred people, a hundred or so people, plusieurs centaines de personnes several hundred people, des centaines de lettres hundreds of letters

centenaire NOUN MASC **centenary**

centième NUMBER **hundredth**

centime NOUN MASC ❶ cent *(one hundredth of a euro)* ❷ centime *(one hundredth of former French currency: the franc)*

centimètre NOUN MASC ❶ centimetre; un centimètre carré a square centimetre, un centimètre cube a cubic centimetre ❷ tape measure

central NOUN MASC un central téléphonique a telephone exchange

central ADJECTIVE MASC (PLURAL centraux) ❶ central ❷ main

centrale NOUN FEM power station; une centrale nucléaire a nuclear power station

centraliser VERB [1] to centralize

centre NOUN MASC centre; au centre de in the centre of, centre de documentation et d'information school library

centre commercial NOUN MASC shopping centre, mall

centre de loisirs NOUN MASC leisure centre

centre sportif NOUN MASC sports centre

centre-ville NOUN MASC town centre, city centre

cependant ADVERB however

cercle NOUN MASC circle; en cercle in a circle

cercueil NOUN MASC coffin

céréale NOUN FEM cereal, grain

cérémonie NOUN FEM ceremony

cerf NOUN MASC stag

cerf-volant NOUN MASC kite

cerise NOUN FEM cherry

cerisier NOUN MASC cherry tree

certain ADJECTIVE ❶ certain, sure; être certain de to be certain (or sure) of ❷ certain; un certain nombre de a certain number of ❸ some; certaines personnes some people

certains PRONOUN some; certains de mes amis some of my friends

certainement ADVERB ❶ most probably ❷ certainly ❸ of course

certes ADVERB admittedly

certificat NOUN MASC certificate

certifier VERB [1] to certify

cerveau NOUN MASC (PLURAL cerveaux) ❶ brain ❷ mind

ces ADJECTIVE ❶ these; c'est Sara qui m'a acheté ces fleurs it was Sara who bought me these flowers ❷ those; ces livres que je t'ai prêtés those books I lent you, ces arbres-là those trees

CES NOUN MASC ; *(Collège d'enseignement secondaire)* secondary school *(from 11 to 15, when students can go on to a 'lycée' for a further 3 years)*

cesse NOUN FEM sans cesse constantly

cesser VERB [1] to stop; cesser de faire to stop doing

cessez-le-feu NOUN MASC ceasefire

c'est-à-dire PHRASE that is, that's to say

cet, cette DETERMINER ▸ SEE ce[1]

ceux, celles PRONOUN the ones; 'quels livres?' – 'ceux qui sont sur la table' 'which books?' – 'the ones

on the table', 'quelles chaussettes?'
– 'celles que tu m'as prêtées hier'
'which socks?' – 'the ones you lent
me yesterday'
► SEE **celui**

ceux-ci, **celles-ci** PRONOUN MASC, FEM
these ones

ceux-là, **celles-là** PRONOUN MASC, FEM
those ones

chacal NOUN MASC jackal

chacun, **chacune** PRONOUN MASC,
FEM ❶ each; ils ont chacun un
billet they each have a ticket
❷ everyone; comme chacun sait
as everyone knows

chagrin NOUN MASC grief

chaîne NOUN FEM ❶ chain ❷ channel
(on TV)

chaîne laser NOUN FEM CD player

chaîne stéréo NOUN FEM stereo
system

chair NOUN FEM ❶ flesh ❷ meat; la
chair à saucisse sausage meat
• avoir la chair de poule to have
goose pimples (literally: to have
hen's flesh)

chaise NOUN FEM chair

châle NOUN MASC shawl

chalet NOUN MASC chalet

chaleur NOUN FEM heat, warmth

chaleureux , **chaleureuse** ADJECTIVE
MASC, FEM warm

chambre NOUN FEM ❶ bedroom;
dans ma chambre in my bedroom
❷ (hotel) room; une chambre
pour une personne a single room,
une chambre pour deux personnes
a double room ❸ la musique de
chambre chamber music

chambre d'amis NOUN FEM spare
bedroom

chambre de commerce NOUN FEM
chamber of commerce

chambres d'hôte PLURAL NOUN FEM
bed and breakfast

chameau NOUN MASC (PLURAL
chameaux) camel

champ NOUN MASC field

champagne NOUN MASC champagne

champ de bataille NOUN MASC
battlefield

champ de courses NOUN MASC
racetrack

champignon NOUN MASC
❶ mushroom; des champignons
de Paris button mushrooms
❷ fungus

champion, **championne** NOUN
MASC, FEM champion

championnat NOUN MASC
championship

chance NOUN FEM ❶ luck; un coup
de chance a stroke of luck, Bonne
chance! Good luck!, j'ai eu la chance
de pouvoir passer un an en France
I was lucky enough to be able to
spend a year in France, avoir de
la chance to be lucky, tu as de la
chance d'avoir une sœur pareille!
you're lucky to have a sister like
that! ❷ chance

chancelier NOUN MASC chancellor

chandail NOUN MASC jumper

chandelier NOUN MASC
❶ candlestick ❷ candelabra

change NOUN MASC exchange rate;
bureau de change bureau de
change (for changing money)

changeant ADJECTIVE **changeable**

changement NOUN MASC **change**

changer VERB [52] ❶ **to change**; tu n'as pas changé you haven't changed ❷ changer quelque chose to change something, changer les draps to change the sheets, changer une prise to change a plug ❸ changer quelque chose to exchange something (in a shop) ❹ changer de to change, changer de train to change trains, changer d'avis to change your mind, j'ai changé d'avis I've changed my mind ❺ se changer to get changed, to change your clothes

chanson NOUN FEM **song**

chant NOUN MASC ❶ **singing** ❷ **song**

chantage NOUN MASC **blackmail**

chanter VERB [1] **to sing**

chanteur, chanteuse NOUN MASC, FEM **singer**

chantier NOUN MASC ❶ **building site** ❷ **roadworks**

chantonner VERB [1] **to hum**

chaos NOUN MASC **chaos**

chaotique ADJECTIVE **chaotic**

chapeau NOUN MASC (PLURAL chapeaux) ❶ **hat** ❷ chapeau! well done!

chapeau melon NOUN MASC **bowler hat**

chapelle NOUN FEM **chapel**

chapelure NOUN FEM **breadcrumbs**

chapiteau NOUN MASC (PLURAL chapiteaux) ❶ **marquee** ❷ **big top** (circus tent)

chapitre NOUN MASC **chapter**

chaque ADJECTIVE **each, every**

char NOUN MASC ❶ **(military) tank** ❷ **carnival float**

charabia NOUN MASC (informal) **gobbledygook, rubbish**

charade NOUN FEM **riddle**

charbon NOUN MASC **coal**

charbon de bois NOUN MASC **charcoal**

charcuterie NOUN FEM ❶ **pork butcher's** (selling salads and ready-prepared dishes as well as pork, bacon, ham, sausages, etc) ❷ **pork products** (ham, salami, pâté, etc)

charcutier, charcutière NOUN MASC, FEM **pork butcher**

chardon NOUN MASC **thistle**

charge NOUN FEM ❶ **load** ❷ **responsibility**; avoir la charge de to be responsible for ❸ charges costs, charges

charger VERB [52] ❶ **to load** ❷ **to charge** (a battery)

chariot NOUN MASC ❶ **trolley** (in a supermarket) ❷ **waggon**

charité NOUN FEM **charity**

charmant ADJECTIVE **charming**

charme NOUN MASC ❶ **charm** ❷ **spell**

charmer VERB [1] **to charm**

charnière NOUN FEM **hinge**

charpentier NOUN MASC **carpenter**

charrette NOUN FEM **cart**

charrue NOUN FEM **plough**

charte NOUN FEM **charter**

a
b
c
d
e
f
g
h
i
j
k
l
m
n
o
p
q
r
s
t
u
v
w
x
y
z

charter *ADJECTIVE* un vol charter a charter flight

chasse *NOUN FEM* hunting, shooting

chasse d'eau *NOUN FEM* (toilet) flush; tirer la chasse d'eau to flush the toilet

chasse-neige *NOUN MASC* snowplough

chasser *VERB* [1] to chase off

chasseur *NOUN MASC* hunter

chat *NOUN MASC* cat

châtaigne *NOUN FEM* sweet chestnut

châtaignier *NOUN MASC* sweet chestnut tree

châtain *ADJECTIVE* les cheveux châtains brown hair

château *NOUN MASC (PLURAL* chateaux) ❶ castle ❷ large country house

château d'eau *NOUN MASC* water tower

chatouiller *VERB* [1] to tickle

chatroom *NOUN MASC* chatroom

chatte *NOUN FEM* (female) cat

chaud *ADJECTIVE* hot, warm; du lait chaud hot milk, un pull chaud a warm jumper, j'ai chaud I'm hot, il fait chaud ici it's hot here

chaudière *NOUN FEM* boiler; une chaudière à gaz a gas boiler

chauffage *NOUN MASC* heating

chauffage central *NOUN MASC* central heating

chauffe-eau *NOUN MASC* water heater

chauffer *VERB* [1] ❶ to heat, to heat up ❷ to warm

chauffeur *NOUN MASC* ❶ driver; un chauffeur de taxi a taxi driver ❷ chauffeur

chaumière *NOUN FEM* thatched cottage

chaussée *NOUN FEM* roadway

chaussette *NOUN FEM* sock

chausson *NOUN MASC* ❶ slipper ❷ ballet shoe

chaussure *NOUN FEM* shoe

chauve *ADJECTIVE* bald

chauve-souris *NOUN FEM* bat

chavirer *VERB* [1] to capsize

chef *NOUN MASC* ❶ leader ❷ head ❸ boss ❹ chef de cuisine chef

chef-d'œuvre *NOUN MASC* masterpiece

chemin *NOUN MASC* ❶ country road ❷ track, path ❸ way; perdre son chemin to lose your way, en chemin on the way

chemin de fer *NOUN MASC* railway

cheminée *NOUN FEM* ❶ chimney ❷ fireplace ❸ mantlepiece

cheminot *NOUN MASC* railway worker

chemise *NOUN FEM* shirt

chemise de nuit *NOUN FEM* nightdress

chemisier *NOUN MASC* blouse

chêne *NOUN MASC* ❶ oak tree ❷ oak; une table en chêne an oak table

chenil NOUN MASC ❶ **dog kennel** ❷ **kennels**

chenille NOUN FEM **caterpillar**

chèque NOUN MASC **cheque**; un carnet de chèques a cheque book

chéquier NOUN MASC **cheque book**

cher, **chère** ADJECTIVE MASC, FEM ❶ **dear**; Chère Anne Dear Anne ❷ **expensive**, **dear**; pas trop cher reasonably priced

cher ADVERB coûter cher to be expensive

chercher VERB [1] ❶ **to look for**; qu'est-ce que tu cherches? what are you looking for?, je cherche mes lunettes I'm looking for my glasses, je cherche un emploi I'm looking for a job ❷ chercher quelque chose to look something up (in a dictionary, for example) ❸ aller chercher to go and get (or fetch) (somebody or something), je vais chercher des verres I'll go and get some glasses ❹ **to pick up**; je viendrai te chercher à l'école I'll come and pick you up from school ❺ chercher à faire to try to do

chercheur, **chercheuse** NOUN MASC, FEM **scientist**

chéri, **chérie** NOUN MASC, FEM **darling**

chérir VERB [2] **to cherish**

cheval NOUN MASC (PLURAL **chevaux**) ❶ **horse**; à cheval on horseback, monter à cheval to ride a horse ❷ faire du cheval to go horseriding

cheval à bascule NOUN MASC **rocking horse**

chevalet NOUN MASC **easel**

chevet NOUN MASC ❶ **bedhead**; au chevet de quelqu'un at somebody's bedside, un livre de chevet a bedside book, une lampe de chevet a bedside lamp ❷ **bedside table**

cheveu (PLURAL **cheveux**) NOUN MASC ❶ un cheveu a hair ❷ les cheveux hair, il a les cheveux blonds he has blond hair
- avoir un cheveu sur la langue to have a lisp (literally: to have a hair on one's tongue)
- couper les cheveux en quatre to split hairs (literally: to cut hairs in four)

cheville NOUN FEM **ankle**

chèvre¹ NOUN FEM **goat**, **nanny-goat**

chèvre² NOUN MASC **goat's cheese**

chèvrefeuille NOUN MASC **honeysuckle**

chevreuil NOUN MASC ❶ **roe deer** ❷ **venison**

chez PREPOSITION ❶ chez quelqu'un at (or to) somebody's house, je vais chez Paul ce soir I'm going to Paul's this evening, elle est chez les Brown she's at the Browns', viens chez moi come round to my place, il est chez lui he's at home, je rentre chez moi maintenant I'm going home now, fais comme chez toi make yourself at home ❷ chez le boucher at (or to) the butcher's, je l'ai rencontrée chez le coiffeur hier I met her at the hairdresser's yesterday, je vais chez le coiffeur demain I'm going to the hairdresser's tomorrow

chic ADJECTIVE ❶ **chic**, **well-dressed** ❷ **nice**; c'était vachement chic de ta part it was really nice of you ❸ Chic! (informal) Cool!

a
b
c
d
e
f
g
h
i
j
k
l
m
n
o
p
q
r
s
t
u
v
w
x
y
z

chicorée NOUN FEM ❶ endive ❷ chicory powder (for adding to coffee)

chien NOUN MASC dog; 'chien méchant' 'beware of the dog'

chien d'aveugle NOUN MASC guide dog

chien de berger NOUN MASC sheepdog

chien de garde NOUN MASC guard dog

chienne NOUN FEM (female) dog, bitch

chiffon NOUN MASC ❶ rag ❷ duster

chiffre NOUN MASC figure; un numéro à cinq chiffres a five-figure number

chignon NOUN MASC bun, chignon

chimie NOUN FEM chemistry

chimique ADJECTIVE chemical

chimpanzé NOUN MASC chimpanzee

Chine NOUN FEM China

chinois NOUN MASC Chinese (language)

chinois ADJECTIVE Chinese

Chinois, Chinoise NOUN MASC, FEM Chinese man, Chinese woman; les Chinois the Chinese

chiot NOUN MASC puppy

chips NOUN FEM crisp; un paquet de chips a packet of crisps

chirurgical ADJECTIVE MASC (PLURAL chirurgicaux) surgical; une intervention chirurgicale an operation

chirurgie NOUN FEM surgery

chirurgie au laser NOUN FEM laser surgery

chirurgien NOUN MASC surgeon

chirurgien-dentiste NOUN MASC dental surgeon

choc NOUN MASC ❶ shock; ça m'a fait un choc it gave me a shock ❷ crash

chocolat NOUN MASC chocolate; chocolat au lait milk chocolate, chocolat blanc white chocolate, chocolat en poudre drinking chocolate, un gâteau au chocolat a chocolate cake, un chocolat chaud a hot chocolate

chœur NOUN MASC ❶ choir (professional) ❷ chorus

choisir VERB [2] to choose

choix NOUN MASC ❶ choice; un bon choix a good choice ❷ un grand choix a wide choice (or variety)

chômage NOUN MASC unemployment; être au chômage to be unemployed

chômeur, chômeuse NOUN MASC, FEM unemployed person

chope NOUN FEM beer mug

choquer VERB [1] to shock

chorale NOUN FEM choir (amateur)

choriste NOUN MASC & FEM ❶ member of a choir ❷ member of a chorus ❸ backing singer

chose NOUN FEM thing; les choses qui m'intéressent the things that interest me, j'ai plusieurs choses à te dire I have several things to tell you, je prends la même chose I'll have the same

chou NOUN MASC (PLURAL **choux**)
cabbage

chouchou[1], **chouchoute** NOUN
MASC, FEM **teacher's pet**

chouchou[2] NOUN MASC **scrunchy** *(for
holding back your hair)*

choucroute NOUN FEM **sauerkraut**
*(pickled cabbage with different types
of sausage, ham, and bacon)*

chou de Bruxelles NOUN MASC
Brussels sprout

chouette NOUN FEM **owl**

chouette ADJECTIVE *(informal)* **great**;
c'est chouette! that's great!, leur
maison est très chouette their
house is really lovely

chou-fleur NOUN MASC (PLURAL
choux-fleurs) **cauliflower**

chrétien, **chrétienne** NOUN MASC,
FEM, ADJECTIVE **Christian**

christianisme NOUN MASC
Christianity

chrome NOUN MASC **chromium**

chronique NOUN FEM ❶ **column**,
page *(devoted to a particular
journalist in a newspaper)* ❷ *(radio)*
programme

chronique ADJECTIVE **chronic**

chronomètre NOUN MASC
stopwatch

chrysanthème NOUN MASC
chrysanthemum

chuchoter VERB [1] **to whisper**

chut EXCLAMATION **shh!**

chute NOUN FEM ❶ **fall**; faire une
chute de 5 mètres to fall 5 metres
❷ chutes de neige snowfall, chutes
de pluie rainfall ❸ **fall**, **drop** *(in
price, value, temperature)*

chuter VERB [1] **to fall**, **to drop**

Chypre NOUN FEM **Cyprus**

ci ADVERB ce mois-ci this month, ces
timbres-ci these stamps, ces jours-
ci these last few days

cible NOUN FEM **target**

ciboulette NOUN FEM
de la ciboulette chives

cicatrice NOUN FEM **scar**

ci-contre ADVERB **opposite**

ci-dessous ADVERB **below**

ci-dessus ADVERB **above**

cidre NOUN MASC **cider**

ciel NOUN MASC (PLURAL **cieux**) ❶ **sky**;
au ciel in the sky ❷ **heaven**

cigale NOUN FEM **cicada**

cigare NOUN MASC **cigar**

cigarette NOUN FEM **cigarette**

cigogne NOUN FEM **stork**

ci-inclus ADJECTIVE **enclosed**; la copie
ci-incluse the enclosed copy

ci-inclus ADVERB **enclosed**

ci-joint ADVERB veuillez trouver
ci-joint please find enclosed *(in a
letter)*

cil NOUN MASC **eyelash**

ciment NOUN MASC **cement**

cimetière NOUN MASC ❶ **cemetery**
❷ **graveyard**

cinéaste NOUN MASC & FEM **film
director**

ciné-club NOUN MASC **film club**

a
b
c
d
e
f
g
h
i
j
k
l
m
n
o
p
q
r
s
t
u
v
w
x
y
z

cinéma NOUN MASC ❶ **cinema**; aller au cinéma **to go to the cinema** ❷ *(informal)* **play-acting**; arrête ton cinéma! **stop that nonsense!**

cinéphile NOUN MASC & FEM **keen cinema-goer**

cinglé ADJECTIVE *(informal)* **crazy**

cinq NUMBER **five**; Lucie a cinq ans **Lucie's five**, à cinq heures **at five o'clock**, le cinq avril **the fifth of April**

cinquantaine NOUN FEM une cinquantaine (de) **about fifty**, une cinquantaine de personnes **about fifty people**, avoir la cinquantaine **to be about fifty**

cinquante NUMBER **fifty**

cinquantième NUMBER **fiftieth**

cinquième NOUN FEM *(in a French school)* **the equivalent of Year 8**

cinquième NOUN MASC au cinquième **on the fifth floor**

cinquième ADJECTIVE **fifth**

cintre NOUN MASC **clothes hanger**

cirage NOUN MASC **shoe polish**

circonférence NOUN FEM **circumference**

circonflexe NOUN MASC un accent circonflexe **a circumflex**

circonstance NOUN FEM **circumstance**

circuit NOUN MASC ❶ **circuit** *(in an athletics stadium)* ❷ **tour** ❸ **(electrical) circuit**

circulaire NOUN FEM, ADJECTIVE **circular**

circulation NOUN FEM ❶ **traffic**; il y a beaucoup de circulation ce soir **there's a lot of traffic this evening** ❷ **circulation**

circuler VERB [1] ❶ **to run** *(of a bus or train)*; ce train ne circule pas le dimanche **that train doesn't run on Sundays** ❷ **to circulate**

cire NOUN FEM **wax**

cirer VERB [1] **to polish**

cirque NOUN MASC **circus**; au cirque **at (or to) the circus**

ciseaux PLURAL NOUN MASC **scissors**; une paire de ciseaux **a pair of scissors**

citadin, citadine NOUN MASC, FEM **city dweller**

citation NOUN FEM **quotation**

cité NOUN FEM ❶ **city, town** ❷ **housing estate** ❸ une cité universitaire **university halls of residence**

citer VERB [1] **to quote**

citerne NOUN FEM **tank**

citoyen, citoyenne NOUN MASC, FEM **citizen**

citron NOUN MASC **lemon**; une tarte au citron **a lemon tart**

citronnade NOUN FEM **still lemonade**

citronnier NOUN MASC **lemon tree**

citron vert NOUN MASC **lime**

citrouille NOUN FEM **pumpkin**

civet NOUN MASC **stew**

civil NOUN MASC ❶ **civilian** ❷ un policier en civil **a plain-clothes policeman**

civil *ADJECTIVE* ❶ civilian ❷ un mariage civil a civil wedding (as opposed to a church wedding)

civilisation *NOUN FEM* civilization

civique *ADJECTIVE* civic

clair *ADJECTIVE* ❶ light; bleu clair light blue ❷ la chambre est très claire the bedroom is very light ❸ clear

clair *ADVERB* clearly; voir clair to see clearly

clair de lune *NOUN MASC* moonlight

clairement *ADVERB* clearly

clapier *NOUN MASC* rabbit hutch

claque *NOUN FEM* slap

claqué *ADJECTIVE* (informal) exhausted, wiped out

claquer *VERB* [1] claquer la porte to slam the door

clarifier *VERB* [1] to clarify

clarinette *NOUN FEM* clarinet; jouer de la clarinette to play the clarinet

clarté *NOUN FEM* ❶ light ❷ clarity

classe *NOUN FEM* ❶ class; elle est dans ma classe à l'école she's in my class (or year) at school, en classe in class ❷ classroom ❸ première/deuxième classe first/second class ❹ (social) class

classement *NOUN MASC* ❶ classification ❷ placing ❸ grading ❹ filing

classer *VERB* [1] ❶ to classify ❷ to grade ❸ to file

classeur *NOUN MASC* ❶ ring binder, file ❷ filing cabinet

classique *ADJECTIVE* ❶ classical ❷ classic ❸ usual; c'est classique! that's typical!

clavier *NOUN MASC* keyboard

clé *NOUN FEM* ❶ key; fermer quelque chose à clé to lock something ❷ spanner

clef ► *SEE* clé

clémentine *NOUN FEM* clementine

clic *NOUN MASC* click (with mouse); un clic sur le bouton droit de la souris a right-click, un clic sur le bouton gauche de la souris a left-click

client, cliente *NOUN MASC, FEM* ❶ customer ❷ client

clientèle *NOUN FEM* customers

cligner *VERB* [1] cligner des yeux to blink

clignotant *NOUN MASC* indicator (on a motor vehicle)

clignoter *VERB* [1] to flash

climat *NOUN MASC* climate

climatisation *NOUN FEM* air-conditioning

climatisé *ADJECTIVE* air-conditioned

clin d'œil *NOUN MASC* wink; faire un clin d'œil à quelqu'un to wink at somebody
- en un clin d'œil in a flash

clinique *NOUN FEM* clinic, private hospital

clip *NOUN MASC* ❶ video clip ❷ clip brooch ❸ clip-on earring

cliquer *VERB* [1] cliquer sur quelque chose to click on something (using a computer mouse)
cliquer en appuyant sur le bouton

a
b
c
d
e
f
g
h
i
j
k
l
m
n
o
p
q
r
s
t
u
v
w
x
y
z

gauche de la souris to left-click
cliquer deux fois sur l'icône to
double-click the icon

cliqueter *VERB* [48] ❶ to jingle ❷ to
rattle

clochard, clocharde *NOUN MASC, FEM*
tramp, down-and-out

cloche *NOUN FEM* bell

clocher *NOUN MASC* ❶ steeple ❷ bell
tower

cloison *NOUN FEM* ❶ partition
❷ partition wall ❸ screen

cloître *NOUN MASC* cloister

clos *ADJECTIVE* closed

clôture *NOUN FEM* ❶ fence ❷ close
❸ closing

clou *NOUN MASC* ❶ nail ❷ stud

clou de girofle *NOUN MASC* clove

clou *NOUN MASC* ❶ nail ❷ stud

clou de girofle *NOUN MASC* clove

clouer *VERB* [1] clouer quelque chose
to nail something down

clown *NOUN MASC* clown

club *NOUN MASC* club; un club de foot
a football club

cobaye *NOUN MASC* guinea pig

Coca *NOUN MASC* Coke

cocaïne *NOUN FEM* cocaine

coccinelle *NOUN FEM* ladybird

cocher *VERB* [1] to tick

cochon *NOUN MASC* pig

cochon, cochonne *ADJECTIVE MASC,
FEM (informal)* dirty *(joke, story)*

cochon d'Inde *NOUN MASC* guinea
pig

cocktail *NOUN MASC* ❶ cocktail
❷ cocktail party

coco *NOUN MASC* une noix de coco a
coconut

cocorico *NOUN MASC* cock-a-doodle-
do

cocotte *NOUN FEM* ❶ casserole
❷ hen *(in baby talk)* ❸ chocolate
hen *(traditionally sold at Easter)*

cocotte-minute *NOUN FEM* pressure
cooker

code *NOUN MASC* ❶ code; le code de
la route the highway code ❷ codes
dipped headlights

code postal *NOUN MASC* postcode

cœur *NOUN MASC* ❶ heart ❷ hearts
(suit of playing cards); le roi de cœur
the king of hearts ❸ par cœur by
heart, apprendre quelque chose
par cœur to learn something by
heart
• avoir mal au cœur to feel sick

coffre *NOUN MASC* ❶ chest ❷ safe
❸ boot *(of a car)*

coffre-fort *NOUN MASC* safe

cogner *VERB* [1] to bump, to bang; se
cogner la tête to bang your head

coiffer *VERB* [1] se coiffer to brush *(or
comb)* your hair

coiffeur, coiffeuse¹ *NOUN MASC, FEM*
hairdresser

coiffeuse² *NOUN FEM* dressing table

coiffure *NOUN* ❶ hairdressing
❷ hairstyle; tu as changé de
coiffure you've changed your
hairstyle

coin *NOUN MASC* ❶ corner; au coin in
the corner, au coin de in the corner

of **②** le café du coin the local cafe, les gens du coin the local people
- au coin du feu by the fireside (*literally: in the corner of the fire*)

coincé *ADJECTIVE* **stuck, jammed**

coincer *VERB* [61] **to jam**

coïncidence *NOUN FEM* **coincidence**

col *NOUN MASC* **❶ collar ❷ neck ❸ (mountain) pass**

colère *NOUN FEM* **anger**; être en colère to be angry

colin *NOUN MASC* **hake**

colique *NOUN FEM* **diarrhoea**

colis *NOUN MASC* **parcel**

collant *NOUN MASC* un collant (a pair of) tights

collant *ADJECTIVE* **sticky**

colle *NOUN FEM* **❶ glue ❷ detention**; une heure de colle an hour's detention

collecte *NOUN FEM* **collection** (*of money*)

collection *NOUN FEM* **collection**

collectionner *VERB* [1] **to collect**

collectionneur, collectionneuse *NOUN MASC, FEM* **collector**

collège *NOUN MASC* **secondary school** (*from 11 to 15, when students can either leave school altogether or go on to a 'lycée' for a further 3 years*)

collégien, collégienne *NOUN MASC, FEM* **schoolboy, schoolgirl**

collègue *NOUN MASC & FEM* **colleague**

coller *VERB* [1] **❶ to stick ❷ to stick down ❸ to glue ❹ to press**

collier *NOUN MASC* **❶ necklace ❷ collar** (*for a dog, cat, etc*)

colline *NOUN FEM* **hill**

collision *NOUN FEM* **collision**

colombe *NOUN FEM* **dove**

colonel *NOUN MASC* **colonel**

colonie *NOUN FEM* **colony**

colonie de vacances *NOUN FEM* **holiday camp** (*for children*)

colonne *NOUN FEM* **column**

colonne vertébrale *NOUN FEM* **spine**

colorant *NOUN MASC* **colouring**

coloré *ADJECTIVE* **❶ coloured ❷ colourful**

colorer *VERB* [1] **to colour**

colorier *VERB* [1] **to colour in**

coloris *NOUN MASC* **colour**; existe en plusieurs coloris several colours available

combat *NOUN MASC* **❶ fighting ❷** un combat de boxe a boxing match

combattant *NOUN MASC* un ancien combattant a war veteran

combattre *VERB* [21] **to fight**

combien *ADVERB* **❶ how much**; tu en veux combien? how much do you want?, c'est combien? how much is it?, ça coûte combien? how much does it cost?, je vous dois combien? how much do I owe you?, how much is that? **❷ how many**; tu en veux combien? how many do you want? **❸** combien de how much, combien d'argent? how much money? **❹** combien de how many, combien de tasses? how many cups?

• nous sommes le combien aujourd'hui? what's the date today? *(literally: we are the how many today?)*

combinaison *NOUN FEM*
❶ **combination** ❷ **jumpsuit**
❸ **overalls** ❹ **slip, petticoat**

combiné *NOUN MASC* **receiver** *(of a telephone)*

comble *NOUN MASC* ❶ **le comble de** the height of, **le comble du luxe** the height of luxury ❷ **ça c'est le comble!** that's the last straw!

comédie *NOUN FEM* **comedy**

comédien, comédienne *NOUN MASC, FEM* **actor, actress**

comestible *ADJECTIVE* **edible**

comique *NOUN MASC* **comic, comedian**

comique *ADJECTIVE* **funny**

comité *NOUN MASC* **committee**

commandant *NOUN MASC*
❶ **major** ❷ **squadron leader**
❸ **commandant-en-chef** commander in chief

commande *NOUN FEM* **order**; **sur commande** to order

commander *VERB* [1] ❶ **to order**; **avez-vous commandé?** have you ordered? ❷ **to be in charge**

comme *PREPOSITION* ❶ **like**; **une montre comme la tienne** a watch like yours ❷ **like**; **comme ça** like this ❸ **as a**; **travailler comme serveur dans un café** to work as a waiter in a cafe ❹ **qu'est-ce que tu veux comme glace?** what kind of ice cream would you like?

comme *CONJUNCTION* ❶ **as**; **comme tu veux** as you like ❷ **as, since**; **comme je suis malade** as (or since) I'm ill ❸ **as**; **comme je fermais la**

porte as I was closing the door
❹ **comme si** as if

comme *ADVERB* **comme il est gentil!** he's so nice!, **comme c'est bon!** it's so good!, **comme il fait chaud!** it's so hot!
• **blanc comme la neige** as white as snow
• **fort comme un bœuf** as strong as an ox

commencement *NOUN MASC* **beginning, start**

commencer *VERB* [61] ❶ **to begin, to start**; **le film a commencé** the film has started ❷ **commencer à faire, commencer de faire** to start (or begin) to do, **elle a commencé à faire ses devoirs** she's started to do her homework, **je commence à comprendre** I'm beginning to understand, **il commence à pleuvoir** it's starting to rain

comment *ADVERB* ❶ **how**; **comment as-tu fait ce gâteau?** how did you make this cake?, **je ne sais pas comment le faire** I don't know how to do it ❷ **comment vas-tu?** how are you?, **comment ça va?** how are you?, **comment va ta mère?** how's your mother? ❸ **comment t'appelles-tu?** what's your name?, **il s'appelle comment, ton frère?** what's your brother's name? ❹ **pardon?** ❺ **comment est leur maison?, elle est comment, leur maison?** what's their house like?

commentaire *NOUN MASC*
❶ **comment** ❷ **commentary**

commenter *VERB* [1] **commenter quelque chose** to comment on something

commerçant, commerçante *NOUN MASC, FEM* **shopkeeper**

commerce NOUN MASC ❶ shop ❷ le commerce business, je fais des études de commerce I'm doing business studies ❸ le commerce trade

commercial ADJECTIVE MASC, (PLURAL commerciaux) ❶ commercial ❷ un centre commercial a shopping centre

commettre VERB [11] ❶ commettre une erreur to make a mistake ❷ commettre un crime to commit a crime

commissariat NOUN MASC police station

commission NOUN FEM ❶ committee ❷ commission ❸ message ❹ errand ❺ faire les commissions to do the shopping

commode NOUN FEM chest of drawers

commode ADJECTIVE ❶ convenient, handy ❷ easy

commun ADJECTIVE ❶ common ❷ shared ❸ joint ❹ en commun in common, ils n'ont rien en commun they have nothing in common ❺ en commun jointly, together ❻ les transports en commun public transport

communauté NOUN FEM community

communication NOUN FEM ❶ une communication téléphonique a telephone call ❷ communication; se mettre en communication avec quelqu'un to get in touch with someone

communion NOUN FEM communion

communiquer VERB [1] ❶ to communicate ❷ communiquer quelque chose to pass something on

communisme NOUN MASC communism

communiste NOUN MASC & FEM, ADJECTIVE communist

compact ADJECTIVE ❶ dense ❷ compact ❸ un disque compact a compact disc, a CD

compagnie NOUN FEM ❶ company, firm ❷ company; elle m'a tenu compagnie she kept me company

compagnie aérienne NOUN FEM airline

compagnon NOUN MASC companion

comparable ADJECTIVE comparable

comparaison NOUN FEM comparison; en comparaison de in comparison with

comparatif, comparative ADJECTIVE MASC, FEM comparative

comparé ADJECTIVE comparé à compared to (or with)

comparer VERB [1] to compare

compartiment NOUN MASC compartment

compas NOUN MASC compass

compatir VERB [2] to sympathize

compensation NOUN FEM compensation

compenser VERB [1] compenser quelque chose to compensate for something

compétence NOUN FEM ❶ ability ❷ skill ❸ competence

compétent ADJECTIVE competent

compétitif, compétitive ADJECTIVE MASC, FEM competitive

compétition NOUN FEM competition

complémentaire ADJECTIVE **further, supplementary**

complet NOUN MASC **suit**

complet, complète ADJECTIVE MASC, FEM ❶ **complete** ❷ **total** ❸ **full** (speaking of a hotel or a train) ❹ le pain complet wholemeal bread

complètement ADVERB **completely**

compléter VERB [24] ❶ **to complete** ❷ **to fill in** (a form)

complexe NOUN MASC, ADJECTIVE **complex**

complication NOUN FEM **complication**

complice NOUN MASC & FEM **accomplice**

compliment NOUN MASC **compliment**; faire des compliments à quelqu'un to compliment somebody

compliqué ADJECTIVE **complicated**

compliquer VERB [1] **to complicate**

complot NOUN MASC **plot**

comportement NOUN MASC **behaviour**

comporter VERB [1] ❶ **to include** ❷ **to consist of** ❸ se comporter to behave

composé ADJECTIVE ❶ composé de made up of ❷ une salade composée a mixed salad

composer VERB [1] ❶ **to make up** ❷ **to put together** ❸ **to compose** (music) ❹ composer un numéro (de téléphone) to dial a (telephone) number, composez le 00 44 pour le Royaume Uni dial 00 44 for the United Kingdom

compositeur, compositrice NOUN MASC, FEM **composer**

composition NOUN FEM **composition**

composter VERB [1] **to punch** (a ticket); 'n'oubliez pas de composter votre billet' remember to punch your ticket (in France you must punch your ticket at the start of your journey in the machine)

compote NOUN FEM **stewed fruit**

compréhensible ADJECTIVE **understandable**

compréhensif, compréhensive ADJECTIVE MASC, FEM **understanding**

compréhension NOUN FEM **comprehension**; un test de compréhension a comprehension test

comprendre VERB [64] ❶ **to understand**; je comprends I understand, j'ai compris I understood, j'ai mal compris I misunderstood ❷ **to include** ❸ se comprendre to understand each other ❹ ça se comprend that's understandable

comprimé NOUN MASC **tablet**

compris ADJECTIVE ❶ **included**; service compris service included, non compris not included ❷ y compris including, tout le monde y compris les enfants everybody including the children

compromis NOUN MASC **compromise**

comptabilité NOUN FEM **accounting, accountancy**

comptable NOUN MASC & FEM **accountant**

compte NOUN MASC **❶ account**; un compte bancaire a bank account, un compte d'épargne a savings account, j'ai cent livres sur mon compte I have a hundred pounds in my account **❷** le compte est bon the amount is correct **❸** se rendre compte de quelque chose to realize something, se rendre compte que to realize that, je me suis rendu compte que j'avais oublié mes clés I realized I had forgotten my keys **❹** tenir compte de quelque chose to take something into account **❺** en fin de compte all things considered

compter VERB [1] **❶ to count**; compter les visiteurs to count the visitors **❷** compter sur quelqu'un to count on somebody **❸ to count** (to be valid); ça ne compte pas that doesn't count

compte rendu NOUN MASC **report**

compteur NOUN MASC **meter**

compteur de vitesse NOUN MASC **speedometer**

comptine NOUN FEM **nursery rhyme**

comptoir NOUN MASC **❶ counter ❷ bar**

concentré ADJECTIVE **concentrated**

concentré de tomate NOUN MASC **tomato puree**

concentrer VERB [1] se concentrer (sur) to concentrate (on)

conception NOUN FEM **design**

concernant PREPOSITION **concerning**

concerner VERB [1] **to concern**; en ce qui me concerne as far as I'm concerned

concert NOUN MASC **concert**; un concert de rock a rock concert

concessionnaire NOUN MASC & FEM **dealer, agent**

concierge NOUN MASC & FEM **caretaker**

conclure VERB [25] **to conclude**

conclusion NOUN FEM **conclusion**

concombre NOUN MASC **cucumber**

concours NOUN MASC **competition**

concret, **concrète** ADJECTIVE MASC, FEM **❶ concrete ❷ practical**

concurrence NOUN FEM **competition**; il y a beaucoup de concurrence there's a lot of competition

concurrent, **concurrente** NOUN MASC, FEM **competitor**

condamner VERB [1] **to sentence** (a criminal)

condition NOUN FEM **❶ condition**; en bonne condition in good condition **❷** à condition de/que provided that, tu peux emprunter mon vélo à condition de me le rendre ce soir you can borrow my bike provided you let me have it back this evening **❸** dans ces conditions in that case

conditionnel NOUN MASC **conditional tense**

conditionner VERB [1] **to package**

conducteur, **conductrice** NOUN MASC, FEM **driver**

conduire VERB [26] **❶ to drive**; apprendre à conduire to learn to drive, un permis de conduire a driving licence, je te conduis à la gare I'll drive you to the station **❷ to take**; je vous conduis à votre chambre I'll take you to your room **❸** se conduire to behave

conduite NOUN FEM **behaviour**;
mauvaise conduite bad behaviour

conférence NOUN FEM ❶ **lecture**
❷ **conference**

confesser VERB [1] se confesser to go
to confession

confiance NOUN FEM ❶ **trust**; avoir
confiance en quelqu'un, faire
confiance à quelqu'un to trust
somebody, je te fais confiance I'll
leave it to you ❷ **confidence**

confiant ADJECTIVE **confident**

confidence NOUN FEM **secret**

confier VERB [1] ❶ confier quelque
chose à quelqu'un to entrust
something to somebody ❷ se
confier à quelqu'un to confide in
somebody

confirmation NOUN FEM
confirmation

confirmer VERB [1] **to confirm**

confiserie NOUN FEM ❶ **sweet shop**
❷ **confectionery**

confisquer VERB [1] **to confiscate**

confit ADJECTIVE les fruits confits
crystallized fruits

confiture NOUN FEM **jam**; la confiture
d'abricots apricot jam

conflit NOUN MASC **conflict**

confondre VERB [69] **to confuse**, to
mix up

confort NOUN MASC **comfort**; tout
confort with all mod cons

confortable ADJECTIVE **comfortable**

confrontation NOUN FEM
❶ **confrontation** ❷ **clash**

confus ADJECTIVE ❶ **confused**
❷ **embarrassed**

confusion NOUN FEM ❶ **confusion**
❷ **embarrassment**

congé NOUN MASC ❶ **holiday** (from
work); Robert est en congé
aujourd'hui Robert's on holiday
today, quel est ton jour de congé?
when's your day off?, je pars en
congé le dix I'm on holiday from
the tenth, prendre une semaine
de congé to take a week's holiday
❷ **leave**; Sylvie est en congé de
maladie Sylvie is on sick leave

congélateur NOUN MASC **freezer**

congeler VERB [45] **to freeze**

congère NOUN FEM **snowdrift**

congestion NOUN FEM **congestion**

congrès NOUN MASC **conference**

conifère NOUN MASC **conifer**

conjoint, **conjointe** NOUN MASC, FEM
spouse (husband or wife)

conjonctive NOUN FEM
conjunctivitis

conjugaison NOUN FEM **conjugation**

connaissance NOUN FEM
❶ **knowledge**; tes connaissances
en français your knowledge
of French ❷ **acquaintance**
❸ **consciousness**; perdre
connaissance to lose consciousness

connaître VERB [27] ❶ **to know**;
est-ce que tu connais Gaby? do
you know Gaby?, je ne connais
pas Londres I don't know London,
je la connais depuis trois ans I've
known her for three years ❷ se

connaître to know each other, on se connaît we know each other ❸ s'y connaître en quelque chose to know about something, je ne m'y connais pas du tout en informatique I know absolutely nothing about computers

connecter VERB [1] **to connect**

connexion NOUN FEM **connection**

connu ADJECTIVE **well-known**; elle est très connue en France she's very well-known in France

consacrer VERB [1] **to devote**

consciemment ADVERB **consciously**

conscience NOUN FEM **conscience**; avoir mauvaise conscience to have a guilty conscience

consciencieux (consciencieuse) ADJECTIVE **conscientious**

conscient ADJECTIVE ❶ **aware**; être conscient de quelque chose to be aware of something ❷ **conscious**

conseil NOUN MASC ❶ **advice**; un conseil a piece of advice, donner un conseil à quelqu'un to give someone a piece of advice, des conseils advice, suivre les conseils de quelqu'un to follow someone's advice ❷ **council**

conseiller¹, **conseillère** NOUN MASC, FEM **adviser**

conseiller² VERB [1] ❶ **to advise**; conseiller à quelqu'un de faire to advise somebody to do, je te conseille de voir un médecin I advise you to see a doctor ❷ **to recommend**; pouvez-vous me conseiller un dentiste? Can you recommend me a dentist?

consentement NOUN MASC **consent**

consentir VERB [58] consentir à quelque chose to agree to something

conséquence NOUN FEM ❶ **consequence** ❷ en conséquence consequently

conséquent ADJECTIVE par conséquent consequently

conservateur, **conservatrice** NOUN MASC, FEM ❶ **conservative** ❷ **(museum) curator**

conservation NOUN FEM ❶ **conservation** ❷ lait longue conservation long-life milk

conserve NOUN FEM ❶ les conserves canned food ❷ en conserve canned, des légumes en conserve canned vegetables

conserver VERB [1] ❶ **to keep**; je t'ai conservé une place I've kept you a seat, 'à conserver au frais' 'keep in a cool place' ❷ se conserver to keep, ce fromage se conserve bien this cheese keeps well

considérable ADJECTIVE **considerable**; un pourcentage considérable des étudiants a considerable percentage of the students

considérablement ADVERB **considerably**

considération NOUN FEM **consideration**

considérer VERB [24] **to consider**

consigne NOUN FEM ❶ **left luggage office** ❷ **deposit** (on a returnable bottle) ❸ **instructions**; consignes à suivre en cas d'incendie fire regulations

consistant *ADJECTIVE* **substantial**; un repas consistant a substantial meal

consister *VERB* [1] consister en to consist of, to consist in

console *NOUN FEM* **console**; une console de jeux a games console

consommateur, consommatrice *NOUN MASC, FEM* ❶ **consumer** ❷ **customer** *(in a cafe)*

consommation *NOUN FEM* ❶ **consumption** *(of fuel, electricity, gas)* ❷ **drink**

consommer *VERB* [1] ❶ **to use** *(fuel)* ❷ **to have a drink** *(in a cafe)*

consonne *NOUN FEM* **consonant**

conspiration *NOUN FEM* **conspiracy**

conspirer *VERB* [1] **to conspire, to plot**

constamment *ADVERB* **constantly**

constant *ADJECTIVE* **constant**

constater *VERB* [1] **to notice**

constipé *ADJECTIVE* **constipated**

construction *NOUN FEM* **construction, building**

construire *VERB* [26] **to build**; construire une maison to build a house, faire construire une maison to have a house built

consul *NOUN MASC* **consul**

consulat *NOUN MASC* **consulate**

consultation *NOUN FEM* ❶ **consultation** ❷ **(doctor's) surgery hours**

consulter *VERB* [1] ❶ **to consult** ❷ **to hold surgery**

contact *NOUN MASC* **contact**; prendre contact avec quelqu'un to contact somebody

contacter *VERB* [1] **to contact**

contagieux, contagieuse *ADJECTIVE MASC, FEM* **infectious**

contamination *NOUN FEM* **contamination**

contaminer *VERB* [1] **to contaminate**

conte *NOUN MASC* **tale, story**; un conte de fées a fairy tale

contempler *VERB* [1] **to look at, to contemplate**

contemporain, contemporaine *NOUN MASC, FEM, ADJECTIVE* **contemporary**

contenant *NOUN MASC* **container**

conteneur *NOUN MASC* **container**

contenir *VERB* [77] **to contain**; 'ne contient pas de sucre' 'does not contain sugar'

content *ADJECTIVE* **pleased, glad, happy**; être content de quelque chose to be pleased with something, elle est très contente de son nouveau travail she's very pleased with her new job, je suis content de te voir I'm pleased to see you

contenter *VERB* [1] ❶ **to satisfy** ❷ se contenter de faire to content oneself with doing

contenu *NOUN MASC* **contents**

contesté *ADJECTIVE* **controversial**

contester *VERB* [1] **to dispute, to challenge, to question**

contexte *NOUN MASC* **context**

continent NOUN MASC **continent**

continu ADJECTIVE **continuous**

continuation NOUN FEM
continuation

continuer VERB [1] **to continue, to
go on (with)**; continue! go on!, elle
a continué son histoire she went
on with her story, continuer à faire,
continuer de faire to go on doing,
elle a continué à parler she went
on talking

contour NOUN MASC **outline, contour**

contourner VERB [1] **to go round**

contraceptif NOUN MASC
contraceptive

contraception NOUN FEM
contraception

contractuel, contractuelle NOUN
MASC, FEM **traffic warden**

contradiction NOUN FEM
contradiction

contradictoire ADJECTIVE
contradictory

contraindre VERB [31] **to force**

contraire NOUN MASC ❶ le contraire
the opposite, c'est le contraire de
ce que je pensais it's the opposite
of what I thought ❷ au contraire on
the contrary

contraire ADJECTIVE **opposite**

contrairement ADVERB
contrairement à contrary to, unlike,
contrairement à ce qu'il nous a dit
contrary to what he told us

contrariant ADJECTIVE **annoying**

contrarier VERB [1] ❶ **to upset** ❷ **to
annoy**

contraste NOUN MASC **contrast**

contraster VERB [1] **to contrast**

contrat NOUN MASC **contract**

contravention NOUN FEM ❶ **parking
ticket** ❷ **speeding ticket**

contre PREPOSITION ❶ **against**; contre
le mur against the wall ❷ être
contre quelque chose to be against
something, je suis plutôt contre on
the whole, I'm against it ❸ jouer
contre quelqu'un to play against
somebody ❹ **versus** ❺ échanger
quelque chose contre to exchange
something for (something else)
❻ par contre on the other hand
• le pour et le contre the pros and
cons

contrebande NOUN FEM
❶ **smuggling** ❷ **smuggled goods**

contrebasse NOUN FEM **double bass**

contredire VERB [47] **to contradict**

contrefaçon NOUN FEM ❶ **forgery**;
méfiez-vous des contrefaçons
beware of forgeries ❷ **forged
signature** ❸ **counterfeit
banknote**

contremaître NOUN MASC **foreman**

contremaîtresse NOUN FEM
supervisor

contreplaqué NOUN MASC **plywood**

contribuable NOUN MASC & FEM
taxpayer

contribuer VERB [1] contribuer à to
contribute to

contribution NOUN FEM
contribution

contrôle NOUN MASC ❶ **control**
❷ **class test** (at school); j'ai un

a
b
c
d
e
f
g
h
i
j
k
l
m
n
o
p
q
r
s
t
u
v
w
x
y
z

contrôle de français cet après-midi
I've got a French test this afternoon
❸ contrôle de police police check
❹ contrôle des passeports passport
control, contrôle des billets ticket
inspection

contrôle continu NOUN MASC
continuous assessment

contrôle des naissances NOUN
MASC **birth control**

contrôler VERB [1] **❶ to check ❷ to
control**

contrôleur, contrôleuse NOUN
MASC, FEM **ticket inspector**

**contrôleur aérien, contrôleuse
aérienne** NOUN MASC, FEM **air traffic
controller**

controversé ADJECTIVE
controversial; une décision
controversée a controversial
decision

convaincant ADJECTIVE **convincing**

convaincre VERB [79] **❶ to convince**;
je ne suis pas convaincu I'm not
convinced **❷ to persuade**; je l'ai
convaincu d'acheter un ordinateur
I persuaded him to buy a computer

convenable ADJECTIVE **❶ suitable
❷ decent**

convenir VERB [81] **❶** convenir à to
suit, to be suitable for, est-ce que
dix heures te convient? does ten
o'clock suit you? **❷** convenir de
faire to agree to do

convention NOUN FEM **❶ agreement
❷ convention**

conversation NOUN FEM
conversation

convertir VERB [2] **to convert**

conviction NOUN FEM **conviction**

convive NOUN MASC & FEM **guest**

convivial ADJECTIVE MASC (PLURAL
conviviaux) **❶ friendly**; une
atmosphère conviviale a friendly
atmosphere **❷ user-friendly**

convoi NOUN MASC **❶ convoy
❷** 'convoi exceptionnel' 'dangerous
load'

convoquer VERB [1] **❶ to invite** (to a
meeting) **❷ to summon**

coopératif, coopérative ADJECTIVE
MASC, FEM **cooperative**

coopération NOUN FEM **cooperation**

coopérative NOUN FEM **cooperative**

coopérer VERB [24] **to cooperate**

coordonnées PLURAL NOUN FEM
address and telephone number

coordonner VERB [1] **to coordinate**

copain NOUN MASC **❶ friend, mate**
(male); je sors avec les copains
I'm going out with my mates
❷ boyfriend; elle est partie en
vacances avec son copain she's
gone on holiday with her boyfriend

copie NOUN FEM **❶ copy ❷ paper** (on
which an exam or class exercise has
been written); j'ai un tas de copies
à corriger ce soir I've got a pile of
marking to do this evening

copier VERB [1] **to copy**

copier-coller VERB [1] **to cut and
paste**; copiez-collez, le tableau cut
and paste the table

copieux, copieuse ADJECTIVE MASC,
FEM **hearty**; un petit déjeuner
copieux a hearty breakfast

copine *NOUN FEM* ❶ **friend, mate** *(female)*; je sors avec les copines I'm going out with my mates ❷ **girlfriend**; il est parti en vacances avec sa copine he's gone on holiday with his girlfriend

coq *NOUN MASC* **cockerel**

coque *NOUN FEM* ❶ **hull** *(of a boat)* ❷ **shell** *(of a nut)* ❸ un œuf à la coque a soft-boiled egg

coquelicot *NOUN MASC* **poppy**

coqueluche *NOUN FEM* **whooping-cough**

coquet, coquette *ADJECTIVE MASC, FEM* ❶ **flirtatious** ❷ **pretty**

coquetier *NOUN MASC* **eggcup**

coquillage *NOUN MASC* ❶ **shellfish** ❷ **seashell**

coquille *NOUN FEM* ❶ **shell** ❷ **misprint**

coquille Saint-Jacques *NOUN FEM* **scallop**

coquin *ADJECTIVE* **cheeky, naughty**

cor *NOUN MASC* **horn** *(musical instrument)*

corail *NOUN MASC (PLURAL* **coraux***)* **coral**

Coran *NOUN MASC* le Coran the Koran

corbeau *NOUN MASC* **crow**

corbeille *NOUN FEM* **basket**; une corbeille à papier a wastepaper basket, une corbeille à linge a linen basket

corbillard *NOUN MASC* **hearse**

corde *NOUN FEM* ❶ **rope** ❷ **string** *(of a racket, a bow, or an instrument such as a guitar or violin)*

- pleuvoir des cordes to be pouring down *(literally: to be raining ropes)*

corde à linge *NOUN FEM* **clothes line**

corde à sauter *NOUN FEM* **skipping rope**

corde d'attache *NOUN FEM* **guy rope**

cordial *ADJECTIVE MASC (PLURAL* cordiaux*)* **warm, cordial**

cordialement *ADVERB* ❶ **warmly** ❷ cordialement à vous Yours sincerely

cordonnerie *NOUN FEM* **shoe repairer's**

cordonnier *NOUN MASC* **shoe repairer**

corne *NOUN FEM* **horn**

cornemuse *NOUN FEM* **bagpipes**; jouer de la cornemuse to play the bagpipes

cornet *NOUN MASC* ❶ un cornet de glace an ice cream cone ❷ un cornet de frites a bag of chips *(in fact sold in a cardboard cornet)*

corniche *NOUN FEM* ❶ **ledge** ❷ **cornice** ❸ (route de) corniche coastal road

cornichon *NOUN MASC* **gherkin**

Cornouailles *NOUN FEM* **Cornwall**

corps *NOUN MASC* **body**

correct *ADJECTIVE* ❶ **correct** ❷ **reasonable, fine**; à un prix correct at a reasonable price, le repas était tout à fait correct the meal was absolutely fine

correctement *ADVERB* ❶ **correctly**; est-ce que vous avez rempli le formulaire correctement? have

you filled in the form correctly?
❷ properly ❸ reasonably well

correcteur orthographique
NOUN MASC spell checker

correction *NOUN FEM* correction

correspondance *NOUN FEM*
❶ letters, correspondence
❷ acheter quelque chose
par correspondance to buy
something by mail order
❸ connection *(a train or flight)*;
j'ai raté ma correspondance I
missed my connection, un vol en
correspondance a connecting flight

**correspondant,
correspondante** *NOUN MASC, FEM*
pen friend

correspondre *VERB* [3] to
correspond

corrida *NOUN FEM* bullfight

corriger *VERB* [52] ❶ to correct ❷ to
mark; elle est en train de corriger
ses copies she's doing her marking

corsage *NOUN MASC* ❶ blouse
❷ bodice

corse *ADJECTIVE* Corsican

Corse¹ *NOUN FEM* Corsica

Corse² *NOUN MASC & FEM* Corsican
(person)

corsé *ADJECTIVE* full-bodied, strong

corvée *NOUN FEM* chore

cosmétiques *PLURAL NOUN MASC*
cosmetics

costaud *ADJECTIVE* strong, sturdy

costume *NOUN MASC* ❶ suit
❷ costume

côte *NOUN FEM* ❶ coast ❷ hill ❸ rib
❹ chop; une côte d'agneau a lamb
chop

côté *NOUN MASC* ❶ side; de l'autre
côté (de) on the other side (of), de
l'autre côté de la rue on the other
side of the street ❷ d'un autre côté
on the other hand ❸ à côté nearby,
mon frère habite à côté my brother
lives nearby ❹ à côté de next to,
beside, elle était assise à côté de
moi she was sitting next to me

Côte d'Azur *NOUN FEM* French
Riviera

côtelette *NOUN FEM* chop; une
côtelette de porc a pork chop

cotisation *NOUN FEM* ❶ subscription
❷ contribution

coton *NOUN MASC* ❶ cotton; un
pull en coton a cotton jumper
❷ sewing cotton ❸ cotton wool

cou *NOUN MASC* neck

couchage *NOUN MASC* un sac de
couchage a sleeping bag

couchant *ADJECTIVE* le soleil couchant
the setting sun, au soleil couchant
at sunset

couche *NOUN FEM* ❶ layer ❷ coat *(of
paint)* ❸ nappy

couche d'ozone *NOUN FEM* ozone
layer

coucher *VERB* [1] ❶ to sleep; tu peux
coucher chez Sophie you can sleep
at Sophie's house ❷ se coucher
to go to bed, elle se couche à dix
heures she goes to bed at ten
o'clock, se coucher avec quelqu'un
to sleep with someone ❸ coucher
un enfant to put a child to bed

coucher de soleil *NOUN MASC*
sunset; un coucher de soleil
magnifique a magnificent sunset

coucou NOUN MASC ❶ cuckoo
❷ cowslip

coude NOUN MASC elbow

coudre VERB [28] to sew; coudre un bouton to sew on a button

couette NOUN FEM duvet, quilt

couler VERB [1] ❶ to flow ❷ avoir le nez qui coule to have a runny nose ❸ faire couler un bain to run a bath ❹ to sink

couleur NOUN FEM colour; de quelle couleur est ta voiture? what colour is your car?

couleuvre NOUN FEM grass snake

coulisses PLURAL NOUN FEM wings (in a theatre)

couloir NOUN MASC corridor

couloir d'autobus NOUN MASC bus lane

coup NOUN MASC blow; il a reçu un coup à l'estomac he was hit in the stomach
- boire un coup (informal) to have a drink
- donner un coup de balai to sweep the floor
- un coup de peinture a lick of paint
- sur le coup at first
- tenir le coup to last out
- tout d'un coup all of a sudden

coupable NOUN MASC & FEM culprit

coupable ADJECTIVE guilty

coup de chance NOUN MASC stroke of luck

coup de feu NOUN MASC (gun)shot

coup de main NOUN MASC donner un coup de main à quelqu'un to give somebody a hand

coup de pied NOUN MASC kick

coup de poing NOUN MASC punch

coup de soleil NOUN MASC attraper un coup de soleil to get sunburnt

coup de téléphone NOUN MASC phone call

coup de tonnerre NOUN MASC clap of thunder

coup de vent NOUN MASC gust of wind

coup d'œil NOUN MASC glance; jeter un coup d'œil à quelque chose to have a quick look at something

coupe NOUN FEM ❶ cup (for sports); la Coupe du Monde the World Cup ❷ haircut ❸ fruit dish

couper VERB [1] ❶ to cut; se faire couper les cheveux to have your hair cut ❷ se couper to cut yourself, se couper le doigt to cut your finger ❸ to cut off, to turn off (gas, electricity) ❹ excuse-moi, je t'ai coupé la parole sorry, I interrupted you

coup franc NOUN MASC free kick

couple NOUN MASC couple

couplet NOUN MASC ❶ verse (of song) ❷ couplet

coupon NOUN MASC ❶ remnant (of fabric) ❷ coupon

coupure NOUN FEM cut; une coupure de courant a power cut

cour NOUN FEM ❶ school playground ❷ inner courtyard (in an apartment block or hotel) ❸ court (of a king or queen) ❹ law court

a
b
c
d
e
f
g
h
i
j
k
l
m
n
o
p
q
r
s
t
u
v
w
x
y
z

courage NOUN MASC ❶ courage, bravery ❷ energy; avoir le courage de faire to have the energy to do ❸ bon courage! good luck!

courageux, courageuse ADJECTIVE MASC, FEM brave

couramment ADVERB fluently

courant NOUN MASC ❶ être au courant de quelque chose to know about something, est-ce que ta sœur est au courant? does your sister know?, je te tiens au courant I'll let you know what happens ❷ current ❸ electricity; couper le courant to cut off (or turn off) the electricity, une panne de courant a power cut

courant ADJECTIVE ❶ common ❷ usual ❸ current

courant d'air NOUN MASC draught

courbe NOUN FEM curve

courber VERB [1] to bend

coureur, coureuse NOUN MASC, FEM runner

courge NOUN FEM (vegetable) marrow

courgette NOUN FEM courgette

courir VERB [29] ❶ to run; traverser la rue en courant to run across the street ❷ courir un risque to run a risk

couronne NOUN FEM crown

courrier NOUN MASC mail, post

courrier électronique NOUN MASC electronic mail, email

cours NOUN MASC ❶ class, lesson; le cours de français the French lesson, suivre des cours d'espagnol to go to Spanish classes ❷ course (of events); au cours de in the course of

course NOUN FEM ❶ race ❷ running

❸ les courses shopping, faire des courses to do some shopping, je fais mes courses à midi I do my shopping at lunchtime

courses hippiques PLURAL NOUN FEM horse racing

court ADJECTIVE short

court-circuit NOUN MASC short-circuit

court de tennis NOUN MASC tennis court

couru VERB ▸ SEE **courir**

cousin, cousine NOUN MASC, FEM cousin; mon cousin germain my first cousin

coussin NOUN MASC cushion

coût NOUN MASC cost; le coût de la vie the cost of living

couteau NOUN MASC (PLURAL couteaux) knife; un couteau à pain a bread knife

coûter VERB [1] to cost; ça coûte combien? how much is it?, ça coûte dix euros it's ten euros, coûter cher to be expensive, est-ce que ça t'a coûté cher? was it expensive?

coutume NOUN FEM custom

couture NOUN FEM ❶ sewing, dressmaking; faire de la couture to sew ❷ seam

couturier NOUN MASC fashion designer

couturière NOUN FEM dressmaker

couvent NOUN MASC convent

couvercle NOUN MASC ❶ lid ❷ screwtop

couvert NOUN MASC place setting; les couverts the cutlery, mettre les couverts to set the table

couvert *ADJECTIVE* ❶ **covered**; un marché couvert a covered market ❷ **couvert de** covered with ❸ **overcast, cloudy**

couverture *NOUN FEM* ❶ **blanket** ❷ **cover** (of a book)

couvre-lit *NOUN MASC* **bedspread**

couvrir *VERB* [30] ❶ **to cover** ❷ **se couvrir to cloud over**, ça s'est couvert dans l'après-midi it clouded over in the afternoon

crabe *NOUN MASC* **crab**

cracher *VERB* [1] **to spit**

crachin *NOUN MASC* **drizzle**

craie *NOUN FEM* **chalk**

craindre *VERB* [31] **to be afraid of**

crainte *NOUN FEM* **fear**

crampe *NOUN FEM* **cramp**

crâne *NOUN MASC* **skull**; avoir mal au crâne (informal) to have a headache

crâner *VERB* [1] (informal) **to show off**

crapaud *NOUN MASC* **toad**

craquement *NOUN MASC* **creak**

craquer *VERB* [1] ❶ **to split** ❷ **to creak** ❸ (informal) **to crack up**
• j'ai craqué I couldn't resist it!

crasse *NOUN FEM* **filth**

cravate *NOUN FEM* **tie**

crawl *NOUN MASC* **crawl** (in swimming); nager le crawl to swim crawl

crayon *NOUN MASC* **pencil**

créatif, créative *ADJECTIVE MASC, FEM* **creative**

création *NOUN FEM* **creation**

créativité *NOUN FEM* **creativity**

crèche *NOUN FEM* ❶ **crèche**, **day nursery** ❷ **nativity scene** (as a Christmas decoration)

crédit *NOUN MASC* ❶ **credit** ❷ **funding**

crédit immobilier *NOUN MASC* **mortgage**

créer *VERB* [32] **to create**

crémaillère *NOUN FEM* **chimney hook** (used in olden times to hang a pot for cooking over the fire)
• pendre la crémaillère to have a house-warming party (literally: to hang the chimney hook)

crème *NOUN FEM, ADJECTIVE* **cream**

crème anglaise *NOUN FEM* **custard**

crème Chantilly *NOUN FEM* **whipped cream**

crémerie *NOUN FEM* **cheese shop**

crémeux, crémeuse *ADJECTIVE MASC, FEM* **creamy**

crêpe *NOUN FEM* **pancake**

crêperie *NOUN FEM* **shop or stall selling** crêpes

crépon *NOUN MASC* **crepe paper**

crépuscule *NOUN MASC* **twilight**

cresson *NOUN MASC* **watercress**

creuser *VERB* [1] ❶ **to dig** ❷ **to hollow out**
• se creuser la cervelle (informal) to rack your brains

creux *NOUN MASC* **hollow**

creux, creuse *ADJECTIVE MASC, FEM* ❶ **hollow** ❷ une assiette creuse a soup plate

crevaison *NOUN FEM* **puncture**

crevé ADJECTIVE ❶ burst ❷ (informal) knackered

crever VERB [50] ❶ to burst; un pneu crevé a burst tyre, a puncture ❷ (informal) to die; je crève de faim! I'm starving!

crevette NOUN FEM prawn

cri NOUN MASC cry, shout

criard ADJECTIVE garish

cric NOUN MASC (car) jack

cricket NOUN MASC cricket; jouer au cricket to play cricket

crier VERB [1] ❶ to shout ❷ to scream

crime NOUN MASC crime

criminel, criminelle NOUN MASC, FEM, ADJECTIVE criminal

crinière NOUN FEM mane

criquet NOUN MASC grasshopper

crise NOUN FEM ❶ crisis ❷ attack (of an illness)

crise cardiaque NOUN FEM heart attack

cristal NOUN MASC (PLURAL cristaux) crystal

critère NOUN MASC criterion

critique[1] NOUN MASC critic

critique[2] NOUN FEM ❶ criticism; les critiques criticism ❷ review (of a film, book, etc)

critique[3] ADJECTIVE critical

critiquer VERB [1] to criticize

Croatie NOUN FEM Croatia

croche-pied NOUN MASC faire un croche-pied à quelqu'un (informal) to trip somebody up

crochet NOUN MASC ❶ hook ❷ detour ❸ crochet

crocodile NOUN MASC crocodile

croire VERB [33] ❶ croire que to think that, je crois qu'il est parti I think he's left, tu crois que c'est trop tard? do you think it's too late?, je ne crois pas I don't think so ❷ to believe; je n'arrive pas à le croire I can't believe it ❸ croire à to believe in ❹ je n'en croyais pas mes yeux! I couldn't believe my eyes!

croiser VERB [1] ❶ to cross; croiser les jambes to cross your legs, croiser les bras to fold your arms ❷ croiser quelqu'un to bump into somebody (meet by chance), j'ai croisé Odile devant la banque I bumped into Odile outside the bank

croisière NOUN FEM cruise

croissance NOUN FEM growth

croissant NOUN MASC croissant

croître VERB [34] to grow

croix NOUN FEM cross

Croix-Rouge NOUN FEM Red Cross

croquant ADJECTIVE crunchy

croque-monsieur NOUN MASC toasted ham sandwich with cheese sauce on top

croque-mort NOUN (informal) MASC undertaker

croquer VERB [1] to munch

croquis NOUN MASC sketch

crottes PLURAL NOUN FEM droppings; des crottes de chien dog dirt

croustillant ADJECTIVE crispy

croûte NOUN FEM ❶ crust ❷ rind (of cheese) ❸ scab

croûton NOUN MASC **crouton**

croyance NOUN FEM **belief**

cru¹ VERB ▸ SEE **croire**

cru² ADJECTIVE **raw, uncooked**

cruauté NOUN FEM **cruelty**; ils ont été traités avec beaucoup de cruauté they were treated with great cruelty

cruche NOUN FEM **(large) jug**

crudités PLURAL NOUN FEM **raw vegetables** (served with dips as a starter)

cruel, cruelle ADJECTIVE MASC, FEM **cruel**

crustacé NOUN MASC **shellfish**

crypte NOUN FEM **crypt**

Cuba NOUN FEM **Cuba**

cubain ADJECTIVE FEM **Cuban**

Cubain, Cubaine NOUN MASC, FEM **Cuban**

cube NOUN MASC **cube**

cube ADJECTIVE **cubic**; un mètre cube a cubic metre

cueillir VERB [35] **to pick** (fruit or flowers)

cuiller NOUN FEM ❶ **spoon** ❷ **spoonful**

cuillère NOUN FEM ▸ SEE **cuiller**

cuillerée NOUN FEM **spoonful**

cuir NOUN MASC **leather**; des chaussures en cuir leather shoes

cuir chevelu NOUN MASC **scalp**

cuire VERB [36] **to cook**

cuisine NOUN FEM ❶ **kitchen** ❷ **cooking**; faire la cuisine to cook, to do the cooking

cuisiner VERB [1] **to cook**

cuisinier, cuisinière¹ NOUN MASC, FEM **cook**

cuisinière² NOUN FEM **cooker**; une cuisinière à gaz a gas cooker, une cuisinière à électrique an electric cooker

cuisse NOUN FEM **thigh**

cuisse de poulet NOUN FEM **chicken leg, chicken thigh**

cuit ADJECTIVE **cooked**; bien cuit well done (meat)

cuivre NOUN MASC **copper**

cuivre jaune NOUN MASC **brass**; un chandelier en cuivre jaune a brass candlestick

culot NOUN MASC (informal) **cheek**; quel culot! what a cheek!, what a nerve!, elle a du culot! she's got a nerve!

culotte NOUN FEM une (petite) culotte **knickers, panties**

culpabilité NOUN FEM **guilt**

cultivateur, cultivatrice NOUN MASC, FEM **farmer**

cultiver VERB [1] ❶ **to grow** ❷ **to cultivate**

culture NOUN FEM ❶ **farming** ❷ **growing**; de culture biologique organically produced ❸ **crop** ❹ **culture**

culturel, culturelle ADJECTIVE MASC, FEM **cultural**

culturisme NOUN MASC **body-building**

cure NOUN FEM **course of treatment**

curé NOUN MASC **parish priest**

cure-dents NOUN MASC **toothpick**

curer VERB [1] se curer les ongles to clean your nails, se curer les dents to pick your teeth

curieux, curieuse ADJECTIVE MASC, FEM ❶ **strange**, **odd** ❷ **curious**, **inquisitive**

curiosité NOUN FEM **curiosity**

curseur NOUN MASC **cursor** (on a computer screen)

cuve NOUN FEM **vat**, **tank**

cuvette NOUN FEM **bowl**; la cuvette des wc the lavatory bowl

cybercafé NOUN MASC **Internet cafe**; où est-ce qu'il y a un cybercafé? where is there an Internet cafe?

cybernaute NOUN MASC & FEM **web surfer**, **cybernaut**

cyclable ADJECTIVE une piste cyclable a cycle track

cycle NOUN MASC **cycle**

cyclisme NOUN MASC **cycling**

cycliste NOUN MASC & FEM **cyclist**

cyclone NOUN MASC **hurricane**

cygne NOUN MASC **swan**

cylindre NOUN MASC ❶ **cylinder** ❷ **roller**

cynique ADJECTIVE **cynical**

cyprès NOUN MASC **cypress (tree)**

d' PREPOSITION ▸ SEE **de**

dactylo NOUN MASC & FEM **typist**

dactylographie NOUN FEM **typing**

daigner VERB [1] to deign

daim NOUN MASC ❶ **suede**; des chaussures en daim suede shoes ❷ **fallow deer**

dalle NOUN FEM **paving slab**

daltonien, daltonienne ADJECTIVE MASC, FEM **colour-blind**

dame NOUN FEM ❶ **lady** ❷ **queen** (in cards or chess)

dames PLURAL NOUN FEM **draughts**; jouer aux dames to play draughts

dancing NOUN MASC **dance hall**

Danemark NOUN MASC **Denmark**; au Danemark to (or in) Denmark

danger NOUN MASC **danger**

dangereux, dangereuse ADJECTIVE MASC, FEM **dangerous**

danois NOUN MASC **Danish** (language)

danois ADJECTIVE **Danish**

Danois, Danoise NOUN MASC, FEM **Danish**

dans PREPOSITION ❶ **in**; elle est dans la cuisine she's in the kitchen ❷ **into**; va dans la cuisine go into the kitchen ❸ dans trois mois in three months' time ❹ boire dans un verre to drink out of a glass

danse NOUN FEM ❶ dance ❷ dancing; faire de la danse to go to dancing classes

danse classique NOUN FEM ballet

danser VERB [1] to dance

danseur, **danseuse** NOUN MASC, FEM dancer

d'après PREPOSITION ❶ according to; d'après le ministre according to the minister ❷ based on; un film d'après le roman de a film based on the novel by ❸ in the style of; un tableau d'après Degas a painting in the style of Degas

date NOUN FEM date

date de naissance NOUN FEM date of birth

date limite NOUN FEM closing date

date limite de vente NOUN FEM sell-by date

datte NOUN FEM date (fruit)

dauphin NOUN MASC dolphin

davantage ADVERB ❶ more ❷ longer

de (d' before a vowel or silent 'h' and de + le becomes 'du' and 'de + les' becomes 'des') PREPOSITION ❶ of; une boîte d'allumettes a box of matches, le pied de la table the leg of the table, the table leg ❷ le père de Marie Marie's father, la maison

de tes parents your parents' house ❸ from; elle vient de Paris she comes from Paris, elle rentre du bureau à six heures she comes home from the office at six o'clock ❹ made from; une table de bois a wooden table ❺ by; le prix a augmenté de vingt euros the price has gone up (by) twenty euros

de DETERMINER du café (some) coffee, veux-tu du café? would you like (some) coffee?, je n'ai pas de café I don't have any coffee, nous avons des pommes et des oranges we have apples and oranges, veux-tu de l'eau? would you like some water?

dé NOUN MASC ❶ dice ❷ un dé à coudre a thimble

dealer NOUN MASC drug pusher

déballer VERB [1] to unpack

débardeur NOUN MASC camisole top, vest-style top

débarquer VERB [1] ❶ to disembark ❷ to land ❸ (informal) to turn up; elle a débarqué chez moi she turned up at my place

débarras NOUN MASC junk room
• bon débarras! good riddance!

débarrasser VERB [1] ❶ to clear out (a room); débarrasser la table to clear the table ❷ se débarrasser de quelque chose to get rid of something, je me suis débarrassé de tous ces vieux bouquins I got rid of all those old books

débat NOUN MASC debate

débattre VERB [21] to discuss, to negotiate; 'prix à débattre' 'price negotiable'

débile ADJECTIVE (informal) **stupid**, **crazy**; tu es débile ou quoi? are you stupid or something?, c'est complètement débile! that's completely crazy!

déblayer VERB [59] **to clear**

débordé ADJECTIVE être débordé to be up to your eyes in work

débordement NOUN MASC ❶ **overflowing** ❷ **flood**

déborder VERB [1] **to overflow**

débouché NOUN MASC **job prospect**; il y a peu de/beaucoup de débouchés pour les jeunes diplômés there are few/many openings for recent graduates

déboucher VERB [1] ❶ **to uncork** (a bottle) ❷ **to unblock** (a drain or pipe) ❸ déboucher sur to lead into

déboussoler VERB [1] (informal) **to confuse**

debout ADVERB ❶ **standing**; rester debout to remain standing, je suis resté debout toute la journée I've been on my feet all day, se mettre debout to stand up, tout le monde s'est mis debout everybody stood up ❷ **upright**; mettre quelque chose debout to stand something upright ❸ **up** (out of bed); je suis debout à six heures tous les jours I'm up at six every day
• ça ne tient pas debout it doesn't make any sense (literally: it doesn't stand upright)

déboutonner VERB [1] **to unbutton**

débrancher VERB [1] ❶ **to unplug** (an iron, a television set, etc) ❷ **to disconnect** (the electricity, gas, water, telephone)

débris NOUN MASC ❶ **fragment** ❷ **piece of wreckage**

débrouiller VERB [1] se débrouiller to manage, je peux me débrouiller tout seul I can manage by myself, débrouille-toi! get on with it!

début NOUN MASC **beginning**, **start**; le début the beginning of, au début at the beginning, to start with, on commencera début mars we'll start at the beginning of March, en début d'après-midi in the early afternoon

débutant, **débutante** NOUN MASC, FEM **beginner**

débuter VERB [1] **to begin**, **to start**

décaféiné ADJECTIVE **decaffeinated**

décalage NOUN MASC ❶ **gap** ❷ **discrepancy**

décalage horaire NOUN MASC **time difference** (between time zones); il y a une heure de décalage horaire entre la France et la Grande-Bretagne there's an hour's time difference between France and Britain

décaler VERB [1] **to move** (forward or back)

décapiter VERB [1] **to behead**

décapotable ADJECTIVE une voiture décapotable a convertible (car)

décapsuleur NOUN MASC **(bottle) opener**

décéder VERB [24] **to die**; elle est décédée au mois de novembre she died in November

décembre NOUN MASC **December**; en décembre, au mois de décembre in December

décemment *ADVERB* **decently**

décennie *NOUN FEM* **decade**

décent *ADJECTIVE* **decent**

déception *NOUN FEM* **disappointment**

décès *NOUN MASC* **death**

décevant *ADJECTIVE* **disappointing**

décevoir *VERB* [66] **to disappoint**

décharge *NOUN FEM* **(public) rubbish tip**

décharger *VERB* [52] **to unload**

déchets *PLURAL NOUN MASC* ❶ **waste**; les déchets nucléaires nuclear waste ❷ **rubbish**

déchiffrer *VERB* [1] **to decipher**

déchirant *ADJECTIVE* **heart-rending**

déchirer *VERB* [1] ❶ **to tear**; j'ai déchiré mon pantalon I've torn my trousers ❷ **to tear up**; déchirer une enveloppe to tear up an envelope ❸ **to tear off**; déchirer une feuille to tear off a sheet of paper ❹ **to tear out**; déchirer une page to tear out a page ❺ se déchirer to tear, to rip

décidé *ADJECTIVE* **determined**

décidément *ADVERB* **really**

décider *VERB* [1] ❶ **to decide**; décider de faire to decide to do, j'ai décidé de vendre mon vélo I've decided to sell my bike ❷ se décider to make up your mind, il faut qu'on se décide une fois pour toutes we must make up our minds once and for all ❸ se décider à faire to decide to do

décimal *NOUN MASC (PLURAL* décimaux*), ADJECTIVE* **decimal**

décimale *NOUN FEM* **decimal**

décision *NOUN FEM* **decision**

déclaration *NOUN FEM* ❶ **statement** ❷ **declaration**

déclarer *VERB* [1] **to declare**

déclencher *VERB* [1] ❶ **to cause** ❷ **to set off**; déclencher l'alarme to set off the alarm

déclic *NOUN MASC* **click**

décliner *VERB* [1] **to decline**

décollage *NOUN MASC* **takeoff** *(of a plane)*

décollé *ADJECTIVE*
• avoir les oreilles décollées to have sticking-out ears *(literally: to have ears which have come unstuck)*

décoller *VERB* [1] ❶ **to take off** *(of a plane)* ❷ décoller quelque chose to peel something off ❸ se décoller to come unstuck, to peel off, le papier peint est en train de se décoller the wallpaper's peeling off

décolleté *ADJECTIVE* **low-cut**

décolorer *VERB* [1] se décolorer to fade, se faire décolorer les cheveux to have your hair lightened

décombres *PLURAL NOUN MASC* **rubble**

décongeler *VERB* [45] **to defrost**

déconseillé *ADJECTIVE* **not recommended**; 'déconseillé pour les enfants' 'not recommended for children'

déconseiller *VERB* [1] déconseiller à quelqu'un de faire to advise somebody not to do, nous lui avons déconseillé de voyager toute seule we advised her not to travel alone

a
b
c
d
e
f
g
h
i
j
k
l
m
n
o
p
q
r
s
t
u
v
w
x
y
z

décontracté ADJECTIVE **relaxed, laid-back**; mon patron est très décontracté my boss is very laid-back

décontracter VERB [1] se décontracter **to relax**

décor NOUN MASC ❶ **decor** ❷ **setting**

décorateur, décoratrice NOUN MASC, FEM **interior designer**

décoratif, décorative ADJECTIVE MASC, FEM ❶ **ornamental** ❷ **decorative**

décoration NOUN FEM ❶ **decorating** ❷ **interior design**

décorer VERB [1] **to decorate**

découper VERB [1] ❶ **to cut out**; découper un article dans un journal to cut an article out of a newspaper ❷ **to carve** (meat); c'est Marie-Laure qui va découper le poulet Marie-Laure's going to carve the chicken

décourageant ADJECTIVE **discouraging**

décourager VERB [52] **to discourage**

découvert NOUN MASC **overdraft**

découverte NOUN FEM **discovery**

découvrir VERB [30] **to discover**

décrire VERB [38] **to describe**

décrocher VERB [1] ❶ **to lift the receiver** (of a telephone); 'décrochez' 'lift the receiver', il faut décrocher avant de composer le numéro you have to lift the receiver before dialling ❷ **to take down** (a picture, curtains, etc)

déçu ADJECTIVE **disappointed**; nous sommes tous très déçus we're all very disappointed

dedans ADVERB ❶ **inside**; elle a ouvert la boîte mais il n'y avait rien dedans she opened the box but there was nothing in it ❷ là-dedans **in there**

dédommager VERB [52] **to compensate**

déduction NOUN FEM **deduction**

déduire VERB [26] ❶ **to deduce** ❷ **to deduct**

déesse NOUN FEM **goddess**

défaire VERB [10] ❶ **to undo, to untie** ❷ se défaire **to come undone** ❸ se défaire de **to get rid of**

défaite NOUN FEM **defeat**

défaut NOUN MASC ❶ **flaw, defect** ❷ à défaut de **for want of**

défavorisé ADJECTIVE **underprivileged**; les défavorisés the underprivileged

défectueux, défectueuse ADJECTIVE MASC, FEM **faulty**; une prise défectueuse a faulty plug

défendre VERB [3] ❶ **to forbid** ❷ **to defend**

défendu ADJECTIVE **forbidden**

défense NOUN ❶ défense de fumer **no smoking** ❷ **defence** ❸ **protection**; la défense de l'environnement the protection of the environment ❹ **tusk** (of an elephant)

défi NOUN MASC **challenge**

déficit NOUN MASC **deficit**

défigurer VERB [1] **to disfigure**

défilé NOUN MASC **❶ parade ❷ procession ❸ march**

défiler VERB [1] **❶ to parade ❷ to march ❸ to come and go**

définir VERB [2] **to define**

définitif, définitive ADJECTIVE MASC, FEM **final, definitive**

définition NOUN FEM **definition**

définitivement ADVERB **❶ for good ❷ definitely**

défoncer VERB [61] **to smash in** (a door)

déformer VERB [1] **❶ to bend out of shape ❷ to distort ❸ to stretch** (a garment or shoes)

défouler VERB [1] **❶ se défouler to let off steam ❷ to unwind**

défunt NOUN MASC **le défunt the deceased**

dégagé ADJECTIVE **❶ clear ❷ casual**

dégager VERB [52] **❶ to clear ❷ to free** (a trapped person)

dégâts PLURAL NOUN MASC **damage**

dégel NOUN MASC **thaw**

dégeler VERB [45] **to thaw**

dégénérer VERB [24] **❶ to degenerate ❷ to go from bad to worse**

dégivrer VERB [1] **❶ to defrost ❷ to de-ice**

dégonfler VERB [1] **to let down** (a tyre, an airbed, etc)

dégouliner VERB [1] **to trickle**

dégourdi ADJECTIVE **smart, bright; un gamin dégourdi a bright kid**

dégoût NOUN MASC **disgust**

dégoûtant ADJECTIVE **❶ filthy; tes mains sont dégoûtantes your hands are filthy ❷ disgusting**

dégoûté ADJECTIVE **disgusted**

dégoûter VERB [1] **❶ to disgust ❷ dégoûter quelqu'un de quelque chose to put somebody off something, ça m'a dégoûté du poisson that put me off fish**

dégrader VERB [1] **❶ to damage ❷ se dégrader to deteriorate**

dégraisser VERB [1] **to dryclean**

degré NOUN MASC **degree**

dégringoler VERB [1] (informal) **to tumble down**

déguisé ADJECTIVE **❶ in fancy dress, in disguise ❷ une soirée déguisée a fancy-dress party ❸ disguised**

déguiser VERB [1] **❶ to disguise ❷ se déguiser to dress up in fancy dress**

dégustation NOUN FEM **tasting; 'dégustation de glaces' 'a fine selection of ice creams'**

déguster VERB [1] **❶ to savour, to enjoy ❷ to taste** (wine, cheese, etc)

dehors ADVERB **❶ outside; je t'attends dehors I'll wait for you outside, j'ai passé toute la journée dehors I've been outside all day ❷ en dehors de apart from, en dehors de la salade, tout est prêt everything's ready apart from the salad**

déjà ADVERB **❶ already; tu pars déjà? are you leaving already?, je t'ai déjà dit de ne pas faire ça! I told you not to do that! ❷ before; tu es déjà venu ici? have you been here before?**

déjeuner NOUN MASC **lunch**; petit déjeuner **breakfast**

déjeuner VERB [1] ❶ **to have lunch**; nous déjeunons à une heure **we have lunch at one o'clock** ❷ **to have breakfast**

délabré ADJECTIVE **dilapidated**

délacer VERB [61] **to unlace**

délai NOUN MASC **period of time, waiting period**

délavé ADJECTIVE ❶ **faded** ❷ **washed-out**

délecter VERB [1] se délecter à faire **to delight in doing**

délégué, déléguée NOUN MASC, FEM ❶ **delegate** ❷ **representative**

délibéré ADJECTIVE **deliberate**

délibérer VERB [24] **to discuss**

délicat ADJECTIVE ❶ **delicate** ❷ **tactful**

délice NOUN MASC **delight**; c'est un vrai délice! **it's absolutely delicious!**

délicieux, délicieuse ADJECTIVE MASC, FEM **delicious**

délinquance NOUN FEM ❶ **crime** ❷ **delinquency**

délinquant, délinquante NOUN MASC, FEM **offender**

délirant ADJECTIVE (informal) **crazy**; c'est complètement délirant! **it's completely crazy!**

délire NOUN MASC ❶ (informal) **madness** ❷ **frenzy**

délirer VERB [1] (informal) **to be crazy**; il délire! **he's crazy!**

délit NOUN MASC **criminal offence**

délivrer VERB [1] **to free, to liberate**

déloyal ADJECTIVE MASC (PLURAL déloyaux) **disloyal**

deltaplane NOUN MASC ❶ **hang-glider** ❷ faire du deltaplane **to go hang-gliding**

déluge NOUN MASC ❶ **downpour** ❷ le Déluge **the Flood** (in the Bible)

demain ADVERB **tomorrow**; à demain! **see you tomorrow!**, après-demain **the day after tomorrow**

demande NOUN FEM ❶ **request** ❷ **demand** ❸ **application**; faire une demande d'emploi **to apply for a job**, 'demandes d'emplois' **'situations wanted'** ❹ **claim**; faire une demande de remboursement auprès d'une compagnie d'assurance **to make a claim on insurance**

demandé ADJECTIVE très demandé **very much in demand, very popular**

demander VERB [1] ❶ demander quelque chose **to ask for something** ❷ demander quelque chose à quelqu'un **to ask somebody (for) something**, demande à ton père! **ask your father!**, il m'a demandé ton adresse **he asked me for your address** ❸ demander à quelqu'un de faire **to ask somebody to do**, elle m'a demandé de téléphoner **she asked me to phone** ❹ se demander **to wonder**, je me demande ce qu'elle est en train de faire **I wonder what she's doing**

demandeur d'emploi NOUN MASC **job-seeker**

démangeaison NOUN FEM **itch**

démanger VERB [52] ça me démange
it itches

démanteler VERB [45] to dismantle

démaquillant NOUN MASC **make-up
remover**

démaquiller VERB [1] se démaquiller
to remove your make-up

démarche NOUN FEM ❶ **walk** ❷ **step**

démarrer VERB [1] ❶ **to start** (of
engine or car); la voiture ne veut pas
démarrer the car won't start ❷ **to
drive off** ❸ **to start up, to start
off**; le projet va démarrer en juin
the project will start up in June

démarreur NOUN MASC **starter** (in
a car)

démêler VERB [1] to untangle

déménagement NOUN MASC **(house)
move, removal**

déménager VERB [52] ❶ **to move
(house)** ❷ **to move out**; nous
déménageons la semaine
prochaine we're moving out next
week ❸ déménager quelque chose
to move something

déménageur NOUN MASC **removal
man**

dément ADJECTIVE **crazy**

démentir VERB [53] ❶ **to deny** ❷ **to
refute**

démesuré ADJECTIVE **excessive**

demeure NOUN FEM **residence,
mansion**

demeurer VERB [1] to reside, to live

demi¹ ADJECTIVE ❶ **half**; trois et demi
three and a half, elle a trois ans et
demi she's three and a half, une
heure et demie an hour and a half

❷ une demi-pomme half an apple,
une demi-bouteille half a bottle ❸ à
deux heures et demie at half past
two, à trois heures et demie at half
past three

demi² NOUN MASC **half** (of beer)

demi-cercle NOUN MASC **semicircle**

demi-douzaine NOUN FEM **half a
dozen**

demie NOUN FEM **half-hour**; à la
demie on the half-hour

demi-écrémé ADJECTIVE **semi-
skimmed**

demi-finale NOUN FEM **semifinal**

demi-frère NOUN MASC **half brother**

demi-heure NOUN FEM une demi-
heure half an hour, toutes les demi-
heures every half hour

demi-journée NOUN FEM **half a day**

demi-litre NOUN MASC **half a litre**

demi-pension NOUN FEM **half board**

demi-sel ADJECTIVE **slightly salted**

demi-sœur NOUN FEM **half sister**

démission NOUN FEM **resignation**;
donner sa démission to resign

démissionner VERB [1] to resign

demi-tarif ADJECTIVE **half-price**

demi-tour NOUN MASC faire demi-
tour to turn back

démocrate NOUN MASC & FEM
democrat

démocrate ADJECTIVE **democratic**

démocratie NOUN FEM **democracy**

démocratique ADJECTIVE
democratic

a
b
c
d
e
f
g
h
i
j
k
l
m
n
o
p
q
r
s
t
u
v
w
x
y
z

démodé *ADJECTIVE* **old-fashioned**

demoiselle *NOUN FEM* **young lady**

demoiselle d'honneur *NOUN FEM* **bridesmaid**

démolir *VERB* [2] **to demolish, to wreck**

démolition *NOUN FEM* **demolition**

démon *NOUN MASC* **demon**

démonstrateur, démonstratrice *NOUN MASC, FEM* **demonstrator** *(for products)*

démonstratif, démonstrative *ADJECTIVE MASC, FEM* **demonstrative**

démonstration *NOUN FEM* ❶ **demonstration** *(of a product, appliance, etc)* ❷ **display**

démonter *VERB* [1] **to dismantle, to take apart**

démontrer *VERB* [1] **to demonstrate, to prove**

démoraliser *VERB* [1] **to demoralize**

démouler *VERB* [1] **to turn out** *(a cake, mousse, etc, from a tin or mould)*

démuni *ADJECTIVE* ❶ **poverty stricken** ❷ **penniless**

dénoncer *VERB* [61] **to denounce**

dénouer *VERB* [1] **to undo**

denrée *NOUN FEM* **foodstuff**

dense *ADJECTIVE* **dense**

densité *NOUN FEM* **density**

dent *NOUN FEM* **tooth**; avoir mal aux dents **to have toothache**

dentaire *ADJECTIVE* **denta**

dent de sagesse *NOUN FEM* **wisdom tooth**

dentelé *ADJECTIVE* ❶ **jagged** ❷ **serrated** ❸ **perforated**

dentelle *NOUN FEM* **lace**

dentier *NOUN MASC* **denture, false teeth**

dentifrice *NOUN MASC* **toothpaste**

dentiste *NOUN MASC & FEM* **dentist**

déodorant *NOUN MASC* **deodorant**

dépannage *NOUN MASC* **repair**; 'dépannages' 'emergency repairs', le service de dépannage the breakdown service, un véhicule de dépannage a breakdown vehicle

dépanner *VERB* [1] ❶ **to fix, to repair** ❷ dépanner quelqu'un *(informal)* **to help somebody out**

dépanneuse *NOUN FEM* **breakdown truck**

départ *NOUN MASC* ❶ **departure**; je t'appellerai avant mon départ I'll phone you before I leave, elle m'a appelé avant son départ she phoned me before she left ❷ au départ at first, to start with

département *NOUN MASC* **department** *(As well as other sorts of department, this is a French numbered administrative area, rather like a county in Britain. The two numbers on the end of vehicle registrations in France show the number of the department where the car is registered)*

dépassé *ADJECTIVE* **outdated, old-fashioned**

dépasser *VERB* [1] ❶ **to overtake** ❷ **to exceed** ❸ ça me dépasse! it's beyond me!

dépêcher VERB [50] se dépêcher to hurry up, dépêche-toi! hurry up!

dépendance NOUN FEM **outbuilding**

dépendre VERB [3] ❶ dépendre de to depend on, ça dépend de l'heure it depends on the time, ça dépend it depends ❷ to be dependent on

dépenser VERB [1] **to spend**

dépenses PLURAL NOUN FEM ❶ **expenses** ❷ **spending**

dépensier, **dépensière** ADJECTIVE MASC, FEM **extravagant**

dépilatoire ADJECTIVE une crème dépilatoire a hair-removing cream

dépistage NOUN MASC **screening**

dépit NOUN MASC en dépit de in spite of

déplacé ADJECTIVE **out of place**

déplacement NOUN MASC **trip**; les frais de déplacement travel expenses

déplacer VERB [61] ❶ to move ❷ se déplacer to travel

déplaire VERB [62] déplaire à quelqu'un to be displeasing to somebody, cela me déplaît I don't like that

déplaisant ADJECTIVE **unpleasant**

dépliant NOUN MASC **leaflet**

déplier VERB [1] **to unfold**

déporter VERB [1] **to deport**

déposer VERB [1] ❶ to put down ❷ to drop off; il m'a déposé à la gare he dropped me off at the station ❸ déposer un chèque to pay in a cheque

dépôt NOUN MASC ❶ **warehouse** ❷ **depot** ❸ **deposit**

dépôt d'ordures NOUN MASC **rubbish tip**

dépoussiérer VERB [24] **to dust**

dépressif, **dépressive** ADJECTIVE MASC, FEM **depressive**

dépression NOUN FEM **depression**; une dépression nerveuse a nervous breakdown

déprimant ADJECTIVE **depressing**

déprimer VERB [1] ❶ to depress ❷ to get depressed; elle déprime en ce moment she's depressed at the moment

depuis PREPOSITION ❶ since; depuis vendredi since Friday, je suis à Paris depuis mardi I've been in Paris since Tuesday, j'habite à Londres depuis avril I've been living in London since April ❷ for; elle habite à Londres depuis cinq ans she's lived in London for five years, je le connais depuis longtemps I've known him for a long time ❸ tu es là depuis combien de temps? how long have you been here?, tu le sais depuis combien de temps? how long have you known?, depuis quand es-tu à Paris? how long have you been in Paris? ❹ depuis que since, depuis que ton frère est à Londres since your brother's been in London

depuis ADVERB since; je ne l'ai pas revu depuis I haven't seen him since

député NOUN MASC **deputy** (the French equivalent of a member of Parliament)

déraciner VERB [1] **to uproot**

a
b
c
d
e
f
g
h
i
j
k
l
m
n
o
p
q
r
s
t
u
v
w
x
y
z

déranger VERB [52] to disturb; 'ne pas déranger' 'do not disturb', excusez-moi de vous déranger sorry to bother you, est-ce que cela vous dérange si j'ouvre la fenêtre? do you mind if I open the window?, cela ne me dérange pas du tout I don't mind at all, ça vous dérange de venir me chercher? do you mind coming to pick me up?

déraper VERB [1] ❶ to skid ❷ to get out of control

dérisoire ADJECTIVE pathetic, trivial; je l'ai acheté pour une somme dérisoire I bought it for next to nothing

dériveur NOUN MASC sailing dinghy

dermatologue NOUN MASC & FEM dermatologist

dernier, dernière ADJECTIVE MASC, FEM ❶ last; le dernier train part à minuit the last train leaves at midnight, jeudi dernier last Thursday, la semaine dernière last week, l'année dernière last year ❷ latest; leur dernier album their latest album ❸ en dernier last, il est arrivé en dernier he arrived last

dernier cri NOUN MASC latest fashion; le dernier cri en matière d'équipement hifi the latest in audio equipment

dernièrement ADVERB recently

dérouler VERB [1] ❶ to unroll, to unwind ❷ se dérouler to take place, ça s'est très bien déroulé it went very well

déroutant ADJECTIVE puzzling

derrière NOUN MASC ❶ back (of an object or a house) ❷ bottom, backside

derrière PREPOSITION behind; derrière la porte behind the door

derrière ADVERB behind; être derrière to be in the back (of the car)

des ARTICLE some, any
▸ SEE **de, un**

dès PREPOSITION ❶ from; dès l'âge de cinq ans from the age of five ❷ dès que as soon as

désagréable ADJECTIVE unpleasant

désarroi NOUN MASC confusion

désastre NOUN MASC disaster

désavantage NOUN MASC disadvantage

désavouer VERB [1] ❶ to deny ❷ to disown

descendre VERB [3] ❶ to go down; descendre les escaliers to go down the stairs ❷ to come down; je descends dans trois secondes! I'll be down in a second! ❸ to get off (a train or bus); je descends à Dijon I'm getting off at Dijon ❹ to get down; pouvez-vous descendre ma valise, s'il vous plaît? could you get my case down for me, please? ❺ to take (or bring) downstairs; je vais descendre mes bagages I'm going to take my luggage downstairs, est-ce que tu peux descendre une chaise de là-haut? could you bring a chair down from upstairs?

descente NOUN FEM descent

descriptif, descriptive ADJECTIVE MASC, FEM descriptive

description NOUN FEM description

déséquilibrer VERB [1] déséquilibrer quelqu'un to throw somebody off balance

désert NOUN MASC **desert**

désert ADJECTIVE **deserted**

déserter VERB [1] **to desert**

désespéré ADJECTIVE ❶ **desperate** ❷ **in despair** ❸ une situation désespérée a hopeless situation

désespérer VERB [24] **to despair, to give up hope**

désespoir NOUN MASC **despair**

déshabiller VERB [1] ❶ se déshabiller to undress, to get undressed ❷ déshabiller quelqu'un to undress somebody

désherbant NOUN MASC **weedkiller**

désherber VERB [1] **to weed**

déshérité NOUN MASC les déshérités the underprivileged

déshériter VERB [1] **to disinherit**

déshydraté ADJECTIVE **dehydrated**

désigner VERB [1] ❶ **to point out** ❷ **to denote**

désinfectant NOUN MASC **disinfectant**

désinfecter VERB [1] **to disinfect**

désir NOUN MASC ❶ **wish** ❷ **desire**

désirer VERB [1] **to want**; que désirez-vous? what would you like?

désobéir VERB [2] ❶ **to be disobedient** ❷ désobéir à quelqu'un to disobey somebody

désobéissant ADJECTIVE **disobedient**

désobligeant ADJECTIVE **unpleasant**

désodorisant NOUN MASC **air freshener**

désolé ADJECTIVE être désolé to be sorry, je suis désolé I'm sorry, désolé de te déranger sorry to disturb you

désopilant ADJECTIVE **hilarious**

désordonné ADJECTIVE **untidy**

désordre NOUN MASC ❶ **untidiness, mess**; être en désordre to be in a mess ❷ **disorder**

désorganisé ADJECTIVE **disorganized**

désorienté ADJECTIVE **disorientated, confused**

désormais ADVERB ❶ **from now on** ❷ **from then on**

desquels, desquelles PRONOUN (de lesquels, de lesquelles) **of which, of whom**

dessécher VERB [24] ❶ **to dry out** ❷ se dessécher to dry out

desserrer VERB [1] **to loosen**

dessert NOUN MASC **dessert, pudding**

desservir VERB [58] le train dessert Vienne et Valence the train calls at Vienne and Valence

dessin NOUN MASC ❶ **drawing**; un cours de dessin a drawing class ❷ un dessin a drawing ❸ **design**

dessin animé NOUN MASC **(animated) cartoon**

dessiner VERB [1] **to draw**

dessin humoristique NOUN MASC **cartoon**

dessous NOUN MASC ❶ **underside**; le dessous du pied the sole of the foot ❷ les voisins du dessous the neighbours below ❸ les dessous underwear ❹ en dessous underneath ❺ en dessous de below

dessous ADVERB **underneath**

dessous-de-plat NOUN MASC **table mat** (for dish)

dessus NOUN MASC ❶ **top**; le dessus du carton the top of the box, un pantalon gris et un dessus rose grey trousers and a pink top ❷ les voisins du dessus the neighbours above ❸ en dessus above ❹ au dessus de above

dessus ADVERB **on top**; quelqu'un a écrit dessus somebody's written on it

dessus-de-lit NOUN MASC **bedspread**

destin NOUN MASC ❶ **fate** ❷ **destiny**

destinataire NOUN MASC & FEM **addressee**

destination NOUN FEM **destination**; le train à destination de Nice the train for Nice, les passagers à destination de Rome passengers travelling to Rome

destiner VERB [1] ❶ destiner quelque chose à to design something for ❷ être destiné à to be intended for ❸ être destiné à faire to be intended to do

détachable ADJECTIVE **detachable**

détachant NOUN MASC **stain remover**

détacher VERB [1] ❶ to untie ❷ to undo ❸ to tear off ❹ to remove ❺ to remove the stains from ❻ se détacher to come off, to come undone

détail NOUN MASC ❶ **detail**; en détail in detail ❷ regarder quelque chose dans le détail to look closely at something ❸ **retail**

détailler VERB [1] **to detail**, **to itemize**; une facture détaillée an itemized bill

détecter VERB [1] **to detect**

détective NOUN MASC **detective**

déteindre VERB [60] ❶ **to fade** ❷ **to run** (in the wash)

détendre VERB [3] ❶ **to be relaxing** ❷ **to relax** ❸ se détendre to relax

détendu ADJECTIVE **relaxed**

détenir VERB [81] ❶ **to detain** ❷ **to keep**

détente NOUN FEM **relaxation**

détenu, **détenue** NOUN MASC, FEM **prisoner**, **detainee**

détergent NOUN MASC **detergent**

détériorer VERB [1] se détériorer to deteriorate

détermination NOUN FEM **determination**

déterminer VERB [1] **to fix**

détestable ADJECTIVE **appalling**, **revolting**

détester VERB [1] **to hate**

détour NOUN MASC **detour**
- ça vaut le détour it's well worth seeing (literally: it's worth the detour)

détournement NOUN MASC un détournement d'avion a highjacking

détourner VERB [1] ❶ **to divert** ❷ détourner un avion to highjack a plane ❸ détourner les yeux to look away

détritus PLURAL NOUN MASC **rubbish**, **refuse**

détruire VERB [26] **to destroy**

dette NOUN FEM debt

deuil NOUN MASC ❶ bereavement ❷ mourning

deux NUMBER ❶ two; deux enfants two children, elle a deux ans she's two, il est deux heures it's two o'clock ❷ deux fois twice ❸ second (in dates); le deux juin the second of June ❹ both; les deux frères both brothers, tous les deux, toutes les deux both, ils sont malades tous les deux, tous les deux sont malades they're both ill, both of them are ill

deuxième NOUN au deuxième on the second floor

deuxième ADJECTIVE pour la deuxième fois for the second time

deuxièmement ADVERB secondly

deux-points NOUN MASC colon

dévaliser VERB [1] to rob

dévaluer VERB [1] to devalue

devant NOUN MASC front

devant PREPOSITION ❶ in front of; elle était devant moi dans la queue she was in front of me in the queue, il l'a dit devant ses parents he said it in front of his parents ❷ outside; devant la boulangerie outside the baker's

développement NOUN MASC development; les pays en voie de développement developing countries

développer VERB [1] ❶ to develop ❷ to expand ❸ se développer to expand, la ville se développe the town is expanding

devenir VERB [81] to become; elle est devenue médecin/infirmière she went into medicine/nursing

déverser VERB [1] ❶ to pour out ❷ to tip out

déviation NOUN FEM diversion

deviner VERB [1] ❶ to guess ❷ to foresee

devinette NOUN FEM riddle

devis NOUN MASC quote, estimate

devises PLURAL NOUN FEM (foreign) currency

dévisser VERB [1] to unscrew

devoir NOUN MASC ❶ exercise, test ❷ devoirs homework, faire ses devoirs to do your homework ❸ duty

devoir VERB [8] ❶ to owe; elle me doit vingt euros she owes me twenty euros, je vous dois combien? how much do I owe you? ❷ to have to; je dois partir à dix heures I have to (or I must) leave at ten o'clock ❸ tu dois être fatigué you must be tired, elle doit avoir quarante ans she must be forty, il a dû oublier he must have forgotten ❹ tu devrais partir you ought to leave, you should leave, tu aurais dû partir you should have left ❺ elle doit arriver à cinq heures she's supposed to arrive at five o'clock

dévorer VERB [1] to devour

dévoué ADJECTIVE devoted

dévouement NOUN MASC devotion

dévouer VERB [1] se dévouer à to devote oneself to

diabète NOUN MASC diabetes

diabétique NOUN MASC & FEM, ADJECTIVE diabetic

diable NOUN MASC devil

a
b
c
d
e
f
g
h
i
j
k
l
m
n
o
p
q
r
s
t
u
v
w
x
y
z

diabolo NOUN MASC **fruit cordial and lemonade**; un diabolo menthe a mint cordial and lemonade

diagnostic NOUN MASC **diagnosis**

diagnostique ADJECTIVE **diagnostic**

diagnostiquer VERB [1] **to diagnose**

diagonal ADJECTIVE MASC (PLURAL diagonaux) **diagonal**

diagonale NOUN FEM **diagonal**; en diagonale diagonally

diagramme NOUN MASC **graph**

dialecte NOUN MASC **dialect**

dialogue NOUN MASC **dialogue**

dialyse NOUN FEM **dialysis**

diamant NOUN MASC **diamond**

diamètre NOUN MASC **diameter**

diapo NOUN FEM (informal) (short for diapositive) **slide**

diapositive NOUN FEM **slide**

diarrhée NOUN FEM **diarrhoea**

dico NOUN MASC (informal) (short for dictionnaire) **dictionary**

dictateur NOUN MASC **dictator**

dictature NOUN FEM **dictatorship**

dictée NOUN FEM **dictation**

dicter VERB [1] **to dictate**

dictionnaire NOUN MASC **dictionary**

dicton NOUN MASC **saying**

diesel NOUN MASC **diesel**

diététique NOUN FEM un magasin de diététique a health-food shop

diététique ADJECTIVE **dietary**

dieu NOUN MASC (PLURAL dieux) **god**

Dieu NOUN MASC **God**; mon Dieu! good heavens!

différemment ADVERB **differently**

différence NOUN FEM ❶ **difference**; quelle est la différence (entre)? what's the difference (between)? ❷ à la différence de unlike

différend NOUN MASC **disagreement**

différent ADJECTIVE ❶ **different**; différent de different from ❷ **various, different**; différentes personnes various people, different people

difficile ADJECTIVE ❶ **difficult, hard**; difficile à faire difficult to do, leur maison est difficile à trouver their house is difficult to find, c'est difficile à imaginer it's hard to imagine ❷ **hard to please, fussy**

difficilement ADVERB **with difficulty**

difficulté NOUN FEM **difficulty**; avoir de la difficulté à faire to have difficulty in doing, j'ai eu de la difficulté à vous joindre I had difficulty getting in touch with you

difforme ADJECTIVE **deformed, misshapen**

difformité NOUN FEM **deformity**

diffuser VERB [1] ❶ **to broadcast** ❷ **to distribute** ❸ **to spread**

digérer VERB [24] **to digest**

digestif NOUN MASC **(after-dinner) liqueur**

digestion NOUN FEM **digestion**

digital ADJECTIVE MASC (PLURAL digitaux) **digital**

digne ADJECTIVE ❶ **worthy**; digne de worthy of, digne de foi trustworthy ❷ **dignified**

dignité NOUN FEM **dignity**

digue NOUN FEM ❶ **sea wall** ❷ **dyke**

dilemme NOUN MASC **dilemma**

diligent ADJECTIVE **diligent**

diluant NOUN MASC **thinner**

diluer VERB [1] ❶ **to dilute** ❷ **to thin** (paint)

dimanche NOUN MASC ❶ **Sunday**; nous sommes dimanche aujourd'hui it's Sunday today, dimanche dernier last Sunday, dimanche prochain next Sunday ❷ **on Sunday**; je t'appellerai dimanche soir I'll ring you on Sunday evening ❸ le dimanche on Sundays, fermé le dimanche closed on Sundays ❹ tous les dimanches every Sunday

dimension NOUN FEM **size**

diminuer VERB [1] ❶ **to reduce** ❷ **to come** (or **go**) **down** ❸ **to decrease** ❹ **to die down**

dinde NOUN FEM **turkey** (as meat)

dindon NOUN MASC **turkey** (when alive)

dîner NOUN MASC **dinner, supper**; inviter quelqu'un à dîner to invite somebody to dinner

dîner VERB [1] **to have dinner**; viens dîner chez nous ce soir come to dinner with us this evening

dingue ADJECTIVE (informal) **crazy**

dinosaure NOUN MASC **dinosaur**

diplomate NOUN MASC & FEM **diplomat**

diplomate ADJECTIVE **diplomatic**

diplomatie NOUN FEM **diplomacy**

diplomatique ADJECTIVE **diplomatic**

diplôme NOUN MASC ❶ **diploma, certificate** ❷ (university) **degree**

diplômé ADJECTIVE **qualified**

dire VERB [9] ❶ **to say**; elle dit qu'elle est malade she says she's ill ❷ **to tell**; dire quelque chose à quelqu'un to tell somebody something, j'ai dit à Anne que tu l'appellerais I told Anne you'd ring her, dire à quelqu'un de faire to tell somebody to do, je leur ai dit de venir à cinq heures I told them to come at five o'clock, on dirait qu'il va pleuvoir it looks like rain, dire la vérité to tell the truth, dire l'heure to tell the time, dire des mensonges to tell lies

direct ADJECTIVE ❶ **direct**; un vol direct a direct flight ❷ (in broadcasting) en direct **de live from**

directement ADVERB ❶ **directly** ❷ aller directement à **to go straight to**

directeur, directrice NOUN MASC, FEM ❶ **director** ❷ **manager** ❸ **head** (of a school)

directeur général, directrice générale NOUN MASC, FEM **managing director**

direction NOUN FEM ❶ **direction**; en direction de towards, in the direction of ❷ **management** ❸ **steering** (of a vehicle)

dirigeant, dirigeante NOUN MASC, FEM **leader**

diriger VERB [52] ❶ **to direct** ❷ **to manage** ❸ **to conduct** (an orchestra) ❹ se diriger vers **to make for**, elle s'est dirigée vers la porte she made for the door

discerner VERB [1] **❶** to make out **❷** to detect

discipline NOUN FEM **❶** discipline **❷** subject (of study)

discipliner VERB [1] **❶** to discipline **❷** to control

disco NOUN MASC **❶** disco **❷** disco music

discothèque NOUN FEM **❶** disco, discotheque **❷** music library

discours NOUN MASC speech

discret, discrète ADJECTIVE MASC, FEM **❶** discreet **❷** quiet **❸** subtle

discrétion NOUN FEM discretion

discrimination NOUN FEM discrimination

discussion NOUN FEM discussion

discutable ADJECTIVE questionable; une décision discutable a questionable decision

discuter VERB [1] **❶** to talk; on peut discuter tranquillement chez moi we can talk in peace at my house **❷** to argue; ça se discute it's arguable **❸** discuter de quelque chose to discuss something, on va en discuter demain we'll discuss it tomorrow

disparaître VERB [27] **❶** to disappear **❷** faire disparaître quelque chose to get rid of something **❸** to die **❹** to die out (traditions, customs)

disparition NOUN FEM **❶** disappearance **❷** une espèce en voie de disparition an endangered species **❸** death

disparu, disparue NOUN MASC, FEM **❶** missing person **❷** les disparus the dead

disparu ADJECTIVE **❶** missing **❷** lost **❸** dead **❹** extinct

dispenser VERB [1] **❶** to hand out **❷** to give **❸** dispenser quelqu'un de to exempt somebody from

disperser VERB [1] **❶** to break up (a crowd or demonstration) **❷** se disperser to break up, la foule s'est dispersée the crowd broke up

disponibilité NOUN FEM availability

disponible ADJECTIVE available

disposé ADJECTIVE **❶** arranged, laid out **❷** être disposé à faire to be willing to do

disposer VERB [1] **❶** to arrange, to lay out **❷** disposer de quelque chose to have something (at your disposal)

dispositif NOUN MASC **❶** device **❷** system

disposition NOUN FEM **❶** arrangement, layout **❷** à ta disposition at your disposal **❸** measure

dispute NOUN FEM argument

disputé ADJECTIVE **❶** contested **❷** controversial

disputer VERB [1] **❶** se disputer to argue, ils se sont disputés they had an argument **❷** se disputer quelque chose to fight over something **❸** se faire disputer (informal) to get told off, je me suis fait disputer par mon patron I got told off by my boss

disqualifier VERB [1] to disqualify

disque NOUN MASC **❶** record; passer un disque to play a record (or CD) **❷** disc **❸** (computer) disk

disque compact NOUN MASC compact disc, CD

disque dur NOUN MASC **hard disk** (of a computer)

disséquer VERB [24] **to dissect**

dissertation NOUN FEM **essay**

dissident, **dissidente** NOUN MASC, FEM **dissident**

dissimuler VERB [1] **to conceal**

dissocier VERB [1] **to separate**

dissolvant NOUN MASC ❶ **nail polish remover** ❷ **solvent**

dissoudre VERB [67] ❶ **dissoudre quelque chose** to dissolve something ❷ **se dissoudre** to dissolve

dissuader VERB [1] ❶ **dissuader quelqu'un de faire** to persuade somebody not to do, to put somebody off doing, **il m'a dissuadé d'y aller** he persuaded me not to go ❷ to deter; **pour dissuader les voleurs** in order to deter thieves

distance NOUN FEM ❶ **distance**; **une distance de cinq kilomètres** a distance of five kilometres, **c'est à quelle distance d'ici?** how far is it from here?, **à distance** from a distance, **l'enseignement à distance** distance learning ❷ **gap**

distant ADJECTIVE **distant**; **distant de** far away from, **un village distant de trois kilomètres** a village three kilometres away

distiller VERB [1] **to distil**

distillerie NOUN FEM **distillery**

distinct ADJECTIVE **distinct**

distinctif, **distinctive** ADJECTIVE MASC, FEM **distinctive**

distinction NOUN FEM **distinction**

distingué ADJECTIVE **distinguished**

distinguer VERB [1] ❶ to make out; **j'ai distingué un bateau à l'horizon** I made out a boat on the horizon ❷ **distinguer entre** to distinguish between

distraction NOUN FEM ❶ **entertainment**; **on a besoin d'un peu de distraction** we need a bit of entertainment ❷ **leisure** ❸ **leisure activity**, **form of entertainment** ❹ **absent-mindedness**

distraire VERB [78] ❶ to amuse, to entertain; **ça m'a distrait un peu** that cheered me up a bit ❷ to distract ❸ **se distraire** to amuse yourself, to enjoy yourself

distrait ADJECTIVE **absent-minded**

distribuer VERB [1] ❶ **to hand out**, **to distribute** ❷ **distribuer les cartes** to deal (in a card game) ❸ **distribuer le courrier** to deliver the mail

distributeur NOUN MASC ❶ **distributor** ❷ **un distributeur automatique** a vending machine ❸ **un distributeur de tickets** a ticket machine ❹ **un distributeur de billets** a cash dispenser

distribution NOUN FEM ❶ **distribution** ❷ **handing out** ❸ **delivery** (of mail) ❹ **cast** (of a play)

diverger VERB [52] **to diverge**

divers ADJECTIVE **various**; **dans divers pays** in various countries

divertir VERB [2] ❶ to amuse, to entertain ❷ **se divertir** to amuse oneself

French—English

A
B
C
D
E
F
G
H
I
J
K
L
M
N
O
P
Q
R
S
T
U
V
W
X
Y
Z

divertissant *ADJECTIVE* **amusing, entertaining**

divin *ADJECTIVE* **divine**

diviser *VERB* [1] **to divide**

division *NOUN FEM* **division**

divorce *NOUN MASC* **divorce**

divorcé *ADJECTIVE* **divorced**; mes parents sont divorcés my parents are divorced

divorcer *VERB* [61] **to get divorced**; ils ont divorcé après dix ans de mariage they got divorced after being married for ten years

dix *NUMBER* **ten**; elle a dix ans she's ten, il est dix heures it's ten o'clock, le dix juillet the tenth of July

dix-huit *NUMBER* **eighteen**; il a dix-huit ans he's eighteen, à dix-huit heures at six p.m

dixième *NOUN MASC* au dixième on the tenth floor

dixième *ADJECTIVE* **tenth**

dix-neuf *NUMBER* **nineteen**; elle a dix-neuf ans she's nineteen, à dix-neuf heures at seven p.m

dix-sept *NUMBER* **seventeen**; elle a dix-sept ans she's seventeen, à dix-sept heures at five p.m

dizaine *NOUN FEM* ❶ **ten** ❷ une dizaine de personnes about ten people

docteur *NOUN MASC* **doctor**

document *NOUN MASC* **document**

documentaire *NOUN MASC, ADJECTIVE* **documentary**

documentaliste *NOUN MASC & FEM* **librarian**

documentation *NOUN FEM* ❶ **documentation** ❷ **material** ❸ **research**

documenter *VERB* [1] se documenter sur quelque chose to gather information on something

dodo *NOUN MASC* faire dodo *(baby talk)* to sleep, on va faire dodo time to tuck up in bed

dogmatique *ADJECTIVE* **dogmatic**

doigt *NOUN MASC* **finger**; se couper le doigt to cut your finger, avoir mal au doigt to have a sore finger
• être à deux doigts de to be within an inch of *(literally: to be two fingers away from)*

doigt de pied *NOUN MASC* **toe**

domaine *NOUN MASC* ❶ **estate** ❷ **field, domain**

dôme *NOUN MASC* **dome**

domestique *NOUN MASC & FEM* **servant**

domestique *ADJECTIVE* **domestic**

domicile *NOUN MASC* ❶ **place of residence** ❷ à domicile at home, travailler à domicile to work at home

dominant *ADJECTIVE* ❶ **dominant** ❷ **main**

dominer *VERB* [1] ❶ **to dominate** ❷ **to control**

dominicain *ADJECTIVE* Dominican, la République dominicaine the Dominican Republic

Dominicain, Dominicaine *NOUN MASC, FEM* **Dominican**

domino *NOUN MASC* **domino**; jouer aux dominos to play dominoes

dommage NOUN MASC ❶ c'est dommage it's a pity, c'est dommage qu'elle n'y soit pas allée it's a pity she didn't go ❷ les dommages damage

dompter VERB [1] to tame

DOM-TOM (short for départements et territoires d'outre-mer) **(French overseas departments and territories)**

don NOUN MASC ❶ gift; faire don de to give ❷ donation; dons en argent cash donations ❸ gift, talent; elle a un don pour les langues she has a gift for languages, avoir le don de faire quelque chose to have the gift of doing something

donc CONJUNCTION so, therefore

donne NOUN FEM deal (in card games)

donné ADJECTIVE given; étant donné que given that

donnée NOUN FEM ❶ fact ❷ données data

donner VERB [1] ❶ to give; donner quelque chose à quelqu'un to give somebody something, elle m'a donné dix euros she gave me ten euros, donne-moi ton adresse give me your address ❷ to give away; il a donné tous ses livres he gave away all his books ❸ ma fenêtre donne sur la rue my window looks onto the street ❹ se donner à quelque chose to devote yourself to something

dont RELATIVE PRONOUN whose, of which; une personne dont j'ai oublié le nom a person whose name I've forgotten, la maison dont je parle the house I'm talking about, six verres dont l'un est cassé six glasses, one of which is broken

doré ADJECTIVE ❶ gold ❷ gilt ❸ golden

dorénavant ADVERB from now on; dorénavant je serai là tous les jours from now on I'll be here every day

dorer VERB [1] ❶ to gild ❷ faire dorer to brown (meat or vegetables)

dormir VERB [37] to sleep; tu as bien dormi? did you sleep well?, elle va dormir chez moi she's going to spend the night at my house, il dort he's asleep

dortoir NOUN MASC dormitory

dos NOUN MASC back; avoir mal au dos to have backache, faire quelque chose dans le dos de quelqu'un to do something behind somebody's back, elle me tournait le dos she had her back to me, il m'a tourné le dos he turned his back on me

dosage NOUN MASC ❶ amount ❷ mixture

dose NOUN FEM ❶ dose ❷ measure

dossier NOUN MASC ❶ file ❷ application form; remplir un dossier to fill in an application form ❸ dossier médical medical records ❹ le dossier d'une chaise the back of a chair

douane NOUN FEM la douane customs, passer la douane to go through customs

douanier NOUN MASC customs officer

double NOUN MASC ❶ le double (de) twice as much, twice as many ❷ copy, duplicate ❸ double

double ADJECTIVE double

doublé ADJECTIVE ❶ lined ❷ dubbed (film)

doublement ADVERB doubly

doubler VERB [1] ❶ to double ❷ to overtake; il m'a doublé dans un virage he overtook me on a bend ❸ to line (a garment) ❹ to dub (a film)

doublure NOUN FEM lining

douce ADJECTIVE ▸ SEE **doux**

doucement ADVERB ❶ gently ❷ slowly ❸ softly

douceur NOUN FEM ❶ softness ❷ gentleness ❸ mildness (of weather)

douche NOUN FEM shower; prendre une douche to take a shower

doucher VERB [1] se doucher to have a shower

doué ADJECTIVE gifted; être doué pour quelque chose to have a gift for something

douillet, douillette ADJECTIVE MASC, FEM cosy

douleur NOUN FEM ❶ pain ❷ grief

douloureux, douloureuse ADJECTIVE MASC, FEM painful

doute NOUN MASC ❶ doubt ❷ sans doute probably

douter VERB [1] ❶ to doubt; douter de to have doubts about ❷ se douter de to suspect, je m'en doutais I thought as much

douteux, douteuse ADJECTIVE MASC, FEM ❶ doubtful ❷ dubious

Douvres NOUN Dover

doux, douce ADJECTIVE MASC, FEM ❶ soft ❷ gentle ❸ mild ❹ sweet

douzaine NOUN FEM ❶ dozen ❷ une douzaine (de) a dozen or so

douze NUMBER twelve; elle a douze ans she's twelve, le douze juillet the twelfth of July

douzième NOUN MASC au douzième on the twelfth floor

douzième ADJECTIVE twelfth

dragée NOUN FEM sugared almond

draguer VERB [1] (informal) draguer quelqu'un to chat somebody up, il est toujours en train de draguer les nanas he's always chatting up the girls, se faire draguer to get chatted up, Carole s'est fait draguer par ton copain Carole got chatted up by your mate

dramatique ADJECTIVE ❶ tragic ❷ dramatic; l'art dramatique drama

drame NOUN MASC ❶ tragedy ❷ drama; il en a fait tout un drame he made a big scene about it

drap NOUN MASC sheet

drapeau NOUN MASC (PLURAL drapeaux) flag

drap-housse NOUN MASC fitted sheet

dresser VERB [1] ❶ to train (an animal) ❷ to put up (a tent) ❸ to draw up (a list) ❹ se dresser to stand up

drogue NOUN FEM drug; la drogue drugs, les drogues douces soft drugs, les drogues dures hard drugs

droguer VERB [1] ❶ to drug, to give drugs to ❷ se droguer to take drugs

droguerie NOUN FEM hardware shop

droit *NOUN MASC* ❶ **right**; les droits de l'homme human rights ❷ avoir le droit de faire to be allowed to do, je n'ai pas le droit de sortir ce soir I'm not allowed to go out tonight ❸ avoir le droit de faire to have the right to do, tu n'as pas le droit de me critiquer you have no right to criticize me ❹ le droit law, un étudiant en droit a law student ❺ fee; les droits d'inscription enrolment fees

droit *ADJECTIVE* ❶ **straight**; une ligne droite a straight line cette ligne n'est pas droite this line is crooked ❷ **right**; ma main droite my right hand ❸ un angle droit a right angle

droit *ADVERB* **straight**; continuez tout droit go straight ahead

droite *NOUN FEM* ❶ **right**; à droite on the right, tourner à droite to turn right, à ta droite on your right ❷ la droite the right *(in politics)*

droitier, droitière *ADJECTIVE MASC, FEM* **right-handed**

drôle *ADJECTIVE* ❶ **funny**; une histoire drôle a funny story, un film très drôle a really funny film ❷ **odd**; un drôle de film an odd film

drôlement *ADVERB* ❶ *(informal)* **really**; c'était drôlement bon! it was really good! ❷ **oddly, peculiarly**

du *ARTICLE* **some, any**
▸ SEE **de**

dû, due, dus *VERB* ▸ SEE **devoir**

duc *NOUN MASC* **duke**

duchesse *NOUN FEM* **duchess**

dune *NOUN FEM* **dune**

duo *NOUN MASC* **duet**

duplex *NOUN MASC* **maisonette**

duquel *PRONOUN*
(short for de lequel)

dur *ADJECTIVE* ❶ **hard** ❷ **tough** *(meat)* ❸ **difficult, hard**

dur *ADVERB* travailler dur to work hard

durant *PREPOSITION* ❶ **for**; des années durant for years ❷ **during**

durcir *VERB* [2] ❶ **to harden** ❷ se durcir to harden

durée *NOUN FEM* **length**

durement *ADVERB* **harshly**

durer *VERB* [1] ❶ **to last** ❷ durer pendant trois mois to go on for three months

dureté *NOUN FEM* ❶ **hardness** ❷ **toughness** ❸ **difficulty**

duvet *NOUN MASC* **sleeping bag**

DVD *NOUN MASC* **DVD**

dynamique *ADJECTIVE* **dynamic, lively**

dyslexique *NOUN MASC & FEM* **dyslexic**

Ee

eau *NOUN FEM* **water**; est-ce que
tu veux de l'eau? would you like
some water?, un verre d'eau
a glass of water, eau gazeuse
sparkling mineral water, eau plate
still mineral water, 'eau potable'
'drinking water', 'eau non potable'
'not drinking water'
• tomber à l'eau to fall through
(*literally: to fall into the water*); nos
projets sont tombés à l'eau our
plans have fallen through
• mettre l'eau à la bouche de
quelqu'un to make somebody's
mouth water; ta sauce sent
tellement bon que ça me met l'eau
à la bouche your sauce smells so
good it's making my mouth water

eau de Javel *NOUN FEM* **bleach**

eau de toilette *NOUN FEM* **toilet
water**

eau minérale *NOUN FEM* **mineral
water**

ébaucher *VERB* [1] ❶ **to sketch** ❷ **to
outline**

ébéniste *NOUN MASC & FEM* **cabinet
maker**

éblouir *VERB* [2] **to dazzle**

éblouissant *ADJECTIVE* **dazzling**

éboueur *NOUN MASC* **refuse collector**

ébouillanter *VERB* [1] **to scald**

ébranler *VERB* [1] **to shake**

ébullition *NOUN FEM* **boiling point**;
porter à ébullition to bring to the
boil

écaille *NOUN FEM* ❶ **scale** (*of a fish or
reptile*) ❷ **tortoiseshell**

écailler *VERB* [1] s'écailler to flake, la
peinture s'écaille the paint's flaking

écart *NOUN MASC* ❶ **gap**, **distance**;
faire un écart to swerve
la voiture a fait un écart pour
éviter le chien the car swerved to
avoid the dog ❷ **difference** ❸ à
l'écart de away from

écarté *ADJECTIVE* ❶ un village écarté
a remote village ❷ les jambes
écartées with legs apart ❸ les bras
écartés with arms outstretched

écarter *VERB* [1] ❶ **to move apart**;
écarter les rideaux to open the
curtains ❷ **to move back**

échafaudage *NOUN MASC*
scaffolding

échalote *NOUN FEM* **shallot**

échange *NOUN MASC* **exchange**; en
échange (de) in exchange (for), in
return (for)

échanger *VERB* [52] **to exchange**,
to swap; nous avons échangé nos
adresses we exchanged addresses

échangeur *NOUN MASC* **(motorway)
interchange**

échantillon *NOUN MASC* **sample**

échapper VERB [1] ❶ échapper à to escape, to escape from, to get away from, le week-end nous échappons à la ville at weekends we get away from the town ❷ s'échapper to escape

écharde NOUN FEM splinter

écharpe NOUN FEM scarf

échasse NOUN FEM stilt

échec NOUN MASC failure

échecs PLURAL NOUN MASC chess; jouer aux échecs to play chess

échelle NOUN FEM ❶ ladder ❷ scale

échelon NOUN MASC ❶ rung ❷ grade

échiquier NOUN MASC chessboard

écho NOUN MASC ❶ echo ❷ des échos rumours

échographie NOUN FEM (medical) scan; passer une échographie to have a scan

échouer VERB [1] to fail; échouer à un examen to fail an exam

éclabousser VERB [1] to splash

éclair NOUN MASC ❶ flash of lightning ❷ un éclair au chocolat a chocolate eclair

éclairage NOUN MASC lighting

éclairagiste NOUN MASC & FEM lighting engineer

éclaircie NOUN FEM sunny interval

éclairer VERB [1] to light (up)

éclat NOUN MASC ❶ splinter, fragment ❷ brightness ❸ splendour ❹ un éclat de rire a roar of laughter

éclatant ADJECTIVE brilliant; des murs d'une blancheur éclatante brilliant white walls

éclater VERB [1] ❶ to burst; un pneu a éclaté a tyre has burst ❷ to shatter; l'ampoule a éclaté the bulb shattered ❸ to break out (war or fighting) ❹ éclater de rire to burst out laughing, éclater en sanglots to burst into tears

éclipse NOUN FEM eclipse

écluse NOUN FEM lock (on a canal or river)

écœurant ADJECTIVE sickly

écœurer VERB [1] to make (somebody) feel sick

école NOUN FEM school; aller à l'école to go to school

école de conduite NOUN FEM driving school

école de langue NOUN FEM language, school

école maternelle NOUN FEM (state) nursery school (age 2-6)

école primaire NOUN FEM primary school (age 6-11)

écolier, écolière NOUN MASC, FEM schoolchild

écologie NOUN FEM ecology

écologique ADJECTIVE ❶ ecological ❷ environmentally friendly

écologiste NOUN MASC & FEM ecologist

économe NOUN MASC potato peeler

économe ADJECTIVE economical

économie NOUN FEM ❶ economy ❷ economics ❸ les économies savings, faire des économies to save up

économique ADJECTIVE ❶ economical ❷ economic

économiser VERB [1] to save

économiste NOUN MASC & FEM economist

écorce NOUN FEM ❶ bark (of a tree) ❷ peel (of an orange or a lemon)

écorcher VERB [1] s'écorcher le genou to graze your knee

écorchure NOUN FEM graze

écossais NOUN MASC tartan (cloth)

écossais ADJECTIVE ❶ Scottish ❷ tartan; une jupe écossaise a tartan skirt

Écossais, Écossaise NOUN MASC, FEM Scotsman, Scotswoman, Scot; les Écossais the Scots

Écosse NOUN FEM Scotland; elle habite en Écosse she lives in Scotland

écourter VERB [1] to shorten

écouter VERB [1] to listen to; j'écoute beaucoup la radio I listen to the radio a lot, écoute-moi listen to me

écouteur NOUN MASC ❶ receiver (on a telephone) ❷ headphones

écran NOUN MASC ❶ screen; à l'écran on the screen, le petit écran television ❷ la crème écran total sun block

écrasant ADJECTIVE crushing, overwhelming; une victoire/ défaite écrasante a crushing victory/defeat

écraser VERB [1] ❶ to crush; écrasez les noix crush the walnuts ❷ to squash; tu vas écraser les pêches! you'll squash the peaches! ❸ écraser une cigarette to stub out a cigarette ❹ se faire écraser to get run over, Attention! Tu vas te faire écraser! Watch out! You'll get run over! ❺ s'écraser to crash, leur voiture s'est écrasée contre un mur their car crashed into a wall

écrémé ADJECTIVE le lait écrémé skimmed milk, le lait demi-écrémé semi-skimmed milk

écrevisse NOUN FEM crayfish

écrire VERB [38] ❶ to write; elle m'a écrit une lettre she wrote me a letter ❷ s'écrire to write to each other, ils s'écrivent tous les jours they write to each other every day ❸ s'écrire to be spelled, comment ça s'écrit? how do you spell it?

écrit NOUN MASC ❶ (piece of) writing ❷ written paper (of an exam); il a réussi à l'oral mais il a raté l'écrit he passed the oral but failed the written paper ❸ à l'écrit in writing

écrit ADJECTIVE written

écriture NOUN FEM handwriting

écrivain NOUN MASC writer

écrou NOUN MASC nut (screwed onto a bolt)

écrouler VERB [1] s'écrouler to collapse

écume NOUN FEM ❶ foam, froth ❷ scum

écureuil NOUN MASC squirrel

écurie NOUN FEM stable

eczéma *NOUN MASC* **eczema**

EDF *(short for Électricité de France)* **French electricity company**

Édimbourg *NOUN* **Edinburgh**

éditer *VERB* [1] **to publish**

éditeur *NOUN MASC* **publisher**

édition *NOUN FEM* ❶ **publishing**; elle travaille dans l'édition she works in publishing ❷ **edition**; une édition de poche a paperback edition

édredon *NOUN MASC* **eiderdown**

éducateur, **éducatrice** *NOUN MASC, FEM* **special needs teacher**

éducatif, **éducative** *ADJECTIVE MASC, FEM* **educational**

éducation *NOUN FEM* **education**; elle a reçu une bonne éducation she had a good education

éducation physique *NOUN FEM* **physical education, PE**

éduquer *VERB* [1] **to educate**

effacer *VERB* [61] **to rub out**

effaceur *NOUN MASC* **correction pen**

effarant *ADJECTIVE* **amazing**

effarer *VERB* [1] **to alarm**

effectivement *ADVERB* **indeed** *(used to show agreement with what someone has just said)*; il est effectivement extrêmement gentil he is indeed extremely nice, oui, elle m'a effectivement téléphoné hier yes, that's right, she did phone me yesterday, 'Tu as oublié tes clés' – 'Ah oui, effectivement!' 'You've left your keys behind' – 'Oh yes, so I

have!', 'Il est maintenant trop tard pour y aller' – 'Oui, effectivement' 'It's too late to go now' – 'Yes, so it is.'

effectuer *VERB* [1] **to make, to carry out**

effet *NOUN MASC* ❶ **effect** ❷ **en effet indeed** *(used to show agreement with what someone has just said)*, elle avait en effet raison she was indeed right, 'il fait très froid' – 'Oui, en effet' 'It's very cold' – 'Yes, it is, isn't it?', 'Tu as laissé la porte ouverte' – 'Oui, en effet' 'You've left the door open' – 'Yes, so I have'

efficace *ADJECTIVE* ❶ **efficient**; elle est très efficace she's very efficient ❷ **effective**; c'est un remède très efficace it's a very effective remedy

efficacité *NOUN FEM* ❶ **efficiency**; il est connu pour son efficacité he's known for his efficiency ❷ **effectiveness**

effondrer *VERB* [1] **s'effondrer to collapse**

efforcer *VERB* [61] **s'efforcer de faire to try hard to do**, elle s'efforce de rester calme she tries hard to remain calm

effort *NOUN MASC* **effort**; faire un effort to make an effort, il n'a même pas fait l'effort de m'appeler he couldn't even be bothered to phone me

effrayant *ADJECTIVE* **frightening**

effrayer *VERB* [59] **to frighten**

effroi *NOUN MASC* **terror**

effronté *ADJECTIVE* **cheeky**

effroyable *ADJECTIVE* **dreadful**

égal, **égale** NOUN MASC (PLURAL égaux) equal

égal ADJECTIVE **❶** equal; une distance égale an equal distance, des quantités égales equal quantities, être égal à to be equal to **❷** ça m'est égal I don't mind, 'Tu veux aller au cinéma ou rester à la maison?' – 'Ça m'est égal' 'Do you want to go to the cinema or stay at home?'- 'I don't mind'

également ADVERB also; elle est également prof d'allemand she's also a German teacher

égaler VERB [1] to equal; trois plus cinq égale huit three plus five equals eight

égaliser VERB [1] to equalize; ils ont égalisé dans la dernière minute they equalized in the last minute

égalité NOUN FEM **❶** equality **❷** les deux joueurs sont à égalité the two players are level

égard NOUN MASC **❶** à l'égard de towards, à mon égard towards me **❷** à cet égard in this respect

égaré ADJECTIVE stray; un chien égaré a stray dog

égarer VERB [1] **❶** to mislay; j'ai égaré mes lunettes I've mislaid my glasses **❷** s'égarer to get lost, nous nous sommes égarés dans les petites rues we got lost in the back streets

égayer VERB [59] **❶** to brighten up; j'ai acheté quelques fleurs pour égayer la pièce I've bought some flowers to brighten up the room **❷** to cheer up; un peu de musique va nous égayer un peu a bit of music will cheer us up a bit

églantine NOUN FEM wild rose

églefin NOUN MASC haddock

église NOUN FEM church; aller à l'église to go to church

égoïsme NOUN MASC selfishness

égoïste ADJECTIVE selfish

égout NOUN MASC sewer

égoutter VERB [1] **❶** to drain (vegetables) **❷** to strain (pasta) **❸** to drip

égratignure NOUN FEM scratch

Égypte NOUN FEM Egypt

eh bien EXCLAMATION well; eh bien, ça me fait plaisir de te revoir well, it's nice to see you again

élancer VERB [61] s'élancer to dash

élargir VERB [2] to widen

élastique NOUN MASC **❶** rubber band **❷** elastic

élastique ADJECTIVE **❶** elastic **❷** elasticated

électeur, **électrice** NOUN MASC, FEM voter

élection NOUN FEM election; une élection présidentielle a presidential election, se présenter aux élections to be a candidate in the elections

électricien, **électricienne** NOUN MASC, FEM electrician

électricité NOUN FEM electricity

électrique ADJECTIVE **❶** electric **❷** electrical

électronique NOUN FEM electronics

électronique ADJECTIVE electronic

élégant ADJECTIVE **elegant**

élément NOUN MASC ❶ **element** ❷ **part**

élémentaire ADJECTIVE **basic**, **elementary**

éléphant NOUN MASC **elephant**

élevage NOUN MASC ❶ **farming** (of livestock) ❷ **farm**; un élevage de porcs a pig farm

élève NOUN MASC & FEM **student**, **pupil**

élevé ADJECTIVE **high**; une note élevée a high mark

élever VERB [50] ❶ élever un enfant to bring up a child, elle a été élevée en Écosse she was brought up in Scotand ❷ **to breed** (animals) ❸ élever la voix to raise one's voice ❹ s'élever **to rise** ❺ s'élever à to amount to, la facture s'élève à cinq cents euros the bill amounts to five hundred euros

éleveur, **éleveuse** NOUN MASC, FEM **breeder**

éliminer VERB [1] ❶ **to eliminate** ❷ **to rule out**; nous ne pouvons pas éliminer cette possibilité we cannot rule out that possibility

élire VERB [51] **to elect**

elle PRONOUN ❶ **she**; où est Sylvie? – elle est dans la cuisine where's Sylvie? – she's in the kitchen ❷ **her**; Paul est avec elle Paul's with her ❸ **it** (when referring to an object which is feminine in French); où est ma tasse? – elle est sur la table where's my cup? – it's on the table

elle-même PRONOUN ❶ **herself**; elle me l'a dit elle-même she told me herself ❷ **itself** (referring to an object which is feminine in French); la pièce elle-même est jolie mais les meubles sont hideux the room itself is pretty but the furniture is hideous

elles PRONOUN ❶ **they** (referring to female people or feminine objects); elles sont arrivées they've arrived ❷ **them**; avec elles with them

elles-mêmes PRONOUN **themselves** (referring to female people or feminine objects)

éloigné ADJECTIVE **distant**; la colline la plus éloignée the most distant hill

éloigner VERB [1] s'éloigner (de) to move away (from)

Élysée NOUN MASC **the Élysée Palace** (the official residence of the French President)

email, **e-mail** NOUN MASC **email**

émail NOUN MASC **enamel**

emballage NOUN MASC **wrapping**

emballer VERB [1] ❶ **to wrap**, **to pack** ❷ (informal) **to get enthusiastic**; elle s'est vraiment emballée pour son nouveau boulot she's got really enthusiastic about her new job, ça ne m'emballe pas vraiment I'm not that keen

embarquement NOUN MASC **boarding**; une carte d'embarquement a boarding card

embarquer VERB [1] ❶ (informal) **to go off with**; elle a embarqué toutes mes chaises she's gone off with all my chairs ❷ s'embarquer to board

embarras NOUN MASC ❶ **embarrassment** ❷ **dilemma**

embarrassé *ADJECTIVE*
❶ embarrassed ❷ cluttered

embarrasser *VERB* [1] ❶ to embarrass ❷ to clutter up

embaucher *VERB* [1] to take on *(an employee)*; ils embauchent en ce moment they're taking people on at the moment

embêtant *ADJECTIVE* annoying; c'est vraiment embêtant! it's really annoying!

embêter *VERB* [1] ❶ to annoy; arrête de m'embêter! stop annoying me! ❷ s'embêter to be bored, on ne s'embête pas ici there's plenty going on here, on ne s'embête pas! we're having a great time!

embouteillage *NOUN MASC* traffic jam

embrasser *VERB* [1] to kiss; je t'embrasse lots of love *(at the end of a letter or said on the phone to a friend)*

embrayage *NOUN MASC* clutch *(in a vehicle)*

émeraude *NOUN FEM* emerald

émerger *VERB* [52] to emerge

émeute *NOUN FEM* riot

émission *NOUN FEM* programme *(on television or radio)*

emménager *VERB* [52] to move in *(to a flat or house)*; nous avons emménagé la semaine dernière we moved in last week

emmener *VERB* [50] to take; c'est sa sœur qui l'emmène à l'école it's his sister who takes him to school, tu veux que je t'emmène? would you like a lift?

émotif, émotive *ADJECTIVE MASC, FEM* emotional

émotion *NOUN FEM* emotion

émouvant *ADJECTIVE* moving

emparer *VERB* [1] s'emparer de to seize

empêcher *VERB* [1] ❶ to prevent, to stop; rien ne t'empêche d'essayer there's nothing to stop you trying ❷ elle n'a pas pu s'empêcher de rire she couldn't help laughing

empereur *NOUN MASC* emperor

empiler *VERB* [1] to pile up

empirer *VERB* [1] to get worse

emplacement *NOUN MASC* site

emploi *NOUN MASC* ❶ job ❷ use; le mode d'emploi instructions for use

emploi du temps *NOUN MASC* timetable *(at school)*

employé, employée *NOUN MASC, FEM* employee

employer *VERB* [39] ❶ to employ ❷ to use

employeur, employeuse *NOUN MASC, FEM* employer

empoisonné *ADJECTIVE* poisoned

empoisonner *VERB* [1] to poison

emporter *VERB* [1] to take (away); 'plats à emporter' 'takeaway meals'

empreinte *NOUN FEM* footprint

empreinte digitale *NOUN FEM* fingerprint

emprisonner *VERB* [1] to imprison

emprunt *NOUN MASC* loan

emprunter *VERB* [1] to borrow

emprunt-logement *NOUN MASC*
mortgage

EMT *NOUN (short for éducation manuelle et technique)* technology *(at school)*

ému *ADJECTIVE* moved

en *PREPOSITION* ❶ in; elle habite en Écosse she lives in Scotland, en été in summer, en avril in April, un livre en anglais a book in English, habillé en noir dressed in black, j'étais en pyjama I was in my pyjamas ❷ into; aller en ville to go into town, traduire en anglais to translate into English ❸ to; aller en Italie to go to Italy ❹ by; en avion by plane ❺ made of; une table en bois a table made of wood, a wooden table ❻ en vacances on holiday ❼ en ami as a friend ❽ en rentrant à la maison j'ai rencontré Tom as I was coming home I met Tom, je me suis brûlé en repassant ma chemise I burned myself (while) ironing my shirt

en *PRONOUN* ❶ j'en ai I've got some, je n'en veux pas I don't want any, tu en as combien? how many (of them) do you have?, how much (of it) do you have?, elle en a quatre she's got four, 'qui a un stylo?' – 'j'en ai un' 'who's got a pen?' – 'I've got one' *(notice that in this sort of expression 'en' is often not translated at all)* ❷ elle m'en a parlé she told me about it ❸ j'ai emprunté ton fer à repasser – est-ce que tu en as besoin? I borrowed your iron – do you need it?

encadrement *NOUN MASC* ❶ frame ❷ framing ❸ door frame

encadrer *VERB* [1] to frame

enceinte *NOUN FEM* ❶ surrounding wall ❷ enclosed space ❸ loudspeaker

enceinte *ADJECTIVE* pregnant

encens *NOUN MASC* incense

encercler *VERB* [1] to surround, to circle

enchanté *ADJECTIVE* ❶ delighted ❷ *(when meeting someone)* enchanté/enchantée pleased to meet you

enchère *NOUN FEM* bid; une vente aux enchères an auction sale

encombrant *ADJECTIVE* bulky

encombrer *VERB* [1] ❶ to clutter ❷ to obstruct

encore *ADVERB* ❶ still; elle est encore au bureau she's still at the office, il reste encore de la viande there's still some meat left ❷ pas encore not yet, il n'est pas encore rentré he hasn't come home yet, he's not home yet ❸ again; je l'ai encore oublié I've forgotten it again ❹ more; encore un peu a little more, encore une fois one more time, attendre encore une semaine to wait for another week ❺ even; encore mieux even better

encourageant *ADJECTIVE* encouraging

encouragement *NOUN MASC* encouragement

encourager *VERB* [52] ❶ to encourage; elle m'a encouragé à suivre des cours de dessin she encouraged me to go to drawing classes ❷ to cheer on *(a team)*

encre *NOUN FEM* ink

encyclopédie *NOUN FEM* encyclopedia

a
b
c
d
e
f
g
h
i
j
k
l
m
n
o
p
q
r
s
t
u
v
w
x
y
z

endive NOUN FEM **chicory**

endommager VERB [52] **to damage**

endormi ADJECTIVE **asleep**

endormir VERB [37] ❶ endormir quelqu'un **to send somebody to sleep** ❷ s'endormir **to fall asleep, to go to sleep**

endroit NOUN MASC ❶ **place**; un bon endroit pour **a good place for** ❷ **the right side** (of a garment) ❸ à l'endroit **the right way up**

énergie NOUN FEM **energy**

énergique ADJECTIVE **energetic**

énervé ADJECTIVE **irritated, annoyed**

énerver VERB [1] ❶ **to irritate, to annoy**; ça m'énerve! **this is getting on my nerves!** ❷ s'énerver **to get annoyed**

enfance NOUN FEM **childhood**

enfant NOUN MASC & FEM **child**; un enfant unique **an only child**

enfantin ADJECTIVE ❶ **easy** ❷ **childish**

enfer NOUN MASC **hell**

enfermer VERB [1] ❶ **to shut up** ❷ s'enfermer **to shut yourself up**, elle s'est enfermée dans sa chambre **she shut herself up in her room**

enfiler VERB [1] ❶ **to put on**; je vais juste enfiler mon pull **I'll just put my jumper on** ❷ enfiler une aiguille **to thread a needle**

enfin ADVERB ❶ **at last**; je l'ai enfin fini **I've finished it at last** ❷ **finally**; elle a enfin réussi **she finally succeeded**

enflé ADJECTIVE **swollen**; il a le genou enflé **his knee is swollen**

enflure NOUN FEM **swelling**

enfoncer VERB [61] ❶ **to push in** ❷ s'enfoncer dans **to sink into**

enfreindre VERB [2] **to disobey**; elle a enfreint les règles **she disobeyed the rules**

engagement NOUN MASC **commitment**

engager VERB [52] ❶ **to take on** (an employee) ❷ **to commit** ❸ s'engager à faire **to promise to do**, je me suis engagé à organiser le repas **I promised to organize the meal**

engelure NOUN FEM **chilblain**

engin NOUN MASC **device**

engourdi ADJECTIVE **numb**; j'ai les doigts engourdis par le froid **my fingers are numb with cold**

engourdir VERB [2] s'engourdir **to go numb**

engrais NOUN MASC **fertilizer**

engueuler VERB [1] (informal) **to tell off**; elle m'a engueulé **she gave me a telling off**, se faire engueuler **to get a telling off**

énième ADJECTIVE **umpteenth**; pour la énième fois **for the umpteenth time**

énigme NOUN FEM **riddle**

enivrer VERB [1] ❶ enivrer quelqu'un **to make somebody drunk** ❷ s'enivrer **to get drunk**

enjeu NOUN MASC (PLURAL enjeux) ❶ **stake** (in a gambling game) ❷ **what is at stake**

enlèvement NOUN MASC **kidnapping**

enlever VERB [50] ❶ to take off (garment); il a enlevé sa veste he took off his jacket ❷ to remove; enlever une tache to remove a stain, tu peux enlever les assiettes you can clear the plates ❸ to kidnap

enneigé ADJECTIVE ❶ snowy ❷ snow-covered

ennemi, ennemie NOUN MASC, FEM enemy

ennui NOUN MASC ❶ boredom ❷ problem; avoir des ennuis to have problems

ennuyé ADJECTIVE ❶ bored ❷ embarrassed

ennuyer VERB [41] ❶ to bore; son discours m'a ennuyé I found his speech boring ❷ to bother; je t'ennuie? am I bothering you? ❸ s'ennuyer to be (or get) bored, j'ai fini par m'ennuyer I got bored in the end, on s'ennuie ici it's boring here

ennuyeux, ennuyeuse ADJECTIVE MASC, FEM ❶ boring ❷ annoying; ça c'est vraiment ennuyeux that's really annoying

énorme ADJECTIVE huge

énormément ADVERB ❶ tremendously ❷ énormément de masses of, j'ai énormément de choses à faire avant de partir I've got masses of things to do before I leave

enquête NOUN FEM ❶ investigation ❷ inquiry ❸ survey

enregistrement NOUN MASC ❶ recording ❷ check-in (at airport)

enregistrer VERB [1] ❶ to record ❷ to register ❸ to check in (at airport)

enrhumer VERB [1] s'enrhumer to catch a cold, être enrhumé to have a cold

enrichir VERB [2] ❶ to make rich ❷ to enrich

enrichissant ADJECTIVE rewarding

enrouler VERB [1] to wind

enseignant, enseignante NOUN MASC, FEM teacher

enseigne NOUN FEM sign; enseigne lumineuse neon sign

enseignement NOUN MASC ❶ teaching ❷ education

enseigner VERB [1] to teach

ensemble NOUN MASC ❶ outfit; j'ai acheté un joli ensemble pour le mariage I've bought a lovely outfit for the wedding ❷ l'ensemble de the whole of ❸ dans l'ensemble on the whole

ensemble ADVERB together; on va y aller ensemble we'll go together, ils sont ensemble depuis trois ans they've been together for three years

ensoleillé ADJECTIVE sunny

ensommeillé ADJECTIVE sleepy

ensuite ADVERB then; on va aller à la banque et ensuite chez Marianne we'll go to the bank and then to Marianne's

entamer VERB [1] to start; ce paquet n'a pas encore été entamé this packet hasn't been started yet

entasser VERB [1] **to pile up**

entendre VERB [3] ❶ **to hear**; est-ce que tu l'entends? can you hear it?, se faire entendre to make yourself heard ❷ j'ai entendu dire que ... I've heard that ... ❸ **to mean**; qu'est-ce que tu entends par là? what do you mean by that? ❹ s'entendre bien to get on well

entendu EXCLAMATION ❶ **okay, fine** ❷ bien entendu of course

entente NOUN FEM ❶ **understanding** ❷ **agreement**

enterrement NOUN MASC **funeral, burial**

enterrer VERB [1] **to bury**

entêté ADJECTIVE **stubborn**

entêter VERB [1] s'entêter à faire to persist in doing

enthousiasme NOUN MASC **enthusiasm**

enthousiasmer VERB [1] s'enthousiasmer to get enthusiastic

enthousiaste ADJECTIVE **enthusiastic**

entier, entière ADJECTIVE MASC, FEM ❶ **whole**; une pomme entière a whole apple, le monde entier the whole world ❷ je n'ai pas lu sa lettre en entier I haven't read his letter right through ❸ le lait entier full-fat milk

entièrement ADVERB **completely, entirely**

entorse NOUN FEM **sprain**; se faire une entorse à la cheville to sprain your ankle

entouré ADJECTIVE entouré de surrounded by, elle est entourée d'amis she's surrounded by friends

entourer VERB [1] **to surround**; entourer de to surround with

entracte NOUN MASC **interval** (at the theatre)

entraînement NOUN MASC ❶ **training** ❷ **practice**

entraîner VERB [1] ❶ **to lead to**; entraîner des problèmes to lead to problems ❷ **to take**; il m'a entraîné chez sa copine he took me off to his girlfriend's ❸ entraîner une équipe to train a team ❹ **to drag** ❺ s'entraîner to train, elle s'entraîne tous les matins she trains every morning

entre PREPOSITION ❶ **between**; entre la porte et la fenêtre between the door and the window, on va le partager entre nous we'll share it between us ❷ **among**; entre eux among themselves ❸ l'un d'entre eux one of them

entrée NOUN FEM ❶ **entrance**; à l'entrée de at the entrance to, billets à l'entrée tickets at the door ❷ **hall(way)** ❸ **admission** ❹ **starter, first course**

entremets NOUN MASC **dessert**

entrepôt NOUN MASC **warehouse**

entreprendre VERB [64] ❶ **to undertake** ❷ **to start**

entreprise NOUN FEM **firm, business**

entrer VERB [1] ❶ **to go in**; entrer dans un magasin to go into a shop, entrer à l'hôpital to go into hospital ❷ **to come in**; entrer dans to come into, Entrez! Come in!

entre-temps ADVERB **meanwhile**

entretenir *VERB* [81] ❶ to maintain (*a building, a road, etc*) ❷ to support

entretien *NOUN MASC* ❶ interview; elle a été convoquée à un entretien she's been invited for interview ❷ discussion; j'ai eu un entretien avec mon patron I had a discussion with my boss ❸ upkeep; l'entretien de la maison the upkeep of the house

entrevue *NOUN FEM* interview

entrouvert *ADJECTIVE* ajar, half-open

envahir *VERB* [2] to invade

enveloppe *NOUN FEM* envelope; une enveloppe matelassée a padded envelope

envelopper *VERB* [1] to wrap up

envers *NOUN MASC* ❶ wrong side ❷ à l'envers upside down, inside out, back to front

envers *PREPOSITION* towards, to

envie *NOUN FEM* ❶ urge; avoir envie de faire to want to do, to feel like doing, j'ai envie de te voir I want to see you, j'ai envie d'aller au cinéma I feel like going to the cinema ❷ avoir envie de quelque chose to feel like something, j'ai envie d'une glace I feel like an ice cream ❸ ces frites me font envie I fancy some of those chips

envier *VERB* [1] to envy

envieux, **envieuse** *ADJECTIVE MASC, FEM* **envious**

environ *ADVERB* about; environ trente personnes about thirty people

environnement *NOUN MASC* environment

environs *PLURAL NOUN MASC* surroundings; aux environs de near

envisager *VERB* [52] envisager de faire to plan to do, qu'est-ce que vous envisagez de faire? what are you planning to do?

envoi *NOUN MASC* ❶ dispatch; faire un envoi de to send ❷ consignment

envoler *VERB* [1] s'envoler to fly away

envoyer *VERB* [40] to send; envoyer quelque chose à quelqu'un to send somebody something, elle m'a envoyé une carte she sent me a card, elle m'a envoyé chercher les verres she sent me to get the glasses

épais, **épaisse** *ADJECTIVE MASC, FEM* **thick**; une tranche épaisse a thick slice

épaisseur *NOUN FEM* thickness

épargne *NOUN FEM* savings; une banque d'épargne a savings bank, un compte d'épargne a savings account

épatant *ADJECTIVE* (*informal*) fantastic, great

épaule *NOUN FEM* shoulder

épaulette *NOUN FEM* ❶ shoulder strap ❷ shoulder pad

épave *NOUN FEM* wreck

épée *NOUN FEM* sword

épeler *VERB* [18] to spell

éphémère *ADJECTIVE* fleeting

épi *NOUN MASC* ear (*of corn*); un épi de maïs a corn cob

a
b
c
d
e
f
g
h
i
j
k
l
m
n
o
p
q
r
s
t
u
v
w
x
y
z

épice NOUN FEM **spice**

épicé ADJECTIVE **spicy, hot**; je n'aime pas les choses épicées I don't like spicy food

épicerie NOUN FEM **grocer's (shop)**; à l'épicerie at the grocer's

épicier, épicière NOUN MASC, FEM **grocer**

épidémie NOUN FEM **epidemic**

épilepsie NOUN FEM **epilepsy**

épiler VERB [1] s'épiler les sourcils to pluck your eyebrows, une pince à épiler eyebrow tweezers, s'épiler les jambes to shave your legs (or use wax or cream to remove hair)

épinards PLURAL NOUN MASC **spinach**; est-ce que tu aimes les épinards? do you like spinach?

épine NOUN FEM **thorn**

épineux, épineuse ADJECTIVE MASC, FEM **prickly**

épingle NOUN FEM **pin**; une épingle de sûreté a safety pin

épingler VERB [1] **to pin**

éplucher VERB [1] **to peel**

épluchures PLURAL NOUN FEM **peelings**

éponge NOUN FEM ❶ **sponge** ❷ **towelling**

éponger VERB [52] ❶ **to mop up** ❷ **to sponge**

époque NOUN FEM **time**; à cette époque-là at that time

épouse NOUN FEM **wife**

épouser VERB [1] **to marry**

épouvantable ADJECTIVE **dreadful**

épouvantail NOUN MASC **scarecrow**

épouvante NOUN FEM **terror**; un film d'épouvante a horror film

épouvanter VERB [1] **to terrify**

époux NOUN MASC **husband**

épreuve NOUN FEM ❶ **test** ❷ **exam**; l'épreuve de français the French exam ❸ **event** (sports) ❹ **ordeal**

éprouver VERB [1] **to feel, to experience**

éprouvette NOUN FEM **test tube**

EPS NOUN (short for éducation physique et sportive) **PE**

épuisant ADJECTIVE **exhausting**; c'est un travail épuisant it's exhausting work

épuisé ADJECTIVE ❶ **exhausted, worn out**; je suis épuisé I'm worn out ❷ **out of stock** ❸ **out of print**

épuiser VERB [1] **to wear out**; cette discussion m'a épuisé that discussion's worn me out

équateur NOUN MASC **equator**

équestre ADJECTIVE un centre équestre a riding school

équilibre NOUN MASC **balance**

équilibré ADJECTIVE **balanced**

équipage NOUN MASC **crew**

équipe NOUN FEM **team**

équipé ADJECTIVE ❶ **equipped** ❷ une cuisine équipée a fitted kitchen

équipement NOUN MASC **equipment**

équipements PLURAL NOUN MASC les équipements sportifs sports facilities

équitation *NOUN FEM* **riding**

équivalent *ADJECTIVE* **equivalent**

érable *NOUN MASC* **maple tree**; le sirop d'érable maple syrup

errer *VERB* [1] **to wander**

erreur *NOUN FEM* **mistake**; par erreur by mistake

es *VERB* ▸ SEE **être²**

escabeau *NOUN MASC* **stepladder**

escalade *NOUN FEM* **rock-climbing**

escalier *NOUN MASC* **❶ stairs**; dans l'escalier on the stairs **❷ staircase ❸** un escalier mécanique, un escalier roulant an escalator

escargot *NOUN MASC* **snail**

escarpin *NOUN MASC* **court shoe**

esclavage *NOUN MASC* **slavery**

esclave *NOUN MASC & FEM* **slave**

escompte *NOUN MASC* **discount**; un escompte de 10% a 10% discount

escorter *VERB* [1] **to escort**

escrime *NOUN FEM* **fencing** *(the sport)*

escroc *NOUN MASC* **crook, swindler**

escroquer *VERB* [1] **to swindle**

escroquerie *NOUN FEM* **swindle**; quelle escroquerie! what a swindle!

espace *NOUN MASC* **space**

espacer *VERB* [61] **to space out**

espadon *NOUN MASC* **swordfish**

espadrille *NOUN FEM* **espadrille**

Espagne *NOUN FEM* **Spain**

espagnol *NOUN MASC* **Spanish** *(language)*

espagnol *ADJECTIVE* **Spanish**

Espagnol, Espagnole *NOUN MASC, FEM* **Spaniard**; les Espagnols the Spanish

espèce *NOUN FEM* **❶ sort**; une espèce de a sort of, on a mangé du poisson avec une espèce de sauce épicée we had fish with a sort of spicy sauce **❷ species ❸** espèce d'idiot! you idiot! **❹** en espèces in cash

espérer *VERB* [24] **to hope**; ils espèrent pouvoir venir they're hoping to be able to come, j'espère qu'elle n'a pas oublié I hope she hasn't forgotten, j'espère bien! I certainly hope so

espiègle *ADJECTIVE* **mischievous**

espion, espionne *NOUN MASC, FEM* **spy**

espionnage *NOUN MASC* **spying, espionage**

espionner *VERB* [1] **to spy on**

espoir *NOUN MASC* **hope**

esprit *NOUN MASC* **❶ mind**; ça ne m'est pas venu à l'esprit it didn't cross my mind **❷ wit**; avoir de l'esprit to be witty

esquimau *NOUN MASC (PLURAL* esquimaux*)* **choc ice**

esquisse *NOUN FEM* **sketch**

esquisser *VERB* [1] **to sketch**

essai *NOUN MASC* **❶ trial ❷ test ❸ attempt, try**

essaim *NOUN MASC* **swarm**

essayer *VERB* [59] **❶ to try**; essayer de faire to try to do, j'ai essayé de t'appeler I tried to phone you **❷ to try on**; essayer une robe to try on a dress, voulez-vous l'essayer? would you like to try it on? ❸ **to test**

essence NOUN FEM ❶ **petrol**; essence sans plomb unleaded petrol ❷ **essential oil**

essentiel, essentielle ADJECTIVE MASC, FEM **essential**; c'est l'essentiel that's the main thing

essentiellement ADVERB ❶ **mainly** ❷ **essentially**

essorage NOUN MASC **spin-dry**

essorer VERB [1] **to spin-dry**

essoufflé ADJECTIVE **out of breath**

essuie-glace NOUN MASC **windscreen wiper**

essuie-tout NOUN MASC **(paper) kitchen towel**

essuyer VERB [41] **to wipe**; essuyer la vaisselle to do the drying-up, s'essuyer les mains to dry your hands

est[1] VERB ▸ SEE **être**[2]

est[2] NOUN MASC **east**; l'est de Paris the east of Paris, dans l'est de la France in the east of France, l'Europe de l'Est Eastern Europe

est ADJECTIVE ❶ **east** ❷ **eastern**

est-ce que (used for asking questions) est-ce qu'il pleut? is it raining?, est-ce que Julie est partie? has Julie left?, où est-ce qu'il habite? where does he live?

esthéticienne NOUN FEM **beautician**

estime NOUN FEM **respect**

estimer VERB [1] ❶ **to esteem** ❷ **to value** ❸ j'estime que ... I think that ...

estival ADJECTIVE MASC (PLURAL estivaux) **summer**

estivant, estivante NOUN MASC, FEM **summer visitor**

estomac NOUN MASC **stomach**; avoir mal à l'estomac to have stomachache

Estonie NOUN FEM **Estonia**

estrade NOUN FEM **platform**

estragon NOUN MASC **tarragon**; une sauce à l'estragon a tarragon sauce

et CONJUNCTION **and**

établir VERB [2] ❶ **to establish** ❷ établir une liste to draw up a list ❸ s'établir à son compte to set up in business

établissement NOUN MASC ❶ **institution**; établissement scolaire school ❷ **organization**

étage NOUN MASC **floor**; au premier étage on the first floor, au dernier étage on the top floor, à l'étage upstairs

étagère NOUN FEM ❶ **shelf** ❷ **set of shelves**

étain NOUN MASC ❶ **tin** ❷ **pewter**

étalage NOUN MASC **window display**

étaler VERB [1] ❶ **to spread** ❷ **spread out** ❸ **to roll out** (pastry)

étanche ADJECTIVE ❶ **watertight** ❷ **waterproof**

étang NOUN MASC **pond**

étape NOUN FEM ❶ **stage** ❷ **stopping place**

état NOUN MASC **state, condition**; en mauvais état in a bad state, en bon état in good condition, en état de marche in working order, être dans tous ses états to be in a state

État NOUN MASC **state, State**

États-Unis PLURAL NOUN MASC **les États-Unis the United States, aux États-Unis in (or to) the United States**

été¹ VERB ▸ SEE **être²**

été² NOUN MASC **summer; en été in summer, l'été dernier last summer, des vêtements d'été summer clothes**

éteindre VERB [60] ❶ **to turn off, to switch off; éteindre la lumière to turn out the lights ❷ to put out (a fire or cigarette) ❸ s'éteindre to go out**

éteint ADJECTIVE **extinct (volcano)**

étendre VERB [3] ❶ **to spread out ❷ to stretch out (your arms or legs) ❸ étendre le linge to hang out the washing ❹ s'étendre to stretch ❺ s'étendre to spread**

éternel, éternelle ADJECTIVE MASC, FEM **eternal**

éternité NOUN FEM **eternity**

éternuement NOUN MASC **sneeze**

éternuer VERB [1] **to sneeze**

êtes VERB ▸ SEE **être²**

ethnie NOUN FEM **ethnic group**

ethnique ADJECTIVE **ethnic**

étinceler VERB [18] **to sparkle, to twinkle**

étincelle NOUN FEM **spark**

étiquette NOUN FEM ❶ **label ❷ etiquette**

étirer VERB [1] **to stretch**

étoffe NOUN FEM **fabric**

étoile NOUN FEM **star; une étoile filante a shooting star**

étonnant ADJECTIVE ❶ **surprising ❷ astonishing**

étonnement NOUN MASC ❶ **surprise ❷ astonishment**

étonner VERB [1] ❶ **to surprise; ça m'a beaucoup étonné that really surprised me, ça ne m'étonne pas du tout that doesn't surprise me at all ❷ s'étonner to be surprised, s'étonner de quelque chose to be surprised at something**

étouffant ADJECTIVE **stifling**

étouffer VERB [1] ❶ **to stifle ❷ to suffocate ❸ s'étouffer to choke**

étourderie NOUN FEM ❶ **absent-mindedness ❷ une étourderie a careless mistake**

étourdi, étourdie NOUN MASC, FEM **scatterbrain**

étourdi ADJECTIVE **scatterbrained**

étourdir VERB [2] **to daze, to stun**

étourneau NOUN MASC **starling**

étrange ADJECTIVE **strange**

étranger¹, étrangère NOUN MASC, FEM ❶ **foreigner ❷ stranger**

étranger, étrangère ADJECTIVE MASC, FEM **foreign; un pays étranger a foreign country**

étranger² NOUN MASC **à l'étranger abroad**

étrangler VERB [1] ❶ **to strangle ❷ to choke**

être¹ NOUN MASC **being; un être humain a human being**

être² VERB [6] **❶ to be**; nous sommes dans la cuisine we're in the kitchen, elle est malade she's ill, c'est moi it's me **❷** elle est infirmière she's a nurse **❸** être à quelqu'un to belong to somebody, to be somebody's, ce livre est à Paul this book is Paul's, ce livre est à moi this book is mine **❹** il est 6 heures it's 6 o'clock **❺** nous sommes le 7 mars it's the 7th of March (today) **❻** (used with certain verbs to form past tenses: for a list of these, see the centre pages) je suis allé à Paris I went to Paris, nous sommes rentrés à 7 heures we got home at 7 o'clock **❼** (used to form the passive of verbs) ses robes sont faites par sa mère her dresses are made by her mother

étroit ADJECTIVE **❶ narrow ❷ close**

étroitement ADVERB **closely**

étude NOUN FEM **❶ study ❷** études studies, faire des études de médecine to study medicine

étudiant, **étudiante** NOUN MASC, FEM **student**

étudier VERB [1] **to study**

étui NOUN MASC **case**

eu VERB ▸ SEE **avoir**

euro NOUN MASC **euro**; l'euro est divisé en cents/centimes the euro is divided into cents

Europe NOUN FEM **Europe**; en Europe in (or to) Europe

européen, **européene** ADJECTIVE MASC, FEM **European**

euthanasie NOUN FEM **euthanasia**

eux PRONOUN **❶ them**; avec eux with them, des amis à eux friends of theirs **❷ they**

eux-mêmes PRONOUN **themselves** (referring to male people or masculine objects)

évacuer VERB [1] **to evacuate**; la police a fait évacuer l'immeuble the police evacuated the building

évader VERB [1] s'évader **to escape**

évaluer VERB [1] **to assess**

évanouir VERB [2] s'évanouir **to faint**

évaporer VERB [1] s'évaporer **to evaporate**

évasion NOUN FEM **escape**

éveillé ADJECTIVE **awake**

éveiller VERB [1] **❶ to arouse ❷ to awaken**

événement NOUN MASC **event**

éventail NOUN MASC **fan**

éventualité NOUN FEM **possibility**

éventuel, **éventuelle** ADJECTIVE MASC, FEM **possible**

éventuellement ADVERB **❶ possibly ❷ if necessary**

évêque NOUN MASC **bishop**

évidemment ADVERB **of course**

évidence NOUN FEM être en évidence to be clearly visible, de toute évidence clearly, de toute évidence il a oublié de venir he's clearly forgotten to come, mettre quelque chose en évidence to reveal something

évident ADJECTIVE **obvious**

évier NOUN MASC **sink**

éviter *VERB* [1] to avoid; éviter de faire to avoid doing, ça t'évitera de sortir that'll save you having to go out

évolué *ADJECTIVE* advanced

évoluer *VERB* [1] ❶ to develop; nous ne savons pas comment la situation va évoluer we do not know how the situation will develop ❷ to progress; l'informatique a beaucoup évolué ces dernières années computer science has progressed a great deal in recent years ❸ to change; les choses ont évolué depuis things have changed since

évolution *NOUN FEM* ❶ development ❷ progress ❸ evolution

exact *ADJECTIVE* ❶ correct; c'est exact that's absolutely right ❷ exact, precise

exactement *ADVERB* exactly

exagéré *ADJECTIVE* ❶ exaggerated ❷ excessive

exagérer *VERB* [24] ❶ to exaggerate ❷ to go too far

examen *NOUN MASC* ❶ exam; passer un examen to sit an exam, réussir à un examen to pass an exam, un examen blanc a mock exam ❷ un examen médical a medical examination

examinateur, examinatrice *NOUN MASC, FEM* examiner

examiner *VERB* [1] to examine

exaspérant *ADJECTIVE* exasperating

exaspérer *VERB* [24] to exasperate

excellence *NOUN FEM* excellence

excellent *ADJECTIVE* excellent

excentrique *NOUN MASC & FEM, ADJECTIVE* eccentric

excepté *PREPOSITION* except

exception *NOUN FEM* exception; à l'exception de with the exception of

exceptionnel, exceptionnelle *ADJECTIVE MASC, FEM* ❶ exceptional ❷ special

exceptionnellement *ADVERB* exceptionally

excès *NOUN MASC* excess

excès de vitesse *NOUN MASC* speeding

excessif, excessive *ADJECTIVE MASC, FEM* excessive

excessivement *ADVERB* excessively; il est excessivement timide he's incredibly shy

excitant *NOUN MASC* stimulant

excitant *ADJECTIVE* exciting

excitation *NOUN FEM* excitement

excité *ADJECTIVE* ❶ frenzied ❷ over-excited ❸ thrilled

exciter *VERB* [1] s'exciter to get excited

exclamation *NOUN FEM* exclamation

exclamer *VERB* [1] s'exclamer to exclaim

exclu *ADJECTIVE* il n'est pas exclu que … it's not impossible that …

exclusif, exclusive *ADJECTIVE MASC, FEM* exclusive

excursion *NOUN FEM* excursion, trip

excuse *NOUN* ❶ apology; présenter ses excuses to apologize ❷ excuse

excuser *VERB* [1] **❶** to forgive; excusez-moi! sorry!, excusez-moi de vous déranger sorry to disturb you **❷** s'excuser to apologize, je m'excuse I'm sorry, je m'excuse d'être en retard sorry I'm late

exécuter *VERB* [1] **❶** to execute **❷** to carry out

exemplaire *NOUN MASC* copy; six exemplaires du dictionnaire six copies of the dictionary

exemple *NOUN MASC* example; par exemple for example, donner l'exemple to set an example

exercer *VERB* [61] **❶** to exercise *(a right)* **❷** to practise *(an art or a profession)* **❸** to exert *(authority)* **❹** s'exercer to practise

exercice *NOUN MASC* exercise; exercices de mise en forme fitness exercises

exhiber *VERB* [1] **❶** to show off **❷** to display

exhibitionniste *NOUN MASC* flasher

exigeant *ADJECTIVE* hard to please

exiger *VERB* [52] **❶** to demand **❷** to require

exil *NOUN MASC* exile

exilé, exilée *NOUN MASC, FEM* exile

existence *NOUN FEM* existence

exister *VERB* [1] to exist

exotique *ADJECTIVE* exotic

expansion *NOUN FEM* **❶** expansion **❷** growth

expédier *VERB* [1] to send (off); expédier un paquet to send off a package

expéditeur, expéditrice *NOUN MASC, FEM* sender

expédition *NOUN FEM* expedition

expérience *NOUN FEM* **❶** experience; avoir de l'expérience to be experienced **❷** experiment; faire une expérience to carry out an experiment

expérimenté *ADJECTIVE* experienced

expert *NOUN MASC* expert

explication *NOUN FEM* explanation

explicite *ADJECTIVE* explicit

expliquer *VERB* [1] to explain

exploit *NOUN MASC* **❶** achievement **❷** feat

exploiter *VERB* [1] **❶** to exploit **❷** to use, to make use of

explorer *VERB* [1] to explore

exploser *VERB* [1] to explode, to blow up

explosif, explosive *ADJECTIVE MASC, FEM* explosive

explosion *NOUN FEM* **❶** explosion **❷** boom

export *NOUN MASC* export

exportateur, exportatrice *NOUN MASC, FEM* exporter

exportation *NOUN FEM* export

exporter *VERB* [1] to export; la Russie exporte beaucoup de pétrole Russia exports a lot of oil

exposé *NOUN MASC* talk; Gaby a fait un exposé sur le Japon Gaby gave a talk about Japan

exposé *ADJECTIVE* **❶** exposed **❷** on display

exposer VERB [1] **❶** to exhibit **❷** to expose **❸** to explain

exposition NOUN FEM **❶** exhibition; une exposition d'art africain an exhibition of African art **❷** exposure

exprès ADJECTIVE express

exprès ADVERB **❶** deliberately; tu l'as fait exprès you did it deliberately, you did it on purpose, il a fait exprès de le casser he broke it on purpose, c'est fait exprès it's meant to be like that **❷** specially; je suis venu exprès pour te voir I've come specially to see you

express NOUN MASC **❶** fast train **❷** espresso coffee

expression NOUN FEM expression

exprimer VERB [1] **❶** to express **❷** s'exprimer to express yourself, je m'exprime mal I'm expressing myself badly

expulser VERB [1] **❶** to evict **❷** to expel

exquis ADJECTIVE exquisite, delightful

extase NOUN FEM ecstasy

extensif (extensive) ADJECTIVE extensive

extension NOUN FEM extension

extérieur NOUN MASC **❶** outside; à l'extérieur outside **❷** exterior

extérieur ADJECTIVE **❶** outside **❷** outer

externat NOUN MASC day school

externe NOUN MASC & FEM day pupil

extincteur NOUN MASC fire extinguisher

extinction NOUN FEM extinction; une espèce en voie d'extinction an endangered species

extra ADJECTIVE (informal) great, fantastic; ta sauce est vraiment extra! your sauce is really fantastic!

extraction NOUN FEM **❶** extraction **❷** mining

extraire VERB [78] **❶** to extract **❷** to mine

extrait NOUN MASC extract

extraordinaire ADJECTIVE extraordinary, amazing

extra-terrestre NOUN MASC & FEM extra-terrestrial, alien (from outer space)

extravagant ADJECTIVE **❶** eccentric; des vêtements extravagants eccentric clothes **❷** extravagant

extrême NOUN MASC, ADJECTIVE extreme

extrêmement ADVERB extremely

Extrême-Orient NOUN MASC the Far East

extrémité NOUN FEM **❶** end **❷** tip **❸** edge **❹** extreme

a
b
c
d
e
f
g
h
i
j
k
l
m
n
o
p
q
r
s
t
u
v
w
x
y
z

French—English

F *(short for francs)* 30 F 30 francs

fabricant NOUN MASC **manufacturer**

fabrication NOUN FEM **manufacture**

fabriquer VERB [1] **to make**; fabriqué en France made in France, qu'est-ce que tu fabriques? *(informal)* what are you up to?

fabuleux, **fabuleuse** ADJECTIVE MASC, FEM **fabulous**

fac NOUN FEM *(informal)* **university**; être en fac d'anglais to be doing a degree in English

face NOUN FEM ❶ **face**; face à face face to face ❷ en face opposite, en face de l'école opposite the school, la maison d'en face the house opposite, le magasin en face de chez nous the shop opposite our house ❸ faire face à quelque chose to face up to something ❹ face à facing, face au mur facing the wall ❺ pile ou face? heads or tails?

fâché ADJECTIVE ❶ **angry**; elle est fâchée contre moi she's angry with me ❷ il est fâché avec son frère he's fallen out with his brother

fâcher VERB [1] ❶ se fâcher to get angry, se fâcher contre quelqu'un to get angry with somebody, elle s'est fâchée contre moi she got angry with me ❷ se fâcher avec quelqu'un to fall out with somebody

facile ADJECTIVE **easy**; c'est facile it's easy, c'est facile à comprendre it's easy to understand

facilement ADVERB **easily**

facilité NOUN FEM **easiness**

faciliter VERB [1] **to make (something) easier**; ça devrait nous faciliter les choses that should make things easier for us

façon NOUN FEM ❶ **way**; il y a plusieurs façons de le faire there are several ways of doing it, d'une façon extraordinaire in an extraordinary way, de quelle façon? in what way? ❷ de toute façon anyway

façonner VERB [1] ❶ **to make** ❷ **to shape**

facteur[1] NOUN MASC **factor**

facteur[2] NOUN MASC **postman**; est-ce que le facteur est passé? has the postman been?

factrice NOUN FEM **postwoman**

facture NOUN FEM **bill**; la facture d'électricité the electricity bill

facultatif, **facultative** ADJECTIVE MASC, FEM **optional**

faculté NOUN FEM **faculty**

fade ADJECTIVE **tasteless**; la sauce est un peu fade the sauce is a bit tasteless

faible NOUN MASC avoir un faible pour to have a soft spot for

faible ADJECTIVE ❶ **weak**; elle est encore très faible she's still very weak ❷ elle est faible en chimie she's not very good at chemistry ❸ un faible bruit a faint noise

faiblesse NOUN FEM **weakness**

faiblir VERB [2] ❶ **to weaken** ❷ le vent a faibli the wind's died down a bit

faïence NOUN FEM **earthenware**; des assiettes en faïence earthenware plates

faillir VERB [42] faillir faire to nearly do, j'ai failli tomber I nearly fell, j'ai failli rater le train I nearly missed the train

faillite NOUN FEM **bankruptcy**; faire faillite to go bankrupt

faim NOUN FEM **hunger**; avoir faim to be hungry, j'ai très faim I'm really hungry, je meurs de faim! I'm starving!, je n'ai plus faim I've had enough to eat, ces gâteaux me donnent faim those cakes make me feel hungry

fainéant ADJECTIVE **lazy**

faire VERB [10] ❶ **to make**; faire un gâteau to make a cake, je vais me faire un café I'm going to make myself a coffee, faire du bruit to make a noise ❷ **to do**; qu'est-ce que tu fais? what are you doing?, il est en train de faire ses devoirs he's doing his homework, faire du français to do French, fais comme tu veux do as you like ❸ qu'as-tu fait du couteau? what have you done with the knife? ❹ il fait froid it's cold, il fait chaud it's hot ❺ quel temps fait-il? what's the weather like?, il fait beau it's a nice day, il fait beau en été ici the weather's

nice here in summer ❻ ça ne fait rien it doesn't matter ❼ faire faire quelque chose to have (or get) something done, elle a fait réparer son vélo she got her bike repaired, il s'est fait couper les cheveux he's had his hair cut ❽ faire chauffer de l'eau to heat some water, faire cuire quelque chose to cook something ❾ ne t'en fais pas don't worry

faire-part NOUN MASC **announcement** (of birth, marriage, or death)

fais VERB ▸ SEE **faire**

faisan NOUN MASC **pheasant**

faisons VERB ▸ SEE **faire**

fait[1] VERB ▸ SEE **faire**

fait[2] NOUN MASC ❶ **fact**; en fait actually, en fait je l'ai vu hier in fact I saw him yesterday ❷ au fait by the way, au fait, est-ce que tu as fermé la porte? by the way, did you shut the door?

fait d'actualité NOUN MASC **news item**

faites VERB ▸ SEE **faire**

falaise NOUN FEM **cliff**

fallait VERB ▸ SEE **falloir**

falloir IMPERSONAL VERB [43] ❶ il faut le faire it has to be done, you must do it, il ne faut pas faire ça you mustn't do that, il ne fallait pas faire ça you shouldn't have done that, il faudra partir à six heures we'll have to leave at six o'clock ❷ il me faut un stylo I need a pen, il leur faut une voiture they need a car, qu'est-ce qu'il te faut? what do you need? ❸ il faut que tu le fasses (subjunctive) you must do it, il faut que tu prennes tes clés

A
B
C
D
E
F
G
H
I
J
K
L
M
N
O
P
Q
R
S
T
U
V
W
X
Y
Z

you must take your keys ❹ comme il faut properly, tu ne l'as pas fait comme il faut you haven't done it properly, marche comme il faut! walk properly

famé ADJECTIVE un quartier mal famé a rough area

fameux, fameuse ADJECTIVE MASC, FEM **first-rate**; le repas n'était pas fameux the meal wasn't great

familial ADJECTIVE MASC (PLURAL familiaux) **family**; la vie familiale family life, les allocations familiales child benefit

familiariser VERB [1] se familiariser avec to become familiar with

familiarité NOUN FEM **familiarity**

familier, familière ADJECTIVE MASC, FEM **familiar**; un endroit familier a familiar place

famille NOUN FEM ❶ **family**; un déjeuner en famille a family lunch, une famille nombreuse a big family ❷ **relatives**; j'ai de la famille à Londres I have relatives in London

famille monoparentale NOUN FEM **single-parent family**

fanatique NOUN MASC & FEM **fanatic**

faneé ADJECTIVE **withered**; les fleurs sont fanées the flowers are withered

fanfare NOUN FEM **brass band**

fantaisie NOUN FEM ❶ **imagination** ❷ des bijoux de fantaisie costume jewellery

fantaisiste ADJECTIVE ❶ **unreliable**; il est un peu fantaisiste he's rather unreliable ❷ une idée fantaisiste a wild idea

fantastique ADJECTIVE **fantastic**

fantôme NOUN MASC **ghost**

farce NOUN FEM ❶ **practical joke**; un magasin de farces et attrapes a joke shop ❷ **stuffing** (for a chicken, for example)

farci ADJECTIVE **stuffed**; des tomates farcies stuffed tomatoes

farcir VERB [2] **to stuff** (a chicken, for example)

fard à paupières NOUN MASC **eye shadow**

fardeau NOUN MASC (PLURAL fardeaux) **burden**

farfelu ADJECTIVE **bizarre**; c'est un type farfelu he's a bizarre bloke, elle a toujours des idées farfelues she always has crazy ideas

farine NOUN FEM ❶ **flour** ❷ **baby cereal**

fascinant ADJECTIVE **fascinating**; son histoire était absolument fascinante his story was absolutely fascinating

fascination NOUN FEM **fascination**

fasciner VERB [1] **to fascinate**; ça me fascine I find that fascinating

fascisme NOUN MASC **fascism**

fast-food NOUN FEM **fast food**

fastidieux, fastidieuse ADJECTIVE MASC, FEM **tedious**; c'est un travail fastidieux it's tedious work

fatal *ADJECTIVE* ❶ inevitable; c'était fatal it was bound to happen ❷ fatal

fatalité *NOUN FEM* fate

fatidique *ADJECTIVE* fateful

fatigant *ADJECTIVE* tiring

fatigue *NOUN FEM* tiredness

fatigué *ADJECTIVE* tired; je suis fatigué I'm tired, tu as l'air fatigué you look tired

fatiguer *VERB* [1] ❶ to tire (somebody) out; la promenade m'a fatigué the walk tired me out ❷ se fatiguer to get tired

faubourg *NOUN MASC* suburb

fauché *ADJECTIVE* (informal) broke; je suis fauché cette semaine I'm broke this week

faucher *VERB* [1] ❶ to mow, to scythe ❷ (informal) to nick; quelqu'un m'a fauché mon vélo somebody's nicked my bike

faucon *NOUN MASC* falcon, hawk

faudra, faudrait *VERB* ▸ SEE **falloir**

faufiler *VERB* [1] se faufiler à travers la foule to thread your way through the crowd

faune *NOUN FEM* wildlife

fausse *ADJECTIVE* ▸ SEE **faux¹**

faussement *ADVERB* wrongly

fausser *VERB* [1] ❶ to distort ❷ to bend

faut *VERB* ▸ SEE **falloir**

faute *NOUN FEM* ❶ mistake, error; faire une faute to make a mistake, une faute d'orthographe a spelling

mistake ❷ fault; c'est (de) ma faute it's my fault, c'est la faute de Sophie it's Sophie's fault ❸ faute de for lack of, faute de temps for lack of time, faute de mieux for want of anything better ❹ sans faute without fail

fauteuil *NOUN MASC* armchair

fauteuil roulant *NOUN MASC* wheelchair

fautif, fautive *ADJECTIVE MASC, FEM* faulty

fauve *NOUN MASC* wild animal

fauve *ADJECTIVE* tawny

faux¹, fausse *ADJECTIVE MASC, FEM* ❶ wrong; c'est faux it's wrong ❷ untrue; c'est totalement faux it's totally untrue ❸ false; une fausse barbe a false beard ❹ imitation; une table en faux marbre an imitation marble table ❺ chanter faux to sing out of tune

faux² *NOUN MASC* fake, forgery; cette pièce est un faux this coin's a forgery

faux³ *NOUN FEM* scythe

faux ami *NOUN MASC* false friend (a word in a foreign language which looks very like a word in your own language but does not mean the same thing at all)

faux-filet *NOUN MASC* sirloin

faveur *NOUN FEM* favour; en faveur de in favour of

favorable *ADJECTIVE* favourable

favorablement *ADVERB* favourably

favori, favorite ADJECTIVE MASC, FEM
favourite

favoriser VERB [1] **to favour**

fédéral ADJECTIVE MASC (PLURAL
fédéraux) **federal**

fédération NOUN FEM **federation**

fée NOUN FEM **fairy**
• avoir des doigts de fée to have
  nimble fingers (literally: to have the
  fingers of a fairy)

féerique ADJECTIVE **magical**

feignant ADJECTIVE (informal) **lazy**

fêler VERB [1] se fêler **to crack**

félicitations PLURAL NOUN FEM
congratulations

féliciter VERB [1] **to congratulate**

fêlure NOUN FEM **crack**

femelle NOUN FEM, ADJECTIVE **female**
(animal)

féminin NOUN MASC le féminin the
feminine (in French and other
grammars), au féminin in the
feminine

féminin ADJECTIVE ❶ **female**; le
sexe féminin the female sex
❷ **feminine**; elle est très féminine
she's very feminine ❸ **women's**;
les vêtements féminins women's
clothing, la presse féminine
women's magazines, les questions
féminines women's issues

féministe NOUN MASC & FEM **feminist**

femme NOUN FEM ❶ **woman**; c'est
une femme très intéressante she's
a very interesting woman ❷ **wife**; la
femme de David David's wife

femme au foyer NOUN FEM
housewife

femme d'affaires NOUN FEM
businesswoman

femme de ménage NOUN FEM
cleaning lady

fendre VERB [3] ❶ **to split** ❷ **to crack**

fenêtre NOUN FEM **window**; regarder
par la fenêtre to look out the
window
• jeter l'argent par les fenêtres to
  throw your money away (literally: to
  throw money out of the windows)

fenouil NOUN MASC **fennel**

fente NOUN FEM ❶ **slit** ❷ **slot** ❸ **crack**

fer NOUN MASC **iron**

fer à cheval NOUN MASC **horseshoe**

fer à repasser NOUN MASC **iron** (for
ironing things with)

fer forgé NOUN MASC **wrought iron**

férié ADJECTIVE un jour férié a public
holiday

ferme¹ NOUN FEM ❶ **farm**
❷ **farmhouse**

ferme² ADJECTIVE **firm**

fermé ADJECTIVE **closed**; 'fermé le
dimanche' closed on Sundays

ferme d'éoliennes NOUN FEM **wind
farm**

fermenter VERB [1] **to ferment**

fermer VERB [1] ❶ **to close, to shut**;
peux-tu fermer la porte, s'il te
plaît shut the door please, il a
fermé les yeux he closed his eyes
❷ **to turn off** (the lights, the tap, the
water, etc); n'oublie pas de fermer
les robinets don't forget to turn
off the taps ❸ se fermer to close,
to shut

fermeture NOUN FEM ❶ **closing**; heures de fermeture closing times ❷ **fastening** (on a garment)

fermeture annuelle NOUN FEM **annual closure**

fermeture éclair NOUN FEM **zip**

fermier, fermière NOUN MASC, FEM ❶ **farmer** ❷ la fermière the farmer's wife

fermière ADJECTIVE **farm**; produits fermiers farm produce, un poulet fermier a free-range chicken

fermoir NOUN MASC **clasp**

féroce ADJECTIVE ❶ **fierce** ❷ **ferocious**

ferraille NOUN FEM **scrap metal**

ferroviaire ADJECTIVE **rail**; le réseau ferroviaire the rail network

fertile ADJECTIVE **fertile**

fertilité NOUN FEM **fertility**

fesse NOUN FEM **buttock**; fesses bottom

festin NOUN MASC **feast**

festival NOUN MASC **festival**

fête NOUN FEM ❶ **public holiday** ❷ **party**; faire la fête to celebrate ❸ les fêtes de fin d'année the festive season ❹ fête, fair ❺ saint's name day (in France each day of the year is associated with the name of a saint and many people still celebrate the day of the saint they are named after)

fête des Mères NOUN FEM **Mother's Day** (in France on the last Sunday in May)

fête des Pères NOUN FEM **Father's Day**

fête foraine NOUN FEM **funfair**

Fête Nationale NOUN FEM **Bastille Day**

fêter VERB [1] **to celebrate**

feu NOUN MASC ❶ **fire**; faire du feu to light a fire, prendre feu to catch fire ❷ **light**; as-tu du feu? have you got a light? ❸ les feux de signalisation the traffic lights, un feu rouge a red light ❹ faire cuire à feu doux cook on a gentle heat
• il n'y a pas le feu there's no hurry (literally: there isn't a fire)

feu d'artifice NOUN MASC ❶ **firework** ❷ **firework display**

feuillage NOUN MASC **leaves**

feuille NOUN FEM ❶ **leaf** ❷ une feuille de papier a sheet of paper

feuilleté NOUN MASC **savoury pasty**

feuilleté ADJECTIVE de la pâte feuilletée puff pastry

feuilleter VERB [48] feuilleter un livre to leaf through a book

feuilleton NOUN MASC **serial**, **soap** (on television)

feutre NOUN MASC ❶ **felt** ❷ un feutre a felt-tip pen

fève NOUN FEM **broad bean**

février NOUN MASC **February**; en février, au mois de février in February

fiable ADJECTIVE **reliable**

fiançailles PLURAL NOUN FEM **engagement** (to be married)

fiancé, fiancée NOUN MASC, FEM **fiancé, fiancée**

fiancé *ADJECTIVE* être fiancé à quelqu'un to be engaged to somebody

fiancer *VERB* [61] se fiancer to get engaged

fibre *NOUN FEM* fibre

ficeler *VERB* [18] to tie up

ficelle *NOUN FEM* ❶ string ❷ thin baguette *(of French bread)*

fiche *NOUN FEM* ❶ form; remplir une fiche to fill in a form ❷ index card ❸ plug

fiche d'inscription *NOUN FEM* registration form

ficher *VERB* [1] *(informal)* ❶ to do; qu'est-ce que tu fiches? what do you think you're doing? ❷ je m'en fiche! I don't care! ❸ fiche-moi la paix! leave me alone!

fichier *NOUN MASC* file

fichu *ADJECTIVE* *(informal)* done for; ma voiture est fichue my car's had it

fiction *NOUN FEM* fiction

fidèle *ADJECTIVE* ❶ faithful ❷ loyal

fier[1], **fière** *ADJECTIVE MASC, FEM* proud

fier[2] *VERB* [1] se fier à to trust

fierté *NOUN FEM* pride

fièvre *NOUN FEM* fever; avoir de la fièvre to have a temperature

figer *VERB* [52] ❶ se figer to congeal ❷ to freeze to the spot

figue *NOUN FEM* fig

figuier *NOUN MASC* fig tree

figure *NOUN FEM* ❶ face ❷ figure

figurer *VERB* [1] ❶ to appear ❷ se figurer to imagine

fil *NOUN MASC* ❶ thread; du fil à coudre sewing thread ❷ wire, flex *(of a telephone or electrical appliance)* ❸ un coup de fil *(informal)* a phone call, passer un coup de fil to make a phone call, passe-moi un coup de fil give me a ring

fil de fer *NOUN MASC* wire; fil de fer barbelé barbed wire

file *NOUN FEM* ❶ une file d'attente a queue ❷ lane *(on a road)*

filer *VERB* [1] ❶ to speed along ❷ *(informal)* to give; elle m'a filé deux CD she gave me two CDs *(which she didn't want any more)*

filet *NOUN MASC* ❶ net ❷ fillet; un filet de poisson a fish fillet

fille *NOUN FEM* ❶ girl; une petite fille a little girl, une jeune fille a young woman ❷ daughter

fillette *NOUN FEM* little girl

filleul, **filleule** *NOUN MASC, FEM* godson, goddaughter

film *NOUN MASC* film

film comique *NOUN MASC* comedy *(film)*

film d'épouvante *NOUN MASC* horror film

filmer *VERB* [1] to film

film policier *NOUN MASC* thriller

fils *NOUN MASC* son

filtre *NOUN FEM* filter

filtrer *VERB* [1] to filter

fin[1] *NOUN FEM* **end**; à la fin in the end, à la fin du film at the end of the film, sans fin endless

fin[2] *ADJECTIVE* ❶ **fine** ❷ **slender**

final *ADJECTIVE MASC (PLURAL* **finaux***)* **final**

finale *NOUN FEM* **final, cup final**

finalement *ADVERB* ❶ **in the end, finally** ❷ **after all**

finance *NOUN FEM* **finance**

financer *VERB* [61] **to finance**

fines herbes *PLURAL NOUN FEM* **mixed herbs**

finir *VERB* [2] ❶ **to finish, to end**; le film finit à dix heures the film finishes at ten o'clock ❷ finir de faire to finish doing, j'ai fini de faire la vaisselle I've finished doing the washing-up ❸ finir quelque chose to finish something, as-tu fini tes devoirs? have you finished your homework?, j'ai fini le sucre I've finished the sugar, I've used up all the sugar ❹ finir par faire to end up doing, il a fini par accepter he accepted in the end

finlandais *NOUN MASC* **Finnish** *(language)*

finlandais *ADJECTIVE* **Finnish**

Finlande *NOUN FEM* **Finland**

firme *NOUN FEM* **firm**

fisc *NOUN MASC* **tax office**

fissure *NOUN FEM* **crack**

fixe *ADJECTIVE* ❶ **fixed** ❷ un emploi fixe a steady job ❸ aux heures fixes at set times

fixer *VERB* [1] ❶ **to fix** *(to attach)* ❷ **to set** *(a date, a price)*; fixer les

élections legislatives to set the date for the general elections

flacon *NOUN MASC* **(small) bottle**

flamand *NOUN MASC* **Flemish** *(language)*

flamand *ADJECTIVE* **Flemish**

Flamand, Flamande *NOUN MASC, FEM* **Fleming** *(Dutch-speaking Belgian)*

flamant *NOUN MASC* **flamingo**

flamber *VERB* [1] **to blaze**

flamme *NOUN FEM* **flame**

flan *NOUN MASC* **custard tart**

flanc *NOUN MASC* **side**

flâner *VERB* [1] **to stroll**

flaque *NOUN FEM* une flaque d'eau a puddle

flash *NOUN MASC* ❶ **flash** *(on a camera)* ❷ **newsflash**

flatter *VERB* [1] **to flatter**

flatteur, flatteuse *ADJECTIVE MASC, FEM* **flattering**

flèche *NOUN FEM* ❶ **arrow** ❷ **spire**

fléchette *NOUN FEM* **dart**; jouer aux fléchettes to play darts

fléchir *VERB* [2] ❶ **to bend** ❷ **to weaken**

fleur *NOUN FEM* **flower**; un tissu à fleurs a flower-patterned fabric, étre en fleurs to be in flower

fleuri *ADJECTIVE* ❶ **flowery**; du tissu fleuri flowery material ❷ ton jardin est très fleuri you've got lots of flowers in your garden

fleurir *VERB* [2] ❶ **to flower, to blossom** ❷ **to flourish**

fleuriste NOUN MASC & FEM **florist**

fleuve NOUN MASC **river**

flexible ADJECTIVE **flexible**

flic NOUN MASC (informal) **policeman**, **cop**

flipper NOUN MASC **pinball machine**

flirter VERB [1] **to flirt**

flocon NOUN MASC **flake**; un flocon de neige a snowflake

flocons d'avoine PLURAL NOUN MASC **porridge oats**

floral ADJECTIVE MASC (PLURAL **floraux**) **floral**

flotte NOUN FEM **fleet** (of ships)

flotter VERB [1] **to float**

flou ADJECTIVE ❶ **blurred**; une image floue a blurred image ❷ **vague**; ses projets sont un peu flous her plans are a bit vague

fluide NOUN MASC, ADJECTIVE **fluid**

fluo ADJECTIVE (informal) **fluorescent**; vert fluo fluorescent green

fluor NOUN MASC **fluorine**

fluorescent ADJECTIVE **fluorescent**

flûte NOUN FEM **flute**; jouer de la flûte to play the flute

flûte à bec NOUN FEM **recorder**

focaliser VERB [1] **to focus**

foi NOUN FEM **faith**

foie NOUN MASC **liver**; une crise de foie an upset stomach

foin NOUN MASC **hay**

foire NOUN FEM **fair**

fois NOUN FEM ❶ **time**; une fois once, deux fois twice, trois fois three times, trois fois dix three times ten, plusieurs fois several times, la première fois the first time, trois fois plus grand three times as big ❷ à la fois at the same time, trois à la fois three at a time ❸ une fois que once, une fois que j'aurai pris une douche once I've had a shower ❹ j'ai vu une fois ... I once saw ..., il était une fois ... once upon a time ... ❺ à chaque fois whenever, each time, à chaque fois que nous sortons, nous verrouillons la porte whenever we go out, we lock the door

folie NOUN FEM **madness**; c'est de la folie! it's crazy!

folk NOUN MASC **folk music**

folle NOUN FEM, ADJECTIVE ▸ SEE **fou**

foncer VERB [61] (informal) **to rush**; tout le monde a foncé vers la porte everybody rushed for the door

fonction NOUN FEM ❶ **job**; une voiture de fonction a company car ❷ **function**

fonctionnaire NOUN MASC & FEM **civil servant**

fonctionnel, fonctionnelle ADJECTIVE MASC, FEM **functional**

fonctionnement NOUN MASC **working**; comprendre le fonctionnement de quelque chose to understand how something works

fonctionner VERB [1] **to work**

fonction publique NOUN FEM **civil service**

fond NOUN MASC ❶ **bottom**; au fond du lac at the bottom of the lake, au fond de la bouteille in the bottom of the bottle ❷ back; au fond du tiroir at the back of the drawer, au fond de la salle at the back of the room ❸ end; au fond du couloir at the end of the corridor ❹ background ❺ au fond basically

fondamental ADJECTIVE MASC (PLURAL **fondamentaux**) **basic**, **fundamental**

fondateur, **fondatrice** NOUN MASC, FEM **founder**

fondation NOUN FEM **foundation**

fond de teint NOUN MASC **make-up**, **foundation**

fonder VERB [1] ❶ **to found** ❷ **to base**

fondre VERB [3] **to melt**

fondu ADJECTIVE **melted**

font VERB ▸ SEE **faire**

fontaine NOUN FEM ❶ **fountain** ❷ **drinking fountain**

fonte NOUN FEM ❶ **cast iron**; une poêle en fonte a cast iron frying pan ❷ **melting** (of metal) ❸ **thawing** (of ice)

foot NOUN (informal) un match de foot a football match, jouer au foot to play football

football NOUN MASC **football**

footballeur NOUN MASC **footballer**

footing NOUN MASC **jogging**; faire du footing to go jogging

forain NOUN MASC **fairground worker**

forain ADJECTIVE une fête foraine a funfair

force NOUN FEM ❶ **strength** ❷ **force**; de force by force ❸ **force**; force de vente sales force ❹ à force de by, à force de travailler toute la nuit, elle a fini sa dissertation she finished her essay by working all night

forcément ADVERB ❶ **inevitably**; il y a forcément une solution there has to be a solution ❷ pas forcément not necessarily

forcer VERB [61] ❶ **to force** ❷ se forcer to force yourself

forêt NOUN FEM **forest**

forfait NOUN MASC **fixed price**

forgeron NOUN MASC **blacksmith**

formalité NOUN FEM **formality**

format NOUN MASC **format**, **size**

formation NOUN FEM **training**; elle a une formation d'infirmière she's a trained nurse

formation continue NOUN FEM **continuing education**

forme NOUN FEM ❶ **shape**, **form** ❷ être en forme to be on form, se mettre en forme to get fit, tu as l'air en forme you're looking well

formel, **formelle** ADJECTIVE MASC, FEM ❶ **positive**, **categorical** ❷ **formal**

formellement ADVERB **strictly**; formellement interdit strictly forbidden

former VERB [1] ❶ **to form** ❷ **to train**, **to educate**

formidable ADJECTIVE (informal) **great**, **fantastic**; le film était formidable the film was fantastic

formulaire NOUN MASC **form**; remplir un formulaire to fill in a form

a
b
c
d
e
f
g
h
i
j
k
l
m
n
o
p
q
r
s
t
u
v
w
x
y
z

formule NOUN FEM ❶ **formula**; Formule Un Formula One (car racing) ❷ **form** ❸ **format**

fort ADJECTIVE ❶ **strong**; il est très fort he's very strong, le café est très fort the coffee's very strong ❷ être fort en quelque chose to be good at something, elle est très forte en maths she's very good at maths ❸ **stout**

fort ADVERB ❶ **extremely**; c'était fort bon it was extremely good ❷ **hard**; frapper fort to knock (or hit) hard ❸ **loudly**; chanter fort to sing loudly, parle plus fort speak louder

forteresse NOUN FEM **fortress**

fortifiant NOUN MASC **tonic**

fortifier VERB [1] ❶ **to strengthen** ❷ **to fortify**

fortuit ADJECTIVE **accidental**

fortune NOUN FEM ❶ **fortune**; faire fortune to make a fortune ❷ de fortune makeshift, un lit de fortune a makeshift bed

fossé NOUN MASC **ditch**

fossette NOUN FEM **dimple**

fou, folle NOUN MASC, FEM **madman, madwoman**; un fou m'a doublé dans un virage a madman overtook me on a bend

fou, folle ADJECTIVE MASC, FEM ❶ **mad**; devenir fou to go mad ❷ **crazy, amazing**; on a passé une soirée folle we had an amazing evening, il y avait un monde fou there were masses of people ❸ être fou de to be mad about
• attraper un fou rire to get the giggles

• **foudre** NOUN FEM **lightning**; être frappé par la foudre to be struck by lightning

fouet NOUN MASC ❶ **whip** ❷ **whisk** (for eggs, cream, etc)

fouetter VERB [1] ❶ **to whip** ❷ **to whisk** (eggs, cream, etc)
• avoir d'autres chats à fouetter to have other fish to fry (literally: to have other cats to whip)

fougère NOUN FEM ❶ **fern** ❷ **bracken**

fouille NOUN FEM **search**

fouiller VERB [1] ❶ **to search**; fouiller quelqu'un to search somebody, la police a fouillé la chambre/la maison the police searched the room/house ❷ fouiller dans quelque chose to rummage through something

fouillis NOUN MASC **mess**

foulard NOUN MASC **scarf**

foule NOUN FEM ❶ **crowd** ❷ une foule de masses of

four NOUN MASC **oven**; cuit au four roasted, baked

four à micro-ondes NOUN MASC **microwave oven**

fourche NOUN FEM **garden fork, pitchfork**

fourchette NOUN FEM **fork**

fourgon NOUN MASC **van**

fourgonnette NOUN FEM (small) **van**

fourmi NOUN FEM **ant**
• avoir des fourmis dans les jambes to have pins and needles in your legs (literally: to have ants in your legs)

fourmiller *VERB* [1] fourmiller de to be swarming with

fourneau *NOUN MASC* (*PLURAL* fourneaux) stove

fournée *NOUN FEM* batch (*of cakes, bread*)

fournir *VERB* [2] to supply

fournisseur *NOUN MASC* supplier

fournitures *PLURAL NOUN FEM* stationery; les fournitures de bureau office stationery, les fournitures scolaires school equipment (*stationery, school bags etc*)

fourré *ADJECTIVE* ❶ filled; fourré au chocolat with a chocolate filling ❷ fur-lined

fourrure *NOUN FEM* ❶ fur ❷ fur coat

foyer *NOUN MASC* ❶ home; rester au foyer to stay at home (*rather than going out to work*), une femme au foyer a housewife ❷ hearth ❸ household ❹ hostel

fracas *NOUN MASC* crash

fracasser *VERB* [1] to smash

fraction *NOUN FEM* fraction

fracture *NOUN FEM* fracture

fracturer *VERB* [1] ❶ to break open ❷ to fracture

fragile *ADJECTIVE* ❶ fragile ❷ frail

fragment *NOUN MASC* fragment

fraîche *ADJECTIVE* ▸ SEE **frais²**

fraîcheur *NOUN FEM* ❶ coolness ❷ freshness

frais¹ *PLURAL NOUN MASC* ❶ expenses; les frais de déplacement travel expenses ❷ costs

frais², **fraîche** *ADJECTIVE MASC, FEM* ❶ cool, cold; il fait frais ce matin it's a chilly morning ❷ cool; 'boissons fraîches' 'cool drinks', servir frais serve chilled, conserver au frais keep in a cool place ❸ fresh; des légumes frais fresh vegetables, 'peinture fraîche' 'wet paint'

fraise *NOUN FEM* strawberry; une glace à la fraise a strawberry ice cream

framboise *NOUN FEM* raspberry; un yaourt à la framboise a raspberry yoghurt

franc¹ *NOUN MASC* franc (*the currency of Switzerland; name of the currencies used in France, Belgium and Luxembourg until replaced by the euro; 100 French francs = 15.24 euros*)

franc², **franche** *ADJECTIVE MASC, FEM* frank

français *NOUN MASC* French; j'apprends le français I'm learning French, Laura parle français Laura speaks French

français *ADJECTIVE* French; un film français a French film

Français, **Française** *NOUN MASC, FEM* Frenchman, Frenchwoman; les Français the French

France *NOUN FEM* France; aller en France to go to France, habiter en France to live in France

franche *ADJECTIVE* ▸ SEE **franc²**

franchement ADVERB ❶ frankly; franchement, je ne le crois pas frankly, I don't believe him ❷ really; le film était franchement nul the film was really awful

franchir VERB [2] to cross

franchise NOUN FEM ❶ frankness, honesty ❷ franchise

francophone ADJECTIVE French-speaking

frange NOUN FEM fringe

frangin NOUN MASC (informal) brother

frangine NOUN FEM (informal) sister

frangipane NOUN FEM almond cream

franglais NOUN MASC Franglais (a mixture of French and English)

frapper VERB [1] ❶ to hit ❷ frapper à la porte to knock on the door ❸ to strike; être frappé par to be struck by, ça m'a beaucoup frappé that made a big impression on me ❹ frappé par le chômage hit by unemployment

fraude NOUN FEM ❶ fraud ❷ cheating

fredonner VERB [1] to hum

freezer NOUN MASC freezer compartment (in a fridge)

frein NOUN MASC brake; les freins the brakes, le frein à main the handbrake

freiner VERB [1] ❶ to brake ❷ to slow down

frêle ADJECTIVE frail

frelon NOUN MASC hornet

frémir VERB [2] ❶ to shudder ❷ to tremble

frêne NOUN MASC ash tree

fréquemment ADVERB frequently

fréquence NOUN FEM frequency

fréquenté ADJECTIVE ❶ busy; un restaurant très fréquenté a very busy restaurant ❷ un quartier mal fréquenté a rough area

fréquenter VERB [1] ❶ to go around with (people) ❷ to go often to (a place)

frère NOUN MASC brother

fric NOUN MASC (informal) money

frictionner VERB [1] to rub

frigidaire NOUN MASC fridge

frigo NOUN MASC (informal) fridge; au frigo in the fridge

frileux, frileuse ADJECTIVE MASC, FEM être frileux to feel the cold, je ne suis pas frileuse I don't feel the cold

frime NOUN FEM (informal) c'est de la frime! it's all show!

fringues PLURAL NOUN FEM (informal) clothes

fripé ADJECTIVE crumpled

frire VERB [74] faire frire quelque chose to fry something

frisé ADJECTIVE ❶ curly ❷ curly-haired

frisée NOUN FEM curly endive, frisée (a sort of lettuce)

friser VERB [1] to curl

frisson NOUN MASC shiver

frissonner VERB [1] ❶ to shiver ❷ to shudder

frit ADJECTIVE fried

frite NOUN FEM **chip, French fry**; steak frites steak and chips

friture NOUN FEM friture de poissons fried fish

froid NOUN MASC ❶ le froid the cold ❷ avoir froid to be cold, j'ai froid I'm cold ❸ il fait froid aujourd'hui it's cold today ❹ prendre froid to catch a chill

froid ADJECTIVE **cold**; tes mains sont froides your hands are cold

froidement ADVERB **coldly**

froideur NOUN FEM **coldness**

froisser VERB [1] ❶ **to crease** ❷ se froisser to crease, la soie se froisse facilement silk crushes easily ❸ se froisser to take offence ❹ se froisser to strain (a muscle)

frôler VERB [1] **to brush against**

fromage NOUN MASC **cheese**

fromagerie NOUN FEM **cheese shop**

froment NOUN MASC **wheat**

froncer VERB [61] froncer les sourcils to frown

front NOUN MASC ❶ **forehead** ❷ faire front à to face up to

frontière NOUN FEM **border**; nous avons passé la frontière à Bâle we crossed the border at Basle

frotter VERB [1] **to rub**; se frotter les yeux to rub your eyes

fruit NOUN MASC les fruits fruit, acheter des fruits to buy some fruit, un fruit a piece of fruit, veux-tu un fruit? would you like some fruit?

fruité ADJECTIVE **fruity**

fruits de mer PLURAL NOUN MASC

seafood; une omelette aux fruits de mer a seafood omelette

frustrant ADJECTIVE **frustrating**

frustrer VERB [1] ❶ **to thwart** ❷ **to frustrate**

fugue NOUN FEM ❶ faire une fugue to run away ❷ **fugue**

fuir VERB [44] ❶ **to run away, to flee** ❷ fuir quelque chose to run away from something ❸ **to leak**; la bouilloire fuit the kettle's leaking

fuite NOUN FEM ❶ **flight** ❷ prendre la fuite to flee ❸ **leak**

fulgurant ADJECTIVE **dazzling**

fumé ADJECTIVE **smoked**; du saumon fumé smoked salmon

fumée NOUN FEM **smoke**
• il n'y a pas de fumée sans feu there's no smoke without fire

fumer VERB [1] ❶ **to smoke** ❷ fumer une cigarette to smoke a cigarette, il fume la pipe he smokes a pipe
• fumer comme un pompier to smoke like a chimney (literally: to smoke like a fireman)

fumeur, fumeuse NOUN MASC, FEM **smoker**; zone non-fumeur no-smoking area

fumier NOUN MASC **manure**

funambule NOUN MASC & FEM **tightrope walker**

funèbre ADJECTIVE ❶ **funeral**; pompes funèbres undertaker's ❷ **gloomy**

funérailles PLURAL NOUN FEM **funeral**

funiculaire NOUN MASC **funicular**

fur NOUN MASC ❶ au fur et à mesure as you go along, je corrige les erreurs au fur et à mesure I correct the

a
b
c
d
e
f
g
h
i
j
k
l
m
n
o
p
q
r
s
t
u
v
w
x
y
z

mistakes as I go along ❷ au fur et à mesure que as

furet NOUN MASC **ferret**

fureur NOUN FEM ❶ **rage, fury** ❷ **frenzy**
- faire fureur to be all the rage; ces boucles d'oreilles font fureur en ce moment these earrings are all the rage at the moment

furibond ADJECTIVE **furious**

furieusement ADVERB **furiously**

furieux, furieuse ADJECTIVE MASC, FEM **furious**; elle est furieuse contre son copain she's furious with her boyfriend

furoncle NOUN MASC **boil**

fusain NOUN MASC **charcoal** (for drawing)

fuseau NOUN MASC **ski pants**

fusée NOUN FEM **rocket**

fusible NOUN MASC **fuse**

fusil NOUN MASC **gun**

fusiller VERB [1] to **shoot**

fusionner VERB [1] to **merge**

fût NOUN MASC **cask, barrel**

futé ADJECTIVE ❶ **crafty** ❷ **bright, clever**

futur NOUN MASC **future** (tense)

futur ADJECTIVE **future**; son futur mari her husband-to-be

gâcher VERB [1] ❶ to **waste**; gâcher la nourriture to waste food ❷ to **spoil**; ça m'a gâché la journée! that's spoiled my day!

gâchis NOUN MASC **waste**

gadget NOUN MASC **gadget**

gaffe NOUN FEM (informal) **blunder**; j'ai fait une gaffe I've done something stupid
- fais gaffe! watch out!

gage NOUN MASC **forfeit** (in a game)

gagnant, gagnante NOUN MASC, FEM **winner**

gagnant ADJECTIVE **winning**

gagner VERB [1] ❶ to **win**; il a gagné he's won, gagner le match to win the match ❷ to **earn** (money); elle gagne bien sa vie she makes a good living ❸ gagner du temps to save time

gai ADJECTIVE **cheerful**

gaieté NOUN FEM **cheerfulness**

gain NOUN MASC ❶ **earnings** ❷ c'est un gain de temps it saves time

galaxie NOUN FEM **galaxy**

galerie NOUN FEM **gallery**

galerie marchande NOUN FEM **shopping arcade**

galet NOUN MASC **pebble**

galette NOUN FEM ❶ **biscuit** ❷ **round flat cake or loaf**

galette des Rois NOUN FEM **Twelfth Night cake** (a cake eaten on Twelfth Night; it contains a 'fève', literally a bean, but usually a small ceramic figure; the person who gets this is the king or queen and is given a cardboard crown to wear)

galipette NOUN FEM **somersault** (child's)

Galles NOUN **le pays de Galles Wales**

gallois NOUN MASC **Welsh** (language)

gallois ADJECTIVE **Welsh**

Gallois, Galloise NOUN MASC, FEM **Welshman, Welshwoman; les Gallois the Welsh**

galoper VERB [1] **to galop**

gamba NOUN FEM **king prawn**

gamin, gamine NOUN MASC, FEM (informal) **kid; elle a trois gamins she has three kids**

gamme NOUN FEM ❶ **range; la nouvelle gamme de produits de beauté the new range of beauty products** ❷ **scale** (in music)

gammé ADJECTIVE **la croix gammée the swastika**

gangster NOUN MASC **gangster**

gant NOUN MASC **glove**

gant de boxe NOUN MASC **boxing glove**

gant de ménage NOUN MASC **rubber glove**

gant de toilette NOUN MASC **faceloth**

garage NOUN MASC **garage**

garagiste NOUN MASC & FEM ❶ **garage owner** ❷ **motor mechanic**

garantie NOUN FEM **guarantee**

garantir VERB [2] **to guarantee**

garçon NOUN MASC ❶ **boy** ❷ **young man; un brave garçon a nice chap** ❸ **waiter** ❹ **un vieux garçon a bachelor**

garçon de café NOUN MASC **waiter** (in a cafe)

garde NOUN MASC & FEM ❶ **guard** ❷ **nurse** ❸ **être de garde to be on duty, la pharmacie de garde the duty chemist's, mettre quelqu'un en garde to warn somebody**
• **prends garde! watch out, be careful!**

garder VERB [1] ❶ **to keep; est-ce que tu peux garder mon sac? can you keep my bag for me?, je t'ai gardé du gâteau I've kept you some cake, je t'ai gardé une place I've kept you a seat** ❷ **to keep on; elle a gardé son manteau she kept her coat on** ❸ **to look after; je garde mon petit-fils ce soir I'm looking after my grandson this evening** ❹ **garder la maison to guard the house**

garderie NOUN FEM **day nursery**

garde-robe NOUN FEM **wardrobe**

gardien, gardienne NOUN MASC, FEM ❶ **security guard** ❷ **caretaker** ❸ **attendant** (in a car park or museum)

gardien de but NOUN MASC **goalkeeper**

gardien de la paix NOUN MASC **policeman**

gare *NOUN FEM* (railway) station

garer *VERB* [1] ❶ garer une voiture to park a car ❷ se garer to park

gare routière *NOUN FEM* coach station

garni *ADJECTIVE* bien garni full, well-stocked

garnir *VERB* [2] ❶ to decorate ❷ to stock (shelves, fridge)

garniture *NOUN FEM* ❶ side-dish ❷ filling (for sandwich) ❸ topping (for pizza) ❹ trimming, decoration

gars *NOUN MASC* (informal) guy

Gascogne *NOUN FEM* Gascony

gasoil *NOUN MASC* diesel (oil)

gaspiller *VERB* [1] to waste

gastronome *NOUN MASC & FEM* gourmet

gastronomie *NOUN FEM* gastronomy

gâteau *NOUN MASC (PLURAL* gâteaux) cake; un gâteau au chocolat a chocolate cake

gâter *VERB* [1] ❶ to spoil ❷ se gâter to go bad, la viande se gâte the meat is going bad, le temps se gâte the weather's breaking

gauche *NOUN FEM* ❶ left; à gauche on the left, les Anglais conduisent à gauche the English drive on the left, tournez à gauche turn left, à ma gauche on my left ❷ la gauche the Left (in politics), des idées de gauche left-wing ideas

gauche *ADJECTIVE* left, left-hand; sa main gauche his left hand

gaucher, gauchère *ADJECTIVE MASC, FEM* left-handed

gaufre *NOUN FEM* waffle

gaufrette *NOUN FEM* wafer

gaz *NOUN MASC* gas; le chauffage à gaz gas central heating, nous nous chauffons au gaz we have gas heating

gazeux, gazeuse *ADJECTIVE MASC, FEM* fizzy; eau gazeuse fizzy mineral water

gazole *NOUN MASC* diesel (oil)

gazon *NOUN MASC* grass, lawn

géant, géante *NOUN MASC, FEM* giant

géant *ADJECTIVE* huge

gel *NOUN MASC* ❶ frost ❷ le gel des prix the price freeze ❸ gel

gelé *ADJECTIVE* frozen

gelée *NOUN FEM* ❶ jelly; œuf en gelée egg in aspic ❷ frost

geler *VERB* [45] to freeze; il gèle dehors it's freezing outside

gélule *NOUN FEM* capsule

Gémeaux *PLURAL NOUN MASC* Gemini (sign of the Zodiac)

gémir *VERB* [2] to moan

gênant *ADJECTIVE* ❶ annoying; ce bruit est très gênant that noise is very annoying ❷ awkward; c'est une situation gênante it's an awkward situation

gencive *NOUN FEM* gum (part of your mouth)

gendarme *NOUN MASC* policeman

gendarmerie *NOUN FEM* police station

gendarmerie nationale *NOUN FEM* (French) national police force

gendre NOUN MASC **son-in-law**

gêne NOUN FEM ❶ **embarrassment** ❷ **inconvenience** ❸ **discomfort**

gêné ADJECTIVE **embarrassed**

gêner VERB [1] ❶ **to bother**; est-ce que mon sac vous gêne? is my bag in your way? ❷ **to embarrass** ❸ **to block** (traffic); ta voiture gêne your car's in the way

général NOUN MASC (PLURAL généraux) **general**; le général Dubois General Dubois

général ADJECTIVE MASC (PLURAL généraux) **general**; en général in general, generally, de façon générale generally

généralement ADVERB **generally**

génération NOUN FEM **generation**

généreux, généreuse ADJECTIVE MASC, FEM **generous**

générique NOUN MASC (film) **credits**

générosité NOUN FEM **generosity**

genêt NOUN MASC **broom** (the bush)

génétique NOUN FEM **genetics**

Genève NOUN **Geneva**

génial ADJECTIVE MASC (PLURAL géniaux) ❶ **brilliant**; une idée géniale a brilliant idea ❷ (informal) **great**; c'était génial! it was great!

génie NOUN MASC ❶ **genius** ❷ **engineering**

genou NOUN MASC (PLURAL **genoux**) **knee**; avoir mal au genou to have a sore knee, être à genoux to be kneeling, se mettre à genoux to kneel down, sur mes genoux on my lap

genre NOUN MASC **kind**; un genre de sauce épicée a kind of spicy sauce, un peu dans le genre de ton pull a bit like your sweater

gens PLURAL NOUN MASC **people**; beaucoup de gens lots of people, les gens disent que ... people say that ...

gentil, gentille ADJECTIVE MASC, FEM ❶ **kind, nice**; elle est très gentille she's really nice ❷ **kind**; c'est très gentil de ta part it's very kind of you ❸ **good**; sois gentil et mange ta viande be a good boy and eat up your meat

gentillesse NOUN FEM **kindness**

gentiment ADVERB ❶ **nicely**; demande gentiment ask nicely ❷ **kindly**

géographie NOUN FEM **geography**

géologie NOUN FEM **geology**

géométrie NOUN FEM **geometry**

gérant, gérante NOUN MASC, FEM **manager, manageress**

gérer VERB [24] **to manage, to run**

germain ADJECTIVE un cousin germain a first cousin

gésier NOUN MASC **gizzard**

geste NOUN MASC **gesture**

gestion NOUN FEM **management**; gestion de fichiers file management (on a computer)

gibier NOUN MASC **game** (for example, venison, pheasant)

gifle NOUN FEM **slap** (in the face)

gifler VERB [1] **to slap** (in the face)

gigantesque ADJECTIVE **huge, gigantic**; un repas gigantesque a huge meal

a
b
c
d
e
f
g
h
i
j
k
l
m
n
o
p
q
r
s
t
u
v
w
x
y
z

gigaoctet NOUN MASC **gigabyte**; un disque dur de 20 gigaoctets a twenty gigabyte hard disk

gigot NOUN MASC **leg of lamb**

gilet NOUN MASC ❶ **cardigan** ❷ **waistcoat**

gilet de sauvetage NOUN MASC **life-jacket**

gingembre NOUN MASC **ginger**

girafe NOUN FEM **giraffe**

gitan, gitane NOUN MASC, FEM **gipsy**

gîte (rural) NOUN MASC **holiday house**

glaçage NOUN MASC ❶ **glazing** ❷ **icing**

glace NOUN FEM ❶ **ice cream**; une glace au chocolat a chocolate ice cream ❷ **ice** ❸ **mirror**; se regarder dans la glace to look at yourself in the mirror ❹ **window** (in a car)

glacé ADJECTIVE ❶ **icy cold**; j'ai les mains glacées my hands are freezing ❷ un thé glacé an iced tea

glacier NOUN MASC **glacier**

glacière NOUN FEM **cool-box**

glaçon NOUN MASC **ice cube**

glissant ADJECTIVE **slippery**

glisser VERB [1] to slip, to slide; attention, ça glisse! be careful, it's slippery!

global NOUN MASC (PLURAL globaux), ADJECTIVE **total**

globalisation NOUN FEM **globalization**

gloire NOUN FEM **fame, glory**

glorieux, glorieuse ADJECTIVE MASC, FEM **glorious**

glossaire NOUN MASC **glossary**

gobelet NOUN MASC **cup, tumbler**; un gobelet en carton a paper cup

godasse NOUN FEM (informal) **shoe**

gogo (informal) à gogo as much as you like, pizza à gogo as much pizza as you can eat

golden NOUN FEM **Golden Delicious (apple)**

golf NOUN MASC ❶ **golf**; jouer au golf to play golf ❷ **golf course**

golfe NOUN MASC **gulf**

golfeur, golfeuse NOUN MASC, FEM **golfer**

gomme NOUN FEM **rubber**

gommer VERB [1] to rub out

gonfler VERB [1] ❶ to pump up (tyres) ❷ to blow up (a balloon)

gorge NOUN FEM ❶ **throat**; j'ai mal à la gorge I've got a sore throat, j'avais la gorge serrée I had a lump in my throat, il chantait à pleine gorge he was singing at the top of his voice ❷ **gorge**

gorgée NOUN FEM **sip**; une gorgée de thé a sip of tea

gorille NOUN MASC **gorilla**

gosse NOUN MASC & FEM **kid**

goudron NOUN MASC **tar**

gourde NOUN FEM **water bottle**

gourmand ADJECTIVE **greedy**

gourmandise NOUN FEM ❶ **greed** ❷ elle aime les gourmandises she likes sweet things

gousse NOUN FEM une gousse d'ail a clove of garlic

goût NOUN MASC **taste**; ça a un goût bizarre it has a strange taste, de bon goût in good taste
• chacun ses goûts it takes all sorts to make a world

goûter NOUN MASC ❶ **teatime snack** ❷ **children's party**

goûter VERB [1] ❶ **to taste, to try**; est-ce que tu as goûté le gâteau? have you tried the cake? ❷ **to have a teatime snack**

goutte NOUN FEM **drop**; une goutte de a drop of, goutte à goutte drop by drop

gouvernement NOUN MASC **government**

gouverner VERB [1] **to govern, to rule**

grâce NOUN FEM grâce à **thanks to**, la soirée a été un grand succès grâce à toi the evening was a great success thanks to you

gracieux, gracieuse ADJECTIVE MASC, FEM **graceful**

grade NOUN MASC **rank**; monter en grade to be promoted

gradins PLURAL NOUN MASC **terraces** (in a stadium)

graduel, graduelle ADJECTIVE MASC, FEM **gradual**

graffiti PLURAL NOUN MASC **graffiti**

grain NOUN MASC ❶ **grain**; un grain de sable a grain of sand ❷ du poivre en grains peppercorns ❸ du café en grains coffee beans ❹ un grain de beauté a beauty spot ❺ un grain de raisin a grape

graine NOUN FEM **seed**

graisse NOUN FEM **fat, grease**

grammaire NOUN FEM **grammar**

gramme NOUN MASC **gramme**

grand ADJECTIVE ❶ **big**; une grande maison a big house, c'est ma grande sœur she's my big sister ❷ **tall**; un grand arbre a tall tree, ton frère est très grand your brother's very tall, elle est plus grande que moi she's taller than me ❸ **great**; un grand artiste a great artist, un grand ami a great friend ❹ **main**; les grandes lignes main (railway) lines

grand ADVERB **wide**; la porte était grande ouverte the door was wide open

grand bassin NOUN MASC **main pool** (for experienced swimmers)

grand-chose PRONOUN **much**; pas grand-chose not much, il ne reste pas grand-chose there's not much left

Grande-Bretagne NOUN FEM **Great Britain**

grande personne NOUN FEM **grown-up**

grande surface NOUN FEM **hypermarket**

grandes vacances PLURAL NOUN FEM **summer holidays**

grandeur NOUN FEM **size**; grandeur nature life-size

grandir VERB [2] **to grow, to grow up**

grand magasin NOUN MASC **department store**

grand-mère NOUN FEM (PLURAL grands-mères) **grandmother**

grand-père NOUN MASC (PLURAL grands-pères) **grandfather**

grands espaces PLURAL NOUN MASC **open spaces**

grands-parents PLURAL NOUN MASC **grandparents**

grange NOUN FEM **barn**

graphiste NOUN MASC & FEM **graphic designer**

grappe NOUN FEM une grappe de raisin a bunch of grapes

gras, grasse ADJECTIVE MASC, FEM **❶ fatty, greasy**; 40% matière grasse 40% fat (on cheese or yoghurt label) **❷** une peau grasse oily skin
• faire la grasse matinée to have a lie-in

gratitude NOUN FEM **gratitude**

gratte-ciel NOUN MASC **skyscraper**

gratter VERB [1] **❶** gratter quelque chose to scratch something **❷** se gratter to scratch (yourself) **❸ to itch**; ça gratte it itches

gratuit ADJECTIVE **free**; le concert est gratuit the concert's free, 'entrée gratuite' 'admission free'

grave ADJECTIVE **❶ serious**; un grave accident a serious accident **❷** ce n'est pas grave it doesn't matter **❸ serious**; une expression grave a serious expression **❹ deep**; une voix grave a deep voice

gravement ADVERB **seriously**; elle est gravement malade she's seriously ill

gravure NOUN FEM **engraving, print**

gré NOUN MASC contre son gré against his will

grec NOUN MASC **Greek** (language)

grec, grecque ADJECTIVE MASC, FEM **Greek**

Grec, Grecque NOUN MASC, FEM **Greek** (person)

Grèce NOUN FEM **Greece**

grêle NOUN FEM **hail**

grelotter VERB [1] **to shiver**

grenade NOUN FEM **❶ grenade ❷ pomegranate**

grenadine NOUN FEM **grenadine** (pomegranate cordial)

grenier NOUN MASC **attic, loft**; au grenier in the attic

grenouille NOUN FEM **frog**; les cuisses de grenouille frogs' legs

grève NOUN FEM **strike**; une grève des trains a train strike, le métro est en grève the underground's on strike, faire grève to go (or be) on strike

gréviste NOUN MASC & FEM **striker**

grièvement ADVERB **seriously**; grièvement blessé seriously injured

griffe NOUN FEM **claw**

griffonner VERB [1] **to scribble**

grillade NOUN FEM **grilled meat, meat for grilling**; une grillade de porc a pork steak

grillage NOUN MASC **wire netting**

grille NOUN FEM **❶ metal gate ❷ railings ❸ wire fence**

grillé ADJECTIVE **❶ grilled ❷ toasted**; du pain grillé toast

grille-pain NOUN MASC **toaster**

griller VERB [1] **❶ to grill ❷ to toast**

grillon NOUN MASC **cricket** (the creature not the game)

grimace NOUN FEM **faire des grimaces** to make faces

grimper VERB [1] **to climb**; grimper dans un arbre to climb a tree

grincer VERB [61] **to creak**, **to squeak**

grincheux, **grincheuse** ADJECTIVE MASC, FEM **grumpy**

grippe NOUN FEM **flu**; avoir la grippe to have flu, une grippe intestinale gastric flu

gris ADJECTIVE **grey**

grisaille NOUN FEM **dull overcast weather**

grogner VERB [1] ❶ **to growl** ❷ **to grumble**

gronder VERB [1] ❶ gronder quelqu'un to tell somebody off, se faire gronder to get a telling-off ❷ **to rumble** (thunder, for example)

gros, **grosse** ADJECTIVE MASC, FEM ❶ **big**; un gros morceau a big piece, un gros problème a big problem ❷ **fat**; un gros monsieur a fat man ❸ un gros rhume a bad cold ❹ un gros fumeur a heavy smoker ❺ un gros mot a swear word ❻ en gros roughly

groseille NOUN FEM **redcurrant**

groseille à maquereau NOUN FEM **gooseberry**

grosse ADJECTIVE ▸ SEE **gros**

grossesse NOUN FEM **pregnancy**

grosseur NOUN FEM ❶ **lump** ❷ **size**

grossier, **grossière** ADJECTIVE MASC, FEM ❶ **rude** ❷ **crude**; une idée grossière a rough idea of, une erreur grossière a bad mistake

grossir VERB [2] **to put on weight**; il a beaucoup grossi he's put on a lot of weight

grosso modo ADVERB **roughly**

grotesque ADJECTIVE **ridiculous**

grotte NOUN FEM **cave**

groupe NOUN MASC **group**; travailler/ voyager en groupe to work/travel in a group

grouper VERB [1] ❶ **to group** ❷ se grouper to gather, to form a group

groupe sanguin NOUN MASC **blood group**

grue NOUN FEM **crane**

guépard NOUN MASC **cheetah**

guêpe NOUN FEM **wasp**

guère ADVERB ne ... guère hardly, je ne l'ai guère vu depuis Noël I've hardly seen him since Christmas

guérir VERB [2] ❶ **to cure**; le médecin l'a guéri the doctor cured him ❷ **to get better**; j'ai été malade mais je suis maintenant guéri I've been ill but I'm better now

guérison NOUN FEM **recovery** (from an illness or injury) .

guerre NOUN FEM **war**; le pays est actuellement en guerre the country is at war at the moment, la Seconde Guerre mondiale World War II

guetter VERB [1] **to watch out for**

gueule NOUN FEM **mouth** (of an animal; considered rude if used of a person); (ferme) ta gueule! (rude) shut up!

gueule de bois *NOUN FEM (informal)*
avoir la gueule de bois to have a
hangover

gueuler *VERB* [1] *(informal)* **to yell**

gui *NOUN MASC* **mistletoe**

guichet *NOUN MASC* ❶ **ticket office** *(in
a station or museum)* ❷ **box office**
(in a theatre or cinema) ❸ **counter**,
window *(in a bank or post office)*

guichet automatique *NOUN MASC*
cashpoint

guide *NOUN MASC* **guide**

guider *VERB* [1] **to guide**

guidon *NOUN MASC* **handlebars**

guillemets *PLURAL NOUN MASC*
inverted commas; entre
guillemets in inverted commas

guirlande *NOUN FEM* des guirlandes
tinsel, des guirlandes en papier
paper chains

guirlande électrique *NOUN FEM*
fairy lights, **Christmas-tree lights**

guitare *NOUN FEM* **guitar**; jouer de la
guitare to play the guitar

guitariste *NOUN MASC & FEM* **guitarist**

gym *NOUN FEM (informal)* **PE**,
gymnastics

gymnase *NOUN MASC* **gym**; je te
verrai au gymnase I'll see you in
the gym

gymnastique *NOUN FEM*
gymnastics, **exercises**

habile *ADJECTIVE* **clever**; elle est habile
de ses mains she's clever with her
hands, de manière habile cleverly

habillé *ADJECTIVE* ❶ **dressed**; je ne
suis pas encore habillé I'm not
dressed yet ❷ **smart** *(for example, a
dress or suit)*

habiller *VERB* [1] ❶ habiller quelqu'un
to dress somebody ❷ s'habiller to
get dressed, habille-toi vite! get
dressed quick! ❸ s'habiller to dress
up, s'habiller en clown to dress up
as a clown

habitant, **habitante** *NOUN MASC, FEM*
inhabitant

habitation *NOUN FEM* **house**

habiter *VERB* [1] **to live**; ils habitent à
Paris they live in Paris

habitude *NOUN FEM* ❶ **habit**; c'est
une mauvaise habitude it's a
bad habit ❷ d'habitude usually,
d'habitude il arrive à midi he
usually arrives at twelve ❸ comme
d'habitude as usual, j'ai pris le bus
comme d'habitude I took the bus
as usual ❹ avoir l'habitude de faire
to be used to doing, j'ai l'habitude
de travailler le soir I'm used to
working in the evening

habitué, **habituée** *NOUN MASC, FEM*
regular *(in a cafe, shop, etc)*

habitué *ADJECTIVE* être habitué à quelque chose to be accustomed to something

habituel, **habituelle** *ADJECTIVE MASC, FEM* usual

habituer *VERB* [1] s'habituer à quelque chose to get used to something, je m'y suis habituée I've got used to it

hache *NOUN FEM* axe

haché *ADJECTIVE* chopped; du bœuf haché mince

hacher *VERB* [1] ❶ to chop *(vegetables)* ❷ to mince *(meat)*

hachis Parmentier *NOUN MASC* shepherd's pie

haddock *NOUN MASC* smoked haddock

haie *NOUN FEM* ❶ hedge ❷ les haies hurdles *(sport)*

haine *NOUN FEM* hatred

haïr *VERB* [46] to hate

Haïti *NOUN MASC* Haiti

haïtien *FEM* haïtienne *ADJECTIVE* Haitian

Haïtien, **Haïtienne** *NOUN MASC, FEM* Haitian

haleine *NOUN FEM* breath; être hors d'haleine to be out of breath

hall *NOUN MASC* ❶ (entrance) hall ❷ concourse *(in a station)*

halles *PLURAL NOUN FEM* covered market

halogène *ADJECTIVE* halogen; une lampe halogène a halogen lamp

halte *NOUN FEM* stop; halte! stop!, faire une halte to stop somewhere

halte-garderie *NOUN FEM* playgroup

haltérophilie *NOUN FEM* weightlifting

hamac *NOUN MASC* hammock

hameau *NOUN MASC (PLURAL* hameaux*)* group of houses

hameçon *NOUN MASC* fish hook

hamster *NOUN MASC* hamster

hanche *NOUN FEM* hip

handball *NOUN MASC* handball; jouer au handball to play handball

handicapé *ADJECTIVE* disabled

hanté *ADJECTIVE* haunted

harceler *VERB* [45] ❶ to pester ❷ to harass

hareng *NOUN MASC* herring

haricot *NOUN MASC* bean; haricot vert French bean, haricot blanc haricot bean

harmonica *NOUN MASC* mouth organ; jouer de l'harmonica to play the mouth organ

harmonie *NOUN FEM* harmony

harmoniser *VERB* [1] to coordinate, to harmonize

harnais *NOUN MASC* harness

harpe *NOUN FEM* harp

hasard *NOUN MASC* ❶ chance; par hasard by chance, je l'ai rencontré par hasard I met him by chance ❷ au hasard at random, elle a choisi un livre au hasard she chose a book at random ❸ à tout hasard just in case, prends un manteau à tout hasard take a coat just in case ❹ à tout hasard on the off chance

hasardeux, hasardeuse *ADJECTIVE MASC, FEM* **risky**

hâte *NOUN FEM* à la hâte **hurriedly**, elle est partie à la hâte she left in a rush

hausse *NOUN FEM* **increase, rise**; une hausse des prix a rise in prices, les prix sont en hausse prices are rising

hausser *VERB* [1] ❶ **to raise** ❷ hausser les épaules to shrug your shoulders

haut *NOUN MASC* ❶ **top**; le haut de l'échelle the top of the ladder, regarder quelqu'un de haut en bas to look somebody up and down ❷ l'arbre fait 10 mètres de haut the tree is 10 metres high ❸ en haut **upstairs**, elle est en haut she's upstairs ❹ en haut de at the top of, en haut de l'escalier at the top of the stairs

haut *ADJECTIVE* ❶ **high**; la branche la plus haute the highest branch ❷ à haute voix **aloud**, lire à haute voix to read aloud

haut *ADVERB* **high**; plus haut dans l'arbre higher up the tree, 'voir plus haut' 'see above' *(in a book)*, haut les mains! hands up!

hautbois *NOUN MASC* **oboe**

hauteur *NOUN FEM* **height**; la hauteur de la pièce the height of the room, dans le sens de la hauteur upright, l'avion prend de la hauteur the plane's gaining height, il n'est pas

à la hauteur de son travail he's not up to his job

haut-parleur *NOUN MASC* **loudspeaker**

Haye *NOUN* La Haye **The Hague**

hebdomadaire *NOUN MASC* **weekly magazine**

héberger *VERB* [52] **to put up**; Jess va nous héberger Jess'll put us up

hein *EXCLAMATION (informal)* **what?, eh?**

hélas *EXCLAMATION* **unfortunately**; elle est déjà partie, hélas she's already left, unfortunately, hélas non I'm afraid not

hélicoptère *NOUN MASC* **helicopter**

hémorragie *NOUN FEM* **haemorrhage**

hennir *VERB* [2] **to neigh**

herbe *NOUN FEM* ❶ l'herbe **grass** ❷ **herb**; les fines herbes mixed herbs, les herbes de Provence mixed herbs ❸ une mauvaise herbe a weed

hérisson *NOUN MASC* **hedgehog**

héritage *NOUN MASC* **inheritance**

hériter *VERB* [1] **to inherit**

hermétique *ADJECTIVE* **airtight**

héroïne *NOUN FEM* ❶ **heroine** ❷ **heroin**

héros *NOUN MASC* **hero**

hésitation *NOUN FEM* **hesitation**

hésiter *VERB* [1] **to hesitate**; à ta place, je n'hésiterais pas! if I were you, I wouldn't hesitate!, j'ai beaucoup hésité avant d'accepter I thought about it for a long time before I agreed, j'hésite entre le poulet et le poisson I can't decide whether to have the chicken or the fish

hêtre NOUN MASC ❶ **beech tree** ❷ **beech wood**

heure NOUN FEM ❶ **hour**; une heure plus tard an hour later, deux heures de train two hours in the train, une demi-heure half an hour, une heure et demie an hour and a half, Londres est à une heure d'avion de Paris London is an hour from Paris by air, toutes les quatre heures every four hours, toutes les heures: il y a des trains toutes les heures there are trains every hour, payé à l'heure paid by the hour, cent kilomètres à l'heure a hundred kilometres an hour ❷ **time**; quelle heure est-il? what time is it?, il est sept heures it's seven o'clock, à huit heures du matin at eight o'clock in the morning, tu te lèves à quelle heure demain? what time are you getting up tomorrow?, à neuf heures at nine o'clock, à six heures et demie at half past six ❸ être à l'heure to be on time ❹ à l'heure du déjeuner at lunchtime
• de bonne heure early; je me lève de bonne heure demain I'm getting up early tomorrow

heures d'affluence PLURAL NOUN FEM **peak time, rush hour**

heureusement ADVERB **fortunately**

heureux, heureuse ADJECTIVE MASC, FEM ❶ **happy**; elle est heureuse d'être ici she's happy to be here ❷ **lucky, fortunate**

heurter VERB [1] **to hit, to bump into**; la voiture a heurté un camion the car collided with a lorry

heurtoir NOUN MASC **(door) knocker**

hexagone NOUN MASC ❶ **hexagon** ❷ l'Hexagone France (French journalists often refer to France as l'Hexagone as it has a six-sided shape on the map)

hibou NOUN MASC (PLURAL hiboux) **owl**

hideux, hideuse ADJECTIVE MASC, FEM **hideous**

hier ADVERB **yesterday**; je l'ai vue hier I saw her yesterday, hier matin yesterday morning, avant-hier the day before yesterday

hi-fi NOUN FEM **hi-fi**; une chaîne hi-fi a stereo system

hippique ADJECTIVE **equestrian**; un concours hippique a horse show, un club hippique a riding school

hippodrome NOUN MASC **racecourse**

hippopotame NOUN MASC **hippopotamus**

hirondelle NOUN FEM **swallow**

histoire NOUN FEM ❶ **history**; l'histoire française French history ❷ **story**; l'histoire de ma vie the story of my life ❸ **matter**; c'est une histoire d'argent it's a matter of money
• faire des histoires to kick up a fuss

historique ADJECTIVE ❶ **historic**; un monument historique a historic monument ❷ **historical**

hit-parade NOUN MASC le hit-parade the charts (pop music)

hiver NOUN MASC **winter**; en hiver in winter

HLM NOUN MASC & FEM (short for habitation à loyer modéré) **council flat**; nous habitons dans un HLM à

French—English

Valence we live in a council flat in Valence, les HLM council housing

hocher VERB [1] hocher la tête to shake your head, to nod

hockey NOUN MASC **hockey**; jouer au hockey to play hockey, le hockey sur glace ice hockey

hollandais NOUN MASC **Dutch** (language)

hollandais ADJECTIVE **Dutch**

Hollandais, Hollandaise NOUN MASC, FEM **Dutchman, Dutchwoman**; les Hollandais the Dutch

Hollande NOUN FEM **Holland**; en Hollande in (or to) Holland

homard NOUN MASC **lobster**

homéopathique ADJECTIVE **homeopathic**

hommage NOUN MASC **tribute, homage**; rendre hommage à quelqu'un/quelque chose to pay tribute to someone/something

homme NOUN MASC **man**; l'homme de la rue the man in the street, l'homme moderne est plus grand que ses ancêtres modern man is taller than his ancestors

homme d'affaires NOUN MASC **businessman**

homme d'État NOUN MASC **statesman**

homogénéisé ADJECTIVE **homogenized**

homosexuel, homosexuelle NOUN MASC, FEM, ADJECTIVE **homosexual**

Hongrie NOUN FEM **Hungary**

hongrois NOUN MASC **Hungarian** (language)

hongrois ADJECTIVE **Hungarian**

honnête ADJECTIVE **honest, respectable**

honnêtement ADVERB **honestly, frankly**; honnêtement je ne sais pas ce que tu veux dire I honestly don't know what you mean

honnêteté NOUN FEM **honesty**; en toute honnêteté in all honesty

honneur NOUN MASC **honour**

honorer VERB [1] **to honour**

honte NOUN FEM **shame**; avoir honte de quelque chose to be ashamed of something, j'ai vraiment honte I'm really ashamed of myself, tu n'as pas honte! what a thing to say (or do)!

honteux, honteuse ADJECTIVE MASC, FEM **disgraceful**

hôpital NOUN MASC **hospital**; être à l'hôpital to be in hospital

hoquet NOUN MASC **hiccup**; avoir le hoquet to have hiccups

horaire NOUN MASC **timetable, schedule**; les horaires de train the train timetable

horizon NOUN MASC **horizon**; à l'horizon on the horizon

horizontal ADJECTIVE MASC (PLURAL horizontaux) **horizontal**

horloge NOUN FEM **clock**

horodateur NOUN MASC **parking ticket machine**

horoscope NOUN MASC **horoscope**

horreur NOUN FEM ❶ horror; quelle horreur! how awful! ❷ avoir horreur de quelque chose to hate something, j'ai horreur d'être en retard I hate being late, j'ai horreur des escargots! I can't stand snails!

horrible ADJECTIVE horrible

horrifier VERB [1] to horrify

hors PREPOSITION ❶ hors de outside, hors de France outside France ❷ être hors jeu to be offside ❸ les boutiques hors taxe the duty-free shops
• être hors de soi to be beside yourself; j'étais hors de moi I was beside myself

hors-d'œuvre NOUN MASC starter (to a meal)

hortensia NOUN MASC hydrangea

hospitalier ADJECTIVE un centre hospitalier a hospital

hospitaliser VERB [1] elle a été hospitalisée she's been taken into hospital

hospitalité NOUN FEM hospitality

hostilité NOUN FEM hostility

hôte¹ NOUN MASC host

hôte² NOUN MASC, FEM ❶ guest; hôte payant paying guest ❷ host

hôtel NOUN MASC hotel; un hôtel de luxe a luxury hotel, passer deux nuits à l'hôtel to spend two nights in a hotel

hôtel de ville NOUN MASC town hall

hôtesse NOUN FEM ❶ hostess ❷ receptionist

hôtesse d'accueil NOUN FEM receptionist

hôtesse de l'air NOUN FEM flight attendant

housse NOUN FEM cover (for a chair or a machine); une housse de couette a duvet cover

houx NOUN MASC holly

hublot NOUN MASC ❶ window (in a plane) ❷ porthole (in a boat)

huer VERB [1] to boo; la foule a hué l'arbitre the crowd booed the referee

huile NOUN FEM oil; huile de tournesol sunflower oil, huile d'olive olive oil, huile solaire suntan oil

huit NUMBER ❶ eight; Paul a huit ans Paul's eight, le huit juillet the eighth of July ❷ huit jours a week, il y a huit jours a week ago

huitième NOUN MASC au huitième on the eighth floor

huitième ADJECTIVE eighth

huître NOUN FEM oyster

humain ADJECTIVE human

humanitaire ADJECTIVE humanitarian

humeur NOUN FEM mood; il est de bonne humeur he's in a good mood, elle est de mauvaise humeur she's in a bad mood, je ne suis pas d'humeur à faire ça I'm not in the mood to do that

humide ADJECTIVE damp

humidité NOUN FEM damp

humoristique ADJECTIVE humorous; un dessin humoristique a cartoon

humour NOUN MASC humour; avoir de l'humour to have a sense of humour

hurler *VERB* [1] **to yell, to howl**

hutte *NOUN FEM* **hut**

hydratant *ADJECTIVE* **moisturizing**

hygiène *NOUN FEM* **hygiene**

hygiénique *ADJECTIVE* ❶ **hygienic** ❷ **une serviette hygiénique a sanitary towel** ❸ **du papier hygiénique toilet paper**

hymne *NOUN MASC* **hymn**; **l'hymne national the national anthem**

hypermarché *NOUN MASC* **hypermarket**

hypermétrope *ADJECTIVE* **long-sighted**

hypertension *NOUN FEM* **high blood pressure**

hypnotiser *VERB* [1] **to hypnotize**

hypocondriaque *NOUN MASC & FEM* *ADJECTIVE,* **hypochondriac**

hypocrite *NOUN MASC & FEM* **hypocrite**

hypothèse *NOUN FEM* **hypothesis**

hystérie *NOUN FEM* **hysteria**

iceberg *NOUN MASC* **iceberg**

ici *ADVERB* ❶ **here**; **il y a trop de monde ici there are too many people here, les gens d'ici the local people** ❷ **jusqu'ici this far, les bus ne viennent pas jusqu'ici the buses don't come this far** ❸ **jusqu'ici so far, jusqu'ici il a fait beau so far the weather's been good**

icône *NOUN FEM* **icon**

idéal *ADJECTIVE MASC (PLURAL* **idéaux)** **ideal**; **l'idéal serait de louer une voiture the ideal thing would be to hire a car**

idée *NOUN FEM* **idea**; **quelle bonne idée! what a good idea!, je n'ai aucune idée I've no idea, se faire des idées to imagine things**

identifier *VERB* [1] **to identify**

identique *ADJECTIVE* **identical**

identité *NOUN FEM* **identity**; **une carte d'identité an identity card**

idiot, idiote *NOUN MASC, FEM* **idiot**; **ne fais pas l'idiot! don't fool around!**

idiot *ADJECTIVE* **stupid**; **c'est vraiment idiot! it's really stupid!**

ignorance *NOUN FEM* **ignorance**

ignorant *ADJECTIVE* **ignorant**

ignorer *VERB* [1] ❶ **not to know**; **j'ignore leur adresse I don't know their address, j'ignore les détails I**

don't know the details **②** to ignore; ils l'ont ignoré they ignored him

il *PRONOUN* **①** he; il parle français he speaks French **②** it; 'où est mon sac?' – 'il est sur la chaise' 'where's my bag?' – 'it's on the chair, il pleut it's raining

île *NOUN FEM* **island**

illégal *ADJECTIVE MASC (PLURAL* illégaux) **illegal**

illimité *ADJECTIVE* **unlimited**

illisible *ADJECTIVE* **illegible**

illumination *NOUN FEM* **floodlighting**; les illuminations de Noël the Christmas lights

illuminer *VERB* [1] **to floodlight**

illusion *NOUN FEM* **illusion**; elle se fait des illusions she's fooling herself

illustration *NOUN FEM* **illustration**

illustré *NOUN MASC* **comic**

illustré *ADJECTIVE* **illustrated**

illustrer *VERB* [1] **to illustrate**

ils *PRONOUN* **they**; ils sont en vacances they're on holiday

il y a ▸ SEE **avoir**

image *NOUN FEM* **picture**; il y a de belles images dans ton livre there are some lovely pictures in your book

imaginaire *ADJECTIVE* **imaginary**

imagination *NOUN FEM* **imagination**

imaginer *VERB* [1] **to imagine**; je n'arrive pas à l'imaginer I can't imagine it, elle va appeler, j'imagine I suppose she'll phone

imbattable *ADJECTIVE* **unbeatable**

imbécile *NOUN MASC & FEM* **fool**; faire l'imbécile to fool around

imbécile *ADJECTIVE* **idiotic**

imitation *NOUN FEM* **imitation**

imiter *VERB* [1] **to imitate**

immangeable *ADJECTIVE* **inedible**

immanquablement *ADVERB* **inevitably**

immatriculation *NOUN FEM* **registration** (of a car); une plaque d'immatriculation a numberplate

immédiat *ADJECTIVE* **immediate**; dans l'immédiat for the time being, je n'ai pas de projets dans l'immédiat I don't have any plans for the time being

immédiatement *ADVERB* **immediately**

immense *ADJECTIVE* **huge**

immeuble *NOUN MASC* **①** block of flats **②** building; un immeuble de six étages a six-storey building **③** un immeuble de bureaux an office block

immigration *NOUN FEM* **immigration**

immigré, **immigrée** *NOUN MASC, FEM* **immigrant**

immobile *ADJECTIVE* **motionless**

immobilier, **immobilière** *NOUN MASC, FEM* une agence immobilière an estate agent's

immobiliser *VERB* [1] **to immobilize**

immodéré *ADJECTIVE* **excessive**

immoral *ADJECTIVE MASC (PLURAL* immoraux) **immoral**

a
b
c
d
e
f
g
h
i
j
k
l
m
n
o
p
q
r
s
t
u
v
w
x
y
z

immuniser VERB [1] **to immunize**

impact NOUN MASC **impact**

impair ADJECTIVE **odd**; un nombre impair an odd number

impardonnable ADJECTIVE **unforgivable**

imparfait NOUN MASC **imperfect (tense)**; à l'imparfait in the imperfect

imparfait ADJECTIVE **imperfect**

impasse NOUN FEM **dead end**

impatience NOUN FEM **impatience**

impatient ADJECTIVE **impatient**

impeccable ADJECTIVE **❶ perfect**; un accent français impeccable a perfect French accent **❷ spotless**; l'appartement est impeccable the flat's spotless **❸** (informal) **great**; 'je viendrai te chercher chez toi à midi' – 'impeccable!' 'I'll come and pick you up at your place at twelve' – 'great!'

impensable ADJECTIVE **unthinkable**

imper NOUN MASC (informal) (short for impermeéable) **raincoat**

impératif NOUN MASC **imperative**; à l'impératif in the imperative

impératrice NOUN FEM **empress**

imperfection NOUN FEM **imperfection**

imperméable NOUN MASC **raincoat**

impertinent ADJECTIVE **cheeky**

impitoyable ADJECTIVE **merciless**

impliquer VERB [1] **❶ to mean**; cela implique que nous n'aurons pas assez d'argent this means that we won't have enough money **❷** être impliqué dans quelque chose to be involved in something

impoli ADJECTIVE **rude**

importance NOUN FEM **importance**; ça n'a pas d'importance it doesn't matter

important ADJECTIVE **❶ important**; il est important de savoir que ... it's important to know that ... **❷ considerable**; une réduction importante a considerable reduction, il y aura des retards importants there will be considerable delays

importations PLURAL NOUN FEM **imports**

importer VERB [1] **❶ to import** (goods) **❷ to matter**; 'lequel veux-tu?' – 'n'importe!' 'which one do you want?' – 'it doesn't matter!', n'importe où anywhere, viens n'importe quand come any time, n'importe qui sait faire ça anyone can do that, il dit n'importe quoi he's talking nonsense, elle le fait n'importe comment she does it any old how

imposant ADJECTIVE **imposing**

imposer VERB [1] **❶ to impose**; imposer à quelqu'un de faire quelque chose to make somebody do something, la maman de Katy lui a imposé de rester à la maison Katy's mum made her stay at home **❷** s'imposer to establish oneself

impossibilité NOUN FEM **impossibility**

impossible ADJECTIVE **impossible**

impossible NOUN faire l'impossible to do your utmost, nous ferons

l'impossible pour les contacter
we'll do our utmost to contact them

impôt NOUN MASC **tax**

imprécis ADJECTIVE **vague**

impression NOUN FEM **impression**;
sa première impression his first
impression, elle a fait très bonne
impression she made a very good
impression, j'ai l'impression qu'il
n'est pas heureux I have a feeling
he's not happy

impressionnant ADJECTIVE
impressive

impressionner VERB [1] **to impress**

imprévisible ADJECTIVE
unpredictable

imprévu ADJECTIVE **unexpected**

imprimante NOUN FEM **printer** (for a
computer)

imprimante laser NOUN FEM **laser
printer**

imprimé NOUN MASC **form** (to fill in)

imprimé ADJECTIVE **printed**

imprimer VERB [1] **to print**

improviser VERB [1] **to improvise**

improviste NOUN à l'improviste
unexpectedly, mon oncle est arrivé
à l'improviste my uncle arrived
unexpectedly

imprudent ADJECTIVE ❶ **careless**
❷ **rash**

impuissant ADJECTIVE **helpless**

impulsif, impulsive ADJECTIVE MASC,
FEM **impulsive**

inabordable ADJECTIVE
❶ **inaccessible** ❷ des prix
inabordables **prohibitive prices**

inacceptable ADJECTIVE
unacceptable

inaccessible ADJECTIVE **inaccessible**

inachevé ADJECTIVE **unfinished**

inadapté ADJECTIVE **unsuitable**

inadmissible ADJECTIVE **intolerable**

inaperçu ADJECTIVE passer inaperçu
to go unnoticed, son départ est
passé inaperçu her departure went
unnoticed

inattendu ADJECTIVE **unexpected**;
une visite inattendue an
unexpected visit

inattention NOUN FEM **lack of
attention**; une faute d'inattention
a careless mistake

inaudible ADJECTIVE **inaudible**

inauguration NOUN FEM
inauguration, opening

inaugurer VERB [1] ❶ **to open** (an
exhibition, a new building) ❷ **to
unveil** (a monument)

incapable ADJECTIVE ❶ **incapable**;
je suis incapable de bouger!
I'm incapable of moving!
❷ **incompetent**; il est
complètement incapable he's
completely incompetent

incassable ADJECTIVE **unbreakable**

incendiaire NOUN MASC & FEM **arsonist**

incendiaire ADJECTIVE une bombe
incendiaire an incendiary bomb

incendie NOUN MASC **fire**; l'incendie
a détruit l'église the fire destroyed
the church

incertain ADJECTIVE ❶ **uncertain**; le
résultat est toujours incertain the
result is still uncertain ❷ **unsettled**
(weather)

a
b
c
d
e
f
g
h
i
j
k
l
m
n
o
p
q
r
s
t
u
v
w
x
y
z

incertitude NOUN FEM **uncertainty**

incident NOUN MASC **incident**; en cas d'incident if anything should happen

inciter VERB [1] **to encourage**; le père d'André l'a incité à apprendre la guitare André's father encouraged him to learn to play the guitar

inclure VERB [25] ❶ **to include** ❷ **to enclose**

inclus ADJECTIVE **including**; il y aura trente invités, enfants inclus there will be thirty guests, including children, jusqu'à samedi inclus up to and including Saturday

incollable ADJECTIVE le riz incollable easy-cook rice

incolore ADJECTIVE **colourless**

incommode ADJECTIVE ❶ **awkward** ❷ **uncomfortable**

incomparable ADJECTIVE **incomparable**

incompétent ADJECTIVE **incompetent**

incompréhensible ADJECTIVE **incomprehensible**

inconditionnel, inconditionnelle NOUN MASC, FEM **devotee**; c'est un inconditionnel du jazz he's a real jazz fan

inconditionnel, inconditionnelle ADJECTIVE MASC, FEM **unconditional**

inconfortable ADJECTIVE **uncomfortable**

inconnu, inconnue NOUN MASC, FEM **stranger**

inconnu ADJECTIVE **unknown**; elle m'est inconnue I don't know her

inconsciemment ADVERB **unconsciously**

inconscient ADJECTIVE ❶ **unthinking** ❷ **unconscious** (in a faint)

incontestable ADJECTIVE **unquestionable**

incontournable ADJECTIVE **unavoidable**; c'est un fait incontournable it's an undeniable fact

inconvénient NOUN MASC ❶ **drawback**; il y a plusieurs inconvénients there are several drawbacks ❷ l'inconvénient, c'est que ... the difficulty is that ... ❸ si vous n'y voyez pas d'inconvénient if you have no objection

incorporer VERB [1] **to blend in** (ingredients in cooking); incorporez l'huile une goutte à la fois blend in the oil drop by drop

incorrect ADJECTIVE ❶ **incorrect** ❷ **rude**

incrédule ADJECTIVE **incredulous**

incroyable ADJECTIVE **incredible**; elle a des connaissances incroyables her knowledge is incredible

inculper VERB [1] inculper quelqu'un de to charge somebody with (a crime), elle a été inculpée de vol she was charged with theft

Inde NOUN FEM **India**; en Inde in (or to) India

indécis ADJECTIVE ❶ **undecided**; elle est toujours indécise she hasn't decided yet ❷ **indecisive**

indemne ADJECTIVE **unharmed**

indemnisation NOUN FEM
compensation; une demande
d'indemnisation a claim for
compensation

indemniser VERB [1] to
compensate; demander à
être indemnisé to demand
compensation

indéniable ADJECTIVE **undeniable**

indépendamment ADVERB
independently

indépendance NOUN FEM
independence

indépendant ADJECTIVE
❶ **independent** ❷ cuisine
indépendante separate kitchen
❸ une maison indépendante a
detached house

index NOUN MASC ❶ **index**
❷ **forefinger**

indicateur NOUN MASC ❶ **timetable**
(in a rail or coach station);
l'indicateur des départs the
departures board ❷ **street**
directory ❸ **gauge** (for example,
for oil levels) ❹ un panneau
indicateur a road sign

indicateur de pression NOUN MASC
pressure gauge

indicatif NOUN MASC ❶ **dialling code**;
l'indicatif pour l'Espagne est 34
the dialling code for Spain is 34
❷ **theme tune** ❸ **indicative** (of
a verb)

indications PLURAL NOUN FEM
directions

indice NOUN MASC **clue**

indien, indienne ADJECTIVE MASC, FEM
Indian

Indien, Indienne NOUN MASC, FEM
Indian (person)

indifférent ADJECTIVE **indifferent**

indigène ADJECTIVE **native**; les
indigènes the locals

indigeste ADJECTIVE **indigestible**

indigestion NOUN FEM **indigestion**;
avoir une indigestion to have
indigestion

indignation NOUN FEM **indignation**

indigne ADJECTIVE ❶ **unworthy**
❷ **disgraceful**

indigner VERB [1] s'indigner to get
indignant

indiqué ADJECTIVE **recommended**; ce
n'est pas très indiqué it's not a very
good idea

indiquer VERB [1] **to point out, to**
show; pouvez-vous m'indiquer la
gare? can you show me the way to
the station?, le nom est indiqué sur
un grand panneau the name is on
a big sign, cela indique que ... this
shows that ...

indirect ADJECTIVE **indirect**

indiscipliné ADJECTIVE **unruly**

indiscret, indiscrète ADJECTIVE MASC,
FEM ❶ **indiscreet**; ne le lui dis pas,
elle est très indiscrète don't tell
her, she can't keep a secret ❷ si ce
n'est pas indiscret if it's not being
nosy

indiscutable ADJECTIVE
unquestionable

indispensable ADJECTIVE **essential**;
les vêtements indispensables
essential clothing, il est
indispensable it's essential

a
b
c
d
e
f
g
h
i
j
k
l
m
n
o
p
q
r
s
t
u
v
w
x
y
z

indisposé ADJECTIVE **unwell**

individu NOUN MASC **individual**; c'est un drôle d'individu he's a funny bloke

individuel, individuelle ADJECTIVE MASC, FEM ❶ **individual** ❷ **separate**; une chambre individuelle a single room, une maison individuelle a detached house

indolore ADJECTIVE **painless**

indulgent ADJECTIVE **indulgent**; notre prof de maths est trop indulgent avec nous our maths teacher isn't strict enough with us

industrialisé ADJECTIVE les pays industrialisés the industrialized countries

industrie NOUN FEM **industry**

industriel, industrielle ADJECTIVE MASC, FEM **industrial**; une ville industrielle an industrial city

inédit ADJECTIVE ❶ **unpublished** ❷ **new**

inefficace ADJECTIVE ❶ **inefficient**; en tant que patron il est très inefficace as a boss he's very inefficient ❷ **ineffective**; un remède inefficace an ineffective remedy

inégal ADJECTIVE MASC (PLURAL **inégaux**) ❶ **uneven** ❷ **unequal**

inespéré ADJECTIVE **unhoped-for**; un succès inespéré an unhoped-for success

inévitable ADJECTIVE ❶ **inevitable**; c'était inévitable it was bound to happen ❷ **unavoidable**; des problèmes inévitables unavoidable problems

inexact ADJECTIVE ❶ **incorrect** ❷ **inaccurate**

inexpérimenté ADJECTIVE **inexperienced**

infarctus NOUN MASC **heart attack**

infect ADJECTIVE **foul**; le repas était infect! the meal was foul!

infecter VERB [1] ❶ **to infect** ❷ s'infecter to go septic

infection NOUN FEM **infection**

inférieur ADJECTIVE ❶ **lower**; sur une marche inférieure on a lower step, des prix inférieurs à la moyenne lower than average prices ❷ **smaller**; la taille inférieure the smaller size ❸ **inferior, worse**; de qualité inférieure of inferior quality

infernal ADJECTIVE MASC (PLURAL infernaux) **frightful, dreadful**

infini ADJECTIVE **infinite**

infinitif NOUN MASC **infinitive** (in grammar); à l'infinitif in the infinitive

infirme NOUN les infirmes the disabled

infirme ADJECTIVE **disabled**; est-il infirme? does he have a disability?

infirmerie NOUN FEM **medical room**

infirmier, infirmière NOUN MASC, FEM **nurse**

infirmité NOUN FEM **disability**

inflammable ADJECTIVE **flammable**

inflation NOUN FEM **inflation**

influence NOUN FEM **influence**; il a une bonne influence sur son frère he's a good influence on his brother

influencer *VERB* [61] **to influence**

informaticien, **informaticienne** *NOUN MASC, FEM* **computer scientist**

information *NOUN FEM*
❶ **information**; une information très utile a very useful piece of information ❷ les informations the news *(on TV or radio)*, les informations sont à vingt heures the news is at eight o'clock

informatique *NOUN FEM* **computer science**, **IT**

informatique *ADJECTIVE* **computer**; un système informatique a computer system

informatiser *VERB* [1] **to computerize**

informer *VERB* [1] ❶ **to inform** ❷ s'informer to find out, je peux m'informer si tu veux I can find out if you like

infos *PLURAL NOUN FEM* les infos the news *(on TV or radio)*

infrarouge *ADJECTIVE* **infra-red**

infusion *NOUN FEM* **herbal tea**

ingénierie *NOUN FEM* **engineering**

ingénieur *NOUN MASC* **engineer**; faire des études d'ingénieur to study engineering

ingénieux, **ingénieuse** *ADJECTIVE MASC, FEM* **ingenious**; c'était très ingénieux de sa part that was very ingenious of her

ingrat *ADJECTIVE* ❶ **ungrateful** ❷ un travail ingrat unrewarding work

ingrédient *NOUN MASC* **ingredient**

inhabité *ADJECTIVE* **uninhabited**

inhabituel, **inhabituelle** *ADJECTIVE MASC, FEM* **unusual**

inhalateur *NOUN MASC* **inhaler**

inhumain *ADJECTIVE* **inhuman**

inimaginable *ADJECTIVE* **unimaginable**, **unthinkable**

ininterrompu *ADJECTIVE* ❶ **uninterrupted** ❷ **continuous**

initial *ADJECTIVE MASC (PLURAL* **initiaux***)* **initial**

initiale *NOUN FEM* **initial**; mes initiales sont là-dessus my initials are on it

initiation *NOUN FEM* **introduction** *(to a new place or skill)*; une journée d'initiation an introductory day *(to a course, for example)*, une initiation à l'anglais an introduction to English

initiative *NOUN FEM* **initiative**

initier *VERB* [1] ❶ initier quelqu'un à to introduce somebody to *(a skill)* ❷ **to initiate** *(an idea or plan)* ❸ s'initier à quelque chose to learn about something, elle s'initie à la photo she's starting to learn photography

injecter *VERB* [1] **to inject**

injection *NOUN FEM* **injection**

injure *NOUN FEM* **insult**

injurier *VERB* [1] **to insult**; il m'a injurié he swore at me

injuste *ADJECTIVE* **unfair**

innocent *ADJECTIVE* **innocent**

innombrable *ADJECTIVE* **countless**

innovation *NOUN FEM* **innovation**

a b c d e f g h i j k l m n o p q r s t u v w x y z

innover VERB [1] **to break new ground**

inoccupé ADJECTIVE **empty**

inondation NOUN FEM **flood**; des inondations flooding

inonder VERB [1] **to flood**

inoubliable ADJECTIVE **unforgettable**

inouï ADJECTIVE **incredible**

inox NOUN MASC **stainless steel**; une casserole en inox a stainless steel pan

inoxydable ADJECTIVE un évier en acier inoxydable a stainless steel sink

inquiet, **inquiète** ADJECTIVE MASC, FEM **anxious**, **worried**

inquiétant ADJECTIVE **worrying**

inquiéter VERB [24] ❶ **to worry**; je ne veux pas t'inquiéter I don't want to worry you, ça m'inquiète un peu I find that a bit worrying, ce qui m'inquiète, c'est qu'elle n'a pas téléphoné what I find worrying is the fact that she hasn't phoned ❷ s'inquiéter **to worry, to be worried**, elle va s'inquiéter si nous sommes en retard she'll worry if we're late, ne t'inquiète pas! don't worry!

inquiétude NOUN FEM **anxiety**

insatisfait ADJECTIVE **dissatisfied**

inscription NOUN FEM ❶ **enrolment** (for a course or in a school) ❷ **registration**

inscrire VERB [38] ❶ **to enrol, to register** (someone for a course or school); elle m'a inscrit pour l'examen she's entered me for the exam ❷ s'inscrire **to enrol, to**

s'inscrire au club de foot to join the football club

insecte NOUN MASC **insect**

insérer VERB [24] **to, insert**

insertion NOUN FEM ❶ **insertion** (of an advertisement in a paper, for example) ❷ **integration** (when somebody joins a new community); l'insertion des jeunes dans la société the integration of young people into society

insignifiant ADJECTIVE **insignificant**

insister VERB [1] **to insist**; il faut insister keep on trying, la clé est un peu tordue, il faut insister un peu the key's a bit bent, you have to push it really hard

insolation NOUN FEM **sunstroke**; attraper une insolation to get sunstroke

insolent ADJECTIVE **insolent**

insoutenable ADJECTIVE **unbearable**

inspecter VERB [1] **to inspect**

inspecteur, **inspectrice** NOUN MASC, FEM **inspector**

inspection NOUN FEM ❶ **inspection** ❷ **inspectorate** (an official department)

inspiration NOUN FEM **inspiration**

inspirer VERB [1] ❶ **to inspire**; ça ne m'inspire pas that doesn't appeal to me ❷ **to breathe in**; inspire fort! breathe in deep! ❸ s'inspirer **to be inspired by**, il s'est inspiré de Picasso he was inspired by Picasso

instable ADJECTIVE **unstable**; il fait un temps instable the weather's unsettled

installation NOUN FEM
❶ installation, putting in
❷ move (to a house or town); avant son installation à Paris before he moved to Paris ❸ des installations sportives sports facilities

installer VERB [1] ❶ to install, to put in (central heating or a dishwasher, for example) ❷ to connect (gas, electricity, a phone) ❸ s'installer to settle, to settle in, installez-vous do sit down, je me suis installée à mon bureau I settled down at my desk

instant NOUN MASC moment; pour l'instant for the moment, à tout instant all the time

instantané ADJECTIVE instant; du café instantané instant coffee

instinct NOUN MASC instinct

institut NOUN MASC institute; un institut de beauté a beautician's

instituteur, institutrice NOUN MASC, FEM primary school teacher

institution NOUN FEM ❶ institution ❷ private school

institutrice NOUN FEM ▶ SEE **instituteur**

instructeur, instructrice NOUN MASC, FEM instructor

instruction NOUN FEM ❶ education; instruction civique civics ❷ instructions instructions, instructions de lavage washing instructions

instruire VERB [26] ❶ to teach, to train ❷ s'instruire to learn

instruit ADJECTIVE educated

instrument NOUN MASC
❶ instrument; un instrument de mesure a measuring instrument, les instruments de bord the controls ❷ un instrument de musique a musical instrument, un instrument à cordes a string instrument

insu NOUN MASC à mon insu without my knowing

insuffisance NOUN FEM shortage

insuffisant ADJECTIVE ❶ insufficient ❷ inadequate; c'est insuffisant it's not good enough

insultant ADJECTIVE insulting

insulte NOUN FEM insult

insulter VERB [1] to insult

insupportable ADJECTIVE unbearable; je la trouve insupportable I can't stand her

intact ADJECTIVE intact

intégral ADJECTIVE MASC (PLURAL intégraux) complete

intégrale NOUN FEM complete works (usually music); l'intégrale des Beatles the complete Beatles collection

intellectuel, intellectuelle NOUN MASC, FEM, ADJECTIVE intellectual

intelligence NOUN FEM intelligence

intelligent ADJECTIVE clever, intelligent

intendance NOUN FEM administration (in a school)

intense ADJECTIVE intense

intensif, intensive ADJECTIVE MASC, FEM intensive

intention NOUN FEM intention; avoir l'intention de faire to mean to do, j'avais l'intention d'y aller mais je n'ai pas pu I meant to go but I wasn't able to

interdiction NOUN FEM **ban**; 'interdiction de fumer' 'no smoking'

interdire VERB [47] **to forbid**; je t'interdis de le faire I forbid you to do it

interdit ADJECTIVE **forbidden**; 'entrée interdite' 'no entry', il est interdit de fumer dans la salle smoking is forbidden in the theatre

intéressant ADJECTIVE ❶ **interesting**; c'est un film très intéressant it's a very interesting film ❷ à un prix intéressant at a good price

intéressé[1] ADJECTIVE **interested**; être intéressé par quelque chose to be interested in something

intéressé[2], **intéressée** NOUN MASC, FEM **person concerned**

intéresser VERB [1] ❶ **to interest**; ça ne m'intéresse pas that doesn't interest me ❷ s'intéresser à to be interested in, elle s'intéresse beaucoup à l'informatique she's very interested in computing

intérêt NOUN MASC ❶ **interest**; ce livre est sans intérêt this book is really boring ❷ tu as intérêt à faire you'd better do, tu as intérêt à le finir avant ce soir! you'd better get it finished by this evening!

intérieur NOUN MASC **inside**, **interior**; l'intérieur du placard the inside of the cupboard, où est-elle? – à l'intérieur where is she? – inside (in the house)

intérieur ADJECTIVE **inside**, **internal**; le côté intérieur the inside

intermédiaire NOUN MASC & FEM **go-between**

intermédiaire ADJECTIVE **intermediate**; avez-vous la taille intermédiaire? do you have the size in between?

internat NOUN MASC **boarding school**

international ADJECTIVE MASC (PLURAL internationaux) **international**

interne NOUN MASC & FEM **boarder** (in a school)

interne ADJECTIVE **internal**

Internet NOUN MASC **Internet**; sur Internet on the Internet

interpeller VERB [1] ❶ **to call out to** ❷ la police l'a interpellé the police have taken him in for questioning

interphone NOUN MASC **entry phone**

interprète NOUN MASC & FEM ❶ (in the theatre) **actor**, (in music) **performer**, **soloist** ❷ **interpreter**

interpréter VERB [24] ❶ **to perform**, **to play** (a role in the theatre or a piece of music), **to sing** (a song) ❷ **to interpret** (a language or a remark)

interrogatif NOUN MASC **interrogative**

interrogation NOUN FEM ❶ **test** (at school) ❷ **questioning**

interroger VERB [52] ❶ **to question**, **to ask**; il m'a interrogé sur mon séjour en France he asked me about my stay in France ❷ **to test** (at school)

interrompre VERB [69] **to interrupt**; interrompre quelqu'un to interrupt somebody, il a interrompu son travail he broke off his work

interrupteur NOUN MASC **switch**

interruption NOUN FEM
❶ **interruption** ❷ **sans interruption** without stopping

intervalle NOUN MASC ❶ **interval**
❷ **dans l'intervalle** in the meantime

intervenir VERB [81] **to intervene**

intervention NOUN FEM
intervention

interview NOUN FEM **interview** (on TV, radio, for a magazine)

intestin NOUN MASC **intestine**

intime ADJECTIVE **intimate**; **un journal intime** a diary (kept by somebody)

intimider VERB [1] **to intimidate**

intimité NOUN FEM **intimacy**; **dans l'intimité** in private

intolérable ADJECTIVE **intolerable**

intolérant ADJECTIVE **intolerant**

intoxication NOUN FEM **poisoning**

intoxiquer VERB [1] **to poison**

intrigue NOUN FEM **plot** (of a novel, play, etc)

introduction NOUN FEM
introduction

introduire VERB [26] ❶ **to introduce** (an idea, a measure, a new product)
❷ **s'introduire** to get into, **un cambrioleur s'est introduit dans l'appartement** a burglar got into the flat

intrus, **intruse** NOUN MASC, FEM
intruder

intuitif, **intuitive** ADJECTIVE MASC, FEM
intuitive

intuition NOUN FEM **intuition**

inusable ADJECTIVE **hard-wearing**

inutile ADJECTIVE **pointless**; **il est inutile de l'appeler** there's no point telephoning him, **inutile de dire que ...** needless to say ...

inutilement ADVERB **pointlessly**; **je l'ai cherché inutilement** I looked for it in vain

inutilisable ADJECTIVE **unusable**

invalide NOUN MASC & FEM **disabled person**

invasion NOUN FEM **invasion**

inventer VERB [1] **to invent**

invention NOUN FEM **invention**

inverse NOUN MASC **l'inverse** the opposite, **l'inverse est vrai** the opposite is true

inverse ADJECTIVE **opposite**; **en sens inverse** in the opposite direction, **dans l'ordre inverse** in reverse order

investigation NOUN FEM
investigation

investissement NOUN MASC
investment

invisible ADJECTIVE **invisible**

invitation NOUN FEM **invitation**

invité, **invitée** NOUN MASC, FEM **guest**; **nous avons des invités ce soir** we have people coming round this evening

inviter VERB [1] **to invite**; **ils m'ont invité à dîner** they invited me to dinner

involontaire ADJECTIVE
unintentional

invraisemblable *ADJECTIVE*
❶ unlikely; une explication invraisemblable an unlikely explanation **❷** *(informal)* **amazing**

ira, irai, iraient, irais, irait, iras *VERB ▸ SEE* **aller¹**

iris *NOUN MASC* **iris**

irlandais *NOUN MASC*

irlandais *ADJECTIVE* **Irish**

Irlandais, Irlandaise *NOUN MASC, FEM* **Irishman, Irishwoman**; les Irlandais the Irish

Irlande *NOUN FEM* **Ireland**; la République d'Irlande the Republic of Ireland

Irlande du Nord *NOUN FEM* **Northern Ireland**

ironie *NOUN FEM* **irony**

ironique *ADJECTIVE* **ironic**

irons, iront *VERB ▸ SEE* **aller¹**

irradier *VERB* [1] **to irradiate**

irréel, irréelle *MASC, FEM ADJECTIVE* **unreal**

irréfléchi *ADJECTIVE* **thoughtless**

irrégularité *NOUN FEM* **irregularity**

irrégulier, irrégulière *ADJECTIVE MASC, FEM* **irregular**

irrésistible *ADJECTIVE* **irresistible**

irresponsable *ADJECTIVE* **irresponsible**

irritable *ADJECTIVE* **irritable**

irritation *NOUN FEM* **irritation**

irriter *VERB* [1] **❶ to irritate**; cela m'irrite that makes me cross **❷** s'irriter to get irritated

islamique *ADJECTIVE* **Islamic**

isolation *NOUN FEM* **insulation**; isolation acoustique soundproofing

isolé *ADJECTIVE* **❶ remote ❷ lonely**

isoler *VERB* [1] **❶ to insulate** *(a room or building)* **❷ to isolate** *(a sick person or a prisoner)*

Israël *NOUN MASC* **Israel**

israélien, israélienne *ADJECTIVE MASC, FEM* **Israeli**

issue *NOUN FEM* **exit**; issue de secours emergency exit, une rue sans issue a dead end

Italie *NOUN FEM* **Italy**; en Italie in (or to) Italy

italien *NOUN MASC* **Italian** *(language)*

italien *ADJECTIVE* **Italian**

Italien, Italienne *NOUN MASC, FEM* **Italian** *(person)*

itinéraire *NOUN MASC* **route**

itinérant *ADJECTIVE* **travelling**

ivoire *NOUN MASC, ADJECTIVE* **ivory**

ivre *ADJECTIVE* **drunk**

ivresse *NOUN FEM* **drunkenness**

ivrogne *NOUN MASC & FEM* **drunkard**

j' *PRONOUN* ▸ SEE **je**

jacinthe *NOUN FEM* hyacinth

jalousie *NOUN FEM* ❶ jealousy ❷ slatted blind

jaloux, **jalouse** *ADJECTIVE MASC, FEM* jealous; elle est jalouse de mes résultats d'examen she's jealous of my exam results

jamaïquain *ADJECTIVE* Jamaican

Jamaïquain, **Jamaïquaine** *NOUN MASC, FEM* Jamaican

Jamaïque *NOUN FEM* Jamaica

jamais *ADVERB* ❶ never; elle ne fume jamais she never smokes, on ne sait jamais you never know, jamais plus! never again! ❷ ever; plus grand que jamais bigger than ever, si jamais il pleut if by any chance it rains, à jamais forever

jambe *NOUN FEM* leg; se casser la jambe to break your leg

jambon *NOUN MASC* ham; jambon blanc cooked ham, jambon de pays cured raw ham

janvier *NOUN MASC* January; en janvier, au mois de janvier in January

Japon *NOUN MASC* Japan; au Japon in (or to) Japan

japonais *NOUN MASC* Japanese *(language)*

japonais *ADJECTIVE* Japanese

Japonais, **Japonaise** *NOUN MASC, FEM* Japanese *(person)*

jardin *NOUN MASC* garden; Patrick est au jardin Patrick's in the garden, une chaise de jardin a garden chair

jardinage *NOUN MASC* gardening

jardinier, **jardinière**¹ *NOUN MASC, FEM* gardener

jardinière² *NOUN FEM* (large) plant pot

jardin public *NOUN MASC* park (in a town)

jaune *NOUN MASC* ❶ yellow ❷ un jaune d'œuf an egg-yolk

jaune *ADJECTIVE* yellow; une robe jaune a yellow dress

jaunisse *NOUN FEM* jaundice

Javel *NOUN* eau de Javel bleach

jazz *NOUN MASC* jazz; j'aime le jazz I like jazz

J.-C. *NOUN MASC* (short for Jésus-Christ); 200 avant J.-C. 200 BC, 400 après J.-C. 400 AD

je (j' before a vowel or silent 'h') *PRONOUN* I; je sais où il habite I know where he lives, j'habite à Lyon I live in Lyons

jean *NOUN MASC* ❶ (pair of) jeans; j'ai acheté un jean I've bought some jeans ❷ denim; une jupe en jean a denim skirt

jet *NOUN MASC* ❶ jet (of water or steam); les jets d'eau de Versailles the fountains at Versailles ❷ jet (plane)

a
b
c
d
e
f
g
h
i
j
k
l
m
n
o
p
q
r
s
t
u
v
w
x
y
z

jetée NOUN FEM **jetty**

jeter VERB [48] **❶ to throw**; jette-moi le ballon throw me the ball **❷ to throw away**; j'ai jeté ces vieilles chaussures I've thrown away those old shoes **❸** jeter un coup d'œil to have a look, est-ce que tu peux jeter un coup d'œil aux pommes de terre? can you have a look at the potatoes?

jeton NOUN MASC **❶ counter** (for a board game) **❷ token** (for a machine)

jeu NOUN MASC (PLURAL **jeux**) **❶ game**; faire un jeu to play a game, gagner par trois jeux à deux to win by three games to two **❷ gambling** **❸ acting**
• ce n'est pas du jeu! (informal) that's not fair!

jeu-concours NOUN MASC **competition**

jeu de cartes NOUN MASC **❶ pack of cards ❷ game of cards**

jeu de hasard NOUN MASC **game of chance**

jeu de mots NOUN MASC **pun**

jeu de société NOUN MASC **board game**

jeudi NOUN MASC **❶ Thursday**; nous sommes jeudi aujourd'hui it's Thursday today, jeudi prochain next Thursday, jeudi dernier last Thursday **❷ on Thursday**; je l'ai vu jeudi soir I saw him on Thursday evening **❸** le jeudi on Thursdays, fermé le jeudi closed on Thursdays **❹** tous les jeudis every Thursday

jeune NOUN MASC & FEM **young person**; une émission destinée aux jeunes a programme aimed at young people

jeune ADJECTIVE **young**; un jeune homme a young man, une jeune femme a young woman, une jeune fille a girl

jeunesse NOUN FEM **❶ young people**; la jeunesse d'aujourd'hui young people today **❷ youth**; dans ma jeunesse in my youth

jeu-vidéo NOUN MASC **video game**

Jeux Olympiques PLURAL NOUN MASC **Olympic Games**

jogging NOUN MASC **❶** faire du jogging to go jogging **❷** un jogging a track-suit

joie NOUN FEM **joy**

joindre VERB [49] **❶ to get hold of** (often by telephone); je n'ai pas pu la joindre I wasn't able to get hold of her **❷ to enclose** (in a letter or parcel) **❸ to put together**; les pieds joints feet together
• joindre les deux bouts to make ends meet (financially)

joli ADJECTIVE **pretty**

jongler VERB [1] **to juggle**

jongleur, jongleuse NOUN MASC, FEM **juggler**

jonquille NOUN FEM **daffodil**

joue NOUN FEM **cheek**

jouer VERB [1] **❶ to play**; elle joue avec le chien she's playing with the dog, à toi de jouer! your go!, bien joué! well done! **❷** jouer à to play (a sport), on va jouer au foot we're going to play football **❸** jouer de to play (an instrument), Robert joue de la guitare Robert plays the guitar **❹ to act**; il joue bien dans ce film he's really good in this film

jouet NOUN MASC **toy**

joueur, **joueuse** NOUN MASC, FEM
player

jour NOUN MASC ❶ **day**; les jours de
la semaine the days of the week,
trois jours plus tard three days
later, le jour où the day when, un
de ces jours one of these days ❷ de
nos jours nowadays, de nos jours,
ils sont assez fréquents nowadays
they are quite common ❸ mettre
quelque chose à jour to bring
something up to date ❹ **daylight**,
light; il fait jour it's daylight, en
plein jour in broad daylight, jour et
nuit night and day

jour de l'an NOUN MASC **New Year's
Day**

jour férié NOUN MASC **public holiday**

journal NOUN MASC (PLURAL **journaux**)
❶ **newspaper**, **magazine**; le
journal du soir the evening paper,
du papier journal newspaper (for
wrapping) ❷ **news** (on TV or radio);
le journal de vingt-deux heures
the ten o'clock news ❸ un journal
intime a diary

journalisme NOUN MASC **journalism**

journaliste NOUN MASC & FEM
journalist

journée NOUN FEM **day**; toute la
journée all day, the whole day, il
est payé à la journée he's paid by
the day

jour ouvrable NOUN MASC **working
day**

joyeux, **joyeuse** ADJECTIVE MASC, FEM
happy; Joyeux Anniversaire
Happy Birthday, Joyeux Noël Merry
Christmas

judaïsme NOUN MASC **Judaism**

judicieux, **judicieuse** ADJECTIVE
MASC, FEM **sensible**; un choix
judicieux a wise choice

judo NOUN MASC **judo**

juge NOUN MASC **judge**

juge de ligne NOUN MASC **line judge**
(in tennis)

juge de touche NOUN MASC
linesman (in football, rugby)

juge d'instruction NOUN MASC
examining magistrate

jugement NOUN MASC **judgement**

juger VERB [52] **to judge**

juif, **juive** NOUN MASC, FEM **Jew**

juif, **juive** ADJECTIVE MASC, FEM **Jewish**

juillet NOUN MASC **July**; en juillet, au
mois de juillet in July, le quatorze
juillet Bastille Day (July 14, a
national holiday to celebrate the
taking of the Bastille prison in Paris
by the people at the beginning of the
French Revolution in 1789)

juin NOUN MASC **June**; en juin, au mois
de juin in June

juive NOUN FEM, ADJECTIVE ▸ SEE **juif**

jumeau, **jumelle** NOUN MASC, FEM
(PLURAL **jumeaux**) **twin**; des vrais
jumeaux identical twins

jumeler VERB [18] **to twin** (towns);
Oxford est jumelé avec Grenoble
Oxford is twinned with Grenoble

jumelles PLURAL NOUN FEM
❶ **binoculars** ❷ ▸ SEE **jumeau**

jument NOUN FEM **mare**

jungle NOUN FEM **jungle**

jupe NOUN FEM **skirt**

jupon NOUN MASC **petticoat**

jurer VERB [1] **to swear**

juridique ADJECTIVE **legal**; le système juridique the legal system

jury NOUN MASC ❶ **jury** ❷ **board of examiners**

jus NOUN MASC ❶ **juice**; un jus d'orange an orange juice ❷ **gravy**

jus de fruits NOUN MASC **fruit juice**

jusqu'à PREPOSITION ❶ **as far as** *(a place)*; ce train va jusqu'à Paris this train goes as far as Paris, nous avons marché jusqu'à la mer we walked as far as the sea, il m'a accompagné jusqu'à chez moi he took me all the way home ❷ **until**; elle reste jusqu'à mardi she's staying until Tuesday, jusqu'à quand reste-t-il? how long is he staying for?, jusqu'à présent, jusqu'à maintenant up to now ❸ jusqu'à ce que until

juste ADJECTIVE ❶ **right, correct**; le mot juste the right word, ce que tu dis est juste what you say is right ❷ **fair**; ce n'est pas juste! it's not fair! ❸ **in tune**; elle chante juste she sings in tune ❹ c'est un peu juste it's a bit tight, une heure est un peu juste an hour's a bit tight

juste ADVERB **just**; juste à temps just in time, il vient tout juste d'arriver he's only just arrived

justement ADVERB ❶ **precisely** ❷ **just**; je parlais justement de toi I was just talking about you ❸ **correctly**; comme elle a dit très justement as she so rightly said

justesse NOUN FEM ❶ **correctness** ❷ de justesse only just, il a eu son avion, mais de justesse he caught his plane, but only just

justice NOUN FEM **justice**

justifier VERB [1] **to justify**

juteux, juteuse ADJECTIVE MASC, FEM **juicy**

juvénile ADJECTIVE **youthful**

Kk

kaki NOUN MASC **persimmon**

kaki ADJECTIVE **khaki**

kangourou NOUN MASC **kangaroo**

karaté NOUN MASC **karate**

karting NOUN MASC **go-karting**

kascher ADJECTIVE **kosher**

kermesse NOUN FEM **(school) fête**

ketchup NOUN MASC **ketchup**

kidnapper VERB [1] **to kidnap**

kidnappeur, kidnappeuse NOUN MASC, FEM **kidnapper**

kilo NOUN MASC **kilo**; deux kilos de pommes two kilos of apples, j'ai pris trois kilos I've put on three kilos

kilogramme *NOUN MASC*
kilogramme

kilométrage *NOUN MASC* **mileage**

kilomètre *NOUN MASC* **kilometre**; à dix kilomètres d'ici ten kilometres from here, Paris est à combien de kilomètres de Dijon? how many kilometres is it from Paris to Dijon?, elle a combien de kilomètres votre voiture? what's the mileage on your car?

kinésithérapeute *NOUN MASC & FEM*
physiotherapist

kinésithérapie *NOUN FEM*
physiotherapy

kiosque *NOUN MASC* **kiosk**

kiwi *NOUN MASC* **kiwi** *(the bird and the fruit)*

klaxon *NOUN MASC* **horn** *(on a car)*

klaxonner *VERB* [1] **to sound the horn** *(in a car)*

km *(short for kilomètre)* km/h kph *(kilometres per hour)*

K.O. *ADJECTIVE* ❶ mettre quelqu'un K.O. to knock somebody out *(in boxing)* ❷ je suis complètement K.O. *(informal)* I'm completely knocked out

koala *NOUN MASC* **koala bear**

kraft *NOUN MASC* le papier kraft brown paper

K-way *NOUN MASC* **cagoule**

la *(l' before a vowel or silent 'h')*
DETERMINER, PRONOUN ▸ SEE **le**

là *ADVERB* ❶ **there**; est-ce que Paul est là? is Paul there?, c'est là qu'habite mon frère that's where my brother lives ❷ **here**; viens là come here, Danielle n'est pas là en ce moment Danielle's not here at the moment ❸ **then**; c'est là que j'ai pensé à toi that's when I thought of you

-là *ADVERB* cette maison-là that house, ces gens-là those people, à ce moment-là at that moment

là-bas *ADVERB* ❶ **there**; qu'est-ce que vous avez fait là-bas? what did you do there? ❷ **over there**; notre maison est là-bas our house is over there

labo *NOUN MASC (informal)* **lab**

laboratoire *NOUN MASC* **laboratory**

laboratoire de langues *NOUN MASC*
language laboratory

labourer *VERB* [1] **to plough**

labyrinthe *NOUN MASC* **maze, labyrinth**

lac *NOUN MASC* **lake**; le lac d'Annecy Lake Annecy

lacer *VERB* [61] lacer ses chaussures to tie your shoelaces

lacet *NOUN MASC* **lace** *(for shoes)*; des chaussures à lacets lace-up shoes

lâche ADJECTIVE ❶ **cowardly** ❷ **loose** *(a belt or rope, for example)*

lâcher VERB [1] ❶ **to drop** *(an object)*, **to let go of** *(a rope or branch)*; lâche-moi! let go of me!, ne lâche pas la corde! don't let go of the rope! ❷ **to drop**; elle a lâché son sac she dropped her bag ❸ **to give way**; la corde a lâché the rope gave way

lâcheté NOUN FEM **cowardice**

lacrymogène ADJECTIVE le gaz lacrymogène teargas

là-dedans ADVERB **in there**; il y a un oiseau là-dedans there's a bird in there, il n'y a rien là-dedans there's nothing inside

là-dessous ADVERB **under there**; les verres sont là-dessous the glasses are under there

là-dessus ADVERB ❶ **on there**; tu peux mettre les assiettes là-dessus you can put the plates on there ❷ **about it**; ils sont d'accord là-dessus they agree about it, a-t-il dit quelque chose là-dessus? did he say anything about it? ❸ **with that**; là-dessus il est sorti with that, he went out

là-haut ADVERB ❶ **up here**, **up there**; il est là-haut dans l'arbre he's up there in the tree ❷ **upstairs**; maman est là-haut Mum's upstairs

laid ADJECTIVE **ugly**

laideur NOUN FEM **ugliness**

laine NOUN FEM **wool**; un pull en laine a woollen jumper

laine vierge NOUN FEM **pure new wool**

laïque ADJECTIVE une école laïque a state school

laisse NOUN FEM **lead** *(for a dog)*

laisser VERB [1] ❶ **to leave**; j'ai laissé mes clés chez toi I've left my keys at your house, bon, je vous laisse right, I must be off now ❷ laisser quelqu'un faire to let somebody do, laisse-le parler! let him speak!, laissez-la faire, elle reviendra leave her alone, she'll come back ❸ il se laisse insulter he puts up with being insulted, elle s'est laissée aller she's let herself go

laisser-aller NOUN MASC **carelessness**

lait NOUN MASC **milk**; un thé au lait a cup of tea with milk, un café au lait a white coffee

lait demi-écrémé NOUN MASC **semi-skimmed milk**

lait écrémé NOUN MASC **skimmed milk**

laitier, laitière ADJECTIVE MASC, FEM les produits laitiers milk products *(such as yoghurt)*

laiton NOUN MASC **brass**

laitue NOUN FEM **lettuce**

lame NOUN FEM **blade**

lamelle NOUN FEM **thin strip**

lamentable ADJECTIVE **awful**

lampadaire NOUN MASC ❶ **standard lamp** ❷ **street lamp**

lampe *NOUN FEM* **lamp**, **light**; allumer la lampe to turn on the lamp

lampe de poche *NOUN FEM* **torch**

lampe électrique *NOUN FEM* **torch**

lance *NOUN FEM* **spear**

lancement *NOUN MASC* **launch**

lancer *VERB* [61] ❶ **to throw**; il m'a lancé le ballon he threw the ball to me ❷ **to launch** *(a product, a spacecraft)*; ils vont lancer leur nouveau produit en juin they're going to launch their new product in June ❸ se lancer dans quelque chose to embark on something

landau *NOUN MASC* **pram**

lande *NOUN FEM* **moor**

langage *NOUN MASC* **language**, **type of language**; le langage administratif official jargon

langouste *NOUN FEM* **crayfish**

langue *NOUN FEM* ❶ **tongue**; tirer la langue to stick your tongue out ❷ **language**; une langue étrangère a foreign language, ma langue maternelle my mother tongue
• je l'ai sur le bout de la langue it's on the tip of my tongue

lanière *NOUN FEM* **strap**

lapin *NOUN MASC* **rabbit**
• il m'a posé un lapin *(informal)* he stood me up

laque *NOUN FEM* ❶ **hairspray** ❷ **lacquer**, **gloss paint**

laquelle *PRONOUN* ▸ SEE **lequel**

lard *NOUN MASC* **streaky bacon**

lardons *PLURAL NOUN MASC* **diced bacon**; salade aux lardons fumés green salad with diced smoked bacon

La Réunion *NOUN FEM* **Réunion**, **Réunion Island**

large *NOUN MASC* **open sea**; au large offshore

large *ADJECTIVE* **wide**; un large sourire a broad smile, être large de deux mètres to be two metres wide

largement *ADVERB* c'est largement suffisant that's more than enough, j'ai largement le temps I've got plenty of time

largeur *NOUN FEM* **width**

larme *NOUN FEM* **tear**; en larmes in tears, rire aux larmes to laugh till you cry

laryngite *NOUN FEM* **laryngitis**

lasagnes *PLURAL NOUN FEM* **lasagna**; manger des lasagnes to eat lasagna

laser *NOUN MASC* **laser**; une platine laser a compact disc player

lasser *VERB* [1] se lasser to get tired

lassitude *NOUN FEM* **weariness**

latin *NOUN MASC*, *ADJECTIVE* **Latin**

lauréat, **lauréate** *NOUN MASC, FEM* **winner**; un lauréat du prix Nobel a Nobel Prize winner

laurier *NOUN MASC* **laurel**; un laurier commun a bay tree, une feuille de laurier a bay leaf

laurier-rose *NOUN MASC* **oleander**

a
b
c
d
e
f
g
h
i
j
k
l
m
n
o
p
q
r
s
t
u
v
w
x
y
z

lavable ADJECTIVE **washable**; lavable en machine machine-washable

lavabo NOUN MASC **washbasin**

lavage NOUN MASC ❶ **washing** ❷ **wash** (on a washing-machine programme) ❸ **car wash**

lavande NOUN FEM **lavender**

lave-linge NOUN MASC **washing machine**

laver VERB [1] ❶ **to wash** ❷ se laver to wash, se laver les mains to wash your hands, se laver les dents to brush your teeth

laverie NOUN FEM **launderette**

lave-vaisselle NOUN MASC **dish washer**

le, la, l', les DETERMINER ❶ **the**; le chat the cat, la maison the house, les enfants the children, 'quelle chemise?' – 'la verte' 'which shirt?' – 'the green one' ❷ ('les is often not translated) je n'aime pas les chiens I don't like dogs, elle se lave les cheveux she's washing her hair ❸ le père de mon ami my friend's father ❹ a, an; cinq euros le kilo five euros a kilo

le, la, l', les PRONOUN **him, her, it, them**; je la vois tous les soirs I see her every evening, je le vois tous les soirs I see him every evening, où est-ce que tu les as mis? where did you put them?, il l'a acheté chez Meyer he bought it at Meyer's

lécher VERB [24] **to lick**

lèche-vitrines NOUN MASC faire du lèche-vitrines to go window-shopping

leçon NOUN FEM **lesson**; une leçon de géographie a geography lesson

lecteur, lectrice NOUN MASC, FEM ❶ **reader** (of a book) ❷ **foreign language assistant** (in a university)

lecteur laser NOUN MASC **CD player**

lecture NOUN FEM **reading**; j'aime la lecture I like reading, le soir il fait de la lecture he reads in the evenings

légal ADJECTIVE MASC (PLURAL **légaux**) **legal**

légende NOUN FEM ❶ **caption** (to a picture) ❷ **key** (to a map) ❸ **legend**

léger, légère ADJECTIVE MASC, FEM ❶ **light**; une veste légère a light jacket, un repas léger a light meal ❷ **slight**; un léger retard a slight delay ❸ **weak**; un café léger a weak coffee
• faire quelque chose à la légère to do something without thinking

légèrement ADVERB ❶ **lightly**; légèrement parfumé lightly perfumed ❷ **slightly**; il est légèrement blessé he's slightly hurt, elle est légèrement plus grande que moi she's slightly taller than me

légèreté NOUN FEM **lightness**

législatif, législative ADJECTIVE MASC, FEM **legislative**; les élections législatives the general election

légume NOUN MASC **vegetable**; des légumes verts green vegetables

lendemain NOUN MASC le lendemain the next day, Marc est arrivé le lendemain Marc arrived the next day, le lendemain matin the next morning, le lendemain de l'accident the day after the accident

lent ADJECTIVE **slow**

lentement ADVERB **slowly**

lenteur NOUN FEM **slowness**; avec lenteur slowly

lentille NOUN FEM ❶ **lentil**; soupe aux lentilles lentil soup ❷ **lens**; lentilles de contact contact lenses, elle met ses lentilles she's putting in her contact lenses

léopard NOUN MASC **leopard**

lequel, laquelle, lesquels, lesquelles PRONOUN ❶ **which one?, which?**; 'passe-moi les verres' – 'lesquels?' 'pass me the glasses' – 'which ones?' ❷ **which, who**; la voiture dans laquelle ils roulaient the car they were driving in, the car in which they were driving, le monsieur avec lequel je discutais the man to whom I was talking (often not translated), the man I was talking to

les DETERMINER, PRONOUN ▸ SEE **le**

lesquelles, lesquelles ▸ SEE **lequel**

lessive NOUN FEM ❶ **washing**; faire la lessive to do the washing ❷ **washing powder, washing liquid**

lettre NOUN FEM ❶ **letter**; écrire une lettre to write a letter ❷ **letter** (of the alphabet); une lettre minuscule a small letter, une lettre majuscule a capital letter

• il prend tout ce qu'on lui dit à la lettre he takes everything you say literally

lettres PLURAL NOUN FEM **arts** (at university)

leur PRONOUN **them** (meaning 'to them'); je leur donne de l'argent I give them money

leur DETERMINER (PLURAL **leurs**) **their**; leur voiture their car, leurs enfants their children

leur PRONOUN le leur, la leur, les leurs **theirs**, ça, c'est notre maison, et ça, c'est la leur that's our house and that's theirs, nous avons appelé nos parents et ils ont appelé les leurs we phoned our parents and they phoned theirs

levant ADJECTIVE le soleil levant the rising sun

lever[1] VERB [50] ❶ **to lift, to raise**; levons nos verres! let's raise our glasses!, levez la main! put your hand up!, il a levé les yeux he looked up ❷ se lever **to get up** (out of bed or from a chair); je me lève à sept heures I get up at seven o'clock, nous nous sommes levés tôt we got up early, quand le soleil se lève when the sun rises

lever[2] NOUN MASC au lever du soleil at sunrise

lève-tard NOUN MASC **late riser**

lève-tôt NOUN MASC **early riser**

levier NOUN MASC **lever**

lèvre NOUN FEM **lip**

lévrier NOUN MASC **greyhound**

levure NOUN FEM **yeast**

lexique NOUN MASC **word list**

lézard NOUN MASC **lizard**

liaison NOUN FEM ❶ link, connection; une liaison routière a road link, une liaison radio radio contact, une liaison satellite a satellite link ❷ (love) affair

liasse NOUN FEM wad, bundle (of papers or banknotes)

libellule NOUN FEM dragonfly

libération NOUN FEM release, liberation; la libération des femmes women's liberation, la Libération (de 1944) the Liberation (of 1944) (the end of the German occupation of France)

libérer VERB [24] ❶ to free, to release (a prisoner or hostage) ❷ to vacate (a hotel room or flat)

liberté NOUN FEM freedom

libraire NOUN MASC & FEM bookseller

librairie NOUN FEM bookshop

librairie-papeterie NOUN FEM bookseller's and stationer's

libre ADJECTIVE ❶ free; vous êtes libre de partir you are free to go ❷ free (of a seat or telephone); est-ce que cette place est libre? is this seat free?

librement ADVERB freely

libre-service NOUN MASC self service, self-service shop or restaurant; un libre-service bancaire a cash dispenser

licence NOUN FEM degree (at university); elle a une licence de chimie she has a chemistry degree

licencier VERB [1] licencier quelqu'un to make somebody redundant

lien NOUN MASC link; mes liens avec la famille my links with my family, un lien d'amitié a bond of friendship

lierre NOUN MASC ivy

lieu NOUN MASC (PLURAL lieux) ❶ place; un lieu public a public place, date et lieu de naissance date and place of birth, lieu de travail place of work ❷ en premier lieu in the first place ❸ avoir lieu to take place, le mariage aura lieu en juin the marriage will take place in June ❹ au lieu de instead of, au lieu de prendre le bus, il est parti à pied instead of taking the bus, he went off on foot ❺ les lieux the premises, peut-on visiter les lieux? can one visit the premises?, la police est arrivée sur les lieux the police are now at the scene

lieutenant NOUN MASC lieutenant

lièvre NOUN MASC hare

lifting NOUN MASC face-lift

ligne NOUN FEM ❶ line; une ligne droite a straight line, une ligne blanche a white line (on the road), à la ligne! new paragraph! (in a dictation) ❷ line (of a bus or train); la ligne Paris-Dijon the Paris-Dijon line, une ligne de chemin de fer a railway line, les grandes lignes the main lines (sign at a railway station) ❸ cable; ligne électrique electric cable ❹ (telephone) line; la ligne est mauvaise it's a bad line, restez en ligne, monsieur hold the line, sir ❺ figure; pour garder la ligne to keep your figure, to stay slim ❻ fishing line

ligne d'arrivée NOUN FEM finishing line

ligne de touche NOUN FEM **touch line**

lilas NOUN MASC **lilac**

limace NOUN FEM **slug**

lime NOUN FEM **file**; une lime à ongles a nail file

limitation de vitesse NOUN FEM **speed limit**

limite NOUN FEM ❶ **limit**; une limite d'âge an age limit ❷ la date limite the closing date ❸ sans limites endless, une patience sans limites endless patience ❹ à la limite if it comes to it, at a pinch, à la limite, je peux te prêter l'argent if it comes to it, I can lend you the money ❺ dans la limite de within the limits of, dans la limite des places disponibles subject to available seating space, dans la limite du possible as far as possible ❻ **boundary**; les limites du village the village boundaries ❼ **maximum, last**; vitesse limite maximum speed, âge limite maximum age, date limite de vente sell-by date

limiter VERB [1] ❶ **to limit** ❷ se limiter to limit oneself, je me limite à deux cafés par jour I limit myself to two coffees a day

limonade NOUN FEM **lemonade**

lin NOUN MASC **linen**; une jupe en lin a linen skirt

linge NOUN MASC ❶ **linen** (sheets, towels, etc); linge de maison household linen, du linge sale dirty linen ❷ **washing**; as-tu du linge pour la machine? have you any washing for the machine?, une

corde à linge a washing line
• elle était blanche comme un linge she was white as a sheet

lingerie NOUN FEM **lingerie**

lion NOUN MASC **lion**

Lion NOUN MASC **Leo** (sign of the Zodiac)

lionne NOUN FEM **lioness**

liqueur NOUN FEM **liqueur**

liquidation NOUN FEM **clearance sale, closing-down sale**; 'liquidation totale!' 'everything must go!'

liquide NOUN MASC ❶ **liquid** ❷ **cash**; payer quelque chose en liquide to pay cash for something

liquide ADJECTIVE **liquid**

lire VERB [51] **to read**; lire un roman to read a novel, elle sait lire maintenant she can read now, elle m'a lu une histoire she read me a story, un auteur qui est très lu a popular author, lire à haute voix to read aloud
• lire entre les lignes to read between the lines

lis VERB ▸ SEE **lire**

lisible ADJECTIVE **legible**

lisse ADJECTIVE **smooth**

liste NOUN FEM **list**; faire une liste to make a list, faire la liste de to make a list of

liste d'attente NOUN FEM **waiting list**

lit[1] VERB ▸ SEE **lire**

lit[2] NOUN MASC **bed**; aller au lit to go to bed, faire son lit to make one's bed, un lit à une place a single bed, un lit à deux places a double bed, une chambre à deux lits a twin-bedded room, au lit! bedtime!

literie NOUN FEM **bedding**

litière NOUN FEM **litter** (for an animal's bed); la litière pour chat cat litter

litre NOUN MASC **litre**; un litre d'eau a litre of water

littéralement ADVERB **literally**

littérature NOUN FEM **literature**; la littérature française French literature

livraison NOUN FEM **delivery**; 'livraisons à toute heure' 'we deliver any time', 'livraisons à domicile' 'we deliver'

livre¹ NOUN MASC **book**; un livre pour enfants a children's book, un livre de poche a paperback

livre² NOUN FEM ❶ **pound** (in money); une livre sterling a pound sterling ❷ **pound** (in France = 500 grammes); une livre de tomates a pound of tomatoes

livrer VERB [1] ❶ **to deliver** ❷ **to hand over** ❸ se livrer **to surrender**

livret NOUN MASC **booklet**

livret de famille, **livret de famille** NOUN MASC, FEM **family record book** (with details of births, marriages, and deaths)

livret scolaire NOUN MASC **school report book**

local NOUN MASC (PLURAL **locaux**) **place** (usually a building); locaux commerciaux business premises, dans les locaux du lycée on school premises

local ADJECTIVE MASC (PLURAL **locaux**) **local**; un journal local a local paper,

dix heures heure locale ten a.m. local time

localement ADVERB **locally**

locataire NOUN MASC & FEM **tenant**

location NOUN FEM ❶ **renting**; un appartement de location a rented flat, 'locations' 'to rent' ❷ **hire**, **rental**; location de voitures car hire, location de vidéos video rental ❸ **reservation**, **booking** (of theatre seats)

locomotive NOUN FEM **engine**, **locomotive**

loge NOUN FEM ❶ **lodge** (for the caretaker in a block of flats) ❷ (in a theatre) **dressing-room** (for an actor), **box** (for a spectator)

logement NOUN MASC ❶ **accommodation**; il a trouvé un logement tout près he's found somewhere to live just nearby ❷ **housing**; la crise du logement the housing crisis

loger VERB [52] ❶ **to put up**; peux-tu me loger ce soir? can you put me up tonight? ❷ **to stay**; pour l'instant elle loge chez mes parents for the moment she's staying with my parents

logiciel NOUN MASC ❶ **software** ❷ **program** (for a computer); un logiciel de jeux a games program, un logiciel antivirus antivirus software

logique NOUN FEM **logic**

logique ADJECTIVE **logical**

loi NOUN FEM **law**

loin ADVERB ❶ (in distance) **a long way**, **far off**; c'est loin it's a long way, c'est trop loin it's too far, c'est

170

loin d'ici it's a long way from here, le cinéma est plus loin the cinema is further on, nous ne sommes pas allés plus loin that's the farthest we went ❷ *(in time)* **far off**; les vacances sont loin the holidays are a long way off, il n'est pas loin de midi it's almost twelve ❸ de loin from a long way off, on voit leur maison de loin you can see their house from a long way off ❹ de loin by far, c'est de loin le plus cher it's by far the most expensive ❺ au loin in the distance

lointain ADJECTIVE **distant**

loisirs PLURAL NOUN MASC ❶ **spare time**; je dessine pendant mes loisirs I draw in my spare time ❷ **spare-time activities**

Londonien, Londonienne NOUN MASC, FEM **Londoner**

Londres NOUN **London**; à Londres in (or to) London, les rues de Londres the streets of London

long NOUN MASC ❶ une corde de cinq mètres de long a rope five metres long ❷ le long de all along, le long de la route all along the road ❸ tout le long du film all the way through the film

long, longue ADJECTIVE MASC, FEM **long**; une longue vie a long life, un long silence a long silence, un long voyage a long journey, la rue la plus longue de Paris the longest street in Paris, une chemise à manches longues a long-sleeved shirt, la pièce est longue de quatre mètres, la pièce fait quatre mètres de long the room is four metres long
• marcher de long en large to walk up and down
• à la longue in the long run

longtemps ADVERB **(for) a long time**; elle est restée longtemps she stayed for a long time, longtemps après a long time after, elle est là depuis longtemps she's been here for a long time, j'y suis allé, mais il y a longtemps I've been there, but a long time ago, ça fait longtemps qu'on ne s'est pas vu! it's ages since we've seen each other!, je n'en ai pas pour longtemps I won't be long

longuement ADVERB **for a long time**

longueur NOUN FEM ❶ **length**; de quelle longueur est le couloir? how long is the corridor? ❷ avoir des longueurs to drag, le film est intéressant mais il a des longueurs it's an interesting film but it drags in places

longueur d'onde NOUN FEM **wavelength**

lorsque (*lorsqu'* before a vowel or silent 'h') CONJUNCTION **when**; lorsque j'étais petite when I was a little girl

lot NOUN MASC ❶ **batch**; un lot de trois boîtes a pack of three cans ❷ **prize** *(in a lottery)*; elle a gagné le gros lot she won the jackpot

lot NOUN MASC **batch** *(in computing)*

loterie NOUN FEM ❶ **lottery** ❷ **raffle**

lotion NOUN FEM **lotion**

lotissement NOUN MASC **housing estate**

loto NOUN MASC **lottery**

lotte NOUN FEM **monkfish**

louche[1] NOUN FEM **ladle**

louche[2] ADJECTIVE **fishy**; il y a un type

louche à la porte there's a fishy-looking guy at the door

louer VERB [1] ❶ **to let** (a house or flat); pendant mon absence j'ai loué mon appartement while I was away I let my flat, 'à louer' 'to let' ❷ **to rent**; nous avons loué un appartement à Lille we've rented a flat in Lille ❸ **to hire**; nous avons loué une voiture we hired a car ❹ **to praise**

loup NOUN MASC **wolf**
- j'ai une faim de loup I'm absolutely starving (literally: I'm as hungry as a wolf)
- quand on parle du loup (on en voit la queue) speak of the devil (literally: when you speak of the wolf (you see its tail))

loupe NOUN FEM **magnifying glass**

louper VERB [1] (informal) ❶ **to miss** (a train); on a loupé le train de dix heures we missed the ten o'clock train ❷ **to fail**; elle a loupé son permis she failed her driving test

loup-garou NOUN MASC **werewolf**

lourd ADJECTIVE ❶ **heavy**; ta valise est très lourde your case is very heavy, le repas était un peu lourd the meal was a bit heavy ❷ une lourde erreur a serious mistake

loutre NOUN FEM **otter**

loyal ADJECTIVE MASC (PLURAL loyaux) **faithful**

loyauté NOUN FEM **loyalty**

loyer NOUN MASC **rent**; payer le loyer to pay the rent

lu VERB ▸ SEE **lire**

lucarne NOUN FEM **skylight**

luge NOUN FEM **sledge**

lugubre ADJECTIVE **gloomy**

lui PRONOUN ❶ **him**; c'est lui it's him, Hélène travaille avec lui Hélène works with him, est-ce qu'il a aimé le bouquin que je lui ai prêté? did he like the book I lent him? ❷ **to him**; Pierre est en colère – qu'est-ce que tu lui as dit? Pierre's angry – what did you say to him? ❸ **to her**; Nadine est en colère – qu'est-ce que tu lui as dit? Nadine's angry – what did you say to her? ❹ (for emphasis) lui, il n'est jamais content! he's never pleased!

lui-même PRONOUN ❶ **himself**; il l'a fait lui-même he did it himself ❷ (on telephone) 'Monsieur Dubois?' – 'lui-même' 'Monsieur Dubois?' – 'speaking'

lumière NOUN FEM **light**

lumineux, lumineuse ADJECTIVE MASC, FEM **luminous**; un panneau lumineux an electronic display board, une enseigne lumineuse a neon sign

lunch NOUN MASC **buffet** (lunch or supper)

lundi NOUN MASC ❶ **Monday**; nous sommes lundi aujourd'hui it's Monday today, lundi prochain next Monday, lundi dernier last Monday ❷ **on Monday**; je l'ai vu lundi soir I saw him on Monday evening ❸ le lundi on Mondays, fermé le lundi closed on Mondays ❹ tous les lundis every Monday

lune NOUN FEM **moon**
- il est dans la lune he's got his head in the clouds
- il m'a promis la lune he promised me the earth

lune de miel *NOUN FEM* **honeymoon**

lunettes *PLURAL NOUN FEM* **glasses**; une paire de lunettes a pair of glasses, mets tes lunettes! put on your glasses!, je porte des lunettes pour lire I wear glasses for reading

lunettes de natation *PLURAL NOUN FEM* **swimming goggles**

lunettes de soleil *PLURAL NOUN FEM* **sun-glasses**

lutte *NOUN FEM* **fight**, **struggle**; la lutte contre la drogue the fight against drugs

lutter *VERB* [1] **to fight**, **to struggle**; ils luttaient pour la liberté et contre l'oppression they were fighting for freedom and against oppression

luxe *NOUN MASC* **luxury**; une voiture de luxe a luxury car

luxueux, **luxueuse** *ADJECTIVE MASC, FEM* **luxurious**

lycée *NOUN MASC* **secondary school** (for ages 15-18)

lycéen, **lycéenne** *NOUN MASC, FEM* **secondary school student**

M. (short for Monsieur) M. Dupont Mr Dupont

ma *DETERMINER* **my** ▸ SEE **mon**

macaronis *PLURAL NOUN MASC* **macaroni**; manger des macaronis to have macaroni

mâche *NOUN FEM* **lamb's lettuce**

mâcher *VERB* [1] **to chew**

machin *NOUN MASC* (informal) **whatsit**, **thingumajig**; tu n'as pas un machin pour ouvrir les enveloppes? don't you have a whatsit for opening envelopes with?

machine *NOUN FEM* ❶ **machine** ❷ taper à la machine to type

machine à coudre *NOUN FEM* **sewing machine**

machine à écrire *NOUN FEM* **typewriter**

machine à laver *NOUN FEM* **washing machine**

machine à sous *NOUN FEM* **fruit machine**

mâchoire *NOUN FEM* **jaw**

mâchonner *VERB* [1] **to chew**

maçon *NOUN MASC* ❶ **builder** ❷ **bricklayer**

a
b
c
d
e
f
g
h
i
j
k
l
m
n
o
p
q
r
s
t
u
v
w
x
y
z

Madame NOUN FEM (PLURAL **Mesdames**) ❶ Madame Jones Ms Jones, Mrs Jones ❷ Madame, … Dear Madam, … ❸ bonsoir madame good evening (when greeting a person you do not know well in French, it is polite to add 'Madame', 'Monsieur', or 'Mademoiselle' to the greeting)

Mademoiselle NOUN FEM (PLURAL **Mesdemoiselles**) ❶ Miss, Ms ❷ bonsoir mademoiselle good evening
▶ SEE **Madame**

magasin NOUN MASC **shop**; un grand magasin a department store, un magasin de vêtements a clothes shop, un magasin de sport a sports shop, faire les magasins to go round the shops

magazine NOUN MASC **magazine**

maghrébin ADJECTIVE **North African**

Maghrébin, Maghrébine NOUN MASC, FEM **North African**

magicien, magicienne NOUN MASC, FEM **magician**

magie NOUN FEM **magic**

magique ADJECTIVE ❶ **magic** ❷ **magical**

magistral ADJECTIVE MASC (PLURAL **magistraux**) un cours magistral a lecture (at university)

magnétique ADJECTIVE **magnetic**

magnétiser VERB [1] ❶ to **magnetize** ❷ to **hypnotize**

magnétophone NOUN MASC **tape recorder**

magnétoscope NOUN MASC **video recorder**

magnifique ADJECTIVE **splendid**

magouille NOUN FEM (informal) **fiddling**

magret de canard NOUN MASC **duck breast**

mai NOUN MASC **May**; en mai, au mois de mai in May, le premier mai May Day

maigre ADJECTIVE **thin, skinny**
• maigre comme un clou as thin as a rake (literally: as thin as a nail)

maigrir VERB [2] **to lose weight**; il a beaucoup maigri he's lost a lot of weight

maille NOUN FEM **stitch** (in knitting)

maillot NOUN MASC ❶ **shirt, jersey** (in sports such as football) ❷ maillot (de corps) vest

maillot de bain NOUN MASC ❶ **swimsuit** ❷ **swimming trunks**

main NOUN FEM **hand**; avoir quelque chose à la main to have something in your hand, serrer la main à quelqu'un to shake hands with somebody, se serrer la main to shake hands, nous nous sommes serré la main we shook hands, se donner la main to hold hands, haut les mains! hands up!, donner un coup de main à quelqu'un to give somebody a hand, tu veux un coup de main? do you want a hand?, fait à la main handmade

main-d'œuvre NOUN FEM **labour**

maintenant ADVERB ❶ **now**; il est maintenant trop tard pour sortir it's too late to go out now ❷ **nowadays**; maintenant presque tout le monde a le téléphone nowadays nearly everybody has a phone

maintenir *VERB* [81] ❶ to maintain ❷ to support

maire *NOUN MASC* mayor

mairesse *NOUN FEM* mayoress

mairie *NOUN FEM* ❶ town hall ❷ town council

mais *CONJUNCTION* ❶ but; j'ai essayé de t'appeler mais tu n'étais pas là I tried to phone you but you weren't there ❷ mais oui yes of course, mais non of course not

maïs *NOUN MASC* ❶ maize ❷ sweetcorn ❸ des épis de maïs corn on the cob

maison *NOUN FEM* ❶ house; leur maison est petite mais très confortable their house is small but very comfortable ❷ home; rester à la maison to stay at home, rentrer à la maison to go home

maison de la culture *NOUN FEM* cultural centre, arts centre

maison de retraite *NOUN FEM* old people's home

maître, maîtresse *NOUN MASC, FEM* ❶ master, mistress ❷ teacher

maître-nageur *NOUN MASC* swimming instructor

maîtresse *NOUN FEM* ❶ ▸ SEE **maître** ❷ lover

maîtrise *NOUN FEM* ❶ mastery ❷ command; la maîtrise de soi self-control ❸ master's degree

maîtriser *VERB* [1] ❶ to control ❷ to master

majestueux, majestueuse *ADJECTIVE MASC, FEM* majestic

majeur *ADJECTIVE* ❶ major ❷ être majeur to be over 18

majeur *NOUN* middle finger

majorité *NOUN FEM* majority

majuscule *NOUN FEM* capital (letter); en majuscules in block capitals, un R majuscule a capital R

mal *NOUN MASC (PLURAL* maux) ❶ pain, ache; faire mal to hurt, se faire mal to hurt yourself, avoir mal à la gorge to have a sore throat, j'ai mal au dos my back hurts, ça fait mal it hurts ❷ faire mal à quelqu'un to hurt somebody, aïe! tu me fais mal! ouch! you're hurting me! ❸ avoir du mal à faire to have difficulty in doing, j'ai du mal à comprendre ce qu'il dit I have difficulty in understanding what he says, se donner du mal à faire to go to a lot of trouble to do, elle s'est donné beaucoup de mal pour contacter tout le monde she went to a lot of trouble to contact everybody ❹ evil

mal *ADJECTIVE* ❶ pas mal not bad ❷ être mal to be uncomfortable

mal *ADVERB* ❶ badly; écrire mal to write badly ❷ je t'entends mal I can't hear you very well ❸ j'ai mal compris I misunderstood ❹ être mal à l'aise to feel uncomfortable

malade *NOUN MASC & FEM* patient

malade *ADJECTIVE* ill, sick; tomber malade to fall ill

maladie *NOUN FEM* ❶ illness ❷ disease

maladresse *NOUN FEM* ❶ clumsiness ❷ blunder

maladroit *ADJECTIVE* clumsy

malaise *NOUN MASC* ❶ avoir un malaise to feel faint, to pass out ❷ créer un malaise to make people feel uncomfortable, ça a créé un malaise it made everybody feel uncomfortable

malaxer VERB [1] ❶ to knead ❷ to cream

malchance NOUN FEM bad luck

mal de mer NOUN MASC avoir le mal de mer to be seasick

mal du pays NOUN MASC avoir le mal du pays to be homesick

mâle NOUN MASC, ADJECTIVE male

malédiction NOUN FEM curse

malencontreux, malencontreuse ADJECTIVE MASC, FEM unfortunate

malentendu NOUN MASC misunderstanding

malfaiteur NOUN MASC criminal

mal famé ADJECTIVE un quartier mal famé a rough area

malgré PREPOSITION ❶ in spite of; malgré le froid in spite of the cold ❷ malgré tout all the same, mais malgré tout nous avons décidé d'y aller but we decided to go all the same

malheur NOUN MASC misfortune; porter malheur to bring bad luck

malheureusement ADVERB unfortunately; Vincent était déjà parti, malheureusement unfortunately, Vincent had already left

malheureux, malheureuse NOUN MASC, FEM poor thing; la malheureuse! poor woman!

malheureux, malheureuse ADJECTIVE MASC, FEM ❶ unhappy; avoir l'air malheureux to look unhappy, rendre quelqu'un malheureux to make somebody unhappy ❷ unfortunate; un choix malheureux an unfortunate choice

malhonnête ADJECTIVE dishonest

malice NOUN FEM mischief

malicieux, malicieuse ADJECTIVE MASC, FEM mischievous

malin, maligne ADJECTIVE MASC, FEM ❶ clever; ce n'était pas très malin ça that wasn't very clever, elle se croit maligne she thinks she's clever ❷ malignant (tumour)

malle NOUN FEM trunk

malodorant ADJECTIVE smelly

malpoli ADJECTIVE rude

malpropre ADJECTIVE dirty

malsain ADJECTIVE unhealthy

maltraiter VERB [1] to ill-treat; les enfants maltraités battered children

malveillance NOUN FEM malice

malveillant ADJECTIVE malicious

maman NOUN FEM mum, mummy

mamie NOUN FEM granny, gran, nan

mammifère NOUN MASC mammal

manager VERB [52] to manage

manageur NOUN MASC manager

manche¹ NOUN MASC handle (of a tool)

manche² NOUN FEM ❶ sleeve; une chemise à manches courtes a short-sleeved shirt, sans manches sleeveless ❷ leg (of a match)

Manche NOUN FEM la Manche the Channel, le tunnel sous la Manche the Channel Tunnel

mandarine NOUN FEM **mandarin orange**

mandat NOUN MASC **money order**

manège NOUN MASC ❶ **merry-go-round** ❷ **riding school**

manette NOUN FEM **lever**

mangeable ADJECTIVE **edible**

manger NOUN MASC **food**

manger VERB [52] **to eat**; qu'est-ce qu'on va manger? what shall we have to eat?, manger au restaurant to go out for a meal, j'ai déjà mangé I've already eaten, j'ai assez mangé I'm full, I've had enough, donner à manger à to feed, ils mangent trois fois par jour they have three meals a day
• manger ses mots to mumble (literally: to eat your words)

mangue NOUN FEM **mango**

maniaque NOUN MASC & FEM **fusspot**

maniaque ADJECTIVE **extremely fussy**

manie NOUN FEM ❶ **odd habit** ❷ **mania**

manier VERB [1] **to handle**

manière NOUN FEM ❶ **way**; une manière plus facile an easier way, on ne peut pas le faire d'une manière plus facile? isn't there an easier way of doing it?, de cette manière like this, like that, d'une autre manière in another way, d'une manière ou d'une autre one way or another, d'une certaine manière in a way ❷ de toute manière in any case ❸ de manière à faire so as to do, de manière à éviter de dépenser de l'argent so as to avoid spending money

❹ manières manners, ne fais pas de manières! don't make a fuss!

manifestant, **manifestante** NOUN MASC, FEM **demonstrator**

manifestation NOUN FEM **demonstration**; une manifestation contre le racisme a demonstration against racism

manifester VERB [1] ❶ **to demonstrate**, **to take part in a demonstration** ❷ manifester quelque chose to express something

manipuler VERB [1] ❶ **to handle** ❷ **to manipulate**

manivelle NOUN FEM **handle**

mannequin NOUN MASC ❶ **fashion model** ❷ **dummy** (either in a shop window or as used by a dressmaker)

manoir NOUN MASC **manor house**

manque NOUN MASC manque de lack of, shortage of, leur manque d'imagination their lack of imagination, être en manque d'affection to be in need of affection

manqué ADJECTIVE ❶ **failed**; un acteur manqué a failed actor ❷ **missed**; une occasion manquée a missed opportunity

manquer VERB [1] ❶ manquer quelque chose to miss something, il a manqué son train he missed his train ❷ manquer un examen to fail an exam ❸ manquer à quelqu'un to be missed by somebody, tu me manques I miss you, Londres leur manque they miss London ❹ il manque quelque chose something's missing, il manque trois fourchettes there are three forks missing, we're three forks short ❺ **manquer de** to lack, nous ne manquons pas de verres there's no shortage of glasses ❻ **manquer de faire** to fail to do, il a manqué de fermer la porte à clé he failed to lock the door

mansarde NOUN FEM **attic room**

manteau NOUN MASC (PLURAL manteaux) **coat**

manuel, manuelle ADJECTIVE MASC, FEM ❶ **manual** ❷ **textbook**; un manuel scolaire a school book

manuel (manuelle) ADJECTIVE **manual**

manufacture NOUN FEM ❶ **factory** ❷ **manufacture**

manuscrit NOUN MASC **manuscript**

manuscrit ADJECTIVE **handwritten**; un petit mot manuscrit a handwritten note

maquereau NOUN MASC (PLURAL maquereaux) **mackerel**

maquette NOUN FEM **scale model**

maquillage NOUN MASC **make-up**

maquiller VERB [1] se maquiller to put on your make-up

marais NOUN MASC **marsh**

marathon NOUN MASC **marathon**

marbre NOUN MASC **marble**; une cheminée en marbre a marble fireplace

marc de café NOUN MASC **coffee grounds**

marchand, marchande NOUN MASC, FEM ❶ **shopkeeper**; la marchande de fromage the woman in the cheese shop ❷ **stallholder** (on a market)

marchand de journaux NOUN MASC **newsagent**

marchander VERB [1] to haggle (over)

marchandise NOUN FEM **goods**

marche NOUN FEM ❶ **walking**; faire de la marche to go walking ❷ **march** ❸ **step**; les marches d'escalier the stairs, attention à la marche mind the step ❹ mettre en marche to start up (a machine), être en état de marche to be in working order

marché NOUN MASC ❶ **market**; aller au marché to go to market, le marché aux fleurs the flower market, un marché aux puces a flea market, le marché de l'emploi the job market ❷ **deal**

marche arrière NOUN FEM **reverse**; faire marche arrière to reverse

marchepied NOUN MASC **step** (on a train)

marcher VERB [1] ❶ **to walk**; on va marcher jusqu'à la gare we'll walk as far as the station ❷ **marcher dans quelque chose** to tread in something, marcher sur quelque chose to tread on something ❸ **to march** ❹ **to work**; ça a marché it worked, la machine à laver ne marche pas the washing machine doesn't work, les trains ne marchent pas aujourd'hui the trains are not running today ❺ et ton boulot, ça marche? (informal) and is your job going all right?
• faire marcher quelqu'un to pull somebody's leg

marcheur, marcheuse NOUN MASC, FEM **walker**

mardi NOUN MASC ❶ **Tuesday**; nous sommes mardi aujourd'hui it's

Tuesday today, mardi prochain next Tuesday, mardi dernier last Tuesday ❷ on Tuesday; je t'appellerai mardi soir I'll ring you on Tuesday evening ❸ le mardi on Tuesdays, c'est fermé le mardi it's closed on Tuesdays ❹ tous les mardis every Tuesday

Mardi gras NOUN MASC **Shrove Tuesday**

mare NOUN FEM **pond**

marécage NOUN MASC **swamp**

marée NOUN FEM **tide**; la marée monte the tide's coming in, la marée descend the tide's going out

marée noire NOUN FEM **oil slick**

margarine NOUN FEM **margarine**

marge NOUN FEM ❶ **margin** ❷ en marge de on the fringe of

marguerite NOUN FEM ❶ **marguerite** ❷ **oxeye daisy**

mari NOUN MASC **husband**; le mari de Claire Claire's husband

mariage NOUN MASC ❶ **marriage** ❷ **wedding**; être invité à un mariage to be invited to a wedding

Marianne NOUN FEM **Marianne** (a female figure representing the French Republic in statues and paintings)

marié, mariée NOUN MASC, FEM **bridegroom, bride**; les jeunes mariés the newlyweds

marié ADJECTIVE **married**

marier VERB [1] ❶ se marier to get married, ils se sont mariés à Londres they got married in London, elle s'est mariée avec Frank she married Frank ❷ le prêtre qui les a mariés the priest who married them

marin NOUN MASC **sailor**

marin ADJECTIVE **sea**

marine ADJECTIVE bleu marine navy blue

mariner VERB [1] **to marinate**

marionnette NOUN FEM **puppet**

marjolaine NOUN FEM **marjoram**

marketing NOUN MASC **marketing**

marmelade NOUN FEM marmelade d'oranges amères orange marmalade

marmite NOUN FEM **cooking pot**

marmonner VERB [1] **to mutter, to mumble**

Maroc NOUN MASC **Morocco**

marocain ADJECTIVE **Moroccan**

Marocain, Marocaine NOUN MASC, FEM **Moroccan** (person)

maroquinerie NOUN FEM ❶ **leather shop** ❷ **leather goods**

marquant ADJECTIVE **outstanding**

marque NOUN FEM ❶ **brand**; une marque de nourriture pour chats a brand of cat food ❷ **make**; c'est une marque de jean bien connue it's a well-known make of jeans ❸ **mark** ❹ **point**

marque déposée NOUN FEM **registered trademark**

marquer VERB [1] ❶ **to mark** ❷ **to write down**; j'ai marqué ton nom I've written down your name ❸ marquer un but to score a goal

marqueur NOUN MASC **marker pen**

marraine NOUN FEM **godmother**

marrant ADJECTIVE (informal) **funny**

marre ADVERB (informal) j'en ai marre I'm fed up, j'en ai marrre d'écrire I'm fed up with writing

marrer VERB [1] ❶ se marrer to have a great time ❷ se marrer to have a good laugh

marron NOUN MASC ❶ (sweet) chestnut ❷ (horse) chestnut

marron ADJECTIVE **brown**; des chaussures marron brown shoes, marron clair light brown, marron foncé dark brown

marronnier NOUN MASC **chestnut tree**

mars NOUN MASC **March**; en mars, au mois de mars in March

Marseillaise NOUN FEM la Marseillaise the Marseillaise (the French national anthem)

Marseille NOUN **Marseilles**

marteau NOUN MASC (PLURAL marteaux) ❶ **hammer** ❷ **doorknocker**

marteau piqueur NOUN MASC **pneumatic drill**

marteler VERB [45] to **hammer**

martinet NOUN MASC **swift**

martin-pêcheur NOUN MASC **kingfisher**

martyrisé ADJECTIVE un enfant martyrisé a battered child

mascotte NOUN FEM **mascot**

masculin NOUN MASC **masculine** (in French and other grammars); au masculin in the masculine

masculin ADJECTIVE ❶ **male**; le sexe masculin the male sex ❷ **men's**; les vêtements masculins men's clothing ❸ **masculine**

masque NOUN MASC **mask**

masquer VERB [1] to **hide**

massacre NOUN MASC **massacre**

massacrer VERB [1] to **massacre**

massage NOUN MASC **massage**; faire un massage à quelqu'un to give somebody a massage

masse NOUN FEM ❶ **mass** ❷ une masse de (informal) masses of, j'ai une masse de boulot à faire avant lundi I've got masses of work to do for Monday

masser VERB [1] ❶ to **massage** ❷ se masser to assemble

massif, massive ADJECTIVE MASC, FEM ❶ **solid**; une table en pin massif a solid pine table ❷ **massive**

mass media PLURAL NOUN MASC les mass media the mass media

mastic NOUN MASC ❶ **putty** ❷ **filler**

mastiquer VERB [1] ❶ to **chew** ❷ to **putty** (a window) ❸ to **fill** (a crack)

mat ADJECTIVE **matt**

mât NOUN MASC ❶ **mast** ❷ **pole**

match NOUN MASC **match**; un match de foot a football match, faire match nul to draw

matelas NOUN MASC **mattress**

matelassé ADJECTIVE **quilted**

matelot NOUN MASC **sailor**

matériaux *PLURAL NOUN MASC* **materials**; les matériaux de construction building materials

matériel *NOUN MASC* **equipment**; matériel de sport sports equipment

maternel, maternelle *ADJECTIVE MASC, FEM* ❶ **motherly** ❷ **maternal**; ma tante maternelle my aunt on my mother's side of the family

maternelle *NOUN FEM* **(state) nursery school** *(for ages 2-6)*; aller en maternelle to go to nursery school

maternité *NOUN FEM* ❶ **motherhood** ❷ **pregnancy**; être en congé de maternité to be on maternity leave ❸ **maternity unit**

mathématiques *PLURAL NOUN FEM* **mathematics**

matheux, matheuse *NOUN MASC, FEM* **maths genius**

maths *PLURAL NOUN FEM* **maths**

matière *NOUN FEM* **subject**; la matière que j'aime le mieux c'est l'histoire the subject I like best is history, en matière de: la politique du gouvernement en matière de l'éducation the government's education policy

matières grasses *PLURAL NOUN FEM* **fat** *(in food)*

matin *NOUN MASC* **morning**; à quelle heure est-ce que tu te lèves le matin? what time do you get up in the morning?, à six heures du matin at six o'clock in the morning, du matin au soir from morning till night, de bon matin early in the morning

matinal *ADJECTIVE MASC (PLURAL matinaux)* ❶ **morning** ❷ être matinal to be an early riser

matinée *NOUN FEM* ❶ **morning**; au cours de la matinée during the morning ❷ **matinée**

matou *NOUN MASC* **tomcat**

matraque *NOUN FEM* **truncheon, club**

matrimonial *ADJECTIVE MASC (PLURAL matrimoniaux)* une agence matrimoniale a marriage bureau

maturité *NOUN FEM* **maturity**

maudire *VERB* **to curse**

maussade *ADJECTIVE* ❶ **sullen** ❷ **dull, dreary** *(weather)*

mauvais *ADJECTIVE* ❶ **bad**; une mauvaise expérience a bad experience, ça sent mauvais ici there's a nasty smell here, ça a mauvais goût it tastes horrible, c'est du mauvais goût it's bad taste ❷ **wrong**; le mauvais numéro the wrong number, la mauvaise adresse the wrong address ❸ il fait mauvais the weather's bad ❹ elle a mauvaise mine she doesn't look well

mauvaise herbe *NOUN FEM* **weed**

maux *PLURAL NOUN MASC* ▸ SEE **mal**

maximum *NOUN MASC, ADJECTIVE* **maximum**; au maximum as much as possible, au maximum at the most, faire le maximum to do your utmost

mayonnaise *NOUN FEM* **mayonnaise**

mazout *NOUN MASC* **fuel oil**

me (m' before a vowel or silent 'h')
PRONOUN ❶ me; elle me déteste
she hates me, il m'a vu he saw me
❷ to me; elle ne me parle jamais
she never speaks to me, elle m'a
donné son adresse she gave me her
address, il me l'a donné he gave
it to me ❸ myself; je me fais une
salade I'm making myself a salad, je
me suis blessé I hurt myself, je me
lève à sept heures I get up at seven
o'clock, je me brosse les dents I
brush my teeth (literally: I brush to
myself the teeth)

mec NOUN MASC (informal) guy

mécanicien, mécanicienne NOUN
MASC, FEM ❶ mechanic ❷ train
driver

mécanique NOUN FEM ❶ mechanics
❷ mechanism

mécanique ADJECTIVE ❶ mechanical
❷ clockwork

mécanisme NOUN MASC mechanism

méchamment ADVERB spitefully,
nastily

méchanceté NOUN FEM ❶ nastiness
❷ spite

méchant ADJECTIVE ❶ nasty; elle a été
vraiment méchante avec moi she
was really nasty to me ❷ spiteful
❸ vicious; 'chien méchant' 'beware
of the dog'

mèche NOUN FEM ❶ lock (of hair)
❷ wick

méconnaissable ADJECTIVE
unrecognizable

mécontent ADJECTIVE dissatisfied

mécontentement NOUN MASC
❶ annoyance ❷ displeasure

médaille NOUN FEM medal

médecin NOUN MASC doctor; aller
chez le médecin to go to the
doctor's

médecine NOUN FEM medicine; faire
des études de médecine to go to
medical school

médias PLURAL NOUN MASC les médias
the media

médiathèque NOUN FEM
multimedia library

médical ADJECTIVE MASC (PLURAL
médicaux) medical

médicament NOUN MASC drug

médiéval ADJECTIVE MASC (PLURAL
médiévaux) medieval

médiocre ADJECTIVE second-rate,
poor; un travail médiocre a second-
rate piece of work

méditation NOUN FEM meditation

méditer VERB [1] ❶ to meditate
❷ méditer quelque chose to mull
something over

Méditerranée NOUN FEM la
Méditerranée the Mediterranean

**méditerranéen,
méditerranéenne** ADJECTIVE MASC,
FEM Mediterranean; la cuisine
méditerranéenne Mediterranean
cooking

méduse NOUN FEM jellyfish

méfait NOUN MASC ❶ crime
❷ les méfaits de la pollution the
detrimental effects of pollution

méfiance NOUN FEM suspicion

méfiant ADJECTIVE suspicious

méfier VERB [1] se méfier de
quelqu'un not to trust somebody,
méfie-toi! watch out!

mégère NOUN FEM **shrew**

mégot NOUN MASC **cigarette end**

meilleur NOUN MASC **best**; c'est le meilleur it's the best one, le meilleur des deux the better of the two

meilleur ADJECTIVE ❶ **better**; le climat est bien meilleur au sud the climate's much better in the south, meilleur que better than, ton écriture est meilleure que la mienne your writing's better than mine, c'est meilleur que l'autre it's better than the other one ❷ **best**; le meilleur the best moment, c'est ma meilleure amie she's my best friend, meilleurs voeux best wishes

mélange NOUN MASC **mixture**

mélanger VERB [52] ❶ **to mix** ❷ **to mix up**; j'ai mélangé les dates I got the dates mixed up

mélasse NOUN FEM **black treacle**

mêlée NOUN FEM **scrum**

mêler VERB [1] ❶ se mêler à to mingle with ❷ se mêler de to meddle in
• mêle-toi de ce qui te regarde! mind your own business!

mélodie NOUN FEM **melody**, **tune**

mélomane NOUN MASC & FEM **music lover**

melon NOUN MASC ❶ **melon** ❷ un chapeau melon a bowler hat

membre NOUN MASC ❶ **member** ❷ **limb**

même ADJECTIVE ❶ **same**; j'ai le même anniversaire que toi I have the same birthday as you, ils avaient des chapeaux de la même couleur they had the same colour hats ❷ en

même temps at the same time ❸ tout de même all the same

même ADVERB **even**; il n'a même pas demandé he didn't even ask

mémé NOUN (informal) FEM ❶ **granny**, **gran**, **nan** ❷ une vieille mémé an old lady

mémoire NOUN FEM **memory**

mémoriser VERB [1] **to memorize**

menace NOUN FEM **threat**

menacer VERB [61] **to threaten**

ménage NOUN MASC ❶ **housework**; faire le ménage to do the cleaning, une femme de ménage a cleaning lady ❷ **household**

ménager[1], **ménagère** ADJECTIVE MASC, FEM quelqu'un to handle somebody tactfully

ménager[2] (ménagère) ADJECTIVE **household**; les appareils ménagers household appliances, les travaux ménagers housework

mendiant, **mendiante** NOUN MASC, FEM **beggar**

mendier VERB [1] **to beg**

mener VERB [50] ❶ **to lead**; mener à to lead to, le chemin qui mène à la ferme the track which leads to the farm ❷ mener une société to run a company ❸ mener une campagne to conduct a campaign

méningite NOUN FEM **meningitis**

menottes PLURAL NOUN FEM **handcuffs**

mensonge NOUN MASC **lie**; dire des mensonges to tell lies

mensualité NOUN FEM **monthly payment**

mensuel, mensuelle *ADJECTIVE MASC, FEM* **monthly**

mental *ADJECTIVE MASC (PLURAL* **mentaux)** **mental**

mentalité *NOUN FEM* **mentality**

menteur, menteuse *NOUN MASC, FEM* **liar**

menteur, menteuse *ADJECTIVE MASC, FEM* **untruthful**

menthe *NOUN FEM* **mint**; le sirop de menthe mint cordial

mention *NOUN FEM* ❶ **mention** ❷ **grade** *(in an exam or a degree)*; elle a eu son bac avec mention bien she got a grade B plus pass in her baccalaureate

mentionner *VERB* [1] **to mention**

mentir *VERB* [53] **to lie, to tell lies**

menton *NOUN MASC* **chin**

menu[1] *NOUN MASC* **menu**; qu'est-ce qu'il y a au menu? what's on the menu?, le menu du jour today's menu, est-ce qu'il y a un menu à prix fixe? is there a set menu?

menu[2] *ADJECTIVE* **very small**

menuiserie *NOUN FEM* **woodwork**

menuisier *NOUN MASC* **joiner**

mépris *NOUN MASC* **contempt**

mépriser *VERB* [1] **to despise**

mer *NOUN FEM* **sea**; aller à la mer to go to the seaside, au bord de la mer at the seaside, la mer du Nord the North Sea, la mer des Antilles the Caribbean (Sea)

mercerie *NOUN FEM* **haberdashery**

merci[1] *EXCLAMATION* **thank you,** **thanks**; merci beaucoup, merci bien thank you very much, merci de m'avoir rappelé thank you for calling me back

merci[2] *NOUN FEM* **mercy**

mercredi *NOUN MASC* ❶ **Wednesday**; nous sommes mercredi aujourd'hui it's Wednesday today, mercredi prochain next Wednesday, mercredi dernier last Wednesday ❷ **on Wednesday**; je t'appellerai mercredi soir I'll ring you on Wednesday evening ❸ le mercredi on Wednesdays, c'est fermé le mercredi it's closed on Wednesdays, tous les mercredis every Wednesday

mercure *NOUN MASC* **mercury**

mère *NOUN FEM* **mother**; la mère de Sophie Sophie's mother

merguez *NOUN FEM* **spicy lamb sausage**

méridional *ADJECTIVE MASC (PLURAL* **méridionaux)** **southern**

meringue *NOUN FEM* **meringue**

mérite *NOUN FEM* **merit**

mériter *VERB* [1] **to deserve**

merlan *NOUN MASC* **whiting**

merle *NOUN MASC* **blackbird**

merveille *NOUN FEM* ❶ **wonder**; ton gâteau est une vraie merveille your cake's absolutely wonderful ❷ à merveille wonderfully

merveilleux, merveilleuse *ADJECTIVE MASC, FEM* **marvellous**

mes *DETERMINER* ▸ SEE **mon**

Mesdames *NOUN* ▸ SEE **Madame**

Mesdemoiselles *NOUN* ▸ SEE **Mademoiselle**

mesquin *ADJECTIVE* **petty**, **mean**

message *NOUN MASC* **message**

messager, **messagère** *NOUN MASC,
FEM* **messenger**

messagerie vocale *NOUN FEM*
voicemail

messe *NOUN FEM* **mass**; aller à la
messe to go to mass

Messieurs *NOUN* ▸ SEE **Monsieur**

mesure *NOUN FEM* ❶ **measurement**;
prendre les mesures de la pièce
to take the measurements of the
room ❷ sur mesure tailor-made
❸ **measure**; prendre des mesures
pour faire to take measures to do,
le conseil municipal va prendre
des mesures pour contrôler la
pollution the town council is
going to take measures to control
pollution ❹ être en mesure de faire
to be in a position to do, nous ne
sommes pas en mesure de vous
aider we are not in a position to
help you

mesurer *VERB* [1] to measure

met *VERB* ▸ SEE **mettre**

métal *NOUN MASC (PLURAL* métaux*)*
metal

métallique *ADJECTIVE* **metallic**

métallisé *ADJECTIVE* **metallic**; bleu
métallisé metallic blue

météo *NOUN FEM* **weather forecast**

méthode *NOUN FEM* ❶ **method**; une
méthode de faire a method of
doing ❷ **manual, tutor**

métier *NOUN MASC* ❶ **job** ❷ un métier
à tisser a weaving loom

mètre *NOUN MASC* ❶ **metre** ❷ **metre
rule**

métrique *ADJECTIVE* **metric**

métro *NOUN MASC* **underground**; une
station de métro an underground
station

mets *VERB* ▸ SEE **mettre**

metteur en scène *NOUN MASC*
❶ **director** *(of a film)* ❷ **producer**
(of a play)

mettre *VERB* [11] ❶ to put; où as-tu
mis le sel? where have you put the
salt? ❷ to put on; je vais mettre
mon manteau I'm going to put my
coat on ❸ to wear; mets ta jupe
rose wear your pink skirt ❹ to
turn on *(radio, television, heating)*;
mettre le réveil to set the alarm
clock ❺ mettre quelqu'un en colère
to make somebody angry ❻ j'ai
mis trois heures pour le faire it
took me three hours to do it ❼ se
mettre quelque part to stand (or
sit) somewhere ❽ se mettre debout
to stand up ❾ se mettre à faire to
start to do, elle s'est mise à chanter
she started to sing

meuble *NOUN MASC* ❶ des meubles
furniture ❷ un meuble a piece of
furniture

meublé *ADJECTIVE* **furnished**

meule *NOUN FEM* ❶ **millstone** ❷ une
meule de foin a haystack

meurtre *NOUN MASC* **murder**

meurtrier, **meurtrière** *NOUN MASC,
FEM* **murderer**

meurtrier, **meurtrière** *ADJECTIVE
MASC, FEM* ❶ **deadly** ❷ **fatal**

a
b
c
d
e
f
g
h
i
j
k
l
m
n
o
p
q
r
s
t
u
v
w
x
y
z

mexicain ADJECTIVE **Mexican**

Mexicain, **Mexicaine** NOUN MASC, FEM **Mexican**

Mexico NOUN **Mexico City**

Mexique NOUN MASC **Mexico**; aller au Mexique to go to Mexico

mi- PREFIX ❶ **half-**; mi-clos half-shut ❷ **mid-**; à la mi-février in mid-February

mi-bas NOUN MASC **knee sock**

mi-chemin NOUN à mi-chemin halfway

micro NOUN MASC **microphone**

microbe NOUN MASC **germ**

micro-ondes NOUN MASC **microwave**; faire cuire quelque chose au micro-ondes to cook something in the microwave

micro-ordinateur NOUN MASC **microcomputer**

microscope NOUN MASC **microscope**

midi NOUN MASC ❶ **midday, noon**; il est midi vingt it's twenty past twelve, je viendrai vers midi I'll come around twelve ❷ **lunchtime**; je fais mes courses à midi I do my shopping in my lunch hour

Midi NOUN MASC le Midi the South of France

miel NOUN MASC **honey**

mien, mienne, miens, miennes PRONOUN le mien, la mienne, les miens, les miennes mine, 'à qui sont ces chaussures?' – 'ce sont les miennes' 'whose shoes are these?' – 'they're mine', puis-je t'emprunter ton vélo? le mien est chez moi can I borrow your bike? mine's at home

miette NOUN FEM **crumb**

mieux ADJECTIVE, ADVERB ❶ **better**; tu la connais mieux que moi you know her better than I do, je me sens mieux I feel better, mon père va mieux maintenant my father's better now, c'est mieux comme ça it's better like that ❷ il vaut mieux que tu restes chez toi it would be better if you stayed at home ❸ **best**; c'est le rouge que j'aime le mieux I like the red one best, I prefer the red one

mieux NOUN MASC le mieux est de revenir the best thing is to come back, au mieux at best, at least, pour le mieux for the best

mignon, mignonne ADJECTIVE MASC, FEM **sweet**

migraine NOUN FEM **headache, migraine**

mijoter VERB [1] to simmer

milieu NOUN MASC ❶ **middle**; au milieu de in the middle of ❷ **background**; il vient d'un milieu pauvre he comes from a poor background ❸ **environment**

militaire NOUN MASC **serviceman**

militaire ADJECTIVE **military**; le service militaire military service

mille NUMBER **a thousand**; mille personnes a thousand people, deux mille personnes two thousand people

millefeuille *NOUN MASC* **vanilla slice**

millénaire *NOUN MASC* **millennium**

mille-pattes *NOUN MASC* **centipede**

milliard *NOUN MASC* **thousand million**

milliardaire *NOUN MASC & FEM* **multimillionaire**

millier *NOUN MASC* **thousand**; des milliers de euros thousands of euros

milligramme *NOUN MASC* **milligramme**

millimètre *NOUN MASC* **millimetre**

million *NOUN MASC* **million**; deux millions de euros two million euros

millionnaire *NOUN MASC & FEM* **millionaire**

mime *NOUN MASC & FEM* **mime artist**

mimer *VERB* [1] ❶ to mime ❷ to mimic

minable *ADJECTIVE* (informal) ❶ **pathetic**; ses plaisanteries sont minables her jokes are pathetic ❷ **crummy**; un film minable a crummy film

mince *ADJECTIVE* ❶ **thin**; une mince tranche de viande a thin slice of meat ❷ **slim** ❸ mince alors! (informal) oh bother!

minceur *NOUN FEM* ❶ **thinness** ❷ **slimness**

mine *NOUN FEM* ❶ avoir bonne mine to look well, tu as mauvaise mine you don't look well ❷ **expression** ❸ **mine**; une mine de charbon a coal mine ❹ **pencil lead**

minéral *NOUN MASC (PLURAL* minéraux*)* **mineral**

minéral *ADJECTIVE* **mineral**; eau minérale mineral water

minet, minette *NOUN MASC, FEM* **pussycat**

mineur¹ *NOUN MASC* **miner**

mineur², **mineure** *NOUN MASC, FEM* **minor, person under 18**

mineure *ADJECTIVE* ❶ **minor** ❷ **under 18**

minijupe *NOUN FEM* **mini-skirt**

minimal *ADJECTIVE MASC (PLURAL* minimaux*)* **minimal**

minimiser *VERB* [1] ❶ to minimize ❷ to play down

minimum *NOUN MASC, ADJECTIVE* **minimum**; au minimum at the very least

ministère *NOUN MASC* **ministry**

ministre *NOUN MASC* **minister**

Minitel *NOUN MASC (Minitel is France Telecom's online data service; subscribers have a small computer linked to the telephone and can use it to access a large number of services including the telephone directories)*

minorité *NOUN FEM* **minority**

minou *NOUN MASC* **pussycat**

minuit *NOUN MASC* **midnight**; à minuit at midnight

minuscule *NOUN FEM* **small letter** (as opposed to a capital letter)

minuscule *ADJECTIVE* **tiny**

minute NOUN FEM **minute**; dans dix minutes in ten minutes, dix minutes plus tard ten minutes later, d'une minute à l'autre any minute now

minuterie NOUN FEM **time-switch**

minutieux, minutieuse ADJECTIVE MASC, FEM **thorough**

mirabelle NOUN FEM **small yellow plum**

miracle NOUN MASC **miracle**; par miracle miraculously

miracle ADJECTIVE **wonder**

miraculeux, miraculeuse ADJECTIVE MASC, FEM **miraculous**

miroir NOUN MASC **mirror**; au miroir in the mirror

mis VERB ▸ SEE **mettre**

miser VERB [1] **to bet**

misérable ADJECTIVE **poor**

misère NOUN FEM **destitution, extreme poverty**

missile NOUN MASC **missile**

missionnaire NOUN MASC & FEM **missionary**

mistral NOUN MASC **mistral** (a strong cold north wind which blows down the Rhône valley to the Mediterranean)

mite NOUN FEM **clothes moth**

mi-temps¹ NOUN MASC **part-time job**; travailler à mi-temps to work part-time

mi-temps² NOUN FEM **half-time** (in a match)

miteux, miteuse ADJECTIVE MASC, FEM **seedy, shabby**

mitraillette NOUN FEM **submachine gun**

mixage NOUN MASC **sound mixing**

mixer VERB [1] **to mix**

mixte ADJECTIVE ❶ **mixed** ❷ **coeducational**

Mlle (short for Mademoiselle)

Mme (short for Madame)

mobile NOUN MASC ❶ **motive** ❷ **mobile**

mobile ADJECTIVE ❶ **mobile** ❷ feuilles mobiles loose sheets (as opposed to a pad of paper)

mobilier NOUN MASC **furniture**

mobylette NOUN FEM **moped**

mocassin NOUN MASC ❶ **loafer** ❷ **moccasin**

moche ADJECTIVE (informal) ❶ **awful** ❷ **ugly**

mode¹ NOUN FEM **fashion**; être à la mode to be fashionable

mode² NOUN MASC **way, mode**

mode d'emploi NOUN MASC **instructions for use**

mode de vie NOUN MASC **way of life**

modèle NOUN MASC ❶ **model** ❷ **style**; ce modèle existe en plusieurs coloris this style is available in several colours

modéré ADJECTIVE **moderate**

moderne ADJECTIVE **modern**

moderniser VERB [1] **to modernize**

modernité NOUN FEM **modernity**

modeste *ADJECTIVE* ❶ modest
❷ humble

modestie *NOUN FEM* modesty

modifier *VERB* [1] to change

modiste *NOUN FEM* milliner

module *NOUN MASC* ❶ module
❷ kitchen unit

moelle *NOUN FEM* marrow *(of bone)*

moelleux, moelleuse *ADJECTIVE
MASC, FEM* ❶ soft ❷ mellow

mœurs *PLURAL NOUN FEM* ❶ customs
❷ morals

moi *PRONOUN* ❶ me; c'est pour moi
it's for me, pas moi not me ❷ moi,
je pense que … I think that … ❸ à
moi mine, ce n'est pas à moi it's not
mine, un ami à moi a friend of mine

moi-même *PRONOUN* myself; je l'ai
fait moi-même I did it myself

moindre *ADJECTIVE* slightest; le
moindre problème the slightest
problem, je n'ai pas la moindre idée
I haven't the slightest idea

moine *NOUN MASC* monk

moineau *NOUN MASC (PLURAL*
moineaux*)* sparrow

moins *PREPOSITION* ❶ minus; sept
moins deux égale cinq seven minus
two equals five ❷ il est dix heures
moins cinq it's five to ten

moins *ADVERB* ❶ less; tu en as moins
que moi you've got less than me, de
moins en moins less and less, il est
moins grand que son frère he's not
as tall as his brother, c'est moins
loin it's not as far, j'aime moins
le bleu I don't like the blue one as
much ❷ le moins the least, le moins
difficile the least difficult, le moins

gros the smallest ❸ moins de less,
fewer, moins de beurre less butter,
moins de voitures fewer cars ❹ au
moins at least ❺ du moins at least
❻ à moins que *(+ subjunctive)*
unless, à moins qu'elle soit malade
unless she's ill

mois *NOUN MASC* month; au mois
de mai in May, le mois dernier
last month, le mois prochain next
month

moisi *NOUN MASC* mould

moisi *ADJECTIVE* mouldy

moisir *VERB* [2] to go mouldy

moisson *NOUN FEM* harvest

moite *ADJECTIVE* ❶ damp ❷ muggy

moitié *NOUN FEM* ❶ half; la moitié
d'une pomme half an apple, donne-
moi la moitié give me half, la moitié
du temps half the time ❷ à moitié
half, à moitié vide half empty

moitié-moitié *ADVERB* half-and-
half; partager moitié-moitié to go
halves

molaire *NOUN FEM* molar, back tooth

molle *ADJECTIVE* ▸ SEE **mou**

mollet *NOUN MASC* calf *(of the leg)*

mollet *ADJECTIVE* un œuf mollet a soft-
boiled egg

molleton *NOUN MASC* flannel,
flannelette

môme *NOUN MASC & FEM* *(informal)* kid

moment *NOUN MASC* moment; un
moment, s'il vous plaît just a
moment please, en ce moment
at the moment, par moments at
times, pour le moment for the
moment, au moment où just

when, à ce moment-là just at that moment, just then, j'ai attendu un bon moment I waited for a good while

mon, **ma**, **mes** DETERMINER **my**; mon fils my son, ma fille my daughter, mes enfants my children

monarchie NOUN FEM **monarchy**

monastère NOUN MASC **monastery**

monde NOUN MASC ❶ **world** ❷ **people**; il y a beaucoup de monde there are a lot of people, peu de monde not many people, tout le monde everybody

mondial ADJECTIVE MASC (PLURAL mondiaux) ❶ **world**; la Seconde Guerre mondiale the Second World War ❷ **worldwide**

monétique NOUN FEM **electronic banking**

moniteur[1] NOUN MASC **monitor**

moniteur[2], **monitrice** NOUN MASC, FEM ❶ **instructor** (sports or driving); un moniteur de ski a ski instructor ❷ **camp leader**

monnaie NOUN FEM ❶ **currency** ❷ une pièce de monnaie a coin ❸ **change**; je n'ai pas de monnaie I don't have any change

monopoliser VERB [1] to **monopolize**

monotone ADJECTIVE **monotonous**

Monsieur NOUN MASC (PLURAL Messieurs) ❶ Monsieur Lejay Mr Lejay, bonsoir monsieur good evening (when greeting somebody you do not know well in French it is polite to add 'Monsieur', 'Madame',

or 'Mademoiselle' to the greeting) ❷ **man**; un grand monsieur a tall man, les deux messieurs assis à la table the two men sitting at the table

monstre NOUN MASC **monster**

monstre ADJECTIVE **huge**; un travail monstre a huge amount of work

monstrueux, **monstrueuse** ADJECTIVE MASC, FEM **monstrous**

mont NOUN MASC **mountain**; le mont Blanc Mont Blanc

montagne NOUN FEM ❶ **mountain**; la montagne the mountains ❷ une montagne de a mountain of

montagneux, **montagneuse** ADJECTIVE MASC, FEM **mountainous**

montant NOUN MASC **sum**

montant ADJECTIVE **rising**

montée NOUN FEM ❶ **ascent, way up** ❷ **rise, increase** ❸ **slope**; en montée uphill

monter VERB [1] ❶ to **go up**, to **come up**; monter l'escalier to go (or come) up the stairs, monter la colline to go up the hill, monter se coucher to go up to bed ❷ monter dans to get on (a bus, train, etc) ❸ monter quelque chose to bring (or take) something up, je vais monter tes valises I'll take your cases up ❹ to **assemble** (a kit) ❺ to **rise**; les prix ont monté prices have risen ❻ to **increase** ❼ monter à cheval to ride a horse

montgolfière NOUN FEM **hot-air balloon**

montre NOUN FEM **watch**

montrer VERB [1] ❶ to **show**;

montrer quelque chose à quelqu'un to show somebody something, montre-moi ton cadeau show me your present ❷ **to point out**; montrer quelque chose du doigt to point to something

monture NOUN FEM **frames** (of glasses)

monument NOUN MASC
❶ **monument**; un monument aux morts a war memorial ❷ **historic building**

moquer VERB [1] ❶ se moquer de to make fun of, tout le monde s'est moqué de moi everybody made fun of me ❷ se moquer de not to care about, je m'en moque I couldn't care less

moquette NOUN FEM **fitted carpet**

moqueur, moqueuse ADJECTIVE MASC, FEM **mocking**

moral NOUN MASC (PLURAL **moraux**) **morale**; je n'ai pas le moral I'm feeling really down

moral ADJECTIVE MASC (PLURAL **moraux**) ❶ **moral** ❷ **mental**

morale NOUN FEM ❶ **moral** ❷ **morality**

morceau NOUN MASC (PLURAL **morceaux**) **piece**, **bit**; un morceau de pain a piece of bread, un morceau de sucre a sugar lump

mordre VERB [3] **to bite**

mordu ADJECTIVE être mordu de quelque chose (informal) to be mad about something

morne ADJECTIVE ❶ **gloomy** ❷ **dismal**, **dreary**

morsure NOUN FEM **bite**

mort¹ NOUN FEM **death**; trois mois avant sa mort three months before he died

mort², **morte** NOUN MASC, FEM **dead man**, **dead woman**

mort ADJECTIVE **dead**

mort-aux-rats NOUN FEM **rat poison**

mortel, mortelle ADJECTIVE MASC, FEM ❶ **deadly** ❷ **fatal**

morue NOUN FEM ❶ **cod** ❷ **salt cod**

mosaïque NOUN FEM **mosaic**

Moscou NOUN **Moscow**

mosquée NOUN FEM **mosque**

mot NOUN MASC ❶ **word**; mot à mot word for word ❷ un petit mot a note

motard, motarde NOUN MASC, FEM (informal) **motorcyclist**

mot de passe NOUN MASC **password**

moteur NOUN MASC **engine**

motif NOUN MASC ❶ **motive** ❷ **pattern**

motiver VERB [1] **to motivate**

moto NOUN FEM **motorbike**; je suis venu en moto I came by motorbike

motocycliste NOUN MASC & FEM **motorcyclist**

mots croisés PLURAL NOUN MASC **crossword**

motte NOUN FEM ❶ **lump** ❷ **slab**

mou (mol before a vowel) ADJECTIVE **molle** FEM ❶ **soft** ❷ **flabby**

mouche NOUN FEM **fly**

moucher VERB [1] **se moucher** to blow your nose

moucheron NOUN MASC **midge**

mouchoir NOUN MASC
❶ **handkerchief** ❷ **tissue**

moue NOUN FEM **pout**; **faire la moue** to pout

mouette NOUN FEM **seagull**

moufle NOUN FEM **mitten**

mouillé ADJECTIVE **wet**

mouiller VERB [1] ❶ **to wet** ❷ **se mouiller** to get wet

moulant ADJECTIVE **tight-fitting**

moule¹ NOUN MASC **mould**

moule² NOUN FEM **mussel**

mouler VERB [1] **to mould**

moulin NOUN MASC **mill**

moulin à vent NOUN MASC **windmill**

moulu ADJECTIVE **ground**; **le café moulu** ground coffee

moulure NOUN FEM **moulding**

mourir VERB [54] **to die**; **elle est morte en février** she died in February, **je meurs de faim!** I'm starving!, **je meurs d'envie d'y aller** I'm dying to go there

mousquetaire NOUN MASC **musketeer**

moussant ADJECTIVE **foaming**

mousse NOUN FEM ❶ **foam**; **mousse à raser** shaving foam ❷ **lather** ❸ **froth** ❹ **mousse au chocolat** chocolate mousse ❺ **moss**

mousser VERB [1] **to foam**

mousseux, mousseuse ADJECTIVE MASC, FEM **du vin mousseux** sparkling wine

moustache NOUN FEM **moustache**

moustique NOUN MASC **mosquito**

moutarde NOUN FEM **mustard**

mouton NOUN MASC ❶ **sheep** ❷ **mutton**

mouvement NOUN MASC
❶ **movement** ❷ **activity, bustle**

mouvementé ADJECTIVE **hectic, eventful**; **j'ai eu une semaine mouvementée** I've had a hectic week

moyen NOUN MASC ❶ **means**; **un moyen de transport** a means of transport, **un moyen de faire** a means of doing, **je n'ai aucun moyen de le contacter** I have no means of contacting him ❷ **les moyens** the means, the wherewithal, **je n'ai pas les moyens de m'acheter un ordinateur** I can't afford to buy a computer ❸ **way**

moyen, moyenne ADJECTIVE MASC, FEM ❶ **medium** ❷ **medium-sized** ❸ **average**; **un équipe de niveau très moyen** a very average team

Moyen-Âge NOUN MASC **Middle Ages**

moyenne NOUN FEM ❶ **average**; **en moyenne** on average ❷ **avoir la moyenne** to pass (an exam)

Moyen-Orient NOUN MASC **Middle East**

muet, muette ADJECTIVE MASC, FEM ❶ **speechless, dumb** ❷ **silent**

muguet NOUN MASC lily of the valley

mulet NOUN MASC mule

multifonction ADJECTIVE multipurpose

multiple ADJECTIVE ❶ multiple ❷ various

multiplication NOUN FEM ❶ multiplication ❷ multiplication de increase in the number of

multiplier VERB [1] ❶ to multiply ❷ to increase

municipal ADJECTIVE MASC (PLURAL municipaux) ❶ local, town ❷ municipal

municipalité NOUN FEM ❶ town (or local) council ❷ municipality

munition NOUN FEM ammunition

mur NOUN MASC wall

mûr ADJECTIVE ❶ ripe ❷ mature

muraille NOUN FEM (defensive) wall; la Grande Muraille de Chine the Great Wall of China

mûre NOUN FEM blackberry

mûrir VERB [2] ❶ to ripen ❷ to mature ❸ to develop

murmure NOUN MASC murmur

murmurer VERB [1] to murmur

musc NOUN MASC musk

muscade NOUN FEM nutmeg; une noix de muscade a nutmeg

muscle NOUN MASC muscle

musclé ADJECTIVE muscular

musculation NOUN FEM bodybuilding

museau NOUN MASC (PLURAL museaux) muzzle, snout

musée NOUN MASC museum

musical ADJECTIVE MASC (PLURAL musicaux) musical

musicien, **musicienne** NOUN MASC, FEM musician

musique NOUN FEM music; mettre de la musique to put on some music

musulman, **musulmane** NOUN MASC, FEM, ADJECTIVE Muslim

mutuel, **mutuelle** ADJECTIVE MASC, FEM mutual

myope ADJECTIVE short-sighted
• être myope comme une taupe to be as blind as a bat (literally: to be as short-sighted as a mole)

myopie NOUN FEM short-sightedness

myosotis NOUN MASC forget-me-not

myrtille NOUN FEM bilberry

mystère NOUN MASC mystery

mystérieux ADJECTIVE MASC (PLURAL mystérieuse) mysterious

mystifier VERB [1] to fool

mystique ADJECTIVE mystical

mythe NOUN MASC myth

mythologie NOUN FEM mythology

Nn

n' ADVERB ▸ SEE **ne**

nacre NOUN FEM **mother-of-pearl**

nage NOUN FEM **swimming**

nager VERB [52] **to swim**

nageur, nageuse NOUN MASC, FEM **swimmer**

naïf, naïve ADJECTIVE MASC, FEM **naïve**

nain, naine NOUN MASC, FEM, ADJECTIVE **dwarf**

naissance NOUN FEM **birth**; date de naissance date of birth

naître VERB [55] **to be born**; elle est née en 1975 she was born in 1975

nana NOUN FEM (informal) **girl**

naphtaline NOUN FEM **mothballs**

nappe NOUN FEM **tablecloth**

narcisse NOUN MASC **narcissus**

narine NOUN FEM **nostril**

natal ADJECTIVE **native**; mon pays natal my native country

natalité NOUN FEM le taux de natalité the birthrate

natation NOUN FEM **swimming**; faire de la natation to go swimming

natif, native ADJECTIVE MASC, FEM **native**

nation NOUN FEM **nation**

national ADJECTIVE MASC (PLURAL nationaux) **national**

nationaliser VERB [1] **to nationalize**

nationalité NOUN FEM **nationality**

nativité NOUN FEM **Nativity**

natte NOUN FEM ❶ **plait** ❷ **mat**

nature NOUN FEM **nature**

nature ADJECTIVE yaourt nature plain yoghurt, un thé nature a cup of tea without milk or sugar

naturel NOUN MASC ❶ **nature** ❷ au naturel plain

naturel, naturelle ADJECTIVE MASC, FEM **natural**

naturellement ADVERB **of course**

nausée NOUN FEM **nausea**; avoir la nausée to feel sick

nautique ADJECTIVE **water**; faire du ski nautique to go water-skiing

navet NOUN MASC **turnip**

navette NOUN FEM **shuttle**; j'ai pris la navette de l'aéroport I took the shuttle from the airport, faire la navette to travel back and forth

navigateur NOUN MASC **browser**

naviguer VERB [1] **to sail**

navire NOUN MASC **ship**

navire-citerne NOUN MASC **oil tanker**

navire-école NOUN MASC **training ship**

navré ADJECTIVE **sorry**; je suis vraiment navré I'm terribly sorry

ne (n' before a vowel or silent 'h') ADVERB ❶ ne + pas not, je n'aime

pas le lait I don't like milk **②** ne +
jamais never, je ne vais jamais à
Londres I never go to London **③** ne
+ que only, je n'ai que dix euros I
only have ten euros **④** ne + plus no
longer, elle n'habite plus à Londres
she no longer lives in London **⑤**
ne + rien nothing, il ne mange rien he
eats nothing, rien ne t'empêche
d'y aller there's nothing to stop you
going **⑥** ne + personne nobody,
il n'y a personne there's nobody,
personne n'a compris nobody
understood

né, née *VERB* ▸ SEE **naître**

néanmoins *ADVERB* **nevertheless**

nécessaire *NOUN MASC* faire le
nécessaire to do the necessary

nécessaire *ADJECTIVE* **necessary**;
il est nécessaire de faire it is
necessary to do, est-ce qu'il est
nécessaire de réserver? is it
necessary to book?

nécessairement *ADVERB*
necessarily

nécessité *NOUN FEM* **necessity**

nécessiter *VERB* [1] **to require**

nectarine *NOUN FEM* **nectarine**

néerlandais *NOUN MASC* **Dutch**
(language)

néerlandais *ADJECTIVE* **Dutch**

nef *NOUN FEM* **nave** *(of a church)*

négatif *NOUN MASC* **negative**

négatif, négative *ADJECTIVE MASC, FEM*
negative

négligé *ADJECTIVE* **scruffy**

négligent *ADJECTIVE* **careless**

négliger *VERB* [52] **①** to neglect
② il a négligé de le faire he didn't
bother to do it

négociant *NOUN MASC* **merchant**

négocier *VERB* [1] **to negotiate**

neige *NOUN FEM* **snow**; un bonhomme
de neige a snowman

neiger *VERB* [52] **to snow**; il neige it's
snowing

neigeux, neigeuse *ADJECTIVE MASC,
FEM* **snowy**

nénuphar *NOUN MASC* **waterlily**

néon *NOUN MASC* **neon**

néo-zélandais *ADJECTIVE* **New
Zealand**

Néo-Zélandais, Néo-Zélandaise
NOUN MASC, FEM **New Zealander**

nerf *NOUN MASC* **nerve**

nerveux, nerveuse *ADJECTIVE MASC,
FEM* **nervous**

n'est-ce pas? *ADVERB* il fait froid
ce soir, n'est-ce pas? it's cold this
evening, isn't it?, il habite à Paris,
n'est ce pas? he lives in Paris,
doesn't he?, tu as déjà mangé,
n'est-ce pas? you've already eaten,
haven't you?

net, nette *ADJECTIVE MASC, FEM*
① clear; c'est très net it's quite
clear **②** distinct; une nette
différence a distinct difference,
une nette amélioration a distinct
improvement

net *ADVERB* **①** s'arrêter net to stop
dead **②** refuser net to refuse flatly

nettement *ADVERB* **far**; nettement
meilleur much better

nettoyage *NOUN MASC* **cleaning**; le
nettoyage à sec dry cleaning

nettoyer *VERB* [39] **to clean**

neuf[1] *NUMBER* **nine**; il est neuf heures du matin it's nine o'clock in the morning, Julie a neuf ans Julie's nine, le neuf juillet the ninth of July

neuf[2], **neuve** *ADJECTIVE MASC, FEM* **new**; une voiture toute neuve a brand new car

neutre *ADJECTIVE* **neutral**

neuvième *NOUN MASC* au neuvième on the ninth floor

neuvième *ADJECTIVE* **ninth**

neveu *NOUN MASC (PLURAL* **neveux)** **nephew**

nez *NOUN MASC* **nose**

ni *CONJUNCTION* ni ... ni neither ... nor, ni lui ni son frère neither he nor his brother, il n'y a ni pain ni lait there's neither bread nor milk, ni Frank ni Paul ne le sait neither Frank nor Paul knows, ni moi non plus me neither

niche *NOUN FEM* ❶ **kennel** ❷ **niche**

nid *NOUN MASC* **nest**

nièce *NOUN FEM* **niece**

nier *VERB* [1] **to deny**

n'importe *ADVERB* ❶ **either, it doesn't matter**; 'tu veux une aile ou une cuisse?' – 'n'importe' 'do you want a wing or a leg?' – 'either, it doesn't matter' ❷ n'importe qui anybody, n'importe qui peut le faire anybody can do it ❸ n'importe quoi anything, je ferai n'importe quoi pour t'aider I'll do absolutely anything to help you, elle a fait n'importe quoi she's made a real mess of it, tu dis n'importe quoi you're talking complete rubbish ❹ n'importe quand any time, tu peux m'appeler n'importe quand you can ring me any time

❺ n'importe comment any old how, tu peux jeter tous ces papiers dans un tiroir n'importe comment you can throw all these papers into a drawer any old how ❻ n'importe où anywhere, pose tes valises n'importe où put your cases down anywhere you like, je ne peux pas habiter n'importe où I can't live just anywhere

niveau *NOUN MASC (PLURAL* **niveau)** **level**; au même niveau at the same level

niveau de vie *NOUN MASC* **standard of living**

noble *ADJECTIVE* **noble**

noces *PLURAL NOUN FEM* **wedding**

nocif, **nocive** *ADJECTIVE MASC, FEM* **harmful**

nocturne *NOUN FEM* **late-night opening**

nocturne *ADJECTIVE* **nocturnal**

Noël *NOUN MASC* **Christmas**; Joyeux Noël Merry Christmas, un cadeau de Noël a Christmas present, le sapin de Noël the Christmas tree

nœud *NOUN MASC* **knot**; faire un nœud to tie a knot

nœud ferroviaire *NOUN MASC* **(railway) junction**

noir *NOUN MASC* ❶ **black** ❷ le noir the dark

noir *ADJECTIVE* ❶ **black** ❷ **dark**; il fait noir it's dark

Noir, **Noire** *NOUN MASC, FEM* **black man, black woman**; les Noirs black people

noirceur *NOUN FEM* **blackness**

noircir VERB [2] **to blacken**

noisette NOUN FEM **hazelnut**

noix NOUN FEM ❶ **walnut** ❷ une noix de beurre a knob of butter

noix de cajou NOUN FEM **cashew nut**

noix de coco NOUN FEM **coconut**

nom NOUN MASC ❶ **name**; nom de famille surname, nom de jeune fille maiden name ❷ au nom de: au nom de la famille Dupont on behalf of the Dupont family ❸ **noun**

nombre NOUN MASC **number**; bon nombre de a good many, le nombre de victimes s'élève à 25 the number of dead is 25

nombreux, **nombreuse** ADJECTIVE MASC, FEM **many**; de nombreuses personnes many people, ils étaient nombreux there were a lot of them, ils étaient peu nombreux there weren't many of them, une famille nombreuse a big family

nombril NOUN MASC **navel**

nommer VERB [1] ❶ **to appoint** ❷ **to name**

non ADVERB ❶ **no**; elle a dit non she said no ❷ non seulement not only, non loin de not far from, moi non plus me neither

non- COMBINING FORM un non-fumeur a nonsmoker

nord NOUN MASC **north**; le nord de l'Espagne northern Spain, le vent du nord the north wind

nord ADJECTIVE **north**, **northern**; le côté nord the north side

nord-américain ADJECTIVE **North American**

Nord-Américain, **Nord-Américaine** NOUN MASC, FEM **North American**

nord-est NOUN MASC **north-east**

nord-ouest NOUN MASC **north-west**

normal ADJECTIVE MASC (PLURAL normaux) ❶ **normal** ❷ c'est normal it's natural ❸ ce n'est pas normal it's not right

normalement ADVERB ❶ **normally** ❷ **according to plan**; normalement, elle doit être à Rome actuellement if things have gone according to plan, she should be in Rome at the moment

normand ADJECTIVE **Norman**; la côte normande the Normandy coast

Normand, **Normande** NOUN MASC, FEM **Norman**

Normandie NOUN FEM **Normandy**

norme NOUN FEM ❶ **norm** ❷ **standard**; selon les normes européennes according to European standards

Norvège NOUN FEM **Norway**

norvégien, **norvégienne** ADJECTIVE MASC, FEM **Norwegian**

nos ADJECTIVE ▸ SEE **notre**

notaire NOUN MASC **notary public**

notamment ADVERB **in particular**

note NOUN FEM ❶ **bill**; la note, s'il vous plaît can I have the bill please ❷ **mark**; j'ai eu une bonne note en allemand I got a good mark in German ❸ prendre des notes to take notes

noter VERB [1] ❶ **to write down** ❷ **to notice**

notice NOUN FEM **instructions**

notion NOUN FEM ❶ **idea** ❷ **des notions basic knowledge**, **j'ai des notions d'espagnol** I have a basic knowledge of Spanish

notre ADJECTIVE (PLURAL **nos**) **our**; **notre fille** our daughter, **nos enfants** our children

nôtre PRONOUN **le nôtre**, **la nôtre**, **les nôtres ours**

nouer VERB [1] **to tie**, **to knot**

nougat NOUN MASC **nougat**

nouilles PLURAL NOUN FEM **noodles**, **pasta**

nounours NOUN MASC (baby talk) **teddy bear**

nourrice NOUN FEM **childminder**

nourrir VERB [2] **to feed**

nourrissant ADJECTIVE **nourishing**

nourrisson NOUN MASC **infant**

nourriture NOUN FEM **food**

nous PRONOUN ❶ **we**; **nous apprenons le français** we are learning French ❷ **us**; **viens avec nous** come with us, **elle nous aide** she helps us, **elle nous a aidés** she helped us ❸ **to us**; **elle ne nous a pas parlé** she didn't speak to us, **elle nous a donné son adresse** she gave us her address ❹ **ourselves**; **nous nous ferons une salade** we'll make ourselves a salad ❺ reflexive **nous nous levons à sept heures** we get up at seven o'clock

nous-mêmes PRONOUN **ourselves**

nouveau (**nouvel** before a vowel or silent 'h') ADJECTIVE MASC, **nouvelle** FEM (PLURAL **nouveaux**) ❶ **new**; **viens**

voir mon nouvel appartement come and see my new flat ❷ **à nouveau**, **de nouveau again**

nouveauté NOUN FEM ❶ **novelty** ❷ **new release**

Nouvel An NOUN MASC **New Year**

nouvelle ADJECTIVE ▸ SEE **nouveau**

nouvelle NOUN FEM ❶ **une nouvelle news**, **j'ai une bonne nouvelle!** I've got good news! ❷ **short story**; **nous étudions une nouvelle de Camus** we're doing a Camus short story ❸ **des nouvelles news**, **nous n'avons pas de nouvelles pour l'instant** we have no news for the moment, **as-tu des nouvelles de lui?** have you heard from him?

Nouvelle-Calédonie NOUN FEM **New Caledonia** (French island territory in the Pacific)

Nouvelle-Zélande NOUN FEM **New Zealand**

novembre NOUN MASC **November**; **en novembre**, **au mois de novembre** in November

noyau NOUN MASC (PLURAL **noyaux**) ❶ **stone** (in fruit) ❷ **nucleus**

noyer[1] VERB [39] ❶ **to drown** ❷ **se noyer to drown**, **to drown oneself**

noyer[2] NOUN MASC ❶ **walnut tree** ❷ **walnut**; **une table en noyer** a walnut table

nu ADJECTIVE ❶ **naked** ❷ **bare**

nuage NOUN MASC **cloud**

nuageux, **nuageuse** ADJECTIVE MASC, FEM **cloudy**

nuance NOUN FEM ❶ **shade** (of a colour) ❷ **nuance**

nucléaire ADJECTIVE **nuclear**; **l'énergie nucléaire nuclear power**

nuisible *ADJECTIVE* **harmful**

nuit *NOUN FEM* ❶ **night**; cette nuit last night, tonight, dans la nuit in the night, toute la nuit all night, travailler la nuit to work at night ❷ il fait nuit it's dark, avant la nuit before dark, la nuit tombe à sept heures it gets dark at seven o'clock

nul, nulle *ADJECTIVE MASC, FEM* ❶ (informal) **hopeless, awful**; le film était nul the film was awful, je suis nul en histoire I'm hopeless at history ❷ un match nul a draw

nulle part *ADVERB* **nowhere**; je ne trouve nulle part mon dictionnaire I can't find my dictionary anywhere

numérique *ADJECTIVE* **digital**

numéro *NOUN MASC* **number**; ils habitent au numéro vingt-cinq they live at number twenty-five

numéro de téléphone *NOUN MASC* **telephone number**

nu-pied *NOUN MASC* **open sandal**

nurse *NOUN FEM* **nanny**

nutritif, nutritive *ADJECTIVE MASC, FEM* **nourishing, nutritious**; valeur nutritive nutritional value

nutrition *NOUN FEM* **nutrition**

nylon *NOUN MASC* **nylon**

oasis *NOUN FEM* **oasis**

obéir *VERB* [2] obéir à to **obey**

obéissance *NOUN FEM* **obedience**

obéissant *ADJECTIVE* **obedient**

obèse *ADJECTIVE* **obese**

obésité *NOUN FEM* **obesity**

objectif *NOUN MASC* **objective**

objectif, objective *ADJECTIVE MASC, FEM* **objective**

objection *NOUN FEM* **objection**

objet *NOUN MASC* **object**

objets trouvés *PLURAL NOUN MASC* **lost property**; aller aux objets trouvés to go to the lost property office

obligatoire *ADJECTIVE* **compulsory**

obligé *ADJECTIVE* être obligé de faire to **have to do**, je suis obligé de partir I have to go

obliger *VERB* [52] obliger quelqu'un à faire to **force somebody to do**

obscène *ADJECTIVE* **obscene**

obscur *ADJECTIVE* ❶ **dark** ❷ **obscure**

obscurité *NOUN FEM* ❶ **darkness**; dans l'obscurité in the dark ❷ **obscurity**

obséder *VERB* [24] to **obsess**; être obsédé par quelque chose to be obsessed by something

a b c d e f g h i j k l m n o p q r s t u v w x y z

obsèques *PLURAL NOUN FEM* **funeral**

observateur, **observatrice** *NOUN MASC, FEM* **observer**

observateur, **observatrice** *ADJECTIVE MASC, FEM* **observant**

observation *NOUN FEM* **❶ comment ❷ remark**

observatoire *NOUN MASC* **observatory**

observer *VERB* [1] **❶ to watch**; elle nous observait de loin she was watching us from a distance **❷ to observe** (rules)

obsession *NOUN FEM* **obsession**

obstacle *NOUN MASC* **obstacle**

obstination *NOUN FEM* **obstinacy**

obstiné *ADJECTIVE* **stubborn**

obtenir *VERB* [77] **to get**

occasion *NOUN FEM* **❶ opportunity**; avoir l'occasion de faire to have the opportunity to do **❷** acheter quelque chose d'occasion to buy something second hand, une voiture d'occasion a second-hand car **❸ bargain**; une bonne occasion a good bargain **❹ occasion**; à l'occasion de on the occasion of **❺** à l'occasion some time

occasionner *VERB* [1] **to cause**

Occident *NOUN MASC* **l'Occident the West**

occidental *ADJECTIVE MASC (PLURAL* occidentaux) **western**

occupation *NOUN FEM* **occupation**; trouver une occupation to find something to do

occupé *ADJECTIVE* **❶ busy**; je suis occupé en ce moment I'm busy at the moment **❷ engaged** (of a telephone line or toilet) **❸** cette place est occupée this seat is taken

occuper *VERB* [1] **❶ to occupy ❷** s'occuper to keep yourself busy **❸** s'occuper de to deal with, to see to, je vais m'occuper du dîner I'll go and see to dinner, je m'en occupe I'll see to it **❹** s'occuper de quelqu'un to attend to somebody, est-ce qu'on s'occupe de vous? are you being attended to?

occurrence *NOUN FEM* **❶ case**; plusieurs occurrences de typhoïde several cases of typhoid **❷ occurrence**

océan *NOUN MASC* **ocean**

octet *NOUN MASC* **byte** (in computing)

octobre *NOUN MASC* **October**; en octobre, au mois d'octobre in October

odeur *NOUN FEM* **smell**; des odeurs de cuisine cooking smells

odorat *NOUN MASC* **sense of smell**

œil *NOUN MASC (PLURAL* yeux) **eye**
• cela saute aux yeux it's obvious (literally: it jumps into your eyes)

œillet *NOUN MASC* **carnation**

œuf *NOUN MASC* **egg**; un œuf à la coque a boiled egg, un œuf dur a hard-boiled egg, un œuf mollet a soft-boiled egg, un œuf sur le plat a fried egg, des œufs brouillés scrambled eggs

œuvre *NOUN FEM* **work** (of art or literature); une œuvre d'art a work of art

offenser *VERB* [1] **to offend**

office *NOUN MASC* **❶ office ❷** office religieux religious service

officiel NOUN MASC **official**

officiel, **officielle** ADJECTIVE MASC, FEM **official**

officier NOUN MASC **officer**

offre NOUN FEM ❶ **offer** ❷ 'offres d'emploi' 'situations vacant'

offrir VERB [56] ❶ offrir quelque chose à quelqu'un to give something to somebody, elle m'a offert une montre pour mon anniversaire she gave me a watch for my birthday ❷ s'offrir quelque chose to treat yourself to something, je vais m'offrir un nouveau dictionnaire I'm going to treat myself to a new dictionary ❸ to offer

oie NOUN FEM **goose**

oignon NOUN MASC **onion**

oiseau NOUN MASC (PLURAL oiseaux) **bird**

olive NOUN FEM **olive**; l'huile d'olive olive oil

olivier NOUN MASC **olive tree**

ombragé ADJECTIVE **shaded** (from the sun)

ombre NOUN FEM ❶ **shade**; à l'ombre in the shade ❷ **shadow**

ombre à paupières NOUN FEM **eyeshadow**

ombrelle NOUN FEM **sun umbrella**

omelette NOUN FEM **omelette**; une omelette aux champignons a mushroom omelette

omettre VERB [11] **to omit**, **to leave out**; omettre de faire quelque chose to fail to do something

omoplate NOUN FEM **shoulder blade**

on PRONOUN ❶ **we**; on va au cinéma we're going to the cinema, on a oublié de fermer la porte we forgot to shut the door ❷ **you**; de la terrasse on voit la mer from the terrace you can see the sea, on ne devrait pas mentir you shouldn't tell lies ❸ on leur a dit que ... they were told that ..., on a volé leur voiture their car's been stolen

oncle NOUN MASC **uncle**

onde NOUN FEM **wave** (on radio)

ondée NOUN FEM **shower** (of rain)

onéreux, **onéreuse** ADJECTIVE MASC, FEM **costly**

ongle NOUN MASC **nail**; se faire les ongles to do your nails, je me suis coupé les ongles I've cut my nails

ongle de pied NOUN MASC **toenail**

ONU NOUN FEM (short for Organisation des Nations) unies UN, United Nations

onze NUMBER **eleven**; onze personnes eleven people, Marie-Ange a onze ans Marie-Ange is eleven, le onze juillet the eleventh of July

onzième NOUN MASC au onzième on the eleventh floor

onzième ADJECTIVE **eleventh**

opéra NOUN MASC ❶ **opera** ❷ **opera house**

opérateur, **opératrice** NOUN MASC, FEM **operator**

opération NOUN FEM ❶ **operation** ❷ **calculation**

opérer VERB [24] **to operate**; opérer quelqu'un to operate on somebody, est-ce qu'il va falloir opérer? will they have to operate, se faire opérer to have an operation

opinion NOUN FEM **opinion**

opposant, **opposante** NOUN MASC, FEM **opponent**

opposé NOUN **l'opposé the opposite**

opposé ADJECTIVE ❶ **opposite** ❷ **être opposé à quelque chose to be opposed to something**

opposer VERB [1] ❶ **le match de samedi prochain oppose les Anglais et les Français the English are playing the French in next Saturday's match** ❷ **s'opposer à quelque chose to oppose something, ils s'opposent à un changement des règles they are opposed to a change in the rules**

opposition NOUN FEM **opposition**

opter VERB [1] **to opt**

opticien, **opticienne** NOUN MASC, FEM **optician**

optimisme NOUN MASC **optimism**

optimiste NOUN MASC & FEM **optimist**

optimiste ADJECTIVE **optimistic**

option NOUN FEM **option**

optionnel, **optionnelle** ADJECTIVE MASC, FEM **optional**

or[1] NOUN MASC ❶ **gold**; **une montre en or a gold watch** ❷ **une occasion en or a golden opportunity**

or[2] CONJUNCTION **now**

orage NOUN MASC **storm**

orageux, **orageuse** ADJECTIVE MASC, FEM ❶ **stormy** ❷ **thundery**

oral NOUN MASC (PLURAL **oraux**) **oral (exam)**; **l'oral de français the French oral**

oral ADJECTIVE MASC (PLURAL **oraux**) **oral**; **une épreuve orale an oral exam**

orange NOUN FEM, ADJECTIVE **orange**

oranger NOUN MASC **orange tree**

orbite NOUN FEM **orbit**

orchestral ADJECTIVE MASC (PLURAL **orchestraux**) **orchestral**

orchestre NOUN MASC ❶ **orchestra** ❷ **band**

orchidée NOUN FEM **orchid**

ordinaire NOUN MASC ❶ **2-star petrol** ❷ **sortir de l'ordinaire to be out of the ordinary, ça sort un peu de l'ordinaire it's a bit out of the ordinary** ❸ **à l'ordinaire, d'ordinaire usually**

ordinaire ADJECTIVE **ordinary**; **une journée ordinaire an ordinary day**

ordinateur NOUN MASC **computer**; **un ordinateur portable a portable computer**

ordonnance NOUN FEM **prescription**

ordonné ADJECTIVE **tidy**

ordonner VERB [1] **to order**

ordre NOUN MASC ❶ **order**; **donner des ordres to give orders** ❷ **order**; **par ordre alphabétique in alphabetical order, mettre de l'ordre to tidy up, mettre en ordre to tidy**

ordures PLURAL NOUN FEM **rubbish**

oreille NOUN FEM **ear**

oreiller NOUN MASC **pillow**

oreillons PLURAL NOUN MASC **mumps**

organe NOUN MASC **organ** (of the body)

organique ADJECTIVE **organic**

organisateur, organisatrice NOUN MASC, FEM **organizer**

organisation NOUN FEM **organization**

organiser VERB [1] ❶ to organize ❷ s'organiser to get organized

organisme NOUN MASC ❶ organization ❷ body ❸ organism

organiste NOUN MASC & FEM **organist**

orge NOUN FEM **barley**; le sucre d'orge barley sugar

orgeat NOUN MASC le sirop d'orgeat barley water

orgue NOUN FEM **organ**; jouer de l'orgue to play the organ

orgueil NOUN MASC **pride**

orgueilleux, orgueilleuse ADJECTIVE MASC, FEM **proud**

Orient NOUN MASC l'Orient the East

oriental ADJECTIVE MASC (PLURAL orientaux) ❶ eastern ❷ oriental

orientation NOUN FEM ❶ orientation ❷ l'orientation professionnelle careers advice ❸ avoir le sens de l'orientation to have a good sense of direction

orienter VERB [1] ❶ to position ❷ to direct ❸ s'orienter to get one's bearings ❹ s'orienter vers to move towards, Bernard s'oriente vers les langues Bernard's going in for languages

originaire ADJECTIVE être originaire de to be a native of, Giselle est originaire de Dijon Giselle comes from Dijon

original ADJECTIVE MASC (PLURAL originaux) **original**

original ADJECTIVE MASC (PLURAL originaux) ❶ original; le film est en version originale the film isn't dubbed ❷ eccentric; c'est une vieille dame assez originale she's rather an eccentric old lady

originalité NOUN FEM ❶ originality ❷ eccentricity

origine NOUN FEM ❶ origin ❷ elle est d'origine écossaise she's Scottish ❸ à l'origine originally, à l'origine la maison appartenait à mon oncle the house originally belonged to my uncle

orme NOUN MASC **elm tree**

orné ADJECTIVE orné de decorated with

ornemental ADJECTIVE MASC (PLURAL ornementaux) **ornamental**

orphelin, orpheline NOUN MASC, FEM **orphan**

orphelinat NOUN MASC **orphanage**

orteil NOUN MASC **toe**; gros orteil big toe

orthographe NOUN FEM **spelling**

ortie NOUN FEM **nettle**

os NOUN MASC **bone**

osé ADJECTIVE **daring**; c'était un peu osé de dire ça it was a bit daring to say that

a
b
c
d
e
f
g
h
i
j
k
l
m
n
o
p
q
r
s
t
u
v
w
x
y
z

oseille NOUN FEM **sorrel**

oser VERB [1] **to dare**

osier NOUN MASC **wicker**; un panier en osier a wicker basket

osseux, osseuse ADJECTIVE MASC, FEM **bony** (knees, arms)

otage NOUN MASC **hostage**; être pris en otage to be taken hostage

OTAN NOUN FEM (short for Organisation du traité de l'Atlantique Nord) **NATO**

ôter VERB [1] ❶ **to take off**; je vais ôter ma veste I'll take off my jacket ❷ **to take away** ❸ **to remove**

otite NOUN FEM **earache**; avoir une otite to have earache

ou CONJUNCTION ❶ **or**; est-ce que vous voulez le fromage ou le dessert? would you like cheese or dessert? ❷ ou … ou **either … or**, c'est ou dans ma chambre ou dans le salon it's either in my bedroom or in the sitting-room ❸ ou bien **or else**, on peut se retrouver au cinéma ou bien chez moi, si tu veux we can meet at the cinema or else at my place, if you like

où ADVERB **where**; où es-tu? where are you?, ton frère habite où? where does your brother live?, tu l'as trouvé où ton sac? where did you find your bag?, je sais où elle habite I know where she lives

où PRONOUN ❶ **where**; le village où elle habite the village where she lives, la ville d'où il vient the town he comes from ❷ **when, that**; le jour où je suis arrivé the day I arrived

ouate NOUN FEM **cotton wool**

oubli NOUN MASC ❶ **forgetfulness** ❷ l'oubli de quelque chose forgetting something ❸ **oversight**; c'était un oubli I (or you, etc.) forgot about it

oublier VERB [1] ❶ **to forget**; j'ai oublié leur adresse I've forgotten their address ❷ **to leave**; j'ai oublié mes clefs chez Jérôme I've left my keys at Jérôme's

ouest NOUN MASC **west**; à l'ouest de Paris west of Paris, dans l'ouest de la France in the west of France, l'Ouest the West, l'Europe de l'Ouest Western Europe

ouest ADJECTIVE ❶ **west**; le côté ouest the west coast ❷ **western**

ouf EXCLAMATION **phew!**

oui ADVERB **yes**; elle a dit oui she said yes, dire oui de la tête to nod

ouragan NOUN MASC **hurricane**

ourlet NOUN MASC **hem**

ours NOUN MASC **bear**

oursin NOUN MASC **sea urchin**

outil NOUN MASC **tool**

outre PREPOSITION **in addition to**

outré ADJECTIVE **outraged**

outremer NOUN MASC, ADJECTIVE **ultramarine**

outre-mer ADVERB **overseas**

ouvert ADJECTIVE ❶ **open**; laisse la porte ouverte leave the door open, 'ouvert le dimanche' 'open on Sundays' ❷ laisser le robinet ouvert to leave the tap on

ouvertement *ADVERB* **openly**

ouverture *NOUN FEM* ❶ **opening**; les heures d'ouverture opening hours ❷ **openness**; ouverture d'esprit open-mindedness

ouvre-boîte *NOUN MASC* **tin-opener**

ouvre-bouteille *NOUN MASC* **bottle-opener**

ouvrier, ouvrière *NOUN MASC, FEM* **worker**

ouvrier, ouvrière *ADJECTIVE MASC, FEM* la classe ouvrière the working class

ouvrir *VERB* [30] ❶ **to open**; ouvrir la fenêtre to open the window ❷ ouvrir le robinet to turn on the tap ❸ elle n'a pas ouvert la bouche she didn't say a word ❹ s'ouvrir to open, ça s'ouvre comment? how do you open it?

ovale *ADJECTIVE* **oval**

ovni *NOUN MASC* (*short for volant non identifié*) **UFO**

oxygène *NOUN MASC* **oxygen**

ozone *NOUN FEM* **ozone**

Pacifique *NOUN MASC* l'océan Pacifique the Pacific Ocean

pagaille *NOUN FEM* (*informal*) **mess**; quelle pagaille! what a mess!

page *NOUN FEM* **page**; à la première/ dernière page on the first/last page, les Pages Jaunes the Yellow Pages

paie *NOUN FEM* **pay**; un bulletin de paie, une fiche de paie a payslip

paiement *NOUN MASC* **payment**

paillasson *NOUN MASC* **doormat**

paille *NOUN FEM* **straw**

pain *NOUN MASC* ❶ **bread**; une tranche de pain a slice of bread ❷ un pain a loaf of bread, trois pains three loaves of bread, un petit pain a roll
• ils se vendent comme des petits pains they're selling like hot cakes (*literally: like rolls*)

pain au chocolat *NOUN MASC* **chocolate pastry**

pain complet *NOUN MASC* **wholemeal bread**

pain de mie *NOUN MASC* **sandwich loaf**

pain d'épices *NOUN MASC* **gingerbread**

pain de seigle *NOUN MASC* **rye bread**

pain grillé *NOUN MASC* **toast**

a
b
c
d
e
f
g
h
i
j
k
l
m
n
o
p
q
r
s
t
u
v
w
x
y
z

pair ADJECTIVE ❶ even (number) ❷ au pair au pair, une jeune fille au pair an au pair, travailler au pair to work as an au pair

paire NOUN FEM pair; une paire de chaussures a pair of shoes

paix NOUN FEM peace

pakistanais ADJECTIVE Pakistani

Pakistanais, **Pakistanaise** NOUN MASC, FEM Pakistani

palais NOUN MASC ❶ palace ❷ palate

palais de justice NOUN MASC law courts

pâle ADJECTIVE pale; bleu pâle pale blue

Palestine NOUN FEM Palestine

palier NOUN MASC landing (on a staircase)

pâlir VERB [2] ❶ to turn pale ❷ to fade

palme NOUN FEM flipper (for swimming)

palmier NOUN MASC palm tree

palpitant ADJECTIVE thrilling

pamplemousse NOUN MASC grapefruit

panaché NOUN MASC shandy

panaché ADJECTIVE une salade panachée a mixed salad

pancarte NOUN FEM notice, sign

pané ADJECTIVE coated in breadcrumbs

panier NOUN MASC basket

panier à salade NOUN MASC salad shaker

panique NOUN FEM panic

paniquer VERB [1] to panic

panne NOUN FEM breakdown (of a car or machine); la voiture est en panne the car's broken down, la photocopieuse est en panne the photocopier's not working, tomber en panne to break down, nous sommes en panne d'essence we've run out of petrol, une panne de courant a power cut

panneau NOUN MASC (PLURAL panneaux) sign, notice board

panneau indicateur NOUN MASC signpost

panneau publicitaire NOUN MASC advertisement hoarding

panorama NOUN MASC ❶ panorama ❷ viewpoint

pansement NOUN MASC ❶ sticking plaster ❷ dressing

panser VERB [1] to put a dressing on (a wound)

pantalon NOUN MASC trousers; mon pantalon gris my grey trousers, un pantalon neuf a new pair of trousers, deux pantalons two pairs of trousers

panthère NOUN FEM panther

pantoufle NOUN FEM slipper

paon NOUN MASC peacock

papa NOUN MASC Dad, Daddy, father

pape NOUN MASC pope

paperasse NOUN FEM (informal) paperwork, bumph

papeterie NOUN FEM ❶ stationer's shop ❷ stationery

papi NOUN MASC (informal) **granddad**

papier NOUN MASC **paper**; du papier blanc white paper, vos papiers, s'il vous plaît monsieur your (identity) papers please, sir

papier à lettres NOUN MASC **writing paper**

papier aluminium NOUN MASC **kitchen foil**

papier cadeau NOUN MASC **gift wrap**

papier-calque NOUN MASC **tracing paper**

papier hygiénique NOUN MASC **toilet paper**

papier peint NOUN MASC **wallpaper**

papiers d'identité PLURAL NOUN MASC **identity papers**

papillon NOUN MASC **butterfly**

papy NOUN MASC (informal) **granddad**

paquebot NOUN MASC **liner**

pâquerette NOUN FEM **daisy**

Pâques NOUN MASC **Easter**; à Pâques at Easter, un œuf de Pâques an Easter egg, les vacances de Pâques the Easter holidays, le lundi de Pâques Easter Monday

paquet NOUN MASC ❶ **packet**; un paquet de sucre a packet of sugar ❷ **parcel**; il y a un paquet pour vous there's a parcel for you ❸ **bundle** (of clothes or papers)

paquet-cadeau NOUN MASC **gift-wrapped parcel**; est-ce que je vous fais un paquet-cadeau? shall I gift-wrap it for you?

par PREPOSITION ❶ **by**; par moi by me, par la poste by post, payer par chèque to pay by cheque, par accident by accident, par hasard by chance, deux par deux two by two, jeter quelque chose par la fenêtre to throw something out of the window, aller par Paris to go via (or by) Paris, par ennui out of boredom ❷ **in**; par endroits in places, par cette chaleur in this heat ❸ **per**; 50 euros par personne 50 euros per person, deux repas par jour two meals a day, deux fois par semaine twice a week

parachute NOUN MASC **parachute**

parachutiste NOUN MASC & FEM **parachutist**

paradis NOUN MASC **heaven**

paragraphe NOUN MASC **paragraph**

paraître VERB [57] ❶ **to seem**; ça me paraît étrange that seems strange to me, il paraît qu'il est mort it seems he's dead ❷ paraît-il apparently, elle est à Nice, paraît-il she's in Nice, apparently ❸ **to appear**; paraître en public to appear in public ❹ (of a book) **to come out, to be published**; le roman va paraître en juin the novel will come out in June

parallèle ADJECTIVE **parallel**

paralysé ADJECTIVE **paralysed**

parapente NOUN MASC ❶ **paraglider** ❷ **paragliding**

parapluie NOUN MASC **umbrella**

parasite NOUN MASC ❶ **parasite** ❷ des parasites interference (on TV or radio)

parasol NOUN MASC **parasol**

parc NOUN MASC ❶ **park**; aller au parc to go to the park ❷ **grounds** (of a large house) ❸ **fleet** (of vehicles)

parc d'attractions NOUN MASC **amusement park**

parce que CONJUNCTION **because**; parce qu'elle est malade because she's ill, c'est parce que je t'aime it's because I love you

par-ci ADVERB par-ci par-là here and there

parcmètre NOUN MASC **parking meter**

parc naturel NOUN MASC **nature park**

parcourir VERB [29] **to go all over, to travel all over**; j'ai parcouru l'Europe I travelled all over Europe

parcours NOUN MASC ❶ **route** (for a bus or a traveller) ❷ **course** (for a race)

par-derrière ADVERB **from the back, behind**; elle est passée par-derrière she went round the back

par-dessous ADVERB **underneath**

pardessus NOUN MASC **overcoat**

par-dessus ADVERB ❶ **on top** ❷ **over it**; il a sauté par-dessus he jumped over it

par-dessus PREPOSITION **over**; elle a sauté par-dessus le ruisseau she jumped over the stream, j'aime ça par-dessus tout! I like that best of all!

par-devant ADVERB **by the front**

pardon NOUN MASC ❶ **pardon, forgiveness**; je te demande pardon I'm sorry ❷ **excuse me, sorry**

pardonner VERB [1] **to forgive**; je ne lui pardonnerai jamais I'll never forgive him

pare-balles ADJECTIVE **bullet-proof**; un gilet pare-balles a bullet-proof vest

pare-brise NOUN MASC **windscreen**

pare-chocs NOUN MASC **bumper** (on a car)

pareil, pareille ADJECTIVE MASC, FEM ❶ **the same**; les deux voitures sont presque pareilles the two cars are almost the same, c'est toujours pareil it's always the same, mais ce n'est pas du tout pareil! but it's not the same at all! ❷ **such**; je n'ai jamais dit une chose pareille I never said any such thing, tu ne peux pas sortir par un temps pareil you can't go out in weather like this

parent NOUN MASC ❶ **parent**; mes parents my parents ❷ **relation**; parents et amis friends and relations

parenthèse NOUN FEM **bracket**; entre parenthèses in brackets

paresse NOUN FEM **laziness**

paresseux, paresseuse ADJECTIVE MASC, FEM **lazy**

parfait ADJECTIVE **perfect**

parfaitement ADVERB ❶ **perfectly**; tu le sais parfaitement! you know perfectly well!, parfaitement faux totally wrong ❷ parfaitement! **absolutely!**

parfois ADVERB **sometimes**

parfum NOUN MASC ❶ **perfume** ❷ **flavour**; tu veux quel parfum de yaourt? what flavour yoghurt would you like?

parfumé ADJECTIVE ❶ **perfumed, fragrant**; parfumé à la lavande lavender-scented ❷ **flavoured**; une glace parfumée au chocolat a chocolate ice cream

parfumerie *NOUN FEM* **perfume shop**

pari *NOUN MASC* **bet**; faire un pari to make a bet

parier *VERB* [1] **to bet**

Paris *NOUN* **Paris**; à Paris in (*or* to) Paris

parisien, parisienne *ADJECTIVE MASC, FEM* ❶ **Parisian** ❷ **Paris**; un restaurant parisien a Paris restaurant

Parisien, Parisienne *NOUN MASC, FEM* **Parisian**

parking *NOUN MASC* **car park**; dans le parking in the car park

Parlement *NOUN MASC* **parliament**

parler *VERB* [1] ❶ **to speak**; parler (le) français to speak French, parler en italien to speak in Italian, parler fort/doucement to speak loudly/softly, parler à quelqu'un to speak to someone ❷ **to talk**; il parle très vite he talks very fast, parler cinéma to talk (about) films ❸ parler de to talk about, to mention, tout le monde en parle everyone's talking about it, non, il n'en a pas parlé no, he didn't mention it, n'en parlons plus! let's say no more about it! ❹ se parler to talk to each other
• tu parles! *(informal)* you must be joking!

parmi *PREPOSITION* **among**; parmi les invités among the guests

parole *NOUN FEM* ❶ les paroles the lyrics, les paroles de la chanson the lyrics of the song ❷ elle m'a donné sa parole she gave me her word ❸ **speech**; perdre la parole to lose the power of speech

parquet *NOUN MASC* ❶ **wooden floor** ❷ **parquet**

parrain *NOUN MASC* **godfather**

parrainer *VERB* [1] **to sponsor**

parsemer *VERB* [50] **to sprinkle**

part *NOUN FEM* ❶ **portion, helping**; une part de pizza a portion of pizza ❷ **share**; il a payé sa part he paid his share, elle a fait sa part du travail she did her share of the work ❸ **side**; de toutes parts from all sides ❹ pour ma part, je pense que ... for my part, I think that ... ❺ à part separate, separately, une chambre à part a separate bedroom, j'ai mis l'argent à part I put the money aside, à part ça, qu'est-ce qu'il t'a dit? apart from that, what did he tell you? ❻ de la part de quelqu'un on behalf of somebody, for somebody, c'est de la part de qui? who's calling?, dis-lui bonjour de ma part say hello to him from me

partager *VERB* [52] ❶ **to share** (*possessions or food*) ❷ **to divide**; je partage mon temps entre mon travail et les enfants I divide my time between my job and the children

partenaire *NOUN MASC & FEM* **partner**

parterre *NOUN MASC* ❶ **flower bed** ❷ **stalls** (*in a theatre*)

parti *NOUN MASC* ❶ **party, group**; le parti communiste the communist party ❷ **side**

participation *NOUN FEM* **participation**

participe *NOUN MASC* **participle**; participe passé past participle

participer VERB [1] participer à quelque chose to take part in something

particulier NOUN MASC **private individual**

particulier, particulière ADJECTIVE MASC, FEM ❶ **special**; rien de particulier nothing special ❷ **private**; une voiture particulière a private car ❸ en particulier in particular, rien en particulier nothing in particular ❹ en particulier in private

particulièrement ADVERB **particularly**

partie NOUN FEM ❶ **part**; une partie de ma vie part of of my life, la première partie the first part ❷ en partie partly ❸ faire partie de quelque chose to be part of something, ce bâtiment fait partie du musée this building is part of the museum, elle fait partie de la famille she's one of the family ❹ **game**; faire une partie de tennis to have a game of tennis, gagner la partie to win the game

partir VERB [58] ❶ **to leave, to go**; partir à pied to go on foot, tu pars déjà? are you leaving already?, elle est partie en Italie she's gone to Italy, il est parti à Londres he's gone to London, elle est partie au travail she's left for work, partir en vacances to go away on holiday, elle est partie pour huit jours she's gone away for a week, ils sont partis en courant they ran off ❷ à partir de from, à partir de lundi from Monday (onwards)

partition NOUN FEM **score** (in music)

partout ADVERB ❶ **everywhere**; j'ai cherché partout I've looked everywhere ❷ un peu partout: ça se trouve un peu partout you can find it/them almost anywhere ❸ trois buts partout three goals all

parvenir VERB [81] ❶ parvenir à to reach ❷ parvenir à faire to manage to do, il est parvenu à ouvrir la porte he managed to open the door

pas¹ ADVERB ❶ (used with 'ne' to put verbs into the negative) je ne suis pas I am not, je n'ai pas de stylo I don't have a pen, je ne pense pas I don't think so, ils n'ont pas le téléphone they're not on the phone ❷ **not**; c'est lui qui paie, pas moi he's paying, not me, pas du tout not at all, pas vraiment not really, une radio pas chère a cheap radio, pas de chance! bad luck!, pas possible! I don't believe it!

pas² NOUN MASC ❶ **step**; faire un grand/petit pas to take a big/small step, j'habite à deux pas d'ici I live very near here ❷ **pace**; ralentir le pas to slow down, 'roulez au pas!' 'dead slow' (road sign)

passage NOUN MASC ❶ **traffic**; une rue où il y a beaucoup de passage a street where there's a lot of traffic, passage interdit no through traffic ❷ **visit**; je peux te prendre au passage I can pick you up on my way

passage à niveau NOUN MASC **level crossing**

passage pour piétons NOUN MASC **pedestrian crossing**

passager, passagère NOUN MASC, FEM **passenger**

passager, passagère ADJECTIVE MASC, FEM **passing, temporary**

passage souterrain NOUN MASC **subway** (under a road)

passant, **passante** NOUN MASC, FEM
passer-by

passé NOUN MASC ❶ past; c'est dans le passé it's in the past now ❷ past tense; le passé composé the present perfect

passé ADJECTIVE ❶ l'année passée last year ❷ past; il est dix heures passées it's past ten o'clock

passeport NOUN MASC passport

passer VERB [1] ❶ to pass; le temps passe vite time passes quickly ❷ to spend (time); j'ai passé deux jours à Paris I spent two days in Paris ❸ en passant in passing ❹ passer quelque chose à quelqu'un to pass somebody something, passe-moi le sel pass me the salt ❺ to cross; passer le pont to cross the bridge ❻ to drop in; Pierre est passé ce matin Pierre dropped in this morning, est-ce que le facteur est passé? has the postman been?, je passerai te prendre à huit heures I'll pick you up at eight ❼ to get through; laissez passer l'ambulance! let the ambulance through! ❽ to be on, to be showing (films); le film est passé à la télé lundi the film was on telly on Monday ❾ to go; passer à la caisse to go to the checkout, passons au salon let's go through to the sitting room ❿ to give; il m'a passé son vélo he gave me his bike ⓫ to put through, to hand over to (on the telephone); je vous passe le responsable I'll put you through to the manager ⓬ to put (on) (a garment) ⓭ passer l'aspirateur to vacuum ⓮ to take, to sit (a test or an exam) ⓯ passer par to go through, nous sommes passés par Paris we went through (or via) Paris ⓰ se passer to happen, qu'est-ce qui se passe? what's happening?, ça s'est passé en Chine it happened in China ⓱ se passer de to do without, se passer d'un manteau to do without a coat

passerelle NOUN FEM ❶ footbridge ❷ gangway

passe-temps NOUN MASC hobby

passif NOUN MASC passive (in grammar)

passif, **passive** ADJECTIVE MASC, FEM passive

passion NOUN FEM passion

passionnant ADJECTIVE exciting

passionné, **passionnée** NOUN MASC, FEM enthusiast; c'est un passionné de tennis he's a tennis enthusiast

passionné ADJECTIVE keen; c'est une musicienne passionnée she's a keen musician

passionner VERB [1] l'histoire me passionne history fascinates me

passoire NOUN FEM strainer

pastille NOUN FEM throat sweet

patate NOUN FEM (informal) potato

pâte NOUN FEM ❶ pastry; pâte feuilletée puff pastry ❷ dough ❸ batter; à crêpes pancake batter ❹ paste ❺ les pâtes pasta, on va manger des pâtes ce soir we're having pasta tonight

pâté NOUN MASC pâté

pâte à modeler NOUN FEM Plasticine

patience NOUN FEM patience

patient, **patiente** NOUN MASC, FEM, ADJECTIVE patient

patienter VERB [1] to wait; patientez, s'il vous plaît please hold the line?

patin NOUN MASC skate

patinage NOUN MASC skating; patinage artistique figure skating

patin à glace NOUN MASC ❶ ice skate ❷ ice skating

patin à roulettes NOUN MASC roller skate

patiner VERB [1] to skate

patineur, patineuse NOUN MASC, FEM skater

patinoire NOUN FEM ice rink

pâtisserie NOUN FEM ❶ cake shop ❷ cake

patois NOUN MASC dialect

patrie NOUN FEM homeland, country

patron[1] NOUN MASC pattern (for dressmaking)

patron[2]**, patronne** NOUN MASC, FEM boss

patronner VERB [1] to sponsor

patrouille NOUN FEM patrol

patte NOUN FEM ❶ paw ❷ leg (of an animal)
• à quatre pattes on all fours

paume NOUN FEM palm (of the hand)

paumer VERB [1] (informal) ❶ to lose ❷ se paumer to get lost

paupière NOUN FEM eyelid; le fard à paupières eyeshadow

pause NOUN FEM ❶ break; faire une pause to take a break, la pause café the coffee break ❷ pause

pauvre NOUN MASC & FEM poor man, poor woman; les pauvres the poor, le pauvre! poor thing!

pauvre ADJECTIVE poor

pauvreté NOUN FEM poverty

pavé NOUN MASC cobblestone

pavillon NOUN MASC ❶ detached house; un pavillon de banlieue a house in the suburbs ❷ wing (in a hospital)

payant ADJECTIVE ❶ (of a show or event) not free; c'est payant? do you have to pay to get in?, un parking payant a pay-and-display car park ❷ un hôte payant a paying guest

paye NOUN FEM wages

payer VERB [59] ❶ to pay (a bill or a person); c'est moi qui paie I'm paying, être mal payé to be badly paid, être payé à l'heure to be paid by the hour ❷ to pay for; il a payé le repas he paid for the meal ❸ (informal) je te paie à boire I'll buy you a drink ❹ je me suis payé une semaine à Paris I treated myself to a week in Paris

pays NOUN MASC ❶ country; la France est un beau pays France is a beautiful country ❷ region; des fruits du pays locally grown fruit

paysage NOUN MASC landscape

paysan, paysanne NOUN MASC, FEM farmer

Pays-Bas PLURAL NOUN MASC les Pays-Bas the Netherlands

pays de Galles NOUN MASC Wales; au pays de Galles in (or to) Wales

PC NOUN MASC PC, personal computer

péage NOUN MASC ❶ **toll**; autoroute à péage toll motorway (*motorists have to pay to travel on motorways in France*) ❷ **tollbooth**

peau NOUN FEM (*PLURAL* **peaux**) ❶ **skin**; avoir la peau sèche to have dry skin ❷ **peel** (*of fruit*); peau d'orange orange peel

pêche NOUN FEM ❶ **peach** ❷ **fishing**; aller à la pêche to go fishing

péché NOUN MASC **sin**

pêcher[1] VERB [1] ❶ **to fish for** (*trout, salmon, etc*) ❷ **to catch**; Denise a pêché trois truites Denise caught three trout

pêcher[2] NOUN MASC **peach tree**

pêcheur NOUN MASC **fisherman**

pédagogique ADJECTIVE **educational**; méthode pédagogique teaching method

pédale NOUN FEM **pedal**
• perdre les pédales (*informal*) to lose your grip

pédaler VERB [1] **to pedal**

pédalo NOUN MASC **pedalo, pedal boat**

pédestre ADJECTIVE faire une randonnée pédestre to go walking (*on a long-distance public footpath*)

peigne NOUN MASC **comb**

peigner VERB [1] ❶ **to comb** ❷ se peigner to comb your hair

peindre VERB [60] **to paint**

peine NOUN FEM ❶ **effort, trouble**; se donner de la peine to go to a lot of trouble, il n'a même pas pris la peine d'appeler he didn't even take the trouble to ring ❷ ce n'est pas la peine it's not worth it ❸ **difficulty**; elle a eu beaucoup de peine à trouver un logement she had a lot of difficulty finding somewhere to live ❹ faire de la peine à quelqu'un to upset somebody ❺ **penalty** (*in law*); sous peine d'amende offenders will be fined ❻ à peine hardly, scarcely, je le connais à peine I hardly know him, il était à peine cinq heures it was barely five o'clock

peine de mort NOUN FEM **death penalty**

peintre NOUN MASC **painter**

peintre-décorateur NOUN MASC **decorator**

peinture NOUN FEM ❶ **paint**; 'peinture fraîche' 'wet paint' ❷ **painting**; faire de la peinture to paint ❸ une peinture a painting

pèlerin NOUN MASC **pilgrim**

pèlerinage NOUN MASC **pilgrimage**; faire un pèlerinage to go on a pilgrimage

pelle NOUN FEM ❶ **spade** ❷ **shovel**

pelle à poussière NOUN FEM **dustpan**

pelle mécanique NOUN FEM **mechanical digger**

pellicule NOUN FEM ❶ **film** (*for a camera*); une pellicule couleur a colour film ❷ les pellicules dandruff

pelouse NOUN FEM **lawn**; 'pelouse interdite' 'keep off the grass'

peluche NOUN FEM **soft toy**

pencher VERB [1] ❶ **to tilt** ❷ **to lean** ❸ se pencher to bend down ❹ se pencher par la fenêtre to lean out of the window

pendant PREPOSITION ❶ **for**; je t'ai attendu pendant deux heures I waited for you for two hours ❷ **during**; pendant l'hiver during the winter ❸ **pendant que** while, pendant que les enfants sont à l'école while the children are at school ❹ **pendant ce temps là** meanwhile, pendant ce temps là elle attendait à la gare meanwhile she was waiting at the station

pendentif NOUN MASC **pendant**

penderie NOUN FEM **wardrobe, hanging cupboard**

pendre VERB [3] ❶ **to hang** ❷ pendre quelque chose to hang something up ❸ **to hang down**

pendule NOUN FEM **clock**

pénétrer VERB [24] ❶ pénétrer dans to enter, un voleur a pénétré dans le bureau a thief got into the office ❷ **to penetrate**

pénible ADJECTIVE ❶ **difficult, hard** ❷ il est pénible he's a pain

péniche NOUN FEM **barge**

pénis NOUN MASC **penis**

pensée NOUN FEM ❶ **thought** ❷ **pansy**

penser VERB [1] ❶ **to think**; je pense que tu as raison I think you're right, oui, je pense yes, I think so, je ne pense pas I don't think so ❷ **to intend**; il pense arriver mardi he's intending to arrive on Tuesday ❸ penser de to think of, qu'est-ce que tu penses de mon idée? what do you think of my idea? ❹ penser à to think about, à quoi penses-tu? what are you thinking about? ❺ cette chanson me fait penser à ta mère this song

reminds me of your mother ❻ **to remember**; pendant que j'y pense while I remember, fais-moi penser à acheter des citrons remind me to buy lemons

pension NOUN FEM ❶ **boarding school** ❷ **boarding house** ❸ **pension** ❹ pension complète full board, demi-pension half board, dinner, bed and breakfast

pension de famille NOUN FEM **family hotel**

pensionnaire NOUN MASC & FEM **boarder**

pensionnat NOUN MASC **boarding school**

pente NOUN FEM **slope**; en pente sloping

Pentecôte NOUN FEM **Whitsun**; à la Pentecôte at Whitsun

pépé NOUN MASC (informal) **granddad**

pépin NOUN MASC ❶ **(grape) pip** ❷ (informal) **slight problem**

perçant ADJECTIVE ❶ **piercing** ❷ **sharp**

perce-neige NOUN MASC & FEM **snowdrop**

percer VERB [61] **to pierce**; avoir les oreilles percées to have pierced ears, se faire percer les oreilles to have your ears pierced, percer un trou to make a hole

perceuse NOUN FEM **drill**

perdant, perdante NOUN MASC, FEM **loser**

perdre VERB [3] ❶ **to lose**; notre équipe a perdu our team lost ❷ perdre quelque chose to lose something, j'ai perdu mes clefs I've lost my keys, j'ai perdu mon chemin I've lost my way ❸ être perdu to be lost ❹ se perdre to get lost, je me suis perdu dans les petites rues I got lost in the back streets ❺ perdre du temps to waste time

perdrix NOUN FEM INVARIABLE **partridge**

perdu ADJECTIVE ❶ **lost**; un enfant perdu a lost child, je suis perdu I'm lost, vous êtes perdu? are you lost? ❷ **stray**; un chien perdu a stray dog ❸ c'est du temps perdu it's a waste of time

père NOUN MASC **father**; le père Noël Father Christmas

perfectionner VERB [1] **to perfect**

performant ADJECTIVE ❶ **efficient** ❷ **high-performance**

périmé ADJECTIVE **out-of-date**

période NOUN FEM **period**

périphérique NOUN MASC **ring road**

perle NOUN FEM ❶ **pearl** ❷ **bead**

permanence NOUN FEM ❶ **service**; 'permanence de 8h à 19h' 'open from 8 a.m. to 7 p.m.' ❷ en permanence permanently, all the time

permanent ADJECTIVE ❶ **permanent** ❷ **continuous**

permettre VERB [11] permettre à quelqu'un de faire to allow someone to do, elle leur a permis de partir she allowed them to leave, permettez-moi de vous aider let me help you

permis NOUN MASC **permit, licence**

permis de conduire NOUN MASC **driving licence**; passer son permis to sit your driving test

permission NOUN FEM ❶ **permission** ❷ **leave** *(from the army)*

perroquet NOUN MASC **parrot**

perruche NOUN FEM **budgie**

perruque NOUN FEM **wig**

persécution NOUN FEM **persecution**

persévérer VERB [24] **to persevere**

persil NOUN MASC **parsley**

persister VERB [1] **to persist**

personnage NOUN MASC ❶ **character** *(in a book, film, or play)* ❷ **figure**, **person**; un personnage célèbre a famous person

personnalité NOUN FEM **personality**

personne[1] PRONOUN ❶ **nobody**; personne ne sait nobody knows ❷ **anybody**; je ne vois personne I can't see anybody, je n'ai parlé à personne I didn't speak to anybody

personne[2] NOUN FEM **person**; vingt personnes twenty people, les personnes âgées the elderly, en personne in person

personnel NOUN MASC ❶ **staff** ❷ le service du personnel the personnel department

personnel, personnelle ADJECTIVE MASC, FEM **personal**

personnellement ADVERB **personally**

perspective NOUN FEM ❶ **perspective** ❷ **view** ❸ **prospect**

persuader VERB [1] ❶ **to persuade**; persuader quelqu'un de faire to persuade somebody to do ❷ être persuadé to be sure

perte NOUN FEM ❶ loss ❷ waste; une perte de temps a waste of time

perturber VERB [1] to disrupt

pesanteur NOUN FEM gravity

pèse-personne NOUN MASC bathroom scales

peser VERB [50] ❶ peser quelque chose to weigh something ❷ to weigh; je pèse 60 kilos I weigh 60 kilos

pessimiste NOUN MASC & FEM pessimist

pessimiste ADJECTIVE pessimistic

pétale NOUN MASC petal

pétanque NOUN FEM bowls (the French version, played outdoors with metal bowls; also called 'boules')

pétard NOUN MASC firecracker, banger

pétillant ADJECTIVE sparkling (wine or mineral water)

petit[1] ADJECTIVE ❶ little, small; une petite fille a little girl, une toute petite maison a tiny house ❷ short; une petite distance a short distance
• petit à petit little by little

petit[2] NOUN MASC little boy; les petits the children

petit ami NOUN MASC boyfriend

petit bassin NOUN MASC shallow pool (for non-swimmers)

petit déjeuner NOUN MASC breakfast

petite NOUN FEM little girl; les petites the little girls

petite amie NOUN FEM girlfriend

petite annonce NOUN FEM small ad

petite-fille NOUN FEM granddaughter

petit-fils NOUN MASC grandson

petit mot NOUN MASC note

petit pois NOUN MASC garden pea

petits-enfants PLURAL NOUN MASC grandchildren

pétrole NOUN MASC ❶ oil, petroleum ❷ paraffin

pétrolier NOUN MASC ❶ oil tanker, ship ❷ petroleum engineer

peu ADVERB ❶ not much; il dort peu he doesn't sleep much, elle gagne très peu she earns very little ❷ not very; peu intéressant not very interesting, peu réaliste unrealistic ❸ peu de not much, not many, il reste peu de temps there's not much time left, peu de voitures not many cars ❹ un peu de a little, a bit, il reste un peu de café there's a bit of coffee left, un tout petit peu de sel a tiny amount of salt ❺ parle un peu plus fort speak a little louder, juste un petit peu just a little ❻ à peu près about, il y avait à peu près vingt personnes there were about twenty people

peuple NOUN MASC people, nation

peuplier NOUN MASC poplar

peur NOUN FEM fear; avoir peur de to be afraid of, Nadine a peur des souris Nadine's afraid of mice, n'ayez pas peur! don't be afraid!, faire peur à quelqu'un to frighten somebody, tu m'as fait peur! you gave me a fright!

A B C D E F G H I J K L M N O P Q R S T U V W X Y Z

peut *VERB* ▸ SEE **pouvoir**[1]

peut-être *ADVERB* **perhaps**

peuvent, peux *VERB* ▸ SEE **pouvoir**[1]

phare *NOUN MASC* ❶ **headlight**; allumer les phares to turn the headlights on ❷ **lighthouse**

pharmacie *NOUN FEM* **chemist's**

pharmacien, pharmacienne *NOUN MASC, FEM* **chemist, pharmacist**

phénomène *NOUN MASC* **phenomenon**

philo *NOUN FEM* (informal) (short for *philosophie*) **philosophy**

philosophie *NOUN FEM* **philosophy**

phoque *NOUN MASC* **seal**

photo *NOUN FEM* ❶ **photo, photograph**; une photo d'identité a passport photo ❷ **photography**

photocopie *NOUN FEM* **photocopy**

photocopier *VERB* [1] **to photocopy**

photocopieuse *NOUN FEM* **photocopier**

photographe *NOUN MASC & FEM* **photographer**; Sean est photographe Sean's a photographer

photographie *NOUN FEM* ❶ **photography** ❷ **photograph**

photographier *VERB* [1] **to photograph**

photomaton *NOUN MASC* **photo booth**

phrase *NOUN FEM* **sentence**

physique[1] *NOUN FEM* **physics**

physique[2] *ADJECTIVE* **physical**

pianiste *NOUN MASC & FEM* **pianist**

piano *NOUN MASC* **piano**; jouer du piano to play the piano

piano à queue *NOUN MASC* **grand piano**

pichet *NOUN MASC* **jug**

pièce *NOUN FEM* ❶ **room**; notre maison a quatre pièces our house has four rooms ❷ **coin**; une pièce de deux euros a two-euro coin ❸ **play**; une pièce de Molière a play by Molière ❹ **bit, piece**; les pièces d'un puzzle the pieces of a jigsaw ❺ **item**; dix euros (la) pièce ten euros each ❻ **patch** (for repairs)

pièce détachée *NOUN FEM* **spare part**

pièce de théâtre *NOUN FEM* **play**

pièce d'identité *NOUN FEM* **identification** (such as a passport or identity card)

pièce jointe *NOUN FEM* **attachment**

pied *NOUN MASC* ❶ **foot**; être pieds nus to be barefoot, aller à pied to go on foot, un coup de pied a kick, donner un coup de pied à quelqu'un to kick someone ❷ **bottom, foot**; au pied du lit at the foot of the bed ❸ le pied de la table the table leg ❹ *in swimming* j'ai pied I can touch the bottom, je n'ai plus pied I'm out of my depth

piège *NOUN MASC* **trap**

piéger *VERB* [15] **to trap**; une voiture piégée a car bomb

pierre *NOUN FEM* **stone**

pierre précieuse *NOUN FEM* **precious stone**

piéton, piétonne *NOUN MASC, FEM* **pedestrian**; un passage pour piétons a pedestrian crossing

piétonnier, piétonnière *ADJECTIVE MASC, FEM* **pedestrian**; une rue piétonnière a pedestrian street

pieuvre *NOUN FEM* **octopus**

pigeon *NOUN MASC* **pigeon**

pile[1] *NOUN FEM* ❶ **battery** ❷ **pile**; une pile de vêtements a pile of clothes ❸ **tails** (when tossing a coin); pile ou face? heads or tails?

pile[2] *ADVERB* (informal) ❶ **exactly**; à dix heures pile at ten o'clock on the dot ❷ s'arrêter pile to stop dead

pilône *NOUN MASC* **pylon**

pilote *NOUN MASC* ❶ **pilot** ❷ un pilote de course a racing driver

piloter *VERB* [1] to **fly** (a plane)

pilule *NOUN FEM* **pill**

piment *NOUN MASC* **chilli**

pin *NOUN MASC* **pine tree**; une pomme de pin a pine cone

pince *NOUN FEM* ❶ une pince a pair of pliers ❷ **dart** (in a garment) ❸ **pincer** (of a crab)

pince à épiler *NOUN FEM* **tweezers**

pince à linge *NOUN FEM* **clothes peg**

pinceau *NOUN MASC* (PLURAL pinceaux) **paintbrush**

pincée *NOUN FEM* **pinch** (of salt, for example)

pincer *VERB* [61] to **pinch**

pingouin *NOUN MASC* **penguin**

ping-pong *NOUN MASC* **ping-pong**

pintade *NOUN FEM* **guinea fowl**

pion[1] *NOUN MASC* ❶ **counter** (in a board game) ❷ **pawn** (in chess) ❸ **piece** (in draughts)

pion[2] *NOUN MASC & FEM* **student supervisor of school pupils** (colloquial)
▸ SEE **surveillant**

pipe *NOUN FEM* **pipe**; fumer la pipe to smoke a pipe

pipi *NOUN MASC* (informal) **wee**; faire pipi to have a wee

piquant *ADJECTIVE* ❶ **prickly** ❷ **spicy**

pique *NOUN MASC* **spades** (in a pack of cards); le trois de pique the three of spades

pique-nique *NOUN MASC* **picnic**

pique-niquer *VERB* [1] to **have a picnic**

piquer *VERB* [1] ❶ to **sting**; j'ai été piqué par une guêpe I've been stung by a wasp ❷ to **bite**; piqué par des moustiques bitten by mosquitoes ❸ se piquer to prick yourself, je me suis piqué le doigt I've pricked my finger ❹ (informal) to **pinch**; quelqu'un a piqué mon stylo somebody's pinched my pen
• piquer une crise (de nerfs) (informal) to throw a fit

piquet *NOUN MASC* ❶ **post** ❷ **peg**

piqûre *NOUN FEM* ❶ **injection**; faire une piqûre à quelqu'un to give somebody an injection ❷ **bite**, **sting** (of an insect)

pirate *NOUN MASC* **pirate**

pirate de l'air *NOUN MASC* **hijacker** (of plane)

pirate de la route *NOUN MASC* **hijacker** (of lorry)

pirate informatique NOUN MASC
computer hacker

pire ADJECTIVE **❶** worse; pire que
worse than, c'est pire que ça! it's
worse than that!, c'est encore pire
it's even worse **❷** worst; le pire
the worst, au pire if the worst comes
to the worst

pis IN PHRASE tant pis too bad, tant pis
pour lui! that's his bad luck!

piscine NOUN FEM swimming-pool;
est-ce que la piscine est surveillée?
is there a lifeguard at the swimming
pool?

pissenlit NOUN MASC dandelion

pistache NOUN FEM pistachio

piste NOUN FEM **❶** trail (left by an
animal or fugitive); la police est sur
sa piste the police are on his trail
❷ track (for racing or sport); faire
un tour de piste to do a lap **❸** piste,
trail (in skiing) **❹** runway (at an
airport)

piste cyclable NOUN FEM cycle lane

pistolet NOUN MASC pistol

pitié NOUN FEM pity; avoir pitié de
quelqu'un to feel sorry for someone

pittoresque ADJECTIVE picturesque

pizza NOUN FEM pizza; vous voulez
une pizza à quoi? what kind of
pizza would you like?

placard NOUN MASC cupboard

place NOUN FEM **❶** space, room; il y
a assez de place pour deux there's
enough room for two **❷** seat (in a
theatre, cinema, train, or bus); trois
places pour ce soir three seats
for this evening's performance
❸ place; remettez tous les livres
à leur place! put all the books back
in their places!, si j'étais à ta place
if I were you **❹** place; en troisième
place in third place **❺** square; la
place Rouge the Red Square, la
place du village the village square
❻ à la place de instead of, il y est
allé à ma place he went instead of
me **❼** être sur place to be on the
spot

placer VERB [61] **❶** to place **❷** to seat
(a person); elle m'a placé à côté de
Louis she put me next to Louis

plafond NOUN MASC ceiling

plage NOUN FEM beach; on va à la
plage we're going to the beach

plaie NOUN FEM wound

plaindre VERB [31] **❶** to feel sorry
for; je te plains I feel sorry for you
❷ se plaindre to complain, je ne
me plains pas I'm not complaining,
elle s'est plainte de la qualité du
service auprès du responsable she
complained to the manager about
the standard of service

plaine NOUN FEM plain

plainte NOUN FEM complaint; porter
plainte to complain

plaire VERB [62] **❶** s'il te plaît, s'il
vous plaît please, deux billets, s'il
vous plaît two tickets, please **❷** le
tissu me plaît I like the material,
la chambre vous plaît? do you like
your room?, le film a beaucoup plu
à mon père my father liked the film
very much

plaisanter VERB [1] to joke

plaisanterie NOUN FEM joke

plaisir NOUN MASC pleasure; le plaisir
de lire the pleasure of reading,
'vous venez avec nous?' – 'oui,

avec plaisir' 'will you come too?'
– 'yes, with pleasure', faire plaisir
à quelqu'un to please someone,
j'y suis allé pour faire plaisir à ma
mère I went to please my mother

plan NOUN MASC ❶ **map** (of a town
or underground system); le plan
du métro the underground map
❷ **plan**; le plan du bâtiment the
plan of the building ❸ au premier
plan in the foreground, in the
forefront

planche NOUN FEM **plank**

planche à repasser NOUN FEM
ironing board

planche à roulettes NOUN FEM
skateboard

planche à voile NOUN FEM
❶ **windsurfing board**
❷ **windsurfing**; faire de la planche
à voile to go windsurfing

plancher NOUN MASC **floor**

plan d'eau NOUN MASC **artificial lake**
(often for swimming and other water
sports)

planer VERB [1] ❶ **to glide**
❷ (informal) **to have your head in
the clouds**

planète NOUN FEM **planet**

plante NOUN FEM **plant**; une plante
verte a house-plant

planter VERB [1] ❶ **to plant** (a tree,
shrub, or plant) ❷ **to hammer in** (a
nail) ❸ se planter (informal) to make
a blunder

plaquage NOUN MASC ❶ **tackle**
❷ **tackling**

plaque NOUN FEM ❶ **patch** (of damp
or ice) ❷ **plate**, **sheet** (of metal or
glass)

plaqué ADJECTIVE plaqué or gold-
plated, plaqué argent silver-plated

plaque d'immatriculation NOUN
FEM **number plate** (on a car)

plastique NOUN MASC **plastic**; un sac
en plastique a plastic bag

plat NOUN MASC ❶ **dish**; un plat chaud/
froid a hot/cold dish, le plat du jour
the dish of the day ❷ **course** (of
a meal); le plat principal the main
course
• faire tout un plat de quelque chose
(informal) to make a big deal of
something

plat ADJECTIVE ❶ **flat**; à plat ventre
flat on your stomach ❷ l'eau plate
still water

platane NOUN MASC **plane tree**

plateau NOUN MASC (PLURAL **plateaux**)
❶ **tray** ❷ **plateau**

plate-bande NOUN FEM **flower bed**

plâtre NOUN MASC **plaster**; il a une
jambe dans le plâtre he has a leg
in plaster

plein ADJECTIVE ❶ **full**; le panier est
plein the basket's full, elle est
pleine d'idées she's full of ideas
❷ en pleine nuit in the middle of
the night, en plein été at the height
of summer, en plein centre-ville
right in the middle of town, en
pleine mer on the open sea

plein NOUN MASC faire le plein to fill up
(a car with petrol), le plein, s'il vous
plaît a full tank, please

plein ADVERB plein de (informal) loads
of, elle a plein d'amis she's got
loads of friends

pleurer *VERB* [1] **to cry**

pleut *VERB* ▸ SEE **pleuvoir**

pleuvoir *VERB* [63] **to rain**; il pleut it's raining, il va pleuvoir it's going to rain, il a plu cette nuit it rained last night

pli *NOUN MASC* ❶ **fold** ❷ **pleat** ❸ **crease** (in trousers)

plier *VERB* [1] ❶ **to fold** ❷ **to bend** (your arm or leg, or a stem)
• être plié en deux/en quatre (informal) to be doubled up (with laughter or pain)

plomb *NOUN MASC* ❶ **lead**; de l'essence sans plomb unleaded petrol ❷ **fuse**; faire sauter les plombs to blow the fuses

plombage *NOUN MASC* **filling** (in a tooth)

plombier *NOUN MASC* **plumber**

plongée *NOUN FEM* **diving**; faire de la plongée to go diving

plongeoir *NOUN MASC* **diving board**

plonger *VERB* [52] ❶ **to dive** ❷ **to plunge**

plongeur, plongeuse *NOUN MASC, FEM* ❶ **diver** ❷ **washer-up**

plu *VERB* ▸ SEE **plaire; pleuvoir**

pluie *NOUN FEM* **rain**; un jour de pluie a rainy day, sous la pluie in the rain

plume *NOUN FEM* ❶ **feather** ❷ **ink pen**

plupart *NOUN FEM* la plupart de **most**, la plupart des gens most people, la plupart du temps most of the time

pluriel *NOUN MASC* **plural**; au pluriel in the plural

plus *ADVERB* ❶ plus de **more**, voulez-vous un peu plus de fromage? would you like a little more cheese? ❷ plus de **more than**, il y avait plus de cent personnes there were more than a hundred people ❸ plus que **more than**, il mange plus que moi he eats more than I do, le film est plus intéressant que le livre the film's more interesting than the book, leur maison est plus grande que la nôtre their house is bigger than ours ❹ le plus rapide **the fastest**, le plus joli **the prettiest** ❺ plus ... plus **the more ... the more**, plus je gagne, plus je dépense the more I earn the more I spend ❻ en plus **more**, il nous faut trois côtelettes en plus we need three more chops ❼ de plus **more**, trois chaises de plus three more chairs, une fois de plus one more time ❽ de plus en plus **more and more**, elle fume de plus en plus she smokes more and more, je deviens de plus en plus fatigué I'm getting more and more tired, il fait de plus en plus chaud it's getting hotter and hotter ❾ plus ou moins **more or less**, la cuisine est plus ou moins propre the kitchen's more or less clean ❿ le plus **the most**, c'est lui qui gagne le plus he earns the most, au plus at the most ⓫ ne ... plus **no longer**, elle n'habite plus ici she no longer lives here ⓬ je ne veux plus y aller I don't want to go there any more ⓭ il n'y a plus de lait there's no milk left ⓮ **plus**; deux plus trois égalent cinq two plus three is five

plusieurs *ADJECTIVE* **several**; plusieurs personnes several people, plusieurs fois several times

plutôt *ADVERB* ❶ **rather**; prends le jaune plutôt que le vert take the

a
b
c
d
e
f
g
h
i
j
k
l
m
n
o
p
q
r
s
t
u
v
w
x
y
z

yellow one rather than the green one ❷ **instead**; demande plutôt à Anne ask Anne instead ❸ **pretty**; le repas était plutôt bon the meal was pretty good, plutôt bien pretty good ❹ **rather**; elle est plutôt maigre she's rather thin

pluvieux, **pluvieuse** ADJECTIVE MASC, FEM **rainy**

pneu NOUN MASC **tyre**

pneumopathie atypique NOUN FEM **SARS** (the disease)

poche NOUN FEM **pocket**; un livre de poche a paperback, l'argent de poche pocket money
• c'est dans la poche (informal) it's in the bag
• je connais Paris comme ma poche (informal) I know Paris like the back of my hand

poêle¹ NOUN MASC **stove** (for heating); un poêle à bois a wood-burning stove

poêle² NOUN FEM **frying pan**

poème NOUN MASC **poem**

poésie NOUN FEM **poetry**

poète NOUN MASC **poet**

poids NOUN MASC **weight**; prendre du poids to put on weight, perdre du poids to lose weight

poids lourd NOUN MASC **lorry**

poignée NOUN FEM ❶ **handful**; une poignée de cailloux a handful of pebbles ❷ **handle** ❸ une poignée de main a handshake

poignet NOUN MASC **wrist**

poil NOUN MASC **hair**; un poil a hair, le chat perd ses poils the cat's moulting
• être de bon/mauvais poil to be in a good/bad mood

poilu ADJECTIVE **hairy**

poing NOUN MASC **fist**; un coup de poing a punch

point NOUN MASC ❶ **point**; et mon dernier point and my last point, un point de détail a minor point, un point faible a weak point ❷ un point de rencontre a meeting-place ❸ être sur le point de faire to be just about to do, j'étais sur le point de t'appeler I was on the point of phoning you ❹ **dot**; un petit point sur la carte a tiny dot on the map ❺ **full stop** ❻ **point** (when scoring); six points contre sept six points to seven, marquer/perdre des points to win/lose points ❼ **mark** (in a test) ❽ à point just in time, tu es arrivé à point you arrived just in time, un steak cuit à point a medium-rare steak

point chaud NOUN MASC **trouble spot**

point de départ NOUN MASC **starting point**

point de vue NOUN MASC **point of view**; d'un point de vue politique from a political point of view

point d'exclamation NOUN MASC **exclamation mark**

point d'interrogation NOUN MASC **question mark**

pointe NOUN FEM ❶ **point**; la pointe d'un couteau the point of a knife, sur la pointe des pieds on tip-toe, être en pointe to be pointed ❷ les heures de pointe the rush hour, peak time ❸ une pointe de a touch of, une pointe d'ail a touch of garlic
• être à la pointe du progrès to be in the forefront of progress

pointillé NOUN MASC **dotted line**

point mort NOUN MASC **neutral** (*gear*); tu es au point mort you're in neutral

pointu ADJECTIVE **pointed**

pointure NOUN FEM **size** (*of shoes*); quelle est votre pointure? what size do you take?

point-virgule NOUN MASC **semicolon**

poire NOUN FEM **pear**

poireau NOUN MASC (*PLURAL* poireaux) **leek**

poirier NOUN MASC **pear tree**; faire le poirier to stand on your head

pois NOUN MASC ❶ **pea**; des petits pois (garden) peas ❷ à pois spotted, un tissu à pois a spotted fabric

pois chiche NOUN MASC **chick pea**

pois de senteur NOUN MASC **sweet pea**

poison NOUN MASC **poison**

poisson NOUN MASC **fish**; j'aime le poisson I like fish

poisson d'avril NOUN MASC **April fool**; il m'a fait un poisson d'avril he played an April fool trick on me

poissonnerie NOUN FEM **fishmonger's**

poissonnier, poissonnière NOUN MASC, FEM **fishmonger**

poisson rouge NOUN MASC **goldfish**

Poissons PLURAL NOUN MASC **Pisces** (*sign of the Zodiac*)

poitrine NOUN FEM ❶ **chest** ❷ **bust**; quel est votre tour de poitrine? what is your bust size?

poivre NOUN MASC **pepper**; poivre noir en grains whole black peppercorns

poivrier NOUN MASC **pepper pot**

poivron NOUN MASC **pepper** (*red, green, or yellow*)

poker NOUN MASC **poker**

polar NOUN MASC (*informal*) **detective story**

pôle NOUN MASC **pole**; le pôle Nord/ Sud the North/South Pole

poli ADJECTIVE **polite**; être poli avec quelqu'un to be polite to somebody

police NOUN FEM ❶ **police**; appeler la police to call the police ❷ (*insurance*) **policy**

policier NOUN MASC **police officer**; une femme policier a woman police officer

policier ADJECTIVE un roman policier a detective story

poliment ADVERB **politely**

politesse NOUN FEM **politeness**; par politesse out of politeness

politicien, politicienne NOUN MASC, FEM **politician**

politique NOUN FEM ❶ **politics** ❷ **policy**; la politique sociale/ étrangère social/foreign policy

politique ADJECTIVE ❶ **political** ❷ un homme politique a politician

polluer VERB [1] **to pollute**

pollution NOUN FEM **pollution**

polo NOUN MASC **polo shirt**

Pologne NOUN FEM **Poland**; en Pologne in (*or* to) Poland

polonais NOUN MASC **Polish** (language)

polonais ADJECTIVE **Polish**

Polonais, Polonaise NOUN MASC, FEM **Pole**

pommade NOUN FEM **ointment**

pomme NOUN FEM ❶ **apple**; une tarte aux pommes an apple tart ❷ **potato**; pommes frites chips
• tomber dans les pommes (informal) to faint (literally: to fall into the apples)

pomme de terre NOUN FEM **potato**

pommier NOUN MASC **apple tree**

pompe NOUN FEM **pump**

pompe à essence NOUN FEM **petrol pump**

pompes funèbres PLURAL NOUN FEM **undertaker's**

pompier NOUN MASC **fire fighter**; appeler les pompiers to call the fire brigade

pompiste NOUN MASC & FEM **petrol pump attendant**

poncer VERB [61] **to sand** (wood)

ponctuation NOUN FEM **punctuation**

poney NOUN MASC **pony**

pont NOUN MASC ❶ **bridge** ❷ **deck** (of a ship)
• faire le pont to take a long weekend (usually when the Thursday before or the Tuesday after is a public holiday)

populaire ADJECTIVE ❶ **working-class** (family, housing, or area) ❷ **popular** (art or writing) ❸ **folk**; la culture populaire folk culture ❹ **popular**

population NOUN FEM **population**

porc NOUN MASC ❶ **pig**; un élevage de porcs a pig farm ❷ **pork**; manger un rôti de porc to have roast pork

porcelaine NOUN FEM **china, porcelain**

porcherie NOUN FEM **pigsty**; ta chambre est une vraie porcherie your room is a real pigsty

port NOUN MASC ❶ **port** ❷ **harbour**

portable ADJECTIVE **portable**; un ordinateur portable a laptop computer

portail NOUN MASC **gate**

portatif, portative ADJECTIVE MASC, FEM **portable**

porte NOUN FEM ❶ **door**; la porte d'entrée the front door ❷ **gate** (in an airport); la porte numéro douze gate number twelve ❸ l'entreprise a fermé ses portes the business has closed down, mettre quelqu'un à la porte to sack somebody

porte-bagages NOUN MASC **luggage rack**

porte-clés NOUN MASC **key-ring**

portée NOUN FEM à portée de main within reach

porte-fenêtre NOUN FEM **French window**

portefeuille NOUN MASC **wallet**; une jupe en portefeuille a wrapover skirt

porte-jarretelles NOUN MASC **suspender belt**

portemanteau NOUN MASC (PLURAL portemanteaux) **coat rack**

portemine NOUN MASC **propelling pencil**

porte-monnaie NOUN MASC **purse**

porte-parole NOUN MASC **spokesperson**

porter VERB [1] **❶ to carry**; porter une valise to carry a suitcase **❷ to take**; porter un paquet à la poste to take a parcel to the post office **❸ to wear**; elle portait une robe bleue she was wearing a blue dress **❹** se porter bien to be well, se porter mal to be in a bad way
• porter bonheur/malheur to bring good/bad luck

portière NOUN FEM **door** (of a car)

portion NOUN FEM **portion, helping**

porto NOUN MASC **port** (wine)

portoricain ADJECTIVE **Puerto Rican**

Portoricain, Portoricaine NOUN MASC, FEM **Puerto Rican** (person)

Porto Rico NOUN FEM **Puerto Rico**

portrait NOUN MASC **portrait**

portugais NOUN MASC **Portuguese** (language)

portugais ADJECTIVE **Portuguese**

Portugais, Portugaise NOUN MASC, FEM **Portuguese** (person)

Portugal NOUN MASC **Portugal**; au Portugal in (or to) Portugal

poser VERB [1] **❶ to put down**; il a posé sa tasse sur la table he put his cup down on the table, pose ta valise put your case down **❷** cela nous pose un problème that's a problem for us **❸** poser une question to ask a question

positif, positive ADJECTIVE MASC, FEM **positive**

position NOUN FEM **position**

posséder VERB [24] **to own**

possessif, possessive ADJECTIVE MASC, FEM **possessive**

possibilité NOUN FEM **❶ possibility**; c'est une possibilité it's a possibility **❷ opportunity**; la possibilité de voyager the opportunity to travel

possible ADJECTIVE **possible**; aussi grand que possible as big as possible, le moins possible as little as possible, dès que possible as soon as possible, ce n'est pas possible! I don't believe it!
• faire tout son possible to do your best

poste¹ NOUN MASC **❶ job, post**; un poste de secrétaire a job as a secretary **❷** un poste de radio/ télévision a radio/television set **❸ extension** (on a telephone system); le poste 578, s'il vous plaît extension 578, please

poste² NOUN FEM **post office**; il travaille pour la poste he works for the post office, mettre quelque chose à la poste to post something

poste de police NOUN MASC **police station**

poster NOUN MASC **poster**

pot NOUN MASC **❶ jar**; un pot de confiture a jar of jam **❷ carton**; un pot de crème a carton of cream **❸** un pot de peinture a tin of paint
• prendre un pot to have a drink

potable ADJECTIVE eau (non) potable (not) drinking water

potage NOUN MASC **soup**; potage aux légumes vegetable soup

potager NOUN MASC **vegetable garden**

pot-au-feu NOUN MASC **boiled beef with vegetables**

pot d'échappement NOUN MASC **exhaust**, **silencer** (for a car)

poteau NOUN MASC (PLURAL **poteaux**) **post**

poteau télégraphique NOUN MASC **telegraph pole**

potelé ADJECTIVE **chubby**

poterie NOUN FEM ❶ **pottery** ❷ **piece of pottery**

pou NOUN MASC (PLURAL **poux**) **louse**
• chercher des poux (informal) to nitpick

poubelle NOUN FEM **dustbin**; mettre quelque chose à la poubelle to throw something in the dustbin

pouce NOUN MASC ❶ **thumb** ❷ **inch**
• se tourner les pouces (informal) to twiddle your thumbs

poudre NOUN FEM **powder**

pouffer VERB [1] pouffer de rire to burst out laughing

poulain NOUN MASC **foal**

poule NOUN FEM **hen**
• quand les poules auront des dents (informal) when pigs can fly (literally: when hens have teeth)

poulet NOUN MASC **chicken**; une cuisse de poulet a chicken leg, du poulet rôti roast chicken

poulet fermier NOUN MASC **free-range chicken**

pouls NOUN MASC **pulse**; le médecin a pris mon pouls the doctor took my pulse

poumon NOUN MASC **lung**; crier à pleins poumons to shout at the top of your voice

poupée NOUN FEM **doll**

pour PREPOSITION ❶ **for**; un cadeau pour Marie-Laure a present for Marie-Laure, un billet pour Calais a ticket for Calais, le train pour Londres the train for London, ce sera prêt pour samedi? will it be ready for Saturday?, être pour to be in favour, je n'y suis pour rien I had nothing to do with it, je n'en ai pas pour longtemps it won't take long ❷ pour faire cela in order to do that, je suis allé au marché pour acheter des légumes I went to the market to buy some vegetables, je suis là pour t'aider I'm here to help you, c'était juste pour rire! it was only meant as a joke!, pour ainsi dire so to speak
• le pour et le contre the pros and cons

pourboire NOUN MASC **tip**

pour cent NOUN MASC **per cent**; dix pour cent ten per cent

pourcentage NOUN MASC **percentage**

pourquoi ADVERB **why**; pourquoi ont-ils refusé? why did they refuse?, je veux savoir pourquoi I want to know why, pourquoi pas? why not?

pourri ADJECTIVE **rotten**

pourrir VERB [2] **to go bad**

poursuivre VERB [75] ❶ **to chase** ❷ **to continue**

pourtant ADVERB ❶ **though**; et pourtant c'est vrai it's true though ❷ **yet**; et pourtant ça aurait pu être bien and yet it could have been good

pourvu que CONJUNCTION ❶ (followed by subjunctive) **providing**, **as**

long as; **pourvu que tu reviennes samedi** providing you come back on Saturday ❷ let's hope that; **pourvu que ça dure!** let's hope it lasts!

pousser *VERB* [1] ❶ to push; **elle a poussé la porte** she pushed the door shut (*or* open) ❷ **pousser un cri** to let out a cry, to cry out ❸ to grow (*of a child, hair, or a plant*); **mes tomates poussent bien** my tomatoes are growing well ❹ **se pousser** to move over, **pousse-toi!** move over!

poussette *NOUN FEM* pushchair

poussière *NOUN FEM* dust
- **dix euros et des poussières** ten euros something, just over 10 euros

poutre *NOUN FEM* beam

pouvez *VERB* ▸ SEE **pouvoir**¹

pouvoir¹ *VERB* [12] can; **je peux être là à dix heures** I can be there at ten, **peux-tu m'aider?** can you help me?, **je ne peux pas l'ouvrir** I can't open it, **ils ne pouvaient pas téléphoner avant** they couldn't phone before, **je n'ai pas pu réserver** I wasn't able to book, **elle aurait pu nous le dire** she could have told us, **puis-je parler à Cécile, s'il vous plaît** may I speak to Cécile, please, **tu peux toujours essayer** there's no harm in trying

pouvoir² *NOUN MASC* power; **après dix ans au pouvoir** after ten years in power

pouvons *VERB* ▸ SEE **pouvoir**¹

prairie *NOUN FEM* meadow

pratique *NOUN FEM* practice; **mettre quelque chose en pratique** to put something into practice, **il manque de pratique** he lacks practical experience

pratique *ADJECTIVE* practical, convenient; **cet ouvre-boîte n'est pas très pratique** this can opener isn't very practical, **le nouvel appartement est très pratique pour les magasins** the new flat's very handy for the shops

pratiquement *ADVERB* practically; **c'est pratiquement fini** it's practically finished

pratiquer *VERB* [1] ❶ to play, to do (*a sport or hobby*); **je pratique le yoga** I do yoga ❷ to practise; **pendant mon séjour à Lille j'aurai la possibilité de pratiquer mon français** during my stay in Lille I'll be able to practise my French

pré *NOUN MASC* meadow

préalable *ADJECTIVE* prior; **une condition préalable** a prior condition

précaution *NOUN FEM* precaution; **par précaution** as a precaution, **prendre ses précautions** to take precautions

précédent *ADJECTIVE* previous; **l'année précédente** the previous year, the year before

précieux, **précieuse** *ADJECTIVE MASC, FEM* precious, valuable; **une pierre précieuse** a precious stone, **des renseignements précieux** extremely useful information

précipice *NOUN MASC* precipice

précipitation *NOUN FEM* ❶ haste ❷ **précipitations** rainfall

précipiter *VERB* [1] **se précipiter** to rush, **ils se sont précipités vers la porte** they rushed for the door

a
b
c
d
e
f
g
h
i
j
k
l
m
n
o
p
q
r
s
t
u
v
w
x
y
z

précis ADJECTIVE ❶ precise ❷ accurate ❸ specific

précisément ADVERB precisely

préciser VERB [1] ❶ to specify (details or one's intentions) ❷ to explain; pouvez-vous préciser comment? could you explain exactly how?

précision NOUN FEM ❶ precision ❷ detail; voici quelques précisions sur le voyage here are some details about the journey

précuit ADJECTIVE precooked

préfecture NOUN FEM prefecture (France is divided into 96 'départements', which are roughly equivalent to British counties. The administration of each of these is done at the local level from the prefecture)

préfecture de police NOUN FEM (local) police headquarters

préférable ADJECTIVE preferable

préféré ADJECTIVE favourite; mon plat préféré my favourite dish

préférence NOUN FEM ❶ preference ❷ de préférence preferably, de préférence avant le dix mai preferably before the tenth of May

préférer VERB [24] to prefer; elle préfère le poisson à la viande she prefers fish to meat

préfet NOUN MASC prefect (official with overall responsibility for running a French territorial department); le préfet de police the chief of police ▸ SEE **préfecture**

préjugé NOUN MASC prejudice

prélavage NOUN MASC prewash

prématuré ADJECTIVE premature

premier, première ADJECTIVE MASC, FEM ❶ first; la première fois the first time, c'est la première fois que je le fais it's the first time I've done it, Michel, tu passes le premier Michel, you go first, le premier juin the first of June ❷ top; de première qualité top quality ❸ au premier étage on the first floor ❹ en premier first, arriver en premier to arrive first

première NOUN FEM ❶ première (of a film or play) ❷ une première mondiale a world first (an important event or achievement) ❸ voyager en première to travel first-class ❹ (in a French school) the equivalent of Year 12

premièrement ADVERB firstly

premier ministre NOUN MASC prime minister

prendre VERB [64] ❶ to take; prends celui-ci! take this one!, prendre un taxi to take a taxi ❷ prendre quelque chose à quelqu'un to take something from somebody, qui m'a pris mon vélo? who's taken my bike? ❸ to have (something to eat or drink); je prends une bière I'll have a beer, qu'est-ce que tu prends? what would you like? ❹ to bring; est-ce que tu as pris ton parapluie? did you bring your umbrella? ❺ passer prendre quelqu'un to pick somebody up, je passerai te prendre à dix heures I'll pick you up at ten
• c'est à prendre ou à laisser take it or leave it

prénom NOUN MASC first name

préparatifs PLURAL NOUN MASC preparations; les préparatifs du voyage the preparations for the journey

préparation *NOUN FEM* **preparation**, **training**

préparer *VERB* [1] ❶ **to prepare**; je vais préparer les légumes I'll go and prepare the vegetables, Françoise est en train de préparer le dîner Françoise is busy making dinner, as-tu préparé tes affaires pour le matin? have you got your things ready for the morning?, on a préparé une petite surprise pour elle we've got a little surprise ready for her, des plats préparés ready-to-eat meals ❷ **se préparer** to get ready, je vais me préparer pour partir I'll go and get ready to leave

préposition *NOUN FEM* **preposition**

près *ADVERB* ❶ **nearby**; il y a un village tout près there's a village nearby ❷ près de near, près de la gare near the station, près de toi near you, près de chez nous near our house, near where we live ❸ près de nearly, almost, près de mille euros nearly a thousand euros ❹ de près closely, regarder quelque chose de près to look closely at something ❺ à peu près more or less, à peu près deux heures two hours, more or less, j'ai à peu près fini I've more or less finished

prescrire *VERB* [38] ❶ **to prescribe** ❷ **to stipulate**

présence *NOUN FEM* **presence**

présent *NOUN MASC* ❶ **present (tense)**; au présent in the present ❷ à présent now, à présent je n'ai pas le temps I haven't got time just now

présent *ADJECTIVE* **present** *(at an event)*; toute la famille était présente the whole family was there

présentateur, présentatrice *NOUN MASC, FEM* ❶ **presenter** *(of a broadcast or programme)* ❷ **newsreader**

présentation *NOUN FEM* ❶ **presentation** ❷ **introduction** *(to someone you haven't met before)*

présenter *VERB* [1] ❶ **to introduce**; je vous présente mon père may I introduce my father?, Alain, je te présente Raphaël Alain, this is Raphaël ❷ **to present** *(a ticket, pass, or document)*; il faut présenter votre passeport you must show your passport ❸ présenter ses excuses to apologize ❹ se présenter to go, to come, en arrivant, présentez-vous à la réception when you get there (or here), go (or come) to reception ❺ se présenter à quelqu'un to introduce yourself to somebody

préservatif *NOUN MASC* **condom**

préservation *NOUN FEM* ❶ **preservation** ❷ **conservation**

préserver *VERB* [1] **to protect**, **to preserve**

président *NOUN MASC* ❶ **president** ❷ **chairman**

présidente *NOUN FEM* ❶ **president** ❷ **chairwoman**

présidentielles *PLURAL NOUN FEM* les présidentielles the presidential elections

presque *ADVERB* ❶ **nearly**; j'ai presque fini I've nearly finished ❷ presque rien hardly anything, il ne reste presque rien there's hardly anything left ❸ presque pas de hardly any, il ne reste presque pas de lait there's hardly any milk left

a
b
c
d
e
f
g
h
i
j
k
l
m
n
o
p
q
r
s
t
u
v
w
x
y
z

presqu'île *NOUN FEM* **peninsula**

pressant *ADJECTIVE* **urgent**

presse *NOUN FEM* **la presse the press, the newspapers, que dit la presse?** what do the papers say?

pressé *ADJECTIVE* ❶ **être pressé to be in a hurry** ❷ **urgent; ce n'est pas pressé it's not urgent** ❸ **un citron pressé a fresh lemon juice** *(served with water and sugar)*

presser *VERB* [1] ❶ **to urge** *(someone to do something)* ❷ **to squeeze; presser une orange to squeeze an orange** ❸ **ça ne presse pas there's no hurry, presser le pas to hurry (on)** ❹ **se presser to hurry**

pressing *NOUN MASC* **dry cleaner's**

pression *NOUN FEM* ❶ **pressure; sous pression pressurized** ❷ **press stud** ❸ *(informal)* **draught beer; un demi pression a half of draught beer**

prestidigitateur, **prestidigitatrice** *NOUN MASC, FEM* **conjurer**

prestige *NOUN MASC* **prestige**

prestigieux, **prestigieuse** *ADJECTIVE MASC, FEM* **prestigious**

présumer *VERB* [1] **to assume, to presume**

prêt *NOUN MASC* **loan**

prêt *ADJECTIVE* **ready; le dîner est prêt! dinner's ready!, être prêt à partir to be ready to leave**

prêt-à-porter *NOUN MASC* **ready-to-wear (clothes)**

prétendre *VERB* [3] **to claim; elle prétend que ce n'est pas sa faute she claims it's not her fault**

prêter *VERB* [1] ❶ **to lend; prêter quelque chose à quelqu'un to lend somebody something, je te prêterai mon vélo I'll lend you my bike** ❷ **prêter attention to pay attention** ❸ **prêter l'oreille to listen**

prétexte *NOUN MASC* **excuse**

prêtre *NOUN MASC* **priest**

preuve *NOUN FEM* ❶ **proof; la preuve, c'est que ... the proof is that ...** ❷ **faire preuve de to show, ils ont fait preuve de beaucoup d'intelligence they showed considerable intelligence**

prévenir *VERB* [81] ❶ **to tell** *(in advance)*; **préviens-moi de ta visite tell me when you're coming, ils arrivent toujours sans nous prévenir they always arrive without letting us know** ❷ **to call** *(the police or a doctor)* ❸ **to warn; je te préviens I warn you**

prévention *NOUN FEM* **prevention**

prévision *NOUN FEM* **forecast, forecasting; les prévisions météorologiques the weather forecast**

prévoir *VERB* [65] ❶ **to predict** *(an event or change)* ❷ **to plan** *(a journey or an arrangement)* ❸ **tout a été prévu everything's been taken care of** ❹ **le départ est prévu pour huit heures departure is scheduled for eight o'clock** ❺ **to allow** *(time or money)*; **prévoyez 10 euros pour le taxi allow 10 euros for the taxi**

prier *VERB* [1] ❶ **prier quelqu'un de faire to ask someone to do, il m'a prié d'excuser son retard he asked me to forgive him for being late, les clients sont priés de ne pas fumer customers are kindly requested**

not to smoke ❷ je vous en prie you're welcome, it's nothing, 'merci beaucoup' – 'je vous en prie' 'thank you very much' – 'you're welcome' ❸ to pray

prière *NOUN FEM* ❶ prayer ❷ request; 'prière de fermer la porte' 'please close the door'

primaire *ADJECTIVE* primary; l'école primaire primary school

prime *NOUN FEM* ❶ bonus ❷ free gift

primevère *NOUN FEM* primrose

prince *NOUN MASC* prince; le prince Charles Prince Charles

princesse *NOUN FEM* princess

principal *ADJECTIVE MASC* (PLURAL principaux) principal, chief

principe *NOUN MASC* ❶ principle ❷ en principe as a rule, en principe je rentre à six heures as a rule I get back at six ❸ en principe in theory, en principe tout le monde a été informé in theory, everybody's been informed

printanier, printanière *ADJECTIVE MASC, FEM* spring-like (weather)

printemps *NOUN MASC* spring; au printemps in (the) spring

priorité *NOUN FEM* ❶ priority ❷ right of way; 'vous n'avez pas la priorité' 'you do not have right of way' (sign at a roundabout)

pris *VERB* ▶ SEE **prendre**

pris *ADJECTIVE* ❶ busy; je suis très prise ce matin I'm very busy this morning ❷ taken; toutes les places sont prises all the seats are taken ❸ overcome (with an emotion or a feeling); être pris de panique to be panic-stricken

prise *NOUN FEM* ❶ socket, plug (for an electric appliance) ❷ capture; la prise de la Bastille the storming of the Bastille

prise de courant *NOUN FEM* power point

prise de sang *NOUN FEM* blood test

prise multiple *NOUN FEM* adaptor plug

prison *NOUN FEM* prison

prisonnier, prisonnière *NOUN MASC, FEM* prisoner

privé *NOUN MASC* ❶ private sector (of business or the school system) ❷ en privé in private, off the record

privé *ADJECTIVE* ❶ private; 'propriété privée' 'private property' ❷ without; nous sommes privés d'électricité we are without electricity, privé de sens senseless

priver *VERB* [1] ❶ priver quelqu'un de quelque chose to deprive someone of something ❷ se priver de quelque chose to do without something

privilège *NOUN MASC* privilege

privilégié *ADJECTIVE* privileged, special, fortunate

privilégier *VERB* [1] ❶ to favour ❷ to give priority to

prix *NOUN MASC* ❶ price; quel est le prix des places? what price are the seats?, le prix a augmenté the price has gone up ❷ à tout prix at all costs ❸ prize; le premier prix first prize

probable *ADJECTIVE* likely; c'est peu probable it's unlikely

A
B
C
D
E
F
G
H
I
J
K
L
M
N
O
P
Q
R
S
T
U
V
W
X
Y
Z

probablement *ADVERB* **probably**

problème *NOUN MASC* **problem**; sans problème! no problem!

procédé *NOUN MASC* **process**

procès *NOUN MASC* ❶ **trial** ❷ **lawsuit**

procession *NOUN FEM* **procession**

prochain *ADJECTIVE* **next**; la prochaine fois the next time, le mois prochain next month, jeudi prochain next Thursday, à la prochaine! see you soon!

prochainement *ADVERB* **soon**

proche *ADJECTIVE* ❶ **near**; la ville la plus proche est Valence the nearest town is Valence ❷ **close**; c'est une amie très proche de Julie she' a very close friend of Julie's ❸ proche de near, ils ont acheté une maison proche de Nice they've bought a house near Nice

Proche-Orient *NOUN MASC* le Proche-Orient the Middle East

proches *PLURAL NOUN MASC* **close family and friends**

procurer *VERB* [1] se procurer quelque chose to get something

producteur, **productrice** *NOUN MASC, FEM* **producer**

production *NOUN FEM* **production**

produire *VERB* [26] ❶ **to produce** ❷ se produire to happen, ça s'est produit au mois de mai that happened in May

produit *NOUN MASC* **product**; les produits de beauté beauty products, les produits d'entretien household products, les produits laitiers dairy produce, les produits congelés frozen foods, les produits d'exportation export products

prof *NOUN MASC (informal) (short for professeur)* **teacher**; notre prof de français our French teacher

professeur *NOUN MASC* ❶ **teacher**; ma sœur est professeur de physique my sister's a physics teacher ❷ **university lecturer** ❸ **university professor**

profession *NOUN FEM* **profession, occupation**

professionnel, **professionnelle** *ADJECTIVE MASC, FEM* **professional**

profil *NOUN MASC* **profile**

profit *NOUN MASC* ❶ **profit**; les profits de la société the company's profits ❷ au profit de in aid of, au profit des sans-abri in aid of the homeless

profiter *VERB* [1] ❶ profiter de to take advantage of *(an opportunity)*, j'ai profité des soldes pour m'acheter un manteau I took advantage of the sales to buy myself a coat ❷ **to make the most of**; profite bien de tes vacances! make the most of your holiday! ❸ profiter à to benefit

profond *ADJECTIVE* **deep**; un trou profond de 3 mètres a hole three metres deep, la France profonde provincial France

profondément *ADVERB* **deeply, profoundly**

profondeur *NOUN FEM* **depth**; la piscine a une profondeur de 3 mètres the swimming pool is 3 metres deep, étudier quelque chose en profondeur to study something in depth

programmateur[1] *NOUN MASC* ❶ **timer** ❷ **programme selector** *(on appliance)*

programmateur², **programmatrice** NOUN MASC, FEM **programmer** (on radio, tv)

programme NOUN MASC ❶ **programme**; ce n'est pas au programme it's not on the programme ❷ **program** (for a computer) ❸ **syllabus**; le programme de maths the maths syllabus

programmer VERB [1] ❶ **to schedule** ❷ **to program** (on a computer)

programmeur, **programmeuse** NOUN MASC, FEM **(computer) programmer**

progrès NOUN MASC **progress**; les progrès de l'informatique advances in computer science, faire des progrès to make progress

progresser VERB [1] ❶ **to progress** ❷ **to make progress**

projecteur NOUN MASC ❶ **floodlight** ❷ **spotlight** ❸ **projector**

projet NOUN MASC ❶ **plan**; mes projets pour l'été my plans for the summer ❷ **project** ❸ **rough draft**

projeter VERB [48] ❶ **to throw, to hurl**; le choc l'a projeté de sa voiture the impact hurled him out of his car ❷ **to show** (a film) ❸ **to cast** (a shadow) ❹ projeter de faire to plan to do

prolongation NOUN FEM ❶ **continuation** ❷ **extension** ❸ **extra time**; jouer les prolongations to go into extra time

prolongé ADJECTIVE **lengthy**; une discussion prolongée a lengthy discussion

prolonger VERB [52] ❶ **to extend**; elle a prolongé son congé de maladie she's extended her sick leave ❷ se prolonger to go on, les discussions se sont prolongées jusqu'à 23 h discussions went on till 11 p.m

promenade NOUN FEM ❶ **walk**; faire une promenade to go for a walk, une promenade en voiture a drive, une promenade à vélo a bike ride, une promenade en bateau a boat trip ❷ **promenade** (by the sea)

promener VERB [50] ❶ promener un enfant to take a child for a walk, promener le chien to walk the dog ❷ promener quelque chose to carry something around ❸ se promener to go for a walk, se promener en voiture to go for a drive, se promener à vélo to go for a bike ride

promesse NOUN FEM **promise**; il m'a fait une promesse he made me a promise, tenir sa promesse to keep your promise

prometteur, **prometteuse** ADJECTIVE MASC, FEM **promising**

promettre VERB [11] **to promise**; promettre de faire to promise to do, il a promis de téléphoner ce soir he promised to ring this evening, j'ai promis à ma mère de lui écrire une fois par semaine I promised my mother I would write to her once a week

promotion NOUN FEM ❶ **special offer**; les fraises sont en promotion cette semaine strawberries are on special offer this week ❷ **promotion** (to a higher job); avoir une promotion to be promoted

pronom NOUN MASC **pronoun**

prononcer VERB [61] ❶ to pronounce (a word) ❷ to mention (a name), to say (a word or phrase) ❸ to make (a speech) ❹ se prononcer pour/contre quelque chose to declare oneself for/against something

prononciation NOUN FEM **pronunciation**

propagande NOUN FEM **propaganda**

proportion NOUN FEM **proportion**; en proportion de in proportion to

propos NOUN MASC ❶ à propos by the way, à propos, as-tu appelé maman? by the way, did you ring Mum? ❷ à propos de about, il n'a rien dit à propos de son père he said nothing about his father ❸ des propos remarks

proposer VERB [1] ❶ proposer quelque chose à quelqu'un to suggest something to somebody, je leur ai proposé une petite promenade I suggested we went for a little walk ❷ proposer quelque chose à quelqu'un to offer somebody something, on lui a proposé un poste de technicien she (or he) has been offered a job as a technician

proposition NOUN FEM **offer**

propre ADJECTIVE ❶ (when it comes after the noun) **clean**; une chemise propre a clean shirt ❷ (when it comes before the noun) **own**; ma propre voiture my own car, leurs propres enfants their own children

proprement ADVERB ❶ **properly**; mange proprement! eat properly! ❷ à proprement parler strictly speaking

propreté NOUN FEM **cleanliness**

propriétaire NOUN MASC & FEM ❶ **owner** (usually of a building or a business) ❷ **landlord**, **landlady**

propriété NOUN FEM ❶ **property**; propriété privée private property ❷ **ownership**

prospectus NOUN MASC **leaflet**

prospère ADJECTIVE **prosperous**

prostituée NOUN FEM **prostitute**

protecteur, **protectrice** NOUN MASC, FEM **protector**

protecteur, **protectrice** ADJECTIVE MASC, FEM **protective**; une crème protectrice protective cream

protection NOUN FEM **protection**; des lunettes de protection protective goggles

protéger VERB [15] to **protect**; pour protéger l'environnement to protect the environment, se protéger du soleil to protect yourself from the sun

protestant, **protestante** NOUN MASC, FEM, ADJECTIVE **Protestant**

protestation NOUN FEM **protest**

protester VERB [1] to **protest**; protester contre quelque chose to protest against something

prouver VERB [1] to **prove**

provenance NOUN FEM **origin**; du fromage en provenance de France cheese from France, un passager en provenance de Madrid a passenger arriving from Madrid

provençal ADJECTIVE MASC (PLURAL provençaux) from Provence, **Provençal**

proverbe NOUN MASC **proverb**

province NOUN FEM **province**; en province in the provinces, une ville de province a provincial town

provision NOUN FEM ❶ **supply**; nous avons fait provision de bois we've laid in a supply of wood ❷ des provisions food, maman est partie prendre des provisions Mum's gone off shopping for food

provisoire ADJECTIVE **temporary**

provocateur, **provocatrice** NOUN MASC, FEM **agitator**

provocateur, **provocatrice** ADJECTIVE MASC, FEM **provocative**

provoquer VERB [1] ❶ **to cause**; provoquer un accident to cause an accident, provoquer une discussion to spark off a discussion ❷ provoquer quelqu'un to provoke somebody

proximité NOUN FEM **nearness**; à proximité de near

prudemment ADJECTIVE **carefully**

prudence NOUN FEM **caution**; conduisez avec prudence! drive carefully!

prudent ADJECTIVE ❶ **careful**; soyez prudents par mauvais temps! be careful in bad weather! ❷ **wise**; il est plus prudent de réserver it's wiser to book

prune NOUN FEM **plum**

pruneau NOUN MASC (PLURAL pruneaux) **prune**

prunier NOUN MASC **plum tree**

psychanalyste NOUN MASC & FEM **psychoanalyst**

psychiatre NOUN MASC & FEM **psychiatrist**

psychologie NOUN FEM **psychology**

psychologique ADJECTIVE **psychological**

psychologue NOUN MASC & FEM **psychologist**

pu VERB ▶ SEE **pouvoir**[1]

pub NOUN FEM (informal) (short for publicité) **advert**

public NOUN MASC ❶ **public**; en public in public, ouvert au public open to the public, 'interdit au public' 'no admission' ❷ **audience**, **spectators**; pour un public jeune for a young audience ❸ **fans** (of a performer)

public, **publique** ADJECTIVE MASC, FEM **public**; dans un lieu public in a public place, une école publique a state school

publicitaire ADJECTIVE ❶ **advertising**; une campagne publicitaire an advertising campaign ❷ **promotional** (material)

publicité NOUN FEM ❶ **advertising**; elle travaille dans la publicité she works in advertising, faire de la publicité to advertise ❷ **advertisement**, **ad** (in a magazine, a newspaper, on television, or at the cinema)

publier VERB [1] **to publish**

puce NOUN FEM ❶ une puce électronique a microchip, une carte à puce a smart card ❷ **flea**; un marché aux puces a fleamarket

puer VERB [1] **to stink**

puis ADVERB **then**; nous allons à Cannes, puis à Nice we're going to Cannes, then Nice

A
B
C
D
E
F
G
H
I
J
K
L
M
N
O
P
Q
R
S
T
U
V
W
X
Y
Z

puisque (*puisqu'* before a vowel or silent 'h') CONJUNCTION **since**; puisqu'il pleut je prendrai le bus since it's raining I'll take the bus

puissance NOUN FEM **power**; un moteur d'une forte puissance a high-power engine, une puissance étrangère a foreign power

puissant ADJECTIVE **powerful, strong**

puits NOUN MASC **well**

pull, pull-over NOUN MASC **jumper**

pulvérisateur NOUN MASC **spray**

punaise NOUN FEM ❶ **drawing-pin** ❷ **bug**

punir VERB [2] **to punish**

punition NOUN FEM **punishment**

pur ADJECTIVE ❶ **pure**; un shampooing très doux, très pur an ultra-mild, ultra-pure shampoo, un croissant pur beurre an all-butter croissant ❷ **sheer, total**; c'est de la folie pure it's sheer madness

purée NOUN FEM **mashed potatoes**

puzzle NOUN MASC **jigsaw puzzle**

PV NOUN MASC (short for *procès verbal*) **parking ticket**

pyjama NOUN MASC **(pair of) pyjamas**; où est mon pyjama? where are my pyjamas?, un pyjama propre a clean pair of pyjamas

pyramide NOUN FEM **pyramid**

Pyrénées PLURAL NOUN FEM **Pyrenees**

Qq

quai NOUN MASC ❶ **platform**; le train à destination de Paris va arriver au quai numéro trois the train for Paris is about to arrive at platform number three ❷ **quay**

qualifié ADJECTIVE ❶ **qualified** ❷ **skilled**

qualifier VERB [1] **to qualify**

qualité NOUN FEM **quality**; des fruits de première qualité top quality fruit

quand CONJUNCTION, ADVERB **when**; quand est-ce que ton frère arrive? when is your brother arriving?, quand tu auras dix-sept ans, tu pourras apprendre à conduire when you're seventeen you'll be able to learn to drive

quand même ADVERB **all the same**; il pleut mais je vais sortir quand même it's raining but I'm going to go out all the same, quand même! honestly!

quant à PREPOSITION **as for**; quant à moi, je reste as for me, I'm staying here

quantité NOUN FEM **amount**

quarantaine NOUN FEM ❶ **about forty**; une quarantaine de personnes about forty people, j'approche la quarantaine I'll soon be forty ❷ **quarantine**

quarante NUMBER **forty**

quart NOUN MASC ❶ (in time expressions) **quarter**; un quart d'heure a quarter of an hour, dix heures et quart quarter past ten ❷ **quarter**; le quart du gâteau a quarter of the cake, un quart d'eau minérale a quarter-litre bottle of mineral water, trois quarts three quarters, les trois quarts du temps most of the time

quart de finale NOUN MASC **quarter-final**

quartier NOUN MASC **area** (of a town); un quartier résidentiel a residential area, les gens du quartier the local people

quartier général MASC **headquarters**

quartz NOUN MASC **quartz**

quasi ADVERB **almost**; quasi parfait almost perfect

quasiment ADVERB ❶ **practically**; c'est quasiment neuf it's practically new ❷ quasiment jamais hardly ever, il n'est quasiment jamais chez lui he's hardly ever at home

quatorze NUMBER **fourteen**; Céline a quatorze ans Céline's fourteen, le quatorze juin the fourteenth of June

quatre NUMBER **four**; Louis a quatre ans Louis is four, le quatre mars the fourth of March

quatre-vingt-dix NUMBER **ninety**; quatre-vingt-dix-neuf ninety-nine

quatre-vingts NUMBER **eighty**; quatre-vingts personnes eighty people, quatre-vingt-trois eighty-three (note that the 's' is dropped when another number is added), quatre-vingt-seize ninety-six

quatrième NOUN FEM (in a French school) **the equivalent of Year 9**

quatrième NOUN MASC au quatrième on the fourth floor

quatrième ADJECTIVE **fourth**

que CONJUNCTION, PRONOUN, ADVERB ❶ **that** (often left out in English); elle dit que c'est vrai she says (that) it's true, je sais qu'il y habite I know he lives there, je veux que tu sois heureux I want you to be happy ❷ **whether**; qu'ils arrivent demain ou mardi, n'importe whether they come tomorrow or on Tuesday, it doesn't matter ❸ que tout le monde se lève! everybody stand up! ❹ plus ... que more ... than, elle est plus grande que Marie she's taller than Marie ❺ aussi ... que as ... as, elle est aussi grande que moi she's as tall as me ❻ ne ... que only, je n'ai que dix euros I've only got ten euros ❼ **that**, **which**, **whom** (often left out in English); le livre que je lis the book (that) I'm reading, la chemise qu'il a achetée the shirt (which) he's bought ❽ **what**; que veut-il? what does he want?, je ne sais pas ce qu'il veut I don't know what he wants ❾ qu'est-ce que ...? what ...?, qu'est-ce que tu as trouvé? what have you found?, qu'est-ce que c'est? what's that?, qu'est-ce qu'il y a? what's the matter?, qu'est-ce qu'elle a? what's the matter with her? ❿ **how** (in an exclamation); que tu as grandi! how you've grown!

237

Québec *NOUN MASC* le Québec Quebec

québécois *NOUN MASC* **Canadian French** *(language)*

québécois *ADJECTIVE* **from Quebec, Quebecker**

Québécois, Québécoise *NOUN MASC, FEM* **French Canadian, Quebecker**; les Québécois the French Canadians, the Quebeckers

quel, quelle *DETERMINER* **❶** *(in a question)* **what, which**; quel livre? which book?, quelle voiture? which car?, quelle heure est-il? what time is it?, quel âge as-tu? how old are you?, dans quels pays? in which countries?, pour quelles raisons? for what reasons? **❷** *(in an exclamation)* **what**; quel beau temps! what lovely weather!, quelle coïncidence! what a coincidence!, quelle horreur! how dreadful!

quelconque *ADJECTIVE* **any**; si tu as un problème quelconque if you have any sort of a problem, si pour une raison quelconque if for any reason

quelle *DETERMINER* ▸ SEE **quel**

quelque chose *PRONOUN* **❶ something**; il faut manger quelque chose, Claire you must eat something, Claire, il y a quelque chose de bizarre there's something strange, voulez-vous boire quelque chose? would you like something to drink? **❷ anything**; est-ce que tu as vu quelque chose? did you see anything?

quelquefois *ADVERB* **sometimes**

quelque part *ADVERB* **❶ somewhere**; quelque part dans le jardin somewhere in the garden **❷ anywhere**; est-ce que tu as vu mes lunettes quelque part? have you seen my glasses anywhere?

quelques *PLURAL DETERMINER* **❶ some**; je vais te donner quelques cerises I'll give you some cherries **❷ a few**; il reste quelques fraises there are a few strawberries left, elle est partie pour quelques jours she's gone away for a few days

quelques-uns, quelques-unes *PLURAL PRONOUN* **some**; quelques-uns des enfants some of the children

quelqu'un *PRONOUN* **❶ somebody**; quelqu'un a appelé pour toi somebody rang for you, quelqu'un d'autre somebody else **❷ anybody**; il y a quelqu'un? is there anybody there?

quels, quelles ▸ SEE **quel**

querelle *NOUN FEM* **quarrel**

qu'est-ce que ▸ SEE **que**

qu'est-ce qui ▸ SEE **qui**

question *NOUN FEM* **❶ question**; poser une question à quelqu'un to ask somebody a question, elle n'a pas répondu à mes questions she didn't answer my questions **❷ matter, question**; c'est une question de goût it's a matter of taste, c'est hors de question it's out of the question, pas question! no way!

questionnaire *NOUN MASC* **questionnaire**

questionner *VERB* [1] **to question**

queue *NOUN FEM* ❶ **tail**; la queue du chat the cat's tail ❷ **queue**; faire la queue to queue ❸ la queue du train the rear of the train ❹ **stalk** *(of a flower or a fruit)*

queue de cheval *NOUN FEM* **ponytail**

qui *PRONOUN* ❶ **who**; qui a fermé la porte? who closed the door?, qui voulez-vous voir? who do you want to see?, la personne qui vous a écrit n'est pas là aujourd'hui the person who wrote to you is not here today ❷ **that**; prends la casserole qui est sur l'évier take the pan that's on the sink ❸ à qui? whose?, à qui est ce pull? whose is this jumper? ❹ à qui parles-tu? who are you talking to? ❺ qu'est-ce qui ...? what ...?, qu'est-ce qui t'amène? what brings you here?

quincaillerie *NOUN FEM* **hardware shop**

quinzaine *NOUN FEM* ❶ **about fifteen**; une quinzaine d'enfants about fifteen children ❷ une quinzaine de jours a fortnight, dans une quinzaine two weeks from now

quinze *NUMBER* ❶ **fifteen**; Marise a quinze ans Marise is fifteen, le quinze juillet the fifteenth of July ❷ quinze jours two weeks, tous les quinze jours every two weeks

quitter *VERB* [1] ❶ **to leave**; je quitte le bureau à cinq heures I leave the office at five, j'ai quitté l'école à seize ans I left school at sixteen ❷ se quitter to part ❸ ne quittez pas hold the line please *(on the telephone)*

quoi *PRONOUN* ❶ **what**; quoi encore? what now?, tu es sourd ou quoi? are you deaf or what?, à quoi penses-tu? what are you thinking about?, pour quoi faire? what for?, à quoi bon continuer? what's the point in going on?, il n'y a pas de quoi se fâcher there's no reason to get angry, il n'y a pas de quoi don't mention it ❷ **which**; après quoi, il est parti after which, he left

quoique *CONJUNCTION* **although, though**; quoique petit, il est fort although he's small he's strong

quotidien, quotidienne *ADJECTIVE MASC, FEM* **daily**; la vie quotidienne daily life, sa visite quotidienne her daily visit

quotidien *NOUN MASC* **daily newspaper**

quotidiennement *ADVERB* **daily**; les livraisons s'effectuent quotidiennement deliveries are made daily

rabais NOUN MASC **discount**; au rabais at a discount

raccompagner VERB [1] raccompagner quelqu'un to see somebody home

raccourci NOUN MASC **short cut**

raccourcir VERB [2] to shorten

raccrocher VERB [1] to hang up (telephone)

race NOUN FEM ❶ **race**; la race humaine the human race ❷ **breed**; un chien de race a pedigree dog

racheter VERB [16] ❶ to buy more; il faut racheter du pain we'll have to buy more bread ❷ il m'a racheté ma voiture he bought my car off me

racine NOUN FEM **root**

raciste NOUN MASC & FEM, ADJECTIVE **racist**; des propos racistes racist remarks

racler VERB [1] to scrape

raconter VERB [1] to tell (a story); raconte-nous ce qui s'est passé tell us what happened

radar NOUN MASC **radar**

radeau NOUN MASC (PLURAL **radeaux**) **raft**

radiateur NOUN MASC **radiator**

radio NOUN FEM ❶ **radio**; je l'ai entendu à la radio I heard it on the radio ❷ **X-ray**; passer une radio to have an X-ray

radio-réveil NOUN MASC **clock radio**

radis NOUN MASC **radish**

rafale NOUN FEM **gust** (of wind or rain), **flurry** (of snow)

raffoler VERB [1] raffoler de to be mad about, je ne raffole pas des huîtres I'm not mad about oysters

rafraîchir VERB [2] ❶ le temps se rafraîchit the weather's getting cooler ❷ to cool (somebody) down

rafraîchissement NOUN MASC ❶ **refreshment** ❷ **drop in temperature**

rage NOUN FEM ❶ **rabies** ❷ une rage de dents raging toothache

ragoût NOUN MASC **stew**

raide ADJECTIVE ❶ **stiff** (body, arm, leg) ❷ **straight** (hair) ❸ une pente raide a steep slope

raie NOUN FEM ❶ **parting** (in your hair) ❷ **skate** (the fish)

rail NOUN MASC **rail** (for trains)
• remettre quelque chose sur les rails to put something back on the right track

raisin NOUN MASC **grapes**; j'ai acheté du raisin noir I bought some black grapes, une grappe de raisin a bunch of grapes, un grain de raisin a grape, le jus de raisin grape juice

raisin de Corinthe NOUN MASC **currant**

raisin sec NOUN MASC **raisin**

raison NOUN FEM ❶ **reason**; pour cette raison for this reason, pour raisons de santé for health reasons ❷ avoir raison to be right, oui, tu as raison yes, you're right

raisonnable ADJECTIVE **sensible**

raisonnement NOUN MASC **reasoning**

rajouter VERB [1] **to add**; on peut rajouter de l'eau si on veut you can add water if you want

ralentir VERB [2] **to slow down**

ralentissement NOUN MASC **slowing down**

ralentisseur NOUN MASC **speed bump**

râler VERB [1] (informal) **to moan**; arrête de râler! stop moaning!

rallonge NOUN FEM ❶ **extension cord** ❷ **extra leaf** (for a table)

ramasser VERB [1] ❶ **to pick up**; est-ce que tu peux ramasser tous ces papiers, s'il te plaît can you pick up all these papers please ❷ **to pick** (fruit); ils ont déjà ramassé les framboises they've already picked the raspberries ❸ **to collect**; on va ramasser des châtaignes dans les bois we're going to go and collect chestnuts in the woods ❹ **collect in** (books, homework); Anne, veux-tu ramasser tous les cahiers? Anne, would you collect in all the exercise books?

rame NOUN FEM ❶ **oar** ❷ une rame de métro an underground train

rameau NOUN MASC (PLURAL **rameaux**) **branch**; le dimanche des Rameaux Palm Sunday

ramener VERB [50] ❶ ramener quelqu'un (en voiture) to give somebody a lift home, tu veux que je te ramène? do you want a lift home?, elle m'a ramené en voiture she gave me a lift back ❷ **to take**

back; je dois ramener les livres à la bibliothèque I must take these books back to the library

ramer VERB [1] **to row**

rampe NOUN FEM ❶ **banister** ❷ **ramp**

rançon NOUN FEM **ransom**

rancune NOUN FEM **resentment, grudge**

randonnée NOUN FEM **hike, walk**; faire une randonnée pédestre to go on a hike (on public footpaths), on a fait une randonnée de vingt kilomètres we did a twenty-kilometre walk, faire une randonnée à cheval to go pony-trekking, une randonnée à vélo a long-distance bike ride

randonneur, **randonneuse** NOUN MASC, FEM ❶ **hiker, walker, rambler** ❷ **touring cyclist**

rang NOUN MASC **row**; au cinquième rang in the fifth row

rangée NOUN FEM **row**; une rangée de maisons a row of houses

ranger VERB [52] ❶ **to put away**; ranger la vaisselle to put away the dishes ❷ **to tidy**; je vais ranger ma chambre I'm going to tidy my room ❸ **to arrange**; il range ses livres par ordre alphabétique he arranges his books alphabetically

râper VERB [1] **to grate**; le fromage râpé grated cheese

rapide NOUN MASC **express train**

rapide ADJECTIVE **quick**; prends le métro, c'est plus rapide take the underground, it's quicker

a
b
c
d
e
f
g
h
i
j
k
l
m
n
o
p
q
r
s
t
u
v
w
x
y
z

rapidement ADVERB **quickly, rapidly**

rappel NOUN MASC **❶ reminder** (for a bill); 'dernier rappel' 'final demand' **❷ booster** (vaccination)

rappeler VERB [18] **❶ to remind**; rappelle-moi de passer par la banque remind me to go to the bank, le paysage me rappelle la France the countryside reminds me of France **❷ to ring back** (on the telephone); il va te rappeler dans une heure he'll ring you back in a hour **❸ se rappeler to remember**, je ne me rappelle plus I can't remember, je me rappelle qu'elle avait les cheveux longs I remember she had long hair

rapport NOUN MASC **❶ report**; un rapport officiel an official report **❷ connection**; je ne vois pas le rapport I don't see the connection **❸ être en rapport avec quelqu'un** to be in touch with someone **❹ avoir de bons/mauvais rapports avec quelqu'un** to be on good/bad relations with someone **❺ par rapport à** compared with, il a fait très beau par rapport à l'année dernière the weather's been very good compared with last year

rapporter VERB [1] **❶ to bring back**; est-ce que tu peux le rapporter demain? can you bring it back tomorrow? **❷ to bring in**; son travail ne rapporte pas beaucoup her job doesn't bring in much money

rapprocher VERB [1] **❶ to move (something) closer**; peux-tu rapprocher la lampe de ma chaise? can you move the lamp closer to my chair? **❷ to bring together** (different people); des efforts pour rapprocher les deux pays efforts to

bring the two countries together **❸ se rapprocher to come** (or go) **closer**, elle s'est rapprochée de la table she moved closer to the table

raquette NOUN FEM **❶ racket** (for tennis) **❷ bat** (for ping-pong)

rare ADJECTIVE **rare**; une fleur rare a rare flower, il est rare qu'elle arrive à l'heure she hardly ever arrives on time

rarement ADVERB **rarely**

ras ADJECTIVE **❶ short** (hair or fur); il a les cheveux coupés ras his hair is cut short **❷ en rase campagne in open country ❸ au ras de l'eau/du sol** at water/ground level
• **j'en ai ras le bol!** (informal) **I'm fed up!**

raser VERB [1] **❶ to shave, to shave off**; il a rasé sa barbe he's shaved off his beard, la mousse à raser shaving foam **❷ se raser to shave**, se raser les jambes to shave your legs

ras-le-cou NOUN MASC **crew-neck sweater**

rasoir NOUN MASC **razor**

rassemblement NOUN MASC **meeting, rally**

rassembler VERB [1] **to gather (together)**; j'ai rassemblé les enfants près de l'entrée I gathered all the children together by the main entrance, tout le village s'est rassemblé pour l'écouter the whole village gathered to listen to him

rassis ADJECTIVE du pain rassis stale bread

rassurer VERB [1] **❶ to reassure**; ah, cela me rassure! oh, that sets my mind at rest! **❷ rassure-toi don't worry**

rat NOUN MASC **rat**

râteau NOUN MASC (PLURAL **râteaux**) **rake**

rater VERB [1] **❶** to fail; Sophie a raté son permis Sophie failed her driving test **❷** to miss; j'ai raté mon train I've missed my train

rationner VERB [1] **to ration**

RATP NOUN FEM (short for Régie autonome des transports parisiens) **Paris city-transport system**

rattacher VERB [1] **❶** to (re)fasten; rattache ta ceinture (re)fasten your seat-belt **❷** to attach; plus rien ne me rattache ici I no longer have any ties here

rattraper VERB [1] **❶** to catch up with (a person); ne t'inquiète pas, ils nous rattraperont don't worry, they'll catch up with us **❷** to make up for (lost time) **❸** se rattraper to make up for it, j'ai très peu joué cet été mais je vais me rattraper I've played very little this summer but I'll make up for it

rature NOUN FEM **crossing-out**

ravi ADJECTIVE **delighted**; je suis ravi de vous voir I'm delighted to see you

ravisseur, **ravisseuse** NOUN MASC, FEM **kidnapper**

rayé ADJECTIVE **striped** (fabric)

rayer VERB [59] **❶** to cross out (a mistake); j'ai rayé ton nom de la liste I crossed your name off the list **❷** to scratch (a surface)

rayon NOUN MASC **❶** shelf; un rayon pour mes livres a shelf for my books **❷** department (in a department store), section (in a supermarket); au rayon fraîcheur in the chilled foods section **❸** ray; un rayon de soleil a ray of sunshine, un rayon laser a laser beam, les rayons X X-rays **❹** radius

rayure NOUN FEM **❶** stripe **❷** scratch

RC NOUN MASC (short for rez-de-chaussée) **ground floor**

réacteur NOUN MASC **❶** un réacteur nucléaire a nuclear reactor **❷** jet engine

réaction NOUN FEM **reaction**

réagir VERB [2] **to react**; elle n'a pas réagi she didn't react

réalisateur, **réalisatrice** NOUN MASC, FEM **director** (of a film or TV programme)

réalisation NOUN FEM **❶** carrying out (of a plan or project) **❷** production (of a film or a radio/TV programme)

réaliser VERB [1] **❶** to carry out (a project) **❷** to fulfil; réaliser un rêve to fulfil a dream **❸** to make (a film) **❹** to realize

réaliste ADJECTIVE **realistic**

réalité NOUN FEM **reality**; en réalité in reality

réanimation NOUN FEM **resuscitation**; (service de) réanimation intensive care (unit)

rebelle NOUN MASC & FEM **rebel**

rébellion NOUN FEM **rebellion**

rebondir VERB [2] **to bounce**

rebord NOUN MASC **❶** le rebord de la fenêtre the window ledge **❷** edge; le rebord de la baignoire the edge of the bath

récemment ADVERB **recently**

récent ADJECTIVE **recent**

réception NOUN FEM ❶ **reception desk**; demandez la clé à la réception ask for the key at the reception desk ❷ **reception** (party)

réceptionniste NOUN MASC & FEM **receptionist**

recette NOUN FEM **recipe**; la recette du gâteau the recipe for the cake

recevoir VERB [66] ❶ **to receive**, **to get**; j'ai reçu ta lettre I got your letter ❷ **to welcome** (a visitor or guest) ❸ **to see** (a patient or client); le dentiste reçoit entre 9h et 17h the dentist sees patients between 9 a.m. and 5 p.m. ❹ être reçu à un examen to pass an exam, elle a été reçue première à l'examen she came top in the exam

rechange NOUN MASC de rechange **spare**, une pièce de rechange a spare part

recharge NOUN FEM **refill**

réchaud NOUN MASC **stove**

réchauffement planétaire NOUN MASC **global warming**

réchauffer VERB [1] ❶ **to warm up** (food); peux-tu mettre la soupe à réchauffer? can you put the soup on to warm? ❷ **to warm** (hands or feet) ❸ se réchauffer **to get warm**, va te réchauffer près du feu go and get warm by the fire

recherche NOUN FEM ❶ **research** ❷ être à la recherche de quelque chose to be looking for something, je suis à la recherche d'un logement I'm looking for somewhere to live

rechercher VERB [1] **to look for**; la police le recherche the police are looking for him, elle recherche un travail plus flexible she's looking for a more flexible job

récipient NOUN MASC **container**

réciproque ADJECTIVE **mutual**

récit NOUN MASC **story**; il nous a fait le récit de son voyage he told us all about his journey

récitation NOUN FEM **recitation**

réciter VERB [1] **to recite**

réclamation NOUN FEM **claim** (for compensation)

réclame NOUN FEM ❶ **advertisement**; une réclame pour le nouveau modèle an advertisement for the new model ❷ en réclame on (special) offer, le jambon est en réclame cette semaine the ham is on special offer this week

réclamer VERB [1] **to demand**; ils réclament trois jours de plus de vacances they're demanding three more days' holiday

récolte NOUN FEM ❶ **harvest** ❷ **crop**; faire la récolte to get the harvest in

récolter VERB [1] ❶ **to harvest**; récolter le blé to harvest the wheat ❷ **to collect** (money) ❸ (informal) **to get**; récolter une amende to get a fine

recommandation NOUN FEM **recommendation**

recommandé ADJECTIVE **registered**; une lettre recommandée a registered letter, je voudrais l'envoyer en recommandé I'd like to send it by registered post

recommander VERB [1] ❶ **to advise**; je te recommande de ne rien dire I advise you to say nothing ❷ **to recommend**

recommencer VERB [61] ❶ **to start again**; j'ai recommencé ma lettre I started my letter again, il a recommencé à neiger it's started snowing again ❷ **to do it again**; si tu ne fais pas attention, elle va recommencer if you don't watch out, she'll do it again, ça recommence! here we go again!

récompense NOUN FEM **reward**

récompenser VERB [1] **to reward**

réconcilier VERB [1] se réconcilier avec quelqu'un to make it up with somebody

réconfortant ADJECTIVE **comforting**

reconnaissable ADJECTIVE **recognizable**

reconnaissance NOUN FEM ❶ **gratitude**; en reconnaissance de in appreciation of ❷ **recognition**

reconnaissant ADJECTIVE **grateful**

reconnaître VERB [27] ❶ **to recognize**; je ne l'ai pas reconnue I didn't recognize her, je l'ai reconnu à sa voix I recognized him by his voice ❷ **to admit**; il faut reconnaître que c'est difficile it must be admitted that it's difficult, elle reconnaît qu'elle a menti she admits she lied

reconstruire VERB [26] **to rebuild**

recopier VERB [1] **to copy out**

record NOUN MASC **record**; un record mondial a world record, battre un record to break a record

recouvrir VERB [30] **to cover**

récré NOUN FEM (informal) **break**

récréation NOUN FEM **break**; la cour de récréation the playground

rectangle NOUN MASC **rectangle**

rectangulaire ADJECTIVE **rectangular**

rectifier VERB [1] **to correct**

reçu NOUN MASC **receipt**

reçu VERB ▸ SEE **recevoir**

recueil NOUN MASC **collection** (of poems or essays)

reculer VERB [1] ❶ **to move back**; elle a reculé de quelques pas she moved back a few steps ❷ **to reverse** (in a car) ❸ reculer la date d'une réunion to postpone a meeting

reculons IN PHRASE à reculons backwards

récupérer VERB [24] ❶ **to get back**; je vais chez Brigitte pour récupérer le bouquin que je lui ai prêté I'm going round to Brigitte's to get back the book I lent her ❷ **to recover** (from an illness)

recyclage NOUN MASC **recycling**; faire du recyclage to recycle

recycler VERB [1] **to recycle**

rédaction NOUN FEM **essay**

redemander VERB [1] ❶ **to ask again**; tu devrais redemander you should ask again ❷ **to ask for more**; il faut qu'on redemande des cahiers we'll have to ask for more exercise books

a
b
c
d
e
f
g
h
i
j
k
l
m
n
o
p
q
r
s
t
u
v
w
x
y
z

redescendre VERB [3] ❶ **to go (or come) back down**; elle est redescendue à la cave she went back down to the cellar, je monte à Glasgow demain et je redescends lundi I'm going up to Glasgow tomorrow and I'm coming back down on Monday ❷ **to bring or take back down**; est-ce que tu peux redescendre ma valise? can you bring my suitcase back down?

rédiger VERB [52] **to write** (an article), **to write up** (notes)

redonner VERB [1] **to give again**; je leur ai redonné mon adresse I gave them my address again, est-ce que je te redonne un peu de salade? can I give you a bit more salad?

redoubler VERB [1] **to repeat a year** (at school)

redresser VERB [1] ❶ **to straighten up** ❷ **to put right** ❸ se redresser **to recover**

réduction NOUN FEM ❶ **reduction**; une réduction du nombre d'étudiants a reduction in the number of students ❷ **(price) reduction**; une réduction de 20% a 20% reduction

réduire VERB [68] **to cut** (prices); réduire les impôts to cut taxes, des vêtements à prix réduits cut-price clothing

rééducation NOUN FEM **physiotherapy**

réel, réelle ADJECTIVE MASC, FEM **real**

réellement ADVERB **really**

refaire VERB [10] ❶ **to redo**; je dois refaire mon devoir de maths I have to redo my maths homework, c'est tout à refaire it has to be completely redone, il ne faut pas refaire la même erreur we mustn't make the same mistake again ❷ **to make more**; elle est en train de refaire du café she's making some more coffee

référence NOUN FEM **reference**; faire référence à quelque chose to refer to something

réfléchi ADJECTIVE ❶ **reflexive** (verb) ❷ **considered** (decision)

réfléchir VERB [2] **to think**; il faut bien réfléchir avant d'accepter you should think carefully before accepting, j'ai réfléchi au problème I've thought about the problem

reflet NOUN MASC ❶ **reflection** ❷ des cheveux aux reflets blonds hair with blond highlights

refléter VERB [24] **to reflect**

réflexe NOUN MASC, ADJECTIVE **reflex**

réflexion NOUN FEM ❶ **thought** ❷ **comment**; il m'a fait des réflexions désagréables he made some nasty comments to me

refrain NOUN MASC **chorus**

réfrigérateur NOUN MASC **refrigerator**

refroidir VERB [2] **to cool down**

refroidissement NOUN MASC **drop in temperature**

refuge NOUN MASC ❶ **mountain hut** (for climbers) ❷ **animal sanctuary** ❸ **traffic island** ❹ **refuge**

réfugié, réfugiée NOUN MASC, FEM **refugee**

réfugier VERB [1] se réfugier **to take shelter, to take refuge**

refus NOUN MASC **refusal**
- ce n'est pas de refus I wouldn't say no; 'veux-tu boire quelque chose?' – 'ce n'est pas de refus' 'would you like a drink?' – 'I wouldn't say no'

refuser VERB [1] **① to refuse**; refuser de faire to refuse to do, elle a refusé de répondre she refused to answer **② to turn down**; ils ont refusé sa candidature they turned him down for the job

regagner VERB [1] nous avons regagné nos places we went back to our seats

régal NOUN MASC **feast**; ça a été un véritable régal it was a real feast

régaler VERB [1] on s'est vraiment régalé! the food was absolutely wonderful!

regard NOUN MASC **look**

regarder VERB [1] **① to look at**; je vais regarder la carte I'll look at the map **② to watch**; regarder la télé to watch telly, veux-tu regarder le film? do you want to watch the film? **③ to look**; regarder par la fenêtre to look out of the window, regarde! look! **④ to concern**; cela ne nous regarde pas that doesn't concern us, cela ne le regarde pas that's none of his business

régate NOUN FEM **regatta**

régime NOUN MASC **① diet**; un régime sans sel a salt-free diet, je fais un régime I'm on a diet **② un régime de bananes a bunch of bananas **③ régime

région NOUN FEM **region**; les vins de la région the local wines

régional ADJECTIVE MASC (PLURAL régioneaux) **regional**

registre NOUN MASC **register**

réglable ADJECTIVE **adjustable**

règle NOUN FEM **① ruler ② rule**; selon les règles according to the rules, les règles de sécurité the safety regulations, en règle générale as a general rule **③ en règle in order** (valid) **④ les règles period** (menstruation), j'ai mes règles I've got my period

règlement NOUN MASC **regulations**

régler VERB [24] **① to pay** (a debt or a bill); vous réglez comment, monsieur? how would you like to pay, sir? **② to sort out** (details or a problem) **③ to adjust**; on peut régler la hauteur you can adjust the height

réglisse NOUN FEM **liquorice**

règne NOUN MASC **reign**

régner VERB [24] **to reign**

regret NOUN MASC **regret**; avec/sans regret with/without regret, mille regrets I'm terribly sorry

regretter VERB [1] **① to be sorry**; je regrette I'm sorry, nous regrettons beaucoup de partir we're very sorry to be leaving **② to regret**; elles regrettent avoir quitté Paris they regret having left Paris, je ne regrette rien I have no regrets **③ to miss**; je regrette la vie à Paris I miss the Parisian way of life

regrouper VERB [1] **① to group together**; les débutants sont regroupés ensemble beginners are grouped together **② se regrouper to regroup**, les enfants se sont regroupés autour d'elle the children gathered around her

a
b
c
d
e
f
g
h
i
j
k
l
m
n
o
p
q
r
s
t
u
v
w
x
y
z

régularité NOUN FEM **regularity**

régulier, régulière ADJECTIVE MASC, FEM ❶ **regular**; à intervalles réguliers at regular intervals ❷ vols réguliers à New York scheduled flights to New York

régulièrement ADVERB **regularly**

rein NOUN MASC ❶ **kidney** ❷ les reins the back, j'ai mal aux reins I've got back-ache

reine NOUN FEM **queen**; la reine Elisabeth Queen Elizabeth

reine-claude NOUN FEM **greengage**

rejeter VERB [48] **to reject**

rejoindre VERB [49] ❶ **to meet up with**; je vous rejoins au bar I'll meet you in the bar ❷ **to join** (other people, a group, or a movement) ❸ se rejoindre to meet up, alors on se rejoint à onze heures? so shall we meet up at eleven? ❹ se rejoindre to merge (motorways, lanes)

rejouer VERB [1] **to replay**

relâcher VERB [1] ❶ **to loosen** (a grip or hold) ❷ **to set free** (a prisoner, hostage, or animal) ❸ **to relax** (your attention or discipline)

relais NOUN MASC ❶ **restaurant, hotel** ❷ prendre le relais (de quelqu'un) to take over (from someone), il a pris le relais au volant he took over the driving ❸ **relay race**

relatif, relative ADJECTIVE MASC, FEM **relative**

relation NOUN FEM ❶ **connection**; en relation avec in connection with ❷ **acquaintance**; une relation de mon frère an acquaintance of my brother's ❸ **relationship**; il a de

bonnes relations avec son patron he has a good relationship with his boss ❹ les relations publiques public relations

relativement ADVERB **relatively**; relativement à in relation to

relax ADJECTIVE (informal) **casual, laid back**

relaxer VERB [1] **to relax**

relent NOUN MASC **lingering smell**

relevé NOUN MASC ❶ faire le relevé de quelque chose to make a list of something ❷ un relevé de compte a bank statement

relever VERB [50] ❶ **to raise** ❷ relever la tête to look up ❸ **to notice** (details, mistakes, or interesting facts) ❹ relever le compteur to read the meter ❺ se relever to pick yourself up (after a fall)

relier VERB [1] ❶ **to link** ❷ **to match up**

religieux, religieuse NOUN MASC, FEM **monk, nun**

religieux, religeuse ADJECTIVE MASC, FEM **religious**

religion NOUN FEM **religion**

relire VERB [51] **to re-read, to read over**

remarié ADJECTIVE **remarried**

remarquable ADJECTIVE **remarkable, striking**

remarque NOUN FEM **remark, comment**

remarquer VERB [1] ❶ **to notice**; je n'ai rien remarqué I didn't notice anything, j'ai remarqué qu'elle

est arrivée en retard I noticed she
arrived late **②** se faire remarquer to
draw attention to yourself, il n'aime
pas se faire remarquer he doesn't
like drawing attention to himself
③ faire remarquer quelque chose
à quelqu'un to point something
out to somebody, elle lui a fait
remarquer que c'était déjà trop
tard she pointed out to him that it
was already too late

rembobiner *VERB* [1] **to rewind**

remboursement *NOUN MASC*
repayment, **refund**

rembourser *VERB* [1] **①** **to pay
back**; je te rembourserai demain
I'll pay you back tomorrow **②** **to
refund the price of**; ils m'ont
remboursé les billets they
refunded me the price of the
tickets **③** **to reimburse**; nous vous
rembourserons le voyage we'll pay
your travelling expenses

remède *NOUN MASC* **remedy**

remerciement *NOUN MASC* **thanks**;
tous mes remerciements many
thanks, une lettre de remerciement
a thank-you letter

remercier *VERB* [1] **①** **to thank**; je l'ai
remerciée pour les fleurs I thanked
her for the flowers **②** remercier
quelqu'un d'avoir fait quelque
chose to thank somebody for doing
something, il nous a remerciés
de l'avoir aidé he thanked us for
helping him

remettre *VERB* [11] **①** **to put back**;
remets la bouteille au frigo put the
bottle back in the fridge, il a remis
la photo sur la table he put the
photo back on the table, as-tu remis
tous les livres à leur place? have
you put all the books back in their

place? **②** **to put back on**; je vais
remettre ma veste I'm going to put
my jacket back on **③** **to hand over**;
pouvez-vous me remettre les clés
demain? can you hand over the keys
to me tomorrow? **④** **to put off**; ils
ont remis la réunion à jeudi they've
put the meeting off until Thursday
⑤ se remettre to start again, elle
s'est remise au piano she's started
playing the piano again, il s'est
remis à pleuvoir it's started raining
again **⑥** se remettre de to recover,
ils ne se sont toujours pas remis
du choc they still haven't recovered
from the shock

remise *NOUN FEM* **①** **handing out**;
la remise des prix the prizegiving
② **discount**; nous faisons une
remise de 20% sur tous les CD
we're giving a 20% discount on all
CDs **③** **garden shed**

remonte-pente *NOUN MASC* **ski lift**

remonter *VERB* [1] **①** **to go** (or
come) **back up**; Nathalie est
remontée dans sa chambre
Nathalie's gone back up to her
room, je descends à Londres ce soir
et je remonte lundi I'm going down
to London tonight and coming back
up on Monday **②** **to take** (or **bring**)
back up; veux-tu remonter les
chaises? would you take the chairs
back upstairs? **③** **to put back up**;
il m'a remonté ma valise au filet he
put my case up in the luggage rack
for me **④** remonter la pente to go
back up the hill **⑤** **to get** or **climb
back in**; ils sont remontés dans le
car they got back into the coach
⑥ remonter quelqu'un, remonter
le moral à quelqu'un to cheer
someone up

remords *NOUN MASC* **remorse**

remorque NOUN FEM ❶ **trailer** (for a car) ❷ **tow-rope**

remplaçant, **remplaçante** NOUN MASC, FEM ❶ **replacement** (for another person) ❷ **supply teacher**

remplacer VERB [61] ❶ **to stand in for** (a person) ❷ **to replace**; il faut remplacer les piles you need to replace the batteries

remplir VERB [2] ❶ **to fill**; il a rempli son verre de vin he filled his glass with wine, la salle était remplie de jeunes the hall was full of young people ❷ remplir un formulaire to fill in a form ❸ **to carry out** (a duty or a role)

remue-ménage NOUN MASC **commotion**

remuer VERB [1] ❶ **to move** (your head or hand, for example); le vent remuait les branches the wind was shaking the branches ❷ **to stir**; peux-tu remuer la sauce, s'il te plaît? can you stir the sauce, please?

rémunérer VERB [24] **to pay** (a person), **to pay for** (work)

renard NOUN MASC **fox**

rencontre NOUN FEM ❶ **meeting**; elle est venue à ma rencontre she came to meet me ❷ (in sport) **match**; la rencontre entre la France et l'Allemagne the match between France and Germany

rencontrer VERB [1] ❶ **to meet** (a person); je l'ai rencontrée en 1993 I met her in 1993 ❷ **to play** (an opponent or a team) ❸ se rencontrer to meet, nous nous sommes rencontrés à Londres we met in London

rendez-vous NOUN MASC
❶ **appointment**; prendre rendez-vous to make an appointment, j'ai rendez-vous chez le dentiste I've got a dentist's appointment, le médecin voit les malades sur rendez-vous the doctor sees patients by appointment ❷ **date**; Marc a rendez-vous avec sa copine à trois heures Marc's got a date with his girlfriend at three ❸ donner rendez-vous à quelqu'un to arrange to meet somebody, il m'a donné rendez-vous au café he arranged to meet me at the cafe

rendormir VERB [37] se rendormir to go back to sleep, elle s'est rendormie she went back to sleep

rendre VERB [3] ❶ **to give back**; je te rendrai les clés demain I'll give you back the keys tomorrow ❷ rendre quelqu'un heureux to make somebody happy ❸ **to hand in** (homework) ❹ se rendre to give oneself up, to surrender, les voleurs se sont rendus à la police the thieves gave themselves up to the police ❺ se rendre compte de quelque chose to realize something, je me suis rendu compte du fait que j'avais oublié mes clés I realized I had forgotten my keys

renifler VERB [1] **to sniff**

renne NOUN MASC **reindeer**

renommé ADJECTIVE **famous**

renoncer VERB [61] ❶ **to give up**; c'est trop difficile, je renonce! it's too difficult, I give up! ❷ renoncer à quelque chose to give something up

renouveler VERB [18] **to renew** (a passport or a subscription, for example)

rénover *VERB* [1] ❶ **to renovate** *(a house)* ❷ **to restore** *(furniture)*

renseignement *NOUN MASC*
❶ un renseignement a piece of information, un renseignement utile a useful piece of information ❷ les renseignements information, je cherche des renseignements I'm looking for information, adressez-vous aux renseignements ask at the information desk ❸ renseignements directory enquiries

renseigner *VERB* [1] ❶ renseigner quelqu'un to give someone information, la brochure vous renseigne sur les horaires the brochure gives you timetable information, il était très bien renseigné sur le projet he was very well-informed about the project ❷ se renseigner to find out, je vais me renseigner au bureau de tourisme I'm going to find out at the tourist office

rentable *ADJECTIVE* **profitable**

rentrée *NOUN FEM* la rentrée (des classes) the start of the new school year

rentrer *VERB* [1] ❶ **to get home**; Maman rentre à dix-huit heures Mum will be home at six, je vais rentrer chez moi I'm going home ❷ **to get back**; ils rentrent de Paris jeudi they'll be back from Paris on Thursday ❸ **to come** *(or go)* **in**; rentrez! do come in!, elles sont rentrées dans un magasin they've gone into a shop ❹ rentrer dans quelque chose to go in something, tout ça ne rentrera jamais dans ton sac! all that will never go in your bag! ❺ rentrer dans quelque chose to crash into something, la voiture

est rentrée dans un mur the car crashed into a wall ❻ rentrer quelque chose to bring something in *(from outside)*, rentre les chaises, il pleut! bring the chairs in, it's raining!

renverser *VERB* [1] ❶ **to knock over**; il a renversé sa chaise he knocked his chair over ❷ être renversé par une voiture to be knocked down by a car ❸ **to spill**; j'ai renversé mon thé I've spilled my tea

renvoyer *VERB* [40] ❶ **to send back**; as-tu renvoyé le formulaire? have you sent back the form?, on m'a renvoyé à l'hôpital they sent me back to hospital ❷ **to throw back** *(a ball)* ❸ **to dismiss**; la secrétaire a été renvoyée the secretary has been dismissed

réouverture *NOUN FEM* **reopening**

répandu *ADJECTIVE* **widespread**

réparation *NOUN FEM* **repair**

réparer *VERB* [1] **to repair**

repartir *VERB* [58] ❶ **to go off again**; ils ont déposé les enfants et ils sont repartis they dropped the children and went off again ❷ **to go again**; je suis reparti chez moi I went home again ❸ repartir à zéro to start from scratch

repas *NOUN MASC* **meal**; le repas de midi lunch, le repas du soir the evening meal

repassage *NOUN MASC* **ironing**

repasser *VERB* [1] ❶ **to drop in again**; il a dit qu'il repasserait demain he said he'd drop in again tomorrow ❷ **to iron**; Frank est en train de repasser sa chemise Frank's busy ironing his shirt, une planche à repasser an ironing board ❸ **to resit** *(an exam or test)* ❹ **to replay** *(a video)*

repeindre *VERB* [60] **to repaint**

repère *NOUN MASC* un point de repère a landmark, a reference point

repérer *VERB* [24] ❶ *(informal)* **to spot**; j'ai repéré trois erreurs dans son article I spotted three mistakes in his article ❷ **to locate** *(a place)*

répertoire *NOUN MASC* **notebook** *(with a thumb index)*; un répertoire d'adresses an address book

répéter *VERB* [24] ❶ **to repeat**; elle l'a répété trois fois she repeated it three times, faire des essais répétés to make repeated attempts ❷ **to rehearse** *(a play)* ❸ **to practise** *(a piece of music)* ❹ se répéter to repeat oneself ❺ se répéter to happen again, espérons que cela ne se répètera pas let's hope it doesn't happen again

répétition *NOUN FEM* ❶ **rehearsal**; la répétition générale the dress rehearsal ❷ **repetition**

replier *VERB* [1] ❶ **to fold up**; elle a replié la carte she folded up the map *(a sheet)* ❷ elle a replié ses jambes she tucked her legs up *(under her)*

répondeur *NOUN MASC* **answering machine**; j'ai laissé un message sur le répondeur I left a message on the answering machine

répondre *VERB* [3] ❶ **to answer**; il n'a pas répondu he didn't answer, je ne lui ai pas répondu I didn't answer him ❷ répondre à une question to answer a question ❸ répondre à une lettre to reply to a letter

réponse *NOUN FEM* **answer**; donner la bonne/mauvaise réponse to give the right/wrong answer

reportage *NOUN MASC* ❶ **report**; un reportage sur la drogue a report on drugs ❷ **(news) story**

reporter¹ *VERB* [1] **to postpone**; on a reporté le match à jeudi the match has been postponed until Thursday

reporter² *NOUN MASC* **reporter**

repos *NOUN MASC* **rest**; dix jours de repos ten days' rest

reposant *ADJECTIVE* **restful**

reposer *VERB* [1] ❶ reposer quelque chose to put something back down, elle a reposé le livre sur la table she put the book back down on the table ❷ se reposer to have a rest, j'ai besoin de me reposer I need a rest, repose-toi bien! have a good rest!

repousser *VERB* [1] ❶ **to grow again**; tes cheveux ont vite repoussé your hair's grown quickly ❷ **to push back** ❸ **to postpone**; le match a été repoussé the match has been postponed

reprendre *VERB* [64] ❶ **to have some more** *(food or drink)*; reprends du poulet have some more chicken ❷ **to take back**; est-ce que je peux reprendre les verres que je t'avais prêtés? can I take back the glasses I lent you? ❸ **to start again**; l'école reprend en septembre school starts again in September ❹ reprendre le travail to go back to work, j'ai repris le travail lundi I went back to work on Monday ❺ reprendre la route to set off again

représentant, **représentante** *NOUN MASC, FEM* **sales rep**

représentation *NOUN FEM* **performance** *(of a play)*; prochaine représentation à 20h next performance 8 p.m

représenter *VERB* [1] ❶ **to depict** ❷ **to represent**

réprimander *VERB* [1] **to tell off, to reprimand**

réprimer *VERB* [1] **to suppress**

reprise *NOUN FEM* ❶ **resumption** *(of work or discussions)* ❷ **rerun** *(of a play or film)*, **repeat** *(of a broadcast)* ❸ à plusieurs reprises **on several occasions**

reproche *NOUN MASC* **criticism**; il m'a fait des reproches he criticized me

reprocher *VERB* [1] ❶ **to criticize**; il a reproché à son fils de ne pas travailler he criticized his son for not working ❷ se reprocher **to blame oneself**

reproduction *NOUN FEM* **reproduction**

reproduire *VERB* [26] ❶ **to reproduce** ❷ se reproduire **to happen again**

républicain *ADJECTIVE* **republican**

république *NOUN FEM* **republic**; la République française the French Republic

répugnant *ADJECTIVE* **revolting**

réputation *NOUN FEM* **reputation**; il a la réputation d'être très sévère he has a reputation for being very strict

requin *NOUN MASC* **shark**

RER *NOUN MASC (short for réseau express régional)* **the fast suburban network on the Paris underground**

rescousse *NOUN FEM* aller à la rescousse de quelqu'un to go to someone's rescue

réseau *NOUN MASC (PLURAL* réseaux*)* **network**

réservation *NOUN FEM* **reservation**

réserve *NOUN FEM* ❶ **stock**; des réserves de charbon stocks of coal, j'ai deux bouteilles en réserve I have put aside two bottles ❷ **reserve** *(for birds or animals)*; une réserve ornithologique a bird sanctuary

réservé *ADJECTIVE* **reserved**

réserver *VERB* [1] ❶ **to reserve, to book**; j'ai réservé deux places pour ce soir I've booked two seats for this evening ❷ **to keep**; Philippe t'a réservé du poulet Philippe's kept some chicken for you

réservoir *NOUN MASC* ❶ **tank**; réservoir à essence petrol tank ❷ **reservoir**

résidence *NOUN FEM* ❶ **home, residence**; une résidence secondaire a holiday home ❷ **block of flats**

résidence universitaire *NOUN FEM* **hall of residence**

résident, **résidente** *NOUN MASC, FEM* **resident**

résidentiel, **résidentielle** *ADJECTIVE MASC, FEM* **residential**

résistant, **résistante** *NOUN MASC, FEM* **Resistance fighter** *(in France during World War II)*

a
b
c
d
e
f
g
h
i
j
k
l
m
n
o
p
q
r
s
t
u
v
w
x
y
z

résistant ADJECTIVE **tough**

résister VERB [1] résister à to resist

résolu ADJECTIVE **❶ determined**; elle est résolue à démissionner she is determined to resign **❷ resolved**; le problème est résolu the problem is resolved

résoudre VERB [67] **❶ to solve** *(a problem)* **❷** se résoudre à faire to make up one's mind to do, elle s'est résolue à partir she made up her mind to leave

respect NOUN MASC **respect**

respecter VERB [1] **to respect**

respectueux, respectueuse ADJECTIVE MASC, FEM **respectful**

respiration NOUN FEM **breathing**

respirer VERB [1] **to breathe**

responsabilité NOUN FEM **❶ responsibility ❷** avoir la responsabilité de quelque chose to be responsible for something, il a la responsabilité des livraisons he's responsible for deliveries

responsable NOUN MASC & FEM **❶ person in charge**; le responsable du projet the person in charge of the project **❷ person responsible**; les responsables de la catastrophe those responsible for the disaster

responsable ADJECTIVE **responsible**; il est responsable de l'accident he's responsible for the accident

ressemblance NOUN FEM **similarity**

ressembler VERB [1] **❶** ressembler à to look like, elle ressemble beaucoup à sa mère she looks very like her mother, cela ressemble à

du bois mais c'est du plastique it looks like wood but it's plastic **❷** se ressembler to be alike, les deux sœurs ne se ressemblent pas du tout the two sisters are not at all alike

ressentiment NOUN MASC **resentment**

resserrer VERB [1] **❶ to tighten** *(a knot or screw, for example)* **❷** se resserrer to move closer together, resserrez-vous un peu! squeeze up a bit!

resservir VERB [58] **❶ to give another helping**; je vous ressers un peu? shall I give you a little more? **❷** se resservir to help yourself to more, ressers-toi de la salade help yourself to some more salad, je me suis déjà resservi, merci I've already helped myself to more, thank you

ressort NOUN MASC **spring** *(in a bed or a chair)*

ressortir VERB [58] **to go out again**; il est revenu pour les clés et il est ressorti he came back for the keys and went out again

ressource NOUN FEM **❶ resource**; des ressources énergétiques energy resources **❷** il est sans ressources he has no means of support

restaurant NOUN MASC **restaurant**; on mange au restaurant ce soir we're going out for a meal tonight

restauration NOUN FEM **❶ catering**; la restauration rapide the fast-food industry **❷ restoration**

restaurer VERB [1] **to restore**

reste NOUN MASC **❶** le reste the rest, le reste du temps the rest of the time, et tout le reste, tu le sais déjà and you know all the rest already ❷ les restes the leftovers, j'ai fait un curry avec les restes du poulet I made a curry with the leftover chicken

rester *VERB* [1] ❶ **to stay**; reste là, je reviens tout de suite! stay there, I'll be right back!, Camille est restée à la maison Camille stayed at home, je ne peux pas rester longtemps I can't stay long, hier je suis resté sans manger I didn't have anything to eat yesterday ❷ rester debout to remain standing, je préfère rester debout I prefer to stand ❸ rester assis to remain seated, je suis resté assis toute la journée I've been sitting down all day ❹ **to be left**; il reste du fromage there's some cheese left, il nous reste combien d'argent? how much money have we got left?, il ne reste pas beaucoup à faire there's not much left to do

restriction *NOUN FEM* **restriction**

résultat *NOUN MASC* **result**; les résultats des examens the exam results

résulter *VERB* [1] résulter de to result from

résumé *NOUN MASC* **summary, résumé**

résumer *VERB* [1] **to summarize, to sum up**

rétablir *VERB* [2] ❶ **to restore** ❷ se rétablir to recover *(after an illness)*

retaper *VERB* [1] **to do up** *(a house)*

retard *NOUN MASC* ❶ **delay**; ils annoncent un retard d'une heure sur notre vol they say there's an hour's delay on our flight, sans

retard without delay ❷ avoir du retard to be late, excusez mon retard I'm sorry I'm late, ils sont arrivés avec trois heures de retard they arrived three hours late ❸ être en retard to be late, nous sommes en retard we're late

retarder *VERB* [1] ❶ **to hold up, to delay**; la grève nous a retardés the strike held us up, l'avion était retardé the plane was delayed ❷ **to put off, to postpone**; il a retardé son départ he put off his departure

retenir *VERB* [77] ❶ **to hold up**; j'ai été retenu au bureau I was held up at the office, je ne vous retiendrai pas longtemps I won't keep you long ❷ retenir son souffle to hold your breath, elle ne pouvait pas retenir ses larmes she couldn't hold back her tears ❸ **to book**; j'ai retenu des places I've booked seats ❹ **to remember**; je ne retiens jamais leur adresse I can never remember their address

retenue *NOUN FEM* **detention**

réticence *NOUN FEM* ❶ **reluctance** ❷ **reticence**

retirer *VERB* [1] ❶ **to take off**; je vais d'abord retirer ma veste I'll take my jacket off first ❷ **to take away**; ils ont retiré son permis they took away his licence ❸ retirer de l'argent to take out some money *(from your bank account)*

retouche *NOUN FEM* **alteration** *(to a garment)*

retour *NOUN MASC* ❶ **return**; un billet aller-retour a return ticket, dès mon retour as soon as I get back ❷ être de retour to be back, elle sera de retour vers onze heures she'll be back about eleven

retourner VERB [1] ❶ to go back; elle est retournée à l'école she went back to school, je n'y suis jamais retourné I've never been back there ❷ to turn over; est-ce que je retourne les steaks? shall I turn the steaks over? ❸ to overturn

retraite NOUN FEM retirement; prendre sa retraite to retire, une maison de retraite an old people's home

retraité, retraitée NOUN MASC, FEM pensioner

rétrécir VERB [2] to shrink

retrousser VERB [1] ❶ to hitch up ❷ to roll up; il a retroussé ses manches he rolled up his sleeves

retrouver VERB [1] ❶ to find; as-tu retrouvé tes clés? did you find your keys? ❷ to meet; je te retrouve à la sortie I'll meet you at the exit ❸ se retrouver to meet, on se retrouve devant le cinéma? shall we meet outside the cinema?, on se retrouvera à Noël we'll see each other again at Christmas ❹ se retrouver to end up, on s'est retrouvé chez Amanda we ended up at Amanda's place ❺ se retrouver to find one's way around, je n'arrive jamais à me retrouver à Londres I can never find my way around London

rétroviseur, rétro NOUN MASC rearview mirror

réunion NOUN FEM ❶ meeting ❷ reunion ❸ gathering ❹ reunification

réunir VERB [2] se réunir to meet, on s'est réuni pour discuter du problème we met to discuss the problem

réussi ADJECTIVE successful

réussir VERB [2] ❶ to succeed; j'espère qu'elle va réussir I hope she'll succeed ❷ réussir un examen to pass an exam ❸ to be successful; ça a très bien réussi that was very successful ❹ réussir à faire to manage to do, je n'ai pas réussi à les persuader I didn't manage to persuade them

réussite NOUN FEM success

réutilisable ADJECTIVE reusable

revanche NOUN FEM ❶ return match ❷ prendre sa revanche to get your own back ❸ en revanche on the other hand

rêve NOUN MASC dream; faire un rêve to have a dream, votre maison de rêve your dream house

réveil NOUN MASC alarm clock

réveille-matin NOUN MASC alarm clock

réveiller VERB [1] ❶ réveiller quelqu'un to wake somebody up, elle m'a réveillé à sept heures she woke me at seven ❷ se réveiller to wake up, d'habitude je me réveille à sept heures I usually wake up at seven

réveillon NOUN MASC le réveillon du Nouvel An the New Year's Eve celebrations

réveillonner VERB [1] ❶ to celebrate Christmas Eve ❷ to see the New Year in

révéler VERB [24] to reveal

revenant, revenante NOUN MASC, FEM ghost

revendre VERB [3] to sell, to resell

revenir *VERB* [81] ❶ to come back; elles sont revenues très tard they came back very late, tu reviendras nous voir? will you come back and see us? ❷ to come to; ça revient à quinze euros that comes to fifteen euros, ça revient au même it comes to the same thing ❸ je n'en reviens pas! I can't get over it!

revenu *NOUN MASC* income

rêver *VERB* [1] to dream

réverbère *NOUN MASC* street lamp

revers *NOUN MASC* ❶ lapel (on a jacket), turn-up (of trousers), cuff (on a sleeve) ❷ backhand (in tennis) ❸ setback ❹ le revers de la médaille the other side of the coin

réviser *VERB* [1] ❶ to revise ❷ to service (a car or machine)

révision *NOUN FEM* ❶ revision ❷ service (for a car)

revoici *PREPOSITION* (informal) me revoici! here I am again!

revoir[1] *VERB* [13] ❶ to see again; et nous ne l'avons jamais revue and we never saw her again ❷ to revise; je dois revoir ma chimie I have to revise my chemistry

revoir[2] *NOUN MASC* au revoir goodbye

révoltant *ADJECTIVE* appalling

révolte *NOUN FEM* revolt, rebellion

révolter *VERB* [1] to appal

révolution *NOUN FEM* revolution

révolutionner *VERB* [1] to revolutionize

revolver *NOUN MASC* revolver, handgun

revouloir *VERB* [14] to have a second helping of; est-ce que tu reveux des frites? would you like a second helping of chips?

revue *NOUN FEM* magazine; une revue d'art an art magazine, une revue scientifique a scientific journal

rez-de-chaussée *NOUN MASC* ground floor (literally: level with the road); la réception est au rez-de-chaussée reception is on the ground floor

RF *ABBREVIATION* (short for République française) French Republic

Rhin *NOUN MASC* le Rhin the Rhine

rhinocéros *NOUN MASC* rhinoceros

rhubarbe *NOUN FEM* rhubarb

rhum *NOUN MASC* rum

rhume *NOUN MASC* cold; attraper un rhume to catch a cold, un rhume de cerveau a head cold

rhume des foins *NOUN MASC* hay fever

ri *VERB* ▸ SEE **rire**

ricaner *VERB* [1] to snigger, to giggle

riche *ADJECTIVE* ❶ well-off; nous ne sommes pas très riches we're not terribly well-off ❷ rich; riche en vitamines rich in vitamins

richesse *NOUN FEM* ❶ wealth ❷ les richesses naturelles natural resources

ride *NOUN FEM* wrinkle (on skin), ripple (on water)

rideau *NOUN MASC* (PLURAL rideaux) curtain

ridicule *ADJECTIVE* ridiculous; mais c'est totalement ridicule! but that's completely ridiculous!

rien[1] *PRONOUN* **❶ nothing**; 'qu'est-ce qu'elle a dit?' – 'rien' 'what did she say?' – 'nothing', il n'a rien he has nothing, je n'ai rien vu I didn't see anything, ce n'est rien it's nothing, il ne reste plus rien there's nothing left, rien du tout nothing at all, 'merci' – 'de rien' 'thank you' – 'it's nothing', rien d'autre nothing else, rien de bon nothing good **❷ rien que** just, rien que les livres pèsent 20 kilos the books by themselves weigh 20 kilos, 'que reste-t-il à faire?' – 'rien que la vaisselle' 'what's left to do?' – 'just the washing-up'
• rien à faire! it's no good!

rien[2] *NOUN MASC* **little thing**; elle se met à hurler pour un rien the slightest thing starts her shouting

rigide *ADJECTIVE* **rigid, stiff**

rigoler *VERB* [1] (informal) **❶ to laugh**; elle en a beaucoup rigolé she had a good laugh about it **❷ to have a good time**; nous avons bien rigolé we had a great time **❸ to be joking**; je rigolais! I was only joking!

rigolo, rigolote *ADJECTIVE MASC, FEM* (informal) **funny**

rigoureux, rigoureuse *ADJECTIVE MASC, FEM* **❶ rigorous ❷ strict ❸ harsh**

rillettes *PLURAL NOUN FEM* les rillettes de porc potted pork

rime *NOUN FEM* **rhyme**

rimer *VERB* [1] **to rhyme**

rincer *VERB* [61] **to rinse**; se rincer les cheveux to rinse one's hair

rire *NOUN MASC* **laughter**; un rire a laugh

rire *VERB* [68] **❶ to laugh**; il nous fait rire he makes us laugh **❷ to have fun**; on va rire ce soir we'll have some fun this evening, c'était pour rire it was meant as a joke

ris *NOUN MASC* les ris de veau calf's sweetbreads

risque *NOUN MASC* **risk**; risque d'incendie fire risk, c'est sans risque it's safe

risqué *ADJECTIVE* **risky**

risquer *VERB* [1] **❶ to risk**; vas-y, tu ne risques rien go on, it's quite safe **❷** il risque de pleuvoir it might well rain, tu risques de te brûler you might burn yourself

rivage *NOUN MASC* **shore**

rival, rivale *NOUN MASC, FEM* (PLURAL rivaux) **rival**

rive *NOUN FEM* **❶ bank** (of a river); la Rive gauche the Left Bank (when talking about the Seine in Paris and other rivers which flow through cities, the left bank is the left side of the river when you are facing downstream) **❷ shore** (by the sea)

rivière *NOUN FEM* **river**

riz *NOUN MASC* **rice**; riz cantonais fried rice, gâteau de riz rice pudding

RN *ABBREVIATION FEM* (short for route nationale) **A road**

robe *NOUN FEM* **dress**; une robe d'été a summer dress, une robe de mariée a wedding dress

robe de chambre *NOUN FEM* **dressing gown**

robinet *NOUN MASC* **tap**; l'eau du robinet tap water

robot *NOUN MASC* **robot**; robot ménager food processor

robuste *ADJECTIVE* **robust**, **sturdy**

roche *NOUN FEM* **rock**

rocher *NOUN MASC* **rock**

rock *NOUN MASC* **rock (music)**

rôder *VERB* [1] **to prowl**

rognons *PLURAL NOUN MASC* **kidneys** *(for cooking)*

roi *NOUN MASC* **king**; le roi Charles King Charles, les Rois mages the Three Wise Men, la fête des Rois Twelfth Night

rôle *NOUN MASC* **role**

roller *NOUN MASC* **❶ roller-skating ❷ roller-skate**

romain *ADJECTIVE* **Roman**

roman *NOUN MASC* **novel**; un roman policier a detective story

romancier, romancière *NOUN MASC, FEM* **novelist**

romantique *ADJECTIVE* **romantic**

romarin *NOUN MASC* **rosemary**

rompre *VERB* [69] **to split up**; Claire et David ont rompu Claire and David have split up, Anne a rompu avec son copain Anne's broken up with her boyfriend, rompre ses fiançailles to break off your engagement

ronce *NOUN FEM* **bramble**

rond *NOUN MASC* **circle**; tourner en rond to go round in circles

rond *ADJECTIVE* **round**

rondelle *NOUN FEM* **❶ slice**; une rondelle de tomate a slice of tomato **❷ washer** *(for a tap or screw)*

rond-point *NOUN MASC* **roundabout**

ronfler *VERB* [1] **to snore**

ronger *VERB* [52] **❶ to gnaw ❷** se ronger les ongles to bite one's nails

ronronner *VERB* [1] **to purr**

rosbif *NOUN MASC* **roast beef**

rose *NOUN FEM* **rose**

rose *ADJECTIVE* **pink**; rose pâle pale pink

rosé *NOUN MASC* **rosé (wine)**; un verre de rosé a glass of rosé

rosée *NOUN FEM* **dew**

rosier *NOUN MASC* **rosebush**

rossignol *NOUN MASC* **nightingale**

rôti *NOUN MASC* **roast**; du rôti de bœuf roast beef, un rôti de bœuf a joint of beef

rôtir *VERB* [2] **to roast**

roucouler *VERB* [1] **to coo**

roue *NOUN FEM* **wheel**; la roue de secours the spare wheel
• faire la roue to turn a cartwheel

rouge *NOUN MASC* **❶ (the colour) red**; le rouge ne me va pas red doesn't suit me **❷ red traffic light**; il est passé au rouge he jumped the lights, le feu est passé au rouge the light changed to red **❸ red wine**; un verre de rouge a glass of red wine

rouge *ADJECTIVE* **red**; tes chaussettes rouges your red socks

rouge à lèvres *NOUN MASC* **lipstick**

rouge-gorge *NOUN MASC* **robin**

rougeur *NOUN FEM* **redness**

a
b
c
d
e
f
g
h
i
j
k
l
m
n
o
p
q
r
s
t
u
v
w
x
y
z

rougir VERB [2] ❶ to blush ❷ to turn red

rouille NOUN FEM rust

rouillé ADJECTIVE rusty

rouiller, se rouiller VERB [1] to go rusty

roulade NOUN FEM ❶ stuffed rolled meat ❷ somersault, roll

roulant ADJECTIVE un fauteuil roulant a wheelchair

rouleau NOUN MASC (PLURAL **rouleaux**) roll; un rouleau d'essuie-tout a roll of kitchen towel

rouleau à pâtisserie NOUN MASC rolling pin

rouler VERB [1] ❶ to go; nous roulons très vite we're going very fast ❷ to drive; il faut rouler à droite en France in France you must drive on the right, nous avons roulé toute la nuit we drove all night ❸ to roll ❹ to roll up; il faut rouler le tapis we must roll up the carpet ❺ (informal) to cheat; on m'a roulé! I've been done!

Roumanie NOUN FEM Romania

rousse ADJECTIVE ▸ SEE **roux**

route NOUN FEM ❶ road; une grande route a main road, un accident de la route a road accident, Rouen est à trois heures de route d'ici Rouen is three hours' drive from here ❷ route; il a changé de route à cause de la neige he changed his route because of the snow ❸ en route on the way, être en route to be on the way, nous sommes en route pour Nice we're on our way to Nice ❹ se mettre en route to set off ❺ bonne route! safe journey!

route à quatre voies NOUN FEM dual carriageway

route départementale NOUN FEM secondary road, B road

route nationale NOUN FEM A road

routier, routière NOUN MASC, FEM lorry driver

routier, routière ADJECTIVE MASC, FEM road; le transport routier road transport, la gare routière the bus station

routine NOUN FEM routine

roux, rousse ADJECTIVE MASC, FEM red-haired, ginger

royal ADJECTIVE MASC (PLURAL **royaux**) royal

royaume NOUN MASC kingdom

Royaume-Uni NOUN MASC United Kingdom

ruban NOUN MASC ribbon

ruban adhésif NOUN MASC sticky tape

rubéole NOUN FEM German measles

ruche NOUN FEM beehive

rudement ADVERB (informal) really; il est rudement bon ton gâteau your cake's really good

rue NOUN FEM street; une rue piétonne a pedestrian street
• mettre quelqu'un à la rue to put someone out on the street

rugby NOUN MASC rugby; jouer au rugby to play rugby

rugbyman NOUN MASC (PLURAL rugbymen) rugby player

ruine NOUN FEM **ruin**; une maison en ruine(s) a ruined house

ruiner VERB [1] **to ruin**

ruisseau NOUN MASC (PLURAL ruisseaux) **stream**

rumeur NOUN FEM ❶ **rumour** ❷ **murmur**

rumsteck NOUN MASC **rump steak**

rupture NOUN FEM **break-up**

rural ADJECTIVE MASC (PLURAL ruraux) **country**; la vie rurale country life

ruse NOUN FEM ❶ **trick**; les ruses du métier the tricks of the trade ❷ **cunning**

rusé ADJECTIVE **cunning**, **crafty**

russe NOUN MASC **Russian** (language)

russe ADJECTIVE **Russian**

Russe NOUN MASC, FEM **Russian** (person)

Russie NOUN FEM **Russia**

rythme NOUN MASC **rhythm**; marquer le rythme to beat time

Ss

s' PRONOUN ▸ SEE **se**

sa ADJECTIVE ▸ SEE **son**[1]

sable NOUN MASC **sand**

sablé NOUN MASC **shortbread biscuit**

sablé ADJECTIVE la pâte sablée shortcrust pastry

sac NOUN MASC ❶ **bag**; un sac de sucre a bag of sugar, un sac de sport a sports bag ❷ **sack**; un sac de charbon a sack of coal
- vider son sac (informal) to get something off one's chest (literally: to empty one's bag)

sac à dos NOUN MASC **rucksack**

sac à main NOUN MASC **handbag**

sac de congélation NOUN MASC **freezer bag**

sac de couchage NOUN MASC **sleeping bag**

sachet NOUN MASC **sachet**; un sachet de thé a teabag

sacoche NOUN FEM ❶ **bag**; la sacoche du facteur the postman's bag ❷ **pannier** (for a bike)

sacré ADJECTIVE ❶ (informal) c'est un sacré problème it's a hell of a problem, elle a eu une sacrée chance she's been damn lucky ❷ **sacred**

a
b
c
d
e
f
g
h
i
j
k
l
m
n
o
p
q
r
s
t
u
v
w
x
y
z

sacrifice NOUN MASC **sacrifice**

sacrifier VERB [1] **to sacrifice**

sage ADJECTIVE ❶ **good, well-behaved**; Tom, sois sage be a good boy, Tom ❷ **wise, sensible**; il serait sage de se renseigner sur le prix it would be wise to enquire about the price

sage-femme NOUN FEM **midwife**

sagesse NOUN FEM **wisdom**; une dent de sagesse a wisdom tooth

Sagittaire NOUN MASC **Sagittarius** (sign of the Zodiac)

saignant ADJECTIVE **rare** (beef)

saigner VERB [1] **to bleed**

sain ADJECTIVE **healthy**
• sain et sauf safe and sound

saint, sainte NOUN MASC, FEM **saint**

saint ADJECTIVE **holy**; le Saint-Esprit the Holy Spirit, le vendredi saint Good Friday, la Sainte Vierge the Virgin Mary

Saint-Jacques NOUN une coquille Saint-Jacques a scallop

Saint-Jean NOUN FEM **Midsummer's Day** (June 24th)

Saint-Sylvestre NOUN FEM **New Year's Eve**

Saint-Valentin NOUN FEM **St Valentine's Day**

sais VERB ▸ SEE **savoir**[1]

saisir VERB [2] ❶ **to grab**; il m'a saisi par le bras he grabbed my arm ❷ saisir l'occasion **to seize the opportunity** ❸ **to understand**; je n'ai pas tout à fait saisi ... I didn't entirely understand ... ❹ **to catch** (to hear); je n'ai pas saisi votre nom I didn't catch your name

saison NOUN FEM **season**; il fait froid pour la saison it's cold for the time of year

sait VERB ▸ SEE **savoir**[1]

salade NOUN FEM ❶ **lettuce**; une salade a lettuce ❷ **salad**; une salade de fruits a fruit salad

saladier NOUN MASC **salad bowl**

salaire NOUN MASC **salary, wages**

salarié, salariée NOUN MASC, FEM **salaried employee**

sale ADJECTIVE ❶ (after the noun) **dirty**; les mains sales dirty hands ❷ (before the noun) (informal) **horrible**; quel sale temps! what horrible weather!, il a une sale tête he looks awful

salé ADJECTIVE ❶ **salty**; la sauce est un peu trop salée the sauce is a bit salty ❷ **savoury**; des petits gâteaux salés savoury biscuits ❸ du beurre salé salt butter

saler VERB [1] **to salt**

saleté NOUN FEM **dirt**

salir VERB [2] **to dirty, to get (something) dirty**; tu vas salir ta robe you'll get your dress dirty

salive NOUN FEM **saliva**

salle NOUN FEM ❶ **room** ('salle' by itself is no longer used to mean a room in a house) ❷ **dining-room** (in a restaurant) ❸ **hall** ❹ **auditorium** (in a theatre or cinema)

salle à manger NOUN FEM ❶ **dining room** ❷ **dining-room suite**

salle d'attente NOUN FEM **waiting room**

salle d'eau NOUN FEM **shower room**

salle de bains NOUN FEM **bathroom**

salle de classe NOUN FEM **classroom**

salle de jeux NOUN FEM **games room**

salle d'embarquement NOUN FEM **departure lounge**

salle de séjour NOUN FEM **living room**

salle des fêtes NOUN FEM **community centre**

salon NOUN MASC ❶ **sitting room** ❷ **living-room suite** ❸ **trade fair** ❹ **salon**; salon de coiffure hair salon

salon de thé NOUN MASC **tea-room**

salopette NOUN FEM ❶ **dungarees** ❷ **overalls**

saluer VERB [1] ❶ **to say hello to**; je l'ai salué, mais il ne m'a pas entendu I said hello to him but he didn't hear, elle l'a salué de la main she waved at him ❷ **to say goodbye to**

salut GREETING MASC **Hi!**

samedi NOUN MASC ❶ **Saturday**; samedi prochain next Saturday, samedi dernier last Saturday ❷ **on Saturday**; samedi soir on Saturday evening ❸ le samedi on Saturdays, fermé le samedi closed on Saturdays ❹ tous les samedis every Saturday

SAMU NOUN MASC (short for Service d'assistance médicale d'urgence) **ambulance service**

sandale NOUN FEM **sandal**

sandwich NOUN MASC **sandwich**; un sandwich au jambon a ham sandwich

sandwicherie NOUN FEM **snack bar**

sang NOUN MASC **blood**; être en sang to be covered in blood

sang-froid NOUN MASC **calm**

sanglier NOUN MASC **wild boar**

sanglot NOUN MASC **sob**; éclater en sanglots to burst into tears

sanisette NOUN FEM **automatic public lavatory**

sanitaire ADJECTIVE les conditions sanitaires sanitary conditions, les règlements sanitaires health regulations

sanitaire NOUN MASC les sanitaires the toilet block (in a campsite)

sans PREPOSITION **without**; une maison sans téléphone a house without a telephone, un café sans sucre a coffee with no sugar, sans hésiter without hesitating

sans-abri NOUN MASC & FEM **homeless person**; les sans-abri the homeless

sans-emploi NOUN MASC & FEM **unemployed person**; les sans-emploi the unemployed

santé NOUN FEM ❶ **health**; être en bonne santé to be in good health ❷ à votre santé! cheers!

sapeur-pompier NOUN MASC **fireman**; appeler les sapeurs-pompiers to call the fire brigade

sapin NOUN MASC **fir tree**; un sapin de Noël a Christmas tree

sarcasme NOUN MASC **sarcasm**

sardine NOUN FEM **sardine**

satellite NOUN MASC **satellite**

satin NOUN MASC **satin**

satisfaction NOUN FEM **satisfaction**

satisfaire VERB [10] **to satisfy**

satisfaisant ADJECTIVE **satisfactory**

satisfait ADJECTIVE **satisfied**; êtes-vous satisfaits de votre séjour? are you satisfied with your stay?

sauce NOUN FEM ❶ **sauce** ❷ **gravy**

saucisse NOUN FEM **sausage**

saucisson NOUN MASC **salami**

sauf¹ PREPOSITION ❶ **except**; tous les jours sauf le lundi every day except Monday, sauf quand il pleut except when it rains ❷ sauf si **unless**, c'est tout, sauf s'il y a des questions? that's all, unless there are any questions? ❸ sauf que **except that**, tout va bien, sauf que ta sœur n'est pas encore arrivée everything's fine, except that your sister hasn't arrived yet

sauf² ADJECTIVE ▸ SEE **sain**

saule NOUN MASC **willow**; un saule pleureur a weeping willow

saumon NOUN MASC **salmon**

saupoudrer VERB [1] **to sprinkle**

saut NOUN MASC **jump**

saut à la perche NOUN MASC **pole vault**

saut à l'élastique NOUN MASC **bungee jumping**

saut en hauteur NOUN MASC **high jump**

saut en longueur NOUN MASC **long jump**

sauter VERB [1] ❶ **to jump, to jump over**; elle a sauté la barrière she jumped over the gate, elle a sauté dans un taxi she jumped into a taxi ❷ sauter à la corde **to skip** (with a rope) ❸ **to skip**; nous avons sauté trois pages we've skipped three pages ❹ **to blow up**; les terroristes ont fait sauter l'avion the terrorists blew up the plane, faire sauter les plombs to blow the fuses
• ça saute aux yeux! it's blindingly obvious!

sauterelle NOUN FEM **grasshopper**

sauvage NOUN MASC, FEM **savage**

sauvage ADJECTIVE ❶ **wild** ❷ **savage**

sauvegarder VERB [1] ❶ **to safeguard** ❷ **to save, to back up** (on a computer)

sauver VERB [1] ❶ **to save**; vous m'avez sauvé la vie you saved my life ❷ se sauver **to run away**, ils se sont sauvés they ran away ❸ je me sauve! (informal) I'm off!

sauvetage NOUN MASC **rescue, life-saving**

savent, savez VERB ▸ SEE **savoir**¹

savoir¹ VERB [70] ❶ **to know**; je sais qu'il habite à Londres I know he lives in London, je ne savais pas qu'elle était médecin I didn't know she was a doctor, tu sais très bien que ... you know very well that ..., je n'en sais rien I know nothing about it, comment l'avez-vous su? how did you find out about it?, allez savoir! who knows! ❷ savoir faire **to know how to do**, je ne sais pas le faire I don't know how to do it, savoir lire et écrire to be able to read and write, tu sais jouer du piano? can you play the piano?

savoir² NOUN MASC **knowledge**

savoir-faire NOUN MASC **know-how**

savon NOUN MASC **soap**

savonnette NOUN FEM **cake of soap**

savons VERB ▶ SEE **savoir**[1]

savoureux, **savoureuse** ADJECTIVE MASC, FEM **tasty**

scandale NOUN MASC **scandal**; le discours du ministre a fait scandale the minister's speech caused a scandal

scandinave ADJECTIVE **Scandinavian**

Scandinavie NOUN FEM **Scandinavia**

scanner NOUN MASC **scanner** (in medicine and for documents); passer un scanneur to have a scan

scarabée NOUN MASC **beetle**

scénariste NOUN MASC & FEM **scriptwriter**

scène NOUN FEM ❶ **stage** (in a theatre); être sur scène to be on stage, mettre en scène to stage (a play), to direct (a film) ❷ **scene**; sur la scène politique on the political scene, des scènes de panique scenes of panic, faire (toute) une scène to throw a fit

sceptique ADJECTIVE **sceptical**

schéma NOUN MASC **diagram**

scie NOUN FEM **saw**

science NOUN FEM **science**

sciences naturelles PLURAL NOUN FEM **biology**

scientifique NOUN MASC & FEM **scientist**

scientifique ADJECTIVE **scientific**

scier VERB [1] **to saw**

scolaire ADJECTIVE **school**; les vacances scolaires the school holidays, le livret scolaire the school report

scolarité NOUN FEM **schooling**, **education**

Scorpion NOUN MASC **Scorpio** (sign of the Zodiac)

Scotch NOUN MASC **Sellotape**

scout, **scoute** NOUN MASC, FEM **boy scout**, **girl guide**

scrutin NOUN MASC ❶ **ballot** ❷ **polls**; le jour du scrutin polling day

sculpteur NOUN MASC **sculptor**

sculpteuse NOUN FEM **sculptress**

sculpture NOUN FEM **sculpture**

SDF NOUN MASC & FEM (short for sans domicile fixe) **of no fixed abode**; les SDF the homeless

se (s' before a vowel or silent 'h') REFLEXIVE PRONOUN ❶ **himself**; il se regarde he's looking at himself ❷ **herself**; elle se regarde she's looking at herself ❸ **itself**; le chien s'est fait mal the dog has hurt itself ❹ **themselves**; ils se sont fait mal they've hurt themselves ❺ **each other**; ils se regardaient they were looking at each other ❻ **yourself**, **oneself**; se faire mal to hurt yourself (or oneself) ❼ (sometimes not translated) Claudie se lave les cheveux Claudie's washing her hair, Jules se brosse les dents Jules is brushing his teeth

séance NOUN FEM ❶ **session** ❷ **showing** (of a film); la séance de vingt heures the eight o'clock showing

seau NOUN MASC (PLURAL **seaux**) **bucket**

sec, sèche ADJECTIVE MASC, FEM ❶ dry; mes cheveux ne sont pas secs my hair's not dry, un vin blanc sec a dry white wine ❷ dried; des abricots secs dried apricots

sèche-cheveux NOUN MASC hair dryer

sèche-linge NOUN MASC tumble dryer

sèche-mains NOUN MASC hand dryer

sécher VERB [1] to dry; des fleurs séchées dried flowers

sécheresse NOUN FEM drought

second NOUN MASC au second on the second floor, il est arrivé en second he arrived second

second ADJECTIVE second; la seconde fois the second time

secondaire ADJECTIVE secondary; une école secondaire a secondary school, des effets secondaires side effects

seconde NOUN FEM ❶ second; je reviens dans une seconde I'll be back in a moment ❷ second class; voyager en seconde to travel second class, un billet de seconde a second class ticket ❸ (in a French school) the equivalent of Year 11

secouer VERB [1] to shake; secouer la tête to shake your head

secourir VERB [29] to rescue

secourisme NOUN MASC first aid

secouriste NOUN MASC & FEM first aider

secours NOUN MASC ❶ help; au secours! help!, elle a crié au secours she shouted for help ❷ les premiers secours first aid ❸ une sortie de secours an emergency exit ❹ la roue de secours the spare wheel

secret NOUN MASC secret; garder un secret to keep a secret, en secret in secret

secret, secrète ADJECTIVE MASC, FEM secret

secrétaire¹ NOUN MASC, FEM secretary

secrétaire² NOUN MASC writing desk

secrétariat NOUN MASC secretary's office

secteur NOUN MASC sector; dans le secteur privé in the private sector, dans le secteur public in the public sector

sécu NOUN FEM (informal) (short for Sécurité sociale) Social Security

sécurité NOUN FEM ❶ safety; pour votre sécurité for your own safety, les règles de sécurité safety regulations, la sécurité routière road safety, une ceinture de sécurité a seatbelt ❷ être en sécurité to be safe ❸ security; un système de sécurité a security system, la sécurité de l'emploi job security

Sécurité sociale NOUN FEM Social Security

séduisant ADJECTIVE attractive, appealing

seigle NOUN MASC rye; le pain de seigle rye bread

seigneur NOUN MASC lord; le Seigneur the Lord

sein NOUN MASC ❶ breast; avoir un cancer du sein to have breast cancer ❷ within; au sein du gouvernement within the government

seize NUMBER **sixteen**; Corinne a seize ans Corinne's sixteen, le seize juillet the sixteenth of July

seizième NUMBER **sixteenth**

séjour NOUN MASC ❶ **stay**; pendant votre séjour en France during your stay in France ❷ la salle de séjour the living room

sel NOUN MASC **salt**; une pincée de sel a pinch of salt

sélection NOUN FEM ❶ **selection** ❷ **choice** ❸ **team**; la sélection française the French team

sélectionner VERB [1] **to select**

self NOUN MASC (informal) **self-service restaurant**

self-service NOUN MASC (informal) **self-service restaurant**

selle NOUN FEM **saddle**

selon PREPOSITION **according to**; selon la météo, il va pleuvoir according to the forecast, it's going to rain

semaine NOUN FEM **week**; cette semaine this week, la semaine prochaine/dernière next/last week, une/deux fois par semaine once/ twice a week, elle est payée à la semaine she's paid by the week

semblable ADJECTIVE **similar**

semblant NOUN MASC faire semblant de faire to pretend to do, elle fait semblant de ne pas entendre she's pretending not to hear

sembler VERB [1] **to seem**; la maison semble vide the house seems empty, il semble bon d'attendre leur retour it seems a good idea to wait till they get back

semelle NOUN FEM **sole** (of a shoe)

semer VERB [1] ❶ **to sow** (seeds) ❷ semer la panique to spread panic

semestre NOUN MASC **semester**

semi-remorque NOUN MASC **articulated truck**

semoule NOUN FEM **semolina**; le sucre semoule caster sugar

sens NOUN MASC ❶ **direction**; dans les deux sens in both directions, dans le sens Calais-Paris in the Calais-Paris direction, dans tous les sens in all directions, sens dessus dessous upside down, mets-le dans le bon sens! put it the right way up! ❷ **meaning**; le sens d'un mot the meaning of a word, cela n'a pas de sens it doesn't make sense, it's absurd

sensation NOUN FEM ❶ **feeling** ❷ **sensation**; le film a fait sensation à Cannes the film was a sensation at Cannes

sensationnel, **sensationnelle** ADJECTIVE MASC, FEM **sensational**, **fantastic**

sens commun NOUN MASC **common sense**

sens de l'humour NOUN MASC **sense of humour**; avoir le sens de l'humour to have a sense of humour

sensé ADJECTIVE **sensible**

sensibiliser VERB [1] sensibiliser les gens à un problème to increase people's awareness of a problem

sensibilité NOUN FEM ❶ **sensitivity** ❷ **sensibility**

sensible ADJECTIVE ❶ **sensitive**; c'est une fille très sensible she's a very sensitive girl, je suis sensible au froid I feel the cold ❷ **noticeable**; une différence sensible a noticeable difference

sensiblement ADVERB **noticeably**

sens interdit NOUN MASC **no entry sign, one-way street**

sens unique NOUN MASC **one-way street**

sentier NOUN MASC **path**

sentier de randonnée NOUN MASC **long-distance footpath** (a marked route for ramblers)

sentiment NOUN MASC **feeling**; sentiments affectueux best wishes, veuillez croire à mes sentiments les meilleurs yours sincerely, yours faithfully (one of a number of fixed formulae for ending a formal letter)

sentimental ADJECTIVE MASC (PLURAL sentimentaux) **sentimental**

sentir VERB [58] ❶ **to smell**; ça sent bon! that smells good! ❷ **to smell of**; ça sent les roses it smells of roses, tu sens la cigarette you smell of cigarettes ❸ **to feel**; je ne sens rien I can't feel anything, on sent que l'hiver s'approche you can feel it will soon be winter, je sens qu'elle est sincère I feel she's sincere ❹ se sentir to feel, je ne me sens pas bien I don't feel well

• je ne peux pas le sentir! I can't stand him!

séparé ADJECTIVE ❶ **separated**; mes parents sont séparés my parents are separated ❷ **separate**; dans une chambre séparée in a separate bedroom

séparément ADVERB **separately**

séparer VERB [1] ❶ **to separate**; séparez les œufs separate the eggs, séparer les filles des garçons to separate the girls from the boys ❷ se séparer to separate, to split up, mes parents se sont séparés my parents have separated

sept NUMBER **seven**; Yasmin a sept ans Yasmin's seven, il est sept heures it's seven o'clock, le sept mars the seventh of March

septante NUMBER **seventy** (used in Belgium and Switzerland, instead of soixante-dix); septante-sept seventy-seven

septembre NOUN MASC **September**; en septembre, au mois de septembre in September

septième NOUN MASC au septième on the seventh floor

septième ADJECTIVE **seventh**

sera, serai, seras, serez VERB ▸ SEE être[1]

série NOUN FEM **series**

sérieusement ADVERB **seriously**

sérieux NOUN prendre quelque chose au sérieux to take something seriously

sérieux, sérieuse ADJECTIVE MASC, FEM ❶ **serious**; vraiment? tu es sérieux? really? are you serious? ❷ **responsible**; Camilla est une jeune fille sérieuse Camilla is a responsible young woman ❸ **reliable**; il n'est pas sérieux he's unreliable ❹ un travail sérieux a careful piece of work

• garder son sérieux to keep a straight face

serin NOUN MASC **canary**

seringue NOUN FEM **syringe**

séronégatif, séronégative ADJECTIVE MASC, FEM **HIV-negative**

serons, **seront** VERB ▸ SEE **être**[1]

séropositif, **séropositive** ADJECTIVE MASC, FEM HIV-positive

serpent NOUN MASC snake

serpillière NOUN FEM floorcloth

serre NOUN FEM greenhouse; l'effet de serre the greenhouse effect

serré ADJECTIVE ❶ tight; ma jupe est trop serrée my skirt's too tight, un budget serré a tight budget ❷ close (match or competition)

serrer VERB [1] ❶ to grip; elle serrait le volant she gripped the steering wheel, il m'a serrée dans ses bras he hugged me ❷ serrer la main à quelqu'un to shake somebody's hand, nous nous sommes serré la main we shook hands ❸ serrer quelqu'un dans ses bras to hug somebody ❹ serrer les poings to clench your fists ❺ to tighten (a screw or belt) ❻ to be too tight; mes chaussures me serrent my shoes are too tight ❼ to push closer together; serrez les tables move the tables closer together ❽ se serrer to squeeze up, serrez-vous un peu! squeeze up a bit!

serrure NOUN FEM lock

serveur, **serveuse** NOUN MASC, FEM waiter, waitress

service NOUN MASC ❶ favour; peux-tu me rendre un petit service? could you do me a small favour? ❷ service (bus, train); service de dimanche Sunday service ❸ être en service to be working, il n'y a qu'un ascenseur en service there's only one lift working, être hors service to be out of order, l'ascenseur est hors service the lift is out of order ❹ duty, service; la pharmacie de service the duty chemist, je suis de service ce soir I am on duty this evening, le service militaire national service ❺ service (charge); le service est compris service is included ❻ department (in a town hall or hospital, for example); le service des urgences the casualty department

service après-vente NOUN MASC after-sales service

service clientèle NOUN MASC customer services

serviette NOUN FEM ❶ towel; une serviette de bain a bath towel ❷ napkin ❸ briefcase

serviette hygiénique NOUN FEM sanitary towel

servir VERB [71] ❶ to serve (in a shop, for example); merci, on me sert thank you, I'm being served ❷ to serve (with food or drink); est-ce que je peux vous servir du poulet? can I give you some chicken?, 'servir frais' 'serve chilled' ❸ se servir to help yourself, sers-toi de riz help yourself to rice ❹ se servir de to use, est-ce que tu sais te servir d'une machine à coudre? do you know how to use a sewing machine? ❺ to serve (in tennis or in the army); à toi de servir! your service! ❻ servir à to be used for, à quoi ça sert? what's it for?, ça ne sert à rien! it's no use!, ça ne sert à rien de pleurer there's no point in crying ❼ se servir to be served (food or drink), ce vin se sert frais this wine should be served chilled

ses ADJECTIVE ▸ SEE **son**[1]

set de table NOUN MASC place mat

seul ADJECTIVE ❶ **only**; la seule personne the only person, c'est le seul Anglais que je connaisse he's the only English person I know, j'étais le seul à aimer le film I was the only one who liked the film ❷ **alone**; il ne faut pas y aller seul you mustn't go there alone, j'étais tout seul à la maison I was all alone in the house ❸ se sentir seul to feel lonely ❹ tout seul all by yourself, il l'a fait tout seul he did it all by himself, Sophie sait s'habiller toute seule maintenant Sophie can get dressed all by herself now

seulement ADVERB ❶ **only**; trois fois seulement only three times ❷ **non seulement … mais not only …**; but, non seulement elle n'est pas venue, mais elle n'a même pas appelé not only did she not come, but she didn't even phone ❸ si seulement je l'avais su if only I'd known

sévère ADJECTIVE **strict**

sexe NOUN MASC ❶ **sex** ❷ **genitals**

sexuel, sexuelle ADJECTIVE MASC, FEM ❶ **sexual** ❷ l'éducation sexuelle sex education

shampooing NOUN MASC **shampoo**

short NOUN MASC **(pair of) shorts**; où est mon short? where are my shorts?, trois shorts three pairs of shorts

si (s' before 'il' or 'ils') CONJUNCTION **if**; si tu veux if you like, s'il pleut if it rains

si ADVERB ❶ **so**; je suis si fatigué! I'm so tired!, tu chantes si bien! you sing so well! ❷ **yes** (when you are contradicting somebody); 'tu ne viens pas avec nous?' – 'si!' 'you're

not coming with us?' – 'yes I am!', 'il ne reste pas manger' – 'mais si!' 'he's not staying for a meal' – 'of course he is!', elle ne les aime pas du tout, moi si she doesn't like them at all, but I do

Sicile NOUN FEM **Sicily**

sida NOUN MASC (short for syndrome immuno-déficitaire acquis) **AIDS**; avoir le sida to have AIDS

siècle NOUN MASC **century**; au vingtième siècle in the twentieth century

siège NOUN MASC ❶ **seat**; le siège d'avant the front seat ❷ **head office** (of a company) ❸ **siege** (in war)

sien, sienne, siens, siennes PRONOUN le sien, la sienne, les siens, les siennes ❶ **his**; j'ai prêté mon vélo à Paul, le sien est chez lui I've lent Paul my bike, his is at home, 'est-ce que ces chaussures sont à Bernard?' – 'oui, ce sont les siennes' 'are these shoes Bernard's?' – 'yes, they're his' ❷ **hers**; j'ai prêté mon vélo à Annie, le sien est chez elle I've lent Annie my bike, hers is at home, 'est-ce que ces chaussures sont à Nathalie?' – 'oui, ce sont les siennes' 'are these shoes Nathalie's?' – 'yes, they're hers'

sieste NOUN FEM **nap**; faire la sieste to have a nap

siffler VERB [1] **to whistle**

sifflet NOUN MASC **whistle**

signal NOUN MASC (PLURAL **signaux**) **signal**

signaler VERB [1] ❶ **to point out**; je vous signale que je serai absent ce jour-là I'd like to point out that I shall be away that day **②** to report **③** to indicate (*roadworks or danger, for example*)

signalisation NOUN FEM **signalling, signals**

signalisation routière NOUN FEM **road signs and markings**

signature NOUN FEM **signature**; je vous demande une petite signature just sign here, would you?

signe NOUN MASC **sign**; c'est bon/mauvais signe it's a good/bad sign, faire signe à quelqu'un to wave to someone, il m'a fait signe de m'approcher he beckoned me over to him, d'un signe de main elle a montré la sortie she pointed to the exit, de quel signe êtes-vous? what star sign are you?

signe astrologique NOUN MASC **star sign**

signer VERB [1] **①** to sign **②** se signer to cross oneself

signification NOUN FEM **meaning**

signifier VERB [1] to mean

silence NOUN MASC **silence**; en silence in silence

silencieux, silencieuse ADJECTIVE MASC, FEM **silent**

silhouette NOUN FEM **①** silhouette, outline **②** figure

similarité NOUN FEM **similarity**

simple NOUN MASC le simple messieurs/dames the men's/women's singles (*in tennis*)

simple ADJECTIVE **simple**; un repas simple a simple meal, un simple coup de téléphone just one telephone call

simplement ADVERB **simply**

simplicité NOUN FEM **simplicity**

simplifier VERB [1] to simplify

simuler VERB [1] to simulate

simultané ADJECTIVE **simultaneous**

sincère ADJECTIVE **sincere**

sincérité NOUN FEM **sincerity**

singe NOUN MASC **monkey**; un grand singe an ape

singulier NOUN MASC **singular**; au singulier in the singular

sinistre NOUN MASC **accident, disaster** (*for example, a fire or flood*)

sinistre ADJECTIVE **①** sinister **②** gloomy

sinistré, sinistrée NOUN MASC, FEM **disaster victim**

sinistrée ADJECTIVE **stricken**; de l'aide pour les familles sinistrées help for the families stricken by the disaster

sinon CONJUNCTION **otherwise**; il faut partir, sinon on sera en retard we must leave, otherwise we'll be late

sirène NOUN FEM **①** siren; une sirène d'alarme a fire alarm **②** mermaid

sirop NOUN MASC **①** syrup; sirop pectoral cough mixture **②** sirop de menthe mint cordial

site NOUN MASC **site, area**; site touristique place of interest (*to visit*), site classé conservation area

site internet NOUN MASC **web site**

sitôt ADVERB **as soon as**; sitôt rentrée, elle s'est couchée as soon as she got home, she went to bed, sitôt après immediately afterwards

a
b
c
d
e
f
g
h
i
j
k
l
m
n
o
p
q
r
s
t
u
v
w
x
y
z

- sitôt dit, sitôt fait no sooner said than done

situation NOUN FEM ❶ situation ❷ job; il a perdu sa situation he's lost his job

situer VERB [1] ❶ être situé to be situated, l'hôtel est situé au bord de la mer the hotel is situated by the sea, bien situé well situated ❷ se situer to be situated, la maison se situe dans un quartier résidentiel the house is in a residential area ❸ se situer to be set, le roman se situe à Moscou the novel is set in Moscow

six NUMBER six; Rosie a six ans Rosie's six, il est six heures it's six o'clock, le six juillet the sixth of July

sixième NOUN FEM (in a French school) the equivalent of Year 7

sixième NOUN MASC au sixième on the sixth floor

sixième ADJECTIVE sixth

skate NOUN MASC ❶ skate-boarding ❷ skate-board

ski NOUN MASC ❶ ski; où sont mes skis? where are my skis? ❷ skiing; il adore le ski he loves skiing, on va faire du ski ce week-end we're going skiing this weekend

ski de fond NOUN MASC cross-country skiing

ski de piste NOUN MASC downhill skiing

skier VERB [1] to ski; il skie plutôt bien he skis pretty well, skier hors piste to ski off-piste

skieur, skieuse NOUN MASC, FEM skier

ski nautique NOUN MASC water-skiing

slip NOUN MASC ❶ underpants ❷ knickers

Slovaquie NOUN FEM Slovakia

Slovénie NOUN FEM Slovenia

SMIC NOUN MASC (short for Salaire minimum interprofessionnel de croissance) guaranteed minimum wage; elle touche le SMIC she's on the legal minimum wage

smoking NOUN MASC dinner jacket

snack NOUN MASC snack bar

SNCF NOUN FEM (short for Société nationale des chemins de fer français) French national railways

snob NOUN MASC & FEM snob

snob ADJECTIVE snobbish (of a person), posh (of a restaurant)

sobre ADJECTIVE sober

sociable ADJECTIVE friendly, sociable

social ADJECTIVE MASC (PLURAL sociaux) social

socialiste NOUN MASC & FEM, ADJECTIVE socialist

société NOUN FEM ❶ society; dans notre société in our society ❷ company; il travaille pour une grande société he works for a big company

société anonyme NOUN FEM public company

sociologie NOUN FEM sociology

socquette NOUN FEM ankle sock

sœur NOUN FEM sister; ma grande sœur my big sister, my older sister

soi PRONOUN ❶ one, oneself; des amis autour de soi friends around one

❷ avoir confiance en soi to have confidence in oneself ❸ **itself**; pas très intéressant en soi not very interesting in itself, cela va de soi that goes without saying

soi-disant ADJECTIVE ❶ **so-called**; c'est le soi-disant champion he's the so-called champion ❷ **supposedly**; elle est soi-disant malade she's supposedly ill

soie NOUN FEM **silk**; un foulard en soie a silk scarf, le papier de soie tissue paper

soif NOUN MASC **thirst**; avoir soif to be thirsty

soigner VERB [1] to look after

soigneusement ADVERB **carefully**

soi-même PRONOUN **yourself**, **oneself**; il faut le faire soi-même you have to do it yourself

soin NOUN MASC ❶ **care** ❷ prendre soin de quelque chose to take care of something ❸ les soins treatment ❹ les premiers soins first aid

soir NOUN MASC **evening**, **night**; ce soir tonight, hier soir last night, demain soir tomorrow night, je sors tous les samedis soirs I go out every Saturday night, par un beau soir d'été one fine summer's evening, à six heures du soir at six in the evening, à ce soir! see you tonight!

soirée NOUN FEM ❶ **evening**; pendant la soirée during the evening ❷ **party**; elle donne une petite soirée she's having a little party ❸ en tenue de soirée in evening dress

soirée dansante NOUN FEM **dance**

sois VERB ▸ SEE **être**[1] sois gentil be good

soit CONJUNCTION soit … soit either … or, soit demain, soit jeudi either tomorrow or Thursday

soixantaine NOUN FEM ❶ **about sixty**; une soixantaine de personnes about sixty people ❷ avoir la soixantaine to be in your sixties

soixante NUMBER **sixty**

soixante-dix NUMBER **seventy**; soixante-dix-huit seventy-eight

soja NOUN MASC **soya bean**; la sauce de soja soy sauce

sol NOUN MASC ❶ **floor** ❷ **soil**

solaire ADJECTIVE ❶ **solar** ❷ la crème solaire sun cream

soldat NOUN MASC **soldier**

solde NOUN MASC ❶ les soldes the sales, faire les soldes to go round the sales ❷ être en solde to be reduced, les pulls sont en solde the jumpers are reduced ❸ **balance** (in a bank account)

soldé ADJECTIVE **reduced**

sole NOUN FEM **sole** (fish)

soleil NOUN MASC **sun**; au soleil in the sun, il fait soleil it's sunny, en plein soleil in full sun, attraper un coup de soleil to get sunburnt

solfège NOUN MASC **musical theory**

solide ADJECTIVE ❶ **strong** ❷ **solid**

soliste NOUN MASC & FEM **soloist**

solitaire ADJECTIVE ❶ **lonely**, **isolated** ❷ un navigateur solitaire a solo yachtsman

solitude NOUN FEM ❶ **loneliness** ❷ **solitude**

solution NOUN FEM **solution**

sombre ADJECTIVE **dark**, **gloomy**

somme[1] NOUN FEM **sum**; une somme d'argent a sum of money

somme[2] NOUN MASC **nap**; faire un somme to have a nap

sommeil NOUN MASC **sleep**; avoir sommeil to feel sleepy, je n'ai plus sommeil I'm not sleepy any more

sommes VERB ▸ SEE **être**[1]

sommet NOUN MASC **summit**

somnambule NOUN MASC & FEM **sleepwalker**; être somnambule to walk in your sleep

son[1], **sa**, **ses** ADJECTIVE ❶ **his**; son fils his son, sa fille his daughter, ses enfants his children ❷ **her**; son fils her son, sa fille her daughter, ses enfants her children ❸ **its**; le chat a perdu son collier the cat's lost its collar

son[2] NOUN MASC ❶ **sound**; le son d'un piano the sound of a piano ❷ **volume** (on a radio or hi-fi); baisser le son to turn the volume down ❸ **bran**

sondage NOUN MASC **survey**; un sondage d'opinion an opinion poll

sonner VERB [1] **to ring**; le téléphone sonne the phone's ringing, on sonne à la porte somebody's ringing the doorbell

sonnerie NOUN FEM **bell**; la sonnerie d'alarme the alarm bell, la sonnerie du téléphone the ring of the telephone

sonnette NOUN FEM **bell**, **doorbell**

sono NOUN FEM (informal) **sound system**

Sonotone NOUN MASC **hearing aid**

sophistiqué ADJECTIVE **sophisticated**

sorbet NOUN MASC **sorbet**; un sorbet au cassis a blackcurrant sorbet

sorcière NOUN FEM **witch**

sort NOUN MASC **fate**
• tirer au sort to draw lots

sorte NOUN FEM **sort**; c'est une sorte de poudre it's a sort of powder, toutes sortes d'activités all sorts of activities

sortie NOUN FEM ❶ **exit**; il nous attend à la sortie he's waiting for us at the exit, sortie de secours emergency exit ❷ **outing** ❸ **launch** (of a new product), **release** (of a film), **publication** (of a book)

sortir VERB [72] ❶ **to go out**; tout le monde est sorti dans la rue everybody went out into the street, ils sont sortis déjeuner they've gone out for lunch, elle est sortie en courant she ran out ❷ **to come out**; c'est l'heure où les gens sortent du cinéma it's the time when people are coming out of the cinema, son nouveau film sortira en mai her new film is coming out in May ❸ **to go out** (for pleasure); mes parents sortent peu my parents don't go out much ❹ sortir avec to be going out with; il sort avec ma sœur he's going out with my sister ❺ **to take out**; elle a sorti une bouteille du frigo she took a bottle out of the fridge, j'ai oublié de sortir le chien I forgot to take the dog out ❻ s'en sortir to manage, je m'en sortirai d'une manière ou d'une autre I'll manage one way or another

sottise NOUN FEM ❶ **silliness** ❷ dire des sottises to talk nonsense, ne fais pas de sottises don't do anything silly

sou NOUN MASC j'ai dépensé tous mes sous I've spent all my money, je n'ai pas un sou I'm broke, une machine à sous a fruit machine
• être près de ses sous to be tight-fisted

souci NOUN MASC ❶ **worry**; se faire du souci to worry, mon fils me donne bien des soucis my son's a great worry to me, j'ai d'autres soucis à présent I've got other problems just now ❷ **marigold**

soucieux, soucieuse ADJECTIVE MASC, FEM **worried**

soucoupe NOUN FEM **saucer**

soudain ADJECTIVE **sudden**

soudain ADVERB **suddenly**

souffle NOUN MASC **breath**; être à bout de souffle to be out of breath, couper le souffle à quelqu'un to take someone's breath away

soufflé NOUN MASC **soufflé**; un soufflé au fromage a cheese soufflé

souffler VERB [1] ❶ **to blow**; le vent soufflait fort there was a strong wind ❷ **to blow out** (a candle) ❸ **to whisper**; elle me soufflait quelque chose à l'oreille she was whispering something in my ear
• souffler dans le ballon (informal) to be breathalysed

souffrance NOUN FEM ❶ **suffering** ❷ **misery**

souffrir VERB [73] ❶ **to suffer**; a-t-elle beaucoup souffert? did she suffer much?, il souffre souvent du dos he often has back pain ❷ je ne peux pas le souffrir! (informal) I can't stand him!

souhait NOUN MASC **wish**
• à tes souhaits! bless you! (when somebody sneezes)

souhaiter VERB [1] **to wish**; je te souhaite bonne chance I wish you luck, il nous a souhaité la bienvenue he welcomed us, il souhaite se marier he'd like to get married

soûl ADJECTIVE **drunk**

soulagé ADJECTIVE **relieved**

soulagement NOUN MASC **relief**

soulager VERB [52] **to relieve**

soulever VERB [50] ❶ **to lift**; je n'arrive pas à soulever ta valise I can't lift your case ❷ **to raise** (problems, objections, or difficulties); personne n'a soulevé la question nobody raised the question

soulier NOUN MASC **shoe**

souligner VERB [1] ❶ **to underline** ❷ **to emphasize**

soupçon NOUN MASC ❶ **suspicion** ❷ **spot, drop** (of food or drink); juste un soupçon de lait just a drop of milk

soupçonner VERB [1] **to suspect**

soupe NOUN FEM **soup**; la soupe aux oignons onion soup

souper VERB [1] **to have supper**

soupir NOUN MASC **sigh**

soupirer VERB [1] **to sigh**

souple ADJECTIVE ❶ **supple** (person) ❷ **flexible** (system) ❸ **soft** (hair or clean washing)

source NOUN FEM **spring**; l'eau de source spring water

sourcil NOUN MASC **eyebrow**

sourd ADJECTIVE ❶ **deaf** ❷ **dull, muffled** (noise)
- faire la sourde oreille to turn a deaf ear

souriant ADJECTIVE **cheerful**

sourire NOUN MASC **smile**; il faut garder le sourire you must keep smiling

sourire VERB [68] **to smile**; sourire à quelqu'un to smile at somebody

souris NOUN FEM **mouse** (also for a computer)

sous PREPOSITION **under, underneath**; sous la chaise under the chair, sortir sous la pluie to go out in the rain, sous terre underground
- sous peu before long

sous-entendu NOUN MASC **innuendo**

sous-entendu ADJECTIVE **implied**

sous-estimer VERB [1] **to underestimate**

sous-marin NOUN MASC **submarine**

sous-marin ADJECTIVE **under-water, deep-sea**

sous-sol NOUN MASC **basement**; au sous-sol in the basement

sous-tasse NOUN FEM **saucer**

sous-titre NOUN MASC **subtitle**

soustraction NOUN FEM **subtraction**

sous-vêtements PLURAL NOUN MASC **underwear**

soutenir VERB [77] ❶ **to support**; elle m'a soutenu à la réunion

she supported me at the meeting ❷ soutenir que to maintain that ❸ soutenir une conversation to keep up a conversation ❹ **to withstand** (a shock or attack)

souterrain ADJECTIVE **underground**

soutien NOUN MASC **support**

soutien-gorge NOUN MASC **bra**

soutif NOUN MASC (informal) **bra**

souvenir NOUN MASC ❶ **memory**; mes souvenirs de Londres my memories of London, garder un bon souvenir de quelque chose to have happy memories of something, je n'ai aucun souvenir de l'avoir rencontrée I have no memory of meeting her ❷ souvenir

souvenir VERB [81] se souvenir de **to remember**, je me souviens d'elle I remember her, je me souviens de l'avoir rencontrée I remember meeting her, t'en souviens-tu? do you remember that?

souvent ADVERB **often**; je ne la vois pas très souvent I don't see her very often, le plus souvent more often than not

spacieux, **spacieuse** ADJECTIVE MASC, FEM **spacious**

spaghettis PLURAL NOUN MASC **spaghetti**; manger des spaghettis to have spaghetti

sparadrap NOUN MASC **sticking plaster**

speaker, **speakerine** NOUN MASC, FEM **announcer**

spécial ADJECTIVE MASC (PLURAL spéciaux) ❶ **special**; rien de spécial nothing special, les effets spéciaux special effects ❷ **odd**; il est vraiment très spécial he's really very odd

spécialement ADVERB specially

spécialiser VERB [1] se spécialiser to specialize, elle se spécialise dans la génétique she's specializing in genetics

spécialiste NOUN MASC & FEM specialist

spécialité NOUN FEM speciality

spécifier VERB [1] to specify

spectacle NOUN MASC show

spectaculaire ADJECTIVE spectacular

spectateur, spectatrice NOUN MASC, FEM ❶ member of the audience ❷ spectator

spéléologie NOUN FEM potholing

spirituel, spirituelle ADJECTIVE MASC, FEM ❶ witty ❷ spiritual

splendeur NOUN FEM splendour

splendide ADJECTIVE magnificent

sponsoriser VERB [1] to sponsor

spontané ADJECTIVE spontaneous

sport NOUN MASC sport, sports; aimez-vous le sport? do you like sport?, il fait beaucoup de sport he does a lot of sport, mon maillot de sport my sports shirt, les sports d'hiver winter sports, être bon en sport to be good at sports

sportif, sportive NOUN MASC, FEM sportsman, sportswoman

sportif, sportive ADJECTIVE MASC, FEM ❶ sports; un club sportif a sports club, une rencontre sportive a sports meeting ❷ sporty, athletic

spot NOUN MASC ❶ spotlight ❷ un spot publicitaire a commercial

square NOUN MASC public garden

squelette NOUN MASC skeleton

stable ADJECTIVE ❶ stable ❷ un emploi stable a steady job

stade NOUN MASC stadium

stage NOUN MASC ❶ course; un stage intensif d'anglais an intensive English course, faire un stage de formation to go on a training course ❷ un stage professionnel work experience, j'aimerais faire un stage professionnel dans une société française I'd like to do work experience in a French company

stagiaire NOUN MASC & FEM ❶ trainee ❷ person on a work experience placement

stand NOUN MASC ❶ stand (in a market or an exhibition) ❷ stall (in a fairground)

standard NOUN MASC switchboard; il faut passer par le standard you have to go through the switchboard

standardiste NOUN MASC & FEM switchboard operator

standing NOUN MASC un appartement de standing a luxury flat

star NOUN FEM star (in a film or show)

starter NOUN MASC choke (in a car)

station NOUN FEM ❶ une station de métro an underground station ❷ une station de taxis a taxi rank ❸ resort; une station de ski a ski resort ❹ une station de radio a radio station

station de travail NOUN FEM (computer) work station

stationnaire ADJECTIVE ❶ stationary ❷ stable

stationnement NOUN MASC parking; 'stationnement interdit' 'no parking'

stationner VERB [1] to park

station-service NOUN FEM service station

statistique NOUN FEM statistic(s)

statue NOUN FEM statue

statut NOUN MASC ❶ statute ❷ status

steak NOUN MASC steak; un steak frites steak and chips, un steak haché a burger steak

sténodactylo NOUN MASC & FEM shorthand typist

stéréo NOUN FEM, ADJECTIVE stereo

stérile ADJECTIVE sterile

stériliser VERB [1] to sterilize

steward NOUN MASC flight attendant (male)

stimulant ADJECTIVE stimulating

stock NOUN MASC stock; en stock in stock

stop NOUN MASC ❶ stop sign ❷ faire du stop to hitch-hike

stopper VERB [1] to stop

store NOUN MASC ❶ blind ❷ awning

strapontin NOUN MASC fold-down seat

stratégie NOUN FEM strategy

stratégique ADJECTIVE strategic

stress NOUN MASC stress

stressant ADJECTIVE stressful

stressé ADJECTIVE stressed; elle avait l'air stressé she looked stressed, je suis très stressé en ce moment I'm stressed out at the moment

strict ADJECTIVE ❶ strict ❷ severe

studieux, studieuse ADJECTIVE MASC, FEM studious

studio NOUN MASC ❶ studio flat ❷ studio

stupéfait ADJECTIVE astounded

stupéfiants PLURAL NOUN MASC narcotics

stupeur NOUN FEM astonishment

stupide ADJECTIVE stupid

stupidité NOUN FEM stupidity

style NOUN MASC style; c'est bien son style! that's just like him!

styliste NOUN MASC & FEM designer

stylo NOUN MASC pen

stylo-bille NOUN MASC ball-point pen

stylo-feutre NOUN MASC felt pen

stylo-plume NOUN MASC fountain pen

su VERB ▸ SEE **savoir**[1]

subir VERB [2] ❶ to be subjected to (change, violence, or pressure) ❷ to suffer (defeat or damage) ❸ subir une opération to have an operation

subitement ADVERB suddenly

subjonctif NOUN MASC subjunctive; au subjonctif in the subjunctive

subordonné, subordonnée NOUN MASC, FEM subordinate

substituer VERB [1] to substitute

subtil ADJECTIVE subtle

subvention NOUN FEM **subsidy**

succès NOUN MASC **success**; c'est un grand succès! it's a great success!

succursale NOUN FEM **branch** (of a company)

sucer VERB [61] **to suck**

sucette NOUN FEM **lollipop**

sucre NOUN MASC ❶ **sugar**; du jus d'orange sans sucre unsweetened orange juice ❷ un sucre a lump of sugar

sucré ADJECTIVE **sweet**; c'est trop sucré pour moi it's too sweet for me

sucre cristallisé NOUN MASC **granulated sugar**

sucre d'orge NOUN MASC **barley sugar**

sucre en morceaux NOUN MASC **sugar lumps**

sucre en poudre NOUN MASC **caster sugar**

sucre glace NOUN MASC **icing sugar**

sucrerie NOUN FEM des sucreries sweet things

sucre roux NOUN MASC **brown sugar**

sucrier NOUN MASC **sugar bowl**

sud NOUN MASC **south**; au sud de l'Écosse in the south of Scotland, au sud de Calais south of Calais, un vent du sud a south wind

sud ADJECTIVE ❶ **south**; la côte sud the south coast ❷ **southern**; la partie sud the southern part

sud-africain ADJECTIVE **South African**

Sud-Africain, Sud-Africaine NOUN MASC, FEM **South African**

sud-américain ADJECTIVE **South American**

Sud-Américain, Sud-Américaine NOUN MASC, FEM **South American**

sud-est NOUN MASC, ADJECTIVE **south-east**

sud-ouest NOUN MASC, ADJECTIVE **south-west**

Suède NOUN FEM **Sweden**

suédois NOUN MASC **Swedish** (language)

suédois ADJECTIVE **Swedish**

Suédois, Suédoise NOUN MASC, FEM **Swede**

suer VERB [1] **to sweat**

sueur NOUN FEM **sweat**; je suis en sueur I'm sweating

suffire VERB [74] ❶ **to be enough**; un kilo suffit one kilo's enough, ça suffit! that's enough! ❷ il suffit de faire all you have to do is, il suffit de nous téléphoner all you have to do is give us a call

suffisamment ADVERB **enough**; ce n'est pas suffisamment cuit it's not cooked enough, il n'y a pas suffisamment de verres there aren't enough glasses

suffisant ADJECTIVE ❶ **sufficient**; c'est bien suffisant! that's quite enough! ❷ **smug**; je la trouve un peu suffisante I find her a bit smug

suffoquer VERB [1] **to suffocate**, **to choke**

suggérer VERB [24] **to suggest**

suggestion NOUN FEM **suggestion**

suicider VERB [1] se suicider to commit suicide

suis VERB ▸ SEE **être**¹
▸ SEE **suivre**

suisse ADJECTIVE **Swiss**

Suisse NOUN FEM **Switzerland**; en Suisse in (or to) Switzerland, la Suisse romande French-speaking Switzerland, la Suisse allemande German-speaking Switzerland

suite NOUN FEM ❶ **rest**; je te raconterai la suite plus tard I'll tell you the rest later, et on connaît la suite we all know what happened next ❷ **continuation**; 'suite page 67' 'continued on page 67', regardez la suite jeudi watch the next instalment on Thursday ❸ **suite** (in a hotel) ❹ **in succession**; trois fois de suite three times in succession ❺ tout de suite straightaway, j'arrive tout de suite! I'll be right there! ❻ par la suite later, on s'est rendu compte par la suite que c'était une erreur we realized later that it was a mistake

suivant, **suivante** NOUN MASC, FEM **next one**; pas ce lundi mais le suivant not this Monday but the next

suivant ADJECTIVE **following**; le jour suivant the following day

suivre VERB [75] ❶ **to follow**; suivez-moi follow me ❷ suivre l'actualité to keep up with the news ❸ 'à suivre' 'to be continued' ❹ faire suivre son courrier to have your mail forwarded ❺ suivre un cours to do a course ❻ suivre un régime to be on a diet

sujet NOUN MASC ❶ **subject**; au sujet de about, c'est au sujet de votre fils it's about your son, c'est à quel sujet? what's it about?, un sujet de conversation a topic of conversation ❷ un sujet d'examen an exam question

sujet, **sujette** ADJECTIVE MASC, FEM être sujet à to suffer from, elle est sujette à des crises d'asthme she suffers from asthma attacks

super NOUN MASC **four-star petrol**

super ADJECTIVE (informal) **fantastic**; mais c'est super! but that's fantastic!

superficie NOUN FEM **area**

superficiel, **superficielle** ADJECTIVE MASC, FEM **superficial**

supérieur, **supérieure** NOUN MASC, FEM **superior**

supérieur ADJECTIVE ❶ **upper**; l'étage supérieur the upper floor, la lèvre supérieure the upper lip ❷ **greater**; la taille supérieure the bigger size, à une vitesse supérieure at a faster speed, à une température supérieure at a higher temperature, un prix supérieur a higher price ❸ **better**, **superior** (work, quality); c'est de loin supérieur à l'autre! it's much better than the other one! ❹ supérieur à greater than, un nombre supérieur à trois a number higher than three

superlatif NOUN MASC **superlative**

supermarché NOUN MASC **supermarket**

superposer VERB [1] ❶ **to stack up**; des lits superposés bunk beds ❷ **to superimpose** (an image)

superstitieux, **superstitieuse** ADJECTIVE MASC, FEM **superstitious**

superstition NOUN FEM **superstition**

supplément NOUN MASC **extra charge**; le vin est en supplément wine is extra

supplémentaire ADJECTIVE **❶ additional ❷** faire des heures supplémentaires to do overtime

supplice NOUN MASC **torture**

supplier VERB [1] **to beg**

support NOUN MASC **❶ support ❷ back-up** (material); un support audiovisuel audiovisual aids

supportable ADJECTIVE **bearable**

supporter VERB [1] **❶ to stand**; il ne supporte pas qu'on le critique he can't stand being criticized, je ne peux plus la supporter! I can't stand any more of her! **❷ to support** (a weight)

supposer VERB [1] **to suppose**

supprimer VERB [1] **❶ to get rid of ❷** supprimer des emplois to cut jobs, supprimer un train to cancel a train

sur PREPOSITION **❶ on**; c'est sur ton lit it's on your bed, un débat sur le racisme a discussion on racism, le cinéma est sur la droite the cinema's on the right **❷ over**; un pont sur la Loire a bridge over the Loire **❸ by** (in measurements); c'est deux mètres sur trois it's two metres by three **❹ out of**; trois femmes sur cinq three women out of five **❺ out of**; j'ai eu douze sur vingt en géographie I got twelve out of twenty in geography

sûr ADJECTIVE **❶ sure**; tu es sûr? are you sure?, oui, bien sûr! yes, of course!, sûr et certain certain, j'en étais sûr! I knew it! **❷** sûr de soi, de lui, d'elle (etc) self-confident, elle est très sûre d'elle she's very self-confident **❸ safe**; en lieu sûr in a safe place, le plus sûr est de tout fermer à clé the safest thing is to lock everything

surcharger VERB [52] **to overload**

surdité NOUN FEM **deafness**

surdose NOUN FEM **overdose** (of medicine)

sûrement ADVERB **❶ certainly**; sûrement pas! certainly not! **❷** il doit sûrement arriver à tout instant he's bound to arrive at any moment, elle est sûrement partie she's bound to have left

sûreté NOUN FEM **safety**, **security**

surf NOUN MASC **surfing**; faire du surf to go surfing

surface NOUN FEM **❶ surface ❷ area ❸** une grande surface a hypermarket

surface de réparation NOUN FEM **penalty area**

surf des neiges NOUN MASC **snowboarding**; faire du surf des neiges to go snowboarding

surfer VERB [1] surfer Internet/le web to surf the Net/Web

surfeur, **surfeuse** NOUN MASC, FEM **surfer** (on the sea)

surgelé NOUN MASC les surgelés frozen food

surgelé ADJECTIVE **frozen**; les légumes surgelés frozen vegetables

sur-le-champ ADVERB **right away**

surlendemain NOUN MASC elle est arrivée le surlendemain she arrived two days later

surmonter VERB [1] to overcome

surnaturel, **surnaturelle** ADJECTIVE MASC, FEM **supernatural**

surnom NOUN MASC nickname

surnommer VERB [1] to nickname

surpeuplé ADJECTIVE overpopulated

surprenant ADJECTIVE surprising

surprendre VERB [64] ❶ to surprise; ça m'a beaucoup surpris I found that really surprising ❷ surprendre quelqu'un en train de faire quelque chose to catch somebody doing something, je l'ai surprise en train de lire mon courrier I caught her reading my mail

surpris ADJECTIVE surprised; je suis surpris de te voir I'm surprised to see you

surprise NOUN FEM surprise; quelle surprise! what a surprise!, à ma grande surprise elle a accepté to my great surprise she agreed, faire une surprise à quelqu'un to give somebody a surprise

surréaliste NOUN MASC & FEM surrealist

surréaliste ADJECTIVE surreal

surtout ADVERB ❶ especially; il y a beaucoup de touristes, surtout en été there are lots of tourists, especially in the summer ❷ above all; il faut surtout rester calme above all, we must stay calm

surveillant, **surveillante** NOUN MASC, FEM **supervisor** (in a school, responsible for maintaining school discipline outside the classroom)

surveiller VERB [1] ❶ to watch, to keep an eye on; est-ce que tu peux surveiller mon sac deux secondes? can you keep an eye on my bag for a couple of minutes? ❷ surveiller une maison to keep a house under surveillance ❸ to supervise; surveiller le travail des élèves to supervise the students' work (work or progress) ❹ surveiller un examen to invigilate an exam ❺ je surveille ma ligne I'm watching my figure

survêtement NOUN MASC tracksuit

survie NOUN FEM survival

survivant, **survivante** NOUN MASC, FEM **survivor**

survivre VERB [82] to survive; survivre à un accident to survive an accident

survoler VERB [1] to fly over

suspect, **suspecte** NOUN MASC, FEM suspect

suspect ADJECTIVE suspicious

suspense NOUN MASC suspense (as in a thriller)

suture NOUN FEM un point de suture a stitch (in a wound)

svelte ADJECTIVE slender

SVP ABBREVIATION (short for s'il vous plaît) please

sweat NOUN MASC ▸ SEE sweatshirt

sweatshirt NOUN MASC sweatshirt

syllabe NOUN FEM syllable

symbole NOUN MASC symbol

symbolique *ADJECTIVE* **symbolic**; un geste symbolique a token gesture

sympa *ADJECTIVE (informal)* **nice**; je le trouve très sympa, ton copain he's really nice, your boyfriend

sympathie *NOUN FEM* j'ai beaucoup de sympathie pour elle I like her a lot

sympathique *ADJECTIVE* **nice**; c'est un type sympathique he's a nice guy

sympathiser *VERB* [1] sympathiser avec quelqu'un to get on well with someone

symptôme *NOUN MASC* **symptom**

synagogue *NOUN FEM* **synagogue**

syndicat *NOUN MASC* **trade union**

syndicat d'initiative *NOUN MASC* **tourist information office**

synthétique *ADJECTIVE* **synthetic**

synthétiseur *NOUN MASC* **synthesizer**

système *NOUN MASC* **system**; un système d'éclairage a lighting system

ta *ADJECTIVE* ▸ SEE **ton**[1]

tabac *NOUN MASC* ❶ **tobacco** ❷ un bureau de tabac a tobacconist's

tabagisme *NOUN MASC* **addiction to tobacco**

table *NOUN FEM* **table**; à table! dinner's ready!, se mettre à table to sit down to eat, mettre la table to lay the table

tableau *NOUN MASC* ❶ **painting**; un tableau de Renoir a painting by Renoir ❷ le tableau noir the blackboard ❸ le tableau d'affichage the notice board

tableau de bord *NOUN MASC* **dashboard**

table de chevet, **table de nuit** *NOUN FEM* **bedside table**

table des matières *NOUN FEM* **(list of) contents** *(in a book)*

tablette *NOUN FEM* une tablette de chocolat a bar of chocolate

tablier *NOUN MASC* **apron**

tabouret *NOUN MASC* **stool**

tache *NOUN FEM* ❶ **stain** ❷ **spot**

tâche *NOUN FEM* **task**

a
b
c
d
e
f
g
h
i
j
k
l
m
n
o
p
q
r
s
t
u
v
w
x
y
z

tache de rousseur NOUN FEM freckle

tacher VERB [1] to stain

tacle NOUN MASC **tackle** (in rugby)

tact NOUN MASC **tact**; il l'a fait avec beaucoup de tact he did it very tactfully

tactique NOUN FEM **tactics**

tactique ADJECTIVE **tactical**

tagueur NOUN MASC **graffiti artist**

taie NOUN FEM une taie d'oreiller a pillowcase

taille NOUN FEM ❶ **size**; qu'est-ce que vous avez à ma taille? what have you got in my size?, quelle taille faites-vous? what size are you?, 'taille unique' 'one size', la taille au-dessus/au-dessous the next size up/down ❷ **height**; un homme de grande taille a tall man ❸ **waist**; avoir la taille fine to have a slim waist

taille-crayon NOUN MASC **pencil sharpener**

tailler VERB [1] ❶ to cut ❷ to carve ❸ to prune ❹ to sharpen (a pencil)

tailleur NOUN MASC ❶ **suit** (for a woman) ❷ **tailor**
- s'asseoir en tailleur to sit cross-legged (literally: like a tailor)

taire VERB [76] se taire to stop talking, taisez-vous! be quiet!

talent NOUN MASC **talent**; c'est un jeune musicien de talent he's a talented young musician

talon NOUN MASC ❶ **heel** (of your foot or a shoe) ❷ **stub** (of a ticket or cheque book)

talon aiguille NOUN MASC **stiletto heel**

tambour NOUN MASC **drum**

tambourin NOUN MASC **tambourine**

Tamise NOUN FEM la Tamise the Thames

tampon NOUN MASC ❶ **pad** (for sponging); un tampon à récurer a scouring pad ❷ un tampon (hygiénique) a tampon

tamponneuse ADJECTIVE les autos tamponneuses the dodgems

tandis que CONJUNCTION **while**

tant ADVERB ❶ **so much**; j'ai tant mangé que ... I've eaten so much that ..., ce qu'elle avait tant espéré what she had so much hoped for, je ne les aime pas tant que ça I don't like them as much as that ❷ tant de so much, so many, tant d'argent so much money, tant d'amis so many friends, tant de monde so many people ❸ tant pis never mind ❹ tant mieux so much the better ❺ tant que while, tant que tu y es, passe-moi un stylo while you're there, pass me a pen ❻ tant que as long as, tant que Jacques ne sera pas rentré, je ne peux pas sortir I can't go out until Jacques gets back

tante NOUN FEM **aunt**

tantôt ADVERB **sometimes**; tantôt chez elle, tantôt chez moi sometimes at her place and sometimes at mine

taper *VERB* [1] ❶ taper quelqu'un to hit somebody, ça tape aujourd'hui the sun's really beating down today ❷ taper à la machine to type, taper une lettre to type a letter ❸ taper des mains to clap your hands, taper du pied to tap your foot ❹ taper à la porte to knock on the door ❺ (informal) se taper dessus to knock each other about

tapis *NOUN MASC* **carpet**

tapis de bain *NOUN MASC* **bathmat**

tapis roulant *NOUN MASC*
❶ **walkway** ❷ **carousel** (for airport luggage) ❸ **conveyor belt**

tapisser *VERB* [1] ❶ **to wallpaper**
❷ **to upholster**

tapisserie *NOUN FEM* ❶ **tapestry**
❷ **wallpaper**

taquiner *VERB* [1] **to tease**

tard *ADVERB* **late**; couche-toi, il est tard go to bed, it's late, plus tard later, trop tard too late, pas plus tard que mardi no later than Tuesday, ce sera pour plus tard there'll be other times

tarder *VERB* [1] **to be a long time**; ta mère ne va pas tarder your mother won't be long

tardif, tardive *ADJECTIVE MASC, FEM*
late

tarif *NOUN MASC* ❶ **rate**; tarif de nuit night rate (for the phone) ❷ **fare**; plein tarif full fare, tarif réduit reduced fare ❸ **price list**

tarte *NOUN FEM* **tart**; une tarte aux abricots an apricot tart

tartine *NOUN FEM* **slice of bread and butter** (and/or jam)

tartiner *VERB* [1] **to spread** (on bread)

tas *NOUN MASC* ❶ **pile**; un tas de bois a pile of wood ❷ **batch**; un tas de lettres a batch of letters ❸ (informal) un tas de **stacks of**, j'ai un tas de choses à faire ce soir I've got stacks of things to do tonight

tasse *NOUN FEM* **cup**; une tasse de thé a cup of tea

tatie *NOUN FEM* (informal) **auntie**

taupe *NOUN FEM* **mole** (animal)

taupinière *NOUN FEM* **mole hill**

taureau *NOUN MASC* (PLURAL taureaux) **bull**

Taureau *NOUN MASC* **Taurus** (sign of the Zodiac)

taux *NOUN MASC* **rate**; le taux mensuel the monthly rate, le taux de change the exchange rate

taxe *NOUN FEM* **tax**; la boutique hors taxes the duty-free shop

taxi *NOUN MASC* **taxi**; appeler un taxi to call a taxi

tchèque *ADJECTIVE* **Czech**; la République tchèque the Czech Republic

te (t' before a vowel or silent 'h') *PRONOUN* ❶ **you**; Gaby te cherche Gaby's looking for you, il t'a vu he saw you, il te l'a donné he gave it to you ❷ **to you** ❸ **yourself**; tu peux te faire une salade you can make yourself a salad, tu t'es blessé? have you hurt yourself?, tu te lèves quand? what time do you get up?

technicien, technicienne NOUN MASC, FEM **technician**

technique NOUN FEM **technique**

technique ADJECTIVE **technical**

technologie NOUN FEM **technology**

teckel NOUN MASC **dachshund**

tee-shirt NOUN MASC **T-shirt**

teint NOUN MASC **complexion**; avoir le teint clair to have a fair complexion

teinturier, teinturière NOUN MASC, FEM **dry-cleaner's**

tel, telle ADJECTIVE MASC, FEM ❶ **such**; avec un tel intérêt with such interest, une telle aventure such an adventure, de tels mensonges such lies ❷ tel que such as, les grandes villes telles que Paris et Lyon large towns such as Paris and Lyons ❸ rien de tel que nothing like, il n'y a rien de tel qu'un bon repas there's nothing like a good meal ❹ servir le saumon tel quel serve the salmon just as it is, je l'ai acheté tel quel I bought it just as it was

télé NOUN FEM (informal) **telly**; je l'ai vu à la télé I saw it on telly

télécabine NOUN MASC **cable car**

télécarte NOUN FEM **phonecard**

télécharger VERB [52] **to download**

télécommande NOUN FEM **remote control**

télécopie NOUN FEM **fax**

télécopieur NOUN MASC **fax machine, fax**

téléphérique NOUN MASC **cable car**

téléphone NOUN MASC **telephone**; un numéro de téléphone a phone number, Bruno est au téléphone Bruno's on the phone

téléphone portable NOUN MASC **mobile phone**

téléphoner VERB [1] **to phone**; je vais téléphoner à Robert I'll phone Robert

téléphone sans fil NOUN MASC **cordless phone**

téléphonique ADJECTIVE une cabine téléphonique a phone box, un appel téléphonique a phone call

télé-réalité NOUN FEM **reality TV**

télésiège NOUN MASC **chairlift**

téléski NOUN MASC **ski-tow**

téléspectateur, téléspectatrice NOUN MASC, FEM **viewer** (of TV)

téléviser VERB [1] **to televize**

téléviseur NOUN MASC **television (set)**; un téléviseur couleur a colour television

télévision NOUN FEM **television**; à la télévision on television

telle ADJECTIVE ▶ SEE **tel**

tellement ADVERB ❶ **so**; c'est tellement compliqué! it's so complicated! ❷ **so much**; c'est tellement mieux payé it's so much better paid, 'tu aimes lire?' – 'pas tellement' 'do you like reading?' – 'not much' ❸ tellement de so much, so many, j'ai tellement de travail! I've got so much work!, il y a tellement de choses à voir! there are so many things to see!, il y avait tellement de monde there were so many people there

tels, **telles** ADJECTIVE ▸ SEE **tel**

témoignage NOUN MASC ❶ **story**, **account**; selon les témoignages de l'accident according to accounts of the accident ❷ **evidence** (in court) ❸ un témoignage d'amitié a token of friendship

témoigner VERB [1] **to give evidence**

témoin NOUN MASC **witness**

température NOUN FEM **temperature**

tempête NOUN FEM **storm**

temple NOUN MASC ❶ **temple** ❷ **(Protestant) church**

temporaire ADJECTIVE **temporary**

temps NOUN MASC ❶ **weather**; quel temps fait-il? what's the weather like?, par temps de pluie in rainy weather ❷ **time**; je n'ai pas le temps I haven't got time, il est temps de partir it's time to go, arriver à temps to arrive in (or on) time, de temps en temps from time to time, en même temps at the same time, ça a pris beaucoup de temps it took a long time, il nous reste combien de temps? how much time do we have left?, c'est du temps perdu it's a waste of time, il était temps! about time too!, ces derniers temps recently, un travail à plein temps a full-time job, un travail à temps partiel a part-time job ❸ **tense** (of a verb)

tendance NOUN FEM ❶ **tendency**; avoir tendance à faire to tend to do ❷ **trend**

tendre¹ VERB [3] ❶ **to stretch** (something elastic) ❷ **to hold out**; elle m'a tendu un crayon she held out a pencil to me, tendre la main à quelqu'un to hold out one's hand to someone ❸ tendre le bras to reach out

tendre² ADJECTIVE **tender**

tendresse NOUN FEM **tenderness**

tendu ADJECTIVE **tense**

tenir VERB [77] ❶ **to hold**; peux-tu tenir la corde? can you hold the rope?, elle tenait l'enfant par la main she was holding the child by the hand ❷ **to run** (a shop, a business); le stand est tenu par des bénévoles the stand is run by volunteers ❸ **to keep**; elle tenait les yeux baissés she kept her eyes down, 'tenir hors de la portée des enfants' 'keep out of reach of children' ❹ **to take up**; cela tient la place de deux personnes it takes up the space of two people ❺ tenir à **to be attached to**, elle tient beaucoup à ses petits-enfants she's very attached to her grandchildren ❻ tenir à faire quelque chose **to be determined to do something**, je tiens à le finir aujourd'hui I'm determined to finish it today ❼ tiens! oh!, tiens, il est déjà midi! oh, it's twelve already!, tiens! est-ce que je t'ai raconté ...? listen! have I told you ...?, tiens, tiens, c'est toi! well, well, it's you!, tiens, prends le mien here, take mine ❽ tenir de quelqu'un **to take after someone**, elle tient de sa mère

she takes after her mother **⑨** se
tenir to hold, ils se tenaient par la
main they were holding each other
by the hand **⑩** se tenir to stand,
elle se tenait devant l'entrée she
was standing by the entrance,
tiens-toi tranquille! be quiet!,
tiens-toi droit! stand up straight!
⑪ se tenir pour to think yourself,
il se tient pour un génie he thinks
he's a genius

tennis NOUN MASC **①** tennis; jouer
au tennis to play tennis, un terrain
de tennis, un tennis a tennis
court, tennis de table table tennis
② tennis shoe

tension NOUN FEM **①** tension
② blood pressure

tentant ADJECTIVE **tempting**

tentation NOUN FEM **temptation**

tentative NOUN FEM **attempt**

tente NOUN FEM **tent**

tenter VERB [1] **①** to attempt; il a
tenté de s'échapper he tried to
escape, tenter sa chance, tenter le
coup (informal) to give it a try **②** to
tempt

tenu ADJECTIVE **①** bien/mal tenu well/
badly cared for **②** être tenu de faire
to be required to do

tenue NOUN FEM **clothes**; être en
tenue de sport to be in sports kit,
en tenue de soirée in evening dress

terme NOUN MASC **①** word, term; un
terme technique a technical term,
les termes du contrat the terms of
the contract **②** end; à court terme
short-term, à long terme long-term

terminaison NOUN FEM **ending**

terminale NOUN FEM (in a French
school) **the equivalent of Year 13**

terminer VERB [1] **①** to finish **②** to
end; la réunion s'est terminée à
dix-huit heures the meeting ended
at six p.m., ça va mal se terminer!
it'll end in tears!

terminus NOUN MASC **terminus**

terrain NOUN MASC **①** ground, land;
il a acheté du terrain he's bought
some land **②** pitch, ground (for
sports); un terrain de football a
football pitch, un terrain de golf a
golf course **③** piece of ground; un
terrain à bâtir a building plot

terrain de camping NOUN MASC
campsite

terrain de jeu(x) NOUN MASC
playground

terrain de sport(s) NOUN MASC
sports ground

terrain vague NOUN MASC **waste
ground**

terrasse NOUN FEM **terrace**

terre NOUN FEM **①** ground; s'asseoir
par terre to sit on the floor, tomber
par terre to fall down **②** la Terre the
Earth **③** soil **④** land (not sea); aller à
terre to go ashore

terre cuite NOUN FEM **terracotta**

terrible ADJECTIVE **①** terrible; des
événements terribles terrible
events **②** (informal) terrific; 'c'était
bien, le film?' – 'pas terrible' 'was
the film any good?' – 'not great'

terrifiant ADJECTIVE **terrifying**

terrifier VERB [1] **terrify**

terrine NOUN FEM **pâté**

territoire NOUN MASC ❶ **territory** ❷ **country**; il fera beau sur l'ensemble du territoire the weather will be fine throughout the country

terrorisme NOUN MASC **terrorism**

terroriste NOUN MASC & FEM **terrorist**

tes ADJECTIVE **your**
  ▸ SEE **ton**[1]

test NOUN MASC **test**

testament NOUN MASC **will**

tester VERB [1] **to test**

tétanos NOUN MASC **tetanus**

têtard NOUN MASC **tadpole**

tête NOUN FEM ❶ **head**; se laver la tête to wash your hair, j'ai la tête qui tourne my head's spinning ❷ **face**; je n'aime pas sa tête I don't like his face ❸ **top**; tu es en tête de la liste you're first on the list ❹ **mind**; j'ai quelque chose en tête I have something in mind, où avais-tu la tête? what were you thinking of? ❺ **front** (of a train); les deux wagons de tête sont à destination de Bourges the two front coaches are for Bourges
• faire la tête to sulk
• un dîner en tête à tête a private dinner for two
• j'en ai par-dessus la tête! I'm fed up to the back teeth!

têtu ADJECTIVE **stubborn**

texte NOUN MASC **text**

texto NOUN MASC **text message**; envoyer un texto à quelqu'un to text someone

TGV NOUN MASC (short for train à grande vitesse) **high-speed train**

thalassothérapie NOUN FEM **sea-water treatment** (at a health spa)

thé NOUN MASC **tea**; un thé au lait tea with milk

théâtre NOUN MASC ❶ **theatre**; des costumes de théâtre stage costumes, un coup de théâtre a dramatic turn of events ❷ **plays**; le théâtre de Molière Molière's plays ❸ faire du théâtre to belong to a drama group

théière NOUN FEM **teapot**

thème NOUN MASC ❶ **subject** ❷ **prose** (a text to translate into the foreign language)

théorie NOUN FEM **theory**

thérapie NOUN FEM ❶ **(medical) treatment** ❷ **therapy**

thermal ADJECTIVE MASC (PLURAL thermaux) **thermal**; une station thermale a spa

thermomètre NOUN MASC **thermometer**

thermos NOUN MASC **vacuum flask, thermos**

thon NOUN MASC **tuna**

thym NOUN MASC **thyme**

tibia NOUN MASC ❶ **shin** ❷ **shinbone**

tic NOUN MASC **nervous twitch**

ticket NOUN MASC ❶ **ticket**; un ticket de métro an underground ticket ❷ un ticket de caisse a till receipt

A
B
C
D
E
F
G
H
I
J
K
L
M
N
O
P
Q
R
S
T
U
V
W
X
Y
Z

tiède *ADJECTIVE* ❶ **warm** ❷ **lukewarm**

tien, tienne, tiens, tiennes
PRONOUN le tien, la tienne, les tiens,
les tiennes yours, est-ce que ce
stylo est le tien? is this pen yours?,
ma voiture et la tienne my car and
yours, mes lettres et les tiennes my
letters and yours

tiens *VERB* ▸ SEE **tenir**

tiens *PRONOUN* ▸ SEE **tien**

tiers *NOUN MASC* **third**; les deux tiers
de la population two-thirds of the
population

tiers , **tierce** *ADJECTIVE MASC, FEM* **third**

tiers-monde *NOUN MASC* **Third
World**

tige *NOUN FEM* **stem**

tigre *NOUN MASC* **tiger**

tilleul *NOUN MASC* ❶ **lime tree** ❷ **lime
flower tea**

timbre *NOUN MASC* **stamp**

timide *ADJECTIVE* ❶ **shy** ❷ **self-
conscious**

timidité *NOUN FEM* **shyness**

tiquer *VERB* [1] sans tiquer without
batting an eyelid

tir *NOUN MASC* ❶ **shooting** ❷ **shot** *(in
football)*

tirage *NOUN MASC* le tirage au sort the
draw *(in a lottery, for example)*, par
tirage au sort by drawing lots

tir à l'arc *NOUN MASC* **archery**

tire-bouchon *NOUN MASC* **corkscrew**

tirelire *NOUN FEM* **money box**

tirer *VERB* [1] ❶ **to pull**; il m'a tiré
par le bras he pulled my arm, elle
m'a tiré les cheveux she pulled my
hair ❷ **to draw**; tirer les rideaux to
draw the curtains, il a tiré la lettre
de sa poche he drew the letter from
his pocket, tirer un trait to draw a
line, tirer des conclusions to draw
conclusions, tirer au sort to draw
lots ❸ **to fire**; ils ont tiré sur les
policiers they fired on the police,
tirer plusieurs coups de feu to fire
several shots

tiret *NOUN MASC* **dash**

tiroir *NOUN MASC* **drawer**

tisane *NOUN FEM* **herbal tea**

tisonnier *NOUN MASC* **poker** *(for fire)*

tissu *NOUN MASC* **material, fabric**

titre *NOUN MASC* ❶ **title** ❷ **headline**;
les titres de l'actualité the news
headlines ❸ à juste titre quite
rightly, à titre d'exemple as an
example

titre de transport *NOUN MASC*
travel ticket

tituber *VERB* [1] **to stagger**

toast *NOUN MASC* ❶ **piece of toast**;
servir avec des toasts serve with
toast ❷ **toast** *(to someone's health)*

toboggan *NOUN MASC* **slide**

toi *PRONOUN* **you**; c'est toi! it's you!,
avec toi with you, plus grand
que toi bigger than you, c'est à
toi de jouer it's your turn,
assieds-toi sit down, est-ce
que ces chaussettes sont à toi?
are these socks yours?

toile NOUN FEM ❶ **cloth**; toile de lin linen, une toile cirée an oilcloth ❷ **painting**, **canvas**; une toile de Picasso a painting by Picasso

Toile NOUN FEM la Toile the **Web**

toile d'araignée NOUN FEM **spider's web**, **cobweb**

toilette NOUN FEM ❶ faire sa toilette to have a wash ❷ **outfit**; je me suis acheté une toilette pour le mariage de ma sœur I've bought an outfit for my sister's wedding

toilettes PLURAL NOUN FEM **toilet**; aller aux toilettes to go to the toilet

toi-même PRONOUN **yourself**; l'as-tu fait toi-même? did you make it yourself?

toit NOUN MASC **roof**

tolérant ADJECTIVE **tolerant**

tolérer VERB [24] to **tolerate**

tomate NOUN FEM **tomato**; une salade de tomates a tomato salad

tombe NOUN FEM **grave**

tombeau NOUN MASC (PLURAL tombeaux) **tomb**

tomber VERB [1] ❶ to **fall**; attention, tu vas tomber! careful, you'll fall!, la chaise est tombée the chair fell over, Noël tombe un lundi Christmas falls on a Monday ❷ laisser tomber to drop, j'ai laissé tomber mon porte-monnaie I've dropped my purse ❸ laisser tomber to give up (an activity), elle a laissé tomber l'espagnol she's given up Spanish ❹ tomber malade to fall ill, tomber amoureux to fall in love ❺ tomber sur to bump into, je suis tombé sur Georges devant la poste I bumped into Georges outside the

post office ❻ ça tombe bien that's lucky
• je tombe de sommeil I can't keep my eyes open (literally: I'm dropping with sleep)

tombola NOUN FEM **tombola**, **lottery**

ton¹, **ta**, **tes** ADJECTIVE **your**; ton chat your cat, ta sœur your sister, tes pieds your feet

ton² NOUN MASC ❶ **tone of voice** ❷ **colour**

tondeuse NOUN FEM **lawnmower**

tondre VERB [3] to **mow**

tongs PLURAL NOUN FEM **flip-flops**

tonique ADJECTIVE **bracing**

tonne NOUN FEM **tonne**, **metric ton** (1,000 kg)
• j'ai des tonnes de choses à faire (informal) I've loads of things to do

tonneau NOUN MASC (PLURAL tonneaux) **barrel**

tonnerre NOUN MASC **thunder**

tonton NOUN MASC (informal) **uncle**

tonus NOUN MASC ❶ **energy** (for a person) ❷ **tone** (for your muscles)

toque NOUN FEM **chef's hat**

torchon NOUN MASC **cloth**, **tea towel**

tordre VERB [3] to **twist**; se tordre la cheville to twist your ankle

tordu ADJECTIVE ❶ **bent** ❷ **crooked** ❸ **weird**; une histoire tordue a weird story

tornade NOUN FEM **tornado**

torrent NOUN MASC **waterfall**, **mountain stream**

torse NOUN MASC **chest**, **upper body**;

il s'est mis torse nu he stripped to the waist

tort NOUN MASC ❶ avoir tort to be wrong, je crois que tu as tort I think you're wrong, il a tort de dire ça he's wrong to say that ❷ à tort wrongly, à tort ou à raison rightly or wrongly

torticolis NOUN MASC **stiff neck**; avoir le torticolis to have a stiff neck

tortiller VERB [1] se tortiller to wriggle

tortue NOUN FEM **tortoise, turtle**

torture NOUN FEM **tortur**

torturer VERB [1] **to torture**

tôt ADVERB ❶ **early**; on va partir tôt we're leaving early, tôt le matin early in the morning ❷ **soon**; le plus tôt possible as soon as possible, tôt ou tard sooner or later

total NOUN MASC (PLURAL **totaux**) **total**; au total in total

total ADJECTIVE MASC (PLURAL **totaux**) **total**

totalement ADVERB **totally**

totalité NOUN FEM la totalité des élèves all the pupils, la totalité du groupe the whole group

touchant ADJECTIVE **touching**

touche NOUN FEM ❶ **key** (on a piano or keyboard) ❷ **button** (on a machine); la touche d'enregistrement the record button, appuyez sur la touche press the button ❸ (ligne de) touche touchline

toucher VERB [1] ❶ **to touch**; ne touche pas à ma peinture don't touch my painting ❷ **to touch**;

cette histoire m'a beaucoup touché that story really touched me ❸ **to affect, to concern**; ce problème nous touche tous this problem affects us all ❹ **to get** (money or wages); il touche 350 euros par semaine he's getting 350 euros a week

touffu ADJECTIVE **bushy, thick**

toujours ADVERB ❶ **always**; il est toujours en retard he's always late, comme toujours as always ❷ **still**; nous habitons toujours au même endroit we're still living in the same place, ton paquet n'est toujours pas arrivé your parcel still hasn't come ❸ pour toujours for ever

tour¹ NOUN MASC ❶ faire le tour de to go round, faire le tour des magasins to go round all the shops, faire le tour du monde to go round the world ❷ faire un tour to go for a walk, on va faire un petit tour we'll go for a little walk ❸ faire un tour à vélo to go for a bike ride ❹ faire un tour en voiture to go for a drive ❺ **turn**; c'est ton tour de jouer it's your turn to play, à qui le tour? whose turn is it?

tour² NOUN FEM ❶ **tower**; la tour Eiffel the Eiffel Tower ❷ **tower block** ❸ **castle, rook** (in chess)

tourbillon NOUN MASC **whirlwind, whirlpool**

tourisme NOUN MASC **tourism**

touriste NOUN MASC & FEM **tourist**

touristique ADJECTIVE un guide touristique a tourist guide(book), une ville touristique a town which attracts tourists

tourmenter *VERB* [1] **to tease**

tournant *NOUN MASC* ❶ **bend** *(in a road)* ❷ **turning-point**

tourne-disque *NOUN MASC* **record player**

tournée *NOUN FEM* ❶ **round** *(of a postman or baker, for example)* ❷ **round** *(of drinks)*; c'est ma tournée it's my round ❸ **tour** *(of a performer)*; être en tournée to be on tour

tourner *VERB* [1] ❶ **to turn**; tournez à gauche à l'église turn left at the church ❷ **to toss** *(a salad)* ❸ mal tourner to go wrong ❹ se tourner to turn, elle s'est tournée vers moi she turned to face me ❺ tourner le dos à quelqu'un to have your back to somebody

tournesol *NOUN MASC* **sunflower**

tournevis *NOUN MASC* **screwdriver**

tournis *NOUN MASC* avoir le tournis to feel dizzy, j'ai le tournis I'm feeling dizzy

tournoi *NOUN MASC* **tournament**

tourterelle *NOUN FEM* **turtle dove**

tous *ADJECTIVE, PRONOUN* ▸ SEE **tout**

Toussaint *NOUN FEM* **All Saints' Day** *(November 1st)*

tousser *VERB* [1] **to cough**

tout, **toute**, **tous**, **toutes** *ADJECTIVE* ❶ **all**; tout le pain all the bread, toute la classe all the class, the whole class, tous les garçons all the boys, toutes les filles all the girls, tout le monde everybody, toute la journée all day, tous les deux both, je les achète tous les trois I'll buy all three of them, pendant toute une année for a whole year ❷ **any**; à tout âge at any age, à tout instant at any moment, 'service à toute heure' 'service at any time' ❸ **every**; tous les jours every day, prenez un comprimé toutes les quatre heures take one pill every four hours

tout, **toutes**, **tous**, **toutes** *PRONOUN* ❶ **everything**; ils ont tout pris they took everything, tout va bien everything's fine ❷ **all**; tous ensemble all together, elles étaient toutes là they were all there, 54 en tout 54 in all, et tout ça and all that, tout ce que je sais, c'est que … all I know is that … ❸ pas du tout not at all

tout *ADVERB* c'est tout prêt it's all ready, il est tout seul he's all alone, tout doucement very slowly, tout droit straight ahead

tout à coup *ADVERB* **suddenly**

tout à fait *ADVERB* **completely**, **absolutely**; ce n'est pas tout à fait sec it's not absolutely dry

tout à l'heure *ADVERB* ❶ **just now**; je l'ai vu tout à l'heure I saw him just now ❷ **in a little while**; à tout à l'heure! see you later!

tout de même *ADVERB* **all the same**; c'est tout de même bizarre all the same, it is odd

tout de suite *ADVERB* **at once**; fais-le tout de suite! do it at once!

tout d'un coup *ADVERB* **suddenly**

toutefois *ADVERB* **however**

toutes *ADJECTIVE, PRONOUN* ▸ SEE **tout**

toux *NOUN FEM* **cough**

toxicomane NOUN MASC & FEM **drug addict**

toxique ADJECTIVE **poisonous, toxic**

trac NOUN MASC (informal) avoir le trac to feel nervous

trace NOUN FEM ❶ **tracks**; des traces de skis ski-tracks, des traces de pas footprints ❷ **mark**; des traces de doigts finger marks

tracer VERB [61] **to draw**

tracteur NOUN MASC **tractor**

tradition NOUN FEM **tradition**

traditionnel, traditionnelle ADJECTIVE MASC, FEM **traditional**

traducteur, traductrice NOUN MASC, FEM **translator**

traduction NOUN FEM **translation**

traduire VERB [26] **to translate**; traduire en français to translate into French

trafic NOUN MASC ❶ le trafic de drogue drug dealing ❷ **traffic**

trafiquant, trafiquante NOUN MASC, FEM **dealer** (in drugs or arms)

tragédie NOUN FEM **tragedy**

tragique ADJECTIVE **tragic**

trahir VERB [2] **to betray**

trahison NOUN FEM **betrayal**

train NOUN MASC ❶ **train**; monter dans le train to get on the train, descendre du train to get off the train, le train de dix heures the ten o'clock train ❷ être en train de faire to be (busy) doing, Henri est en train de faire la vaisselle Henri's doing the washing-up

traîner VERB [1] ❶ **to wander round** ❷ **to lie around**; il laisse ses affaires traîner partout he leaves his things lying around everywhere ❸ **to dawdle**; ne traînez pas, le train arrive don't be long, the train's coming ❹ **to drag on**; j'ai des projets qui traînent I've got some projects that are dragging on ❺ **to drag**; elle traînait sa valise derrière elle she was dragging her suitcase behind her ❻ traîner les pieds to drag your feet

traire VERB [78] **to milk**

trait NOUN MASC ❶ **line** ❷ les traits features (of a face), avoir les traits fins to have delicate features ❸ d'un seul trait at one go, il l'a bu d'un seul trait he drank it all at one go

trait d'union NOUN MASC **hyphen**

traité NOUN MASC **treaty**

traitement NOUN MASC ❶ **treatment** ❷ **processing**; le traitement de texte word processing ❸ **salary**

traiter VERB [1] ❶ **to treat**; il la traite très mal he treats her very badly, le médecin qui me traite the doctor who's treating me ❷ **to deal with** (a question or problem) ❸ traiter de to call, il m'a traité de menteur he called me a liar

traiteur NOUN MASC **caterer**

trajet NOUN MASC ❶ **journey**; c'est un trajet de deux heures it's a two-hour journey ❷ **route**

trampoline NOUN MASC
trampoline; faire du trampoline
to trampoline

tramway NOUN MASC **tram, tramway**

tranchant ADJECTIVE **sharp**

tranche NOUN FEM ❶ **slice**; deux
tranches de jambon two slices of
ham ❷ **phase, period** (of time)

trancher VERB [1] ❶ **to slice** ❷ **to
decide**

tranquille ADJECTIVE ❶ **quiet**; une rue
tranquille a quiet street, tiens-toi
tranquille! be quiet! ❷ laisse-
moi tranquille! leave me alone!
❸ maman n'est pas tranquille si
je n'appelle pas Mum worries if I
don't ring

tranquillité NOUN FEM **peace**

transat NOUN MASC (informal) **deck
chair**

transférer VERB [24] **to transfer**

transfert NOUN MASC **transfer**

transformer VERB [1] ❶ **to change**;
ils ont transformé leur jardin
they've completely changed their
garden, nous avons transformé
cette chambre en bureau we've
turned this bedroom into a study
❷ se transformer en to change
into, le têtard se transforme en
grenouille the tadpole changes into
a frog

transfusion NOUN FEM une
transfusion sanguine a blood
transfusion

transistor NOUN MASC **transistor**

transmettre VERB [11]
❶ transmettre quelque chose à

quelqu'un to pass something on to
somebody ❷ **to transmit**

transpiration NOUN FEM
perspiration, sweat

transpirer VERB [1] **to sweat**

transplantation NOUN FEM
❶ **transplant** (medical)
❷ **transplantation** (of plants)

transport NOUN MASC ❶ **transport**;
les frais de transport transport
costs ❷ les transports en commun
public transport

transporter VERB [1] ❶ **to transport**
❷ **to carry**

trappe NOUN FEM **trap door**

travail NOUN MASC (PLURAL **travaux**)
❶ **work**; j'ai beaucoup de travail
à faire I've got a lot of work to do
❷ **job**; je cherche un travail I'm
looking for a job

travailler VERB [1] **to work**; travailler
dans la banque to work in banking

travailleur, travailleuse NOUN
MASC, FEM **worker**

travailleur, travailleuse ADJECTIVE
MASC, FEM **hard-working**

travailliste ADJECTIVE **Labour**; le
parti travailliste the Labour party
(in Britain)

travaux PLURAL NOUN MASC ❶ **work**;
des travaux de construction
building work, ils font faire des
travaux chez eux they're having
some work done on the house
❷ **roadworks** ❸ les travaux
ménagers housework ❹ les travaux
dirigés classwork, les travaux
manuels handicrafts

travée NOUN FEM **bay** (for coaches)

travers NOUN ❶ à travers **through**, j'ai regardé à travers les rideaux **I looked through the curtains**, voyager à travers le monde **to travel all over the world** ❷ de travers **crooked**, le tableau est de travers **the picture's crooked** ❸ de travers **wrongly**, c'est boutonné de travers **it's buttoned up wrongly**

traversée NOUN FEM **crossing**; une traversée de l'Atlantique an **Atlantic crossing**

traverser VERB [1] ❶ to **cross**; regarde avant de traverser la rue **look before you cross the road** ❷ to **go through**; traverser la France pour aller en Italie **to go through France on the way to Italy**, la pluie a traversé ma veste **the rain's gone right through my jacket**, ils ont traversé une crise **they went through a crisis**

traversin NOUN MASC **bolster**

trébucher VERB [1] to **stumble**

trèfle NOUN MASC ❶ **clover** ❷ **clubs** (in cards); la dame de trèfle **the queen of clubs**

treize NUMBER **thirteen**; Aurélie a treize ans **Aurélie's thirteen**, à treize heures **at one p.m.**, le treize juillet **the thirteenth of July**

treizième NUMBER **thirteenth**

tremblement de terre NOUN MASC **earthquake**

trembler VERB [1] to **shake**, to **tremble**

trempé ADJECTIVE **soaked**

tremper VERB [1] to **soak**

tremplin NOUN MASC **springboard**

trentaine NOUN FEM ❶ **about thirty**; une trentaine de personnes **about thirty people** ❷ elle a la trentaine **she's in her thirties**

trente NUMBER **thirty**; elle a trente ans **she's thirty**, le trente juillet **the thirtieth of July**

très ADVERB **very**; très heureux **very happy**, j'ai très faim **I'm very hungry**, très bien fait **very well done**

trésor NOUN MASC **treasure**

tresse NOUN FEM **plait**

tréteau NOUN MASC (PLURAL **tréteaux**) **trestle**

triangulaire ADJECTIVE **triangular**

tribu NOUN FEM **tribe**

tribunal NOUN MASC (PLURAL **tribunaux**) **court**; paraître devant le tribunal **to appear in court** (on a charge)

tricher VERB [1] to **cheat**

tricolore ADJECTIVE **three-coloured**; le drapeau tricolore **the French flag** (which is three-coloured, blue, white, and red, in vertical stripes)

tricoter VERB [1] to **knit**

trier VERB [1] **to sort (out)**; hier soir nous avons trié toutes les photos last night we sorted out all the photographs

trimestre NOUN MASC **term**

trinidadien, **trinidadienne** ADJECTIVE MASC, FEM **Trinidadian**

Trinidadien, **Trinidadienne** NOUN MASC, FEM **Trinidadian**

Trinité NOUN FEM (l'île de) la Trinité **Trinidad**

triomphe NOUN MASC **triumph**

triompher VERB [1] **to triumph**

tripes PLURAL NOUN FEM **tripe**

triple NOUN MASC le triple **three times as much**

tripler VERB [1] **to treble**; le prix a triplé the price has tripled

triplés PLURAL NOUN MASC **triplets**

triste ADJECTIVE **sad**

tristesse NOUN FEM **sadness**

trognon NOUN MASC un trognon de pomme an apple core

trois NUMBER **three**; Tom a trois ans Tom's three, à trois heures at three o'clock, le trois mars the third of March

être haut comme trois pommes **to be knee-high to a grasshopper** (literally: as tall as three apples)

troisième NOUN FEM (in a French school) **the equivalent of Year 10**

troisième NOUN MASC au troisième on the third floor

troisième ADJECTIVE **third**

trombone NOUN MASC ❶ **trombone** ❷ **paperclip** (because of its shape)

trompe NOUN FEM **trunk** (elephant's)

tromper VERB [1] ❶ **to deceive** ❷ se tromper **to make a mistake**, il s'est trompé he made a mistake, je me suis trompé de train I got the wrong train, vous vous êtes trompé de numéro you've got the wrong number

trompette NOUN FEM **trumpet**; jouer de la trompette to play the trumpet

tronc NOUN MASC **trunk** (of a tree)

tronçonneuse NOUN FEM **chain saw**

trop ADVERB ❶ **too**; c'est trop loin it's too far, c'est beaucoup trop cher it's much too expensive ❷ **too much**; j'ai trop mangé I've eaten too much, tu m'en as donné trop you've given me too much ❸ trop de **too much, too many**, trop de pain too much bread, trop de tomates too many tomatoes, trop de monde too many people ❹ de trop **too many, too much**, il y a une chaise de trop there's one chair too many, il y a dix euros de trop that's ten euros too much

tropique NOUN MASC **tropic**

trottoir NOUN MASC **pavement**

trou NOUN MASC **hole**; le trou dans la couche d'ozone the hole in the ozone layer

troublant ADJECTIVE **disturbing**

trou de serrure NOUN MASC **keyhole**

trou d'incendie NOUN MASC **fire hydrant**

trouer VERB [1] **to make a hole in**; des chaussettes trouées socks with holes in them

trouille NOUN FEM avoir la trouille (informal) to be scared

troupe NOUN FEM ❶ une troupe de théâtre a theatre company ❷ **flock** (of birds) ❸ **troop** (of tourists or children)

troupeau NOUN MASC (PLURAL **troupeaux**) **herd** (of cattle), **flock** (of sheep)

trousse NOUN FEM **pencil case**

trousseau NOUN MASC (PLURAL **trousseaux**) un trousseau de clés a bunch of keys

trousse de maquillage NOUN FEM **make-up bag**

trousse de secours NOUN FEM **first-aid kit**

trousse de toilette NOUN FEM **toilet bag**

trouver VERB [1] ❶ **to find**; as-tu trouvé ton passeport? did you find your passeport? ❷ **to think**; j'ai trouvé le film passionnant I thought the film was wonderful ❸ se trouver to be (in a place), les gens qui se trouvaient autour de moi the people who were around me, savez-vous où se trouve la gare routière? do you know where the bus station is?

truc NOUN MASC (informal) ❶ **thing**; un petit truc en bois a little thing made of wood, il y a un truc qui ne va pas something's wrong, le jazz, ce n'est pas mon truc jazz just isn't my thing ❷ **trick**; il doit y avoir un truc there must be a trick to it

truite NOUN FEM **trout**

tsigane NOUN MASC & FEM **gipsy**

TSVP ABBREVIATION (short for tournez s'il vous plaît) **PTO** (please turn over)

TTC short for toutes taxes comprises **inclusive of tax**

tu PRONOUN **you** ('tu' is used when talking to family members, people you know well, and people of your own age; otherwise 'vous' is used for 'you')

tube NOUN MASC ❶ **tube** ❷ (informal) **hit** (a pop song)

tuer VERB [1] ❶ **to kill** ❷ se tuer to be killed, elle s'est tuée dans un accident de voiture she was killed in a car accident ❸ se tuer to kill yourself

tue-tête IN PHRASE crier à tue-tête to shout at the top of your voice

tuile NOUN FEM ❶ **tile** ❷ **thin almond biscuit**

tulipe NOUN FEM **tulip**

Tunisie NOUN FEM **Tunisia**

tunisien, **tunisienne** ADJECTIVE MASC, FEM **Tunisian**

tunnel NOUN MASC **tunnel**; le tunnel sous la Manche the Channel Tunnel

turban NOUN MASC **turban**

turc NOUN MASC **Turkish** (language)

turc, **turque** ADJECTIVE MASC, FEM **Turkish**

Turc, **Turque** *NOUN MASC, FEM* **Turk**

Turquie *NOUN FEM* **Turkey**

tuteur, **tutrice** *NOUN MASC, FEM*
❶ **guardian** ❷ **tutor**

tutoyer *VERB* [39] **to address somebody as 'tu'** *(rather than 'vous')*; il ne faut pas tutoyer ton professeur you mustn't address your teacher as 'tu', et si on se tutoyait? shall we say 'tu' to each other?

tuyau *NOUN MASC* *(PLURAL* **tuyaux***)* ❶ **pipe** ❷ *(informal)* **tip** *(a helpful hint)*

tuyau d'arrosage *NOUN MASC* **hosepipe**

TVA *NOUN FEM (short for taxe à la valeur ajoutée)* **VAT**

type *NOUN MASC* ❶ **kind**; quel type de papier? what type of paper? ❷ *(informal)* **guy**; le type qui a ouvert la porte the guy who opened the door

typique *ADJECTIVE* **typical**

tyranniser *VERB* [1] **to bully**

tzigane *NOUN MASC & FEM, ADJECTIVE* **gypsy**

Uu

ulcère *NOUN MASC* **ulcer**

un, **une**, *des DETERMINER, PRONOUN, NUMBER* ❶ **a**, **an**; un lion a lion, une fraise a strawberry, des cerises (some) cherries ❷ **one**; un pour moi one for me, un par un one by one, trente et une personnes thirty-one people, les uns pensent que ... some think that ..., un jour sur deux every other day ❸ l'un(e) et l'autre the one and the other, l'un est français et l'autre est allemand one's French and the other's German ❹ l'un(e) ou l'autre either of them, tu peux prendre l'un ou l'autre, ça n'a pas d'importance you can take either of them, it doesn't matter

uni *ADJECTIVE* ❶ **close-knit** *(family or group)* ❷ **plain** *(not patterned)*; un tissu uni a plain fabric

uniforme *NOUN MASC* **uniform**

union *NOUN FEM* **union**; l'ex-Union soviétique the former Soviet Union

Union européenne *NOUN FEM* **European Union**

unique *ADJECTIVE* ❶ **only**; elle est fille unique she's an only child, il est fils unique he's an only child, l'unique raison the only reason ❷ **single**; 'prix unique' 'all one price' ❸ **unique**

uniquement ADVERB **only**

unité NOUN FEM ❶ **unity** ❷ **unit** (of currency, measurement, etc)

unité de disques NOUN FEM **disk drive**

univers NOUN MASC **universe**

universitaire ADJECTIVE **university** (degree, town), **academic** (work)

université NOUN FEM **university**

urbanisme NOUN MASC **town planning**

urgence NOUN FEM ❶ **urgency**; il y a urgence! it's urgent! ❷ d'urgence **immediately, at once** il faut téléphoner d'urgence you must phone at once ❸ **emergency**; les urgences, le service des urgences **accident and emergency, the casualty department**

urgent ADJECTIVE **urgent**

USA PLURAL NOUN MASC **USA**; aux USA in (or to) the USA

usage NOUN MASC ❶ **use**; à l'usage **with use**, en usage **in use**, à usage externe **for external use only** ❷ 'hors d'usage' 'not in service'

usagé ADJECTIVE ❶ **worn** ❷ **used**

usager NOUN MASC **user**

usé ADJECTIVE **worn**

user VERB [1] **to wear out** (shoes, clothing)

usine NOUN FEM **factory**

ustensile NOUN MASC **utensil**

utile ADJECTIVE **useful**

utilisable ADJECTIVE **usable**

utilisateur, utilisatrice NOUN MASC, FEM **user**

utiliser VERB [1] **to use**

utilité NOUN FEM **usefulness**; un livre d'une grande utilité a very useful book

va VERB ▸ SEE **aller¹**

vacances PLURAL NOUN FEM **holidays**; les vacances scolaires the school holidays, les grandes vacances the summer holidays, être en vacances to be on holiday, bonnes vacances! have a good holiday!

vacancier, vacancière NOUN MASC, FEM **holiday-maker**

vacarme NOUN MASC **din**; ils faisaient un vacarme pas possible! they were making an amazing din!

vaccination NOUN FEM **vaccination**

vacciner VERB [1] **to vaccinate**; se faire vacciner to be vaccinated

vache NOUN FEM **cow**

vache ADJECTIVE **mean**

vachement ADVERB (informal) **really**; c'était vachement bien! it was really good!

va-et-vient NOUN MASC **coming and going**

vagabond NOUN MASC **tramp**

vagin NOUN MASC **vagina**

vague[1] NOUN FEM **wave** *(in the sea)*

vague[2] ADJECTIVE **vague**

vaguement ADVERB **vaguely**

vain ADJECTIVE ❶ **useless** ❷ en vain
in vain

vaincre VERB [79] ❶ **to defeat** ❷ **to overcome**

vainqueur NOUN MASC **winner**

vais VERB ▸ SEE **aller**[1]

vaisseau NOUN MASC *(PLURAL* vaisseaux*)* **vessel**

vaisselle NOUN FEM **dishes**; faire la vaisselle to do the washing-up

valable ADJECTIVE **valid**

valet NOUN MASC **jack**; le valet de pique the jack of spades

valeur NOUN FEM **value**; des objets de valeur valuables, c'est sans valeur it's of no value

valider VERB [1] **to stamp** *(a ticket)*

valise NOUN FEM **suitcase**; faire ses valises to pack

vallée NOUN FEM **valley**

valoir VERB [80] ❶ **to be worth**; ça vaut combien? how much is it worth?, ce tableau vaut cher that painting's worth a lot ❷ valoir la peine to be worth it, ça ne vaut pas la peine d'y aller s'il pleut it's not worth going if it's raining, ça vaudrait la peine d'essayer it would be worth a try ❸ il vaut mieux faire it would be better to do, il vaut mieux téléphoner avant it would be better to phone first

valse NOUN FEM **waltz**

vampire NOUN MASC **vampire**

vandalisme NOUN MASC **vandalism**

vanille NOUN FEM **vanilla**; une glace à la vanille a vanilla ice cream

vanter VERB [1] se vanter to boast

vapeur NOUN FEM **steam**; faire cuire des légumes à la vapeur to steam vegetables

vaporisateur NOUN MASC **(perfume) spray**

variable ADJECTIVE **variable, changeable**

varicelle NOUN FEM **chickenpox**; avoir la varicelle to have chickenpox

varié ADJECTIVE **varied, various**; 'sandwichs variés' 'a selection of sandwiches'

varier VERB [1] **to vary**

variété NOUN FEM ❶ **variety** ❷ un spectacle de variétés a variety show

vas VERB ▸ SEE **aller**[1]

vase[1] NOUN MASC **vase**

vase[2] NOUN FEM **mud**

vaste ADJECTIVE **large, enormous**

va-vite ADVERB FEM à la va-vite in a rush

veau NOUN MASC *(PLURAL* veaux*)* ❶ **calf** ❷ **veal**

vécu VERB ▸ SEE **vivre**

vedette NOUN FEM **star**; une vedette de cinéma a film star

A
B
C
D
E
F
G
H
I
J
K
L
M
N
O
P
Q
R
S
T
U
V
W
X
Y
Z

végétal *ADJECTIVE* **vegetable**; l'huile végétale vegetable oil

végétarien, végétarienne *NOUN MASC, FEM*

végétarien, végétarienne *ADJECTIVE MASC, FEM* **vegetarian**

véhicule *NOUN MASC* **vehicle**

veille *NOUN FEM* la veille the day before, je l'avais rencontrée la veille de mon départ I met her the day before my departure, la veille de Noël Christmas Eve, la veille du jour de l'an New Year's Eve

veilleuse *NOUN FEM* ❶ **night-light** ❷ **pilot light**

veinard *NOUN MASC* (informal) petit veinard! you lucky little devil!

veine *NOUN FEM* ❶ avoir de la veine (informal) to be lucky ❷ **vein**

vélo *NOUN MASC* **bike**; je suis venu à vélo I came by bike, faire du vélo to go cycling

vélodrome *NOUN MASC* **cycle-racing track, velodrome**

vélomoteur *NOUN MASC* **moped**

vélo tout-terrain *NOUN MASC* **mountain bike**

velours *NOUN MASC* ❶ **velvet** ❷ **corduroy**

velouté *NOUN MASC* **cream soup**; velouté de champignons cream of mushroom soup

vendanges *PLURAL NOUN FEM* **grape harvest**

vendeur, vendeuse *NOUN MASC, FEM* ❶ **shop assistant** ❷ **salesperson** ❸ **seller**

vendre *VERB* [3] **to sell**; vendre quelque chose à quelqu'un to sell somebody something, j'ai vendu mon ordinateur à Colette I've sold my computer to Colette, 'à vendre' 'for sale', 'vendu' 'sold'

vendredi *NOUN MASC* ❶ **Friday**; nous sommes vendredi aujourd'hui it's Friday today, vendredi dernier last Friday, vendredi prochain next Friday ❷ **on Friday**; je l'ai vu vendredi soir I saw him on Friday evening ❸ **on Fridays**; fermé le vendredi closed on Fridays ❹ tous les vendredis every Friday, le vendredi saint Good Friday

vénéneux, vénéneuse *ADJECTIVE MASC, FEM* **poisonous** (plant)

vengeance *NOUN FEM* **revenge**

venger *VERB* [52] se venger to have your revenge

venimeux, venimeuse *ADJECTIVE MASC, FEM* **poisonous** (snake, spider)

venir *VERB* [81] ❶ **to come**; il vient de Provence he comes from Provence, elles sont venues mardi they came on Tuesday, viens voir! come and see! ❷ faire venir to send for, il faut faire venir le médecin we must send for the doctor ❸ venir de faire to have just done, ils viennent d'arriver they have just arrived, elle venait de partir she had just left

vent *NOUN MASC* **wind**; un vent du sud a south wind

vente *NOUN FEM* **sale**; être en vente to be on sale

vente aux enchères *NOUN FEM* **auction sale**

ventilateur NOUN MASC **fan**

ventre NOUN MASC **stomach**; avoir mal au ventre to have stomachache

venu VERB ▸ SEE **venir**

ver NOUN MASC **worm**

verbe NOUN MASC **verb**

verdict NOUN MASC **verdict**

verger NOUN MASC **orchard**

verglas NOUN MASC **black ice**

vérifier VERB [1] **to check**

véritable ADJECTIVE **real**

vérité NOUN FEM **truth**

vernir VERB [2] **to varnish**

vernis à ongles NOUN MASC **nail varnish**

verre NOUN MASC ❶ **glass**; un verre de vin a glass of wine ❷ **glass**; un vase en verre a glass vase ❸ **lens** (of spectacles)

verrou NOUN MASC **bolt** (on a door)

verrouiller VERB [1] **to bolt** (a door)

verrue NOUN FEM **wart**

vers¹ PREPOSITION ❶ **towards**; il montait vers l'église he was going up towards the church ❷ **about** (a time); vers midi about twelve, vers la fin du mois around the end of the month

vers² NOUN MASC **line of poetry**; des vers poetry

Verseau NOUN MASC **Aquarius** (sign of the Zodiac)

versement NOUN MASC **payment**

verser VERB [1] ❶ **to pour**; Sylvie m'a versé une tasse de thé Sylvie poured me a cup of tea ❷ **to pay in**; j'ai versé 300 euros sur mon compte I paid 300 euros into my account

version NOUN FEM ❶ **version** ❷ **translation** (into your own language)

verso NOUN MASC **back** (of a piece of paper); voir au verso see overleaf

vert ADJECTIVE **green**
• avoir la main verte to have green fingers

vertical ADJECTIVE MASC (PLURAL verticaux) **vertical, upright**

vertige NOUN MASC **vertigo**

verveine NOUN FEM **verbena tea**

veste NOUN FEM **jacket**

vestiaire NOUN MASC ❶ **cloakroom** (in a theatre, restaurant, etc) ❷ **changing room** (in a gym, sports ground)

vêtement NOUN MASC **garment**; les vêtements clothes, 'vêtements pour enfants' 'children's wear'

vétérinaire NOUN MASC & FEM **vet**

veuf, veuve NOUN MASC, FEM **widower, widow**

vexer VERB [1] **to annoy, to offend**

viande NOUN FEM **meat**

vibrer VERB [1] **to vibrate**

victime NOUN FEM **victim**

victoire NOUN FEM **victory**

vide ADJECTIVE **empty**

a b c d e f g h i j k l m n o p q r s t u **v** w x y z

vide NOUN MASC **❶ space**; dans le vide in(to) space **❷ vacuum**; emballé sous vide vacuum-packed

vidéo NOUN FEM **video**; une caméra vidéo a video camera, un jeu vidéo a video game

vidéoclip NOUN MASC **music video**

vidéoclub NOUN MASC **video shop**

vidéothèque NOUN FEM **video library**

vider VERB [1] **to empty**

vie NOUN FEM **life**; toute ma vie all my life, il est encore en vie he's still alive, ton mode de vie your lifestyle
• c'est la vie that's life, that's the way it goes

vieil ADJECTIVE ▸ SEE **vieux**

vieillard, vieillarde NOUN MASC, FEM **old man, old woman**

vieille ADJECTIVE ▸ SEE **vieux**

vieillesse NOUN FEM **old age**

vieillir VERB [2] **to age**; il a beaucoup vieilli récemment he's aged a lot recently

vierge NOUN FEM **virgin**; la Sainte Vierge the Virgin Mary

vierge ADJECTIVE **❶ blank**; une cassette vierge a blank cassette **❷** laine vierge pure new wool, l'huile d'olive vierge virgin olive oil

Vierge NOUN FEM **Virgo** (sign of the Zodiac)

vieux ADJECTIVE (vieil before a noun or silent 'h') **vieille** FEM (PLURAL vieaux) **old**; une vieille ville an old town, un vieil arbre an old tree

vieux, vieux NOUN MASC, FEM un vieux an old man, une vieille an old woman

vieux garçon NOUN MASC **bachelor**

vif, vive ADJECTIVE MASC, FEM **❶ bright**; rose vif bright pink **❷ lively**; une vive discussion a lively discussion **❸** avoir l'esprit vif to be quick-witted

vigne NOUN FEM **vine, vineyard**

vigneron, vigneronne NOUN MASC, FEM **wine-grower**

vignette NOUN FEM **❶ label ❷ tax disc**

vignoble NOUN MASC **vineyard**

vilain ADJECTIVE **❶ ugly ❷ naughty**; c'est vilain, ça! that's naughty!

villa NOUN FEM **detached house, villa**

village NOUN MASC **village**

ville NOUN FEM **town, city**; une grande ville a city, en ville in (or into) town

vin NOUN MASC **wine**

vinaigre NOUN MASC **vinegar**

vinaigrette NOUN FEM **French dressing**

vingt NUMBER **twenty**; Marion a vingt ans Marion's twenty, le vingt juillet the twentieth of July, à vingt heures at 8 p.m., vingt et un twenty-one

vingtaine NOUN FEM **about twenty**; une vingtaine de personnes about twenty people

vingtième ADJECTIVE **twentieth**

viol NOUN MASC **rape**

violemment ADJECTIVE **violently**

violence NOUN FEM **violence**

violent ADJECTIVE **violent**

violer VERB [1] **to rape**

violet, violette[1] ADJECTIVE MASC, FEM **purple**

violette[2] NOUN FEM **violet** *(the flower)*

violon NOUN MASC **violin**; jouer du violon to play the violin

violoncelle NOUN MASC **cello**; jouer du violoncelle to play the cello

vipère NOUN FEM **adder, viper**

virage NOUN MASC **bend** *(in the road)*

virement NOUN MASC **transfer** *(of money)*

virer VERB [1] ❶ **to transfer** *(money)* ❷ **to turn** ❸ **to turn (right) around**

virgule NOUN FEM ❶ **comma** ❷ **decimal point**; sept virgule trois seven point three

virus NOUN MASC **virus**

vis[1] VERB ▸ SEE **vivre**

vis[2] NOUN FEM **screw**

visa NOUN MASC **visa**

visage NOUN MASC **face**

viser VERB [1] ❶ **to aim** ❷ **to aim at** *(a target)*

visibilité NOUN FEM **visibility**

visible ADJECTIVE **visible, obvious**

visite NOUN FEM **visite**; une visite chez nos cousins a visit to our cousins, rendre visite à quelqu'un to visit somebody, elle a de la visite she's got visitors

visiter VERB [1] **to visit** *(a place)*; on peut visiter l'appartement? can we see round the flat?

visiteur, visiteuse NOUN MASC, FEM **visitor**

visualisation graphique NOUN FEM **graphics**

vit VERB ▸ SEE **vivre**

vitamine NOUN FEM **vitamin**

vite ADVERB ❶ **fast**; tu conduis trop vite you drive too fast, parle moins vite speak more slowly ❷ **quick**; vite! le bus arrive! quick! here's the bus!, ce sera vite fait it won't take long ❸ **soon**; on sera vite arrivé we'll soon be there, elle a vite compris she understood immediately

vitesse NOUN FEM ❶ **speed**; elle est partie à toute vitesse she rushed off ❷ **gear**; en deuxième vitesse in second gear

vitrail NOUN MASC *(PLURAL* **vitraux**) **stained glass window**

vitre NOUN FEM **window**

vitrine NOUN FEM **shop window**

vivant ADJECTIVE ❶ **living** ❷ **lively**

vive[1] ADJECTIVE ▸ SEE **vif**

vive[2] EXCLAMATION Vive le roi! Long live the king!

vivement ADVERB ❶ réagir vivement to react strongly ❷ vivement les vacances! roll on the holidays!

vivre VERB [82] **to live**; ils vivent ensemble they live together, ils ont vécu dans plusieurs pays différents they've lived in several different countries

vocabulaire NOUN MASC **vocabulary**

vœu *(vœux)* NOUN MASC ❶ **wish**; faire un vœu to make a wish, meilleurs

a b c d e f g h i j k l m n o p q r s t u v w x y z

vœux! best wishes! *(especially at the New Year)* ❷ **vow**

vogue NOUN FEM **fashion**; en vogue in fashion

voici PREPOSITION ❶ **here is, here are**; voici l'addition here's the bill, voici les clés here are the keys, me voici! here I am! ❷ **this is**; voici ma sœur this is my sister

voie NOUN FEM ❶ **way**; être sur la bonne voie to be on the right track ❷ **track** *(for trains)*; la voie ferrée the railway track, le train de Bourges entre en gare voie dix the train from Bourges is now arriving at platform ten ❸ **lane** *(on a main road)*; une route à trois voies a three-lane road

voilà PREPOSITION ❶ **there is, there are**; voilà tes lunettes, là-bas sur la table there are your glasses, over there on the table, la voilà devant la boulangerie there she is outside the baker's ❷ **here is, here are**; voilà Anna qui arrive here's Anna coming now, voilà ton café here's your coffee, voilà, c'est tout right, that's all ❸ **that is**; voilà ma fille that's my daughter, et voilà pourquoi and that's why

voile¹ NOUN MASC **veil**

voile² NOUN FEM **sail**; des cours de voile sailing lessons

voilier NOUN MASC **sailing boat**

voir VERB [13] ❶ **to see**; je ne vois rien I can't see anything, je viendrai te voir un de ces jours I'll come and see you one of these days, oui, je vois, tu veux dire que ... yes, I see, you mean that ..., un film à voir a film worth seeing, peut-être, on

verra perhaps, we'll see ❷ **se voir to be noticeable**, ça ne se verra pas nobody will notice ❸ **se voir to see each other**, ils se voient à Noël they see each other at Christmas ❹ **faire voir quelque chose à quelqu'un to show somebody something**, je te ferai voir mes photos de vacances I'll show you my holiday photos, fais voir! let's have a look! ❺ **ça n'a rien à voir avec mon problème that's got nothing to do with my problem**
- il ne voit pas plus loin que le bout de son nez he can't see any further than the end of his nose
- elle ne peut pas le voir (en peinture) she can't stand him *(literally: she can't bear to see him (in a painting))*
- j'en ai vu d'autres I've seen worse

voisin, voisine NOUN MASC, FEM **neighbour**; Claire est chez les voisins Claire's round at the neighbours', ma voisine de table the girl sitting next to me at table

voisinage NOUN MASC **neighbourhood**

voiture NOUN FEM ❶ **car**; en voiture by car ❷ **carriage** *(on a train)*

voix NOUN FEM ❶ **voice**; à haute voix aloud, à voix basse softly ❷ **vote**; elle a eu 20 voix she got 20 votes

vol NOUN MASC ❶ **flight**; le vol pour Milan the Milan flight ❷ **theft**
- à vol d'oiseau as the crow flies *(literally: by bird flight)*

volaille NOUN FEM **poultry**; les foies de volaille chicken livers

volant NOUN MASC ❶ **steering wheel**; qui était au volant? who was driving? ❷ **shuttlecock**

volant ADJECTIVE **flying**

volcan NOUN MASC **volcano**

volée NOUN FEM **volley**

voler VERB [1] ❶ **to fly** ❷ **to steal**; voler quelque chose à quelqu'un to steal something from someone, on leur a volé leur voiture their car's been stolen ❸ voler quelqu'un to rob somebody

volet NOUN MASC **shutter**

voleur, voleuse NOUN MASC, FEM **thief**

volley NOUN MASC **volleyball**; jouer au volley to play volleyball

volontaire NOUN MASC & FEM **volunteer**

volonté NOUN FEM ❶ **will**; la bonne volonté goodwill ❷ à volonté unlimited, 'pizza à volonté' 'as much pizza as you want'

volontiers ADVERB **gladly**; 'tu viens avec nous?' – 'volontiers' 'will you come too?' – 'I'd love to', 'tu me le prêtes?' – 'volontiers' 'will you lend it to me?' – 'of course'

volume NOUN MASC **volume**

vomir VERB [2] **to be sick, to vomit**

vos ADJECTIVE ▸ SEE **votre**

voter VERB [1] **to vote**; elle vote toujours pour les Verts she always votes for the Greens

votre ADJECTIVE (PLURAL vos) **your**; nous connaissons votre fils we know your son, vos billets, monsieur your tickets, sir

vôtre PRONOUN le vôtre, la vôtre, les vôtres yours, une maison comme la vôtre a house like yours, mes parents et les vôtres my parents and yours
• à la vôtre! cheers!

vouloir VERB [14] ❶ **to want**; elle ne veut rien she doesn't want anything, veux-tu venir avec nous?, do you want to come with us?, je n'ai pas voulu arriver trop tôt I didn't want to arrive too early, il veut qu'elle l'appelle he wants her to phone him, il m'a vexé sans le vouloir he annoyed me without meaning to ❷ **to like**; si tu veux if you like, je voudrais visiter Versailles I'd like to go to Versailles, 'encore du café?' – 'oui, je veux bien' 'more coffee?' – 'yes, I'd love some' ❸ voulez-vous m'excuser? would you excuse me?, veux-tu fermer la porte? would you shut the door?, veux-tu te taire! will you be quiet! ❹ vouloir dire to mean, qu'est-ce que tu veux dire? what do you mean?, si tu vois ce que je veux dire if you see what I mean, qu'est-ce que ce mot veut dire? what does this word mean? ❺ en vouloir à quelqu'un to bear a grudge against someone, elle leur en veut she's never forgiven them
• vouloir c'est pouvoir where there's a will there's a way (literally: to want is to be able)

voulu VERB ▸ SEE **vouloir**

vous PRONOUN ❶ **you**; avec vous with you, est-ce que ce sac est à vous? is this your bag?, à vous de jouer! your turn to play! ❷ **to you**; je vous écrirai I'll write to you ❸ **yourself**; ne vous coupez pas! don't cut yourself!

vous-même(s) PRONOUN **yourself,**

yourselves; vous me l'avez dit vous-même you told me yourself, est-ce que vous l'avez fait vous-mêmes? did you make it yourselves?

voûte NOUN FEM **vault, arch**

vouvoyer VERB [39] **to use 'vous' to mean 'you'** (rather than 'tu' which you use when talking to friends, family, and people of your own age); ils se connaissent depuis des années mais ils continuent à se vouvoyer they've known each other for years but they still address each other as 'vous'

voyage NOUN MASC **journey**; bon voyage! have a good trip!

voyage organisé NOUN MASC **package tour**

voyager VERB [52] **to travel**

voyageur, voyageuse NOUN MASC, FEM **passenger**

voyelle NOUN FEM **vowel**

voyou NOUN MASC **hooligan**

vrac ADVERB acheter des olives en vrac to buy olives loose (as opposed to pre-packaged)

vrai ADJECTIVE ❶ **true**; c'est une histoire vraie it's a true story ❷ **real**; c'est un vrai problème it's a real problem, c'est vrai? really?, pour de vrai for real ❸ à vrai dire to tell the truth

vraiment ADVERB **really**

vraisemblable ADJECTIVE **likely**; peu vraisemblable unlikely

vraisemblablement ADVERB **probably**

VTT NOUN MASC (short for vélo tout-terrain) **mountain bike**

vu VERB ▸ SEE **voir**

vu ADJECTIVE ❶ vu que seeing that, vu qu'il pleut, ce n'est pas la peine d'y aller seeing it's raining, there's no point in going ❷ être mal vu to be disapproved of, il est plutôt mal vu people don't think much of him, c'est mal vu de faire beaucoup de bruit they don't like people making a lot of noise, cette critique a été mal vue this criticism didn't go down well ❸ être bien vu to be well thought of, elle est très bien vue dans la société people in the company think highly of her

vue NOUN FEM ❶ **eyesight**; perdre la vue to lose your eyesight ❷ **sight**; je le connais de vue I know him by sight, nous l'avons perdue de vue we've lost touch with her, rien qu'à la vue de la viande at the very sight of meat ❸ **view**; une chambre avec vue sur le lac a room with a view of the lake

vulgaire ADJECTIVE ❶ **vulgar** ❷ **common**

Ww

wagon *NOUN MASC* ❶ **railway carriage** ❷ **waggon**

wagon-lit *NOUN MASC* **sleeper** *(on a train)*

wagon-restaurant *NOUN MASC* **restaurant car**

wallon *NOUN MASC* **Wallon** *(language)*

wallon, wallonne *ADJECTIVE MASC, FEM* **Wallon** *(of French-speaking Belgium)*

Wallon, Wallone *NOUN MASC, FEM* **Wallon** *(French-speaking Belgian)*

WC *(pronounced 'vaysay')* *PLURAL NOUN MASC* **toilet**; aller aux WC to go to the toilet, il est aux WC he's in the loo

web *NOUN MASC* **le web the Web**

weekend, week-end *NOUN MASC* **weekend** ; le weekend prochain next weekend, le weekend dernier last weekend, bon weekend! have a good weekend!

Xx

xylophone *NOUN MASC* **xylophone**; jouer du xylophone to play the xylophone

Yy

y *PRONOUN, ADVERB* ❶ **there**; j'y vais demain I'm going there tomorrow ❷ il y a there is, there are, il y a un café à côté there's a cafe next door, il y a des tomates dans le frigo there are some tomatoes in the fridge ❸ j'y pensais I was thinking of it, tu n'y peux rien you can't do anything about it

yaourt *NOUN MASC* **yoghurt**

yeux *PLURAL NOUN MASC* ▸ SEE **œil**

yoga *NOUN MASC* **yoga**

yougoslave *ADJECTIVE* **Yugoslavian**

Yougoslavie *NOUN FEM* **Yugoslavia**; l'ex-Yougoslavie the former Yugoslavia

a
b
c
d
e
f
g
h
i
j
k
l
m
n
o
p
q
r
s
t
u
v
w
x
y
z

French—English

Zz

zapper *VERB* [1] **to channel hop**

zèbre *NOUN MASC* **zebra**

zéro *NOUN MASC* **zero, nil, love** *(in tennis)*; **trois à zéro** three-nil, **zéro heure** midnight, **elle a le moral à zéro** she's really depressed
- **il faut tout reprendre à zéro** we'll have to start again from scratch

zézayer *VERB* [59] **to lisp**

zigzag *NOUN MASC* **zigzag**; **une route en zigzag** a winding road, **faire des zigzags** to zigzag

zodiaque *NOUN MASC* **zodiac**

zone *NOUN FEM* **❶ zone, area ❷ la zone** the slums, **un enfant de la zone** a child who grew up in the slums

zone euro *NOUN FEM* **eurozone**

zone industrielle *NOUN FEM* **industrial estate**

zoo *NOUN MASC* **zoo**

zoologique *ADJECTIVE* **zoological**

zut *EXCLAMATION* *(informal)* **damn!**

A
B
C
D
E
F
G
H
I
J
K
L
M
N
O
P
Q
R
S
T
U
V
W
X
Y
Z

VERB TABLES

Using the verb tables

French regular verbs (pages 314–317)

There are three regular verb families in French: **-er**, **-ir**, and **-re** verbs.
When you look up an entry in this dictionary, you will see a number in square brackets ([1], [2], etc.). This number tells you which verb model you need to follow for that verb.

[1]	-er	e.g. parler	to speak
[2]	-ir	e.g. finir	to finish
[3]	-re	e.g. attendre	to wait
[4]	reflexive (-er)	e.g. se laver	to wash (oneself)

Main French irregular verbs (pages 318–327)

The following verbs are unlike the regular verbs. They are irregular and don't follow a particular pattern so their forms are given for you.
Again, when you look up an entry, use the number in square brackets to bring you to these tables to see how to form the parts of the verb you need.

[5]	avoir	to have
[6]	être	to be

- -

[7]	aller	to go
[8]	devoir	to have to
[9]	dire	to say
[10]	faire	to do or to make
[11]	mettre	to put
[12]	pouvoir	to be able
[13]	voir	to see
[14]	vouloir	to want

Other French irregular verbs (pages 328–330)

il/elle/on and ils/elles/on

Use the **il** form in the tables for **il/elle** and **on**. Use the **ils** form for **ils/elles** forms.

Perfect tense

Some verbs take **avoir** in the perfect tense and some take **être**. In these tables the ✢ reminds you which ones take **être**.

[1]
parler
to speak

Imperative

parle	speak
parlons	let's speak
parlez	speak

Past participle

| parlé | spoken |

Present

je parle	I speak or I am speaking
tu parles	
il parle	
nous parl**ons**	
vous parl**ez**	
ils parl**ent**	

Perfect ★

j' ai parlé	I have spoken or I spoke
tu as parlé	
il a parlé	
nous avons parlé	
vous avez parlé	
ils ont parlé	

Future

je parler**ai**	I will speak
tu parler**as**	
il parler**a**	
nous parler**ons**	
vous parler**ez**	
ils parler**ont**	

Present subjunctive ☆

je parle	I speak or I am speaking
tu parles	
il parle	
nous parl**ions**	
vous parl**iez**	
ils parlent	

Imperfect ☉

je parl**ais**	I spoke or I used to speak or I was speaking
tu parl**ais**	
il parl**ait**	
nous parl**ions**	
vous parl**iez**	
ils parl**aient**	

Conditional

je parler**ais**	I would speak
tu parler**ais**	
il parler**ait**	
nous parler**ions**	
vous parler**iez**	
ils parler**aient**	

★ uses *avoir* plus the past participle to describe completed events in the past

☆ usually used after *que*: **Il est possible que tu aimes le film.** It is possible that you will like the film.

☉ used to describe what something was like, what used to happen, or what was happening

Imperative

finis	finish
finissons	let's finish
finissez	finish

Past participle

| fini | finished |

[2]
finir
to finish

Present

je finis	I finish or I am finishing
tu finis	
il finit	
nous finissons	
vous finissez	
ils finissent	

Perfect ★

j' ai fini	I have finished or I finished
tu as fini	
il a fini	
nous avons fini	
vous avez fini	
ils ont fini	

Future

je finirai	I will finish
tu finiras	
il finira	
nous finirons	
vous finirez	
ils finiront	

Present subjunctive ☆

je finisse	I finish or I am finishing
tu finisses	
il finisse	
nous finissions	
vous finissiez	
ils finissent	

Imperfect ☉

je finissais	I finished or I used to finish or I was finishing
tu finissais	
il finissait	
nous finissions	
vous finissiez	
ils finissaient	

Conditional

je finirais	I would finish
tu finirais	
il finirait	
nous finirions	
vous finiriez	
ils finiraient	

★ uses *avoir* plus the past participle to describe completed events in the past

☆ usually used after *que*: **Le prof veut que je finisse ça pour demain.** The teacher wants me to finish this for tomorrow.

☉ used to describe what something was like, what used to happen, or what was happening

[3]
attendre
to wait

Imperative
attend<u>s</u> wait
attend<u>ons</u> let's wait
attend<u>ez</u> wait

Past participle
attend<u>u</u> waited

Present

j'	attend<u>s</u>	I wait or I am waiting
tu	attend<u>s</u>	
il	attend	
nous	attend<u>ons</u>	
vous	attend<u>ez</u>	
ils	attend<u>ent</u>	

Present subjunctive ☆

j'	attend<u>e</u>	I wait or I am waiting
tu	attend<u>es</u>	
il	attend<u>e</u>	
nous	attend<u>ions</u>	
vous	attend<u>iez</u>	
ils	attend<u>ent</u>	

Perfect ★

j'	ai attend<u>u</u>	I have waited or I waited
tu	as attend<u>u</u>	
il	a attend<u>u</u>	
nous	avons attend<u>u</u>	
vous	avez attend<u>u</u>	
ils	ont attendu	

Imperfect ✪

j'	attend<u>ais</u>	I waited or I used to wait or I was waiting
tu	attend<u>ais</u>	
il	attend<u>ait</u>	
nous	attend<u>ions</u>	
vous	attend<u>iez</u>	
ils	attend<u>aient</u>	

Future

j'	attendr<u>ai</u>	I will wait
tu	attendr<u>as</u>	
il	attendr<u>a</u>	
nous	attendr<u>ons</u>	
vous	attendr<u>ez</u>	
ils	attendr<u>ont</u>	

Conditional

j'	attendr<u>ais</u>	I would wait
tu	attendr<u>ais</u>	
il	attendr<u>ait</u>	
nous	attendr<u>ions</u>	
vous	attendr<u>iez</u>	
ils	attendr<u>aient</u>	

★ uses *avoir* plus the past participle to describe completed events in the past
☆ usually used after *que*: **Il faut que tu attendes les autres.** You must wait for the others.
✪ used to describe what something was like, what used to happen, or what was happening

Imperative

lave-toi wash (yourself)
or have a wash
lavons-nous
let's wash (ourselves) or let's
have a wash
lavez-vous
wash (yourselves) or wash (yourself)
or have a wash

Past participle

lavé washed

Present

je	me lave	I wash (myself) or I am washing (myself)
tu	te laves	
il	se lave	
nous	nous lavons	
vous	vous lavez	
ils	se lavent	

Perfect ✢

je	me suis lavé	I have washed (myself) or I washed (myself)
tu	t'es lavé	
il	s'est lavé	
elle	s'est lavée	
nous	nous sommes lave(e)s	
vous	vous êtes lave(e)s	
ils	se sont lavés	
elles	se sont lavées	

Future

je	me laverai	I will wash (myself)
tu	te laveras	
il	se lavera	
nous	nous laverons	
vous	vous laverez	
ils	se laveront	

Present subjunctive ☆

je	me lave	I wash (myself) or I am washing (myself)
tu	te laves	
il	se lave	
nous	nous lavions	
vous	vous laviez	
ils	se lavent	

Imperfect ✪

je	me lavais	I washed (myself) or I used to wash (myself) or I was washing (myself)
tu	te lavais	
il	se lavait	
nous	nous lavions	
vous	vous laviez	
ils	se lavaient	

Conditional

je	me laverais	I would wash (myself)
tu	te laverais	
il	se laverait	
nous	nous laverions	
vous	vous laveriez	
ils	se laveraient	

✢ uses *être* plus the past participle to describe completed events in the past
☆ usually used after *que*: **Il est important que vous vous laviez les mains.**
It is important that you wash your hands.
✪ used to describe what something was like, what used to happen, or what was happening

[5]

avoir
to have

Imperative

<u>aie</u>   have
<u>ayons</u> let's have
<u>ayez</u> have

Past participle

<u>eu</u>   had

Present

j'	<u>ai</u>	I have or I am having
tu	<u>as</u>	
il	<u>a</u>	
nous	av<u>ons</u>	
vous	av<u>ez</u>	
ils	<u>ont</u>	

Perfect ★

j'	ai <u>eu</u>	I have had or I had
tu	as <u>eu</u>	
il	a <u>eu</u>	
nous	avons <u>eu</u>	
vous	avez <u>eu</u>	
ils	ont <u>eu</u>	

Future

j'	<u>aurai</u>	I will have
tu	<u>auras</u>	
il	<u>aura</u>	
nous	<u>aurons</u>	
vous	<u>aurez</u>	
ils	<u>auront</u>	

Present subjunctive ☆

j'	<u>aie</u>	I have or I am having
tu	<u>aies</u>	
il	<u>ait</u>	
nous	<u>ayons</u>	
vous	<u>ayez</u>	
ils	<u>aient</u>	

Imperfect ✪

j'	av<u>ais</u>	I had or I used to have or I was having
tu	av<u>ais</u>	
il	av<u>ait</u>	
nous	av<u>ions</u>	
vous	av<u>iez</u>	
ils	av<u>aient</u>	

Conditional

j'	<u>aurais</u>	I would have
tu	<u>aurais</u>	
il	<u>aurait</u>	
nous	<u>aurions</u>	
vous	<u>auriez</u>	
ils	<u>auraient</u>	

★ uses *avoir* plus the past participle to describe completed events in the past
☆ usually used after *que*: **Il faut que j'aie ce jeu.** I must have that game.
✪ used to describe what something was like, what used to happen, or what was happening

Imperative

<u>sois</u>	be
<u>soyons</u>	let's be
<u>soyez</u>	be

Past participle

<u>été</u>	been

Present

je	<u>suis</u>	I am
tu	<u>es</u>	
il	<u>est</u>	
nous	<u>sommes</u>	
vous	<u>êtes</u>	
ils	<u>sont</u>	

Present subjunctive ☆

je	<u>sois</u>	I am
tu	<u>sois</u>	
il	<u>soit</u>	
nous	<u>soyons</u>	
vous	<u>soyez</u>	
ils	<u>soient</u>	

Perfect ★

j'	ai <u>été</u>	I have been or I was
tu	as <u>été</u>	
il	a <u>été</u>	
nous	avons <u>été</u>	
vous	avez <u>été</u>	
ils	ont <u>été</u>	

Imperfect ☺

j'	<u>étais</u>	I was or I used to be or I was being
tu	<u>étais</u>	
il	<u>était</u>	
nous	<u>étions</u>	
vous	<u>étiez</u>	
ils	<u>étaient</u>	

Future

je	<u>serai</u>	I will be
tu	<u>seras</u>	
il	<u>sera</u>	
nous	<u>serons</u>	
vous	<u>serez</u>	
ils	<u>seront</u>	

Conditional

je	<u>serais</u>	I would be
tu	<u>serais</u>	
il	<u>serait</u>	
nous	<u>serions</u>	
vous	<u>seriez</u>	
ils	<u>seraient</u>	

★ uses *avoir* plus the past participle to describe completed events in the past
☆ usually used after *que*: **J'ai peur qu'elle soit là**. I'm afraid she may be there.
☺ used to describe what something was like, what used to happen, or what was happening

[7] aller
to go

Imperative

va	go
allons	let's go
allez	go

Past participle

allé — gone

Present

je	vais	I go *or* I am going
tu	vas	
il	va	
nous	allons	
vous	allez	
ils	vont	

Perfect ✤

je	suis allé	I have gone *or* I went
tu	es allé	
il	est allé	
elle	est allée	
nous	sommes alle(e)s	
vous	êtes alle(e)s	
ils	sont allés	
elles	sont allées	

Future

j'	irai	I will go
tu	iras	
il	ira	
nous	irons	
vous	irez	
ils	iront	

Present subjunctive ☆

j'	aille	I go *or* I am going
tu	ailles	
il	aille	
nous	allions	
vous	alliez	
ils	aillent	

Imperfect ✪

j'	allais	I went *or* I used to go *or* I was going
tu	allais	
il	allait	
nous	allions	
vous	alliez	
ils	allaient	

Conditional

j'	irais	I would go
tu	irais	
il	irait	
nous	irions	
vous	iriez	
ils	iraient	

✤ uses *être* plus the past participle to describe completed events in the past

☆ usually used after *que*: **Mamie veut que tu ailles faire les courses avec elle.** Gran wants you to go shopping with her.

✪ used to describe what something was like, what used to happen, or what was happening

Imperative
The imperative of
<u>devoir</u> is not used.

Past participle
<u>dû</u>   had to

[8]

devoir
to have to

Present

je	<u>dois</u>	I have to *or* I must
tu	<u>dois</u>	
il	<u>doit</u>	
nous	dev<u>ons</u>	
vous	dev<u>ez</u>	
ils	<u>doivent</u>	

Perfect ★

j'	ai <u>dû</u>	I have had to *or* I had to
tu	as <u>dû</u>	
il	a <u>dû</u>	
nous	avons <u>dû</u>	
vous	avez <u>dû</u>	
ils	ont <u>dû</u>	

Future

je	devr<u>ai</u>	I will have to
tu	devr<u>as</u>	
il	devr<u>a</u>	
nous	devr<u>ons</u>	
vous	devr<u>ez</u>	
ils	devr<u>ont</u>	

Present subjunctive ☆

je	<u>doive</u>	I have to *or* I must
tu	<u>doives</u>	
il	<u>doive</u>	
nous	dev<u>ions</u>	
vous	dev<u>iez</u>	
ils	<u>doivent</u>	

Imperfect ☉

je	dev<u>ais</u>	I had to *or* I used to have to
tu	dev<u>ais</u>	
il	dev<u>ait</u>	
nous	dev<u>ions</u>	
vous	dev<u>iez</u>	
ils	dev<u>aient</u>	

Conditional

je	devr<u>ais</u>	I ought to
tu	devr<u>ais</u>	
il	devr<u>ait</u>	
nous	devr<u>ions</u>	
vous	devr<u>iez</u>	
ils	devr<u>aient</u>	

★ uses *avoir* plus the past participle to describe completed events in the past
☆ usually used after *que*: **J'ai bien peur que nous devions aller le voir.** I'm afraid we may have to visit him.
☉ used to describe what something was like, what used to happen, or what was happening

[9]

dire
to say

Imperative

<u>dis</u>   say
<u>disons</u>   let's say
<u>dites</u>   say

Past participle

<u>dit</u>   said

Present

je	<u>dis</u>	I say *or* I am saying
tu	<u>dis</u>	
il	<u>dit</u>	
nous	<u>disons</u>	
vous	<u>dites</u>	
ils	<u>disent</u>	

Perfect ★

j'	ai <u>dit</u>	I have said *or* I said
tu	as <u>dit</u>	
il	a <u>dit</u>	
nous	avons <u>dit</u>	
vous	avez <u>dit</u>	
ils	ont <u>dit</u>	

Future

je	dir<u>ai</u>	I will say
tu	dir<u>as</u>	
il	dir<u>a</u>	
nous	dir<u>ons</u>	
vous	dir<u>ez</u>	
ils	dir<u>ont</u>	

Present subjunctive ☆

je	<u>dise</u>	I say *or* I am saying
tu	<u>dises</u>	
il	<u>dise</u>	
nous	<u>disions</u>	
vous	<u>disiez</u>	
ils	<u>disent</u>	

Imperfect ✪

je	<u>disais</u>	I said *or* I used to say *or* I was saying
tu	<u>disais</u>	
il	<u>disait</u>	
nous	<u>disions</u>	
vous	<u>disiez</u>	
ils	<u>disaient</u>	

Conditional

je	dir<u>ais</u>	I would say
tu	dir<u>ais</u>	
il	dir<u>ait</u>	
nous	dir<u>ions</u>	
vous	dir<u>iez</u>	
ils	dir<u>aient</u>	

★ uses *avoir* plus the past participle to describe completed events in the past
☆ usually used after *que*: **Il faut que tu le lui dises.** You must tell her.
✪ used to describe what something was like, what used to happen, or what was happening

Imperative

fais	do or make
faisons	let's do or let's make
faites	do or make

Past participle

| fait | done or made |

Present

je	fais	I do or I make or I am doing or I am making
tu	fais	
il	fait	
nous	faisons	
vous	faites	
ils	font	

Perfect ★

j'	ai fait	I have done or I have made or I did or I made
tu	as fait	
il	a fait	
nous	avons fait	
vous	avez fait	
ils	ont fait	

Future

je	ferai	I will do or I will make
tu	feras	
il	fera	
nous	ferons	
vous	ferez	
ils	feront	

Present subjunctive ☆

je	fasse	I do or I make or I am doing or I am making
tu	fasses	
il	fasse	
nous	fassions	
vous	fassiez	
ils	fassent	

Imperfect ☉

je	faisais	I did or I made or I used to do or I used to make or I was doing or I was making
tu	faisais	
il	faisait	
nous	faisions	
vous	faisiez	
ils	faisaient	

Conditional

je	ferais	I would do or I would make
tu	ferais	
il	ferait	
nous	ferions	
vous	feriez	
ils	feraient	

★ uses *avoir* plus the past participle to describe completed events in the past
☆ usually used after *que*: **Le prof veut que nous fassions tous nos devoirs.**
The teacher wants us to do all our homework.
☉ used to describe what something was like, what used to happen, or what was happening

Verb tables

[11]

mettre
to put

Imperative

mets	put
mettons	let's put
mettez	put

Past participle

| mis | put |

Present

je	mets	I put *or* I am putting
tu	mets	
il	met	
nous	mettons	
vous	mettez	
ils	mettent	

Perfect ★

j'	ai mis	I have put *or* I put
tu	as mis	
il	a mis	
nous	avons mis	
vous	avez mis	
ils	ont mis	

Future

je	mettrai	I will put
tu	mettras	
il	mettra	
nous	mettrons	
vous	mettrez	
ils	mettront	

Present subjunctive ☆

je	mette	I put *or* I am putting
tu	mettes	
il	mette	
nous	mettions	
vous	mettiez	
ils	mettent	

Imperfect ○

je	mettais	I put *or* I used to put *or* I was putting
tu	mettais	
il	mettait	
nous	mettions	
vous	mettiez	
ils	mettaient	

Conditional

je	mettrais	I would put
tu	mettrais	
il	mettrait	
nous	mettrions	
vous	mettriez	
ils	mettraient	

★ uses *avoir* plus the past participle to describe completed events in the past

☆ usually used after *que*: Il faut qu'elle mette aussi un casque. She must also wear a helmet.

○ used to describe what something was like, what used to happen, or what was happening

324

Imperative

The imperative of
<u>pouvoir</u> is not used.

Past participle

<u>pu</u>   been able to

[12]

pouvoir
to be able to

Present

je	<u>peux</u>	I am able to *or* I can
tu	<u>peux</u>	
il	<u>peut</u>	
nous	pouv<u>ons</u>	
vous	pouv<u>ez</u>	
ils	<u>peuvent</u>	

Perfect ★

j'	ai <u>pu</u>	I have been able to *or* I was able to *or* I could
tu	as <u>pu</u>	
il	a <u>pu</u>	
nous	avons <u>pu</u>	
vous	avez <u>pu</u>	
ils	ont <u>pu</u>	

Future

je	<u>pourrai</u>	I will be able to
tu	<u>pourras</u>	
il	<u>pourra</u>	
nous	<u>pourrons</u>	
vous	<u>pourrez</u>	
ils	<u>pourront</u>	

Present subjunctive ☆

je	<u>puisse</u>	I am able to *or* I can
tu	<u>puisses</u>	
il	<u>puisse</u>	
nous	<u>puissions</u>	
vous	<u>puissiez</u>	
ils	<u>puissent</u>	

Imperfect ○

je	pouv<u>ais</u>	I was able to *or* I could *or* I used to be able to
tu	pouv<u>ais</u>	
il	pouv<u>ait</u>	
nous	pouv<u>ions</u>	
vous	pouv<u>iez</u>	
ils	pouv<u>aient</u>	

Conditional

je	<u>pourrais</u>	I would be able to *or* I could
tu	<u>pourrais</u>	
il	<u>pourrait</u>	
nous	<u>pourrions</u>	
vous	<u>pourriez</u>	
ils	<u>pourraient</u>	

★ uses *avoir* plus the past participle to describe completed events in the past
☆ usually used after *que*: **Ça m'étonnerait qu'elle puisse le faire.** I'd be surprised if she could do it.
○ used to describe what something was like, what used to happen, or what was happening

[13]
voir
to see

Imperative

voi<u>s</u>   see
<u>voyons</u>   let's see
<u>voyez</u>   see

Past participle

<u>vu</u>   seen

Present

je	voi<u>s</u>	I see or I am seeing
tu	voi<u>s</u>	
il	voi<u>t</u>	
nous	<u>voyons</u>	
vous	<u>voyez</u>	
ils	<u>voient</u>	

Present subjunctive ☆

je	<u>voie</u>	I see or I am seeing
tu	<u>voies</u>	
il	<u>voie</u>	
nous	<u>voyions</u>	
vous	<u>voyiez</u>	
ils	<u>voient</u>	

Perfect ★

j'	ai <u>vu</u>	I have seen or I saw
tu	as <u>vu</u>	
il	a <u>vu</u>	
nous	avons <u>vu</u>	
vous	avez <u>vu</u>	
ils	ont <u>vu</u>	

Imperfect ☉

je	<u>voyais</u>	I saw or I used to see or I was seeing
tu	<u>voyais</u>	
il	<u>voyait</u>	
nous	<u>voyions</u>	
vous	<u>voyiez</u>	
ils	<u>voyaient</u>	

Future

je	<u>verrai</u>	I will see
tu	<u>verras</u>	
il	<u>verra</u>	
nous	<u>verrons</u>	
vous	<u>verrez</u>	
ils	<u>verront</u>	

Conditional

je	<u>verrais</u>	I would see
tu	<u>verrais</u>	
il	<u>verrait</u>	
nous	<u>verrions</u>	
vous	<u>verriez</u>	
ils	<u>verraient</u>	

★ uses *avoir* plus the past participle to describe completed events in the past
☆ usually used after *que*: **Il faut que vous voyiez mon nouveau VTT.** You must see my new mountain bike.
☉ used to describe what something was like, what used to happen, or what was happening

Imperative
The veuille and the
veuillons form of the
imperative are not used.
veuillez please

Past participle
voulu   wanted

Present

je	veux	I want or I am wanting
tu	veux	
il	veut	
nous	voulons	
vous	voulez	
ils	veulent	

wanting

Perfect ★

j'	ai voulu	I have wanted or I wanted
tu	as voulu	
il	a voulu	
nous	avons voulu	
vous	avez voulu	
ils	ont voulu	

Future

je	voudrai	I will want
tu	voudras	
il	voudra	
nous	voudrons	
vous	voudrez	
ils	voudront	

Present subjunctive ☆

je	veuille	I want or I am wanting
tu	veuilles	
il	veuille	
nous	voulions	
vous	vouliez	
ils	veuillent	

Imperfect ☉

je	voulais	I wanted or I used to want or I was wanting
tu	voulais	
il	voulait	
nous	voulions	
vous	vouliez	
ils	voulaient	

Conditional

je	voudrais	I would like
tu	voudrais	
il	voudrait	
nous	voudrions	
vous	voudriez	
ils	voudraient	

★ uses *avoir* plus the past participle to describe completed events in the past
☆ usually used after *que*: **Ça m'étonnerait qu'il veuille venir avec nous.** I'd be surprised if he wanted to come.
☉ used to describe what something was like, what used to happen, or what was happening

Other French irregular verbs

The list shows the main forms of other irregular verbs. The number before the infinitive is the number given after verbs in the dictionary which follow this pattern.

1 = Present
2 = Past participle
3 = Imperfect
4 = Future
5 = Subjunctive present

[15] **abréger** 1 j'abrège, nous abrégeons, ils abrègent 2 abrégé 3 j'abrégeais 4 j'abrégerai

[16] **acheter** 1 j'achète, nous achetons, ils achètent 2 acheté 3 j'achetais 4 j'achèterai

[17] **acquérir** 1 j'acquiers, il acquiert, nous acquérons, vous acquérez, ils acquièrent 2 acquis 3 j'acquérais 4 j'acquerrai

[18] **appeler** 1 j'appelle, nous appelons 2 appelé 3 j'appelais 4 j'appellerai

[19] **apprendre** 1 j'apprends, nous apprenons, vous apprenez, ils apprennent 2 appris 3 j'apprenais 4 j'apprendrai

[20] **s'asseoir** 1 je m'assieds, nous nous asseyons, vous vous asseyez, ils s'asseyent 2 assis 3 je m'asseyais 4 je m'assiérai

[21] **battre** 1 je bats, il bat, nous battons 2 battu 3 je battais 4 je battrai

[22] **boire** 1 je bois, nous buvons, ils boivent 2 bu 3 je buvais 4 je boirai

[23] **bouillir** 1 je bous, nous bouillons 2 bouilli 3 je bouillais 4 je bouillirai

[24] **céder** 1 je cède, nous cédons, ils cèdent 2 cédé 3 je cédais 4 je céderai

[25] **conclure** 1 je conclus, nous concluons 2 conclu 3 je concluais 4 je conclurai

[26] **conduire** 1 je conduis, nous conduisons 2 conduit 3 je conduisais 4 je conduirai

[27] **connaître** 1 je connais, nous connaissons 2 connu 3 je connaissais 4 je connaîtrai

[28] **coudre** 1 je couds, nous cousons, vous cousez, ils cousent 2 cousu 3 je cousais 4 je coudrai

[29] **courir** 1 je cours, nous courons 2 couru 3 je courais 4 je courrai

[30] **couvrir** 1 je couvre, nous couvrons 2 couvert 3 je couvrais 4 je couvrirai

[31] **craindre** 1 je crains, nous craignons 2 craint 3 je craignais 4 je craindrai

[32] **créer** 1 je crée, nous créons 2 créé 3 je créais 4 je créerai

[33] **croire** 1 je crois, nous croyons, ils croient 2 cru 3 je croyais 4 je croirai

[34] **croître 1** je croîs, nous croissons **2** crû, crue **3** je croissais **4** je croîtrai

[35] **cueillir 1** je cueille, nous cueillons **2** cueilli **3** je cueillais **4** je cueillerai

[36] **cuire 1** je cuis, nous cuisons, ils cuisent **2** cuit **3** je cuisais **4** je cuirai

[37] **dormir 1** je dors, nous dormons **2** dormi **3** je dormais **4** je dormirai

[38] **écrire 1** j'écris, nous écrivons **2** écrit **3** j'écrivais **4** j'écrirai

[39] **employer 1** j'emploie, nous employons, vous employez, ils emploient **2** employé **3** j'employais **4** j'emploierai

[40] **envoyer 1** j'envoie, nous envoyons, vous envoyez, ils envoient **2** envoyé **3** j'envoyais **4** j'enverrai

[41] **essuyer 1** j'essuie, nous essuyons, vous essuyez, ils essuient **2** essuyé **3** j'essuyais **4** j'essuierai

[42] **faillir 1** je faux **2** failli

[43] **falloir 1** il faut **2** fallu **3** il fallait **4** il faudra

[44] **fuir 1** je fuis, nous fuyons, ils fuient **2** fui **3** je fuyais **4** je fuirai

[45] **geler 1** je gèle, nous gelons, vous gelez, ils gèlent **2** gelé **3** je gelais **4** je gèlerai

[46] **haïr 1** je hais, nous haïssons, ils haïssent **2** haï **3** je haïssais **4** je haïrai

[47] **interdire 1** j'interdis, nous interdisons, vous interdisez **2** interdit **3** j'interdisais **4** j'interdirai

[48] **jeter 1** je jette, nous jetons, ils jettent **2** jeté **3** je jetais **4** je jetterai

[49] **joindre 1** je joins, nous joignons **2** joint **3** je joignais **4** je joindrai

[50] **lever 1** je lève, nous levons, ils lèvent **2** levé **3** je levais **4** je lèverai

[51] **lire 1** je lis, nous lisons **2** lu **3** je lisais **4** je lirai

[52] **manger 1** je mange, nous mangeons **2** mangé **3** je mangeais **4** je mangerai

[53] **mentir 1** je mens, nous mentons **2** menti **3** je mentais **4** je mentirai

[54] **mourir 1** je meurs, nous mourons, ils meurent **2** mort **3** je mourais **4** je mourrai

[55] **naître 1** je nais, il naît, nous naissons **2** né **3** je naissais **4** je naîtrai

[56] **offrir 1** j'offre, nous offrons **2** offert **3** j'offrais **4** j'offrirai

[57] **paraître 1** je parais, il paraît, nous paraissons **2** paru **3** je paraissais **4** je paraîtrai

[58] **partir** 1 je pars, nous partons 2 parti 3 je partais 4 je partirai

[59] **payer** 1 je paie/je paye, nous payons, vous payez, ils paient/ils payent 2 payé 3 je payais 4 je paierai/je payerai

[60] **peindre** 1 je peins, nous peignons 2 peint 3 je peignais 4 je peindrai

[61] **placer** 1 place, nous plaçons 2 placé 3 je plaçais 4 je placerai

[62] **plaire** 1 je plais, il plaît, nous plaisons 2 plu 3 je plaisais 4 je plairai

[63] **pleuvoir** 1 il pleut 2 plu 3 il pleuvait 4 il pleuvra

[64] **prendre** 1 je prends, nous prenons, ils prennent 2 pris 3 je prenais 4 je prendrai

[65] **prévoir** 1 je prévois, nous prévoyons, vous prévoyez, ils prévoient 2 prévu 3 je prévoyais 4 je prévoirai

[66] **recevoir** 1 je reçois, il reçoit, ils reçoivent 2 reçu 3 je recevais 4 je recevrai

[67] **résoudre** 1 je résous, nous résolvons, vous résolvez, ils résolvent 2 résolu 3 je résolvais 4 je résoudrai

[68] **rire** 1 je ris, nous rions 2 ri 3 je riais 4 je rirai

[69] **rompre** 1 je romps, il rompt, nous rompons 2 rompu 3 je rompais 4 je romprai

[70] **savoir** 1 je sais, nous savons, ils savent 2 su 3 je savais 4 je saurai 5 je sache

[71] **servir** 1 je sers, nous servons 2 servi 3 je servais 4 je servirai

[72] **sortir** 1 je sors, nous sortons 2 sorti 3 je sortais 4 je sortirai

[73] **souffrir** 1 je souffre, nous souffrons 2 souffert 3 je souffrais 4 je souffrirai

[74] **suffire** 1 je suffis, nous suffisons 2 suffi 3 je suffisais 4 je suffirai

[75] **suivre** 1 je suis, nous suivons 2 suivi 3 je suivais 4 je suivrai

[76] **se taire** 1 je me tais, nous nous taisons 2 tu 3 je me taisais 4 je me tairai

[77] **tenir** 1 je tiens, nous tenons, ils tiennent 2 tenu 3 je tenais 4 je tiendrai

[78] **traire** 1 je trais, nous trayons, ils traient 2 trait 3 je trayais 4 je trairai

[79] **vaincre** 1 je vaincs, il vainc, nous vainquons 2 vaincu 3 je vainquais 4 je vaincrai

[80] **valoir** 1 je vaux, il vaut, nous valons 2 valu 3 je valais 4 je vaudrai

[81] **venir** 1 je viens, nous venons, ils viennent 2 venu 3 je venais 4 je viendrai

[82] **vivre** 1 je vis, nous vivons 2 vécu 3 je vivais 4 je vivrai

a DETERMINER **❶** (before a noun which is masculine in French) un; **a tree** un arbre **❷** (before a noun which is feminine in French) une; **a table** une table **❸** **five euros a kilo** cinq euros le kilo **❹** **fifty kilometres an hour** cinquante kilomètres l'heure **❺** **three times a day** trois fois par jour

abandon VERB abandonner [1]

abbey NOUN abbaye FEM; **Westminster Abbey** l'Abbaye de Westminster

abbreviation NOUN abréviation FEM

abide VERB **I can't abide ...** je ne supporte pas ...

ability NOUN capacité FEM; **the ability to do** la capacité de faire

able ADJECTIVE **to be able to do** pouvoir [12] faire, **she wasn't able to come** elle n'a pas pu venir

abnormal ADJECTIVE anormal MASC (PLURAL anormaux)

abolish VERB abolir [2]

abortion NOUN avortement MASC

about PREPOSITION **❶** (on the subject of) sur; **a film about Picasso** un film sur Picasso **❷** **what's it about?** de quoi s'agit-il? **❸** (concerning or in relation to) au sujet de; **he wants to talk to you about your exam** il veut te parler au sujet de ton examen **❹** to

talk about something parler de quelque chose, **what is she talking about?** de quoi parle-t-elle? **❺** **to think about something/somebody** penser à quelque chose/quelqu'un, **I'm thinking about you** je pense à toi

about ADVERB **❶** (approximately) environ, à peu près; **there are about sixty people** il y a environ soixante personnes, il y a à peu près soixante personnes **❷** (when talking about the time) vers; **about three o'clock** vers trois heures
• **to be about to do** être sur le point de faire; **I'm (just) about to leave** je suis sur le point de partir

above PREPOSITION **❶** au dessus de; **above the table** au dessus de la table **❷** **above all** surtout

abroad ADVERB à l'étranger; **to go abroad** aller à l'étranger, **to live abroad** vivre à l'étranger

abscess NOUN abcès MASC

abseiling NOUN descente (FEM) en rappel

absent ADJECTIVE absent; **to be absent from** être absent de

absent-minded ADJECTIVE distrait

absolute ADJECTIVE complet (FEM complète); **an absolute disaster** un désastre complet

absolutely ADVERB **❶** absolument; **it's absolutely dreadful** c'est absolument affreux **❷** tout à fait; **you're absolutely right** tu as tout à fait raison

absorb VERB absorber [1]

abuse NOUN **❶** **alcohol abuse** abus (MASC) d'alcool, **drug abuse** usage (MASC) des stupéfiants **❷** (violent *treatment of a person)* **mauvais traitement** *MASC* ❸ *(insulting words)* **injures** *FEM PLURAL*

abuse *VERB* **to abuse somebody** maltraiter [1] quelqu'un

academic *ADJECTIVE* **the academic year** l'année universitaire

accelerate *VERB* accélérer [24]

accelerator *NOUN* accélérateur *MASC*

accent *NOUN* accent *MASC*; **she has a French accent** elle a l'accent français

accept *VERB* accepter [1]

acceptable *ADJECTIVE* acceptable

acceptance *NOUN* acceptation *FEM*

access *NOUN* accès *MASC*

access *VERB* **to access something** accéder [24] à quelque chose

accessory *NOUN* accessoire *MASC*

accident *NOUN* ❶ accident *MASC*; **to have an accident** avoir un accident, **a road accident** un accident de la route, **a car accident** un accident de voiture ❷ *(chance)* hasard *MASC*; **by accident** par hasard, **I found it by accident** je l'ai trouvé par hasard

accident & emergency *NOUN* **les urgences** *FEM PLURAL*

accidental *ADJECTIVE* fortuit; **an accidental discovery** une découverte fortuite

accidentally *ADVERB* ❶ *(without meaning to)* accidentellement; **I accidentally knocked over his glass** j'ai accidentellement renversé son verre ❷ *(by chance)* par hasard; **I accidentally discovered that …** j'ai découvert par hasard que …

accommodate *VERB* recevoir [66]; **the centre can accommodate sixty people** le centre peut recevoir soixante personnes

accommodation *NOUN* logement *MASC*; **I'm looking for accommodation** je cherche un logement

accompany *VERB* **to accompany somebody** accompagner [1] quelqu'un

according *ADVERB* **according to** selon, **according to Sophie** selon Sophie

accordion *NOUN* accordéon *MASC*

account *NOUN* ❶ *(in a bank, shop, or post office)* compte *MASC*; **a bank account** un compte bancaire, **to open an account** ouvrir un compte, **I have fifty pounds in my account** j'ai cinquante livres sur mon compte ❷ *(a description of an experience or event)* compte rendu *MASC* ❸ **on account of** à cause de, **the station is closed on account of the strike** la gare est fermée à cause de la grève ❹ **to take something into account** tenir compte de quelque chose, **we will take his illness into account** nous tiendrons compte de sa maladie

accountant *NOUN* comptable *MASC & FEM*; **she is an accountant** elle est comptable

accuracy *NOUN* précision *FEM*

accurate *ADJECTIVE* précis

accurately *ADVERB* avec précision

accuse *VERB* accuser [1]; **to accuse somebody of something** accuser quelqu'un de quelque chose, **to accuse someone of doing**

something accuser quelqu'un d'avoir fait quelque chose, **she accused me of stealing her pen** elle m'a accusé d'avoir volé son stylo

accustomed to ADJECTIVE **to be accustomed to something** être [6] habitué à, **she's accustomed to having lots of homework** elle a l'habitude d'avoir beaucoup de devoirs

ace NOUN as MASC; **the ace of hearts** l'as de cœur

ace ADJECTIVE super (informal); **he's an ace drummer** c'est un super batteur

ache VERB **my arm aches** j'ai mal au bras, **my head aches** j'ai mal à la tête

achieve VERB ❶ accomplir [2]; **she's achieved a great deal** elle a beaucoup accompli ❷ **to achieve an ambition** réaliser [1] une ambition ❸ **to achieve an aim** atteindre [60] un objectif ❹ **to achieve success** réussir [2]

achievement NOUN ❶ réussite FEM; **it's a great achievement** c'est une grande réussite ❷ **a sense of achievement** un sentiment de satisfaction

acid NOUN acide MASC

acid rain NOUN pluies (FEM PLURAL) acides

acne NOUN acné FEM

acorn NOUN gland MASC

acrobat NOUN acrobate MASC & FEM

across PREPOSITION ❶ (over to the other side of) **to walk across something** traverser [1] quelque chose, **we walked across the park** nous avons traversé le parc, **to run across the road** traverser la route en courant ❷ (on the other side of) de

l'autre côté de; **the house across the street** la maison de l'autre côté de la rue ❸ **across from** en face de, **she was sitting across from me** elle était assise en face de moi

acrylic NOUN acrylique MASC

act NOUN acte MASC

act VERB ❶ (in a play or film) **jouer** [1]; **to act the part of** jouer le rôle de ❷ (to take action) agir [2]

acting NOUN jeu MASC; **she wants to go into acting** elle veut devenir actrice, **the acting was terrible/ sensational** les acteurs jouaient très mal/bien

action NOUN action FEM

action replay NOUN répétition (FEM) d'une séquence

active ADJECTIVE actif (FEM active)

activity NOUN activité FEM

activity holiday NOUN vacances (FEM PLURAL) sportives

actor NOUN acteur MASC; **who's your favourite actor?** qui est votre acteur préféré?

actress NOUN actrice FEM; **she's my favourite actress** c'est mon actrice préférée

actual ADJECTIVE **his actual words** ses paroles précises
• **in actual fact** en fait

actually ADVERB ❶ (in fact, as it happens)) en fait; **actually, I've changed my mind** en fait, j'ai changé d'avis, **he's not actually here at the moment** en fait il n'est pas là en ce moment ❷ (really and truly) vraiment; **did she actually say that?** est-ce qu'elle a vraiment dit ça?

acupuncture NOUN acupuncture FEM

acute ADJECTIVE ❶ (pain) vif (FEM vive) ❷ an acute accent un accent aigu

ad NOUN ❶ pub FEM (informal) ❷ (in a newspaper) annonce FEM; to put an ad in the paper mettre une annonce dans le journal, the small ads les petites annonces

AD ABBREVIATION après Jésus-Christ, apr. J-C; in 400 AD en quatre cents après Jésus-Christ

adapt VERB ❶ to adapt something adapter [1] quelque chose (a book or film) ❷ to adapt to something s'adapter [1] à quelque chose, she's adapted to the new system elle s'est adaptée au nouveau système

adaptor NOUN adaptateur MASC

add VERB ajouter [1]; add three eggs ajoutez trois œufs
• to add something up additionner [1] quelque chose

addict NOUN ❶ (drug addict) drogué, droguée MASC, FEM ❷ accro MASC & FEM (informal); she's a telly addict c'est une accro de la télé, he's a football addict c'est un accro du foot

addicted ADJECTIVE ❶ to become addicted to heroin former une dépendance à l'héroïne ❷ I'm addicted to tomatoes je raffole des tomates

addition NOUN ❶ (adding up) addition FEM ❷ in addition en plus ❸ in addition to en plus de

additional ADJECTIVE supplémentaire; additional costs les frais supplémentaires

additive NOUN additif MASC

address NOUN adresse FEM; what's your address? quelle est ton adresse?, to change address changer d'adresse

address book NOUN carnet (MASC) d'adresses

adequate ADJECTIVE suffisant

adhesive NOUN colle FEM

adhesive ADJECTIVE collant; adhesive tape du papier collant

adjective NOUN adjectif MASC

adjust VERB ❶ to adjust something régler [24] quelque chose, to adjust the height régler la hauteur ❷ to adjust to something s'adapter [1] à quelque chose

adjustable ADJECTIVE réglable

administration NOUN administration FEM

admiral NOUN amiral MASC

admiration NOUN admiration FEM

admire VERB admirer [1]

admission NOUN entrée FEM; 'no admission' 'entrée interdite', 'admission free' 'entrée gratuite'

admit VERB ❶ (confess) reconnaître [27]; she admits she lied elle reconnaît qu'elle a menti ❷ (concede) admettre [11]; I must admit that ... j'admets que ... ❸ (allow to enter) laisser [1] entrer; to admit somebody to a restaurant laisser entrer quelqu'un dans un restaurant ❹ to be admitted to hospital être [6] hospitalisé

adolescence NOUN adolescence FEM

adolescent NOUN adolescent MASC, adolescente FEM

adopt VERB adopter [1]

adopted ADJECTIVE adoptif (FEM adoptive)

adoption NOUN adoption FEM

adore VERB adorer [1]

Adriatic Sea NOUN the Adriatic Sea la mer Adriatique

adult NOUN adulte MASC & FEM

adult ADJECTIVE adulte; **the adult population** la population adulte

Adult Education NOUN enseignement (MASC) pour adultes

advance NOUN progrès MASC; **advances in technology** des progrès dans le domaine de la technologie

advance VERB ❶ (make progress) progresser [1] ❷ (move forward) avancer [61]

advanced ADJECTIVE avancé

advantage NOUN ❶ avantage MASC; **there are several advantages** il y a plusieurs avantages ❷ **to take advantage of something** profiter de quelque chose, **I took advantage of the sales to buy myself some shoes** j'ai profité des soldes pour m'acheter des chaussures ❸ **to take advantage of somebody** (unfairly) exploiter quelqu'un

Advent NOUN Avent MASC

adventure NOUN aventure FEM

adventurous ADJECTIVE aventureux (FEM aventureuse)

adverb NOUN adverbe MASC

advert, **advertisement** NOUN ❶ (at the cinema or on television) publicité FEM ❷ (commercial advertisement in a newspaper) annonce FEM ❸ (small ad in a newspaper advertising a job, an article for sale, etc) petite annonce FEM

advertise VERB ❶ **to advertise something in the newspaper** (in the small ads) mettre [11] une annonce pour quelque chose dans le journal, **I saw a bike advertised in the paper** j'ai vu une annonce pour un vélo dans le journal ❷ **to advertise a product** faire [10] de la publicité pour un produit

advertising NOUN publicité FEM

advice NOUN conseils MASC PLURAL; **to ask for advice about something** demander des conseils à propos de quelque chose, **a piece of advice** un conseil

advise VERB conseiller [1]; **to advise somebody to do** conseiller à quelqu'un de faire, **I advised him to stop** je lui ai conseillé d'arrêter, **I advised her not to wait** je lui ai conseillé de ne pas attendre

adviser NOUN conseiller MASC, conseillère FEM

aerial NOUN antenne FEM

aerobics NOUN aérobic MASC; **to do aerobics** faire de l'aérobic

aeroplane NOUN avion MASC

aerosol NOUN an aerosol can une bombe

affair NOUN ❶ (event) affaire FEM; **international affairs** les affaires internationales ❷ **a love affair** une aventure amoureuse

affect VERB affecter [1]

a b c d e f g h i j k l m n o p q r s t u v w x y z

affectionate ADJECTIVE **affectueux**
(FEM **affectueuse**)

afford VERB **to be able to afford to
do** avoir [5] **les moyens de faire, we
can't afford to go out much** nous
n'avons pas les moyens de sortir
beaucoup, **I can't afford a new bike**
je n'ai pas les moyens de m'acheter
un nouveau vélo

afraid ADJECTIVE ❶ **to be afraid of
something** avoir peur de quelque
chose, **she's afraid of dogs** elle a
peur des chiens ❷ **I'm afraid there's
no milk left** je suis désolé mais il ne
reste plus de lait, **I'm afraid so** hélas
oui, **I'm afraid not** hélas non

Africa NOUN **Afrique** FEM; **in Africa** en
Afrique, **to Africa** en Afrique

African NOUN **Africain** MASC,
Africaine FEM

African ADJECTIVE **africain** (FEM
africaine)

after PREPOSITION, ADVERB, CONJUNCTION
après; after 10 o'clock après
dix heures, **after lunch** après le
déjeuner, **after school** après l'école,
the day after tomorrow après-
demain, **soon after** peu après, **after
I've finished my homework** après
que j'aurai fini mes devoirs, **to
run after somebody** courir après
quelqu'un

after all ADVERB **après tout; after all,
she's only six** elle n'a que six ans
après tout

afternoon NOUN **après-midi** MASC &
FEM; **this afternoon** cet après-midi,
tomorrow afternoon demain après-
midi, **yesterday afternoon** hier
après-midi, **on Saturday afternoon**
samedi après-midi, **on Saturday
afternoons** le samedi après-midi,
at four o'clock in the afternoon à

quatre heures de l'après-midi, **every
afternoon** tous les après-midi

afters NOUN **dessert** MASC

after-shave NOUN **après-rasage**
MASC

afterwards ADVERB **après; shortly
afterwards** peu de temps après

again ADVERB ❶ (one more time)
encore une fois; try again essaie
encore une fois, **I've forgotten
it again** je l'ai oublié encore une
fois ❷ (once more) **de nouveau;
she's ill again** elle est de nouveau
malade ❸ **I saw her again yesterday**
je l'ai revue hier, **you should ask
again** tu devrais redemander ❹ **I
don't want to see her again** je ne
veux plus la revoir, **never again!**
jamais plus!

against PREPOSITION **contre; against
the wall** contre le mur, **to lean
against the wall** s'appuyer contre
le mur, **I'm against the idea** je suis
contre l'idée, **the fight against
racism** la lutte contre le racisme

age NOUN ❶ **âge** MASC; **at the age of
fifteen** à l'âge de quinze ans, **she's
the same age as me** elle a le même
âge que moi, **to be under age** être
mineur ❷ **I haven't seen Johnny for
ages** ça fait une éternité que je n'ai
pas vu Johnny, **I haven't been to
London for ages** ça fait une éternité
que je ne suis pas allé à Londres

aged ADJECTIVE **âgé de; a woman aged
thirty** une femme âgée de trente ans

agenda NOUN **ordre** (MASC) **du jour**

agent NOUN **agent** MASC; **an estate
agent** un agent immobilier, **a travel
agent's** une agence de voyage

aggressive ADJECTIVE **agressif** (FEM
agressive)

ago ADVERB **an hour ago** il y a une heure, **three days ago** il y a trois jours, **five years ago** il y a cinq ans, **a long time ago** il y a longtemps, **not long ago** il n'y a pas longtemps, **how long ago was it?** c'était il y a combien de temps?

agree VERB ❶ **to agree with somebody** être [6] d'accord avec quelqu'un, **I agree with Laura** je suis d'accord avec Laura, **I don't agree** je ne suis pas d'accord ❷ **I agree that ...** je suis d'accord sur le fait que ..., **I agree that it's too late now** je suis d'accord sur le fait qu'il est maintenant trop tard ❸ **to agree to do** accepter [1] de faire, **Steve's agreed to help me** Steve a accepté de m'aider ❹ **coffee doesn't agree with me** je ne supporte pas le café

agreement NOUN accord MASC

agricultural ADJECTIVE agricole

agriculture NOUN agriculture FEM

ahead ADVERB ❶ **go ahead!** allez-y! ❷ **straight ahead** tout droit, **go straight ahead until you get to the crossroads** allez tout droit jusqu'au carrefour ❸ **our team was ten points ahead** notre équipe avait dix points d'avance ❹ **to be ahead of time** être en avance

aid NOUN ❶ aide FEM; **aid to developing countries** l'aide aux pays en voie de développement ❷ **in aid of** au profit de, **in aid of the homeless** au profit des sans-abri

AIDS NOUN sida MASC (*short for syndrome immunodéficitaire acquis*); **to have AIDS** avoir le sida

aim NOUN objectif MASC; **their aim is to control pollution** leur objectif est de contrôler la pollution

aim VERB ❶ **to aim to do** avoir [5] l'intention de faire, **we're aiming to finish it today** nous avons l'intention de le finir aujourd'hui ❷ **a campaign aimed at young people** une campagne qui vise les jeunes ❸ **to aim a gun at somebody** braquer [1] un révolver sur quelqu'un

air NOUN ❶ air MASC; **in the open air** en plein air, **to go out for a breath of air** sortir prendre l'air ❷ **to travel by air** voyager en avion

airbag NOUN (*in a car*) airbag MASC

air-conditioned ADJECTIVE climatisé

air conditioning NOUN climatisation FEM

Air Force NOUN Armée (*FEM*) de l'air

air hostess NOUN hôtesse (*FEM*) de l'air; **she's an air hostess** elle est hôtesse de l'air

airline NOUN compagnie (*FEM*) aérienne

airmail NOUN **by airmail** par avion

airport NOUN aéroport MASC

aisle NOUN allée (*FEM*) centrale

alarm NOUN alarme FEM; **a fire alarm** une alarme incendie, **a burglar alarm** une alarme contre le vol

alarm clock NOUN réveil MASC

album NOUN album MASC

alcohol NOUN alcool MASC

alcoholic NOUN alcoolique MASC & FEM

alcoholic ADJECTIVE alcoolisé; **alcoholic drinks** les boissons alcoolisées

alert ADJECTIVE vif (*FEM* vive)

A
B
C
D
E
F
G
H
I
J
K
L
M
N
O
P
Q
R
S
T
U
V
W
X
Y
Z

alert NOUN on the alert you must be on the alert for pickpockets faites attention aux pickpockets

A levels NOUN PLURAL baccalauréat MASC, bac MASC (informal) (Students take 'le bac' at the same age as A levels are taken in Britain. You can explain A levels briefly as follows: Les A levels sont répartis en deux niveaux, AS et A2. On passe les examens AS au bout d'une année de préparation, généralement dans quatre ou cinq matières. On passe les examens A2 un an plus tard, dans un plus petit nombre de matières, en choisissant parmi celles qui ont déjà fait l'objet d'un examen AS. La meilleure note que l'on peut obtenir est A et la note la plus basse est N. Les A levels permettent de s'inscrire à l'université)
► SEE baccalauréat

Algeria NOUN Algérie FEM; to Algeria en Algérie, in Algeria en Algérie

alibi NOUN alibi MASC

alien NOUN ❶ (foreigner) étranger MASC, étrangère FEM ❷ (from outer space) extra-terrestre MASC & FEM

alike ADJECTIVE ❶ pareil (FEM pareille); they're all alike ils sont tous pareils ❷ to look alike se ressembler, the two brothers look alike les deux frères se ressemblent

alive ADJECTIVE vivant

all along ADVERB depuis le début; I knew it all along je le savais depuis le début

allergic ADJECTIVE allergique; to be allergic to something être allergique à quelque chose

allergy NOUN allergie FEM; she has an allergy to cats elle est allergique aux chats

alligator NOUN alligator MASC

allow VERB ❶ to allow somebody to do permettre [11] à quelqu'un de faire, the teacher allowed them to go out le prof leur a permis de sortir ❷ to be allowed to do avoir [5] le droit de faire, I'm not allowed to go out during the week je n'ai pas le droit de sortir en semaine

all right ADVERB ❶ (yes) d'accord; 'come round to my house around six' – 'all right' 'passe chez moi vers six heures' – 'd'accord' ❷ (fine) bien; is everything all right? est-ce que tout va bien?, she's all right now elle va bien maintenant, it's all right by me ça ne me dérange pas ❸ (not bad) pas mal; the meal was all right le repas n'était pas mal ❹ are you all right? ça va? ❺ is it all right to ...? est-ce qu'on peut ...?, is it all right to leave the door open? est-ce qu'on peut laisser la porte ouverte?

ally NOUN allié MASC, alliée FEM

almond NOUN amande FEM

almost ADVERB presque; almost every day presque tous les jours, almost everybody presque tout le monde, she's almost five elle a presque cinq ans

alone ADJECTIVE ❶ seul; he lives alone il habite seul ❷ leave me alone! laisse-moi tranquille! ❸ leave these papers alone! ne touche pas à ces papiers!

along PREPOSITION ❶ le long de; there are trees all along the road il y a des arbres tout le long de la route ❷ (there is often no direct translation for 'along' so the sentence has to be expressed differently) **she lives along the road from me** elle habite dans la même rue que moi, **to go for a walk along the beach** aller se promener sur la plage

aloud ADVERB à haute voix; **to read something aloud** lire quelque chose à haute voix

alphabet NOUN alphabet MASC

alphabetical ADJECTIVE alphabétique; **in alphabetical order** par ordre alphabétique

Alps PLURAL NOUN **the Alps** les Alpes

already ADVERB déjà; **they've already left** ils sont déjà partis, **it's six o'clock already!** il est déjà six heures!

Alsatian NOUN (dog) berger (MASC) allemand

also ADVERB aussi; **I've also invited Karen** j'ai aussi invité Karen

alter VERB changer [52]

alternate ADJECTIVE **on alternate days** un jour sur deux

alternative NOUN ❶ possibilité FEM; **there are several alternatives** il y a plusieurs possibilités ❷ **we have no alternative** nous n'avons pas le choix

alternative ADJECTIVE autre; **to find an alternative solution** trouver une autre solution

alternatively ADVERB sinon; **alternatively, we could go together on Saturday** sinon, on pourrait y aller ensemble samedi

alternative medicine NOUN médecine (FEM) douce

although CONJUNCTION bien que

(followed by subjunctive); **although she's ill, she's willing to help us** bien qu'elle soit malade, elle est prête à nous aider

altitude NOUN altitude FEM

altogether ADVERB ❶ en tout; **I've spent thirty pounds altogether** j'ai dépensé trente livres en tout ❷ (completely) complètement; **I'm not altogether convinced** je ne suis pas complètement convaincu

aluminium NOUN aluminium MASC

always ADVERB toujours; **I always leave at five** je pars toujours à cinq heures

am VERB ▸ SEE **be**

a.m. ABBREVIATION du matin; **at 8 a.m.** à huit heures du matin

amateur NOUN amateur MASC; **amateur dramatics** théâtre (MASC) amateur

amaze VERB surprendre [64]; **what amazes me is ...** ce qui me surprend c'est ...

amazed ADJECTIVE stupéfait; **I was amazed to see her** j'étais stupéfait de la voir

amazement NOUN stupéfaction FEM; **to my amazement to my amazement she agreed** à ma grande surprise elle s'est mise d'accord

amazing ADJECTIVE ❶ (terrific) fantastique; **your dress is amazing!** ta robe est fantastique!, **they've got an amazing house** ils ont une maison fantastique ❷ (extraordinary) extraordinaire; **she has an amazing number of friends** elle a

a
b
c
d
e
f
g
h
i
j
k
l
m
n
o
p
q
r
s
t
u
v
w
x
y
z

un nombre extraordinaire d'amis, **he told me an amazing story** il m'a raconté une histoire extraordinaire

ambassador NOUN ambassadeur MASC, ambassadrice FEM

ambition NOUN ambition FEM

ambitious ADJECTIVE ambitieux (FEM ambitieuse)

ambulance NOUN ambulance FEM

ambulance driver NOUN ambulancier MASC, ambulancière FEM

amenities PLURAL NOUN équipements MASC PLURAL

America NOUN Amérique FEM; **in America** en Amérique, **to America** en Amérique

American NOUN Américain MASC, Américaine FEM

American ADJECTIVE américain (FEM américaine)

ammunition NOUN munition FEM

among, amongst
PREPOSITION ❶ parmi; **I found it amongst my books** je l'ai trouveé parmi mes livres ❷ (between) entre; **you can decide amongst yourselves** vous pouvez décider entre vous

amount NOUN ❶ quantité FEM; **an enormous amount of bread** une énorme quantité de pain, **a huge amount of work** un travail énorme ❷ (of money) somme FEM; **a large amount of money** une grosse somme d'argent

amount VERB **to amount to** s'élever [50] à, **the bill amounts to five hundred euros** la facture s'élève à cinq cents euros

amp NOUN ❶ (electricity) ampère MASC ❷ (amplifier) ampli MASC (informal)

amplifier NOUN amplificateur MASC

amuse VERB amuser [1]

amusement arcade NOUN salle (FEM) de jeux électroniques

amusing ADJECTIVE amusant

an ARTICLE ▸ SEE **a**

anaesthetic NOUN anesthésie FEM

analyse VERB analyser [1]

analysis NOUN analyse FEM

ancestor NOUN ancêtre MASC & FEM

anchor NOUN ancre FEM

anchovy NOUN anchois MASC

ancient ADJECTIVE ❶ (historic) ancien (FEM ancienne); **an ancient abbey** une abbaye ancienne ❷ (very old) très vieux (FEM très vieille); **an ancient pair of jeans** un très vieux jean ❸ **ancient Greece** la Grèce antique

and CONJUNCTION ❶ et; **Sean and Anna** Sean et Anna, **Rosie and I** Rosie et moi, **your shoes and socks** tes chaussures et tes chaussettes ❷ **louder and louder** de plus en plus fort

angel NOUN ange MASC

anger NOUN colère FEM

angle NOUN angle MASC

angrily ADVERB avec colère

angry ADJECTIVE **to be angry** être en colère, **she was angry with me** elle était en colère contre moi, **to get angry** se fâcher [1]

animal NOUN animal MASC (PLURAL animaux)

ankle NOUN cheville FEM; **to break your ankle** se casser la cheville

anniversary NOUN anniversaire MASC; **a wedding anniversary** un anniversaire de mariage

announce VERB annoncer [61]

announcement NOUN annonce FEM

annoy VERB agacer [61]; **to be annoyed** être [6] agacé, **to get annoyed** se fâcher [1], **she got annoyed** elle s'est fâchée

annoying ADJECTIVE agaçant

annual ADJECTIVE annuel (FEM annuelle)

anorak NOUN anorak MASC

anorexia NOUN anorexie FEM

another ADJECTIVE ❶ un autre (FEM une autre); **would you like another cup of tea?** voulez-vous une autre tasse de thé? ❷ encore; **another two years** encore deux ans, **we need another three chairs** il nous faut encore trois chaises

answer NOUN ❶ réponse FEM; **the right answer** la bonne réponse, **the wrong answer** la mauvaise réponse ❷ **the answer to a problem** la solution à un problème

answer VERB ❶ répondre [3] à; **he hasn't answered our letter** il n'a pas répondu à notre lettre ❷ **to answer the door** aller [5] ouvrir la porte

answering machine NOUN répondeur MASC; **to leave a message on the answering machine** laisser un message au répondeur

ant NOUN fourmi FEM

Antarctic NOUN Antarctique MASC

anthem NOUN **the national anthem** l'hymne national

antibiotic NOUN antibiotique FEM

antique NOUN **antiques** les antiquités FEM

antique ADJECTIVE ancien (FEM ancienne); **an antique table** une table ancienne

antique shop NOUN magasin (MASC) d'antiquités

antiseptic NOUN antiseptique MASC

anxious ADJECTIVE inquiet (FEM inquiète)

anxiously ADVERB avec inquiétude

any DETERMINER, ADVERB, PRONOUN ❶ du, de l', de la, des; **is there any butter?** y a-t-il du beurre?, **is there any oil?** y a-t-il de l'huile?, **is there any flour?** y a-t-il de la farine?, **are there any eggs?** y a-t-il des œufs? ❷ de (used in negative sentences); **there isn't any flour** il n'y a pas de farine, **there aren't any eggs** il n'y a pas d'œufs ❸ en (when 'any' is used on its own without a noun); **I don't want any** je n'en veux pas ❹ **not … any more** ne … plus, **there isn't any more butter** il n'y a plus de beurre, **I don't go there any more** je n'y vais plus

anybody, **anyone** PRONOUN ❶ (in questions and after 'if') quelqu'un; **is anybody in?** est-ce qu'il y a quelqu'un?, **if anybody wants some beer, it's in the fridge** si quelqu'un veut de la bière, elle au au frigo, **does anybody want some tea?** qui veut du thé? ❷ not … anybody ne … personne, **there isn't anybody**

in her office il n'y a personne dans son bureau ❸ *(absolutely anybody)* n'importe qui; **anybody can go** n'importe qui peut y aller

anyhow ADVERB ▸ SEE **anyway**

anyone PRONOUN ▸ SEE **anybody**

anything PRONOUN ❶ *(in questions)* quelque chose; **is there anything I can do to help?** est-ce que je peux faire quelque chose pour t'aider? ❷ **not … anything** ne … rien, **there isn't anything on the table** il n'y a rien sur la table ❸ *(anything at all)* n'importe quoi; **anything could happen** il pourrait arriver n'importe quoi

anyway, **anyhow** ADVERB de toute façon; **anyway, I'll ring you before I leave** de toute façon, je t'appellerai avant de partir

anywhere ADVERB ❶ *(in questions)* quelque part; **have you seen my keys anywhere?** est-ce que tu as vu mes clés quelque part?, **are you going anywhere tomorrow?** est-ce que tu vas quelque part demain? ❷ **not … anywhere** ne … nulle part, **I can't find my keys anywhere** je ne trouve nulle part mes clés ❸ *(absolutely anywhere)* n'importe où; **put your cases down anywhere** pose tes valises n'importe où

apart ADJECTIVE, ADVERB ❶ *(separate)* séparé; **we don't like being apart** nous n'aimons pas être séparés ❷ **to be two metres apart** être à deux mètres l'un de l'autre ❸ **apart from** à part, **apart from Judy everybody was there** à part Judy tout le monde y était

apartheid NOUN apartheid MASC

apartment NOUN appartement MASC

ape NOUN (grand) singe MASC

apologize VERB s'excuser [1]; **he apologizes for his behaviour** il s'excuse de son comportement, **he apologized to Tanya** il s'est excusé auprès de Tanya

apology NOUN excuses FEM PLURAL

apostrophe NOUN apostrophe FEM

apparatus NOUN ❶ *(in a gym)* agrès MASC PLURAL ❷ *(in a lab)* matériel MASC

apparent ADJECTIVE apparent

apparently ADVERB apparemment

appeal NOUN appel MASC

appeal VERB ❶ **to appeal for** lancer [61] un appel pour ❷ **to appeal to somebody** tenter [1] quelqu'un, **horror films don't appeal to me** les films d'épouvante ne me tentent pas

appear VERB ❶ apparaître [57]; **Mick appeared at the door** Mick est apparu à la porte ❷ **to appear on television** passer [1] à la télévision ❸ *(seem)* paraître [57]; **it appears that somebody has stolen the key** il paraît que quelqu'un a volé la clé

appendicitis NOUN appendicite FEM

appendix NOUN ❶ *(of book)* annexe FEM ❷ *(organ)* appendice MASC

appetite NOUN appétit MASC; **it'll spoil your appetite** ça te coupera l'appétit

applaud VERB applaudir [2]

applause NOUN applaudissements MASC PLURAL

apple NOUN pomme FEM

apple core NOUN trognon (MASC) de pomme

apple tree NOUN pommier MASC

applicant NOUN candidat MASC, candidate FEM

application NOUN a job application une candidature

application form NOUN (for a job) dossier (MASC) de candidature

apply VERB ❶ to apply for a job poser [1] sa candidature à un poste ❷ to apply for a course faire [10] une demande d'inscription à un cours ❸ to apply to s'appliquer [1] à, that doesn't apply to students cela ne s'applique pas aux étudiants

appointment NOUN rendez-vous MASC; to make a dental appointment prendre rendez-vous chez le dentiste, I've got a hair appointment at four j'ai rendez-vous chez le coiffeur à seize heures

appreciate VERB I appreciate your advice je vous suis reconnaissant de vos conseils, I'd appreciate it if you could tidy up afterwards je te serais reconnaissant de ranger après

apprentice NOUN apprenti MASC, apprentie FEM

apprenticeship NOUN apprentissage MASC

approach VERB ❶ (come near to) s'approcher de [1]; we were approaching Paris nous nous approchions de Paris ❷ (tackle) aborder [1] (a task or problem)

appropriate ADJECTIVE approprié

approval NOUN approbation FEM

approve VERB to approve of apprécier [1], they don't approve of her friends ils n'apprécient pas ses amis

approximate ADJECTIVE approximatif (FEM approximative)

approximately ADVERB environ; approximately fifty people environ cinquante personnes

apricot NOUN abricot MASC

apricot tree NOUN abricotier MASC

April NOUN avril MASC; in April en avril

April Fool NOUN poisson (MASC) d'avril

April Fool's Day NOUN le premier avril

apron NOUN tablier MASC

aquarium NOUN aquarium MASC

Aquarius NOUN Verseau MASC; Sharon's Aquarius Sharon est Verseau

Arab NOUN Arabe MASC & FEM

Arab ADJECTIVE arabe; the Arab countries les pays arabes

arch NOUN arche FEM

archaeologist NOUN archéologue MASC & FEM; she's an archaeologist elle est archéologue

archaeology NOUN archéologie FEM

archbishop NOUN archevêque MASC

architect NOUN architecte MASC & FEM; he's an architect il est architecte

architecture NOUN architecture FEM

Arctic NOUN Arctique MASC

are VERB ▸ SEE **be**

area NOUN ❶ (part of a town) quartier; a nice area un quartier bien, **a rough area** un quartier mal fréquenté ❷ *(region)* **région** FEM; **in the Leeds area** dans la région de Leeds

argue VERB ❶ se disputer [1]; **there's no point in arguing** ce n'est pas la peine de se disputer ❷ **to argue about something** discuter [1] de quelque chose, **they're arguing about the result** ils sont en train de discuter du résultat

argument NOUN dispute FEM; **to have an argument** se disputer

Aries NOUN Bélier MASC; **Pauline's Aries** Pauline est Bélier

arithmetic NOUN arithmétique FEM

arm NOUN bras MASC; **to fold your arms** croiser les bras, **arm in arm** bras dessus bras dessous, **to break your arm** se casser le bras

armchair NOUN fauteuil MASC

armed ADJECTIVE armé

armpit NOUN aisselle FEM

army NOUN armée FEM; **to join the army** s'engager dans l'armée

around PREPOSITION, ADVERB ❶ *(with time)* vers; **we'll be there around ten** on va arriver vers dix heures ❷ *(with ages or amounts)* environ; **she's around fifteen** elle a environ quinze ans, **we need around six kilos** il nous faut environ six kilos ❸ *(surrounding)* autour de; **the countryside around Edinburgh** le paysage autour d'Édimbourg ❹ *(near)* **is there a post office around here?** est-ce qu'il y a un bureau de poste près d'ici?, **is Phil around?** est-ce que Phil est là? ❺ *(wrapped around)* autour de; **she had a scarf around her neck** elle avait une écharpe autour du cou

arrange VERB **to arrange to do** prévoir [65] de faire, **we've arranged to see a film on Saturday** nous avons prévu de voir un film samedi

arrangement NOUN ❶ *(of things)* disposition FEM ❷ *(agreement)* accord MASC

arrest NOUN **to be under arrest** être en état d'arrestation

arrest VERB arrêter [1]

arrival NOUN arrivée FEM

arrive VERB arriver [1]; **they arrived at 3 p.m.** ils sont arrivés à quinze heures

arrow NOUN flèche FEM

art NOUN ❶ art MASC; **modern art** l'art moderne ❷ *(school subject)* dessin MASC; **the art class** le cours de dessin

artery NOUN artère FEM

art gallery NOUN *(public)* musée *(MASC)* des beaux arts

artichoke NOUN artichaut MASC

article NOUN article MASC

artificial ADJECTIVE artificiel *(FEM artificielle)*

artist NOUN artiste MASC & FEM; **he's an artist** c'est un artiste

artistic ADJECTIVE artistique

art school NOUN école *(FEM)* de beaux arts

as CONJUNCTION, ADVERB, PREPOSITION ❶ comme; **as you know** comme vous le savez, **as usual** comme d'habitude, **as I told you** comme je t'avais dit ❷ *(because)* puisque; **as there were no trains, we took the bus** puisqu'il n'y avait pas de trains, nous avons pris le bus ❸ **as ... as** aussi ... que, **he's as tall as his brother** il est aussi grand que son frère, **you must be as tired as I am** tu dois être aussi fatigué que moi ❹ **as much ... as** autant de ... que, **you have as much time as I do** tu as autant de temps que moi ❺ **as many ... as** autant de ... que, **we have as many problems as he does** nous avons autant de problèmes que lui ❻ **as long as** pourvu que *(with subjunctive)*, **we'll go tomorrow, as long as it's a nice day** on va y aller demain, pourvu qu'il fasse beau ❼ **for as long as** aussi longtemps que, **you can stay for as long as you like** tu peux rester aussi longtemps que tu veux ❽ **as soon as possible** dès que possible ❾ **to work as** travailler comme, **he works as a taxi driver in the evenings** il travaille comme chauffeur de taxi le soir

asbestos NOUN **amiante** FEM

ash NOUN **cendre** FEM

ashamed ADJECTIVE **to be ashamed** avoir honte, **you should be ashamed of yourself!** tu devrais avoir honte!

ashtray NOUN **cendrier** MASC

Asia NOUN **Asie** FEM; **in Asia** en Asie

Asian NOUN ❶ *(from the Far East)* **Asiatique** MASC & FEM ❷ *(from India)* **Indien** MASC, **Indienne** FEM ❸ *(from Pakistan)* **Pakistanais** MASC, **Pakistanaise** FEM

Asian ADJECTIVE ❶ **asiatique** *(from Asia)* ❷ *(from India)* **indien** *(FEM indienne)* ❸ *(from Pakistan)* **pakistanais** *(FEM pakistanaise)*

ask VERB ❶ **demander** [1]; **you can ask at reception** tu peux demander

à l'accueil, **to ask somebody something** demander quelque chose à quelqu'un, **I asked him where he lives** je lui ai demandé où il habite, **to ask for something** demander quelque chose, **I asked for three coffees** j'ai demandé trois cafés, **to ask somebody for something** demander quelque chose à quelqu'un, **to ask somebody to do** demander à quelqu'un de faire, **ask Danny to give you a hand** demande à Danny de te donner un coup de main ❷ **to ask somebody a question** poser [1] une question à quelqu'un, **I asked you a question!** je t'ai posé une question! ❸ **inviter** [1]; **they've asked us to a party at their house** ils nous ont invité à une soirée chez eux ❹ **Paul's asked Janie out on Friday** Paul a invité Janie à sortir avec lui vendredi

asleep ADJECTIVE **to be asleep** dormir [37], **the baby's asleep** le bébé dort, **to fall asleep** s'endormir [37]

asparagus NOUN **asperges** FEM PLURAL

aspirin NOUN **aspirine** FEM

assembly NOUN *(at school)* **rassemblement** MASC

assess VERB **évaluer** [1]

assignment NOUN *(at school)* **devoir** MASC

assist VERB **aider** [1]

assistance NOUN **aide** FEM

assistant NOUN ❶ **assistant** MASC, **assistante** FEM ❷ **a shop assistant** un vendeur, une vendeuse

association NOUN **association** FEM

assorted ADJECTIVE **variés** *(FEM variées)*

a
b
c
d
e
f
g
h
i
j
k
l
m
n
o
p
q
r
s
t
u
v
w
x
y
z

A
B
C
D
E
F
G
H
I
J
K
L
M
N
O
P
Q
R
S
T
U
V
W
X
Y
Z

assortment NOUN mélange MASC

assume VERB supposer [1]

assure VERB assurer [1]

asterisk NOUN astérisque MASC

asthma NOUN asthme MASC; she has asthma elle souffre de l'asthme

astonishing ADJECTIVE étonnant; her knowledge is astonishing elle a des connaissances incroyables

astrologer NOUN astrologue MASC & FEM

astrology NOUN astrologie FEM

astronaut NOUN astronaute MASC & FEM

astronomer NOUN astronome MASC & FEM

astronomy NOUN astronomie FEM

at PREPOSITION ❶ à (note that 'à + le' always becomes 'au' and 'à + les' always becomes 'aux'); at home à la maison, at school à l'école, at my office à mon bureau, at the market au marché, at meetings aux réunions ❷ (talking about the time) à; at eight o'clock à huit heures ❸ at night la nuit, at the weekend le weekend ❹ at Emma's house chez Emma, she's at her brother's this evening elle est chez son frère ce soir, at the hairdresser's chez le coiffeur ❺ at last enfin, he's found a job at last il a enfin trouvé un emploi ❻ (@ in e-mail addresses) arobase MASC; john-dot-smith@easycom-dot-com john-point-smith-arobase-easycom-point-com

athlete NOUN athlète MASC & FEM

athletic ADJECTIVE athlétique

athletics NOUN athlétisme MASC

Atlantic NOUN Atlantique MASC

atlas NOUN atlas MASC

atmosphere NOUN atmosphère FEM

atom NOUN atome MASC

atomic ADJECTIVE atomique

attach VERB attacher [1]

attached ADJECTIVE to be attached to être [6] attaché à

attachment NOUN pièce (FEM) jointe

attack NOUN attaque FEM

attack VERB attaquer [1]

attacker NOUN agresseur MASC

attempt NOUN tentative FEM; at the first attempt à la première tentative

attempt VERB to attempt to do essayer [59] de faire

attend VERB assister [1] à; to attend a class assister à un cours

attention NOUN attention FEM; to pay attention to faire attention à, I wasn't paying attention je ne faisais pas attention

attic NOUN grenier MASC; in the attic au grenier

attitude NOUN attitude FEM

attract VERB attirer [1]

attraction NOUN attraction FEM

attractive ADJECTIVE séduisant

aubergine NOUN aubergine FEM

auction NOUN vente (FEM) aux enchères

audience NOUN public MASC

August NOUN août MASC; in August en août

aunt, **auntie** NOUN tante FEM

au pair NOUN jeune fille (FEM) au pair; **I'm looking for a job as an au pair** je cherche un emploi de jeune fille au pair

Australia NOUN Australie FEM; **in Australia** en Australie, **to Australia** en Australie

Australian NOUN Australien MASC, Australienne FEM

Australian ADJECTIVE australien (FEM australienne)

Austria NOUN Autriche FEM; **in Austria** en Autriche, **to Austria** en Autriche

Austrian NOUN Autrichien MASC, Autrichienne FEM

Austrian ADJECTIVE autrichien (FEM autrichienne)

author NOUN auteur MASC

autobiography NOUN autobiographie FEM

autograph NOUN autographe MASC

automatic ADJECTIVE automatique

automatically ADVERB automatiquement

autumn NOUN automne MASC; **in autumn** en automne

availability NOUN disponibilité FEM

available ADJECTIVE disponible

avalanche NOUN avalanche FEM

avenue NOUN avenue FEM

average NOUN moyenne FEM; **on average** en moyenne, **above average** au-dessus de la moyenne

average ADJECTIVE moyen (FEM moyenne); **the average height** la hauteur moyenne

avocado NOUN avocat MASC

avoid VERB éviter [1]; **she avoided me** elle m'a évité, **to avoid doing** éviter de faire, **I avoid speaking to him** j'évite de lui parler

awake ADJECTIVE **to be awake** être réveillé, **is Lola awake?** est-ce que Lola est réveillée?, **are you still awake?** tu ne dors pas?

award NOUN prix MASC; **to win an award** remporter un prix

aware ADJECTIVE **to be aware of a noise** être conscient d'un bruit, **to be aware of a problem** être au courant d'un problème, **as far as I'm aware** à ma connaissance

away ADVERB ❶ **to be away** être absent, **I'll be away next week** je serai absent la semaine prochaine ❷ **to go away** partir, **Laura's gone away for a week** Laura est partie pour une semaine, **go away!** va-t-en! ❸ **to run away** partir en courant, **the thieves ran away** les voleurs sont partis en courant ❹ **the school is two kilometres away** l'école est à deux kilomètres d'ici, **how far away is it?** c'est à quelle distance d'ici?, **not far away** pas loin d'ici ❺ **to put something away** ranger quelque chose, **I'll just put my books away** je vais juste ranger mes livres ❻ **to give something away** donner quelque chose, **she's given away all her books** elle a donné toutes ses livres

away match NOUN match (MASC) à l'extérieur

awful ADJECTIVE ❶ affreux (FEM affreuse); **the film was awful!** le film était affreux! ❷ **I feel awful** (ill) je ne me sens pas bien du tout ❸ **I feel awful about it** ça m'ennuie vraiment ❹ **an awful lot of** énormément de

awkward ADJECTIVE ❶ difficile; **it's an awkward situation** c'est une situation difficile, **it's a bit awkward** c'est un peu difficile, **an awkward child** un enfant difficile ❷ **an awkward question** une question gênante

axe NOUN hache FEM

baby NOUN bébé MASC

babysit VERB faire [10] du babysitting

babysitter NOUN babysitter MASC & FEM

babysitting NOUN babysitting MASC

bachelor NOUN célibataire MASC

back NOUN ❶ (of a person or animal) dos MASC; **to do something behind someone's back** faire quelque chose dans le dos de quelqu'un ❷ (of a piece of paper, your hand, or a garment) dos MASC; **on the back** au dos ❸ (of a car, a plane, or a building) arrière MASC; **we have seats at the back** nous avons des places à l'arrière, **a garden at the back of the house** un jardin à l'arrière de la maison ❹ **the children at the back of the room** les enfants au fond de la salle ❺ (of a chair or sofa) dossier MASC ❻ (in football or hockey) arrière MASC; **left back** arrière gauche

back ADJECTIVE ❶ arrière (a wheel or seat); **the back seat of the car** le siège arrière de la voiture ❷ **the back gate** la porte de derrière, **the back garden** le jardin de derrière

back ADVERB ❶ **to go back** rentrer, **to go back to school** rentrer à l'école, **Lisa's gone back to London** Lisa est rentrée à Londres ❷ **to come back** rentrer, **they've come back from Italy** ils sont rentrés d'Italie, **she's back at work** elle a repris le travail, **Sue's not back yet** Sue n'est pas encore rentrée, **we went by bus and walked back** nous avons pris le bus pour y aller et nous sommes rentrés à pied ❸ **to phone back** rappeler, **I'll ring back later** je rappellerai plus tard ❹ **to give something back to somebody** rendre quelque chose à quelqu'un, **I gave him back his socks** je lui ai rendu ses chausettes, **give it back!** rends-le-moi!

back VERB ❶ (to support) soutenir [81] (a candidate, for example) ❷ (to bet on) parier [1] sur (a horse)
• **to back up** (computing) **to back up a file** sauvegarder [1] un fichier sur disquette
• **to back somebody up** soutenir [77] quelqu'un

backache NOUN mal (MASC) de dos

backbone NOUN colonne (FEM) vertébrale

A
B
C
D
E
F
G
H
I
J
K
L
M
N
O
P
Q
R
S
T
U
V
W
X
Y
Z

back door NOUN ❶ (of a building) porte (FEM) de derrière ❷ (of a car) porte (FEM) arrière

backfire VERB (turn out badly) échouer [1]

background NOUN ❶ (of a person) (social) milieu MASC ❷ (of events or a situation) contexte MASC ❸ (in a picture or view) arrière-plan MASC; **the trees in the background** les arbres à l'arrière-plan ❹ **background music** la musique d'ambiance ❺ **background noise** les bruits (MASC PLURAL) de fond

backhand NOUN revers MASC

backing NOUN ❶ (on sticky-back plastic, for example) revêtement (MASC) intérieur ❷ (moral support) soutien MASC ❸ (in music) **a backing group** un groupe d'accompagnement

backpack NOUN sac (MASC) à dos

backpack VERB **to go backpacking** partir [58] en voyage avec son sac à dos

back seat NOUN siège (MASC) arrière

backside NOUN derrière MASC

backstage ADVERB **to go backstage** aller dans les coulisses

backstroke NOUN dos (MASC) crawlé

back to front ADVERB à l'envers; **your jumper's back to front** ton pull est à l'envers

backup NOUN ❶ (support) soutien MASC ❷ (in computing) **a backup disk** un disque de sauvegarde

backwards ADVERB (to lean or fall) en arrière

bacon NOUN ❶ (French streaky bacon) lard MASC ❷ (thin-sliced British-type) bacon MASC; **bacon and eggs** œufs au bacon

bad ADJECTIVE ❶ (not good) mauvais (goes before the noun); **bad work** du mauvais travail, **a bad meal** un mauvais repas, **his new film's not bad** son nouveau film n'est pas mauvais, **it's bad for your health** c'est mauvais pour la santé, **I'm bad at physics** je suis mauvais en physique ❷ (serious) grave; **a bad accident** un accident grave, **a bad cold** un gros rhume ❸ (rotten) pourri; **a bad apple** une pomme pourrie, **to go bad** se gâter ❹ (rude) **bad language** du langage grossier ❺ (naughty) vilain; **bad dog!** vilain!, **bad girl!** vilaine!
• **too bad!** (I'm sorry for you) pas de chance!, (I don't care) tant pis!

badge NOUN badge MASC

badly ADVERB ❶ mal; **he writes badly** il écrit mal, **I slept badly** j'ai mal dormi, **the exam went badly** l'examen s'est mal passé ❷ (seriously) (to hurt or damage) gravement; **the car was badly damaged** la voiture a été gravement endommagée, **badly hurt** grièvement blessé

bad-mannered ADJECTIVE mal élevé

badminton NOUN badminton MASC; **to play badminton** jouer au badminton

bad-tempered ADJECTIVE ❶ (for a little while) irrité ❷ (always) **she's very bad-tempered** elle a très mauvais caractère

bag NOUN sac MASC

baggage NOUN bagages MASC PLURAL

baggage allowance NOUN franchise (FEM) de bagages

baggage reclaim NOUN réception (FEM) des bagages

bagpipes PLURAL NOUN cornemuse FEM; **to play the bagpipes** jouer de la cornemuse

bags PLURAL NOUN bagages MASC PLURAL; **to pack your bags** faire ses bagages
• **to have bags under your eyes** avoir des valises sous les yeux (informal)

Bahaman ADJECTIVE des Bahamas

Bahamas NOUN (plural) **the Bahamas** les Bahamas, **the Bahamas Islands** les îles Bahamas

bake VERB **to bake a cake** faire [10] un gâteau, **to bake vegetables** faire [10] cuire des légumes au four

baked ADJECTIVE ❶ (fish or fruit) au four; **baked apples** les pommes au four ❷ **a baked potato** une pomme de terre au four

baked beans PLURAL NOUN les haricots blancs à la sauce tomate

baker NOUN boulanger MASC, boulangère FEM; **to go to the baker's** aller à la boulangerie

bakery NOUN boulangerie FEM

balance NOUN ❶ équilibre MASC; **to lose your balance** perdre l'équilibre ❷ (money in your bank account) solde MASC

balanced ADJECTIVE équilibré

balcony NOUN balcon MASC

bald ADJECTIVE chauve

ball NOUN ❶ (for tennis or golf) balle FEM ❷ (for football or volleyball) ballon MASC ❸ (of string or wool) pelote FEM

ballet NOUN ballet MASC

ballet dancer NOUN danseur (MASC) de ballet, danseuse (FEM) de ballet

ballet shoe NOUN chausson (MASC) de danse

balloon NOUN ❶ ballon MASC ❷ (hot air) montgolfière FEM

ballot NOUN scrutin MASC

ballpoint (pen) NOUN stylo (MASC) à bille

ban NOUN interdiction FEM; **a ban on smoking** une interdiction de fumer

ban VERB interdire [47]

banana NOUN banane FEM; **a banana yoghurt** un yaourt à la banane

band NOUN ❶ (playing music) groupe MASC; **a rock band** un groupe de rock ❷ **a jazz band** un orchestre de jazz ❸ **a brass band** une fanfare ❹ **a rubber band** un élastique

bandage NOUN bandage MASC

bandage VERB mettre [11] un bandage à

bang NOUN ❶ (noise) boum MASC ❷ (of a door, shutter, or window, etc) claquement MASC

bang VERB ❶ (to hit) taper [1] sur (a drum, for example); **he banged his fist on the table** il a tapé du poing sur la table ❷ (to knock) cogner [1]; **to bang on the door** cogner à la porte, **I banged my head on the door** je me suis cogné la tête contre la porte, **I banged into the table** j'ai heurté la table ❸ **to bang the door** claquer [1] la porte

bang EXCLAMATION (like a gun) pan!

bangle NOUN bracelet MASC

banister(s), **bannister(s)** (PLURAL) NOUN rampe FEM (d'escalier)

bank NOUN ❶ (for money) banque FEM; **I'm going to the bank** je vais à la banque ❷ (of a river or lake) bord MASC

bank account NOUN compte (MASC) bancaire

bank balance NOUN solde (MASC) bancaire

bank card NOUN carte (FEM) bancaire

bank holiday NOUN jour (MASC) férié

banking NOUN banque (FEM), milieu (MASC) bancaire

banknote NOUN billet (MASC) de banque

bank statement NOUN relevé (MASC) de compte

baptize VERB baptiser [1]

bar NOUN ❶ (selling drinks) bar MASC; **Janet works in a bar** Janet travaille dans un bar ❷ (the counter) comptoir MASC; **on the bar** sur le bar ❸ a bar of chocolate une tablette de chocolat ❹ a bar of soap une savonnette ❺ (made of wood or metal) barre FEM; **a metal bar** une barre en métal ❻ (in music) mesure FEM

bar VERB ❶ (to block physically) barrer [1]; **to bar someone's way** barrer le passage à quelqu'un ❷ (to ban from an activity) exclure [25]

Barbadian NOUN Barbadien MASC, Barbadienne FEM

Barbadian ADJECTIVE de la Barbade

Barbados NOUN la Barbade

barbecue NOUN barbecue MASC; **there's a barbecue tonight** il y a un barbecue ce soir

barbecue VERB to barbecue a chicken faire [10] griller un poulet au barbecue, **barbecued chicken** du poulet grillé au barbecue

barbed wire NOUN barbelé MASC

bare ADJECTIVE nu

barefoot ADJECTIVE to be barefoot être nu-pieds, **to walk barefoot** marcher pieds nus

bargain NOUN (a good buy) affaire FEM; **I got a bargain** j'ai fait une affaire, **it's a bargain!** c'est une bonne affaire!

barge NOUN péniche FEM

bark NOUN ❶ (of a tree) écorce FEM ❷ (of a dog) aboiement MASC

bark VERB aboyer [39]

barley NOUN orge MASC

barmaid NOUN barmaid FEM

barman NOUN barman MASC

barn NOUN grange FEM

barometer NOUN baromètre MASC

barrel NOUN tonneau MASC (PLURAL tonneaux)

barrier NOUN barrière FEM

base NOUN base FEM

baseball NOUN base-ball MASC; **a baseball cap** une casquette de base-ball

based ADJECTIVE ❶ to be based on être fondé sur, **the film is based on a true story** le film est fondé sur une histoire vraie ❷ to be based in être basé à, **he's based in Bristol** il est basé à Bristol

basement NOUN sous-sol MASC; **in the basement** au sous-sol

bash NOUN ❶ bosse FEM; **it's got a bash on the wing** il y a une bosse à l'aile ❷ **I'll have a bash** je vais essayer un coup

bash VERB cogner [1]; **I bashed my head** je me suis cogné la tête

basic ADJECTIVE ❶ de base; **basic knowledge** des connaissances de base, **her basic salary** son salaire de base ❷ **the basic facts** les faits essentiels ❸ (not luxurious) rudimentaire; **the flat's a bit basic** l'appartement est un peu rudimentaire

basically ADVERB ❶ au fond; **it's basically all right** au fond ça va ❷ à vrai dire; **basically, I don't want to go** à vrai dire, je ne veux pas y aller

basics NOUN rudiments MASC PLURAL

basin NOUN (washbasin) lavabo MASC

basis NOUN ❶ base FEM ❷ **on the basis of** sur la base de, **on a regular basis** régulièrement

basket NOUN ❶ (for shopping) panier MASC ❷ (other) corbeille FEM; **a waste-paper basket** une corbeille à papier, **a linen basket** une corbeille à linge

basketball NOUN basketball MASC; **to play basketball** jouer au basketball

bass NOUN ❶ basse FEM; **to play bass** jouer de la basse ❷ **a double bass** une contrebasse

bass drum NOUN grosse caisse FEM

bass guitar NOUN guitare (FEM) basse

bassoon NOUN basson MASC; **to play the bassoon** jouer du basson

bat NOUN ❶ (for cricket or baseball) batte FEM ❷ (for table tennis) raquette FEM ❸ (animal) chauve-souris FEM

batch NOUN ❶ (of cakes) fournée FEM ❷ (of letters) tas MASC; **a batch of letters** un tas de lettres ❸ (in computing) lot MASC

bath NOUN ❶ bain MASC; **to have a bath** prendre un bain, **I was in the bath** j'étais dans mon bain ❷ (bathtub) baignoire FEM; **the bath's pink** la baignoire est rose

bathe VERB ❶ laver [1] (a wound) ❷ (go swimming) se baigner [1]

bathroom NOUN salle (FEM) de bains (PLURAL salles de bains)

baths PLURAL NOUN piscine FEM

bath towel NOUN serviette (FEM) de bain

batter NOUN (for frying) pâte (FEM) à frire; **fish in batter** des beignets de poisson, **pancake batter** la pâte à crêpes

battery NOUN ❶ (for a torch or radio, for example) pile FEM ❷ (for a car) batterie FEM

battle NOUN bataille FEM

bay NOUN ❶ (on the coast) baie FEM ❷ (for coaches) travée FEM

BC ABBREVIATION (short for **before Christ**) av. J.-C

be VERB ❶ être [6]; **Melanie is in the kitchen** Melanie est dans la cuisine, **where is the butter?** où est le beurre?, **I'm tired** je suis fatigué, **when we were in France** quand nous étions en France ❷ (with jobs and professions) être; **she's a**

teacher elle est professeur *(note that 'a' is not translated)*, **he's a taxi driver** il est chauffeur de taxi ❸ *(in clock times)* être; **it's three o'clock** il est trois heures, **it's half past five** il est cinq heures et demie ❹ *(days of the week and dates)* **what day is it today?** nous sommes quel jour aujourd'hui?, **it's Tuesday today** nous sommes mardi aujourd'hui, **it's the twentieth of May** nous sommes le vingt mai ❺ *(talking about age)* avoir [5]; **how old are you?** quel âge as-tu?, **I'm fifteen** j'ai quinze ans, **Harry's twenty** Harry a vingt ans ❻ *(cold, hot, hungry)* avoir [5]; **I'm hot** j'ai chaud, **I'm cold** j'ai froid, **I'm hungry** j'ai faim ❼ *(weather)* faire [10]; **it's cold today** il fait froid aujourd'hui, **it's a nice day** il fait beau ❽ **I've never been to Paris** je ne suis jamais allé à Paris, **have you been to Britain before?** est-ce que tu es déjà venu en Grande Bretagne? ❾ **to be loved** être aimé, **he has been killed** il a été tué

beach NOUN plage FEM; **to go to the beach** aller à la plage, **on the beach** sur la plage

bead NOUN perle FEM

beak NOUN bec MASC

beam NOUN ❶ *(of light)* rayon MASC ❷ *(for a roof)* poutre FEM

bean NOUN haricot MASC; **baked beans** les haricots à la sauce tomate, **green beans** les haricots verts

bear NOUN ours MASC

bear VERB ❶ supporter [1]; **I can't bear him** je ne peux pas le supporter, **I can't bear the idea** je ne supporte pas l'idée ❷ **to bear something in mind** tenir [77]

compte de quelque chose, **I'll bear it in mind** je ne l'oublierai pas
• **to bear up** tenir [77] le coup

beard NOUN barbe FEM

bearded ADJECTIVE barbu

bearings PLURAL NOUN **to get one's bearings** se repérer [24]

beast NOUN ❶ *(animal)* bête FEM ❷ **you beast!** chameau!

beat NOUN rythme MASC

beat VERB ❶ *(defeat)* battre [21]; **we beat them!** on les a battus! ❷ **to beat the eggs** battre les œufs ❸ **you can't beat a good meal** rien ne vaut un bon repas
• **to beat somebody up** tabasser [1] quelqu'un *(informal)*

beautician NOUN esthéticien MASC, esthéticienne FEM

beautiful ADJECTIVE beau MASC, belle FEM *(PLURAL* beaux*) (goes before the noun)*; **a beautiful day** un beau jour, **a beautiful girl** une belle fille, **beautiful pictures** de beaux tableaux, **a beautiful place** un bel endroit *('bel' for masculine nouns beginning with a vowel or silent 'h')*

beautifully ADVERB admirablement

beauty NOUN beauté FEM

beauty spot NOUN *(for tourists)* beau site MASC

because CONJUNCTION ❶ parce que; **because it's you** parce que c'est toi, **because it's cold** parce qu'il fait froid ❷ **because of** à cause de, **because of the accident** à cause de l'accident

become VERB devenir [81]

a
b
c
d
e
f
g
h
i
j
k
l
m
n
o
p
q
r
s
t
u
v
w
x
y
z

A B C D E F G H I J K L M N O P Q R S T U V W X Y Z

bed NOUN ❶ lit MASC; **a double bed** un grand lit, **in bed** au lit, **to go to bed** aller se coucher ❷ (flower bed) parterre MASC

bedclothes PLURAL NOUN couvertures FEM PLURAL

bedding NOUN literie FEM

bedroom NOUN chambre FEM; **bedroom furniture** les meubles de chambre, **my bedroom window** la fenêtre de ma chambre

bedside NOUN **a bedside table** une table de chevet

bedsit, **bedsitter** NOUN chambre (FEM) meublée

bedspread NOUN dessus-de-lit MASC

bedtime NOUN **it's bedtime** c'est l'heure d'aller se coucher

bee NOUN abeille FEM

beech NOUN hêtre MASC

beef NOUN bœuf MASC; **we had roast beef** on a mangé du rôti de bœuf

beefburger NOUN hamburger MASC

beer NOUN bière FEM; **two beers please** deux bières s'il vous plaît, **a beer can** une canette de bière

beetle NOUN scarabée MASC

beetroot NOUN betterave FEM

before PREPOSITION, ADVERB ❶ avant; **before Monday** avant lundi, **he left before me** il est parti avant moi ❷ **the day before** la veille, **the day before the wedding** la veille du mariage, **the day before yesterday** avant-hier, **the week before** la semaine d'avant ❸ (already) déjà; **I've seen him before somewhere** je l'ai déjà vu quelque part, **I had seen the film before** j'avais déjà vu le film

before CONJUNCTION ❶ avant de; **before doing** avant de faire, **I closed the windows before leaving** (or **before I left**) j'ai fermé les fenêtres avant de partir ❷ avant que; **phone me before they leave** appelle-moi avant qu'ils s'en aillent, **oh, before I forget ...** avant que j'oublie ...

beforehand ADVERB (ahead of time) à l'avance; **phone beforehand** appelle à l'avance

beg VERB ❶ (ask for money) mendier [1] ❷ (ask) supplier [1]; **she begged me not to leave** elle m'a supplié de ne pas partir, **I beg your pardon** je vous demande pardon

begin VERB ❶ commencer [61]; **the meeting begins at ten** la réunion commence à dix heures, **the words beginning with P** les mots qui commencent par un P ❷ **to begin to do** commencer à faire, **I'm beginning to understand** je commence à comprendre

beginner NOUN débutant MASC, débutante FEM

beginning NOUN début MASC; **at the beginning** au début, **at the beginning of the holidays** au début des vacances

behalf NOUN **on behalf of** pour

behave VERB ❶ se comporter [1]; **he behaved badly** il s'est mal comporté ❷ **to behave yourself** être sage, **behave yourselves!** soyez sages!

behaviour NOUN comportement MASC

behind ADVERB, PREPOSITION ❶ derrière; **behind the sofa** derrière le canapé, **behind them** derrière eux, **the car behind**

la voiture de derrière ❷ *(not making progress)* he's behind in class il a du retard en classe ❸ to leave something behind oublier quelque chose, I've left my keys behind j'ai oublié mes clés

behind *NOUN* derrière *MASC*

beige *ADJECTIVE* beige

Belgian *NOUN* Belge *MASC & FEM*

Belgian *ADJECTIVE* belge

Belgium *NOUN* Belgique *FEM*; to Belgium en Belgique, in Belgium en Belgique

belief *NOUN* conviction *FEM*; his political beliefs ses convictions politiques

believe *VERB* ❶ croire [33]; I believe you je te crois, they believed what I said ils ont cru ce que j'ai dit, I don't believe you! ce n'est pas vrai! ❷ to believe in croire à, to believe in ghosts croire aux fantômes, to believe in God croire en Dieu

bell *NOUN* ❶ *(in a church)* cloche *FEM* ❷ *(on a door)* sonnette *FEM*; ring the bell! appuyez sur la sonnette! ❸ *(for a cat or toy)* grelot *MASC*
• that name rings a bell ce nom me dit quelque chose *(literally: says something to me)*

belong *VERB* ❶ to belong to appartenir [81] à, that belongs to Richard cela appartient à Richard ❷ to belong to a club faire [10] partie d'un club ❸ *(go)* aller [5]; that chair belongs in the study cette chaise va dans le bureau, where does this vase belong? ce vase va où?

belongings *PLURAL NOUN* affaires *FEM PLURAL*; all my belongings are in

London toutes mes affaires sont à Londres

below *PREPOSITION* au-dessous de; below the window au-dessous de la fenêtre, the flat below yours l'appartement au-dessous du tien

below *ADVERB* ❶ *(further down)* en bas; shouts came from below des cris venaient d'en bas ❷ the flat below l'appartement de dessous

belt *NOUN* ceinture *FEM*

bench *NOUN* banc *MASC*

bend *NOUN* ❶ *(in a road)* virage *MASC* ❷ *(in a river)* courbe *FEM*

bend *VERB* ❶ *(to make a bend in)* plier [1] *(your arm or leg, or a wire)* ❷ *(to curve) (a road or path)* tourner [1] ❸ to bend down or forwards se pencher [1], she bent down to look elle s'est penchée pour regarder

beneath *PREPOSITION* sous

benefit *NOUN* ❶ avantage *MASC* ❷ unemployment benefit les allocations *(FEM PLURAL)* de chômage

bent *ADJECTIVE* tordu

beret *NOUN* béret *MASC*

berry *NOUN* baie *FEM*

berth *NOUN* couchette *FEM*

beside *PREPOSITION* *(next to)* à côté de; she was sitting beside me elle était assise à côté de moi
• that's beside the point ça n'a rien à voir

besides *ADVERB* ❶ *(anyway)* d'ailleurs; besides, it's too late d'ailleurs, il est trop tard ❷ *(as well)* en plus; four dogs, and six cats besides quatre chiens et six chats en plus

best ADJECTIVE ❶ meilleur; it's the best c'est le meilleur, that's the best car cette voiture-là est la meilleure, she's my best friend c'est ma meilleure amie ❷ she's the best at tennis c'est elle la meilleure en tennis, the best thing to do is to phone them la meilleure chose à faire, c'est de les appeler

best ADVERB le mieux; he plays best il joue le mieux, I like Paris best c'est Paris que j'aime le mieux, best of all mieux que tout
• all the best! (good luck) bonne chance!, (cheers) à ta santé!
• it's the best I can do je ne peux pas faire mieux
• to do your best to do faire de son mieux pour faire; I did my best to help her j'ai fait de mon mieux pour l'aider

best man NOUN garçon (MASC) d'honneur

bet NOUN pari MASC

bet VERB parier [1]; to bet on a horse parier sur un cheval, I bet you he'll forget! je te parie qu'il va oublier!

better ADJECTIVE, ADVERB ❶ meilleur; she's found a better flat elle a trouvé un meilleur appartement, this road's better than the other one cette route est meilleure que l'autre ❷ mieux; this pen writes better ce stylo écrit mieux, it works better than the other one ça fonctionne mieux que l'autre ❸ even better encore mieux, it's even better than before c'est encore mieux qu'avant ❹ (less ill) to be better aller mieux, he's a bit better today il va un peu mieux aujourd'hui, to feel better se sentir mieux, I feel better je me sens mieux ❺ to get better s'améliorer,

my French is getting better mon français s'améliore ❻ so much the better tant mieux, the sooner the better le plus vite possible

better ADVERB you had better phone at once tu ferais mieux d'appeler tout de suite, he'd better not go il ferait mieux de ne pas y aller, I'd better go now je dois partir maintenant

better off ADJECTIVE ❶ (richer) plus riche; they're better off than us ils sont plus riches que nous ❷ (more comfortable) mieux; you'd be better off in bed tu serais mieux au lit

between PREPOSITION entre; between London and Dover entre Londres et Douvres, between Monday and Friday entre lundi et vendredi, between the two entre les deux

beware VERB beware of the dog! attention au chien!

beyond PREPOSITION ❶ (in space and time) au-delà de; beyond the border au-delà de la frontière ❷ it's beyond me! ça me dépasse!

Bible NOUN the Bible la Bible

bicycle NOUN vélo MASC; by bicycle à vélo

bicycle lane NOUN piste (FEM) cyclable

big ADJECTIVE ❶ grand (goes before the noun); a big house une grande maison, a big city une grande ville, my big sister ma grande sœur, it's too big for me c'est trop grand pour moi ❷ gros (FEM grosse) (before the noun); a big dog un gros chien, a big car une grosse voiture, a big mistake une grosse erreur

bigheaded ADJECTIVE **to be bigheaded** avoir la grosse tête

big screen NOUN **grand écran** MASC

big toe NOUN **gros orteil** MASC

bike NOUN ❶ *(with pedals)* **vélo** MASC; **by bike** à vélo ❷ *(with motor)* **moto** FEM

bikini NOUN **bikini** MASC

bilingual ADJECTIVE **bilingue**

bill NOUN ❶ *(in a restaurant)* **addition** FEM; **can we have the bill, please** l'addition, s'il vous plaît ❷ *(for gas, electricity, etc.)* **facture** FEM

billiards NOUN **billard** MASC; **to play billiards** jouer au billard

billion NOUN **milliard** MASC

bin NOUN **poubelle** FEM

binoculars NOUN **jumelles** FEM PLURAL

biochemistry NOUN **biochimie** FEM

biography NOUN **biographie** FEM

biologist NOUN **biologiste** MASC & FEM

biology NOUN **biologie** FEM

bird NOUN **oiseau** MASC *(PLURAL* **oiseaux***)*

bird sanctuary NOUN **réserve** *(FEM)* **ornithologique**

birdwatching NOUN **to go birdwatching** observer les oiseaux

Biro NOUN **bic** MASC

birth NOUN **naissance** FEM

birth certificate NOUN **acte** *(MASC)* **de naissance**

birth control NOUN **contraception** FEM

birthday NOUN ❶ **anniversaire** MASC; **happy birthday!** joyeux anniversaire! ❷ **a birthday present** un cadeau d'anniversaire

birthday party NOUN ❶ *(for a child)* **goûter** *(MASC)* **d'anniversaire** ❷ *(for an adult)* **soirée** *(FEM)* **d'anniversaire**

biscuit NOUN **biscuit** MASC

bishop NOUN **évêque** MASC

bit NOUN ❶ *(of bread, cheese, wood)* **morceau** MASC; **a bit of chocolate** un morceau de chocolat ❷ *(of string, paper, garden)* **bout** MASC; **a bit of string** un bout de ficelle, **with a little bit of garden** avec un petit bout de jardin ❸ *(a small amount)* **a bit of** un peu de, **a bit of sugar** un peu de sucre, **with a bit of luck** avec un peu de chance, **a bit of news** une nouvelle, **to have a bit of trouble with** avoir un petit problème avec ❹ *(in a book or film, for example)* **passage** MASC; **this bit is brilliant!** ce passage est génial! ❺ **to fall to bits** tomber en morceaux ❻ **a bit** un peu, **a bit hot** un peu chaud, **a bit early** un peu trop tôt, **wait a bit!** attends un peu! ❼ *(for a horse)* **mors** MASC
• **bit by bit** petit à petit

bite NOUN ❶ *(snack)* **morceau** MASC; **I'll just have a bite before I go** je vais juste manger un morceau avant de partir ❷ *(from an insect)* **piqûre** FEM; **a mosquito bite** une piqûre de moustique ❸ *(from a dog)* **morsure** FEM

bite VERB ❶ *(a person or a dog)* **mordre** [3] ❷ *(an insect)* **piquer** [1]
• **to bite one's nails** se ronger [52] les ongles

bitter ADJECTIVE (taste) amer (FEM amère)

black ADJECTIVE ❶ noir; my black jacket ma veste noire, to turn black noircir [2] ❷ a Black man un Noir, a Black woman une Noire ❸ a black coffee un café noir

blackberry NOUN mûre FEM

blackbird NOUN merle MASC

blackboard NOUN tableau (MASC) noir

blackcurrant NOUN cassis MASC

black eye NOUN œil (MASC) au beurre noir

black pudding NOUN boudin (MASC) noir

blade NOUN lame FEM

blame NOUN responsabilité FEM; to take the blame for something prendre la responsabilité de quelque chose

blame VERB to blame someone for something tenir [77] quelqu'un responsable de quelque chose, they blamed him for the accident ils l'ont tenu responsable de l'accident, she is to blame for it elle en est responsable, I blame the parents! à mon avis c'est la faute des parents!, I don't blame you! je te comprends!

blank NOUN blanc MASC

blank ADJECTIVE ❶ (a page or piece of paper, or a cheque) blanc (FEM blanche), (a tape or disk) vierge (a screen), vide ❷ my mind went blank j'ai eu un trou de mémoire

blanket NOUN couverture FEM

blast NOUN ❶ (an explosion) explosion FEM ❷ (of air) souffle MASC ❸ to play music at full blast jouer de la musique à plein volume

blaze NOUN incendie MASC

blaze VERB brûler [1]

blazer NOUN blazer MASC

bleach NOUN eau (FEM) de javel

bleed VERB saigner [1]; my nose is bleeding je saigne du nez

blend NOUN mélange MASC

blender NOUN mixer MASC

bless VERB bénir [2]; bless you! (after a sneeze) à tes souhaits!

blind NOUN (in a window) store MASC

blind ADJECTIVE aveugle; to go blind perdre la vue

blindness NOUN cécité FEM

blink VERB (your eyes) cligner [1] des yeux

blister NOUN ampoule FEM

blizzard NOUN tempête (FEM) de neige

blob NOUN goutte FEM

block NOUN ❶ a block of flats un immeuble, an office block un immeuble de bureaux ❷ (a square group of buildings) to run (or drive) round the block faire le tour du pâté de maisons

block VERB ❶ bloquer [1] (an exit or a road) ❷ boucher [1] (a drain or a hole); the sink's blocked l'évier est bouché

blonde ADJECTIVE blond

blood NOUN sang MASC

blood test NOUN prise (FEM) de sang

blossom NOUN fleurs FEM PLURAL; **to be in blossom** être en fleurs

blot NOUN tache FEM

blotchy ADJECTIVE (skin) marbré

blouse NOUN chemisier MASC

blow NOUN coup MASC

blow VERB ❶ (the wind or a person) souffler [1] ❷ (in an explosion) **the bomb blew a hole in the wall** la bombe a fait un trou dans le mur ❸ **to blow your nose** se moucher [1]
• **to blow something out** souffler [1] (a candle), éteindre [60] (flames)
• **to blow up** (explode) exploser [1]
• **to blow something up** gonfler [1] (a balloon or tyre), faire [10] sauter (a building); **they blew up the president's residence** ils ont fait sauter la résidence du président

blow-dry NOUN brushing MASC; **a cut and blow dry** une coupe brushing

blue ADJECTIVE bleu; **blue eyes** les yeux bleus

bluebell NOUN jacinthe (FEM) des bois

blues PLURAL NOUN le blues MASC SINGULAR

blunder NOUN gaffe FEM

blunt ADJECTIVE ❶ (a knife or scissors) émoussé ❷ (a pencil) mal taillé ❸ (person) brusque

blurred ADJECTIVE ❶ indistinct ❷ (photo) flou

blush VERB rougir [2]

board NOUN ❶ (plank) planche FEM ❷ (blackboard) tableau (MASC) noir ❸ (notice board) panneau (MASC) d'affichage ❹ (for a board game) jeu MASC ❺ **a chess board** un échiquier ❻ (accommodation in a hotel) **full board** pension (FEM) complète, **half board** demi-pension FEM ❼ **on board** à bord, **they were on board the ferry** ils étaient à bord du ferry

boarder NOUN (in a school) interne MASC & FEM

board game NOUN jeu (MASC) de société (PLURAL jeux de société)

boarding NOUN embarquement MASC

boarding card NOUN carte (FEM) d'embarquement

boarding school NOUN école (FEM) privée avec internat

boast VERB se vanter [1]; **he was boasting about his new bike** il se vantait de son nouveau vélo

boat NOUN ❶ (in general) bateau MASC ❷ (sailing boat) voilier MASC ❸ (rowing boat) barque FEM

body NOUN ❶ corps MASC ❷ (corpse) cadavre MASC

bodybuilding NOUN culturisme MASC

bodyguard NOUN garde (MASC) du corps

boil NOUN ❶ **bring the water to the boil** portez l'eau à ébullition ❷ (swelling) furoncle MASC

boil VERB ❶ bouillir [23]; **the water's boiling** l'eau bout ❷ faire [10] bouillir; **I'm going to boil some water** je vais faire bouillir de l'eau, **to boil vegetables** faire [10] cuire des légumes à l'eau bouillante, **to boil an egg** faire cuire un œuf
• **to boil over** déborder [1]

a
b
c
d
e
f
g
h
i
j
k
l
m
n
o
p
q
r
s
t
u
v
w
x
y
z

boiled egg NOUN œuf (MASC) à la coque

boiler NOUN (for central heating) chaudière FEM

boiling ADJECTIVE ❶ (water) bouillant ❷ it's boiling hot today! il fait une chaleur infernale aujourd'hui!

bolt NOUN (on a door) verrou MASC

bolt VERB (to lock) verrouiller [1] (a door)

bomb NOUN bombe FEM

bomb VERB bombarder [1]

bombing NOUN ❶ (in a war) bombardement MASC ❷ (a terrorist attack) attentat (MASC) à la bombe

bone NOUN ❶ os MASC ❷ (of a fish) arête FEM

bonfire NOUN ❶ (for rubbish) feu (MASC) de jardin ❷ (for a celebration) feu (MASC) de joie

bonnet NOUN capot MASC (of a car)

bony ADJECTIVE ❶ (fish) plein d'arêtes ❷ (body) anguleux (FEM anguleuse) ❸ (knee) osseux (FEM osseuse)

boo VERB huer [1]; the crowd booed the referee la foule a hué l'arbitre

book NOUN ❶ (that you read) livre MASC; a book about dinosaurs un livre sur les dinosaures, a biology book un livre de biologie ❷ an exercise book un cahier ❸ (of cheques, stamps, tickets, etc) carnet MASC; a cheque book un carnet de chèques

book VERB réserver [1]; I booked a table for 8 p.m. j'ai réservé une table pour vingt heures

bookcase NOUN bibliothèque FEM

booking NOUN (for a theatre or a holiday, for example) réservation FEM

booking office NOUN bureau (MASC) de location

booklet NOUN brochure FEM

bookshelf NOUN étagère FEM

bookshop NOUN librairie FEM

boom NOUN ❶ (of a sail) bôme FEM ❷ (time of prosperity) boom MASC

boot NOUN ❶ (for football, walking, climbing, or skiing) chaussure FEM; walking boots des chaussures de randonnée ❷ (short fashion boot) bottine FEM ❸ (knee-high boots or wellingtons) botte FEM ❹ (of a car) coffre MASC

border NOUN (between countries) frontière FEM; we crossed the border at Basel nous avons passé la frontière à Bâle

bore NOUN ❶ (a boring person) raseur MASC, raseuse FEM, (informal) ❷ (a nuisance) what a bore! quelle barbe!

bored ADJECTIVE to be bored s'ennuyer, je m'ennuie I'm bored, to get bored s'ennuyer

boring ADJECTIVE ennuyeux (FEM ennuyeuse)

born ADJECTIVE né; to be born naître [55], she was born in June elle est née en juin

borrow VERB emprunter [1]; can I borrow your bike? puis-je t'emprunter ton vélo?, to borrow something from someone emprunter quelque chose à quelqu'un, I'll borrow some money from Dad je vais emprunter de l'argent à Papa

Bosnia NOUN Bosnie FEM

boss NOUN patron MASC, patronne FEM

bossy ADJECTIVE autoritaire

both PRONOUN ❶ (of people) tous les deux (FEM toutes les deux); **they both came** ils sont venus tous les deux, **both my sisters were there** mes sœurs y étaient toutes les deux ❷ (of things) les deux; **they are both sold** les deux sont vendus, **both my feet** mes deux pieds ❸ **both at home and at school** à la maison comme à l'école, **both in summer and in winter** en été comme en hiver

bother NOUN ennui MASC; **I've had a lot of bother with the car** j'ai eu beaucoup d'ennuis avec la voiture, **it's too much bother** c'est trop de tracas, **it's no bother** ce n'est pas un problème, **without any bother** sans aucune difficulté

bother VERB ❶ (to disturb) déranger [52]; **I'm sorry to bother you** je suis désolé de vous déranger ❷ (to worry) inquiéter [24]; **that doesn't bother me at all** ça ne m'inquiète pas du tout, **don't bother about dinner** ne t'inquiète pas pour le dîner ❸ **she didn't even bother to come** elle n'a même pas pris la peine de venir, **don't bother!** ce n'est pas la peine!

bottle NOUN bouteille FEM

bottle bank NOUN conteneur (MASC) à verre

bottle opener NOUN ouvre-bouteille MASC

bottom NOUN ❶ (of a hill, a wall, or steps) pied MASC; **at the bottom of the ladder** au pied de l'échelle ❷ (of a bag or a bottle, a hole, a stretch of water, or a garden) fond MASC; **at the bottom of the lake** au fond du lac ❸ **at the bottom of the page** en bas de la page ❹ (buttocks) derrière MASC

bottom ADJECTIVE ❶ inférieur; **the bottom shelf** le rayon inférieur ❷ (a division, team, or place) dernier (FEM dernière) ❸ **the bottom sheet** le drap de dessous, **the bottom flat** l'appartement du rez-de-chaussée

bounce VERB rebondir [2]

bouncer NOUN videur MASC

bound ADJECTIVE (certain) **he's bound to be late** il va sûrement être en retard, **that was bound to happen** cela devait arriver

boundary NOUN limite FEM; (for sports) limites (FEM PLURAL) du terrain

bow NOUN ❶ (in a shoelace or ribbon) nœud MASC ❷ (for a violin) archet MASC ❸ **a bow and arrow** un arc et une flèche

bowels PLURAL NOUN intestins MASC PLURAL

bowl NOUN ❶ (for cereal, for example) bol MASC ❷ (larger, for salad or mixing) saladier MASC ❸ (for washing up) cuvette FEM

bowl VERB lancer [61] (a ball)

bowler NOUN (in cricket) lanceur MASC

bowling NOUN (tenpin) bowling MASC; **to go bowling** jouer au bowling

bow tie NOUN nœud (MASC) papillon

A
B
C
D
E
F
G
H
I
J
K
L
M
N
O
P
Q
R
S
T
U
V
W
X
Y
Z

box NOUN ❶ boîte FEM; **a box of chocolates** une boîte de chocolats ❷ **a cardboard box** un carton ❸ (on an application form) case FEM

boxer NOUN ❶ (fighter) boxeur MASC ❷ (dog) boxer MASC

boxer shorts PLURAL NOUN caleçon MASC SINGULAR

boxing NOUN ❶ boxe FEM ❷ **a boxing match** un match de boxe

Boxing Day NOUN le lendemain de Noël

box office NOUN guichet MASC

boy NOUN garçon MASC; **a little boy** un petit garçon

boyfriend NOUN copain MASC

bra NOUN soutien-gorge MASC

brace NOUN (for teeth) appareil MASC

bracelet NOUN bracelet MASC

bracket NOUN **in brackets** entre parenthèses

brain NOUN cerveau MASC (PLURAL cerveaux)

brainwave NOUN idée (FEM) géniale

brake NOUN frein MASC

brake VERB freiner [1]

bramble NOUN ronce FEM

branch NOUN ❶ (of a tree) branche FEM ❷ (of a shop) succursale FEM; **our Oxford branch** notre succursale à Oxford ❸ (of a bank) agence FEM

brand NOUN marque FEM

brand new ADJECTIVE tout neuf (FEM toute neuve)

brandy NOUN cognac MASC

brass NOUN laiton MASC, cuivre (MASC) jaune; **a brass candlestick** un chandelier en cuivre jaune

brass band NOUN fanfare FEM

brave ADJECTIVE courageux (FEM courageuse)

bravery NOUN courage MASC

Brazilian NOUN Brésilien MASC, Brésilienne FEM

Brazilian ADJECTIVE brésilien (FEM brésilienne)

bread NOUN pain MASC; **a slice of bread** une tranche de pain

break NOUN ❶ (a short rest) pause FEM; **fifteen minutes' break** une pause de quinze minutes, **to take a break** faire une pause ❷ (in school) récréation FEM, récré FEM ❸ **the Christmas break** les vacances de Noël

break VERB ❶ casser [1]; **he broke a glass** il a cassé un verre, **I broke a tooth/my arm** je me suis cassé une dent/le bras ❷ se casser [1]; **the eggs broke** les œufs se sont cassés ❸ **to break your arm** se casser le bras ❹ **to break your promise** manquer [1] à sa promesse, **he broke the rules** il n'a pas respecté les règlements, **you mustn't break the rules** il faut respecter les règlements ❺ **to break a record** battre [21] un record ❻ **to break the news** annoncer [61] la nouvelle
- **to break down** tomber [1] en panne; **the car broke down** la voiture est tombée en panne
- **to break in** (a thief) entrer [1] par effraction
- **to break out** ❶ (a fire) se déclarer [1] ❷ (a fight or a storm) éclater [1] ❸ (a prisoner) s'évader [1]

- **to break up** *(a family or couple)* se séparer [1] ❷ *(a crowd or clouds)* se disperser [1] ❸ *(for the holidays)* **we break up on Thursday** les cours finissent jeudi

breakdown NOUN ❶ *(of a vehicle)* panne FEM; **we had a breakdown on the motorway** nous sommes tombés en panne sur l'autoroute ❷ *(in talks or negotiations)* rupture FEM ❸ *(a nervous collapse)* dépression FEM; **to have a (nervous) breakdown** faire une dépression

breakdown truck NOUN camion (MASC) de dépannage

breakfast NOUN petit déjeuner MASC; **we have breakfast at eight** nous prenons le petit déjeuner à huit heures

break-in NOUN cambriolage MASC

breast NOUN ❶ *(a woman's)* sein MASC ❷ *(of a chicken or other fowl)* blanc MASC

breaststroke NOUN brasse FEM

breath NOUN ❶ *(when you breathe in)* souffle MASC; **out of breath** à bout de souffle, **to get one's breath** reprendre son souffle, **to take a deep breath** respirer profondément ❷ *(when you breathe out)* haleine FEM; **to have bad breath** avoir mauvaise haleine

breathe VERB respirer [1]

breathing NOUN respiration FEM

breed NOUN *(of dog, for example)* race FEM

breed VERB ❶ élever [50] *(animals)* ❷ *(to have babies)* se reproduire [26]; **rabbits breed fast** les lapins se reproduisent vite

breeze NOUN brise FEM

brew VERB ❶ préparer [1] *(tea)* ❷ brasser [1] *(beer)*

brewery NOUN brasserie FEM

brick NOUN brique FEM; **a brick wall** un mur de briques

bride NOUN mariée FEM; **the bride and groom** les mariés MASC PLURAL

bridegroom NOUN marié MASC

bridesmaid NOUN demoiselle (FEM) d'honneur

bridge NOUN ❶ *(over a river)* pont MASC; **a bridge over the Thames** un pont sur la Tamise ❷ *(card game)* bridge MASC; **to play bridge** jouer au bridge

bridle NOUN bride FEM

brief ADJECTIVE bref *(FEM* brève*)*

briefcase NOUN serviette FEM

briefly ADJECTIVE brièvement

briefs PLURAL NOUN slip MASC

bright ADJECTIVE ❶ *(colour, light)* vif *(FEM* vive*)*; **bright green socks** des chaussettes vert vif ❷ **bright sunshine** un soleil éclatant ❸ *(clever)* intelligent; **she's not very bright** elle n'est pas très intelligente
- **to look on the bright side** voir le bon côté des choses

brighten up VERB **the weather's brightening up** le temps s'éclaircit

brilliant ADJECTIVE ❶ *(very clever)* brillant; **a brilliant surgeon** un chirurgien brillant, **he's brilliant at maths** il est très doué en maths ❷ *(wonderful)* génial MASC *(PLURAL* géniaux*) (informal)*; **the party was brilliant!** la boum était géniale!

bring VERB ❶ apporter [1] (something you carry); **they brought a present** ils ont apporté un cadeau, **bring your camera!** apporte ton appareil-photo!, **it brings good luck** ça porte bonheur ❷ amener [50] (a person or an animal); **she's bringing all the children** elle va amener tous les enfants ❸ **to bring something back** rapporter [1] quelque chose ❹ **to bring up** élever [50] (children), **he was brought up by his aunt** il a été élevé par sa tante

bristle NOUN poil MASC

Britain, **Great Britain** NOUN Grande-Bretagne FEM; **in Britain** en Grande-Bretagne, **to Britain** en Grande-Bretagne, **Britain is sending aid** la Grande-Bretagne envoie de l'aide

British PLURAL NOUN **the British** les Britanniques, **the British love animals** les Britanniques adorent les animaux

British ADJECTIVE britannique; **the British army** l'armée britannique, **the British Isles** les îles Britanniques

Brittany NOUN Bretagne FEM; **in Brittany** en Bretagne, **to Brittany** en Bretagne

broad ADJECTIVE (wide) large

broad bean NOUN fève FEM

broadcast NOUN émission FEM

broadcast VERB diffuser [1] (a programme)

broccoli NOUN brocolis MASC PLURAL; **to eat broccoli** manger des brocolis

brochure NOUN brochure FEM

broke ADJECTIVE **to be broke** (no money) être fauché (informal)

broken ADJECTIVE cassé; **the window's broken** la vitre est cassée, **to have a broken leg** avoir la jambe cassée

bronchitis NOUN bronchite FEM; **to have bronchitis** avoir une bronchite

brooch NOUN broche FEM

broom NOUN ❶ (for sweeping) balai MASC ❷ (bush) genêt MASC

brother NOUN frère MASC; **my little brother** mon petit frère, **my mother's brother** le frère de ma mère

brother-in-law NOUN beau-frère MASC (PLURAL beaux-frères)

brown ADJECTIVE ❶ marron (does not change in the feminine or plural); **my brown jacket** ma veste marron, **your brown shoes** tes chaussures marron, **light brown** marron clair, **dark brown** marron foncé ❷ châtain (hair) ❸ (tanned in the sun) bronzé; **to go brown** bronzer

brown bread NOUN pain (MASC) complet

brown sugar NOUN sucre (MASC) brun

browser NOUN navigateur MASC

bruise NOUN ❶ (on a person) bleu MASC ❷ (on fruit) tache FEM

brush NOUN ❶ (for your hair, clothes, nails, or shoes) brosse FEM; **my hair brush** ma brosse à cheveux ❷ (for sweeping) balai MASC ❸ (paintbrush) pinceau MASC

brush VERB brosser [1] (the floor or your clothes); **to brush your hair** se brosser les cheveux, **she brushed her hair** elle s'est brossé les cheveux, **to brush your teeth** se brosser les dents

Brussels NOUN Bruxelles

Brussels sprout NOUN chou (MASC) de Bruxelles

bubble NOUN bulle FEM

bubble bath NOUN bain (MASC) moussant

bucket NOUN seau MASC (PLURAL seaux)

buckle NOUN boucle FEM

Buddhism NOUN bouddhisme MASC

Buddhist NOUN bouddhiste MASC & FEM

budget NOUN budget MASC

budgie NOUN perruche FEM

buffet NOUN buffet MASC

buffet car NOUN voiture (FEM) bar

bug NOUN ❶ (insect) bestiole FEM (informal) ❷ (germ) microbe FEM; **a stomach bug** une gastroentérite ❸ (in a computer) bug MASC

build VERB construire [26]; **they are building three houses over there** ils construisent trois maisons là-bas

builder NOUN maçon MASC

building NOUN bâtiment MASC, (with offices or flats) immeuble MASC

building site NOUN chantier MASC

building society NOUN société (FEM) d'investissement et de crédit immobilier

built-up ADJECTIVE urbanisé; **a built-up area** une agglomération

bulb NOUN ❶ (for a light) ampoule FEM ❷ (that you plant) bulbe MASC

bull NOUN taureau MASC (PLURAL taureaux)

bulldozer NOUN bulldozer MASC

bullet NOUN balle FEM

bulletin NOUN bulletin MASC; **a news bulletin** un bulletin d'informations

bullfight NOUN corrida FEM

bully NOUN brute FEM; **he's a bully** c'est une brute

bully VERB tyranniser [1]

bum NOUN (bottom) derrière MASC

bump NOUN ❶ (that sticks up) bosse FEM; **a bump on the head** une bosse à la tête, **a bump in the road** une bosse sur la route ❷ (jolt) secousse FEM ❸ (noise) bruit (MASC) sourd

bump VERB ❶ (to bang) cogner [1]; **I bumped my head** je me suis cogné la tête ❷ **to bump into something** rentrer [1] dans quelque chose ❸ **to bump into somebody** (meet by chance) croiser [1] quelqu'un

bumper NOUN pare-chocs MASC

bumpy ADJECTIVE ❶ accidenté (road) ❷ agité (plane landing)

bun NOUN ❶ (for a burger) petit pain MASC ❷ (sugary) petit cake MASC

bunch NOUN ❶ (of flowers) bouquet MASC ❷ (of carrots or radishes) botte FEM ❸ (of keys) trousseau MASC ❹ **a bunch of grapes** une grappe de raisin

bundle NOUN tas MASC

bungalow NOUN pavillon MASC

bunk NOUN ❶ (on a train or boat) couchette FEM ❷ **bunk beds** des lits superposés

bureau NOUN agence FEM

burger NOUN hamburger MASC

burglar NOUN **cambrioleur** MASC

burglar alarm NOUN **sonnerie** (FEM) **d'alarme**

burglary NOUN **cambriolage** MASC

burn NOUN **brûlure** FEM

burn VERB ❶ **brûler** [1]; **I've burned the rubbish** j'ai brûlé les ordures, **the fire's burning well** le feu brûle bien, **she burnt herself on the grill** elle s'est brûlée au grill, **you'll burn your finger!** tu vas te brûler le doigt! ❷ **laisser** [1] **brûler** (something you're cooking); **Mum's burnt her cake** maman a laissé brûler son gâteau ❸ (through sunburn) **I burn easily** j'attrape facilement des coups de soleil

burnt ADJECTIVE **brûlé**

burst VERB ❶ **crever** [50] (a balloon or tyre, for example); **a burst tyre** un pneu crevé ❷ **to burst out laughing** éclater [1] de rire ❸ **to burst into tears** fondre [3] en larmes ❹ **to burst into flames** prendre [64] feu

bury VERB **enterrer** [1]

bus NOUN ❶ (public transport) **autobus** MASC, **bus** MASC; **we'll take the bus** on va prendre le bus, **on the bus** dans le bus, **a bus ticket** un ticket de bus ❷ (coach) **car** MASC; **to go to London by bus** aller à Londres en car

bus conductor NOUN **receveur** (MASC) **d'autobus**

bus driver NOUN **conducteur de bus** MASC, **conductrice de bus** FEM

bush NOUN **buisson** MASC

business NOUN ❶ (commercial dealings) **affaires** FEM PLURAL; **to be in business** être dans les affaires, **he's**

in Leeds on business il est à Leeds en voyage d'affaires, **he's in the insurance business** il travaille dans l'assurance, **a business letter** une lettre d'affaires ❷ (firm or company) **entreprise** FEM; **small businesses** les petites entreprises ❸ **mind your own business!** occupe-toi de tes affaires!, **that's my business!** ça me regarde!

business class NOUN **classe** (FEM) **affaires**

businessman NOUN **homme** (MASC) **d'affaires**

business trip NOUN **voyage** (MASC) **d'affaires**

businesswoman NOUN **femme** (FEM) **d'affaires**

bus lane NOUN **couloir** (MASC) **d'autobus**

bus pass NOUN **carte** (FEM) **de bus**

bus route NOUN **ligne** (FEM) **d'autobus**

bus shelter NOUN **abribus** MASC

bus station NOUN **gare** (FEM) **routière**

bus stop NOUN **arrêt** (MASC) **de bus**

bust NOUN **bust size tour** (MASC) **de poitrine**

busy ADJECTIVE ❶ **occupé** (a person), **chargé** (a day or week) ❷ **don't disturb him, he's busy** ne le dérange pas, il est occupé, **a busy day** une journée chargée ❸ (full of cars or people) **très fréquenté** (a road); **the shops were busy** il y avait beaucoup de monde dans les magasins ❹ (phone) **the line's busy** la ligne est occupée

but CONJUNCTION mais; small but strong petit mais fort, not Thursday but Friday pas jeudi mais vendredi, I'll try, but it's difficult j'essaierai, mais c'est difficile

but PREPOSITION sauf; anything but that tout, sauf ça, everyone but Roger tout le monde sauf Roger, the last but one l'avant-dernier

butcher NOUN boucher MASC; he's a butcher il est boucher, the butcher's la boucherie

butter NOUN beurre MASC

butter VERB beurrer [1]

buttercup NOUN bouton (MASC) d'or

butterfly NOUN papillon MASC

button NOUN bouton MASC; the record button la touche d'enregistrement

buttonhole NOUN boutonnière FEM

buy NOUN a good buy une bonne affaire, a bad buy une mauvaise affaire

buy VERB acheter [16]; I bought the tickets j'ai acheté les billets, to buy something for somebody acheter quelque chose à quelqu'un, Sarah bought him a sweater Sarah lui a acheté un pull, to buy something from someone acheter quelque chose à quelqu'un, I bought my bike from Tim j'ai acheté mon vélo à Tim

buyer NOUN acheteur MASC, acheteuse FEM

buzz VERB (a fly or bee) bourdonner [1]

buzzer NOUN sonnerie FEM

by PREPOSITION ❶ par; by telephone par téléphone, to take somebody by the hand prendre quelqu'un par la main, eaten by a dog mangé par un chien, by mistake par erreur ❷ (travel) en; to come by bus venir en bus, to leave by train partir en train, by bike en vélo ❸ (near) à côté de; by the fire à côté du feu, by the sea au bord de la mer, close by tout près ❹ (before) avant; ready by Monday prêt avant lundi, Kevin was back by four Kevin est rentré avant quatre heures ❺ by yourself tout seul, I was by myself in the house j'étais tout seul chez moi, she did it by herself elle l'a fait toute seule ❻ by the way au fait ❼ to go by passer

bye EXCLAMATION au revoir; bye for now! à bientôt!

bypass NOUN rocade FEM

Cc

cab NOUN ❶ taxi MASC; to call a cab appeler un taxi ❷ (on a lorry) cabine FEM

cabbage NOUN chou MASC (PLURAL choux)

cabin NOUN cabine FEM

cable NOUN câble MASC

cable car NOUN téléphérique MASC

cable television NOUN télévision (FEM) par câble

cactus NOUN cactus MASC

cafe NOUN café MASC

cage NOUN cage FEM

cagoule NOUN K-way MASC

cake NOUN gâteau MASC (PLURAL gâteaux); **would you like a piece of cake?** veux-tu un morceau de gâteau?

calculate VERB calculer [1]

calculation NOUN calcul MASC

calculator NOUN calculatrice FEM

calendar NOUN calendrier MASC

calf NOUN ❶ (animal) veau MASC ❷ (of your leg) mollet

call NOUN (telephone) appel MASC; **I had several calls this morning** j'ai eu plusieurs appels ce matin, **thank you for your call** merci de votre appel, **a phone call** un coup de téléphone

call VERB ❶ appeler [18]; **to call a taxi** appeler un taxi, **to call the doctor** appeler le médecin, **they called the police** ils ont appelé la police, **call this number** appelez ce numéro, **thank you for calling** merci de votre appel, **I'll call you back later** je te rappellerai plus tard ❷ appeler [18]; **they've called the baby Julie** ils ont appelé le bébé Julie ❸ **to be called** s'appeler [18], **she has a brother called Dan** elle a un frère qui s'appelle Dan, **what's he called?** il s'appelle comment?
• **to call in** passer [1]; **I'll call in on the way back from school** je passerai en rentrant de l'école

call box NOUN cabine (FEM) téléphonique

calm ADJECTIVE calme

calm VERB calmer [1]
• **to calm down** se calmer; **he's calmed down a bit** il s'est calmé un peu
• **to calm somebody down** calmer quelqu'un; **I tried to calm her down** j'ai essayé de la calmer

calmly ADVERB calmement

calorie NOUN calorie FEM

camcorder NOUN caméscope MASC

camel NOUN chameau MASC (PLURAL chameaux)

camera NOUN ❶ appareil (MASC) photo (PLURAL appareils photo) ❷ (film or TV camera) caméra

cameraman NOUN caméraman MASC

camp NOUN camp MASC

camp VERB camper [1]

campaign NOUN campagne FEM

camper van NOUN camping-car MASC

camping NOUN camping MASC; **to go camping** faire du camping, **we're going camping in Brittany this summer** nous allons faire du camping en Bretagne cet été

campsite NOUN terrain (MASC) de camping

can¹ NOUN ❶ boîte FEM; **a can of tomatoes** une boîte de tomates ❷ (for petrol or oil) bidon MASC

can² VERB ❶ pouvoir [12]; **I can't/cannot be there before ten** je ne peux pas y être avant dix heures, **you can leave your bag here** tu peux laisser ton sac ici, **can you open the door, please?** peux-tu ouvrir la porte, s'il te plaît?, **can I**

help you? est-ce que je peux vous aider?, **they couldn't come** ils n'ont pas pu venir, **you could ring back tomorrow** tu pourrais rappeler demain, **you could have told me** tu aurais pu me le dire ❷ *(not translated)* **can you hear me?** est-ce que tu m'entends?, **I can't see him** je ne le vois pas, **I can't remember** je ne me souviens pas, **I can't find my keys** je ne trouve pas mes clés ❸ *(know how to)* savoir [70]; **she can't drive** elle ne sait pas conduire, **can you play the piano?** est-ce que tu sais jouer du piano?

Canada NOUN Canada MASC; **to Canada** au Canada, **in Canada** au Canada

Canadian NOUN Canadien MASC, Canadienne FEM

Canadian ADJECTIVE canadien (FEM canadienne)

canal NOUN canal MASC (PLURAL canaux)

canary NOUN canari MASC

cancel VERB annuler [1]; **the concert's been cancelled** le concert a été annulé

cancer NOUN cancer MASC; **to have lung cancer** avoir un cancer du poumon

Cancer NOUN Cancer MASC; **I'm Cancer** je suis Cancer

candidate NOUN candidat MASC, candidate FEM

candle NOUN bougie FEM

candlestick NOUN bougeoir MASC

candyfloss NOUN barbe *(FEM)* à papa

canned ADJECTIVE en conserve; **canned tomatoes** les tomates en conserve

cannon NOUN canon MASC

cannot VERB ▸ SEE **can²**

canoe NOUN canoë MASC

canoeing NOUN **to go canoeing** faire du canoë, **I like canoeing** j'aime faire du canoë

can-opener NOUN ouvre-boîte MASC

canteen NOUN cantine FEM

canvas NOUN toile FEM

cap NOUN ❶ *(hat)* casquette FEM; **a baseball cap** une casquette de baseball ❷ *(on a bottle or tube)* bouchon MASC

capable ADJECTIVE capable

capacity NOUN capacité FEM

capital NOUN ❶ *(city)* capitale FEM; **Paris is the capital of France** Paris est la capitale de la France ❷ *(letter)* majuscule FEM; **in capitals** en majuscules

capitalism NOUN capitalisme MASC

Capricorn NOUN Capricorne MASC; **Linda's Capricorn** Linda est Capricorne

capsize VERB chavirer [1]

captain NOUN capitaine MASC

captivity NOUN captivité FEM; **to be kept in captivity** être gardé en captivité

capture VERB capturer [1]

car NOUN voiture FEM; **in the car** dans la voiture, **to park the car** garer la voiture, **we're going by car** nous y allons en voiture, **a car crash** un accident de voiture

caramel NOUN caramel MASC

caravan NOUN caravane FEM

A
B
C
D
E
F
G
H
I
J
K
L
M
N
O
P
Q
R
S
T
U
V
W
X
Y
Z

card NOUN carte FEM; **un jeu de cartes** a card game, a pack of cards, **faire une partie de cartes** to have a game of cards

cardboard NOUN carton MASC

cardigan NOUN cardigan MASC

care NOUN ❶ soin MASC; **to take care to do** prendre soin de faire ❷ **to take care of somebody** s'occuper de quelqu'un ❸ **take care!** *(be careful)* fais attention!, *(when saying goodbye)* à bientôt!

care VERB ❶ **to care about** se soucier de [1], **to care about pollution** se soucier de la pollution ❷ **she doesn't care** ça lui est égal, **I couldn't care less!** ça m'est complètement égal!

career NOUN carrière FEM

careful ADJECTIVE ❶ prudent; **a careful driver** un conducteur prudent ❷ **be careful!** fais attention!

carefully ADVERB ❶ **read the instructions carefully** lisez attentivement les instructions, **listen carefully** écoutez bien ❷ *(handle)* avec précaution; **she put the vase down carefully** elle a posé le vase avec précaution ❸ **to copy something carefully** recopier soigneusement quelque chose ❹ **drive carefully!** sois prudent!

careless ADJECTIVE ❶ **he's very careless** il ne fait pas du tout attention à ce qu'il fait ❷ **this is careless work** c'est du travail peu soigné, **a careless mistake** une faute d'inattention ❸ **careless driving** la conduite imprudente

caretaker NOUN gardien MASC, gardienne FEM

car ferry NOUN ferry MASC

cargo NOUN cargaison FEM

car hire NOUN location *(FEM)* de voitures

Caribbean NOUN ❶ **the Caribbean (islands)** les Caraïbes ❷ **the Caribbean** *(sea)* la mer des Caraïbes

carnation NOUN œillet MASC

carnival NOUN carnaval MASC

car park NOUN parking MASC

carpenter NOUN menuisier MASC

carpentry NOUN menuiserie FEM

carpet NOUN ❶ *(fitted)* moquette FEM ❷ *(loose)* tapis MASC

car radio NOUN autoradio MASC

carriage NOUN *(of a train)* voiture FEM

carrier bag NOUN sac *(MASC)* en plastique

carrot NOUN carotte FEM

carry VERB ❶ porter [1]; **she was carrying a parcel** elle portait un paquet ❷ *(vehicle, plane)* transporter [1]; **the coach was carrying schoolchildren** le car transportait des écoliers
• **to carry on** continuer [1]; **they carried on talking** ils ont continué à parler

carrycot NOUN porte-bébé MASC

carsick ADJECTIVE **to be carsick** avoir le mal de la route

cart NOUN charrette FEM

carton NOUN ❶ *(of cream or yoghurt)* pot MASC ❷ *(of milk or orange)* brique FEM

cartoon NOUN ❶ *(a film)* dessin *(MASC)* animé ❷ *(a comic strip)* bande *(FEM)*

dessinée ❸ (an amusing drawing)
dessin (MASC) humoristique

cartridge NOUN (for a pen or a video)
cartouche FEM

carve VERB découper [1] (meat)

case¹ NOUN ❶ (suitcase) valise FEM;
to pack a case faire une valise ❷ (a
large wooden box, for wine for
example) caisse FEM ❸ (for spectacles
or small things) étui MASC

case² NOUN ❶ cas MASC; **in that case**
en ce cas, **that's not the case** ce
n'est pas le cas, **a case of flu** un
cas de grippe ❷ **in case** au cas où,
in case he's late au cas où il serait
en retard, **check first, just in case**
vérifie d'abord, au cas où ❸ **in any
case** de toute façon, **in any case,
it's too late** de toute façon, c'est
trop tard

cash NOUN ❶ (money in general)
argent MASC; **I haven't any cash on
me** je n'ai pas d'argent ❷ (money
rather than a cheque) espèces FEM
PLURAL; **to pay in cash** payer en
espèces, **£50 in cash** cinquante
livres en espèces

cash card NOUN carte (FEM) de
retrait

cash desk NOUN caisse FEM; **pay at
the cash desk** payez à la caisse

cash dispenser NOUN guichet (MASC)
automatique

cashew NOUN cajou MASC

cashier NOUN caissier MASC,
caissière FEM

cash point NOUN distributeur
automatique MASC

cast NOUN les acteurs MASC PLURAL;
the cast were on stage les acteurs
étaient sur scène

castle NOUN ❶ château MASC (PLURAL
châteaux) ❷ (in chess) tour FEM

casual ADJECTIVE décontracté

casualty NOUN ❶ (in an accident)
victime FEM; **there are 47 casualties**
il y a 47 victimes ❷ (hospital
department) urgences FEM PLURAL;
he's in casualty il est aux urgences

cat NOUN chat MASC (female) chatte
FEM; **a big black cat** un gros chat noir
• **it's raining cats and dogs** il pleut
des cordes (literally: it's raining in
ropes)

catalogue NOUN catalogue MASC

catastrophe NOUN catastrophe FEM

catch NOUN ❶ (on a door) fermeture
FEM ❷ (a drawback) piège MASC;
what's the catch? où est le piège?

catch VERB ❶ attraper [1]; **Tom
caught the ball** Tom a attrapé
le ballon, **you can't catch me!**
vous ne m'attraperez pas!, **can
you catch hold of the branch?**
peux-tu attraper la branche? ❷ **to
catch somebody doing** attraper
quelqu'un en train de faire, **he
was caught stealing money** il
a été attrapé en train de voler
de l'argent ❸ prendre [64] (a
bus or plane); **did Tim catch his
plane?** est-ce que Tim a pris son
avion? ❹ attraper [1] (an illness);
he's caught chickenpox il a attrapé
la varicelle, **I've caught a cold** j'ai
attrapé un rhume ❺ saisir [2] (what
somebody says); **I didn't catch your
name** je n'ai pas saisi votre nom
• **to catch up with somebody**
rattraper [1] quelqu'un

category NOUN catégorie FEM

catering NOUN restauration FEM

caterpillar NOUN chenille FEM

cathedral NOUN cathédrale FEM; **Winchester cathedral** la cathédrale de Winchester

Catholic NOUN, ADJECTIVE catholique MASC & FEM

cattle PLURAL NOUN bétail MASC SINGULAR

cauliflower NOUN chou-fleur MASC (PLURAL choux-fleurs); **cauliflower cheese** un gratin de chou-fleur

cause NOUN cause FEM; **the cause of the accident** la cause de l'accident, **for a good cause** pour une bonne cause

cause VERB ❶ causer [1] (damage or problems); **to cause problems** causer des problèmes ❷ provoquer [1] (chaos or disease); **the strike caused delays** la grève a provoqué des retards

caution NOUN prudence FEM

cautious ADJECTIVE prudent

cave NOUN grotte FEM

caving NOUN spéléologie FEM; **to go caving** faire de la spéléologie

CD NOUN CD MASC

CD player NOUN platine (FEM) laser

CD-ROM NOUN CD-ROM MASC

ceiling NOUN plafond MASC; **on the ceiling** au plafond

celebrate VERB fêter [1]; **I'm celebrating my birthday** je fête mon anniversaire

celebrity NOUN célébrité FEM

celery NOUN céleri MASC

cell NOUN cellule FEM

cellar NOUN cave FEM

cello NOUN violoncelle MASC; **to play the cello** jouer du violoncelle

cement NOUN ciment MASC

cemetery NOUN cimetière MASC

cent NOUN ❶ (in euro system) centime (MASC) (d'euro), (unofficial term), cent MASC (official term) ❷ (in dollar system) cent MASC

centenary NOUN centenaire MASC

centigrade ADJECTIVE centigrade; **ten degrees centigrade** dix degrés centigrade

centimetre NOUN centimètre MASC

central ADJECTIVE central MASC (PLURAL centraux); **central London** le centre de Londres, **the office is very central** le bureau est en plein centre-ville

central heating NOUN chauffage (MASC) central

centre NOUN centre MASC; **in the centre of** au centre de, **in the town centre** en centre-ville, **a shopping centre** un centre commercial

century NOUN siècle MASC; **in the twentieth century** au vingtième siècle, **the twenty-first century** le vingt-et-unième siècle

cereal NOUN breakfast cereal céréales (FEM PLURAL) pour le petit déjeuner, **to have cereal for breakfast** prendre des céréales au petit déjeuner

ceremony NOUN cérémonie FEM

certain ADJECTIVE certain; **a certain number of** un certain nombre de, **are you certain of the address?** es-tu certain de l'adresse?, **I'm certain of it** j'en suis certain, **to be certain that** être sûr que, **Nicola's certain you're wrong** Nicola est sûre que tu as tort, **nobody knows for certain** personne ne sait au juste

certainly ADVERB **certainement**; **certainly not** certainement pas

certificate NOUN ❶ **certificat** MASC ❷ **a birth certificate** un acte de naissance

chain NOUN **chaîne** FEM

chair NOUN ❶ (upright) **chaise** FEM; **a kitchen chair** une chaise de cuisine ❷ (with arms) **fauteuil** MASC

chair lift NOUN **télésiège** MASC

chalet NOUN ❶ (in the mountains) **chalet** MASC ❷ (in a holiday camp) **bungalow** MASC

chalk NOUN **craie** FEM

challenge NOUN ❶ (that excites you) **challenge** MASC; **the challenge of new ideas** le challenge des nouvelles idées ❷ (that is difficult) **épreuve** FEM; **the exam was a real challenge** l'examen était une vraie épreuve

champion NOUN **champion** MASC, **championne** FEM; **world champion** champion du monde

chance NOUN ❶ (an opportunity) **occasion** FEM; **to have the chance to do** avoir l'occasion de faire, **if you have the chance to go to New York** si tu as l'occasion d'aller à New York, **I haven't had the chance to write to him** je n'ai pas eu l'occasion de lui écrire ❷ (likelihood) **chance** FEM; **there's little chance of winning** il y a peu de chance de gagner ❸ (luck) **by chance** par hasard, **do you have her address, by any chance?** aurais-tu par hasard son adresse?

change NOUN ❶ **changement** MASC; **a change of plan** un changement de programme, **they've made some changes to the house** ils ont fait des changements dans la maison, **for a change, let's eat out** mangeons au restaurant pour changer, **it makes a change from hamburgers** cela change un peu des hamburgers ❷ **a change of clothes** des vêtements de rechange ❸ (cash) **monnaie** FEM; **I haven't any change** je n'ai pas de monnaie

change VERB ❶ (transform completely) **changer** [52]; **it changed my life** cela m'a changé la vie, **Liz never changes** Liz ne change jamais ❷ (to switch from one thing to another) **changer** [52] de; **we changed trains at Crewe** nous avons changé de train à Crewe, **I must change my shirt** je dois changer de chemise, **they changed places** ils ont changé de place, **to change your mind** changer d'avis ❸ (to exchange in a shop) **échanger** [52]; **can I change it for the next size?** puis-je l'échanger contre la taille au-dessus? ❹ (to change your clothes) **se changer** [52]; **Mike's gone up to change** Mike est monté se changer

changing room NOUN (for sport or swimming) ❶ **vestiaire** MASC ❷ (in a shop) **salon** (MASC) **d'essayage**

channel NOUN ❶ (on TV) **chaîne** FEM; **to change channels** changer de chaîne ❷ **the Channel** la Manche

Channel Islands PLURAL NOUN **îles** (FEM PLURAL) **Anglo-Normandes**

Channel Tunnel NOUN **tunnel** (MASC) **sous la Manche**

chaos NOUN **pagaille** FEM (informal); **it was chaos!** c'était la pagaille!

chapel NOUN chapelle FEM

chapter NOUN chapitre MASC; **in chapter two** au chapitre deux

character NOUN ① (personality) caractère MASC; **a house with a lot of character** une maison qui a du caractère ② (somebody in a book, play, or film) personnage MASC; **the main character** le personnage principal

characteristic ADJECTIVE caractéristique

charcoal NOUN ① (for burning) charbon (MASC) de bois ② (for drawing) fusain MASC

charge NOUN ① (what you pay) frais MASC PLURAL; **a booking charge** des frais de réservation, **an extra or additional charge** un supplément, **there's no charge** c'est gratuit ② **to be in charge** être responsable, **who's in charge of these children?** qui est responsable de ces enfants? ③ **to be on a charge of theft** être inculpé de vol

charge VERB ① (to ask a specific sum) prendre [64]; **they charge fifteen pounds an hour** ils prennent quinze livres de l'heure, **how much do you charge for one day?** combien prenez-vous pour une journée? ② (to ask people to pay) faire [10] payer; **we don't charge, it's free** nous ne faisons pas payer les gens, c'est gratuit ③ **to charge somebody with** inculper [1] quelqu'un de (a crime)

charity NOUN organisation (FEM) caritative

charm NOUN charme MASC

charming ADJECTIVE charmant

chart NOUN ① (table) tableau MASC ② **the weather chart** la carte du temps ③ **the charts** le hit-parade, **number one in the charts** numéro un au hit-parade

charter flight NOUN vol (MASC) charter

chase NOUN poursuite FEM; **a car chase** une poursuite en voiture

chase VERB pourchasser [1] (a person or animal)

chat NOUN conversation FEM; **to have a chat with somebody** bavarder avec quelqu'un

chatroom NOUN chatroom MASC

chat show NOUN talk-show MASC

chatter VERB ① (gossip) bavarder [1] ② **my teeth are chattering** je claque des dents

cheap ADJECTIVE pas cher (FEM pas chère); **cheap shoes** des chaussures pas chères, **that's very cheap!** ce n'est vraiment pas cher!

cheaper ADJECTIVE moins cher (FEM moins chère)

cheaply ADVERB pas cher; **to eat cheaply** manger pas cher

cheap rate ADJECTIVE à tarif réduit; **a cheap rate phone call** un appel à tarif réduit

cheat NOUN tricheur MASC, tricheuse FEM

cheat VERB tricher [1]

check NOUN ① (in a factory or at border controls) contrôle MASC; **passport check** contrôle des passeports ② (by a doctor) examen MASC ③ (in chess) **check!** échec au roi!

check VERB (to make sure) **vérifier** [1]; **he checked the time** il a vérifié l'heure, **check they're all back** vérifiez qu'ils sont tous rentrés, **check with your father** demande à ton père
- **to check in ❶** (at the airport) enregistrer [1] **❷** (at a hotel) arriver [1] à l'hôtel; **he checked in at five o'clock** il est arrivé à l'hôtel à cinq heures
- **to check out** quitter [1] l'hôtel; **he checked out at 8.30** il a quitté l'hôtel à 8h30

check-in NOUN **enregistrement** MASC

checkout NOUN **caisse** FEM; **at the checkout** à la caisse

check-up NOUN **examen** (MASC) **médical**

cheek NOUN **❶** (part of face) **joue** FEM **❷** (nerve) **what a cheek!** quel culot! (informal)

cheeky ADJECTIVE **❶ coquin ❷** (rude) **impoli**

cheer NOUN **❶ three cheers for Tom!** faisons un ban à Tom! **❷** (when you have a drink) **cheers!** à la vôtre!

cheer VERB (to shout hurray) **applaudir** [2]
- **to cheer on** encourager
- **to cheer up cheer up!** courage!
- **to cheer somebody up** remonter [1] le moral à quelqu'un; **your visit's cheered me up** ta visite m'a remonté le moral

cheerful ADJECTIVE **gai**

cheese NOUN **fromage** MASC; **blue cheese** le fromage bleu, **a cheese sandwich** un sandwich au fromage

cheesecake NOUN **cheesecake** MASC

chef NOUN **chef** (MASC) **cuisinier**

chemical NOUN **produit** (MASC) **chimique**

chemical ADJECTIVE **chimique**

chemist NOUN **❶ pharmacien** MASC, **pharmacienne** FEM **❷ chemist's pharmacie** FEM, **at the chemist's** à la pharmacie **❸** (scientist) **chimiste** MASC & FEM

chemistry NOUN **chimie** FEM

cheque NOUN **chèque** MASC; **to pay by cheque** payer par chèque, **to write a cheque** faire un chèque

chequebook NOUN **carnet** (MASC) **de chèques**

cherry NOUN **cerise** FEM

chess NOUN **échecs** MASC PLURAL; **to play chess** jouer aux échecs

chessboard NOUN **échiquier** MASC

chest NOUN **❶** (part of the body) **poitrine** FEM **❷** (box) **coffre** MASC **❸ a chest of drawers** une commode

chestnut NOUN **marron** MASC

chestnut tree NOUN **❶** (horse-chestnut) **marronnier** MASC **❷** (sweet chestnut) **châtaignier** MASC

chew VERB **mâcher** [1] (food)

chewing gum NOUN **chewing-gum** MASC

chick NOUN (of a hen) **poussin** MASC

chicken NOUN **poulet** MASC; **roast chicken** du poulet rôti, **chicken thighs** des cuisses de poulet, **a chicken sandwich** un sandwich au poulet

chickenpox NOUN **varicelle** FEM

chicory NOUN **endive** FEM

chief NOUN chef MASC; **the chief of police** le préfet de police

child NOUN enfant MASC & FEM; **Jenny's children** les enfants de Jenny

childish ADJECTIVE puéril

child-minder NOUN nourrice FEM

chill NOUN fraîcheur FEM

chilled ADJECTIVE (wine) bien frais

chilli NOUN piment MASC

chilly ADJECTIVE frisquet (FEM frisquette); **it's chilly today** il fait frisquet aujourd'hui

chimney NOUN cheminée FEM

chimpanzee NOUN chimpanzé MASC

chin NOUN menton MASC

china NOUN porcelaine FEM; **a china plate** une assiette en porcelaine

China NOUN Chine FEM; **in China** en Chine

Chinese NOUN ❶ **the Chinese** (people) les Chinois ❷ (language) chinois MASC

Chinese ADJECTIVE chinois; **a Chinese man** un Chinois, **a Chinese woman** une Chinoise, **a Chinese meal** un repas chinois

chip NOUN ❶ (fried potato) frite FEM; **I'd like some chips** j'aimerais des frites ❷ (microchip) puce FEM ❸ (in glass or china) ébréchure FEM

chipped ADJECTIVE ébréché

chives NOUN ciboulette FEM SINGULAR

choc ice NOUN esquimau MASC

chocolate NOUN chocolat MASC; **a chocolate ice cream** une glace au chocolat, **hot chocolate** chocolat (MASC) chaud, **a box of chocolates** une boîte de chocolats

choice NOUN choix MASC; **you have a choice of two flights** vous avez le choix entre deux vols

choir NOUN ❶ (in a school) chorale FEM; **I sing in the choir** je fais partie de la chorale ❷ (professional) chœur MASC

choke NOUN (on a car) starter MASC

choke VERB ❶ (by yourself) s'étouffer [1]; **she was choking on a bone** elle s'étouffait avec une arête ❷ (smoke or fumes) étouffer [1]

choose VERB choisir [2]; **you chose well** tu as bien choisi, **Cathy chose the red one** Cathy a choisi le rouge, **it's hard to choose from all these colours** il est difficile de choisir parmi toutes ces couleurs

chop NOUN côtelette FEM; **a lamb chop** une côtelette d'agneau

chop VERB hacher [1]

chopstick NOUN baguette FEM

chord NOUN accord MASC

chorus NOUN ❶ (when you all join in the song) refrain MASC ❷ (a group of singers) chœur MASC

Christ NOUN le Christ

christening NOUN baptême MASC

Christian NOUN, ADJECTIVE chrétien MASC, chrétienne FEM

Christian name NOUN prénom MASC

Christmas NOUN Noël MASC; **at Christmas** à Noël, **Happy Christmas!** Joyeux Noël!

Christmas card NOUN carte (FEM) de Noël

Christmas carol NOUN chant (MASC) de Noël

Christmas cracker NOUN diablotin MASC

Christmas Day NOUN jour (MASC) de Noël

Christmas dinner NOUN repas (MASC) de Noël

Christmas Eve NOUN veille (FEM) de Noël; **on Christmas Eve** la veille de Noël

Christmas present NOUN cadeau (MASC) de Noël

Christmas tree NOUN sapin (MASC) de Noël

chunk NOUN morceau MASC

church NOUN église FEM; **to go to church** aller à l'église

churchyard NOUN cimetière MASC

chute NOUN (in a swimming pool or playground) toboggan MASC

cider NOUN cidre MASC

cigar NOUN cigare MASC

cigarette NOUN cigarette FEM; **to light a cigarette** allumer une cigarette

cinema NOUN cinéma MASC; **to go to the cinema** aller au cinéma

circle NOUN cercle MASC; **to sit in a circle** s'asseoir en cercle, **to go round in circles** tourner en rond

circuit NOUN ❶ (for athletes) piste FEM ❷ (for cars) circuit MASC

circumference NOUN circonférence FEM

circumflex NOUN accent (MASC) circonflexe

circumstances PLURAL NOUN **under the circumstances** dans ces circonstances

circus NOUN cirque MASC

citizen NOUN citoyen MASC, citoyenne FEM

city NOUN (grande) ville FEM; **the city of Paris** la ville de Paris

city centre NOUN centre-ville MASC; **in the city centre** au centre-ville

civilian NOUN civil MASC, civile FEM

civilization NOUN civilisation FEM

civil servant NOUN fonctionnaire MASC & FEM; **he's a civil servant** il est fonctionnaire

civil service NOUN fonction (FEM) publique

civil war NOUN guerre (FEM) civile

claim NOUN ❶ (statement) déclaration FEM ❷ (for compensation) réclamation FEM; **to make a claim on insurance** faire une demande de remboursement d'une compagnie d'assurance

claim VERB prétendre [3]; **he claimed to know** il prétendait savoir

clap VERB ❶ applaudir [2]; **everyone clapped** tout le monde a applaudi ❷ **to clap your hands** battre [21] des mains

clapping NOUN applaudissements MASC PLURAL

clarinet NOUN clarinette FEM; **to play the clarinet** jouer de la clarinette

clash NOUN (for example, between police and demonstrators) affrontement MASC

clash VERB ❶ (rival groups) s'affronter [1] ❷ (colours) jurer [1]; **the curtains clash with the wallpaper** les rideaux jurent avec le papier peint

clasp NOUN (of a necklace) **fermoir** MASC

class NOUN ❶ (a group of students or pupils) **classe** FEM; **she's in the same class as me** elle est dans la même classe que moi ❷ (a lesson) **cours** MASC; **an art class** un cours de dessin, **in class** en cours ❸ (division) **classe** FEM; **a social class** une classe sociale

classic ADJECTIVE **classique**

classical ADJECTIVE **classique**; **classical music** la musique classique

classmate NOUN **camarade** (MASC & FEM) **de classe**

classroom NOUN **classe** FEM

claw NOUN ❶ (of a cat or dog) **griffe** FEM ❷ (of a crab) **pince** FEM

clay NOUN ❶ (for modelling) **argile** FEM ❷ **a clay court** (in tennis) un terrain en terre battue

clean ADJECTIVE ❶ **propre**; **a clean shirt** une chemise propre, **my hands are clean** j'ai les mains propres ❷ (germ-free) **pur** (air or water)

clean VERB ❶ **nettoyer** [39]; **I cleaned the whole house** j'ai nettoyé toute la maison ❷ **to clean your teeth** se laver [1] les dents, **I'm going to clean my teeth** je vais me laver les dents

cleaner NOUN ❶ (in a public place) **agent** (MASC) **de nettoyage** ❷ (cleaning lady) **femme** (FEM) **de ménage** ❸ **a dry cleaner's** un pressing

cleaning NOUN **to do the cleaning** faire le ménage

cleanser NOUN ❶ (for the house) **produit** (MASC) **d'entretien** ❷ (for your face) **démaquillant** MASC

clear ADJECTIVE ❶ (that you can see through) **transparent**; **clear glass** du verre transparent ❷ (cloudless) **clair** ❸ (easy to understand) **clair**; **clear instructions** des instructions claires, **is that clear?** est-ce que c'est clair?, **it's clear that …** il est clair que …

clear VERB ❶ **enlever** [50] (papers, rubbish, or clothes); **have you cleared your stuff out of your room?** as-tu enlevé tes affaires de ta chambre? ❷ **débarrasser** [1] (a table or a room); **can I clear the table?** puis-je débarrasser la table? ❸ **dégager** [52] (a road or path) ❹ (fog or snow) **se dissiper** [1]; **and then the fog cleared** et puis le brouillard s'est dissipé ❺ **to clear your throat** se racler [1] la gorge
• **to clear something up** **ranger** [52] quelque chose; **I'll just clear up my books** je vais juste ranger mes livres

clearly ADJECTIVE ❶ (to think, speak, or hear) **clairement** ❷ (obviously) **manifestement**; **she was clearly worried** manifestement, elle était inquiète

clementine NOUN **clémentine** FEM

clever ADJECTIVE ❶ **intelligent**; **their children are all very clever** leurs enfants sont tous très intelligents ❷ (ingenious) **astucieux** (FEM **astucieuse**); **a clever idea** une idée astucieuse

click NOUN ❶ (noise) **petit bruit** MASC, **déclic** MASC ❷ (with mouse) **clic** MASC; **a double-click** un double-clic

click VERB **to click on something** cliquer [1] sur quelque chose; **click on the icon twice** cliquer deux fois sur l'icône

client NOUN client (MASC), cliente FEM

cliff NOUN falaise FEM

climate NOUN climat MASC

climb VERB ❶ monter [1] (a hill, stairs) ❷ faire [10] l'escalade de (a mountain); **we climbed Mont Blanc** nous avons fait l'escalade du Mont Blanc

climber NOUN alpiniste MASC & FEM

climbing NOUN escalade FEM; **they go climbing in Italy** ils font de l'escalade en Italie

clinic NOUN centre (MASC) médical (PLURAL centres médicaux)

clip NOUN ❶ (from a film) extrait MASC ❷ (for your hair) barrette FEM

clip VERB ❶ (to cut) couper [1] ❷ (to fasten) attacher [1]

cloakroom NOUN (for coats) vestiaire MASC

clock NOUN (large) horloge FEM, (smaller) pendule FEM; **an alarm clock** un réveil, **to put the clocks forward an hour** avancer les pendules d'une heure, **to put the clocks back** reculer les pendules

clock radio NOUN radio-réveil MASC

clockwise ADVERB dans le sens des aiguilles d'une montre; **it turns clockwise** ça tourne dans le sens des aiguilles d'une montre

close¹ ADJECTIVE, ADVERB ❶ (result) serré ❷ (friend or relation) proche ❸ (near) près; **the station's very close** la gare est tout près, **she lives close by** elle habite tout près, **close to the cinema** près du cinéma, **not very close** pas très près

close² NOUN fin FEM; **at the close** à la fin

close VERB fermer [1]; **close your eyes!** ferme les yeux!, **she closed the door** elle a fermé la porte, **the post office closes at six** la poste ferme à six heures

closed ADJECTIVE fermé; **'closed on Mondays'** 'fermé le lundi'

closely ADVERB de près; **to examine something closely** regarder quelque chose de près

closing date NOUN date (FEM) limite; **the closing date for entries** la date limite pour les inscriptions

closing-down sale NOUN liquidation FEM

closing time NOUN heure (FEM) de fermeture

cloth NOUN ❶ (for the floor) serpillière FEM ❷ (for polishing) chiffon MASC ❸ (for drying up) torchon MASC ❹ (fabric by the metre) tissu MASC

clothes PLURAL NOUN vêtements MASC PLURAL; **to put your clothes on** s'habiller, **to take your clothes off** se déshabiller, **to change your clothes** se changer

clothes hanger NOUN cintre MASC

clothes line NOUN corde (FEM) à linge

clothes peg NOUN pince (FEM) à linge

clothing NOUN vêtements MASC PLURAL

cloud NOUN nuage MASC
• **to cloud over** se couvrir [30]; **it clouded over in the afternoon** ça s'est couvert dans l'après-midi

cloudy ADJECTIVE nuageux (FEM nuageuse)

clove NOUN ❶ clou (MASC) de girofle ❷ a clove of garlic une gousse d'ail

clown NOUN clown MASC

club NOUN ❶ (association) club MASC; he's in the football club il fait partie du club de foot ❷ (in cards) trèfle MASC; the four of clubs le quatre de trèfle ❸ (golfing iron) crosse FEM

clue NOUN ❶ indice MASC; they have a few clues ils ont quelques indices ❷ (in a crossword) définition FEM
• I haven't a clue je n'ai aucune idée

clumsy ADJECTIVE maladroit

clutch NOUN (in a car) embrayage MASC

clutch VERB to clutch something tenir [77] quelque chose fermement

coach NOUN ❶ (bus) car MASC; by coach en car, on the coach dans le car, to travel by coach voyager en car ❷ (sports trainer) entraîneur MASC, entraîneuse FEM ❸ (railway carriage) wagon MASC

coach station NOUN gare (FEM) routière

coach trip NOUN excursion (FEM) en car; to go on a coach trip faire une excursion en car

coal NOUN charbon MASC

coal mine NOUN mine (FEM) de charbon

coal miner NOUN mineur MASC

coarse ADJECTIVE grossier (FEM grossière)

coast NOUN côte FEM; on the east coast sur la côte est

coat NOUN ❶ manteau MASC (PLURAL manteaux) ❷ a coat of paint une couche de peinture

coat hanger NOUN cintre MASC

cobweb NOUN toile (FEM) d'araignée

cockerel NOUN coq MASC

cocoa NOUN (drink) chocolat MASC (chaud), (powder) cacao MASC

coconut NOUN noix (FEM) de coco

cod NOUN cabillaud MASC

code NOUN ❶ code MASC; the highway code le code de la route ❷ the dialling code for Cambridge l'indicatif pour Cambridge

coffee NOUN café MASC; a cup of coffee un café, a black coffee, please un café, s'il vous plaît, a white coffee un café au lait

coffee break NOUN pause-café FEM

coffee cup NOUN tasse (FEM) à café

coffee machine NOUN cafetière FEM (electric) cafetière (FEM) électrique

coffee table NOUN table (FEM) basse

coffin NOUN cercueil MASC

coin NOUN pièce (FEM) de monnaie; a pound coin une pièce d'une livre

coincidence NOUN coïncidence FEM

Coke NOUN coca MASC; two Cokes please deux cocas s'il vous plaît

colander NOUN passoire FEM

cold NOUN ❶ (cold weather) froid MASC; to be out in the cold être dehors dans le froid ❷ (illness) rhume MASC; to have a cold être enrhumé, Carol's got a cold Carol est enrhumée, a bad cold un gros rhume

cold ADJECTIVE ❶ froid; your hands

are cold tu as les mains froides, **cold milk** du lait froid ➋ *(weather, temperature)* **it's cold today** il fait froid aujourd'hui, **it's cold in the kitchen** il fait froid dans la cuisine ➌ *(feeling)* **I'm cold** j'ai froid

cold sore *NOUN* bouton *(MASC)* de fièvre

collapse *VERB* ➊ *(a roof or a wall)* s'écrouler [1] ➋ *(a person)* **he collapsed in his office** il a eu un malaise dans son bureau

collar *NOUN* ➊ *(on a garment)* col *MASC* ➋ *(for a dog)* collier *MASC*

collarbone *NOUN* clavicule *FEM*

colleague *NOUN* collègue *MASC & FEM*

collect *VERB* ➊ *(as a hobby)* collectionner [1]; **I collect stamps** je collectionne les timbres ➋ aller [7] chercher *(a person)*; **she collects the children from school** elle va chercher les enfants à la sortie de l'école ➌ passer [64] prendre *(thing)*; **I have to collect a book at the library** je dois passer prendre un livre à la bibliothèque ➍ encaisser [1] *(fares or money)* ➎ **to collect in the exercise books** ramasser [1] les cahiers

collection *NOUN* ➊ *(of stamps, CDs, etc)* collection *FEM* ➋ *(of money)* collecte *FEM*

collector *NOUN* collectionneur *MASC*, collectionneuse *FEM*

college *NOUN* ➊ *(for higher education)* établissement *(MASC)* d'études supérieures; **to go to college** faire des études supérieures ➋ *(a school)* collège *MASC*

collie *NOUN* colley *MASC*

collision *NOUN* collision *FEM*

colonel *NOUN* colonel *MASC*

colour *NOUN* couleur *FEM*; **what colour is your car?** de quelle couleur est ta voiture?, **what colour is it?** c'est de quelle couleur?, **do you have it in a different colour?** est-ce que vous l'avez dans une autre couleur?

colour *VERB* *(with paints or crayons)* colorier [1]; **to colour something red** colorier quelque chose en rouge

colour blind *ADJECTIVE* daltonien *(FEM* daltonienne*)*

colour film *NOUN* pellicule *(FEM)* couleur *(PLURAL* pellicules couleur*)*

colourful *ADJECTIVE* en couleurs vives

colouring book *NOUN* album *(MASC)* à colorier

colour scheme *NOUN* couleurs *FEM PLURAL*

colour supplement *NOUN* supplément *(MASC)* illustré

column *NOUN* colonne *FEM*

comb *NOUN* peigne *MASC*

comb *VERB* **to comb your hair** se peigner [1], **I'll just comb my hair** je vais juste me peigner

combination *NOUN* combinaison *FEM*

combine *VERB* combiner [1] *(two separate things)*; **they don't combine well** ils ne se combinent pas bien

come *VERB* ➊ venir [81]; **come quick!** viens vite!, **come and see!** venez voir!, **Nick came by bike** Nick est venu à vélo, **did Jess come to school yesterday?** est-ce que Jess est venue à l'école hier?, **Alan comes from Scotland** Alan vient de l'Ecosse, **can you come over for a coffee?** peux-tu venir prendre un café? ❷ **arriver** [1]; **coming!** j'arrive!, **the bus is coming** le bus arrive ❸ **to come down** descendre [3] *(the stairs or the street)* ❹ **to come up** monter [1], **can you come up a moment?** peux-tu monter un instant? ❺ **to come in** entrer [1], **come in!** entrez!, **she came into the kitchen** elle est entrée dans la cuisine ❻ **to come for** passer [1] prendre *(a person)*, **my father's coming for me** mon père passe me prendre ❼ **come along!** dépêche-toi!

• **to come apart** *(to break)* se casser [1]; **the door handle came apart in my hands** la poignée m'est restée dans la main *(a book)* se déchirer [1]
• **to come back** revenir [81]; **he's coming back to collect us** il revient nous chercher
• **to come off** *(a button or handle, for example)* se détacher [1], *(a lid)* s'enlever [50]
• **to come out** ❶ sortir [72]; **they came out when I called** ils sont sortis quand j'ai appelé, **the album comes out soon** l'album sort bientôt ❷ *(the sun or moon)* se montrer [1]
• **to come up to somebody** aborder [1] quelqu'un

comedian NOUN comique MASC

comedy NOUN comédie FEM

comfortable
ADJECTIVE ❶ confortable; **this chair's really comfortable** ce fauteuil est très confortable ❷ **to feel comfortable** *(a person)* se sentir à l'aise, **are you comfortable there?** êtes-vous bien là?

comfortably ADVERB

confortablement

comic NOUN *(magazine)* illustré MASC

comic strip NOUN bande *(FEM)* dessinée

comma NOUN virgule FEM

command NOUN ordre MASC

comment NOUN *(in a conversation)* remarque FEM; **he made some rude comments about my friends** il a fait des remarques impolies sur mes amis

commentary NOUN reportage *(MASC)* en direct; **the commentary of the match** le reportage du match

commentator NOUN commentateur MASC, commentatrice FEM; **a sports commentator** un commentateur sportif

commercial NOUN spot *(MASC)* publicitaire

commercial ADJECTIVE commercial MASC *(PLURAL* commerciaux*)*

commit VERB ❶ commettre [11] *(a crime)* ❷ **to commit yourself** s'engager [52]

committee NOUN comité MASC

common ADJECTIVE ❶ courant; **it's a common problem** c'est un problème courant ❷ **in common** en commun, **they have nothing in common** ils n'ont rien en commun

common sense NOUN bon sens MASC

communicate VERB communiquer [1]

communication NOUN ❶ *(message)* communication FEM ❷ **communications** communications FEM PLURAL, **the communications are good** les communications sont bonnes

communion NOUN communion FEM

communism NOUN communisme MASC

communist NOUN, ADJECTIVE communiste MASC & FEM

community NOUN communauté FEM; **the European Community** la Communauté Européenne

commute VERB to commute between Oxford and London faire [10] le trajet entre Oxford et Londres tous les jours

commuter NOUN navetteur MASC, navetteuse FEM

compact disc NOUN disque (MASC) compact

compact disc player NOUN platine (FEM) laser

company NOUN ❶ (business) société FEM; **an insurance company** une société d'assurances, **she's set up a company** elle a monté une société ❷ compagnie FEM; **an airline company** une compagnie aérienne, **a theatre company** une compagnie théâtrale ❸ **to keep somebody company** tenir compagnie à quelqu'un, **the dog keeps me company** le chien me tient compagnie

comparatively ADVERB relativement

compare VERB comparer [1]; **if you compare the French with the English** si on compare les Français aux Anglais, **our house is small compared with yours** notre maison est petite par rapport à la vôtre

comparison NOUN comparaison FEM; **in comparison with** par rapport à

compartment NOUN compartiment MASC

compass NOUN boussole FEM

compatible ADJECTIVE (computing) compatible

compensation NOUN indemnisation FEM

compete VERB ❶ to compete in something participer [1] à quelque chose (race, event) ❷ to compete for something se disputer [1] quelque chose (jobs, places), **thirty people competing for one job** trente personnes qui se disputent un seul emploi

competent ADJECTIVE compétent

competition NOUN concours MASC; **a fishing competition** un concours de pêche

competitor NOUN concurrent MASC, concurrente FEM

complain VERB se plaindre [31]; **we complained about the hotel and the meals** nous nous sommes plaints de l'hôtel et des repas

complaint NOUN plainte FEM; **to make a complaint** se plaindre [31], **she made a complaint to the manager about the poor service** elle s'est plainte de la qualité du service auprès du responsable

complete ADJECTIVE complet (FEM complète); **the complete collection** la collection complète

complete VERB (to finish) compléter [24]

completely ADVERB complètement

a
b
c
d
e
f
g
h
i
j
k
l
m
n
o
p
q
r
s
t
u
v
w
x
y
z

complexion NOUN teint MASC

complicated ADJECTIVE compliqué

compliment NOUN compliment MASC; **to pay somebody a compliment** faire un compliment à quelqu'un

compose VERB composer [1]; **composed of** composé de

composer NOUN compositeur MASC, compositrice FEM

comprehension NOUN compréhension FEM; **a comprehension test** un test de compréhension

compromise NOUN compromis MASC

compulsory ADJECTIVE obligatoire

computer NOUN ordinateur MASC; **to work on a computer** travailler sur ordinateur, **to have something on computer** avoir quelque chose sur ordinateur

computer engineer NOUN technicien (MASC) en informatique, technicienne (FEM) en informatique

computer game NOUN jeu (MASC) électronique (PLURAL jeux électroniques)

computer program NOUN programme (MASC) informatique, logiciel MASC

computer programmer NOUN programmeur MASC, programmeuse FEM

computer science NOUN informatique FEM

computing NOUN informatique FEM

conceited ADJECTIVE vaniteux (FEM vaniteuse)

concentrate VERB se concentrer [1]; **I can't concentrate** je n'arrive pas à me concentrer, **I was concentrating on the film** je me concentrais sur le film

concentration NOUN concentration FEM

concern NOUN (worry) inquiétude FEM; **there is no cause for concern** il n'y a pas lieu de s'inquiéter

concern VERB ❶ (to affect) concerner [1]; **this doesn't concern you** ceci ne te concerne pas ❷ **as far as I'm concerned** en ce qui me concerne

concert NOUN ❶ concert MASC; **to go to a concert** aller à un concert ❷ **a concert ticket** un billet de concert

conclusion NOUN conclusion FEM

concrete NOUN béton MASC; **a concrete floor** un sol en béton

condemn VERB condamner [1]

condition NOUN ❶ condition FEM; **in good condition** en bonne condition, **weather conditions** les conditions météorologiques ❷ (something you agree to) condition FEM; **the conditions of sale** les conditions de vente, **on condition that you let me pay** à condition que tu me laisses payer

conditional NOUN conditionnel MASC

conditioner NOUN (for your hair) après-shampooing MASC

condom NOUN préservatif MASC

conduct NOUN conduite FEM

conduct VERB diriger [52] (an orchestra or a piece of music)

conductor NOUN (of an orchestra) chef (MASC) d'orchestre

cone NOUN ❶ (for ice cream) cornet MASC ❷ (for traffic) balise FEM

confectionery NOUN confiserie FEM

conference NOUN conférence FEM

confess VERB avouer [1]

confession NOUN confession FEM

confidence NOUN ❶ (self-confidence) assurance FEM; **to be lacking in confidence** manquer d'assurance ❷ (faith in somebody else) confiance FEM; **to have confidence in somebody** avoir confiance en quelqu'un

confident ADJECTIVE ❶ (sure of yourself) assuré ❷ (sure that something will happen) sûr

confirm VERB confirmer [1]; **we'll confirm the date** nous confirmerons la date

confuse VERB ❶ troubler [1] (a person) ❷ confondre [69]; **I confuse him with his brother** je le confonds avec son frère

confused ADJECTIVE ❶ confus; **he gave us a confused story** il nous a raconté une histoire confuse ❷ **I'm confused about the holiday dates** je ne comprends pas bien les dates des vacances, **now I'm completely confused!** là je ne comprends plus rien!

confusing ADJECTIVE pas clair; **the instructions are confusing** les instructions ne sont pas claires

confusion NOUN confusion FEM

congratulate VERB féliciter [1]; **I congratulated Tim on his success** j'ai félicité Tim de son succès, **we congratulate you on winning** nous vous félicitons d'avoir gagné

congratulations PLURAL NOUN félicitations FEM PLURAL; **congratulations on the baby!** félicitations pour le bébé!

conjurer NOUN prestidigitateur MASC

connect VERB (to plug in to the mains) brancher [1] (a dishwasher or TV, for example)

connection NOUN ❶ (between two ideas or events) rapport MASC; **there's no connection between his letter and my decision** il n'y a aucun rapport entre sa lettre et ma décision ❷ (between trains or planes) correspondance FEM; **Sally missed her connection** Sally a raté sa correspondance ❸ (electrical) contact; **a faulty connection** un mauvais contact

conscience NOUN conscience FEM; **to have a guilty conscience** avoir mauvaise conscience

conscious ADJECTIVE conscient

consequence NOUN conséquence FEM

consequently ADVERB par conséquent

conservation NOUN (of nature) protection FEM

conservative NOUN, ADJECTIVE conservateur MASC, conservatrice FEM

conservatory NOUN jardin (MASC) d'hiver

consider VERB ❶ (to give thought to) considérer [24] (a suggestion or idea) ❷ (to think you might do) envisager [52]; **we are considering buying a flat** nous envisageons d'acheter un appartement ❸ **all things considered** tout compte fait

considerable ADJECTIVE considérable; **a considerable number of the students** un pourcentage considérable des étudiants

considerate ADJECTIVE attentionné (person)

consideration NOUN considération FEM; **no consideration was given to their safety** on ne s'est pas soucié de leur sécurité

considering PREPOSITION étant donné; **considering her age** étant donné son âge, **considering he did it all himself** étant donné qu'il a tout fait lui-même

consist VERB **to consist of** être [6] composé de

consistent ADJECTIVE régulier, constant

console NOUN console FEM; **a games console** une console de jeux

consonant NOUN consonne FEM

constant ADJECTIVE permanent

constipated ADJECTIVE constipé

construct VERB construire [26]

construction NOUN construction FEM

consul NOUN consul MASC

consulate NOUN consulat MASC

consult VERB consulter [1]

consumer NOUN consommateur MASC, consommatrice FEM

consumption NOUN consommation FEM

contact NOUN ❶ (touch) contact MASC; **to be in contact with somebody** être en contact avec quelqu'un, **we've lost contact** nous avons perdu contact ❷ (a person you know) connaissance FEM; **Rob has contacts in the music business** Rob a des connaissances dans le monde de la musique

contact VERB contacter [1]; **I'll contact you tomorrow** je te contacterai demain

contact lens NOUN lentille (FEM) de contact (PLURAL lentilles de contact)

contain VERB contenir [77]

container NOUN récipient MASC

contaminate VERB contaminer [1]

contemporary ADJECTIVE ❶ (around today) contemporain ❷ (modern) moderne

contents PLURAL NOUN contenu MASC; **the contents of my suitcase** le contenu de ma valise

contest NOUN concours MASC

contestant NOUN concurrent MASC, concurrente FEM

context NOUN contexte MASC

continent NOUN continent MASC; **on the Continent** en Europe continentale

continental ADJECTIVE **a continental holiday** des vacances en Europe continentale

continue VERB continuer [1]; **we continued (with) our journey** nous avons continué notre voyage, **Jill continued chatting** Jill a continué de bavarder, **'to be continued'** 'à suivre'

continuous ADJECTIVE continu;
continuous assessment le contrôle
continu

contraception NOUN
contraception FEM

contraceptive NOUN contraceptif
MASC

contract NOUN contrat MASC

contradict VERB contredire [47]

contradiction NOUN contradiction
FEM

contrary NOUN contraire MASC; on
the contrary au contraire

contrast NOUN contraste MASC

contribute VERB donner [1] (money)

contribution NOUN (to charity or an
appeal) don MASC

control NOUN (of a crowd or animals)
contrôle MASC; the police have lost
control la police a perdu le contrôle,
keep your dogs under control
maîtrisez vos chiens, everything's
under control tout va bien, the fire
was out of control on ne maîtrisait
plus l'incendie

control VERB ❶ maîtriser [1]
(a crowd, animals, or a fire, for
example) ❷ to control oneself se
contrôler [1]

controversial ADJECTIVE discutable;
a controversial decision une
décision discutable

convenient ADJECTIVE ❶ commode;
frozen vegetables are very
convenient les légumes congelés
sont très commodes ❷ to be
convenient for somebody convenir
à quelqu'un, if that's convenient
for you si cela vous convient ❸ the
house is convenient for shops and
schools la maison est bien située
par rapport aux magasins et aux
écoles

convent NOUN couvent MASC

conventional
ADJECTIVE ❶ conventionnel (FEM
conventionnelle) ❷ (person)
conformiste

conversation NOUN conversation
FEM

convert VERB transformer [1]; we're
going to convert the garage into a
workshop nous allons transformer
le garage en atelier

convince VERB convaincre [79]; I'm
convinced you're wrong je suis
convaincu que tu as tort

convincing ADJECTIVE convaincant

cook NOUN cuisinier MASC,
cuisinière FEM

cook VERB ❶ faire [10] la cuisine;
who's cooking tonight? qui fait
la cuisine ce soir?, I like cooking
j'aime faire la cuisine ❷ faire [10]
cuire (vegetables, pasta, etc); cook
the carrots for five minutes faites
cuire les carottes pendant cinq
minutes ❸ préparer [1] (a meal)
Fran's busy cooking supper Fran est
en train de préparer le dîner ❹ (food)
cuire [36]; the sausages are cooking
les saucisses sont en train de cuire,
is the chicken cooked? est-ce que le
poulet est cuit?

cooker NOUN cuisinière FEM; an
electric cooker une cuisinière
électrique, a gas cooker une
cuisinière à gaz

cookery NOUN cuisine FEM

cookery book NOUN livre (MASC) de
cuisine

cooking NOUN cuisine FEM; **to do the cooking** faire la cuisine, **Italian cooking** la cuisine italienne

cool NOUN ❶ (coldness) fraîcheur FEM; **stay in the cool** reste à la fraîcheur ❷ (calm) **to lose one's cool** perdre son sang-froid, **he kept his cool** il a gardé son sang-froid

cool ADJECTIVE ❶ (cold) frais (FEM fraîche); **a cool drink** une boisson fraîche, **it's cool inside** il fait frais dans la maison ❷ (laid-back) décontracté ❸ (sophisticated) branché (informal)

cool VERB refroidir [2]; **while the engine was cooling (down)** pendant que le moteur refroidissait

cooperate VERB coopérer [24]

cop NOUN flic MASC (informal)

cope VERB ❶ (to manage) se débrouiller [1]; **she copes well** elle se débrouille bien ❷ **to cope with** s'occuper [1] de (children or work), **I'll cope with the dishes** je m'occuperai de la vaisselle ❸ faire [10] face à (problems); **she's had a lot to cope with** elle a été obligée de faire face à beaucoup de choses, **he can't cope any more** il n'arrive plus à faire face

copper NOUN cuivre MASC

copy NOUN ❶ copie FEM; **make ten copies of this letter** faites dix copies de cette lettre ❷ (of a book) exemplaire MASC

copy VERB copier [1]; **I copied (down) the address** j'ai copié l'adresse

cord NOUN (for a blind, for example) cordon MASC

cordless telephone NOUN téléphone (MASC) sans fil

core NOUN (of an apple or a pear) trognon MASC

cork NOUN ❶ (in a bottle) bouchon MASC ❷ (material) liège MASC

corkscrew NOUN tire-bouchon MASC

corn NOUN ❶ (wheat) blé MASC ❷ (sweetcorn) maïs MASC

corner NOUN coin MASC; **in a corner of the kitchen** dans un coin de la cuisine, **at the corner of the street** au coin de la rue, **out of the corner of your eye** du coin de l'œil, **it's just round the corner** c'est tout près

cornflakes NOUN corn-flakes MASC PLURAL

Cornwall NOUN Cornouailles FEM; **in Cornwall** en Cornouailles

corpse NOUN cadavre MASC

correct ADJECTIVE ❶ exact; **yes, that's correct** oui, c'est exact ❷ bon (FEM bonne); **the correct sum** la bonne somme, **the correct answer** la bonne réponse, **the correct choice** le bon choix

correct VERB corriger [52]

correction NOUN correction FEM

correctly ADVERB correctement; **have you filled in the form correctly?** est-ce que vous avez rempli le formulaire correctement?, **she answered correctly** elle a donné la bonne réponse

correspond VERB correspondre [3]

corridor NOUN couloir MASC

Corsica NOUN Corse FEM; **to Corsica** en Corse

cosmetics PLURAL NOUN **produits** (MASC PLURAL) **de beauté**

cost NOUN **prix** MASC; **the cost of a new computer** le prix d'un nouvel ordinateur, **the cost of living** le coût de la vie

cost VERB **coûter** [1]; **how much does it cost?** combien est-ce que ça coûte?, **the tickets cost £10** les billets coûtent dix livres, **it costs too much** cela coûte trop cher

costume NOUN **costume** MASC

cosy ADJECTIVE (a bed or room) **douillet** (FEM **douillette**); **it's cosy by the fire** on est bien à côté du feu

cot NOUN **lit** (MASC) **d'enfant**

cottage NOUN **petite maison** FEM

cotton NOUN ❶ (fabric) **coton** MASC; **a cotton shirt** une chemise en coton ❷ (thread) **fil** (MASC) **de coton**

cotton wool NOUN **ouate** (FEM) **de coton**

couch NOUN **canapé** MASC

cough NOUN **toux** FEM; **a nasty cough** une mauvaise toux, **to have a cough** tousser

cough VERB **tousser** [1]

could VERB ❶ if he could pay s'il pouvait payer, **I couldn't open it** je ne pouvais pas l'ouvrir, **they couldn't smoke there** ils ne pouvaient pas fumer là, **she did all she could** elle a fait tout ce qu'elle pouvait ❷ (knew how to) **he couldn't drive** il ne savait pas conduire, **I couldn't swim** je ne savais pas nager ❸ (with seeing, hearing, or smelling) **I could hear the police car** j'entendais la voiture de police, **she couldn't see anything**

elle ne voyait rien ❹ (might) **could I speak to David?** pourrais-je parler à David?, **you could try telephoning** tu pourrais téléphoner

council NOUN **conseil** MASC; **the town council** le conseil municipal

councillor NOUN ❶ (of town council) **membre** (MASC) **du conseil municipal** ❷ (local council) **membre** (MASC) **du conseil régional**

count VERB ❶ (reckon up) **compter** [1]; **I counted my money** j'ai compté mon argent, **thirty-five not counting the children** trente-cinq sans compter les enfants ❷ **to count as** être [6] **considéré comme**, **children over twelve count as adults** les enfants au-dessus de douze ans sont considérés comme adultes ❸ (to be allowed) **compter** [1]; **that doesn't count** ça ne compte pas

counter NOUN ❶ (in a shop or cafe) **comptoir** MASC ❷ (in a post office or bank) **guichet** MASC ❸ (in a big store) **rayon** MASC; **on the cheese counter** au rayon fromagerie ❹ (for board games) **jeton** MASC

country NOUN ❶ (France, England, etc) **pays** MASC; **a foreign country** un pays étranger, **from another country** d'un autre pays ❷ (not town) **campagne** FEM; **to live in the country** vivre à la campagne, **a country walk** une promenade à la campagne, **a country road** une route de campagne

country dancing NOUN **danse** (FEM) **folklorique**

countryside NOUN **campagne** FEM

county NOUN **comté** MASC

couple NOUN ❶ *(a pair)* couple MASC ❷ **a couple of** deux ou trois, **a couple of times** deux ou trois fois, **I've got a couple of things to do** j'ai deux ou trois choses à faire

courage NOUN courage MASC

courgette NOUN courgette FEM

courier NOUN ❶ *(on a package holiday)* accompagnateur MASC, accompagnatrice FEM ❷ *(delivery service)* coursier MASC; **by courier** par coursier

course NOUN ❶ *(lessons)* cours MASC; **a beginners' course** un cours pour débutants, **a computer course** un cours d'informatique, **to go on a course** suivre un cours ❷ *(part of a meal)* plat MASC; **the main course** le plat principal, **a golf course** un golf ❸ **of course** bien sûr, **yes, of course!** oui, bien sûr!, **he's forgotten, of course** il a oublié, bien sûr

court NOUN ❶ *(for tennis or squash)* court MASC ❷ *(for basketball)* terrain MASC

courtyard NOUN cour FEM

cousin NOUN cousin MASC, cousine FEM; **my cousin Sonia** ma cousine Sonia

cover NOUN ❶ *(for a book)* couverture FEM ❷ *(for a duvet or cushion)* housse FEM; **a duvet cover** une housse de couette

cover VERB ❶ *(to protect or cover up)* couvrir [30]; **cover the wound** couvrez la blessure, **he was covered in spots** il était couvert de boutons ❷ *(with leaves, snow, or fabric)* recouvrir [30]; **the ground was covered with snow** le sol était recouvert de neige

cow NOUN vache FEM; **mad cow disease** maladie *(FEM)* de la vache folle

coward NOUN lâche MASC & FEM

cowboy NOUN cowboy MASC

crab NOUN crabe MASC

crack NOUN ❶ *(in a wall or cup)* fêlure FEM ❷ *(a cracking noise)* craquement MASC

crack VERB ❶ *(to make a crack in)* fêler [1] *(a cup, a chair, or a bone)* ❷ *(to break)* casser [1] *(a nut or an egg)* ❸ *(to split by itself: ice, for example)* se fêler [1] ❹ *(to make a noise) (a twig)* craquer [1]

cracker NOUN ❶ *(biscuit)* cracker MASC ❷ *(Christmas cracker)* diablotin MASC

crackle VERB crépiter [1]

craft NOUN *(at school)* travaux *(MASC PLURAL)* manuels

crafty ADJECTIVE ingénieux *(FEM ingénieuse)*; **that was very crafty of her** c'était très ingénieux de sa part

cramp NOUN crampe FEM; **to have cramp in your leg** avoir une crampe à la jambe

crane NOUN grue FEM

crash NOUN ❶ *(an accident)* accident MASC; **a car crash** un accident de voiture ❷ *(smashing noise)* fracas MASC; **a crash of broken glass** un fracas de verre brisé

crash VERB ❶ *(a car or plane)* s'écraser [1]; **the plane crashed** l'avion s'est écrasé ❷ **to crash into something** rentrer [1] dans quelque chose, **the car crashed into a tree** la voiture est rentrée dans un arbre

A B C D E F G H I J K L M N O P Q R S T U V W X Y Z

crash course NOUN cours (MASC) intensif

crash helmet NOUN casque MASC

crate NOUN ❶ (for bottles or china) caisse FEM ❷ (for fruit) cageot MASC

crawl NOUN (in swimming) crawl MASC

crawl VERB ❶ (a person, a baby) marcher [1] à quatre pattes ❷ (cars in a jam) rouler [1] au pas; **we were crawling along** nous roulions au pas

crayon NOUN ❶ (wax) crayon (MASC) gras ❷ (coloured pencil) crayon (MASC) de couleur

craze NOUN vogue FEM; **the craze for rollerblades** la vogue des rollers

crazy ADJECTIVE fou (FEM folle)

creak VERB (a hinge) grincer [61] (a floorboard) craquer [1]

cream NOUN crème FEM; **strawberries and cream** des fraises à la crème

cream cheese NOUN fromage (MASC) à tartiner

crease NOUN pli MASC

creased ADJECTIVE froissé

create VERB créer [32]

creative ADJECTIVE créatif (FEM créative) (a person)

creature NOUN créature FEM

crèche NOUN crèche FEM

credit NOUN crédit MASC; **to buy something on credit** acheter quelque chose à crédit

credit card NOUN carte (FEM) de crédit

cress NOUN cresson MASC

crew NOUN ❶ (on a ship or plane) équipage MASC ❷ (rowing or filming) équipe FEM

crew cut NOUN cheveux (MASC PLURAL) en brosse

cricket NOUN ❶ (game) cricket MASC; **to play cricket** jouer au cricket ❷ (insect) grillon MASC

cricket bat NOUN batte (FEM) de cricket

crime NOUN ❶ crime MASC; **murder is a crime** le meurtre est un crime ❷ (within society) criminalité FEM; **the fight against crime** la lutte contre la criminalité

criminal NOUN, ADJECTIVE criminel MASC, criminelle FEM

crimson ADJECTIVE pourpre

crisis NOUN crise FEM

crisp NOUN chip FEM; **a packet of (potato) crisps** un sachet de chips

crisp ADJECTIVE ❶ (biscuit) croustillant ❷ (apple) croquant

critical ADJECTIVE ❶ critique (a remark or somebody's condition) ❷ décisif (FEM décisive) (a moment)

criticism NOUN critique FEM

criticize VERB critiquer [1]

Croatia NOUN Croatie FEM

crockery NOUN vaisselle FEM

crocodile NOUN crocodile MASC

crook NOUN (criminal) escroc MASC

crooked ADJECTIVE de travers; **the picture is crooked** le tableau est de travers, **a crooked line** une ligne pas droite

crop NOUN récolte FEM

cross NOUN **croix** FEM

cross ADJECTIVE **fâché**; she's very cross elle est très fâchée, **I'm cross with you** je suis fâché contre toi

cross VERB ❶ (to cross over) **traverser** [1]; **to cross the road** traverser la rue ❷ **to cross your legs croiser** [1] **les jambes** ❸ **to cross into Italy passer** [1] **en Italie** ❹ (to cross each other) **se croiser** [1]; **the two roads cross here** les deux routes se croisent ici
• **to cross out rayer** [59] (a mistake, for example)

cross-Channel ADJECTIVE **trans-Manche**; **a cross-Channel ferry** un ferry trans-Manche

cross-country NOUN ❶ **cross** MASC ❷ **cross-country skiing** le ski de fond

crossing NOUN ❶ (from one place to another) **traversée** FEM; **a Channel crossing** une traversée trans-Manche ❷ **a pedestrian crossing** un passage piétons, **a level crossing** un passage à niveau

cross-legged ADJECTIVE **to sit cross-legged** être assis en tailleur

crossroads NOUN **carrefour** MASC; **at the crossroads** au carrefour

crossword NOUN **mots** (MASC PLURAL) **croisés**; **to do the crossword** faire les mots croisés

crouch VERB **s'accroupir** [2]

crow NOUN **corbeau** MASC
• **ten kilometres as the crow flies** dix kilomètres à vol d'oiseau

crow VERB (a cock) **chanter** [1]

crowd NOUN **foule** FEM; **in the crowd** dans la foule, **a crowd of 5,000** une foule de cinq mille

crowd VERB **to crowd into** or **onto s'entasser** [1] **dans** (a room or bus, for example), **we all crowded into the train** nous nous sommes tous entassés dans le train

crowded ADJECTIVE **bondé**

crown NOUN **couronne** FEM

crude ADJECTIVE ❶ (rough and ready) **rudimentaire** ❷ (vulgar) **grossier** (FEM **grossière**)

cruel ADJECTIVE **cruel** (FEM **cruelle**)

cruelty NOUN **cruauté** FEM; **they were treated with great cruelty** ils ont été traités avec beaucoup de cruauté

cruise NOUN **croisière** FEM; **to go on a cruise** faire une croisière

crumb NOUN **miette** FEM

crumple VERB **froisser** [1]

crunch VERB **croquer** [1] (an apple)

crunchy ADJECTIVE **croquant**

crush VERB **écraser** [1]

crust NOUN **croûte** FEM

crusty ADJECTIVE **croustillant** (bread)

crutch NOUN **béquille** FEM; **to be on crutches** marcher avec des béquilles

cry NOUN **cri** MASC

cry VERB ❶ (weep) **pleurer** [1] ❷ (call out) **crier** [1]

crystal NOUN **cristal** MASC

cub NOUN ❶ (animal) **petit** MASC ❷ (scout) **louveteau** MASC

Cuba NOUN **Cuba** FEM

Cuban NOUN Cubain MASC, Cubaine FEM

Cuban ADJECTIVE cubain

cube NOUN cube MASC; **an ice cube** un glaçon

cubic ADJECTIVE (for measurements) cube; **three cubic metres** trois mètres cube

cubicle NOUN ❶ (in a changing room) cabine FEM ❷ (in a public lavatory) cabinet MASC

cuckoo NOUN coucou MASC

cucumber NOUN concombre MASC

cuddle NOUN **to give somebody a cuddle** faire un câlin à quelqu'un

cuddle VERB câliner [1]

cue NOUN (billiards, pool, snooker) queue (FEM) de billard

cuff NOUN (on a shirt) manchette FEM

cul-de-sac NOUN impasse FEM

culture NOUN culture FEM

cunning ADJECTIVE rusé

cup NOUN ❶ (for drinking) tasse FEM; **a cup of tea** une tasse de thé ❷ (a trophy) coupe FEM

cupboard NOUN placard MASC; **in the kitchen cupboard** dans le placard de la cuisine

cup tie NOUN match (MASC) de coupe

cure NOUN remède MASC

cure VERB guérir [2]

curiosity NOUN curiosité FEM

curious ADJECTIVE curieux (FEM curieuse)

curl NOUN boucle FEM

curl VERB friser [1] (hair)

currant NOUN raisin (MASC) de Corinthe

currency NOUN **foreign currency** les devises étrangères

current NOUN (of electricity or water) courant MASC

current ADJECTIVE actuel (FEM actuelle) (a situation, for example)

current affairs NOUN actualité FEM

curriculum NOUN programme MASC

curry NOUN curry MASC; **chicken curry** le curry de poulet

cursor NOUN curseur MASC

curtain NOUN rideau MASC (PLURAL rideaux)

cushion NOUN coussin MASC

custard NOUN ❶ (runny) crème (FEM) anglaise ❷ (baked) flan MASC

custom NOUN coutume FEM

customer NOUN client MASC, cliente FEM; **customer services** le service clientèle

customs PLURAL NOUN douane FEM SINGULAR; **to go through customs** passer à la douane

customs hall NOUN douane FEM

customs officer NOUN douanier MASC, douanière FEM

cut NOUN ❶ (injury) coupure FEM ❷ (haircut) coupe FEM

cut VERB ❶ couper [1]; **I've cut the bread** j'ai coupé le pain, **you'll cut yourself!** tu vas te couper!, **Kevin's cut his finger** Kevin s'est coupé le doigt ❷ **to cut the grass** tondre [3] le gazon ❸ **to get your hair cut** se

a
b
c
d
e
f
g
h
i
j
k
l
m
n
o
p
q
r
s
t
u
v
w
x
y
z

faire [10] couper les cheveux, **Anne's had her hair cut** Anne s'est fait couper les cheveux ❹ **to cut prices** baisser les prix
- **to cut down something** abattre [21] *(a tree)*
- **to cut out something** ❶ découper [1] *(a shape, a newspaper article)* ❷ supprimer *(sugar, fatty food, etc.)*
- **to cut up something** couper [1] *(food)*

cutlery NOUN **couverts** MASC PLURAL

CV NOUN **CV** MASC

cycle NOUN *(bike)* **vélo** MASC

cycle VERB **faire [10] du vélo**; **do you like cycling?** est-ce que tu aimes faire du vélo?, **we cycle to school** nous allons à l'école à vélo

cycle lane NOUN **piste** *(FEM)* **cyclable**

cycle race NOUN **course** *(FEM)* **cycliste**

cycling NOUN **cyclisme** MASC

cycling holiday NOUN **vacances** *(FEM PLURAL)* **à vélo**

cyclist NOUN **cycliste** MASC & FEM

cylinder NOUN **cylindre** MASC

Dd

dad NOUN ❶ **père** MASC; **Anna's dad** le père d'Anna, **my dad works in a bank** mon père travaille dans une banque ❷ *(within the family)* **papa** MASC; **Dad's not home yet** Papa n'est pas encore rentré

daffodil NOUN **jonquille** FEM

daily ADJECTIVE **quotidien** *(FEM* **quotidienne**); **his daily visit** sa visite quotidienne

daily ADVERB **quotidiennement**; **she visits him daily** elle lui rend visite tous les jours

dairy products PLURAL NOUN **les produits** *(MASC PLURAL)* **laitiers**

daisy NOUN **paquerette** FEM

dam NOUN **barrage** MASC

damage VERB **abîmer [1]**

damage NOUN **dégâts** MASC PLURAL; **there's no damage** il n'y a pas de dégâts

damage VERB **endommager [52]**

damn NOUN **he doesn't give a damn** il s'en fiche complètement *(informal)*

damn EXCLAMATION **damn!** zut! *(informal)*

damp ADJECTIVE **humide**

damp NOUN **humidité** FEM; **because of the damp** à cause de l'humidité

dance NOUN ❶ (art form) danse
FEM; **a folk dance** une danse
traditionnelle ❷ (occasion) soirée
(FEM) dansante

dance VERB danser [1]

dancer NOUN danseur MASC,
danseuse FEM

dancing NOUN danse FEM; **I like
dancing** j'aime danser

dancing class NOUN cours (MASC)
de danse; **to go to dancing classes**
suivre des cours de danse

dandruff NOUN pellicules FEM PLURAL

danger NOUN danger MASC; **to be in
danger** être en danger

dangerous ADJECTIVE dangereux
(FEM dangereuse); **it's dangerous
to drive too fast** il est dangereux de
conduire trop vite

Danish NOUN danois MASC

Danish ADJECTIVE danois

dare VERB ❶ oser [1]; **to dare to do**
oser faire, **I didn't dare suggest it** je
n'ai pas osé le suggérer ❷ **don't you
dare tell her I'm here!** je t'interdis
de lui dire que je suis là! ❸ **I dare
you!** chiche que tu y vas! (informal),
I dare you to tell him! chiche que tu
le lui dises! (informal)

daring ADJECTIVE osé; **that was a bit
daring!** c'était un peu osé!

dark NOUN **in the dark** dans
l'obscurité, **after dark** après la
tombée de la nuit, **to be afraid of
the dark** avoir peur du noir

dark ADJECTIVE ❶ (colour) foncé;
a dark blue skirt une jupe bleu
foncé ❷ **she has dark brown hair**
elle est brune ❸ **it's dark already** il
fait nuit déjà, **it gets dark around**

five la nuit commence à tomber
vers cinq heures ❹ (room) sombre;
the kitchen's a bit dark la cuisine
est plutôt sombre, **it's dark in here**
il fait sombre ici

darkness NOUN obscurité FEM; **in
darkness** dans l'obscurité

darling NOUN chéri (MASC), chérie
FEM; **see you later, darling!** à tout à
l'heure, chéri!

dart NOUN fléchette FEM; **to play
darts** jouer aux fléchettes

data PLURAL NOUN données FEM PLURAL

database NOUN base (FEM) de
données

date NOUN ❶ date FEM; **the date
of the meeting** la date de la
réunion, **to fix a date for** fixer
une date pour ❷ **what's the
date today?** nous sommes le
combien aujourd'hui? ❸ **out
of date** (passport, driving
licence, etc) périmé, (technology,
method, information, etc)
dépassé, **my passport's out
of date** mon passeport est
périmé ❹ (appointment) **Laura's got
a date with Frank tonight** Laura
sort avec Frank ce soir ❺ (fruit)
datte FEM

date of birth NOUN date (FEM) de
naissance

daughter NOUN fille FEM; **Tina's
daughter** la fille de Tina

daughter-in-law NOUN belle-fille
FEM (PLURAL belles-filles)

dawn NOUN aube FEM

day NOUN ❶ jour MASC; **three days
later** trois jours plus tard, **the
day I went to London** le jour où
je suis allé à Londres ❷ (just from

morning until evening) **journée** FEM;
we spent the day in London nous
avons passé la journée à Londres,
it rained all day il a plu pendant
toute la journée ❸ **it's going to
be a nice day tomorrow** il va faire
beau demain ❹ **the day after**
le lendemain, **the day after the
wedding** le lendemain du mariage,
the day after tomorrow après-
demain, **my sister's arriving the
day after tomorrow** ma sœur arrive
après-demain ❺ **the day before** la
veille, **the day before the wedding**
la veille du mariage, **the day before
yesterday** avant-hier, **my sister
arrived the day before yesterday**
ma sœur est arrivée avant-hier

day off NOUN jour (MASC) de congé;
when's your day off? quel est ton
jour de congé?

dead ADJECTIVE **mort;** her father's
dead son père est mort

dead ADVERB *(really)* **vachement**
(informal); **he's dead nice** il est
vachement gentil, **it was dead good**
c'était vachement bien, **it's dead
easy** c'est vachement facile, **you're
dead right** tu as absolument raison,
she arrived dead on time elle est
arrivée à l'heure pile

dead end NOUN impasse FEM

deadline NOUN date (FEM) limite

deaf ADJECTIVE **sourd**

deafening ADJECTIVE **assourdissant**

deal NOUN ❶ *(involving money)*
affaire; it's a good deal c'est une
bonne affaire ❷ **marché** MASC; **I'll
make a deal with you** je ferai un
marché avec toi, **it's a deal!** marché
conclu! ❸ **a great deal of** beaucoup
de, **I don't have a great deal of time**
je n'ai pas beaucoup de temps

deal VERB *(in cards)* **donner** [1]; **it's
you to deal** c'est à toi de donner
• **to deal with something** s'occuper
[1] de quelque chose; **Linda deals
with the accounts** Linda s'occupe
de la comptabilité, **I'll deal with
it as soon as possible** je m'en
occuperai dès que possible

dear ADJECTIVE ❶ **cher** (FEM
chère); Dear Sylvie Chère
Sylvie ❷ *(expensive)* **cher** (FEM **chère)**

death NOUN **mort** FEM; **after his
father's death** après la mort de son
père
• **you'll frighten him to death** tu lui
feras une peur bleue
• **I'm bored to death** je m'ennuie à
mourir
• **I'm sick to death of it** j'en ai marre
(informal)

death penalty NOUN **peine** (FEM)
de mort

debate NOUN **débat** MASC

debate VERB **débattre** [21]

debt NOUN **dette** FEM; **to get into debt**
s'endetter

decade NOUN **décennie** FEM

decaffeinated ADJECTIVE **décaféiné**

deceive VERB **tromper** [1]

December NOUN **décembre** MASC; **in
December** en décembre

decent ADJECTIVE ❶ **convenable;
a decent salary** un salaire
convenable ❷ **a decent meal** un bon
repas ❸ **he seems a decent enough
guy** il semble être un type plutôt
bien *(informal)*

decide VERB **décider** [1]; **to decide to
do** décider de faire, **she's decided
to buy a car** elle a décidé d'acheter

une voiture, **she's decided not to buy a car** elle a décidé de ne pas acheter une voiture

decimal ADJECTIVE décimal MASC (PLURAL décimaux)

decimal point NOUN virgule FEM

decision NOUN décision FEM; **the right decision** la bonne décision, **the wrong decision** la mauvaise décision, **to make a decision** prendre une décision

deck NOUN (on a ship) pont MASC

deckchair NOUN transat MASC

declare VERB déclarer [1]

decorate VERB ❶ décorer [1]; **to decorate the Christmas tree** décorer le sapin de Noël ❷ peindre; **we're decorating the kitchen this weekend** on va peindre la cuisine ce weekend

decoration NOUN décoration FEM

decorator NOUN peintre-décorateur MASC

decrease NOUN diminution FEM; **a decrease in the number of** une diminution du nombre de

decrease VERB diminuer [1]

deduct VERB déduire [26]

deep ADJECTIVE profond; **a deep feeling of gratitude** un profond sentiment de reconnaissance, **the river is very deep here** la rivière est très profonde ici, **how deep is the swimming pool?** quelle est la profondeur de la piscine?, **a hole two metres deep** un trou de deux mètres de profondeur

deep end NOUN **the deep end** (of a swimming pool) le grand bassin

deep freeze NOUN congélateur MASC

deeply ADVERB profondément

deer NOUN ❶ (red deer) cerf MASC ❷ (roe deer) chevreuil MASC ❸ (fallow deer) daim MASC

defeat NOUN défaite FEM

defeat VERB battre [21]

defect NOUN défaut MASC

defence NOUN défense FEM

defend VERB défendre [3]

defender NOUN défenseur MASC

define VERB définir [2]

definite ADJECTIVE ❶ net (FEM nette) (before the noun); **a definite change** un net changement, **a definite improvement** une nette amélioration ❷ (certain) sûr; **it's not definite yet** ce n'est pas encore sûr ❸ (exact) précis; **a definite answer** une réponse précise, **I don't have a definite idea of what I want** je n'ai pas une idée précise de ce que je veux

definite article NOUN article (MASC) défini

definitely ADVERB ❶ (when giving your opinion about something) sans aucun doute; **the blue one is definitely the biggest** le bleu est sans aucun doute le plus grand, **your French is definitely better than mine** ton français est sans aucun doute meilleur que le mien, **'are you sure you like this one better?' – 'definitely!'** 'tu es sûr que tu préfères celui-ci?' – 'sans aucun doute!' ❷ **she's definitely going to be there** elle va y être, c'est sûr, **I'm definitely not going** c'est décidé, je n'y vais pas

definition NOUN définition FEM

degree NOUN ❶ degré MASC; **thirty degrees** trente degrés ❷ **a university degree** un diplôme universitaire

delay NOUN retard MASC; **a two-hour delay** un retard de deux heures

delay VERB ❶ (make late) retarder [1]; **the flight was delayed by bad weather** le vol a été retardé par le mauvais temps ❷ (postpone) différer [24]; **the decision has been delayed until Thursday** la décision a été différée juqu'à jeudi

delete VERB effacer [61]

deliberate ADJECTIVE délibéré

deliberately ADVERB exprès; **you did it deliberately** tu l'as fait exprès, **he left it there deliberately** il a fait exprès de le laisser là

delicate ADJECTIVE délicat

delicatessen NOUN épicerie (FEM) fine

delicious ADJECTIVE délicieux (FEM délicieuse)

delighted ADJECTIVE ravi; **they're delighted with their new flat** ils sont ravis de leur nouvel appartement, **I'm delighted to hear you can come** je suis ravi d'apprendre que vous pouvez venir

deliver VERB ❶ livrer [1]; **they're delivering the washing machine tomorrow** ils vont livrer la machine à laver demain ❷ distribuer [1] (mail)

delivery NOUN livraison FEM

demand NOUN demande FEM

demand VERB exiger [52]

demo NOUN (protest) manif FEM (informal)

democracy NOUN démocratie FEM

democratic ADJECTIVE démocratique

demolish VERB démolir [2]

demonstrate VERB ❶ faire [10] la démonstration de (a machine, product, or technique) ❷ (protest) manifester [1]; **to demonstrate against something** manifester contre quelque chose

demonstration NOUN ❶ (of machine, product, technique) démonstration FEM ❷ (protest) manifestation

demonstrator NOUN (in protest) manifestant MASC, manifestante FEM

denim NOUN jean MASC; **a denim jacket** un blouson en jean

Denmark NOUN Danemark MASC; **in Denmark** au Danemark, **to Denmark** au Danemark

dense ADJECTIVE dense

dent NOUN bosse FEM

dent VERB cabosser [1]

dental ADJECTIVE ❶ dentaire; **dental floss** du fil dentaire, **dental hygiene** l'hygiène dentaire ❷ **a dental appointment** un rendez-vous chez le dentiste

dental surgeon NOUN chirurgien-dentiste MASC

dentist NOUN dentiste MASC & FEM; **my mum's a dentist** ma mère est dentiste

deny VERB nier [1]

deodorant NOUN déodorant MASC

depart VERB partir [58]

department NOUN ❶ (in school, university) département MASC; **the language department** le département de langues ❷ (in a shop) rayon MASC; **the men's department** le rayon hommes

department store NOUN grand magasin MASC

departure NOUN départ MASC

departure lounge NOUN salle (FEM) d'embarquement

depend VERB to depend on dépendre [3] de, **it depends on the price** ça dépend du prix, **it depends on what you want** ça dépend de ce que tu veux, **it depends** ça dépend

deposit NOUN ❶ (when renting or hiring) caution FEM ❷ (when booking a holiday or hotel room) arrhes FEM PLURAL; **to pay a deposit** verser des arrhes ❸ (on a bottle) consigne FEM

depressed ADJECTIVE déprimé

depressing ADJECTIVE déprimant

depth NOUN profondeur FEM

deputy NOUN adjoint MASC, adjointe FEM

deputy head NOUN directeur (MASC) adjoint, directrice (FEM) adjointe

descend VERB descendre [3]

describe VERB décrire [38]

description NOUN description FEM

desert NOUN désert MASC; **in the desert** dans le désert

desert island NOUN île (FEM) déserte

deserve VERB mériter [1]

design NOUN ❶ conception FEM; the design of the plane la conception de l'avion ❷ (artistic design) design MASC; **fashion design** le stylisme ❸ (pattern) motif MASC; **a floral design** un motif floral

design VERB ❶ concevoir [66] (a machine, plane, system) ❷ créer [32] (costumes, clothes, fabric, scenery)

designer NOUN ❶ (fashion designer) styliste MASC & FEM ❷ (graphic designer) graphiste MASC & FEM

desire NOUN désir MASC

desire VERB désirer [1]

desk NOUN ❶ (in office or at home) bureau MASC ❷ (pupil's) table FEM ❸ the reception desk la réception, **the information desk** le bureau des renseignements

despair NOUN désespoir MASC

despair VERB to despair of doing désespérer [24] de faire

desperate ADJECTIVE ❶ désespéré; **a desperate attempt** une tentative désespérée ❷ to be desperate to do avoir très envie de faire, **I'm desperate to see you** j'ai très envie de te voir

despise VERB mépriser [1]

dessert NOUN dessert MASC; **what's for dessert?** qu'est-ce qu'il y a comme dessert?

destination NOUN destination FEM

destroy VERB détruire [26]

destruction NOUN destruction FEM

detached house NOUN maison (FEM) individuelle

detail NOUN détail MASC

detailed ADJECTIVE détaillé

detective NOUN ❶ (police) inspecteur (MASC) de police ❷ a private detective un détective

detective story NOUN roman (MASC) policier

detention NOUN retenue FEM

detergent NOUN détergent MASC

determined ADJECTIVE résolu; he's determined to leave il est résolu de partir

detour NOUN détour MASC

develop VERB ❶ développer [1]; to get a film developed faire développer une pellicule ❷ se développer; how children develop comment les enfants se développent

developing country NOUN pays (MASC) en voie de développement

development NOUN développement MASC

devil NOUN diable MASC

devoted ADJECTIVE dévoué

dew NOUN rosée FEM

diabetes NOUN diabète MASC

diabetic NOUN, ADJECTIVE diabète MASC & FEM; to be (a) diabetic être diabète

diaeresis NOUN tréma MASC

diagnosis NOUN diagnostic MASC

diagonal ADJECTIVE diagonal MASC (PLURAL diagonaux)

diagram NOUN schéma MASC

dial VERB composer [1] le numéro; lift the receiver and dial 142

décrochez et composez le 142, **dial 00 33 for France** faites le 00 33 pour la France

dialling tone NOUN tonalité FEM

dialogue NOUN dialogue MASC

diameter NOUN diamètre MASC

diamond NOUN ❶ diamant MASC ❷ (in cards) carreau; the jack of diamonds le valet de carreau ❸ (shape) losange MASC

diarrhoea NOUN diarrhée FEM; to have diarrhoea avoir la diarrhoée

diary NOUN ❶ agenda MASC; j'ai marqué la date de la réunion dans mon agenda I've noted the date of the meeting in my diary ❷ journal intime; to keep a diary tenir un journal (intime)

dice NOUN dé MASC; to throw the dice jeter le dé

dictation NOUN dictée FEM

dictionary NOUN dictionnaire MASC; to look up a word in the dictionary chercher un mot dans le dictionnaire

did VERB ▸ SEE **do**

die VERB ❶ mourir [54]; my grannie died in January ma grand-mère est morte en janvier ❷ to be dying to do mourir d'envie de faire, I'm dying to see them! je meurs d'envie de les voir!
• to die out disparaître [27]

diesel NOUN ❶ gazole MASC ❷ a diesel engine un moteur diesel, a diesel car une voiture diesel

diet NOUN ❶ alimentation FEM; to have a healthy diet avoir une alimentation saine ❷ (slimming or special) régime MASC; to be on a diet être au régime, **a salt-free diet** un régime sans sel

difference NOUN ❶ différence FEM; **I can't see any difference between the two** je ne vois pas la différence entre les deux, **what's the difference between ...?** quelle est la différence entre ...? ❷ **it makes a difference** ça change quelque chose, **it makes no difference** ça ne change rien, **it makes no difference what I say** je peux dire ce que je veux, ça ne change rien

different ADJECTIVE différent; **the two sisters are very different** les deux sœurs sont très différentes, **she's very different from her sister** elle est très différente de sa sœur

difficult ADJECTIVE difficile; **it's really difficult** c'est vraiment difficile, **it's difficult to decide** il est difficile de décider

difficulty NOUN ❶ difficulté FEM ❷ **to have difficulty doing** avoir du mal à faire, **I had difficulty finding your house** j'ai eu du mal à trouver ta maison

dig VERB **to dig a hole** creuser [1] un trou

digestion NOUN digestion FEM

digital ADJECTIVE numérique; **a digital recording** un enregistrement numérique, **a digital watch** une montre à affichage numérique

dim ADJECTIVE ❶ **a dim light** une lumière faible ❷ **she's a bit dim** elle est un peu bouchée (informal)

dimension NOUN dimension FEM

din NOUN vacarme MASC; **they were making a dreadful din** ils faisaient un vacarme pas possible, **stop making such a din!** arrêtez de faire ce vacarme!

dinghy NOUN ❶ **a sailing dinghy** un dériveur ❷ **a rubber dinghy** un canot pneumatique

dining room NOUN salle (FEM) à manger; **in the dining room** dans la salle à manger

dinner NOUN ❶ (evening) dîner MASC; **to invite somebody to dinner** inviter quelqu'un à dîner ❷ (midday) déjeuner MASC; **to have school dinner** manger à la cantine

dinner party NOUN dîner MASC

dinner time NOUN ❶ (evening) l'heure du dîner ❷ (midday) l'heure du déjeuner

dinosaur NOUN dinosaure MASC

diploma NOUN diplôme MASC

direct ADJECTIVE direct; **a direct flight** un vol direct

direct ADVERB directement; **the bus goes direct to the airport** le bus est direct pour l'aéroport

direct VERB ❶ réaliser [1] (programme, film) ❷ mettre en scène (play) ❸ régler (traffic)

direction NOUN ❶ direction FEM; **in the other direction** dans l'autre direction ❷ **to ask somebody for directions** demander son chemin à quelqu'un ❸ **directions for use** mode (MASC) d'emploi

directly ADVERB ❶ directement ❷ **directly afterwards** immédiatement après

director NOUN ❶ (of a company) directeur MASC, directrice FEM ❷ (of a programme or film) réalisateur MASC, réalisatrice FEM ❸ (of a play) metteur (MASC) en scène

directory NOUN annuaire MASC; **to be ex-directory** être sur la liste rouge

dirt NOUN saleté FEM

dirty ADJECTIVE sale; **my hands are dirty** j'ai les mains sales, **to get something dirty** salir quelque chose, **you'll get your dress dirty** tu vas salir ta robe, **to get dirty** se salir, **the curtains get dirty quickly** les rideaux se salissent vite

disability NOUN infirmité FEM, **does he have a disability?** est-il infirme?

disabled ADJECTIVE handicapé; **disabled people** les handicapés

disadvantage NOUN ❶ désavantage MASC ❷ **to be at a disadvantage** être désavantagé

disagree VERB **I disagree** je ne suis pas d'accord, **I disagree with James** je ne suis pas d'accord avec James

disappear VERB disparaître [27]

disappearance NOUN disparition FEM

disappointed ADJECTIVE déçu; **I was disappointed with my marks** j'ai été déçu par mes notes

disappointment NOUN déception FEM

disaster NOUN désastre MASC; **it was a complete disaster** ça a été un désastre complet

disastrous ADJECTIVE désastreux (FEM désastreuse)

disc NOUN ❶ **a compact disc** un disque compact ❷ **a slipped disc** une hernie discale ❸ **a tax disc** (for a vehicle) une vignette

discipline NOUN discipline FEM

disc-jockey NOUN disc-jockey MASC

disco NOUN ❶ soirée (FEM) disco; **they're having a disco** ils font une soirée disco ❷ (club) discothèque

disconnect VERB ❶ (the telephone, electricity) couper [1]; **have you disconnected the electricity?** est-ce que vous avez coupé l'électricité? ❷ (appliance) débrancher [1]

discount NOUN réduction FEM

discourage VERB décourager [52]

discover VERB découvrir [30]

discovery NOUN découverte FEM

discreet ADJECTIVE discret (FEM discrète)

discrimination NOUN discrimination FEM; **racial discrimination** la discrimination raciale

discuss VERB **to discuss something** discuter [1] de quelque chose, **we'll discuss the problem tomorrow** nous discuterons du problème demain, **I'm going to discuss it with Phil** je vais en discuter avec Phil

discussion NOUN discussion FEM

disease NOUN maladie FEM

disgraceful ADJECTIVE scandaleux (FEM scandaleuse)

disguise NOUN déguisement MASC; **to be in disguise** être déguisé

disguise VERB déguiser [1]; **disguised as a woman** déguisé en femme

disgust NOUN dégoût MASC

disgusted ADJECTIVE dégoûté

disgusting ADJECTIVE dégoûtant

dish NOUN ❶ plat MASC; **a large white dish** un grand plat blanc, **he cooked my favourite dish** il a préparé mon plat favori ❷ **to do the dishes** faire la vaisselle

dishcloth NOUN (for drying up) torchon MASC

dishonest ADJECTIVE malhonnête

dishonesty NOUN malhonnêteté FEM

dish towel NOUN torchon MASC

dishwasher NOUN lave-vaisselle MASC

disinfect VERB désinfecter [1]

disinfectant NOUN désinfectant MASC

disk NOUN disque MASC; **the hard disk** le disque dur

disk drive NOUN unité (FEM) de disque

dislike VERB ne pas aimer [1]; **I dislike sport** je n'aime pas le sport

dismay NOUN consternation FEM

dismiss VERB licencier [1] (an employee)

disobedient ADJECTIVE désobéissant

disobey VERB désobéir à [2] (a person), enfreindre [60] (a rule); **she disobeyed the rules** elle a enfreint les régles

display NOUN ❶ exposition FEM; **a handicrafts display** une exposition d'artisanat, **to be on display** être exposé ❷ **a window display** une vitrine ❸ **a firework display** un feu d'artifice

display VERB exposer [1]

disposable ADJECTIVE jetable

dispute NOUN dispute FEM

disqualify VERB disqualifier [1]

disrupt VERB perturber [1]

dissolve VERB dissoudre [67]

distance NOUN distance FEM; **from a distance** de loin, **in the distance** au loin, **it's within walking distance** on peut y aller à pied

distant ADJECTIVE lointain

distinct ADJECTIVE net (FEM nette)

distinctly ADVERB ❶ distinctement ❷ **it's distinctly odd** c'est vraiment bizarre

distract VERB distraire [78]

distribute VERB distribuer [1]

district NOUN ❶ (in town) quartier MASC; **a poor district of Paris** un quartier pauvre de Paris ❷ (in the country) région FEM

disturb VERB déranger [52]; **sorry to disturb you** je suis désolé de vous déranger, **do not disturb** ne pas déranger

ditch NOUN fossé MASC

ditch VERB **to ditch somebody** plaquer [1] quelqu'un (informal)

dive NOUN plongeon MASC

dive VERB plonger [52]

diver NOUN plongeur MASC, plongeuse FEM

diversion NOUN (traffic) déviation FEM

divide VERB diviser [1]

diving NOUN plongée FEM

diving board NOUN plongeoir MASC

division NOUN division FEM

divorce NOUN divorce MASC

divorce VERB divorcer [61]; **they divorced in Mexico** ils ont divorcé au Mexique

divorced ADJECTIVE divorcé; **my parents are divorced** mes parents sont divorcés

DIY NOUN bricolage MASC; **to do DIY** faire du bricolage, **a DIY shop** un magasin de bricolage

dizzy ADJECTIVE **I feel dizzy** j'ai la tête qui tourne

DJ NOUN disc jockey MASC

do VERB ❶ faire [10]; **what are you doing?** qu'est-ce que tu fais?, **I'm doing my homework** je fais mes devoirs, **what have you done with the hammer?** qu'est-ce que tu as fait du marteau? ❷ *(questions in French are formed either with 'est-ce que' or by putting the pronoun subject after the verb and a hyphen between them)* **do you want some strawberries?** est-ce que tu veux des fraises?, veux-tu des fraises?, **when does it start?** quand est-ce que ça commence?, **how did you open the door?** comment as-tu ouvert la porte? ❸ *(in negative sentences)* **don't**, **doesn't**, **didn't** ne ... pas, **I don't like mushrooms** je n'aime pas les champignons, **Rosie doesn't like spinach** Rosie n'aime pas les épinards, **you didn't shut the door** tu n'as pas fermé la porte, **it doesn't matter** ça ne fait rien ❹ *(when it refers back to another verb, 'do' is not translated)* **'do you live here?' – 'yes, I do'** est-ce que tu habites ici?' – 'oui', **she has more money than I do** elle a plus d'argent que moi, **'I live in Oxford' – 'so do I'** j'habite à Oxford' – 'moi aussi', **'I didn't**

phone Gemma' – 'neither did I' 'je n'ai pas appelé Gemma' – 'moi non plus' ❺ **don't you?**, **doesn't he? etc.** n'est-ce pas?, **you know Helen, don't you?** tu connais Helen, n'est-ce pas?, **she left on Thursday, didn't she?** elle est partie jeudi, n'est-ce pas? ❻ **that'll do** ça ira, **it'll do like that** ça ira comme ça

• **to do something up** ❶ lacer [61] *(shoes)* ❷ boutonner [1] *(cardigan, jacket)* ❸ retaper [1] *(house)*

• **to do with** ❶ regarder [1]; **it has nothing to do with him/you** ça ne le/te regarde pas ❷ **to do with something I could do with a rest** j'aurai bien besoin de me reposer

• **to do without** se passer [1] de; **we can do without knives** on peut se passer de couteaux

doctor NOUN médecin MASC; **her mother's a doctor** sa mère est médecin

document NOUN document MASC

documentary NOUN documentaire MASC

dodgems PLURAL NOUN **the dodgems** les autos *(FEM PLURAL)* tamponneuses

dog NOUN chien MASC, *(female)* chienne FEM

do-it-yourself NOUN bricolage MASC

dole NOUN allocations *(FEM PLURAL)* chômage; **to be on the dole** être au chômage

doll NOUN poupée FEM

dollar NOUN dollar MASC

dolphin NOUN dauphin MASC

Dominican NOUN Dominicain MASC, Dominicaine FEM

Dominican ADJECTIVE dominicain

Dominican Republic NOUN
République (FEM) dominicaine

domino NOUN domino MASC; **to play
dominoes** jouer aux dominos

donation NOUN don MASC

donkey NOUN âne MASC

don't ▸ SEE **do**

door NOUN ❶ porte FEM; **to open the
door** ouvrir la porte, **to shut the
door** fermer la porte ❷ (of a vehicle
or train) portière FEM

doorbell NOUN sonnerie FEM; **to ring
the doorbell** sonner à la porte,
there's the doorbell! on sonne!

doorstep NOUN pas (MASC) de la
porte

dormitory NOUN dortoir MASC

dot NOUN ❶ (written) point MASC ❷ (on
fabric) pois MASC ❸ **at ten on the dot**
à dix heures pile

double ADJECTIVE, ADVERB ❶ double;
a double helping une double
portion, **a double whisky** un double
whisky ❷ le double; **double the
time** le double du temps, **double
the price** le double du prix ❸ **a
double room** une chambre pour
deux personnes ❹ **a double bed** un
grand lit

double bass NOUN contrebasse FEM;
to play the double bass jouer de la
contrebasse

double-breasted ADJECTIVE **a
double-breasted jacket** une veste
croisée

double-decker bus NOUN autobus
(MASC) à impériale

double glazing NOUN double
vitrage MASC

doubles NOUN (in tennis) double
MASC; **to play a game of doubles**
faire un double

doubt NOUN doute MASC; **there's no
doubt about it** il n'y a aucun doute
là-dessus, **I have my doubts** j'ai des
doutes

doubt VERB **to doubt something**
douter [1] de quelque chose, **I doubt
it** j'en doute, **I doubt that** douter
que (+ subjunctive), **I doubt they'll
do it** je doute qu'il le fassent

doubtful ADJECTIVE ❶ pas sûr; **it's
doubtful** ce n'est pas sûr ❷ **to be
doubtful about doing** hésiter à
faire, **I'm doubtful about inviting
them together** j'hésite à les inviter
ensemble

dough NOUN pâte FEM

doughnut NOUN beignet MASC

Dover NOUN Douvres; **to Dover** à
Douvres

down ADVERB, PREPOSITION ❶ en bas;
he's down in the cellar il est en
bas dans la cave ❷ **down the road**
(nearby) à côté, **there's a chemist's
just down the road** il y a une
pharmacie juste à côté ❸ **to go
down** descendre, **I went down to
the kitchen** je suis descendu dans
la cuisine, **to walk down the street**
descendre la rue, **to run down
the stairs** descendre les escaliers
en courant ❹ **to come down**
descendre, **she came down from
her bedroom** elle est descendue de
sa chambre ❺ **to sit down** s'asseoir,
she sat down on the sofa elle s'est
assise sur le canapé

download VERB télécharger [52]

downstairs ADVERB ❶ en bas; **she's
downstairs in the sitting-room**

a
b
c
d
e
f
g
h
i
j
k
l
m
n
o
p
q
r
s
t
u
v
w
x
y
z

elle est en bas dans le salon, **the dog sleeps downstairs** le chien dort en bas ❷ **du dessous; the flat downstairs** l'appartement du dessous, **the people downstairs** les voisins du dessous

doze VERB **sommeiller** [1]

dozen NOUN **douzaine** FEM; **a dozen eggs** une douzaine d'œufs

drag NOUN **what a drag!** quelle barbe! *(informal)*, **she's a bit of a drag** elle n'est pas marrante *(informal)*

drag VERB **traîner** [1]

dragon NOUN **dragon** MASC

drain NOUN **égout** MASC

drain VERB **égoutter** [1] *(vegetables)*

drama NOUN ❶ *(subject)* **art** *(MASC)* **dramatique** ❷ **he made a big drama about it** il en a fait tout un cinéma *(informal)*

dramatic ADJECTIVE **spectaculaire**

draught NOUN **courant** *(MASC)* **d'air**

draughts NOUN **dames** FEM PLURAL; **to play draughts** jouer aux dames

draw NOUN ❶ *(in a match)* **match nul** MASC; **it was a draw** ils ont fait match nul ❷ *(lottery)* **tirage** *(MASC)* **au sort**

draw VERB ❶ **dessiner** [1]; **I can't draw horses** je ne sais pas dessiner les chevaux, **she can draw really well** elle dessine vraiment bien ❷ **to draw a picture** faire [10] un dessin ❸ **to draw the curtains** tirer [1] les rideaux ❹ **to draw a crowd** attirer [1] une foule de spectateurs ❺ *(in a match)* **faire** [10] **match nul; we drew three all** nous avons fait match nul trois à trois ❻ **to draw lots** tirer [1] au sort

drawback NOUN **inconvénient** MASC

drawer NOUN **tiroir** MASC

drawing NOUN **dessin** MASC

drawing pin NOUN **punaise** FEM

dreadful ADJECTIVE **affreux** *(FEM* **affreuse)*

dreadfully ADVERB **terriblement; I'm dreadfully late** je suis terriblement en retard, **I'm dreadfully sorry** je suis vraiment navré

dream NOUN **rêve** MASC; **to have a dream** faire un rêve, **I had a horrible dream last night** j'ai fait un rêve horrible cette nuit

dream VERB **rêver** [1]; **to dream about something** rêver de quelque chose

drenched ADJECTIVE **trempé; to get drenched** se faire tremper, **we got drenched on the way home** on s'est fait tremper en rentrant

dress NOUN **robe** FEM

dress VERB **to dress a child** habiller [1] un enfant
• **to dress up** se déguiser [1]; **to dress up as a vampire** se déguiser en vampire

dressed ADJECTIVE ❶ **habillé; is Tom dressed yet?** est-ce que Tom est habillé?, **she was dressed in black trousers and a yellow shirt** elle était habillée d'un pantalon noir et d'une chemise jaune ❷ **to get dressed** s'habiller, **I got dressed quickly** je me suis vite habillé

dresser NOUN *(for dishes)* **vaisselier** MASC

dressing gown NOUN **robe** *(FEM)* **de chambre**

dressing table NOUN coiffeuse FEM

drier NOUN **a hair drier** un sèche-cheveux, **a tumble drier** un sèche-linge

drift NOUN **a snow drift** une congère

drill NOUN perceuse FEM

drink NOUN ❶ boisson FEM; **a hot drink** une boisson chaude, **a cold drink** une boisson fraîche ❷ **would you like a drink?** tu veux boire quelque chose? ❸ **to go out for a drink** aller prendre un pot (informal)

drink VERB boire [22]; **he drank a glass of water** il a bu un verre d'eau

drive NOUN ❶ **to go for a drive** faire un tour en voiture ❷ (up to a house) allée FEM

drive VERB ❶ conduire [26]; **she drives very fast** elle conduit très vite, **to drive a car** conduire une voiture, **I'd like to learn to drive** j'aimerais apprendre à conduire, **can you drive?** tu sais conduire? ❷ aller en voiture; **we drove to Paris** nous sommes allés à Paris en voiture ❸ **to drive somebody (to a place)** emmener [50] quelqu'un en voiture, **Mum drove me to the station** Maman m'a emmené en voiture à la gare, **to drive somebody home** raccompagner [1] quelqu'un
• **she drives me mad!** elle me rend folle!

driver NOUN ❶ conducteur MASC, conductrice FEM ❷ (of a taxi or bus) chauffeur MASC

driving instructor NOUN moniteur (MASC) d'auto-école

driving lesson NOUN leçon (FEM) de conduite

driving licence NOUN permis (MASC) de conduire

driving school NOUN école (FEM) de conduite

driving test NOUN permis (MASC) de conduire; **to take your driving test** passer son permis, **Jenny's passed her driving test** Jenny a eu son permis

drop NOUN goutte FEM

drop VERB ❶ **to drop something** laisser [1] tomber quelque chose, **I dropped my glasses** j'ai laissé tomber mes lunettes, **I'm going to drop history next year** je vais laisser tomber l'histoire l'année prochaine, **drop it!** laisse tomber! ❷ déposer [1] (a person); **could you drop me at the station?** est-ce que tu peux me déposer à la gare?

drought NOUN sécheresse FEM

drown VERB se noyer [39]; **she drowned in the lake** elle s'est noyée dans le lac

drug NOUN ❶ (medicine) médicament MASC ❷ (illegal) **drugs** la drogue

drug abuse NOUN usage (MASC) des stupéfiants

drug addict NOUN toxicomane MASC & FEM

drug addiction NOUN toxicomanie FEM

drum NOUN ❶ tambour MASC ❷ **drums** la batterie, **to play drums** jouer de la batterie

drum kit NOUN batterie FEM

drummer NOUN batteur MASC, batteuse FEM

drunk NOUN ivrogne MASC & FEM

drunk ADJECTIVE ivre

dry ADJECTIVE sec (FEM sèche)

dry VERB ❶ sécher [24]; to let something dry laisser [1] sécher quelque chose ❷ to dry your hair se sécher les cheveux ❸ to dry your hands s'essuyer [41] les mains, to dry the dishes s'essuyer [41] la vaisselle ❹ to dry the washing faire [10] sécher le linge

dry cleaner's NOUN teinturerie FEM

dryer NOUN ▸ SEE **drier**

dual carriageway NOUN route (FEM) à quatre voies

dubbed ADJECTIVE a dubbed film un film doublé

duck NOUN canard MASC

due ADJECTIVE, ADVERB ❶ to be due to do devoir faire, we're due to leave on Thursday nous devons partir jeudi, Paul's due back soon Paul doit bientôt revenir ❷ due to en raison de, the match has been cancelled due to bad weather le match a été annulé en raison du mauvais temps

duke NOUN duc MASC

dull ADJECTIVE ❶ dull weather un temps maussade, it's a dull day today il fait un temps maussade aujourd'hui ❷ (boring) ennuyeux (FEM ennuyeuse)

dumb ADJECTIVE ❶ muet (FEM muette); to be deaf and dumb être sourd-muet ❷ (stupid) bête; he asked some dumb questions il a posé des questions bêtes

dummy NOUN (for a baby) tétine FEM

dump VERB ❶ jeter [48] (rubbish) ❷ plaquer [1] (a person)

(informal); she's dumped her boyfriend elle a plaqué son copain

dune NOUN dune FEM

dungarees PLURAL NOUN salopette FEM SINGULAR

dungeon NOUN cachot MASC

Dunkirk NOUN Dunkerque

during PREPOSITION pendant; during the night pendant la nuit, I saw her during the holidays je l'ai vue pendant les vacances

dusk NOUN at dusk à la nuit tombante

dust NOUN poussière FEM

dust VERB épousseter [48]

dustbin NOUN poubelle FEM; to put something in the dustbin jeter quelque chose à la poubelle

dustman NOUN éboueur MASC

dusty ADJECTIVE poussiéreux (FEM poussiéreuse)

Dutch NOUN ❶ (language) hollandais MASC ❷ the Dutch (people) les Hollandais MASC PLURAL

Dutch ADJECTIVE hollandais

duty NOUN ❶ devoir MASC; to have a duty to do avoir le devoir de faire, you have a duty to inform us vous avez le devoir de nous informer ❷ to be on duty être de service, to be on night duty être de service de nuit, I'm off duty tonight je ne suis pas de service ce soir

duty-free ADJECTIVE hors taxes; the duty-free shops les boutiques hors taxes, duty-free purchases les achats hors taxes

duvet NOUN couette FEM

duvet cover NOUN housse (FEM) de couette

DVD NOUN DVD MASC

dwarf NOUN nain MASC, naine FEM

dye NOUN teinture FEM

dye VERB teindre [60]; **to dye your hair** se teindre les cheveux, **I'm going to dye my hair pink** je vais me teindre les cheveux en rose

dynamic ADJECTIVE dynamique

dyslexia NOUN dyslexie FEM

dyslexic ADJECTIVE dyslexique

Ee

each ADJECTIVE chaque; **each time** chaque fois, **curtains for each window** des rideaux pour chaque fenêtre

each PRONOUN chacun (FEM chacune); **my sisters each have a computer** mes sœurs ont chacune un ordinateur, **she gave us an apple each** elle nous a donné une pomme à chacun, **each of you** chacun de vous, chacune de vous, **we each got a present** chacun de nous a reçu un cadeau, **the tickets cost ten pounds each** les billets coûtent dix livres chacun

each other PRONOUN ('each other' is usually translated using a reflexive pronoun) **they love each other** ils

s'aiment, **we know each other** nous nous connaissons, **do you often see each other?** est-ce que vous vous voyez souvent?

eagle NOUN aigle MASC

ear NOUN oreille FEM

earache NOUN **to have earache** avoir une otite

earlier ADVERB ❶ (a while ago) tout à l'heure; **your brother phoned earlier** ton frère a appelé tout à l'heure ❷ (not as late) plus tôt; **we should have started earlier** nous aurions dû commencer plus tôt, **earlier in the morning** plus tôt le matin

early ADVERB ❶ (in the morning) tôt; **to get up early** se lever tôt, **it's too early** il est trop tôt ❷ (for an appointment) en avance; **we're early, the train doesn't leave until ten** nous sommes en avance, le train ne part qu'à dix heures, **Grandma likes to be early** Grand-mère aime être en avance

early ADJECTIVE ❶ (one of the first) premier (FEM première); **in the early months** pendant les premiers mois, **I'm getting the early train** je prends le premier train ❷ **to have an early lunch** déjeuner tôt, **Jan's having an early night** Jan va se coucher tôt, **we're making an early start** nous partons tôt ❸ **in the early afternoon** en début d'après-midi, **in the early hours** au petit matin

earn VERB gagner [1] (money); **Richard earns four pounds an hour** Richard gagne quatre livres de l'heure

earnings PLURAL NOUN salaire MASC

earphones NOUN casque MASC

earring NOUN boucle (FEM) d'oreille

earth NOUN terre FEM; **life on earth** la vie sur terre
• **what on earth are you doing?** mais qu'est-ce que tu fais là?

earthquake NOUN tremblement (MASC) de terre

easily ADVERB ❶ (without difficulty) facilement ❷ (by far) de loin; **he's easily the best** il est de loin le meilleur

east NOUN est MASC; **in the east** à l'est

east ADJECTIVE, ADVERB est; **the east side** le côté est, **an east wind** un vent d'est, **east of Paris** à l'est de Paris

Easter NOUN Pâques MASC; **they're coming at Easter** ils viennent à Pâques, **Happy Easter** Joyeuses Pâques

Easter Day NOUN dimanche (MASC) de Pâques

Easter egg NOUN œuf (MASC) de Pâques

Eastern Europe NOUN Europe (FEM) de l'Est

easy ADJECTIVE facile; **it's easy!** c'est facile!, **it was easy to make** c'était facile à faire

eat VERB ❶ manger [52]; **he was eating a banana** il mangeait une banane, **we're going to have something to eat** nous allons manger quelque chose ❷ prendre [64] (a meal); **we were eating breakfast** nous prenions le petit déjeuner ❸ **to eat out** manger au restaurant

EC NOUN (short for **European Community**) CE FEM, Communauté (FEM) européenne

echo NOUN écho MASC

echo VERB retentir [2]

eclipse NOUN éclipse FEM

ecological ADJECTIVE écologique

ecologist NOUN écologiste MASC & FEM

ecology NOUN écologie FEM

economic ADJECTIVE ❶ (to do with the economy) économique ❷ (profitable) rentable

economical ADJECTIVE ❶ économe (a person) ❷ économique (way of doing something); **it's more economical to buy a big one** c'est plus économique d'acheter un grand

economics NOUN économie FEM

economy NOUN économie FEM

eczema NOUN eczéma MASC

edge NOUN ❶ bord MASC; **the edge of the table** le bord de la table, **at the edge of the lake** au bord du lac ❷ **to be on edge** être énervé

edible ADJECTIVE comestible

Edinburgh NOUN Édimbourg

edit VERB éditer [1]

editor NOUN (of a newspaper) rédacteur (MASC) en chef, rédactrice (FEM) en chef

educate VERB (a teacher) instruire [26]

education NOUN éducation FEM

educational ADJECTIVE éducatif (FEM éducative)

effect NOUN effet MASC; **the effect of the accident** l'effet de l'accident, **to have an effect on** avoir un effet sur,

it had a good effect on the whole family ça a eu un bon effet sur toute la famille, **special effects** les effets spéciaux

effective ADJECTIVE **efficace**

efficient ADJECTIVE **efficace**

effort NOUN **effort** MASC; **to make an effort** faire un effort, **David made an effort to help us** David a fait un effort pour nous aider, **he didn't even make the effort to apologize** il n'a même pas fait l'effort pour s'excuser

e.g. ABBREVIATION **par ex**

egg NOUN **œuf** MASC; **a dozen eggs** une douzaine d'œufs, **a fried egg** un œuf au plat, **two boiled eggs** deux œufs à la coque, **a hard-boiled egg** un œuf dur, **scrambled eggs** les œufs brouillés

egg-cup NOUN **coquetier** MASC

eggshell NOUN **coquille** (FEM) **d'œuf**

egg-white NOUN **blanc** (MASC) **d'œuf**

egg-yolk NOUN **jaune** (MASC) **d'œuf**

eight NUMBER **huit** MASC; **Maya's eight** Maya a huit ans, **at eight o'clock** à huit heures

eighteen NUMBER **dix-huit** MASC; **Jason's eighteen** Jason a dix-huit ans

eighth NUMBER ❶ **huitième** ❷ **the eighth of July** le huit juillet, **on the eighth floor** au huitième étage

eighty NUMBER **quatre-vingts**; **eighty-five** quatre-vingt-cinq (note that the 's' disappears when another number follows)

Eire NOUN **la République d'Irlande**; **in Eire** en République d'Irlande

either PRONOUN ❶ (one or the other)

l'un ou l'autre; **choose either (of them)** choisis l'un ou l'autre, **I don't like either (of them)** je n'aime ni l'un ni l'autre ❷ (both) **les deux**; **either is possible** tous les deux sont possibles

either CONJUNCTION ❶ **either … or** ou … ou, **either Thursday or Friday** ou jeudi ou vendredi, **either Susie or Judy** ou Susie ou Judy, **he either wrote or phoned** il a ou écrit ou appelé ❷ (with a negative) **non plus**; **he doesn't want to either** il ne veut pas non plus, **I don't know them either** je ne les connais pas non plus

elastic NOUN, ADJECTIVE **élastique** MASC

elastic band NOUN **élastique** MASC

elbow NOUN **coude** MASC

elder ADJECTIVE **aîné**; **her elder brother** son frère aîné

elderly ADJECTIVE **âgé**; **the elderly** les personnes (FEM PLURAL) âgées

eldest ADJECTIVE **aîné**; **her eldest brother** son frère aîné

elect VERB **élire** [51]; **she has been elected** elle a été élue

election NOUN **élection** FEM; **in the election** aux élections, **to call a general election** fixer les élections législatives

electric ADJECTIVE **électrique**

electrical ADJECTIVE **électrique**

electrician NOUN **électricien** MASC, **électricienne** FEM

electricity NOUN **électricité** FEM; **to turn off the electricity** couper le courant

electronic ADJECTIVE **électronique**

electronics NOUN **électronique** FEM

a
b
c
d
e
f
g
h
i
j
k
l
m
n
o
p
q
r
s
t
u
v
w
x
y
z

elegant ADJECTIVE **élégant**

element NOUN **élément** MASC

elephant NOUN **éléphant** MASC

eleven NUMBER **onze** MASC; **Josh is eleven** Josh a onze ans, **at eleven o'clock** à onze heures, **a football eleven** une équipe de football

eleventh NUMBER **onzième**; **the eleventh of May** le onze mai, **on the eleventh floor** à l'onzième étage

eliminate VERB **éliminer** [1]

else ADVERB ❶ **d'autre**; **somebody else** quelqu'un d'autre, **did you see anyone else?** as-tu vu quelqu'un d'autre?, **nothing else** rien d'autre, **I don't want anything else** je ne veux rien d'autre ❷ **something else** autre chose, **would you like something else?** désirez-vous autre chose? ❸ **somewhere else** ailleurs ❹ **or else** sinon, **hurry up, or else we'll be late** dépêche-toi, sinon nous serons en retard

email NOUN **email** MASC, **courrier** (MASC) **électronique**

embankment NOUN ❶ (by a river) **quai** MASC ❷ (by a railway) **remblai** MASC

embarrassed ADJECTIVE **gêné**; **I was terribly embarrassed** j'étais très gêné

embarrassing ADJECTIVE **gênant**

embarrassment NOUN **embarras** MASC, **gêne** FEM

embassy NOUN **ambassade** FEM; **the French Embassy** l'ambassade de France

embroider VERB **broder** [1]

embroidery NOUN **broderie** FEM

emergency NOUN **cas** (MASC) **d'urgence**; **in an emergency, break the glass** en cas d'urgence, cassez la vitre, **it's an emergency!** c'est urgent!

emergency exit NOUN **sortie** (FEM) **de secours**

emergency landing NOUN **atterrissage** (MASC) **d'urgence**

emotion NOUN **émotion** FEM

emotional ADJECTIVE ❶ **ému** (a person); **she was quite emotional** elle était tout émue ❷ (a speech or an occasion) **chargé d'émotion**

emperor NOUN **empereur** MASC

emphasis NOUN **accent** MASC

emphasize VERB **he emphasized that it wasn't compulsory** il a insisté sur le fait que ce n'était pas obligatoire

empire NOUN **empire** MASC; **the Roman Empire** l'Empire Romain

employ VERB **employer** [39]

employee NOUN **salarié** MASC, **salariée** FEM

employer NOUN **employeur** MASC, **employeuse** FEM

employment NOUN **travail** MASC

empress NOUN **impératrice** FEM

empty ADJECTIVE **vide**; **an empty bottle** une bouteille vide, **the room was empty** la pièce était vide

empty VERB **vider** [1]; **I emptied the teapot into the sink** j'ai vidé la théière dans l'évier

enchanting ADJECTIVE **ravissant**

enclose VERB (in a letter) **joindre** [49]; **please find enclosed a cheque** veuillez trouver ci-joint un chèque

encore NOUN **bis** MASC; **to give an encore** jouer un bis

encourage VERB **encourager** [52]; **to encourage somebody to do something** encourager quelqu'un à faire quelque chose, **Mum encouraged me to try again** Maman m'a encouragé à recommencer

encouragement NOUN **encouragement** MASC

encouraging ADJECTIVE **encourageant**

encyclopedia NOUN **encyclopédie** FEM

end NOUN ❶ (last part) **fin** FEM; '**The End**' 'Fin', **at the end of the film** à la fin du film, **by the end of the day** à la fin de la journée, **in the end I went home** finalement je suis rentré chez moi, **Sally's coming at the end of June** Sally viendra fin juin ❷ (of a table, garden, stick, or road, for example) **bout** MASC; **hold the other end** tiens l'autre bout, **at the end of the street** au bout de la rue ❸ (in tennis or football) **côté** MASC; **to change ends** changer de côté

end VERB ❶ (to put an end to) **mettre** [11] **fin à** (an arrangement); **they've ended the strike** ils ont mis fin à la grève ❷ (to come to an end) **se terminer** [1]; **the day ended with a dinner** la journée s'est terminée par un dîner

• **to end up** ❶ **to end up doing** finir [2] par faire, **we ended up taking a taxi** nous avons fini par prendre un taxi ❷ **to end up somewhere** se retrouver [1] quelque part, **Rob ended up in San Francisco** Rob s'est retrouvé à San Francisco

endangered ADJECTIVE **menacé**; **an endangered species** une espèce en voie d'extinction

ending NOUN **fin** FEM

endless ADJECTIVE **interminable** (a day or a journey, for example)

enemy NOUN **ennemi** MASC, **ennemie** FEM; **to make enemies** se faire des ennemis

energetic ADJECTIVE **énergique**

energy NOUN **énergie** FEM

engaged ADJECTIVE ❶ (to be married) **fiancé**; **they're engaged** ils sont fiancés, **to get engaged** se fiancer [61] ❷ (a phone or toilet) **occupé**; **it's engaged, I'll ring later** c'est occupé, j'appellerai plus tard

engagement NOUN (to marry) **fiançailles** FEM PLURAL

engagement ring NOUN **bague** (FEM) **de fiançailles**

engine NOUN ❶ (in a car) **moteur** MASC ❷ (pulling a train) **locomotive** FEM

engineer NOUN ❶ (who comes for repairs) **technicien** MASC ❷ (who builds roads and bridges) **ingénieur** MASC

engineering NOUN **ingénierie** FEM; **to study engineering** faire des études d'ingénieur

England NOUN **Angleterre** FEM; **in England** en Angleterre, **to England** en Angleterre, **I am from England** je suis anglais

English NOUN ❶ (the language) **anglais** MASC; **do you speak English?** parlez-vous anglais?, **he answered in English** il a répondu en anglais ❷ (English people) **the English** les Anglais MASC PLURAL

English ADJECTIVE ❶ (of or from England) anglais; **the English team** l'équipe anglaise ❷ **an English lesson** un cours d'anglais, **our English teacher** notre professeur d'anglais

English Channel NOUN **the English Channel** la Manche

Englishman NOUN Anglais MASC

Englishwoman NOUN Anglaise FEM

enjoy VERB ❶ aimer [1]; **did you enjoy the party?** as-tu aimé la soirée?, **we really enjoyed the concert** nous avons beaucoup aimé le concert ❷ **to enjoy doing** aimer faire, **I enjoy swimming** j'aime nager, **do you enjoy living in York?** aimez-vous vivre à York? ❸ **to enjoy oneself** s'amuser [1], **we really enjoyed ourselves** nous nous sommes très bien amusés, **enjoy yourselves!** amusez-vous bien!, **did you enjoy yourself?** tu t'es bien amusé?

enjoyable ADJECTIVE agréable

enlarge VERB agrandir [2] (a photo, for example)

enlargement NOUN (of a photo) agrandissement MASC

enormous ADJECTIVE énorme

enough ADVERB, PRONOUN ❶ assez; **there's enough for everyone** il y en a assez pour tout le monde ❷ (followed by a noun) assez de; **is there enough bread?** est-ce qu'il y a assez de pain? ❸ (followed by an adjective or adverb) suffisamment; **big enough** suffisamment grand, **slowly enough** suffisamment lentement ❹ **that's enough** ça suffit

enquire VERB se renseigner [1]; **I'm going to enquire about the trains** je vais me renseigner sur les trains

enquiry NOUN demande (FEM) de renseignements; **to make enquiries about something** demander des renseignements sur quelque chose

enrol VERB s'inscrire [38]; **I want to enrol on the course** je veux m'inscrire au cours

enter VERB ❶ (to go inside) entrer [1] dans (a room or building); **we all entered the church** nous sommes tous entrés dans l'église ❷ **to enter for** s'inscrire [38] à (an exam or competition) **s'inscrire pour** (a race)

entertain VERB ❶ (to keep amused) divertir [2]; **something to entertain the children** quelque chose pour divertir les enfants ❷ (to have people round) recevoir [66]; **they don't entertain much** ils reçoivent peu

entertaining NOUN **they do a lot of entertaining** ils reçoivent beaucoup

entertaining ADJECTIVE amusant

entertainment NOUN (fun) distractions FEM PLURAL; **there wasn't much entertainment in the evenings** il n'y avait pas beaucoup de distractions le soir

enthusiasm NOUN enthousiasme MASC

enthusiast NOUN passionné MASC, passionnée FEM; **he's a rugby enthusiast** c'est un passionné de rugby

enthusiastic ADJECTIVE enthousiaste

entire ADJECTIVE entier (FEM entière); **the entire class** la classe entière

entirely ADVERB complètement

entrance NOUN entrée FEM

entry NOUN *(the way in)* entrée FEM; 'no entry' 'défense d'entrer'

entry phone NOUN interphone MASC

envelope NOUN enveloppe FEM

envious ADJECTIVE envieux *(FEM envieuse)*; **he's envious of my exam results** il est jaloux de mes résultats d'examen

environment NOUN environnement MASC

environmental ADJECTIVE écologique

environment-friendly ADJECTIVE écologique

envy NOUN envie FEM

epidemic NOUN épidémie FEM

epileptic NOUN épileptique MASC & FEM

episode NOUN épisode MASC

equal ADJECTIVE égal MASC *(PLURAL égaux)*; **in equal quantities** en quantités égales

equal VERB égaler [1]

equality NOUN égalité FEM

equalize VERB égaliser [1]; **they equalized in the last minute** ils ont égalisé dans la dernière minute

equally ADVERB *(to share)* en parts égales; **we divided it equally** nous l'avons divisé en parts égales

equator NOUN équateur MASC

equip VERB équiper [1]; **well equipped for the hike** bien équipé pour la randonnée, **equipped with rucksacks** équipés de sacs à dos

equipment NOUN ❶ *(for sport)* équipement MASC ❷ matériel MASC; **laboratory equipment** le matériel de laboratoire ❸ *(for sports)* équipement MASC

equivalent ADJECTIVE **to be equivalent to** être équivalent à

error NOUN ❶ *(in spelling or typing)* faute FEM; **a spelling error** une faute d'orthographe ❷ *(in maths or on a computer)* erreur FEM

error message NOUN message *(MASC)* d'erreur

escalator NOUN escalier *(MASC)* mécanique

escape NOUN *(from prison)* évasion FEM

escape VERB ❶ *(a person)* s'évader [1] ❷ *(an animal)* s'échapper [1]

escort NOUN escorte FEM; **a police escort** une escorte de police

especially ADJECTIVE ❶ *(above all)* surtout; **there are lots of tourists, especially in August** il y a beaucoup de touristes, surtout en août ❷ *(unusually)* particulièrement; **'is he rich?' – 'not especially'** 'est-il riche?' – 'pas particulièrement'

essay NOUN rédaction FEM; **an essay on pollution** une rédaction sur la pollution

essential ADJECTIVE essentiel *(FEM essentielle)*; **it's essential to reply quickly** il est essentiel de répondre vite

establishment NOUN *(an organization)* établissement MASC

estate NOUN ❶ *(a housing estate)* cité FEM ❷ *(a big house and grounds)* domaine MASC

a b c d e f g h i j k l m n o p q r s t u v w x y z

estate agent's NOUN agence (FEM) immobilière

estate car NOUN break MASC

estimate NOUN ❶ (a quote for work) devis MASC ❷ (a rough guess) estimation FEM

estimate VERB évaluer [1]

etc ABBREVIATION etc

ethnic ADJECTIVE ethnique; an ethnic minority une minorité ethnique

EU NOUN (short for **European Union**) Union (FEM) européenne

euro NOUN euro MASC; the euro is divided into cents l'euro est divisé en centimes

Europe NOUN Europe FEM; in Europe en Europe, to Europe en Europe

European NOUN Européen MASC, Européenne FEM

European ADJECTIVE européen (FEM européenne)

European Union NOUN Union (FEM) européenne

eurozone NOUN zone (FEM) euro

evacuate VERB faire [10] évacuer; the police evacuated the building la police a fait évacuer l'immeuble

evaporate VERB s'évaporer [1]

eve NOUN Christmas Eve la veille de Noël, New Year's Eve la Saint-Sylvestre

even[1] ADVERB ❶ même; even Lisa didn't like it même Lisa ne l'a pas aimé, without even asking sans même demander ❷ even if même si, even if they arrive même s'ils arrivent ❸ not even même pas, I don't like animals, not even dogs

je n'aime pas les animaux, même pas les chiens ❹ even bigger encore plus grand, even more embarrassing encore plus gênant, even faster encore plus vite ❺ even more than encore plus que, I liked the song even more than their last one j'ai aimé la chanson encore plus que leur dernière ❻ even so quand même, even so, we had a good time nous nous sommes bien amusés quand même

even[2] ADJECTIVE ❶ (a surface or layer) régulier (FEM régulière) ❷ (a number) pair; six is an even number six est un numéro pair ❸ (with the same score) à égalité (competitors); Lee and Blair are even Lee et Blair sont à égalité

evening NOUN ❶ soir MASC; this evening ce soir, at six o'clock in the evening à six heures du soir, tomorrow evening demain soir, on Thursday evening jeudi soir, the evening before la veille au soir, every evening tous les soirs, I work in the evening(s) je travaille le soir, the evening meal le repas du soir ❷ (from beginning to end) soirée FEM; during the evening pendant la soirée, an evening with Pavarotti une soirée avec Pavarotti

evening class NOUN cours (MASC) du soir

event NOUN ❶ (a happening) évènement MASC ❷ (in athletics) épreuve FEM; track events les épreuves de vitesse ❸ in any event, at all events de toute façon

eventful ADJECTIVE mouvementé (a day or an outing)

eventually ADVERB finalement

ever ADVERB ❶ (at any time) jamais; **hardly ever** presque jamais, **have you ever noticed that?** as-tu jamais remarqué ça?, **no-one ever came** personne n'est jamais venu, **hotter than ever** plus chaud que jamais, **more slowly than ever** plus lentement que jamais ❷ (always) toujours; **as cheerful as ever** toujours aussi gai, **the same as ever** toujours le même ❸ **ever since** depuis, **and it's been raining ever since** et depuis il pleut tout le temps

every ADJECTIVE ❶ tous (FEM toutes); **every house has a garden** toutes les maisons ont un jardin, **every day** tous les jours, **every Monday** tous les lundis, **every ten kilometres** tous les dix kilomètres, **I've seen every one of his films** j'ai vu tous ses films ❷ (each) chaque; **every time** chaque fois ❸ **every now and then** de temps en temps

everybody, **everyone** PRONOUN tout le monde; **everybody knows that ...** tout le monde sait que ..., **everyone else** tous les autres

everything PRONOUN tout; **everything is ready** tout est prêt, **everything's fine** tout va bien, **everything else** tout le reste, **everything you said** tout ce que tu as dit

everywhere ADVERB partout; **there was mud everywhere** il y avait de la boue partout, **everywhere she went** partout où elle allait, **everywhere else** partout ailleurs

evidently ADVERB manifestement

evil NOUN mal MASC

evil ADJECTIVE mauvais

exact ADJECTIVE exact; **the exact amount** la somme exacte, **it's the**

exact opposite c'est exactement le contraire

exactly ADVERB exactement; **they're exactly the same age** ils ont exactement le même âge, **yes, exactly** oui, exactement

exaggerate VERB exagérer [24]

exaggeration NOUN exagération FEM

exam NOUN examen MASC; **a history exam** un examen d'histoire, **to sit an exam** passer un examen, **to pass an exam** réussir un examen, **to fail an exam** échouer à un examen

examination NOUN examen MASC

examine VERB examiner [1]

examiner NOUN examinateur MASC, examinatrice FEM

example NOUN exemple MASC; **for example** par exemple, **to set a good example** donner l'exemple

excellent ADJECTIVE excellent

except PREPOSITION ❶ sauf; **except in March** sauf au mois de mars, **every day except Tuesday** tous les jours sauf le mardi, **except when it rains** sauf quand il pleut ❷ **except for** sauf, **except for the children** sauf les enfants

exception NOUN exception FEM; **without exception** sans exception, **with the exception of** à l'exception de

exchange NOUN échange MASC; **in exchange for his help** en échange de son aide, **an exchange visit** un voyage d'échange

exchange VERB échanger [52]; **can I exchange this shirt for a smaller one?** puis-je échanger cette chemise contre une plus petite?

A
B
C
D
E
F
G
H
I
J
K
L
M
N
O
P
Q
R
S
T
U
V
W
X
Y
Z

exchange rate NOUN taux (MASC) d'échange

excite VERB exciter [1]

excited ADJECTIVE ❶ excité (a person or animal); **the children are excited** les enfants sont excités ❷ **to get excited** s'exciter, **the dogs get excited when they hear the car** les chiens s'excitent quand ils entendent la voiture

excitement NOUN excitation FEM

exciting ADJECTIVE passionnant; **a really exciting film** un film vraiment passionnant

exclamation mark NOUN point (MASC) d'exclamation

excursion NOUN excursion FEM

excuse NOUN excuse FEM; **Gary has a good excuse** Gary a une bonne excuse, **that's no excuse** ce n'est pas une excuse

excuse VERB (apologizing) **excuse me!** excusez-moi!

execute VERB exécuter [1]

exercise NOUN exercice MASC; **a maths exercise** un exercice de maths, **physical exercise** l'exercice physique

exercise bicycle NOUN vélo (MASC) d'appartement

exercise book NOUN cahier MASC; **my French exercise book** mon cahier de français

exhaust (pipe) NOUN pot (MASC) d'échappement

exhausted ADJECTIVE épuisé

exhaust fumes NOUN gaz (MASC PLURAL) d'échappement

exhibition NOUN exposition FEM; **the Cézanne exhibition** l'exposition Cézanne

exist VERB exister [1]

exit NOUN sortie FEM

expand VERB s'agrandir [2]; **the town is expanding** la ville se développe

expect VERB ❶ attendre [3] (guests or a baby); **we're expecting thirty people** nous attendons trente personnes ❷ s'attendre [3] à (something to happen); **I didn't expect that** je ne m'attendais pas à ça, **I didn't expect it at all** je ne m'y attendais pas du tout ❸ (as a supposition) imaginer [1]; **I expect you're tired** j'imagine que tu es fatigué, **I expect she'll bring her boyfriend** j'imagine qu'elle amènera son copain, **yes, I expect so** oui, j'imagine

expedition NOUN expédition FEM

expel VERB **to be expelled** (from school) se faire [10] renvoyer

expenses NOUN frais MASC PLURAL

expensive ADJECTIVE cher (FEM chère); **those shoes are too expensive for me** ces chaussures sont trop chères pour moi, **the most expensive dresses** les robes les plus chers

experience NOUN expérience FEM

experienced ADJECTIVE expérimenté

experiment NOUN expérience FEM; **to do an experiment** faire une expérience

expert NOUN spécialiste MASC & FEM; **he's a computer expert** c'est un spécialiste en informatique

expire VERB expirer [1]

expiry date NOUN date (FEM) d'expiration

explain VERB expliquer [1]

explanation NOUN explication FEM

explode VERB exploser [1]

explore VERB explorer [1]

explosion NOUN explosion FEM

export NOUN exportation FEM; **our chief export is wool** la laine est notre premier produit d'exportation

export VERB exporter [1]; **Russia exports a lot of oil and timber** la Russie exporte beaucoup de pétrole et de bois

exposure NOUN (of a film) pose FEM; **a 24-exposure film** une pellicule de vingt-quatre poses

express NOUN (a train) rapide MASC

express VERB ❶ exprimer [1] ❷ **to express yourself** s'exprimer

expression NOUN expression FEM

extend VERB agrandir [2] (a building)

extension NOUN ❶ (to a house) addition FEM ❷ (telephone) poste MASC; **can I have extension 2347 please?** est-ce que je peux avoir le poste vingt-trois quarante-sept, s'il vous plaît? (note that in spoken French telephone numbers are usually broken down into groups of two figures; this applies to longer numbers as well) ❸ (electrical) rallonge FEM

extension lead NOUN rallonge FEM

extension number NOUN numéro (MASC) de poste

exterior ADJECTIVE extérieur

extinct ADJECTIVE ❶ (species) disparu ❷ (volcano) éteint

extinguish VERB éteindre [60]

extinguisher NOUN (fire extinguisher) extincteur MASC

extra ADJECTIVE supplémentaire; **extra homework** des devoirs supplémentaires, **wine is extra** le vin est en supplément, **you have to pay extra** il faut payer un supplément, **at no extra charge** sans supplément

extra ADVERB **extra hot** extra-chaud, **extra large** extra-grand

extraordinary ADJECTIVE extraordinaire

extra-special ADJECTIVE exceptionnel (FEM exceptionnelle)

extra time NOUN (in football) prolongation FEM; **to go into extra time** jouer les prolongations

extravagant ADJECTIVE dépensier (FEM dépensière) (a person)

extreme NOUN extrême MASC; **to go to extremes** pousser les choses à l'extrême

extreme ADJECTIVE extrême

extremely ADVERB extrêmement; **extremely fast** extrêmement vite

eye NOUN œil MASC (PLURAL yeux); **my left eye** mon œil gauche, **a girl with blue eyes** une fille aux yeux bleus, **shut your eyes!** ferme les yeux!
- **to keep an eye on something** surveiller quelque chose
- **to make eyes at somebody** faire les yeux doux à quelqu'un

eyebrow NOUN sourcil MASC

eyelash NOUN cil MASC

eyelid NOUN paupière FEM

eyeliner NOUN eye-liner MASC

eye make-up NOUN maquillage (MASC) pour les yeux

eye shadow NOUN fard (MASC) à paupières

eyesight NOUN vue FEM

fabric NOUN (cloth) tissu MASC

fabulous ADJECTIVE sensationnel (FEM sensationnelle)

face NOUN ❶ (of a person) visage MASC; **you've got chocolate on your face** tu as du chocolat sur le visage ❷ **to pull a face** faire une grimace ❸ (of a clock or watch) cadran MASC

face VERB ❶ (a person) faire [10] face à; **she faced her attacker** elle a fait face à son agresseur ❷ **the house faces the park** la maison donne sur le jardin public ❸ (to stand the idea of) avoir [5] le courage de; **I can't face going back** je n'ai pas le courage de rentrer ❹ **to face up to something** faire face à quelque chose

face cloth NOUN gant (MASC) de toilette

facilities PLURAL NOUN ❶ **the school has good sports facilities** l'école dispose d'un bon ensemble sportif ❷ **the flat has cooking facilities** l'appartement a une cuisine équipée

fact NOUN fait MASC; **the fact is that ...** le fait est que ..., **in fact** en fait, **is that a fact?** vraiment?

factory NOUN usine FEM

fade VERB ❶ (fabric) se décolorer [1]; **faded jeans** un jean délavé ❷ **the colours have faded** les couleurs ont passé

fail VERB ❶ rater [1] (a test or exam); **I failed my driving test** j'ai raté mon permis ❷ échouer [1]; **three students failed** trois étudiants ont échoué ❸ (not to do) **to fail to do** manquer [1] de faire, **he failed to contact us** il a manqué de nous contacter
- **without fail** sans faute; **ring me without fail** appelle-moi sans faute

failure NOUN ❶ échec MASC; **it was a terrible failure** c'était un échec terrible ❷ (a breakdown in a machine) panne FEM; **a power failure** une panne de courant

faint ADJECTIVE ❶ **to feel faint** se sentir [58] mal ❷ (slight) léger (FEM légère); **a faint smell of gas** une légère odeur de gaz, **I haven't the faintest idea** je n'en ai pas la moindre idée ❸ (a voice or sound) faible

faint VERB s'évanouir [2]; **Lisa fainted** Lisa s'est évanouie

fair NOUN foire FEM

fair ADJECTIVE ❶ (not unfair) juste; **it's not fair!** ce n'est pas juste! ❷ (hair) blond; **he's fair-haired** il a les cheveux blonds ❸ (skin) clair; **people with fair skin** les gens qui ont la peau claire ❹ (fairly good) assez bon *(FEM* assez bonne) *(a chance, condition, or performance)*; **her history is fair** son histoire est assez bonne ❺ *(weather)* **if it's fair tomorrow** s'il ne pleut pas demain

fairground *NOUN* champ *(MASC)* de foire

fairly *ADVERB (quite)* assez; **she's fairly happy** elle est assez contente

fairy *NOUN* fée *FEM*

fairy tale *NOUN* conte *(MASC)* de fées

faith *NOUN* ❶ *(trust)* confiance *FEM*; **to have faith in somebody** avoir confiance en quelqu'un ❷ *(religious belief)* foi *FEM*

faithful *ADJECTIVE* fidèle

faithfully *ADVERB* **yours faithfully** veuillez agréer, Monsieur *(or* Madame) mes salutations distinguées

fake *NOUN* faux *MASC*; **the diamonds were fakes** les diamants étaient des faux

fake *ADJECTIVE* faux *(FEM* fausse) *(goes before the noun)*; **a fake passport** un faux passeport

fall *NOUN* chute *FEM*; **to have a fall** tomber

fall *VERB* ❶ tomber [1]; **mind, you'll fall** attention, tu vas tomber, **Tony fell off his bike** Tony est tombé de son vélo, **she fell downstairs** elle est tombée dans l'escalier, **my jacket fell on the floor** ma veste est tombée par terre ❷ *(the temperature)* descendre [3]; **it fell to minus eleven last night** il est descendu à moins onze cette nuit ❸ *(prices)* baisser [1]

false *ADJECTIVE* faux *(FEM* fausse) *(goes before the noun)*; **a false alarm** une fausse alerte

false teeth *PLURAL NOUN* dentier *MASC*

fame *NOUN* renommée *FEM*

familiar *ADJECTIVE* familier *(FEM* familière); **your face is familiar** votre visage m'est familier

family *NOUN* famille *FEM*; **a family of six** une famille de six personnes, **Ben's one of the family** Ben fait partie de la famille, **the Barnes family** la famille Barnes

family name *NOUN* nom *(MASC)* de famille

famous *ADJECTIVE* célèbre

fan *NOUN* ❶ fan *MASC & FEM (informal)*; **Diana's an Oasis fan** Diana est une fan de Oasis ❷ *(of a team)* supporter *MASC*; **Brian's a Chelsea fan** Brian est un supporter de Chelsea ❸ *(electric, for cooling)* ventilateur *MASC* ❹ *(that you hold in your hand)* éventail *MASC*

fanatic *NOUN* fanatique *MASC & FEM*

fancy *NOUN* **to take someone's fancy** faire envie à quelqu'un, **the picture took his fancy** le tableau lui a fait envie

fancy *ADJECTIVE (equipment)* sophistiqué

fancy *VERB* ❶ *(to want)* **(do you) fancy a coffee?** tu veux un café?, **do you fancy going to the new film?** ça te dirait d'aller voir le nouveau film? ❷ **I really fancy him** il me plaît beaucoup ❸ *(just)* **fancy that!** pas possible!, **fancy you being here!** tiens donc, toi ici!

fancy dress NOUN in fancy dress déguisé, a fancy-dress party une soirée déguisée

fantastic ADJECTIVE génial MASC (PLURAL géniaux) (informal); really? that's fantastic! vraiment? c'est génial!, a fantastic holiday des vacances géniales

far ADVERB, ADJECTIVE ❶ loin; it's not far ce n'est pas loin, is it far to Carlisle? est-ce que Carlisle est loin d'ici?, how far is it to Bristol? Bristol est à quelle distance d'ici?, he took us as far as Newport il nous a accompagnés jusqu'à Newport ❷ by far de loin, the prettiest by far de loin le plus joli ❸ (much) beaucoup; far better beaucoup mieux, far faster beaucoup plus vite, far too many people beaucoup trop de monde ❹ so far jusqu'ici, so far everything's going well jusqu'ici tout va bien
• as far as I know pour autant que je sache

fare NOUN ❶ (on a bus or the underground) prix (MASC) du ticket ❷ (on a train or plane) prix (MASC) du billet; half fare demi-tarif MASC, full fare plein tarif MASC, the return fare to Cardiff le prix d'un aller-retour à Cardiff

Far East NOUN Extrême-Orient MASC

farm NOUN ferme FEM

farmer NOUN agriculteur MASC, agricultrice FEM

farmhouse NOUN ferme FEM

farming NOUN agriculture FEM

farthest ADJECTIVE le plus éloigné; the farthest hill la colline la plus éloignée

farthest ADVERB le plus loin; that's the farthest we went that day nous ne sommes pas allés plus loin ce jour-là

fascinating ADJECTIVE fascinant

fashion NOUN mode FEM; in fashion à la mode, out of fashion démodé

fashionable ADJECTIVE à la mode

fashion model NOUN mannequin MASC

fashion show NOUN présentation (FEM) de collection

fast ADJECTIVE ❶ rapide; a fast car une voiture rapide ❷ my watch is fast ma montre avance, you're ten minutes fast ta montre avance de dix minutes

fast ADVERB ❶ vite; he swims fast il nage vite ❷ to be fast asleep être profondément endormi

fast food NOUN fast-food MASC

fast forward NOUN avance (FEM) rapide

fat NOUN ❶ (butter, cream, etc) matières, grasses FEM PLURAL ❷ (on meat) gras MASC ❸ (on your body) graisse FEM

fat ADJECTIVE gros (FEM grosse) (goes before the noun); a fat man un gros monsieur, to get fat grossir

fatal ADJECTIVE (accident) mortel (FEM mortelle)

father NOUN père MASC; my father's office le bureau de mon père

Father Christmas NOUN le père Noël

father-in-law NOUN beau-père MASC

Father's Day NOUN fête (FEM) des Pères

fault NOUN ❶ *(when you are responsible)* **faute** FEM; **it's Stephen's fault** c'est la faute de Stephen, **it's not my fault** ce n'est pas ma faute ❷ *(a defect)* **défaut** MASC; **there's a fault in this sweater** il y a un défaut dans ce pull ❸ *(in tennis)* **faute** FEM

favour NOUN ❶ *(a kindness)* **service** MASC; **to do somebody a favour** rendre service à quelqu'un, **can you do me a favour?** peux-tu me rendre service?, **to ask a favour of somebody** demander un service à quelqu'un ❷ **to be in favour of something** être pour quelque chose

favourite ADJECTIVE **préféré**; **my favourite band** mon groupe préféré

fear NOUN **peur** FEM

fear VERB **craindre** [31]; **to fear the worst** craindre le pire

feather NOUN **plume** FEM

feature NOUN ❶ *(of your face)* **trait** MASC; **to have delicate features** avoir les traits délicats ❷ *(of a car or a machine)* **caractéristique** FEM

February NOUN **février** MASC; **in February** en février

fed up ADJECTIVE **I'm fed up** j'en ai marre *(informal)*, **I'm fed up with working every day** j'en ai marre de travailler tous les jours

feed VERB **donner** [1] **à manger à**; **have you fed the dog?** est-ce que tu as donné à manger au chien?

feel VERB ❶ **se sentir** [58]; **I feel tired** je me sens fatigué, **I don't feel well** je ne me sens pas bien ❷ **sentir** [58]; **I didn't feel a thing** je n'ai rien senti ❸ **to feel afraid** avoir [5] peur, **to feel cold** avoir froid,

to feel thirsty avoir soif ❹ **to feel like doing** avoir envie de faire, **I feel like going to the cinema** j'ai envie d'aller au cinéma ❺ *(touch)* **toucher** [1]

feeling NOUN ❶ *(in your mind)* **sentiment** MASC; **a feeling of embarrassment** un sentiment de gêne, **to show your feelings** montrer ses sentiments, **to hurt somebody's feelings** blesser quelqu'un ❷ *(in your body)* **sensation** FEM; **a dizzy feeling** une sensation de vertige ❸ *(an impression or intuition)* **impression** FEM; **I have the feeling James doesn't like me** j'ai l'impression que James ne m'aime pas

felt-tip (pen) NOUN **feutre** MASC

female NOUN *(animal)* **femelle** FEM

female ADJECTIVE ❶ **féminin** *(person, population)* ❷ **femelle** *(animal, insect)*

feminine ADJECTIVE **féminin**

feminist NOUN, ADJECTIVE **féministe** MASC & FEM

fence NOUN *(round a field)* **clôture** FEM

fern NOUN **fougère** FEM

ferry NOUN **ferry** MASC

fertilizer NOUN **engrais** MASC

festival NOUN *(for films, art, or music)* **festival** MASC

fetch VERB **aller** [7] **chercher**; **Tom's fetching the children** Tom est allé chercher les enfants, **fetch me the other knife!** va me chercher l'autre couteau!

fever ADJECTIVE **fièvre** FEM

A B C D E F G H I J K L M N O P Q R S T U V W X Y Z

few ADJECTIVE, PRONOUN ❶ peu de; **few people think that ...** peu de gens pensent que ..., **very few houses have a swimming-pool** très peu de maisons ont une piscine ❷ **a few** (followed by a noun) quelques, **a few weeks earlier** quelques semaines plus tôt, **in a few minutes** dans quelques minutes ❸ **a few** (by itself) quelques-uns (FEM quelques-unes), **have you any tomatoes? we want a few for the salad** avez-vous des tomates? nous en voulons quelques-unes pour la salade ❹ **quite a few** pas mal de, **there were quite a few questions** il y avait pas mal de questions

fewer ADJECTIVE moins de; **there are fewer tourists this year** il y a moins de touristes cette année

fiancé NOUN fiancé MASC

fiancée NOUN fiancée FEM

fiction NOUN **I read a lot of fiction** je lis beacoup de romans

field NOUN ❶ (with grass or crops) champ MASC; **a field of wheat** un champ de blé ❷ (for sport) terrain MASC ❸ (the kind of work you do) domaine MASC

fierce ADJECTIVE ❶ féroce (an animal or person) ❷ violent (a storm or a battle)

fifteen NUMBER quinze; **Lara's fifteen** Lara a quinze ans

fifth NUMBER cinquième; **the fifth of January** le cinq janvier, **on the fifth floor** au cinquième étage

fifty NUMBER cinquante MASC; **my uncle's fifty** mon oncle a cinquante ans

fig NOUN figue FEM

fight NOUN ❶ (a scuffle) bagarre FEM ❷ (in boxing) combat MASC ❸ (against illness) lutte FEM

fight VERB ❶ (to have a fight) se battre [21]; **they were fighting** ils se battaient ❷ (to quarrel) se disputer [1]; **they're always fighting** ils sont toujours en train de se disputer ❸ (struggle against) lutter [1] contre (poverty or a disease)

fighting NOUN ❶ (in the streets or a pub, for example) bagarre FEM ❷ (in war) combat MASC

figure NOUN ❶ (number) chiffre MASC; **a four-figure number** un nombre de quatre chiffres ❷ (body shape) ligne FEM; **good for your figure** bon pour la ligne ❸ (a person) personnage MASC; **a familiar figure** un personnage familier ❹ (diagram) figure FEM

file NOUN ❶ (for records of a person or case) dossier MASC ❷ (ring binder) classeur MASC ❸ (cardboard folder) chemise FEM ❹ (on a computer) fichier MASC ❺ **a nail file** une lime

file VERB ❶ classer [1] (documents) ❷ **to file your nails** se limer [1] les ongles

fill VERB remplir [2] (a container); **she filled my glass** elle a rempli mon verre, **a smoke-filled room** une pièce remplie de fumée

* **to fill in** remplir [2] (a form)
* **to fill in for someone** remplacer [61] quelqu'un

filling NOUN ❶ (for a sandwich) garniture FEM, (of meat, vegetables) farce FEM; **with an apricot filling** fourré à l'abricot ❷ (in tooth) plombage MASC

film NOUN ❶ *(in a cinema)* **film** MASC; **shall we go and see a film?** si on allait voir un film?, **the new film about Picasso** le nouveau film au sujet de Picasso ❷ *(for a camera)* **pellicule** FEM; **a 24-exposure colour film** une pellicule couleur de 24 poses

film star NOUN **vedette** *(FEM)* **de cinéma**

filter NOUN **filtre** MASC

filthy ADJECTIVE **dégoûtant**

fin NOUN **nageoire** FEM

final NOUN *(in sport)* **finale** FEM

final ADJECTIVE **dernier** *(FEM* **dernière***)*; **the final instalment** le dernier épisode, **the final result** le résultat final

finally ADVERB **finalement**

find VERB **trouver** [1]; **did you find your passport?** as-tu trouvé ton passeport?, **I can't find my keys** je ne trouve pas mes clefs
• **to find out** ❶ *(to enquire)* se **renseigner** [1]; **I don't know, I'll find out** je ne sais pas, je me renseignerai ❷ **to find something out** découvrir [30] *(the facts or an answer)*, **when Lucy found out the truth** quand Lucy a découvert la vérité

fine NOUN **amende** FEM *(for parking or speeding)*, **contravention** FEM

fine ADJECTIVE ❶ *(in good health)* **bien**; **'how are you?' – 'fine, thanks'** 'comment ça va?' – 'très bien merci' ❷ *(very good)* **excellent**; **she's a fine athlete** c'est une excellente athlète ❸ *(convenient)* **très bien**; **ten o'clock? yes, that's fine** dix heures? oui, très bien,

Friday will be fine vendredi sera très bien ❹ *(sunny)* **beau** *(FEM* **belle***)* *(weather or a day)*; **if it's fine** s'il fait beau ❺ *(not coarse or thick)* **fin**; **in fine wool** en laine fine

finely ADJECTIVE *(chopped or grated)* **finement**

finger NOUN **doigt** MASC
• **I'll keep my fingers crossed for you** je croise les doigts pour toi

fingernail NOUN **ongle** MASC

finish NOUN ❶ *(end)* **fin** FEM ❷ *(in a race)* **arrivée** FEM

finish VERB ❶ **finir** [2]; **wait, I haven't finished** attends, je n'ai pas fini, **when does school finish?** à quelle heure finit l'école? ❷ *(to finish off)* **terminer** [1] *(work or a project)*; **have you finished the book?** est-ce que tu as terminé le livre? ❸ **to finish doing** finir de faire, **have you finished telephoning?** as-tu fini de téléphoner?
• **to finish with** finir avec; **have you finished with the computer?** as-tu fini avec l'ordinateur?

finishing line NOUN **ligne** *(FEM)* **d'arrivée**

Finland NOUN **Finlande** FEM; **in Finland** en Finlande, **to Finland** en Finlande

Finnish NOUN **finnois** MASC *(the language)*

Finnish ADJECTIVE **finlandais**

fire NOUN ❶ *(in a grate)* **feu** MASC; **to light a fire** allumer un feu, **sitting by the fire** assis près du feu ❷ **to catch fire** prendre feu ❸ *(accidental)* **incendie** MASC; **a fire in a factory** un incendie dans une usine

fire VERB ❶ (to shoot) tirer [1]; **the soldiers were firing** les soldats tiraient, **to fire at somebody** tirer sur quelqu'un ❷ décharger (a gun)

fire alarm NOUN alarme (FEM) incendie

fire brigade NOUN pompiers MASC PLURAL

fire engine NOUN voiture (FEM) des pompiers

fire escape NOUN escalier (MASC) de secours

fire extinguisher NOUN extincteur MASC

fire fighter NOUN pompier MASC

fireplace NOUN cheminée FEM

fire station NOUN caserne (FEM) de pompiers

firework NOUN feu (MASC) d'artifice (PLURAL feux d'artifice); **there will be a firework display** il y aura un feu d'artifice

firm NOUN (business) entreprise FEM

firm ADJECTIVE ferme

first ADJECTIVE, ADVERB ❶ premier (FEM première); **Susan's the first** Susan est la première, **the first of May** le premier mai, **for the first time** pour la première fois, **I came first in the 200 metres** je suis arrivé premier aux 200 mètres ❷ (to begin with) d'abord; **first, I'm going to make some tea** d'abord je vais faire du thé ❸ at first au début, **at first he was shy** au début il était timide

first aid NOUN premiers secours MASC PLURAL

first-aid kit NOUN trousse (FEM) de secours

first class ADJECTIVE ❶ de première classe (a ticket, carriage, or hotel); **a first-class compartment** un compartiment de première classe, **he always travels first class** il voyage toujours en première ❷ au tarif rapide (a letter or stamp); **six first-class stamps** six timbres au tarif rapide

first floor NOUN premier étage MASC; **on the first floor** au premier étage

firstly ADVERB premièrement

first name NOUN prénom MASC

fir tree NOUN sapin MASC

fish NOUN poisson MASC; **do you like fish?** aimez-vous le poisson?

fish VERB pêcher [1]; **Dad was fishing for trout** Papa pêchait la truite

fish and chips NOUN poisson (MASC) frit avec des frites

fisherman NOUN pêcheur MASC

fishing NOUN pêche FEM; **I love fishing** j'adore la pêche, **to go fishing** aller à la pêche

fishing rod NOUN canne (FEM) à pêche

fishing tackle NOUN matériel (MASC) de pêche

fist NOUN poing MASC

fit NOUN ❶ (of rage) **to have a fit** piquer une crise, **your dad'll have a fit when he sees your hair!** ton père va piquer une crise quand il va voir tes cheveux! ❷ an epileptic fit une crise d'épilepsie

fit ADJECTIVE (healthy) en forme; **I feel really fit** je me sens vraiment en forme, **to keep fit** se maintenir en forme

fit VERB ❶ (to be the right size for) (a garment) être [6] de la taille de (a person), (shoes) être à la pointure de; **this skirt doesn't fit me** cette jupe n'est pas à ma taille ❷ (be able to be put into) aller [7] dans; **will my cases all fit in the car?** est-ce que mes valises iront dans la voiture?, **the key doesn't fit in the lock** la clé ne va pas dans la serrure ❸ (install) installer [1]; **they've fitted an alarm** ils ont installé une alarme

fitness NOUN forme FEM; **fitness training** exercices (MASC PLURAL) de mise en forme

fitted carpet NOUN moquette FEM

fitted kitchen NOUN cuisine (FEM) intégrée

fitting room NOUN cabine (FEM) d'essayage

five NUMBER cinq MASC; **Belinda's five** Belinda a cinq ans, **it's five o'clock** il est cinq heures

fix VERB ❶ (repair) réparer [1]; **Mum's fixed the computer** Maman a réparé l'ordinateur ❷ (to decide on) fixer [1]; **to fix a date** fixer une date, **at a fixed price** à prix fixe ❸ préparer [1] (a meal); **I'll fix supper** c'est moi qui vais préparer le repas du soir

fizzy ADJECTIVE gazeux (FEM gazeuse); **fizzy water** eau (FEM) gazeuse

flag NOUN drapeau MASC (PLURAL drapeaux)

flame NOUN flamme FEM

flamingo NOUN flamant (MASC) rose

flan NOUN tarte FEM; **an onion flan** une tarte à l'oignon

flap VERB battre [21]; **the bird flapped its wings** l'oiseau battait des ailes

flash NOUN ❶ **a flash of lightning** un éclair ❷ **to do something in a flash** faire quelque chose en un clin d'œil ❸ (on a camera) flash MASC

flash VERB ❶ (a light) clignoter [1] ❷ **to flash by or past** passer [1] comme un éclair ❸ **to flash your headlights** faire [10] un appel de phares

flashback NOUN flash-back MASC

flask NOUN ❶ (insulated bottle) thermos® MASC OR FEM ❷ (container) flacon MASC

flat NOUN appartement MASC; **a third-floor flat** un appartement au troisième étage

flat ADJECTIVE ❶ plat; **flat shoes** des chaussures plates, **a flat landscape** un paysage plat ❷ **a flat tyre** un pneu crevé

flatmate NOUN colocataire MASC & FEM

flatter VERB flatter [1]

flattering ADJECTIVE flatteur (FEM flatteuse)

flavour NOUN ❶ (taste) goût MASC; **the sauce had no flavour** la sauce n'avait aucun goût ❷ (of drink, ice cream, etc.) parfum MASC; **what flavour of ice cream would you like?** tu veux quel parfum de glace?

flavour VERB parfumer [1]; **vanilla-flavoured** parfumé à la vanille

flea NOUN puce FEM

flea market NOUN marché (MASC) aux puces

fleet NOUN ❶ (of ships) flotte FEM ❷ (of vehicles) parc MASC

flesh NOUN **chair** FEM

flex NOUN **fil** MASC

flexible ADJECTIVE **flexible** (an arrangement)

flight NOUN ❶ **vol** MASC; **a charter flight** un vol charter, **the flight from Moscow is delayed** le vol de Moscou est retardé ❷ **a flight of stairs** un escalier, **four flights of stairs** quatre étages

flight attendant NOUN ❶ (male) **steward** MASC ❷ (female) **hôtesse** (FEM) **de l'air**

fling VERB **lancer** [61]

flip-flops PLURAL NOUN **tongs** FEM PLURAL

flipper NOUN (for a swimmer) **palme** FEM

flirt VERB **flirter** [1]

float VERB **flotter** [1]

flood NOUN ❶ (of water) **inondation** FEM; **the floods in the south** les inondations au sud, **to be in floods of tears** verser des torrents de larmes ❷ (of letters or complaints) **déluge** MASC

flood VERB **inonder** [1]

floodlight NOUN **projecteur** MASC

floor NOUN ❶ (wooden) **plancher** MASC, (concrete) **sol** MASC; **to sweep the floor** balayer, **to sweep the kitchen floor** balayer la cuisine, **your glasses are on the floor** tes lunettes sont par terre ❷ (a storey) **étage** MASC; **on the second floor** au deuxième étage

florist NOUN **fleuriste** MASC & FEM

flour NOUN **farine** FEM

flow VERB **couler** [1]

flower NOUN **fleur** FEM; **a bunch of flowers** un bouquet

flower VERB **fleurir** [2]

flu NOUN **grippe** FEM; **to have flu** avoir la grippe

fluent ADJECTIVE **she speaks fluent Italian** elle parle couramment l'italien

fluently ADVERB **couramment**

fluid NOUN **liquide** MASC

flush VERB ❶ (to go red) **rougir** [2] ❷ **to flush the lavatory** tirer [1] la chasse

flute NOUN **flûte** FEM; **to play the flute** jouer de la flûte

fly NOUN **mouche** FEM

fly VERB ❶ (a bird, a bee, or a plane) **voler** [1] ❷ (in a plane) **prendre** [64] **l'avion**; **we flew to Edinburgh** nous sommes allés à Édimbourg en avion, **we flew from Gatwick** nous sommes partis de Gatwick ❸ **faire** [10] **voler** (a kite) ❹ (to pass quickly) (time) **passer** [1] **très vite**

fly spray NOUN **bombe** (FEM) **insecticide**

foam NOUN ❶ (foam rubber) **mousse** FEM; **a foam mattress** un matelas mousse ❷ (on a drink) **mousse** FEM

focus NOUN **to be in focus** être au point, **to be out of focus** être flou

focus VERB **mettre** [11] **au point** (a camera)

fog NOUN **brouillard** MASC

foggy ADJECTIVE **brumeux** (FEM **brumeuse**) (weather); **it was foggy** il y avait du brouillard

foil NOUN (kitchen foil) papier (MASC) aluminium

fold NOUN pli MASC

fold VERB ❶ plier [1]; **to fold something up** plier quelque chose ❷ **to fold your arms** croiser [1] les bras

folder NOUN chemise FEM

folding ADJECTIVE pliant; **a folding table** une table pliante

follow VERB suivre [75]; **follow me!** suivez-moi!, **followed by a dinner** suivi d'un dîner, **do you follow me?** vous me suivez?

following ADJECTIVE suivant; **the following year** l'année suivante

fond ADJECTIVE **to be fond of somebody** aimer beaucoup quelqu'un, **I'm very fond of him** je l'aime beaucoup

food NOUN ❶ nourriture FEM; **to buy food** acheter à manger, **I like French food** j'aime la cuisine française ❷ (stocks) provisions FEM PLURAL; **we bought food for the holiday** nous avons acheté des provisions pour les vacances

food poisoning NOUN intoxication (FEM) alimentaire

fool NOUN idiot MASC, idiote FEM

foot NOUN ❶ pied MASC; **Lucy came on foot** Lucy est venue à pied ❷ (the bottom) **at the foot of the stairs** en bas de l'escalier

football NOUN ❶ (the game) football MASC; **to play football** jouer au football ❷ (ball) ballon (MASC) de football

footballer NOUN joueur (MASC) de football, joueuse (FEM) de football

footpath NOUN sentier MASC

footprint NOUN empreinte FEM

footstep NOUN pas MASC

for PREPOSITION ❶ pour; **a present for my mother** un cadeau pour ma mère, **petrol for the car** de l'essence pour la voiture, **sausages for lunch** des saucisses pour le déjeuner, **it's for cleaning** c'est pour nettoyer, **what's it for?** c'est pour quoi faire? ❷ (time expressions in the past or future) pendant; **I studied French for six years** (but I no longer do) j'ai étudié le français pendant six ans, **I'll be away for four days** je serai absent pendant quatre jours ❸ (time expressions in the past but continuing in the present) depuis; **I've been waiting here for an hour** (and I'm still waiting) j'attends ici depuis une heure, **my brother's been living in Paris for three years** (and he still lives there) mon frère habite à Paris depuis trois ans ❹ **I sold my bike for fifty pounds** j'ai vendu mon vélo cinquante livres ❺ **what's the French for 'bee'?** comment dit-on 'bee' en français?

forbid VERB défendre [3]; **to forbid somebody to do something** défendre à quelqu'un de faire quelque chose, **I forbid you to go out** je te défends de sortir

forbidden ADJECTIVE défendu

force NOUN force FEM

force VERB forcer [61]; **to force somebody to do** forcer quelqu'un à faire

forecast NOUN (weather forecast) météo FEM

forefinger NOUN index MASC

foreground NOUN **premier plan** MASC; **in the foreground** au premier plan

forehead NOUN **front** MASC

foreign ADJECTIVE **étranger** (FEM étrangère); **in a foreign country** dans un pays étranger

foreigner NOUN **étranger** MASC, **étrangère** FEM

foresee VERB **prévoir** [65]

forest NOUN **forêt** FEM

forever ADVERB ❶ **pour toujours**; **I'd like to stay here forever** j'aimerais rester là pour toujours ❷ (non-stop) **sans arrêt**; **he's forever asking questions** il pose sans arrêt des questions

forgery NOUN ❶ (picture) **faux** MASC ❷ (signature, banknote) **contrefaçon** FEM

forget VERB **oublier** [1]; **I forget his name** j'oublie son nom, **we've forgotten the bread!** nous avons oublié le pain!, **to forget to do** oublier de faire, **I forgot to phone** j'ai oublié d'appeler, **to forget about something** oublier quelque chose

forgive VERB **pardonner** [1] à; **to forgive somebody** pardonner à quelqu'un, **I forgave him** je lui ai pardonné, **to forgive somebody for doing** pardonner à quelqu'un d'avoir fait, **I forgave her for losing my ring** je lui ai pardonné d'avoir perdu ma bague

fork NOUN **fourchette** FEM

form NOUN ❶ **formulaire** MASC; **to fill in a form** remplir un formulaire ❷ (shape or kind) **forme** FEM; **in the form of** sous

form de ❸ **to be on form** être en forme ❹ (in school) **classe** FEM

form VERB **former** [1]

formal ADJECTIVE **officiel** (FEM officielle) (invitation, event, complaint, etc.)

format NOUN **format** MASC

former ADJECTIVE **ancien** (FEM ancienne) (goes before the noun); **a former pupil** un ancien élève

formula NOUN **formule** FEM

fortnight NOUN **quinze jours** MASC PLURAL; **we're going to Spain for a fortnight** nous allons passer quinze jours en Espagne

fortress NOUN **forteresse** FEM

fortunate ADJECTIVE **to be fortunate** avoir [5] de la chance

fortunately ADVERB **heureusement**

fortune NOUN **fortune** FEM; **to make a fortune** gagner [1] beaucoup d'argent

forty NUMBER **quarante**; **my aunt's forty** ma tante a quarante ans

forward NOUN (in sport) **avant** MASC

forward ADVERB **to move forward** avancer, **a seat further forward** une place plus en avant

foster child NOUN **enfant** (MASC) **adoptif, enfant** (FEM) **adoptive**

foul NOUN (in sport) **faute** FEM

foul ADJECTIVE **infect**; **the weather's foul** il fait un temps infect

fountain NOUN **fontaine** FEM

fountain pen NOUN **stylo** (MASC) **à encre**

four NUMBER quatre MASC; **Simon's four** Simon a quatre ans, **it's four o'clock** il est quatre heures
• **on all fours** à quatre pattes

fourteen NUMBER quatorze MASC; **Susie's fourteen** Susie a quatorze ans

fourth NUMBER quatrième; **the fourth of July** le quatre juillet, **on the fourth floor** au quatrième étage

fox NOUN renard MASC

fracture NOUN fracture FEM

fragile ADJECTIVE fragile

frame NOUN ❶ (of picture) cadre MASC ❷ (of door) encadrement MASC

franc NOUN franc MASC; (the currency of Switzerland; name of the currencies used in France, Belgium and Luxembourg until replaced by the euro; 100 French francs = 15.24 euros)

France NOUN France FEM; **in France** en France, **to France** en France, **I like France** j'aime la France, **Nadine's from France** Nadine est française

frantic ADJECTIVE ❶ (very upset) fou (FEM folle); **Mum was frantic with worry** Maman était folle d'inquiétude ❷ (desperate) désespéré (efforts or a search)

freckle NOUN tache (FEM) de rousseur

free ADJECTIVE ❶ (when you don't pay) gratuit; **the bus is free** le bus est gratuit, **a free ticket** un billet gratuit ❷ (not occupied) libre; **are you free on Thursday?** es-tu libre jeudi? ❸ sugar-free sans sucre, lead-free sans plomb

free VERB libérer [24]

freedom NOUN liberté FEM

free gift NOUN cadeau MASC (PLURAL cadeaux)

free kick NOUN coup (MASC) franc

freeze VERB ❶ (in a freezer) congeler [45]; **frozen peas** des petits pois congelés ❷ (in cold weather) geler [45]; **it's freezing outside** il gèle dehors

freezer NOUN congélateur MASC

freezing NOUN zéro MASC; **three degrees below freezing** trois degrés en-dessous de zéro

freezing ADJECTIVE **I'm freezing** je suis gelé (informal), **it's freezing outside** il fait très froid dehors

French NOUN ❶ (the language) français MASC; **to speak French** parler français, **say it in French** dis-le en français, **to learn French** apprendre le français ❷ (the people) **the French** les Français MASC PLURAL, **most of the French** la plupart des Français

French ADJECTIVE ❶ français; **Jean-Marc is French** Jean-Marc est français ❷ de français (a teacher or a lesson); **the French class** le cours de français

French bean NOUN haricot (MASC) vert

French dressing NOUN vinaigrette FEM

French fries PLURAL NOUN frites FEM PLURAL

Frenchman NOUN Français MASC

French stick NOUN baguette FEM

French window NOUN porte-fenêtre FEM (PLURAL portes-fenêtres)

Frenchwoman NOUN Française FEM

frequent ADJECTIVE fréquent

frequently ADVERB souvent

fresh ADJECTIVE frais (FEM fraîche); **fresh eggs** des œufs frais, **I'm going out for some fresh air** je vais prendre de l'air

Friday NOUN vendredi MASC; **next Friday** vendredi prochain, **last Friday** vendredi dernier, **on Friday** vendredi, **I'll phone you on Friday evening** je t'appellerai vendredi soir, **on Fridays** le vendredi, **closed on Fridays** fermé le vendredi, **every Friday** tous les vendredis, **Good Friday** le Vendredi saint

fridge NOUN frigo MASC (informal); **put it in the fridge** mets-le au frigo

friend NOUN ami MASC, amie FEM; **a friend of mine** un ami (or une amie) à moi, **to make friends** (in a general way) se faire des amis, **he made friends with Danny** il est devenu ami avec Danny

friendly ADJECTIVE sympathique

friendship NOUN amitié FEM

fries PLURAL NOUN frites FEM PLURAL

fright NOUN peur FEM; **to have** or **get a fright** avoir peur, **you gave me a fright!** tu m'as fait peur!

frighten VERB effrayer [59]

frightened ADJECTIVE **to be frightened** avoir peur, **Martin's frightened of snakes** Martin a peur des serpents

frightening ADJECTIVE effrayant

fringe NOUN frange FEM

frog NOUN grenouille FEM

from PREPOSITION de; **a letter from Tom** une lettre de Tom, **100 metres from the cinema** à cent mètres du cinéma, **from Monday to Friday** du lundi jusqu'au vendredi, **he comes from Dublin** il vient de Dublin, **two years from now** d'ici deux ans, **from seven o'clock onwards** à partir de sept heures

front NOUN ❶ (of a building, a garment, or a cupboard) devant MASC ❷ (of a car) avant MASC; **sitting in the front** assis à l'avant ❸ (of a train or a queue) tête FEM; **there are seats at the front of the train** il y a des places en tête du train ❹ (of a card or envelope) recto MASC; **the address is on the front** l'adresse est au recto ❺ (in a theatre, cinema, or class) premier rang MASC; **seats at the front** des places au premier rang ❻ in front de devant, **in front of the TV** devant la télé, **in front of me** devant moi

front ADJECTIVE ❶ de devant; **his front paw** sa patte de devant, **in the front row** au premier rang ❷ avant; **the front seat** (of a car) le siège avant, **the front wheel** la roue avant

front door NOUN porte (FEM) d'entrée

frontier NOUN frontière FEM

frost NOUN gel MASC

frosty ADJECTIVE ❶ **it's frosty this morning** il gèle ce matin ❷ couvert de givre (windscreen, grass, etc.)

frown VERB froncer [61] les sourcils; **he frowned at us** il nous a regardés en fronçant les sourcils

frozen *ADJECTIVE* (in a freezer) surgelé; **a frozen pizza** une pizza surgelée

fruit *NOUN* fruits *MASC PLURAL* (note that in French 'un fruit' is a piece of fruit, whereas 'fruit' in English meaning several pieces of fruit always has to be 'fruits' in the plural in French); **we bought cheese and fruit** nous avons acheté du fromage et des fruits, **fruit juice** le jus de fruits

fruit machine *NOUN* machine (FEM) à sous

fruit salad *NOUN* salade (FEM) de fruits

frustrated *ADJECTIVE* frustré

frustrating *ADJECTIVE* frustrant

fry *VERB* faire [10] frire; **we fried the fish** nous avons fait frire les poissons, **a fried egg** un œuf au plat

frying pan *NOUN* poêle *FEM*

fuel *NOUN* (for a vehicle or plane) carburant *MASC*

full *ADJECTIVE* ❶ plein; **this glass is full** ce verre est plein, **the train was full of tourists** le train était plein de touristes ❷ complet (FEM complète) (a hotel or flight) ❸ (top) **at full speed** à toute vitesse, **at full volume** à plein volume ❹ **I'm full** j'ai assez mangé ❺ **to write something out in full** écrire quelque chose en toutes lettres

full stop *NOUN* point *MASC*

full-time *ADJECTIVE* **a full-time job** un travail à plein temps

full time *NOUN* (in sport) fin (FEM) du match

fully *ADJECTIVE* entièrement

fun *NOUN* plaisir *MASC*; **to have fun** s'amuser, **have fun!** amusez-vous bien!, **we had fun catching the ponies** nous nous sommes beaucoup amusés en attrapant les poneys, **skiing is fun** c'est amusant de faire du ski, **I do it for fun** je le fais pour m'amuser
- **to make fun of somebody** se moquer de quelqu'un

funds *PLURAL NOUN* fonds *MASC PLURAL*

funeral *NOUN* enterrement *MASC*

funfair *NOUN* fête (FEM) foraine

funny *ADJECTIVE* ❶ (when you laugh) drôle; **how funny you are!** que tu es drôle!, **a funny story** une histoire drôle ❷ (strange) bizarre; **that's funny, I'm sure I paid** c'est bizarre, je suis certain que j'ai payé, **a funny noise** un bruit bizarre

fur *NOUN* ❶ (on an animal) poils *MASC PLURAL* ❷ (for a coat) fourrure *FEM*; **a fur coat** un manteau de fourrure

furious *ADJECTIVE* furieux (FEM furieuse); **she was furious with Steve** elle était furieuse contre Steve

furniture *NOUN* meubles *MASC PLURAL*; **to buy some furniture** acheter des meubles, **a piece of furniture** un meuble

further *ADVERB* plus loin; **further than the station** plus loin que la gare, **ten kilometres further on** dix kilomètres plus loin, **further forward** plus en avant, **further back** plus en arrière

fuse *NOUN* fusible *MASC*

a
b
c
d
e
f
g
h
i
j
k
l
m
n
o
p
q
r
s
t
u
v
w
x
y
z

fuss NOUN histoires FEM PLURAL; **to make a fuss** faire des histoires, **to make a fuss about the bill** faire toute une histoire à propos de l'addition

fussy ADJECTIVE **to be fussy about something** être difficile sur quelque chose (food, for example)

future NOUN ❶ avenir MASC; **in future** à l'avenir, **in the future** dans l'avenir ❷ (in grammar) futur MASC; **a verb in the future** un verbe au futur

gadget NOUN gadget MASC

gain VERB ❶ gagner [1]; **in order to gain time** pour gagner du temps, **we have nothing to gain** nous n'avons rien à gagner ❷ **to gain speed** prendre de la vitesse, **to gain weight** prendre du poids

galaxy NOUN galaxie FEM

gale NOUN vent (MASC) violent

gallery NOUN **an art gallery** (public) un musée, (private) une galerie

gamble VERB jouer [1]

gambling NOUN jeu MASC

game NOUN ❶ jeu MASC; **children's games** les jeux d'enfant, **a game of chance** un jeu de hasard, **a board game** un jeu de société ❷ a

game of une partie de, **to have a game of cards** faire une partie de cartes ❸ match MASC; **a game of football** un match de foot, **to be good at games Jack's very good at games** Jack est très bon en sport

gang NOUN bande FEM; **all the gang were there** toute la bande y était

gangster NOUN gangster MASC

gap NOUN ❶ (hole) trou MASC ❷ (in time) intervalle MASC; **a two-year gap** un intervalle de deux ans ❸ **an age gap** une différence d'âge

gap year NOUN année (FEM) sabbatique avant d'entrer à l'université

garage NOUN garage MASC

garden NOUN jardin MASC

gardener NOUN jardinier MASC; **he wants to be a gardener** il veut être jardinier

gardening NOUN jardinage MASC

garlic NOUN ail MASC

garlic mayonnaise NOUN aïoli MASC

garment NOUN vêtement MASC

gas NOUN gaz MASC

gas cooker NOUN cuisinière (FEM) à gaz

gas fire NOUN radiateur (MASC) à gaz

gas meter NOUN compteur (MASC) à gaz

gate NOUN ❶ (garden) portail MASC ❷ (field) barrière FEM ❸ (at the airport) porte FEM

gather VERB ❶ (people) se rassembler [1]; **a crowd gathered** une foule s'est rassemblée ❷ cueillir [35] (fruit, *vegetables, flowers)* ❸ as far as I can **gather** autant que je sache

gay *ADJECTIVE* homosexuel *(FEM* homosexuelle)

gaze *VERB* **to gaze at something** regarder [1] quelque chose

GCSEs *NOUN PLURAL (You can explain GCSEs briefly as follows: Ce sont des examens que l'on passe à environ 16 ans dans un certain nombre de matières (12 au maximum). La meilleure note que l'on peut obtenir est A-star et la note la plus basse est N. Une fois qu'ils ont obtenu leurs GCSEs, de nombreux étudiants se préparent pour les A levels)*
▸ SEE **A levels**

gear *NOUN* ❶ *(in a car)* **vitesse** *FEM*; **to change gear** changer de vitesse ❷ *(equipment)* **matériel** *MASC*; **camping gear** du matériel de camping ❸ *(things)* **affaires** *FEM*; **I've left all my gear at Gary's** j'ai laissé toutes mes affaires chez Gary

gear lever *NOUN* **levier** *(MASC)* **de vitesses**

gel *NOUN* **hair gel** le gel pour les cheveux

Gemini *NOUN* **Gémeaux** *MASC PLURAL*; **Steph's Gemini** Steph est Gémeaux

gender *NOUN (of a word)* **genre** *MASC*; **what is the gender of** 'maison'? quel est le genre de 'maison'?

general *NOUN* **général** *MASC (PLURAL* généraux)*; **General Jackson** le général Jackson

general *ADJECTIVE* **général** *MASC (PLURAL* généraux)*; **in general** en général

general election *NOUN* **élections** *(FEM PLURAL)* **législatives**

general knowledge *NOUN* **connaissances** *(FEM PLURAL)* **générales**

generally *ADVERB* généralement

generation *NOUN* génération *FEM*

generator *NOUN* générateur *MASC*

generous *ADJECTIVE* **généreux** *(FEM* généreuse)*

genetics *NOUN* génétique *FEM*

Geneva *NOUN* **Genève**; **to Geneva** à Genève, **in Geneva** à Genève, **Lake Geneva** le lac Léman

genius *NOUN* **génie** *MASC*; **Lisa, you're a genius!** Lisa, tu es un génie!

gentle *ADJECTIVE* **doux** *(FEM* douce)*

gentleman *NOUN* **monsieur** *MASC (PLURAL* messieurs)*; **ladies and gentlemen** mesdames et messieurs

gently *ADVERB* doucement

gents *NOUN* **toilettes** *FEM PLURAL*, *(marked on the door)* 'Messieurs'; **where's the gents?** où sont les toilettes?

genuine *ADJECTIVE* ❶ *(real)* **véritable**; **a genuine diamond** un véritable diamant ❷ *(authentic)* **authentique**; **a genuine signature** une signature authentique ❸ **sincère** *(person)*; **she's very genuine** elle est très sincère

geography *NOUN* géographie *FEM*

geology *NOUN* géologie *FEM*

geometry *NOUN* géométrie *FEM*

germ *NOUN* **microbe** *MASC*

German *NOUN* ❶ **Allemand** *MASC*, **Allemande** *FEM* ❷ *(language)* **allemand**

German ADJECTIVE **allemand**

Germany NOUN **Allemagne** FEM; **to Germany** en Allemagne, **in Germany** en Allemagne

get VERB ❶ (have, receive) **avoir** [5]; **he's got lots of money** il a beaucoup d'argent, **she's got long hair** elle a les cheveux longs, **I got a bike for my birthday** j'ai eu un véo pour mon anniversaire, **I got your letter yesterday** j'ai eu ta lettre hier, **I got fifteen for my French homework** j'ai eu quinze pour mon devoir français ❷ (fetch) **chercher** [1]; **I'll go and get some bread** j'irai chercher du pain, **I'll get your bag for you** je te chercherai ton sac ❸ (obtain) **trouver** [1]; **Fred's got a job** Fred a trouvé un emploi, **where did you get that jacket?** où est-ce que tu as trouvé cette veste? ❹ **to have got to do** devoir [8] faire, **I've got to phone before midday** je dois appeler avant midi ❺ **to get to somewhere** arriver [1] quelque part, **when we got to London** quand nous sommes arrivés à Londres, **to get here** (or **there**) arriver, **we got here this morning** nous sommes arrivés ce matin, **what time did they get there?** ils sont arrivés à quelle heure? ❻ (become) **commencer** [61] à être; **I'm getting tired** je commence à être fatigué, **it's getting late** il commence à être tard, **it's getting dark** il commence à faire nuit, **I'm getting hungry** je commence à avoir faim ❼ **to get something done** faire [10] faire quelque chose, **I'm getting my hair cut this afternoon** je vais me faire couper les cheveux cet après-midi

- **to get back** rentrer [1]; **Mum gets back at six** Maman rentre à six heures
- **to get something back** récupérer [24] quelque chose; **did you get your books back?** est-ce que tu as récupéré tes livres?
- **to get into something** monter [1] dans quelque chose (a vehicle); **he got into the car** il est monté dans la voiture
- **to get off something** descendre [3] de quelque chose; **I got off the train at Banbury** je suis descendu du train à Banbury
- **to get on** aller [7]; **how's Amanda getting on?** comment va Amanda?
- **to get on something** monter [1] dans quelque chose (vehicle); **she got on the train at Reading** elle est montée dans le train à Reading
- **to get on with somebody** s'entendre [3] avec quelqu'un; **she doesn't get on with her brother** elle ne s'entend pas avec son frère
- **to get out of something** descendre [3] de quelque chose (vehicle); **Laura got out of the car** Laura est descendue de la voiture
- **to get something out** sortir [72] quelque chose; **Robert got his guitar out** Robert a sorti sa guitare
- **to get together** se voir; [13]; **we must get together soon** il faut qu'on se voie bientôt
- **to get up** se lever; [50]; **I get up at seven** je me lève à sept heures

ghost NOUN **fantôme** MASC

giant NOUN **géant** MASC, **géante** FEM

giant ADJECTIVE **énorme**; **a giant lorry** un énorme camion

giddy ADJECTIVE **to feel giddy** avoir [5] le tournis, **I'm feeling giddy** j'ai le tournis

gift NOUN ❶ **cadeau** MASC (PLURAL **cadeaux**); **a Christmas gift** un cadeau de Noël ❷ **to have a gift**

for something être doué pour quelque chose, **Jo has a real gift for languages** Jo est vraiment douée pour les langues

gifted ADJECTIVE **doué**

gig NOUN **concert** (MASC) **de rock**

gigabyte NOUN **gigaoctet** MASC; **a twenty gigabyte hard disk** un disque dur de 20 gigaoctets

gigantic ADJECTIVE **gigantesque**

gin NOUN **gin** MASC

ginger NOUN **gingembre** MASC

gipsy NOUN ❶ (in general) **bohémien** MASC, **bohémienne** FEM ❷ (from Spain) **gitan** MASC, **gitane** FEM ❸ (from Eastern Europe) **tsigane** MASC & FEM

giraffe NOUN **giraffe** FEM

girl NOUN ❶ **fille** FEM; **three boys and four girls** trois garçons et quatre filles, **a little girl** une petite fille, **when I was a little girl** quand j'étais petite ❷ (a teenager or young woman) **jeune fille** FEM; **an eighteen-year-old girl** une jeune fille de dix-huit ans

girlfriend NOUN **copine** FEM; **Darren's gone out with his girlfriend** Darren est sorti avec sa copine, **Lizzie and her girlfriends have gone to the cinema** Lizzie et ses copines sont allées au cinéma

give VERB **donner** [1]; **to give something to somebody** donner quelque chose à quelqu'un, **I'll give you my address** je te donnerai mon adresse, **give me the key** donne-moi la clé, **Yasmin's dad gave her the money** le père de Yasmin lui a donné l'argent

• **to give something away** donner

quelque chose; **she's given away all her books** elle a donné tous ses livres

• **to give something back to somebody** rendre [3] quelque chose à qulqu'un; **I gave her back the keys** je lui ai rendu les clés

• **to give in** céder [24]; **my mum said no but she gave in in the end** maman a dit non, mais elle a fini par céder

• **to give up** abandonner [1]; **I give up!** j'abandonne!

• **to give up doing** arrêter [1] de faire; **she's given up smoking** elle a arrêté de fumer

glacier NOUN **glacier** MASC

glad ADJECTIVE **content**; **I'm glad to hear he's better** je suis content d'apprendre qu'il va mieux, **I'm glad to be back** je suis content d'être de retour

glamorous ADJECTIVE ❶ (life) **luxueux** (FEM **luxueuse**) ❷ (job) **prestigieux** (FEM **prestigieuse**) ❸ (woman) **élégant**

glance NOUN **coup d'œil** MASC

glance VERB **to glance at something** jeter [48] un coup d'œil à quelque chose, **Sara glanced at the envelope** Sara a jeté un coup d'œil à l'enveloppe

glass NOUN **verre** MASC; **a glass of water** un verre d'eau, **a glass table** une table en verre

glasses PLURAL NOUN **lunettes** FEM PLURAL; **to wear glasses** porter des lunettes

glider NOUN **planeur** MASC

global ADJECTIVE **mondial** MASC (PLURAL **mondiaux**); **global warming** réchauffement (MASC) planétaire

global warming NOUN le réchauffement de la planète

globe NOUN globe MASC

gloomy ADJECTIVE ❶ (expression) lugubre ❷ (weather) déprimant

glory NOUN gloire FEM

glove NOUN gant MASC; **a pair of gloves** une paire de gants

glove compartment NOUN boîte (FEM) à gants

glue NOUN colle FEM

go NOUN ❶ (in a game) whose go is it? c'est à qui de jouer?, **it's my go** c'est à moi de jouer ❷ **to have a go at doing** essayer de faire, **I'll have a go at mending it for you** j'essaierai de le réparer pour toi

go VERB ❶ aller [7]; **we're going to London tomorrow** nous allons à Londres demain, **Mark's gone to the dentist** Mark est allé chez le dentiste, **to go for a walk** aller se promener ❷ (with another verb) aller; **I'm going to make some tea** je vais faire du thé, **he was going to phone me** il allait m'appeler ❸ (leave) partir [58]; **Pauline's already gone** Pauline est déjà partie, **we're going on holiday tomorrow** nous partons en vacances demain ❹ (an event) se passer [1]; **did the party go well?** est-ce que la soirée s'est bien passée?
- **to go away** s'en aller [7]; **go away!** va-t-en!
- **to go back** ❶ retourner [1]; **I'm going back to France in March** je retourne en France en mars, **I'm not going back there again!** je n'y retourne plus! ❷ (to home, school, office) rentrer [1]; **I went back home** je suis rentré chez moi

- **to go down** ❶ descendre [3]; **she's gone down to the kitchen** elle est descendue dans la cuisine, **to go down the stairs** descendre l'escalier ❷ (price, temperature) baisser [1]; **prices have gone down** les prix ont baissé ❸ (tyre, balloon, airbed) se dégonfler [1]
- **to go in** entrer [1]; **he went in and shut the door** il est entré et il a fermé la porte
- **to go into** ❶ (person) entrer dans; **Fran went into the kitchen** Fran est entrée dans la cuisine ❷ (object) rentrer [1] dans; **this file won't go into my bag** ce classeur ne rentre pas dans mon sac
- **to go off** ❶ (bomb) exploser [1] ❷ (alarm clock) sonner [1]; **my alarm clock went off at six** mon réveil a sonné à six heures ❸ (fire or burglar alarm) se déclencher [1]; **the fire alarm went off** l'alarme d'incendie s'est déclenchée
- **to go on** ❶ se passer [1]; **what's going on?** qu'est-ce qui se passe? ❷ **to go on doing** continuer [1] à faire, **she went on talking** elle a continué à parler ❸ **to go on about something** ne pas arrêter [1] de parler de quelque chose, **he's always going on about his dog** il n'arrête pas de parler de son chien
- **to go out** ❶ sortir [72]; **I'm going out tonight** je sors ce soir, **she went out of the kitchen** elle est sortie de la cuisine ❷ **to be going out with somebody** sortir avec quelqu'un, **she's going out with my brother** elle sort avec mon frère ❸ (light, fire) s'éteindre [60]; **the light went out** la lumière s'est éteinte
- **to go past something** passer [1] devant quelque chose; **we went past your house** nous sommes passés devant chez toi
- **to go round** to go round to

somebody's house aller [7] chez quelqu'un, **I went round to Fred's last night** je suis allé chez Fred hier soir
- **to go round something ❶** faire [10] le tour de *(building, park, garden)* **❷** visiter [1] *(museum, monument)*
- **to go through** passer [1] par; **the train went through Dijon** le train est passé par Dijon, **you can go through my office** tu peux passer par mon bureau
- **to go up ❶** *(person)* monter [1]; **she's gone up to her room** elle est montée dans sa chambre, **to go up the stairs** monter l'escalier **❷** *(prices)* augmenter [1]; **the price of petrol has gone up** le prix de l'essence a augmenté

goal NOUN but MASC; **to score a goal** marquer un but, **to win by three goals to two** gagner trois buts à deux

goalkeeper NOUN gardien *(MASC)* de but

goat NOUN chèvre FEM; **goat's cheese** le fromage de chèvre

god NOUN dieu MASC *(PLURAL dieux)*

God NOUN Dieu MASC; **to believe in God** croire en Dieu

godchild NOUN filleul MASC, filleule FEM

goddaughter NOUN filleule FEM

goddess NOUN déesse FEM

godfather NOUN parrain MASC

godmother NOUN marraine FEM

godson NOUN filleul MASC

goggles PLURAL NOUN lunettes FEM PLURAL; **swimming goggles** les lunettes de plongée, **skiing goggles** les lunettes de ski

go-karting NOUN karting MASC; **to go go-karting** faire du karting

gold NOUN or MASC; **a gold bracelet** un bracelet en or

goldfish NOUN poisson *(MASC)* rouge

golf NOUN golf MASC; **to play golf** jouer au golf

golf club NOUN **❶** *(place)* club *(MASC)* de golf **❷** *(iron)* crosse *(FEM)* de golf

golf course NOUN terrain *(MASC)* de golf

golfer NOUN golfeur MASC, golfeuse FEM

good ADJECTIVE **❶** bon *(FEM bonne)*; **she's a good teacher** c'est un bon professeur, **the cherries are very good** les cerises sont très bonnes **❷ to be good for you** être bon pour la santé, **tomatoes are good for you** les tomates sont bonnes pour la santé **❸ to be good at** être bon en, **she's good at art** elle est bonne en dessin **❹** *(well-behaved)* sage; **be good!** sois sage! **❺** *(kind)* gentil *(FEM gentille)*; **she's been very good to me** elle a été très gentille avec moi **❻ for good** pour de bon, **I've stopped smoking for good** j'ai arrêté de fumer pour de bon

good afternoon EXCLAMATION bonjour

goodbye EXCLAMATION au revoir

good evening EXCLAMATION bonsoir

Good Friday NOUN le Vendredi saint

good-looking ADJECTIVE beau MASC, belle FEM *(PLURAL beaux)*; **Maya's boyfriend's really good-looking** le copain de Maya est très beau

good morning EXCLAMATION
bonjour

goodness EXCLAMATION mon Dieu!;
for goodness sake! au nom du ciel!

goodnight EXCLAMATION bonne nuit

goods PLURAL NOUN marchandises
FEM PLURAL

goods train NOUN train (MASC) de
marchandises

goose NOUN oie FEM

goose pimples NOUN chair (FEM) de
poule

gorgeous ADJECTIVE superbe; a
gorgeous dress une robe superbe,
it's a gorgeous day il fait un temps
superbe

gorilla NOUN gorille MASC

gorse NOUN ajoncs MASC PLURAL

gosh EXCLAMATION ça alors!

gossip NOUN ❶ (person) bavard MASC,
bavarde FEM ❷ (news) nouvelles
FEM PLURAL; what's the latest gossip?
quoi de neuf?

gossip VERB bavarder [1]

government NOUN gouvernement
MASC

grab VERB ❶ saisir [2]; she grabbed
my arm elle m'a saisi par le
bras ❷ to grab something from
somebody arracher [1] quelque
chose à quelqu'un, he grabbed the
book from me il m'a arraché le livre

graceful ADJECTIVE élégant

grade NOUN (mark) note FEM; to get
good grades avoir de bonnes notes

gradual ADJECTIVE progressif (FEM
progressive)

gradually ADVERB petit à petit; the
weather got gradually better le
temps s'est amélioré petit à petit

graffiti PLURAL NOUN graffiti MASC
PLURAL

grain NOUN grain MASC

grammar NOUN grammaire FEM

grammar school NOUN (from age 11
to 15) collège MASC, (from age 15 to
18) lycée MASC

grammatical ADJECTIVE a
grammatical error une faute de
grammaire

gramme NOUN gramme MASC

gran NOUN mamie FEM (informal)

grandchildren PLURAL NOUN petits-
enfants MASC PLURAL

granddad NOUN papy MASC (informal)

granddaughter NOUN petite-fille
FEM

grandfather NOUN grand-père MASC

grandma NOUN mamie FEM (informal)

grandmother NOUN grand-mère
FEM

grandpa NOUN papi MASC (informal)

grandparents PLURAL NOUN
grandparents MASC PLURAL

grandson NOUN petit-fils MASC

granny NOUN mamie FEM (informal)

grape NOUN a grape un grain de
raisin, to buy some grapes acheter
du raisin, do you like grapes? est-ce
que tu aimes le raisin?, a bunch of
grapes une grappe de raisin

grapefruit NOUN pamplemousse MASC

graph NOUN graphique MASC

graphic designer NOUN graphiste MASC & FEM

graphics NOUN visualisation (FEM) graphique

grasp VERB saisir [2]

grass NOUN ❶ herbe FEM; **sitting on the grass** assis sur l'herbe ❷ (lawn) pelouse FEM; **to cut the grass** tondre la pelouse

grasshopper NOUN sauterelle FEM

grate VERB râper [1]; **grated cheese** du fromage râpé

grateful ADJECTIVE reconnaissant

grater NOUN râpe FEM

grave[1] NOUN tombe FEM

grave[2] NOUN accent (MASC) grave

gravel NOUN gravillons MASC PLURAL

graveyard NOUN cimetière MASC

gravity NOUN pesanteur FEM

gravy NOUN sauce (FEM) au jus de rôti

grease NOUN graisse FEM

greasy ADJECTIVE gras (FEM grasse); **to have greasy skin** avoir la peau grasse, **I hate greasy food** je déteste la nourriture grasse

great ADJECTIVE ❶ grand; **a great poet** un grand poète ❷ (terrific) génial MASC (PLURAL géniaux); **it was a great party!** ça a été une soirée géniale!, **great!** génial! ❸ **a great deal of** beaucoup de, **a great many** beaucoup de, **there are a great many things still to be done** il reste beaucoup de choses à faire

Great Britain NOUN Grande-Bretagne FEM; **in Great Britain** en Grande-Bretagne, **to Great Britain** en Grande-Bretagne, **to be from Great Britain** être britannique

Greece NOUN Grèce FEM; **to Greece** en Grèce, **in Greece** en Grèce

greedy ADJECTIVE (with food) gourmand

Greek NOUN ❶ (person) Grec MASC, Grecque FEM ❷ (language) grec MASC

Greek ADJECTIVE grec (FEM grecque)

green NOUN ❶ (colour) vert MASC; **a pale green** un vert pâle ❷ **greens** (vegetables) les légumes verts ❸ **the Greens** (ecologists) les Verts MASC PLURAL

green ADJECTIVE ❶ vert; **a green door** une porte verte ❷ écologiste; **the Green Party** le parti écologiste

greengrocer NOUN marchand (MASC) de fruits et légumes

greenhouse NOUN serre FEM

greenhouse effect NOUN effet (MASC) de serre

greetings PLURAL NOUN **Season's Greetings** meilleurs vœux MASC PLURAL

greetings card NOUN carte (FEM) de vœux

grey ADJECTIVE gris; **a grey skirt** une jupe grise, **to have grey hair** avoir les cheveux gris

greyhound NOUN lévrier MASC

grid NOUN ❶ (grating) grille FEM ❷ (network) réseau MASC (PLURAL réseaux)

grief NOUN chagrin MASC

grill NOUN (of a cooker) gril MASC

grill VERB to grill something faire [10] griller quelque chose, **I grilled the sausages** j'ai fait griller les saucisses

grim ADJECTIVE sinistre

grin NOUN sourire MASC

grin VERB sourire [68]

grip NOUN prise FEM

grip VERB serrer [1]

grit NOUN (for roads) gravillons MASC PLURAL

groan NOUN ❶ (of pain) gémissement MASC ❷ (of disgust, boredom) grognement MASC

groan VERB ❶ (in pain) gémir [2] ❷ (in disgust, boredom) grogner [1]

grocer NOUN épicier MASC; **my dad's a grocer** mon père est épicier

groceries PLURAL NOUN provisions FEM PLURAL; **to buy some groceries** acheter des provisions

grocer's NOUN épicerie FEM; **I met Jake in the grocer's** j'ai rencontré Jake à l'épicerie

groom NOUN (bridegroom) marié MASC; **the bride and groom** les jeunes mariés

gross ADJECTIVE ❶ **a gross injustice** une injustice flagrante ❷ **a gross error** une erreur grossière ❸ (disgusting) dégoûtant; **the food was gross!** la nourriture était dégoûtante!

ground NOUN ❶ terre FEM; **to sit on the ground** s'asseoir par terre, **to throw something on the ground** jeter quelque chose par terre ❷ (for sport) terrain MASC; **a football ground** un terrain de foot

ground ADJECTIVE moulu; **ground coffee** du café moulu

ground floor NOUN rez-de-chaussée MASC; **they live on the ground floor** ils habitent au rez-de-chaussée

group NOUN groupe MASC

grow VERB ❶ (plant, hair) pousser [1]; **you hair's grown!** tes cheveux ont poussé! ❷ (person) grandir [2]; **my little sister's grown a lot this year** ma petite sœur a beaucoup grandi cette année ❸ (number) augmenter [1]; **the number of students has grown** le nombre d'étudiants a augmenté ❹ faire [10] pousser (fruit, vegetables); **our neighbours grow strawberries** nos voisins font pousser des fraises ❺ **to grow a beard** se laisser [1] pousser la barbe ❻ **to grow old** vieillir [2]
• **to grow up** grandir [2]; **the children are growing up** les enfants grandissent, **she grew up in Scotland** elle a grandi en Écosse

growl VERB grogner [1]

grown-up NOUN adulte MASC & FEM

growth NOUN croissance FEM

grudge NOUN **to bear a grudge against somebody** en vouloir à quelqu'un, **she bears me a grudge** elle m'en veut

gruesome ADJECTIVE horrible

grumble VERB se plaindre [31]; **she's always grumbling** elle est toujours en train de se plaindre, **to grumble about something** se plaindre de quelque chose

guarantee NOUN garantie FEM; **a year's guarantee** une garantie d'un an

guarantee VERB garantir [2]

guard NOUN ❶ **a prison guard** un gardien de prison ❷ (on a train) chef (MASC) de train ❸ **a security guard** un vigile

guard VERB surveiller [1]

guard dog NOUN chien (MASC) de garde

guardian NOUN (of child) tuteur MASC, tutrice FEM

guess NOUN **have a guess!** devine!, **it's a good guess** tu as deviné

guess VERB deviner [1]; **guess who I saw last night!** devine qui j'ai vu hier soir!, **you'll never guess!** tu ne devineras jamais!

guest NOUN ❶ invité MASC, invitée FEM; **we've got guests coming tonight** nous avons des invités ce soir ❷ (in a hotel) client MASC, cliente FEM ❸ **a paying guest** un hôte payant

guesthouse NOUN pension (FEM) de famille

guide NOUN ❶ (person or book) guide MASC ❷ (girl guide) guide FEM, (belonging to a church company of girl guides) éclaireuse FEM

guidebook NOUN guide MASC

guide dog NOUN chien (MASC) d'aveugle

guideline NOUN indication FEM

guilty ADJECTIVE coupable; **to feel guilty** se sentir coupable

guinea pig NOUN (pet) cochon (MASC) d'Inde, (in an experiment) cobaye MASC; **they want me to be a guinea pig** ils veulent que je serve de cobaye

guitar NOUN guitare FEM; **to play the guitar** jouer de la guitare, **on the guitar** à la guitare

guitarist NOUN guitariste MASC & FEM

gum NOUN ❶ (in mouth) gencive FEM ❷ (chewing gum) chewing-gum MASC

gun NOUN ❶ revolver MASC ❷ (rifle) fusil MASC

gust NOUN **a gust of wind** une rafale de vent

gutter NOUN (in the street) caniveau (PLURAL caniveaux)

guy NOUN type MASC (informal); **he's a nice guy** c'est un type sympa, **a guy from Newcastle** un type qui vient de Newcastle

guy rope NOUN corde (FEM) d'attache

gym NOUN gym FEM; **to go to the gym** aller à la gym

gymnasium NOUN gymnase MASC

gymnast NOUN gymnaste MASC & FEM

gymnastics NOUN gymnastique FEM

gym shoe NOUN tennis MASC

a
b
c
d
e
f
g
h
i
j
k
l
m
n
o
p
q
r
s
t
u
v
w
x
y
z

habit NOUN habitude FEM; **to be in
the habit of doing** avoir l'habitude
de faire, **it's a bad habit** c'est une
mauvaise habitude

haddock NOUN églefin MASC; **smoked
haddock** haddock MASC

hail NOUN grêle FEM

hailstone NOUN grêlon MASC

hailstorm NOUN averse (FEM) de grêle

hair NOUN ❶ cheveux MASC PLURAL; **to
have short hair** avoir les cheveux
courts, **to brush your hair** se
brosser les cheveux, **to wash your
hair** se laver les cheveux, **to have
your hair cut** se faire couper les
cheveux, **she's had her hair cut** elle
s'est fait couper les cheveux ❷ **a
hair** (from the head) un cheveu,
(from the body) un poil

hairbrush NOUN brosse (FEM) à
cheveux

haircut NOUN ❶ coupe FEM; **I like
your new haircut** j'aime bien ta
nouvelle coupe ❷ **to have a haircut**
se faire couper les cheveux

hairdresser NOUN coiffeur
MASC, coiffeuse FEM; **she's a
hairdresser** elle est coiffeuse, **at the
hairdresser's** chez le coiffeur

hair drier NOUN sèche-cheveux MASC

hair gel NOUN gel (MASC) pour les
cheveux

hairgrip NOUN pince (FEM) à cheveux

hair remover NOUN crème (FEM)
dépilatoire

hairslide NOUN barrette FEM

hairspray NOUN laque FEM

hairstyle NOUN coiffure FEM

hairy ADJECTIVE poilu

Haiti NOUN Haïti MASC

Haitian NOUN Haïtien MASC,
Haïtienne FEM

Haitian ADJECTIVE haïtien (FEM
haïtienne)

half NOUN ❶ moitié FEM; **half of** la
moitié de, **I gave him half of the
money** je lui ai donné la moitié de
l'argent, **half an apple** la moitié
d'une pomme, **you've only eaten
half of it** tu n'en as mangé que la
moitié, **half the people** la moitié
des gens ❷ **to cut something in half**
couper quelque chose en deux ❸ (as
a fraction) demi; **three and a half**
trois et demi, **she's five and a half**
elle a cinq ans et demi ❹ (in time)
demi, demie; **half an hour** une
demi-heure, **an hour and a half** une
heure et demie, **it's half past three**
il est trois heures et demie ❺ (in
weights and measures) demi,
demie; **half a litre** un demi-litre,
half a cup une demi-tasse

half hour NOUN demi-heure FEM;
every half hour toutes les demi-
heures

half price ADJECTIVE, ADVERB à moitié
prix; **half-price CDs** des CD à moitié
prix, **I bought it half price** je l'ai
acheté à moitié prix

half-time NOUN mi-temps FEM; **at
half-time** à la mi-temps

halfway ADVERB ❶ à mi-chemin; **halfway between Paris and Dijon** à mi-chemin entre Paris et Dijon ❷ **to be halfway through doing** avoir à moitié fini de faire, **I'm halfway through my homework** j'ai à moitié fini mes devoirs

hall NOUN ❶ (in a house) entrée FEM ❷ (public) salle FEM; **the village hall** la salle des fêtes, **a concert hall** une salle de concert

Hallowe'en NOUN la veille de la Toussaint (the French do not have any particular customs for this date)

ham NOUN jambon MASC; **a slice of ham** une tranche de jambon, **a ham sandwich** un sandwich au jambon

hamburger NOUN hamburger MASC

hammer NOUN marteau MASC (PLURAL marteaux)

hammock NOUN hamac MASC

hamster NOUN hamster MASC

hand NOUN ❶ main FEM; **to have something in your hand** avoir quelque chose à la main, **to hold somebody's hand** tenir quelqu'un par la main ❷ **to give somebody a hand** donner un coup de main à quelqu'un, **can you give me a hand to move the table?** est-ce que tu peux me donner un coup de main pour déplacer la table?, **do you need a hand?** est-ce que tu as besoin d'un coup de main? ❸ **on the other hand ...** par contre ... ❹ (of a watch or clock) aiguille FEM; **the hour hand** l'aiguille des heures

hand VERB **to hand something to somebody** passer [1] quelque chose à quelqu'un, **I handed him the keys** je lui ai passé les clés
• **to hand something in** rendre [3]

quelque chose; **I've handed in my homework** j'ai rendu mon devoir
• **to hand something out** distribuer [1] quelque chose; **Claire handed out the exercise books** Claire a distribué les cahiers

handbag NOUN sac (MASC) à main (PLURAL sacs à main)

handcuffs PLURAL NOUN menottes FEM PLURAL

handful NOUN **a handful of** une poignée de

handkerchief NOUN mouchoir MASC

handle NOUN ❶ (of a door or drawer) poignée FEM ❷ (on a cup or basket) anse FEM ❸ (of a knife, tool, or saucepan) manche MASC ❹ (of a frying pan) queue FEM

handle VERB ❶ s'occuper [1] de; **Gina handles the accounts** Gina s'occupe de la comptabilité ❷ **she's good at handling people** elle a un bon contact avec les gens ❸ **I can't handle any more problems!** j'ai assez de problèmes comme ça!

handlebars PLURAL NOUN guidon MASC

hand luggage NOUN bagages (MASC PLURAL) à main

handmade ADJECTIVE fait à la main

handsome ADJECTIVE beau (FEM belle); **he's a handsome guy** c'est un beau type

handwriting NOUN écriture FEM

handy ADJECTIVE ❶ pratique; **this little knife's very handy** ce petit couteau est très pratique ❷ sous la main; **I always keep a notebook handy** je garde toujours un calepin sous la main

a
b
c
d
e
f
g
h
i
j
k
l
m
n
o
p
q
r
s
t
u
v
w
x
y
z

hang VERB ❶ être [6] accroché; **there was a mirror hanging on the wall** il y avait un miroir accroché au mur ❷ **to hang something** accrocher [1] quelque chose, **we hung the mirror on the wall** nous avons accroché le miroir au mur
- **to hang around** traîner [1]; **we were hanging around outside the cinema** on traînait devant le cinéma
- **to hang down** pendre [3]
- **to hang on** attendre [3]; **hang on a second!** attends une seconde!
- **to hang up** (on the phone) raccrocher [1]; **she hung up on me** elle m'a raccroché au nez (literally: she hung up on my nose)
- **to hang something up** accrocher [1] quelque chose; **you can hang your coat up in the hall** tu peux accrocher ton manteau dans l'entrée

hang-gliding NOUN deltaplane MASC; **to go hang-gliding** faire du deltaplane

hangover NOUN gueule (FEM) de bois; **to have a hangover** avoir la gueule de bois

happen VERB ❶ se passer [1]; **what's happening?** qu'est-ce qui se passe?, **it happened in June** ça s'est passé en juin ❷ **what's happened to the can-opener?** où est l'ouvre-boîte? ❸ **if you happen to see Jill** si par hasard tu vois Jill

happily ADVERB ❶ joyeusement; **she smiled happily** elle a souri joyeusement ❷ (willingly) volontiers; **I'll happily do it for you** je le ferai pour toi volontiers

happiness NOUN bonheur MASC

happy ADJECTIVE heureux (FEM heureuse); **a happy child** un enfant heureux, **Happy Birthday!** Bon anniversaire!

harbour NOUN port MASC

hard ADJECTIVE ❶ dur; **to go hard** durcir ❷ (difficult) difficile; **a hard question** une question difficile, **it's hard to know ...** il est difficile de savoir ...

hard ADVERB ❶ **to work hard** travailler dur ❷ **to try hard** faire beaucoup d'efforts

hard-boiled egg NOUN œuf (MASC) dur

hard disk NOUN (in a computer) disque (MASC) dur

hardly ADVERB ❶ à peine; **I can hardly hear him** je l'entends à peine ❷ **hardly any** presque pas de, **there's hardly any milk** il n'y a presque pas de lait ❸ **hardly ever** presque jamais, **I hardly ever see them** je ne les vois presque jamais ❹ **there was hardly anybody** il n'y avait presque personne

hard up ADJECTIVE fauché (informal)

hare NOUN lièvre MASC

harm NOUN **it won't do you any harm** ça ne te fera pas de mal

harm VERB **to harm somebody** faire [10] du mal à quelqu'un, **they did not harm him** ils ne lui ont pas fait de mal, **a cup of coffee won't harm you** une tasse de café ne te fera pas de mal

harmful ADJECTIVE nuisible

harmless ADJECTIVE inoffensif (FEM inoffensive)

harvest NOUN récolte FEM; **to get the harvest in** faire [10] la récolte

hat NOUN chapeau MASC (PLURAL chapeaux)

hate VERB détester [1]; **I hate geography** je déteste la géographie

hatred NOUN haine FEM

haunted ADJECTIVE hanté

have VERB ❶ avoir [5]; **Anna has three brothers** Anna a trois frères, **how many sisters do you have?** tu as combien de sœurs? ❷ **to have got** avoir [5], **we've got a dog** nous avons un chien, **what have you got in your hand?** qu'est-ce que tu as à la main? ❸ *(to form past tenses, some verbs in French take 'avoir' and some 'être')* **I've finished** j'ai fini, **have you seen the film?** est-ce que tu as vu le film?, **Rosie hasn't arrived yet** Rosie n'est pas encore arrivée, **he had left** il était parti ❹ **to have to do** devoir [8] faire, **I have to phone my mum** je dois appeler ma mère ❺ **prendre** [64] *(food, drink, a shower)*; **we had a coffee** nous avons pris un café, **what will you have?** qu'est-ce que tu prends?, **I'll have an omelette** je prends une omelette, **I'm going to have a shower** je vais prendre une douche ❻ **to have lunch** déjeuner [1], **to have dinner** *(in the evening)* dîner [1] ❼ **to have something done** faire [10] faire quelque chose, **I'm going to have my hair cut** je vais me faire couper les cheveux

hawk NOUN faucon MASC

hay NOUN foin MASC

hay fever NOUN rhume *(MASC)* des foins

hazelnut NOUN noisette FEM

he PRONOUN il; **he lives in Manchester** il habite à Manchester, **he's my brother** c'est mon frère

head NOUN ❶ tête FEM; **he had a cap on his head** il avait une casquette sur la tête, **at the head of the queue** à la tête de la queue ❷ *(of school)* directeur MASC, directrice FEM ❸ *(when tossing a coin)* **'heads or tails?' – 'heads'** 'pile ou face?' – 'face' *(note that it is in fact 'tails or heads' in French)*
• **to head for something** se diriger [52] vers quelque chose; **Liz headed for the door** Liz s'est dirigée vers la porte

headache NOUN **I've got a headache** j'ai mal à la tête

headlight NOUN phare MASC

headline NOUN gros titre MASC; **to hit the headlines** faire la une

headmaster NOUN directeur MASC

headmistress NOUN directrice FEM

headphones PLURAL NOUN casque MASC SINGULAR

headquarters NOUN ❶ *(of organization)* siège *(MASC)* social ❷ *(military)* quartier *(MASC)* général

headteacher NOUN directeur MASC, directrice FEM

health NOUN santé FEM

health centre NOUN centre *(MASC)* médico-social

healthy ADJECTIVE ❶ *(person)* **to be healthy** être en bonne santé ❷ **a healthy diet** une alimentation saine

heap NOUN tas MASC; **I've got heaps of things to do** j'ai un tas de choses à faire

hear VERB ❶ entendre [3]; **I can't hear you** je ne t'entends pas, **I can't hear anything** je n'entends rien ❷ apprendre [64] (news); **I hear you've bought a dog** j'apprends que tu as acheté un chien
• **to hear about something** entendre [3] parler de quelque chose; **have you heard about the concert?** as-tu entendu parler du concert?
• **to hear from somebody** avoir [5] des nouvelles de quelqu'un; **have you heard from Amanda?** as-tu des nouvelles d'Amanda?

hearing aid NOUN Sonotone MASC

heart NOUN ❶ cœur MASC; **to learn something by heart** apprendre quelque chose par cœur ❷ (in cards) cœur; **the jack of hearts** le valet de cœur

heart attack NOUN crise (FEM) cardiaque

heat NOUN chaleur FEM

heat VERB ❶ chauffer [1]; **the soup's heating** la soupe est en train de chauffer ❷ **to heat something** faire [10] chauffer quelque chose, **I'll go and heat the soup** je vais faire chauffer la soupe
• **to heat something up** faire [10] réchauffer quelque chose; **I'm heating up the sauce** je fais réchauffer la sauce

heater NOUN radiateur MASC

heather NOUN bruyère FEM

heating NOUN chauffage MASC

heatwave NOUN vague (FEM) de chaleur

heaven NOUN paradis MASC

heavy ADJECTIVE ❶ lourd; **my rucksack's really heavy** mon sac à dos est très lourd ❷ (busy) chargé; **I've got a heavy day tomorrow** j'ai une journée chargée demain ❸ **heavy rain** des pluies fortes

heavy metal NOUN (music) hard rock MASC

hectic ADJECTIVE **a hectic day** une journée mouvementée

hedge NOUN haie FEM

hedgehog NOUN hérisson MASC

heel NOUN talon MASC

height NOUN ❶ (of a person) taille FEM ❷ (of a building) hauteur FEM ❸ (of a mountain) altitude FEM

helicopter NOUN hélicoptère MASC

hell NOUN enfer MASC; **it's hell here!** c'est infernal ici!

hello EXCLAMATION ❶ (polite) bonjour! ❷ (informal) salut! ❸ (on the telephone) allô!

helmet NOUN casque MASC

help NOUN aide FEM; **do you need any help?** est-ce que tu as besoin d'aide?

help VERB ❶ aider [1]; **to help somebody to do** aider quelqu'un à faire, **can you help me move the table?** peux-tu m'aider à déplacer la table? ❷ **to help yourself to something** se servir [71] de quelque chose, **help yourselves to vegetables** servez-vous de légumes, **help yourself!** sers-toi! ❸ **help!** au secours!

helper NOUN aide MASC & FEM; **helpers are needed to run charity stalls** on a besoin de bénévoles pour tenir les stands de la fête de charité

helpful ADJECTIVE (person) serviable

helping NOUN portion FEM; **would you like a second helping of chips?** est-ce que tu veux reprendre des frites?

hem NOUN ourlet MASC

hen NOUN poule FEM

her PRONOUN ❶ la (l' before a vowel or silent 'h'); **I know her** je la connais, **I can hear her** je l'entends, **listen to her!** écoute-la!, **I saw her last week** je l'ai vue la semaine dernière ❷ (to her) lui; **I gave her my address** je lui ai donné mon adresse ❸ (after a preposition) elle; **with her** avec elle, **without her** sans elle, (in comparisons) **he's older than her** il est plus âgé qu'elle

her ADJECTIVE ❶ (before a masculine noun) son; **her brother** son frère, **her book** son livre ❷ (before a feminine noun) sa; **her sister** sa sœur, **her house** sa maison (but 'sa' becomes 'son' before a feminine noun beginning with a vowel or silent 'h') **her address** son adresse ❸ (before a plural noun) ses; **her children** ses enfants ❹ (with parts of the body) le, la, les; **she had a glass in her hand** elle avait un verre à la main, **she's washing her hands** elle se lave les mains

herb NOUN herbe FEM

herd NOUN troupeau MASC (PLURAL troupeaux)

here ADVERB ❶ ici; **not far from here** pas loin d'ici ❷ là; **Tom isn't here at the moment** Tom n'est pas là en ce moment ❸ **here is** voilà, **here's my address** voilà mon adresse ❹ **here are** voilà, **here are the photos** voilà les photos, **and here they are!** et les voilà!

hero NOUN héros MASC

heroin NOUN héroïne FEM

heroine NOUN héroïne FEM

herring NOUN hareng MASC

hers PRONOUN ❶ (for a masculine noun) le sien; **I took my hat and she took hers** j'ai pris mon chapeau et elle a pris le sien ❷ (for a feminine noun) la sienne; **I gave her my address and she gave me hers** je lui ai donné mon adresse et elle m'a donné la sienne ❸ (for a masculine plural noun) les siens; **I've invited my parents and Karen's invited hers** j'ai invité mes parents et Karen a invité les siens ❹ (for a feminine plural noun) les siennes; **I showed her my photos and she showed me hers** je lui ai montré mes photos et elle m'a montré les siennes ❺ à elle; **the green one's hers** le vert est à elle, **it's hers** c'est à elle

herself PRONOUN ❶ **she's hurt herself** elle s'est blessée ❷ **she said it herself** elle l'a dit elle-même ❸ **she did it by herself** elle l'a fait toute seule

hesitate VERB hésiter [1]; **to hesitate to do** hésiter à faire

heterosexual ADJECTIVE, NOUN hétérosexuel MASC, hétérosexuelle FEM

hi EXCLAMATION salut!

hiccups PLURAL NOUN **to have the hiccups** avoir le hoquet

hidden ADJECTIVE caché

hide VERB ❶ (person) se cacher [1]; **she hid behind the door** elle s'est cachée derrière la porte ❷ **to hide something** cacher [1] quelque chose, **who's hidden the chocolate?** qui a caché le chocolat?

hide-and-seek NOUN **to play hide-and-seek** jouer à cache-cache

hi-fi NOUN chaîne (FEM) hi-fi

high ADJECTIVE ❶ haut; **on a high shelf** sur une étagère haute, **the wall is very high** le mur est très haut, **how high is the wall?** quelle est la hauteur du mur?, **the wall is two metres high** le mur fait deux mètres de hauteur ❷ (number, price, temperature) élevé; **food prices are very high** les prix de la nourriture sont très élevés ❸ **at high speed** à grande vitesse ❹ **high winds** des vents violents ❺ **a high voice** une voix aiguë

Highers, Advanced Highers NOUN PLURAL baccalauréat MASC, bac MASC (informal) (Students take 'le bac' at the end of their secondary education. You can explain Highers briefly as follows: Les Highers sont un examen qui sanctionne l'avant-dernière année d'école secondaire en Écosse. On passe les Highers dans cinq matières au maximum. En dernière année, certains lycéens passent également les Advance Highers dans un maximum de trois matières, qui ont déjà fait l'objet de l'un de leurs Highers. Ces deux examens sont notés de A à C et permettent de s'inscrire à l'université)

high-heeled ADJECTIVE à hauts talons; **high-heeled shoes** des chaussures à hauts talons

high jump NOUN saut (MASC) en hauteur

highly ADVERB extrêmement

hijack VERB **to hijack a plane** détourner [1] un avion

hijacker NOUN pirate (MASC) de l'air

hijacking NOUN détournement MASC

hike NOUN randonnée FEM; **to go on a hike** faire une randonnée

hiker NOUN randonneur MASC, randonneuse FEM

hiking NOUN randonnée FEM

hilarious ADJECTIVE hilarant

hill NOUN ❶ (in landscape) colline FEM; **you can see the hills** on voit les collines ❷ (hillside) coteau MASC (PLURAL coteaux); **the houses on the hill** les maisons sur le coteau ❸ (sloping street or road) **to go up the hill** monter, **you go up the hill to the church and then turn right** vous montez jusqu'à l'église et vous tournez à droite

him PRONOUN ❶ le (l' before a vowel or silent 'h'); **I know him** je le connais, **I can hear him** je l'entends, **listen to him!** écoute-le!, **I saw him last week** je l'ai vu la semaine dernière ❷ (to him) lui; **I gave him my address** je lui ai donné mon adresse ❸ (after a preposition) lui; **with him** avec lui, **without him** sans lui, (in comparisons) **she's older than him** elle est plus âgée que lui

himself PRONOUN ❶ **he's hurt himself** il s'est blessé ❷ **he said it himself** il l'a dit lui-même ❸ **he did it by himself** il l'a fait tout seul

Hindu ADJECTIVE hindou

hip NOUN hanche FEM

hippie NOUN hippie MASC & FEM

hippopotamus NOUN
hippopotame MASC

hire NOUN location FEM; **car hire**
location de voitures, **for hire** à louer

hire VERB louer [1]; **we're going to
hire a car** nous allons louer une
voiture

his DETERMINER ❶ (before a masculine
noun) son; **his brother** son frère, **his
book** son livre ❷ (before a feminine
noun) sa; **his sister** sa sœur, **his
house** sa maison (but 'sa' becomes
'son' before a feminine noun
beginning with a vowel or silent 'h')
his address son adresse ❸ (before
a plural noun) ses; **his children** ses
enfants ❹ (with parts of the body)
le, la, les; **he had a glass in his
hand** il avait un verre à la main,
he's washing his hands il se lave
les mains

his PRONOUN ❶ (for a masculine noun)
le sien; **I took my hat and he took
his** j'ai pris mon chapeau et il a
pris le sien ❷ (for a feminine noun)
la sienne; **I gave him my address
and he gave me his** je lui ai donné
mon adresse et il m'a donné la
sienne ❸ (for a masculine plural
noun) les siens; **I've invited my
parents and Steve's invited his** j'ai
invité mes parents et Steve a invité
les siens ❹ (for a feminine plural
noun) les siennes; **I showed him
my photos and he showed me his**
je lui ai montré mes photos et il
m'a montré les siennes ❺ à lui; **the
green car's his** la voiture verte est la
lui, **it's his** c'est à lui

historic ADJECTIVE historique

history NOUN histoire FEM

hit NOUN ❶ (song) tube MASC
(informal); **their latest hit** leur
dernier tube ❷ (success) succès
MASC; **the film is a huge hit** le film a
un succès fou

hit VERB ❶ frapper [1]; **to hit the ball**
frapper la balle ❷ **to hit your head
on something** se cogner [1] la tête
contre quelque chose ❸ heurter
[1]; **the car hit a tree** la voiture a
heurté un arbre ❹ **to be hit by a car**
(person) être [6] renversé par une
voiture

hitch NOUN problème MASC; **there's
been a slight hitch** il y a eu un petit
problème

hitch VERB **to hitch a lift** faire [10] du
stop (informal)

hitchhike VERB faire [10] du stop
(informal); **we hitchhiked to Dijon**
nous sommes allés à Dijon en stop

hitchhiker NOUN autostoppeur
MASC, autostoppeuse FEM

hitchhiking NOUN autostop MASC

HIV-negative ADJECTIVE séronégatif
(FEM séronégative)

HIV-positive ADJECTIVE séropositif
(FEM séropositive)

hobby NOUN passe-temps MASC

hockey NOUN hockey MASC; **to play
hockey** jouer au hockey

hockey stick NOUN crosse (FEM) de
hockey

hold VERB ❶ tenir [77]; **to hold
something in your hand** tenir
quelque chose à la main, **can you
hold the torch?** est-ce que tu peux
tenir la lampe? ❷ (contain) contenir
[77]; **a jug which holds a litre** un
pichet qui contient un litre ❸ **to**

hold a meeting organiser [1] une réunion ❹ **can you hold the line, please** ne quittez pas, s'il vous plaît ❺ **hold on!** *(wait)* attends!, *(on telephone)* ne quittez pas!
- **to hold somebody up** *(delay)* retenir [77] quelqu'un; **I was held up at the dentist's** j'ai été retenu chez le dentiste
- **to hold something up** *(raise)* lever [50] quelque chose; **he held up his glass** il a levé son verre

hold-up NOUN ❶ **retard** MASC ❷ *(traffic jam)* **bouchon** MASC ❸ *(robbery)* **hold-up** MASC

hole NOUN **trou** MASC

holiday NOUN ❶ **vacances** FEM PLURAL; **where are you going for your holiday?** où est-ce que vous partez en vacances?, **have a good holiday!** bonnes vacances!, **to be away on holiday** être en vacances, **to go on holiday** partir en vacances, **the school holidays** les vacances scolaires ❷ *(from work)* **congé** MASC; **I'm taking two days' holiday next week** je prends deux jours de congé la semaine prochaine ❸ **a public holiday** un jour férié, **Monday's a holiday** lundi est férié

holiday home NOUN **résidence** *(FEM)* **secondaire**

Holland NOUN **Hollande** FEM; **to Holland** en Hollande, **in Holland** en Hollande

hollow ADJECTIVE **creux** *(FEM* **creuse)**

holly NOUN **houx** MASC

holy ADJECTIVE **saint**

home NOUN **maison** FEM; **I was at home** j'étais à la maison, **to stay at home** rester à la maison, **make yourself at home** fais comme chez toi

home ADVERB ❶ **chez soi**; **Susie's gone home** Susie est rentrée chez elle, **I'll call in and see you on my way home** je passerai te voir en rentrant chez moi ❷ **to get home** rentrer, **we got home at midnight** nous sommes rentrés à minuit

homeless ADJECTIVE **sans abri**; **the homeless** les sans-abri MASC PLURAL

homemade ADJECTIVE **fait maison**; **homemade cakes** des gâteaux faits maison

home match NOUN **match** *(MASC)* **à domicile**

homeopathic ADJECTIVE **homéopathique**

homesick ADJECTIVE **to be homesick** avoir le mal du pays

homework NOUN **devoirs** MASC PLURAL; **I did my homework** j'ai fait mes devoirs, **my French homework** mes devoirs de français, *(written)* mon devoir de français

homosexual ADJECTIVE, NOUN **homosexuel** *(FEM* **homosexuelle)**

honest ADJECTIVE **honnête**

honestly ADVERB **franchement**

honesty NOUN **honnêteté** FEM

honey NOUN **miel** MASC

honeymoon NOUN **voyage** *(MASC)* **de noces**; **they're going to Paris on their honeymoon** ils partent à Paris en voyage de noces

honeysuckle NOUN **chèvrefeuille** MASC

honour NOUN **honneur** MASC

hood NOUN **capuchon** MASC

hook NOUN ❶ crochet MASC ❷ to take the phone of the hook décrocher le téléphone

hooligan NOUN voyou MASC

hooray EXCLAMATION hourra!

hoover VERB passer [1] l'aspirateur; I hoovered my bedroom j'ai passé l'aspirateur dans ma chambre

Hoover NOUN aspirateur MASC

hope NOUN espoir MASC; to give up hope perdre espoir

hope VERB espérer [24]; we hope you'll be able to come nous espérons que vous allez pouvoir venir, hoping to see you on Friday en espérant te voir vendredi, here's hoping! espérons que ça marchera!, I hope so je l'espère, I hope not j'espère que non

hopefully ADVERB avec un peu de chance; hopefully, the film won't have started avec un peu de chance, le film n'aura pas commencé

hopeless ADJECTIVE nul (FEM nulle) (informal); I'm completely hopeless at geography je suis complètement nul en géographie

horizon NOUN horizon MASC

horizontal ADJECTIVE horizontal MASC (PLURAL horizontaux)

horn NOUN ❶ (of an animal) corne FEM ❷ (of a car) klaxon MASC; to sound your horn klaxonner ❸ (musical instrument) cor; to play the horn jouer du cor

horoscope NOUN horoscope MASC

horrible ADJECTIVE ❶ affreux (FEM affreuse); the weather was horrible il a fait un temps

affreux ❷ (person) désagréable; she's really horrible! elle est vraiment désagréable, he was really horrible to me il a été vraiment désagréable avec moi

horrific ADJECTIVE terrible; a horrific accident un terrible accident

horror NOUN horreur FEM

horror film NOUN film (MASC) d'épouvante

horse NOUN cheval MASC (PLURAL chevaux)

horse chestnut NOUN ❶ (tree) marronnier MASC ❷ (nut) marron MASC

horse racing NOUN courses (FEM PLURAL) hippiques

horseshoe NOUN fer (MASC) à cheval

hose NOUN tuyau MASC (PLURAL tuyaux)

hosepipe NOUN tuyau (MASC) d'arrosage

hospital NOUN hôpital MASC (PLURAL hôpitaux); to be in hospital être à l'hôpital, to be taken into hospital être hospitalisé

hospitality NOUN hospitalité FEM

host NOUN hôte MASC, hôtesse FEM; my host family is very nice ma famille d'accueil est très sympathique

hostage NOUN otage MASC

hostel NOUN youth hostel auberge (FEM) de jeunesse

hostess NOUN hôtesse FEM; an air hostess une hôtesse de l'air

hot ADJECTIVE ❶ chaud; a hot drink une boisson chaude, be careful, the plates are hot! fais attention, les assiettes sont très chaudes! ❷ *(a person)* **to be hot** avoir chaud, **I'm hot** j'ai chaud, **I'm very hot** j'ai très chaud, **I'm too hot** j'ai trop chaud ❸ *(the weather or temperature in a room)* **it's hot today** il fait chaud aujourd'hui, **it's very hot in the kitchen** il fait très chaud dans la cuisine ❹ *(food: spicy)* épicé; **the curry's too hot for me** le curry est trop épicé pour moi

hot dog NOUN **hot-dog** MASC

hotel NOUN **hôtel** MASC

hour NOUN **heure** FEM; **two hours later** deux heures plus tard, **we waited for two hours** nous avons attendu pendant deux heures, **two hours ago** il y a deux heures, **to be paid by the hour** être payé à l'heure, **every hour** toutes les heures, **half an hour** une demi-heure, **a quarter of an hour** un quart d'heure, **an hour and a half** une heure et demie

hourly ADJECTIVE **toutes les heures**; **there is an hourly bus** il y a un bus par heure
the trains leave hourly il y a des trains toutes les heures

house NOUN ❶ **maison** FEM; **to buy a house** acheter une maison ❷ **at somebody's house** chez quelqu'un, **I'm at Judy's house** je suis chez Judy, **I'm going to Judy's house tonight** je vais chez Judy ce soir, **I phoned from Judy's house** j'ai téléphoné de chez Judy

housewife NOUN **femme** *(FEM)* **au foyer**

housework NOUN **ménage** MASC; **to do the housework** faire le ménage

how ADVERB ❶ **comment**; **how did you do it?** comment l'as-tu fait?,

how are you? comment allez-vous? ❷ **how much?** combien?, **how much money do you have?** tu as combien d'argent?, **how much is it?** *(price)* ça coûte combien? ❸ **how many?** combien?, **how many brothers do you have?** tu as combien de frères? ❹ **how old are you?** quel âge as-tu? ❺ **how far is it?** c'est à quelle distance d'ici?, **how far is it to Paris?** Paris est à quelle distance d'ici? ❻ **how long will it take?** ça va prendre combien de temps?, **how long have you known her?** tu la connais depuis combien de temps?

however ADVERB **cependant**

hug NOUN **to give somebody a hug** serrer quelqu'un dans ses bras; **she gave me a hug** elle m'a serré dans ses bras

huge ADJECTIVE **immense**

hum VERB **fredonner** [1]

human ADJECTIVE **humain**

human being NOUN **être** *(MASC)* **humain**

humour NOUN **humour** MASC; **to have a sense of humour** avoir le sens de l'humour

hundred NUMBER ❶ **cent**; **two hundred** deux cents, **two hundred and ten** deux cent dix *(note that there is no 's' on 'cent' when it is followed by another number)*, **a hundred people** cent personnes ❷ **about a hundred** une centaine, **about a hundred people** une centaine de personnes, **hundreds of people** des centaines de personnes

Hungary NOUN **Hongrie** FEM

hunger NOUN **faim** FEM

English—French

hungry ADJECTIVE **to be hungry** avoir faim, **I'm hungry** j'ai faim

hunt VERB ❶ chasser [1] *(an animal)* ❷ rechercher [1] *(person)*

hunting NOUN chasse FEM; **fox-hunting** la chasse au renard

hurricane NOUN ouragan MASC

hurry NOUN **to be in a hurry** être pressé, **I'm in a hurry** je suis pressé

hurry VERB se dépêcher [50]; **I must hurry** je dois me dépêcher, **he hurried home** il s'est dépêché de rentrer chez lui, **hurry up!** dépêche-toi!

hurt VERB ❶ **to hurt somebody** faire [10] mal à quelqu'un, **you're hurting me!** tu me fais mal!, **that hurts!** ça fait mal! ❷ **my back hurts** j'ai mal au dos ❸ **to hurt yourself** se faire [10] mal, **did you hurt yourself?** est-ce que tu t'es fait mal?

hurt ADJECTIVE ❶ *(in an accident)* blessé; **three people were hurt** trois personnes ont été blessées ❷ *(in feelings)* blessé; **she felt hurt** elle était blessée

husband NOUN mari MASC

hutch NOUN clapier MASC

hygienic ADJECTIVE hygiénique

hymn NOUN cantique MASC

hypermarket NOUN hypermarché MASC

hyphen NOUN trait *(MASC)* d'union

hypnotize VERB hypnotiser [1]

I PRONOUN ❶ je *(j' before a vowel or a silent 'h')*; **I am Scottish** je suis écossais, **I have two sisters** j'ai deux sœurs ❷ moi; **Robert and I** Robert et moi, **Tony and I left before you** Tony et moi sommes partis avant vous

ice NOUN ❶ glace FEM ❷ *(on the roads)* verglas MASC ❸ *(in a drink)* glaçons MASC PLURAL

iceberg NOUN iceberg MASC

ice cream NOUN glace FEM; **a chocolate ice cream** une glace au chocolat

ice-cube NOUN glaçon MASC

ice hockey NOUN hockey *(MASC)* sur glace

ice rink NOUN patinoire FEM

ice-skating NOUN **to go ice-skating** faire [10] du patin à glace

icing NOUN glaçage MASC

icon NOUN icône FEM

icy ADJECTIVE ❶ verglacé *(a road)* ❷ *(very cold)* glacial; **an icy wind** un vent glacial

idea NOUN idée FEM; **what a good idea!** quelle bonne idée!, **I've no idea** je n'ai aucune idée

ideal ADJECTIVE idéal MASC *(PLURAL* idéaux*)*

identical ADJECTIVE identique; **identical twins** des vrais jumeaux

a
b
c
d
e
f
g
h
i
j
k
l
m
n
o
p
q
r
s
t
u
v
w
x
y
z

identification NOUN identification FEM

identify VERB identifier [1]

identity card NOUN carte (FEM) d'identité

idiom NOUN idiome MASC

idiot NOUN idiot MASC, idiote FEM

idiotic ADJECTIVE bête

idyllic ADJECTIVE idyllique

i.e. c-à-d (short for c'est-à-dire)

if CONJUNCTION ❶ si (s' before 'il' and 'ils'); if Sue's there si Sue est là, if it rains s'il pleut, if I won the lottery si je gagnais la loterie, if not sinon ❷ if only … si seulement …, if only you'd told me si seulement tu me l'avais dit ❸ even if même si, even if it snows même s'il neige ❹ if I were you … à ta place …, if I were you, I'd forget it à ta place je n'y penserais plus

ignore VERB ❶ ignorer [1] (a person) ❷ ne pas écouter [1] (what somebody says) ❸ just ignore it ne fais pas attention

ill ADJECTIVE malade; to fall ill, to be taken ill tomber [1] malade, I feel ill je ne me sens pas bien

illegal ADJECTIVE illégal MASC (PLURAL illégaux)

illegible ADJECTIVE illisible

illness NOUN maladie FEM

illusion NOUN illusion FEM

illustrated ADJECTIVE illustré

illustration NOUN illustration FEM

image NOUN image FEM
• he's the spitting image of his father c'est son père tout craché

imagination NOUN imagination FEM; to show imagination faire preuve d'imagination

imaginative ADJECTIVE plein d'imagination

imagine VERB imaginer [1]; imagine that you're very rich imagine que tu es très riche, you can't imagine how hard it was! tu ne peux pas t'imaginer combien c'était difficile!

imitate VERB imiter [1]

imitation NOUN imitation FEM

immediate ADJECTIVE immédiat

immediately ADVERB immédiatement; I rang them immediately je les ai appelés immédiatement, immediately before juste avant, immediately after juste après

immigrant NOUN immigré MASC, immigrée FEM

immigration NOUN immigration FEM

impact NOUN impact MASC

impatience NOUN impatience FEM

impatient ADJECTIVE ❶ impatient ❷ to get impatient with somebody s'impatienter [1] contre quelqu'un

impatiently ADVERB avec impatience

imperfect NOUN (of a verb) imparfait MASC; in the imperfect à l'imparfait

import NOUN produit (MASC) importé

import VERB importer [1]

importance NOUN importance FEM

important ADJECTIVE important

impossible *ADJECTIVE* impossible; **it's impossible to find a telephone** il est impossible de trouver un téléphone

impressed *ADJECTIVE* impressionné

impression *NOUN* impression *FEM*; **to make a good impression on somebody** faire bonne impression sur quelqu'un, **I got the impression he was hiding something** j'avais l'impression qu'il cachait quelque chose

impressive *ADJECTIVE* impressionnant

improve *VERB* ❶ to improve something améliorer [1] quelque chose ❷ (get better) s'améliorer [1]; **the weather is improving** le temps s'améliore

improvement *NOUN* ❶ (a clear change for the better) amélioration *FEM* ❷ (gradual progress) progrès *MASC PLURAL* (in schoolwork, for example)

in *PREPOSITION, ADVERB* ❶ dans; **in my pocket** dans ma poche, **in the newspaper** dans le journal, **in the kitchen** dans la cuisine, **in my class** dans ma classe, **I was in the bath** j'étais dans mon bain ❷ à; **in Oxford** à Oxford, **a house in the country** une maison à la campagne, **in school** à l'école, **in the sun** au soleil, **the girl in the pink shirt** la fille à la chemise rose ❸ en; **in France** en France **in Portugal** au Portugal *('en' for feminine countries, 'au' for most masculine countries)*, **in town** en ville, **in French** en français ❹ (time expressions) **in May** en mai, **in '94** en quatre-vingt-quatorze, **in winter** en hiver, **in summer** en été, **in spring** au printemps, **in the morning** le matin, **at eight in the morning** à huit heures du matin, **in the**

night pendant la nuit, **I'll phone you in ten minutes** je t'appellerai dans dix minutes, **she did it in five minutes** elle l'a fait en cinq minutes ❺ (talking about a group) de; **the tallest boy in the class** le garçon le plus grand de la classe, **the biggest city in the world** la ville la plus grande du monde ❻ **in time** à temps ❼ **in the photo** sur la photo ❽ **in the rain** sous la pluie ❾ **dressed in white** habillé en blanc ❿ **to come in** entrer, **to go in** entrer, **we went into the cinema** nous sommes entrés dans le cinéma, **to run in** entrer en courant ⓫ **to be in** être là, **Mick's not in at the moment** Mick n'est pas là en ce moment

incident *NOUN* incident *MASC*

include *VERB* comprendre [64]; **dinner is included in the price** le dîner est compris dans le prix, **service included** service compris

including *PREPOSITION* (y) compris; **£50 including VAT** cinquante livres TVA comprise, **everyone, including children** tout le monde, y compris les enfants, **including Sundays** y compris les dimanches, **not including Sundays** sans compter les dimanches

income *NOUN* revenu *MASC*

income tax *NOUN* impôt *(MASC)* sur le revenu

inconvenient
ADJECTIVE ❶ incommode (a place or an arrangement) ❷ inopportun (a time)

increase *NOUN* augmentation *FEM* (in price, for example)

increase VERB augmenter [1]; **the price has increased by £10** le prix a augmenté de dix livres

incredible ADJECTIVE incroyable

incredibly ADVERB (very) extrêmement; **the film's incredibly boring** le film est extrêmement ennuyeux

indeed ADVERB ❶ (to emphasize) vraiment; **she's very pleased indeed** elle est vraiment très contente, **I'm very hungry indeed** j'ai vraiment très faim, **thank you very much indeed** merci beaucoup ❷ (certainly) bien sûr; **'can you hear his radio?' – 'indeed I can!'** 'entends-tu sa radio?' – 'bien sûr que oui!'

indefinite article NOUN (in grammar) article (MASC) indéfini

independence NOUN indépendance FEM

independent ADJECTIVE indépendant; **an independent school** une école privée

index NOUN index MASC

index finger NOUN index MASC

India NOUN Inde FEM; **in India** en Inde, **to India** en Inde

Indian NOUN Indien MASC, Indienne FEM

Indian ADJECTIVE indien (FEM indienne)

indicate VERB indiquer [1]

indication NOUN indication FEM

indigestion NOUN indigestion FEM; **to have indigestion** avoir une indigestion

indirect ADJECTIVE indirect

individual NOUN individu MASC

individual ADJECTIVE ❶ individuel (FEM individuelle) (a serving or a contribution, for example) ❷ **individual tuition** des cours particuliers

indoor ADJECTIVE couvert; **an indoor swimming pool** une piscine couverte

indoors ADVERB à l'intérieur; **it's cooler indoors** il fait plus frais à l'intérieur, **to go indoors** rentrer

industrial ADJECTIVE industriel (FEM industrielle)

industrial estate NOUN zone (FEM) industrielle

industry NOUN industrie FEM; **the advertising industry** l'industrie de la publicité

inefficient ADJECTIVE inefficace

inevitable ADJECTIVE inévitable

inevitably ADVERB inévitablement

inexperienced ADJECTIVE inexpérimenté

infant school NOUN école (FEM) maternelle

infected ADJECTIVE qui s'est infecté

infection NOUN infection FEM; **an eye infection** une infection de l'œil, **a throat infection** une angine

infectious ADJECTIVE contagieux (FEM contagieuse)

infinitive NOUN infinitif MASC; **in the infinitive** à l'infinitif

inflammable ADJECTIVE inflammable

inflatable *ADJECTIVE* pneumatique *(a mattress or a boat)*

inflate *VERB* gonfler [1] *(a mattress or boat)*

inflation *NOUN* inflation *FEM*

influence *NOUN* influence *FEM*; **to be a good influence on somebody** avoir une bonne influence sur quelqu'un

influence *VERB* influencer [61]

inform *VERB* informer [1]; **to inform somebody that** informer quelqu'un du fait que, **they informed us that there was a problem** ils nous ont informés du fait qu'il y avait un problème, **to inform somebody of something** informer quelqu'un de quelque chose

informal *ADJECTIVE* ❶ simple *(a meal or event, for example)* ❷ *(language)* familier *(FEM* familière*)*; **an informal expression** une expression familière

information *NOUN* renseignements *MASC PLURAL*; **I need some information about flights to Paris** j'ai besoin de quelques renseignements sur les vols vers Paris, **a piece of information** un renseignement

information desk, **information office** *NOUN* bureau *(MASC)* des renseignements

information technology *NOUN* informatique *FEM*

infuriating *ADJECTIVE* exaspérant

ingredient *NOUN* ingrédient *MASC*

inhabitant *NOUN* habitant *MASC*, habitante *FEM*

initials *PLURAL NOUN* initiales *FEM PLURAL*; **put your initials here** marquez vos initiales ici

initiative *NOUN* initiative *FEM*

injection *NOUN* piqûre *FEM*; **to give somebody an injection** faire [10] une piqûre à quelqu'un

injure *VERB* blesser [1]

injured *ADJECTIVE* blessé

injury *NOUN* blessure *FEM*

ink *NOUN* encre *FEM*

in-laws *NOUN* beaux-parents *MASC PLURAL*

inner *ADJECTIVE* intérieur

innocent *ADJECTIVE* innocent

insane *ADJECTIVE* fou *(FEM* folle*)*

inscription *NOUN* inscription *FEM*

insect *NOUN* insecte *MASC*; **an insect bite** une piqûre d'insecte

insect repellent *NOUN* insectifuge *MASC*

insert *VERB* insérer [24]

inside *NOUN* intérieur *MASC*; **the inside of the oven** l'intérieur du four

inside *PREPOSITION* à l'intérieur de; **inside the cinema** à l'intérieur du cinéma

inside *ADVERB* à l'intérieur; **she's inside, I think** elle est à l'intérieur, je crois, **to go inside** rentrer

inside out *ADJECTIVE, ADVERB* à l'envers

insincere *ADJECTIVE* peu sincère

a b c d e f g h i j k l m n o p q r s t u v w x y z

English—French

A B C D E F G H I J K L M N O P Q R S T U V W X Y Z

insist VERB ❶ insister [1]; **if you insist** puisque tu insistes, **to insist on doing** insister pour faire, **he insisted on paying** il a insisté pour payer ❷ **to insist that** affirmer [1] que, **Ruth insisted I was wrong** Ruth a affirmé que j'avais tort

insomnia NOUN insomnie FEM

inspector NOUN inspecteur MASC, inspectrice FEM

install VERB installer [1]

instalment NOUN (of a story or serial) épisode MASC

instance NOUN **for instance** par exemple

instant NOUN instant MASC; **come here this instant!** viens ici tout de suite!

instant ADJECTIVE ❶ instantané (coffee or soup) ❷ (immediate) immédiat (an effect or a success, for example)

instantly ADVERB immédiatement

instead ADVERB ❶ **Ted couldn't go, so I went instead** Ted ne pouvait pas y aller, donc je suis allé à sa place, **we didn't go to the concert, we went to Lucy's instead** au lieu d'aller au concert, nous sommes allés chez Lucy ❷ **instead of** au lieu de, **instead of pudding I had cheese** j'ai pris le fromage au lieu d'un dessert, **instead of playing tennis we went swimming** au lieu de jouer au tennis nous sommes allés à la piscine

instinct NOUN instinct MASC

institute NOUN institut MASC

institution NOUN institution FEM

instruct VERB **to instruct somebody to do** donner [1] l'ordre à quelqu'un de faire, **the teacher instructed us**

to stay together le professeur nous a donné l'ordre de rester en groupe

instructions PLURAL NOUN instructions FEM PLURAL; **follow the instructions on the packet** suivez les instructions sur l'emballage, **'instructions for use'** 'mode d'emploi'

instructor NOUN moniteur MASC, monitrice FEM; **my skiing instructor** mon moniteur de ski

instrument NOUN instrument MASC; **to play an instrument** jouer d'un instrument

insulin NOUN insuline FEM

insult NOUN insulte FEM

insult VERB insulter [1]

insurance NOUN assurance FEM; **travel insurance** l'assurance voyage, **do you have medical insurance?** est-ce que vous avez une assurance maladie?

intelligence NOUN intelligence FEM

intelligent ADJECTIVE intelligent

intend VERB ❶ vouloir [14]; **as I intended** comme je le voulais ❷ **to intend to do** avoir [5] l'intention de faire, **we intend to spend the night in Rome** nous avons l'intention de passer la nuit à Rome

intensive ADJECTIVE intensif (FEM intensive)

intensive care NOUN **in intensive care** en réanimation

intention NOUN intention FEM; **I have no intention of paying** je n'ai aucune intention de payer

interest NOUN ❶ *(hobby)* centre *(MASC)* d'intérêt; **what are your interests?** quels sont vos centres d'intérêt? ❷ *(keenness)* intérêt *MASC*; **he has an interest in jazz** il a un intérêt pour le jazz

interest VERB intéresser [1]; **that doesn't interest me** ça ne m'intéresse pas

interested ADJECTIVE **to be interested in** s'intéresser à, **Sean's very interested in cooking** Sean s'intéresse beaucoup à la cuisine

interesting ADJECTIVE intéressant

interfere VERB ❶ **to interfere with something** *(to fiddle with it)* toucher [1] quelque chose, **don't interfere with my computer!** ne touche pas mon ordinateur ❷ **to interfere in** se mêler [1] à *(someone else's affairs)*

interior ADJECTIVE intérieur

interior designer NOUN designer *MASC & FEM*

international ADJECTIVE international *MASC (PLURAL* internationaux)

Internet NOUN Internet *MASC*; **on the Internet** sur Internet

interpret VERB *(act as an interpreter)* faire [10] l'interprète

interpreter NOUN interprète *MASC & FEM*

interrupt VERB interrompre [69]

interruption NOUN interruption *FEM*

interval NOUN entracte *MASC (in a play or concert)*

interview NOUN ❶ *(for a job)* entretien *MASC*; **a job interview** un entretien ❷ *(in a newspaper, on TV or radio)* interview *FEM*

interview VERB interviewer [1] *(on TV, radio)*

interviewer NOUN interviewer *MASC*

into PREPOSITION ❶ dans; **he's gone into the bank** il est entré dans la banque, **I put the cat into his basket** j'ai mis le chat dans son panier, **we all got into the car** nous sommes tous montés dans la voiture ❷ **to go into town** aller en ville, **Mum's gone into town** Maman est allée en ville, **to get into bed** se mettre au lit, **to translate into French** traduire en français, **to change pounds into euros** changer des livres sterling en euros ❸ **to be into jazz** être fana du jazz *(informal)*

introduce VERB présenter [1]; **she introduced me to her brother** elle m'a présenté à son frère, **can I introduce you to my mother?** je te présente ma mère

introduction NOUN *(in a book)* introduction *FEM*

intuition NOUN intuition *FEM*

invade VERB envahir [2]

invalid NOUN malade *MASC & FEM*

invasion NOUN invasion *FEM*

invent VERB inventer [1]

invention NOUN invention *FEM*

inventor NOUN inventeur *MASC*, inventrice *FEM*

inverted commas PLURAL NOUN guillemets *MASC PLURAL*; **in inverted commas** entre guillemets

investigation NOUN *(by police)* enquête *FEM*; **an investigation into the fire** une enquête sur l'incendie

invisible ADJECTIVE invisible

invitation NOUN invitation FEM; **an invitation to dinner** une invitation à dîner

invite VERB inviter [1]; **Kirsty invited me to lunch** Kirsty m'a invité à déjeuner, **he's invited me out on Tuesday** il m'a invitée à sortir avec lui mardi

inviting ADJECTIVE ❶ appétissant (a meal) ❷ accueillant (a room)

invoice NOUN facture FEM

involve VERB ❶ nécessiter [1]; **it involves a lot of work** cela nécessite beaucoup de travail ❷ (to affect) concerner [1]; **the play will involve everybody** le spectacle va concerner tout le monde, **two cars were involved** deux voitures ont été concernées ❸ **to be involved in** participer [1] à, **I am involved in the new project** je participe au nouveau projet

Iran NOUN Iran MASC

Iraq NOUN Iraq MASC

Ireland NOUN Irlande FEM; **in Ireland** en Irlande, **to Ireland** en Irlande, **the Republic of Ireland** la République d'Irlande

Irish NOUN ❶ (the language) irlandais MASC ❷ (the people) **the Irish** les Irlandais MASC PLURAL

Irish ADJECTIVE irlandais

Irishman NOUN Irlandais MASC

Irish Sea NOUN mer (FEM) d'Irlande

Irishwoman NOUN Irlandaise FEM

iron NOUN ❶ (for clothes) fer (MASC) à repasser ❷ (the metal) fer MASC

iron VERB repasser [1]

ironing NOUN repassage MASC; **to do the ironing** faire le repassage

ironing board NOUN planche (FEM) à repasser

ironmonger's NOUN quincaillerie FEM

irregular ADJECTIVE irrégulier (FEM irrégulière)

irresponsible ADJECTIVE irresponsable

irritable ADJECTIVE irritable

irritate VERB irriter [1]

irritating ADJECTIVE irritant

Islam NOUN Islam MASC

Islamic ADJECTIVE islamique

island NOUN île FEM

isolated ADJECTIVE isolé

Israel NOUN Israël MASC

Israeli NOUN Israélien MASC, Israélienne FEM

Israeli ADJECTIVE israélien (FEM israélienne)

issue NOUN ❶ (something you discuss) question FEM; **a political issue** une question politique ❷ (of a magazine) numéro MASC

issue VERB (hand out) distribuer [1]

it PRONOUN ❶ (as the subject) il (when it stands for a masculine noun), elle (when it stands for a feminine noun); **'where is my bag?' – 'it's in the kitchen'** 'où est mon sac?' – 'il est dans la cuisine', **'how old is your car?' – 'it's five years old'** 'quel âge a ta voiture?' – 'elle a cinq ans' ❷ (as the object) le (when it stands for a masculine noun), la (when it stands for a feminine noun), l' (before a vowel or silent 'h'); **his new book? I know it** son nouveau livre? je le connais, **his address? I know it** son addresse? je la connais, **where's my book? I've lost it** où est mon livre? je l'ai perdu ❸ **yes, it's true** oui, c'est vrai, **it doesn't matter** ça ne fait rien ❹ **who is it?** qui c'est?, **it's me** c'est moi, **what is it?** qu'est-ce que c'est? ❺ **it's raining** il pleut, **it's a nice day** il fait beau, **it's two o'clock** il est deux heures

IT NOUN informatique FEM

Italian NOUN ❶ (the language) italien MASC ❷ (person) Italien MASC, Italienne FEM

Italian ADJECTIVE ❶ italien (FEM italienne); **Italian food** la cuisine italienne ❷ d'italien (a teacher or a lesson); **my Italian class** mon cours d'italien

italics NOUN italique MASC; **in italics** en italique

Italy NOUN Italie FEM; **in Italy** en Italie, **to Italy** en Italie

itch VERB **my back is itching** j'ai le dos qui me démange, **this sweater itches** ce pull me gratte

item NOUN article MASC

its DETERMINER son (before a masculine noun or a feminine noun beginning with a vowel or silent 'h'), sa (before a feminine noun), ses (before a plural noun); **the dog has lost its collar** le chien a perdu son collier, **the dog's in its kennel** le chien est dans sa niche, **its ear** son oreille, **its toys** ses jouets

itself PRONOUN ❶ se (s' before a vowel or silent 'h'); **the cat is washing itself** le chat se lave ❷ **he left the dog by itself** il a laissé le chien tout seul

ivory NOUN ivoire MASC

ivy NOUN lierre MASC

jack NOUN ❶ (in cards) valet MASC; **the jack of clubs** le valet de trèfle ❷ (for a car) cric MASC

jacket NOUN veste FEM

jacket potato NOUN pomme (FEM) de terre en robe des champs

jackpot NOUN gros lot MASC; **to win the jackpot** gagner le gros lot

jagged ADJECTIVE dentelé

jail NOUN prison FEM

jail VERB emprisonner [1]

jam NOUN ❶ (that you eat) confiture FEM; **raspberry jam** la confiture de framboises ❷ **a traffic jam** un embouteillage

Jamaica NOUN Jamaïque FEM

Jamaican NOUN Jamaïquain MASC, Jamaïquaine FEM

Jamaican ADJECTIVE jamaïquain

jammed ADJECTIVE coincé

January NOUN janvier MASC; **in January** en janvier

Japan NOUN Japon MASC; **in Japan** au Japon

Japanese NOUN ❶ (the language) japonais MASC ❷ (person) Japonais MASC, Japonaise FEM; **the Japanese** les Japonais MASC PLURAL

Japanese ADJECTIVE japonais

jar NOUN (small) pot MASC, (large) bocal MASC (PLURAL bocaux); a jar of jam un pot de confiture

javelin NOUN javelot MASC

jaw NOUN mâchoire FEM

jazz NOUN jazz MASC

jealous ADJECTIVE jaloux (FEM jalouse)

jealousy NOUN jalousie FEM

jeans NOUN jean MASC; my jeans mon jean, a pair of jeans un jean

jelly NOUN gelée FEM

jellyfish NOUN méduse FEM

jersey NOUN ❶ (a pullover) pull-over MASC ❷ (for football) maillot MASC

Jersey NOUN Jersey FEM

Jesus NOUN Jésus MASC; Jesus Christ Jésus-Christ

jet NOUN jet MASC

jet lag NOUN décalage (MASC) horaire

jetty NOUN jetée FEM

Jew NOUN Juif MASC, Juive FEM

jewel NOUN bijou MASC (PLURAL bijoux)

jeweller NOUN bijoutier MASC, bijoutière FEM

jeweller's NOUN bijouterie FEM

jewellery NOUN bijoux MASC PLURAL

Jewish ADJECTIVE juif (FEM juive)

jigsaw NOUN puzzle MASC

job NOUN ❶ (paid work) emploi MASC; a job as a secretary un emploi comme secrétaire, he's got a job il a trouvé un emploi, out of a job sans emploi, what's your job? qu'est-ce que vous faites comme travail?, a job offer une offre d'emploi ❷ (a task) travail MASC; it's not an easy job ce n'est pas un travail facile, she made a good job of it elle a fait un bon travail

jobless ADJECTIVE sans emploi

jockey NOUN jockey MASC

jog VERB to go jogging faire [10] du jogging

join VERB ❶ (become a member of) s'inscrire [38] à; I've joined the judo club je me suis inscrit au club de judo ❷ (to meet up with) rejoindre [49]; I'll join you later je vous rejoindrai plus tard
• to join in ❶ participer [1]; Ruth never joins in Ruth ne participe jamais ❷ to join in something participer [1] à quelque chose, won't you join in the game? veux-tu participer au jeu?

joiner NOUN menuisier MASC

joint NOUN ❶ (of meat) rôti MASC; a joint of beef un rôti de bœuf ❷ (in your body) articulation FEM

joint ADJECTIVE the joint winners les lauréats ex aequo

joke NOUN (a funny story) plaisanterie FEM; to tell a joke raconter une plaisanterie

joke VERB plaisanter [1]; you must be joking! tu plaisantes!

joker NOUN (in cards) joker MASC

Jordan NOUN Jordanie FEM

journalism NOUN journalisme MASC

journalist NOUN journaliste MASC & FEM; **Sean's a journalist** Sean est journaliste

journey NOUN ❶ *(a long one)* voyage MASC; **our journey to Turkey** notre voyage en Turquie ❷ *(shorter: to work or school)* trajet MASC; **a bus journey** un trajet en bus

joy NOUN joie FEM

joy-riding NOUN rodéo *(MASC)* à la voiture volée

joystick NOUN *(for computer games)* manette *(FEM)* de jeu

Judaism NOUN judaïsme MASC

judge NOUN juge MASC

judge VERB estimer [1] *(a time or distance)*

judgement NOUN jugement MASC

judo NOUN judo MASC; **he does judo** il fait du judo

jug NOUN pot MASC

juggle VERB jongler [1]

juice NOUN jus MASC; **two orange juices please** deux jus d'orange s'il vous plaît

juicy ADJECTIVE juteux *(FEM* juteuse)

jukebox NOUN jukebox MASC

July NOUN juillet MASC; **in July** en juillet

jumble sale NOUN vente *(FEM)* de charité

jumbo jet NOUN gros-porteur MASC

jump NOUN saut MASC; **a parachute jump** un saut en parachute

jump VERB sauter [1]

jumper NOUN pull MASC

junction NOUN ❶ *(of roads)* carrefour MASC ❷ *(of motorways)* échangeur MASC ❸ *(on railway)* nœud *(MASC)* ferroviaire

June NOUN juin MASC; **in June** en juin

jungle NOUN jungle FEM

junior ADJECTIVE primaire; **a junior school** une école primaire, **the juniors** les élèves du primaire

junk NOUN *(real rubbish)* bric-à-brac MASC

junk food NOUN **you shouldn't eat junk food** tu devrais manger correctement *(there is no word for junk food in French, so you will need to express it differently, according to the context)*

junk shop NOUN magasin *(MASC)* de brocante

jury NOUN jury MASC

just ADVERB ❶ juste; **just before midday** juste avant midi, **just after the church** juste après l'église, **just for fun** juste pour rire ❷ **to have just done** venir de faire, **Tom has just arrived** Tom vient d'arriver, **Helen had just called** Helen venait d'appeler ❸ **to be just doing** être en train de faire, **I'm just finishing the ironing** je suis en train de finir le repassage ❹ *(only)* ne ... que; **he's just a child** il n'est qu'un enfant, **there's just me and Justine** il n'y a que moi et Justine ❺ **just coming!** j'arrive!

justice NOUN justice FEM

justify VERB justifier [1]

kangaroo NOUN **kangourou** MASC

karaoke NOUN **karaoké** MASC

karate NOUN **karaté** MASC

kebab NOUN **brochette** FEM

keen ADJECTIVE ❶ (enthusiastic) **enthousiaste**; you don't look too keen tu n'as pas l'air très enthousiaste ❷ (committed) **passionné**; he's a keen photographer c'est un photographe passionné ❸ I'm not keen on fish je n'aime pas trop le poisson ❹ to be keen on doing (or to do) avoir très envie de faire, I'm not keen on camping je n'ai pas très envie de faire du camping

keep VERB ❶ **garder** [1]; I kept the letter j'ai gardé la lettre, will you keep my seat? veux-tu garder ma place?, they kept her in hospital ils l'ont gardée à l'hôpital, to keep a secret garder un secret ❷ to keep somebody waiting faire [10] attendre quelqu'un ❸ (to store) **ranger** [52]; I keep my bike in the garage je range mon vélo dans le garage, where do you keep saucepans? où rangez-vous les casseroles? ❹ to keep on doing **continuer** [1] à faire, she kept on talking elle a continué à parler, keep straight on continuez tout droit ❺ to keep on doing (time after time) he keeps on ringing me up il n'arrête pas de m'appeler ❻ (stay)

rester [1]; keep calm! restez calme!, keep out of the sun reste à l'abri du soleil ❼ to keep a promise tenir [77] sa promesse

keep fit NOUN **gymnastique** (FEM) **d'entretien**

kennel NOUN ❶ (for one dog) **niche** FEM ❷ (for boarding) **kennels chenil** MASC

kerb NOUN **bord** (MASC) **du trottoir**

ketchup NOUN **ketchup** MASC

kettle NOUN **bouilloire** FEM; to put the kettle on mettre l'eau à chauffer

key NOUN ❶ (for a lock) **clé** FEM; a bunch of keys un trousseau de clés ❷ (on a piano or typewriter) **touche** FEM

keyboard NOUN (for a piano or a computer) **clavier** MASC

keyhole NOUN **trou** (MASC) **de serrure**

keyring NOUN **porte-clés** MASC

kick NOUN ❶ (from a person or a horse) **coup** (MASC) **de pied; to give somebody a kick** donner un coup de pied à quelqu'un ❷ (in football) **tir** MASC
• to get a kick out of doing prendre plaisir à faire

kick VERB to kick somebody donner [1] un coup de pied à quelqu'un, to kick the ball donner un coup de pied dans le ballon
• to kick off donner [1] le coup d'envoi

kick-off NOUN **coup** (MASC) **d'envoi**

kid NOUN **gosse** MASC & FEM (child); Dad's looking after the kids Dad s'occupe des gosses

kidnap VERB **enlever** [50]

kidnapper NOUN ravisseur MASC, ravisseuse FEM

kidney NOUN ❶ (part of your body) rein MASC ❷ (for eating) rognon MASC

kill VERB tuer [1]; she was killed in an accident elle a été tuée dans un accident

killer NOUN (murderer) meurtrier MASC, meurtrière FEM

kilo NOUN kilo MASC; a kilo of sugar un kilo de sucre, five euros a kilo cinq euros le kilo

kilogramme NOUN kilogramme MASC

kilometre NOUN kilomètre MASC

kilt NOUN kilt MASC

kind NOUN sorte FEM; all kinds of people toutes sortes de gens

kind ADJECTIVE gentil (FEM gentille); Marion was very kind to me Marion a été très gentille avec moi

kindness NOUN gentillesse FEM

king NOUN roi MASC; King George le roi Georges, the king of hearts le roi de cœur

kingdom NOUN royaume MASC; the United Kingdom le Royaume-Uni

kiosk NOUN ❶ (for newspapers or snacks) kiosque MASC ❷ (for a phone) cabine FEM

kipper NOUN hareng (MASC) fumé

kiss NOUN baiser MASC; to give somebody a kiss embrasser quelqu'un

kiss VERB embrasser [1]; kiss me! embrasse-moi!, we kissed each other nous nous sommes embrassés

kit NOUN ❶ (of tools) trousse FEM; a tool kit une trousse à outils ❷ (clothes) affaires FEM PLURAL; where's my football kit? où sont mes affaires de foot? ❸ (for making a model, a piece of furniture, etc) kit MASC

kitchen NOUN cuisine FEM; the kitchen table la table de la cuisine

kitchen foil NOUN papier (MASC) d'aluminium

kitchen garden NOUN jardin (MASC) potager

kitchen roll NOUN essuie-tout MASC

kite NOUN (toy) cerf-volant MASC; to fly a kite faire voler un cerf-volant

kitten NOUN chaton MASC

kiwi fruit NOUN kiwi MASC

knack NOUN don MASC

knee NOUN genou MASC (PLURAL genoux); on (your) hands and knees à quatre pattes

kneel VERB se mettre [11] à genoux

knickers PLURAL NOUN petite culotte FEM

knife NOUN couteau MASC (PLURAL couteaux)

knight NOUN (in chess) cavalier MASC

knit VERB tricoter [1]

knitting NOUN tricot MASC

knob NOUN bouton MASC

knock NOUN coup MASC; a knock on the head un coup à la tête, a knock at the door un coup à la porte

knock VERB ❶ (to bang) **cogner** [1]; **I knocked my arm on the table** je me suis cogné le bras contre la table ❷ **to knock on something** (a person) **frapper** [1] à (the door)

• **to knock down** ❶ (in a traffic accident) **renverser** [1] (a person) ❷ (to demolish) **démolir** [2] (an old building)

• **to knock out** ❶ (to make unconscious) **assommer** [1] ❷ (in sport, to eliminate) **éliminer** [1]

knocker NOUN **heurtoir** MASC

knot NOUN **nœud** MASC; **to tie a knot in something nouer** [1] quelque chose

know VERB ❶ (know a fact) **savoir** [70]; **do you know where Tim is?** sais-tu où est Tim?, **I know they've moved house** je sais qu'ils ont déménagé, **he knows it by heart** il le sait par cœur, **yes, I know** oui, je sais, **you never know!** on ne sait jamais! ❷ (be personally acquainted with) **connaître** [27] (a person, place, book, or music, for example); **do you know the Jacksons?** est-ce que tu connais les Jackson?, **all the people I know** tous les gens que je connais, **I don't know his mother** je ne connais pas sa mère ❸ **to know how to do savoir** [70] **faire**, **Steve knows how to make couscous** Steve sait faire du couscous, **Liz knows how to mend it** Liz sait le réparer ❹ **to know about être** [6] **au courant de** (the latest news) ❺ **to know about s'y connaître** [27] **en** (machines, cooking, etc), **Lindy knows about computers** Lindy s'y connaît en informatique

knowledge NOUN **connaissance** FEM

knuckle NOUN **articulation** (FEM) **des doigts**

koala NOUN **koala** MASC

Koran NOUN **Coran** MASC

kosher ADJECTIVE **kascher**

lab NOUN **labo** MASC

label NOUN **étiquette** FEM

laboratory NOUN **laboratoire** MASC

Labour NOUN **les travaillistes** MASC PLURAL; **to vote for the Labour party** voter pour les travaillistes, **the Labour Party** le parti travailliste

lace NOUN ❶ (for a shoe) **lacet** MASC ❷ (for curtains, for example) **dentelle** FEM

lad NOUN **gars** MASC

ladder NOUN (for climbing, or in your tights) **échelle** FEM

ladies NOUN (lavatory) **toilettes** FEM PLURAL; (on a sign) **'Ladies'** 'Dames'

lady NOUN **dame** FEM; **ladies and gentlemen mesdames et messieurs**

ladybird NOUN **coccinelle** FEM

lager NOUN **bière** (FEM) **blonde**

laid-back ADJECTIVE **relaxe**

lake NOUN lac MASC; **Lake Geneva** le lac Léman

lamb NOUN agneau MASC (PLURAL agneaux); **a leg of lamb** un gigot

lame ADJECTIVE boiteux (FEM boiteuse); **he is lame** il boite

lamp NOUN lampe FEM

lamp-post NOUN réverbère MASC

lampshade NOUN abat-jour MASC (PLURAL abat-jour)

land NOUN ❶ terre FEM; **I can see land** je vois la terre ❷ (property) terrain MASC; **a piece of land** un terrain

land VERB ❶ (plane, passenger) atterrir [2] ❷ (leave a ship) débarquer [1]

landing NOUN ❶ (on the stairs) palier MASC ❷ (of a plane) atterrissage MASC ❸ (from a boat) débarquement MASC

landlady NOUN propriétaire FEM

landlord NOUN propriétaire MASC

landscape NOUN paysage MASC

lane NOUN ❶ (a country path) chemin MASC ❷ (of a motorway) voie FEM

language NOUN ❶ (French, Italian, etc) langue FEM; **a foreign language** une langue étrangère ❷ (way of speaking) langage MASC; **bad language** un langage grossier

language lab NOUN laboratoire (MASC) de langues

language school NOUN école (FEM) de langue

lap NOUN ❶ (your knees) genoux MASC PLURAL; **on my lap** sur mes genoux ❷ (in races) tour (MASC) de piste

laptop NOUN portable MASC

larder NOUN garde-manger MASC

large ADJECTIVE ❶ grand (goes before the noun); **a large number** un grand nombre, **a large house** une grande maison ❷ gros (FEM grosse) (a piece, part, animal) (goes before the noun); **a large piece of cake** un gros morceau de gâteau ❸ nombreux (FEM nombreuse) (crowd or family); **I come from a large family** je viens d'une famille nombreuse

laser NOUN laser MASC

laser beam NOUN rayon (MASC) laser

laser printer NOUN imprimante (FEM) laser

last ADJECTIVE dernier (FEM dernière); **the last time** la dernière fois, **last week** la semaine dernière, **last night** (in the evening) hier soir, (in the night) cette nuit

last ADVERB ❶ (in final position) (to arrive or leave) en dernier; **Rob arrived last** Rob est arrivé en dernier, **at last!** enfin! ❷ (most recently) **I last saw him in May** la dernière fois que je l'ai vu était en mai

last VERB durer [1]; **the play lasted two hours** le spectacle a duré deux heures

late ADJECTIVE, ADVERB ❶ en retard; **we're late** nous sommes en retard, **they arrived late** ils sont arrivés en retard, **to be late for something** être en retard pour quelque chose, **we were late for the film** nous étions en retard pour le film ❷ **to be late** (a bus or train) avoir du retard, **the train was an hour late** le train a eu une heure de retard ❸ (late in the day) tard; **we got up late** nous nous sommes levés tard, **the chemist is open late** la pharmacie est ouverte tard, **late last night** tard hier soir, **too late!** trop tard!

lately ADVERB ces derniers temps

later ADVERB plus tard; **I'll explain later** j'expliquerai plus tard, **see you later!** à tout à l'heure!

latest ADJECTIVE ❶ dernier (FEM dernière); **the latest news** les dernières nouvelles ❷ **at the latest** au plus tard

latest NOUN **the latest in audio equipment** le dernier cri en matière d'équipement hifi

Latin NOUN latin MASC

laugh NOUN rire MASC; **to do something for a laugh** faire quelque chose pour rigoler (informal)

laugh VERB ❶ rire [68]; **everybody laughed** tout le monde a ri ❷ **to laugh at** se moquer [1] de, **I tried to explain but they laughed at me** j'ai essayé d'expliquer mais ils se sont moqués de moi

laughter NOUN rire MASC

launch NOUN (of a ship, product, spacecraft) lancement MASC

launch VERB ❶ (product, spacecraft) lancer [61] ❷ (ship) mettre [11] à l'eau

launderette NOUN laverie (FEM) automatique

laundry NOUN ❶ (in hotel etc) laverie FEM ❷ (shop) blanchisserie FEM

lavatory NOUN toilettes FEM PLURAL; **to go to the lavatory** aller aux toilettes

lavender NOUN lavande FEM

law NOUN ❶ loi FEM; **it's against the law** c'est interdit ❷ (subject of study) droit MASC

lawn NOUN pelouse FEM

lawnmower NOUN tondeuse (FEM) à gazon

lawyer NOUN avocat MASC, avocate FEM

lay VERB ❶ (put) poser [1]; **she laid the card on the table** elle a posé la carte sur la table ❷ (spread out) étaler [1]; **we laid newspaper on the floor** nous avons étalé du papier journal sur le parquet ❸ **to lay the table** mettre [11] la table

lay-by NOUN aire (FEM) de stationnement

layer NOUN couche FEM

laziness NOUN paresse FEM

lazy ADJECTIVE paresseux (FEM paresseuse)

lead¹ NOUN ❶ (when you are ahead) **to be in the lead** être en tête, **Baxter's in the lead** Baxter est en tête, **we have a lead of three points** nous avons trois points d'avance ❷ (electric) fil MASC ❸ (for a dog) laisse FEM; **on a lead** en laisse

lead ADJECTIVE (a role or a singer) principal MASC (PLURAL principaux)

lead VERB ❶ mener [50]; **the path leads to the sea** le chemin mène à la mer ❷ **to lead the way** montrer [1] le chemin ❸ **to lead to something** entraîner [1] quelque chose (an accident or problems, for example)

lead² NOUN (the metal) plomb MASC

leader

leader NOUN ❶ *(of a gang)* chef
MASC ❷ *(of a political party)*
dirigeant MASC, dirigeante
FEM ❸ *(in a competition)* premier
MASC, première FEM

lead-free petrol NOUN essence
(FEM) sans plomb

lead singer NOUN chanteur
principal MASC, chanteuse
principale FEM

leaf NOUN feuille FEM

leaflet NOUN dépliant MASC

league NOUN *(in sport)* championnat
MASC

leak NOUN fuite FEM; **a gas leak** une
fuite de gaz

leak VERB *(a bottle or a roof)* fuir [44]

lean ADJECTIVE *(meat)* maigre

lean VERB ❶ **to lean on something**
s'appuyer [41] contre quelque
chose ❷ *(prop)* appuyer [41]; **lean
the ladder against the tree!** appuie
l'échelle contre l'arbre! ❸ *(a person)*
se pencher [1]; **to lean out of the
window** se pencher par la fenêtre,
lean forward a bit penche-toi un
peu en avant

leap VERB sauter [1]

leap year NOUN année *(FEM)*
bissextile

learn VERB apprendre [64]; **to learn
Russian** apprendre le russe, **to
learn (how) to drive** apprendre à
conduire

learner NOUN apprenant MASC,
apprenante FEM; **to be a fast
learner** apprendre vite

learner driver NOUN élève *(MASC &
FEM)* d'auto-école

least ADVERB, DETERMINER, PRONOUN ❶ le
moins; **I like the blue shirt least**
c'est la chemise bleue que j'aime
le moins ❷ *(followed by a noun)*
le moins de; **Tony has the least
money** c'est Tony qui a le moins
d'argent ❸ *(followed by an adjective)*
le moins, la moins, les moins
*(according to the gender and number
of the noun going with the adjective)*;
the least expensive hotel l'hôtel le
moins cher, **the least expensive car**
la voiture la moins chère, **the least
expensive shoes** les chaussures
les moins chères ❹ **the least** *(the
slightest)* le moindre, la moindre
*(according to the gender of the noun
that follows)*, **I haven't the least
idea** je n'ai pas la moindre idée ❺ **at
least** *(at a minimum)* au moins, **at
least twenty people** au moins vingt
personnes ❻ **at least** *(at any rate)*
du moins, **at least, I think she's a
teacher** du moins, je crois qu'elle
est professeur

leather NOUN cuir MASC; **a leather
jacket** un blouson en cuir

leave NOUN congé MASC; **three days'
leave** trois jours de congé

leave VERB ❶ *(go away)* partir [58];
they're leaving tomorrow ils vont
partir demain, **we left at six** nous
sommes partis à six heures ❷ *(go
away from)* quitter [1]; **I left the
office at five** j'ai quitté le bureau
à cinq heures, **Guy left school at
sixteen** Guy a quitté l'école à seize
ans ❸ *(go out of)* sortir [72] de; **she
left the cinema at ten** elle est sortie
du cinéma à dix heures ❹ *(deposit)*
laisser [1]; **you can leave your coats
in the hall** vous pouvez laisser vos
manteaux dans l'entrée ❺ *(not do)*
laisser [1]; **let's leave the washing
up!** laissons la vaisselle! ❻ *(forget)*

oublier [1]; **he left his umbrella on the train** il a oublié son parapluie dans le train **➐ be left** rester [1], **there are two pancakes left** il reste deux crêpes, **we have ten minutes left** il nous reste dix minutes, **I don't have any money left** il ne me reste plus d'argent

lecture NOUN **➊** (at university) cours (MASC) magistral (PLURAL cours magistraux) **➋** (public) conférence FEM

lecturer NOUN professeur (MASC) à l'université

ledge NOUN **➊** (of a window) rebord MASC **➋** (on a cliff) corniche FEM

leek NOUN poireau MASC (PLURAL poireaux)

left NOUN gauche FEM; **to drive on the left** conduire à gauche, **turn left at the church** tournez à gauche à l'église, **on my left** à ma gauche

left ADJECTIVE gauche; **his left foot** son pied gauche

left-click NOUN clic (MASC) sur le bouton gauche de la souris

left-click VERB **to left-click the icon** cliquer [1] en appuyant sur le bouton gauche de la souris

left-hand ADJECTIVE **the left-hand side** la gauche

left-handed ADJECTIVE gaucher MASC, gauchère FEM

left luggage office NOUN consigne FEM

leftovers PLURAL NOUN restes MASC PLURAL

leg NOUN **➊** (of a person or a horse) jambe FEM; **my left leg** ma jambe gauche, **to break your leg** se casser

la jambe **➋** (of other animals) patte FEM **➌** (of a table or chair) pied MASC **➍** (in cooking) **a leg of chicken** une cuisse de poulet, **a leg of lamb** un gigot
• **to pull somebody's leg** faire [10] marcher quelqu'un

legal ADJECTIVE légal MASC (PLURAL légaux)

legend NOUN **➊** (story) légende FEM **➋** (person) légende FEM

leggings PLURAL NOUN caleçon MASC

leisure NOUN loisirs MASC PLURAL; **in my leisure time** pendant mes loisirs

leisure centre NOUN centre (MASC) de loisirs

lemon NOUN citron MASC; **a lemon yoghurt** un yaourt au citron

lemonade NOUN limonade FEM

lemon juice NOUN jus (MASC) de citron

lend VERB prêter [1]; **to lend something to somebody** prêter quelque chose à quelqu'un, **I lent Judy my bike** j'ai prêté mon vélo à Judy, **will you lend it to me?** veux-tu me le prêter?

length NOUN longueur FEM

lens NOUN **➊** (in a camera) objectif MASC **➋** (in spectacles) verre MASC **➌** **contact lenses** les lentilles (FEM PLURAL) de contact

Lent NOUN Carême MASC

lentil NOUN lentille FEM

Leo NOUN Lion MASC; **I'm Leo** je suis Lion

leotard NOUN justaucorps MASC

lesbian NOUN lesbienne FEM

less PRONOUN, DETERMINER, ADVERB
❶ moins; **Richard eats less** Richard mange moins ❷ (before a noun) moins de; **less traffic** moins de circulation, **less time** moins de temps ❸ (before an adjective or adverb) moins; **less interesting** moins intéressant, **less quickly than us** moins vite que nous ❹ **less than** moins de, **less than three hours** moins de trois heures, **less than a kilo** moins d'un kilo ❺ **less than** (in comparisons) moins que, **you spent less than me** tu as dépensé moins que moi

lesson NOUN ❶ (class) cours MASC; **the history lesson** le cours d'histoire, **to take tennis lessons** prendre des cours de tennis ❷ (one in a planned series) leçon FEM; **a driving lesson** une leçon de conduite

let¹ VERB ❶ (allow) **to let somebody do** laisser [1] quelqu'un faire, **she lets me borrow her bike** elle me laisse emprunter son vélo, **will you let me go alone?** veux-tu me laisser y aller toute seule?, **the police let us through** la police nous a laissés passer, **let me see** (show me) laisse-moi voir ❷ (as a suggestion or a command) **let's go!** allons-y!, **let's not talk about it** n'en parlons pas, **let's see, if Tuesday is the third …** voyons, si mardi est le trois …, **let's eat out** si on mangeait au restaurant?
• **to let off** ❶ tirer [1] (fireworks) ❷ faire [10] exploser (a bomb) ❸ (to excuse from) dispenser [1] de (homework)

let² VERB (to rent out) louer [1]; **'flat to let'** appartement à louer

lethal ADJECTIVE **mortel** mortelle

letter NOUN **lettre** FEM; **a letter for you from Delia** une lettre pour toi de Delia, **G is the letter after F** G est la lettre après F

letter box NOUN **boîte** (FEM) **à lettres**

lettuce NOUN **salade** FEM; **two lettuces** deux salades

leukaemia NOUN **leucémie** FEM

level NOUN **niveau** MASC (PLURAL **niveaux**); **at street level** au niveau de la rue

level ADJECTIVE ❶ **droit** (a shelf or floor) ❷ **plat** (ground)

level crossing NOUN **passage** (MASC) **à niveau**

lever NOUN **levier** MASC

liar NOUN **menteur** MASC, **menteuse** FEM

liberal ADJECTIVE **libéral** MASC (PLURAL **libéraux**); **the Liberal Democrats** le parti libéral-démocrate

liberty NOUN **liberté** FEM

Libra NOUN **Balance** FEM; **Sean's Libra** Sean est Balance

librarian NOUN **bibliothécaire** MASC & FEM; **Mark's a librarian** Mark est bibliothécaire

library NOUN **bibliothèque** FEM; **the public library** la bibliothèque municipale

licence NOUN ❶ (for driving or fishing) **permis** MASC; **a driving licence** un permis de conduire ❷ (for a TV) **redevance** FEM

lick VERB **lécher** [24]

lid NOUN **couvercle** MASC; **she took the lid off** elle a enlevé le couvercle

a b c d e f g h i j k l m n o p q r s t u v w x y z

lie NOUN mensonge MASC; **to tell a lie** (*or* **lies**) mentir [53]

lie VERB ❶ (*to be stretched out*) être [6] allongé; **Jimmy was lying on the bed** Jimmy était allongé sur le lit, **my coat lay on the bed** mon manteau était sur le lit ❷ **to lie down** se coucher [1], (*for a little while*) s'allonger [52], **come and lie down in the sun** viens t'allonger au soleil ❸ (*not to tell the truth*) mentir [53]

lie-in NOUN **to have a lie-in** faire la grasse matinée

lieutenant NOUN lieutenant MASC

life NOUN vie FEM; **all her life** toute sa vie, **full of life** plein de vie, **that's life!** c'est la vie!

lifebelt NOUN bouée (FEM) de sauvetage

lifeboat NOUN canot (MASC) de sauvetage

lifeguard NOUN maître nageur MASC; **is there a lifeguard at the pool?** est-ce que la piscine est surveillée?

life jacket NOUN gilet (MASC) de sauvetage

life-style NOUN style (MASC) de vie

lift NOUN ❶ ascenseur MASC; **let's take the lift** prenons l'ascenseur ❷ (*a ride*) **to give somebody a lift to the station** déposer quelqu'un à la gare, **Tom gave me a lift home** Tom m'a déposé chez moi, **can I give you a lift?** puis-je vous déposer quelque part?

lift VERB soulever [50]; **he lifted the box** il a soulevé le carton

light NOUN ❶ (*electric*) lumière FEM; **will you turn the light on?** veux-tu allumer la lumière?, **to turn off the light** éteindre la lumière ❷ (*streetlight*) réverbère MASC ❸ (*a headlight for a car*) phare MASC; **are your lights on?** as-tu allumé tes phares? ❹ (*an indicator on a machine*) voyant MASC ❺ **traffic lights** les feux MASC PLURAL, **the lights were green** le feu était au vert ❻ **have you got a light?** tu as du feu?

light ADJECTIVE ❶ (*in colour*) clair; **light blue eyes** des yeux bleu clair ❷ (*not night*) **it gets light at six** il fait jour à six heures ❸ (*not heavy*) léger (FEM légère); **a light sweater** un pull léger, **a light breeze** une brise légère

light VERB ❶ allumer [1] (*the oven, the fire, or a cigarette*); **we lit a fire** nous avons fait un feu ❷ craquer [1] (*a match*)

light bulb NOUN ampoule FEM

lighter NOUN briquet MASC

lighthouse NOUN phare MASC

lightning NOUN éclairs MASC PLURAL; **a flash of lightning** un éclair, **to be struck by lightning** être frappé par la foudre

light switch NOUN interrupteur MASC

like[1] PREPOSITION, CONJUNCTION ❶ comme; **like me** comme moi, **like this** comme ça, **like a duck** comme un canard, **like I said** comme j'ai dit, **what's it like?** c'est comment?, **what was the weather like?** quel temps faisait-il? **❷ to look like** ressembler [1] à, **Cindy looks like her father** Cindy ressemble à son père

like² VERB **❶** aimer [1] (bien); **I like fish** j'aime bien le poisson, **I don't like snakes** je n'aime pas les serpents, **Mum likes travelling** Maman aime bien voyager, **I like Renoir best** je préfère Renoir **❷ I would like** je voudrais, **would you like a coffee?** est-ce que tu voudrais un café?, **what would you like to eat?** qu'est-ce que tu veux manger?, **yes, if you like** oui, si tu veux

likely ADJECTIVE probable; **it's not very likely** ce n'est pas très probable, **she's likely to phone** elle va probablement appeler

lilac NOUN lilas MASC

lily NOUN lys MASC

lily of the valley NOUN muguet MASC

lime NOUN citron (MASC) vert

limit NOUN limitation FEM; **the speed limit** la limitation de vitesse

limp NOUN **to have a limp** boiter [1]

line NOUN **❶** ligne FEM; **a straight line** une ligne droite, **six lines of text** six lignes de texte, **to draw a line** tirer un trait **❷ a railway line** (from one place to another) une ligne de chemin de fer, **on the railway line** (the track) sur la voie ferrée **❸** (a queue of people or cars) file FEM; **to stand in line** faire la queue **❹** (telephone) ligne FEM; **the line's bad** la ligne est mauvaise, **hold the line, please** ne quittez pas

line VERB doubler [1] (a coat)

linen NOUN lin MASC; **a linen jacket** une veste en lin

lining NOUN doublure FEM

link NOUN rapport MASC; **what's the link between the two?** quel est le rapport entre les deux?

link VERB relier [1] (two places); **the terminals are linked by a shuttle service** les terminaux sont reliés par une navette

lino NOUN linoléum MASC

lion NOUN lion MASC

lioness NOUN lionne FEM

lip NOUN lèvre FEM

lip-read VERB lire [51] sur les lèvres

lipstick NOUN rouge (MASC) à lèvres

liquid NOUN, ADJECTIVE liquide MASC

liquidizer NOUN mixer MASC

list NOUN liste FEM

listen VERB **❶** écouter [1]; **I wasn't listening** je n'écoutais pas **❷ to listen to** écouter [1], **listen to the music** écoutez la musique, **you're not listening to me** tu ne m'écoutes pas

listener NOUN (to the radio) auditeur MASC, auditrice FEM

literally ADVERB littéralement

literature NOUN littérature FEM

litre NOUN litre MASC; **a litre of milk** un litre de lait

litter NOUN (rubbbish) détritus MASC PLURAL

litter bin NOUN poubelle FEM

little ADJECTIVE, PRONOUN ❶ (small) petit (goes before the noun); **a little boy** un petit garçon, **a little break** une petite pause ❷ (not much) peu (de); **they have little money** ils ont peu d'argent, **we have very little time** nous avons très peu de temps ❸ **a little** un peu (de) ❹ **we have a little money** nous avons un peu d'argent, **just a little, please** juste un peu, s'il vous plaît, **it's a little late** c'est un peu tard, **a little more** un peu plus, **a little less** un peu moins
• **little by little** petit à petit

little finger NOUN petit doigt MASC

live¹ VERB ❶ (in a house or town) habiter [1]; **Susan lives in York** Susan habite à York, **we live in a flat** nous habitons dans un appartement, **they live at number 57** ils habitent au numéro cinquante-sept, **we're living in the country now** nous habitons à la campagne maintenant ❷ (be or stay alive, spend one's life) vivre [82]; **lions live in Africa** les lions vivent en Afrique, **they live on fruit** ils vivent de fruits, **they live together** ils vivent ensemble

live² ADJECTIVE ❶ en direct (a broadcast); **a live concert** un concert en direct, **a broadcast live from Wembley** une émission en direct de Wembley ❷ (alive) vivant

lively ADJECTIVE animé (a party or restaurant, for example)

liver NOUN foie MASC

living NOUN vie FEM; **to earn a living** gagner sa vie

living room NOUN salle (FEM) de séjour

lizard NOUN lézard MASC

load NOUN ❶ (on a lorry) chargement MASC; **a (lorry-)load of bricks** un camion de briques ❷ **a bus-load of tourists** un autobus plein de tourists ❸ **loads of** des tas de (informal), **loads of people** des tas de gens, **they've got loads of money** ils sont bourrés de fric (informal)

load VERB charger [52]; **a lorry loaded with wood** un camion chargé de bois

loaf NOUN pain MASC; **a loaf of wholemeal bread** un pain complet

loan NOUN prêt MASC

loan VERB prêter [1]

loathe VERB détester [1]; **I loathe getting up early** je déteste me lever tôt

lobster NOUN homard MASC

local NOUN ❶ (a pub) pub (MASC) du coin ❷ **the locals** (people) les gens du coin

local ADJECTIVE **the local library** la bibliothèque du coin, **the local newspaper** le journal local

locally ADVERB de façon locale; **they only advertise locally** ils ne font de publicité que dans la région

lock NOUN ❶ (with a key) serrure FEM ❷ (on a canal) écluse FEM

lock VERB **to lock the door** fermer [1] la porte à clé, **the door was locked** la porte était fermée à clé

locker NOUN casier MASC

locker room NOUN vestiaire MASC

lodger NOUN locataire MASC & FEM

loft NOUN grenier MASC

log NOUN bûche FEM; **a log fire** un feu de bois

logical ADJECTIVE logique

lollipop NOUN sucette FEM

London NOUN Londres; **to London** à Londres, **a day in London** une journée à Londres, **the London streets** les rues de Londres

Londoner NOUN Londonien MASC, Londonienne FEM

loneliness NOUN solitude FEM

lonely ADJECTIVE ❶ seul; **to feel lonely** se sentir [53] seul ❷ (a place) isolé

long ADJECTIVE, ADVERB ❶ long (FEM longue); **a long film** un film long, **a long day** une longue journée, **it's an hour long** ça dure une heure ❷ **a long time** longtemps, **he stayed for a long time** il est resté longtemps, **I've been here for a long time** je suis là depuis longtemps, **a long time ago** il y a longtemps, **this won't take long** ça ne prendra pas longtemps ❸ **how long?** combien de temps?, **how long have you been here?** tu es là depuis combien de temps?, **long ago** il y a longtemps ❹ **a long way** loin, **it's a long way to the cinema** le cinéma est loin d'ici ❺ **all night long** toute la nuit

long VERB **to long to do** avoir [5] très envie de faire, **I'm longing to see you** j'ai très envie de te voir

long-distance call NOUN (within the country) appel (MASC) interurbain

longer ADVERB **no longer** ne ... plus, **I no longer know** je ne sais plus, **they no longer live here** ils n'habitent plus ici

long jump NOUN saut (MASC) en longueur

longlife milk NOUN lait (MASC) longue conservation

loo NOUN toilettes FEM PLURAL

look NOUN ❶ (a glance) coup (MASC) d'œil; **to have a look at something** jeter un coup d'œil à quelque chose ❷ (a tour) **to have a look round the town** faire un tour dans la ville, **to have a look round the shops** faire les magasins ❸ **to have a look for** chercher (something you've lost)

look VERB ❶ regarder [1]; **I wasn't looking** je ne regardais pas, **to look out of the window** regarder par la fenêtre ❷ **to look at** regarder [1], **Andy was looking at the photos** Andy regardait les photos ❸ (to seem) avoir [5] l'air; **Melanie looks pleased** Melanie a l'air contente, **the salad looks delicious** la salade a l'air délicieuse ❹ **to look like** ressembler [1] à, **Sally looks like her aunt** Sally ressemble à sa tante, **they look like each other** ils se ressemblent, **what does the house look like?** comment est la maison?, **it looks like rain** on dirait qu'il va pleuvoir

- **to look after** ❶ s'occuper [1] de; **Dad's looking after the baby** Papa s'occupe du bébé ❷ surveiller [1] (luggage)

- to look for chercher [1]; **I'm looking for the keys** je cherche les clés
- to look forward to something attendre [3] quelque chose avec impatience *(a party or a trip, for example)*
- to look out *(to be careful)* faire [10] attention; **look out, it's hot!** (fais) attention, c'est chaud!
- to look something up chercher [1] quelque chose *(in a dictionary or directory)*; **you can look it up in the dictionary** tu peux le chercher dans le dictionnaire

loose ADJECTIVE ❶ *(a screw or knot)* desserré ❷ *(a garment)* ample ❸ **loose change** la petite monnaie
- **I'm at a loose end** je ne sais pas trop quoi faire

lorry NOUN camion MASC

lorry driver NOUN routier MASC

lose VERB ❶ perdre [3]; **we lost** nous avons perdu, **we lost the match** nous avons perdu le match, **Sam's lost his watch** Sam a perdu sa montre ❷ **to get lost** se perdre [3], **we got lost in the woods** nous nous sommes perdus dans les bois

loss NOUN perte FEM

lost ADJECTIVE perdu; **I'm lost** je suis perdu, **are you lost?** vous êtes perdu?

lost property NOUN objets (MASC PLURAL) trouvés

lot NOUN ❶ **a lot** beaucoup, **Jason eats a lot** Jason mange beaucoup, **I spent a lot** j'ai beaucoup dépensé, **he's a lot better** il va beaucoup mieux ❷ **a lot of** beaucoup de, **a lot of coffee** beaucoup de café, **lots of people** beaucoup de gens, **'what are you doing tonight?' – 'not a lot'**

'qu'est-ce que tu fais ce soir?' – 'pas grand-chose'

lottery NOUN loterie FEM; **to win the lottery** gagner à la loterie

loud ADJECTIVE ❶ fort; **in a loud voice** d'une voix forte ❷ **to say something out loud** dire quelque chose à haute voix

loudly ADVERB fort

loudspeaker NOUN haut-parleur MASC (PLURAL **haut-parleurs**)

lounge NOUN ❶ *(in a house or hotel)* salon MASC ❷ *(in an airport)* **the departure lounge** la salle d'embarquement

love NOUN ❶ amour MASC; **to be in love with somebody** être amoureux (FEM **amoureuse**) de quelqu'un, **she's in love with Jake** elle est amoureuse de Jake, **Gina sends her love** Gina t'embrasse, **with love from Charlie** amitiés, Charlie ❷ *(in tennis)* zéro MASC

love VERB ❶ aimer [1] *(a person)*; **I love you** je t'aime ❷ aimer beaucoup *(place, suggestion)*; **she loves London** elle aime beaucoup Londres, **I'd love to come** j'aimerais beaucoup venir ❸ adorer [1] *(activity, thing)*; **I love dancing** j'adore danser, **Wayne loves seafood** Wayne adore les fruits de mer

lovely ADJECTIVE ❶ *(to look at)* joli; **a lovely dress** une jolie robe, **their garden is lovely** leur jardin est très joli, **a lovely house** une belle maison ❷ **it's a lovely day** il fait très beau, **we had lovely weather** il a fait très beau ❸ *(food, meal)* délicieux (FEM **délicieuse**)

lover *NOUN* ❶ *(general)* partenaire *MASC & FEM* ❷ *(of married man)* maîtresse *FEM*, *(of married woman)* amant *MASC*

low *ADJECTIVE* bas *(FEM* basse); **a low table** une table basse, **at a low price** à prix bas, **in a low voice** à voix basse

lower *ADJECTIVE (not as high)* inférieur

lower *VERB* baisser [1]

low-fat milk *NOUN* lait *(MASC)* écrémé

loyalty *NOUN* loyauté *FEM*; **loyalty card** carte *(FEM)* de fidélité

luck *NOUN* chance *FEM*; **good luck!** bonne chance!, **bad luck!** pas de chance!, **with a bit of luck** avec un peu de chance

luckily *ADVERB* heureusement; **luckily for them** heureusement pour eux

lucky *ADJECTIVE* ❶ **to be lucky** *(a person)* avoir de la chance, **we were lucky** nous avons eu de la chance ❷ **to be lucky** *(bringing luck)* porter bonheur, **it's supposed to be lucky** c'est censé porter bonheur, **my lucky number** mon numéro porte-bonheur

luggage *NOUN* bagages *MASC PLURAL*; **my luggage is in the boot** mes bagages sont dans le coffre

lump *NOUN* ❶ *(of earth)* motte *FEM* ❷ *(piece)* morceau *MASC (PLURAL* morceaux) ❸ *(swelling)* grosseur *FEM*

lunch *NOUN* déjeuner *MASC*; **to have lunch** déjeuner [1], **we had lunch in Oxford** nous avons déjeuné à Oxford

lunch break *NOUN* pause-déjeuner *FEM*

lunch hour, **lunch time** *NOUN* heure *(FEM)* du déjeuner

lung *NOUN* poumon *MASC*

Luxembourg *NOUN* ❶ *(country)* Luxembourg *MASC*; **to Luxembourg** au Luxembourg, **in Luxembourg** au Luxembourg ❷ *(city)* Luxembourg; **in Luxembourg** à Luxembourg

luxurious *ADJECTIVE* luxueux *(FEM* luxueuse)

luxury *NOUN* luxe *MASC*; **a luxury hotel** un hôtel de luxe

lyrics *PLURAL NOUN* paroles *FEM PLURAL*

mac *NOUN* imper *MASC (informal)*

macaroni *NOUN* macaronis *MASC PLURAL*; **we had macaroni** nous avons mangé des macaronis

machine *NOUN* machine *FEM*

machinery *NOUN* machines *FEM PLURAL*

mackerel *NOUN* maquereau *MASC (PLURAL* maquereaux)

mad *ADJECTIVE* ❶ fou *(FEM* folle); **she's completely mad!** elle est complètement folle! ❷ *(angry)* furieux (FEM furieuse); **my mum will be mad!** ma mère sera furieuse! ❸ **to be mad about something** adorer quelque chose, **she's mad about horses** elle adore les chevaux

madam NOUN madame FEM

madman NOUN fou MASC

madness NOUN folie FEM

magazine NOUN magazine MASC

maggot NOUN asticot MASC

magic NOUN magie FEM

magic ADJECTIVE ❶ magique; **a magic wand** une baguette magique ❷ (great) super

magician NOUN ❶ (wizard) magicien MASC ❷ (conjurer) prestidigitateur MASC

magnet NOUN aimant MASC

magnificent ADJECTIVE magnifique

magnifying glass NOUN loupe FEM

magnolia NOUN magnolia MASC

mahogany NOUN acajou MASC

maiden name NOUN nom (MASC) de jeune fille

mail NOUN courrier MASC; **email** (electronic mail) courrier (MASC) électronique

mail order NOUN **to buy something by mail order** acheter quelque chose par correspondance, **a mail order catalogue** un catalogue de vente par correspondance

main ADJECTIVE principal MASC (PLURAL principaux); **the main entrance** l'entrée principale

main course NOUN plat (MASC) principal

mainly ADVERB principalement

main road NOUN route (FEM) principale

maize NOUN maïs MASC

major ADJECTIVE majeur

major NOUN commandant MASC

Majorca NOUN Majorque FEM

majority NOUN majorité FEM

make NOUN marque FEM; **what make is your bike?** de quelle marque est ton vélo?

make VERB ❶ faire [10]; **I made an omelette** j'ai fait une omelette, **she made her bed** elle a fait son lit, **he made me wait** il m'a fait attendre, **she makes me laugh** elle me fait rire, **two and three make five** deux et trois font cinq ❷ fabriquer [1]; **they make computers** ils fabriquent des ordinateurs, 'made in France' 'fabriqué en France' ❸ rendre [3]; **to make somebody happy** rendre quelqu'un heureux, **that makes me hungry** ça me donne faim ❹ gagner [1] (money); **he makes forty pounds a day** il gagne quarante livres par jour, **to make a living** gagner sa vie ❺ (force) **to make somebody do something** obliger [52] quelqu'un à faire quelque chose, **she made him give the money back** elle l'a obligé à rendre l'argent ❻ **to make a meal** préparer [1] un repas ❼ **to make a phone call** passer [1] un coup de fil, **I have to make a few phone calls** je dois passer quelques coups de fil ❽ I can't make it tonight je ne peux pas venir ce soir

• to make something up ❶ inventer [1] quelque chose; she made up an excuse elle a inventé une excuse ❷ to make it up (after a quarrel) se réconcilier [1], they've made it up now il se sont maintenant réconciliés

make-up NOUN maquillage MASC; to put on your make-up se maquiller, Jo's putting on her make-up Jo est en train de se maquiller, I don't wear make-up je ne me maquille pas

male ADJECTIVE ❶ mâle (animal); a male rat un rat mâle ❷ (sex : on a form) masculin ❸ a male role un rôle pour homme, a male voice une voix d'homme, a male student un étudiant

mall NOUN centre (MASC) commercial

Malta NOUN Malte FEM

mammal NOUN mammifère MASC

man NOUN homme MASC; modern man is taller than his ancestors l'homme moderne est plus grand que ses ancêtres

manage VERB ❶ diriger (52) (business, team); she manages a travel agency elle dirige une agence de voyages ❷ (cope) se débrouiller [1]; I can manage je me débrouille ❸ to manage to do réussir [2] à faire, he managed to open the door il a réussi à ouvrir la porte, I didn't manage to get in touch with her je n'ai pas réussi à la contacter

management NOUN ❶ gestion FEM; a management course un cours de gestion ❷ direction; a meeting

with management une réunion avec la direction

manager NOUN ❶ (of a company or a bank) directeur MASC, directrice FEM ❷ (of a shop or restaurant) gérant MASC, gérante FEM ❸ (in sport and entertainment) manager MASC

manageress NOUN gérante FEM

managing director NOUN directeur (MASC) général, directrice (FEM) générale

mandarin (orange) NOUN mandarine FEM

mango NOUN mangue FEM

mania NOUN manie FEM

maniac NOUN fou MASC, folle FEM; she drives like a maniac! elle conduit comme une folle!

mankind NOUN humanité FEM

man-made ADJECTIVE (fibre) synthétique

manner NOUN ❶ in a manner of speaking pour ainsi dire ❷ to have good manners être poli, it's bad manners to talk like that ce n'est pas poli de parler comme ça

manpower NOUN main-d'œuvre FEM

mansion NOUN demeure FEM

mantelpiece NOUN cheminée FEM

manual NOUN manuel MASC

manufacture VERB fabriquer [1]

manufacturer NOUN fabricant MASC

manure NOUN fumier MASC

many DETERMINER, PRONOUN ❶ beaucoup (de); does she have many friends? est-ce

a
b
c
d
e
f
g
h
i
j
k
l
m
n
o
p
q
r
s
t
u
v
w
x
y
z

A
B
C
D
E
F
G
H
I
J
K
L
M
N
O
P
Q
R
S
T
U
V
W
X
Y
Z

qu'elle a beaucoup d'amis?, **we
didn't see many people** nous
n'avons pas vu beaucoup (de) gens,
not many pas beaucoup, **there
aren't many onions left** il ne reste
pas beaucoup d'oignons, **many of
them forgot** beaucoup d'entre eux
ont oublié ❷ **very many** beaucoup
(de), **there aren't very many glasses**
il n'y a pas beaucoup de verres ❸ **so
many** tant, **I have so many things to
do!** j'ai tant de choses à faire! ❹ **so
many** autant de, **I've never eaten
so many strawberries** je n'ai jamais
mangé autant de fraises ❺ **as
many as** autant que, **you can take
as many as you like** tu peux en
prendre autant que tu veux ❻ **too
many** trop (de), **I've got too many
things to do** j'ai trop de choses à
faire, **there were too many people**
il y avait trop de monde, **that's
far too many!** c'est beaucoup
trop! ❼ **how many?** combien?, **how
many are there?** il y en a combien?,
how many sisters have you got? tu
as combien de sœurs?, **how many
are there left?** il en reste combien?

map NOUN ❶ carte FEM; **a road map**
une carte routière ❷ (of a town)
plan MASC

marathon NOUN marathon MASC

marble NOUN ❶ marbre MASC; **a
marble fireplace** une cheminée en
marbre ❷ bille; **to play marbles**
jouer aux billes

march NOUN (demonstration)
manifestation FEM

march VERB (demonstrators) défiler [1]

March NOUN mars MASC; **in March**
en mars

mare NOUN jument FEM

margarine NOUN margarine FEM

margin NOUN marge FEM

marijuana NOUN marijuana FEM

mark NOUN ❶ (at school) note FEM;
**I got a good mark for my French
homework** j'ai eu une bonne note
pour mon devoir de français, **what
mark did you get for French?** tu as
eu combien en français? ❷ (stain)
tache FEM

mark VERB corriger [52]; **the teacher
marks our homework** le professeur
corrige nos devoirs

market NOUN marché MASC

marketing NOUN marketing MASC

marmalade NOUN confiture (FEM)
d'oranges amères

maroon ADJECTIVE bordeaux; **a
maroon jumper** un pull bordeaux

marriage NOUN mariage MASC

married ADJECTIVE marié; **a married
couple** un couple marié, **they've
been married for twenty years** ils
sont mariés depuis vingt ans

marry VERB ❶ **to marry somebody**
épouser [1] quelqu'un, **she married
a Frenchman** elle a épousé un
Français ❷ **to get married** se marier
[1], **they got married in July** ils se
sont mariés en juillet

marvellous ADJECTIVE merveilleux
(FEM merveilleuse); **the weather's
marvellous** il fait un temps
merveilleux

marzipan NOUN pâte (FEM)
d'amandes

mascara NOUN mascara MASC

masculine NOUN (in French and other grammars) masculin MASC; **in the masculine** au masculin

mash VERB écraser [1] (vegetables)

mashed potatoes NOUN purée (FEM) de pommes de terre

mask NOUN masque MASC

mass NOUN ❶ **a mass of** une masse de ❷ **masses of** beaucoup de, **they've got masses of money** ils ont beaucoup d'argent, **there's masses left over** il en reste beaucoup ❸ (religious) messe FEM; **to go to mass** aller à la messe

massacre NOUN massacre MASC

massage NOUN massage MASC

massive ADJECTIVE énorme

master VERB maîtriser [1]

masterpiece NOUN chef-d'œuvre MASC (PLURAL chefs-d'œuvre)

mat NOUN ❶ (doormat) paillasson MASC ❷ (to put under a hot dish) dessous-de-plat MASC ❸ **a table mat** un set de table

match NOUN ❶ allumette FEM; **a box of matches** une boîte d'allumettes ❷ (sports) match MASC (PLURAL matchs); **a football match** un match de foot, **to watch the match** regarder [1] le match, **to win the match** gagner [1] le match, **to lose the match** perdre [3] le match

match VERB être [6] assorti à; **the jacket matches the skirt** la veste est assortie à la jupe

matching ADJECTIVE **matching curtains and cushions** des rideaux et des coussins assortis

mate NOUN copain MASC, copine FEM (informal); **I'm going out with my mates tonight** je sors avec mes copains ce soir

material NOUN ❶ (fabric) tissu MASC ❷ (information) documentation FEM ❸ (substance) matière FEM; **raw materials** les matières (FEM PLURAL) premières

mathematics NOUN mathématiques FEM PLURAL

maths NOUN maths FEM PLURAL; **I like maths** j'aime bien les maths, **Anna's good at maths** Anna est forte en maths

matter NOUN **what's the matter?** qu'est-ce qu'il y a?

matter VERB ❶ **the things that matter** les choses importantes, **it matters a lot to me** c'est très important pour moi ❷ **it doesn't matter** ça ne fait rien, **it doesn't matter if it rains** ça ne fait rien s'il pleut ❸ **it doesn't matter** (whether one thing or another) ça n'a pas d'importance, **you can write it in French or English, it doesn't matter** tu peux l'écrire en français ou en anglais, ça n'a pas d'importance

mattress NOUN matelas MASC

mature ADJECTIVE mûr

maximum NOUN maximum MASC; **the maximum possible** le maximum possible

maximum ADJECTIVE maximum (does not change in the feminine or plural); **the maximum temperature** la température maximum, **maximum profits** les bénéfices maximum

a
b
c
d
e
f
g
h
i
j
k
l
m
n
o
p
q
r
s
t
u
v
w
x
y
z

may VERB ❶ she may be ill elle est peut-être malade, we may go to Spain nous irons peut-être en Espagne ❷ (asking permission) may I close the door? est-ce que je peux fermer la porte?

May NOUN mai MASC; in May en mai

maybe ADVERB peut-être; maybe not peut-être pas, maybe he's forgotten il a peut-être oublié, maybe they've got lost ils se sont peut-être perdus

May Day NOUN le Premier Mai

mayonnaise NOUN mayonnaise FEM

mayor NOUN maire MASC

mayoress NOUN mairesse FEM

me PRONOUN ❶ me (m' before a vowel or silent 'h'); she knows me elle me connaît, can you help me, please? est-ce que tu peux m'aider, s'il te plaît?, can you lend me a pen? peux-tu me prêter un stylo?, can you give me your address? peux-tu me donner ton adresse? ❷ (after a preposition) moi; I took her with me je l'ai emmenée avec moi, they left without me ils sont partis sans moi ❸ (in commands) moi; listen to me! écoute-moi!, wait for me! attends-moi!, excuse me! excusez-moi! ❹ (in comparisons) than me que moi, she's older than me elle est plus âgée que moi ❺ me too! moi aussi!

meadow NOUN pré MASC

meal NOUN repas MASC; they have three meals a day ils mangent trois fois par jour

mean VERB ❶ vouloir [14] dire; what do you mean? qu'est-ce que tu veux dire?, what does that mean? qu'est-

ce que ça veut dire?, that's not what I meant ce n'est pas ce que je voulais dire ❷ to mean to do avoir [5] l'intention de faire, I meant to phone my mother j'avais l'intention d'appeler ma mère ❸ to be meant to do devoir faire, she was meant to be here at six elle devait être là à six heures

mean ADJECTIVE ❶ (with money) radin (informal) ❷ (unkind) méchant; she's really mean to her brother elle est vraiment méchante avec son frère, what a mean thing to do! c'est vraiment méchant!

meaning NOUN sens MASC

means NOUN moyen MASC; a means of transport un moyen de transport, a means of doing un moyen de faire, we have no means of contacting him nous n'avons aucun moyen de le contacter, by means of au moyen de, by all means certainement

meantime NOUN for the meantime pour le moment, in the meantime pendant ce temps

meanwhile ADVERB pendant ce temps; meanwhile she was waiting at the station pendant ce temps, elle attendait à la gare

measles NOUN rougeole FEM

measure VERB mesurer [1]

measurements PLURAL NOUN ❶ (of a room or an object) dimensions FEM PLURAL; the measurements of the room les dimensions de la pièce ❷ (of a person) mensurations FEM PLURAL; my chest measurement mon tour de poitrine, my waist measurement mon tour de taille

meat NOUN **viande** FEM

Mecca NOUN **Mecque** FEM

mechanic NOUN **mécanicien** MASC; **he's a mechanic** il est mécanicien

mechanical ADJECTIVE **mécanique**

medal NOUN **médaille** FEM; **the gold medal** la médaille d'or

media NOUN **the media** les médias MASC PLURAL

medical NOUN **visite** (FEM) **médicale**; **to have a medical** passer une visite médicale

medical ADJECTIVE **médical** (MASC PLURAL **médicaux**); **do you have medical insurance?** est-ce que vous avez une assurance-maladie?

medicine NOUN ❶ **médicament** MASC; **I'd like some cough medecine** je voudrais un médicament pour la toux ❷ (subject of study) **médecine** FEM; **she's studying medicine** elle fait des études de médecine ❸ **alternative medecine** la médecine douce

medieval ADJECTIVE **médiéval, du moyen-âge**

Mediterranean NOUN **the Mediterranean** la Méditerranée

medium ADJECTIVE **moyen** (FEM **moyenne**)

medium-sized NOUN **de taille moyenne**

meet VERB ❶ (by chance) **rencontrer** [1]; **I met Rosie outside the baker's** j'ai rencontré Rosie devant la boulangerie ❷ (by appointment) **retrouver** [1]; **I'll meet you outside the cinema at six** je te retrouverai devant le cinéma à six heures ❸ **se retrouver** [1]; **we're meeting at**

six nous allons nous retrouver à six heures ❹ (get to know) **faire** [10] **la connaissance de**; **I met a French girl last week** j'ai fait la connaissance d'une Française la semaine dernière ❺ **Tom, have you met Oskar?** Tom, est-ce que tu connais Oskar? ❻ (off a train, bus, etc) **venir** [81] **chercher**; **my dad's meeting me at the station** mon père vient me chercher à la gare

meeting NOUN **réunion** FEM; **there's a meeting at ten o'clock** il y a une réunion à dix heures, **she's in a meeting** elle est en réunion

megabyte NOUN **mégaoctet** MASC

melody NOUN **mélodie** FEM

melon NOUN **melon** MASC

melt VERB ❶ **fondre** [3]; **it melts in your mouth** ça fond dans la bouche ❷ **to melt something** faire [10] **fondre quelque chose**, **melt the butter in a saucepan** faites fondre le beurre dans une casserole

member NOUN **membre** MASC; **she's a member of the Labour Party** elle est membre du parti travailliste

Member of Parliament NOUN **député** MASC

membership NOUN **adhésion** FEM

membership card NOUN **carte** (FEM) **de membre**

membership fee NOUN **cotisation** FEM

memorial NOUN **a war memorial** un monument aux morts

memorial service NOUN **messe** (FEM) **commémorative**

memorize VERB **to memorize something** apprendre [64] quelque chose par cur

memory NOUN ❶ *(of a person or computer)* mémoire FEM; **you have a good memory!** tu as bonne mémoire!, **I have a bad memory** je n'ai pas de mémoire ❷ *(of the past)* souvenir MASC; **I have good memories of my stay in France** j'ai de bons souvenirs de mon séjour en France

mend VERB réparer [1]

meningitis NOUN méningite FEM

mental ADJECTIVE mental MASC (PLURAL mentaux); **a mental illness** une maladie mentale, **a mental hospital** un hôpital psychiatrique

mention VERB mentionner [1]

menu NOUN menu MASC; **on the menu** au menu, **is there a set menu?** est-ce qu'il y a un menu à prix fixe?

mercy NOUN pitié FEM

merge VERB ❶ *(roads)* se rejoindre [49] ❷ *(documents)* fusionner [1]

meringue NOUN meringue FEM

merit NOUN mérite MASC

mermaid NOUN sirène FEM

merry ADJECTIVE ❶ joyeux *(FEM joyeuse)*; **Merry Christmas** Joyeux Noël ❷ *(from drinking)* éméché *(informal)*

merry-go-round NOUN manège MASC

mess NOUN désordre MASC; **my papers are in a mess** mes papiers sont dans le désordre, **to make a mess** mettre du désordre, **to clear up the mess** mettre de l'ordre, **what a mess!** quelle pagaille! *(informal)*
- **to mess about** faire [10] l'imbécile; **stop messing about!** arrête de faire l'imbécile!

- **to mess about with something** jouer [1] avec quelque chose; **it's dangerous to mess about with matches** il est dangereux de jouer avec les allumettes
- **to mess something up** mettre [11] la pagaille dans quelque chose *(informal)*; **you've messed up all my papers** tu as mis la pagaille dans tous mes papiers

message NOUN message MASC; **a telephone message** un message téléphonique

messenger NOUN messager MASC

messy ADJECTIVE ❶ **it's a messy job** c'est un travail salissant ❷ **he's a messy eater** il mange n'importe comment, **her writing's really messy** elle écrit n'importe comment

metal NOUN métal MASC (PLURAL métaux)

meter NOUN ❶ *(electricity, gas, taxi)* compteur MASC; **to read the meter** relever le compteur ❷ **a parking meter** un parcmètre

method NOUN méthode FEM

Methodist NOUN méthodiste MASC & FEM; **I'm a Methodist** je suis méthodiste

metre NOUN mètre MASC

metric ADJECTIVE métrique

Mexican NOUN Mexicain MASC, Mexicaine FEM

Mexican ADJECTIVE mexicain

Mexico NOUN Mexique MASC; **in Mexico** au Mexique, **to Mexico** au Mexique

microchip NOUN puce FEM

microphone NOUN microphone MASC

microscope NOUN microscope MASC

microwave oven NOUN four (MASC) à micro-ondes

midday NOUN midi MASC; **at midday** à midi

middle NOUN ❶ milieu MASC; **in the middle of the room** au milieu de la pièce, **in the middle of the night** au milieu de la nuit ❷ **to be in the middle of doing** être en train de faire, **when she phoned I was in the middle of washing my hair** quand elle a appelé j'étais en train de me laver les cheveux

middle-aged ADJECTIVE d'un certain âge; **a middle-aged lady** une dame d'un certain âge

middle-class ADJECTIVE de la classe moyenne; **a middle-class family** une famille de la classe moyenne

Middle-East NOUN Moyen-Orient MASC; **in the Middle East** au Moyen-Orient

middle finger NOUN majeur MASC

midge NOUN moucheron MASC

midnight NOUN minuit MASC; **at midnight** à minuit

Midsummer's Day NOUN la Saint Jean

midwife NOUN sage-femme FEM

might VERB 'are you going to phone him?' – 'I might' 'est-ce que tu vas l'appeler?' – 'peut-être', **I might invite Jo** j'inviterai peut-être Jo, **Amanda might know** Amanda le saurait peut-être, **he might have forgotten** il a peut-être oublié

migraine NOUN migraine FEM

mike NOUN micro MASC (informal)

mild ADJECTIVE doux (FEM douce); **it's quite mild today** il fait plutôt doux aujourd'hui

mile NOUN ❶ mille MASC (the French use kilometres for distances; to convert miles roughly to kilometres, multiply by 8 and divide by 5); **the village is ten miles from Oxford** le village est à seize kilomètres d'Oxford ❷ **it's miles better!** c'est dix fois meilleur!

mileage NOUN kilométrage MASC; **what's the mileage on your car?** elle a combien de kilomètres, votre voiture?

military ADJECTIVE militaire

milk NOUN lait MASC; **full-cream milk** le lait entier, **skimmed milk** le lait écrémé, **semi-skimmed milk** le lait demi-écrémé

milk VERB traire [78]

milk chocolate NOUN chocolat (MASC) au lait

milk jug NOUN pot (MASC) à lait

milkman NOUN laitier MASC

milk shake NOUN milk-shake MASC

millennium NOUN millénaire MASC

millimetre NOUN millimètre MASC

million NOUN million MASC; **a million people** un million de personnes, **two million people** deux millions de personnes

millionaire NOUN millionnaire MASC

mimic VERB imiter [1]

mince NOUN viande (FEM) hachée

mind NOUN ❶ esprit MASC; **it crossed my mind that ...** il m'est venu à l'esprit que ... ❷ **to change your mind** changer d'avis, **I've changed my mind** j'ai changé d'avis ❸ **to make up your mind** se décider, **I can't make up my mind** je n'arrive pas à me décider

mind VERB ❶ surveiller [1]; **can you mind my bag for me?** est-ce que tu peux surveiller mon sac? ❷ s'occuper [1] de (baby); **could you mind the baby for ten minutes?** est-ce que tu peux t'occuper du bébé pendant dix minutes? ❸ **do you mind if ...?** est-ce que cela vous dérange si ...?, **do you mind if I close the door?** est-ce que cela vous dérange si je ferme la porte?, **I don't mind** cela ne me dérange pas, **I don't mind the heat** la chaleur ne me dérange pas ❹ **mind the step!** attention à la marche! ❺ **never mind!** peu importe!

mine¹ NOUN mine FEM; **a coal mine** une mine de charbon

mine² PRONOUN ❶ (for a masculine noun) le mien; **she took her hat and I took mine** elle a pris son chapeau et j'ai pris le mien ❷ (for a feminine noun) la mienne; **she gave me her address and I gave her mine** elle m'a donné son adresse et je lui ai donné la mienne ❸ (for a masculine plural noun) les miens; **Karen's invited her parents and I've invited mine** Karen a invité ses parents et j'ai invité les miens ❹ (for a feminine plural noun) les miennes; **she showed me her**

photos and I showed her mine elle m'a montré ses photos et je lui ai montré les miennes ❺ à moi; **the green one's mine** le vert est à moi, **it's mine** c'est à moi

miner NOUN mineur MASC

mineral water NOUN eau (FEM) minérale

miniature NOUN, ADJECTIVE miniature FEM

minibus NOUN minibus MASC

minimum NOUN minimum MASC; **a minimum of** un minimum de

minimum ADJECTIVE minimum (does not change in the feminine or plural); **the minimum age** l'âge minimum, **minimum safety measures** des mesures de sécurité minimum, **the minimum amount** le minimum

miniskirt NOUN mini-jupe FEM

minister NOUN ❶ (in government) ministre MASC ❷ (of a church) pasteur MASC

ministry NOUN ministère MASC

minor ADJECTIVE mineur

minority NOUN minorité FEM

mint NOUN ❶ (herb) menthe FEM ❷ (sweet) bonbon (MASC) à la menthe

minus PREPOSITION moins; **seven minus three is four** sept moins trois égale quatre, **it was minus ten this morning** il a fait moins dix ce matin

minute¹ NOUN minute FEM; **just a minute!** une minute!, **I'll be ready in two minutes** je serai prêt dans deux minutes, **it's five minutes' walk from here** c'est à cinq minutes à pied d'ici

minute² *ADJECTIVE* **minuscule; the bedrooms are minute** les chambres sont minuscules

miracle *NOUN* **miracle** *MASC*

mirror *NOUN* ❶ **glace** *FEM*; **I looked at myself in the mirror** je me suis regardé dans la glace ❷ *(rearview mirror in a car)* **rétroviseur** *MASC*

misbehave *VERB* **se conduire** [26] **mal**

mischief *NOUN* **to get up to mischief** faire des bêtises

mischievous *ADJECTIVE* **coquin**

miser *NOUN* **avare** *MASC & FEM*

miserable *ADJECTIVE* ❶ **malheureux** *(FEM* **malheureuse***)*; **he was miserable without her** il était malheureux sans elle, **I feel really miserable today** je n'ai vraiment pas le moral aujourd'hui ❷ **it's miserable weather** il fait un sale temps ❸ **she gets paid a miserable wage** elle gagne un salaire de misère

misery *NOUN* **souffrance** *FEM*; **he was in misery** il était extrêmement malheureux

misfire *VERB* **tomber** [1] **à plat; our plans misfired** nos projets sont tombés à plat

misfortune *NOUN* **malheur** *MASC*

misjudge *VERB* ❶ **mal évaluer** [1]; **she misjudged the distance** elle a mal évalué la distance ❷ **mal juger** [52] *(a person)*; **everybody had misjudged her** tout le monde l'avait mal jugée

mislay *VERB* **égarer** [1]; **I've mislaid my keys** j'ai égaré mes clés

misleading *ADJECTIVE* **trompeur** *(FEM* **trompeuse***)*; **it's a misleading advertisement** c'est une publicité trompeuse

miss *VERB* ❶ **rater** [1]; **she missed her train** elle a raté son train, **I missed the film** j'ai raté le film, **the ball missed the goal** le ballon a raté le but, **missed!** raté! ❷ **manquer** [1]; **he's missed several classes** il a manqué plusieurs cours, **to miss an opportunity** manquer une occasion ❸ **I miss you** tu me manques, **she's missing her sister** sa sœur lui manque, **I miss France** la France me manque

Miss *NOUN* **Mademoiselle; Miss Jones** Mademoiselle Jones, *(written as)* Mlle Jones

missile *NOUN* **missile** *MASC*

missing *ADJECTIVE* ❶ **manquant; she's found the missing pieces** elle a trouvé les pièces manquantes, **the missing link** le chaînon manquant ❷ **there's a plate missing** il manque une assiette, **there are three forks missing** il manque trois fourchettes ❸ **to go missing** disparaître, **several things have gone missing lately** plusieurs choses ont disparu récemment, **three people are missing** trois personnes ont disparu

missionary *NOUN* **missionnaire** *MASC & FEM*

mist *NOUN* **brume** *FEM*

mistake *NOUN* ❶ **erreur** *FEM*; **by mistake** par erreur, **it was my mistake** c'était une erreur de ma part ❷ **faute** *FEM*; **a spelling mistake** une faute d'orthographe, **you've made lots of mistakes** tu as fait beaucoup de fautes ❸ **to make a**

mistake *(be mistaken)* se tromper, **sorry, I made a mistake** je suis désolé, je me suis trompé

mistake *VERB* **I mistook you for your brother** je vous ai pris pour votre frère

mistaken *ADJECTIVE* **to be mistaken** se tromper, **you're mistaken** tu te trompes

mistletoe *NOUN* gui *MASC*

misty *ADJECTIVE* brumeux *(FEM brumeuse)*; **a misty morning** un matin brumeux, **it's misty this morning** il y a de la brume ce matin

misunderstand *VERB* mal comprendre [64]; **I misunderstood** j'ai mal compris

misunderstanding *NOUN* malentendu *MASC*; **there's been a misunderstanding** il y a eu un malentendu

mitten *NOUN* moufle *FEM*

mix *NOUN* ❶ mélange *MASC*; **a good mix of people** un bon mélange de gens ❷ **a cake mix** une préparation pour gâteau

mix *VERB* ❶ mélanger [52]; **mix all the ingredients together** mélangez tous les ingrédients ❷ **to mix with** fréquenter [1], **she mixes with lots of interesting people** elle fréquente beaucoup de gens intéressants

• **to mix up** ❶ mélanger [52]; **you've mixed up all my papers** tu as mélangé tous mes papiers, **you've got it all mixed up!** tu mélanges tout! (*story*) ❷ *(confuse)* confondre [69]; **I get him mixed up with his brother** je le confonds avec son frère

mixed *ADJECTIVE* varié; **a mixed programme** un programme varié

mixed salad *NOUN* salade *(FEM)* composée

mixed school *NOUN* école *(FEM)* mixte

mixer *NOUN* batteur *(MASC)* électrique

mixture *NOUN* mélange *MASC*; **it's a mixture of jazz and rock** c'est un mélange de jazz et de rock

moan *VERB* râler [1] *(informal)*; **stop moaning!** arrête de râler!

mobile home *NOUN* mobile home *MASC*

mobile phone *NOUN* téléphone *(MASC)* portable

mock *NOUN* *(mock exam)* examen *(MASC)* blanc

mock *VERB* se moquer [1] de; **stop mocking me!** arrête de te moquer de moi!

model *NOUN* ❶ *(type)* modèle *MASC*; **the latest model** le dernier modèle ❷ *(fashion model)* mannequin *MASC*; **she's a model** elle est mannequin de luxe ❸ *(of a plane, car, etc)* modèle *(MASC)* réduit; **he makes models** il fait des modèles réduits ❹ *(of a building)* maquette *FEM*; **a model of Westminster Abbey** une maquette de l'Abbaye de Westminster

model aeroplane *NOUN* modèle *(MASC)* réduit d'avion

model railway *NOUN* chemin *(MASC)* de fer miniature

model village *NOUN* village *(MASC)* miniature

modem NOUN modem MASC

moderate ADJECTIVE modéré

modern ADJECTIVE moderne

modernize VERB moderniser [1]

modern languages NOUN langues (FEM PLURAL) vivantes

modest ADJECTIVE modeste

modify VERB modifier [1]

moisture NOUN humidité FEM

moisturizer NOUN ❶ (lotion) lait hydratant MASC ❷ (cream) crème (FEM) hydratante

mole NOUN ❶ (animal) taupe FEM ❷ (on skin) graine (FEM) de beauté

molecule NOUN molécule FEM

molehill NOUN taupinière FEM

moment NOUN ❶ instant MASC; **he'll be here in a moment** il sera là dans un instant, **at any moment** à tout instant ❷ **at the moment** en ce moment, **at the right moment** au bon moment

Monaco NOUN Monaco

monarchy NOUN monarchie FEM

monastery NOUN monastère MASC

Monday NOUN lundi MASC; **on Monday** lundi, **I'm going out on Monday** je sors lundi, **see you on Monday!** à lundi!, **on Mondays** le lundi, **the museum is closed on Mondays** le musée est fermé le lundi, **every Monday** tous les lundis, **last Monday** lundi dernier, **next Monday** lundi prochain

money NOUN argent MASC; **I don't have enough money** je n'ai pas assez d'argent, **to make money**

gagner de l'argent, **they gave me my money back** (in a shop) ils m'ont remboursé

money box NOUN tirelire FEM

mongrel NOUN chien (MASC) bâtard

monitor NOUN (on computer) moniteur MASC

monk NOUN moine MASC

monkey NOUN ❶ singe MASC ❷ **you little monkey!** petit galopin! (informal)

monotonous ADJECTIVE monotone

monster NOUN monstre MASC

month NOUN mois MASC; **in the month of May** au mois de mai, **this month** ce mois-ci, **next month** le mois prochain, **we're leaving next month** nous allons partir le mois prochain, **last month** le mois dernier, **every month** tous les mois, **in two months' time** dans deux mois, **at the end of the month** à la fin du mois

monthly ADJECTIVE mensuel (FEM mensuelle); **a monthly payment** une mensualité

monument NOUN monument MASC

mood NOUN humeur FEM; **to be in a good mood** être de bonne humeur, **to be in a bad mood** être de mauvaise humeur, **I'm not in the mood** ça ne me dit rien

moody ADJECTIVE lunatique

moon NOUN lune FEM; **by the light of the moon** au clair de lune
• **to be over the moon** être aux anges (literally: to be at the level of the angels)

moonlight NOUN clair (MASC) de lune; **by moonlight** au clair de lune

moor NOUN lande FEM; **the Yorkshire moors** les landes du Yorkshire

moor VERB amarrer [1] *(a boat)*

moped NOUN mobylette FEM

moral NOUN morale FEM; **the moral of the story** la morale de l'histoire

moral ADJECTIVE moral MASC (PLURAL moraux)

morale NOUN moral MASC; **to boost somebody's morale** remonter le moral à quelqu'un, **he's been trying to boost morale** il essaie de leur remonter le moral

morals NOUN moralité FEM

more ADVERB ❶ plus; **more interesting** plus intéressant, **more difficult** plus difficile, **more slowly** plus lentement, **more easily** plus facilement ❷ **more ... than** plus ... que, **the book's more interesting than the film** le livre est plus intéressant que le film

more DETERMINER ❶ plus de; **they have more money than we do** ils ont plus d'argent que nous, **I'll have a little more milk** je prendrai un peu plus de lait ❷ *(of something you have already)* encore de; **would you like some more cake?** voulez-vous encore du gâteau?, **a few more glasses** encore quelques verres

more PRONOUN ❶ plus; **he eats more than me** il mange plus que moi ❷ *(of something you have already)* encore; **we need three more** il nous en faut encore trois, **I'll have a little more** je prendrai un peu plus, **I don't want any more** je n'en veux plus ❸ **more and more** de plus en

plus, **books are getting more and more expensive** les livres coûtent de plus en plus cher, **it takes more and more time** ça prend de plus en plus de temps ❹ **more or less** plus ou moins, **it's more or less finished** c'est plus ou moins fini

morning NOUN ❶ matin MASC; **this morning** ce matin, **tomorrow morning** demain matin, **yesterday morning** hier matin, **in the morning** le matin, **she doesn't work in the morning** elle ne travaille pas le matin, **on Friday mornings** le vendredi matin, **at six o'clock in the morning** à six heures du matin ❷ *(as a period of time spent doing something)* matinée; **I spent the whole morning doing the washing-up** j'ai passé toute la matinée à faire la vaisselle

Morocco NOUN Maroc MASC; **to Morocco** au Maroc, **in Morocco** au Maroc

mortgage NOUN crédit MASC (immobilier)

Moscow NOUN Moscou; **in Moscow** à Moscou

Moslem NOUN musulman MASC, musulmane FEM

mosque NOUN mosquée FEM

mosquito NOUN moustique MASC; **a mosquito bite** une piqûre de moustique

most DETERMINER, ADVERB, PRONOUN ❶ *(followed by a plural noun)* la plupart de; **most children like chocolate** la plupart des enfants aiment le chocolat, **most of my friends** la plupart de mes amis ❷ *(followed by a singular noun)* presque tout; **they've eaten most of the chocolate** ils ont mangé presque tout le chocolat ❸ **most of the time** la plupart du temps ❹ **the most** (followed by adjective) le plus, la plus, les plus, **the most interesting film** le film le plus intéressant, **the most exciting story** l'histoire la plus passionnante, **the most boring books** les livres les plus ennuyeux ❺ **the most** (followed by noun) le plus de, **I've got the most time** c'est moi qui ai le plus de temps ❻ **the most** (after verb) le plus, **what I hate most is the noise** ce que je déteste le plus, c'est le bruit

moth NOUN ❶ (butterfly) papillon (MASC) de nuit ❷ (clothes moth) mite FEM

mother NOUN mère FEM; **my mother** ma mère, **Kate's mother** la mère de Kate

mother-in-law NOUN belle-mère FEM (PLURAL belles-mères)

Mother's Day NOUN la fête des Mères (in France the last Sunday in May)

motion NOUN mouvement MASC

motivated ADJECTIVE motivé

motivation NOUN motivation FEM

motor NOUN moteur MASC

motorbike NOUN moto FEM

motorboat NOUN bateau (MASC) à moteur

motorcyclist NOUN motocycliste MASC & FEM

motorist NOUN automobiliste MASC & FEM

motor racing NOUN course (FEM) automobile

motorway NOUN autoroute FEM

mouldy ADJECTIVE moisi

mountain NOUN montagne FEM; **in the mountains** à la montagne

mountain bike NOUN VTT MASC (short for vélo tout-terrain)

mountaineer NOUN alpiniste MASC & FEM

mountaineering NOUN alpinisme MASC; **to go mountaineering** faire de l'alpinisme

mountainous ADJECTIVE montagneux (FEM montagneuse)

mouse NOUN souris FEM (both the animal and for a computer)

mousse NOUN mousse FEM; **chocolate mousse** la mousse au chocolat

moustache NOUN moustache FEM; **a man with a moustache** un moustachu

mouth NOUN bouche FEM

mouthful NOUN bouchée FEM

mouth organ NOUN harmonica MASC; **to play the mouth organ** jouer de l'harmonica

move NOUN ❶ (to a different house) déménagement MASC ❷ (in a game) **your move!** à toi de jouer!

move VERB ❶ bouger [52]; **she didn't move** elle n'a pas bougé ❷ **move up a bit** pousse-toi un peu ❸ enlever [50] (an object); **can you move your bag, please?** peux-tu enlever ton sac, s'il te plaît? ❹ (car, traffic) avancer [61]; **the traffic was moving slowly** la circulation avançait lentement ❺ **to move forward** avancer [61], **he moved forward a step** il s'est avancé d'un pas ❻ *(move house)* **déménager** [52]; **we're moving on Tuesday** nous déménageons mardi, **they've moved to France** ils se sont installés en France

• **to move in** emménager [52]; **when are you moving in?** quand est-ce que tu emménages?

• **to move out** déménager [52]; **we're moving out next week** nous déménageons la semaine prochaine

movement NOUN mouvement MASC

movie NOUN film MASC; **to go to the movies** aller au cinéma

moving ADJECTIVE ❶ en marche; **a moving vehicle** un véhicule en marche ❷ *(emotionally)* émouvant; **it's a very moving film** c'est un film très émouvant

mow VERB tondre [3]; **to mow the grass** tondre la pelouse

mower NOUN tondeuse *(FEM)* à gazon

MP NOUN député MASC; **she is an MP** elle est député

Mr NOUN Monsieur *(usually abbreviated to 'M.')*; **Mr Angus Brown** M. Angus Brown

Mrs NOUN Madame *(usually abbreviated to 'Mme')*; **Mrs Mary Hendry** Mme Mary Hendry

Ms NOUN Madame *(usually abbreviated to 'Mme'; note that there is no direct equivalent for 'Ms' in French, but 'Madame' may be used whether the woman is married or not)*

much ADJECTIVE, ADVERB, PRONOUN ❶ beaucoup; **she doesn't eat much** elle ne mange pas beaucoup, **we don't go out much** nous ne sortons pas beaucoup, **much more** beaucoup

plus, **much shorter** beaucoup plus court ❷ *(followed by a noun)* beaucoup de; **we don't have much time** nous n'avons pas beaucoup de temps, **there isn't much butter left** il ne reste pas beaucoup de beurre ❸ **very much** beaucoup, **thank you very much** merci beaucoup, **I don't watch television very much** je ne regarde pas beaucoup la télé ❹ **very much** *(followed by a noun)* beaucoup de, **there isn't very much milk** il n'y a pas beaucoup de lait ❺ **not much** pas beaucoup, **'do you have a lot of homework?' – 'no, not much'** 'est-ce que tu as beaucoup de devoirs?' – 'non, pas beaucoup' ❻ **so much** tellement, **we liked it so much!** nous l'avons tellement aimé!, **I have so much to do!** j'ai tellement de choses à faire! ❼ **so much** autant, **you shouldn't have given me so much** tu n'aurais pas dû m'en donner autant ❽ **as much as** autant que, **you can take as much as you like** tu peux en prendre autant que tu veux ❾ **too much** trop (de), **her parents give her too much money** ses parents lui donnent trop d'argent, **that's far too much!** c'est beaucoup trop! ❿ **how much?** combien (de)?, **how much is it?** ça coûte combien?, **how much do you want?** tu en veux combien?, **how much sugar do you want?** tu veux combien de sucre?

mud NOUN boue FEM

muddle NOUN désordre MASC; **to be in a muddle** être en désordre

muddy ADJECTIVE ❶ *(path, road)* boueux *(FEM boueuse)* ❷ *(shoes, clothes)* couverts de boue; **your boots are all muddy** tes bottes sont couvertes de boue

mug NOUN grande tasse FEM; **a mug of coffee** une grande tasse de café

mug VERB **to mug somebody** agresser [1] quelqu'un, **to be mugged** se faire [10] agresser, **my brother was mugged in the park** mon frère s'est fait agresser au parc

mugging NOUN agression FEM

multiplication NOUN multiplication FEM

multiply VERB multiplier [1]; **to multiply six by four** multiplier six par quatre

mum, mummy NOUN ❶ mère FEM; **Tom's mum** la mère de Tom, **I'll ask my mum** je vais demander à ma mère ❷ *(within the family or as a name)* maman FEM; **mum's not back yet** maman n'est pas encore rentrée

mumps NOUN oreillons MASC PLURAL

murder NOUN meurtre MASC

murder VERB assassiner [1]

murderer NOUN assassin MASC

muscle NOUN muscle MASC

muscular ADJECTIVE musclé

museum NOUN musée MASC; **to go to the museum** aller au musée

mushroom NOUN champignon MASC; **a mushroom salad** une salade aux champignons

music NOUN musique FEM; **pop music** la musique pop, **classical music** la musique classique

musical NOUN comédie *(FEM)* musicale

musical ADJECTIVE ❶ **a musical instrument** un instrument de musique ❷ **they're a very musical family** ils sont très musiciens dans la famille

musician NOUN musicien MASC, musicienne FEM

Muslim NOUN musulman MASC, musulmane FEM

mussel NOUN moule FEM

must VERB ❶ falloir [43] *(to express obligation 'falloir' is used as an impersonal verb)*; **we must leave now** il faut partir maintenant *(the construction 'il faut que' is followed by a verb in the subjunctive)*, **I must tell you something** il faut que je te dise quelque chose, **you must be there at eight** il faut que tu sois là à huit heures, **you must learn the vocabulary** il faut que tu apprennes le vocabulaire ❷ *(expressing probability)* devoir [8]; **you must be tired** tu dois être fatigué, **it must be five o'clock** il doit être cinq heures, **he must have forgotten** il a dû oublier

mustard NOUN moutarde FEM

mutter VERB marmonner [1]

my ADJECTIVE ❶ *(before a masculine noun)* mon; **my brother** mon frère, **my book** mon livre ❷ *(before a feminine noun)* ma; **my sister** ma sœur, **my house** ma maison *(but 'ma' becomes 'mon' before a feminine noun beginning with a vowel or silent 'h')* **my address** mon adresse ❸ *(before a plural noun)* mes; **my children** mes enfants ❹ *(with parts of the body)* le, la, les; **I had a glass in my hand** j'avais un verre à la main, **I'm washing my hands** je me lave les mains

myself PRONOUN ❶ I've hurt myself je me suis blessé ❷ I said it myself je l'ai dit moi-même ❸ by myself tout seul, I did it by myself je l'ai fait tout seul

mysterious ADJECTIVE mystérieux (FEM mystérieuse)

mystery NOUN ❶ mystère MASC ❷ (book) roman (MASC) policier

myth NOUN mythe MASC

mythology NOUN mythologie FEM

nail NOUN ❶ (on finger or toe) ongle MASC; to bite your nails se ronger [52] les ongles ❷ (metal) clou MASC

nail VERB clouer [1]

nailbrush NOUN brosse (FEM) à ongles

nailfile NOUN lime (FEM) à ongles

nail scissors NOUN ciseaux (MASC PLURAL) à ongles

nail varnish NOUN vernis (MASC) à ongles

nail varnish remover NOUN dissolvant MASC

naked ADJECTIVE nu

name NOUN ❶ nom MASC; I've forgotten her name j'ai oublié son nom, what's your name? comment vous appelez-vous?, my name is Joy je m'appelle Joy ❷ (of a book or film) titre MASC

nanny NOUN nurse FEM

nap NOUN petit somme MASC; to have a nap faire un petit somme

napkin NOUN serviette FEM

nappy NOUN couche FEM

narrow ADJECTIVE étroit; a narrow street une rue étroite

nasty ADJECTIVE ❶ (mean) méchant; that was a nasty thing to do c'était méchant ❷ (unpleasant) désagréable; that's a nasty job c'est une tâche désagréable ❸ (bad) mauvais; a nasty smell une mauvaise odeur

nation NOUN nation FEM

national ADJECTIVE national MASC (PLURAL nationaux)

national anthem NOUN hymne (MASC) national

nationality NOUN nationalité FEM

national park NOUN parc (MASC) national (PLURAL parcs nationaux)

Nativity NOUN nativité FEM

natural ADJECTIVE naturel (FEM naturelle)

naturally ADVERB naturellement

nature NOUN nature FEM

nature reserve NOUN réserve (FEM) naturelle

naughty ADJECTIVE vilain

nausea NOUN nausée FEM

navel NOUN nombril MASC

navigate VERB naviguer [1]

navy NOUN marine FEM; **my uncle's in the navy** mon oncle est dans la marine

navy-blue ADJECTIVE bleu marine; **navy-blue gloves** des gants bleu marine

near ADJECTIVE proche; **the nearest shop** le magasin le plus proche

near ADVERB, PREPOSITION ❶ près; **they live quite near** ils habitent tout près, **to come nearer** s'approcher ❷ **near (to)** près de, **near the station** près de la gare

nearby ADVERB tout près; **there's a park nearby** il y a un parc tout près

nearly ADVERB presque; **nearly empty** presque vide, **we're nearly there** nous sommes presque arrivés

neat ADJECTIVE ❶ (well-organized) bien rangé; **a neat desk** un bureau bien rangé ❷ soigné (a garden, your clothes, or the way you look)

neatly ADVERB avec soin

necessarily ADVERB not necessarily pas forcément

necessary ADJECTIVE nécessaire; **if necessary** si besoin est

neck NOUN ❶ (of a person) cou MASC ❷ (of a garment) encolure FEM

necklace NOUN collier MASC

nectarine NOUN nectarine FEM

need NOUN there's no need, I've done it already inutile, c'est fait, **there's no need to wait** inutile d'attendre

need VERB ❶ avoir [5] besoin de; **we need bread** nous avons besoin de pain, **they need help** ils ont besoin d'aide, **everything you need** tout ce qu'il vous faut ❷ (to have to) devoir [8]; **I need to drop in at the bank** je dois passer par la banque ❸ **you needn't decide today** tu n'es pas obligé de décider aujourd'hui, **you needn't wait** tu n'es pas obligé d'attendre

needle NOUN aiguille FEM

negative NOUN (of a photo) négatif MASC

neglected ADJECTIVE mal entretenu

neighbour NOUN voisin MASC, voisine FEM; **we're going round to the neighbours'** on va chez les voisins

neighbourhood NOUN quartier MASC; **a nice neighbourhood** un quartier agréable

neither CONJUNCTION ❶ neither ... nor ni ... ni, **I have neither the time nor the money** je n'ai ni le temps ni l'argent ❷ neither do I moi non plus, **'I don't like fish'** – 'neither do I' 'je n'aime pas le poisson' – 'moi non plus' (translations using 'non plus' can be used for many similar replies), **'I wasn't invited'** – 'neither was I' 'je n'ai pas été invité' – 'moi non plus', **'I didn't like the film'** – 'neither did Kirsty' 'je n'ai pas aimé le film' – 'Kirsty non plus' ❸ **'which do you like?'** – 'neither' 'lequel aimes-tu?' – 'ni l'un ni l'autre'

nephew NOUN neveu MASC (PLURAL neveux)

nerve NOUN ❶ (in the body) nerf MASC ❷ **to lose one's nerve** perdre son courage ❸ you've got a nerve!

tu as un sacré culot! (*informal*)
- he gets on my nerves il me tape sur les nerfs (*informal*)

nervous ADJECTIVE nerveux (FEM nerveuse); **to feel nervous** (*before a performance or an exam*) avoir le trac (*informal*)

nervous breakdown NOUN dépression (FEM) nerveuse

nest NOUN nid MASC

net NOUN ❶ (*for fishing or in tennis*) filet MASC ❷ (*in football*) filets MASC PLURAL

Netherlands NOUN Pays-Bas MASC PLURAL; **in the Netherlands** aux Pays-Bas

nettle NOUN ortie FEM

network NOUN réseau MASC (PLURAL réseaux)

neutral NOUN (*in a gearbox*) point (MASC) mort; **to be in neutral** être au point mort

neutral ADJECTIVE neutre

never ADJECTIVE ❶ ne ... jamais; **Ben never smokes** Ben ne fume jamais, **I've never seen the film** je n'ai jamais vu le film ❷ jamais; '**have you ever been to Spain?' – 'no, never'** 'est-ce que tu es déjà allé en Espagne?' – 'non, jamais' ❸ **never again** plus jamais ❹ **never mind!** peu importe!

new ADJECTIVE ❶ (*different or unknown to you*) nouveau (FEM nouvelle); **have you seen their new house?** as-tu vu leur nouvelle maison?, **Debbie's new boyfriend** le nouveau copain de Debbie ❷ (*brand new*) neuf (FEM neuve); **it's a new car** c'est une voiture neuve

newcomer NOUN nouveau venu MASC (PLURAL nouveaux venus), nouvelle venue FEM, (PLURAL nouvelles venues)

news PLURAL NOUN ❶ (*everyday gossip*) nouvelle FEM (PLURAL nouvelles); **a piece of good news** une bonne nouvelle, **I've got good news** j'ai de bonnes nouvelles, **any news?** y a-t-il des nouvelles? ❷ (*on TV*) journal MASC; **the midday news** le journal de midi ❸ (*on the radio*) **the news** les informations

newsagent NOUN marchand (MASC) de journaux; **at the newsagent's** chez le marchand de journaux

newspaper NOUN journal MASC (PLURAL journaux)

newsreader NOUN présentateur MASC, présentatrice FEM

New Year NOUN le Nouvel An; **Happy New Year!** Bonne Année!

New Year's Day NOUN le jour de l'An

New Year's Eve NOUN la Saint-Sylvestre

New Zealand NOUN Nouvelle-Zélande FEM

New Zealander NOUN Néo-Zélandais MASC, Néo-Zélandaise FEM

next ADJECTIVE ❶ prochain; **the next train is at ten** le prochain train est à dix heures, **next week** la semaine prochaine, **next Thursday** jeudi prochain, **next year** l'année prochaine, **the next time I see you** la prochaine fois que je te verrai ❷ (*following*) suivant; **I saw her the next week** je l'ai vue la semaine suivante, **the next day** le lendemain, **the letter arrived the next day** la lettre est arrivée le lendemain ❸ *(next-door)* **voisin; in the next room** dans la pièce voisine

next ADVERB ❶ *(afterwards)* ensuite; **what did he say next?** qu'est-ce qu'il a dit ensuite? ❷ *(now)* maintenant; **what shall we do next?** qu'est-ce qu'on fait maintenant? ❸ **next to** à côté de, **the girl next to Pat** la fille à côté de Pat, **it's next to the baker's** c'est à côté de la boulangerie

next door ADVERB à côté; **they live next door** ils habitent à côté, **the girl next door** la fille d'à côté

nice ADJECTIVE ❶ *(pleasant)* agréable; **we had a nice evening** nous avons passé une soirée agréable, **Brighton's a nice town** Brighton est une ville agréable, **have a nice time!** amusez-vous bien! ❷ *(attractive to look at)* joli; **that's a nice dress** elle est jolie, cette robe ❸ *(kind, friendly)* sympathique *(a person)*; **she's really nice** elle est vraiment sympathique ❹ **to be nice to somebody** être gentil avec quelqu'un, **she's been very nice to me** elle a été très gentille avec moi ❺ *(tasting good)* bon *(FEM bonne)*; **let's have a nice cup of tea** si on prenait une bonne tasse de thé ❻ *(weather)* **it's a nice day** il fait beau, **we had nice weather** il a fait beau

nick VERB *(steal)* piquer [1] *(informal)*

nickname NOUN surnom MASC

niece NOUN nièce FEM

night NOUN ❶ *(before you go to bed)* soir MASC; **what are you doing tonight?** qu'est-ce que tu fais ce soir?, **see you tonight!** à ce soir!,

I saw Greg last night j'ai vu Greg hier soir ❷ *(after bedtime)* nuit FEM; **it's cold at night** il fait froid la nuit, **to stay the night with somebody** coucher chez quelqu'un

night club NOUN boîte *(FEM)* de nuit

nightie NOUN chemise *(FEM)* de nuit

nightingale NOUN rossignol MASC

nightmare NOUN cauchemar MASC; **to have a nightmare** faire un cauchemar

night-time NOUN nuit FEM

nil NOUN zéro MASC; **they won four-nil** ils ont gagné quatre à zéro

nine NUMBER neuf MASC; **Jake's nine** Jake a neuf ans

nineteen NUMBER dix-neuf MASC; **Kate's nineteen** Kate a dix-neuf ans

ninety NUMBER quatre-vingt-dix MASC

ninth NUMBER neuvième; **on the ninth floor** au neuvième étage, **the ninth of June** le neuf juin

nitrogen NOUN azote MASC

no ADVERB non; **I said no** j'ai dit non, **no thank you** non merci

no ADJECTIVE ❶ pas de; **we've got no bread** nous n'avons pas de pain, **no problem!** pas de problème! ❷ *(on a notice)* 'no smoking' défense de fumer', 'no parking' 'stationnement interdit'

nobody PRONOUN personne; 'who's there?' – 'nobody' 'qui est là?' – 'personne', **there's nobody in the kitchen** il n'y a personne dans la cuisine, **nobody knows me** personne ne me connaît, **nobody answered** personne n'a répondu

nod VERB *(to say yes)* faire [10] oui de la tête; **he nodded** il a fait oui de la tête

noise NOUN bruit MASC; **to make a noise** faire du bruit

noisy ADJECTIVE bruyant

none PRONOUN ❶ *(not one)* aucun *(FEM* aucune*)*; **'how many students failed the exam?' – 'none'** 'combien d'étudiants ont raté l'examen?' – 'aucun', **none of the girls knows him** aucune des filles ne le connaît ❷ **there's none left** il n'y en a plus, **there are none left** il n'y en a plus

nonsense NOUN bêtises *FEM PLURAL*; **to talk nonsense** dire des bêtises, **nonsense! she's at least thirty!** tu dis des bêtises! elle a au moins trente ans!

non-smoker NOUN non-fumeur MASC

non-stop ADJECTIVE direct *(a train or flight)*

non-stop ADVERB sans arrêt; **she talks non-stop** elle parle sans arrêt

noodles PLURAL NOUN nouilles *FEM PLURAL*

noon NOUN midi MASC; **at (twelve) noon** à midi

no-one PRONOUN personne; **'who's there?' – 'no-one'** 'qui est là?' – 'personne', **there's no-one in the kitchen** il n'y a personne dans la cuisine, **no-one knows me** personne ne me connaît, **no-one answered** personne n'a répondu

nor CONJUNCTION ❶ **neither ... nor** ni ... ni, **I have neither the time nor the money** je n'ai ni le temps ni l'argent ❷ **nor do I** moi non plus, **'I**

don't like fish' – 'nor do I' 'je n'aime pas le poisson' – 'moi non plus', *(translations using 'non plus' can be used for many similar replies)* **'I wasn't invited' – 'nor was I'** je n'ai pas été invité' – 'moi non plus'

normal ADJECTIVE ❶ normal MASC *(PLURAL* normaux*)* ❷ *(usual)* habituel *(FEM* habituelle*)*

normally ADVERB normalement

Normandy NOUN Normandie *FEM*; **in Normandy** en Normandie

north NOUN nord MASC; **in the north** au nord

north ADJECTIVE, ADVERB nord *(never agrees)*; **the north side** le côté nord, **a north wind** un vent du nord, **north of Paris** au nord de Paris

North America NOUN Amérique *(FEM)* du Nord

North American NOUN Nord-Américain MASC, Nord-Américaine *FEM*

North American ADJECTIVE nord-américain

northeast NOUN nord-est MASC

northeast ADJECTIVE **in northeast England** au nord-est de l'Angleterre

Northern Ireland NOUN Irlande *(FEM)* du Nord

North Pole NOUN pôle *(MASC)* Nord

North Sea NOUN **the North Sea** la mer du Nord

northwest NOUN nord-ouest MASC

northwest ADJECTIVE **in northwest England** au nord-ouest de l'Angleterre

Norway NOUN Norvège FEM; **in Norway** en Norvège

Norwegian NOUN ❶ (person) Norvégien MASC, Norvégienne FEM ❷ (language) norvégien MASC

Norwegian ADJECTIVE norvégien (FEM norvégienne)

nose NOUN nez MASC; **to blow your nose** se moucher [1]

nosebleed NOUN **to have a nosebleed** saigner [1] du nez

nostril NOUN narine FEM

not ADVERB ❶ pas; **not on Saturdays** pas le samedi, **not all alone!** pas tout seul!, **not bad** pas mal, **not at all** pas du tout, **not yet** pas encore ❷ (when used with a verb) ne … pas; **it's not my car** ce n'est pas ma voiture, **I don't know** je ne sais pas, **Sam didn't phone** Sam n'a pas appelé, **we decided not to wait** nous avons décidé de ne pas attendre ❸ **I hope not** j'espère que non

note NOUN ❶ (a short letter) mot MASC; **she left me a note** elle m'a laissé un mot ❷ **to take notes** prendre [64] des notes ❸ (a banknote) billet MASC; **a ten-pound note** un billet de dix livres ❹ (in music) note FEM, (on the keyboard) touche FEM

notebook NOUN carnet MASC

notepad NOUN bloc-notes MASC (PLURAL blocs-notes)

nothing PRONOUN ❶ rien; **'what did you say?' – 'nothing'** 'qu'est-ce que tu as dit?' – 'rien' ❷ (with an adjective) **nothing new** rien de nouveau, **there's nothing new** il n'y a rien de nouveau ❸ (when used with a verb) ne … rien; **she knows**

nothing elle ne sait rien, **but there was nothing there** mais il n'y avait rien, **I saw nothing** je n'ai rien vu, **nothing's happening** il ne se passe rien ❹ **nothing has changed** rien n'a changé

notice NOUN ❶ (a sign) panneau MASC (PLURAL panneaux) ❷ (an advertisement) annonce FEM ❸ **don't take any notice of her!** ne fais pas attention à elle! ❹ **to do something at short notice** faire quelque chose à la dernière minute

notice VERB remarquer [1]; **I didn't notice anything** je n'ai rien remarqué

noticeable ADJECTIVE visible

notice board NOUN panneau (MASC) d'affichage

nought NOUN zéro MASC

noun NOUN nom MASC

novel NOUN roman MASC

novelist NOUN romancier MASC, romancière FEM

November NOUN novembre MASC; **in November** en novembre

now ADVERB ❶ maintenant; **where is he now?** où est-il maintenant?, **they've got six children now** ils ont six enfants maintenant ❷ **he's busy just now** il est occupé en ce moment, **I saw her just now in the corridor** je viens de la voir dans le couloir ❸ **do it right now!** fais-le tout de suite! ❹ **now and then** de temps en temps

nowadays ADVERB de nos jours; **nowadays they are quite common** de nos jours, ils sont assez fréquents

nowhere ADJECTIVE ❶ nulle part; **nowhere in France** nulle part en France ❷ **there's nowhere to park** il n'y a pas d'endroit pour se garer

nuclear ADJECTIVE nucléaire; **a nuclear power station** une centrale nucléaire

nude NOUN **in the nude** nu

nude ADJECTIVE nu

nuisance NOUN **it's a nuisance** c'est embêtant

numb ADJECTIVE ❶ (with cold) engourdi; **my fingers are numb with cold** j'ai les doigts engourdis par le froid ❷ (with an anaesthetic) insensible

number NOUN ❶ (of a house, telephone, or account) numéro MASC; **I live at number thirty-one** j'habite au numéro trente-et-un, **my new phone number** mon nouveau numéro de téléphone ❷ (a written figure) chiffre MASC; **the third number is a 7** le troisième chiffre est un 7 ❸ (an amount) nombre MASC; **a large number of visitors** un grand nombre de visiteurs

number plate NOUN plaque (FEM) d'immatriculation

nun NOUN religieuse FEM

nurse NOUN infirmier MASC, infirmière FEM; **Janet's a nurse** Janet est infirmière

nursery NOUN ❶ (for children) crèche FEM ❷ (for plants) pépinière FEM

nursery school NOUN école (FEM) maternelle

nursing NOUN profession (FEM) d'infirmier/d'infirmière; **she went into nursing** elle est devenue infirmière

nut NOUN ❶ (walnut) noix FEM ❷ (almond) amande FEM ❸ (peanut) cacahuète FEM ❹ (for a bolt) écrou MASC

nutmeg NOUN noix (FEM) de muscade

nylon NOUN nylon MASC

oak NOUN chêne MASC

oar NOUN rame FEM

oasis NOUN oasis FEM

oats NOUN avoine FEM; **porridge oats** les flocons d'avoine

obedient ADJECTIVE obéissant

obese ADJECTIVE obèse

obesity NOUN obésité FEM

obey VERB obéir [2] à (a person); **to obey the rules** respecter [1] les règlements

object NOUN objet MASC

object VERB soulever [50] des objections; **if you don't object** si vous n'avez pas d'objection

objection NOUN objection FEM

oblong ADJECTIVE rectangulaire

oboe NOUN hautbois MASC; **to play the oboe** jouer du hautbois

obscene ADJECTIVE obscène

observe VERB observer [1]

obsessed ADJECTIVE obsédé; **she's obsessed with her diet** elle est obsédée par son régime

obsession NOUN obsession FEM; **she has an obsession with cleanliness** elle est obsédée par la propreté

obstacle NOUN obstacle MASC

obstinate ADJECTIVE têtu

obstruct VERB gêner [1] (people or the traffic)

obtain VERB obtenir [77]

obvious ADJECTIVE évident

obviously ADVERB ❶ (of course) évidemment; 'do you want to come too?' – 'obviously, but it's a bit difficult' 'veux-tu nous accompagner?' – 'évidemment, mais c'est un peu difficile' ❷ (looking at something) manifestement; **the house is obviously empty** la maison est manifestement vide

occasion NOUN occasion FEM; **a special occasion** une grande occasion

occasional ADJECTIVE **he sends us the occasional card** il nous envoie une carte de temps en temps

occasionally ADVERB de temps en temps

occupation NOUN ❶ (job) profession FEM ❷ (of territory) occupation FEM

occupied ADJECTIVE occupé

occur VERB ❶ **it occurs to me that my cousins live nearby** il me vient à l'esprit que mes cousins habitent tout près, **it never occurred to me** cela ne m'est pas venu à l'idée ❷ (happen) avoir [5] lieu; **the accident occurred on Monday** l'accident a eu lieu lundi

ocean NOUN océan MASC

o'clock ADVERB **at ten o'clock** à dix heures, **it's three o'clock** il est trois heures

October NOUN octobre MASC; **in October** en octobre

octopus NOUN pieuvre FEM

odd ADJECTIVE ❶ (strange) bizarre; **that's odd, I'm sure I heard the phone** c'est bizarre, je suis sûr d'avoir entendu le téléphone ❷ (number) impair; **three is an odd number** trois est un chiffre impair ❸ **to be the odd one out** être l'exception

odds and ends PLURAL NOUN bricoles FEM PLURAL

of PREPOSITION ❶ de; **a kilo of tomatoes** un kilo de tomates, **the end of my work** la fin de mon travail ❷ (note that 'de le' becomes 'du' and 'de les' becomes 'des') **the beginning of the concert** le début du concert, **the name of the flower** le nom de la fleur, **the parents of the children** les parents des enfants ❸ **Ray has four horses but he's selling three of them** Ray a trois chevaux mais il en vend trois, **we ate a lot of it** nous en avons mangé beaucoup ❹ **two of us** deux d'entre nous ❺ **the sixth of June** le six juin ❻ **made of** en, **a bracelet made of silver** un bracelet en argent

off ADVERB, ADJECTIVE, PREPOSITION
❶ *(switched off)* éteint; **is the telly off?** est-ce que la télé est éteinte?, **to turn off the lights** éteindre la lumière ❷ *(tap, water, gas)* fermé; **to turn off the tap** fermer le robinet ❸ *(turned off at the meter)* coupé; **the gas and electricity were off** le gaz et l'électricité étaient coupés ❹ **to be off** *(to leave)* s'en aller [7], **I'm off** je m'en vais ❺ **a day off** un jour de congé, **Caroline took three days off work** Caroline a pris trois jours de congé, **to be off sick** être malade, **Maya's off school today** Maya n'est pas à l'école aujourd'hui ❻ *(cancelled)* annulé; **the match is off** le match est annulé ❼ **'20% off shoes'** '20% de remise sur les chaussures'

offence NOUN ❶ *(crime)* délit MASC ❷ **to take offence** s'offenser [1], **he takes offence easily** il s'offense facilement

offer NOUN ❶ offre FEM; **a job offer** une offre d'emploi ❷ **'on (special) offer'** 'en promotion'

offer VERB ❶ offrir [56] *(a present, a reward, or a job)*; **he offered her a chair** il lui a offert une chaise ❷ **to offer to do** proposer [1] de faire, **Blake offered to drive me to the station** Blake m'a proposé de me conduire à la gare

office NOUN bureau MASC (PLURAL bureaux); **he's still at the office** il est toujours au bureau, **Sue works in the same office** Sue travaille dans le même bureau

office block, **office building** NOUN immeuble *(MASC)* de bureaux

officer NOUN officier MASC

official ADJECTIVE officiel *(FEM officielle)*; **the official version** la version officielle

off-licence NOUN magasin *(MASC)* de vins et de spiritueux

offside ADJECTIVE hors jeu

often ADVERB souvent; **he's often late** il est souvent en retard, **how often do you see Rosie?** est-ce que tu vois Rosie souvent?, **I'd like to see Eric more often** j'aimerais voir Eric plus souvent

oil NOUN ❶ huile FEM; **olive oil** l'huile d'olive, **suntan oil** l'huile solaire ❷ *(crude oil)* pétrole MASC

oil painting NOUN peinture *(FEM)* à l'huile *(both the activity and the object)*

oil rig NOUN plateforme *(FEM)* pétrolière

oil slick NOUN marée *(FEM)* noire

oil tanker NOUN pétrolier MASC

ointment NOUN pommade FEM

okay ADJECTIVE ❶ d'accord; **okay, tomorrow at ten** d'accord, demain à dix heures, **is it okay with you if I don't come till Friday?** ça te va si je ne viens que vendredi? ❷ *(person)* sympa *(informal)*; **Daisy's okay** Daisy est sympa ❸ *(nothing special)* pas mal; **the film was okay** le film n'était pas mal ❹ *(not ill)* **are you okay?** ça va?, **I've been ill but I'm okay now** j'ai été malade, mais ça va mieux maintenant

old ADJECTIVE ❶ *(not young, not new)* vieux *(vieil before a vowel or silent 'h'), (FEM vieille)*; **an old man** un vieux monsieur, **an old lady** une vieille dame, **an old tree** un vieil arbre, **old people**

les personnes âgées, **bring some old clothes** apporte de vieux vêtements ❷ *(previous)* ancien *(FEM* **ancienne**); **our old car was a Rover** notre ancienne voiture était une Rover, **I've only got their old address** je n'ai que leur ancienne adresse ❸ *(talking about age)* **how old are you?** tu as quel âge?, **James is ten years old** James a dix ans, **a two-year-old child** un enfant de deux ans ❹ **my older sister** ma sœur aînée, **she's older than me** elle est plus âgée que moi, **he's a year older than me** il a un an de plus que moi

old age NOUN **vieillesse** *FEM*

old age pensioner NOUN **retraité** *MASC,* **retraitée** *FEM*

old-fashioned NOUN ❶ *(clothes, music, style)* **démodé** ❷ *(a person)* **vieux jeu** *(NEVER AGREES);* **my parents are so old-fashioned** mes parents sont si vieux jeu

olive NOUN **olive** *FEM*

olive oil NOUN **huile** *(FEM)* **d'olive**

Olympic Games, Olympics PLURAL NOUN **Jeux Olympiques** *MASC PLURAL*

omelette NOUN **omelette** *FEM;* **a cheese omelette** une omelette au fromage

omit VERB **omettre** [11]

on PREPOSITION ❶ **sur**; **on the desk** sur le bureau, **on the road** sur la route, **on the beach** sur la plage ❷ *(in expressions of time)* **on March 21st** le 21 mars, **he's arriving on Tuesday** il arrive mardi, **it's shut on Saturdays** c'est fermé le samedi, **on rainy days** quand il pleut ❸ *(for buses, trains, etc)* **she arrived on the bus** elle est arrivée en bus, **I met Jackie on the bus** j'ai vu Jackie dans le bus, **I slept**

on the plane j'ai dormi dans l'avion, **let's go on our bikes!** allons-y à vélo! ❹ **on TV** à la télé, **on the radio** à la radio, **on video** en vidéo ❺ **on holiday** en vacances, **on strike** en grève

on ADJECTIVE ❶ *(switched on)* **to be on** *(TV, light, oven)* être [6] allumé, *(radio, machine)* être en marche, **all the lights were on** toutes les lumières étaient allumées, **is the radio on?** est-ce que la radio est en marche?, **I've put the oven on** j'ai allumé le four ❷ *(happening)* **what's on on TV?** qu'est-ce qu'il y a à la télé?, **what's on this week at the cinema?** qu'est-ce qui passe cette semaine au cinéma?

once ADVERB ❶ **une fois**; **I've tried once already** j'ai déjà essayé une fois, **try once more** essaie encore une fois, **once a day** une fois par jour, **more than once** plus d'une fois ❷ **at once** *(immediately)* tout de suite, **the doctor came at once** le médecin est venu tout de suite ❸ **at once** *(at the same time)* à la fois, **I can't do two things at once** je ne peux pas faire deux choses à la fois

one NUMBER **un** *(FEM* **une**); **one son** un fils, **one apple** une pomme, **if you want a pen I've got one** si tu veux un stylo j'en ai un, **at one o'clock** à une heure

one PRONOUN ❶ **on**; **one never knows** on ne sait jamais ❷ **this one** celui-ci *(FEM* **celle-ci**), **I like that bike, but this one's cheaper** j'aime bien ce vélo-là, mais celui-ci est moins cher, **do you want the red tie or this one?** veux-tu la cravate rouge ou celle-ci? ❸ **that one** celui-là *(FEM* **celle-là**), **'which video?' – 'that one'** quelle vidéo? – 'celle-là' ❹ **which one?** lequel?

(FEM **laquelle?***)*, **'my foot's hurting'** – **'which one?'** 'j'ai mal au pied' – 'auquel?', **'she borrowed a skirt from me'** – **'which one?'** 'elle m'a emprunté une jupe' – 'laquelle?'

one's *DETERMINER* son, sa, ses; **one does one's best** on fait de son mieux, **to pay for one's car** payer sa voiture, **to love one's children** aimer ses enfants, **to wash one's hands** se laver les mains

oneself *NOUN* ❶ to wash oneself se laver, **to hurt oneself** se blesser ❷ *(for emphasis)* soi-même; **one has to do everything oneself** il faut tout faire soi-même ❸ **(all) by oneself** tout seul *(FEM* **toute seule)**

one-way street *NOUN* sens *(MASC)* unique

onion *NOUN* oignon *MASC*; **onion soup** la soupe à l'oignon

only *ADJECTIVE* ❶ seul; **the only free seat** la seule place libre, **the only thing to do** la seule chose à faire ❷ **an only child** un enfant unique

only *ADVERB, CONJUNCTION* ❶ *(with a verb)* ne … que; **they've only got two bedrooms** ils n'ont que deux chambres, **Anne's only free on Fridays** Anne n'est libre que le vendredi, **there are only three left** il n'en reste que trois ❷ seulement; **'how long did they stay?'** – **'only two days'** 'ils sont restés combien de temps?' – 'deux jours seulement' ❸ *(but)* mais; **I'd walk, only it's raining** j'irais à pied, mais il pleut

onto *PREPOSITION* sur

open *NOUN* **in the open** en plein air

open *ADJECTIVE* ❶ *(not shut)* ouvert; **the door's open** la porte est ouverte, **the baker's is not open** la boulangerie n'est pas ouverte ❷ **in the open air** en plein air

open *VERB* ❶ ouvrir [30]; **can you open the door for me?** est-ce que tu peux ouvrir la porte?, **Sam opened his eyes** Sam a ouvert les yeux, **the bank opens at nine** la banque ouvre à neuf heures ❷ **the door opened slowly** la porte s'est ouverte lentement

open-air *ADJECTIVE* en plein air; **an open-air swimming pool** une piscine en plein air

opener *NOUN* ❶ *(for bottles)* décapsuleur *MASC* ❷ *(for cans)* ouvre-boîte *MASC*

opening *NOUN* ❶ *(space)* ouverture *FEM* ❷ *(opportunity)* occasion *FEM*; **there are few openings for recent graduates** il y a peu de débouchés pour les jeunes diplômés

opera *NOUN* opéra *MASC*

operate *VERB* *(medically)* opérer [24]; **will they have to operate?** est-ce qu'il va falloir qu'ils opèrent?

operation *NOUN* opération *FEM*; **to have an operation** se faire opérer, **she's had an operation** elle s'est fait opérer

opinion *NOUN* avis *MASC*; **in my opinion** à mon avis

opinion poll *NOUN* sondage *MASC*

opponent *NOUN* adversaire *MASC & FEM*

opportunity *NOUN* occasion *FEM*; **to have the opportunity of doing** avoir l'occasion de faire, **I took the opportunity to visit the museum**

j'ai profité de l'occasion pour visiter le musée

opposed ADJECTIVE **to be opposed to something** être [6] opposé à quelque chose, **they are opposed to any change of the rules** ils s'opposent à un changement des règles

opposite NOUN contraire MASC; **no, quite the opposite** non, tout le contraire

opposite ADJECTIVE ❶ opposé (a direction, side, or view, for example); **she went off in the opposite direction** elle est partie dans la direction opposée ❷ (facing) d'en face; **in the house opposite** dans la maison d'en face

opposite ADVERB en face; **they live opposite** ils habitent en face

opposite PREPOSITION en face de; **opposite the station** en face de la gare

opposition NOUN opposition FEM

optician NOUN opticien MASC, opticienne FEM

optimistic ADJECTIVE optimiste

option NOUN choix MASC; **we have no option** nous n'avons pas le choix

optional ADJECTIVE facultatif (FEM facultative)

or CONJUNCTION ❶ ou; **English or French?** anglais ou français?, **today or Tuesday?** aujourd'hui ou mardi? ❷ (in negatives) **I don't have a cat or a dog** je n'ai ni un chat ni un chien, **not in June or July** ni en juin ni en juillet ❸ (or else) sinon; **phone Mum, or she'll worry** appelle maman, sinon elle va s'inquiéter

oral NOUN (an exam) oral MASC (PLURAL oraux); **the French oral** l'oral de français

orange NOUN (the fruit) orange FEM; **an orange juice** un jus d'orange

orange ADJECTIVE orange (never changes); **my orange socks** mes chaussettes orange

orchard NOUN verger MASC

orchestra NOUN orchestre MASC

order NOUN ❶ (arrangement) ordre MASC; **in the right order** dans le bon ordre, **in the wrong order** dans le mauvais ordre, **in alphabetical order** dans l'ordre alphabétique ❷ (in a restaurant or café) commande FEM; **can I take your orders?** puis-je prendre vos commandes? ❸ 'out of order' 'en panne' ❹ **in order to do** pour faire, **we hurried in order to be on time** nous nous sommes dépêchés pour arriver à l'heure

order VERB ❶ (in a restaurant or a shop) commander [1]; **we ordered steaks** nous avons commandé des steaks ❷ réserver [1] (a taxi)

ordinary ADJECTIVE ordinaire

organ NOUN ❶ (in music) orgue MASC; **to play the organ** jouer de l'orgue ❷ (of body) organe MASC

organic ADJECTIVE biologique, bio (food)

organization NOUN organisation FEM

organize VERB organiser [1]

orienteering NOUN course (FEM) d'orientation

original

original ADJECTIVE original MASC (PLURAL originaux); **the original version was better** la version originale était meilleure, **it's a really original novel** c'est un roman très original

originally ADVERB à l'origine; **originally we wanted to take the car** à l'origine nous voulions prendre la voiture

Orkneys PLURAL NOUN **the Orkneys** les Orcades FEM PLURAL

ornament NOUN bibelot MASC

orphan NOUN orphelin MASC, orpheline FEM

ostrich NOUN autruche FEM

other ADJECTIVE ❶ autre; **the other day** l'autre jour, **we took the other road** nous avons pris l'autre route, **give me the other one** donne-moi l'autre, **where are the others?** où sont les autres?, **the other two cars** les deux autres voitures ❷ **every other week** une semaine sur deux ❸ **somebody or other** quelqu'un, **something or other** quelque chose, **somewhere or other** quelque part

otherwise ADVERB (in other ways) à part ça; **the flat's a bit small but otherwise it's lovely** l'appartement n'est pas très grand mais à part ça il est très bien

otherwise CONJUNCTION (or else) sinon; **I'll phone home, otherwise they'll worry** je vais appeler chez moi, sinon ils vont s'inquiéter

ought VERB
('ought' is translated by the conditional tense of 'devoir') [8] **I ought to go now** je devrais partir maintenant, **they ought to know the address** ils devraient savoir

out

l'adresse, **you oughtn't to have any problems** vous ne devriez pas avoir des problèmes

our ADJECTIVE ❶ notre; **our house** notre maison ❷ (before a plural noun) nos; **our parents** nos parents ❸ (with parts of the body) le, la, les; **we'll go and wash our hands** on va se laver les mains

ours PRONOUN ❶ (for a masculine noun) le nôtre; **their garden's bigger than ours** leur jardin est plus grand que le nôtre ❷ (for a feminine noun) la nôtre; **their house is smaller than ours** leur maison est plus petite que la nôtre ❸ (for a plural noun) les nôtres; **they've invited their friends and we've invited ours** ils ont invité leurs amis et nous avons invité les nôtres ❹ à nous; **the green one's ours** le vert est à nous, **it's ours** c'est à nous, **a friend of ours** un ami à nous

ourselves PRONOUN ❶ nous; **we introduced ourselves** nous nous sommes présentés ❷ (for emphasis) nous-mêmes; **in the end we did it ourselves** finalement nous l'avons fait nous-mêmes

out ADVERB ❶ (outside) dehors; **it's cold out there** il fait froid dehors, **out in the rain** sous la pluie, **they're out in the garden** ils sont dans le jardin ❷ **to go out** sortir [72], **she went out an hour ago** elle est sortie il y a une heure, **Mr. Barnes is out** Monsieur Barnes est sorti, **are you going out this evening?** est-ce que tu sors ce soir?, **Alison's going out with Danny at the moment** Alison sort avec Danny en ce moment, **he's asked me out** il m'a invitée à sortir avec lui ❸ **to go out of the room** sortir de la pièce, **he threw it out of the window** il l'a jeté par la fenêtre, to drink out of a glass boire dans un verre, **she took the photo out of her bag** elle a pris la photo dans son sac

out ADJECTIVE *(light, fire)* éteint; **are all the lights out?** est-ce que toutes les lumières sont éteintes?, **the fire was out** le feu était éteint

outdoor ADJECTIVE *(an activity or sport)* de plein air; **an outdoor restaurant** un restaurant en plein air

outdoors ADVERB en plein air

outing NOUN sortie FEM; **to go on an outing** faire une sortie

outline NOUN *(of an object)* contour MASC

out-of-date ADJECTIVE ❶ *(no longer valid)* périmé; **my passport's out of date** mon passeport est périmé ❷ *(old-fashioned)* démodé; **they played out-of-date music** ils ont joué la musique démodée

outside NOUN extérieur MASC; **it's blue on the outside** c'est bleu à l'extérieur

outside ADJECTIVE extérieur

outside ADVERB dehors; **it's cold outside** il fait froid dehors

outside PREPOSITION devant *(a building)*; **I'll meet you outside the cinema** on se retrouve devant le cinéma

outskirts NOUN périphérie FEM; **on the outskirts of York** à la périphérie de York

outstanding ADJECTIVE exceptionnel *(FEM* exceptionnelle*)*

oval ADJECTIVE ovale

oven NOUN four MASC; **I've put it in the oven** je l'ai mis au four

over PREPOSITION ❶ *(above)* au-dessus de; **there's a mirror over the sideboard** il y a un miroir au-dessus du buffet ❷ *(involving movement)* par-dessus; **she jumped over the fence** elle a sauté par-dessus la clôture, **he threw the ball over the wall** il a jeté la balle par-dessus le mur ❸ **over here** par ici, **the drinks are over here** les boissons sont par ici ❹ **over there** là-bas, **she's over there talking to Julian** elle est là-bas en train de discuter avec Julian ❺ *(more than)* plus de; **it will cost over a hundred pounds** ça coûtera plus de cent livres, **he's over sixty** il a plus de soixante ans ❻ *(during)* pendant; **over the weekend** pendant le weekend, **over Christmas** à Noël ❼ *(finished)* terminé; **when the meeting's over** quand la réunion sera terminée, **it's all over now** c'est terminé maintenant ❽ **over the phone** par téléphone, **to ask someone over** inviter quelqu'un, **can you come over on Saturday?** peux-tu venir chez moi samedi? ❾ **all over the place** partout, **all over the house** partout dans la maison

overcast ADJECTIVE couvert

overcrowded ADJECTIVE bondé

overdose NOUN ❶ *(of drugs)* overdose FEM ❷ *(of medicine)* surdose FEM

overflow VERB déborder [1]

overseas ADVERB à l'étranger; **Dave works overseas** Dave travaille à l'étranger

oversleep *VERB* se réveiller [1] trop tard

overtake *VERB* doubler [1] *(another car)*

overtime *NOUN* to work overtime faire [10] des heures supplémentaires

overweight *ADJECTIVE (a person)* trop gros *(FEM* trop grosse*)*

owe *VERB* devoir [8]; **I owe Rick ten pounds** je dois dix livres à Rick

owing *ADJECTIVE* ❶ *(to pay)* à payer; **there's five pounds owing** il y a cinq livres à payer ❷ **owing to** en raison de, **owing to the snow** en raison de la neige

owl *NOUN* hibou *MASC (PLURAL* hiboux*)*

own *ADJECTIVE* ❶ propre *(goes before the noun)*; **my own computer** mon propre ordinateur, **I've got my own room** j'ai une chambre à moi ❷ **on your own** tout seul *(FEM* toute seule*)*, **Annie did it on her own** Annie l'a fait toute seule

own *VERB* posséder [24]

owner *NOUN* propriétaire *MASC & FEM*

oxygen *NOUN* oxygène *MASC*

oyster *NOUN* huître *FEM*

ozone layer *NOUN* couche *(FEM)* d'ozone

pace *NOUN* ❶ *(a step)* pas *MASC* ❷ *(the speed you walk at)* allure *FEM*; **at a brisk pace** à vive allure

Pacific *NOUN* **the Pacific Ocean** l'océan *(MASC)* Pacifique

pack *NOUN* ❶ paquet *MASC* ❷ **a pack of cards** un jeu de cartes

pack *VERB* ❶ faire [10] ses bagages; **I haven't packed yet** je n'ai pas encore fait mes bagages ❷ **I'll pack my case tonight** je ferai ma valise ce soir, **have you packed my red shirt?** as-tu mis ma chemise rouge dans la valise?

package *NOUN* paquet *MASC*

package holiday, **package tour** *NOUN* voyage *(MASC)* organisé

packed lunch *NOUN* panier-repas *MASC*

packet *NOUN* ❶ paquet *MASC*; **a packet of biscuits** un paquet de biscuits ❷ *(bag)* sachet *MASC*; **a packet of crisps** un sachet de chips

packing *NOUN* **to do your packing** faire ses bagages

pad *NOUN (of paper)* bloc-notes *MASC*

paddle *NOUN (for a canoe)* pagaie *FEM*

paddle *VERB (at the seaside)* **to go paddling** faire [10] trempette

padlock NOUN cadenas MASC

page NOUN page FEM; **on page seven** à la page sept

pain NOUN douleur FEM; **I've got a pain in my leg** j'ai mal à la jambe, **to be in pain** souffrir [73]
- **Eric's a real pain (in the neck)** Eric est vraiment pénible

painful ADJECTIVE douloureux (FEM douloureuse)

painkiller NOUN analgésique MASC

paint NOUN peinture FEM; **'wet paint'** 'peinture fraîche'

paint VERB peindre [60]; **to paint something pink** peindre quelque chose en rose

paintbrush NOUN pinceau MASC (PLURAL pinceaux)

painter NOUN peintre MASC

painting NOUN (picture) tableau MASC (PLURAL tableaux); **a painting by Monet** un tableau de Monet

pair NOUN ❶ paire FEM; **a pair of socks** une paire de chaussettes, **a pair of scissors** une paire de ciseaux ❷ a **pair of jeans** un jean, **a pair of trousers** un pantalon, **a pair of knickers** un slip ❸ **to work in pairs** travailler en groupes de deux

Pakistan NOUN Pakistan MASC; **in Pakistan** au Pakistan, **to Pakistan** au Pakistan

Pakistani NOUN Pakistanais MASC, Pakkistanaise FEM

Pakistani ADJECTIVE pakistanais

palace NOUN palais MASC

pale ADJECTIVE pâle; **pale green** vert pâle (never changes), **pale green curtains** des rideaux vert pâle, **to turn pale** pâlir [2]

palm NOUN ❶ (of your hand) paume FEM ❷ (a palm tree) palmier MASC

pan NOUN (saucepan) ❶ casserole FEM; **a pan of water** une casserole d'eau ❷ (frying pan) poêle FEM

pancake NOUN crêpe FEM

panel NOUN ❶ (on radio or TV) (for a discussion) invités MASC PLURAL (i.e. guests), (for a quiz show) jury MASC ❷ (for a wall or a bath, for example) panneau MASC (PLURAL panneaux)

panel game NOUN jeu MASC (PLURAL jeux)

panic NOUN panique FEM

panic VERB s'affoler [1]; **don't panic!** pas de panique!

pannier NOUN (on a bike) sacoche FEM

panther NOUN panthère FEM

panties NOUN petite culotte FEM

pantomime NOUN spectacle (MASC) pour enfants

pants PLURAL NOUN slip MASC

paper NOUN ❶ papier MASC; **a sheet of paper** une feuille de papier ❷ a **paper cup** un gobelet en carton, **a paper hanky** un mouchoir en papier ❸ (newspaper) journal MASC (PLURAL journaux); **it was in the paper** c'était dans le journal

paperback NOUN livre (MASC) de poche

paperclip NOUN trombone MASC (because of its shape)

paper shop NOUN magasin (MASC) de journaux

paper towel NOUN essuie-tout MASC

parachute NOUN parachute MASC

parachuting NOUN parachutisme MASC; **to go parachuting** faire du parachutisme

parade NOUN défilé MASC

paradise NOUN paradis MASC

paraffin NOUN pétrole MASC

paragraph NOUN paragraphe MASC; **'new paragraph'** 'à la ligne'

parallel ADJECTIVE parallèle

paralysed ADJECTIVE paralysé

parcel NOUN paquet MASC

pardon NOUN I beg your pardon pardon, **pardon?** pardon?

parent NOUN parent MASC; **my parents are Scottish** mes parents sont écossais, **a parents' evening** une réunion pour les parents d'élèves

Paris NOUN Paris; **Marie lives in Paris** Marie habite à Paris

Parisian NOUN Parisien MASC, Parisienne FEM

Parisian ADJECTIVE parisien (FEM parisienne)

park NOUN ❶ parc MASC; **a theme park** un parc à thème ❷ **a car park** un parking

park VERB ❶ se garer [1]; **you can park outside the house** vous pouvez vous garer devant la maison ❷ **to park a car** garer [1] une voiture, **where did you park the car?** où as-tu garé la voiture?

parking NOUN stationnement MASC; **'no parking'** 'stationnement interdit'

parking meter NOUN parcmètre MASC

parking space NOUN place FEM

parking ticket NOUN PV MASC (informal)

parliament NOUN parlement MASC

parrot NOUN perroquet MASC

parsley NOUN persil MASC

part NOUN ❶ partie FEM; **part of the garden** une partie du jardin, **the last part of the concert** la dernière partie du concert, **that's part of your job** ça fait partie de votre travail ❷ **to take part in something** participer à quelque chose ❸ (a role in a play) rôle MASC ❹ **spare parts** pièces (FEM PLURAL) détachées

particular ADJECTIVE particulier (FEM particulière); **nothing in particular** rien de particulier

particularly ADVERB ❶ (unusually) spécialement; **not particularly interesting** pas spécialement intéressant ❷ (in particular) surtout; **particularly as it's our last day** surtout que c'est notre dernier jour

parting NOUN (in your hair) raie FEM

partly ADVERB en partie

partner NOUN ❶ (in a game) partenaire MASC ❷ (the person you live with) partenaire MASC & FEM ❸ (in business) associé MASC, associée FEM

partridge NOUN **perdrix** FEM

part-time ADJECTIVE, ADVERB **à temps partiel**; **part-time work** du travail à temps partiel, **to work part-time** travailler à temps partiel

party NOUN ❶ **fête** FEM; **a Christmas party** une fête de Noël, **to have a birthday party** faire une fête d'anniversaire ❷ (more formal, in the evening) **soirée** FEM; **we've been invited to a party at the Smiths' house** nous sommes invités à une soirée chez les Smith ❸ (group) **groupe** MASC; **a party of schoolchildren** un groupe d'élèves, **a rescue party** une équipe de secouristes ❹ (in politics) **parti** MASC; **the Labour party** le parti travailliste

party game NOUN **jeu** (MASC) **de société** (PLURAL **jeux de société**)

pass NOUN ❶ (to let you in) **laisser-passer** MASC (PLURAL **laisser-passer**) ❷ **a bus pass** une carte de bus ❸ (a mountain pass) **col** MASC ❹ (in an exam) **to get a pass in history** être reçu en histoire

pass VERB ❶ (go past) **passer** [1] **devant** (a place or building); **we passed your house** nous sommes passés devant toi ❷ (to overtake) **doubler** [1] (a car) ❸ (give) **passer** [1]; **could you pass me the paper please?** peux-tu me passer le journal s'il te plaît? ❹ (time) **passer** [1]; **the time passed slowly** le temps passait lentement ❺ (in an exam) **être** [6] **reçu**; **did you pass?** as-tu été reçu?, **to pass an exam** être reçu à un examen

passage NOUN ❶ (a corridor) **couloir** MASC ❷ (a piece of text) **passage** MASC

passenger NOUN ❶ (in a car, plane, or ship) **passager** MASC,

passagère FEM ❷ (in a train, bus, or underground) **voyageur** MASC, **voyageuse** FEM

passerby NOUN **passant** MASC, **passante** FEM

passion NOUN **passion** FEM

passionate ADJECTIVE **passionné**

passive NOUN **passif** MASC

passive ADJECTIVE **passif** (FEM **passive**)

Passover NOUN **Pâque** (FEM) **juive**

passport NOUN **passeport** MASC; **an EU passport** un passeport de l'UE

password NOUN **mot** (MASC) **de passe**

past NOUN **passé** MASC; **in the past** au passé

past ADJECTIVE ❶ (recent) **dernier** (FEM **dernière**) (GOES BEFORE THE NOUN); **in the past few weeks** pendant les dernières semaines ❷ (over) **fini**; **winter is past** l'hiver est fini

past PREPOSITION, ADVERB ❶ **to walk or drive past something** passer devant quelque chose, **we went past the school** nous sommes passés devant l'école, **Ray went past in his new car** Ray est passé dans sa nouvelle voiture ❷ (the other side of) **après**; **it's just past the post office** c'est juste après la poste ❸ (talking about time) **ten past six** six heures dix, **half past four** quatre heures et demie, **a quarter past two** deux heures et quart

pasta NOUN **pâtes** FEM PLURAL; **I don't like pasta** je n'aime pas les pâtes

paste VERB **coller** [1]; **to cut and paste the table** copier-coller le tableau

pasteurized ADJECTIVE pasteurisé

pastry NOUN pâte FEM

patch NOUN ❶ (fabric, for mending) pièce FEM ❷ (of snow or ice) plaque FEM ❸ (of blue sky) coin MASC

path NOUN chemin MASC, (very narrow) sentier MASC

pathetic ADJECTIVE (useless, hopeless) lamentable

patience NOUN ❶ patience FEM ❷ (card game) réussite FEM

patient NOUN patient MASC, patiente FEM

patient ADJECTIVE patient

patiently ADVERB avec patience

patio NOUN terrasse FEM

patrol NOUN patrouille FEM

patrol car NOUN voiture (FEM) de police

pattern NOUN ❶ (on wallpaper or fabric) motif MASC ❷ (dressmaking) patron MASC ❸ (knitting) modèle MASC

pause NOUN pause FEM

pavement NOUN trottoir MASC; on the pavement sur le trottoir

paw NOUN patte FEM

pawn NOUN pion MASC

pay NOUN salaire MASC

pay VERB ❶ payer [59]; I'm paying c'est moi qui paie, to pay cash payer comptant ❷ to pay for something payer [59] quelque chose, Tony paid for the drinks Tony a payé les boissons, it's all paid for c'est tout payé ❸ to pay by credit card régler [24] par carte de crédit, to pay by

cheque régler par chèque ❹ to pay somebody back (money) rembourser [1] quelqu'un ❺ to pay attention faire [10] attention ❻ to pay a visit to somebody rendre [3] visite à quelqu'un

paydesk NOUN caisse FEM

payment NOUN paiement MASC (of a bill), règlement MASC

pay phone NOUN téléphone (MASC) public

PC NOUN (computer) PC MASC

pea NOUN petit pois MASC

peace NOUN paix FEM

peaceful ADJECTIVE paisible (day, scene)

peach NOUN pêche FEM

peacock NOUN paon MASC

peak NOUN (of a mountain) pic MASC

peak period (for holidays) période (FEM) de pointe

peak rate NOUN (for phoning) tarif (MASC) rouge

peak time NOUN (for traffic) heures (FEM PLURAL) de pointe

peanut NOUN cacahuète FEM

peanut butter NOUN beurre (MASC) de cacahuètes

pear NOUN poire FEM

pearl NOUN perle FEM

peasant NOUN paysan MASC, paysanne FEM

pebble NOUN ❶ (on the road) caillou MASC (PLURAL cailloux) ❷ (on a beach) galet MASC

peculiar ADJECTIVE bizarre

pedal NOUN pédale FEM

pedal VERB pédaler [1]

pedal boat NOUN pédalo MASC

pedestrian NOUN piéton MASC

pedestrian crossing NOUN passage (MASC) pour piétons

pedestrian precinct NOUN zone (FEM) piétonne

pee NOUN to have a pee faire [10] pipi (informal)

peel NOUN ❶ (of an apple) peau FEM ❷ (of an orange) écorce FEM

peel VERB éplucher [1] (fruit, vegetables)

peer VERB to peer at something regarder [1] quelque chose attentivement

peg NOUN ❶ (hook) patère FEM ❷ a clothes peg une pince à linge ❸ a tent peg un piquet

pen NOUN stylo MASC; a felt pen un stylo-feutre

penalty NOUN ❶ (a fine) amende FEM ❷ (in football) penalty MASC ❸ (in rugby) pénalité FEM

penalty area NOUN surface (FEM) de réparation

pence PLURAL NOUN pence MASC PLURAL

pencil NOUN crayon MASC; to write in pencil écrire au crayon

pencil case NOUN trousse FEM

pencil sharpener NOUN taille-crayon MASC

pendant NOUN pendentif MASC

penfriend NOUN correspondant MASC, correspondante FEM; my French pen-friend is called Christelle ma correspondante française s'appelle Christelle

penguin NOUN pingouin MASC

penis NOUN pénis MASC

penknife NOUN canif MASC

penny NOUN penny MASC

pension NOUN retraite FEM

pensioner NOUN retraité MASC, retraitée FEM

people PLURAL NOUN ❶ gens MASC PLURAL; people round here les gens d'ici, nice people des gens sympathiques ❷ (when you're counting them) personnes FEM PLURAL; ten people dix personnes, several people plusieurs personnes, how many people have you asked? tu as invité combien de personnes? ❸ people say he's very rich on dit qu'il est très riche

pepper NOUN ❶ (spice) poivre MASC ❷ (vegetable) poivron; a green pepper un poivron vert

peppermill NOUN moulin (MASC) à poivre

peppermint NOUN menthe FEM; peppermint tea le thé à la menthe

per PREPOSITION par; ten pounds per person dix livres par personne

per cent ADVERB pour cent; sixty per cent of students soixante pour cent des étudiants

percentage NOUN pourcentage MASC

percussion NOUN percussion FEM; to play percussion jouer des percussions

perfect ADJECTIVE ❶ parfait; she speaks perfect English elle parle un anglais parfait ❷ (ideal) idéal MASC (PLURAL idéaux); the perfect place for a picnic l'endroit idéal pour un pique-nique

perfectly ADVERB parfaitement

perform VERB ❶ jouer [1] (a piece of music or a play) ❷ chanter [1] (a song)

performance NOUN ❶ (playing or acting) interprétation FEM; a wonderful performance of Macbeth une superbe interprétation de Macbeth ❷ (show) spectacle MASC; the performance starts at eight le spectacle commence à huit heures ❸ (the results of a team or company) performance FEM

performer NOUN artiste MASC & FEM

perfume NOUN parfum MASC

perhaps ADVERB peut-être; perhaps it's in the drawer? c'est peut-être dans le tiroir?, perhaps he's missed the train il a peut-être raté le train

period NOUN ❶ période FEM; a two-year period une période de deux ans ❷ (in school) cours MASC; a forty-five-minute period un cours de quarante-cinq minutes ❸ (menstruation) règles FEM PLURAL; during your period pendant vos règles

perm NOUN permanente FEM

permanent ADJECTIVE permanent

permanently ADVERB en permanence

permission NOUN permission FEM; to get permission to do obtenir la permission de faire

permit NOUN permis MASC

permit VERB permettre [11]; to permit somebody to do permettre à quelqu'un de faire, smoking is not permitted il est interdit de fumer, weather permitting si le temps le permet

person NOUN personne FEM; there's room for one more person il y a de la place pour une autre personne, in person en personne

personal ADJECTIVE personnel (FEM personnelle)

personality NOUN personnalité FEM

personally ADVERB personnellement; personally, I'm against it personnellement, je suis contre

personal stereo NOUN baladeur MASC

perspiration NOUN transpiration FEM

persuade VERB persuader [1]; to persuade somebody to do persuader quelqu'un de faire, we persuaded Tim to wait a bit nous avons persuadé Tim d'attendre un peu

pessimistic ADJECTIVE pessimiste

pest NOUN ❶ (greenfly for example) insecte (MASC) nuisible ❷ (annoying person) casse-pieds MASC & FEM

pester VERB harceler [45]

pet NOUN ❶ animal (MASC) de compagnie (PLURAL animaux de compagnie); do you have a pet? avez-vous un animal de compagnie?, a pet dog un chien ❷ (favourite person) chouchou MASC, chouchoute FEM; Julie is teacher's pet Julie est la chouchoute du prof

petal NOUN **pétale** MASC

pet name NOUN **petit nom** MASC

petrol NOUN **essence** FEM; **to fill up with petrol** faire le plein d'essence, **to run out of petrol** tomber en panne d'essence

petrol station NOUN **station** (FEM) **d'essence**

petticoat NOUN **jupon** MASC

pharmacist NOUN **pharmaciste** MASC & FEM

pharmacy NOUN **pharmacie** FEM

pheasant NOUN **faisan** MASC

philosophy NOUN **philosophie** FEM

phone NOUN **téléphone** MASC; **she's on the phone** elle est au téléphone, **I was on the phone to Sophie** j'étais au téléphone avec Sophie, **you can book by phone** on peut réserver par téléphone

phone VERB ❶ **téléphoner** [1]; **while I was phoning** pendant que je téléphonais ❷ **to phone somebody** appeler [18] quelqu'un, **I'll phone you tonight** je t'appellerai ce soir

phone book NOUN **annuaire** MASC

phone box NOUN **cabine** (FEM) **téléphonique**

phone call NOUN **appel** MASC; **phone calls are free** les appels sont gratuits, **to make a phone call** téléphoner

phone number NOUN **numéro** (MASC) **de téléphone**

photo NOUN **photo** FEM; **to take a photo** prendre une photo, **to take a photo of somebody** prendre quelqu'un en photo, **I took a photo**

of their house j'ai pris leur maison en photo

photocopier NOUN **photocopieuse** FEM

photocopy NOUN **photocopie** FEM

photocopy VERB **photocopier** [1]

photograph NOUN **photo** FEM; **to take a photograph** prendre une photo, **to take a photograph of somebody** prendre quelqu'un en photo

photograph VERB **photographier** [1]

photographer NOUN **photographe** MASC & FEM

photography NOUN **photographie** FEM

phrase NOUN **expression** FEM

phrase-book NOUN **manuel** (MASC) **de conversation**

physical ADJECTIVE **physique**

physicist NOUN **physicien** MASC, **physicienne** FEM

physics NOUN **physique** FEM

physiotherapist NOUN **kinésithérapeute** MASC & FEM

physiotherapy NOUN **kinésithérapie** FEM

pianist NOUN **pianiste** MASC & FEM

piano NOUN **piano** MASC; **to play the piano** jouer du piano, **Steve played it on the piano** Steve l'a joué au piano, **a piano lesson** une leçon de piano

pick NOUN **take your pick!** choisis!

pick VERB ❶ (to choose) choisir [2]; **pick a card** choisis une carte ❷ (for a team) sélectionner [1]; **I've been picked for Saturday** j'ai été sélectionné pour samedi ❸ cueillir [35] (fruit or flowers)
• **to pick up** ❶ (lift) prendre [64]; **he picked up the papers and went out** il a pris les papiers et il est sorti ❷ (collect together) ramasser [1]; **I'll pick up the toys** je ramasserai les jouets ❸ (to collect) venir [81] chercher; **I'll pick you up at six** je viendrai te chercher à six heures, **I'll pick up the keys tomorrow** je viendrai chercher les clés demain ❹ (learn) apprendre [64]; **you'll soon pick it up** tu vas vite l'apprendre

pickpocket NOUN pickpocket MASC

picnic NOUN pique-nique MASC; **to have a picnic** pique-niquer

picture NOUN ❶ (a painting) tableau MASC (PLURAL tableaux); **a picture by Renoir** une tableau de Renoir, **he painted a picture of a horse** il a peint un cheval ❷ (a drawing) dessin MASC; **draw me a picture of your little sister** dessine-moi ta petite sœur ❸ (in a book) illustration FEM; **a book with lots of pictures** un livre avec beaucoup d'illustrations ❹ (the cinema) **the pictures** le cinéma, **to go to the pictures** aller au cinéma

pie NOUN ❶ (sweet) tarte FEM; **an apple pie** une tarte aux pommes ❷ (savoury) tourte FEM; **a meat pie** une tourte à la viande

piece NOUN ❶ (a bit) morceau MASC (PLURAL morceaux); **a big piece of cheese** un gros morceau de fromage ❷ (that you fit together) pièce FEM; **the pieces of a jigsaw** les pièces d'un puzzle, **to take something to pieces** démonter [1] quelque chose ❸ **a piece of furniture** un meuble, **four pieces of luggage** quatre valises, **a piece of information** un renseignement, **that's a piece of luck!** c'est un coup de chance! ❹ (coin) pièce FEM; **a two-euro piece** une pièce de deux euros

pier NOUN jetée FEM

pierced ADJECTIVE percé; **to have pierced ears** avoir les oreilles percées

pig NOUN cochon MASC

pigeon NOUN pigeon MASC

piggy bank NOUN tirelire FEM

pigsty NOUN porcherie FEM; **your room is a pigsty** ta chambre est une vraie porcherie

pigtail NOUN natte FEM

pile NOUN ❶ (a neat stack) pile FEM; **a pile of plates** une pile d'assiettes ❷ (a heap) tas MASC; **a pile of dirty shirts** un tas de chemises sales
• **to pile something up** (neatly) empiler [1] quelque chose, (in a heap) entasser [1] quelque chose

pilgrimage NOUN pèlerinage MASC; **to go on a pilgrimage** faire [10] un pèlerinage

pill NOUN comprimé MASC; **the pill** (contraceptive) la pilule

pillar NOUN pilier MASC

pillar box NOUN boîte (FEM) aux lettres

pillow NOUN oreiller MASC

pillowcase NOUN taie (FEM) d'oreiller

pilot NOUN pilote MASC

pimple NOUN bouton MASC

pin NOUN ❶ (for sewing) épingle FEM ❷ a three-pin plug une prise à trois fiches
- **to pin up** ❶ épingler [1] (a hem) ❷ accrocher [1] (a notice)

PIN NOUN (short for **personal identification number**) code (MASC) confidentiel

pinball NOUN flipper MASC; **to play pinball** jouer au flipper, **a pinball machine** un flipper

pinch NOUN (of salt, for example) pincée FEM

pinch VERB ❶ (steal) piquer [1]; **somebody's pinched my bike** on m'a piqué mon vélo ❷ **to pinch somebody** pincer [61] quelqu'un

pine NOUN pin MASC; **a pine table** une table en pin

pineapple NOUN ananas MASC

pine cone NOUN pomme (FEM) de pin

ping-pong NOUN ping-pong MASC; **to play ping-pong** jouer au ping-pong

pink ADJECTIVE rose

pip NOUN (in a fruit) pépin MASC

pipe NOUN ❶ (for gas or water) tuyau MASC (PLURAL tuyaux) ❷ (to smoke) pipe FEM; **he smokes a pipe** il fume la pipe

pirate NOUN pirate MASC

pirated ADJECTIVE piraté; **a pirated video** une vidéo piratée

Pisces NOUN Poissons MASC PLURAL; **Amanda is Pisces** Amanda est Poissons

pistachio NOUN pistache FEM

pit NOUN fosse FEM

pitch NOUN terrain MASC; **a football pitch** un terrain de foot

pitch VERB **to pitch a tent** dresser [1] une tente

pity NOUN ❶ **what a pity!** quel dommage!, **it would be a pity to miss the beginning** ce serait dommage de rater le début ❷ (feeling sorry for somebody) pitié FEM

pity VERB **to pity somebody** plaindre [31] quelqu'un

pizza NOUN pizza FEM

place NOUN ❶ endroit MASC; **in a warm place** dans un endroit chaud, **Rome is a wonderful place** Rome est un endroit merveilleux, **all over the place** partout ❷ (a space) place FEM; **a place for the car** une place pour la voiture, **is there a place for me?** y a-t-il une place pour moi?, **will you keep my place?** veux-tu me garder ma place?, **to change places** changer de place ❸ (in a race) place FEM; **in first place** à la première place ❹ **at your place** chez toi, **we'll go round to Zafir's place** on ira chez Zafir ❺ **to take place** avoir [5] lieu, **the competition will take place at four** le concours aura lieu à quatre heures

place VERB mettre [11]; **he placed his cup on the table** il a mis sa tasse sur la table

plain NOUN plaine FEM

plain ADJECTIVE ❶ simple; **plain cooking** une cuisine simple ❷ (unflavoured) nature; **a plain yoghurt** un yaourt nature ❸ (not patterned) uni; **plain curtains** des rideaux unis

plait NOUN natte FEM

plan NOUN ❶ projet MASC; **what are your plans for this summer?** quels sont vos projets pour cet été?, **to go according to plan** se passer comme prévu, **everything went according to plan** tout s'est passé comme prévu ❷ (a map) plan MASC

plan VERB ❶ **to plan to do** avoir [5] l'intention de faire, **we're planning to leave at eight** nous avons l'intention de partir à huit heures ❷ (make plans for) préparer [1]; **Ricky's planning a trip to Italy** Ricky prépare un voyage en Italie ❸ (organize) organiser [1]; **I'm planning my day** j'organise ma journée ❹ (to design) concevoir [66] (a house or garden); **a well-planned kitchen** une cuisine bien conçue

plane NOUN avion MASC; **we went by plane** nous avons pris l'avion

planet NOUN planète FEM

plank NOUN planche FEM

plant NOUN plante FEM; **a house plant** une plante d'intérieur

plant VERB planter [1]

plaster NOUN ❶ (sticking plaster) pansement (MASC) adhésif ❷ (for walls) plâtre MASC ❸ **to have your leg in plaster** avoir la jambe dans le plâtre

plastic NOUN plastique MASC; **a plastic bag** un sac en plastique

plate NOUN assiette FEM

platform NOUN ❶ (in a station) quai MASC; **the train arriving at platform six** le train qui entre en gare quai numéro six ❷ (for lecturing or performing) estrade FEM

play NOUN pièce FEM; **a play by Molière** une pièce de Molière, **our school is putting on a play** notre école monte une pièce

play VERB ❶ jouer [1]; **the children were playing with a ball** les enfants jouaient avec un ballon, **they play all kinds of music** ils jouent toutes sortes de musique, **who's playing Hamlet?** qui est-ce qui joue Hamlet? ❷ jouer [1] à (a game); **to play tennis** jouer au tennis, **they were playing cards** ils jouaient aux cartes ❸ jouer [1] de (a musical instrument); **Helen plays the violin** Helen joue du violon ❹ mettre [11] (a CD or record); **play me your new album** mets-moi ton nouveau album

player NOUN ❶ (in sport) joueur MASC, joueuse FEM; **a football player** un joueur de foot ❷ (musician) musicien MASC, musicienne FEM

playground NOUN cour (FEM) de récréation

playgroup NOUN halte-garderie FEM

playing card NOUN carte (FEM) à jouer

playing field NOUN terrain (MASC) de sport

playroom NOUN salle (FEM) de jeux

plaza NOUN **a shopping plaza** un centre commercial

pleasant ADJECTIVE agréable

please ADVERB s'il vous plaît, (less formal) s'il te plaît; **two coffees, please** deux cafés, s'il vous plaît, **could you turn the TV off, please?** est-ce que tu peux éteindre la télé s'il te plaît?

pleased ADJECTIVE content; **I was really pleased!** j'étais très content!, **she was pleased with her present** elle était contente de son cadeau, **pleased to meet you!** enchanté!

pleasure NOUN plaisir MASC

plenty PRONOUN ❶ (lots) beaucoup; **there's plenty of bread** il y a beaucoup de pain, **he's got plenty of money** il a beaucoup d'argent ❷ (quite enough) **we've got plenty of time for a coffee** nous avons largement le temps de prendre un café, **thank you, that's plenty!** merci, ça suffit largement!

pliers NOUN pince FEM

plot NOUN (of a film or novel) intrigue FEM

plough VERB labourer [1]

plug NOUN ❶ (electrical) prise FEM ❷ (in a bath or sink) bonde FEM; **to pull out the plug** retirer la bonde

plum NOUN prune FEM; **a plum tart** une tarte aux prunes

plumber NOUN plombier MASC; **he's a plumber** il est plombier

plump ADJECTIVE potelé

plunge VERB plonger [52]

plural NOUN pluriel MASC; **in the plural** au pluriel

plus PREPOSITION plus; **three children plus the baby** trois enfants plus le bébé

p.m. ADVERB
(French people usually express times after midday in terms of the 24-hour clock) ❶ **at two p.m.** à quatorze heures, **at nine p.m.** à vingt-et-une heures ❷ *(however, you can also use 'de l'après-midi', for times up to 6 p.m. and 'du soir' for times after that)* **at two p.m.** à deux heures de l'après-midi, **at nine p.m.** à neuf heures du soir

poached egg NOUN œuf (MASC) poché

pocket NOUN poche FEM

pocket money NOUN ❶ (for child) argent (MASC) de poche ❷ (for small purchases) petites dépenses FEM PLURAL

poem NOUN poème MASC

poet NOUN poète MASC

poetry NOUN poésie FEM

point NOUN ❶ (tip) pointe FEM; **the point of a nail** la pointe d'un clou ❷ (in time) moment MASC; **at that point the police arrived** à ce moment-là, la police est arrivée ❸ **to get the point** comprendre, **I don't get the point** je ne comprends pas, **what's the point of waiting?** à quoi bon attendre?, **there's no point phoning, he's out** ça ne sert à rien d'appeler, il est sorti, **that's not the point** il ne s'agit pas de ça ❹ **that's a good point!** c'est vrai! ❺ **from my point of view** de mon point de vue ❻ **her strong point** son point fort ❼ (in scoring) point MASC; **fifteen points to eleven** quinze points à onze ❽ (in decimals) *(in French, a comma is used for the* decimal point, so 6,75) **6 point 4** 6 virgule 4 *(this is how you say it aloud)*

point *VERB* ❶ indiquer [1]; **a notice pointing to the station** un panneau qui indiquait la gare, **James pointed out the cathedral** James nous a montré la cathédrale ❷ *(with finger)* montrer [1] du doigt; **he pointed at one of the children** il a montré l'un des enfants du doigt ❸ **I'd like to point out that I'm paying** je vous signale que c'est moi qui paie

pointless *ADJECTIVE* inutile; **it's pointless to keep on ringing** c'est inutile de continuer de sonner

poison *NOUN* poison *MASC*

poison *VERB* empoisonner [1]

poisonous *ADJECTIVE* ❶ toxique *(chemical or gas)* ❷ vénéneux *(FEM* vénéneuse*)* *(toadstools or berries)* ❸ venimeux *(FEM* venimeuse*)* *(snake or insect)*

poker *NOUN* ❶ *(for fire)* tisonnier *MASC* ❷ *(card game)* poker *MASC*

Poland *NOUN* Pologne *FEM*; **in Poland** en Pologne

polar bear *NOUN* ours *(MASC)* polaire

pole *NOUN* ❶ *(for a tent)* mât *MASC* ❷ *(for skiing)* bâton *MASC* ❸ **the North Pole** le pôle Nord

Pole *NOUN* *(a Polish person)* Polonais *MASC*, Polonaise *FEM*

police *NOUN* **the police** la police, **the police are coming** la police arrive *(note that a singular verb is used after 'la police')*

police *VERB* surveiller [1]

police car *NOUN* voiture *(FEM)* de police

policeman *NOUN* agent *(MASC)* de police

police station *NOUN* commissariat *(MASC)* de police

policewoman *NOUN* femme *(FEM)* policier

policy *NOUN* ❶ *(plan of action)* politique *FEM* ❷ *(document)* police *FEM*

polish *NOUN* ❶ *(for furniture)* cire *FEM* ❷ *(for shoes)* cirage *MASC*

polish *VERB* cirer [1] *(shoes or furniture)*

Polish *NOUN, ADJECTIVE* polonais *MASC*

polite *ADJECTIVE* poli; **to be polite to somebody** être poli avec quelqu'un

political *ADJECTIVE* politique

politician *NOUN* homme *(MASC)* politique, femme *(FEM)* politique

politics *NOUN* politique *FEM*

polluted *ADJECTIVE* pollué

pollution *NOUN* pollution *FEM*

polo-necked *ADJECTIVE* à col roulé; **a polo-necked jumper** un pull à col roulé

polythene bag *NOUN* sac *(MASC)* en plastique

pond *NOUN* ❶ *(large)* étang *MASC* ❷ *(smaller)* mare *FEM* ❸ *(in a garden)* bassin *MASC*

pony *NOUN* poney *MASC*

ponytail *NOUN* queue *(FEM)* de cheval

poodle *NOUN* caniche *MASC*

pool *NOUN* ❶ *(swimming pool)* piscine *FEM* ❷ *(in the country)* étang *MASC* ❸ *(puddle)* flaque *FEM* ❹ *(game)* billard (MASC) américain; **to have a game of pool** jouer au billard américain ❺ **the football pools** le loto sportif, **to do the pools** jouer au loto sportif

poor ADJECTIVE ❶ pauvre; **a poor area** un quartier pauvre, **a poor family** une famille pauvre, **poor Tanya's failed her exam** la pauvre Tanya a raté son examen ❷ (bad) mauvais; **this is poor work** c'est du mauvais travail, **the weather was pretty poor** le temps était assez mauvais

pop NOUN pop MASC; **a pop concert** un concert de pop, **a pop star** un pop star, **a pop song** une chanson pop
• **to pop into** faire [10] un saut à; **I'll just pop into the bank** je vais juste faire un saut à la banque

popcorn NOUN pop-corn MASC

pope NOUN pape MASC

poppy NOUN coquelicot MASC

popular ADJECTIVE populaire

population NOUN population FEM

porch NOUN porche MASC

pork NOUN porc MASC; **a pork chop** une côtelette de porc

porridge NOUN porridge MASC

port NOUN ❶ port MASC; **the ferry was in port** le ferry était au port ❷ (wine) porto MASC

portable computer NOUN ordinateur (MASC) portable

porter NOUN ❶ (at a station or airport) porteur MASC ❷ (in a hotel) portier MASC

portion NOUN (of food) portion FEM

portrait NOUN portrait MASC

Portugal NOUN Portugal MASC; **to Portugal** au Portugal, **in Portugal** au Portugal

Portuguese NOUN ❶ (language) portugais MASC ❷ (a person) Portugais MASC, Portugaise FEM

Portuguese ADJECTIVE portugais

posh ADJECTIVE chic (never changes); **a posh house** une maison chic

position NOUN position FEM

positive ADJECTIVE ❶ (sure) sûr; **I'm positive he's left** je suis sûr qu'il est parti ❷ (enthusiastic) positif (FEM positive); **her reaction was very positive** sa réaction était très positive, **try to be more positive** essaie d'être plus positif

possess VERB posséder [24]

possessions PLURAL NOUN affaires FEM PLURAL; **all my possessions are in the flat** toutes mes affaires sont dans l'appartement

possibility NOUN possibilité FEM

possible ADJECTIVE possible; **it's possible** c'est possible, **if possible** si possible, **as quickly as possible** le plus vite possible

possibly ADVERB ❶ (maybe) peut-être; **'will you be at home at midday?' – 'possibly'** 'est-ce que tu seras chez toi à midi?' – 'peut – être' ❷ (for emphasis) **how can you possibly believe that?** mais comment donc peux-tu croire ça?, **I can't possibly arrive before Thursday** je ne peux vraiment pas arriver avant jeudi

a
b
c
d
e
f
g
h
i
j
k
l
m
n
o
p
q
r
s
t
u
v
w
x
y
z

post NOUN ❶ poste FEM; **to send something by post** envoyer quelque chose par la poste ❷ *(letters)* courrier MASC; **is there any post for me?** y a-t-il du courrier pour moi? ❸ *(a pole)* poteau MASC ❹ *(a job)* poste MASC

post VERB **to post a letter** mettre [11] une lettre à la poste

postbox NOUN boîte *(FEM)* à lettres

postcard NOUN carte *(FEM)* postale

postcode NOUN code *(MASC)* postal

poster NOUN ❶ *(for decoration)* poster MASC; **I've bought an Oasis poster** j'ai acheté un poster d'Oasis ❷ *(advertising)* affiche FEM; **I saw a poster for the concert** j'ai vu une affiche pour le concert

postman NOUN facteur MASC; **has the postman been?** est-ce que le facteur est passé?

post office NOUN poste FEM; **the post office is on the right** la poste est à droite

postpone VERB **to postpone something** remettre [11] quelque chose à plus tard

postwoman NOUN factrice FEM

pot NOUN ❶ *(jar)* pot MASC; **a pot of honey** un pot de miel ❷ *(teapot)* théière FEM; **I'll make a pot of tea** je vais faire du thé ❸ **the pots and pans** les casseroles FEM PLURAL
• **to take pot luck** manger à la fortune du pot

potato NOUN pomme *(FEM)* de terre; **fried potatoes** des pommes de terre sautées, **mashed potatoes** de la purée

potato crisps PLURAL NOUN chips MASC PLURAL

pottery NOUN poterie FEM

pound NOUN ❶ *(money)* livre FEM; **fourteen pounds** quatorze livres, **how much is that in pounds?** c'est combien en livres sterling? ❷ *(in weight)* livre FEM; **a pound of apples** une livre de pommes

pour VERB ❶ verser [1] *(liquid)*; **he poured the milk into the pan** il a versé le lait dans la casserole ❷ servir [71] *(a drink)*; **to pour the tea** servir le thé, **I poured him a drink** je lui ai servi à boire ❸ *(with rain)* **it's pouring** il pleut à verse

poverty NOUN pauvreté FEM

powder NOUN poudre FEM

power NOUN ❶ *(electricity)* courant MASC ❷ *(energy)* énergie FEM; **nuclear power** l'énergie nucléaire ❸ *(over other people)* pouvoir MASC; **to be in power** être au pouvoir

power cut NOUN coupure *(FEM)* de courant

powerful ADJECTIVE puissant

power point NOUN prise *(FEM)* de courant

power station NOUN centrale *(FEM)* électrique

practical ADJECTIVE pratique

practical joke NOUN farce FEM

practically ADVERB pratiquement

practice NOUN ❶ *(for sport)* entraînement MASC; **hockey practice** l'entraînement de hockey ❷ *(for an instrument)* **to do**

your piano practice travailler [1] son piano ❸ **to be out of practice** être rouillé ❹ **in practice** en pratique

practise VERB ❶ travailler [1] *(music, language, etc)*; **a week in Berlin to practise my German** une semaine à Berlin pour travailler mon allemand ❷ *(in a sport)* s'entraîner [1]; **the team practises on Wednesdays** l'équipe s'entraîne le mercredi

praise VERB **to praise somebody for something** féliciter [1] quelqu'un de quelque chose

pram NOUN landau MASC

prawn NOUN crevette FEM

pray VERB prier [1]

prayer NOUN prière FEM

precaution NOUN précaution FEM; **to take precautions** prendre ses précautions

precinct NOUN **a shopping precinct** un quartier commerçant, **a pedestrian precinct** une zone piétonne

precious ADJECTIVE précieux *(FEM précieuse)*

precise ADJECTIVE précis

precisely ADVERB précisément; **at eleven o'clock precisely** à onze heures précises

preface NOUN préface FEM

prefer VERB préférer [24]; **I prefer coffee to tea** je préfère le café au thé

pregnancy NOUN grossesse FEM

pregnant ADJECTIVE enceinte

prejudice NOUN préjugé MASC; **a prejudice** un préjugé, **to fight against racial prejudice** lutter contre les préjugés raciaux

prejudiced ADJECTIVE **to be prejudiced** avoir des préjugés

preliminary ADJECTIVE préliminaire

première NOUN première FEM *(of a play or film)*

prep NOUN devoirs MASC PLURAL; **my English prep** mes devoirs d'anglais

preparation NOUN ❶ préparation FEM ❷ **the preparations for** les préparatifs *(MASC PLURAL)* pour, **our preparations for Christmas** nos préparatifs pour Noël

prepare VERB préparer [1]; **to prepare somebody for** préparer quelqu'un à *(a surprise or shock)*

prepared ADJECTIVE prêt; **I'm prepared to pay half** je suis prêt à en payer la moitié, **to be prepared for the worst** s'attendre [3] au pire

preposition NOUN préposition FEM

prep school NOUN école *(FEM)* primaire privée

prescribe VERB prescrire [38]

prescription NOUN ordonnance FEM; **on prescription** sur ordonnance

presence NOUN présence FEM; **in my presence** en ma présence

presence of mind NOUN présence *(FEM)* d'esprit

present NOUN ❶ *(a gift)* cadeau MASC *(PLURAL* cadeaux*)*; **to give somebody a present** offrir un cadeau à quelqu'un ❷ *(the time now)* présent MASC; **in the present (tense)** au présent, **that's all for the present** c'est tout pour le moment

present ADJECTIVE ❶ (attending) présent; **is Tracy present?** est-ce que Tracy est présente?, **to be present at** assister [1] à, **fifty people were present at the funeral** cinquante personnes ont assisté à l'enterrement ❷ (existing now) actuel (FEM actuelle); **the present situation** la situation actuelle ❸ **at the present time** actuellement

present VERB ❶ remettre [11] (a prize) ❷ (introduce) présenter [1]

presenter NOUN (on TV) présentateur MASC, présentatrice FEM

presently ADVERB (soon) bientôt

president NOUN président MASC, présidente FEM

press NOUN **the press** la presse

press VERB ❶ (to push) appuyer [41]; **press here to open** appuyez ici pour ouvrir ❷ appuyer [41] sur (a button, switch, or pedal); **he pressed the button** il a appuyé sur le bouton

press conference NOUN conférence (FEM) de presse

pressure NOUN pression FEM

pressure gauge NOUN indicateur (MASC) de pression

pressure group NOUN groupe (MASC) de pression

pretend VERB **to pretend to do** faire [10] semblant de faire, **he's pretending not to hear** il fait semblant de ne pas entendre

pretty ADJECTIVE joli (GOES BEFORE THE NOUN); **a pretty dress** une jolie robe

pretty ADVERB plutôt; **it was pretty silly** c'était plutôt bête

prevent VERB **to prevent somebody from doing** empêcher [1] quelqu'un de faire, **there's nothing to prevent you from leaving** rien ne vous empêche de partir

previous ADJECTIVE précédent

previously ADVERB auparavant

price NOUN prix MASC; **the price per kilo** le prix du kilo, **holidays have gone up in price** les vacances ont augmenté

price list NOUN liste (FEM) des prix

price ticket NOUN étiquette FEM

prick VERB piquer [1]; **to prick your finger** se piquer le doigt

pride NOUN fierté FEM

priest NOUN prêtre MASC

primary (school) teacher NOUN instituteur MASC, institutrice FEM

primary school NOUN école (FEM) primaire

prime minister NOUN Premier ministre MASC

primrose NOUN primevère FEM

prince NOUN prince MASC; **Prince Charles** le prince Charles

princess NOUN princesse FEM; **Princess Anne** la princesse Anne

principal NOUN (of a college) directeur MASC, directrice FEM

principal ADJECTIVE (main) principal MASC (PLURAL principaux)

principle NOUN principe MASC; **on principle** par principe, **that's true in principle** cela est vrai en principe

print NOUN ❶ *(letters)* caractères MASC PLURAL; **in small print** en petits caractères ❷ *(a photo)* tirage MASC; **a colour print** un tirage en couleur

printer NOUN imprimante FEM

print-out NOUN copie *(FEM)* papier

prison NOUN prison FEM; **in prison** en prison

prisoner NOUN prisonnier MASC, prisonnière FEM

private ADJECTIVE ❶ privé; **a private school** une école privée, **'private property'** 'propriété privée' ❷ particulier *(FEM particulière) (lesson)*; **to have private lessons** prendre des cours particuliers

privately ADVERB en privé

prize NOUN prix MASC; **to win a prize** gagner un prix

prize-giving NOUN distribution *(FEM)* des prix

prizewinner NOUN gagnant MASC, gagnante FEM

probable ADJECTIVE probable

probably ADVERB probablement

problem NOUN problème MASC; **it's a serious problem** c'est un grave problème, **no problem!** pas de problème!

process NOUN ❶ processus MASC ❷ **to be in the process of doing** être en train de faire

procession NOUN ❶ *(in parade)* défilé MASC ❷ *(at religious festival)* procession FEM

produce NOUN *(food)* produits MASC PLURAL

produce VERB produire [26]; **I produced my passport** j'ai produit mon passeport, **it produces a lot of heat** ça produit beaucoup de chaleur

producer NOUN *(of a film or programme)* metteur *(MASC)* en scène

product NOUN produit MASC

production NOUN ❶ *(of a film or opera)* production FEM ❷ *(of a play)* mise *(FEM)* en scène; **a new production of Hamlet** une nouvelle mise en scène de Hamlet ❸ *(by a factory)* production FEM

profession NOUN profession FEM

professional NOUN professionnel MASC, professionnelle FEM; **he's a professional** c'est un professionnel

professional ADJECTIVE professionnel *(FEM professionnelle)*; **she's a professional singer** c'est une chanteuse professionnelle

professor NOUN professeur MASC

profile NOUN profil MASC

profit NOUN bénéfice MASC

profitable ADJECTIVE rentable

program NOUN **a computer program** un programme informatique

programme NOUN ❶ *(for a play or an event)* programme MASC ❷ *(on TV or radio)* émission FEM

programmer NOUN programmateur MASC, programmatrice FEM

progress   **Protestant**

progress NOUN ❶ progrès MASC; to make progress faire des progrès ❷ to be in progress être en cours

project NOUN ❶ (at school) dossier MASC ❷ (a plan) projet MASC; a project to build a bridge un projet pour construire un pont

projector NOUN projecteur MASC

promise NOUN promesse FEM; to make a promise faire une promesse, to break a promise manquer à sa promesse, it's a promise! c'est promis!

promise VERB to promise to do promettre [11] de faire, I've promised to be home by ten j'ai promis de rentrer avant dix heures

promote VERB to be promoted être [6] promu

promotion NOUN promotion FEM

prompt ADJECTIVE rapide; a prompt reply une réponse rapide

promptly ADJECTIVE ❶ (at once) immédiatement; he promptly fell off again il est retombé immédiatement ❷ (quickly) rapidement; please reply promptly répondez rapidement s'il vous plaît ❸ promptly at nine o'oclock à neuf heures précises

pronoun NOUN pronom MASC

pronounce VERB prononcer [61]; it's hard to pronounce c'est difficile à prononcer

pronunciation NOUN prononciation FEM

proof NOUN preuve FEM; there's no proof that ... rien ne prouve que ...

propaganda NOUN propagande FEM

propeller NOUN hélice FEM

proper ADJECTIVE ❶ (real, genuine) vrai; a proper doctor un vrai médecin, I need a proper meal j'ai besoin d'un vrai repas ❷ (correct) bon (FEM bonne); the proper answer la bonne réponse, the proper tool le bon outil, in its proper place à sa place

properly ADVERB comme il faut; hold it properly tiens-le comme il faut, is it properly wrapped? est-ce que c'est emballé comme il faut?

property NOUN (your belongings) affaires (FEM PLURAL), propriété FEM; 'private property' 'propriété privée'

proposal NOUN proposition FEM

propose VERB ❶ (suggest) proposer [1] ❷ (marriage) he proposed to her il l'a demandée en mariage

prostitute NOUN prostituée FEM

protect VERB protéger [15]

protection NOUN protection FEM

protein NOUN protéine FEM

protest NOUN protestation FEM; in spite of their protests malgré leurs protestations

protest VERB ❶ (to grumble) protester [1]; he protested, but ... il a protesté, mais ... ❷ (demonstrate) manifester [1]

Protestant NOUN, ADJECTIVE protestant MASC, protestante FEM

protester NOUN manifestant MASC, manifestante FEM

protest march NOUN manifestation FEM

proud ADJECTIVE fier (FEM fière)

prove VERB prouver [1]

proverb NOUN proverbe MASC

provide VERB fournir [2]

provided CONJUNCTION à condition que; **provided you do it now** à condition que tu le fasses maintenant (note that a verb in the subjunctive is needed)

province NOUN province FEM

prune NOUN pruneau MASC (PLURAL pruneaux)

P.S. ABBREVIATION (at end of letter) P.S.

psychiatrist NOUN psychiatre MASC & FEM; **he's a psychiatrist** il est psychiatre

psychological ADJECTIVE psychologique

psychologist NOUN psychologue MASC & FEM; **she's a psychologist** ele est psychologue

psychology NOUN psychologie FEM

PTO TSVP (short for tournez s'il vous plaît)

pub NOUN pub MASC

public NOUN the public le public, **in public** en public

public ADJECTIVE ❶ public (FEM publique) ❷ **the public library** la bibliothèque municipale

public address system NOUN sonorisation FEM

public holiday NOUN jour (MASC) férié; **January 1 is a public holiday** le premier janvier est férié

publicity NOUN publicité FEM

public school NOUN école (FEM) privée

public transport NOUN transports (MASC PLURAL) en commun

publish VERB publier [1]

publisher NOUN éditeur MASC

pudding NOUN (dessert) dessert MASC; **for pudding we've got strawberries** comme dessert nous avons des fraises

puddle NOUN flaque FEM

puff NOUN (of smoke) bouffée FEM

puff pastry NOUN pâte (FEM) feuilletée

pull VERB tirer [1]; **pull hard!** tire fort!, **to pull a rope** tirer sur une corde, **he pulled a letter out of his pocket** il a tiré une lettre de sa poche
- **you're pulling my leg!** tu me fais marcher!
- **to pull down** baisser [1] (a blind)
- **to pull in** (at the roadside) s'arrêter [1]

pullover NOUN pull-over MASC

pulse NOUN pouls MASC; **the doctor took my pulse** le médecin a pris mon pouls

pump NOUN pompe FEM; **a bicycle pump** une pompe à vélo

a b c d e f g h i j k l m n o p q r s t u v w x y z

529

pump VERB pomper [1]; **they were pumping the water out of the cellar** ils pompaient l'eau de la cave
• **to pump up** gonfler [1] *(a tyre)*

pumpkin NOUN citrouille FEM

punch NOUN ❶ *(in boxing)* coup *(MASC)* de poing ❷ *(drink)* punch MASC

punch VERB ❶ **to punch somebody** donner [1] un coup de poing à quelqu'un, **he punched me** il m'a donné un coup de poing ❷ composter [1] *(a ticket)*

punctual ADJECTIVE ponctuel *(FEM ponctuelle)*

punctuation NOUN ponctuation FEM

punctuation mark NOUN signe *(MASC)* de ponctuation

puncture NOUN crevaison FEM; **we had a puncture on the way** nous avons crevé en route

punish VERB punir [2]

punishment NOUN punition FEM

pupil NOUN élève MASC & FEM

puppet NOUN marionnette FEM

puppy NOUN chiot MASC; **a labrador puppy** un chiot labrador

pure ADJECTIVE pur

purple ADJECTIVE violet *(FEM violette)*

purpose NOUN ❶ but MASC; **what was the purpose of her call?** quel était le but de son appel? ❷ **on purpose** exprès, **she did it on purpose** elle l'a fait exprès, **he closed the door on purpose** il a fait exprès de fermer la porte

purr VERB ronronner [1]

purse NOUN porte-monnaie MASC *(PLURAL* porte-monnaie*)*

push NOUN **to give something a push** pousser [1] quelque chose

push VERB ❶ pousser [1]; **he pushed me** il m'a poussé ❷ *(to press)* appuyer [41] sur *(a bell or button)* ❸ **to push somebody to do** pousser [1] quelqu'un à faire, **his teacher is pushing him to sit the exam** son prof le pousse à passer l'examen
• **to push something away** repousser [1] quelque chose; **she pushed her plate away** elle a repoussé son assiette

pushchair NOUN poussette FEM

put VERB ❶ mettre [11]; **you can put the cream in the fridge** tu peux mettre la crème au frigo, **where did you put my bag?** où est-ce que tu as mis mon sac?, **put your suitcase here** mets ta valise ici ❷ *(write)* écrire [38]; **put your address here** écris ton adresse ici
• **to put away** ranger [52]; **I'll put the shopping away** je vais ranger les courses
• **to put back** ❶ remettre [11]; **I put it back in the drawer** je l'ai remis dans le tiroir ❷ *(postpone)* remettre [11]; **the meeting has been put back until Thursday** la réunion a été remise à jeudi
• **to put down** poser [1]; **she put the vase down on the table** elle a posé le vase sur la table
• **to put off** ❶ *(postpone)* remettre [11]; **he's put off my lesson till Thursday** il a remis ma leçon à jeudi ❷ *(turn off)* éteindre [60] *(a light or TV)*; **don't forget to put off the lights** n'oublie pas d'éteindre la lumière ❸ **to put somebody off something** dégoûter [1] quelqu'un

de quelque chose, **it really put me off Chinese food!** ça m'a vraiment dégoûté de la nourriture chinoise! ❹ **to be put off** *(doing something)* se décourager [52], **don't be put off!** ne te décourage pas!

- **to put on** ❶ mettre [11] *(clothing, make-up)*; **I'll just put my shoes on** je vais juste mettre mes chaussures, **il a mis Oasis** he's put on Oasis ❷ *(switch on)* allumer [1] *(a light or heating)*; **could you put the lamp on?** est-ce que tu peux allumer la lampe? ❸ monter [1] *(a play)*; **we're putting on a French play** nous sommes en train de monter une pièce française

- **to put out** ❶ *(put outside)* sortir [72]; **have you put the rubbish out?** as-tu sorti les ordures? ❷ éteindre [60] *(a fire, light, or cigarette)*; **I've put the lights out** j'ai éteint la lumière ❸ **to put out your hand** tendre [3] la main

- **to put through** passer [52]; **I'll put you through to the manager** je vous passe le responsable

- **to put up** ❶ lever [50] *(your hand)*; **I put up my hand** j'ai levé la main ❷ mettre [11] *(picture)*; **I've put up some photos in my room** j'ai mis des photos dans ma chambre ❸ afficher [1] *(a notice)* ❹ augmenter [1] *(the price)*; **they've put up the price of the tickets** ils ont augmenté le prix des billets ❺ *(for the night)* héberger [52]; **can you put me up on Friday?** est-ce que tu peux m'héberger vendredi?

- **to put up with something** supporter [1]; **I don't know how she puts up with it** je ne sais pas comment elle le supporte

puzzle NOUN *(jigsaw)* puzzle MASC

puzzled ADJECTIVE perplexe

pyjamas PLURAL NOUN pyjama MASC SINGULAR; **a pair of pyjamas** un pyjama, **where are my pyjamas?** où est mon pyjama?

pylon NOUN pilône MASC

Pyrenees NOUN les Pyrénées FEM PLURAL; **in the Pyrenees** dans les Pyrénées

quail NOUN caille FEM

qualification NOUN ❶ diplôme MASC *(certificate, exam, degree)* ❷ **qualifications** qualifications FEM PLURAL, **vocational qualifications** les qualifications professionnelles

qualified ADJECTIVE ❶ qualifié; **she's a qualified ski instructor** c'est une monitrice de ski qualifiée ❷ *(having a degree or a diploma)* diplômé; **a qualified architect** un architecte diplômé

qualify VERB ❶ *(to be eligible)* avoir [5] droit à; **we don't qualify for a reduction** nous n'avons pas droit à une réduction ❷ *(in sport)* se qualifier [1]

quality NOUN qualité FEM; **good quality vegetables** des légumes de bonne qualité

a b c d e f g h i j k l m n o p q r s t u v w x y z

quantity NOUN quantité FEM

quarantine NOUN quarantaine FEM

quarrel NOUN dispute FEM; **to have a quarrel** se disputer [1]

quarrel VERB se disputer [1]; **they're always quarrelling** ils sont tout le temps en train de se disputer

quarry NOUN carrière FEM

quarter NOUN ❶ quart MASC; **a quarter of the class** le quart de la classe, **three quarters of the class** les trois quarts de la classe ❷ **a quarter past ten** dix heures et quart, **a quarter to ten** dix heures moins le quart, **a quarter of an hour** un quart d'heure, **three quarters of an hour** trois quarts d'heure, **an hour and a quarter** une heure et quart

quarter-final NOUN quart (MASC) de finale

quartet NOUN quatuor MASC; **a jazz quartet** un quatuor de jazz

quay NOUN quai MASC

queen NOUN reine FEM; **Queen Elizabeth** la reine Elizabeth, **the Queen Mother** la reine mère

query NOUN question FEM; **are there any queries?** y a-t-il des questions?

question NOUN question FEM; **to ask a question** poser une question, **I asked her a question** je lui ai posé une question, **it's a question of time** c'est une question de temps, **it's out of the question!** c'est hors de question!

question VERB interroger [52]

question mark NOUN point (MASC) d'interrogation

questionnaire NOUN questionnaire MASC; **to fill in a questionnaire** remplir un questionnaire

queue NOUN ❶ (of people) queue FEM; **to stand in a queue** faire la queue ❷ (of cars) file FEM

queue VERB faire [10] la queue; **we were queueing for check-in** nous faisions la queue pour l'enregistrement

quick ADJECTIVE ❶ rapide; **a quick lunch** un déjeuner rapide, **it's quicker on the motorway** c'est plus rapide par l'autoroute, **to have a quick look at something** jeter un coup d'il rapide à quelque chose ❷ **quick! there's the bus!** vite! voilà le bus!, **be quick!** dépêche-toi!

quickly ADVERB vite; **I'll just quickly phone my mother** je vais vite appeler ma mère

quiet ADJECTIVE ❶ (silent) silencieux (FEM silencieuse); **the children are very quiet** les enfants sont très silencieux ❷ **to keep quiet** se taire [76], **please keep quiet** taisez-vous, s'il vous plaît ❸ (gentle) doux (FEM douce); **some quiet music** de la musique douce, **in a quiet voice** à voix basse ❹ (peaceful) tranquille; **a quiet street** une rue tranquille, **a quiet day at home** une journée tranquille à la maison

quietly ADVERB ❶ (to move) sans bruit; **he got up quietly** il s'est levé sans bruit ❷ (speak) doucement ❸ (read or play) en silence

quilt NOUN couette FEM

quite ADVERB ❶ assez; **it's quite cold outside** il fait assez froid dehors, **that's quite a good idea** c'est une assez bonne idée, **he sings quite**

well il chante assez bien, **quite often** assez souvent ❷ **not quite** pas tout à fait, **the meat's not quite cooked** la viande n'est pas tout à fait cuite ❸ **quite a lot of** pas mal de, **we've got quite a lot of friends here** nous avons pas mal d'amis ici, **quite a few people** pas mal de gens

quiz NOUN quiz MASC

quotation NOUN (from a book) citation FEM

quotation marks PLURAL NOUN guillemets MASC PLURAL; **in quotation marks** entre guillemets

quote NOUN ❶ (from a book) citation FEM ❷ (estimate) devis MASC ❸ **in quotes** entre guillemets

quote VERB citer [1]

rabbi NOUN rabbin MASC

rabbit NOUN lapin MASC

rabbit hutch NOUN clapier MASC

rabies NOUN rage FEM

race NOUN ❶ (a sports event) course FEM; **a cycle race** une course cycliste, **to have a race** faire la course ❷ (an ethnic group) race FEM

racer NOUN (bike) vélo (MASC) de course

racetrack NOUN ❶ (for horses)

champ (MASC) de course ❷ (for cars) circuit MASC ❸ (for cycles) piste FEM

racial ADJECTIVE racial MASC (PLURAL raciaux); **racial discrimination** la discrimination raciale

racing NOUN courses FEM PLURAL

racing car NOUN voiture (FEM) de course

racing driver NOUN pilote (MASC) de course

racism NOUN racisme MASC

racist NOUN, ADJECTIVE raciste MASC & FEM

rack NOUN (for luggage) porte-bagages MASC

racket NOUN ❶ (for tennis) raquette FEM; **here's your tennis racket** voici ta raquette de tennis ❷ (noise) vacarme MASC

radar NOUN radar MASC

radiation NOUN radiation FEM

radiator NOUN radiateur MASC

radio NOUN radio FEM; **to listen to the radio** écouter la radio, **to hear something on the radio** entendre quelque chose à la radio

radioactive ADJECTIVE radioactif (FEM radioactive)

radio-controlled ADJECTIVE téléguidé

radio station NOUN station (FEM) de radio

radish NOUN radis MASC

radius NOUN rayon MASC

raffle NOUN tombola FEM

a b c d e f g h i j k l m n o p **q** **r** s t u v w x y z

raft NOUN radeau MASC

rag NOUN chiffon MASC

rage NOUN colère FEM; **she's in a rage** elle est furieuse
• **it's all the rage** ça fait fureur

raid NOUN ❶ hold-up MASC ❷ (by the police) rafle FEM

rail NOUN ❶ (the railway) **to go by rail** prendre le train ❷ (on a balcony or bridge) balustrade FEM ❸ (on stairs) rampe FEM ❹ (for a train) rail MASC

railing(s) NOUN grille FEM

rail strike NOUN grève (FEM) des cheminots

railway NOUN ❶ (the system) chemin (MASC) de fer; **the railways** les chemins de fer ❷ **a railway line** une ligne de chemin de fer (from one place to another) ❸ **on the railway line** sur la voie ferrée (the rails)

railway carriage NOUN wagon MASC

railway station NOUN gare FEM; **opposite the railway station** en face de la gare

rain NOUN pluie FEM; **in the rain** sous la pluie

rain VERB pleuvoir [63]; **it's raining** il pleut, **it's going to rain** il va pleuvoir

rainbow NOUN arc-en-ciel MASC (PLURAL arcs-en-ciel)

raincoat NOUN imperméable MASC

raindrop NOUN goutte (FEM) de pluie

rainfall NOUN niveau (MASC) de précipitations

rainy ADJECTIVE pluvieux (FEM pluvieuse)

raise VERB ❶ (lift up) lever [50]; **she raised her head** elle a levé la tête ❷ (increase) augmenter [1] (a price or a salary) ❸ **to raise money for something** collecter [1] des fonds pour quelque chose ❹ (to raise the alarm) donner [1] l'alarme ❺ (to raise somebody's spirits) remonter [1] le moral à quelqu'un

raisin NOUN raisin (MASC) sec

rake NOUN rateau MASC (PLURAL rateaux)

rally NOUN ❶ (a meeting) rassemblement MASC ❷ (for sport) rallye MASC ❸ (in tennis) échange MASC

rambler NOUN randonneur MASC, randonneuse FEM

rambling NOUN randonnée FEM

ramp NOUN (for a wheelchair, for example) rampe FEM

ranch NOUN ranch MASC

range NOUN ❶ (a choice) gamme FEM; **we offer a range of sports** nous vous proposons une gamme de sports, **in a wide range of colours** dans un grand choix de coloris, **a top-of-the-range computer** un ordinateur haut de gamme ❷ (of mountains) chaîne FEM

rap NOUN rap MASC (music)

rape NOUN viol MASC

rape VERB violer [1]

rare ADJECTIVE ❶ rare; **a rare bird** un oiseau rare ❷ saignant (a steak); **medium-rare** à point

rarely *ADVERB* rarement

rash *NOUN* rougeurs *FEM PLURAL*; **I've got a rash on my arms** j'ai des rougeurs sur les bras

rash *ADJECTIVE* irréfléchi; **a rash decision** une décision irréfléchie

raspberry *NOUN* framboise *FEM*; **raspberry jam** la confiture de framboises, **a raspberry tart** une tarte aux framboises

rat *NOUN* rat *MASC*

rate *NOUN* ❶ *(a charge)* tarif *MASC*; **what are the rates for children?** quels sont les tarifs pour les enfants?, **reduced rates** les tarifs réduits ❷ *(a level)* taux *MASC*; **a high cancellation rate** un taux élevé d'annulation ❸ **at any rate** en tout cas

rather *ADVERB* ❶ plutôt; **I'm rather busy** je suis plutôt occupé ❷ **rather than** plutôt que, **in summer rather than winter** en été plutôt qu'en hiver ❸ **I'd rather wait** je préfère attendre, **they'd rather come on Thursday** ils préfèrent venir jeudi ❹ **rather a lot of** pas mal de, **I've got rather a lot of shopping to do** j'ai pas mal de courses à faire

rave *NOUN* rave *MASC* *(a party)*

raw *ADJECTIVE* cru

ray *NOUN* rayon *MASC*

razor *NOUN* rasoir *MASC*

razor blade *NOUN* lame *(FEM)* de rasoir

RE *NOUN* éducation *(FEM)* religieuse

reach *NOUN* portée *FEM*; **out of reach** hors de portée, **within reach** *(of your hand)* à portée de main, **within easy reach of the sea** à proximité de la mer

reach *VERB* ❶ arriver [1] à; **when you reach the church** quand vous arrivez à l'église, **to reach a decision** arriver à une décision ❷ **to reach the final** arriver [1] à la finale

react *VERB* réagir [2]

reaction *NOUN* réaction *FEM*

read *VERB* lire [51]; **what are you reading at the moment?** qu'est-ce que tu lis en ce moment?, **I'm reading a detective novel** je lis un roman policier, **he read out the list** il a lu la liste à haute voix

reading *NOUN* lecture *FEM*; **I don't much like reading** je n'aime pas beaucoup la lecture, **some easy reading for the beach** de la lecture facile pour la plage

ready *ADJECTIVE* prêt; **supper's not ready yet** le dîner n'est pas encore prêt, **are you ready to leave?** est-ce que tu es prêt à partir?, **to get ready** se préparer [1], **I'm getting ready to go out** je me prépare pour sortir, **I was getting ready for bed** je me préparais pour me coucher, **I'll get your room ready** je vais préparer ta chambre

real *ADJECTIVE* vrai; **it's a real diamond** c'est un vrai diamant, **he's a real bore** c'est un vrai casse-pieds, **is that his real name?** est-ce que c'est son vrai nom?, **her real father is dead** son vrai père est mort

realistic *ADJECTIVE* réaliste

reality *NOUN* réalité *FEM*; **reality TV** la télé-réalité

realize *VERB* se rendre [3] compte; **I hadn't realized** je ne m'en étais pas rendu compte, **I didn't realize he was French** je ne me suis pas rendu compte qu'il était français, **do you**

a
b
c
d
e
f
g
h
i
j
k
l
m
n
o
p
q
r
s
t
u
v
w
x
y
z

realize what time it is? tu te rends compte de l'heure qu'il est?

really ADVERB **vraiment**; **not really** pas vraiment, **is it really midnight?** est-il vraiment minuit?, **the film was really good** le film était vraiment très bon, **really?** c'est vrai?

rear NOUN **arrière** MASC

rear ADJECTIVE **arrière**; **the rear door** la porte arrière

reason NOUN **raison** FEM; **the reason for the delay** la raison du retard, **the reason why I phoned** la raison pour laquelle j'ai appelé

reasonable ADJECTIVE **raisonnable**

reassure VERB **rassurer** [1]

reassuring ADJECTIVE **rassurant**

rebel NOUN **rebelle** MASC & FEM

rebellion NOUN **rébellion** FEM, **révolte** FEM

rebuild VERB **reconstruire** [26]

receipt NOUN **reçu** MASC

receive VERB **recevoir** [66]

receiver NOUN **combiné** MASC; **to pick up the receiver** décrocher [1]

recent ADJECTIVE **récent**

recently ADVERB **récemment**

reception NOUN ❶ **réception** FEM; **he's waiting at reception** il attend à la réception, **a big wedding reception** une grande réception de mariage ❷ **to get a good reception** avoir un bon accueil

receptionist NOUN **réceptionniste** MASC & FEM

recipe NOUN **recette** FEM; **can I have the recipe for your salad?** est-ce que je peux prendre la recette de ta salade?

reckon VERB **penser** [1]; **I reckon it's a good idea** je pense que c'est une bonne idée

recognize VERB **reconnaître** [27]

recommend VERB **conseiller** [1]; **can you recommend a dentist?** est-ce que vous pouvez me conseiller un dentiste?, **I recommend the fish soup** je vous conseille la soupe de poisson

recommendation NOUN **recommandation** FEM

record NOUN ❶ **record** MASC; **it's a world record** c'est le record mondial, **record sales for the album** des ventes record pour l'album, **the hottest summer on record** l'été le plus chaud qu'on ait jamais enregistré ❷ **to keep a record of something** noter quelque chose ❸ (music) **disque** MASC; **a Miles Davis record** un disque de Miles Davis ❹ (office files) **dossier** MASC; **I'll just check your records** je vais juste vérifier votre dossier

record VERB (on tape) **enregistrer** [1]; **they're recording a new album** ils sont en train d'enregistrer un nouvel album

recorder NOUN ❶ **flûte** (FEM) **à bec**; **to play the recorder** jouer de la flûte à bec ❷ **a video recorder** un magnétoscope

recording NOUN **enregistrement** MASC

record player NOUN **tourne-disque** MASC

recover VERB se remettre [11]; she's recovered now elle s'est maintenant remise

recovery NOUN (from an illness) rétablissement MASC

recovery vehicle NOUN camion (MASC) de dépannage

rectangle NOUN rectangle MASC

rectangular ADJECTIVE rectangulaire

recycle VERB recycler [1]

recycling NOUN recyclage MASC

red ADJECTIVE ❶ rouge; a red shirt une chemise rouge, a bright red car une voiture rouge vif, to go red rougir [2] ❷ roux (FEM rousse) (hair); to have red hair avoir les cheveux roux

Red Cross NOUN the Red Cross la Croix-Rouge

redcurrant NOUN groseille FEM; redcurrant jelly la gelée de groseilles

redecorate VERB refaire [10]; they've redecorated the kitchen ils ont refait la cuisine

redo VERB refaire [10]

reduce VERB réduire [68]; they've reduced the price ils ont réduit le prix, to reduce speed ralentir [2]

reduction NOUN réduction FEM

redundant ADJECTIVE to be made redundant être licencié

reel NOUN (of cotton) bobine FEM

refer VERB refer to parler [1] de, she's referring to you elle parle de vous

referee NOUN (in sport) arbitre MASC

reference NOUN références FEM PLURAL (for a job); she gave me a good reference elle m'a fourni de bonnes références

reference book NOUN ouvrage (MASC) de référence

refill NOUN recharge FEM

reflect VERB refléter [24]

reflection NOUN ❶ (in a mirror) image FEM ❷ (thought) réflexion FEM; on reflection à la réflexion

reflexive ADJECTIVE a reflexive verb un verbe réfléchi

refreshing ADJECTIVE rafraîchissant

refreshment NOUN rafraîchissement MASC

refrigerator NOUN réfrigérateur MASC

refuge NOUN refuge MASC; a mountain refuge un refuge (de montagne), to take refuge in se réfugier [1] dans

refugee NOUN réfugié MASC, réfugiée FEM

refund NOUN remboursement MASC

refund VERB rembourser [1]

refusal NOUN refus MASC

refuse NOUN (rubbish) ordures FEM PLURAL

refuse VERB refuser [1]; I refused j'ai refusé, he refuses to help il refuse de nous aider

regards PLURAL NOUN amitiés FEM PLURAL; 'regards to your parents' 'mes amitiés à vos parents', Nat sends his regards tu as le bonjour de Nat

reggae NOUN reggae MASC

region NOUN région FEM

regional ADJECTIVE régional MASC (PLURAL régionaux)

register NOUN (in school) cahier (MASC) des absences

register VERB s'inscrire [38]

registered letter NOUN lettre (FEM) recommandée

registration number NOUN numéro (MASC) d'immatriculation (of a vehicle)

regret VERB regretter [1]

regular ADJECTIVE régulier (FEM régulière); **regular visits** des visites régulières

regularly ADVERB régulièrement

regulation NOUN règlement MASC

rehearsal NOUN répétition FEM

rehearse VERB répéter [24]

reheat VERB réchauffer [1]

reign NOUN règne MASC

rein NOUN rêne FEM

reject VERB rejeter [48]

related ADJECTIVE apparenté; **we're not related** nous ne sommes pas apparentés

relation NOUN **my relations** ma famille, **there were just relations and close friends** il n'y avait que la famille et des amis proches, **she's got relations in France** elle a de la famille en France

relationship NOUN relations FEM PLURAL; **we have a good relationship** nous avons de bonnes relations

relative NOUN membre (MASC) de la famille; **there were a few relatives at the funeral** il y avait quelques membres de la famille à l'enterrement, **all my relatives** toute ma famille

relatively ADVERB relativement

relax VERB se détendre [3]; **I'm going to relax and watch telly tonight** je vais me détendre en regardant la télé ce soir

relaxation NOUN détente FEM

relaxed ADJECTIVE détendu

relaxing ADJECTIVE reposant

relay race NOUN course (FEM) de relais

release NOUN ❶ nouveauté FEM; **this week's new releases** les nouveautés de la semaine ❷ (of a prisoner or hostage) libération FEM

release VERB ❶ sortir [72] (a record or a video) ❷ libérer [24] (a person)

relevant ADJECTIVE pertinent

reliable ADJECTIVE fiable

relief NOUN soulagement MASC; **what a relief!** quel soulagement!

relieve VERB soulager [52] (pain)

relieved ADJECTIVE soulagé; **I was relieved to hear you'd arrived** j'ai été soulagé d'apprendre que tu étais arrivé

religion NOUN religion FEM

religious ADJECTIVE ❶ croyant (a person); **Jane's not religious** Jane n'est pas croyante ❷ religieux (FEM religieuse) (art or music, for example)

reluctant *ADJ* réticent; **he's reluctant to go** il est peu disposé à y aller

rely *VERB* **to rely on somebody** compter [1] sur quelqu'un, **I'm relying on you for Saturday** je compte sur toi pour samedi

remain *VERB* rester [1]

remains *PLURAL NOUN* restes *MASC PLURAL*; **the remains of the chicken** les restes du poulet, **the remains of a castle** les restes d'un château

remark *NOUN* remarque *FEM*; **to make remarks about** faire des remarques sur

remarkable *ADJECTIVE* remarquable

remarkably *ADVERB* remarquablement

remember *VERB* ❶ se souvenir [81]; **I don't remember** je ne me souviens plus ❷ **to remember something** se souvenir [81] de quelque chose, **I can't remember the number** je ne me souviens pas du numéro ❸ **to remember to do** ne pas oublier [1] de faire, **remember to shut the door** n'oublie pas de fermer la porte, **I remembered to bring the cakes** je n'ai pas oublié d'apporter les gateaux

remind *VERB* ❶ rappeler [18]; **to remind somebody to do** rappeler à quelqu'un de faire, **remind your mother to pick me up** rappelle à ta mère de venir me chercher ❷ faire [10] penser; **it reminds me of Paris** ça me fait penser à Paris, **he reminds me of Frank** il me fait penser à Frank, **oh, that reminds me ...** tiens, j'y pense ...

remote *ADJECTIVE* isolé

remote control *NOUN* télécommande *FEM*

remove *VERB* enlever [50]; **he removed his jacket** il a enlevé sa veste, **the chairs had all been removed** quelqu'un avait enlevé toutes les chaises

renew *VERB* renouveler [18] *(a passport or licence)*

rent *NOUN* loyer *MASC*

rent *VERB* louer [1]; **Simon's rented a flat** Simon a loué un appartement

rental *NOUN* location *FEM*

reorganize *VERB* réorganiser [1]

repair *NOUN* réparation *FEM*

repair *VERB* réparer [1]; **to get something repaired** faire [10] réparer quelque chose, **we've had the television repaired** nous avons fait réparer la télévision

repay *VERB* rembourser [1]; **he repaid me the money he owed me** il m'a remboursé l'argent qu'il me devait

repeat *NOUN* reprise *FEM (of a programme)*

repeat *VERB* répéter [24]

repeatedly *ADVERB* à plusieurs reprises

repertoire *NOUN* répertoire *MASC*

repetitive *ADJECTIVE* répétitif *(FEM* répétitive)

replace *VERB* remplacer [61]

replacement *NOUN* ❶ *(person)* remplaçant *MASC*, remplaçante *FEM* ❷ *(thing)* **can you find me a replacement?** est-ce que vous pouvez le/la remplacer?

replay VERB ❶ (game) rejouer [1] ❷ (video) repasser [1]

reply NOUN réponse FEM; **I didn't get a reply to my letter** je n'ai pas reçu de réponse à ma lettre, **there's no reply** ça ne répond pas (on the telephone)

reply VERB répondre [3]; **I still haven't replied to the letter** je n'ai toujours pas répondu à la lettre

report NOUN ❶ (of an event) compte rendu MASC ❷ (school report) bulletin (MASC) scolaire

report VERB ❶ signaler [1] (a problem or accident); **we've reported the theft** nous avons signalé le vol ❷ se présenter [1]; **I had to report to reception** je devais me présenter à la réception

reporter NOUN journaliste MASC & FEM

represent VERB représenter [1]

representative NOUN représentant MASC, représentante FEM

reproach NOUN reproche MASC

reproach VERB reprocher [1]

reproduction NOUN reproduction FEM

reptile NOUN reptile MASC

republic NOUN république FEM

reputation NOUN réputation FEM; **a good reputation** une bonne réputation, **she has a reputation for honesty** elle a la réputation d'être honnête

request NOUN demande FEM; **on request** sur demande

request VERB demander [1]

rescue NOUN secours MASC; **to come to somebody's rescue** venir au secours de quelqu'un

rescue VERB sauver [1]; **they rescued the dog** ils ont sauvé le chien

rescue party NOUN équipe (FEM) de secours

rescue worker NOUN secouriste MASC & FEM

research NOUN recherche FEM; **for research into Aids** pour la recherche sur le Sida, **to do research** faire des recherches

research VERB **to research into** faire [10] des recherches sur, **a well-researched programme** un programme bien documenté

resemblance NOUN ressemblance FEM

resemble VERB ressembler [1] à; **she resembles her aunt** elle ressemble à sa tante

reservation NOUN (a booking) réservation FEM; **to make a reservation** faire une réservation

reserve NOUN ❶ réserve FEM; **we have some in reserve** nous en avons en réserve ❷ **a nature reserve** une réserve naturelle ❸ (for a match) remplaçant MASC, remplaçante FEM

reserve VERB réserver [1]; **this table is reserved** cette table est réservée

reservoir NOUN réservoir MASC

resident NOUN résident MASC, résidente FEM

residential ADJECTIVE résidentiel (FEM résidentielle); **a residential area** un quartier résidentiel

resign VERB démissionner [1]

resignation NOUN (from a post) démission FEM

resist VERB résister [1] à (an offer or temptation); **I can't resist!** je ne peux pas résister!

resit VERB repasser [1] (an exam)

resort NOUN ❶ (for holidays) **a holiday resort** un lieu de villégiature, **a ski resort** une station de ski, **a seaside resort** une station balnéaire ❷ **as a last resort** en dernier recours

respect NOUN respect MASC

respect VERB respecter [1]

respectable ADJECTIVE respectable

respectful ADJECTIVE respectueux (FEM respectueuse)

responsibility NOUN responsabilité FEM

responsible ADJECTIVE ❶ (to blame) responsable; **he's responsible for the delay** il est responsable du retard ❷ (in charge) responsable; **I'm responsible for booking the rooms** je suis responsable de la réservation des chambres ❸ (reliable) sérieux (FEM sérieuse); **he's not very responsible** il n'est pas très sérieux

rest NOUN ❶ **the rest** le reste, **the rest of the day** le reste du jour, **the rest of the bread** le reste du pain ❷ (the others) **les autres**; **the rest have gone home** les autres sont rentrés ❸ repos MASC; **ten days' complete rest** dix jours de repos total, **to have a rest** se reposer [1] ❹ (a short break) pause FEM; **to stop for a rest** faire une pause

rest VERB (have a rest) se reposer [1]

restaurant NOUN restaurant MASC

restful ADJECTIVE reposant

restless ADJECTIVE nerveux (FEM nerveuse)

restore VERB restaurer [1]

restrain VERB retenir [77]

restrict VERB limiter [1]

restriction NOUN limitation FEM

result NOUN ❶ résultat MASC; **the exam results** les résultats des examens ❷ **as a result** par conséquent, **as a result we missed the ferry** par conséquent nous avons raté le ferry

retire VERB (from work) prendre [64] sa retraite; **she retires in June** elle prend sa retraite en juin, **for retired people** pour les retraités

retirement NOUN retraite FEM

return NOUN ❶ retour MASC; **the return journey** le voyage de retour, **by return of post** par retour de courrier ❷ **in return** en échange, **in return for his help** en échange de son aide
• **many happy returns!** bon anniversaire!

return VERB ❶ (come back) revenir [81]; **he returned ten minutes later** il est revenu dix minutes plus tard ❷ (get home) rentrer [1]; **to return from holiday** rentrer de vacances, **I'll ask her to phone as soon as she returns** je lui demanderai de vous appeler dès qu'elle rentrera ❸ (to give back) rendre [3]; **Gemma's never returned the video** Gemma n'a jamais rendu la vidéo

return fare NOUN prix (MASC) d'un billet aller-retour

return ticket NOUN billet (MASC) aller-retour

reunion NOUN réunion FEM; **a class reunion** une réunion d'anciens élèves

reveal VERB révéler [24]

revenge NOUN vengeance FEM; **to get one's revenge on someone** se venger [52] de quelqu'un

reverse NOUN ❶ (of a coin) revers MASC ❷ (of a page) dos MASC ❸ (opposite) **the reverse is true** le contraire est vrai ❹ (gear) marche (FEM) arrière

reverse VERB ❶ (in a car) faire [10] marche arrière; **he reversed the car out of the garage** il a sorti la voiture du garage en marche arrière ❷ **to reverse the charges** faire [10] un appel en PCV

review NOUN (of a book, play, or film) critique FEM

review VERB faire [10] la critique de (a play or concert); **the film was well reviewed** le film a eu une bonne critique

revise VERB réviser [1]; **Tessa's busy revising for her exams** Tessa est en train de réviser pour ses examens

revision NOUN révision FEM

revive VERB ranimer [1]

revolting ADJECTIVE infect; **the sausages are revolting** les saucisses sont infectes

revolution NOUN révolution FEM; **the Fench Revolution** la Révolution française

revolving door NOUN porte (FEM) à tambour

reward NOUN récompense FEM; **a £100 reward** cent livres de récompense

reward VERB récompenser [1]

rewarding ADJECTIVE enrichissant

rewind VERB rembobiner [1] (a video)

rhinoceros NOUN rhinocéros MASC

rhubarb NOUN rhubarbe FEM

rhyme NOUN rime FEM

rhythm NOUN rythme MASC

rib NOUN côte FEM

ribbon NOUN ruban MASC

rice NOUN riz MASC; **chicken and rice** du poulet au riz, **rice pudding** le riz au lait

rich ADJECTIVE riche; **we're not very rich** nous ne sommes pas très riches, **the rich and the poor** les riches et les pauvres

rid ADJECTIVE **to get rid of something** se débarrasser de quelque chose, **we got rid of the car** nous nous sommes débarrassés de la voiture

riddle NOUN devinette FEM

ride NOUN tour MASC; **to go for a ride (on a bike)** faire [10] un tour à vélo, **to go for a ride (on a horse)** faire une promenade à cheval

ride VERB ❶ **to learn to ride a bike** apprendre [64] à faire du vélo, **can you ride a bike?** sais-tu faire du vélo? ❷ **to learn to ride (a horse)** apprendre [64] à monter à cheval, **I've never ridden a horse** je ne suis jamais monté à cheval

rider NOUN ❶ (on a horse) **cavalier** MASC, **cavalière** FEM ❷ (on a bike) **cycliste** MASC & FEM ❸ (on a motorbike) **motocycliste** MASC & FEM

ridiculous ADJECTIVE **ridicule**

riding NOUN **équitation** FEM; **to go riding** faire [10] de l'équitation

riding school NOUN **école** (FEM) **d'équitation**

rifle NOUN **fusil** MASC

right NOUN ❶ (not left) **droite** FEM; **on the right** à droite, **on my right** à ma droite MASC; **the right to strike** le droit de grève, **you have no right to say that** tu n'as pas le droit de dire ça

right ADJECTIVE ❶ (not left) **droit**; **my right hand** ma main droite ❷ (correct) **bon** (FEM **bonne**); **the right answer** la bonne réponse, **the right telephone number** le bon numéro de téléphone, **the right amount of** la bonne quantité de, **is this the right address?** est-ce que c'est la bonne adresse? ❸ **to be right** (a person) avoir [5] raison, **you see, I was right** tu vois, j'avais raison ❹ **you were right to stay at home** tu as bien fait de rester chez toi, **he was right not to say anything** il a bien fait de ne rien dire ❺ (moral) **bien**; **it's not right to talk like that** ce n'est pas bien de parler comme ça

right ADVERB ❶ (direction) **à droite**; **turn right at the lights** tournez à droite aux feux ❷ (correctly) **comme il faut**; **you're not doing it right** tu ne le fais pas comme il faut ❸ (completely) **tout**; **right at the bottom** tout au fond, **right at the beginning** tout au début, **right now** tout de suite, **right in**

the middle en plein milieu ❹ (okay) **bon**; **right, let's go** bon, allons-y

right-click NOUN **clic** (MASC) **sur le bouton droit de la souris**

right-hand ADJECTIVE **on the right-hand side** à droite

right-handed ADJECTIVE **droitier** (FEM **droitière**)

rind NOUN ❶ (on fruit) **peau** FEM ❷ (on cheese) **croûte** FEM

ring NOUN ❶ (on the phone) **to give somebody a ring** appeler [18] quelqu'un ❷ (for your finger) **bague** FEM ❸ (circle) **cercle** MASC ❹ **there was a ring at the door** on a sonné à la porte

ring VERB ❶ (a bell or phone) **sonner** [1]; **the phone rang** le téléphone a sonné ❷ (phone) **appeler** [18]; **I'll ring you tomorrow** je t'appellerai demain, **could you ring for a taxi?** est-ce que tu peux appeler un taxi?
- **to ring back** rappeler [18]; **I'll ring you back later** je te rappellerai tout à l'heure
- **to ring off** raccrocher [1]

ring road NOUN **rocade** FEM

rinse VERB **rincer** [61]

riot NOUN **émeute** FEM

rioting NOUN **émeutes** FEM PLURAL

rip VERB **déchirer** [1]

ripe ADJECTIVE **mûr**; **are the tomatoes ripe?** est-ce que les tomates sont mûres?

rip-off NOUN **it's a rip-off!** c'est de l'arnaque!

rise NOUN ❶ **hausse** FEM; **a rise in price** une hausse de prix ❷ **a pay rise** une augmentation

rise VERB ❶ *(the sun)* se lever [50]; **when the sun rose** quand le soleil s'est levé ❷ *(prices)* augmenter [1]

risk NOUN risque MASC; **to take risks** prendre des risques

risk VERB risquer [1]; **he risks losing his job** il risque de perdre son emploi

rival NOUN rival MASC *(PLURAL* rivaux*)*, rivale FEM

river NOUN ❶ rivière FEM; **we picnicked on the edge of a river** nous avons pique-niqué au bord d'une rivière ❷ fleuve MASC; **the rivers of Europe** les fleuves de l'Europe *('fleuve' is only used for a river which flows directly into the sea like the Thames in Britain or the Seine in France)*

Riviera NOUN **the French Riviera** la Côte d'Azur

road NOUN ❶ route FEM; **the road to London** la route de Londres ❷ *(in a town)* rue FEM; **the butcher's is on the other side of the road** la boucherie est de l'autre côté de la rue ❸ **across the road** en face, **they live across the road from us** ils habitent en face de chez nous

road accident NOUN accident *(MASC)* de la route

road map NOUN carte *(FEM)* routière

roadside NOUN **by the roadside** au bord de la route

road sign NOUN panneau *(MASC)* de signalisation *(PLURAL* panneaux de signalisation*)*

roadworks PLURAL NOUN travaux MASC PLURAL

roast NOUN rôti MASC

roast ADJECTIVE rôti; **roast potatoes** les pommes de terre rôties, **roast beef** le rôti de bœuf

rob VERB ❶ voler [1] *(a person)* ❷ dévaliser [1] *(a bank)*

robber NOUN voleur MASC, voleuse FEM

robbery NOUN vol MASC; **a bank robbery** un hold-up

robot NOUN robot MASC

rock NOUN ❶ *(a big stone)* rocher MASC; **she was sitting on a rock** elle était assise sur un rocher ❷ *(the material)* roche FEM ❸ *(music)* rock MASC; **a rock band** un groupe de rock, **to dance rock and roll** danser le rock

rock climbing NOUN escalade FEM; **to go rock climbing** faire de l'escalade

rocket NOUN fusée FEM

rocking horse NOUN cheval *(MASC)* à bascule

rock star NOUN rock-star FEM

rocky ADJECTIVE rocailleux *(FEM* rocailleuse*)*

rod NOUN **a fishing rod** une canne à pêche

role NOUN rôle MASC; **to play the role of** jouer le rôle de

roll NOUN ❶ rouleau MASC *(PLURAL* rouleaux*)*; **a roll of fabric** un rouleau de tissu, **a roll of sellotape** un rouleau de scotch, **a toilet roll** un rouleau de papier hygiénique ❷ **a bread roll** un petit pain

roll VERB rouler [1]
- **to roll something up ❶** rouler [1] (*a carpet*) **❷** retrousser [1] (*sleeves*); **he rolled up his sleeves** il a retroussé ses manches

roller NOUN rouleau MASC (PLURAL rouleaux)

rollerblades PLURAL NOUN rollers MASC PLURAL

rollercoaster NOUN montagnes (FEM PLURAL) russes (literally: Russian mountains)

roller skates PLURAL NOUN patins (MASC PLURAL) à roulettes

Roman Catholic NOUN, ADJECTIVE catholique MASC & FEM

romantic ADJECTIVE romantique

roof NOUN toit MASC

roof rack NOUN galerie FEM

rook NOUN **❶** (in chess) tour FEM **❷** (bird) freux MASC

room NOUN **❶** pièce FEM; **she's in the other room** elle est dans l'autre pièce, **it's the biggest room in the house** c'est la pièce la plus grande de la maison, **a three-room flat** un appartement à trois pièces **❷** (a bedroom) chambre FEM; **Freda's in her room** Freda est dans sa chambre, **I tidied my room last night** j'ai rangé ma chambre hier soir **❸** (space) place FEM; **enough room for two** assez de place pour deux, **very little room** très peu de place

roommate NOUN camarade (MASC & FEM) de chambre

root NOUN racine FEM

rope NOUN corde FEM

rose NOUN rose FEM

rosebush NOUN rosier MASC

rot VERB pourrir [2]

rota NOUN tableau (MASC) de service

rotten ADJECTIVE pourri

rough ADJECTIVE **❶** (scratchy) rugueux (FEM rugueuse) **❷** (vague) approximatif (FEM approximative); **a rough idea** une idée approximative **❸** (stormy) agité; **a rough sea** une mer agitée, **in rough weather** par gros temps **❹** (difficult) **to have a rough time** passer par une période dificile **❺** **to sleep rough** dormir à la dure

roughly ADJECTIVE (approximately) **roughly ten per cent** à peu près dix pour cent, **it takes roughly three hours** ça prend à peu près trois heures

round NOUN **❶** (in a tournament) manche FEM **❷** (of cards) partie FEM **❸** **a round of drinks** une tournée, **it's my round** c'est ma tournée

round ADJECTIVE rond; **a round table** une table ronde

round PREPOSITION **❶** autour de; **round the city** autour de la ville, **round my arm** autour de mon bras, **they were sitting round the table** ils étaient assis autour de la table **❷** **to go round the shops** faire les magasins, **to go round a museum** visiter un musée, **it's just round the corner** c'est tout près

round ADVERB ❶ to go round to somebody's house aller chez quelqu'un, **we invited Sally round for lunch** nous avons invité Sally à déjeuner ❷ **all the year round** toute l'année

roundabout NOUN ❶ (for traffic) **rond-point** MASC ❷ (in a fairground) **manège** MASC

route NOUN ❶ (that you plan) **itinéraire** MASC; **the best route is via Calais** le meilleur itinéraire est par Calais ❷ **a bus route** un parcours de bus

routine NOUN **routine** FEM

row[1] NOUN ❶ **rang** MASC; **in the front row** au premier rang, **in the back row** au dernier rang ❷ **rangée** FEM; **a row of books** une rangée de livres ❸ **four times in a row** quatre fois de suite

row[2] VERB (in a boat) **ramer** [1]; **it's your turn to row** c'est à toi de ramer, **we rowed across the lake** nous avons traversé le lac à la rame

row[3] NOUN ❶ (a quarrel) **dispute** FEM; **to have a row** se disputer, **they've had a row** ils se sont disputés, **I had a row with my parents** je me suis disputé avec mes parents ❷ (noise) **vacarme** MASC; **they were making a terrible row!** ils faisaient un vacarme pas possible!

rowing NOUN **aviron** MASC; **to go rowing** faire [10] de l'aviron

rowing boat NOUN **barque** FEM

royal ADJECTIVE **royal** MASC (PLURAL **royaux**); **the royal family** la famille royale

rub VERB **frotter** [1]; **to rub your eyes** se frotter les yeux
• **to rub something out** effacer [61] quelque chose

rubber NOUN ❶ (an eraser) **gomme** FEM ❷ (material) **caoutchouc** MASC; **rubber soles** des semelles en caoutchouc

rubbish NOUN ❶ (for the bin) **ordures** FEM PLURAL ❷ (nonsense) **bêtises** FEM PLURAL; **you're talking rubbish!** tu dis des bêtises!

rubbish ADJECTIVE **nul** (FEM **nulle**); **the film was rubbish** le film était nul, **they're a rubbish band** c'est un groupe nul

rubbish bin NOUN **poubelle** FEM

rucksack NOUN **sac** (MASC) **à dos**

rude ADJECTIVE ❶ **impoli**; **that's rude** c'est impoli ❷ **a rude joke** une plaisanterie grossière, **a rude word** un gros mot

rug NOUN ❶ **tapis** MASC ❷ (a blanket) **couverture** FEM

rugby NOUN **rugby** MASC; **to play rugby** jouer au rugby, **a rugby match** un match de rugby

ruin NOUN **ruine** FEM; **in ruins** en ruines

ruin VERB ❶ **abîmer** [1]; **you'll ruin your jacket** tu vas abîmer ta veste ❷ **gâcher** [1] (day, holiday); **it ruined my evening** ça m'a gâché la soirée

rule NOUN ❶ **règle** FEM; **the rules of the game** les règles du jeu ❷ **the school rules** le règlement de l'école ❸ **as a rule** en général

ruler NOUN règle FEM; **I've lost my ruler** j'ai perdu ma règle

rum NOUN rhum MASC

rumour NOUN rumeur FEM

run NOUN ❶ to go for a run courir [29] ❷ (in cricket) point MASC; **to score fifteen runs** marquer quinze points ❸ in the long run à long terme

run VERB ❶ courir [29]; **I ran ten kilometres** j'ai couru dix kilomètres, **he ran across the pitch** il a traversé le terrain en courant, **Kitty ran for the bus** Kitty a couru pour attraper le bus ❷ (organize) organiser [1]; **who's running this concert?** qui est-ce qui organise ce concert? ❸ diriger [52] (a business); **he ran the firm for forty years** il a dirigé l'entreprise pendant quarante ans ❹ (a train or bus) circuler [1]; **the buses don't run on Sundays** les bus ne circulent pas le dimanche ❺ to run a bath faire [10] couler un bain

- to run away s'enfuir [44]
- to run into rentrer [1] dans; **the car ran into a lamppost** la voiture est rentrée dans un réverbère
- to run out of something we've run out of bread il ne reste plus de pain, **I'm running out of money** je n'ai presque plus d'argent
- to run somebody over écraser [1] quelqu'un; **you'll get run over!** tu vas te faire écraser!

runner NOUN coureur MASC, coureuse FEM

runner-up NOUN second MASC, seconde FEM

running NOUN (for exercise) course FEM

running ADJECTIVE ❶ running water l'eau courante ❷ three days running trois jours de suite, **six times running** six fois de suite

runway NOUN piste FEM

rush NOUN (a hurry) to be in a rush être pressé, **sorry, I'm in a rush** désolé, je suis pressé

rush VERB ❶ (hurry) se dépêcher [1]; **I must rush!** il faut que je me dépêche! ❷ (run) se précipiter [1]; **she rushed into the street** elle s'est précipitée dans la rue ❸ Louise was rushed to hospital on a emmené Louise d'urgence à l'hôpital

rush hour NOUN heures (FEM PLURAL) de pointe; **in the rush hour** aux heures de pointe

Russia NOUN Russie FEM; **in Russia** en Russie

Russian NOUN ❶ (a person) Russe MASC & FEM ❷ (the language) russe MASC

Russian ADJECTIVE russe

rust NOUN rouille FEM

rusty ADJECTIVE rouillé

rye NOUN seigle MASC

a
b
c
d
e
f
g
h
i
j
k
l
m
n
o
p
q
r
s
t
u
v
w
x
y
z

English–French

Ss

Sabbath NOUN ❶ (Jewish) sabbat MASC ❷ (Christian) dimanche MASC

sack NOUN ❶ sac MASC ❷ to get the sack être mis à la porte

sack VERB to sack somebody mettre [11] quelqu'un à la porte

sacred ADJECTIVE sacré

sacrifice NOUN sacrifice MASC

sad ADJECTIVE triste

saddle NOUN selle FEM

saddlebag NOUN sacoche FEM

sadly ADVERB ❶ tristement; she looked at me sadly elle m'a regardé tristement ❷ (unfortunately) malheureusement

safe ADJECTIVE ❶ (out of danger) hors de danger; to feel safe se sentir en sécurité ❷ (not dangerous) pas dangereux (FEM pas dangereuse); the path is safe le sentier n'est pas dangereux, it's not safe c'est dangereux

safety NOUN sécurité FEM

safety belt NOUN ceinture (FEM) de sécurité

safety pin NOUN épingle (FEM) de nourrice

Sagittarius NOUN Sagittaire MASC; Kylie's Sagittarius Kylie est Sagittaire

sail NOUN voile FEM

sailing NOUN voile FEM; to go sailing faire [10] de la voile, she does a lot of sailing elle fait beaucoup de voile

sailing boat NOUN voilier MASC

sailor NOUN marin MASC

saint NOUN saint MASC, sainte FEM

sake NOUN ❶ for your mother's sake par égard pour ta mère ❷ for heaven's sake nom de Dieu!

salad NOUN salade FEM; a tomato salad une salade de tomates

salad dressing NOUN vinaigrette FEM

salami NOUN saucisson MASC

salary NOUN salaire MASC

sale NOUN ❶ (selling) vente FEM; the sale of the house la vente de la maison, 'for sale' à vendre ❷ the sales les soldes FEM PLURAL, I bought it in the sales je l'ai acheté en solde

sales assistant NOUN vendeur MASC, vendeuse FEM

salesman NOUN représentant MASC; he's a salesman il est représentant

saleswoman NOUN représentante FEM

saliva NOUN salive FEM

salmon NOUN saumon MASC

salt NOUN sel MASC

salty ADJECTIVE salé

Salvation Army NOUN armée (FEM) du Salut

same ADJECTIVE ❶ même; she said the same thing elle a dit la même chose, her birthday's the same day as mine son anniversaire est le même jour que le mien, **at the same time** en même temps, **their car's the same as ours** ils ont la même voiture que nous ❷ **the same** *(after verb)* pareil, **the two bikes are not the same** les deux vélos ne sont pas pareils, **it's not the same** ce n'est pas pareil

sample NOUN échantillon MASC; **a free sample** un échantillon gratuit

sand NOUN sable MASC

sandal NOUN sandale FEM; **a pair of sandals** une paire de sandales

sand castle NOUN château *(MASC)* de sable *(PLURAL* châteaux de sable)

sandpaper NOUN papier *(MASC)* de verre

sandwich NOUN sandwich MASC; **a ham sandwich** un sandwich au jambon

sanitary towel NOUN serviette *(FEM)* hygiénique

Santa Claus NOUN le père Noël

sarcasm NOUN sarcasme MASC

sarcastic ADJECTIVE sarcastique

sardine NOUN sardine FEM

SARS NOUN pneumopathie *(FEM)* atypique

satchel NOUN cartable MASC

satellite NOUN satellite MASC

satellite dish NOUN antenne *(FEM)* parabolique

satellite television NOUN télévision *(FEM)* par satellite

satisfactory ADJECTIVE satisfaisant

satisfied ADJECTIVE satisfait

satisfy VERB satisfaire [10]

satisfying ADJECTIVE ❶ *(pleasing)* satisfaisant ❷ **a satisfying meal** un repas consistant

Saturday NOUN samedi MASC; **on Saturday** samedi, **I'm going out on Saturday** je sors samedi, **see you on Saturday!** à samedi, **on Saturdays** le samedi, **the museum is closed on Saturdays** le musée est fermé le samedi, **every Saturday** tous les samedis, **last Saturday** samedi dernier, **next Saturday** samedi prochain, **to have a Saturday job** travailler le samedi

sauce NOUN sauce FEM

saucepan NOUN casserole FEM

saucer NOUN soucoupe FEM

sausage NOUN ❶ saucisse FEM ❷ *(salami)* saucisson MASC

savage NOUN sauvage MASC & FEM

save VERB ❶ *(rescue)* sauver [1]; **to save somebody's life** sauver la vie à quelqu'un, **the doctors saved his life** les médecins lui ont sauvé la vie ❷ mettre [11] de côté *(money, food)*; **I've saved £60** j'ai mis soixante livres de côté ❸ *(avoid spending)* économiser [1]; **I walk to school to save money** je vais à l'école à pied pour économiser de l'argent ❹ **to save time** gagner [1] du temps, **we'll take a taxi to save time** on va prendre un taxi pour gagner du temps ❺ *(on a computer)* sauvegarder [1]
- **to save up** mettre [11] de l'argent de côté; **I'm saving up to go to Spain** je mets de l'argent de côté pour aller en Espagne

savings PLURAL NOUN **économies** FEM
PLURAL; **I've spent all my savings** j'ai
dépensé toutes mes économies

savoury ADJECTIVE **salé**; **I prefer
savoury things to sweet things**
j'aime mieux les choses salées que
les choses sucrées

saw NOUN **scie** FEM

sawdust NOUN **sciure** FEM

sax NOUN **saxo** MASC (informal); **to play
the sax** jouer du saxo

saxophone NOUN **saxophone** MASC;
to play the saxophone jouer du
saxophone

say VERB ❶ **dire** [9]; **what did you
say?** qu'est-ce que tu as dit?, **she
says she's tired** elle dit qu'elle est
fatiguée, **he said to wait here** il
a dit d'attendre ici, **as they say**
comme on dit, **that goes without
saying** cela va sans dire ❷ **to say
something again** répéter [24]
quelque chose

saying NOUN **dicton** MASC; **as the
saying goes** comme on dit

scab NOUN **croûte** FEM

scale NOUN ❶ (of a map or model)
échelle FEM; **large-scale** à grande
échelle ❷ (extent) **ampleur** FEM;
the scale of the disaster l'ampleur
du désastre ❸ (in music) **gamme**
FEM ❹ (of a fish) **écaille** FEM

scales NOUN ❶ **balance** FEM SINGULAR;
kitchen scales une balance de
cuisine ❷ **bathroom scales** un pèse-
personne MASC SINGULAR

scallop NOUN **coquille** (FEM) Saint-
Jacques

scalp NOUN **cuir** (MASC) **chevelu**

scandal NOUN ❶ **scandale**
MASC ❷ (gossip) **ragots** MASC PLURAL

Scandinavia NOUN **Scandinavie** FEM

Scandinavian ADJECTIVE **scandinave**

scanner NOUN **scanner** MASC

scar NOUN **cicatrice** FEM

scarce ADJECTIVE **rare**

scarcely ADVERB **à peine**

scare NOUN ❶ **panique** FEM; **it caused
a scare** cela a provoqué une
panique ❷ **a bomb scare** une alerte
à la bombe

scare VERB **to scare somebody** faire
[10] peur à quelqu'un, **you scared
me!** tu m'as fait peur!

scarecrow NOUN **épouvantail** MASC

scared ADJECTIVE **to be scared** avoir
[5] peur, **I'm scared!** j'ai peur, **to
be scared of** avoir [5] peur de, **he's
scared of dogs** il a peur des chiens,
I'm scared of falling j'ai peur de
tomber

scarf NOUN ❶ (silky) **foulard**
MASC ❷ (long, warm) **écharpe** FEM

scary ADJECTIVE **effrayant**

scene NOUN ❶ (of an incident or a
crime) **lieux** MASC PLURAL; **to be
on the scene** être sur les lieux,
the scene of the crime le lieu du
crime ❷ (world) **monde** MASC; **on
the music scene** dans le monde de
la musique ❸ **scenes of violence**
des incidents violents ❹ **to make a
scene** faire une scène

scenery NOUN ❶ (landscape) **paysage**
MASC ❷ (theatrical) **décors** MASC
PLURAL

scent NOUN parfum MASC

scented ADJECTIVE parfumé

schedule NOUN programme MASC

scheduled flight NOUN vol (MASC) régulier

scheme NOUN projet MASC

scholarship NOUN bourse FEM

school NOUN école FEM; **at school** à l'école, **to go to school** aller à l'école

schoolbook NOUN livre (MASC) scolaire

schoolboy NOUN écolier MASC

schoolchildren PLURAL NOUN écoliers MASC PLURAL

schoolfriend NOUN camarade (MASC & FEM) de classe

schoolgirl NOUN écolière FEM

science NOUN science FEM; **I like science** j'aime la science, **the science teacher** le prof des sciences

science fiction NOUN science-fiction FEM

scientific ADJECTIVE scientifique

scientist NOUN scientifique MASC & FEM

scissors PLURAL NOUN ciseaux MASC PLURAL; **a pair of scissors** une paire de ciseaux

scoff VERB (eat) bouffer [1] (informal)

scoop NOUN ❶ (utensil) cuillère (FEM) à glace ❷ (content) boule FEM; **how many scoops would you like?** vous voulez combien de boules?

scooter NOUN ❶ (motor scooter) scooter MASC ❷ (for a child) trottinette FEM

score NOUN score MASC; **the score was three two** le score était trois à deux

score VERB ❶ marquer [1]; **Lenny scored a goal** Lenny a marqué un but, **I scored three points** j'ai marqué trois points ❷ (keep score) compter [1] les points

Scorpio NOUN Scorpion MASC; **Jess is Scorpio** Jess est Scorpion

Scot NOUN Écossais MASC, Écossaise FEM; **the Scots** les Écossais MASC PLURAL

Scotland NOUN Écosse FEM; **in Scotland** en Écosse, **to Scotland** en Écosse, **Pauline's from Scotland** Pauline est écossaise

Scots ADJECTIVE écossais; **a Scots accent** un accent écossais

Scotsman NOUN Écossais MASC

Scotswoman NOUN Écossaise FEM

Scottish ADJECTIVE écossais; **a Scottish accent** un accent écossais

scout NOUN scout MASC

scrambled eggs NOUN œufs (MASC PLURAL) brouillés

scrap NOUN **a scrap of paper** un bout de papier

scrapbook NOUN album MASC

scrape VERB gratter [1]

scratch NOUN ❶ (on your skin) égratignure FEM ❷ (on a surface) rayure FEM
• **to start from scratch** partir de zéro

scratch VERB (scratch yourself) se gratter [1]; **to scratch your head** se gratter la tête

scream NOUN cri MASC

A
B
C
D
E
F
G
H
I
J
K
L
M
N
O
P
Q
R
S
T
U
V
W
X
Y
Z

scream VERB crier [1]

screen NOUN écran MASC; **on the screen** à l'écran

screw NOUN vis FEM

screw VERB visser [1]

screwdriver NOUN tournevis MASC

scribble VERB griffonner [1]

scrub VERB récurer [1] (a saucepan); **to scrub your nails** se brosser [1] les ongles

scuba diving NOUN plongée (FEM) sous-marine

sculptor NOUN sculpteur MASC, sculpteuse FEM; **Rebecca's a sculptor** Rebecca est sculpteur

sculpture NOUN sculpture FEM

sea NOUN mer FEM

seafood NOUN fruits (MASC PLURAL) de mer; **I love seafood** j'adore les fruits de mer

seagull NOUN mouette FEM

seal NOUN (animal) phoque MASC

seal VERB coller [1] (envelope)

seaman NOUN marin MASC

search VERB ❶ fouiller [1]; **I've searched my desk but I can't find the letter** j'ai fouillé dans mon bureau mais je ne trouve pas la lettre, **the police searched the house/the room** la police a fouillé la maison/la chambre ❷ **to search for** chercher [1], **I've been searching everywhere for the scissors** j'ai cherché les ciseaux partout

search NOUN fouille FEM

seashell NOUN coquillage MASC

seasick ADJECTIVE **to be seasick** avoir le mal de mer

seaside NOUN **at the seaside** au bord de la mer

season NOUN saison FEM; **the rugby season** la saison de rugby, **strawberries are not in season at the moment** ce n'est pas la saison des fraises en ce moment, **off-season prices** des prix hors saison

season ticket NOUN carte (FEM) d'abonnement

seat NOUN ❶ siège MASC; (in a car) **the front seat** le siège avant, **the back seat** le siège arrière, **take a seat** assieds-toi ❷ (in a cinema, theatre, etc) place FEM; **to book a seat** réserver une place, **can you keep my seat?** est-ce que tu peux garder ma place?

seatbelt NOUN ceinture (FEM) de sécurité

seaweed NOUN algues FEM PLURAL

second NOUN seconde FEM; **can you wait a second?** est-ce que tu peux attendre une seconde?

second ADJECTIVE ❶ deuxième; **for the second time** pour la deuxième fois ❷ **the second of July** le deux juillet

secondary school NOUN ❶ collège MASC (up to the end of the equivalent of Year 10) ❷ lycée MASC (for the equivalent of Years 11 to 13)

second class NOUN (category) deuxième classe FEM; **a second class team** une équipe de niveau très moyen

secondhand ADJECTIVE, ADVERB
d'occasion; **a secondhand bike**
un vélo d'occasion, **I bought
it secondhand** je l'ai acheté
d'occasion

secondly ADVERB deuxièmement

secret NOUN secret MASC; **to keep a
secret** garder un secret, **in secret**
en secret

secret ADJECTIVE secret (FEM secrète);
a secret plan un projet secret

secretarial college NOUN école
(FEM) de secrétariat

secretary NOUN secrétaire MASC
& FEM; **she's a secretary** elle est
secrétaire, **the secretary's office**
le secrétariat

secretly ADVERB secrètement

sect NOUN secte FEM

section NOUN section FEM

security NOUN sécurité FEM

security guard NOUN vigile MASC;
he's a security guard il est vigile

see VERB ❶ voir [13]; **I saw Lindy
yesterday** j'ai vu Lindy hier, **have
you seen the film?** est-ce que tu
as vu le film?, **I haven't see her for
ages** ça fait une éternité que je ne
l'ai pas vue, **I'll see what I can do** je
vais voir ce que je peux faire ❷ **to
be able to see** voir [13], **I can't
see anything** je ne vois rien ❸ **see
you!** salut!, **see you on Saturday!** à
samedi!, **see you soon!** à bientôt!
• **to see to something** s'occuper [1]
de quelque chose; **Jo's seeing to the
drinks** Jo s'occupe des boissons

seed NOUN graine FEM; **to plant seeds**
semer des graines

seem VERB ❶ paraître [57]; **it seems
odd to me** ça me paraît bizarre,
it seems he's left il paraît qu'il est
parti ❷ (look, appear to be) avoir
[5] l'air; **he seems a bit shy** il a l'air
un peu timide, **the museum seems
to be closed** le musée a l'air d'être
fermé

seesaw NOUN tapecul MASC

select VERB sélectionner [1]

selection NOUN sélection FEM

self-confidence NOUN confiance
(FEM) en soi; **she doesn't have
much self-confidence** elle n'a pas
beaucoup de confiance en elle

self-confident ADJECTIVE plein
d'assurance; **he's very self-
confident** il est très sûr de lui

self-conscious ADJECTIVE timide

self-contained NOUN **a self-
contained flat** un appartement
indépendant

self-employed NOUN **the self-
employed** les travailleurs
indépendants MASC PLURAL

self-employed ADJECTIVE **to be self-
employed** travailler à son compte,
my parents are self-employed mes
parents travaillent à leur compte

selfish ADJECTIVE égoïste

self-service ADJECTIVE **a self-service
restaurant** un self (informal)

sell VERB vendre [3]; **to sell
something to somebody** vendre
quelque chose à quelqu'un, **I sold
him my bike** je lui ai vendu mon
vélo, **the house has been sold** la
maison a été vendue, **the concert's
sold out** il ne reste plus de billets
pour le concert

sell-by date NOUN date (FEM) limite de vente

seller NOUN vendeur MASC, vendeuse FEM

Sellotape NOUN Scotch MASC

Sellotape VERB to sellotape something scotcher [1] quelque chose (informal)

semi NOUN maison (FEM) jumelée (literally: a twinned house); we live in a semi nous habitons dans une maison jumelée

semicircle NOUN demi-cercle MASC

semicolon NOUN point-virgule MASC

semi-detached house NOUN maison (FEM) jumelée (literally: a twinned house); we live in a semi-detached house nous habitons dans une maison jumelée

semi-final NOUN demi-finale FEM

semi-skimmed milk NOUN lait (MASC) demi-écrémé

send VERB envoyer [40]; to send something to somebody envoyer quelque chose à quelqu'un, I sent her a present for her birthday je lui ai envoyé un cadeau pour son anniversaire
• to send back to send somebody back renvoyer [40] quelqu'un, to send something back renvoyer [40] quelque chose

sender NOUN expéditeur MASC, expéditrice FEM

senior citizen NOUN personne (FEM) du troisième âge

sensation NOUN ❶ (feeling) sensation FEM ❷ (impact) sensation FEM; she caused a sensation elle a fait sensation

sensational ADJECTIVE sensationnel (FEM sensationnelle)

sense NOUN ❶ sens MASC; common sense le bon sens, it doesn't make sense ça n'a pas de sens, it makes sense ça paraît logique, to have a sense of humour avoir le sens de l'humour, she has no sense of humour elle n'a aucun sens de l'humour ❷ the sense of smell l'odorat MASC, the sense of touch le toucher

sensible ADJECTIVE raisonnable; she's very sensible elle est très raisonnable, it's a sensible decision c'est une décision raisonnable

sensitive ADJECTIVE sensible; for sensitive skin pour peaux sensibles

sentence NOUN ❶ phrase FEM; écris une phrase en français write a sentence in French ❷ the death sentence la peine de mort

sentence VERB condamner [1]; to be sentenced to death être condamné à mort

sentimental ADJECTIVE sentimental (MASC PLURAL sentimentaux)

separate ADJECTIVE ❶ à part; in a separate pile dans une pile à part, on a separate sheet of paper sur une feuille à part ❷ (different) autre; that's a separate problem c'est un autre problème ❸ they have separate rooms ils ont chacun leur chambre

separate VERB ❶ séparer [1] ❷ (a couple) se séparer [1]

separately ADVERB séparément

separation NOUN séparation FEM

September NOUN septembre MASC; in September en septembre

sequel NOUN **suite** FEM

sequence NOUN ❶ **série** FEM; **a sequence of events** une série d'événements ❷ **in sequence** dans l'ordre ❸ *(in a film)* **séquence** FEM

sergeant NOUN ❶ *(in the police)* **brigadier** MASC ❷ *(in the army)* **sergent** MASC

serial NOUN **feuilleton** MASC

series NOUN **série** FEM; **a television series** une série télévisée

serious ADJECTIVE ❶ **sérieux** *(FEM sérieuse)*; **a serious discussion** une discussion sérieuse, **are you serious?** sérieusement? ❷ **grave** *(illness, injury, mistake, problem)*; **we have a serious problem** nous avons un grave problème

seriously ADVERB ❶ **sérieusement**; **seriously, I have to go now** sérieusement je dois partir maintenant, **seriously?** vraiment? ❷ **to take somebody seriously** prendre quelqu'un au sérieux ❸ **gravement** *(ill, injured)*; **she is seriously ill** elle est gravement malade

servant NOUN **domestique** MASC & FEM

serve NOUN *(in tennis)* **service** MASC; **it's my serve** c'est à moi de servir

serve VERB ❶ *(in tennis)* **servir** [71] ❷ **servir**; **can you serve the vegetables, please?** est-ce que tu peux servir les légumes, s'il te plaît?, **they served the fish with a lemon sauce** ils ont servi le poisson accompagné d'une sauce au citron
• **it serves him right** c'est bien fait pour lui

service NOUN ❶ *(in a restaurant, from a company, etc)* **service** MASC; **the service is very slow** le service est très lent, **service is included** le service est compris, **is there a maid service?** est-ce qu'il y a une femme de ménage? ❷ **the emergency services** les services des urgences ❸ *(church service)* **office** MASC ❹ *(of a car or machine)* **révision** FEM

service VERB **réviser** [1] *(a car or a machine)*

service area NOUN **aire** *(FEM)* **de services**

service charge NOUN **service** MASC; **what is the service charge?** le service est de combien?, **there is no service charge** le service est compris

service station NOUN **station-service** FEM *(PLURAL stations-service)*

serviette NOUN **serviette** FEM

session NOUN **séance** FEM

set NOUN ❶ *(for playing a game)* **jeu** MASC *(PLURAL* **jeux***)*; **a chess set** un jeu d'échecs ❷ **a train set** un petit train ❸ *(in tennis)* **set** MASC

set ADJECTIVE **fixe**; **at a set time** à une heure fixe, **a set menu** un menu fixe

set VERB ❶ **fixer** [1] *(date, time)* ❷ **établir** [2] *(record)* ❸ **to set the table** mettre [11] la table, **to set an alarm clock** mettre [11] un réveil, **I've set my alarm for seven** j'ai mis mon réveil à sept heures ❹ **to set a watch** régler [24] une montre ❺ *(sun)* **se coucher** [1]
• **to set off** partir [58]; **we're setting off at ten** nous allons partir à dix heures, **they set off for Paris yesterday** ils sont partis pour Paris hier

- to set off something ❶ faire [10] partir *(firework)* ❷ faire [10] exploser *(bomb)* ❸ déclencher [1] *(alarm)*
- to set out partir [58]; **they set out for Paris yesterday** ils sont partis pour Paris hier

settee NOUN canapé MASC

settle VERB régler [24] *(a bill or a problem)*

seven NUMBER sept; **Rosie's seven** Rosie a sept ans

seventeen NUMBER dix-sept; **Jonny's seventeen** Jonny a dix-sept ans

seventh ADJECTIVE septième; **on the seventh floor** au septième étage, **the seventh of July** le sept juillet

seventies PLURAL NOUN **the seventies** les années soixante-dix, **in the seventies** aux années soixante-dix

seventieth ADJECTIVE soixante-dixième; **it's her seventieth birthday** elle fête ses soixante-dix ans

seventy NUMBER soixante-dix; **my grandma's seventy** ma grand-mère a soixante-dix ans

several ADJECTIVE, PRONOUN plusieurs; **I've seen her several times** je l'ai vue plusieurs fois, **I've read several of her novels** j'ai lu plusieurs de ses romans, **he took several** il en a pris plusieurs

severe ADJECTIVE ❶ *(person)* sévère ❷ *(weather)* rigoureux *(FEM rigoureuse)* ❸ *(injuries)* grave

sew VERB coudre [28]

sewer NOUN égout MASC

sewing NOUN couture FEM; **I like sewing** j'aime la couture

sewing machine NOUN machine *(FEM)* à coudre

sex NOUN ❶ *(gender)* sexe MASC ❷ *(intercourse)* rapports *(MASC PLURAL)* sexuels; **to have sex with someone** coucher avec quelqu'un

sex education NOUN éducation *(FEM)* sexuelle

sexism NOUN sexisme MASC

sexist ADJECTIVE sexiste; **sexist remarks** des propos sexistes

sexual ADJECTIVE sexuel *(FEM sexuelle)*

sexual harassment NOUN harcèlement *(MASC)* sexuel

sexuality NOUN sexualité FEM

sexy ADJECTIVE sexy

shabby ADJECTIVE miteux *(FEM miteuse)*

shade NOUN ❶ *(of a colour)* ton MASC; **a pretty shade of green** un joli vert ❷ **in the shade** à l'ombre

shadow NOUN ombre FEM

shake VERB ❶ *(tremble)* trembler [1]; **my hands are shaking** j'ai les mains qui tremblent ❷ **to shake something** secouer [1] quelque chose ❸ **to shake hands with somebody** serrer [1] la main à quelqu'un, **she shook hands with me** elle m'a serré la main, **we shook hands** nous nous sommes serré la main ❹ **to shake your head** *(meaning no)* faire [10] non de la tête

shaken ADJECTIVE bouleversé; **I was shaken by the news** j'ai été bouleversé par la nouvelle

shall VERB **shall I come with you?** tu veux que je t'accompagne?, **shall we stop now?** si on s'arrêtait maintenant?

shallow *ADJECTIVE* **peu profond; the water's very shallow here** l'eau est très peu profonde ici

shallow end *NOUN* **partie** *(FEM)* **la moins profonde de la piscine**

shambles *NOUN* **pagaille** *FEM* *(informal);* **it was a total shambles!** ça a été la pagaille complète!

shame *NOUN* **❶ honte** *FEM;* **shame on you!** tu devrais avoir honte! **❷ what a shame!** quel dommage!, **it's a shame she can't come** c'est dommage qu'elle ne puisse pas venir *(note that 'c'est dommage que' is followed by a verb in the subjunctive)*

shameful *ADJECTIVE* **honteux** *(FEM honteuse)*

shampoo *NOUN* **shampooing** *MASC;* **I bought some shampoo** j'ai acheté du shampooing

shamrock *NOUN* **trèfle** *MASC*

shandy *NOUN* **panaché** *MASC;* **a half of shandy** un demi panaché

shape *NOUN* **forme** *FEM*

share *NOUN* **❶ part** *FEM;* **your share of the money** ta part de l'argent, **he paid his fair share** il a payé sa part **❷** *(in a company)* **action** *FEM*

share *VERB* **partager** [52]; **I'm sharing a room with Emma** je partage une chambre avec Emma
• **to share out** partager [52], répartir [58]

shark *NOUN* **requin** *MASC*

sharp *ADJECTIVE* **❶** *(knife)* **bien aiguisé; this knife isn't very sharp** ce couteau ne coupe pas très bien **❷ a sharp pencil** un crayon bien taillé **❸ a sharp bend** un virage brusque **❹** *(clever)* **intelligent**

sharpen *VERB* **❶** *(a pencil)* **tailler** [1] **❷** *(a knife)* **aiguiser** [1]

sharpener *NOUN* **taille-crayon** *MASC*

shave *VERB* **❶** *(have a shave)* **se raser** [1]; **he's just shaving** il est en train de se raser **❷ to shave your legs** se raser [1] les jambes, **to shave off your beard** se raser la barbe

shaver *NOUN* **an electric shaver** un rasoir électrique

shaving cream *NOUN* **crème** *(FEM)* **à raser**

shaving foam *NOUN* **mousse** *(FEM)* **à raser**

she *PRONOUN* **elle; she's in her room** elle est dans sa chambre, **she's a student** elle est étudiante, **she's a very good teacher** c'est un très bon prof, **here she is!** la voici!, **there she is!** la voilà!

shed *NOUN* **remise** *FEM*

sheep *NOUN* **mouton** *MASC*

sheepdog *NOUN* **chien** *(MASC)* **de berger** *(PLURAL chiens de berger)*

sheer *ADJECTIVE* **❶ pur; it's sheer stupidity!** c'est de la pure bêtise! **❷** *(tights)* **extra-fin**

sheet *NOUN* **❶** *(for a bed)* **drap** *MASC* **❷ a sheet of paper** une feuille de papier, **a blank sheet** une feuille blanche **❸** *(of glass or metal)* **plaque** *FEM*
• **to be as white as a sheet** être blanc comme un linge; **she was as white as a sheet** elle était blanche comme un linge

shelf *NOUN* **❶** *(in the home)* **étagère** *FEM;* **a set of shelves** une étagère **❷** *(in a shop, in a fridge)* **rayon** *MASC*

a
b
c
d
e
f
g
h
i
j
k
l
m
n
o
p
q
r
s
t
u
v
w
x
y
z

A
B
C
D
E
F
G
H
I
J
K
L
M
N
O
P
Q
R
S
T
U
V
W
X
Y
Z

shell NOUN ❶ (of an egg or a nut) coquille FEM ❷ (seashell) coquillage MASC ❸ (explosive) obus MASC

shellfish NOUN fruits (MASC PLURAL) de mer

shelter NOUN ❶ abri MASC; **in the shelter of** à l'abri de, **to take shelter from the rain** se mettre à l'abri de la pluie ❷ **a bus shelter** un abribus

shepherd NOUN berger MASC

sheriff NOUN shérif MASC

sherry NOUN sherry MASC

Shetland Islands NOUN îles (FEM PLURAL) Shetland

shield NOUN bouclier MASC

shift NOUN service MASC; **the night shift** le service de nuit, **to be on night shift** être de nuit

shift VERB **to shift something** déplacer [61] quelque chose, **can you help me shift this table?** est-ce que tu peux m'aider à déplacer cette table?

shifty ADJECTIVE louche; **he looks a bit shifty** il a l'air un peu louche, **a shifty-looking guy** un type un peu louche

shin NOUN tibia MASC

shine VERB briller [1]

shiny ADJECTIVE brillant

ship NOUN ❶ bateau MASC ❷ **a passenger ship** un paquebot ❸ (large naval vessel) navire MASC

shipbuilding NOUN construction (FEM) navale

shipyard NOUN chantier (MASC) naval

shirt NOUN ❶ (man's) chemise FEM ❷ (woman's) chemisier MASC

shiver VERB frissonner [1]

shock NOUN ❶ choc MASC; **it was a shock** ça a été un choc, **it gave me a shock** j'ai eu un choc ❷ **an electric shock** une décharge, **to get an electric shock** prendre une décharge

shock VERB choquer [1]

shocked ADJECTIVE choqué

shocking ADJECTIVE choquant

shoe NOUN chaussure FEM; **a pair of shoes** une paire de chaussures

shoelace NOUN lacet MASC

shoe polish NOUN cirage MASC

shoe shop NOUN magasin (MASC) de chaussures

shoot VERB ❶ (fire) tirer [1]; **to shoot at somebody** tirer sur quelqu'un, **she shot him in the leg** elle lui a tiré une balle dans la jambe, **he was shot in the arm** il a reçu une balle dans le bras ❷ (kill) abattre [21]; **he was shot by terrorists** il a été abattu par des terroristes ❸ (execute) fusiller [1] ❹ (in football, hockey) shooter [1] ❺ **to shoot a film** tourner [1] un film

shooting NOUN tir MASC

shop NOUN magasin MASC; **a shoe shop** un magasin de chaussures, **to go round the shops** faire les magasins

shop assistant NOUN vendeur MASC, vendeuse FEM; **Brad's a shop assistant** Brad est vendeur

shopkeeper NOUN **commerçant** MASC **commerçante** FEM

shoplifter NOUN **voleur** (MASC) **à l'étalage, voleuse** (FEM) **à l'étalage**

shoplifting NOUN **vol** (MASC) **à l'étalage**

shopping NOUN **courses** FEM PLURAL; **can you put the shopping away?** est-ce que tu peux ranger les courses?, **I've got a lot of shopping to do** j'ai beaucoup de courses à faire, **to go shopping** (for food) faire des courses, (for fun, to buy clothes or presents) faire du shopping

shopping bag NOUN **sac** (MASC) **à provisions**

shopping centre NOUN **centre** (MASC) **commercial**

shopping trolley NOUN ❶ (in a supermarket) **chariot** MASC ❷ (personal) **caddie** MASC

shop window NOUN **vitrine** FEM

shore NOUN **côte** FEM

short ADJECTIVE ❶ **court; a short dress** une robe courte, **she has short hair** elle a les cheveux courts ❷ **a short break** une petite pause, **to go for a short walk** faire une petite promenade, **it's a short walk from the station** c'est à quelques minutes à pied de la gare ❸ **to be short of something** ne pas avoir beaucoup de quelque chose, **we're a bit short of money at the moment** nous n'avons pas beaucoup d'argent en ce moment, **we're getting short of time** il ne nous reste pas beaucoup de temps

shortage NOUN **pénurie** FEM

shortbread NOUN **sablé** MASC

shortcrust pastry NOUN **pâte** (FEM) **brisée**

short cut NOUN **raccourci** MASC; **we took a short cut** nous avons pris un raccourci

shorten VERB ❶ (clothes) **raccourcir** [2] ❷ (a stay, journey) **écourter** [1]

shortly ADVERB **bientôt**

shorts PLURAL NOUN **short** MASC SINGULAR; **a pair of shorts** un short, **my red shorts** mon short rouge

short-sighted ADJECTIVE **myope; I'm short-sighted** je suis myope

short story NOUN **nouvelle** FEM

shot NOUN ❶ (from a gun) **coup** (MASC) **de feu** (PLURAL **coups de feu**) ❷ (a photo) **photo** FEM; **I took several shots of the garden** j'ai pris plusieurs photos du jardin

shotgun NOUN **fusil** (MASC) **de chasse** (PLURAL **fusils de chasse**)

should VERB ❶ ('should' meaning 'ought to' is translated by the conditional tense of 'devoir') **devoir** [8]; **you should ask Simon** tu devrais demander à Simon, **the potatoes should be cooked now** les pommes de terre devraient être cuites maintenant ❷ ('should have' is translated by the past conditional tense of 'devoir') **you should have told me** tu aurais dû me le dire, **I shouldn't have stayed** je n'aurais pas dû rester ❸ ('should' meaning 'would' is translated by the conditional tense of the verb) **I should forget it if I were you** à ta place je l'oublierais ❹ **I should think** à mon avis, **I should think he's forgotten** à mon avis, il a oublié

A
B
C
D
E
F
G
H
I
J
K
L
M
N
O
P
Q
R
S
T
U
V
W
X
Y
Z

shoulder NOUN épaule FEM

shoulder bag NOUN sac (MASC) à bandoulière

shout NOUN cri MASC

shout VERB crier [1]; **stop shouting!** arrêtez de crier!, **they shouted at us to come back** ils nous ont crié de revenir

shovel NOUN pelle FEM

show NOUN ❶ (on stage) spectacle MASC; **we went to see a show** nous sommes allés voir un spectacle ❷ (on TV) émission; **he has a TV show** il a une émission à la télé ❸ (exhibition) salon; **the motor show** le salon des automobiles

show VERB ❶ montrer [1]; **to show something to somebody** montrer quelque chose à quelqu'un, **I'll show you my photos** je te montrerai mes photos, **to show somebody how to do** montrer à quelqu'un comment on fait, **he showed me how to make pancakes** il m'a montré comment on fait les crêpes ❷ **it shows!** ça se voit!
• **to show off** frimer [1] (informal)

shower NOUN ❶ (in a bathroom) douche FEM; **to have a shower** prendre une douche ❷ (of rain) averse FEM

show-jumping NOUN saut (MASC) d'obstacles

show-off NOUN frimeur MASC, frimeuse FEM, (informal)

shriek VERB hurler [1]

shrimp NOUN crevette FEM

shrine NOUN autel MASC

shrink VERB rétrécir [2]

Shrove Tuesday NOUN mardi (MASC) gras

shrug VERB **to shrug your shoulders** hausser [1] les épaules

shuffle VERB **to shuffle the cards** battre [21] les cartes

shut ADJECTIVE fermé; **the shops are shut** les magasins sont fermés

shut VERB fermer [1]; **can you shut the door please?** est-ce que tu peux fermer la porte, s'il te plaît?, **the shops shut at six** les magasins ferment à six heures
• **to shut up** (be quiet) se taire [76]; **shut up!** tais-toi!

shutter NOUN volet MASC

shuttle NOUN navette FEM; **there's a shuttle service from the airport** il y a une navette de l'aéroport

shuttlecock NOUN volant MASC

shy ADJECTIVE timide

shyness NOUN timidité FEM

Sicily NOUN Sicile FEM; **to Sicily** en Sicile, **in Sicily** en Sicile

sick ADJECTIVE ❶ (ill) malade ❷ **to be sick** (vomit) vomir [2], **I was sick several times** j'ai vomi plusieurs fois, **to feel sick** avoir [5] mal au cœur ❸ **a sick joke** une plaisanterie malsaine ❹ **to be sick of something** en avoir assez de quelque chose, **I'm sick of staying at home every night** j'en ai assez de rester à la maison tous les soirs

sickness NOUN maladie FEM

side NOUN ❶ côté MASC; **on the other side of the street** de l'autre côté de la rue, **on the wrong side** du mauvais côté, **I'm on your side** (*I agree with you*) je suis de ton côté ❷ (*edge*) **bord** MASC; **at the side of the road** au bord de la route, **by the side of the pool** au bord de la piscine ❸ (*team*) **équipe**; **she plays on our side** elle joue dans notre équipe ❹ **to take sides** prendre parti ❺ **side by side** côte à côte

sideboard NOUN buffet MASC

sideburns NOUN pattes FEM PLURAL

side-effect NOUN effet (MASC) secondaire

side street NOUN petite rue FEM

siege NOUN siège MASC

sieve NOUN passoire FEM

sigh NOUN soupir MASC

sigh VERB pousser [1] un soupir

sight NOUN ❶ spectacle MASC; **it was a marvellous sight** c'était un spectacle merveilleux ❷ **at the sight of** à la vue de ❸ (*eyesight*) **vue** FEM; **to have poor sight** avoir une mauvaise vue, **to know somebody by sight** connaître quelqu'un de vue, **out of sight** caché ❹ **to see the sights** visiter les attractions touristiques

sightseeing NOUN tourisme MASC; **to do some sightseeing** faire du tourisme

sign NOUN ❶ (*notice*) panneau MASC (PLURAL **panneaux**); **there's a sign on the door** il y a un panneau sur la porte ❷ (*trace, indication*) **signe** MASC ❸ (*of the Zodiac*) **signe** MASC; **what sign are you?** tu es de quel signe?

sign VERB ❶ signer [1]; **to sign a cheque** signer un chèque ❷ (*using sign language*) communiquer [1] en langage par signes
• **to sign on** (*as unemployed*) s'inscrire [38] au chômage

signal NOUN signal MASC (PLURAL **signaux**)

signature NOUN signature FEM

significance NOUN importance FEM

significant ADJECTIVE important

sign language NOUN langage (MASC) par signes

signpost NOUN poteau (MASC) indicateur (PLURAL **poteaux indicateurs**)

silence NOUN silence MASC

silent ADJECTIVE silencieux (FEM silencieuse)

silicon chip NOUN puce (FEM) électronique

silk NOUN soie FEM

silk ADJECTIVE en soie; **a silk shirt** une chemise en soie

silky ADJECTIVE soyeux (FEM soyeuse)

silly ADJECTIVE idiot; **it was a really silly thing to do** c'était vraiment idiot

silver NOUN argent MASC

silver ADJECTIVE **a silver spoon** une cuillère en argent, **a silver medal** une médaille d'argent

SIM card NOUN carte (FEM) SIM

similar ADJECTIVE semblable

similarity NOUN ressemblance FEM

a
b
c
d
e
f
g
h
i
j
k
l
m
n
o
p
q
r
s
t
u
v
w
x
y
z

A
B
C
D
E
F
G
H
I
J
K
L
M
N
O
P
Q
R
S
T
U
V
W
X
Y
Z

simmer VERB **to simmer something** faire [10] mijoter quelque chose

simple ADJECTIVE **facile**

simplify VERB **simplifier** [1]

simply ADVERB **simplement**

sin NOUN **péché** MASC

since PREPOSITION, ADVERB, CONJUNCTION **❶ depuis** *(notice that French uses the present tense where English uses 'have done' or 'have been doing')*; **I have been in Paris since Saturday** je suis à Paris depuis samedi, **I've been learning French since last year** j'apprends le français depuis l'année dernière **❷ depuis que** *(the same thing happens with tenses here as above)*; **since I have known him** depuis que je le connais, **since I've been learning French** depuis que j'apprends le français **❸ I haven't seen her since** je ne l'ai pas revue depuis, **I haven't seen her since Monday** je ne l'ai pas revue depuis lundi, **since when?** depuis quand? **❹** *(because)* **puisque**; **since it was raining, the match was cancelled** puisqu'il pleuvait le match a été annulé

sincere ADJECTIVE **sincère**

sincerely ADVERB **Yours sincerely** *(in a business letter)* Veuillez agréer Madame (or Monsieur) l'expression de mes sentiments distingués, *(to somebody you know)* Cordialement *(in French there are very formal and rigid ways of signing letters)*

sing VERB **chanter** [1]

singer NOUN **chanteur** MASC, **chanteuse** FEM

singing NOUN **❶ chant** MASC; **a singing lesson** une leçon de chant **❷ I like singing** j'aime chanter

single NOUN **aller** *(MASC)* **simple**; **a single to Lyons, please** un aller simple pour Lyon, s'il vous plaît

single ADJECTIVE **❶** *(not married)* **célibataire ❷ a single room** une chambre pour une personne, **a single bed** un lit pour une personne **❸ not a single** pas un seul, pas une seule, **I haven't had a single reply** je n'ai pas reçu une seule réponse

single parent NOUN **she's a single parent** elle élève ses enfants toute seule, **a single-parent family** une famille monoparentale

singles PLURAL NOUN *(in tennis)* **simple** MASC SINGULAR; **the women's singles** le simple dames, **the men's singles** le simple messieurs

singular NOUN **singulier** MASC; **in the singular** au singulier

sink NOUN **évier** MASC

sink VERB **couler** [1]

sir NOUN **monsieur** MASC; **yes, sir** oui, Monsieur

siren NOUN **sirène** FEM

sister NOUN **sœur** FEM; **my sister's ten** ma sœur a dix ans

sister-in-law NOUN **belle-sœur** FEM *(PLURAL* **belles-sœurs***)*

sit VERB **❶ s'asseoir** [20]; **you can sit on the sofa** tu peux t'asseoir sur le canapé, **I can sit on the floor** je peux m'asseoir par terre **❷ to be sitting** être [6] assis, **Leila was sitting on the sofa** Leila était assise sur le canapé **❸ to sit an exam** passer [1]

un examen, **she's sitting her driving test on Thursday** elle passe son permis jeudi
- **to sit down** s'asseoir [20]; **he sat down on a chair** il s'est assis sur une chaise, **do sit down** asseyez-vous

sitcom NOUN comédie (FEM) de situation (PLURAL comédies de situation)

site NOUN ❶ **a building site** un chantier ❷ **a camping site** un camping ❸ **an archaeological site** un site archéologique

sitting room NOUN salon MASC

situated ADJECTIVE **to be situated** être situé, **the house is situated in a small village** la maison est située dans un petit village

situation NOUN situation FEM

six NUMBER six; **Harry's six** Harry a six ans

sixteen NUMBER seize; **Alice is sixteen** Alice a seize ans

sixth ADJECTIVE sixième; **on the sixth floor** au sixième étage, **the sixth of July** le six juillet

sixty NUMBER soixante; **she's sixty** elle a soixante ans

size NOUN ❶ grandeur FEM; **it depends on the size of the house** ça dépend de la grandeur de la maison ❷ (precise measurements) dimensions FEM PLURAL; **what size is the window?** quelles sont les dimensions de la fenêtre? ❸ (in clothes) taille FEM; **what size do you take?** quelle taille faites-vous? ❹ (of shoes) pointure; **I take a size thirty-eight** je fais du trente-huit

skate NOUN ❶ **an ice skate** un patin à glace ❷ **a roller skate** un patin à roulettes

skate VERB ❶ (ice-skate) faire [10] du patin à glace ❷ (roller-skate) faire [10] du patin à roulettes

skateboard NOUN skateboard MASC

skateboarding NOUN skateboard MASC; **to do (or go) skateboarding** faire du skateboard

skater NOUN patineur MASC, patineuse FEM

skating NOUN ❶ (ice) patin (MASC) à glace; **to go skating** faire du patin à glace ❷ roller-skating le patin à roulettes, **to go roller-skating** faire du patin à roulettes

skating rink NOUN patinoire FEM

skeleton NOUN squelette MASC

sketch NOUN ❶ (drawing) croquis MASC ❷ (comedy routine) sketch MASC

ski NOUN ski MASC

ski VERB faire [10] du ski; **he can ski** il sait faire du ski

ski boot NOUN chaussure (FEM) de ski

skid VERB déraper [1]; **the car skidded** la voiture a dérapé

skier NOUN skieur MASC, skieuse FEM

skiing NOUN ski MASC; **to go skiing** faire du ski

ski lift NOUN remonte-pente MASC

skill NOUN compétence FEM

skimmed milk NOUN lait (MASC) écrémé

skin *NOUN* **peau** *FEM (PLURAL* **peaux)**

skinhead *NOUN* **skinhead** *MASC & FEM*

skinny *ADJECTIVE* **maigre**

skip *NOUN (for rubbish)* **benne** *FEM*

skip *VERB* ❶ **sauter** [1] *(a meal, part of a book)*; **I skipped a few chapters** j'ai sauté quelques chapitres ❷ **to skip a lesson** sécher un cours *(informal)*

ski pants *NOUN* **fuseau** *MASC SINGULAR*; **I bought some ski pants** j'ai acheté un fuseau

skipping rope *NOUN* **corde** *(FEM)* à **sauter**

skirt *NOUN* **jupe** *FEM*; **a long skirt** une jupe longue, **a straight skirt** une jupe droite, **a mini-skirt** une mini-jupe

ski suit *NOUN* **combinaison** *(FEM)* **de ski**

skittles *PLURAL NOUN* **quilles** *FEM PLURAL*; **to play skittles** jouer aux quilles

skull *NOUN* **crâne** *MASC*

sky *NOUN* **ciel** *MASC*

skyscraper *NOUN* **gratte-ciel** *MASC (PLURAL* **gratte-ciel)**

slam *VERB* **claquer** [1]; **she slammed the door** elle a claqué la porte

slang *NOUN* **argot** *MASC*

slap *NOUN* **claque** *FEM*

slap *VERB* **to slap somebody** donner [1] une claque à quelqu'un

slate *NOUN* **ardoise** *FEM*

slave *NOUN* **esclave** *MASC & FEM*

sledge *NOUN* **luge** *FEM*

sledging *NOUN* **to go sledging** faire [10] de la luge

sleep *NOUN* **sommeil** *MASC*; **I had a good sleep** j'ai bien dormi, **to go to sleep** s'endormir [37]

sleep *VERB* **dormir** [37]; **she's sleeping** elle dort

sleeping bag *NOUN* **sac** *(MASC)* **de couchage**

sleeping pill *NOUN* **somnifère** *MASC*

sleepy *ADJECTIVE* **to be sleepy** avoir [5] **sommeil**, **I feel sleepy** j'ai sommeil, **he was getting sleepy** il commençait à avoir sommeil

sleet *NOUN* **neige** *(FEM)* **fondue**

sleeve *NOUN* **manche** *FEM*; **a long-sleeved jumper** un pull à manches longues, **a short-sleeved shirt** une chemise à manches courtes, **to roll up your sleeves** retrousser ses manches

slice *NOUN* **tranche** *FEM*; **a slice of ham** une tranche de jambon

slice *VERB* **to slice something** couper [1] quelque chose en tranches

slide *NOUN* ❶ *(photo)* **diapositive** *FEM* ❷ *(hairslide)* **barrette** *FEM* ❸ *(for sliding down)* **toboggan** *MASC*

slight *ADJECTIVE* **léger** *(FEM* **légère)**; **there is a slight problem** il y a un léger problème

slightly *ADVERB* **légèrement**

slim *ADJECTIVE* **mince**

slim *VERB* **I'm slimming** je fais un régime

sling NOUN écharpe FEM; **to have your arm in a sling** avoir le bras en écharpe

slip NOUN ❶ (mistake) erreur FEM ❷ (petticoat) (from waist) jupon MASC (full-length) combinaison FEM

slip VERB ❶ (slide) glisser [1] ❷ **it had slipped my mind** j'avais oublié

slipper NOUN pantoufle FEM

slippery ADJECTIVE glissant

slope NOUN pente FEM

slot NOUN fente FEM

slot machine NOUN ❶ (games machine) machine (FEM) à sous ❷ (vending machine) distributeur (MASC) automatique

slow ADJECTIVE ❶ lent; **the service is a bit slow** le service est une peu lent ❷ **my watch is slow** ma montre retarde
• **to slow down** ralentir [2]

slowly ADVERB ❶ lentement; **he got up slowly** il s'est levé lentement ❷ (speak, drive) doucement; **can you speak more slowly, please?** est-ce que vous pouvez parler plus doucement, s'il vous plaît?

slug NOUN limace FEM

slum NOUN quartier (MASC) démuni

slush NOUN neige (FEM) fondue

sly ADJECTIVE (person) rusé
• **on the sly** en douce

smack NOUN claque FEM

smack VERB **to smack somebody** donner [1] une claque à quelqu'un

small ADJECTIVE petit (goes before the noun); **a small dog** un petit chien

smart ADJECTIVE ❶ (well-dressed, posh) chic; **a smart restaurant** un restaurant chic ❷ (clever) intelligent

smash NOUN **a car smash** un accident de voiture

smash VERB casser [1]; **they smashed a window** ils ont cassé une vitre

smashing ADJECTIVE formidable

smell NOUN odeur FEM; **a nasty smell** une mauvaise odeur, **there's a smell of burning** ça sent le brûlé

smell VERB ❶ sentir [58]; **I can't smell anything** je ne sens rien, **I can smell lavender** ça sent la lavande ❷ (smell bad) sentir [58] mauvais; **the drains smell** les égouts sentent mauvais

smelly ADJECTIVE qui sent mauvais; **her smelly dog** son chien qui sent mauvais

smile NOUN sourire MASC

smile VERB sourire [68]

smoke NOUN fumée FEM

smoke VERB fumer [1]; **she doesn't smoke** elle ne fume pas, **he smokes a pipe** il fume la pipe

smoked ADJECTIVE fumé; **smoked salmon** du saumon fumé

smoker NOUN fumeur MASC, fumeuse FEM

smoking NOUN **'no smoking'** 'défense de fumer', **to give up smoking** arrêter de fumer

a b c d e f g h i j k l m n o p q r s t u v w x y z

smooth   **so**

smooth ADJECTIVE ❶ lisse; **a smooth surface** une surface lisse ❷ *(person)* mielleux *(FEM* mielleuse*)*

smug ADJECTIVE suffisant

smuggle VERB **to smuggle something** faire [10] passer quelque chose en contrebande

smuggler NOUN ❶ contrebandier MASC, contrebandière FEM ❷ **a drugs smuggler** un passeur de drogue

smuggling NOUN ❶ contrebande FEM ❷ *(of drugs or arms)* trafic MASC

snack NOUN casse-croûte MASC

snack bar NOUN sandwicherie FEM, snack-bar MASC

snail NOUN escargot MASC

snake NOUN serpent MASC

snap NOUN *(card game)* bataille FEM

snap VERB ❶ *(break)* casser [1] ❷ **to snap your fingers** faire [10] claquer ses doigts

snapshot NOUN photo FEM

snarl VERB gronder [1]

snatch VERB arracher [1]; **to snatch something from somebody** arracher quelque chose à quelqu'un, **he snatched my book** il m'a arraché mon livre, **she had her bag snatched** on lui a arraché son sac

sneak VERB **to sneak in** entrer [1] furtivement, **to sneak out** sortir [72] furtivement, **he sneaked up on me** il s'est approché de moi sans faire de bruit

sneeze VERB éternuer [1]

sniff VERB renifler [1]

snob NOUN snob MASC & FEM

snobbery NOUN snobisme MASC

snooker NOUN snooker MASC; **to play snooker** jouer au snooker

snooze NOUN somme MASC; **to have a snooze** faire un petit somme

snore VERB ronfler [1]

snow NOUN neige FEM

snow VERB neiger [52]; **it's snowing** il neige, **it's going to snow** il va neiger

snowball NOUN boule *(FEM)* de neige *(PLURAL* boules de neige*)*

snowdrift NOUN congère FEM

snowman NOUN bonhomme *(MASC)* de neige *(PLURAL* bonshommes de neige*)*

snowy ADJECTIVE enneigé; **it was very snowy** il y avait beaucoup de neige

so CONJUNCTION, ADVERB ❶ tellement; **he's so lazy** il est tellement paresseux, **the coffee's so hot I can't drink it** le café est tellement chaud que je n'arrive pas à le boire ❷ **not so** moins, **our house is a bit like yours, but not so big** notre maison est un peu comme la vôtre, mais moins grande ❸ **so much** tellement, **I hate it so much!** je le déteste tellement! ❹ **so much, so many** tellement de, **I have so much work to do** j'ai tellement de travail à faire, **we've got so many problems** nous avons tellement de problèmes ❺ *(therefore)* donc; **he got up late, so he missed his train** il s'est levé tard, donc il a raté son train ❻ *(starting a sentence)* alors; **so what's your name?** alors, tu t'appelles comment?, **so what shall we do?** alors, qu'est-ce qu'on fait?, **so what?** et alors? ❼ **so do I, so did I**

moi aussi, **'I live in Leeds'** – **'so do I'** 'j'habite à Leeds' – 'moi aussi', **'I hated the film'** – **'so did I'** 'j'ai détesté le film' – 'moi aussi', **so am I** moi aussi, **so do we** nous aussi ❽ **I think so** je crois, **I hope so** j'espère

soak VERB tremper [1]

soaked ADJECTIVE trempé
• **to be soaked to the skin** être trempé jusqu'aux os (literally: to be soaked to the bones)

soaking ADJECTIVE trempé; **soaking wet** trempé

soap NOUN ❶ savon MASC; **a cake of soap** un savon ❷ (soap opera: on TV) feuilleton MASC

soap powder NOUN lessive FEM

sober ADJECTIVE **to be sober** ne pas avoir bu, **he's sober** il n'a pas bu, **are you sure she's sober?** tu es sûr qu'elle n'a pas bu?

soccer NOUN football MASC; **to play soccer** jouer au football

social ADJECTIVE social MASC (PLURAL sociaux)

socialism NOUN socialisme MASC

socialist NOUN, ADJECTIVE socialiste MASC & FEM

social security NOUN ❶ aide (FEM) sociale; **to be on social security** recevoir de l'aide sociale ❷ **the social security** (the system) sécurité sociale FEM

social worker NOUN travailleur (MASC) social (PLURAL travailleurs sociaux), travailleuse (FEM) sociale; **she's a social worker** elle est travailleuse sociale

society NOUN société FEM

sociology NOUN sociologie FEM

sock NOUN chaussette FEM; **a pair of socks** une paire de chaussettes

socket NOUN (power point) prise (FEM) de courant (PLURAL prises de courant)

sofa NOUN canapé MASC

sofa bed NOUN canapé-lit MASC

soft ADJECTIVE doux (FEM douce)
• **to have a soft spot for somebody** avoir un faible pour quelqu'un

soft drink NOUN boisson (FEM) non alcoolisée

soft toy NOUN peluche FEM

software NOUN logiciel MASC

soil NOUN terre FEM

solar energy NOUN énergie (FEM) solaire

soldier NOUN soldat MASC

solicitor NOUN ❶ (dealing with property or documents) notaire MASC; **she's a solicitor** elle est notaire ❷ (dealing with lawsuits) avocat MASC, avocate FEM; **she's a solicitor** elle est avocate

solid ADJECTIVE ❶ massif (FEM massive); **a table made of solid pine** une table en pin massif, **a solid gold ring** une bague en or massif, **solid silver** argent massif ❷ (not flimsy) solide; **a solid structure** une structure solide

solo NOUN solo MASC; **a guitar solo** un solo de guitare

solo ADJECTIVE, ADVERB en solo; **a solo album** un album en solo, **to play solo** jouer en solo

A B C D E F G H I J K L M N O P Q R S T U V W X Y Z

soloist NOUN **soliste** MASC & FEM

solution NOUN **solution** FEM

solve VERB **résoudre** [67]

some DETERMINER, ADVERB ❶ (followed by a singular noun), **du** (with a masculine noun), **de la** (with a feminine noun), **de l'** (with a noun beginning with a vowel or silent 'h'); **would you like some butter?** voulez-vous du beurre?, **may I have some salad?** puis-je avoir de la salade?, **can you lend me some money?** est-ce que tu peux me prêter de l'argent? ❷ (followed by a plural noun) **des**; **I've bought some apples** j'ai acheté des pommes ❸ (referring to something that has been mentioned) **en**; **'would you like butter?'** – **'thanks, I've got some'** 'veux-tu du beurre?' – 'merci, j'en ai', **he's eaten some of it** il en a mangé un peu ❹ **some people think he's wrong** il y a des gens qui pensent qu'il a tort ❺ **some day** un de ces jours

somebody, someone PRONOUN **quelqu'un**; **there's somebody in the garden** il y a quelqu'un dans le jardin

somehow ADVERB ❶ **d'une manière ou d'une autre**; **I've got to finish this essay somehow** je dois finir cette rédaction d'une manière ou d'une autre ❷ **I somehow think they won't come** quelque chose me dit qu'ils ne viendront pas

somersault NOUN ❶ (child's) **galipette** FEM ❷ (gymnast's) **roulade** FEM ❸ (diver's) **saut** MASC (PLURAL **périlleux**)

something PRONOUN **quelque chose**; **I've got something to tell you** j'ai quelque chose à te dire, **something pretty** quelque chose de joli, **something interesting** quelque chose d'intéressant, **there's something wrong** il y a quelque chose qui ne va pas, **their house is really something!** leur maison c'est vraiment quelque chose!, **a guy called Colin something or other** un type qui s'appelle Colin quelque chose

sometime ADVERB **un de ces jours**; **give me a ring sometime** appelle-moi un de ces jours, **I'll ring you sometime next week** je t'appellerai dans le courant de la semaine prochaine

sometimes ADVERB **quelquefois**; **I sometimes take the train** quelquefois je prends le train

somewhere ADVERB **quelque part**; **I've put my bag down somewhere** j'ai posé mon sac quelque part, **I've met you somewhere before** je vous ai déjà vu quelque part

son NOUN **fils** MASC

song NOUN **chanson** FEM

son-in-law NOUN **gendre** MASC

soon ADVERB ❶ **bientôt**; **it will soon be the holidays** c'est bientôt les vacances, **see you soon!** à bientôt ❷ **as soon as dès que**, **as soon as she arrives** dès qu'elle arrivera, **as soon as possible** dès que possible ❸ **it's too soon** c'est trop tôt

sooner ADVERB ❶ **plus tôt**; **we should have started sooner** nous aurions dû commencer plus tôt ❷ **I'd sooner wait** je préfère attendre
• **sooner or later** tôt ou tard

soprano NOUN **soprano** MASC & FEM

sore NOUN plaie FEM

sore ADJECTIVE **to have a sore leg**
avoir mal à la jambe, **to have a sore
throat** avoir mal à la gorge, **my
arm's sore** j'ai mal au bras
- **it's a sore point** c'est un sujet
délicat

sorry ADJECTIVE ❶ désolé; **I'm really
sorry** je suis vraiment désolé, **sorry
to disturb you** je suis désolé de
vous déranger, **I'm sorry I forgot
your birthday** je suis désolé d'avoir
oublié ton anniversaire ❷ **sorry!**
excusez-moi! ❸ **sorry?** comment?
❹ **to feel sorry for somebody**
plaindre [31] quelqu'un

sort NOUN sorte FEM; **what sort of
music do you like?** tu aimes quelle
sorte de musique?, **all sorts of**
toutes sortes de, **for all sorts of
reasons** pour toutes sortes de
raisons
- **to sort something out** ❶ mettre
[11] de l'ordre dans (room, desk,
papers, possessions); **I must sort out
my room tonight** je dois mettre
de l'ordre dans ma chambre ce
soir ❷ s'occuper [1] de (problem,
arrangement); **Liz is sorting it out**
Liz s'en occupe

so-so ADJECTIVE moyen (FEM
moyenne); **'how was the film?'
– 'so-so'** 'c'était comment le film?'
– 'moyen'

soul NOUN ❶ âme FEM ❷ (music) soul
MASC

sound NOUN ❶ (noise) bruit; **the
sound of voices** le bruit des
voix ❷ (volume) volume; **to turn
down the sound** baisser le volume

sound VERB **it sounds easy** ça a l'air
facile, **it sounds as if she's happy**
elle a l'air d'être heureuse

sound asleep ADJECTIVE
profondément endormi

sound effect NOUN effet (MASC)
sonore

soundtrack NOUN bande (FEM)
sonore

soup NOUN soupe FEM; **mushroom
soup** la soupe aux champignons

soup plate NOUN assiette (FEM)
creuse la soupe

soup spoon NOUN cuillère (FEM) à
soupe

sour ADJECTIVE ❶ (taste) aigre ❷ **the
milk has gone sour** le lait a tourné

south NOUN sud MASC; **in the south**
au sud

south ADJECTIVE, ADVERB sud (never
agrees); **the south side** le côté sud, **a
south wind** un vent du sud, **south of
Paris** au sud de Paris

South Africa NOUN Afrique (FEM)
du Sud

South America NOUN Amérique
(FEM) du Sud

South American NOUN Sud-
Américain MASC, Sud-Américaine
FEM

South American ADJECTIVE sud-
américain

southeast NOUN sud-est MASC

southeast ADJECTIVE **in southeast
England** au sud-est de l'Angleterre

South Pole NOUN pôle (MASC) Sud

southwest NOUN sud-ouest MASC

southwest ADJECTIVE **in southwest
England** au sud-ouest de
l'Angleterre

A
B
C
D
E
F
G
H
I
J
K
L
M
N
O
P
Q
R
S
T
U
V
W
X
Y
Z

souvenir NOUN souvenir MASC

soya NOUN soja MASC

soy sauce NOUN sauce (FEM) de soja

space NOUN ❶ (room) place FEM; **is there enough space?** est-ce qu'il y a de la place?, **there's enough space for two** il y a de la place pour deux ❷ (gap) espace MASC; **leave a space** laissez un espace ❸ (outer space) espace MASC; **in space** dans l'espace

spacecraft NOUN engin (MASC) spatial

spade NOUN ❶ pelle FEM ❷ (in cards) pique MASC; **the queen of spades** la reine de pique

spaghetti NOUN spaghetti MASC PLURAL

Spain NOUN Espagne FEM; **in Spain** en Espagne, **to Spain** en Espagne

Spaniard NOUN Espagnol MASC, Espagnole FEM

spaniel NOUN épagneul MASC

Spanish NOUN ❶ (language) espagnol MASC; **I'm learning Spanish** j'apprends l'espagnol ❷ **the Spanish** (people) les Espagnols MASC PLURAL

Spanish ADJECTIVE espagnol; **Pedro is Spanish** Pedro est espagnol

spank VERB **to spank somebody** donner [1] une fessée à quelqu'un

spanner NOUN clé (FEM) anglaise

spare ADJECTIVE (part, battery) de rechange; **we have a spare ticket** nous avons un billet de trop

spare VERB **I can't spare the time** je n'ai pas le temps, **can you spare a moment?** est-ce que tu as un instant?

spare part NOUN pièce (FEM) de rechange

spare room NOUN chambre (FEM) d'amis

spare time NOUN temps (MASC) libre; **in my spare time** dans mon temps libre

spare wheel NOUN roue (FEM) de secours

sparkling ADJECTIVE **sparkling (mineral) water** l'eau (minérale) pétillante, **sparkling wine** le vin mousseux

sparrow NOUN moineau MASC (PLURAL moineaux)

speak VERB ❶ parler [1]; **do you speak French?** est-ce que vous parlez français?, **spoken French** le français parlé ❷ **to speak to somebody** parler [1] à quelqu'un, **she's speaking to Mike** elle parle à Mike, **I've never spoken to her** je ne lui ai jamais parlé, **I'll speak to him about it** je vais lui en parler ❸ **who's speaking?** (on the phone) c'est qui à l'appareil?

speaker NOUN ❶ (on a music system) enceinte FEM ❷ (at a public lecture) conférencier MASC, conférencière FEM ❸ (of a language) **a French speaker** un/une francophone, **an English speaker** un/une anglophone

spear NOUN lance FEM

special ADJECTIVE spécial MASC (PLURAL spéciaux)

specialist NOUN spécialiste MASC & FEM

specialize VERB **to specialize in** être [6] spécialisé dans, **we specialize in French cars** nous sommes spécialisés dans les voitures françaises

specially ADVERB ❶ spécialement; not specially pas spécialement, **the poems have been specially chosen for small children** les poèmes ont été spécialement choisis pour les petits enfants ❷ (specifically) exprès; **I came specially in order to see you** je suis venu exprès pour te voir, **I made this cake specially for you** j'ai fait ce gâteau exprès pour toi

species NOUN espèce FEM

specific ADJECTIVE précis

spectacles NOUN lunettes FEM PLURAL

spectacular ADJECTIVE spectaculaire

spectator NOUN spectateur MASC, spectatrice FEM

speech NOUN discours MASC; **to make a speech** faire un discours

speechless ADJECTIVE muet (FEM muette); **to be speechless with rage** rester muet de colère, **I was speechless** j'étais stupéfait

speed NOUN vitesse FEM; **at top speed** à toute vitesse, **what speed was he doing?** il roulait à quelle vitesse?, **a twelve-speed bike** un vélo à douze vitesses
• **to speed up** accélérer [24]

speeding NOUN excès (MASC) de vitesse; **he was fined for speeding** il a reçu une contravention pour excès de vitesse

speed limit NOUN limitation (FEM) de vitesse

spell NOUN (of time) période FEM; **a cold spell** une période de temps froid, **sunny spells** des éclaircies FEM PLURAL

spell VERB ❶ (in writing) écrire [38]; **how do you spell it?** ça s'écrit comment?, **how do you spell your surname?** ça s'écrit comment, ton nom de famille? ❷ (out loud) épeler [18]

spell checker NOUN correcteur (MASC) orthographique

spelling NOUN orthographe FEM; **a spelling mistake** une faute d'orthographe

spend VERB ❶ dépenser [1] (money); **I've spent all my money** j'ai dépensé tout mon argent ❷ passer [1] (time); **we spent three days in Paris** nous avons passé trois jours à Paris, **she spends her time writing letters** elle passe son temps à écrire des lettres

spice NOUN épice FEM

spicy ADJECTIVE épicé; **he doesn't like spicy food** il n'aime pas les choses épicées

spider NOUN araignée FEM

spill VERB renverser [1]; **I've spilled my wine on the carpet** j'ai renversé mon vin sur la moquette

spinach NOUN épinards MASC PLURAL; **do you like spinach?** est-ce que tu aimes les épinards?

spine NOUN colonne (FEM) vertébrale

spiral NOUN spirale FEM

spiral staircase NOUN escalier (MASC) en colimaçon

spire NOUN flèche FEM

spirit NOUN ❶ (energy) énergie FEM ❷ **to get into the spirit of the occasion** se mettre dans l'ambiance

spirits NOUN ❶ (alcohol) alcools (MASC PLURAL) forts ❷ to be in good spirits être de bonne humeur

spit VERB cracher [1]; to spit something out cracher quelque chose

spite NOUN ❶ in spite of malgré, we decided to go in spite of the rain nous avons décidé d'y aller malgré la pluie ❷ (nastiness) méchanceté FEM; to do something out of spite faire quelque chose par méchanceté

spiteful ADJECTIVE méchant

splash NOUN ❶ (noise) plouf MASC ❷ a splash of colour une touche de couleur

splash VERB éclabousser [1]

splendid ADJECTIVE splendide

splinter NOUN écharde FEM

split VERB ❶ (with an axe or a knife) fendre [3]; to split a piece of wood fendre un morceau de bois ❷ (come apart) se fendre [3]; the lining has split la doublure s'est fendue ❸ (divide up) partager [52]; they split the money between them ils ont partagé l'argent entre eux
• to split up ❶ (a couple or group) se séparer [1] ❷ she's split up with her boyfriend elle a rompu avec son copain.

spoil VERB ❶ gâcher [1]; it completely spoiled the evening ça a complètement gâché la soirée, to spoil the surprise gâcher la surprise ❷ gâter [1] (a child)

spoiled ADJECTIVE gâté; a spoiled child un enfant gâté

spoilsport NOUN trouble-fête MASC & FEM

spoke NOUN (of a wheel) rayon MASC

spokesman NOUN porte-parole MASC (PLURAL porte-parole)

spokeswoman NOUN porte-parole MASC (PLURAL porte-parole)

sponge NOUN éponge FEM

sponge bag NOUN trousse (FEM) de toilette

sponge cake NOUN génoise FEM

sponsor NOUN sponsor MASC

sponsor VERB sponsoriser [1]

spontaneous ADJECTIVE spontané

spooky ADJECTIVE ❶ (atmosphere) sinistre ❷ a spooky story une histoire qui fait froid dans le dos

spoon NOUN cuillère FEM; a soup spoon une cuillère à soupe, a teaspoon une petite cuillère

spoonful NOUN cuillère FEM

sport NOUN sport MASC; to be good at sport être bon en sport, my favourite sport mon sport préféré

sports bag NOUN sac (MASC) de sport

sports car NOUN voiture (FEM) de sport

sports centre NOUN centre (MASC) sportif

sports club NOUN club (MASC) sportif

sportsman NOUN sportif MASC

sportswear NOUN vêtements (MASC PLURAL) de sport

sportswoman NOUN sportive FEM

sporty ADJECTIVE sportif (FEM sportive); she's very sporty elle est très sportive

spot NOUN ❶ (in fabric) pois MASC; **a red tie with black spots** une cravate rouge aux pois noirs ❷ (on your skin) bouton; **I've got spots** j'ai des boutons, **to be covered in spots** être couvert de boutons ❸ (stain) tache FEM; **you've got a spot on your tie** tu as une tache sur ta cravate ❹ (spotlight) projecteur MASC, (in the home) spot MASC ❺ **on the spot** (immediately) sur-le-champ, **we'll do it for you on the spot** nous le ferons sur-le-champ ❻ (at hand) sur place; **they have experts on the spot** ils ont des experts sur place

spot VERB repérer [24]; **I spotted her in the crowd** je l'ai repérée dans la foule

spotless ADJECTIVE impeccable

spotlight NOUN ❶ projecteur MASC ❷ (in the home) spot MASC

spotty ADJECTIVE (pimply) boutonneux (FEM boutonneuse)

spouse NOUN époux MASC, épouse FEM

sprain NOUN entorse FEM

sprain VERB **to sprain your ankle** se faire [10] une entorse à la cheville

spray NOUN (spray can) bombe FEM

spray VERB vaporiser [1] (liquid)

spread NOUN pâte (FEM) à tartiner; **cheese spread** le fromage à tartiner

spread VERB ❶ (news or a disease) se propager [52] ❷ étaler [1] (butter, jam, cement, glue, etc.)

spreadsheet NOUN (on a computer) tableur MASC

spring NOUN ❶ (the season) printemps MASC; **in the spring** au printemps, **spring flowers** les fleurs du printemps ❷ (made of metal) ressort MASC ❸ (providing water) source FEM

spring-cleaning NOUN grand nettoyage (MASC) de printemps

springtime NOUN printemps MASC; **in springtime** au printemps

spring water NOUN eau (FEM) de source

sprint NOUN sprint MASC

sprint VERB courir [2] à toute vitesse

sprinter NOUN sprinteur MASC, sprinteuse FEM

sprout NOUN (Brussels sprout) chou (MASC) de Bruxelles (PLURAL choux de Bruxelles)

spy NOUN espion MASC, espionne FEM

spy VERB **to spy on somebody** espionner [1] quelqu'un

spying NOUN espionnage MASC

squabble VERB se disputer [1]

square NOUN ❶ (shape) carré ❷ (in a town or village) place FEM; **the village square** la place du village
• **to go back to square one** retourner à la case départ

square ADJECTIVE carré; **a square box** une boîte carrée, **three square metres** trois mètres carrés, **the room is four metres square** la pièce fait quatre mètres carrés

squash NOUN ❶ (drink) sirop MASC; **orange squash** le sirop d'orange ❷ (sport) squash MASC; **to play squash** jouer au squash

squeak VERB ❶ (door, hinge) grincer [61] ❷ (person, animal) pousser [1] un petit cri

squeeze VERB ❶ serrer [1] (somebody's arm, hand, etc) ❷ presser [1] (toothpaste)

squid NOUN calmar MASC

squirrel NOUN écureuil MASC

stab VERB poignarder [1]

stable NOUN écurie FEM

stable ADJECTIVE stable

stack NOUN ❶ (pile) pile FEM ❷ stacks of plein de, **she's got stacks of CDs** elle a plein de CD

stadium NOUN stade MASC

staff NOUN ❶ (of a company) personnel MASC ❷ (in a school) professeurs MASC PLURAL

stage NOUN ❶ (for a performance) scène FEM; **on stage** sur scène ❷ (phase) stade MASC; **at this stage of the project** à ce stade du projet, **at this stage it's hard to know** pour l'instant il est difficile de savoir

staggered ADJECTIVE (amazed) stupéfié

stain NOUN tache FEM

stain VERB tacher [1]

stainless steel NOUN inox MASC; **a stainless steel sink** un évier en inox

stair NOUN ❶ (step) marche FEM ❷ stairs escalier MASC, **I met her on the stairs** je l'ai croisée dans l'escalier

staircase NOUN escalier MASC

stale ADJECTIVE (bread) rassis

stalemate NOUN (in chess) pat MASC

stall NOUN ❶ (at a market or fair) stand MASC ❷ **the stalls** (in a theatre) l'orchestre MASC SINGULAR

stammer NOUN **to have a stammer** bégayer [59]

stammer VERB bégayer [59]

stamp NOUN timbre MASC

stamp VERB ❶ affranchir [2] (a letter) ❷ **to stamp your foot** taper [1] du pied

stamp album NOUN album (MASC) de timbres

stamp collection NOUN collection (FEM) de timbres

stand VERB ❶ être [6] debout; **several people were standing** plusieurs personnes étaient debout ❷ (when you say somebody is standing somewhere 'standing' is not usually translated) **we were standing outside the cinema** nous étions devant le cinéma, **I'm standing here waiting for you** je suis là en train de t'attendre ❸ (bear) supporter [1]; **I can't stand her** je ne la supporte pas, **I can't stand waiting** je ne supporte pas d'attendre

• **to stand for something** (be short for) être [6] l'abréviation de; **'UN' stands for 'United Nations'** 'UN' est l'abréviation de 'United Nations'

• **stand up** se lever [50]; **everybody stood up** tout le monde s'est levé

standard NOUN niveau MASC; **her work is of a high standard** son travail est d'un bon niveau, **the standard of living** le niveau de vie

standard ADJECTIVE standard; **the standard price** le prix standard

Standard grades NOUN PLURAL *(You can explain Standard grades as follows:)* Ce sont des examens que les lycéens écossais passent à l'âge d'environ 16 ans dans six ou sept matières. La meilleure note que l'on peut obtenir est 1 et la note la plus basse est 7. Une fois qu'ils ont obtenu leurs Standard grades, de nombreux étudiants se préparent pour les Highers
▸ SEE **Highers**

stands NOUN *(in a stadium)* tribune FEM SINGULAR

staple NOUN agrafe FEM

staple VERB agrafer [1]; to staple the pages together agrafer les feuilles

stapler NOUN agrafeuse FEM

star NOUN ❶ *(in the sky)* étoile FEM ❷ *(person)* vedette; he's a film star c'est une vedette de cinéma

star VERB to star in a film être [6] la vedette d'un film

stare VERB regarder [1] fixement; he was staring at me il me regardait fixement, what are you staring at? qu'est-ce que tu regardes?

star sign NOUN signe *(MASC)* astrologique; what star sign are you? de quelle signe êtes-vous?

start NOUN ❶ début MASC; at the start au début, at the start of the book au début du livre, from the start dès le début, we knew from the start that it was dangerous nous savions dès le début que c'était dangereux ❷ to make a start on something commencer à faire quelque chose, I've made a start on my homework j'ai commencé à faire mes devoirs ❸ *(of a race)* départ MASC

start VERB ❶ commencer [61]; the film starts at eight le film commence à huit heures, I've started the book j'ai commencé le livre ❷ to start doing commencer [61] à faire, I've started learning Spanish j'ai commencé à apprendre l'espagnol ❸ to start a business créer [32] une entreprise ❹ to start a car faire [10] démarrer une voiture, she started the car elle a fait démarrer la voiture, the car wouldn't start la voiture n'a pas voulu démarrer

starter NOUN *(in a meal)* entrée FEM; what would you like as a starter? qu'est-ce que vous voulez comme entrée?

starve VERB mourir [54] de faim; I'm starving! je meurs de faim!

state NOUN ❶ état MASC; the house is in a very bad state la maison est en très mauvais état ❷ *(administrative)* état MASC; the state l'État ❸ the States les États-Unis MASC PLURAL, they live in the States ils habitent aux États-Unis

state VERB ❶ déclarer [1] *(intention, opinion)* ❷ indiquer [1] *(address, income, occupation, reason, etc.)*

stately home NOUN château MASC *(PLURAL châteaux)*

statement NOUN déclaration FEM

station NOUN gare FEM; the railway station la gare, the bus station la gare routière, the police station le commissariat, a radio station une station de radio

stationary ADJECTIVE à l'arrêt

stationer's NOUN papeterie FEM

stationery NOUN papeterie FEM

statistics NOUN ❶ (subject) statistique FEM ❷ the statistics (figures) les statistiques

statue NOUN statue FEM

status NOUN position FEM

stay NOUN séjour MASC; **our stay in Paris** notre séjour à Paris, **enjoy your stay!** bon séjour!

stay VERB ❶ rester [1]; **I'll stay here** je reste ici, **how long are you staying?** vous restez combien de temps? ❷ (with time) **we're going to stay in Berlin for three days** nous allons passer trois jours à Berlin ❸ (at somebody's house) **to stay with somebody** aller [7] chez quelqu'un, **I'm going to stay with my sister this weekend** je vais chez ma sœur ce weekend ❹ (be temporarily lodged) loger [52]; **where are you staying?** où est-ce que vous logez?
 • **to stay in** rester [1] à la maison; **I'm staying in tonight** je reste à la maison ce soir

steady ADJECTIVE ❶ stable; **a steady job** un emploi stable ❷ régulier (FEM régulière); **a steady increase** une augmentation régulière ❸ (hand, voice) ferme ❹ **to hold something steady** bien tenir quelque chose

steak NOUN steack MASC; **steak and chips** un steack frites

steal VERB voler [1]

steam NOUN vapeur FEM

steam engine NOUN locomotive (FEM) à vapeur

steam iron NOUN fer (MASC) à vapeur

steel NOUN acier MASC

steep ADJECTIVE raide; **a steep slope** une pente raide

steeple NOUN ❶ (spire) flèche FEM ❷ (bell tower) clocher MASC

steering wheel NOUN volant MASC

step NOUN ❶ pas MASC; **to take a step forwards** faire un pas en avant, **to take a step backwards** faire un pas en arrière ❷ (stair) marche FEM; **'mind the step'** 'attention à la marche'
 • **to step back** faire [10] un pas en arrière
 • **to step forward** faire [10] un pas en avant
 • **to step into** entrer [1] dans (a lift)

stepbrother NOUN demi-frère MASC (PLURAL demi-frères)

stepdaughter NOUN belle-fille FEM (PLURAL belles-filles)

stepfather NOUN beau-père MASC

stepladder NOUN escabeau MASC (PLURAL escabeaux)

stepmother NOUN belle-mère FEM

stepsister NOUN demi-sœur FEM (PLURAL demi-sœurs)

stepson NOUN beau-fils MASC (PLURAL beaux-fils)

stereo NOUN chaîne (FEM) stéréo (PLURAL chaînes stéréo)

sterling NOUN sterling MASC; **in sterling** en livres sterling

stew NOUN ragoût MASC

steward NOUN steward MASC

stewardess NOUN hôtesse FEM

stick NOUN ❶ bâton MASC ❷ **a walking stick** une canne ❸ **a hockey stick** une crosse de hockey

stick VERB ❶ *(with glue)* coller [1] ❷ *(put)* mettre [11]; **stick them on my desk** mets-les sur mon bureau

sticker NOUN autocollant MASC

sticky ADJECTIVE ❶ poisseux *(FEM poisseuse)*; **my hands are sticky** j'ai les mains poisseuses ❷ adhésif *(FEM adhésive)*; **sticky paper** le papier adhésif

sticky tape NOUN Scotch MASC

stiff ADJECTIVE ❶ **to feel stiff** avoir [5] des courbatures, **to have stiff legs** avoir des courbatures dans les jambes ❷ **to be bored stiff** s'ennuyer [41] à mourir, **to be scared stiff** être [6] mort de peur

still ADJECTIVE ❶ **sit still!** tiens-toi tranquille!, **keep still!** ne bouge pas! ❷ **still mineral water** l'eau minérale non-gazeuse

still ADVERB ❶ toujours; **do you still live in London?** est-ce que tu habites toujours à Londres?, **I've still not finished** je n'ai toujours pas fini, **he's still working** il est toujours en train de travailler ❷ encore; **there's still a lot of beer left** il reste encore beaucoup de bière ❸ **better still** encore mieux

sting NOUN piqûre FEM; **a wasp sting** une piqûre de guêpe

sting VERB piquer [1]; **I was stung by a bee** je me suis fait piquer par une abeille

stink NOUN odeur FEM; **what a stink!** ça pue!

stink VERB puer [1]; **it stinks of cigarette smoke in here** ça pue la cigarette ici

stir VERB remuer [1]

stitch NOUN ❶ *(in sewing)* point MASC ❷ *(in knitting)* maille FEM ❸ *(surgical)* point *(MASC)* de souture *(PLURAL* points de souture*)*

stock NOUN ❶ *(in a shop)* stock MASC; **to have something in stock** avoir quelque chose en stock ❷ *(supply)* réserve; **I always have a stock of pencils** j'ai toujours une réserve de crayons ❸ *(for cooking)* bouillon; **chicken stock** le bouillon de poulet

stock VERB *(in a shop)* vendre [3]; **they don't stock dictionaries** ils ne vendent pas les dictionnaires

• **to stock up on something** s'approvisionner [1] en quelque chose

stock cube NOUN bouillon-cube MASC

stock exchange NOUN Bourse FEM (des valeurs)

stocking NOUN bas MASC

stomach NOUN estomac MASC

stomachache NOUN **to have stomachache** avoir mal au ventre

stone NOUN ❶ pierre FEM; **a stone wall** un mur en pierre ❷ *(pebble)* caillou MASC ❸ *(in fruit)* noyau MASC *(PLURAL* noyaux*)*

stool NOUN tabouret MASC

stop NOUN arrêt MASC; **the bus stop** l'arrêt de bus

stop VERB ❶ s'arrêter [1]; he stopped in front of the shop il s'est arrêté devant le magasin, the music stopped la musique s'est arrêtée, does the train stop in Dijon? est-ce que le train s'arrête à Dijon? ❷ to stop somebody/something arrêter [1] quelque chose/quelqu'un, she stopped me in the street elle m'a arrêté dans la rue ❸ to stop doing arrêter [1] de faire, he's stopped smoking il a arrêté de fumer, she never stops asking questions elle n'arrête pas de poser des questions ❹ to stop somebody doing empêcher [1] quelqu'un de faire, there's nothing to stop you going on your own rien ne t'empêche d'y aller tout seul

stopwatch NOUN chronomètre MASC

store NOUN (shop) magasin MASC

store VERB ❶ garder [1] ❷ (on a computer) mémoriser [1]

storey NOUN étage MASC; a three-storey house une maison à trois étages

stork NOUN cigogne FEM

storm NOUN ❶ (wind) tempête FEM; a snowstorm une tempête de neige, a rainstorm une tempête de pluie ❷ (thunderstorm) orage MASC

stormy ADJECTIVE orageux (FEM orageuse)

story NOUN histoire FEM; to tell a story raconter une histoire

stove NOUN (cooker) cuisinière FEM

straight ADJECTIVE ❶ droit; a straight line une ligne droite ❷ to have straight hair avoir les cheveux raides

straight ADVERB ❶ (in direction) droit; go straight ahead continuez tout droit ❷ (in time) directement; he went straight to the doctor's il est allé directement chez le médecin ❸ straight away tout de suite

straightforward ADJECTIVE simple

strain NOUN stress MASC; the strain of the last few weeks le stress de ces dernières semaines, to be a strain être stressant

strain VERB ❶ se faire [10] mal à (part of the body); he's strained his back il s'est fait mal au dos ❷ (a muscle) se froisser [1] ❸ (of vegetables, rice) égoutter [1]

strange ADJECTIVE bizarre; a strange situation une situation bizarre

stranger NOUN inconnu MASC, inconnue FEM

strangle VERB étrangler [1]

strap NOUN ❶ (on case, bag, camera) courroie FEM ❷ (on a garment) bretelle FEM ❸ (of a watch) bracelet MASC; a watchstrap un bracelet de montre ❹ (on a shoe) lanière FEM

strapless ADJECTIVE sans bretelles

straw NOUN paille FEM (both the material and for drinking with); a straw hat un chapeau de paille

strawberry NOUN fraise FEM; strawberry jam la confiture de fraises, a strawberry yoghurt un yaourt à la fraise

stray ADJECTIVE a stray dog un chien perdu

stream NOUN (small river) **ruisseau** MASC (PLURAL **ruisseaux**)

street NOUN **rue** FEM; **I met Simon in the street** j'ai croisé Simon dans la rue

streetlamp NOUN **réverbère** MASC

street map NOUN **plan** (MASC) **de la ville**

streetwise ADJECTIVE **dégourdi**

strength NOUN **force** FEM

stress NOUN **stress** MASC

stress VERB (emphasize) **souligner** [1]; **to stress the importance of something** souligner l'importance de quelque chose

stretch VERB ❶ (garment) **se déformer** [1]; **this jumper has stretched** ce pull s'est déformé ❷ (shoes) **s'élargir** [2]

stretcher NOUN **brancard** MASC

stretchy ADJECTIVE **élastique**

strict ADJECTIVE **strict**

strike NOUN **grève** FEM; **to go on strike** faire grève, **to be on strike** être en grève

strike VERB ❶ (hit) **frapper** [1] ❷ (clock) **sonner** [1]; **the clock struck six** l'horloge a sonné six heures ❸ (go on strike) **faire** [10] **grève**

striker NOUN ❶ (in football) **buteur** MASC ❷ (person on strike) **gréviste** MASC & FEM

striking ADJECTIVE **frappant**; **a striking resemblance** une ressemblance frappante

string NOUN ❶ (for tying) **ficelle** FEM ❷ (for a musical instrument) **corde** FEM

strip NOUN **bande** FEM

strip VERB (undress) **se déshabiller** [1]

strip cartoon NOUN **bande** (FEM) **dessinée**

stripe NOUN **rayure** FEM

striped ADJECTIVE **rayé**

stroke NOUN ❶ (style of swimming) **nage** FEM ❷ (medical) **attaque** FEM; **to have a stroke** avoir une attaque
• **a stroke of luck** un coup de chance

stroke VERB **caresser** [1]

stroll NOUN **to go for a stroll** faire une petite promenade

stroll VERB **se promener** [50]

strong ADJECTIVE ❶ (person, drink) **fort** ❷ (feeling) **puissant** ❸ (material) **solide**

strongly ADVERB ❶ (believe) **fermement** ❷ (support) **fortement** ❸ (advise, oppose) **vivement**

struggle NOUN ❶ **lutte** FEM; **the struggle for independence** la lutte pour l'indépendance, **a power struggle** une lutte pour le pouvoir ❷ **it's been a struggle** ça a été très dur

struggle VERB ❶ (to obtain something) **se battre** [21]; **they have struggled to survive** ils se sont battus pour survivre ❷ (physically, in order to escape or reach something) **se débattre** [21] ❸ (have difficulty in doing) **avoir** [5] **du mal à faire**; **I'm struggling to finish my homework** j'ai du mal à finir mes devoirs

stub NOUN a cigarette stub un mégot
• to stub out écraser [1] *(a cigarette)*

stubborn ADJECTIVE têtu

stuck ADJECTIVE ❶ *(jammed)* coincé;
the drawer's stuck le tiroir est
coincé ❷ *(person)* **to get stuck** rester
coincé *(in a lift, traffic jam, or place)*

stud NOUN ❶ *(on a belt or jacket)*
clou MASC ❷ *(on a boot)* clou
MASC ❸ *(earring)* boucle *(FEM)*
d'oreille

student NOUN étudiant MASC,
étudiante FEM

studio NOUN ❶ *(film, TV)* studio
MASC ❷ *(artist's)* atelier MASC

studio flat NOUN studio MASC

study VERB ❶ réviser [1]; **he's
busy studying for his exams**
il est en train de réviser pour ses
examens ❷ faire [10] des études
de *(a subject)*; **she's studying
medicine** elle fait des études de
médecine

stuff NOUN ❶ *(things)* trucs MASC PLURAL
(informal); **we can put all that stuff
in the attic** on peut mettre tous
ces trucs au grenier ❷ *(personal
belongings)* affaires FEM PLURAL;
**you can leave your stuff at my
house** tu peux laisser tes affaires
chez moi ❸ *(substance)* truc MASC
(informal); **some antiseptic stuff** un
truc antiseptique

stuff VERB ❶ *(shove)* fourrer [1]
(informal); **she stuffed some
things into a suitcase** elle a
fourré quelques affaires dans une
valise ❷ farcir [2] *(chicken, turkey,
vegetables)*; **stuffed aubergines** des
aubergines farcies

stuffing NOUN *(for cooking)* farce FEM

stuffy ADJECTIVE *(airless)* étouffant

stumble VERB *(trip)* trébucher [1]

stunned ADJECTIVE *(amazed)* stupéfait

stunning ADJECTIVE sensationnel *(FEM
sensationnelle)*

stunt NOUN *(in a film)* cascade FEM

stuntman NOUN cascadeur MASC

stuntwoman NOUN cascadeuse FEM

stupid ADJECTIVE bête; **that was really
stupid** c'était vraiment bête, **to do
something stupid** faire une bêtise

stutter NOUN to have a stutter
bégayer [59]

stutter VERB bégayer [59]

style NOUN ❶ style MASC; **a style
of living** un style de vie, **he has
his own style** il a son propre
style ❷ *(fashion)* mode FEM; **it's the
latest style** c'est la dernière mode

subject NOUN ❶ sujet MASC; **the
subject of my talk** le sujet de mon
exposé ❷ *(at school)* matière FEM;
my favourite subject is biology ma
matière préférée c'est la biologie

submarine NOUN sous-marin MASC
(PLURAL sous-marins)

subscription NOUN abonnement
MASC; **to take out a subscription to**
s'abonner à

subsidy NOUN subvention FEM

substance NOUN substance FEM

substitute NOUN *(person)*
remplaçant MASC, remplaçante
FEM

substitute VERB substituer [1]

subtitled ADJECTIVE (film) sous-titré

subtitles PLURAL NOUN sous-titres MASC PLURAL

subtle ADJECTIVE subtil

subtract VERB soustraire [78]

suburb NOUN banlieue FEM; **a suburb of Edinburgh** une banlieue d'Édimbourg, **in the suburbs of London** dans la banlieue de Londres

suburban ADJECTIVE de banlieue

subway NOUN (underpass) passage (MASC) souterrain

succeed VERB réussir [2]; **to succeed in doing** réussir à faire, **we've succeeded in contacting her** nous avons réussi à la contacter

success NOUN succès MASC; **a great success** un grand succès

successful ADJECTIVE ❶ réussi; **he's a successful writer** c'est un écrivain à succès ❷ **to be successful in doing** réussir à faire

successfully ADVERB avec succès

such ADVERB ❶ tellement; **they're such nice people!** ils sont tellement gentils!, **I've had such a busy day!** j'ai eu une journée tellement chargée!, **it's such a long way** c'est tellement loin, **it's such a pity** c'est tellement dommage ❷ **such a lot of** tellement de, **I've got such a lot of things to tell you!** j'ai tellement de choses à te dire! ❸ **such as** comme, **in big cities such as Glasgow** dans les grandes villes comme Glasgow ❹ **there's no such thing** ça n'existe pas

suck VERB sucer [61]

sudden ADJECTIVE soudain
• **all of a sudden** tout d'un coup

suddenly ADVERB ❶ tout d'un coup; **he suddenly started to laugh** tout d'un coup il s'est mis à rire, **suddenly the light went out** tout d'un coup la lumière s'est éteinte ❷ **to die suddenly** mourir subitement

suede NOUN daim MASC; **a suede jacket** une veste en daim

suffer VERB souffrir [73]

sufficiently ADVERB suffisamment

sugar NOUN sucre MASC; **would you like sugar?** est-ce que tu veux du sucre?, **brown sugar** le sucre roux

suggest VERB suggérer [24]; **he suggested I should speak to you abou it** il m'a suggéré de vous en parler

suggestion NOUN suggestion FEM; **to make a suggestion** faire une suggestion

suicide NOUN suicide MASC; **to commit suicide** se suicider

suit NOUN ❶ (man's) costume MASC ❷ (woman's) tailleur MASC

suitable ADJECTIVE ❶ (clothing) approprié; **I don't have any suitable shoes** je n'ai pas de chaussures appropriées ❷ convenable; **a suitable hotel** un hôtel convenable ❸ **to be suitable for** convenir à

suitcase NOUN valise FEM

sulk VERB bouder [1]

sum NOUN ❶ somme FEM; **a sum of money** une somme d'argent, **a large sum** une grosse somme ❷ (calculation) calcul MASC
• **to sum up** résumer [1]

a
b
c
d
e
f
g
h
i
j
k
l
m
n
o
p
q
r
s
t
u
v
w
x
y
z

summarize *VERB* résumer [1]

summary *NOUN* résumé *MASC*

summer *NOUN* été *MASC*; **in summer** en été, **summer clothes** les vêtements d'été, **the summer holidays** les grandes vacances

summertime *NOUN* été *MASC*; **in summertime** en été

summit *NOUN* sommet *MASC*

sun *NOUN* soleil *MASC*; **in the sun** au soleil

sunbathe *VERB* se bronzer [1]

sunblock *NOUN* crème *(FEM)* écran total

sunburn *NOUN* coup *(MASC)* de soleil

sunburned *ADJECTIVE* ❶ *(tanned)* bronzé ❷ **to get sunburned** *(burned)* attraper un coup de soleil

Sunday *NOUN* dimanche *MASC*; **on Sunday** dimanche, **I'm going out on Sunday** je sors dimanche, **see you on Sunday!** à dimanche!, **on Sundays** le dimanche, **the museum is closed on Sundays** le musée est fermé le dimanche, **every Sunday** tous les dimanches, **last Sunday** dimanche dernier, **next Sunday** dimanche prochain

sunflower *NOUN* tournesol *MASC*; **sunflower oil** l'huile *(FEM)* de tournesol

sunglasses *PLURAL NOUN* lunettes *(FEM PLURAL)* de soleil

sunlight *NOUN* soleil *MASC*

sunny *ADJECTIVE* ❶ **it's a sunny day** il fait du soleil, **it's going to be sunny** il va faire du soleil ❷ *(place)* ensoleillé; **in a sunny corner of**

the garden dans un coin ensoleillé du jardin

sunrise *NOUN* lever *(MASC)* du soleil

sunroof *NOUN* toit *(MASC)* ouvrant

sunset *NOUN* coucher *(MASC)* du soleil

sunshine *NOUN* soleil *MASC*

sunstroke *NOUN* insolation *FEM*; **to get sunstroke** attraper une insolation

suntan *NOUN* bronzage *MASC*; **to get a suntan** bronzer

suntan lotion *NOUN* lotion *(FEM)* solaire

suntan oil *NOUN* huile *(FEM)* solaire

super *ADJECTIVE* formidable; **we had a super time!** c'était formidable!

supermarket *NOUN* supermarché *MASC*

supernatural *ADJECTIVE* surnaturel *(FEM surnaturelle)*

superstitious *ADJECTIVE* superstitieux *(FEM superstitieuse)*

supervise *VERB* surveiller [1]

supervisor *NOUN* ❶ *(in a shop)* responsable *MASC & FEM* ❷ *(in a factory)* contremaître *MASC*

supper *NOUN* dîner *MASC*; **I had supper at Sandy's** j'ai dîné chez Sandy

supplement *NOUN* supplément *MASC*

supplies *PLURAL NOUN (of food)* provisions *FEM PLURAL*

supply *NOUN* ❶ *(stock)* réserves *FEM PLURAL* ❷ **to be in short supply** être difficile à trouver

supply VERB fournir [2]; **the school supplies the paper** c'est l'école qui fournit le papier, **to supply somebody with something** fournir quelque chose à quelqu'un

supply teacher NOUN suppléant MASC, suppléante FEM

support NOUN soutien MASC; **he has a lot of support** il a beaucoup de soutien

support VERB ❶ (back up) soutenir [77]; **her teachers have really supported her** ses professeurs l'ont vraiment soutenue ❷ être [6] supporter de (a team); **Graeme supports Liverpool** Graeme est supporter de Liverpool ❸ (financially) **to support a family** subvenir [81] aux besoins d'une famille

supporter NOUN supporter MASC; **a Manchester United supporter** un supporter de Manchester United

suppose VERB **I suppose she's forgotten** elle a sans doute oublié

supposed ADJECTIVE **to be supposed to do** être censé faire, **you're supposed to wear a helmet** on est censé porter un casque, **he was supposed to be here at six** il devait être là à six heures

sure ADJECTIVE sûr; **are you sure?** tu es sûr?, **are you sure you've had enough to eat?** tu es sûr que tu as assez mangé?, **are you sure you saw her?** tu es sûr de l'avoir vue?, **'can you shut the door?' – 'sure!'** 'peux-tu fermer la porte?' – 'bien sûr!'

surely ADVERB quand même; **surely she couldn't have forgotten!** elle ne peut pas avoir oublié quand même!

surf NOUN écume FEM

surf VERB **to surf the Net/Web** surfer [1] Internet/le web

surface NOUN surface FEM

surfboard NOUN planche (FEM) de surf (PLURAL planches de surf)

surfer NOUN ❶ (on the sea) surfeur MASC, surfeuse FEM ❷ (on the Net) cybernaute (MASC & FEM), internaute MASC & FEM

surfing NOUN surf MASC; **to go surfing** faire du surf

surgeon NOUN chirurgien MASC; **she's a surgeon** elle est chirurgien

surgery NOUN ❶ (procedure) chirurgie FEM; **to have surgery** se faire opérer, **laser surgery** la chirurgie au laser ❷ (doctor's) cabinet (MASC) médical; **the dentist's surgery** le cabinet dentaire

surname NOUN nom (MASC) de famille (PLURAL noms de famille)

surprise NOUN surprise FEM; **what a surprise!** quelle surprise!

surprised ADJECTIVE étonné; **I was surprised to see her** j'ai été étonné de la voir

surprising ADJECTIVE étonnant

surrender VERB ❶ (soldiers) se rendre [3] ❷ (country) capituler [1] ❸ livrer [1] (a town, castle)

surrender NOUN (by sportsman) abandon MASC, (by army) capitulation FEM

surround VERB ❶ encercler [1] ❷ **to be surrounded by** être [6] entouré de, **she's surrounded by friends** elle est entourée d'amis

survey NOUN enquête FEM

survive VERB survivre [82]

survivor NOUN survivant MASC, survivante FEM

suspect NOUN suspect MASC, suspecte FEM

suspect ADJECTIVE douteux (FEM douteuse)

suspect VERB soupçonner [1]

suspend VERB ❶ (hang) suspendre [3] ❷ to be suspended (from school) être [6] exclu

suspense NOUN suspense MASC

suspicious ADJECTIVE ❶ méfiant; to be suspicious of se méfier de ❷ a suspicious parcel un paquet suspect ❸ a suspicious-looking individual un individu louche

swallow NOUN (bird) hirondelle FEM

swallow VERB avaler

swan NOUN cygne MASC

swap VERB ❶ échanger [52]; do you want to swap? tu veux qu'on échange?, he's swapped his bike for a computer il a échangé son vélo contre un ordinateur ❷ to swap seats with somebody changer [52] de place avec quelqu'un

swear VERB (use bad language) utiliser [1] des gros mots; he swears a lot il utilise beaucoup de gros mots

swearword NOUN gros mot MASC

sweat NOUN transpiration FEM

sweat VERB transpirer [1]

sweater NOUN pull MASC

sweatshirt NOUN sweatshirt MASC

swede NOUN (vegetable) rutabaga MASC

Swede NOUN Suédois MASC, Suédoise FEM

Sweden NOUN Suède FEM; in Sweden en Suède, to Sweden en Suède

Swedish NOUN (language) suédois MASC

Swedish ADJECTIVE suédois

sweep VERB balayer [59]

sweet NOUN ❶ bonbon MASC; I bought her some sweets je lui ai acheté des bonbons ❷ (dessert) dessert MASC

sweet ADJECTIVE ❶ (food) sucré; I try not to eat sweet things j'essaie d'éviter les choses sucrées ❷ (kind) gentil (FEM gentille); she's a really sweet person elle est vraiment gentille, it was really sweet of him c'était vraiment gentil de sa part ❸ (cute) mignon (FEM mignonne); he looks really sweet in that hat! il est mignon avec ce chapeau!

sweetcorn NOUN maïs MASC

swell VERB (part of the body) enfler [1]

swelling NOUN enflure FEM; he has a swelling on his knee il a le genou enflé

swerve VERB faire [10] un écart (MASC); the car swerved to avoid the dog la voiture a fait un écart pour éviter le chien

swim NOUN to go for a swim aller [7] se baigner

swim VERB nager [52]; can he swim? est-ce qu'il sait nager?, to swim across a lake traverser [1] un lac à la nage

swimmer NOUN nageur MASC, nageuse FEM; she's a strong swimmer c'est une bonne nageuse

swimming NOUN natation FEM; to go swimming faire de la natation

swimming cap NOUN bonnet (MASC) de bain

swimming costume NOUN maillot (MASC) de bain

swimming pool NOUN piscine FEM

swimming trunks NOUN maillot (MASC) de bain

swimsuit NOUN maillot (MASC) de bain

swindle NOUN escroquerie FEM; what a swindle! quelle escroquerie!

swing NOUN balançoire FEM

Swiss NOUN (person) Suisse MASC & FEM; the Swiss les Suisses MASC PLURAL

Swiss ADJECTIVE suisse

switch NOUN ❶ (button type: electrical) bouton MASC ❷ (up-down type) interrupteur MASC

switch VERB (change) changer [52] de; to switch places changer de place
• to switch something off éteindre [60] quelque chose

• to switch something on allumer [1] quelque chose

Switzerland NOUN Suisse FEM; in Switzerland en Suisse, to Switzerland en Suisse

swollen ADJECTIVE enflé

swop VERB ▸ SEE **swap**

sword NOUN épée FEM

swordfish NOUN espadon MASC

sycamore NOUN sycomore MASC

syllabus NOUN programme MASC; to be on the syllabus être au programme

symbol NOUN symbole MASC

symbolic ADJECTIVE symbolique

sympathetic ADJECTIVE compréhensif (FEM compréhensive)

sympathize VERB to sympathize with somebody comprendre [64] quelqu'un, I sympathize with her je la comprends

sympathy NOUN compassion FEM

symphony NOUN symphonie FEM

symphony orchestra NOUN orchestre (MASC) symphonique

symptom NOUN symptôme MASC

synagogue NOUN synagogue FEM

synthesizer NOUN synthétiseur MASC

synthetic ADJECTIVE synthétique

syringe NOUN seringue FEM

system NOUN système MASC

a b c d e f g h i j k l m n o p q r s t u v w x y z

table NOUN table FEM; **on the table** sur
la table, **to lay the table** mettre la
table, **to clear the table** débarrasser
la table

tablecloth NOUN nappe FEM

table football NOUN baby-foot MASC

tablemat NOUN ❶ (for individual
plates) set (MASC) de table ❷ (for
dish) dessous-de-plat MASC

tablespoon NOUN grande cuillère
FEM; (in recipes) **a tablespoon of
flour** une cuillère à soupe de farine

tablet NOUN comprimé MASC

table tennis NOUN ping-pong
MASC; **to play table tennis** jouer au
ping-pong

tabloid NOUN quotidien (MASC)
populaire

tackle NOUN ❶ (in football) tacle
MASC ❷ (in rugby) plaquage MASC

tackle VERB ❶ (in football or hockey)
tacler [1] ❷ s'attaquer [1] à (a job
or problem)

tact NOUN tact MASC

tactful ADJECTIVE plein de tact; **that
wasn't very tactful** ça a manqué un
peu de tact

tactic NOUN tactique FEM

tadpole NOUN têtard MASC

tail NOUN ❶ queue FEM ❷ 'heads or
tails?' – 'tails' 'pile ou face?' – 'pile'

tailor NOUN tailleur MASC

take VERB ❶ prendre [64]; **he took a
chocolate** il a pris un chocolat, **take
my hand** prends ma main, **I took
the bus** j'ai pris le bus, **to take a
holiday** prendre des vacances, **do
you take sugar?** est-ce que vous
prenez du sucre?, **who's taken
my keys?** qui a pris mes clefs?, **it
takes two hours** ça prend deux
heures, **he took the news badly**
il a mal pris la nouvelle ❷ (to
accompany) emmener [50] (a
person); **I'm taking Jake to the
doctor's** j'emmène Jake chez le
médecin, **I must take the car to
the garage** je dois emmener la
voiture au garage ❸ (carry away)
emporter [1]; **she's taken some
work to do at home** elle a emporté
du travail pour faire chez elle ❹ to
take something up(stairs) monter
[1] quelque chose, **could you take
these towels up?** est-ce que tu peux
monter ces serviettes? ❺ to take
something down(stairs) descendre
[3] quelque chose, **Cheryl's taken
the cups down** Cheryl a descendu
les tasses ❻ accepter [1] (a credit
card); **do you take cheques?**
est-ce que vous acceptez les
chèques? ❼ passer [1] (an exam);
**she's taking her driving test
tomorrow** elle passe son permis
demain ❽ **it takes a lot of courage**
il faut beaucoup de courage ❾ **what
size do you take?** quelle taille
faites-vous?

• **to take something apart** démonter
[1] quelque chose
• **to take something back** rapporter
[1] quelque chose
• **to take off** ❶ (a plane) décoller
[1] ❷ enlever [50] (clothes or shoes);

he took off his shirt il a enlevé sa chemise ❸ déduire [26] *(money)*; he took five pounds off the price il a déduit cinq livres du prix
• to take out ❶ *(from a bag or pocket)* sortir [72]; Eric took out his wallet Eric a sorti son porte-feuille ❷ he's taking me out to lunch il m'emmène déjeuner, she took me out to the theatre elle m'a emmenée au théâtre

takeaway NOUN ❶ *(a meal)* repas *(MASC)* à emporter; an Indian takeaway un repas indien à emporter ❷ *(where you buy it)* restaurant *(MASC)* qui fait des plats à emporter

take-off NOUN décollage *MASC (of a plane)*

tale NOUN histoire *FEM*

talent NOUN talent *MASC*; to have a talent for something être doué pour quelque chose

talented ADJECTIVE doué; he's really talented il est vraiment doué

talk NOUN ❶ *(a chat)* conversation *FEM*; I had a talk with Roy about it j'ai eu une conversation avec Roy à ce sujet ❷ exposé *MASC*; she's giving a talk on Hungary elle fait un exposé sur la Hongrie

talk VERB ❶ parler [1]; I was talking to Jeevan about football je parlais du foot avec Jeevan, what's he talking about? de quoi parle-t-il?, we'll talk about it later on en parlera plus tard ❷ *(to gossip)* bavarder [1]; they're always talking ils n'arrêtent pas de bavarder

talkative ADJECTIVE bavard; he's not exactly talkative! on ne pourrait pas dire qu'il est bavard!

tall ADJECTIVE ❶ grand; she's very tall elle est très grande, I'm 1.7 metres tall je mesure un mètre soixante-dix ❷ haut *(a building or tree)*

tambourine NOUN tambourin *MASC*

tame ADJECTIVE apprivoisé *(an animal)*

tampon NOUN tampon *MASC*

tan NOUN bronzage *MASC*; to get a tan bronzer

tan VERB bronzer [1]; I tan easily je bronze facilement

tangerine NOUN mandarine *FEM*

tank NOUN ❶ *(for petrol or water)* réservoir *MASC* ❷ a fish tank un aquarium ❸ *(military)* char *MASC*

tanker NOUN ❶ *(ship)* navire-citerne *MASC* ❷ *(on road)* camion-citerne *MASC*

tanned ADJECTIVE bronzé

tap NOUN ❶ robinet *MASC*; to turn on the tap ouvrir le robinet, to turn off the tap fermer le robinet, the hot tap le robinet d'eau chaude ❷ *(a pat)* petite tape *FEM*

tap VERB taper [1]

tap-dancing NOUN claquettes *FEM PLURAL*; to do tap-dancing faire des claquettes

tape NOUN ❶ cassette *FEM*; my tape of the Stones ma cassette des Stones, I've got it on tape je l'ai en cassette ❷ sticky tape scotch

tape VERB enregistrer [1]; I want to tape the film je veux enregistrer le film

tape measure NOUN mètre *(MASC)* à ruban

tape recorder NOUN magnétophone MASC

tapestry NOUN tapisserie FEM

tar NOUN goudron MASC

target NOUN cible FEM

tart NOUN tarte FEM; **a raspberry tart** une tarte aux framboises

tartan ADJECTIVE écossais; **a tartan skirt** une jupe écossaise

task NOUN tâche FEM

taste NOUN goût MASC; **the taste of onions** le goût des oignons, **in bad taste** de mauvais goût

taste VERB ❶ goûter [1]; **do you want to taste?** tu veux goûter?, **the soup tastes horrible** la soupe a un goût infect ❷ **to taste of** avoir [5] un goût de, **it tastes of strawberries** ça a un goût de fraises

tasty ADJECTIVE savoureux (FEM savoureuse)

tattoo NOUN tatouage MASC; **he's got a tattoo on his arm** il a un tatouage sur le bras

Taurus NOUN Taureau MASC; **Josephine's Taurus** Josephine est Taureau

tax NOUN ❶ impôts MASC PLURAL ❷ (on goods) taxe FEM

taxi NOUN taxi MASC; **by taxi** en taxi, **to take a taxi** prendre un taxi

taxi driver NOUN chauffeur (MASC) de taxi

taxi rank NOUN station (FEM) de taxis

TB NOUN tuberculose FEM

tea NOUN ❶ thé MASC; **a cup of tea** une tasse de thé, **to have tea** prendre le thé ❷ (evening meal) dîner MASC

teabag NOUN sachet (MASC) de thé

teach VERB ❶ apprendre [64]; **she's teaching me Italian** elle m'apprend l'italien, **that'll teach you!** ça t'apprendra! ❷ enseigner [1]; **her mum teaches maths** sa mère enseigne les maths ❸ **to teach yourself something** apprendre [64] quelque chose tout seul, **Anne taught herself Italian** Anne a appris l'italien toute seule

teacher NOUN ❶ (in a secondary school) professeur MASC; **my mother's a teacher** ma mère est professeur, **our biology teacher** notre professeur de biologie ❷ (in primary school) instituteur MASC institutrice FEM; **she's a primary school teacher** elle est institutrice

teaching NOUN enseignement MASC

team NOUN équipe FEM; **a football team** une équipe de foot, **our team won** notre équipe a gagné

teapot NOUN théière FEM

tear[1] NOUN (a rip) accroc MASC; **I've got a tear in my jeans** j'ai un accroc dans mon jean

tear VERB ❶ déchirer [1]; **you've torn your shirt** tu as déchiré ta chemise, **she tore up my letter** elle a déchiré ma lettre ❷ se déchirer [1]; **be careful, it tears easily** attention, ça se déchire facilement
- **to tear off to tear open** ❶ (carefully) détacher [1] ❷ (violently) arracher [1]

- **tear²** NOUN *(when you cry)* larme FEM; **to be in tears** être en larmes, **to burst into tears** fondre en larmes

tease VERB ❶ taquiner [1] *(a person)* ❷ tourmenter [1] *(an animal)*

teaspoon NOUN petite cuillère FEM; *(in recipes)* **a teaspoonful of ...** une cuillère à café de ...

teatime NOUN l'heure *(FEM)* du dîner *(evening meal)*

tea towel NOUN torchon MASC

technical ADJECTIVE technique

technical college NOUN lycée *(MASC)* technique

technician NOUN technicien MASC, technicienne FEM

technique NOUN technique FEM

techno NOUN techno FEM *(music)*

technological ADJECTIVE technologique

technology NOUN technologie FEM; **information technology** l'informatique FEM

teddy bear NOUN nounours MASC

teenage ADJECTIVE ❶ adolescent *(FEM adolescente)*; **they have a teenage son** ils ont un fils adolescent ❷ *(films, magazines, etc.)* pour les jeunes; **a teenage magazine** un magazine pour les jeunes

teenager NOUN ❶ jeune MASC & FEM; **a group of teenagers** une bande de jeunes ❷ *(more precisely)* adolescent MASC, adolescente FEM; **when I was a teenager** quand j'étais adolescent

teens PLURAL NOUN adolescence FEM; **he's in his teens** c'est un adolescent

tee-shirt NOUN tee-shirt MASC

telegraph pole NOUN poteau *(MASC)* télégraphique

telephone NOUN téléphone MASC; **on the telephone** au téléphone

telephone VERB appeler [18]; **I'll telephone the bank** je vais appeler la banque

telephone box NOUN cabine *(FEM)* téléphonique

telephone call NOUN coup *(MASC)* de téléphone

telephone card NOUN carte *(FEM)* de téléphone

telephone directory NOUN annuaire MASC

telephone number NOUN numéro *(MASC)* de téléphone

telescope NOUN télescope MASC

televise VERB téléviser [1]; **they're televising the match** on va téléviser le match

television NOUN télévision FEM; **she was watching television** elle regardait la télévision, **I saw it on television** je l'ai vu à la télévision

television programme NOUN émission *(FEM)* de télévision

tell VERB ❶ **to tell somebody something** dire [9] quelque chose à quelqu'un, **that's what she told me** c'est ce qu'elle m'a dit, **I told him it was silly** je lui ai dit que c'était idiot, **have you told Sara?** est-ce que tu l'as dit à Sara? ❷ **to tell somebody to do** dire [9] à quelqu'un de faire, **he told me to do it myself** il m'a dit de le faire moi-même, **she told me not to wait** elle m'a dit de ne pas attendre ❸ *(explain)* **can you tell me how to do it?** est-ce que vous pouvez m'expliquer comment on le fait? ❹ raconter [1] *(a story)*; **tell me about your holiday** raconte-moi tes vacances ❺ *(to see)* voir [13]; **you can tell it's old** on voit bien que c'est ancien, **you can tell she's cross** on voit bien qu'elle est fâchée, **I can't tell them apart** je n'arrive pas à les distinguer

telly NOUN télé FEM; **to watch telly** regarder la télé, **I saw her on telly** je l'ai vue à la télé

temp NOUN intérimaire MASC & FEM

temper NOUN **to be in a temper** être en colère, **to lose your temper** se mettre en colère

temperature NOUN ❶ température FEM; **the oven temperature** la température du four ❷ **to have a temperature** avoir de la fièvre

temple NOUN temple MASC

temporary ADJECTIVE temporaire

temptation NOUN tentation FEM

tempted ADJECTIVE tenté; **I'm really tempted to go** je suis vraiment tenté d'y aller

tempting ADJECTIVE tentant

ten NUMBER dix MASC; **Harry's ten** Harry a dix ans

tend VERB **to tend to do** avoir [5] tendance à faire, **he tends to talk a lot** il a tendance à beaucoup parler

tendency NOUN tendance FEM; **to have a tendency to** avoir [5] tendance à

tender ADJECTIVE tendre

tennis NOUN tennis MASC; **to play tennis** jouer au tennis

tennis ball NOUN balle *(FEM)* de tennis

tennis court NOUN tennis MASC

tennis player NOUN joueur de tennis MASC, joueuse de tennis FEM

tennis racket NOUN raquette *(FEM)* de tennis

tenor NOUN ténor MASC

tenpin bowling NOUN bowling MASC; **to go tenpin bowling** jouer au bowling

tense NOUN **the present tense** le présent, **in the future tense** au futur

tense ADJECTIVE tendu

tent NOUN tente FEM

tenth NUMBER dixième MASC; **on the tenth floor** au dixième étage, **the tenth of April** le dix avril

term NOUN ❶ *(in school)* trimestre MASC ❷ **to be on good terms with somebody** être en bons termes avec quelqu'un

terminal NOUN ❶ *(at an airport)* aérogare FEM; **terminal two** l'aérogare numéro deux ❷ **a ferry terminal** une gare maritime ❸ *(a computer terminal)* terminal MASC *(PLURAL terminaux)*

terrace NOUN ❶ *(of a house or hotel)* terrasse FEM ❷ **the terraces** *(at a stadium)* les gradins MASC PLURAL

terrible ADJECTIVE épouvantable; **the weather was terrible** il a fait un temps épouvantable

terribly ADVERB ❶ (very) très;
not terribly clean pas très
propre ❷ (badly) **affreusement
mal**; **I played terribly** j'ai joué
affreusement mal

terrific ADJECTIVE ❶ **at a terrific speed**
à une vitesse folle, **a terrific amount**
une quantité énorme ❷ **terrific!**
formidable!

terrified ADJECTIVE **terrifié**

terrify VERB **terrifier** [1]

territory NOUN **territoire** MASC

terrorism NOUN **terrorisme** MASC

terrorist NOUN **terroriste** MASC & FEM

test NOUN ❶ (in school) **contrôle** MASC;
we've got a maths test tomorrow
nous avons un contrôle de maths
demain ❷ (of your skills or patience)
test MASC ❸ (medical) **analyse** FEM; **a
blood test** une analyse de sang ❹ **a
driving test** un examen de permis
de conduire, **she's doing her driving
test on Friday** elle passe son permis
vendredi, **he passed his driving test**
il a eu son permis

test VERB ❶ (in school) **contrôler**
[1] ❷ **to test something out** essayer
[59] quelque chose

test tube NOUN **éprouvette** FEM

text NOUN **texte** MASC

text VERB **to text someone** envoyer
[40] un texto à quelqu'un, **I'll text
you tomorrow** je t'enverrai un
texto demain

textbook NOUN **manuel** MASC

text message NOUN **texto** MASC

Thames NOUN **the Thames** la Tamise

than PREPOSITION, CONJUNCTION ❶ **que**;
**their new album's better than
the last one** leur nouveau album
est meilleur que le dernier, **they
have more money than we do** ils
ont plus d'argent que nous ❷ (for
quantities) **de**; **more than forty** plus
de quarante, **more than thirty years**
plus de trente ans

thank VERB **remercier** [1]

thanks PLURAL NOUN ❶ **merci**; **no
thanks** non merci, **thanks a lot**
merci beaucoup, **thanks for your
letter** merci pour ta lettre ❷ **with
thanks for** avec mes remerciements
pour ❸ **thanks to** grâce à, **it was
thanks to Micky** c'était grâce à
Micky

thank you ADVERB **merci**; **thank you
very much for the cheque** merci
beaucoup pour le chèque, **no thank
you** non merci, **a thank-you letter**
une lettre de remerciements

that DETERMINER ❶ **ce** (FEM **cette**) (but
'ce' becomes 'cet' before a masculine
noun beginning with a vowel or a
silent 'h') **that dog** ce chien, **that
man** cet homme, **that blue car**
cette voiture bleue ❷ **that one**
celui-là MASC celle-là FEM, **'which
cake would you like?' – 'that one,
please'** 'tu veux quel gâteau?'
– 'celui-là, s'il te plaît', **I like all the
dresses but I'm going to buy that
one** j'aime toutes les robes mais je
vais acheter celle-là

that ADVERB ❶ **it's not that silly** ce
n'est pas si idiot que ça, **their house
isn't that big** leur maison n'est pas
si grande que ça ❷ **it was that high**
c'était haut comme ça

a
b
c
d
e
f
g
h
i
j
k
l
m
n
o
p
q
r
s
t
u
v
w
x
y
z

that PRONOUN ❶ (before verb 'être') ce (c' before a vowel); **that's not true** ce n'est pas vrai, **that's not what you told me** ce n'est pas ce que tu m'as dit, **what's that?** qu'est-ce que c'est?, **that smells good** ça sent bon, **who's that?** c'est qui?, **where's that?** c'est où?, **is that Mandy?** c'est Mandy? ❷ ça; **did you see that?** tu as vu ça?, **that's my bedroom** ça c'est ma chambre ❸ qui; **the book that's on the table** le livre qui est sur la table ❹ que (qu' before a vowel or a silent 'h'); **the book that I lent you** le livre que je t'ai prêté

that CONJUNCTION que (qu' before a vowel or a silent 'h'); **I knew that he was wrong** je savais qu'il avait tort

thaw NOUN fonte (FEM) des neiges

the DETERMINER ❶ (before a noun which is masculine in French) le (l' before a vowel or silent 'h') **the cat** le chat, **the tree** l'arbre ❷ (before a noun which is feminine in French) la (l' before a vowel or silent 'h') **the table** la table, **the orange** l'orange ❸ les (before all plural nouns); **the windows** les fenêtres

theatre NOUN théâtre MASC; **to go to the theatre** aller au théâtre

theft NOUN vol MASC

their DETERMINER leur (PLURAL leurs); **their flat** leur appartement, **their mother** leur mère, **their presents** leurs cadeaux

theirs PRONOUN ❶ le leur (when standing for a masculine noun); **our garden's smaller than theirs** notre jardin est plus petit que le leur ❷ la leur (when standing for a feminine noun); **your house is bigger than theirs** votre maison est

plus grande que la leur ❸ les leurs (when standing for a plural noun); **our children are older than theirs** nos enfants sont plus âgés que les leurs ❹ à eux, à elles; **the yellow car's theirs** la voiture jaune est à eux, **it's theirs** c'est à eux

them PRONOUN ❶ les; **I know them** je les connais, **I don't know them** je ne les connais pas, **listen to them!** écoute-les!, **I saw them last week** je les ai vus la semaine dernière ❷ (to them) leur; **I gave them my address** je leur ai donné mon adresse ❸ (after a preposition) eux (FEM elles); **I'll go with them** j'irai avec eux, (if they are all female) j'irai avec elles, **without them** sans eux, sans elles, (in comparisons) **she's older than them** elle est plus âgée qu'eux, (if all female) elle est plus âgée qu'elles

theme NOUN thème FEM

theme park NOUN parc (MASC) de loisirs

themselves PRONOUN ❶ se; **they've helped themselves** ils se sont servis ❷ (for emphasis) eux-mêmes MASC, elles-mêmes FEM; **the boys can do it themselves** les garçons peuvent le faire eux-mêmes, **the girls will tell you themselves** les filles vous le diront elles-mêmes

then ADVERB ❶ (next) ensuite; **I wash up and then I make the bed** je fais la vaisselle et ensuite je fais le lit, **I went to the post office and then the bank** je suis allé à la poste et ensuite à la banque ❷ (at that time) à l'époque; **we were living in York then** nous habitions à York à l'époque ❸ (in that case) alors; **then why worry?** alors pourquoi s'inquiéter?, **that's all right then** ça va alors ❹ **by then** déjà, **by then it was too late** il était déjà trop tard

theory NOUN théorie FEM; **in theory** en théorie

there ADVERB ❶ là; **put it there** mets-le là, **stand there** mettez-vous là, **they're in there** ils sont là ❷ **over there** là-bas, **she's over there talking to Mark** elle est là-bas en train de discuter avec Mark, **down there** là-bas ❸ **up there** là-haut, **look up there!** regarde là-haut! ❹ y *(when the place 'there' stands for has already been mentioned)*; **I've seen photos of Oxford but I've never been there** j'ai vu des photos d'Oxford mais je n'y suis jamais allé, **yes, I'm going there on Tuesday** oui, j'y vais mardi ❺ **there is** il y a, **there's a cat in the garden** il y a un chat dans le jardin, **there was no bread** il n'y avait pas de pain, **yes, there's enough** oui, il y en a assez ❻ **there are** il y a, **there are plenty of seats** il y a beaucoup de places ❼ **there they are!** les voilà!, **there she is!** la voilà!, **there's the bus coming!** voilà le bus qui arrive!

therefore ADVERB donc

thermometer NOUN thermomètre MASC

these DETERMINER ces; **these books** ces livres

they PRONOUN ❶ ils *(when standing for a masculine noun)*; **'where are the knives?' – 'they're in the drawer'** 'où sont les couteaux?' – 'ils sont dans le tiroir' ❷ elles *(when standing for a feminine noun)*; **I bought some apples but they're not very nice** j'ai acheté des pommes mais elles ne sont pas très bonnes

thick ADJECTIVE épais *(FEM* épaisse)*; **a thick layer of butter** une couche épaisse de beurre

thickness NOUN épaisseur FEM

thief NOUN voleur MASC, voleuse FEM

thigh NOUN cuisse FEM

thin ADJECTIVE ❶ mince *(a slice or a person)* ❷ *(too thin, skinny)* maigre; **she's got terribly thin** elle a beaucoup maigri

thing NOUN ❶ *(an object)* chose FEM; **shops full of pretty things** des magasins remplis de jolies choses, **she told me some surprising things** elle m'a raconté des choses étonnantes ❷ *(a whatsit)* truc MASC *(informal)*; **tu peux utiliser ce truc-là pour l'ouvrir** you can use that thing to open it, **that thing next to the hammer** ce truc à côté du marteau ❸ **things** *(belongings)* affaires FEM PLURAL, **you can put your things in my room** tu peux mettre tes affaires dans ma chambre ❹ **the best thing to do is …** ce qu'il faut faire, c'est …, **the thing is, I've lost her address** ce qu'il y a, c'est que j'ai perdu son adresse, **how are things with you?** comment ça va?

think VERB ❶ *(believe)* croire [33]; **do you think they'll come?** tu crois qu'ils vont venir?, **no, I don't think so** non, je ne crois pas, **I think he's already left** je crois qu'il est déjà parti ❷ penser [1]; **I'm thinking about you** je pense à toi, **Tony thinks it's silly** Tony pense que c'est bête, **what do you think of my new jacket?** qu'est-ce que tu penses de ma nouvelle veste?, **what do you think of that?** qu'en penses-tu? ❸ *(to think carefully)* réfléchir [2]; **he thought for a moment** il a réfléchi un instant,

I've thought it over carefully j'y ai bien réfléchi ❹ *(imagine)* imaginer [1]; just think! we'll soon be in Spain! imagine! on va bientôt être en Espagne!, I never thought it would be like this! je n'avais jamais imaginé que ce serait comme ça

third NOUN tiers MASC; **a third of the population** un tiers de la population

third ADJECTIVE troisième; **on the third floor** au troisième étage, **the third of March** le trois mars

thirdly ADVERB troisièmement

Third World NOUN tiers-monde MASC

thirst NOUN soif FEM

thirsty ADJECTIVE **to be thirsty** avoir [5] soif, **I'm thirsty** j'ai soif, **we were all thirsty** nous avions tous soif

thirteen NUMBER treize MASC; **Ahmed's thirteen** Ahmed a treize ans

thirty NUMBER trente MASC

this DETERMINER ❶ ce *(before a masculine noun)*, cet *(before a masculine noun beginning with a vowel or a silent 'h')*, cette *(before a feminine noun)*; **this paintbrush** ce pinceau, **this tree** cet arbre, **this cup** cette tasse, **this morning** ce matin, **this evening** ce soir, **this afternoon** cet après-midi ❷ **this one** celui-ci MASC, celle-ci FEM, **if you need a pen you can use this one** si tu as besoin d'un stylo tu peux utiliser celui-ci, **if you want a lamp you can borrow this one** si tu veux une lampe tu peux emprunter celle-ci

this PRONOUN ❶ ça; **can you hold this for a moment?** est-ce que tu peux prendre ça un instant? ❷ **what's this?** qu'est-ce que c'est?, **this is**

Tracy speaking *(on the phone)* c'est Tracy à l'appareil ❸ *(in introductions)* **this is my sister Carla** je te présente ma sœur Carla

thistle NOUN chardon MASC

thorn NOUN épine FEM

thorough ADJECTIVE ❶ *(search)* minutieux *(FEM minutieuse)* ❷ *(person)* consciencieux *(FEM consciencieuse)*

those DETERMINER ces; **those books** ces livres

those PRONOUN ceux-là MASC, celles-là FEM; **if you want some knives you can take those** si tu veux des couteaux tu peux prendre ceux-là, **if you want some plates you can take those** si tu veux des assiettes tu peux prendre celles-là

though CONJUNCTION, ADVERB ❶ bien que *(followed by a verb in the subjunctive)*; **though it's cold** bien qu'il fasse froid, **though he's older than she is** bien qu'il soit plus âgé qu'elle ❷ **it was a good idea, though** et pourtant, c'était une bonne idée

thought NOUN pensée FEM

thoughtful ADJECTIVE ❶ *(considerate)* gentil *(FEM gentille)*; **it was really thoughtful of you** c'était vraiment gentil de ta part ❷ *(deep in thought)* pensif *(FEM pensive)*

thoughtless ADJECTIVE irréfléchi

thousand NUMBER ❶ mille MASC; **a thousand** mille, **three thousand** trois mille ❷ **thousands of** des milliers de, **there were thousands of tourists in Venice** il y avait des milliers de touristes à Venise

thread NOUN fil MASC

thread VERB enfiler [1] *(a needle)*

threat NOUN menace FEM

threaten VERB menacer [61]; **to threaten to do** menacer de faire

three NUMBER trois MASC; **Oskar's three** Oskar a trois ans

three-quarters NOUN trois-quarts MASC PLURAL; **three-quarters full** plein aux trois-quarts

thrilled ADJECTIVE ravi; **I was thrilled to hear from you** j'ai été ravi d'avoir de tes nouvelles

thriller NOUN thriller MASC

thrilling ADJECTIVE palpitant

throat NOUN gorge FEM; **to have a sore throat** avoir mal à la gorge, **a throat sweet** une pastille

through PREPOSITION ❶ *(across)* à travers; **through the forest** à travers la forêt, **the water went right through** l'eau est passée à travers, **the police let us through** la police nous a laissés passer ❷ *(via)* par; **the train went through Leeds** le train est passé par Leeds, **through the window** par la fenêtre, **I know them through my cousins** je les connais par mes cousins ❸ **to go through something** traverser quelque chose, **we went through the park** nous avons traversé le parc ❹ **right through the day** toute la journée

through ADJECTIVE direct *(a train or flight)*

throughout PREPOSITION **throughout the match** pendant tout le match, **throughout the world** partout dans le monde

throw VERB ❶ jeter [48]; **I threw the letter into the bin** j'ai jeté la lettre dans la poubelle, **he threw the book on the floor** il a jeté le livre par terre ❷ *(taking aim)* lancer [61]; **throw me the ball!** lance-moi le ballon!, **we were throwing snowballs** on lançait des boules de neige
- **to throw something away** jeter [48] quelque chose; **I've thrown away the old newspapers** j'ai jeté les vieux journaux
- **to throw somebody out** expulser [1] quelqu'un
- **to throw something out** jeter [48] quelque chose *(rubbish)*
- **to throw up** vomir [2]

thumb NOUN pouce MASC

thump VERB taper [1]

thunder NOUN tonnerre MASC; **a peal of thunder** un roulement de tonnerre

thunderstorm NOUN orage MASC

thundery ADJECTIVE orageux *(FEM orageuse)*

Thursday NOUN jeudi MASC; **on Thursday** jeudi, **I'm going out on Thursday** je sors jeudi, **see you on Thursday!** à jeudi!, **on Thursdays** le jeudi, **the museum is closed on Thursdays** le musée est fermé le jeudi, **every Thursday** tous les jeudis, **last Thursday** jeudi dernier, **next Thursday** jeudi prochain

thyme NOUN thym MASC

tick VERB ❶ *(tick-tock)* faire [10] tic-tac ❷ *(on paper)* cocher [1]; **tick the box** cochez la case

ticket NOUN ❶ billet MASC *(for a plane, a train, an exhibition, a theatre or cinema)* **two tickets for the concert**

a
b
c
d
e
f
g
h
i
j
k
l
m
n
o
p
q
r
s
t
u
v
w
x
y
z

deux billets pour le concert ❷ *(for the underground, the bus, or left luggage)* ticket *MASC*; **a bus ticket** un ticket de bus ❸ **a parking ticket** un PV *(informal)*

ticket inspector *NOUN* contrôleur *MASC*

ticket office *NOUN (at a station)* guichet *MASC*

tickle *VERB* chatouiller [1]

tide *NOUN* marée *FEM*; **at high tide** à marée haute, **the tide is out** c'est la marée basse

tidy *ADJECTIVE* ❶ bien rangé *(a room)* ❷ soigné *(homework)* ❸ ordonné *(a person)*

tidy *VERB* ranger [52]; **I'll tidy (up) the kitchen** je rangerai la cuisine

tie *NOUN* ❶ cravate *FEM*; **a red tie** une cravate rouge ❷ *(in a match)* match *(MASC)* nul

tie *VERB* ❶ nouer [1]; **to tie your shoelaces** nouer ses lacets ❷ **to tie a knot in something** faire [10] un nœud à quelque chose ❸ *(in a match)* **we tied two all** nous avons fait match nul, deux partout

tiger *NOUN* tigre *MASC*

tight *ADJECTIVE* ❶ juste; **the skirt's a bit tight** la jupe est un peu juste, **these shoes are too tight** ces chaussures me serrent ❷ *(close-fitting)* moulant; **she was wearing a tight dress** elle portait une robe moulante

tighten *VERB* serrer [1]

tightly *ADVERB* fermement

tights *PLURAL NOUN* collant *MASC SINGULAR*; **a pair of purple tights** un collant violet

tile *NOUN* ❶ *(on a floor or wall)* carreau *MASC (PLURAL carreaux)* ❷ *(on a roof)* tuile *FEM*

till¹ *PREPOSITION, CONJUNCTION* ❶ jusqu'à; **they're here till Sunday** ils sont là jusqu'à dimanche, **till then** jusque-là, **till now** jusqu'à présent ❷ **not till** pas avant, **she won't be back till ten** elle ne sera pas rentrée avant dix heures, **we won't know till Monday** nous ne le saurons pas avant lundi

till² *NOUN* caisse *FEM*; **pay at the till** payez à la caisse

time *NOUN* ❶ *(on the clock)* heure *FEM*; **what time is it?** quelle heure est-il?, **it's time for lunch** c'est l'heure du déjeuner, **on time** à l'heure, **ten o'clock French time** dix heures heure française ❷ *(an amount of time)* temps *MASC*; **we've got lots of time** nous avons beaucoup de temps, **there's not much time left** il ne reste plus beaucoup de temps, **for a long time** longtemps, **from time to time** de temps en temps ❸ *(moment)* moment *MASC*; **is this a good time to phone?** est-ce que c'est le bon moment pour vous appeler?, **at times** par moments, **for the time being** pour le moment, **any time now** d'un moment à l'autre ❹ *(in a series)* fois *FEM*; **six times** six fois, **the first time** la première fois, **the first time I saw you** la première fois que je t'ai vu, **three times a year** trois fois par an, **three times two is six** trois fois deux égalent six ❺ **to have a good time** bien s'amuser [1], **we had a really good time** nous nous sommes très bien amusés, **have a good time!** amusez-vous bien!

time off NOUN ❶ (free time) temps (MASC) libre ❷ (leave) congé MASC

timetable NOUN ❶ (in school) emploi (MASC) du temps ❷ (for trains or buses) horaire MASC; **the bus timetable** l'horaire des bus

tin NOUN boîte FEM; **a tin of tomatoes** une boîte de tomates

tin-foil NOUN papier (MASC) aluminium

tinned ADJECTIVE en conserve; **tinned peas** des petits pois en conserve

tin opener NOUN ouvre-boîte MASC

tinted ADJECTIVE teinté

tiny ADJECTIVE minuscule

tip NOUN ❶ (the end) bout MASC; **the tip of my finger** le bout de mon doigt ❷ (money) pourboire MASC ❸ (a useful hint) tuyau MASC (PLURAL tuyaux) (informal)

tip VERB ❶ (to give money to) donner [1] un pourboire à; **we tipped the waiter** nous avons donné un pourboire au garçon ❷ verser [1] (liquid)

tiptoe NOUN **on tiptoe** sur la pointe des pieds

tired ADJECTIVE ❶ fatigué; **I'm tired** je suis fatigué, **you look tired** tu as l'air fatigué ❷ **to be tired of** en avoir assez de, **I'm tired of London** j'en ai assez de Londres, **I'm tired of watching TV** j'en ai assez de regarder la télé

tiring ADJECTIVE fatigant

tissue NOUN (a paper hanky) kleenex MASC; **do you have a tissue?** est-ce que tu as un kleenex?

tissue paper NOUN papier (MASC) de soie

title NOUN titre MASC

to PREPOSITION ❶ (to a place or person) à (note that 'à + le' becomes 'au' and 'à + les' becomes 'aux'); **to go to London** aller à Londres, **give the book to Leila** donne le livre à Leila, **I'm going to school** je vais à l'école, **she's gone to the office** elle est partie au bureau, **a letter to parents** une lettre aux parents, **from Monday to Friday** du lundi au vendredi ❷ (with names of countries) **they're going to Spain** ils vont en Espagne, **they're going to Japan** ils vont au Japon ('en' with feminine countries, 'au' with most masculine countries) ❸ à; **I have nothing to do** je n'ai rien à faire, **I had a lot of homework to do** j'avais beacoup de devoirs à faire, **we're ready to go** nous sommes prêts à partir, **it's easy to do** c'est facile à faire ❹ (to somebody's house, shop, surgery) chez; **I went round to Paul's house** je suis allé chez Paul, **we're going to the Browns' for supper** on va dîner chez les Brown, **I'm going to the dentist's tomorrow** je vais chez le dentiste demain, **she's gone to the hairdresser's** elle est allée chez le coiffeur ❺ (talking about the time) **it's ten to nine** il est neuf heures moins dix, **it's twenty to** il est moins vingt ❻ (in order to) pour; **he gave me some money to buy a sandwich** il m'a donné de l'argent pour acheter un sandwich

toad NOUN crapaud MASC

toadstool NOUN champignon MASC; **a poisonous toadstool** un champignon vénéneux

toast NOUN ❶ **pain** (MASC) **grillé; two slices of toast** deux tranches de pain grillé ❷ (to your health) **toast** MASC; **to drink a toast to the future** lever un verre à l'avenir

toaster NOUN **grille-pain** MASC

tobacco NOUN **tabac** MASC

tobacconist's NOUN **bureau** (MASC) **de tabac**

today NOUN **aujourd'hui** MASC; **today's her birthday** c'est son anniversaire aujourd'hui

toe NOUN **doigt** (MASC) **de pied; my big toe** mon gros orteil

toenail NOUN **ongle** (MASC) **de pied**

toffee NOUN **caramel** MASC

together ADVERB ❶ **ensemble; Kate and Lenny arrived together** Kate et Lenny sont arrivés ensemble ❷ (at the same time) **en même temps; they all left together** ils sont tous partis en même temps

toilet NOUN **toilettes** FEM PLURAL; **where's the toilet?** où sont les toilettes?, **she's gone to the toilet** elle est allé aux toilettes

toilet paper NOUN **papier** (MASC) **hygiénique**

toilet roll NOUN **rouleau** (MASC) **de papier hygiénique**

token NOUN (for a machine or game) **jeton** MASC

tolerant ADJECTIVE **tolérant**

toll NOUN ❶ **péage** MASC ❷ (number of dead) **nombre** MASC; **the death toll is now 25** le nombre de victimes s'élève maintenant à 25

tomato NOUN **tomate** FEM; **a tomato salad** une salade de tomates, **tomato sauce** la sauce tomate

tomorrow ADVERB **demain; I'll do it tomorrow** je le ferai demain, **tomorrow afternoon** demain après-midi, **tomorrow morning** demain matin, **tomorrow night** demain soir, **the day after tomorrow** après-demain

ton NOUN **tonne** FEM; **she gets tons of letters** elle reçoit des tonnes de lettres

tone NOUN ❶ (on an answerphone) **tonalité** FEM; **speak after the tone** parlez après la tonalité ❷ (of a voice or a letter) **ton** MASC

tongue NOUN **langue** FEM; **to stick your tongue out** tirer la langue
• **it's on the tip of my tongue** je l'ai sur le bout de la langue

tonic NOUN **Schweppes** MASC; **a gin and tonic** un gin tonic

tonight ADVERB ❶ (this evening) **ce soir; I'm going out with my mates tonight** je sors avec les copains ce soir ❷ (after bedtime) **cette nuit**

tonsillitis NOUN **angine** FEM

too ADVERB ❶ **trop; it's too expensive** c'est trop cher, **too often** trop souvent ❷ **too much, too many** trop, **it takes too much time** ça prend trop de temps, **there are too many accidents** il y a trop d'accidents, **he eats too much** il mange trop ❸ (as well) **aussi; Karen's coming too** Karen vient aussi, **me too!** moi aussi!

tool NOUN **outil** MASC

tool box NOUN **boîte** (FEM) **à outils**

tool kit NOUN **trousse** (FEM) **à outils**

tooth NOUN dent FEM; **to brush your teeth** se brosser les dents

toothache NOUN mal (MASC) de dents; **to have toothache** avoir mal aux dents

toothbrush NOUN brosse (FEM) à dents

toothpaste NOUN dentifrice MASC

top NOUN ❶ haut MASC (of a page, a ladder, or stairs); **at the top of the stairs** en haut de l'escalier ❷ (of a container or box) dessus MASC; **it's on top of the chest-of-drawers** c'est sur la commode ❸ (of a mountain) sommet MASC ❹ (a lid) (of a pen) capuchon MASC, (of a bottle) capsule FEM ❺ (to wear) haut MASC ❻ **to be at the top of the list** être en tête de la liste

top ADJECTIVE ❶ (a step or floor) dernier (FEM dernière); **it's on the top floor** c'est au dernier étage ❷ de haut (a bunk) ❸ du haut (a shelf) ❹ **in the top left-hand corner** en haut à gauche
- **and on top of all that** et par-dessus le marché
- **it was a bit over the top** c'était un peu exagéré

topic NOUN sujet MASC

topping NOUN garniture FEM; **which topping would you like on your pizza?** vous voulez une pizza à quoi?

torch NOUN lampe (FEM) de poche

torn ADJECTIVE déchiré

tornado NOUN tornade FEM

tortoise NOUN tortue FEM

torture NOUN torture FEM

torture VERB torturer [1]

Tory NOUN conservateur MASC, conservatrice FEM

total NOUN total MASC

total ADJECTIVE total MASC (PLURAL totaux)

totally ADVERB complètement

touch NOUN ❶ (contact) **to get in touch with somebody** prendre contact avec quelqu'un, **to stay in touch with somebody** rester en contact avec quelqu'un ❷ **we've lost touch** on s'est perdu de vue, **I've lost touch with her recently** je l'ai perdue de vue récemment ❸ (a little bit) petit peu MASC; **a touch of vanilla** un petit peu de vanille, **it was a touch embarrassing** c'était un petit peu gênant

touch VERB toucher [1]

touched ADJECTIVE touché

touching ADJECTIVE touchant

tough ADJECTIVE ❶ dur; **the meat's a bit tough** la viande est un peu dure, **it's a tough area** c'est un quartier dur, **things are a bit tough at the moment** la vie est un peu dure en ce moment, **a tough guy** un dur ❷ robuste; **you need to be tough to survive** il faut être robuste pour survivre!, **a tough fabric** un tissu robuste ❸ (tough luck) tant pis; **tough, you're too late** tant pis pour toi, tu arrives trop tard

tour NOUN ❶ visite FEM; **we did the tour of the castle** nous avons fait la visite du château, **a tour of the city** une visite de la ville ❷ **a package tour** un voyage organisé ❸ (by a band or theatre group) tournée FEM; **to go on tour** partir en tournée

tour VERB *(performer)* être [6] en tournée; **they're touring the States** ils sont en tournée aux États-Unis

tourism NOUN tourisme MASC

tourist NOUN touriste MASC & FEM

tourist information office NOUN syndicat *(MASC)* d'initiative

tournament NOUN tournoi MASC; **a tennis tournament** un tournoi de tennis

tow VERB **to be towed away** *(by the police)* être [6] emmené à la fourrière, *(by a breakdown truck)* être [6] remorqué

towards PREPOSITION en direction de; **she went off towards the lake** elle est partie en direction du lac

towel NOUN serviette FEM

tower NOUN tour FEM; **the Eiffel Tower** la tour Eiffel

tower block NOUN tour FEM

town NOUN ville FEM; **to go into town** aller en ville

town centre NOUN centre-ville MASC

town hall NOUN mairie FEM

toxic ADJECTIVE toxique

toy NOUN jouet MASC; **a toy car** une petite voiture

toyshop NOUN magasin *(MASC)* de jouets

trace NOUN trace FEM; **there was no trace of it** il n'en restait aucune trace

trace VERB retrouver [1]

tracing paper NOUN papier *(MASC)* calque

track NOUN ❶ *(for sport)* piste FEM; **a track event** une épreuve de vitesse, **a racing track** *(for cars)* un circuit ❷ *(a path)* chemin MASC ❸ *(song)* chanson; **this is my favourite track** c'est ma chanson préférée

track suit NOUN survêtement MASC

tractor NOUN tracteur MASC

trade NOUN *(a profession)* métier MASC

trademark NOUN marque FEM; **registered trademark** marque déposée

trade union NOUN syndicat MASC

tradition NOUN tradition FEM

traditional ADJECTIVE traditionnel *(FEM traditionnelle)*

traffic NOUN circulation FEM

traffic island NOUN refuge MASC

traffic jam NOUN embouteillage MASC

traffic lights PLURAL NOUN feux MASC PLURAL

traffic warden NOUN contractuel MASC, contractuelle FEM

tragedy NOUN tragédie FEM

tragic ADJECTIVE tragique

trail NOUN *(a path)* sentier MASC; **a nature trail** un sentier écologique

trailer NOUN remorque FEM

train NOUN train MASC; **he's coming by train** il prend le train, **I met her on the train** je l'ai rencontrée dans le train, **the train to York** le train pour York

train VERB ❶ former [1] *(a student)* ❷ **to train to be something** suivre [75] une formation de quelque chose, **he's training to be a nurse** il suit une formation d'infirmier ❸ *(in sport)* s'entraîner [1]; **the team trains on Saturdays** l'équipe s'entraîne le samedi

trainee NOUN stagiaire MASC & FEM

trainer NOUN ❶ *(of an athlete or a horse)* entraîneur MASC, entraîneuse FEM ❷ *(shoe)* basket MASC; **my new trainers** mes nouveaux baskets

training NOUN ❶ *(for a career)* formation FEM ❷ *(for sport)* entraînement MASC

train ticket NOUN billet *(MASC)* de train

train timetable NOUN horaire *(MASC)* des trains

tram NOUN tramway MASC

tramp NOUN clochard MASC, clocharde FEM

trampoline NOUN trampoline MASC

transfer NOUN ❶ *(of money)* virement MASC ❷ *(of employee, footballer)* transfert MASC ❸ *(sticker)* décalcomanie FEM

transform VERB transformer [1]

transistor NOUN transistor MASC

translate VERB traduire [26]; **to translate something into French** traduire quelque chose en français

translation NOUN traduction FEM

translator NOUN traducteur MASC, traductrice FEM; **I'd like to be a translator** j'aimerais être traducteur

transparent ADJECTIVE transparent

transplant NOUN ❶ *(operation)* transplantation FEM ❷ *(organ)* transplant MASC

transport NOUN transport MASC; **air transport** le transport aérien, **public transport** les transports en commun

trap NOUN piège MASC

travel NOUN voyages MASC PLURAL; **foreign travel** les voyages à l'étranger, **a travel brochure** une brochure de voyages

travel VERB voyager [52]

travel agency NOUN agence *(FEM)* de voyages

travel agent NOUN agent *(MASC)* de voyages

traveller NOUN ❶ voyageur *(MASC)*, voyageuse FEM ❷ *(gypsy)* nomade MASC & FEM

traveller's cheque NOUN chèque-voyage MASC *(PLURAL* chèques-voyage)

travelling NOUN voyages MASC PLURAL; **I like travelling** j'aime partir en voyage

travel-sick NOUN **to be** or **get travel-sick** souffrir [73] du mal de voyage

tray NOUN plateau MASC *(PLURAL* plateaux)

tread VERB **to tread on something** marcher [1] sur quelque chose

treasure NOUN trésor MASC

treat NOUN ❶ **I took them to the circus as a treat** je les ai emmenés au cirque pour leur faire plaisir ❷ *(food)* gâterie FEM; **it's a little treat** c'est une petite gâterie

treat VERB ❶ traiter [1]; he treats his dog well il traite bien son chien, the doctor who treated you le médecin qui vous a traité ❷ to treat somebody to something offrir [56] quelque chose à quelqu'un, I'll treat you to a drink je vous offre à boire, I treated myself to a new dress je me suis offert une nouvelle robe

treatment NOUN traitement MASC

treaty NOUN traité MASC

tree NOUN arbre MASC

tree trunk NOUN tronc (MASC) d'arbre

tremble VERB trembler [1]

tremendous ADJECTIVE fantastique; a tremendous victory/defeat une victoire/défaite écrasante

trend NOUN ❶ (a fashion) mode FEM ❷ (a tendency) tendance FEM

trendy ADJECTIVE branché

trial NOUN (legal) procès MASC

triangle NOUN triangle MASC

tribe NOUN tribu FEM

tribute NOUN hommage MASC; many tributes were paid to the Pope de nombreuses personnes ont rendu hommage au Pape

trick NOUN ❶ (by a conjuror, or as a joke) tour MASC; to play a trick on somebody jouer un tour à quelqu'un ❷ (a knack) astuce FEM; it doesn't work, there must be a trick to it ça ne marche pas, il doit y avoir une astuce

trick VERB rouler [1]; he tricked me! il m'a roulé!

tricky ADJECTIVE délicat; it's a tricky situation c'est une situation délicate

tricycle NOUN tricycle MASC

trim VERB couper [1] (hair or fabric)

Trinidad NOUN (île de) la Trinité

Trinidadian NOUN Trinidadien MASC, Trinidadienne FEM

Trinidadian ADJECTIVE trinidadien (FEM trinidadienne)

trip NOUN voyage MASC; a trip to Florida un voyage en Floride, he's on a business trip il est en voyage d'affaires, a day trip to France une excursion d'une journée en France

trip VERB (to stumble) trébucher [1]; Nicky tripped over a stone Nicky a trébuché sur un gros caillou

triple VERB tripler [1]; the price has tripled le prix a triplé

triumph NOUN triomphe MASC

trolley NOUN chariot MASC

trombone NOUN trombone MASC; to play the trombone jouer du trombone

troops PLURAL NOUN troupes FEM PLURAL

trophy NOUN trophée MASC

tropical ADJECTIVE tropical MASC (PLURAL tropicaux)

trot VERB trotter [1]

trouble NOUN ❶ problèmes MASC PLURAL; we've had trouble with the car nous avons eu des problèmes avec la voiture, the trouble is, I've forgotten the number le problème, c'est que j'ai oublié le numéro ❷ (personal problems) ennuis MASC PLURAL; Steph's in trouble Steph a des ennuis, what's the trouble? qu'est-ce qui ne va pas? ❸ (difficulty) to have trouble doing avoir du mal à faire, I had

trouble finding a seat j'ai eu du mal à trouver une place, **it's not worth the trouble** cela ne vaut pas la peine, **it's no trouble!** ça ne me dérange pas!

trousers *PLURAL NOUN* **pantalon** *MASC SINGULAR*; **my old trousers** mon vieux pantalon, **a new pair of trousers** un pantalon neuf

trout *NOUN* **truite** *FEM*

truant *NOUN* **to play truant** faire [10] l'école buissonnière, **she's playing truant** elle fait l'école buissonnière

truck *NOUN* **camion** *MASC*

true *ADJECTIVE* **vrai**; **a true story** une histoire vraie, **is that true?** c'est vrai?, **it's true she's absent-minded** c'est vrai qu'elle est distraite

truly *ADVERB* **vraiment**

trump *NOUN* **atout** *MASC*; **spades are trumps** atout pique

trumpet *NOUN* **trompette** *FEM*; **to play the trumpet** jouer de la trompette

trunk *NOUN* **❶** *(of a tree)* **tronc** *MASC* **❷** *(of an elephant)* **trompe** *FEM* **❸** *(a suitcase)* **malle** *FEM*

trunks *PLURAL NOUN* **swimming trunks** maillot *(MASC)* de bain

trust *NOUN* **confiance** *FEM*

trust *VERB* **I trust her** je lui fais confiance

truth *NOUN* **vérité** *FEM*; **to tell the truth, I'd completely forgottten** à vrai dire, j'avais complètement oublié

try *NOUN* **essai** *MASC*; **it's my first try** c'est mon premier essai, **to have a try** essayer [59], **you should give it a try** tu devrais l'essayer

try *VERB* **essayer** [59]; **to try to do** essayer de faire, **I'm trying to open the door** j'essaie d'ouvrir la porte, **to try hard to do** faire [10] de gros efforts pour faire
- **to try something on** essayer [59] quelque chose *(a garment)*

T-shirt *NOUN* **tee-shirt** *MASC*

tub *NOUN* **❶** *(food container)* **pot** *MASC* **❷** *(bath)* **baignoire** *FEM*

tube *NOUN* **tube** *MASC*

tuberculosis *NOUN* **tuberculose** *FEM*

Tuesday *NOUN* **mardi** *MASC*; **on Tuesday** mardi, **I'm going out on Tuesday** je sors mardi, **see you on Tuesday!** à mardi!, **on Tuesdays** le mardi, **the museum is closed on Tuesdays** le musée est fermé le mardi, **every Tuesday** tous les mardis, **last Tuesday** mardi dernier, **next Tuesday** mardi prochain

tug *VERB* **tirer** [1]

tuition *NOUN* **cours** *MASC PLURAL*; **piano tuition** des cours de piano, **private tuition** des cours particuliers

tulip *NOUN* **tulipe** *FEM*

tumble-drier *NOUN* **sèche-linge** *MASC*

tumbler *NOUN* **verre** *(MASC)* **droit**

tummy *NOUN* **estomac** *MASC*

tuna *NOUN* **thon** *MASC*

tune *NOUN* **air** *MASC*

Tunisia *NOUN* **Tunisie** *FEM*; **in Tunisia** en Tunisie

tunnel *NOUN* **tunnel** *MASC*; **the Channel Tunnel** le tunnel sous la Manche

A
B
C
D
E
F
G
H
I
J
K
L
M
N
O
P
Q
R
S
T
U
V
W
X
Y
Z

turban NOUN turban MASC

turf NOUN gazon MASC

turkey NOUN dinde FEM

Turkey NOUN Turquie FEM; **in Turkey** en Turquie, **to Turkey** en Turquie

Turkish NOUN turc MASC (language)

Turkish ADJECTIVE turc (FEM turque)

turn NOUN ❶ (in a game) tour MASC; **it's your turn** c'est ton tour, **whose turn is it?** c'est à qui le tour?, **it's Jane's turn to play** c'est à Jane de jouer, **to take turns driving** conduire à tour de rôle ❷ (in a road) virage MASC

turn VERB ❶ tourner [1]; **turn your chair round** tourne ta chaise, **turn left at the next set of lights** tournez à gauche aux prochains feux ❷ (become) devenir [81]; **she turned red** elle est devenue rouge

- **to turn back** faire [10] demi-tour; **we turned back** nous avons fait demi-tour
- **to turn off** ❶ (from a road) tourner [1] ❷ (switch off) éteindre [60] (a light, an oven, a TV or radio), fermer [1] (a tap) couper [1] (gas or electricity)
- **to turn on** allumer [1] (the oven, TV, radio, or a light) ouvrir [30] (a tap)
- **to turn out** ❶ to turn out well bien se terminer [1], **the holiday turned out badly** les vacances se sont mal terminées, **it all turned out alright in the end** finalement tout s'est arrangé ❷ it turned out that I was wrong il s'est avéré que j'avais tort
- **to turn over** ❶ (roll over) se retourner [1] ❷ tourner [1] (a page)
- **to turn up** ❶ (to arrive) arriver [1]; **they turned up an hour later** ils sont arrivés une heure plus tard ❷ augmenter [1] (the gas or the

heating) ❸ (make louder) **can you turn up the volume?** est-ce que tu peux monter le son?

turning NOUN virage MASC; **take the third turning on the right** prenez la troisième rue à gauche

turnip NOUN navet MASC

turquoise ADJECTIVE turquoise

turtle NOUN tortue (FEM) marine

turtle dove NOUN tourterelle FEM

TV NOUN télé FEM; **I saw her on TV** je l'ai vue à la télé

tweezers NOUN pince (FEM SINGULAR) à épiler

twelfth NUMBER douzième; **on the twelfth floor** au douzième étage, **the twelfth of May** le douze mai

twelve NUMBER ❶ douze MASC; **Tara's twelve** Tara a douze ans ❷ at twelve o'clock (midday) à midi, (midnight) à minuit

twenty NUMBER vingt MASC; **Marie's twenty** Marie a vingt ans, **twenty-one** vingt-et-un, **twenty-five** vingt-cinq

twice ADVERB deux fois; **I've asked him twice** je lui ai demandé deux fois, **twice as much** deux fois plus

twig NOUN brindille FEM

twilight NOUN crépuscule MASC

twin NOUN jumeau MASC (PLURAL jumeaux), jumelle FEM; **Helen and Tim are twins** Helen et Tim sont jumeaux, **her twin sister** sa sœur jumelle

twin VERB Oxford is twinned with Grenoble Oxford est jumelée avec Grenoble

twist VERB tordre [3]

two NUMBER deux MASC; **Ben's two** Ben a deux ans, **two by two** deux par deux

type NOUN type MASC; **what type of computer is it?** c'est quel type d'ordinateur?

type VERB (on a typewriter) taper [1]; **I'm learning to type** j'apprends à taper à la machine, **I was busy typing some letters** j'étais en train de taper des lettres

typical ADJECTIVE typique

typing NOUN dactylographie FEM; **her typing is awful** elle tape très, mal

tyre NOUN pneu MASC

UFO NOUN ovni MASC

ugly ADJECTIVE laid

UK NOUN (short for **United Kingdom**) Royaume-Uni MASC

ulcer NOUN ulcère MASC

Ulster NOUN Irlande (FEM) du Nord

umbrella NOUN parapluie MASC

umpire NOUN arbitre MASC

UN NOUN O.N.U. FEM (short for Organisation des Nations Unies)

unable ADJECTIVE **to be unable to do** ne pas pouvoir faire, **he's unable to come** il ne peut pas venir

unanimous ADJECTIVE unanime

unattractive ADJECTIVE peu attrayant (person, place)

unavoidable ADJECTIVE inévitable

unbearable ADJECTIVE insupportable

unbelievable ADJECTIVE incroyable

uncertain ADJECTIVE incertain; **I'm uncertain whether they're coming** je ne suis pas sûr qu'ils viennent

unchanged ADJECTIVE inchangé

uncivilized ADJECTIVE barbare

uncle NOUN oncle MASC; **my Uncle Julian** mon oncle Julian

uncomfortable ADJECTIVE ❶ inconfortable (shoes or a chair) ❷ pénible (a journey or a situation)

uncommon ADJECTIVE rare

unconscious ADJECTIVE (out cold) sans connaissance; **Tessa's still unconscious** Tessa est toujours sans connaissance

under PREPOSITION ❶ (underneath) sous; **under the bed** sous le lit, **perhaps it's under there** c'est peut-être là-dessous ❷ (less than) moins de; **under £20** moins de vingt livres, **children under five** les enfants de moins de cinq ans

under-age NOUN **to be under-age** être mineur (FEM mineure)

underclothes PLURAL NOUN sous-vêtements MASC PLURAL

undercooked ADJECTIVE pas assez cuit

a
b
c
d
e
f
g
h
i
j
k
l
m
n
o
p
q
r
s
t
u
v
w
x
y
z

underestimate VERB sous-estimer [1]

underground NOUN (a railway) métro MASC; **I saw her on the underground** je l'ai vue dans le métro, **shall we go by underground?** on prend le métro?

underground ADJECTIVE souterrain; **an underground carpark** un parking souterrain

underline VERB souligner [1]

underneath PREPOSITION sous; **it's underneath these papers** c'est sous ces papiers

underneath ADVERB dessous; **look underneath** cherche dessous

underpants PLURAL NOUN slip MASC SINGULAR; **my underpants** mon slip

underpass NOUN ❶ (pedestrian) passage (MASC) souterrain ❷ (for traffic) passage (MASC) inférieur

understand VERB comprendre [64]; **I don't understand** je ne comprends pas, **I couldn't understand what he was saying** je n'ai pas compris ce qu'il disait

understandable ADJECTIVE that's understandable ça se comprend

understanding NOUN compréhension FEM

understanding ADJECTIVE compréhensif (FEM compréhensive); **he was very understanding** il a été très compréhensif

underwear NOUN sous-vêtements MASC PLURAL

undo VERB ❶ défaire [10] (a button or a lock) ❷ ouvrir [30] (a parcel)

undone ADJECTIVE to come undone se défaire [10]

undress VERB to get undressed se déshabiller [1], **I got undressed** je me suis déshabillé

unemployed NOUN the unemployed les chômeurs, **work for the unemployed** du travail pour les chômeurs

unemployed ADJECTIVE au chômage; **she's unemployed** elle est au chômage

unemployment NOUN chômage MASC

uneven ADJECTIVE irrégulier (FEM irrégulière)

unexpected ADJECTIVE imprévu

unexpectedly ADVERB (to happen, arrive) à l'improviste

unfair ADJECTIVE injuste; **it's unfair to young people** c'est injuste pour les jeunes

unfashionable ADJECTIVE démodé

unfasten VERB défaire [10]

unfit ADJECTIVE I'm terribly unfit je ne suis pas du tout en forme

unfold VERB déplier [1]

unforgettable ADJECTIVE inoubliable

unfortunate ADJECTIVE regrettable

unfortunately ADVERB malheureusement

unfriendly ADJECTIVE pas très sympathique

unfurnished ADJECTIVE non meublé

ungrateful ADJECTIVE ingrat

unhappy ADJECTIVE malheureux (FEM malheureuse)

unhealthy ADJECTIVE ❶ maladif (FEM maladive) (a person) ❷ malsain (food)

unhurt ADJECTIVE indemne

uniform NOUN uniforme MASC; **in school uniform** en uniforme scolaire

uninhabited ADJECTIVE inhabité

union NOUN (a trade union) syndicat MASC

Union Jack NOUN the Union Jack le drapeau du Royaume-Uni

unique ADJECTIVE unique

unit NOUN ❶ (for measuring, for example) unité FEM ❷ (in a kitchen) élément MASC ❸ (a hospital department) service MASC

United Kingdom NOUN Royaume-Uni MASC

United Nations NOUN O.N.U (short for Organisation des Nations Unies)

United States (of America) PLURAL NOUN États-Unis MASC PLURAL; **in the United States** aux États-Unis, **to the United States** aux États-Unis

universe NOUN univers MASC

university NOUN université FEM; **to go to university** aller à l'université

unjust ADJECTIVE injuste

unkind ADJECTIVE pas gentil (FEM pas gentille)

unknown ADJECTIVE inconnu

unleaded petrol NOUN essence (FEM) sans plomb

unless CONJUNCTION unless he does it à moins qu'il ne le fasse, **unless you tell her** à moins que tu ne le lui dises (note that 'à moins que' is followed by a subjunctive)

unlike ADJECTIVE ❶ unlike me, she hates dogs contrairement à moi, elle déteste les chiens ❷ it's unlike her to be late ce n'est pas son genre d'être en retard

unlikely ADJECTIVE peu probable; **it's unlikely** c'est peu probable

unlimited ADJECTIVE illimité

unload VERB décharger [52]

unlock VERB ouvrir [30]; **the car's unlocked** la voiture est ouverte

unlucky ADJECTIVE ❶ to be unlucky (a person) ne pas avoir de chance, **I was unlucky, it was shut** je n'ai pas eu de chance, c'était fermé ❷ thirteen is an unlucky number le treize porte malheur

unmarried ADJECTIVE célibataire

unnatural ADJECTIVE anormal MASC (PLURAL anormaux)

unnecessary ADJECTIVE inutile; **it's unnecessary to book** il est inutile de réserver

unpack VERB défaire [10]; **I unpacked my rucksack** j'ai défait mon sac à dos, **I'll just unpack and then come down** je vais juste défaire ma valise et puis je descendrai

unpaid ADJECTIVE ❶ impayé (a bill) ❷ non rémunéré (work)

unpleasant ADJECTIVE désagréable

unplug VERB débrancher [1]

a b c d e f g h i j k l m n o p q r s t u v w x y z

A
B
C
D
E
F
G
H
I
J
K
L
M
N
O
P
Q
R
S
T
U
V
W
X
Y
Z

unpopular *ADJECTIVE* **impopulaire**

unrealistic *ADJECTIVE* **peu réaliste**

unreasonable *ADJECTIVE* **pas raisonnable**; **he's being really unreasonable** il n'est vraiment pas raisonnable

unrecognizable *ADJECTIVE* **méconnaissable**

unreliable *ADJECTIVE* **peu fiable** *(information or equipment)*; **he's unreliable** on ne peut pas compter sur lui

unroll *VERB* **dérouler** [1]

unsafe *ADJECTIVE* **dangereux** *(FEM* **dangereuse)** *(wiring, for instance)*

unsatisfactory *ADJECTIVE* **insatisfaisant**

unscrew *VERB* **dévisser** [1]

unshaven *ADJECTIVE* **pas rasé**

unsuccessful *ADJECTIVE* **to be unsuccessful** ne pas réussir, **I tried, but I was unsuccessful** j'ai essayé mais je n'ai pas réussi, **an unsuccessful attempt** un essai vain

unsuitable *ADJECTIVE* **inapproprié**

untidy *ADJECTIVE* **en désordre**; **the house is always untidy** la maison est toujours en désordre

untie *VERB* **défaire** [10]

until *PREPOSITION* ❶ **jusqu'à**; **until Monday** jusqu'à lundi, **until the tenth** jusqu'au dix, **until now** jusqu'à présent, **until then** jusque-là ❷ **not until** pas avant, **not until September** pas avant septembre, **it won't be finished until Friday** ce ne sera pas fini avant vendredi

unusual *ADJECTIVE* **peu commun**; **an unusual beetle** un scarabée peu commun, **storms are unusual in June** c'est rare d'avoir des orages au mois de juin

unwilling *ADJECTIVE* **to be unwilling to do** ne pas vouloir faire, **he's unwilling to wait** il ne veut pas attendre

unwrap *VERB* **déballer** [1]

up *PREPOSITION, ADVERB* ❶ *(out of bed)* **to be up** être levé, **Liz isn't up yet** Liz n'est pas encore levée, **to get up** se lever [50], **we got up at six** nous nous sommes levés à six heures, **I was up late last night** je me suis couché tard hier soir ❷ *(higher up)* **en haut**; **hands up!** haut les mains!, **up on the roof** en haut sur le toit, **up here** ici, **up there** là-haut, **we went up the road** nous avons remonté la rue, **it's just up the road** c'est tout près, **up in Glasgow** à Glasgow ❸ *(wrong)* **what's up?** qu'est-ce qui se passe?, **what's with him?** qu'est-ce qu'il a? ❹ **up to** jusqu'à, **up to here** jusqu'ici, **up to fifty people** jusqu'à cinquante personnes, **she came up to me** elle s'est approchée de moi ❺ **what's she up to?** qu'est-ce qu'elle fait?, **it's up to you (to decide)** c'est à toi de décider
• **time's up!** c'est l'heure!

update *NOUN* **mise** *(FEM)* **à jour**; **here's an update on the delays** voici une mise à jour des retards

update *VERB* ❶ *(revise)* **mettre** [11] **à jour** *(timetables or information)* ❷ **moderniser** [1] *(styles or furnishings)*

upheaval *NOUN* **bouleversement** *MASC*

uphill *ADVERB* en montée

upright *ADJECTIVE* droit; **put it upright** mets-le droit, **to stand upright** se tenir droit

upset *NOUN* **a stomach upset** une indigestion

upset *ADJECTIVE* contrarié; **he's upset** il est contrarié

upset *VERB* **to upset somebody** contrarier [1] quelqu'un

upside down *ADJECTIVE* à l'envers

upstairs *ADVERB* en haut; **Mum's upstairs** maman est en haut, **to go upstairs** monter [1]

up-to-date *ADJECTIVE* ❶ *(in fashion)* moderne ❷ *(information)* à jour

upwards *ADJECTIVE* vers le haut

urgent *ADJECTIVE* urgent

urgently *ADVERB* d'urgence; **she wants to see you urgently** elle veut vous voir d'urgence

us *PRONOUN* nous; **she knows us** elle nous connaît, **they saw us** ils nous ont vus, **he gave us a cheque** il nous a donné un chèque, **with us** avec nous

US *NOUN* U.S.A. *MASC PLURAL*

USA *NOUN* U.S.A. *MASC PLURAL*

use *NOUN* ❶ emploi *MASC*; **the instructions for use** le mode d'emploi ❷ **it's no use** ça ne sert à rien, **it's no use phoning** ça ne sert à rien de téléphoner

use *VERB* utiliser [1]; **we used the dictionary** nous avons utilisé le dictionnaire, **to use something to do** se servir [71] de quelque chose pour faire, **I used a knife to open the parcel** je me suis servi d'un

couteau pour ouvrir le paquet
- **to use up** ❶ consommer [1] *(food or petrol)* ❷ dépenser [1] *(money)*

used *ADJECTIVE* ❶ **to be used to something** être [6] habitué à quelque chose, **I'm not used to cats** je ne suis pas habitué aux chats, **I'm not used to it!** je n'ai pas l'habitude ❷ **to be used to doing something** avoir [5] l'habitude de faire quelque chose, **I'm not used to eating in restaurants** je n'ai pas l'habitude de manger au restaurant ❸ **to get used to** s'habituer à, **I've got used to living here** je me suis habitué à habiter ici, **you'll get used to it!** tu t'y habitueras!

used *VERB* **they used to live in the country** ils habitaient à la campagne avant, **she used to smoke** elle fumait avant

useful *ADJECTIVE* utile

useless *ADJECTIVE* nul *(FEM* nulle*)*; **this knife's useless** ce couteau est nul, **you're completely useless!** tu es complètement nul!

user *NOUN* utilisateur *MASC*, utilisatrice *FEM*

user-friendly *ADJECTIVE* convivial *MASC (PLURAL* conviviaux*)*

usual *ADJECTIVE* habituel *(FEM* habituelle*)*; **it's the usual problem** c'est le problème habituel, **as usual** comme d'habitude, **it's colder than usual** il fait plus froid que d'habitude

usually *ADJECTIVE* d'habitude; **I usually leave at eight** d'habitude je pars à huit heures

utensil *NOUN* ustensile *MASC*

vacancy NOUN ❶ (in a hotel) 'vacancies' 'chambres libres', 'no vacancies' 'complet' ❷ a job vacancy un poste vacant

vacant ADJECTIVE libre

vaccinate VERB vacciner [1]

vaccination NOUN vaccination FEM

vacuum NOUN vide MASC

vacuum VERB passer [1] l'aspirateur; **I'm going to vacuum my room** je vais passer l'aspirateur dans ma chambre

vacuum cleaner NOUN aspirateur MASC

vagina NOUN vagin MASC

vague ADJECTIVE vague

vaguely ADVERB vaguement

vain ADJECTIVE vaniteux (FEM vaniteuse); **in vain** en vain

valentine card NOUN carte (FEM) pour la Saint-Valentin

Valentine's Day NOUN la Saint-Valentin

valid ADJECTIVE valable

valley NOUN vallée FEM

valuable ADJECTIVE ❶ de valeur; **to be valuable** avoir de la valeur, **that watch is very valuable** cette montre a une grande valeur ❷ (appreciated) précieux

(FEM précieuse); **he gave us some valuable information** il nous a donné des renseignements précieux

value NOUN valeur FEM

value VERB apprécier [1] (somebody's help, opinion, or friendship)

van NOUN (small) fourgon MASC, (large) camionnette FEM

vandal NOUN vandale MASC & FEM

vandalism NOUN vandalisme MASC

vandalize VERB vandaliser [1]

vanilla NOUN vanille FEM; **a vanilla ice cream** une glace à la vanille

vanish VERB disparaître [27]

variety NOUN variété FEM

various ADJECTIVE plusieurs; **there are various ways of doing it** il y a plusieurs façons de le faire

vary VERB varier [1]; **it varies a lot** ça varie beaucoup

vase NOUN vase MASC

VAT NOUN TVA FEM

VCR NOUN magnétoscope MASC

VDU NOUN console FEM

veal NOUN veau MASC

vegan NOUN végétalien MASC, végétalienne FEM

vegetable NOUN légume MASC

vegetarian NOUN, ADJECTIVE végétarien MASC, végétarienne FEM; **he's vegetarian** il est végétarien

vehicle NOUN véhicule MASC

vein NOUN veine FEM

velvet NOUN velours MASC

vending machine NOUN
distributeur (MASC) automatique

ventilation NOUN aération FEM

verb NOUN verbe MASC

verdict NOUN verdict MASC

verge NOUN ❶ (the roadside)
accotement MASC ❷ to be on the
verge of doing être [6] sur le point
de faire, I was on the verge of
leaving j'étais sur le point de partir

version NOUN version FEM

versus PREPOSITION contre; Bath
versus Chelsea Bath contre Chelsea

vertical ADJECTIVE vertical MASC (PLURAL
verticaux)

vertigo NOUN vertige MASC

very ADVERB it's very difficult c'est
très difficile, very well très bien,
very much beaucoup

very ADJECTIVE ❶ the very person I
need! exactement la personne qu'il
me faut!, the very thing he was
looking for exactement ce qu'il
cherchait ❷ in the very middle en
plein milieu, at the very end tout à
la fin, at the very front tout devant

vest NOUN maillot (MASC) de corps

vet NOUN vétérinaire MASC & FEM; she's
a vet elle est vétérinaire

via PREPOSITION to go via passer par,
we're going via Dover nous allons
passer par Douvres, we'll go via the
bank on va passer par la banque

vicar NOUN pasteur MASC

vicious ADJECTIVE ❶ méchant (a
dog) ❷ brutal MASC (PLURAL brutaux)
(an attack)

victim NOUN victime FEM

victory NOUN victoire FEM

video NOUN ❶ (film) vidéo FEM;
to watch a video regarder une
vidéo, I've got it on video je
l'ai en vidéo ❷ (video recorder)
magnétoscope MASC

video VERB enregistrer [1]; I'll video
it for you je te l'enregistrerai

video game NOUN jeu (MASC) vidéo
(PLURAL jeux vidéo)

video recorder NOUN
magnétoscope MASC

view NOUN ❶ vue FEM; a room with a
view of the lake une chambre avec
vue sur le lac ❷ (opinion) avis MASC;
in my view à mon avis, a point of
view un point de vue

viewer NOUN (on TV) téléspectateur
MASC, téléspectatrice FEM

viewpoint NOUN point (MASC) de vue

vigorous ADJECTIVE vigoureux (FEM
vigoureuse)

vile ADJECTIVE abominable

villa NOUN villa FEM

village NOUN village MASC

villager NOUN villageois MASC,
villageoise FEM

vine NOUN vigne FEM

vinegar NOUN vinaigre MASC

vineyard NOUN vignoble MASC

violence NOUN violence FEM

violent ADJECTIVE violent

violin NOUN violon MASC; to play the
violin jouer du violon

violinist NOUN violoniste MASC & FEM

virgin NOUN vierge FEM

Virgo NOUN **Vierge** FEM; **Robert's Virgo** Robert est Vierge

virtual reality NOUN **réalité** (FEM) **virtuelle**

virus NOUN ❶ (in medicine) **virus** MASC ❷ (in computing) **virus** MASC; **anti-virus software** un logiciel antivirus

visa NOUN **visa** MASC

visible ADJECTIVE **visible**

visit NOUN ❶ (stay) **séjour** MASC; **my last visit to France** mon dernier séjour en France ❷ **visite** FEM (to a house, museum)

visit VERB ❶ **visiter** [1] (museum, castle, town) ❷ **aller** [7] **voir** (a person); **we visited Auntie Pat at Christmas** nous sommes allés voir tante Pat à Noël

visitor NOUN ❶ **invité** MASC, **invitée** FEM; **we've got visitors tonight** on a des invités ce soir ❷ (a tourist) **visiteur** MASC, **visiteuse** FEM

visual ADJECTIVE **visuel** (FEM **visuelle**)

vital ADJECTIVE **indispensable**; **it's vital to book** il est indispensable de réserver

vitamin NOUN **vitamine** FEM

vivid ADJECTIVE ❶ (colour) **vif** (FEM **vive**) ❷ **to have a vivid imagination** exagérer

vocabulary NOUN **vocabulaire** MASC

vocational ADJECTIVE **professionnel** (FEM **professionnelle**)

vodka NOUN **vodka** MASC

voice NOUN **voix** FEM

voicemail NOUN **messagerie** (FEM) **vocale**

volcano NOUN **volcan** MASC

volleyball NOUN **volley-ball** MASC; **to play volleyball** jouer au volley-ball

volume NOUN **volume** MASC; **could you turn down the volume?** est-ce que tu peux baisser le volume?

voluntary ADJECTIVE ❶ (not compulsory) **volontaire** ❷ **to do voluntary work** travailler bénévolement

volunteer NOUN ❶ (for a job) **volontaire** MASC & FEM ❷ (in charity work) **bénévole** MASC & FEM

vomit VERB **vomir** [2]

vote NOUN **vote** MASC; **she got 20 votes** elle a obtenu 20 votes

vote VERB **voter** [1]; **she always votes Green** elle vote toujours pour les Verts

voucher NOUN **bon** MASC

vowel NOUN **voyelle** FEM

voyage NOUN **voyage** MASC

vulgar ADJECTIVE **vulgaire**

Ww

waffle NOUN (to eat) gaufre FEM

wage(s) NOUN salaire MASC

wagon NOUN ❶ (for transport) chariot MASC ❷ (on railway) wagon (MASC) de marchandises

waist NOUN taille FEM

waistcoat NOUN gilet MASC

waist measurement NOUN tour (MASC) de taille

wait NOUN attente FEM; **an hour's wait** une heure d'attente

wait VERB ❶ attendre [3]; **they're waiting in the car** ils attendent dans la voiture, **she kept me waiting** elle m'a fait attendre ❷ **to wait for** attendre [3], **wait for me!** attends-moi!, **wait for the signal** attendez le signal ❸ **I can't wait to open it!** j'ai hâte de l'ouvrir!

waiter NOUN serveur MASC

waiting list NOUN liste (FEM) d'attente

waiting room NOUN salle (FEM) d'attente

waitress NOUN serveuse FEM

wake VERB ❶ réveiller [1] (somebody else); **Jess woke me at six** Jess m'a réveillé à six heures ❷ se réveiller [1]; **I woke (up) at six** je me suis réveillé à six heures, **wake up!** réveille-toi!

Wales NOUN pays (MASC) de Galles; **in Wales** au pays de Galles, **to Wales** au pays de Galles

walk NOUN promenade FEM (a little stroll), tour MASC; **to go for a walk** faire une promenade, **we went for a walk in the woods** nous avons fait une promenade dans la forêt, **we'll go for a little walk round the village** on va faire un petit tour au village, **to take the dog for a walk** promener [50] le chien, **it's about five minutes' walk from here** c'est à environ cinq minutes à pied d'ici

walk VERB ❶ marcher [1]; **I like walking on sand** j'aime marcher sur le sable ❷ (walk around) se promener [50]; **we walked around the old town** nous nous sommes promenés dans la vieille ville ❸ (go) aller [7]; **I'll walk to the bus stop with you** j'irai avec toi jusqu'à l'arrêt de bus ❹ (on foot rather than by car or bus) aller [7] à pied; **it's not far, we can walk** ce n'est pas loin, on peut y aller à pied

walkie-talkie NOUN talkie-walkie MASC (PLURAL talkies-walkies)

walking NOUN (hiking) randonnée FEM; **we're going walking in Scotland** nous allons faire de la randonnée en Écosse

walking distance NOUN **it's within walking distance of the sea** c'est à quelques minutes à pied de la mer

walking stick NOUN canne FEM

wall NOUN ❶ (of a house) mur MASC ❷ (of a city) muraille FEM; **the southern wall was destroyed** la muraille sud a été détruite, **the city walls** les fortifications de la ville

a
b
c
d
e
f
g
h
i
j
k
l
m
n
o
p
q
r
s
t
u
v
w
x
y
z

wallet NOUN portefeuille MASC

wallpaper NOUN papier (MASC) peint

walnut NOUN noix FEM (PLURAL noix)

wander VERB to wander around town se balader [1] en ville, to wander off s'éloigner [1]

want NOUN all our wants tous nos besoins

want VERB vouloir [14]; do you want some coffee? tu veux du café?, what do you want to do? qu'est-ce que tu veux faire?, I don't want to bother him je ne veux pas le déranger

war NOUN guerre FEM

ward NOUN salle FEM (in a hospital)

wardrobe NOUN ❶ (cupboard) armoire FEM ❷ (clothes) garde-robe FEM

warehouse NOUN entrepôt MASC

warm ADJECTIVE ❶ chaud; a warm drink une boisson chaude, it's warm today il fait chaud aujourd'hui, I am warm j'ai chaud, are you warm enough? as-tu assez chaud?, I'll keep your dinner warm je tiendrai ton dîner au chaud ❷ (friendly) chaleureux (FEM chaleureuse); a warm welcome un accueil chaleureux

warm VERB chauffer [1]; warm the plates chauffez les assiettes
• to warm up ❶ (the weather) s'adoucir [2] ❷ (an athlete) s'échauffer [1] ❸ (to heat up) réchauffer [1] (food); I'll warm up some soup for you je vous réchaufferai de la soupe

warmth NOUN chaleur FEM

warn VERB prévenir [81]; I warn you, it's expensive je vous préviens que c'est cher, to warn somebody to do conseiller [1] à quelqu'un de faire, he warned me to lock the car il m'a conseillé de fermer la voiture

warning NOUN avertissement MASC

wart NOUN verrue FEM

wash NOUN to give something a wash laver [1] quelque chose, to have a wash se laver

wash VERB laver [1]; I've washed your jeans j'ai lavé ton jean, to wash your hands se laver les mains, I washed my hands je me suis lavé les mains, to wash your hair se laver les cheveux, to get washed se laver, to wash the dishes faire [10] la vaisselle
• to wash up faire [10] la vaisselle

washbasin NOUN lavabo MASC

washing NOUN ❶ (dirty) linge (MASC) sale ❷ (clean) linge MASC

washing machine NOUN machine (FEM) à laver

washing powder NOUN lessive FEM

washing-up NOUN vaisselle FEM; to do the washing-up faire la vaisselle

washing-up liquid NOUN liquide (MASC) à vaisselle

wasp NOUN guêpe FEM

waste NOUN ❶ (of food, money, paper) gaspillage MASC ❷ (of time) perte FEM; it's a waste of time c'est une perte de temps

waste VERB ❶ gaspiller [1] (food, money, paper) ❷ perdre [3] (time); you're wasting your time tu perds ton temps

A B C D E F G H I J K L M N O P Q R S T U V W X Y Z

waste-bin NOUN **poubelle** FEM

wastepaper-basket NOUN **corbeille** (FEM) **à papier**

watch NOUN **montre** FEM; **my watch is fast** ma montre avance, **my watch is slow** ma montre retarde

watch VERB ❶ (to look at) **regarder** [1]; **I was watching TV** je regardais la télé ❷ (keep a check on) **surveiller** [1]; **watch the time** surveille l'heure ❸ (to be careful) **faire** [10] **attention**; **watch you don't spill it** fais attention de ne pas le renverser, **watch out for black ice** faites attention au verglas, **watch out!** attention!

water NOUN **eau** FEM

water VERB **arroser** [1]; **to water the plants** arroser les plantes

watercolours NOUN **peinture** (FEM) **pour aquarelle**

waterfall NOUN **cascade** FEM

watering can NOUN **arrosoir** MASC

water melon NOUN **pastèque** FEM

waterproof ADJECTIVE **imperméable**

water-skiing NOUN **ski** (MASC) **nautique**; **to go water-skiing faire du ski nautique**

water sports PLURAL NOUN **sports** (MASC PLURAL) **nautiques**

wave NOUN ❶ (in the sea) **vague** FEM ❷ (with your hand) **signe** MASC; **she gave him a wave from the bus** elle lui a fait signe du bus

wave VERB ❶ (with your hand) **saluer** [1] **de la main** ❷ (flap) **agiter** [1] (your ticket or the newspaper, for example)

wax NOUN **cire** FEM

way NOUN ❶ (a route or road) **chemin** MASC; **the way to town** le chemin pour aller en ville, **we asked the way to the station** nous avons demandé le chemin pour aller à la gare, **on the way back** sur le chemin de retour, **on the way** en route, **'way in'** 'entrée', **'way out'** 'sortie' ❷ (direction) **direction** FEM; **which way did he go?** en quelle direction est-il parti?, **come this way** venez par ici, **to be in the way** gêner le passage ❸ (side) **sens** MASC; **the right way up** à l'endroit, **the wrong way round** à l'envers ❹ (distance) **it's a long way** c'est loin, **Terry went all the way to York** Terry est allé jusqu'à York ❺ (manner) **façon** FEM; **a way of talking** une façon de parler, **he does it his way** il le fait à sa façon, **either way, she's wrong** de toute façon elle a tort, **do it this way** fais-le comme ceci ❻ **no way!** pas question! ❼ **by the way** à propos

way in NOUN **entrée** FEM

way out NOUN **sortie** FEM

we PRONOUN **nous**, (informally) **on**; **we live in Carlisle** nous habitons Carlisle, **we're going to the cinema tonight** on va au cinéma ce soir

weak ADJECTIVE ❶ (feeble) **faible**; **her voice was weak** sa voix était faible ❷ **léger** (FEM **légère**) (coffee or tea)

wealth NOUN **fortune** FEM; **the wealth of the nation** la richesse de la nation

wealthy ADJECTIVE **riche**

weapon NOUN **arme** FEM

wear NOUN **children's wear** vêtements (MASC PLURAL) pour enfants, **sports wear** vêtements de sport

wear VERB **porter** [1]; **Tamsin's wearing her trainers** Tamsin porte ses baskets, **she often wears red** elle est souvent en rouge, **to wear make-up** se maquiller [1]

weather NOUN **temps** MASC; **what's the weather like?** quel temps fait-il?, **in fine weather** quand il fait beau, **the weather was cold** il faisait froid, **the weather here is terrible** il fait un temps affreux ici

weather forecast NOUN **météo** FEM; **the weather forecast says it will rain** selon la météo il va pleuvoir

web NOUN ❶ (spider's) **toile** FEM ❷ (Internet) **the Web** le web MASC, la Toile FEM

web site NOUN **site** (MASC) internet

wedding NOUN **mariage** MASC

Wednesday NOUN **mercredi** MASC; **on Wednesday** mercredi, **I'm going out on Wednesday** je sors mercredi, **see you on Wednesday!** à mercredi!, **on Wednesdays** le mercredi, **the museum is closed on Wednesdays** le musée est fermé le mercredi, **every Wednesday** tous les mercredis, **last Wednesday** mercredi dernier, **next Wednesday** mercredi prochain

weed NOUN **mauvaise herbe** FEM

week NOUN **semaine** FEM; **last week** la semaine dernière, **next week** la semaine prochaine, **this week** cette semaine, **for weeks** pendant des semaines, **a week today** aujourd'hui en huit

weekday NOUN **on weekdays** en semaine

weekend NOUN **week-end** MASC; **last weekend** le week-end dernier, **next weekend** le week-end prochain, **they're coming for the weekend** ils vont passer le week-end chez nous, **I'll do it at the weekend** je le ferai pendant le week-end, **have a nice weekend!** bon week-end!

weekly ADVERB **une fois par semaine**; **I see her weekly** je la vois toutes les semaines

weekly ADJECTIVE **hebdomadaire**; **a weekly magazine** un magazine hebdomadaire

weigh VERB **peser** [50]; **to weigh something** peser quelque chose, **how much do you weigh?** combien pèses-tu?, **I weigh 50 kilos** je pèse cinquante kilos, **to weigh yourself** se peser

weight NOUN **poids** MASC; **to put on weight** prendre du poids, **to lose weight** perdre du poids

weightlifting NOUN **haltérophilie** FEM

weird ADJECTIVE **bizarre**

welcome NOUN **accueil** MASC; **they gave us a warm welcome** ils nous ont fait un accueil chaleureux, **welcome to Oxford!** bienvenue à Oxford!

welcome ADJECTIVE **bienvenu**; **you're welcome any time** vous êtes toujours les bienvenus, **'thank you!' – 'you're welcome!'** 'merci!' – 'de rien!'

welcome VERB **accueillir** [35]

A B C D E F G H I J K L M N O P Q R S T U V W X Y Z

well¹ NOUN puits MASC

well² ADVERB ❶ to feel well se sentir bien, **I'm very well, thank you** ça va très bien, merci ❷ bien; **Terry played well** Terry a bien joué, **the operation went well** l'opération s'est bien passée, **well done!** bravo! ❸ as well aussi, **Kevin's coming as well** Kevin vient aussi ❹ alors; **well then, what's the problem?** alors, quel est le problème? ❺ very well then, you can go très bien, tu peux y aller

well-behaved ADJECTIVE sage

well-done ADJECTIVE bien cuit (a steak)

wellington (boot) NOUN botte (FEM) en caoutchouc

well-known ADJECTIVE célèbre

well-off ADJECTIVE aisé

Welsh NOUN ❶ the Welsh (people) les Gallois MASC PLURAL ❷ (language) gallois MASC

Welsh ADJECTIVE gallois

Welshman NOUN Gallois MASC

Welshwoman NOUN Galloise FEM

west NOUN ouest MASC; **in the west** à l'ouest

west ADJECTIVE, ADVERB ouest (never agrees); **the west side** le côté ouest, **a west wind** un vent d'ouest, **west of Paris** à l'ouest de Paris

western NOUN (a film) western MASC

West Indian NOUN Antillais MASC, Antillaise FEM

West Indian ADJECTIVE antillais

West Indies PLURAL NOUN Antilles FEM PLURAL; **in the West Indies** aux Antilles

wet ADJECTIVE ❶ (damp) mouillé; **the grass is wet** l'herbe est mouillée, **we got wet** nous nous sommes fait mouiller ❷ a wet day un jour de pluie

whale NOUN baleine FEM

what PRONOUN, ADJECTIVE ❶ qu'est-ce que (in questions as the object of a verb); **what did you say?** qu'est-ce que tu as dit?, **what's she doing?** qu'est-ce qu'elle fait?, **what did you buy?** qu'est-ce que tu as acheté?, **what is it?** qu'est-ce que c'est?, **what's the matter?** qu'est-ce qu'il y a? ❷ qu'est-ce qui (in questions as the subject of the verb); **what's happening?** qu'est-ce qui se passe? ❸ ce que (relative pronoun as the object of the verb); **tell me what you bought** dis-moi ce que tu as acheté ❹ ce qui (relative pronoun as the subject of a verb); **she told me what had happened** elle m'a dit ce qui s'était passé ❺ quel MASC, quelle FEM; **what's your address?** quelle est ton adresse?, **what country is it in?** c'est dans quel pays?, **what colour is it?** c'est de quelle couleur?, **what make is it?** c'est quelle marque? ❻ what's her name? elle s'appelle comment?, **what?** comment?

wheat NOUN blé MASC

wheel NOUN roue FEM; **the spare wheel** la roue de rechange, **the steering wheel** le volant

wheelbarrow NOUN brouette FEM

wheelchair NOUN fauteuil (MASC) roulant

when ADVERB, CONJUNCTION **quand**; **when is she arriving?** quand est-ce qu'elle arrive?, **when's your birthday?** c'est quand, ton anniversaire?, **it was raining when I went out** il pleuvait quand je suis sorti

where ADVERB, CONJUNCTION **où**; **where are the plates?** où sont les assiettes?, **where do you live?** tu habites où?, **where are you going?** où vas-tu?, **I don't know where they live** je ne sais pas où ils habitent

whether **si**; **I don't know whether he's back or not** je ne sais pas s'il est rentré ou non

which ADJECTIVE **quel** (FEM **quelle**); **which hat did you buy?** quel chapeau as-tu acheté?

which PRONOUN ❶ (which one) **lequel** MASC, **laquelle** FEM; '**I saw your brother**' – '**which one?**' 'j'ai vu ton frère – lequel?', '**I saw your sister**' – '**which one?**' 'j'ai vu ta sœur – laquelle?', **which of these jackets is yours?** laquelle de ces vestes est à toi? ❷ (relative pronoun) **qui**, (as the subject of the verb); **the lamp which is on the table** la lampe qui est sur la table ❸ (relative pronoun) **que**, (as object of the verb); **the book which you borrowed from me** le livre que tu m'as emprunté

while NOUN **for a while** pendant quelque temps, **she worked here for a while** elle a travaillé ici pendant quelque temps, **after a while** au bout d'un moment

while CONJUNCTION **pendant que**; **you can make some tea while I'm finishing my homework** tu peux faire du thé pendant que je finirai mes devoirs

whip NOUN (for a horse) **cravache** FEM

whip VERB **fouetter** [1]; **whipped cream** la crème fouettée

whirlpool NOUN **tourbillon** MASC

whiskers PLURAL NOUN **moustaches** FEM PLURAL

whisky NOUN **whisky** MASC

whisper NOUN **chuchotement** MASC; **to speak in a whisper** chuchoter [1]

whisper VERB **chuchoter** [1]

whistle NOUN **sifflet** MASC

whistle VERB **siffler** [1]

white NOUN **blanc** MASC; **an egg white** un blanc d'œuf

white ADJECTIVE **blanc** (FEM **blanche**); **a white shirt** une chemise blanche

white coffee NOUN **café** (MASC) **au lait**

Whitsun NOUN **Pentecôte** FEM

who PRONOUN ❶ (in questions) **qui**; **who wants some chocolate?** qui veut du chocolat? ❷ (relative pronoun) **qui**, (as subject of the verb); **my friend who lives in Paris** mon ami qui habite à Paris ❸ (relative pronoun) **que**, (as object of the verb); **the friends who we invited** les amis que nous avons invités

whole NOUN **the whole of the class** la classe tout entière, **on the whole** dans l'ensemble

whole ADJECTIVE **tout**; **the whole family** toute la famille, **the whole morning** toute la matinée, **the whole time** tout le temps, **the whole world** le monde entier

English—French

wholemeal ADJECTIVE **complet** (FEM **complète**); **wholemeal bread** le pain complet

whom PRONOUN ❶ **que**; **the person whom I saw** la personne que j'ai vue ❷ (after a preposition) **qui**; **the person to whom I wrote** la personne à qui j'ai écrit

whose PRONOUN, ADJECTIVE ❶ **à qui**; **whose is this jacket?** à qui est cette veste?, **whose shoes are these?** à qui sont ces chaussures?, **whose is it?** à qui c'est?, **I know whose it is** je sais à qui c'est ❷ **dont**; **the man whose car has been stolen** le monsieur dont la voiture a été volée

why ADVERB **pourquoi**; **why did she phone?** pourquoi a-t-elle appelé?, **nobody knows why he did it** personne ne sait pourquoi il l'a fait

wicked ADJECTIVE ❶ (bad) **méchant** ❷ (brilliant) **génial** MASC (PLURAL **géniaux**)

wide ADJECTIVE ❶ **large**; **the Thames is very wide here** la Tamise est très large ici, **a piece of paper 20 cm wide** une feuille de papier de vingt centimètres de large ❷ **a wide range** une vaste gamme

wide ADVERB **the door was wide open** la porte était grande ouverte

wide awake ADJECTIVE **complètement éveillé**

widen VERB **élargir** [2]

widow NOUN **veuve** FEM

widower NOUN **veuf** MASC

width NOUN **largeur** FEM

wife NOUN **femme** FEM

wig NOUN **perruque** FEM

wild ADJECTIVE ❶ **sauvage** (an animal or plant); **wild birds** les oiseaux sauvages ❷ (crazy) **fou** (FEM **folle**) (idea, party, person) ❸ **to be wild about something** être un fana de quelque chose

wild life NOUN **a programme on wild life in Africa** un programme sur la nature en Afrique

wild life park NOUN **réserve** (FEM) **naturelle**

will VERB ❶ (if you are unsure of the future tense of a French verb, you can check in the verb tables in the centre of the dictionary) **I'll see you soon** je te reverrai bientôt, **he'll be pleased to see you** il sera content de te voir, **it won't rain** il ne pleuvra pas, **there won't be a problem** il n'y aura pas de problème ❷ **aller** [7] (can be used for the immmediate future); **I'll phone them at once** je vais les appeler tout de suite ❸ (in offers and requests) **will you have a drink?** est-ce que vous prenez quelque chose à boire?, **will you help me?** est-ce que tu peux m'aider?, **'will you write to me?'** – **'of course I will!'** 'est-ce que tu m'écriras?' – 'bien sûr que oui!' ❹ **he won't open the door** il ne veut pas ouvrir la porte, **the car won't start** la voiture ne veut pas démarrer, **the drawer won't open** je n'arrive pas à ouvrir le tiroir

willing ADJECTIVE **to be willing to do** être prêt à faire, **I'm willing to pay half** je suis prêt à payer la moitié

willingly ADVERB **volontiers**

willow NOUN **saule** MASC; **a weeping willow** un saule pleureur

win NOUN **victoire** FEM; **our win over Everton** notre victoire sur Everton

a
b
c
d
e
f
g
h
i
j
k
l
m
n
o
p
q
r
s
t
u
v
w
x
y
z

win VERB gagner [1]; **we won!** nous avons gagné!, **Rovers won by two goals** Rovers ont gagné de deux buts

wind¹ NOUN vent MASC; **the North wind** le vent du nord

wind² VERB ❶ enrouler [1] (a wire or a rope, for example) ❷ remonter [1] (a clock)

wind farm NOUN ferme (FEM) d'éoliennes

wind instrument NOUN instrument (MASC) à vent

window NOUN ❶ (in a building) fenêtre FEM; **to look out of the window** regarder par la fenêtre ❷ (in a car, bus, train) vitre FEM

windscreen NOUN pare-brise MASC (PLURAL pare-brise)

windscreen wipers PLURAL NOUN essuie-glace MASC

windsurfing NOUN planche (FEM) à voile; **to go windsurfing** faire [10] de la planche à voile

windy ADJECTIVE ❶ venteux (FEM venteuse) (a place) ❷ **it's windy today** il fait du vent aujourd'hui

wine NOUN vin MASC; **a glass of white wine** un verre de vin blanc

wing NOUN ❶ aile FEM ❷ (in sport) ailier MASC

wink VERB **to wink at somebody** faire [10] un clin d'œil à quelqu'un

winner NOUN gagnant MASC, gagnante FEM

winning ADJECTIVE gagnant

winnings PLURAL NOUN gains MASC PLURAL

winter NOUN hiver MASC; **in winter** en hiver

wipe VERB essuyer [41]; **I'll just wipe the table** je vais juste essuyer la table, **to wipe your nose** se moucher [1]

• **to wipe up** (dishes) essuyer [41] la vaisselle

wire NOUN fil MASC; **an electric wire** un fil électrique

wire netting NOUN grillage MASC

wise ADJECTIVE sage

wish NOUN ❶ vœu MASC (PLURAL vœux); **make a wish!** fais un vœu! ❷ (a desire) désir MASC ❸ **best wishes on your birthday** meilleurs vœux pour ton anniversaire

wish VERB ❶ **I wish he were here** si seulement il était ici ❷ **I wished him happy birthday** je lui ai souhaité un bon anniversaire

wit NOUN esprit MASC

witch NOUN sorcière FEM

with PREPOSITION ❶ avec; **with James** avec James, **with me** avec moi, **with pleasure** avec plaisir, **beat the eggs with a fork** battez les œufs avec une fourchette, **he took his umbrella with him** il a pris son parapluie ❷ (at the house of) chez; **we're staying the night with Frank** on va passer la nuit chez Frank ❸ (in descriptions) **a girl with red hair** une fille aux cheveux roux, **the boy with the broken arm** le garçon au bras cassé ❹ de; **filled with water** rempli d'eau, **covered with mud** couvert de boue, **red with rage** rouge de colère

without PREPOSITION sans; **without you** sans toi, **without sugar** sans sucre, **without a sweater** sans pull, **without looking** sans regarder

witness NOUN témoin MASC

witty ADJECTIVE spirituel (FEM spirituelle)

wizard NOUN magicien MASC

wolf NOUN loup MASC

woman NOUN femme FEM; **a woman friend** une amie, **a woman doctor** une femme médecin

wonder NOUN ❶ merveille FEM ❷ **it's no wonder you're tired** ce n'est pas étonnant si tu es fatigué

wonder VERB se demander [1]; **I wonder why** je me demande pourquoi, **I wonder where Jake is** je me demande où est Jake

wonderful ADJECTIVE merveilleux (FEM merveilleuse)

wood NOUN bois MASC; **the lamp is made of wood** la lampe est en bois

wooden ADJECTIVE en bois

woodwork NOUN menuiserie FEM

wool NOUN laine FEM

woollen ADJECTIVE en laine

word NOUN ❶ mot MASC; **a long word** un mot long, **what's the French word for 'window'?** comment dit-on 'window' en français?, **in other words** autrement dit, **to have a word with somebody** parler avec quelqu'un ❷ (promise) **to give somebody your word** donner sa parole à quelqu'un, **he broke his word** il n'a pas tenu parole ❸ **the words of a song** les paroles d'une chanson

word processing NOUN traitement (MASC) de texte

word processor NOUN machine (FEM) à traitement de texte

work NOUN travail MASC (PLURAL travaux); **Mum's at work** maman est au travail, **I've got some work to do** j'ai du travail à faire, **he's out of work** il est sans emploi, **Ben's off work** (sick) Ben est en arrêt de travail, (on holiday) Ben est en congé

work VERB ❶ travailler [1]; **she works in an office** elle travaille dans un bureau, **Dad works at home** papa travaille à domicile, **Ruth works in advertising** Ruth travaille dans la publicité, **he works nights** il travaille de nuit ❷ (to operate) se servir [71] de; **can you work the video?** sais-tu te servir du magnétoscope? ❸ (function) marcher [1]; **the dishwasher's not working** le lave-vaisselle est en panne, **that worked really well!** ça a bien marché!

• **to work out** ❶ (understand) comprendre [64]; **I can't work out why** je ne comprends pas pourquoi ❷ (exercise) s'entraîner [1] ❸ (to go well) (a plan) marcher [1] ❹ (calculate) calculer [1]; **I'll work out how much it would cost** je vais calculer combien ç coûterait

worked up ADJECTIVE **to get worked up** s'énerver [1]

worker NOUN (in a factory) ouvrier MASC, ouvrière FEM

worker NOUN ouvrier MASC, ouvrière FEM

work experience NOUN stage MASC; **to do work experience** faire un stage, **to be on work experience** être en stage

a
b
c
d
e
f
g
h
i
j
k
l
m
n
o
p
q
r
s
t
u
v
w
x
y
z

working-class ADJECTIVE ouvrier (FEM ouvrière); **a working-class background** un milieu ouvrier

work of art NOUN œuvre (FEM) d'art

workshop NOUN atelier MASC

workstation NOUN (computer) poste (MASC) de travail (PLURAL postes de travail)

world NOUN monde MASC; **the best in the world** le meilleur du monde, **the Western world** les pays occidentaux

World Cup NOUN **the World Cup** la Coupe du Monde

world war NOUN guerre (FEM) mondiale; **the Second World War** la Seconde Guerre mondiale

worm NOUN ver MASC

worn out ADJECTIVE ❶ (a person) épuisé ❷ (clothes or shoes) complètement usé

worried ADJECTIVE inquiet (FEM inquiète); **they're worried** ils s'inquiètent, **to be worried about** s'inquiéter pour, **we're worried about Susan** nous nous inquiétons pour Susan

worry NOUN soucis MASC PLURAL

worry VERB s'inquiéter [24]; **don't worry!** ne t'inquiète pas!, **there's nothing to worry about** il n'y a pas de quoi s'inquiéter

worrying ADJECTIVE inquiétant

worse ADJECTIVE pire; **it was even worse than the last time** c'était encore pire que la dernière fois, **to get worse** empirer [1], **the weather's getting worse** le temps empire, **things are getting worse and worse** ça va de pire en pire

worst ADJECTIVE **the worst** le plus mauvais, **it was the worst day of my life** ça a été la journée la plus mauvaise de ma vie, **if the worst comes to the worst** au pire

worth ADJECTIVE **to be worth** valoir [80], **how much is it worth?** ça vaut combien?, **to be worth doing** valoir la peine de faire, **it's worth trying** ça vaut la peine d'essayer, **it's not worth it** ça ne vaut pas la peine

would VERB ❶ **would you like something to eat?** voulez-vous quelque chose à manger? ❷ **he wouldn't answer** il n'a pas voulu répondre, **the car wouldn't start** la voiture n'a pas voulu démarrer ❸ **I would like an omelette** je voudrais une omelette, **I'd like to go to the cinema** j'aimerais aller au cinéma, **that would be a good idea** ce serait une bonne idée, **if we asked her she would help us** elle nous aiderait, si nous le lui demandions

wound NOUN blessure FEM

wound VERB blesser [1]

wrap VERB emballer [1]; **I'm going to wrap (up) my presents** je vais emballer mes cadeaux, **could you wrap it for me please?** voulez-vous me faire un paquet cadeau, s'il vous plaît?

wrapping paper NOUN papier (MASC) cadeau

wreck NOUN ❶ (of a crashed car or plane) épave FEM ❷ **I feel a wreck!** je suis une loque!

wreck VERB ❶ détruire [26] ❷ gâcher [1] (plans, occasion); **it completely wrecked my evening!** ça m'a complètement gâché la soirée!

wrestler NOUN catcheur MASC, catcheuse FEM

wrestling NOUN catch MASC

wrinkle NOUN ride FEM

wrinkled ADJECTIVE ridé

wrist NOUN poignet MASC

write VERB écrire [38] *(a letter or a story)*; **I'll write her a letter** je lui écrirai une lettre, **to write to somebody** écrire à quelqu'un, **I wrote to Jean yesterday** j'ai écrit à Jean hier
• **to write down** noter [1]; **I wrote down her name** j'ai noté son nom

writer NOUN écrivain MASC

writing NOUN écriture FEM

wrong ADJECTIVE ❶ *(not correct)* mauvais; **the wrong answer** la mauvaise réponse, **it's the wrong address** ce n'est pas la bonne adresse, **I've brought the wrong file** je n'ai pas apporté le bon classeur, **you've got the wrong number** vous vous êtes trompé de numéro ❷ **to be wrong** *(mistaken)* se tromper, **I was wrong** je me suis trompé, **I was wrong when I said it was finished** je me suis trompé en disant que c'était fini ❸ **what's wrong?** qu'est-ce qu'il y a? ❹ *(false)* faux *(FEM* fausse)*; **the information was wrong** les renseignements étaient faux

xerox NOUN photocopie FEM

xerox VERB photocopier [1]

Xmas NOUN Christmas

X-ray NOUN radio FEM; **I saw the X-rays** j'ai vu les radios

X-ray VERB faire [10] une radio de; **they X-rayed her ankle** ils ont fait une radio de sa cheville

yacht NOUN ❶ *(sailing boat)* voilier MASC ❷ *(large luxury boat)* yacht MASC

yawn VERB bâiller [1]

year NOUN ❶ an MASC, *(the whole period)* année FEM; **six years ago** il y a six ans, **the whole year** toute l'année, **they lived in Moscow for years** ils ont habité Moscou pendant des années ❷ *(for someone's age)* an MASC; **he's seventeen years old** il a dix-sept ans, **a two-year-old child** un enfant de deux ans ❸ *(in* secondary schools in France the years go from 'sixième', the equivalent of Year 7, to 'terminale', the equivalent of Year 13); **I'm in Year 10** je suis en troisième, **I'm in Year 11** je suis en seconde

yearly ADJECTIVE **annuel** (FEM **annuelle**); **a yearly event** un événement annuel

yearly ADVERB **tous les ans**; **he goes to Normandy yearly** il va en Normandie tous les ans

yell VERB **hurler** [1]

yellow ADJECTIVE **jaune**

yes ADVERB ❶ **oui**; **yes, I know** oui, je sais, **'is Tom in his room?' – 'yes, he is'** 'est-ce que Tom est dans sa chambre?' – 'oui' ❷ (answering a negative) **si**; **'you don't want to go, do you?' – 'yes, I do!'** 'tu ne veux pas y aller, n'est-ce pas?' – 'mais si!', **'you haven't finished, have you?' – 'yes, I have'** 'tu n'as pas fini?' – 'si si'

yesterday ADVERB **hier**; **I saw her yesterday** je l'ai vue hier, **yesterday afternoon** hier après-midi, **yesterday morning** hier matin, **the day before yesterday** avant-hier

yet ADVERB **not yet** pas encore, **it's not ready yet** ce n'est pas encore prêt

yoga NOUN **yoga** MASC

yoghurt NOUN **yaourt** MASC; **a banana yoghurt** un yaourt à la banane

yolk NOUN **jaune** (MASC) **d'œuf** (PLURAL **jaunes d'œuf**)

you PRONOUN ❶ **tu** ('tu' is the familiar way of talking to family members, close friends, and people of your own age; 'vous' is more polite); **do you want to go to the cinema tonight?** tu veux aller au cinéma ce soir? ❷ **te**

(the object form of 'tu'); **I'll lend you my bike** je te prêterai mon vélo, **I'll invite you** je t'inviterai, **I'll write to you** je t'écrirai ❸ **toi** (after prepositions and in comparisons); **I'll go with you** j'irai avec toi, **he's older than you** il est plus âgé que toi ❹ (more polite or to several people) **vous**; **can you tell me where the station is, please?** est-ce que vous pouvez m'indiquer la gare, s'il vous plaît?, **I'll invite you all!** je vous inviterai tous!

young ADJECTIVE **jeune**; **he's younger than me** il est plus jeune que moi, **Tessa's two years younger than me** Tessa a deux ans de moins que moi, **young people** les jeunes

your ADJECTIVE ❶ **ton** MASC, **ta** FEM (PLURAL **tes**) (this is the familiar way of talking to family members, close friends, and people of your own age; 'vous' is more polite); **I met your Dad** j'ai rencontré ton père, **I like your skirt!** j'aime bien ta jupe!, **you've forgotten your shoes!** tu as oublié tes chaussures ❷ (more polite or to several people) **votre** (PLURAL **vos**); **thank you for your hospitality** merci pour votre hospitalité, **you can all bring your friends** vous pouvez tous amener vos amis

yours PRONOUN ❶ **le tien** MASC, **la tienne** FEM, (PLURAL **les tiens** MASC, **les tiennes** FEM) (this is the familiar way of talking to somebody of your own age or belonging to your family; otherwise you should use 'vôtre'); **my brother's younger than yours** mon frère est plus jeune que le tien ❷ (formally or to several people) **le vôtre** MASC **la vôtre** FEM, (PLURAL **les vôtres**); **my children are younger than yours** mes enfants sont plus jeunes que les vôtres ❸ **à**

toi, à vous *(polite form)*; **is this pen yours?** est-ce que ce stylo est à toi?

yourself *PRONOUN* ❶ *(informal)* te, *(formal)* vous; **you'll hurt yourself** tu vas te faire mal ❷ *(for emphasis)* toi-même, *(formal)* vous-même; **did you do it yourself?** est-ce que tu l'as fait toi-même? ❸ **all by yourself** tout seul *(FEM* toute seule*)*

yourselves *PRONOUN* ❶ vous; **help yourselves** servez-vous ❷ *(for emphasis)* vous-mêmes; **did you do it yourselves?** est-ce que vous l'avez fait vous-mêmes?

youth *NOUN* ❶ *(stage in life)* jeunesse *FEM* ❷ *(young people)* les jeunes *MASC PLURAL*; **today's youth** les jeunes d'aujourd'hui ❸ *(young male)* jeune *MASC*

youth hostel *NOUN* auberge *(FEM)* de jeunesse *(PLURAL* auberges de jeunesse*)*

Yugoslavia *NOUN* Yougoslavie *FEM*; **the former Yugoslavia** l'ex-Yougoslavie

zany *ADJECTIVE* loufoque

zebra *NOUN* zèbre *MASC*

zebra crossing *NOUN* passage *(MASC)* pour piétons

zero *NOUN* zéro *MASC*

zigzag *VERB* zigzaguer [1]

zip *NOUN* fermeture *(FEM)* éclair

zodiac *NOUN* zodiaque *MASC*; **the signs of the zodiac** les signes du zodiaque

zone *NOUN* zone *FEM*

zoo *NOUN* zoo *MASC*

zoom lens *NOUN* zoom *MASC*

a
b
c
d
e
f
g
h
i
j
k
l
m
n
o
p
q
r
s
t
u
v
w
x
y
z

LIFE AND CULTURE

At school

le bac	the exam taken by students who have stayed at school to the age of 18, bac is short for baccalauréat
le collège	state school for students aged 11-15 years old
le lycée	state school for 15-18 year olds
la journée scolaire	the school day: the length of the day varies, but can be from 8.30 a.m. to 5 p.m.
la rentrée	the return to school in September

Did you know ...?
that students in state schools do not wear uniforms?

Je vais à l'école à pied.	I walk to school.
Je suis en sixième.	I'm in Year 7.
Il y a 25 élèves dans ma classe.	There are 25 students in my class.
Les cours commencent à neuf heures.	Lessons start at 9 o'clock.
À midi, je mange à la cantine.	At lunchtime, I eat in the canteen.
On a beaucoup de devoirs.	We have a lot of homework.
Entrez!	Come in!
Sortez vos cahiers.	Take out your exercise books.
Ouvrez vos livres, page 23.	Open your books at p23.
Travaillez avec un(e) partenaire.	Work in pairs.
Écoutez et répétez.	Listen and repeat.

Il me faut ...
I need ...

mon cahier.	my exercise book.	ma trousse.	my pencil case.
mon crayon.	my pencil.	ma règle.	my ruler

Ma matière préférée, c'est ...
My favourite subject is ...

l'éducation civique.	Citizenship/PSHE.
l'EPS.	PE.

At home

Dans ma famille, nous sommes cinq.	There are five of us in my family.

J'ai ...
I've got ...

un frère / une sœur.	a brother / a sister.
un demi-frère / une demi-sœur.	a half-brother / a half-sister.
un jumeau / une jumelle.	a twin brother / a twin sister.
Je suis fils / fille unique.	I'm an only child.

J'habite ...
I live ...

(dans) une maison.	in a house.	(dans) un appartement.	in a flat.
en Angleterre.	in England.	(à) Londres.	in London.

Il y a ...
There is ...

une cuisine.	a kitchen.	une salle de bains.	a bathroom.
trois chambres.	three bedrooms.	des toilettes / des W.C.	a toilet.
une salle de séjour.	a living room.	un jardin.	a garden.

Mon passe-temps préféré, c'est ...
My favourite hobby is ...

faire du vélo.	cycling.	regarder la télévision.	watching TV.
faire du VTT.	mountain biking.	sortir avec des copains.	going out with friends.
faire du roller.	roller-blading.	jouer au foot / volley.	playing football / volleyball.
lire.	reading.		
écouter de la musique.	listening to music.	faire du skateboard.	skateboarding.

Je vais regarder...
I'm going to watch ...

la télé.	TV.	une émission sportive.	a sports programme.
un jeu.	a game show.	ma série préférée.	my favourite series.

J'ai ...
I have ...

un (lecteur) e-Reader	an e-Reader
un iPad®	an iPad®
une console de jeux	a games console
un (téléphone) portable	a (mobile) phone
un (ordinateur) portable	a laptop
une webcam	a webcam
un appareil photo numérique	a digital camera
un ordinateur	a computer

Sur mon ordinateur ...
On my computer ...

je fais me devoirs.	I do my homework.
je télécharge de la musique.	I download music.
je cherche quelque chose sur Internet / un site web.	I look something up on the internet / a website.
j'envoie des mails.	I send emails.
je twitte.	I tweet.
je vais sur les réseaux sociaux.	I go on social network sites.
je vais sur les chats / forums (de discussion)	I visit chatrooms.

Did you know ...?
- that in email addresses (les adresses électroniques), @ is called arobase and dot is called point?
- that many French Internet sites (les sites Internet français) end with .fr ?

Shopping, food, and eating out

Je fais des courses...
I go shopping (for food) ...

à la pâtisserie.	at the cake shop.	à la charcuterie.	at the delicatessen.
à l'épicerie.	at the grocer's.	au marché.	at the market.
à la boulangerie.	at the baker's.	au supermarché.	at the supermarket.
à la boucherie.	at the butcher's.		
		sur Internet.	on the Internet.

C'est combien?	How much is it?

Je voudrais ...
I'd like ...

un pain.	a loaf of bread.	un kilo de pommes.	a kilo of apples.
quatre petits pains.	four rolls.		

Did you know ...?
- that shops are often closed (fermés) at lunchtime, but are open (ouverts) late into the evening?

Food

les baguettes	**French bread,** slices of baguette spread with butter are called tartines
la crème Chantilly	fresh cream whipped with sugar and vanilla
les chips	crisps, chips (French fries) are called frites
les crêpes	**pancakes,** a crêperie serves both sweet and savoury pancakes
les escargots	These are **snails.** they are considered a treat, not everyday food!
le fromage	**cheese,** the French are famous for their cheeses
les glaces	These are **ice creams.** Flavours include cassis (blackcurrant), pistache (pistachio), noisette (hazelnut), citron vert (lime).
la ratatouille	**a vegetable dish** made with tomatoes, onions, garlic, courgettes, and often aubergine

Meals (les repas)

le petit déjeuner	breakfast	le goûter	afternoon snack
le déjeuner	lunch	le dîner	dinner

Did you know ... ?
that, at breakfast, many French people drink from a bowl (un bol) rather than a cup?

Vous désirez?
What would you like?

Je voudrais ...
I'd like ...

un jus d'orange.	an orange juice.	un café.	a coffee.
un thé.	a cup of tea.	le plat du jour.	the dish of the day.

Vous avez des glaces à la vanille?   Have you got any vanilla ice cream?

Comme plat principal, je voudrais ...
For my main course I'd like ...

le coq au vin.	chicken in wine sauce.
un hamburger.	a burger.

avec ...
with ...

des frites.	chips.
une salade.	salad.

Comme dessert, je voudrais ...
For dessert I'd like ...

la mousse au chocolat.	chocolate mousse.
une glace à la fraise.	strawberry ice cream.

Comme boisson, je vais prendre ...
To drink I'll have ...

de l'eau minérale.	mineral water.
un coca.	a Coke®.

J'ai faim.	I'm hungry.
J'ai soif.	I'm thirsty.
C'est délicieux!	It's delicious!
L'addition, s'il vous plaît.	The bill, please.
J'ai une allergie / Je suis allergique à la / au /aux ...	I'm allergic to ...

On holiday in France

L'été dernier, je suis allé(e) en France.	Last summer, I went to France.
L'été prochain, je vais aller à Paris.	Next summer, I'll be going to Paris.

J'ai logé ...
I stayed ...

à l'hôtel.	in a hotel.
dans un gîte rural.	in a holiday home in the country.
On a fait du camping.	We went camping.

On a voyagé ...
We travelled ...

en avion.	by plane.	en car.	by coach.
en voiture.	by car.	en train.	by train.
en bateau.	by boat / ship.	à vélo.	by bike.

un bal public	Many events end with a bal public: dancing for all in the town or village square.
les boules	(also called la pétanque) the game of bowls
la carte d'identité	**Identity card.** Many French people use their carte d'identité instead of a passport to travel within the EU. (European Union).
les départements	France is divided into 95 départements. Each has a number, e.g. central Paris is 75. This number is used in postcodes and on car number plates.
une fête	**A party.** In summer, many towns and villages have fêtes, with music, stalls, dancing, etc.
l'hôtel de ville	the town hall
le Stade de France	a very large stadium in Paris
le Tour de France	a famous cycle race which takes place every summer. It is divided into sections called étapes. The previous day's winner wears a special yellow jersey (le maillot jaune).

Did you know ...?

- that you often have to validate your train / bus ticket by putting it into a machine at the train station or on the bus? The machine will punch (composter) your ticket.
- that some main railway lines operate high-speed trains called le TGV® (train à grande vitesse)?
- that the Channel Tunnel is known as le tunnel sous la Manche? (La Manche – 'the sleeve' – is the French name for the Channel.)
- that the Paris underground is called le métro?
- that most French motorways (autoroutes) charge a toll (péage)?
- that French motorways have service stations (aires de services) and rest areas (aires de repos)?

Places of interest

L'Arc de Triomphe	a grand arch in Paris, at the end of the Champs-Élysées
la Bretagne	Brittany: a popular tourist area in northwestern France, with a rocky coast and sandy beaches
les Champs Élysées	the grandest street in Paris, lined with luxury shops, cafes, and hotels
la Côte d'Azur	the French Riviera: the most fashionable stretch of the French Mediterranean coast, including St Tropez, Cannes, Nice, and Monte Carlo
Disneyland Paris®	This is one of two well-known theme parks (parcs d'attractions) near Paris. The other one is le Parc Astérix.
Le musée du Louvre	the most famous museum in Paris
le Midi	the south of France
le mont Blanc	This is western Europe's highest mountain. Mont Blanc is in the Alps.
le Mont-Saint-Michel	a tiny island off the northwestern coast of France, joined to the mainland by a causeway
la tour Eiffel	The Eiffel Tower was built in 1889, 100 years after the French Revolution.
Versailles	a magnificent royal palace built in the town of Versailles, near Paris